LEO ING
682-7876

Second Edition

Operations Management

CONCEPTS, METHODS, AND STRATEGIES

Second Edition

Operations Management

CONCEPTS, METHODS, AND STRATEGIES

Mark A. Vonderembse
University of Toledo

Gregory P. White
Southern Illinois University—Carbondale

West Publishing Company
St. Paul New York Los Angeles San Francisco

Copyediting: Sherry Goldbecker
Text Design: Peter Thiel
Composition: Carlisle Communications, Inc.
Illustration: Asterisk Group
Cover photo: Mel Lindstrom

50 W. Kellogg Boulevard
P.O. Box 64526
St. Paul, MN 55164–0526

Printed in the United States of America

98 97 96 95 94 93 92 91 8 7 6 5 4 3 2 1 0

Library of Congress Cataloging-in-Publication Data

Vonderembse, Mark A., 1948–
Operations management: concepts, methods, and strategies / Mark A. Vonderembse, Gregory P. White.—2nd ed.
p. cm.
Includes bibliographical references (p. 00) and index.
ISBN 0–314–78148-X (hard)
1. Production management. I. White, Gregory P., 1948– .
II. Title.
TS155.V66 1991
658.5—dc20

90–12922
CIP

Dedicated with love to:

Sandra, Anthony, and Elaine

Ruth and Paul

Pat

Martha and Tom

Contents in Brief

Contents

PART II Planning the System

Chapter 10 Transforming Strategic Plans into Business and Operations Plans 382

Chapter 10 Supplement Linear Programming 416

Chapter 11 Planning for Material and Resource Requirements 428

Chapter 12 Just-in-Time and Synchronous Operations 474

Chapter 13 Scheduling 518

Chapter 13 Supplement Management-Science Tools and Scheduling 552

Preface

Our approach to writing *Operations Management: Concepts, Methods, and Strategies* is based on four related ideas. First, an organization should be viewed as a system of interrelated functions such as accounting, marketing, finance, and operations. To have a full understanding of organizations and operations, managers must see the impact that operations has on other parts of the organization and vice versa. Second, decisions made by operations managers can have a major impact on an organization's competitive performance and students should understand the importance of operations in an organization's strategy. Third, all students in an introductory operations management course, regardless of their individual majors, should be brought up to the cutting edge of operations management as it is practiced by today's successful organizations. And fourth, quantitative methods should be integrated into the conceptual material and presented as tools for solving specific problems.

These ideas, which were the foundation of the first edition, are carried forward in the second edition because we still believe that putting these ideas into practice is vitally important to improving organizational performance in the growing and highly competitive international marketplace. The strong response to the first edition and highly favorable comments made by reviewers of the second edition support this belief.

Within this framework, many enhancements have been made in the second edition. Coverage of forecasting concepts and techniques has been expanded and forecasting is now presented in a separate chapter. There is also expanded coverage of facility location and project management, both of which now appear in separate chapters. Current topics like quality functional deployment, synchronous manufacturing, teamwork approach to product and process design (sometimes call concurrent engineering or interactive product and process design), and design for manufacturing and assembly have been added. In fact, every chapter has been carefully reviewed and updated with current material.

Responding to changes in the external environment, the second edition has increased coverage of the international dimension and examines the impact that global markets can have on the organization and, more specifically, on operations. We have also increased coverage of service operations, a growing part of the U.S. and world economies. In line with the AACSB's emphasis on ethics, coverage of ethical issues has been included where appropriate.

Intended Audience

We have written this text for use in the introductory course in operations management for undergraduates and MBA students. The text is designed so that students in any business-related major will find it relevant. Thus, prior training in management science is not required to read and understand the text. However, it is assumed that students have had an introductory course in statistics.

Special Topics

This text covers the standard operations management topics. However, we have gone beyond that standard fare and included new chapters and some new topics in standard chapters. For instance, in Chapter 2 we discuss the use of operations to gain competitive advantage and also present new ideas about technology and computer-integrated manufacturing. In addition, the concepts of using operations to gain a competitive advantage and computer-based technological advancements are integrated throughout the text. This enables readers to relate these concepts to day-to-day operating decisions. In discussing new product development in Chapter 4, we view it as a team effort that should include marketing, engineering, operations, finance, accounting, and management information systems. This illustrates a major theme of the text, which is understanding that an organization is a system of interrelated parts, and that operations is one part of that organization. Operations must interact effectively with other functional areas if the organization is to achieve its objectives. Chapter 5, on capacity, emphasizes the impact that bottlenecks have on system capacity and illustrates how to determine the bottleneck. Chapters 11 and 12 are thoroughly up-to-date in their discussion of material requirements planning, just-in-time operations, and synchronous manufacturing. Chapter 15 provides a more thorough coverage of purchasing concepts than usually found because material costs are often the most significant cost factor in any operation. Chapter 17 emphasizes the latest concepts of quality management, including total quality control and quality functional deployment. In our Chapter 18 discussion of technology, we include the often overlooked human aspects of improving operations through automation. Chapter 19 breaks new ground by discussing information systems for managing and controlling operations.

Integration of Services and Manufacturing

Operations exist in a variety of organizations. Thus, we have been careful to include numerous examples and problems from both service and manufacturing operations. While striving to point out how service and manufacturing operations are different, we have also avoided covering them as totally separate topics. The result, we believe, achieves a reasonable balance between the two.

Computer Applications and Automation

In today's rapidly changing environment, computer applications and automation have an important role in operations. Thus, we have devoted a significant part of this book to discussion of those topics as they relate to both services and manufacturers. The automation topics presented include automated guided vehicles, automated storage and retrieval systems, robotics, cellular manufacturing, and flexible manufacturing systems. The computerization topics discussed include computer-aided design and manufacturing, computer-aided process planning, computer-integrated manufacturing, computer numerical control, data base, MRP, decision support systems and expert systems.

The Role of Quantitative Methods

We understand the important role that quantitative methods, both statistics and management science, have in operations. That is why these topics have been carefully woven throughout the text so their application can follow logically from, and be close to, the discussion of managerial issues. The result is that students are motivated to learn quantitative techniques because the managerial applications are readily apparent.

Because these quantitative methods are integrated throughout the text, instead of being presented as separate chapters, we have listed below the chapters in which each method appears.

Subject	Chapter
Acceptance Sampling for Quality Management	17
Aggregate Planning	10
Assembly Line Balancing	8
Cost-Volume-Profit Model	7
Project Scheduling	14
Decision Trees	5
Distribution Requirements Planning	11
Forecasting	3
Job Shop Layout	8
Learning Curves	9
Linear Programming for Aggregate Planning	Supplement to Chapter 11
Lot Sizing Models	16
Make versus Buy Decisions	15
Material Requirements Planning	11
Modeling, An Introduction	3
Safety Stock Determination	16
Scheduling of Production	13
Simulation of Waiting Lines and Machine Failure	Supplement to Chapter 13
Statistical Process Control	17
Transportation Method	6
Waiting Line Models	Supplement to Chapter 13

Chapter Features

Many pedagogical features have been incorporated into this text as a means of achieving our overall objectives. These features include:

Learning Objectives. A list of performance-based Learning Objectives is provided at the beginning of each chapter so that students will know what will be expected of them after completing the chapter.

Operations in Action Boxes. This feature begins, and is found throughout, each chapter. It is designed to provide students with examples of current problems and issues found in operations and to illustrate how they are being solved by actual companies such as General Motors, Florida Power and Light, Harley-Davidson, and Federal Express. Our intent is to tie together concepts and techniques discussed in this text with the practice of business and industry.

Gaining Strategic Advantage Boxes. There is one of these in each chapter. Its purpose is to supplement the Operations in Action boxes by focusing on how today's successful organizations use operations to gain an advantage over their competitors. Each is tied to the concepts or techniques discussed within the chapter in which it appears.

Integrating the System Boxes. They describe the interactions between two areas or subsystems within the same operations department, or between two different functional areas of an organization. Their purpose is to reinforce the theme of this text by stressing the integrative nature of this field and to highlight the importance of operations to other functional areas.

Examples. In order to help students understand the more quantitative material we have provided frequent numerical examples throughout the book.

Summary. Each chapter ends with a summary of key points that reflect the learning objectives listed at the beginning of the chapter.

Career Profile. Because most students in an introductory course have little, if any, idea of the jobs available in operations management, we have provided a career profile at the end of each chapter. This material highlights a *real person* whose job is related to topics discussed in the chapter. The career profile describes each person's background, the career path he or she has followed, what they do now, and the next career step for them.

Solved Problems. In addition to the extensive examples located throughout each chapter, we have provided solved problems at the end of the chapters. These should serve as a model for students working the homework problems on their own.

Questions. Each chapter concludes with an extensive set of review and discussion questions.

Problems. We have also provided a large number of numerical practice problems. Those problems that are especially appropriate for computer solution have been flagged with a special microcomputer logo, although they can also be solved by hand. Solutions to these problems using the STORM software are available in the instructor's manual.

Data Sets for Computer Solution. To give students a feel for the real-world problems that can only be solved on a computer, we have provided separate problems with larger and/or more complex data sets. Solutions to these problems using the STORM software are available in the instructor's manual.

Mini-Cases. Each chapter includes mini-cases. These are more extensive problem situations that either rely more on subjective judgement or require considerable calculations. These may be assigned as extensive homework problems or used as the basis for class discussions.

Selected Bibliography. Each chapter contains a list of books and articles that are related to the topics discussed in the chapter. These can be used by readers who want to know more about a topic.

Glossary. Key terms have been highlighted in bold type throughout the book. However, these terms, along with their definitions, are also arranged alphabetically at the end of the text.

Summary of Formulas. To help students find a formula even though they may not recall in which chapter that formula appeared, we have provided a summary of formulas. These formulas, arranged alphabetically, appear at the end of the text.

Supporting Material

Instructors' Manual. The Instructor's Manual, prepared by the text authors, includes teaching suggestions as well as answers and solutions to all end of chapter questions, problems, mini-cases, and data sets for computer solution.

Computer Software. There are two options for those who wish to have computer software application as a part of the learning experience. *STORM Personal Version 2.0* software written by Emmons, Flowers, Khot, and Mathur can be used with the text. In certain chapters, problems identified with a micro-computer logo and the data sets for computer solution can be solved using the STORM software. Diskettes are available. These diskettes contain the data for these problems in a format that is readable by the STORM software and a solution to each of these problems. In the appropriate chapter in the instructors manual, a hard-copy solution to each problem using STORM can be found.

For faculty who prefer a spreadsheet approach, *Structuring and Solving Operations Management Problems Using Lotus 1–2–3, Second Edition* by Zimmerman and Zimmerman can be selected. Many of the problems in our text are solved in the Zimmerman and Zimmerman book. More details including a list of problems that can be solved with the Zimmerman and Zimmerman software can be found near the end of the instructor's manual. It is highly likely that alternatives to STORM and the Zimmerman and Zimmerman software can be used, but we have verified that these packages will work.

Test Bank. The test bank, developed by M. Jill Austin of Middle Tennessee State University, has been completely revised. It contains over 1,000 questions (with answers) and is also available on West's Computerized Testing Program, WESTEST. The questions are a mixture of multiple choice, problems, and essay.

Video "Plant Tours". Throughout the text we have stressed the fact that real companies are using the techniques and concepts presented. However, since one picture is worth a thousand words, and because most students do not have an opportunity to experience operations first-hand, we have assembled a video "plant tour." Available free of charge to qualified adopter, this ½" VHS tape consists of nearly 20 segments produced by such companies as Allen-Bradley, Longview Fibre, U.S. Postal Service, Mercury Marine, John Deere, USA Today, Federal Express, General Motors, and Harley-Davidson. These video plant tours take students right inside a company's operations to see how operations management techniques and concepts are applied. Through a specially prepared set of instructor notes, these video clips are tied directly to appropriate chapters of the text by discussion questions and key points.

Transparency Masters. A separate set of transparency masters is available for most exhibits in the text as well as for other important concepts. There are well over 300 transparency masters in the set.

Study Guide. A Study Guide, developed by M. Jill Austin of Middle Tennessee State University, can be purchased by the students. It includes an overview of the chapter's concepts as well as sample problems and sample questions with correct answers.

Acknowledgments

We wish to thank the following people who gave freely of their time and talents in the first edition. Their many constructive criticisms and helpful suggestions are greatly appreciated. They are:

Harold C. Allen, University of South Florida
M. Jill Austin, Middle Tennessee State University
Thomas D. Best, California State University
Martin W. Broin, University of Texas–Dallas
Karen Brown, Seattle University
Dave Christy, Pennsylvania State University
Charles W. Dane, Oregon State University
William Darrow, Towson State University
Stephen Goodman, University of Central Florida
Forrest B. Green, Radford University
Kenneth Jenkins, Portland State University
Barry King, Ohio State University
Burt Madden, University of Arkansas at Little Rock
Paul K. Makens, Vanderbilt University
Donald W. McCaskey, University of Wisconsin at Madison
Craig McLanahan, Salem State University
George E. Monahan, University of Illinois at Urbana
Richard Penlesky, Marquette University
Ronald Satterfield, University of Wisconsin at Eau Claire
Carl R. Schultz, University of New Mexico
Pitner Traughber, Indiana University at South Bend
Michael Umble, Baylor University
Gus A. Vargas, California State University at Fullerton
Ramiro Villeda, San Jose State University.

We also wish to thank the following people who gave freely of their time and talents to review earlier drafts of the second edition. Their many comments and suggestions greatly improved the manuscript. They are:

Sid Moody
Our Lady of the Lake University

Charles W. Dane
Oregon State University

Ricardo Ernst
Georgetown University

James R. Sisak
University of Wisconsin-Whitewater

Donald R. Edwards
Baylor University

R. Anthony Inman
Louisiana Tech University

Edward Fisher
Central Michigan University

Richard A. Sandbothe
SUNY-Binghamton

Elizabeth B. Booth
Louisiana State University

Ellen Dumond
Miami University

Alfred L. Guiffrida
Canisius College

Robert Taylor
University of Colorado at Boulder

Sanford Temkin
Rider College

John Bushnell
University of Colorado at Boulder

J. Roberta Minifie Walden
Southwest Texas State University

Gus A. Vargas
California State University-Fullerton

Sal Agnihothri
SUNY-Binghamton

Paul H. Randolph
Texas Tech University

L. W. Shell
Nicholls State University

Paul Swamidass
University of Missouri-Columbia

David Donnan
University of Toronto

John Boyd
Baylor University

Glenn T. Wilson
Middle Tennessee State University

Fredrik P. Williams
University of North Texas

We also want to thank the many operations management practitioners and their companies that have allowed us to use them for career profiles, to describe their organizations in the text, and to include their videotapes as part of our Video "Plant Tours." Those organizations are:

Allen-Bradley
Cincinnati Milacron
Continental Airlines
Coopers & Lybrand
Dana Corporation
Digital Equipment Company
Exide Electronics
Federal Express
Ford Motor Company
Frito-Lay
General Motors
Harley-Davidson Motor Co.
Inland Steel Corporation
Hewlett Packard
Honeywell Space and Strategic Avionics Division
International Business Machines Corporation
Kawasaki Motors Manufacturing
Longview Fibre Company
McDonnell Douglas Corporation
Mercury Marine Division of Brunswick Corporation
Motorola
Society Bank and Trust
Steelcase Inc.
Toledo Hospital
TriNova Corporation
USA Today
United States Postal Service
WCI Laundry Division
Weirton Steel Corporation
Wendy's International
Weyerhaeuser Corporation
Xerox

In addition, we wish to thank William Ruud of the University of Toledo for his detailed comments on Chapter 18; Joe Scazzero of the University of Toledo for his detailed comments on Chapter 3; Keri Dixon and David Liu of the University of Toledo and Barbara McArthur and Janice Fry of Southern Illinois University for their help in preparing the instructor's manual; and the people at West Publishing Company, especially Mélina Brown and Rick Leyh for their helpful comments and hard work. We also thank Jill Austin for her excellent work in preparing the Study Guide and Test Bank. We also wish to acknowledge the support of the University of Toledo and Southern Illinois University at Carbondale. Finally, we want to thank our families for their understanding and patience as we took many evenings and weekends away from them while preparing the second edition.

Mark A. Vonderembse
Gregory P. White

Second Edition

Operations Management

CONCEPTS, METHODS, AND STRATEGIES

Chapter 1

Introduction to Operations Management

CHAPTER OUTLINE

LEARNING OBJECTIVES

After completing this chapter, you should be able to

- Discuss the role of operations in the organization.
- Describe the differences between producers of services and producers of goods.
- Explain why the approach to managing operations should grow from the organization's goals.
- Define systems theory and discuss the relationships between operations and the other functional areas in the organization, including marketing and engineering.
- Describe how operations can be divided into several parts or subsystems, including facility layout, scheduling, purchasing, inventory control, and quality management.
- Explain how this framework helps to define the relationships among the subsystems of operations: designing operations, planning operations, and managing and controlling operations.

General Electric: Emphasis on Operations

General Electric is pursuing a path that could lead the company to prominence as a world-class manufacturer. To do this, top management has cut back middle-management staffing levels and sold parts of the organization that did not meet tough productivity, cost, and profit criteria. A GE business unit is expected to be number one or two in profit in its industry.

Top management realizes that an organization like GE is a system of interrelated parts that need to be effectively coordinated and managed to achieve the desired results. When these layers of middle management were eliminated, decision making and responsibility were transferred to the operating divisions. This has promoted a feeling of ownership, inspiring managers to act as entrepreneurs instead of employees. These changes have created an atmosphere in which managers are not fearful of crossing traditional departmental boundaries to solve problems. Marketing managers and operations managers are more likely to work together to solve problems involving product design, scheduling, and quality.

In addition, GE is investing heavily in facilities and equipment to build some of the most productive factories in the United States. With a streamlined organization and efficient operations capable of producing high-quality products to meet changing customer needs, GE can gain an edge on the competition. Early efforts have paid dividends for GE. The first result of the automation effort was the dishwasher facility built in Louisville, Kentucky. GE increased market share by 12 percent by achieving low-cost, high-quality products. GE has moved into the refrigerator market with an innovative compressor that is smaller, takes less space away from storage, and will be cheaper to manufacture. The efficiencies at the compressor plant are such that costs are lower and quality is better than compressors produced by foreign competitors. In 1988, GE nearly doubled its capacity at the refrigerator plant by investing $238 million.

Effective management of operations will allow GE and companies like it to become leaders in today's competitive international markets. They will accomplish this by lowering costs, reducing lead time, improving production quality, and responding to customer requirements with high-quality product designs. Operations can be used to gain an edge on the competition when management understands the importance of operations and is willing to integrate operations with the overall strategy of the organization.

DEFINING OPERATIONS MANAGEMENT

Organizations exist to meet the needs of society that people working alone cannot. Only organizations can produce the tremendous array of products in the vast quantities consumed each day. Operations play a critical role in all organizations. Operations are the means by which organizations in this country produce 10 million cars and light trucks, 1.8 million residences, billions of bank transactions, and many other products each year.

Operations are the processes by which people, capital, and material (inputs) are combined to produce the services and goods consumed by the public (outputs), shown in Exhibit 1.1. Operations employ labor and management (people) and use facilities and equipment (capital) to change materials into finished goods (e.g., farm tractors) or to provide services (e.g., computer software develop-

sum of the individual effects (that is, the whole is greater than the sum of its parts). For example, the feat of putting a man on the moon required a co-operative effort that a part of the team could not have achieved.

2. Flexibility in operations permits rapid and inexpensive response to changing customer demand. Customer satisfaction increases, and delivery lead time is reduced.
3. Improved productivity provides the basis for competing in world markets.
4. High product quality has become necessary in order for firms to remain competitive in today's markets. To remain cost competitive, organizations must find ways to improve product quality without increasing costs. Technological advancements can help firms not only improve quality, but also reduce costs.
5. Computers provide opportunities for improving operations. It is important to integrate computers and operations.

These topics are the key points discussed in the remainder of the chapter. They are also part of the theme of operations for competitive advantage, which is woven throughout this text. These and other important integrative points are highlighted in sections called Integrating the System.

STRATEGIC IMPORTANCE

Strategy begins with the organization's goals and includes the key policies that are established to provide direction for meeting those goals. Operating advantages should be pursued because they fit the organization's goals, not because they fit some narrowly defined operating objective, such as minimizing transportation costs. In fact, minimizing transportation costs may not be in the best interests of an organization if inventory holding or other costs would increase too much, or if product quality or on-time delivery would be negatively affected. Operational goals should be important only when they help the organization reach its objectives.

Importance of Linking Strategy and Operations

Operations can become a positive factor that contributes to organizational success, rather than a negative or neutral factor. To make this happen, facilities equipment, and training should be viewed as a means to achieve organizational rather than operational objectives. Consider the Midas Muffler and the Genoa Motors Operations in Action. These organizations, both involved in car repair, have adopted different strategies and have tailored their operations to fit those strategies.

Steps in Linking Strategy and Operations

How do organizations successfully link organizational and operational goals? Management needs a strategic, top-down view of operations. As indicated in the list on page 33, this begins with analyzing the competitive environment and ends with managing and controlling operations.

Midas Muffler: Linking Strategy and Operations

Midas Muffler is in the automotive repair business. Its strategy is to provide a narrow range of services at low cost. National advertising is used to develop wide geographical coverage. The company is not a full-service repair shop, but concentrates on muffler repair, brakes, and shock absorbers. It is successful because it delivers quality service quickly and at low cost. How are operations important to Midas Muffler?

1. Limited service permits special design of the equipment and the shop so that the employees can be more productive.
2. Limited service requires a limited inventory that allows convenient storage close to the point where materials are needed.
3. Multiple shops and limited service permit careful engineering of the necessary hand tools and the work procedures. These special tools and work procedures make the shop employees more efficient. Midas can apply the same tools and methods to a large number of shops, so that initial engineering costs are easily covered.
4. Because employees have few variations in service, they learn how to do these jobs more quickly.
5. Workers' skill levels and knowledge requirements focus on a limited area of service, so they quickly become experts in a particular area.

Genoa Motors: Linking Strategy and Operations

As part of an automobile dealership, Genoa Motors provides a full line of automobile service. In contrast to Midas Muffler, Genoa Motors' service operations compete without advertising or national appeal; it also has a different operating strategy. As a requirement to maintain the dealership, Genoa Motors must be able to satisfy a variety of customer needs. The dealership does wheel alignments, body repair work, engine overhauls, and other tasks in addition to working on brakes, shocks, and mufflers. How does Genoa Motors design operations to match its objectives?

1. The facility is adaptable to changing needs. For example, on one day a stall may be used to wash a new car, repair a door lock, fix an air conditioning leak, or tune up an engine.
2. Genoa Motors has more tools than a specialist like Midas Muffler does because Genoa Motors does a greater variety of jobs.
3. There is some job specialization. Not everyone will be able to do everything, but employees still need a wide range of skills because Genoa Motors does not have enough of one particular job to allow everyone to specialize. Cross-training is necessary.
4. The workers' skill levels and pay rates are higher than those of workers at Midas Muffler.
5. A significant inventory of many different parts is maintained. These parts are physically separated from the repair stalls and controlled by specialists in parts.

As a result of its strategy, Genoa Motors has higher costs and charges higher prices than Midas Muffler does for comparable work. When your car needs routine exhaust system work, you will most likely take it to a national chain like Midas Muffler. The generalists like Genoa Motors will do the more difficult jobs and warranty work.

Exhibit 1.1 Operations

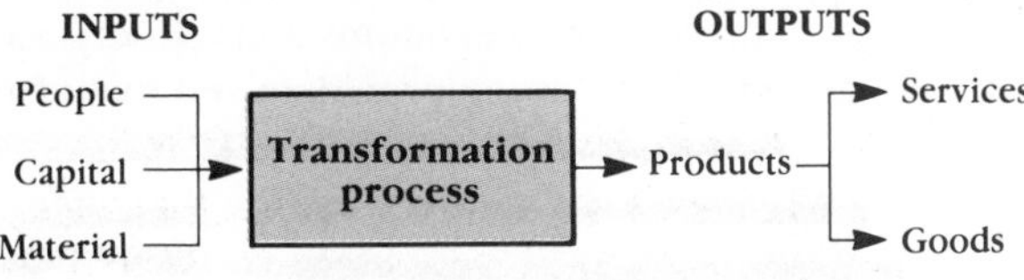

ment). The outputs of the operation should be worth more to the consumer than the total cost of the inputs. In this way, organizations create wealth for society.

Services are intangible products, and **goods** are physical products. According to classification schemes used by the U.S. Departments of Commerce and Labor, the service sector includes transportation, utilities, lodging, entertainment, health care, legal services, education, communications, wholesale and retail trade, banking and finance, public administration, insurance, real estate, and other miscellaneous services. Goods are defined as articles of trade, merchandise, or wares. **Manufacturing** is a specific term referring to the production of goods. Throughout the text, the term **product** is used to refer to services or goods.

Operations are part of both private-sector (profit-driven) and public-sector (not-for-profit) organizations. Exhibit 1.2 lists many different services and goods produced by organizations.

The distinction between services and goods is not as clear as the definitions and examples used in the preceding paragraphs imply. Some operations classified as services actually provide both services and goods. For example, automotive repair services sell and install parts, so customers are purchasing something tangible as well as the labor to install it. At a restaurant, customers purchase not only food, but also food preparation. If we examine the distinctions between services and goods more closely, we discover that the demands for goods and services are interwoven. The purchase of a good contains some measure of service, and the purchase of a service involves the purchase of goods, either directly or indirectly. When a consumer buys a dishwasher, part of the purchase price is

Exhibit 1.2 Examples of Goods and Services Produced by Organizations

Goods		Services	
Profit	**Not-for-Profit**	**Profit**	**Not-for Profit**
Starter motors	Highways	Banking	Police protection
Electronics	Dams	Health care	Health care
Oil refining	Flood control projects	Stock brokerage	Public welfare
Air conditioners	License plates (made in prisons)	Telephone services	Parks and recreation
Appliances		Repair services	Fire protection
Hair driers	Workshops for handicapped	Education	Education
Furniture		Retailing	

used to pay for retail services, external audits of the manufacturer's books by accountants, and consulting services. When consumers pay for a taxi cab or bus ride, part of the money is used to pay for the purchase of vehicles that provide the service. A thriving economy and an increasing standard of living depend on strong and efficient service providers and manufacturers.

Operations management is decision making involving the design, planning, and control of the many factors that affect operations. Decisions include which products to produce, how large a facility to build, how many people to hire, and what methods to use to improve quality. Operations managers apply ideas and knowledge to increase productivity and reduce costs, improve flexibility to meet rapidly changing customer needs, enhance product quality, and improve customer service. An organization that can achieve these advantages through operations will gain a competitive edge.

Operations should be viewed as a part of the total organization, which may also include such departments as accounting, finance, marketing, information systems, engineering, and personnel. When relationships among operations, marketing, and engineering are strong, it is possible to design high-quality products that are well liked by customers and cheaper and easier to produce. Understanding these links between functions in an organization is critical to an employee's advancement beyond an entry-level position. Middle- and upper-level managers have broad responsibilities and a great deal of interaction with other disciplines.

Understanding Operations

Organizations produce and deliver the services and goods demanded by customers. If an organization can produce and deliver high-quality, low-cost products that meet customer needs, and if it can do so in a timely manner, its probability of success is greatly increased. Operations and operations managers play an important role in achieving these objectives, because their effectiveness in organizing, planning, and managing operations shapes the firm's competitiveness. The Operations in Action example at the beginning of the chapter illustrates the importance of operations to General Electric's rise in status to become a world-class manufacturer.

To understand operations and how they can contribute to the success of an organization, it is important to understand (1) the differences and similarities between producing services and producing goods, (2) the value-added nature of operations, (3) the impact that technology can have on performance, (4) the increasing level of international competition, and (5) the importance of teamwork in achieving operating and organizational objectives.

Comparing Goods and Services

Service-producing organizations and goods-producing organizations have many similarities. The Lima Fire Department and Air-Temp Corporation Operations in Action illustrate many of these similarities. Both are concerned with product improvements. For a fire department, product improvements are measured by response time, the quality of its fire prevention program, and the dependability of the service. For Air-Temp, improvements are measured by the power of the air conditioning unit to cool and the unit's special features. Both the Lima Fire

Lima, Ohio, Fire Department: Operating Decisions

A fire department is an excellent example of a service operation. The Lima Fire Department should deliver fast, dependable, high-quality service to customers in a wide area. Its managers should address many questions directly related to operations. What is the maximum time that should elapse between a fire signal and the arrival of the fire equipment? How many fire stations are required? Where should these stations be located to maximize effectiveness? What type of and how much equipment should be purchased? How many firefighters will be required? What should be their qualifications, and how will they be trained?

The answers to these questions shape the service provided and determine the capital required to build facilities, purchase equipment, and train personnel. Operating decisions also determine the costs of providing the service.

Air-Temp Corporation: Operating Decisions

Air-Temp Corporation produces room air conditioners. Developing high-quality, competitively priced products is the result of carefully investigating many related questions. When Air-Temp decided to improve its operations, it considered the following questions: How is the product designed? What are its performance level and special features—thermostat control, multiple-speed blower, and so on? How many air conditioners should be produced? What type of and how much equipment is needed for efficient production? How many employees will be required? What type of training will they need? How many plants will there be, and where will they be located?

Answers to these questions had a significant impact on the company's ability to compete. Changes made resulted in a 10 percent reduction in production costs and improved product quality and reliability. In addition, the product became easier to produce, and planned customer maintenance was reduced by 30 percent. Air-Temp used operations to gain a competitive advantage.

Department and Air-Temp are concerned with their ability to provide products through acquiring equipment, designing facilities, and training employees.

Although operating decisions for services and goods have many similarities, there is one important difference between the two products: a good is tangible, and a service is not. This has two important consequences. First, a service operation cannot inventory finished goods because a service is intangible and is performed on demand. (Most service organizations, however, do have supporting inventory. Hospitals have linens, drugs, and food; banks have forms, ribbons, and other supplies; telephone companies have spare parts and equipment.) Second, because a good is tangible, the product designer must deal with physical characteristics (height, strength, elasticity, durability, etc.).

Some Service Operations Cannot Have Finished Goods Inventory

Not having inventory might seem to be an advantage because inventory is expensive to maintain and time-consuming to manage. But the inability of service organizations to maintain finished goods inventory can be a disadvantage as well. Service organizations cannot separate production from consumption. A customer can buy a car on Saturday, even though the assembly plant is closed, because the dealer can sell one from inventory. But this is not so for services like banking and telephone communications. The telephone company cannot perform services in anticipation of demand because it has no finished goods inventory. Banks cannot perform transactions before a request is made. Customers of service organizations must do without the service or wait until it can be performed.

Banks have reacted by installing computerized tellers to extend service hours and relieve pressure on branch banks. Telephone companies offer discounts on calls made during nonpeak hours. In contrast, Air-Temp can build air conditioners during the slow winter months to offset demand in the spring and summer.

Clearly, then, the planning implications of not having finished goods inventory can be significant. During the morning rush, if seventy people want to ride a public bus with a capacity of fifty, then twenty must wait or be turned away. The possible solution of adding another bus may not be cost-effective because the extra bus will not be heavily used. The consequences of turning customers away are the short-term loss of revenue and the potential long-term loss of customers caused by dissatisfaction with the present service level.

Many bus lines try to relieve the capacity problem by shifting demand to off-peak periods. Senior-citizen discounts are often given during late morning and early afternoon hours. The use of public transportation by high school students is scheduled so it will not conflict with the morning or afternoon demand peaks. Thus, when managers of service operations consider capacity, they should focus on maximum demand, not average demand. They cannot use inventory to smooth peak demand, not even the peaks that occur from hour to hour.

Physical Design Requirement for Goods

As mentioned previously, because goods are tangible and services are not, designing goods requires consideration of physical properties that services simply do not have. Usually, designing goods requires training in engineering because strength, durability, and performance are important. There are also strong implications for marketing in styling and consumer perception of shape and usefulness.

Operations Add Value

Consumers are willing to pay more for an organization's services and goods than the total cost of the inputs. In essence, operations add value to the final product over and above the product's cost. In the private sector, the difference between the price consumers pay and the cost is profit that can be reinvested to build new and better products, thus creating wealth for society.

Without profits, a company cannot raise capital to continue its operations and will eventually become a casualty of competition. With profits, organizations like Allen Bradley and General Electric are able to invest in new technology and new facilities, which lead to improved operations and lower prices. More efficient production of services and goods frees resources (people, capital, and materials) for new product development and innovation. This makes an organization stronger and more competitive.

In the public sector which is not-for-profit, the value added to products represents improved wealth to society. For example, value-added fire protection saves more dollar value (in homes and businesses) than the cost of the service. The wealth created or preserved by such value-added operations contributes to economic growth and makes more resources available for other wealth-creating activities. This ultimately improves our living standard because more wealth is preserved than consumed.

Technology and Operations

Technology is the application of knowledge—usually in the form of recently developed tools, processes, and procedures—to solve problems. Advances in technology make it possible to build better products using fewer resources. The change from the mechanical typewriter to the electronic typewriter is one example of using technology to improve product design. **Product design** is the determination of the characteristics, features, and performance of the product. (**Product technology** is the application of knowledge to improve the product. As product technology improves, the product also improves.) Changes in typewriter technology from the 1900s to the present are illustrated by the following example.

Technology of the Typewriter

Product Technology	Period of Dominant Use	Cost	Significant Features
Mechanical	1900–1950	$150	Manual carriage return, limited features
Electric power assist (IBM Selectric III)	1950–1980	$995	Electric carriage return, easy correction, many type styles, easy-to-set margins
Electronic (IBM Wheelwriter)	1980–	$795	Microprocessor for memory, programmable, spell checking

Today's electronic typewriter is much different from its purely mechanical predecessor. Although it has many more features, it has fewer moving parts and is simpler to assemble. As electronic typewriters become more popular, the unit price will continue to decline. For example, the electric motor and the print mechanism will cost less as production volume increases. Labor costs will be reduced as new methods of assembly are developed. These method improvements are called process improvements. **Process** refers to how the product is made, and **process technology** is the application of knowledge to improve process. Improvements in process permit the same product to be made using fewer resources. As we approach the twenty-first century, microcomputers and inexpensive laser printers may greatly reduce the demand for electronic typewriters.

Technology can often be applied to problems outside of product and process design. For example, research that produced the computer chip has had a revolutionary impact on organizations. Computers and information systems have the potential to improve decision making significantly. Allen Bradley uses microcomputer chips to allow its automated assembly operation to recognize and respond to 125 product variations, and many routine operating decisions are made by computer.

An organization can gain a competitive edge by managing more information with less people. Newspaper publishers now use computer-based information systems to manage the tremendous amount of information that goes into the paper each day. Think for a moment about the effort required to organize and produce just the classified section of your daily newspaper. Without computer-based word processing and typesetting, this would require many more hours of effort.

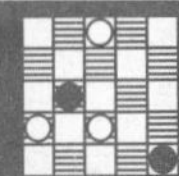

GAINING STRATEGIC ADVANTAGE AT ALLEN BRADLEY

Using Automated Assembly Lines to Increase Market Share

"A computer integrated manufacturing facility was necessary to allow us to sell world-class products anywhere in the world and still make a profit." These are the words of J. Tracy O'Rourke, president and chief executive officer at Allen Bradley. Allen Bradley is using one of the world's smartest automated assembly lines to capture a bigger share of the international market for contactors and relays used in electric starter motors for cars and trucks. Its totally automated facility cost $15 million, and the new assembly lines have reduced production costs by 35 percent. Allen Bradley believes it is the lowest-cost producer of contactors in the world. This is an important strategic advantage in an expanding international marketplace.

A contact insertion machine automatically places lower contact and pressure plates in the correct configuration on relays and contactors made in the World Contactor Assembly facility. *Courtesy: Allen Bradley.*

Allen Bradley's Milwaukee complex has been producing motor contactors and control relays for the world market in a fully automated facility. These contactors and relays can be made in 125 variations and in lot sizes as small as one. The only human intervention in the production line is provided by six attendants who stand by to solve problems; they are rarely needed. This automation effort is an alternative to locating the facility in a foreign country where labor costs are lower.

Allen Bradley elected to automate because management saw two important strategic advantages. First, their market research indicated that a global market was emerging. To stay competitive, they had to offer attractively priced world-class products. In addition, their strategic directions were changing. Among their five-year goals were objectives to increase market share and develop high-quality products. Second, as a major player in automated machine tool controls, they had the productivity concept and the automation control technology necessary to make a fully automated factory a reality, but they did not have a working model. The development of this automated factory has become an important tool for marketing their technology to other companies.

The new facility has allowed Allen Bradley to take orders away from competitors because of lower cost, improved quality, and the ability to meet changing customer needs. Allen Bradley capitalized on the opportunity to start a new facility by designing the product and process in tandem. The employees label each product at the outset with a computer bar code, allowing them to program the assembly line to vary product specifications. (The uniform product codes found on most items in supermarkets are another example of bar codes.) As a result, contactors and relays can be tailored without slowing the line. This imaginative approach enabled Allen Bradley to increase market share.

International Trade and Competition

A country that wants to enhance the living standard of its people will engage in international trade. The country will import those goods and services that are not available locally, or that cost more to make at home than their foreign-made counterparts. Even when a country is the most efficient producer of all goods and services, it can be demonstrated that the country would be better off engaging in international trade. The reason the country should trade is that its relative advantage in one product—for example, pitchforks—would be greater than its relative advantage in another product—say, furniture. **Relative advantage** is defined as the difference between the lowest-cost producer and the next-lowest-cost producer. The country with the pitchfork production advantage should produce pitchforks for the international market and may import to meet all or some of its furniture needs.

As barriers to trade such as import quotas and tariffs decline and countries better understand the benefits of international trade, the level of trade between nations will continue to climb. Recently, international trade in goods and services reported by governments outpaced growth in the world's total production. This means that the percentage of world production moving between nations is increasing. This does not include products made for domestic consumption by firms that are foreign owned.

This increase in trade has resulted in increased international competition, and the effects of this competition can be seen in nearly every industry. Markets for many items, such as those produced by the electronics, steel, automotive, textile, and photographic equipment industries, are world markets dominated by multinational firms. In order for firms to compete, they must be among the best in the world, not simply the best in the nation. These firms must compete with firms from other countries where the labor costs, material costs, material availability, culture, and sociopolitical environment are substantially different. These differences makes a manager's job more difficult. For example, when Ford Motor Company's primary competitors were General Motors and Chrysler, Ford had the same work force and labor cost per hour, virtually the same material costs, and the same set of government regulations as its national competitors. In many cases, these national firms traded executives back and forth so these organizations had similar ideas and approaches to management. Now, Ford faces foreign competitors that have substantially different cost factors and management styles.

Organizations that will be successful in the nineties and into the twenty-first century will develop an understanding of marketing, distribution systems, financial and capital markets, accounting, and operations that is global rather than national. International competition has had and will continue to have a tremendous impact on operations and operations managers. Product performance, product quality, efficiency, and delivery lead time are all elements of competition affected by operations. The impact of international competition on operations is discussed throughout the text.

Operations and Teamwork

Well-managed, teamwork-oriented operations provide services and goods of high quality at prices that consumers can afford. This is good for the organization, labor, consumers, and management.

1. For the organization, the ability to meet the increasing demand for high-quality, low-cost products can lead to greater success in competitive world markets.
2. For labor, well-managed operations provide continuing job opportunities. An inefficient operation drives prices up and makes the service or good subject to competitive pressure from efficient producers, both foreign and domestic. Increases in efficiency allow noninflationary increases in wages, which give labor increased purchasing power.
3. For consumers, a lower price means that more people will be able to buy the product. In addition, consumers will have money left for other purchases.
4. For management, lower production costs can lead to increased sales and higher profit.

UNDERSTANDING THE SYSTEMS APPROACH TO OPERATIONS

Operations management is only one part of the organization, which in turn is a part of the larger economic and government system.

A **system** is a group of items, events, or actions in which no item, event, or action occurs independently. Thus, no item studied in isolation will act in the same way as it would in the system. For example, a study that focuses on minimizing transportation costs might suggest that materials be ordered in larger quantities to reduce the number of trips and save transportation costs. However, larger shipments will require more storage capacity, and the increase in storage costs could be greater than the decrease in transportation costs. When making decisions, a manager should consider these important relationships.

In a system, all items, events, or actions are somehow related. A system can be divided into a series of parts or subsystems, and any system is a part of a larger system. Understanding the relationship among the various subsystems is an integral part of the study of operations management. We will examine relationships between the organization and its environment, relationships between operations and the rest of the organization, and relationships within operations.

Exhibit 1.3 illustrates that an organization is part of the total economic and government system. In turn, the organization is composed of several subsystems, one of which is operations. Operations managers work with managers in marketing, finance, accounting, engineering, and other areas to reach the goals set by top management.

Finally, the operations subsystem is itself divided into a series of subsystems because of the many functions it encompasses. When studying the operations management subsystem, it is important to keep in mind the larger picture of operations, the organization, and the external environment. The systems approach is a central theme that is reinforced at other points in the text.

In order to effectively design, plan, and manage and control operations, managers should be aware that:

1. An organization is part of the total economic and government system.
2. Operations are an integral part of the organization.
3. Operations are composed of a series of related subsystems.

Exhibit 1.3 A Systems View of Operations, the Organization, and the Organization's Environment

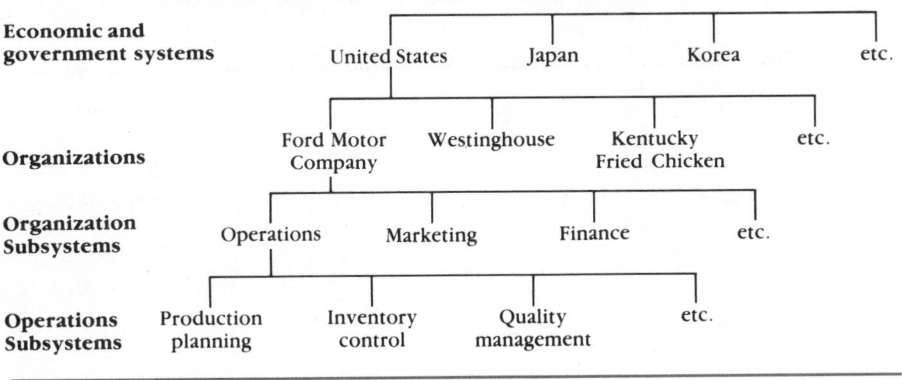

The remainder of this chapter focuses on these three levels in a systems view of operations. It is important to understand the impact that decisions made by operations managers can have on the other parts of the organization and on overall organizational performance.

The Organization as Part of the Economic and Government System

Organizations operate in an environment that includes several interest groups—stockholders, management, labor, consumers, and the general public. Business leaders have realized that to achieve long-term success and to be good corporate neighbors, they should serve all of these interests. Thus, they should be responsive to issues involving wage rates, working conditions, pollution, product safety, and international competition, in addition to the stockholders' return on investment. All of these factors are part of the larger economic and government system within which organizations operate.

The importances of these broader issues becomes clear as the following factors are discussed.

Factor	Interest Group	Impact of Operations Decisions
Wage rates and working conditions	Labor and middle management	Good working conditions and fair wages can be positive factors in employee performance.
Pollution	General public	Well-managed operations should not cause pollution.
Product safety	Consumers	When products are well designed, consumers are safer and more satisfied.
International competition	Stockholders, labor, and middle management	When operations are well managed, costs are not excessive. This, coupled with high quality, discourages foreign competitors.

History provides interesting insights into the impact of operating decisions on a business's external environment.

OPERATIONS IN ACTION

Owens-Illinois, Inc.: Understanding the System

Owens-Illinois, Inc. (OI), produces glass containers for the beverage industry in plants throughout the United States. When decisions are made, OI should consider customer needs and environmental concerns, as well as internal operating issues.

Response to Customer Needs

1. Beverage bottlers, such as Coca-Cola and Miller Brewing Co., want low-cost packaging because the bottle can cost as much as the beverage. High-priced bottles significantly reduce profits.
2. Bottlers want dependable and frequent delivery. They need dependable delivery because they do not want to stop the filling line. They need frequent deliveries because neither OI nor the bottler wants too many bottles in inventory; bottles take a large amount of space and are easily broken.
3. The bottles should be of high quality. If bottles break in the filling lines, the filling process slows, reducing capacity and increasing costs.

Response to Environmental Concerns

1. Development work on a container made of glass and plastic required close cooperation with the Environmental Protection Agency. OI's efforts focused on convincing the agency that the container did not pose additional threats to the environment.
2. The introduction of the all-plastic bottle required working with government agencies to ensure that no health problems would result.
3. As recycling glass and plastic became a concern, OI developed recycling programs and supported recycling stations. This experience became important when some states began requiring deposits on nonrefillable bottles.

Approach to Problem Solving

OI makes a strong effort to develop products of superior quality and low cost and to provide dependable delivery systems. Thus, it has formed teams made up of engineers, marketing managers, and operations managers to solve customer problems. A team's first charge is to solve immediate customer complaints. However, it is not satisfactory to simply send more bottles to replace defective ones. The team must find the cause of the problem and solve it at the source. OI makes a strong effort to understand problems at a system level and to use teamwork to increase success in problem solving.

Labor Relations

As late as the 1930s in the United States, many developing businesses required their production employees to work long hours for low pay. These businesses wanted to keep costs low and to increase their return on investment. In addition, many plants had poor or unsafe working conditions. In many cases, workers rebelled against management. They fought hard and often engaged in battles with management for better pay, better working conditions, and the right to form unions. Eventually labor was able to unionize because the federal government passed laws in the late 1930s that permitted and protected unions. From these conflicts, labor unions and businesses developed an adversarial relationship that exists today.

Both groups need to learn that their security lies in cooperative efforts, primarily in the effort to make better-quality products with better performance at a lower unit cost. Such quality and productivity improvements will help secure jobs in the United States and make our products competitive in world markets. Business leaders therefore need to focus on long-term consequences of operating decisions, not simply on short-term cost savings.

Environmental Impact

In the 1920s and 1930s, many business leaders did not consider pollution a problem because few people fully understood its consequences. Waste from operations was something to dispose of at the least cost. When pollution problems began to surface in the 1950s and 1960s, some businesses were reluctant to change their position. As a result, businesses in this country operate under one of the most restrictive sets of environmental pollution laws and reporting procedures in the world.

Product Safety

Because product design and manufacturing are part of operations, operations management decisions clearly play a significant role in determining product

OPERATIONS IN ACTION

The Steel Industry and the Paper Industry: Two Approaches to Environmental Protection

The steel industry, which has long fought pollution control, now faces laws with tougher standards than might have existed with voluntary compliance. More important, the industry has had to add equipment to control emission to existing plants. "Adding on"—as opposed to "designing in"—results in greater operating and investment costs. The steel industry still faces substantial investments to meet new, tougher standards.

In contrast, the paper industry has taken a positive stance toward pollution control. It has actively pursued programs to reduce emissions from its operations for more than thirty years, and these programs have consistently surpassed the legislative requirements for emissions. The industry accomplished this by a consistent management policy to eliminate pollution at the source. How has the paper industry benefited? First, it has created a positive working relationship with government agencies. Second, new plant construction has included designed-in pollution control as part of the system, rather than as an add-on. As a result, plants operate more efficiently. Third, some of the pollution control programs have paid a full or partial return on their investment by recovering and recycling valuable resources from waste water.

It is clear that the steel industry and the paper industry represent two different approaches to the problem of pollution control. The paper industry in this country is strong and competitive and is not threatened by foreign competition. The steel industry is suffering seriously from the import of low-cost foreign steel. Part of the cost disadvantage for domestic steel can be traced to expensive retrofitting of existing production facilities with pollution control devices. These retrofitted devices add more to the operating cost than devices that are built into the system design do. Also, the unplanned investment in these devices took capital away from other projects that could have improved productivity.

safety. Companies such as Kodak, General Electric, Black and Decker, and Procter and Gamble owe their excellent reputations partly to their concern for product safety. These companies realize that high product quality and safety are compatible with high profits and long-term success.

If foreign and domestic competition is not sufficient to keep out unsafe products, then consumer groups and legislative action will. The past twenty years have seen the rising power of consumer advocates and efforts to protect consumer interests, evaluate products, and educate consumers.

Product Quality and International Competition

In the early 1960s, the product label "Made in Japan" was a synonym for low quality. Today, it means top quality and low price. The Japanese have gained market shares in steel, automobiles, electronics, and other industries by showing domestic firms that high quality and low cost actually go together. Recently, other countries along the Asian rim, including South Korea and Taiwan, have followed the lead of the Japanese and are aggressively increasing exports.

How did certain industries get into an unfavorable competitive position while others did not? The answer is complex, but it can be partially understood by reviewing our earlier points on labor relations, the environment, and the customer. Some organizations have attempted to maximize short-term earnings per share to the stockholder by minimizing costs. These actions have separated management from labor, the consumer, and the general public.

In the longer term, such actions alienated these interest groups and forced them to take action. The actions, often legislative, helped to create an environment that is not conducive to competition in today's world markets. Eventually this environment forced costs up and made some industries vulnerable to foreign competition. In the authors' view, one reason that foreign competition has not hurt industries like paper and oil is that these industries have a balanced view, focusing on both long-term objectives and short-term performance.

A solution to the problem of world competition is difficult and will require significant time to implement. To meet this challenge, management should consider labor, the general public, and the consumer in decision making. Labor and management must work together to build better facilities and better products and to improve productivity. Organizations should use each employee's full range of physical and mental skills. The cooperation and mutual respect between labor and management will be a positive factor in improving operations and building better working relationships.

Operations as Part of the Organization

Exhibit 1.3 illustrated that although an organization is part of the larger economic and government system, it is also a system containing such subsystems as marketing, finance, accounting, personnel, and engineering, in addition to operations. These subsystems, often called **functional areas,** should be linked by common organizational goals and a means of communicating these goals. These common goals are part of an organization's strategy. **Strategy** consists of the organizational goals and the methods for implementing the goals, called **key policies.** Strategy defines how the organization chooses to compete within the framework dictated by the external environment. The usual means of implementing and communicating strategy is the budgeting and planning process which most organizations go through annually.

Strategy

Operations should be linked to the organization by developing operating strategies consistent with the organization's overall strategy. Links between operations and the rest of the organization can be built into the planning process. A **plan** is a list of actions that management expects to take. A plan is a basis for allocating the organization's resources to deal with opportunities and problems present in the environment. Resources allocated by operations managers should help the organization achieve its goals.

The links between strategy and operations can be illustrated by comparing a fast-food restaurant with a four-star restaurant. Customers expect fast-food restaurants to deliver good-quality food at a low price, with a wait of only a few minutes. This implies a limited menu, some advance preparation, and a service operation with a smooth and simple means of communicating orders and delivering food. The training of counter workers and cooks should emphasize speed, efficient movement, and uniform performance of duties.

Compare these requirements with those of a four-star restaurant with a heavy tourist trade. Here, customers expect food of exceptional quality and variety; fine wine, imported beer, and the best liquor; high prices; and a leisurely dinner. This implies a wide selection on the menu, comfortable and pleasant surroundings, entertainment, and little or no advance food preparation. All operations, from training cooks to food procurement, are different from those in a fast-food restaurant. Four-star restaurants do not have counter help. The emphasis is on service to the individual customer rather than on uniformity and quick response.

This comparison illustrates two different approaches to operating a restaurant successfully. Success in a fast-food restaurant is based on providing quality products at low prices and maintaining high customer volume. Success in a four-star restaurant is based on providing entertainment and atmosphere, as well as quality food. The allocation of resources in the design and planning of these restaurants should reflect the differences.

Structure

The development of strategy leads to the question of organizational structure. **Organizational structure** is the formal relationship between different functions or subsystems. The marketing function is responsible for investigating demand for services and goods and for establishing a distribution chain that delivers these products to customers. The operations function is responsible for producing these services and goods. The operations manager's role is essential because without product (output) the organization has no means of achieving its purpose.

Understanding the Operations and Marketing Interface. Exhibit 1.4 illustrates the operations and marketing interface. Let us begin with **market re-**

Exhibit 1.4 The Operations and Marketing Interface

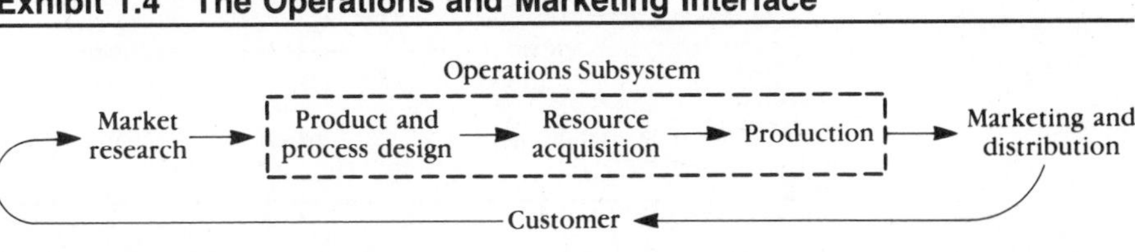

search, which is an effort to measure customers' needs and preferences. The goals of market research are to determine new markets for existing products and to discover demand for new products. Market research leads to product designs that can satisfy consumers' needs at a reasonable cost and a high level of quality.

As the product is being designed, the process for making the product should also be designed. Process design is concerned with how the services or goods are actually produced. For example, if a teacher requires a "typed" term paper, either a conventional typewriter or a computer-based word processing system can be used. Each approach requires different methods and equipment (a different process), but each delivers a document that meets the specification (a "typed" term paper).

After the process has been designed, it is necessary to acquire resources—material, trained people, and equipment. The production of the product includes concern for quality, cost, and on-time completion. Finally, marketing and distribution of the product take place. At this point, the customer's reaction to the product is measured, and another round of market research to monitor changing needs should occur.

Exhibit 1.5 illustrates how decisions in operations can affect marketing. Product cost must be covered by the market price with enough left over to cover overhead, administrative, and selling expenses, and to provide the organization's profit. Effective scheduling helps the organization to make timely delivery. Flexibility permits operations to deliver specially designed products at low cost, making marketing's job easier. High-quality products pay dividends in repeat sales and new customers.

Exhibit 1.5 Marketing and Operations Are Important Subsystems in an Organization

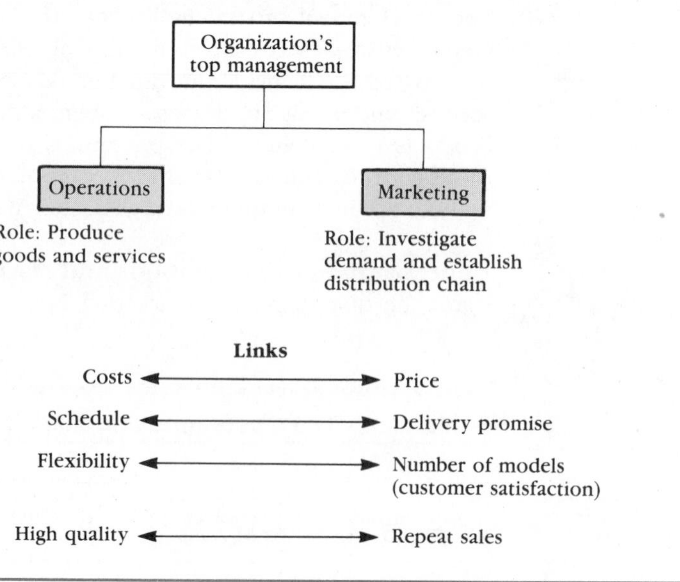

Organization Chart: Line and Staff Relationships. Operations and marketing are line functions within the organization. **Line functions** transfer authority and decision-making responsibility from top management to the level of plant supervisor in operations and the salesperson in marketing. The organizational subsystems of finance, accounting, computers and information systems, and engineering are **staff functions,** and they assist operations and marketing from product development through product distribution. When the staff functions are added to the line functions of marketing and operations, the organization's structure may take the shape shown in Exhibit 1.6.

Communications

An organization should have (1) a strategy (goals and methods for attaining them), (2) key policies (broad guidelines as to how the objectives might be achieved), and (3) a structure (a logical way to organize its resources). To be effective, an organization must develop a means of communicating its strategic direction and key policies to all areas or subsystems of the organization.

In a one-person firm, communication is obviously not a problem. Even in a small business, face-to-face meetings among all personnel can be held regularly to discuss important ideas and establish policies and procedures. However, communication problems become significant in large organizations, where communications among the parts must be formally maintained. Such companies as General Electric, Champion International, and Ford have thousands of employees. As a result, they have developed formal procedures to communicate within the organization.

How do these companies communicate with and coordinate the different functional areas in business? How can a manager in a plant in Atlanta, Georgia, work toward the same goals as a marketing representative in Denver, Colorado? To do this, the goals and objectives are formulated by top management and flow down from the top of the organization. This is illustrated by the colored arrows

Exhibit 1.6 The Business System

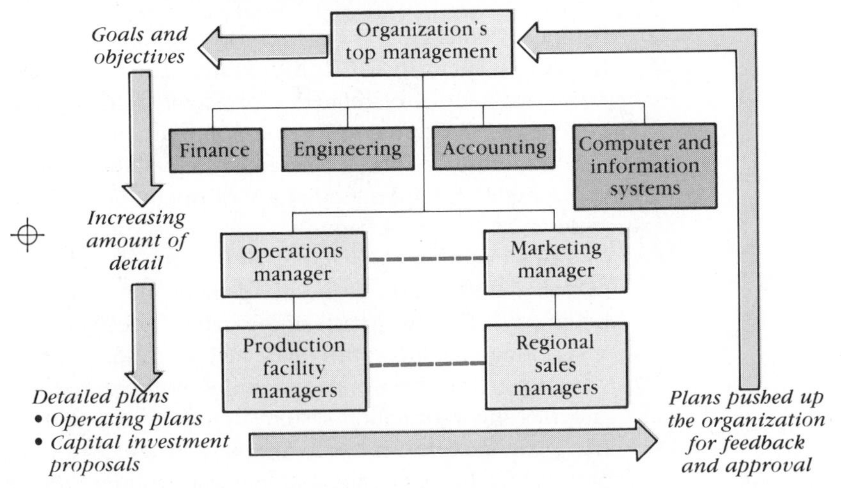

shown in Exhibit 1.6. The information flow represented by the arrows passes through each level of the organization, down to the facility manager.

The goals and objectives formulated by top management are usually general statements. Line functions, operations, and marketing implement these general statements by preparing production and sales goals for products. Operations and marketing managers work from the same general statements. Operations and marketing must work across functions (i.e., develop lateral relations, shown as dashed lines in Exhibit 1.6) to ensure that production plans are consistent with present market conditions. It would be unreasonable to prepare a plan that could not be supported by market demand, or that had sales of 50,000 units when operations can produce only 5,000 units.

Exhibit 1.6 shows the operations manager passing these plans along to the facility managers, who prepare detailed plans for each facility or plant. Part of the product plan is called an **operating budget.** It includes estimates of the costs of the material, labor, and other facilities necessary to meet the forecasted production goal.

Facility managers may request capital improvements. A **capital budget** is the organization's plan for spending money to improve facilities. These improvements are justified by returns to the organization, including increases in output, lower costs, and improvements in quality. These capital improvement requests become part of the capital budget, which includes items that have an impact on the organization that exceeds one year. For example, adding another assembly line to increase dishwasher production or replacing equipment that will improve product quality would be part of a capital budget.

After they are prepared, operating and capital budgets are passed to higher levels in the organization, as shown in Exhibit 1.6. The plans are coordinated and evaluated at each level, with feedback to the facility manager. The plans may have to be reformulated before tentative approval is given and before the plans are given to top management for final approval. This planning and budgeting process occurs annually and is a typical method of coordination and communication in many organizations.

Operations as a Series of Related Subsystems

Earlier sections have described the relationships between the organization and the environment in which it operates. These sections also described an organization as a series of related subsystems, with operations as one of those subsystems. As illustrated in Exhibit 1.3, operations, in turn, can be subdivided into different parts or subsystems, including quality management, inventory control, and scheduling. A detailed study of operations requires that each of these subsystems be treated separately.

To facilitate understanding of the subsystems, and to make the relationships between these parts clear, we provide the overview of operations shown in Exhibit 1.7. The three parts of the exhibit (designing, planning, and managing and controlling) comprise the three major sections of the text.

Designing the system includes all the decisions necessary to establish the facilities and information systems required to produce the service or good. **Planning the system** relates to the way in which the organization expects to use physical facilities, people, and materials to meet the estimated demand. **Manag-**

Exhibit 1.7 Overview of the Systems Approach to Operations

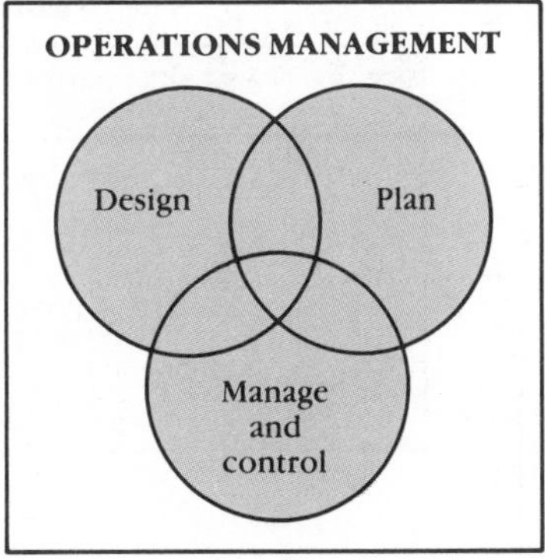

ing and controlling the system includes executing production plans and measuring, evaluating, and providing feedback on performance.

Each part of this overview can be discussed by dividing it into the series of related topics shown in the detailed framework in Exhibit 1.8. The topics in this framework correspond to the chapters within each major part of the text. Following is a summary of the topics covered in the text.

Designing the System

As shown in Exhibit 1.8, good/service design, the first step in systems design, is the determination of the characteristics and features of the product. It includes the preparation of plans and specifications for building the good or providing the service. Products should be designed to deliver high-quality performance. Efforts to reduce costs should be based on the cost over the life of the product, including original purchase price, maintenance costs, operating expense, and downtime for unplanned repairs. This concept, called **life cycle costing,** is important to the organization's customers. Product development is discussed in Chapter 4.

Product design has a direct impact on both system capacity and process design. **Capacity** is the maximum number of units that can be produced in a given time period. Process design determines how the product will be produced. Capacity decisions are covered in Chapter 5, and process selection is discussed in Chapter 7.

Selecting the location of a facility is part of system design. In some organizations, especially service industries, marketing and distribution issues override operating decisions. In these cases, facilities are numerous and are usually located close to markets. Restaurants, banks, and retail stores are good examples. In other cases, operating questions are more critical. Hospitals, oil refineries, and appliance manufacturers have a limited number of facilities because construction and operating costs override market convenience. Facility location is discussed in Chapter 6.

Facility layout is the physical relationship of machines and departments. Material flow, inventory, and the use of people in the facility are coordinated with

Exhibit 1.9 **Framework for Operations Management**

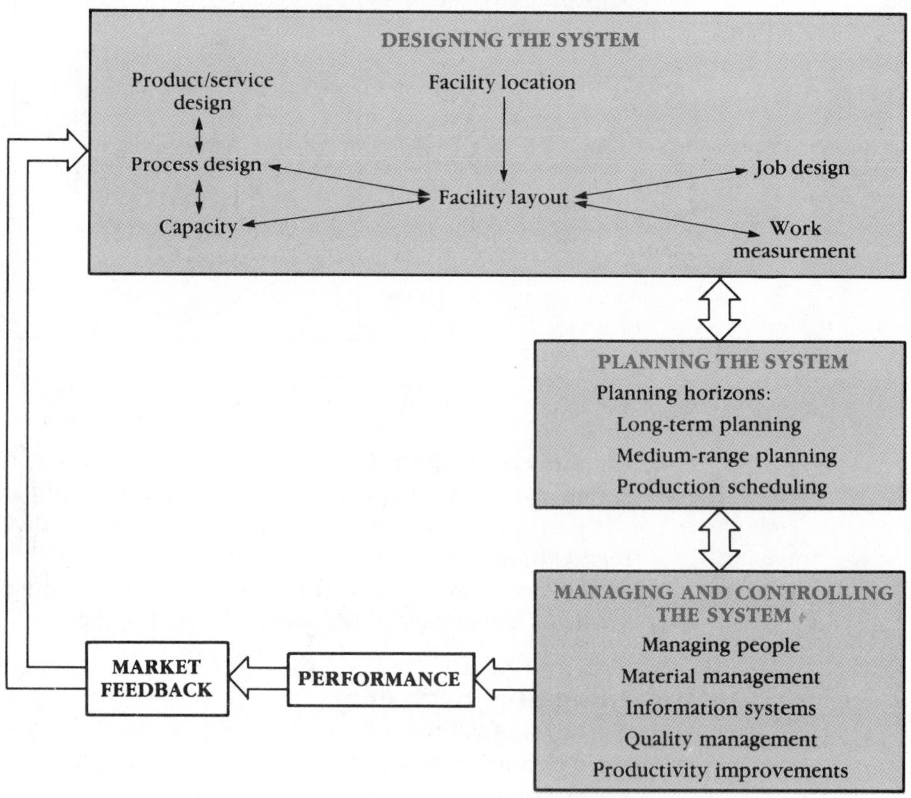

the equipment to provide an effective and efficient layout. Facility layout is discussed in Chapter 8. The details of the facility design include describing individual jobs to be performed and determining operating standards to measure performance. These job design and work measurement issues are important in both service and manufacturing organizations. They are discussed in Chapter 9.

Designing the production system requires a careful look at the information requirements for managing operations. Providing this information should be an integral part of the production system. For example, does the organization need computer technology in designing products or processes? How will maintenance be tracked? How detailed should the information be, and how will the reports be organized? What cost data will be collected? These are only a few of the questions that should be addressed if the system design is to integrate information effectively.

Planning the System

The next major portion of Exhibit 1.8 is planning. Planning operations involve considering how present facilities can be used to meet customer demand in order to satisfy organizational goals. This may lead back to the design phase because existing facilities may require changes to become more effective. This presents a fundamental problem for planners because a firm's productive assets are fixed and are not easily or cheaply changed. On the other hand, demand changes continually and is difficult to forecast. Thus, the problem is how to satisfy changing demand with fixed production resources. Two solutions are

1. Building flexibility into the facilities so that changes can be made easily.
2. Examining facilities to find ways to modify them easily.

What horizon or length of time should a plan cover? Because planning and system design are strongly linked, planning for operations should consider a horizon that is at least as distant as the time required to replace the firm's assets. Otherwise, even an organization with a perfect forecast would not have sufficient lead time to react to market, technological, and environmental changes. How far into the future should an organization plan? The answer is a function of the industry in which it competes.

Although the phases of planning are somewhat arbitrary, long-range planning, middle-range planning, and production scheduling are commonly used. Generally, **long-range production planning** involves examination of the organization's ability to adapt to change. In this phase of planning, all aspects of the firm's production capabilities are candidates for revision. The framework for transforming strategic plans into business and operating plans is discussed in Chapter 10.

Medium-range planning involves a shorter time period than long-range planning. It is usually limited to making minor changes in the facilities and equipment used to produce the services and goods. Changes can be made to improve productivity, enhance quality, or incrementally increase capacity. Medium-range planning focuses on resource planning and allocation. Manufacturing resource planning and material requirement planning are discussed in Chapter 11. Chapter 12 describes just-in-time.

In **production scheduling,** even more severe limits are placed on changing the production system because the plan (schedule) may be executed in only a

OPERATIONS IN ACTION

Toledo Edison: Planning Horizon

Toledo Edison generates electricity for commercial and residential customers. The company should prepare production plans that have a fifteen- to twenty-year time horizon because construction of new facilities to generate electricity can take ten to fifteen years. A shorter time horizon could put Toledo Edison in a position of not having sufficient capacity to meet its customer needs.

Suppose Toledo Edison uses only a five-year horizon for planning production and therefore only estimates demand for five years in the future. If the company discovers that demand will exceed its capacity at the end of five years, then the company will not have sufficient time to build new capacity.

In other industries, the time required to build new facilities may be only one or two years. In these cases, a production planning horizon of four or five years may be satisfactory.

few days or a few hours. The purpose of production scheduling is to coordinate people, material, and equipment to produce the services and goods demanded. Production scheduling is discussed in Chapter 13. Project management is discussed in Chapter 14.

Managing and Controlling Operations

After a system is designed and planned, it can produce services and goods. Thus, the next area illustrated in Exhibit 1.8 is managing and controlling the system. Plans and schedules should be communicated within the organization and the results of production measured so that results tie back to the plan for operations and ultimately to the organization's goals.

In some organizations, more than 50 percent of the finished product cost is material. Material management and inventory control deserve special attention because of the tremendous impact they can have on organizational performance. Chapter 15 discusses material management issues, including purchasing, material flow in the facility, warehousing, and distribution. Chapter 16 discusses lot-sizing models and inventory control.

Quality management, which is discussed in Chapter 17, has become a key factor in today's international marketplace. High quality is essential to maintain competitiveness. Managing and controlling operations includes managing human resources effectively. People *are* the organization. Without people, an organization ceases to exist. Human resource topics are discussed in Chapter 18.

To manage operations, information systems should provide timely data for decision making. Performance and cost data, the monitoring of material flows, and information links to other subsystems in the organization are described in Chapter 19.

Finally, Exhibit 1.8 illustrates that the true test of an organization's success in operations is determined in the marketplace. Feedback can be gathered from customers and used to improve product and process designs, production planning and scheduling practices, quality management systems, and other vital areas within operations and the organization.

SUMMARY

- Operations are the processes by which people, capital, and material are combined to produce the services and goods consumed by the public.
- Products should be value added; that is, the services and goods are worth more to the customer than the cost of the inputs.
- Operations can be designed and used in a manner to gain competitive advantage.
- A system is a group of items, events, or actions in which no item, event, or action occurs independently. The systems approach is a central theme that runs through the text.
- The organization must compete within the constraints presented by its external environment. These constraints include competitors, economic conditions, and government regulation.
- Successful operations management requires teamwork between operations

and other functional areas (subsystems) within an organization. These areas include marketing, finance, accounting, engineering, and information systems.

- Operations are composed of many parts or subsystems, which should be effectively coordinated to build the organization's competitive position. This includes responsibility for material procurement, quality, production planning, and facility layout.

CAREER PROFILE

Ken Wallers

Plant Manager
Sheller-Globe Corp.

Ken Wallers manages a plant that produces parts for office equipment. He is responsible for plotting the future direction of the plant and achieving a top performance rating. Top management evaluates his performance based on product quality, delivery lead time to the customer, and costs. Wallers is responsible for preparing a detailed operating budget for the next year, as well as for preparing capital requests for the next several years. To gain approval for the capital request, Wallers must convince his boss that his requests will help the organization reach its goals.

In addition to operating responsibility, Wallers works with government regulators from the Environmental Protection Agency on plant emissions and from the Occupational Safety and Health Administration (OSHA) on plant safety. He meets with the village council to request a change in zoning and with a local group that would like the corporation to donate funds to improve the county library system.

Work Experience and Opportunities

Before he was appointed plant manager, Wallers worked as a first-shift supervisor responsible for the performance of the stamping department. He also spent time in plant scheduling and as material manager. He was assigned to corporate staff for two years as a financial analyst. There, his responsibilities included preliminary analysis of plant managers' requests for capital. A likely promotion for Wallers would be to division operations manager. In this position, he would have several plants reporting to him. Beyond that lies the vice-presidency of operations and other high-level corporate assignments.

QUESTIONS

1. What is the role of operations in the organization?

2. What does value-added operations mean? How would it apply to not-for-profit organizations?

3. Explain the major differences between producers of services and producers of goods? How do these differences affect operations?

4. Agree or disagree with this statement and support your position: Operations management issues and problems should be narrowly focused on for-profit producers of goods, such as General Motors, Westinghouse, and General Electric.

5. What impact has international competition had on operations?

6. What is meant by the systems approach to operations?

7. Why should an organization have a strategy? How is the strategy communicated within the rest of the organization?

8. What is the basic framework for operations management presented in this chapter?

9. What are the issues in designing a production system? Give a brief description of each.

10. What are the issues in planning a production system? Give a brief description of each.

11. What are the issues in managing and controlling a production system? Give a brief description of each.

12. Find an article about labor relations. Summarize the article in one paragraph. In a second paragraph, describe how the findings in the article affect operations. Provide the article reference or a copy of the article.

13. Find an article that discusses environmental problems. Summarize the article in one paragraph. In a second paragraph, describe how the findings in the article affect operations. Provide the article reference or a copy of the article.

14. Find an article that discusses product safety. Summarize the article in one paragraph. In a second paragraph, describe how the findings in the article affect operations. Provide the article reference or a copy of the article.

15. Find an article that discusses product quality. Summarize the article in one paragraph. In a second paragraph, describe how the findings in the article affect operations. Provide the article reference or a copy of the article.

16. Find an article that discusses international competition. Summarize the article in one paragraph. In a second paragraph, describe how the findings in the article impact operations. Provide the article reference or a copy of the article.

MINI-CASES

Our Lady of Lourdes Hospital

As a management trainee for a large consulting firm, you are part of a team that has been assigned to study operations at Our Lady of Lourdes Hospital (OLL). Recently, OLL was purchased by a for-profit health care provider. The team is to report on operations and to make recommendations to enhance revenues and reduce expenses.

Before it was sold, OLL had begun many of the outreach programs that are common today in health care. An alcohol and drug rehabilitation center, a women's center, and a sleep therapy center already exist, but all have lost money.

Following are summaries of key points from interviews the team had with the directors of marketing, operations, and medicine.

Director of Marketing:

1. A major problem has been the lack of a budget for advertising these centers. These projects need large sums of up-front money for advertising and promotion.

2. We are having trouble getting the kind of cooperation necessary to make these programs work. Things from meal preparation to cleaning and maintenance have not been done well. Medical problems at these centers are given a lower priority by the medical staff because the patients "aren't really sick."

3. What we need is time to work the kinks out of these programs.

Director of Operations:

1. I don't have any problems that could not be solved if I had an unlimited supply of money. Major renovation efforts are needed to improve food preparation areas, the laundry, and the heating system. These three improvements could probably save enough to cover OLL's annual deficit.

2. If these problems aren't bad enough, my people are saddled with several new responsibilities. These new centers require more work than the administrators think. Sufficient operating funds were not allocated to cover the expenses. Several of the centers are off the main site, making it difficult for my supervisors to do a proper job.

3. In my opinion, these centers are a drain on resources.

Director of Medicine:

1. The medical staff requires better support. Certain key medical equipment requires immediate replacement, and the laboratories need updating. To attract the best doctors, we need to purchase equipment we have never had before.

2. The new centers are taking time away from the medical staff. We don't get proper credit for the work we do in those centers.

3. We need to pull back and re-examine our commitment to these new efforts.

The leader for the consultants has asked each member of the team to review the interview summaries and to report on the following points by tomorrow:

1. What are the major areas of conflict that exist in the organization?

2. Do you think having scarce resources is typical of most organizations?

3. Are key administrators working together to make these new centers successful?

4. How would you propose to move all parts of the organization toward common goals?

Flick Fabrication, Inc.

Flick Fabrication, Inc., is responsible for providing sheet metal parts to assembly plants in the home appliance industry. One set of parts used in the door of a dishwasher passes through a stamping department, where the metal is bent into the proper shape. Next, the welding department attaches threaded fasteners that will accept a bolt during final assembly at a customer's plant.

Engineers at Flick, working to improve productivity and reduce manufacturing costs, have redesigned the threaded fastener to eliminate the welding operation. The new equipment will cost Flick $100,000. In addition, there will be a $.05 increase in material costs for each set of parts. Attaching the new threaded fastener to the sheet metal will increase assembly costs by $.01. Also, modification to the dies used in the stamping press will require an additional investment of $25,000.

Savings generated by this change include a $.035 reduction in welding labor and a $.005 reduction in welding materials. Operating expenses for stamping will decline by $.03 per set of parts. Engineering estimates that changing the fastener will allow Flick's customers to reduce their assembly labor by $.06 because quicker location and fastening techniques can be used. Flick's engineers also believe this method will provide a better-quality product with less chance of failure in assembly at customers' plants and after the dishwasher is purchased for home use.

Prepare a report that addresses the following:

1. List the benefits and costs that will result if this change is implemented. Do not limit your search for benefits to Flick's operations.

2. What are the risks to Flick if it proceeds with this process improvement? What are the risks if it does not?

3. If Flick produces 2 million sets of parts in a year, can it recover the total investment in five years? (Consider only those savings internal to Flick.)

4. With the costs and benefits given in the case, how long will it take Flick to pay for the investment? (Hint: How many units have to be sold to earn back the $125,000 investment?)

5. Why is it important to understand the systems concept to work effectively within the organization?

6. How should Flick consider the savings generated for its customers?

SELECTED BIBLIOGRAPHY

Abernathy, William J., and Clark, Kim B. "Innovation: Mapping the Winds of Creative Destruction." *Research Policy North-Holland* 14 (1985): 3–22.

Abernathy, W. J.; Clark, K. B.; and Kantrow, A. M. "The New Industrial Competition." *Harvard Business Review* 59 (September–October 1981): 68–81.

Ball, Donald A., and McCulloch, Wendell H., Jr. *International Business: Introduction and Essentials*. Plano, Tex.: Business Publications, 1985.

Galbraith, J. *Designing Complex Organizations*. Reading, Mass.: Addison-Wesley, 1973.

Hayes, R. H., and Wheelright, S. C. *Restoring Our Competitive Edge: Competing Through Manufacturing*. New York: Wiley, 1984.

Kantrow, A. M. "Keeping Informed: The Strategy-Technology Connection." *Harvard Business Review* 58 (July–August 1980): 6–21.

Limprecht, Joseph A., and Hayes, Robert H. "Germany's World-Class Manufacturers." *Harvard Business Review* 58 (July–August 1980): 137–145.

Miller, Jeffrey G., and Vollmann, Thomas E. "The Hidden Factory." *Harvard Business Review* 63 (September–October 1985): 142–150.

Pascarella, P. "Beyond Market Share." *Industry Week*, June 25, 1984, pp. 40–47.

Pascarella, P. "Rolling Out a Rusty Weapon." *Industry Week*, October 29, 1984, pp. 33–38.

Poza, Ernesto J. "Twelve Actions to Build Strong U. S. Factories." *Sloan Management Review* (Fall 1983): 27–38.

Richardson, Peter R., and Gordon, John R. M. "Measuring Total Manufacturing Performance." *Sloan Management Review* 21 (Winter 1980): 47–58.

Robinson, Richard D. *Internationalization of Business: An Introduction*. Chicago: Dryden Press, 1984.

Rothberg, Robert R. *Corporate Strategy and Product Innovation*. New York: Free Press, 1976.

Sasser, W. Earl; Olsen, R. Paul; and Wyckoff, D. Daryl. *Management of Service Operations: Text, Cases, and Readings*. Boston: Allyn and Bacon, 1978.

Skinner, Wickham. "Getting Physical: New Strategic Leverage from Operations." *Journal of Business Strategy* 3 (Spring 1983): 74–79.

Van Gigch, John P. *Applied General Systems Theory*. New York: Harper & Row, 1978.

Wheelright, S. "Japan—Where Operations Really Are Strategic." *Harvard Business Review* (July–August 1981): 67–74.

Wheelright, S. "Reflecting Corporate Strategy in Manufacturing Decisions." *Business Horizons* 21 (February 1978): 57–66.

Chapter 2

Operations for Competitive Advantage

CHAPTER OUTLINE

LEARNING OBJECTIVES

After completing this chapter, you should be able to

- Explain how operations management can maintain an organization's competitive edge by producing products of high quality, providing convenient delivery and effective customer service, and producing these products at a level of cost and investment that allows the organization to achieve a competitive return.
- Discuss why operations are strategically important.
- List and define the steps necessary to link operations to corporate strategy.
- Describe how operations managers are using computers and related technology to increase productivity, improve quality, provide a safer environment, and reduce costs.
- Identify the component technologies of computer-integrated manufacturing (CIM) and explain how they are related.
- Discuss how computer and information technology affect operations.

OPERATIONS IN ACTION

LTV Aircraft Products Group: How Automation Enhances Flexibility and Increases Productivity

The application of computer and manufacturing technology is giving U.S. firms the advantages necessary to make them competitive in world markets. Rapid and effective implementation of these existing technologies could halt, and eventually reverse, the trend toward foreign production of cars, electronics, steel, and other key industrial goods. This can be accomplished because the automated factory is becoming a reality. Great strides are being made in getting different computers and machine tools to communicate with one another. This will allow the application of flexible manufacturing systems that are capable of efficiently producing a large variety of products to meet changing customer requirements.

In 1984, LTV installed a flexible manufacturing system (FMS), which was designed and built by Cincinnati Milacron, to produce 1,300 different parts used in the assembly of the Rockwell B1-B bomber. By 1988, the system paid for itself in inventory savings alone. The enhanced flexibility of the system allowed LTV to produce each of the 1,300 parts as needed, which often implied a batch size of one. As a result, LTV did not maintain an extensive inventory of parts to feed the assembly operation. In addition to the inventory cost reductions, labor costs were reduced, and product quality increased. With the initial contract for 100 aircraft complete, LTV can easily use the FMS to make parts for other aircraft or products for other industries.

In the decade of the nineties, LTV is investing in another FMS, this one is designed to run without people tending the equipment. The new FMS will offer a two-to-one improvement over the existing FMS, which itself was a three-to-one improvement over traditional methods. The system will include a flexible composite center, which will automatically assemble the "skin" of the aircraft wing, and a 2,000-mile-per-hour abrasive water jet for cutting titanium.

The new FMS will allow LTV to operate efficiently with three shifts a day, six days a week. The company can switch between products easily, and it can quickly and economically produce parts that were made twenty years ago. For customers, this means not having to carry spare parts because LTV can quickly make them. The system gives LTV a competitive advantage.[1]

INTRODUCTION

Operations presents top management with many opportunities to develop competitive advantages. A **competitive advantage** is a capability, such as short delivery lead time or high product quality, that gives an organization an edge on its competition. When properly used, operations can be an important tool for improving profits, increasing market share, and developing new markets. A firm's **market share** is its percentage of sales in a particular market—that is, its sales divided by total sales for all organizations competing in a market.

The following advantages can be gained by carefully managing and coordinating operations:

1. When operational plans are linked to financial, marketing, and information system development plans, synergy can result. **Synergy** involves cooperative (teamwork) actions in which the total effect of the actions is greater than the

1. Analyzing the competitive environment (external environment)
2. Appraising the organization's skills and resources (internal environment)
3. Formulating corporate strategy
4. Determining the implications of corporate strategy for operating strategy
5. Examining the limitations economics and technology place on operations
6. Designing systems for operations
7. Planning for operations
8. Managing and controlling operations

Each of these steps raises questions that should be addressed by management in the organization. Questions that should be asked about these steps are listed in the following sections.

Analyzing the Competitive Environment

All organizations operate within an environment that is shaped by external factors and forces over which they have limited control. These factors include the level of technology, the social and political environment, and the array of competitors and potential competitors, both domestic and international. The application of technology to develop new products and/or processes can impact on an organization's ability to compete. Environmental legislation may dramatically alter an organization's cost of doing business in a way that leaves competitors unaffected. New entrants into the market may possess strengths that give them a competitive advantage over firms already in the market.

To be successful, an organization should know about the market in which it will compete and about its environment. In what market or markets is the organization planning to compete? Who are the present competitors, and what are their strengths? Who are the potential entrants? What changes in government regulations or business conditions might alter the competitive environment?

Appraising the Organization's Skills and Resources

What strengths does an organization possess? How might these be used to take advantage of certain opportunities in the environment? What technological expertise and production capabilities are available? What markets or channels of distribution are open?

Formulating Corporate Strategy

An organization should formulate a strategy by applying its skills and resources to the opportunities present in the environment. What are the goals and objectives of the organization? Suppose an organization wants to lead the state or region in providing financial services to the home via microcomputer connections. What are the key policies for achieving these goals? What policies will be set for minimizing security risks?

Determining the Implications of Corporate Strategy for Operating Strategy

What are the strategic operating decisions? For example, where should the facility be located to provide rapid response to customer needs at an acceptable level of cost? What process technology will be employed and at what capacity? What is the level of product quality? Is there really a trade-off between product cost and quality? What level of flexibility is required to produce services and goods for this market? Is the market likely to change, making flexibility important?

The corporate strategy should be the guidepost for production planning. It should set the stage for the short-term operating budget, which is a detailed annual plan for spending, and for the longer-term capital budget, which is a plan for facility improvements and expansion.

Examining the Limitations of Economics and Technology on Operations

What are the specific limitations of the existing operations? What resources need to be improved or obtained in order to meet the organizational objectives? How large will any one facility be? How should the production resources be distributed? Should there be only a few large facilities with their associated economies of scale? Or would several smaller facilities that are easier to manage be better?

Smaller facilities are part of the focused-factory concept described by Wickham Skinner, a leading expert in operations. **Focused factories** are smaller operations that produce fewer products. They do not attempt to achieve low costs through economies of scale (e.g., by spreading fixed costs over a large volume). Focused factories achieve low costs through better control (for example, by eliminating waste) and ease of managing a smaller operation (because fewer people are involved).[2]

Designing Systems for Operations

How should operations be designed in order to meet the organization's objectives? To answer this question, management must consider product design, capacity, process selection, facility location and layout, job design, and work measurement. How can flexibility be designed into the system in anticipation of changing needs? What are the information-processing capabilities necessary to provide management with useful information for decision making?

Planning for Operations

How can the organization use the resources available to meet present and projected customer needs? These plans should move the organization toward its objectives as defined by the corporate strategy. How might those resources be changed through additional capital expenditures to satisfy changing demands? Planning for operations ranges from short-term decisions involving what products to make this week to long-term decisions regarding future changes in technology or shifts in customer demand.

Managing and Controlling Operations

How well has the operations function performed in meeting the plans established in the previous step? Has it been successful at moving the organization toward its short- and long-term objectives? Has operations made the organization stronger and given it a competitive advantage by making better-quality products, providing improved service and shorter delivery lead times, or reducing costs? Costs refer to total organizational costs, not just production costs.

INTEGRATING THE SYSTEM

Linking Operations to the Organization

The last three steps in the top-down view of operations given here are the same key elements that define the framework for this text. These concepts—system design, planning, and managing and controlling operations—were defined in Chapter 1 and will be discussed in greater detail throughout the book.

It is important to see how these three concepts can be linked to organizational strategy. This view allows managers to see how an organization should use its resources to deal with its environment. It shows management how to develop and define the strengths of an organization in order to build competitive advantage through operations.

The strategic importance of operations should be recognized by organizations competing in today's tough international markets. Firms that utilize the links described in this section and build operations for competitive advantage are more likely to be successful.

A Changing International Environment

In 1992, Belgium, Denmark, France, Germany, Greece, Ireland, Italy, Luxembourg, the Netherlands, Portugal, Spain, and the United Kingdom will join to form the European Economic Community (EEC). The EEC will unite these countries in a single internal market. It is designed to make trade between countries as easy as trade between California and Oregon. One effect of the EEC will be to promote trade among its member countries, but it will also create a powerful new force in the international marketplace. If its membership remains at twelve countries, and it is likely to grow to fifteen or eighteen by the year 2000, the EC will have more than 325 million consumers in 1992. The U.S. market will have about 250 million consumers, and the Japanese market will have about 125 million consumers.

This could have several impacts on the production and distribution of services and goods in the growing global economy. With a unified market and free trade within the market, organizations may be more likely to locate new production facilities in the EEC countries. The pooling of resources and joint ventures are more likely to occur within the EEC, making it a major force in developing, producing, marketing, and distributing products on a worldwide basis. The EEC is likely to stimulate international trade, making it more important for all organizations to think globally when developing strategies and plans for implementing those strategies.

FLEXIBILITY

Flexibility, as defined for operations, is the ability to change between products or customers with minimal costs and delays. Flexibility in operations may be as simple as a barber's chair that can be adjusted for a customer's height. It may be an employee at Wendy's who can run the cash register, the grill, or the drive-up window. It may be a metal-bending press that can quickly be changed from producing a van door panel to producing a car hood. Consider how an organization can use flexibility to gain a competitive advantage.

1. With a wide variety of products, marketing can meet specific customer demand more closely.
2. Timely deliveries are possible because flexibility implies that inexpensive and quick changes can be made from one product to another.
3. Changeover costs are reduced, thereby reducing operating costs as well.
4. When sudden shifts in market preference occur, the cost of redesigning facilities and equipment is reduced because the system can more easily adapt to producing new and different products.

Using Flexibility to Satisfy a Variety of Customer Needs

Marketing would like to satisfy all demands made by customers because selling is part of its job. Sales can be more easily achieved when a wide variety of products is available for customer choice. Marketing would also like to avoid any unnecessary delays in delivering the service or good. One approach would be to request that operations keep adequate stocks of inventory for all items. Inventory, how-

Flint Auto Stamping: Flexibility as a Competitive Advantage

Stamping involves sending flat sheets of steel through a series of large presses that shape the metal by hitting it with dies (molds). The dies are formed to the shape of the finished product. Flint Auto Stamping produces left-front and right-front quarter panels (fenders) for cars. To change from left to right quarter panels, the press must be stopped, and the dies that shape the metal must be changed. At Flint Auto Stamping, it takes four to eight hours to change dies. How will management choose to operate? If they try to change dies each day, they will spend four to eight hours each day with no production. Because of these delays, management will probably choose long production runs so the changeover times and costs will not be excessive. These longer runs will lead to greater inventory. Demand for the quarter panel not being produced must be satisfied from inventory because car assembly requires both front quarter panels at the same time.

If it takes only 15 minutes to change the dies (typical of some producers), how will management choose to operate? They can afford more changeovers because they take less time away from actual production. More changes mean less inventory buildup because the time until the next change is short and less inventory is needed to supply the part that is not being produced.

Greater flexibility is a result of the following factors:

1. Better planning and organization of the changeover procedure
2. Dedicated people willing to work together, including engineering, management, and labor
3. Using more recent technology in the stamping operation

WORLDWIDE SERVICE AND MANUFACTURING OPERATIONS

Service Operations

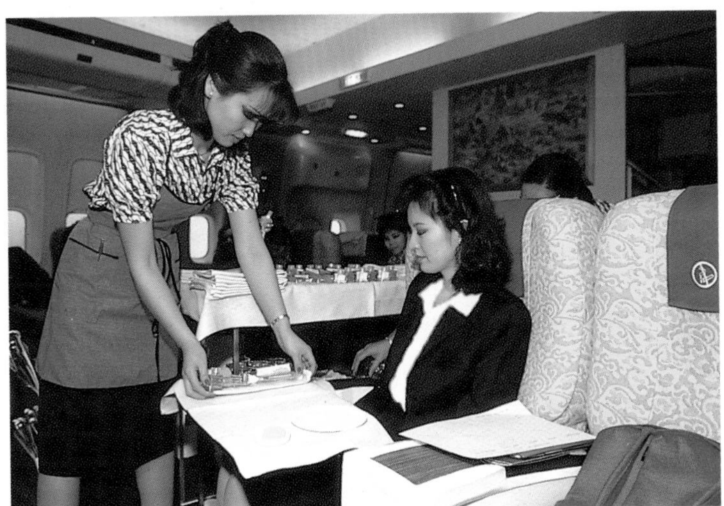

Service operations involve a high degree of interaction between employees and customers, as between this flight attendant and passenger on Cathay Pacific Airlines. ***Photo by Richard Tompkins, Gamma-Liaison.***

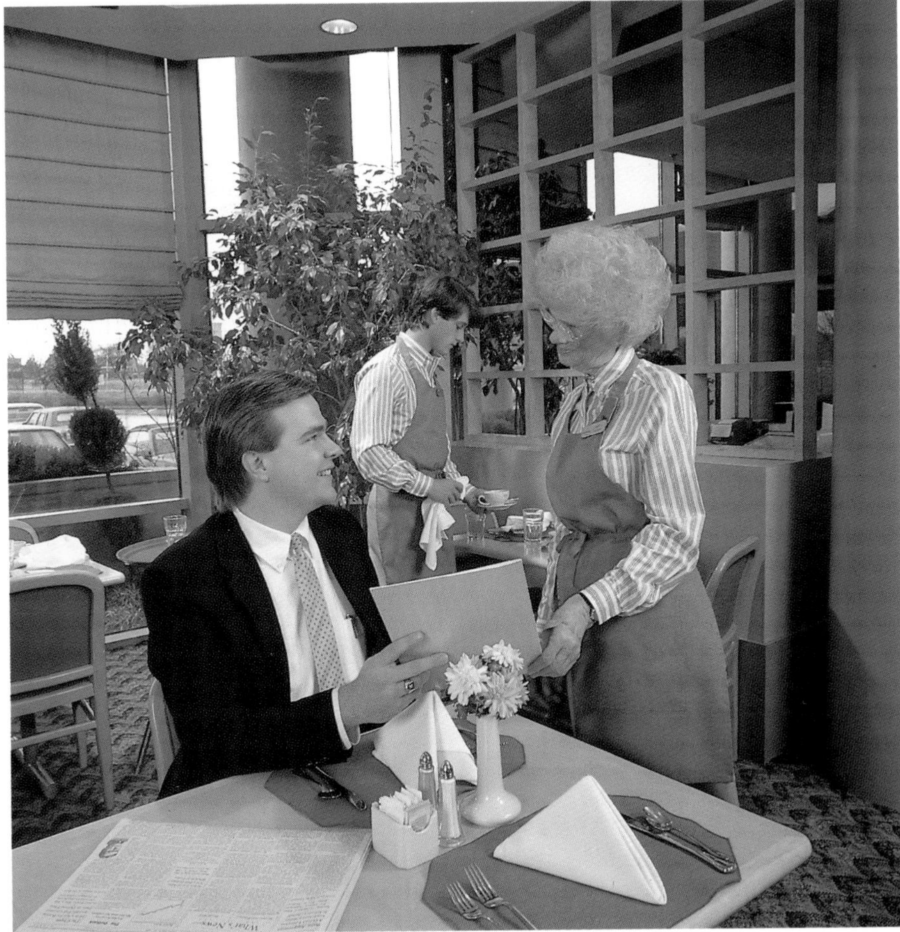

The quality of the service is often based on customer perceptions of the surroundings, friendliness of employees, and other intangible factors. ***Courtesy of Holiday Inns, Inc.***

Some service operations separate the customer from the employees. Here, at the Hamburg, Germany, stock exchange, trades are executed for customers who may be thousands of miles away.
Photo by Kevin Forest, The Image Bank.

Automation in services can further separate the customer and employees. However, automation can also enable a company to serve a worldwide market, as in this Wall Street brokerage house.
Photo by Claudio Edinger, Gamma-Liaison.

Services have used automation to decrease costs and improve service. The Chicago branch of the U.S. Postal Service, shown here, handles 65,000 bundles per hour.
Courtesy of Tony Wilhight, U.S. Postal Service, Chicago Division.

Automation has enabled Federal Express to compete effectively by offering overnight service at low cost.
Courtesy of Federal Express Corporation. All rights reserved.

Federal Express has used the computer to improve its service. This employee uses a hand-held scanner to enter information about a package, enabling Federal Express to track that package every step of the way to its destination.
Courtesy of Federal Express Corporation. All rights reserved.

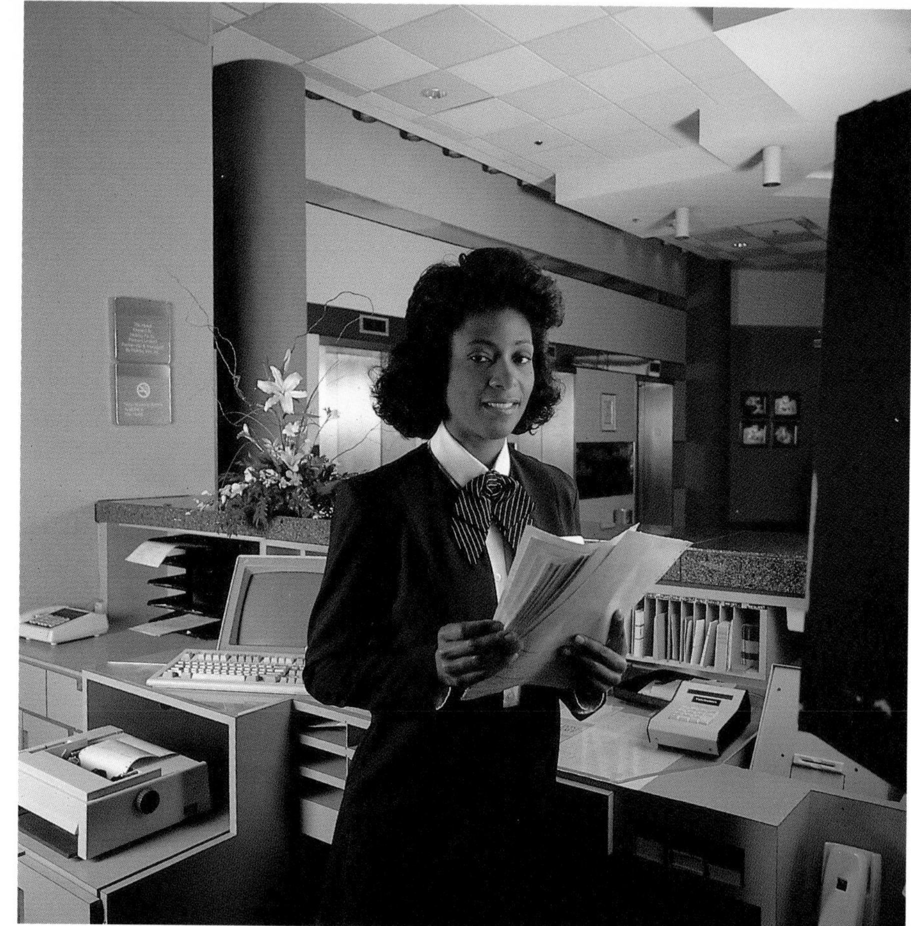

Computers can bring employees and customers together, as does this computer at a Holiday Inn. The desk clerk can quickly access information about each guest, enabling her to provide personalized service.
Courtesy of Holiday Inns, Inc.

Some service operations begin to resemble complex manufacturing operations. This cardiovascular laboratory uses high-tech equipment and a team of trained professionals to provide high-quality health care.
Photo by Jeffrey Grosscup.

Operations with outdated technology and high labor costs, such as this grist mill in Pennsylvania, cannot compete in the world market and will soon cease to exist.
Photo by Sobel/Klonsky, The Image Bank.

The labor-intensive process of crystal-cutting by skilled artisans still exists today because consumers are willing to pay extra for such individualized items.
Photo by Charles Mahaux, The Image Bank.

The assembly line has enabled automobile companies to be very productive, as at this Ford Taurus assembly plant in Chicago—where 3,000 employees produce 1,048 cars per day.
Ford Motor Company Photo.

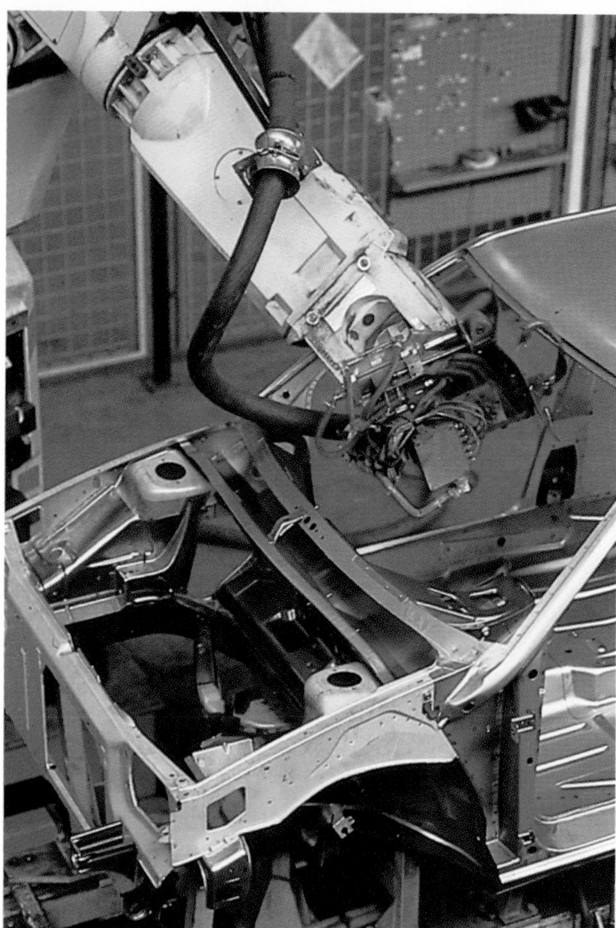

Labor costs have been further decreased and quality improved through extensive use of automation, as demonstrated by the use of a robot to assemble car bodies at this plant in Paris, France.
Photo by Romilly Lockyer, The Image Bank.

South Korea has developed a highly-competitive automotive industry. Note the smaller number of workers and better working position for the employee compared to the Ford Taurus assembly plant.
Photo by Robin Moyer, Gamma-Liaison.

Labor costs have been further decreased and quality improved through extensive use of automation. This new Ford assembly plant uses over 250 robots to perform nearly all body welding on the Ford Escort.
Ford Motor Company Photo.

Manufacture of some electronics products requires highly-specialized facilities, such as this clean room for making microchips in Durham, North Carolina. *Photo by Steve Dunwell, The Image Bank.*

Although automation is used extensively, many electronics operations are labor-intensive. This worker is inspecting integrated circuits. *Photo by Brownie Harris, The Stock Market.*

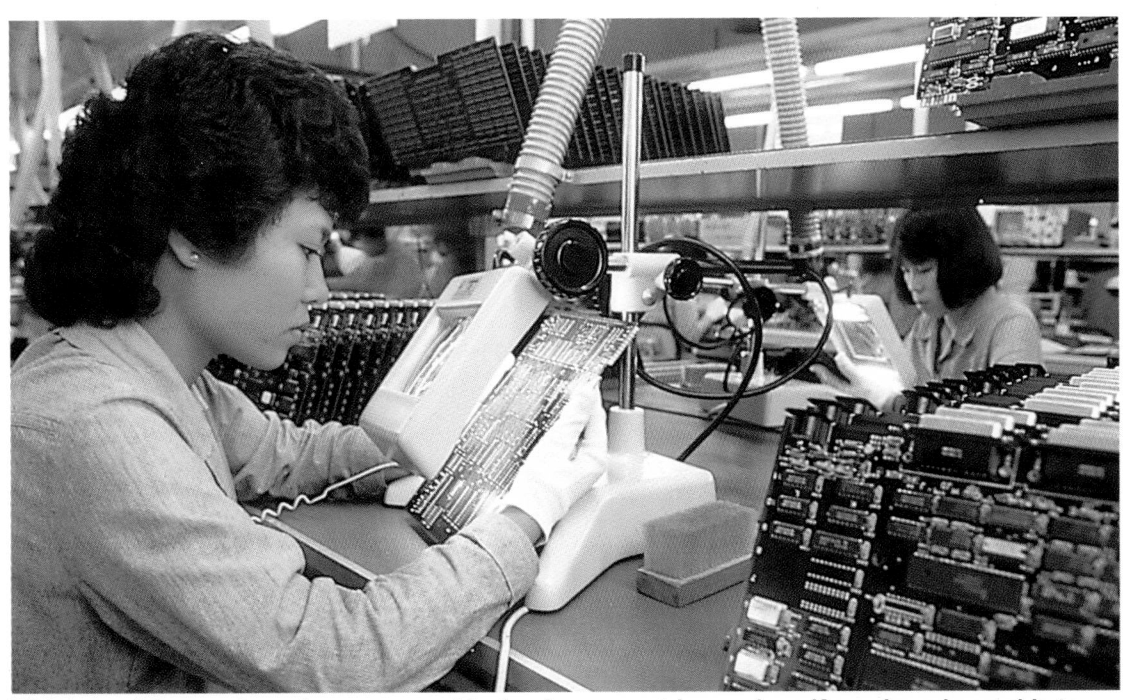

With lower labor costs and more current technology, countries such as Korea have been able to take over much of the world electronics market. *Photo by Steve Niedorf, The Image Bank.*

Food processing has traditionally been very labor intensive, as at this Dim Sum factory in Hong Kong. *Photo by Steve Niedorf, The Image Bank.*

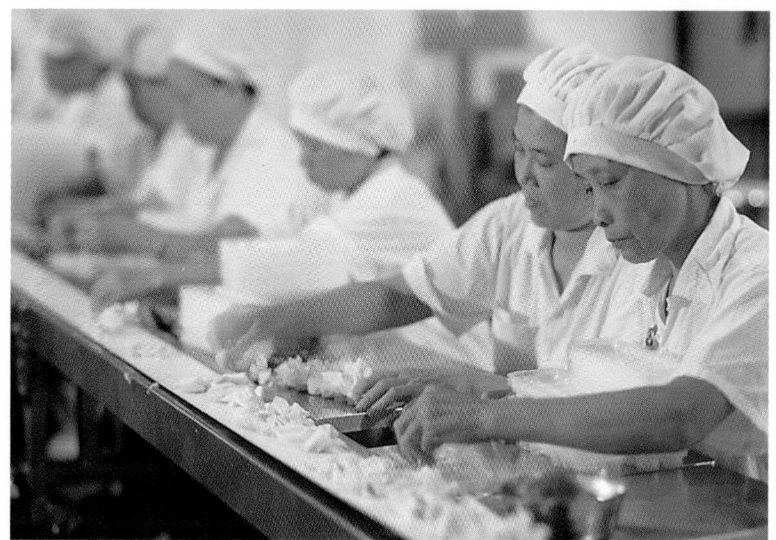

This frozen-potato packaging line demonstrates how automation can decrease the number of workers needed, thus lowering product costs—an important consideration for food products. *Photo by Alvis Upitis, The Image Bank.*

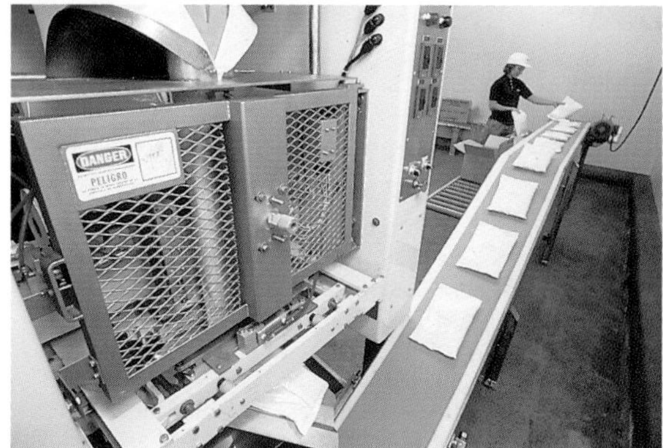

Inspection is important to ensure product quality—even for a product such as the popsicles shown here. *Photo by Walter Bibikow, The Image Bank.*

ever, is very expensive. How can an organization maintain quick delivery and still keep finished-goods inventory low? The answer is to reduce the time for changeover between products.

Using Flexibility to Meet Sudden Market Changes

Flexibility in the production process also permits facilities to adapt to sudden market changes. Consider the U.S. automobile industry. Since 1973, the time of the first Arab oil embargo, it has faced five major switches in market preference between large cars and small cars. These switches have dramatically changed the demand for eight-cylinder engines. If a transfer line, which machines engine blocks, is set up to produce eight-cylinder engines, can it easily be changed to produce six-cylinder engines? That is a function of the design of the transfer line. If it was designed to produce only eight-cylinder engines, than a major investment in time and money would be required to switch to six-cylinder engines.

Flexibility has many facets and affects many different parts of the production system. In determining whether to have flexibility, the automobile industry should consider the trade-off between (1) the extra costs of designing and operating flexible machining centers for engine blocks and (2) the costs of having to convert inflexible transfer lines each time crude-oil prices change dramatically.

PRODUCTIVITY

A business system should be both effective and efficient. A system is **effective** if it achieves the desired results, and a system is **efficient** if it uses a "reasonable" amount of effort (inputs) to achieve the desired outputs. Defining what is reasonable is sometimes difficult. Chapter 9, on job design and work measurement, describes some procedures for estimating a reasonable time for doing a job. For now, however, consider this example. If a fry cook is required to cook a quarter-pound hamburger patty so it is medium rare and the cook accomplishes the task, then the cook was effective. If it took four wasted patties and 15 minutes, then the cook was not efficient. Efficiency is a measurement of outputs versus inputs, and productivity is a measure of efficiency. Productivity can be calculated as shown in the following equation:

$$\text{Productivity} = \frac{\text{output}}{\text{input}}$$

As an example, you might measure your own productivity in completing homework problems as the number of problems you can complete correctly each hour. The more correct homework solutions you can "crank out" per hour, the more productive you are.

Inputs include labor, capital, and raw materials. For measurement purposes, these inputs are usually stated in terms of market value or constant dollars related to some base year. Thus, the labor input would generally be measured in terms of total salary paid to production workers. Raw materials are measured as the cost of all services and raw materials used to generate the output.

The measurement of capital inputs is somewhat more difficult, and a complete discussion of the procedure goes beyond the scope of this book. Suffice it to say, however, that this input is also usually measured in dollar terms and should represent the value of all capital resources used in generating the good or service. Outputs include the goods or services that an organization produces for final sale to its customers. Again, these outputs are usually stated in dollar terms, often as the market value of the outputs.

Changes in Productivity

While the exact measurement of productivity is difficult, it is relatively easy to determine when changes in productivity have occurred. For instance, if a company can double its output without adding more employees or buying more equipment, then productivity has obviously increased. We can say so without knowing precisely what the previous or new productivity levels are. All we know is that the company is now producing more output without changing the inputs. By the same token, if a company can maintain the same output level with fewer employees and without adding more equipment, then we can say that productivity has also increased. Further, if a company can maintain the same level of output while using fewer raw materials, then its productivity has also increased. Thus, it is not necessary to measure productivity precisely to determine whether a change in productivity has occurred.

Productivity of Labor

Labor productivity, the most often cited reference to productivity, is the number of units produced per labor hour or per unit of labor cost. Labor productivity is directly affected by the amount of invested capital, by management policies, by the amount of energy consumed, and by the quantity and quality of raw materials. For example, at IBM's laptop microcomputer assembly plant in Austin, Texas, each of the two no-hands assembly lines, containing 13 robots, turns out a computer every two minutes. Each robot work station requires an investment of about $50,000 plus the hardware and software to coordinate the system. Labor productivity in the plant is very high because of the significant capital investment in automation.

We have already mentioned the situations in which productivity is increased either by producing more without changing the work-force size or by producing the same amount with fewer employees. These are the two most obvious ways that labor can influence productivity, and this type of effect has been occurring in U.S. manufacturing over the last few years, as shown in Exhibit 2.1. The exhibit shows that while manufacturing output has been increasing, total employment in manufacturing has tended to decline since 1985. Part of that effect may be accounted for by the substitution of another input, capital, for labor.

Productivity of Capital

A second major component of the productivity inputs is capital. This usually includes all machinery and other equipment, land, buildings, and inventories. Once again, a company can increase its productivity by producing more with the same amount of capital input; by producing a constant amount, but with less capital; or by making any other change that results in a relative increase in the output to capital ratio.

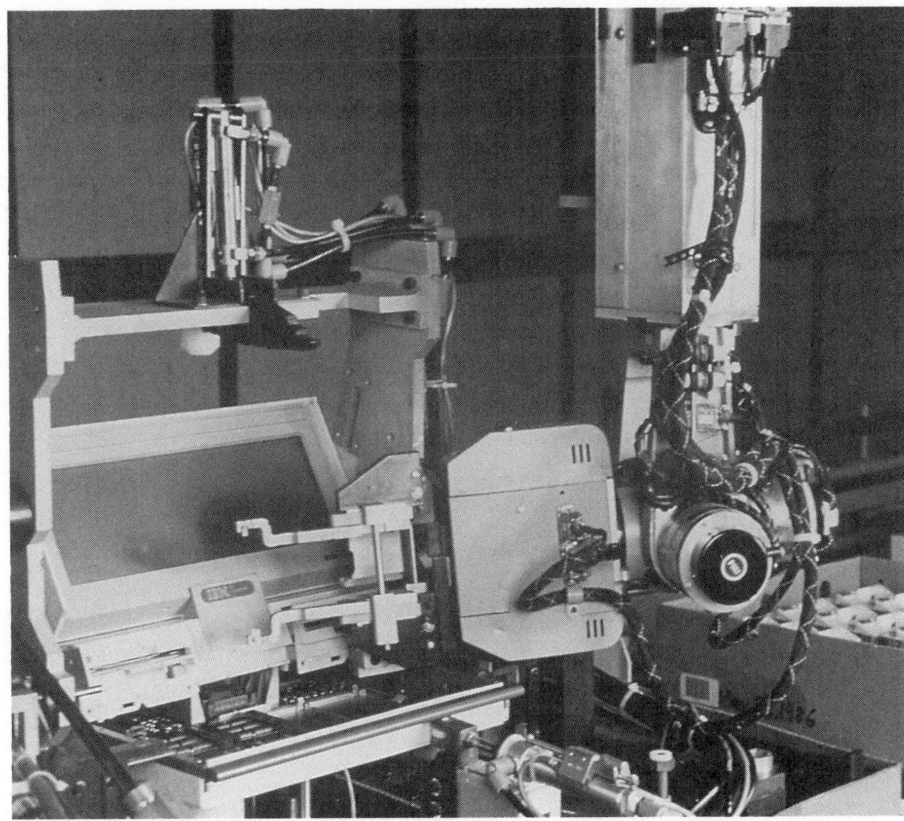

Robot assembly station for IBM's laptop microcomputer. *Courtesy: IBM.*

For example, if a company is able to produce the same output as previously, but reduce its inventory level, then productivity of capital has increased. Similar improvements in productivity can also be brought about by producing the same output using less equipment, less land, or a smaller building. On the other hand, using more equipment to produce the same output will mean that the productivity of capital has decreased.

This brings up an important point. We had mentioned previously that many companies are concerned only with the productivity of labor. However, such an orientation misses possible substitution effects that can occur. For example, many organizations today are using machines to replace employees—a substitution of capital for labor. This produces an increase in the productivity of labor because fewer workers are needed. But the productivity of capital will decrease if output remains the same.

Productivity of Materials

Many organizations find that materials and purchased services account for more than half, often as much as 75 percent, of their production costs. The productivity of materials and services is determined by dividing output by the total value of all materials and services (energy, business services, etc.) used in producing that output.

As was true for the other inputs, any decrease in the required materials and services, without decreasing the output, will mean an increase in productivity.

Exhibit 2.1 Change in Output Versus Labor for U.S. Manufacturing

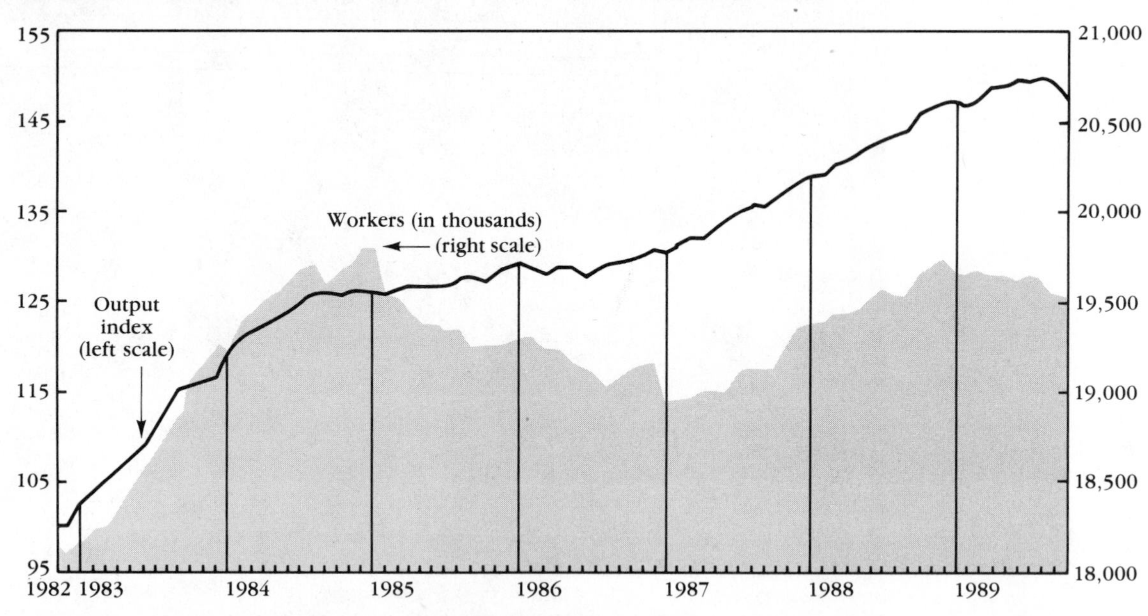

Source: Survey of Current Business, United States Department of Commerce Bureau of Economic Analysis, vol. 62 no. 11–vol. 69 no. 10.

For example, if a company can maintain its level of output, but use less energy in doing so, productivity will increase. Likewise, using less materials to produce the same or more output will generate an increase in productivity.

Productivity Improvements Free Resources for Innovation

Productivity improvements are beneficial to an organization, to consumers, and to workers (labor). In any situation, there are limits on resources, on capital and equipment, on material, and on energy and labor. Additionally, none of these resources is free. If an organization can produce more and better-quality products with less resources, it will achieve two significant advantages. First, the unit cost of the product will decline because less labor and/or fewer materials are required to produce each unit. This makes the product more competitive. Second, there will be unused resources that can be used to develop and produce new and better products. When significant increases in productivity have been achieved, revolutionary changes in resource allocation have occurred.

The First Revolution. Increases in farming productivity have caused farm labor to decline from 95 percent of the labor force in the early 1800s to less than 5 percent today. This freed an army of workers for the task of creating and producing the vast array of consumer goods now available. At the same time, the prices consumers pay for food as a percentage of income have declined dramatically. Such consumer goods as automobiles, home appliances, and electronic gadgets were developed and produced by labor freed from farming tasks. This has improved business opportunities, created new jobs, and improved our living standards. These changes would not have been possible without the development of better methods and machinery that allowed the United States to reallocate its human and physical resources from farming to the production of goods.

The Second Revolution. In the 1900s, improvements in manufacturing productivity have freed resources for rapid expansion in service operations. Banking, health care, insurance, and other service industries have grown because of the labor freed by mechanizing operations. This explosion of opportunity for services is possible because improvements in labor productivity allow us to do more with fewer people and less resources. This is how real improvement in living standards can be made.

The Third Revolution. The next wave of productivity improvements will be caused by the application of computer and information technology to create new "smart" automation systems. As this technology is applied to problems in decision making on the factory floor and in the office, the productivity of blue- and white-collar workers will increase. This technology will allow fewer people, both labor and management, to do more work.

Although service industries may find it more difficult to apply robots and other equipment used in manufacturing, they are ahead of manufacturing in applying the soft side of automation. Service industries such as airlines, health care, insurance, and banking are using information technology to improve service quality, lower costs, and make their workers more productive. Health insurers such as Blue Cross have developed sophisticated computer-based information systems to process claims and to handle subscriber inquiries.

Productivity and Costs

Many factors influence productivity and product cost, as shown below.

Factor	Influence
Product design	A more sophisticated and complicated product tends to cost more. Effective product design can eliminate complexity and increase productivity.
Process design	How the service or good is produced determines costs. Facility and equipment will also affect costs.
Material	The amount and types of material affect costs.
Facility layout	An efficient layout will eliminate wasted movements in production.
Facility location	Many costs, such as labor, transportation, and utility rates, are dependent on the location of a facility.

Inputs to the production process can affect productivity. The quality of materials, the reliability and precision of the equipment, and the skill of management all affect productivity. In seeking productivity improvement, management needs to examine the overall impact of changes in the production system, rather than focusing narrowly on reductions in labor costs.

Labor Costs and International Competition

For several years, some business analysts have attempted to blame declining U.S. competitiveness on the high wage rates that U.S. workers enjoy. Today, the U.S. worker is not the highest or even the second highest paid worker in the world.

In fact, over half of our trade deficit now comes from foreign industries that pay higher wages than U.S. workers receive in the same industry.

Foreign firms are not frightened by our "high" wages when they invest billions of dollars in production facilities in this country. The automotive industry is the best example. The Japanese acquired nine automobile assembly plants in the United States during the 1980s, along with many more supplier facilities. They find doing business in the United States a good deal.

COST, QUALITY, AND TECHNOLOGY

Technological advances can lead to reduced costs, improved product performance, and enhanced quality. Enhancements in quality can result from applying new technology (such as integrated circuits in televisions), developing new materials (such as high-strength plastics to replace steel), and improving operations through better management and training.

High Quality and Low Costs: The Ideal

At one time, many consumers took literally the old adage "You get what you pay for." As a result, consumers believed they had to pay more to get high quality. Although this statement has intuitive appeal, recent history has shown that improvements in quality can be achieved while costs are held constant or reduced.

It is true that high quality can be achieved with high costs and that there will always be a market for exclusive products. But mass-market appeal requires the right blend of improved quality and lower costs, as illustrated in Exhibit 2.2. Organizations that can come closest to achieving this ideal product will have a

OPERATIONS IN ACTION

Motorola, Inc.: Improving Quality and Lowering Costs

At Motorola, Inc., improving quality and lowering costs have become important goals. Motorola produces electronic components, two-way and cellular radio gear, data communication equipment, and computers for the highly competitive electronics and communications markets. The company has been increasing productivity and improving quality by a return to the "basics" of production. Motorola has concentrated on better execution of existing plans, has developed new training programs, has reduced inventory, and has improved delivery and service to the customer. As a result of these improvements, Motorola is challenging the Japanese in markets around the world, including their home market. It is one of the few U.S. companies that supply significant amounts of equipment to Nippon Telegraph and Telephone Company.

Recently, Motorola has assigned key executives to form an Asian task force. This effort is aimed at studying the actions of foreign competition. These executives hope to apply what they learn to further improve product quality and performance, reduce costs, and make Motorola more competitive in world markets.[3]

Exhibit 2.2 Blending Quality and Costs

Cost	Quality: High	Quality: Low
High	Limited market appeal because of cost	Complete failure
Low	Ideal product	Limited market appeal because of quality

tremendous advantage over the competition. Products from many organizations such as Motorola and Electrolux enjoy that advantage.

Moving Toward the Ideal Through Technology

To move toward the ideal of high quality and low costs, improvements in product and process technology should be considered. **Product technology** refers to the way the product functions, and **process technology** refers to the way the product is made. The change from the electromechanical adding machines of the 1960s to the multifunction electronic calculators of today is an example of a change in product technology. Electronic calculators do far more in less time and for a small fraction of the cost of the adding machine.

Another example of improvement in product technology is the television. In the mid-1950s, when color television was first introduced, a set cost over $600. Refinements in technology have allowed producers to reduce costs and significantly improve quality. Today's televisions offer a vastly improved picture, longer life, and more and better features, such as automatic fine tuning. A 25-inch remote-control console can be purchased for less than $500, and a 19-inch color set can sell for less than $200.

Process technology is the method of making a product. Improvements in process include the use of machines to do difficult and demanding jobs. Mechanized welding is an example of a process improvement. It is usually faster and cheaper than manual welding, and it produces stronger welds.

Moving Toward the Ideal Through Better Management

Higher quality and lower costs can also be achieved through better management practices, including quality- and cost-management programs that trim waste from operations, better training and motivation for employees, and greater attention to machine maintenance. Motorola's achievement came as a result of better execution of existing plans or, as Motorola's management put it, "a return to basics." These improvements can have a dramatic impact.

Which should be first, new technology or improved management practices? Improved management practices come first. Full benefits from implementing new technology will result when existing operations are well understood and running properly. Placing high technology on top of poor management understanding of

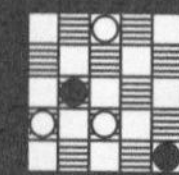

GAINING STRATEGIC ADVANTAGE AT ELECTROLUX CORPORATION

Using Operations for Competitive Advantage

Electrolux makes the Cadillac of vacuum cleaners, but the production facilities in Greenwich, Connecticut, had become antiquated. Because of inefficiencies in manufacturing, the price of its basic model reached $599 in 1982, and sales were declining. After a leveraged buyout by management in the mid-1980s, executives of Electrolux took swift and decisive actions that substantially improved organizational performance and restored the company's competitiveness. In a little over fourteen months, vacuum cleaner sales increased eightfold. How did management achieve this dramatic turnaround?

The vacuum cleaner was redesigned to improve quality and reliability, and to make it easier for customers to operate by switching from a tank design to an upright. The redesign also enhanced the manufacturability of the products and thus increased productivity, reduced cost, and simplify assembly. As a result, six vacuum cleaner models can be assembled on a single production line. Flexibility allows Electrolux to lower operating costs because only one production line is needed and to switch quickly from one model to another so customer demand can be satisfied without maintaining excessive inventory.

A multistory wood building at Greenwich, Connecticut, was closed, and an existing facility at Bristol, Virginia, was expanded. The Greenwich plant was so antiquated that automating it may have been impossible. Parts were piled everywhere, and the product flow snaked throughout the plant. Then the Bristol facility was automated, using much of the existing equipment, and the material-handling system and procedures were improved. The vacuum cleaner that sold for $599 in 1982 can now be purchased for $299.

Electrolux's efforts to improve operations and to gain a strategic advantage over its competitors had multiple facets. The company applied technology and automation to lower material-handling costs, reduce labor costs, and partially eliminate work-in-process inventory. The company redesigned the product to lower costs and increase flexibility in production. Electrolux gave workers control of the line. The work piece does not move from one work station to the next until the worker is satisfied that his or her job is done correctly. The improved performance of the Bristol facility is enabling Electrolux to sell vacuum cleaners in Japan, one of the toughest markets in the world.[4]

the existing system would be disastrous. If managers are having trouble coping with existing operations, it is unlikely that they will be able to understand and control more sophisticated technology and operations.

THE ROLE OF COMPUTER AND INFORMATION TECHNOLOGY IN OPERATIONS

The use of computers in service and manufacturing operations is not new. In accounting, computers perform payroll, accounts receivable, and accounts payable functions. Computers monitor inventory levels and help to control quality. They are used by airlines and hotels to take reservations and to schedule flight crews and housekeeping. Computers are also used to monitor flow process in paper making and oil refining. In these situations, computers provide feedback on operations and can take corrective action. Also, computers are used to control metal-cutting machines that shape parts needed in automobile engines and refrigerator compressors.

Today, many organizations are expanding the use of computers and information systems in ways that could provide them with a competitive advantage. Organizations such as American Airlines have invested heavily in computer-based reservation systems that enhance their ability to serve customers and to maximize the use of their airplanes. Devilbiss Corporation has developed a computer-based expert system to help customers select the correct adhesive or paint for their

The refining operation for the Lima, Ohio, operations of Sohio. *Courtesy: Sohio Division, BP Oil Company.*

specific application. This section discusses expert systems and decision support systems which can be widely applied in service operations or in manufacturing. The next section discusses the application of computers and information systems to manufacturing, especially computer-integrated manufacturing. The final section in the chapter discusses the role of computers and information systems in service operations.

Expert Systems

An **expert system** employs human knowledge that has been captured in a computer to solve complex problems. To be considered an expert system, the system must have (1) a method of acquiring knowledge, (2) a knowledge base (memory), and (3) an inference engine (brain) so it can reason. Knowledge acquisition is the accumulation, transfer, and transformation of problem-solving expertise from some source, usually a human expert. Often the human expert is overloaded or is close to retirement, so the idea of capturing the person's knowledge in a computer-based expert system is very appealing. Someone called a **knowledge engineer** helps the human expert structure the problem by interpreting and integrating human answers, drawing analogies, posing examples, and bringing out conceptual difficulties.

The knowledge base can be thought of as a powerful data base that contains such facts as the problem situation and theory in the problem area, as well as special rules that direct the use of the knowledge. The inference engine is a computer program that provides a methodology for reasoning. This component makes decisions about how to use the knowledge in the system. The inference engine interprets rules, maintains control over the problem, and enforces consistency as the recommended solution emerges.

There are many potential applications of expert systems, including advising on tax-sheltered annuities and scheduling production. La-Courtier is a computer-based expert system in financial planning which was developed by Cognitive Systems, Inc., for a major Belgian bank. The system gives advice on stock purchases and portfolio distribution (how a client's money should be invested) and answers factual questions about the Belgian stock market. For a new customer, La-Courtier conducts an interview to collect information about the user's financial situation. According to the user's current portfolio and market conditions, the system gives advice about which stocks to buy or sell.

Decision Support Systems

A **decision support system (DSS)** is a model-based set of procedures for processing data to assist managers in decision making. A DSS allows managers easy access to information stored in a data base and provides easy-to-use tools for analysis. With these supporting tools, management can more easily control complicated manufacturing and service operations. A DSS is different from an expert system because an expert system has a rule base and an inference engine for decision making and a DSS does not. Once an expert system has been constructed, it can make a decision. On the other hand, a DSS assists managers in making decisions; the manager provides the logic to structure the problem and ultimately makes the decision.

A DSS can help a manager to relate the demand for a product to the correct quantities of materials to be ordered to make that product. If a manager has received an order for 10,000 hair dryers for next month, how does he or she know the number of electric motors, wire connectors, and plastic parts to order? How does the order fit into the production schedule? Does the organization have sufficient capacity? What are the impacts on cost and quality if the orders are processed on certain machines? It becomes necessary to link these decisions by using the computer as a tool to assist managers with information collection and organization.

THE ROLE OF COMPUTER AND INFORMATION TECHNOLOGY IN MANUFACTURING

Computer-based control systems can be combined with manufacturing technology, such as robots, machine tools, and automated guided vehicles (AGVs), to improve manufacturing operations. In this role, the computer can assist in integrating these technologies into a "factory of the future" that is capable of competing in world markets. Allen Bradley and General Electric, which are described in the Chapter 1, are two companies that have used information technology and factory automation to improve manufacturing operations. This combination of information technology and factory automation is often called computer-integrated manufacturing.

Computer-integrated manufacturing (CIM) blends recent developments in manufacturing with information technology to achieve competitive advantage. Exhibit 2.3 defines CIM's component technologies and identifies the stand-alone objectives of each.

When properly organized, CIM offers more than its component technologies. Exhibit 2.4 describes CIM as having engineering design, flexible manufacturing, and production planning and control components. Each component is described briefly here and in greater detail in later sections.

1. Engineering design through computer-aided design (CAD) allows an organization to make high-quality, specialized designs rapidly. The designs can be tailored to meet individual customer needs.
2. Flexible manufacturing systems (FMSs) can quickly produce a variety of high-quality products efficiently. An FMS allows an organization to use specialized designs to produce low-cost, high-quality products quickly.
3. Computer-based production planning and control systems allow an organization to cope with the complexity of managing facilities that produce a wide variety of specialized products without losing efficiency.

When properly combined, these components can yield synergistic results. An organization can have more flexible and integrated operations, be better equipped to manage complex operations, and exercise better control than can a company that operates without CIM.

To merge these components into one coordinated whole, staff from the information systems function need to integrate engineering, manufacturing, and business data bases into a cross-functional decision support system. Once accom-

Exhibit 2.3 CIM Component Technologies

Components	Definition	Stand-Alone Objectives
Computer-aided design (CAD)	Computer-aided design is the application of computer technology to automate the design process including geometric modeling, analyzing stress and strain, drafting, storing specifications, and allowing simulation of a mechanism's parts.	• Improve design productivity • Reduce design lead-time • Improve design quality • Improve access to and storage of product designs • Increase capability to design a variety of products
Flexible manufacturing system (FMS)	Flexible manufacturing systems can react quickly to product and design changes. An FMS includes a number of work stations, an automated material-handling system, and system supervisory computer control. Central computer control provides real-time routing, load balancing, and production scheduling logic. An FMS can incorporate AGV, AS/RS, and robotics to decrease time to change tools and fixtures, load and unload machines, and move materials to and from manufacturing cells.	• Increase capability to produce a variety of products while at the same time reducing delivery lead times and inventory requirements • Enable manufacturing to build volume across products to achieve economies of scope • Enable firms to produce specialized designs for more finely tuned market segments • Respond more rapidly to frequent changes in product design, production requirements, and market demands • Ensure more consistent product quality
Cellular manufacturing	Cellular manufacturing is the physical layout of the factory into product-oriented work centers. Each center or cell includes the machines and tools necessary to efficiently produce a family of parts.	• Reduce material handling • Simplify tool control • Reduce expediting and in-process inventory • Improve operator expertise
Group technology (GT)	Group technology is a process of coding and classifying families of parts according to similarities in their geometric characteristics or in their material or manufacturing requirements.	• Enable scheduling within families of parts to: • Reduce setup time • Reduce lead time • Improve productivity • Simplify process planning (reduce complexity of sequencing operations, simplify routings, eliminate unnecessary routings)
Computer numerical control (CNC)	Computer numerical control is the application of computer technology to numerical controlled (NC) machines by utilizing computer hardware and software to control machine operation.	• Reduce direct labor costs • Improve product quality/precision • Reduce time to load NC software
Computer-aided manufacturing (CAM)	Computer-aided manufacturing is the application of computer and communications technology to enhance manufacturing by linking CNC machines, monitoring the production process, and providing automatic feedback to control operations.	• Improve manufacturing control and reporting • Enhance coordination of material flow between machines • Enhance rerouting capabilities

Exhibit 2.3 continued

Components	Definition	Stand-Alone Objectives
Computer-aided process planning (CAPP)	Computer-aided process planning is a decision support system which generates instructions for the production of parts. Based on information concerning machining requirements and machine capabilities, CAPP plans machining operations and determines routings between machines.	• Enable manufacturing to cope with the complexity of process planning in a multiple-product environment • Reduce the cost and effort required to create and revise process plans
Automated materials handling Automated guided vehicles (AGV) Automated storage and retrieval system (AS/RS)	Material-handling systems may include AGV and AS/RS components. An AGV is a computerized cart system capable of delivering parts and tools to and from multiple work centers. AGVs may be used with an AS/RS which is a computerized system for storing and retrieving parts or tools.	• Reduce material-handling costs • Improve inventory control • Reduce land and building costs. • Improve safety and control of material movement • Reduce work-in-process inventory on the shop floor
Robotics	An industrial robot is a general-purpose, programmable machine possessing certain human-like capabilities (e.g., grasping, sensing, and vision).	• Reduce direct labor costs • Improve quality/precision in repetitive tasks • Avoid risk to humans in hazardous working conditions • Increase throughput
Just-in-time (JIT)	Just-in-time is a business strategy for designing manufacturing systems that are more responsive to precisely timed customer delivery requirements. This strategy focuses on reducing lead times, reducing setup times, and improving product quality.	• Improve customer service • Reduce delivery lead time • Reduce setup time • Improve product quality • Reduce work-in-process, raw-material, and finished-goods inventories • Improve factory design (i.e., distance between work centers and factory floor space requirements) • Uncover work-flow problems hidden by work-in-process inventory
Manufacturing resource planning (MRP II)	Manufacturing resource planning is an integrated decision support system for planning and controlling manufacturing operations. MRP II provides feedback from the shop floor to manage equipment, personnel, material, and information resources. MRP II also includes the data and software capabilities to interface manufacturing decisions with marketing and finance.	• Improve customer service • Improve production and cost control • Enhance decision making • Improve inventory control • Improve coordination among purchasing, receiving, scheduling, production, and shipping

Exhibit 2.4 The CIM Partnership

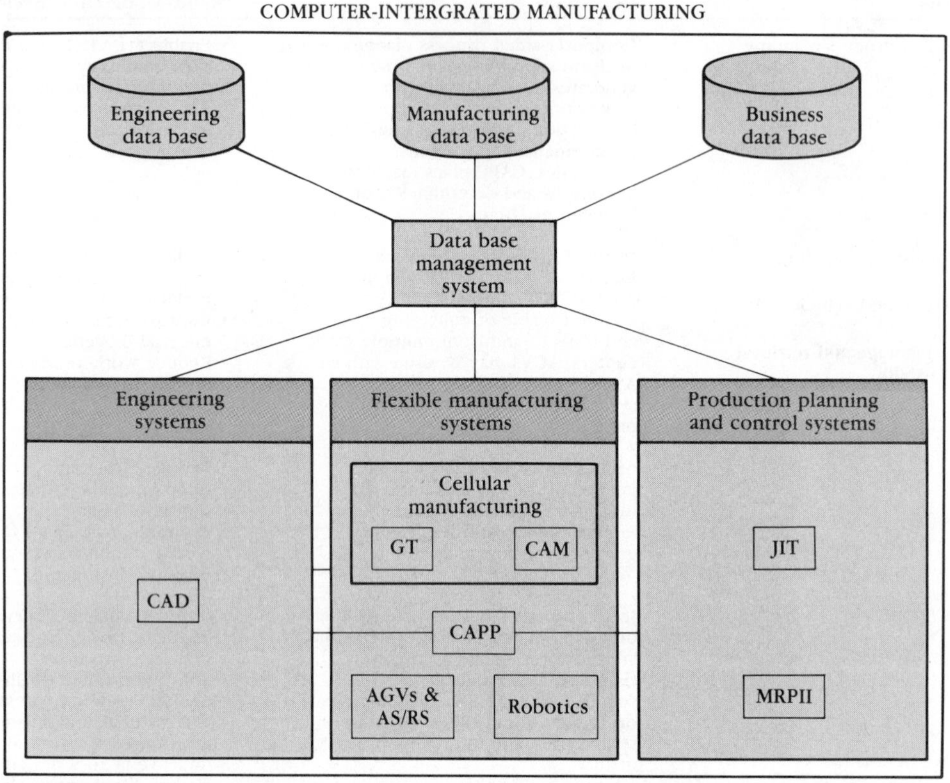

COMPUTER-INTERGRATED MANUFACTURING

Engineering data base

Manufacturing data base

Business data base

Data base management system

Engineering systems

CAD

Flexible manufacturing systems

Cellular manufacturing

GT

CAM

CAPP

AGVs & AS/RS

Robotics

Production planning and control systems

JIT

MRPII

Source: Reprinted by special permission of the *MIS Quarterly,* Volume II, Number 2, June 1987. Copyright 1987 by the Society for Information Management and the Management Information Systems Research Center.

plished, the flexibility to respond to customer demands with low-cost, high-quality specialized products becomes a powerful competitive advantage.

Engineering Design with CAD

Computer-aided design (CAD) is the effective use of a computer to create or modify an engineering design, including geometric modeling, stress and strain analysis, and simulation of part movement. An interactive CAD terminal can be used for dimensional analysis, interference checking between two or more objects, and examination of cross-sections of a part. This is accomplished without building a physical model or making drawings. With computer power and speed, design changes can be made in a matter of seconds.

The major advantages of CAD are that it greatly improves the designer's productivity, it significantly reduces design errors, and it cuts the lead time for designing new parts from weeks to days or even hours. Connecting the computer with an appropriate plotting device permits the user to generate finished drawings in a very short time. These improvements enable the firm to change designs

INTEGRATING THE SYSTEM

Using CAD in a Teamwork Approach

When you read Chapter 4 on new product development, you will see that CAD plays an important role in developing a teamwork approach. CAD's flexibility allows product designers to consider many alternatives. CAD makes it possible for design engineers to sit down with marketing managers to determine if a design meets the anticipated consumer need. If changes are suggested, their impact on costs, durability, and ease of production can quickly be estimated using the "what-if" powers of CAD. Input from operations managers, financial analysts, and cost accountants can be integrated in a decision-making process that can improve the part's manufacturability, costs, and quality.

quickly in response to customer need. CAD is a very good example of applying computer and information technology to improve performance.

Flexible Manufacturing Systems

Flexible manufacturing systems (FMSs) use computer and information technology to integrate material handling, robotics, and computer-aided process planning (CAPP) with cellular manufacturing, which is defined in Exhibits 2.3 and 2.4. The manufacturing cell and its associated family of parts provide the base around which an FMS can be built. A **family of parts** is a group of parts that require similar machining operations. Parts are placed in families based on similarities in size, shape, use, type of material, and/or method of manufacturing. An FMS has flexibility to produce this family of parts using "smart" automation. As a result, an FMS can quickly and efficiently make switches among a family of parts.

Flexibility in an FMS is achieved through the use of two or more reprogrammable computer numerically controlled machines coupled with automated material handling. **Computer numerical control (CNC)** is a machining system that utilizes a dedicated computer to store programs. The programs control the machine so it can shape the finished part. For example, the compressor in a refrigerator has machined surfaces that must fit together precisely. These finished surfaces are probably formed on CNC machines. The control program holds the detailed instructions required to process a part. As a result, a CNC machine with an automatic feed for parts can run without an operator. A CNC machine can repeat the same operation many times over, or a new control program can be down-loaded from a dedicated computer to machine a different part.

CNC machines can be connected to an integrated computer network that provides information, including data about which parts to process, the tools that require changing, and the computer program for the next part. Robots can provide flexibility for loading and unloading parts and changing tools. Automated guided vehicles can move material to and from the cell. As technology improves, FMSs will have increased flexibility and be capable of accepting wider variations in the parts included in a family.

A flexible manufacturing system with several work stations. ***Courtesy: Cincinnati Milacron Inc.***

A computer-controlled drill press at Aeroqulp's Jackson, Michigan, plant. Notice the turret on the right that can hold several different drills (tools). The turret can rotate in a matter of seconds, and a different big can be brought into action. ***Courtesy: Aeroquip a TRINOVA Company.***

Computer-Aided Manufacturing

Computer-aided manufacturing (CAM) is the effective use of computer technology in the management, control, and operation of the production facility through either direct or indirect computer interface with physical and human resources.[5] CAM systems can monitor the production process and the operation of machines by machines.

In metal shaping, CAM goes beyond the usual advantages of CNC machines to provide monitoring and automatic feedback. For example, the quality of a part can be routinely checked against a standard. The results can be given to the computer controlling the machine, and adjustments can be made automatically, without human intervention. CAM implies communication links between CNC machines that enable them to function as a coordinated whole.

By establishing links between CAD and CAM, engineering designs located in the CAD computer can quickly be converted to the specific instructions required by the CNC machine. These instructions for shaping the part can be transferred directly and quickly, often within a few minutes, from the CAD computer to the computer controlling the CNC machine.

Group Technology and Cellular Manufacturing

In **group technology (GT)**, families of parts that require similar machining operations are identified. Production managers have long realized the scheduling advantages of grouping parts into families with similar setup and machining requirements. **Setup** prepares the machine for the required operations on a part. As an example, the setup on a CNC machine could include loading a new program and changing a tool.

With GT, parts can be grouped into families for design as well as manufacturing. These groupings are based on similarity in size, shape, use, and/or method of manufacturing, as illustrated in Exhibits 2.5 and 2.6. Once these families of parts are established, duplicate parts can be eliminated. Parts can also be redesigned and substituted for similar parts. Group technology thus has several advantages.

Exhibit 2.5 Similar Parts Based on Shape

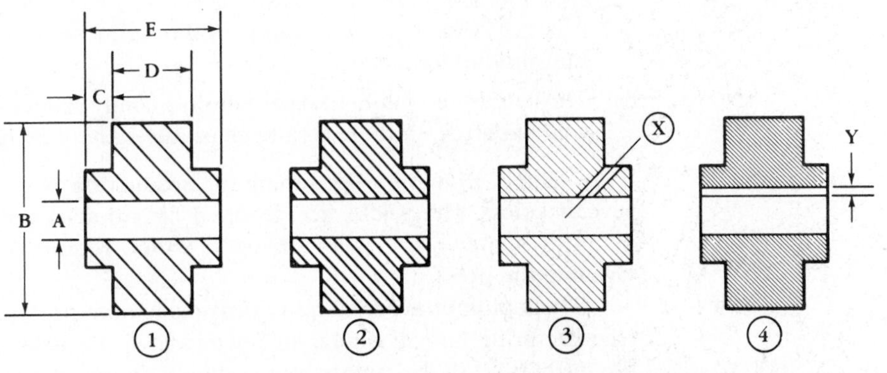

Source: Reprinted courtesy of the Society of Manufacturing Engineers. Copyright 1982, from the CASA/SME Westec '82 Conference Proceedings.

Exhibit 2.6 Similar Parts Based on Manufacturing Process

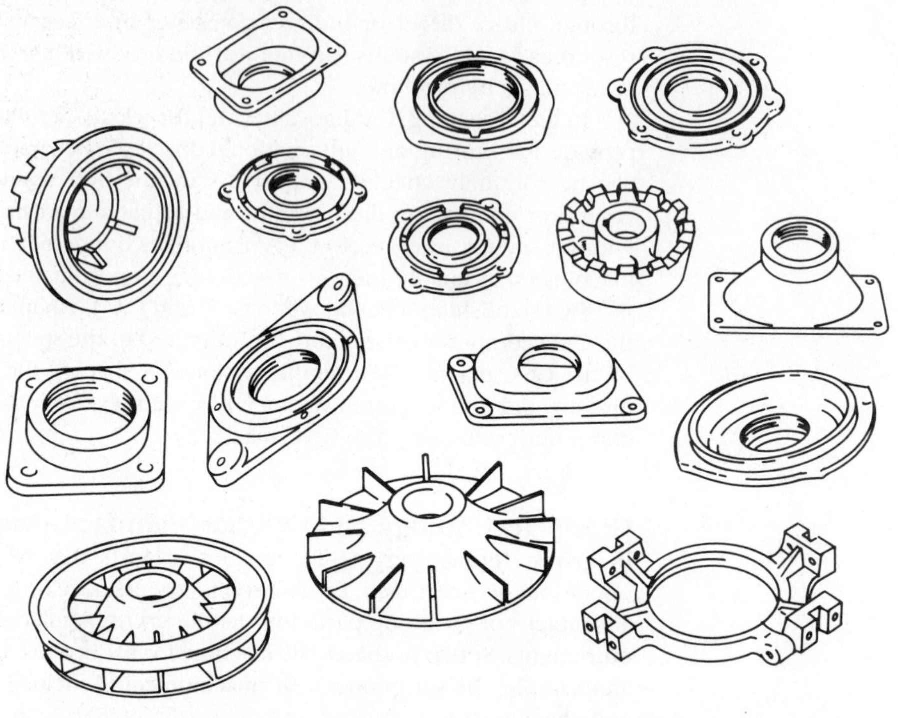

Source: Reprinted courtesy of the Society of Manufacturing Engineers. Copyright 1982, from the CASA/SME Westec '82 Conference Proceedings.

1. Designs can be organized into families so they can easily be retrieved.
2. Some parts that were thought to be different can be eliminated.
3. One manufacturing system or cell can be designed to make an entire family of parts.
4. Robots can be programmed and reprogrammed to adapt to differences within a family.
5. A larger volume of parts can pass through a set of machines, thus reducing unit production costs.
6. The batch scheduling of parts within a family reduces setup time, and people gain expertise in their area because the parts they handle are similar.

A simple example of grouping for production is a print shop that prints in several colors. Here, jobs are grouped by color to reduce setup time and to eliminate unnecessary color changes, which require extensive downtime for cleaning the press.

GT simplifies the problems of organizing both product design (CAD) and the manufacturing floor (cellular manufacturing). **Cellular manufacturing** is the physical layout of the facility into compact groups of machines that will produce

John Deere: Applying Group Technology to the Factory Floor

John Deere has been involved with the implementation of GT for several years. In a recent application of GT to metal-shaping operations at its tractor works, the following results were achieved:

- A 70 percent reduction in the number of departments involved in handling the part
- A 25 percent reduction in the number of machines required for processing
- A reduction in setup time
- An improvement in material handling and a reduction in material-handling costs
- A great reduction in lead time for parts production

These operating improvements have allowed John Deere to enhance its competitive position with respect to other domestic and foreign competitors. These actions also helped Deere withstand the slump in farm implement sales and prepare the organization for more profitable times when demand for farming equipment began to grow again. This occurred in 1990 as the demand for farm equipment rebounded and the demand for lawn tractors remained strong.

families of parts. Within each compact cell, material-handling costs are reduced. Throughput time, work-in-process inventory, and expediting needs are reduced. Storing the tools necessary to produce a family of parts at the cell simplifies tool storage, transportation, and control procedures.

Computer-Aided Process Planning

Computer-aided process planning (CAPP) is an expert system that can generate routings and machining instructions for parts. An expert system is capable of remembering large amounts of data, has rapid recall, and is capable of remembering complex patterns of logic without error. It does not get tired, forget, or go home early. Computers have proved to be very dependable. What sets an expert system apart from other computer-based information systems is its ability to learn from its successes and its mistakes.

A **routing** is a sequence of machines or processes through which a part travels. **Machining instructions** are the procedures and specifications for each machine in the sequence. In a complex multiple-product facility, process planning requires a tremendous amount of detailed information on cell layouts, machining requirements for each part, and the capabilities of each machine. A quality CAPP data base captures the special expertise the work force has developed through years of working with particular parts.

GT can play an important role in helping to organize and standardize routings. Properly applied, GT will group parts with the same or similar routing. Thus, GT is important for good process planning.

Robotics and Automated Material Handling

A **robot** is a reprogrammable, multifunctional manipulator designed to move materials, parts, tools, or specialized devices through variable programmed motions for the performance of a variety of tasks. The use of robots in strenuous, dirty, or dangerous jobs is common today. Robots work in foundries and in welding, forging, machine-tool loading, and spray-painting applications. In the future, robots will become part of integrated manufacturing systems that will move materials and assemble finished products.

Cellular manufacturing reduces and organizes the flow of material. Robots can improve material handling within a cell by loading and unloading machines. Robots should be carefully designed and applied to solve problems in a way that avoids injury to people. Robots do not understand human frailties and have caused injuries when used improperly.

Pressure to cut inventory and material-handling costs has increased interest in low-cost and flexible means of transporting material to and from manufacturing cells. **Automated guided vehicles (AGVs)** are driverless and flexible transportation devices, resembling forklift trucks, that can transport parts between manufacturing cells. Under computer control, AGVs can interface with automated storage and retrieval systems (AS/RS) to coordinate the flow of tools and parts from storage to the manufacturing cell.

Presently, technology is available for computerized control and delivery of materials to the production process. Guided vehicle systems and computerized storage and handling systems allow materials to be delivered to and removed from a work area untouched by human hands. Linking these systems with robotized manufacturing centers presents the opportunity for facilities without direct labor. People would be responsible for other jobs, including carrying out preventive maintenance, repairing machines, and planning.

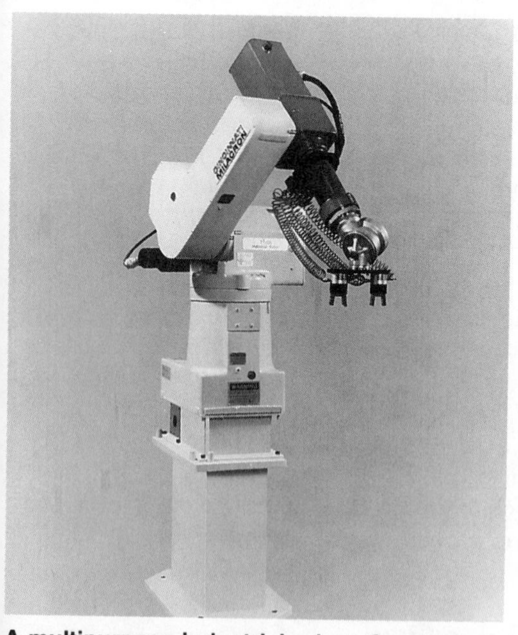

A multipurpose industrial robot. *Courtesy: Cincinnati Milacron Inc.*

A driverless automated guided vehicle can be used to move materials through the facility. *Courtesy: Cincinnati Milacron Inc.*

Automated storage and retrieval system with major components: a terminal for access to computer control, storage bins stacked one on top of the other, and a mechanical device (near top of photo) for storing and retrieving parts.
Courtesy: Cincinnati Milacron, Inc.

Production Planning and Control Systems

Flexibility to quickly and easily change to produce different products enables firms to match production with customer requirements. Organizations should be able to deliver a large number of different products with a short lead time if they are to fully realize the benefits of an FMS. An organization needs to develop information systems for managing customer orders, purchasing, material flow, scheduling, and shipping.

INTEGRATING THE SYSTEM

People and Technology

This portion of the chapter has a heavy emphasis on things (technology) rather than on people. That should not be interpreted to mean that people will be unimportant in the factory of the future. In fact, the opposite is true. The systems described above are heavily dependent on people who understand automation and how it can be implemented. True, there will be little, if any, heavy manual labor. Instead, people will be free to use their creativity and intelligence so that we can all enjoy the fruits of their greater productivity.

To see the results of efforts that lack attention to the human side of automation, read ahead in Chapter 18, on technology and human resources. The first part of the chapter has several interesting examples that illustrate the importance of a strong marriage between people and technology.

Just-in-time (JIT) and manufacturing resource planning (MRP II) are two approaches to designing such systems, and they can be combined in a complementary manner. JIT can be used for short-term scheduling to match precisely timed customer delivery requirements. In contrast, MRP II is useful for longer-term planning of labor availability, material procurements, and capacity requirements. JIT works best in an environment where these longer-term requirements can be estimated accurately.

Although it can be used as a basis for planning and scheduling, **just-in-time** is more properly viewed as a strategy for designing manufacturing systems that are responsive to customer requirements. Applying JIT forces a re-examination of operating philosophy. The JIT philosophy focuses on reducing lead times, reducing setup times, and improving product quality to minimize raw-material, work-in-process, and finished-goods inventories. Minimizing inventory uncovers hidden work-flow problems, reduces working capital requirements, and reduces floor space requirements. It also requires a more reliable manufacturing system.

Manufacturing resource planning (MRP II) provides an integrated decision support system that ties together such departments as engineering, finance, personnel, manufacturing, and marketing via a computer-based dynamic simulation model. MRP II works within the limits of an organization's present production system and with known orders and demand forecasts. JIT and MRP II are discussed in more detail in later chapters.

THE ROLE OF COMPUTER AND INFORMATION TECHNOLOGY IN SERVICE OPERATIONS

Service, by its definition, does not have a physical dimension. However, many operations categorized as service operations are really combinations of services

Kroger Supermarkets: Automated Warehousing

Retail food sales is a competitive business with low profit margins. To remain price competitive, Kroger must cut inventories and warehousing costs, but maintain adequate supplies of thousands of products. To achieve these goals, Kroger and others have implemented automated warehouses and point-of-sale tracking of inventory. The process begins when an item is purchased by a customer. An electronic scanner reads the bar code on the product. The cash register, which is really a computer terminal, records the sale of that item in the computer's data base. At the end of the day, or at any other time, a store manager can run the program that tabulates sales by product. Orders can be sent electronically to the automated warehouse. The orders are filled using automated stock pickers and shipped the next day. At the warehouse, computers help to track shipments to the stores and place orders to suppliers, so that inventory costs in the warehouse are low, yet product availability is high. Kroger gets fast turnaround for orders and efficient, low-cost operations.

and goods. These hybrid operations include restaurants, which both sell food (a good) and prepare it (a service); department stores, which sell products as well as the retailing service; and shops that sell parts and offer repair services. These operations can use some of the manufacturing technologies described in the previous section.

For many services, the tangible part of the product is not significant. With these operations, managers cannot buffer customer demand from the production process with finished-goods inventory. Managers in service operations must find other ways to provide better and faster customer service. This has led managers to implement information systems that provide up-to-date and accurate information about availability of the service and how customers can acquire it. Applications of computer technology in service operations can also provide better information for decision making.

For example, airline registration systems allow ticket agents to determine the availability of flights on any airline. If a flight is booked, the agent can quickly determine another flight that would satisfy a customer's needs. Major hotel chains, such as Holiday Inn, have nationwide registration systems. These computer-based information systems allow travelers to book all their lodging for a cross-country trip with one phone call. If one Holiday Inn is booked for a particular night, reservation agents can quickly check the system for the closest available Holiday Inn.

Many opportunities exist for using computer and information technology to improve operations and to gain competitive advantage. These opportunities will increase as the flow of lower-cost technologies provides significant new capabilities. In order to remain competitive, future managers should understand these technologies and be capable of implementing them. Tomorrow's managers will be expected to do more and better work with these improving tools.

Service Businesses: Applying Information Technology

American Hospital Supply (AHS) is a leading distributor of a broad line of medical products to doctors, laboratories, and hospitals. AHS has developed an order-entry system that links its customers with its mainframe computer. Customers have computer terminals and can place orders at any time. For customers, the computer system simplifies ordering and helps control inventories. For AHS, it reduces costs and provides a competitive edge over rival companies. Once customers have learned AHS's system, they are reluctant to change.

USA Today is the first attempt at a national newspaper. It was made possible by the application of computer-based word processing and communication technology. The text of the paper is transmitted via satellite to geographically dispersed printing plants. Information technology allows an edition to be created, transmitted, and printed in color each day. *USA Today's* use of technology allows it to publish a national daily newspaper, something that others have been unable to duplicate.

Merrill Lynch and Company, a stock brokerage firm, established the cash management account (CMA), which shattered traditional differences between banks and brokerage firms. A CMA is a combination of charge card, checking account, and brokerage service. Implementation of CMAs required the development of communication and data-processing capabilities that link each Merrill Lynch office with the central check-clearing and charge-processing facilities. This system provides customers with up-to-date information on account balances and transfers excess funds from low-paying accounts into higher-interest money-market accounts. Being the first to implement this technology gave Merrill Lynch an advantage over its competition.

SUMMARY

- Operations should be viewed by top management as an opportunity to develop competitive advantage. When properly designed, operations can increase an organization's flexibility, reduce costs, enhance quality, and improve productivity.
- Operations are strategically important to an organization's success. Without this strategic view, an organization can never reach its full potential.
- Links that connect operations to an organization's strategy begin with analysis of the competitive environment and include an appraisal of the organization's skills, the implications of corporate strategy for operations, and the economic and technological limits of operations.
- Computer and information technology helps an organization to achieve a competitive advantage. These systems provide information to enhance decision making and improve control by integrating various parts of the production process.
- The integration of CAD, CAM, GT, cellular manufacturing, CAPP, robotics, automated material handling, FMSs, and computerized production planning and control systems can allow producers to improve their competitive position.

- Applications of information technology in service operations are important ways to achieve a competitive advantage. These applications will tend to be centered on improved systems to support decision making.

CAREER PROFILE

Donna R. Gordon

Vice-President
Toledo Hospital

Donna R. Gordon is the vice-president in charge of support service operations at the Toledo Hospital, an 813-bed teaching hospital and tertiary referral center for northwestern Ohio and southeastern Michigan. She is responsible for directing and administering administrative representatives, central supply, the child care center, dietary services, distribution, educational support services, environmental services, laundry, maintenance and plant operations, purchasing, reprographics, security, and transportation. She is also responsible for implementing a total quality improvement program throughout the hospital's operations. The quality improvement program is based on the theories of Dr. Juran and Dr. Deming and is similar to models used in industry. Donna's areas employ approximately 750 people and have an annual budget of almost $40 million.

Work Experience

Previously, Donna was executive director of Xavier Park and director of planning for Mercy Health Center in Dubuque, Iowa, and before that she was assistant hospital director–support services for the University of Missouri Hospital and Clinics in Columbia, Missouri. She earned a Master's degree in public health with a certificate in hospital administration from the University of Missouri in 1980 and before that held a number of positions in education.

Personal Views

Donna believes that people are the key to the success of any endeavor. Leadership that enlists and encourages the full commitment of empowered employees, whose efforts are coordinated toward the achievement of a well-planned goal, is essential to that success. As technology becomes more complex, human relations skills become even more important. As she and many in this country continue to discover, doing the right thing right the first time is also the least expensive and most profitable method of operation. It falls on administration then to establish clear direction for the organization and to empower employees at all levels to achieve these goals.

QUESTIONS

1. Describe what is meant by the phrase "operations for competitive advantage."

2. How and why are operations strategically important?

3. How can an organization link corporate strategy and operations? Describe the process.

4. How can the following attributes help an organization achieve competitive advantage?

a. Flexibility
b. Increases in productivity
c. Enhanced quality
d. Refinements in product and process technology

5. Describe the role of computer and information technology in improving manufacturing operations.

6. How can CAD increase an organization's ability to compete?

7. An FMS includes several component technologies. Describe these technologies, and discuss how they are related.

8. Production planning and control systems are necessary to manage operations. How do MRP II and JIT complement each other in filling this need?

9. How does CIM offer opportunities for achieving competitive advantage?

10. Describe some ways that service operations can use computer and information technology to gain competitive advantage. Why are these means different from those used by manufacturers?

11. Find an article that discusses CIM. Summarize the article in one paragraph. In a second paragraph, describe how the company used CIM to improve operations. Provide the article reference or a copy of the article.

12. Find an article that discusses the use of information technology to gain competitive advantage. Summarize the article in one paragraph. In a second paragraph, describe how the company used information technology to improve operations. Provide the article reference or a copy of the article.

MINI-CASES

Midas Muffler

Assume that Midas Muffler is considering adding engine tune-ups to its existing product line. Top management has called you in as a consultant to help them to analyze this opportunity. The first thing they ask you to do is read their Operations in Action segment in this chapter.

Management is concerned about the impact that this new service will have on existing operations. Presently, the company has a policy that customers will not wait longer than 30 minutes for muffler service. How can Midas maintain that pledge? What methods of scheduling tune-up service might make it easier for Midas to keep its pledge? If reaction to the new service is great, the shops may not have the capacity to satisfy demand. Should the company add capacity to existing shops to take the extra load, or should it add more shops? How will the shop owners react to the new proposal? Assume that most of the shops are very profitable. Will the owners want higher profits?

Midas Muffler's management is looking for help in organizing their thinking and has asked you to respond to the following questions in a two-page report. Your responses should include the critical issues raised in the previous paragraph.

1. What are the anticipated impacts on operating efficiency? How would you attempt to minimize the negative impacts?

2. Should some operating practices be changed to accommodate the tune-ups?

3. Should input be gathered from the shop owners? If so, what?

4. If it decides to launch this new program, how should Midas begin?

Schoonover Bank and Trust, Inc.

Schoonover Bank and Trust, Inc., has recently installed automated teller machines (ATMs) at several locations in its marketing area. Response to the machines has been weaker than anticipated. Schoonover had hoped to use the computerized tellers to take the pressure off many of their branch banks, which have been experiencing an overload at peak times. The lines of customers have exceeded the desired maximum on many occasions, and service times have been excessive. Bank management likes to see ten or fewer customers waiting at a branch and prefers that service time, including the time in line, be no more than twelve minutes for most customers. Bank management has defined "most" to mean that 95 percent of the customers will spend twelve minutes or less waiting in line and being served. In addition to improved service and reduced investment, ATMs reduce the cost of processing transactions.

Steve Hogan, the operations manager for Schoonover, has asked you to help solve the problem. Should the ATMs be considered a mistake, and should efforts be made to expand branch bank capacity? Expanding branch banking capacity is far more expensive than installing ATMs.

1. What are the strategic implications of retreating from ATMs? How will the competition view such a retreat?

2. How will this decision impact Schoonover's plans to automate other services and eventually to offer banking from home via personal computers?

3. Assuming Schoonover decides to continue with ATMs, what should be done to increase customer use? Do not limit the discussion to operating issues.

SELECTED BIBLIOGRAPHY

Abernathy, William J., and Townsend, Phillip L. "Technology, Productivity and Process Change." *Technology Forecasting and Social Change* 7 (1975): 379–396.

Benjamin, R. I.; Rockart, J. F.; Morton, M. S.; and Wyman, J. "Information Technology: A Strategic Opportunity." *Sloan Management Review* 25, no. 3 (Spring 1984): 3–10.

Black, J. T. "Cellular Manufacturing Systems Reduce Setup Time, Make Small Lot Production Economical." *Industrial Engineering* 15, no. 11 (November 1983): 36–48.

Boddy, D., and Buchanan, D. A. "Information Technology and Productivity: Myths and Realities." *Omega: International Journal of Management Science* 12, no. 3 (1984): 233–240.

Burbidge, J. L., and Dale, B. G. "Planning the Introduction and Predicting the Benefits of Group Technology." *Engineering Costs and Production Economics* 8, no. 1 (1984): 117–128.

Choobineh, F. "Optimum Loading for GT/MRP Manufacturing Systems." *Computer and Industrial Engineering* 8, no. 3/4 (1984): 197–206.

Cyert, R., "Saving the Smokestack Industries." *Bell Atlantic Quarterly* 2, no. 3 (Autumn 1985): 17–24.

Doll, William, and Vonderembse, Mark. "Forging a Partnership to Achieve Competitive Advantage: The CIM Challenge." *MIS Quarterly* 11, no. 2 (June 1987): 205–220.

Frohman, A. L. "Technology as a Competitive Weapon." *Harvard Business Review* 60, no. 1 (January–February 1982): 97–104.

Gale, Bradley T. "Can More Capital Buy Higher Productivity?" *Harvard Business Review* 59, no. 4 (July–August 1980): 78–86.

Gold, Bela. "CAM Sets New Rules for Production." *Harvard Business Review* 60, no. 6 (November–December 1982): 88–94.

Goldhar, J. D., and Jelinek, M. "Plan for Economies of Scope." *Harvard Business Review* 61, no. 6 (November–December 1983): 141–148.

Greene, T. J., and Sadowski, R. P. "A Review of Cellular Manufacturing Assumptions, Advantages and Design Techniques." *Journal of Operations Management* 4, no. 2 (February 1984): 85–97.

Jelinek, Mariann. "Technology, Organizations, and Contingency." *Academy of Management Review* (January 1977): 17–26.

Lewin, Arie, and Minton, John W. "Determining Organizational Effectiveness: Another Look, and an Agenda for Research." *Management Science* 32, no. 5 (May 1986): 514–538.

McFarlan, F. W. "Information Technology Changes the Way You Compete." *Harvard Business Review* 62, no. 3 (May–June 1984): 98–103.

Parsons, G. L. "Information Technology: A New Competitive Weapon." *Sloan Management Review* 25, no. 1 (Fall 1983): 3–13.

Porter, M. E. *Competitive Advantage: Creating and Sustaining Superior Performance*. New York: Free Press, 1985.

Rosenthal, S. R. "Progress Towards the 'Factory of the Future.'" *Journal of Operations Management* 4, no. 3 (May 1984): 203–229.

Sadowski, R. P. "Computer-Integrated Manufacturing Series Will Apply Systems Approach to Factory of Future." *Industrial Engineering* 16, no. 1 (January 1984): 35–40.

Skinner, W. "Manufacturing—Missing Link in Corporate Strategy." *Harvard Business Review* 47, no. 3 (May–June 1969): 136–145.

Skinner, W. "Wanted: Managers for the Factory of the Future." *Annals of the American Academy of Political and Social Science* (November 1983): 102–114.

Skinner, W. "Operations Technology: Blind Spot in Strategic Management." *Interfaces* 14, no. 1 (January–February 1984): 116–125.

Skinner, W. *Manufacturing: The Formidable Competitive Weapon*. New York: Wiley, 1985.

Skinner, W. "The Productivity Paradox." *Harvard Business Review* 64, no. 4 (July–August 1986): 55–59.

Slautterback, William H., and Werther, William B. "The Third Revolution: Computer Integrated Manufacturing." *National Productivity Review* (Autumn 1984): 367–374.

Turban, Efraim. *Decision Support and Expert Systems: Management Support Systems*. New York: Macmillan, 1990.

U. S. Department of Commerce, International Trade Administration, Office of Capital Goods and International Construction Sector Group. *A Competitive Assessment of the U. S. Flexible Manufacturing System Industry.* Washington D. C.: U. S. Government Printing Office, July 1985.

Vandermerwe, Sandra, and L'Huillier, Marc-André. "Euro-Consumers in 1992." *Business Horizons* 32, no. 1 (January–February 1989): 34–40.

Zisk, B. I. "Flexibility is Key to Automated Material Transport System for Manufacturing Cells." *Industrial Engineering* 15, no. 11 (November 1983): 58–64.

Chapter 3

Models and Forecasting

CHAPTER OUTLINE

LEARNING OBJECTIVES

After completing this chapter, you should be able to

- Define a model and describe how models can be used to analyze operating problems.
- Define forecasting and discuss the nature of forecasting.
- Explain how forecasting can be applied to various problems in operations and in the organization.
- Describe methods of forecasting, including judgment and experience, time-series analysis, and regression and correlation.
- Construct forecasting models and estimate forecasting error.
- Discuss tracking signals and how they can be used to verify that a forecasting model is accurate.

The Oil Drilling Industry: When Will Demand Pick Up?

After the oil embargo of the early 1970s, the demand for oil exploration skyrocketed. Drilling activity reached its peak in the early 1980s and then declined steadily until the beginning of the 1990s. The industry that once counted 20,000 independent drillers now has about 12,000, and forty-six of sixty-two big public companies have disappeared. What caused the buildup of drilling operations?

After the oil embargo, the price of gasoline increased from about $.30 per gallon to a little over $.50 per gallon in a few weeks. The price was forecasted to increase to over $1 per gallon. Based on the actual and the forecasted price increases and on a forecasted increase in consumption for gasoline and other crude oil derivatives, drillers purchased new oil drilling rigs, and many new organizations were formed to search for oil. By the end of the 1970s, the price for gasoline approached $1 per gallon and eventually reached a peak of about $1.30 per gallon. At that time, many oil industry executives were forecasting a $2-per-gallon price for gasoline. Drilling operations continued at a feverous pitch. What went wrong?

Several factors caused the prices of crude oil and of the products made from crude oil to decline. Conservation efforts substantially altered consumption patterns. People lowered thermostat settings in their homes and offices, added insulation, replaced drafty windows, and replaced less-efficient heating systems. Automotive companies built more fuel efficient cars to meet federally mandated mileage standards. In 1973, the typical U.S.-produced car got about twelve miles per gallon. Today, cars average about twenty-six miles per gallon. If these changing relationships are not accounted for in the forecast, then the demand for crude oil is likely to be overestimated.

On the production side, exploration efforts found oil, and some oil-producing countries expanded output from existing oil fields to take advantage of the skyrocketing price for crude oil. This increase in output should have indicated to oil industry forecasters that the price of oil on the world market would decline. By 1985, the price of crude oil reached $31 per barrel, significantly above its pre-embargo price of about $3 per barrel. In 1986, when supply substantially outstripped demand, the price temporarily dropped to less than $10 per barrel. In 1990, the price stood at a little over $20 per barrel and was expected to hold steady or decline.

What does the future hold for oil drillers? Much depends on the outlook (forecast) for crude oil prices, which are based on the forecasted demand for gasoline, heating oil, and other products refined from crude oil. It also depends on the forecasted output of oil-producing operations throughout the world.[1]

INTRODUCTION

The purposes of this chapter are to discuss models and describe how they can be applied to business problems and to explain forecasting and its role in operations. A **model** is an abstraction from the real problem of the key variables and relationships in order to simplify the problem. The purpose of modeling is to provide the user with a better understanding of the problem and with a means of manipulating the results for what-if analysis.

A **forecast** is a prediction of the future. It often examines historical data to determine relationships between the key variables in a problem and uses those relationships to make statements about the future. Used in that way, a forecast is one type of model. Forecasting is discussed in more detail in a later section of this chapter.

MODELS AND DECISION MAKING

Organizational performance is a result of the decisions that management makes over a period of time: decisions about what markets to enter, what products to produce, what types of equipment and facilities to acquire, and where to locate facilities. The quality of the decision is a function of how well managers do the following:

1. *Define the problem and the factors that influence it.* If a hospital is having difficulty maintaining high-quality, low-cost food service, it should define that clearly and describe what factors might affect it, such as the quality and cost of incoming food and the training of staff.
2. *Select criteria to guide the decision, and establish objectives.* The hospital may select cost per meal and patient satisfaction as the criteria. The objectives could be to reduce meal costs by 15 percent and to improve patient satisfaction to 90 percent, based on the hospital's weekly surveys.
3. *Formulate a model or models that help the manager understand the relationships between the factors that influence the problem and the objectives that he or she is trying to achieve.* Develop mathematical relationships (one type of model) that indicate how materials (food) and labor are converted into meals. This could include analysis of the amount of food wasted and the standard amount of labor required to prepare a meal.
4. *Collect relevant data.* Data on food cost, the amount of food consumed, the number of meals served, and the amount of labor would be collected. Also, patient preferences would be investigated so that meals would not only meet nutritional requirements, but also taste good.
5. *Identify and evaluate alternatives.* There may be many alternatives, including subcontracting food preparation, considering new food suppliers, establishing better training programs for the staff, and changing management.
6. *Select the best alternative.* One of these alternatives, another alternative, or some combination of alternatives would be selected.
7. *Implement the alternative, and re-evaluate.* The selected alternative(s) would be implemented, and the problem would be re-evaluated. This re-evaluation would include monitoring the accounting cost reports and the patient survey data to see if the objectives have been achieved.

A model is a very important way of thinking about a problem. Decision makers use models to increase their understanding of the problem that they are considering. A model helps managers simplify the problem by focusing on the key variables and relationships in the problem. The model also allows managers to try different options quickly and inexpensively. In these ways, decision making can be improved.

Types of Models

Most of us have seen model airplanes, models of dams, or models of other structures. These models can be used to test design characteristics. Model airplanes can be tested in wind tunnels to determine aerodynamic properties, and a model of a hydroelectric dam can help architects and engineers find ways of integrating the structure with the landscape. These models have physical characteristics similar to those of the "real thing" that is being studied. Experiments can be performed on this type of model to see how it might perform under actual operating conditions. Models also include the drawings of a building that display the physical relationships between the various parts of the structure. All of these models are simplifications of the real thing and help designers make better decisions.

On the other hand, managers and others use mathematical abstraction to model important relationships. The break-even-point calculation that many of you performed in accounting is an example of applying a mathematical model. The use of drawings and diagrams is also modeling. The CAD system that describes product features on a computer screen is a model. The graph in the newspaper that illustrates stock market price changes in the last six months is a way to help the reader see trends in the market. Models do not have to be sophisticated to be useful.

Most models can be grouped into four categories.

1. *Mathematical models* include algebraic models such as break-even analysis, statistical models used in forecasting and quality control, mathematical programming models such as linear programming, and calculus-based models such as the economic order quantity. Mathematical models are widely used in all areas within an organization.
2. *Graphs and charts* are pictorial representations of mathematical relationships. They include a graphical representation of break-even analysis, a pie chart that illustrates market share in an industry, a graph of an organization's stock price over the past six months, and a bar chart that indicates the demand for energy for the past five years.
3. *Diagrams and drawings* are pictorial representations of conceptual relationships. They include a precedence diagram that represents the sequence required to assemble a building, a drawing of a gear that is part of a transmission in a car, a diagram that represents the logic of a computer program, and the drawing of an aircraft carrier.
4. *Scale models and prototypes* are physical representations of the item. They include a scale model of an airplane and the first part produced (prototype) which is normally used for testing purposes.

The Application of Models

You use models frequently without realizing it. If you invite friends over for pizza, you will probably determine how much pizza to order by multiplying the number of people you anticipate are coming by the amount of pizza you expect each person to consume, on the average. You will probably take that one step farther and multiply the anticipated cost per pizza by the number of pizzas required to determine if you have enough money. This is a simple mathematical model that can be used to plan a simple party or expanded to plan a major social event.

In mathematical models, symbols and algebra are often used to show relationships. Mathematical models can be simple or complex. For example, suppose a family is planning a trip to Disney World in Orlando, Florida. To estimate gasoline costs for the trip, family members check a road atlas (one type of model). They determine that Orlando is approximately a 2,200-mile round trip from their home. From records (a data base) kept on the family car, the family estimates that the car will achieve 23 miles per gallon (mpg) on the highway. The average cost of a gallon of gasoline is estimated at \$.95. Using the following model, they make an estimate of gasoline cost.

$$\text{Cost} = (\text{trip miles})(\text{cost per gallon})/\text{miles per gallon}$$

$$= \frac{(2{,}200 \text{ miles})(\$.95 \text{ per gallon})}{23 \text{ mpg}}$$

$$= \$90.87$$

Using Models to Answer What-If Questions

A mathematical model can be used to answer what-if questions. In the previous example, costs could be estimated for a side trip to Tampa or for a 10-cent increase in the price of a gallon of gas, as shown below.

$$\text{Cost} = \frac{(2{,}200 \text{ miles})(\$1.05 \text{ per gallon})}{23 \text{ mpg}}$$

$$= \$100.43$$

The model could also be used to estimate the cost of the trip if the car averaged only 20 miles per gallon, as shown below.

$$\text{Cost} = \frac{(2{,}200 \text{ miles})(\$.95 \text{ per gallon})}{20 \text{ mpg}}$$

$$= \$104.50$$

Building Models That Are Easy to Understand

Models cannot include all factors that affect the outcome because many factors cannot be defined precisely. Also, adding too many variables complicates the model without significantly increasing the accuracy of the prediction. For example, on the trip to Florida the number of miles driven is affected by the number of rest stops made, the number of unexpected detours taken, and even the number of lane changes made. The number of miles per gallon is influenced by the car's speed, the rate of acceleration, and the amount of time spent idling in traffic. These variables are not in the model. The model builder should ask if adding them would significantly improve the model's accuracy.

Why Modeling Is Important

The purpose of modeling is to learn about the item being investigated by manipulating the model and by subjecting it to a changing set of assumptions. The use of a model to determine the gasoline cost for the trip to Disney World is one example. What are the alternatives to modeling? In the example, if no modeling is done, the travelers do not know how much money to allocate to gasoline and how much they can spend on food, lodging, and sightseeing. A manager who is trying to decide how much inventory to maintain or how much to spend on advertising would not seriously consider the do-nothing option. Another option would be to take a practice trip to Florida so that an accurate estimate of fuel costs could be obtained. A manager is unlikely to seriously consider this option because of the time and expense required to make the practice trip. Modeling becomes an important way to examine decisions and to gather information to assist in decision making. As managers use models and gain experience through the practice of business, they build an experience base that is helpful in decision making.

To summarize, models are useful because they allow managers to

1. Simplify complex problems for analysis. The graphical representation of a product or a facility layout on a CAD terminal is one example.
2. See quickly and inexpensively the results of a decision without doing the task. A supermarket manager may want to see the impact on customer service when another checkout stand is added. Instead of investing the money to build another stand, the manager builds a model which can be analyzed with and without the extra stand. The model can be constructed in a day or two, using a few hours of the manager's time. The manager can manipulate the model to learn how adding another stand improves customer service.
3. Answer what-if questions concerning parameters in the model. For the trip to Florida, for example, what happens to gasoline costs if the price of gasoline increases?

Models Used in Business and Operations

Models are widely used in operations and in other areas within organizations. Financial managers use net present value and internal rate of return procedures to analyze investment alternatives. Information systems personnel use flow diagrams to better understand the logic needed to develop a computerized order-entry system. Accountants have developed ratios such as the current ratio and the quick ratio to quickly grasp an organization's ability to pay its short-term bills. Marketing managers use the product life cycle to help them understand the phases that products pass through. Each of these is a model that allows management to simplify a complex idea so the important relationships can be examined.

In operations, models are commonly used to understand concepts. The following list contains a few of the models discussed in this book:

Model	Chapter	Purpose
Forecasting	3	Projects future demand, cost, etc.
Precedence Diagram	4	Illustrates the sequence of operations in assembling a finished product
Decision Tree	5	Explains the decision alternatives and allows managers to evaluate the alternatives
Cost-Volume-Profit	7	Uses estimates of costs, revenue, volume sold, and volume produced to determine profit
Assembly Line Balancing	8	Assigns tasks to work stations in order to minimize idle time
Material Requirements Planning	11	Provides a basis for planning material acquisition and for scheduling production
Critical Path Method	14	Determines the shortest time to complete a job or project

Model	Chapter	Purpose
Make or Buy	15	Determines the point at which the cost to buy a good or service equals the cost to make it
Lot Sizing	16	Calculates the amount of inventory to order
Acceptance Sampling	17	Determines the sample size for a quality control inspection plan

FORECASTING

Forecasting is an attempt to predict the future. Forecasts are usually the result of examining past experiences to gain insights into the future. These insights often take the form of mathematical models that are used to project future sales, product costs, advertising costs, etc. The application of forecasting is not limited to predicting factors needed to operate a business. Forecasting can also be used to estimate the cost of living, housing prices, and the average family income in the year 2020. For organizations, forecasts are an essential part of planning. It would be illogical to plan for tomorrow without some vision of what might happen.

The critical word in the last sentence is *might.* Any competent forecaster knows that the future holds many alternatives and that a forecast is only one of those possibilities. Management should recognize the need to proceed with planning using the best possible forecast and should have contingency plans to deal with uncertainty. Management should not assume that the future is predetermined, but should realize that its actions can help to shape future events. With the proper plans and execution of those plans, an organization can have some control of its future.

INTEGRATING THE SYSTEM

Forecasting for Capacity Decision Making, Production Planning, and Marketing

To be prepared for the future, an organization should plan to acquire the facilities necessary to satisfy future demand. Before deciding to expand capacity, an organization should know its existing capacity and have a forecast of demand. This chapter describes forecasting and illustrates the use of several forecasting techniques. The next chapter illustrates ways to estimate capacity and discusses capacity decision making.

Forecasts are essential in other parts of operations and in other parts of the organization. For example, in production planning, a forecast of customer demand is necessary to prepare schedules and to procure raw materials. How does an organization know how many people to have trained for production or how many machines to have ready if it does not know how many units it is expected to produce?

Marketing plans, advertising and promotional campaigns, and the funds for these projects come from sales revenue. A forecast allows marketing to anticipate the amount of money available for these projects. Also, marketing may target efforts to promote products based on their anticipated sales. A product early in the growth stage may get substantially more for advertising than will a product nearing the end of its life cycle.

Forecasting Applications

Forecasting is something that many of us do daily without realizing it. When we consider a plan for the future, we do so with some understanding of what the future might hold. For example, in planning for college, we forecast expenses, the time commitment, and the anticipated benefits. When a car or a home is purchased on credit, plans are made for repaying the loan based on income in the future. Forecasting is part of planning for any organization, whether it is public or private, whether it produces services or goods, whether it operates in the global economy or in a neighborhood. Marketing managers, financial managers, accountants, information systems specialists, engineers, etc., use forecasts. Forecasting impacts on operations managers, too. The following list contains examples of some of the items that impact on operations managers:

Item Forecasted	Used by Managers to
Demand for the product	Determine if sufficient capacity is available to satisfy demand Prepare plan and schedules for production
Labor and material costs	Prepare budgets for planning Estimate profit from operations
Productivity	Determine the work force required to do the job

The Nature of Forecasting

The forecasting process consists of the following steps: determining the objectives of the forecast, developing and testing a model, applying the model, considering real-world constraints on the model's application, and revising and evaluating the forecast (human judgment). Exhibit 3.1 illustrates these steps.

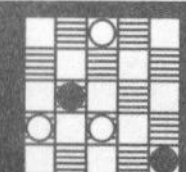

GAINING STRATEGIC ADVANTAGE WITH FORECASTING

Planning for the Future

The U.S. aluminum industry is taking a big gamble. Five years ago, the industry closed 1.2 million tons of old aluminum smelting capacity and has invested $4.5 billion in new plants and equipment. The gamble was based, in part, on a forecast that the U.S. dollar would drop when compared to foreign currency. The decline in the dollar caused U.S.-produced aluminum to be less costly to foreign consumers, and exports increased. At the same time, worldwide demand for aluminum climbed as predicted. Profits at Alcoa, Reynolds, and Alcan rose 63 percent.

Dow Jones & Company, publishers of *The Wall Street Journal* and *Barron's*, has seen its advertising sales decline and the operating profit from its business publications fall since the 1987 stock market crash. In 1989, Dow Jones executives forecasted no growth in advertising for the rest of the year and the beginning of the next year. Plans had to be developed to deal with the forecast and to improve future revenues.

Guinness Peat Aviation (GPA) is one of the largest lessors of commercial aircraft in the world. Based on a forecast for continued growth in the demand for air travel, GPA announced orders and options for 308 aircraft worth $17 billion. This is the largest aircraft order ever. Most aircraft producers have large backlogs of orders, so airlines that have not planned ahead may have to deal with GPA to lease the aircraft needed to meet the forecasted demand for air travel. This puts GPA in a position to earn premium prices for those leases.[2]

Exhibit 3.1 Steps in Forecasting

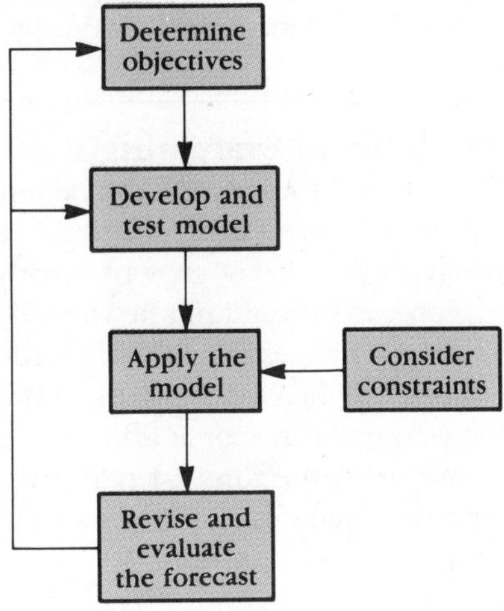

Determining the Objectives

What kind of information is needed by the manager? From a meeting between the analyst and the manager, a list of needs is determined. The following questions should be considered:

1. What is the purpose of the forecast?
2. What variables are to be forecast?
3. Who will use the forecast?
4. What is the time frame of the forecast—long or short term?
5. How accurate should the forecast be?
6. When is the forecast needed?

Developing and Testing a Model

A model should be developed and then tested to ensure that it is as accurate as possible. Moving average, weighted moving average, exponential smoothing, time series analysis, and regression analysis techniques for developing forecasting models are discussed later in this chapter. Often the help of a technical analyst is needed at this point.

Applying the Model

After the model is tested, historical data about the problem are collected. These data are applied to the model, and the forecast is obtained. Great care should be taken so that the proper data are used and the model is applied correctly.

Considering Real-World Constraints

Applying any model requires consideration of real-world constraints. For example, a model may predict that sales will double in the next three years. Management therefore expands the plant, but does not think of the impact this increase will have on the distribution system. What if the company cannot move the increased volume? What about raw-material availability, actions such as price cutting taken by competitors, and the availability of skilled labor? Application of the forecast should be grounded in reality. These factors are within management's control, and management action is required if a workable solution is to be obtained.

Revising and Evaluating the Forecast

The technical forecast should be tempered with human judgment. What relationships might have changed? In the case of the electricity industry, a fundamental change in the rate of growth greatly affected the accuracy of the forecast.

Forecasts should not be treated as sacred or static. Revisions should be made in light of changes taking place within the firm or the environment. The need for revision may be occasioned by changes in price, product characteristics, advertising expenditures, or actions by competitors. Evaluation is the ongoing exercise of comparing the forecast with the actual results. This control process is necessary to maintain quality estimates in the future.

FORECASTING METHODS

Before becoming immersed in the details involved with actually preparing a forecast, it is important to know that there is more to forecasting than developing the model and doing the analysis. The results from the model should be tempered with human judgment. The future is never perfectly represented by the past, and relationships change over time. Thus, the forecast should take into account judgment and experience.

Many techniques exist for developing a forecast. It is impossible to effectively cover all the techniques in one section or even in an entire chapter. Books are

OPERATIONS IN ACTION

The Electric Power Generation Industry: Changing Relationships

As described in the Operations in Action that began this chapter, the 1973 oil embargo caused the price of a barrel of crude oil to climb dramatically in a short period of time. There were some obvious dislocations as the prices of all energy climbed. Shortages of gasoline in various parts of the country were common.

This event, coupled with further price increases, caused a nationwide effort to conserve energy. The impact on the growth of electrical utilities was significant. Instead of growing at about 3 percent annually, the rate of growth plummeted to near zero and since has rebounded somewhat. The embargo changed the pattern of growth in the industry. Electrical utilities had planned for a significantly higher growth rate and did not react quickly enough to the change. Many utilities continued to build new power plants. The results were a surplus of electrical generation capacity and the cancellation of orders for many nuclear power plants. Even today, this surplus capacity is creating problems for some utilities.

devoted to forecasting, and some students major in forecasting as others major in marketing, accounting, or operations. In this section, forecasts based on judgment and experience are discussed, and time-series analysis is addressed, including the simple moving average, the weighted moving average, exponential smoothing, and time-series decomposition. Regression and correlation analysis, forecasting error, and tracking signals are also discussed. A list of additional readings is provided in the Selected Bibliography.

Qualitative Approaches to Forecasting

Although mathematical models are useful in helping management make predictions, qualitative approaches can also be helpful. In fact, qualitative forecasts that are based on subjective interpretation of historical data and observations are frequently used. A homeowner who decides to refinance his or her home has made an implicit prediction that home mortgage rates have hit the bottom and are likely to increase in the future. Similarly, a manager who decides to purchase extra materials because of uncertainty in supply has made an implicit prediction that a strike or other action may disrupt the flow of materials.

There are many different qualitative methods for making forecasts. We discuss briefly the buildup method for predicting sales, surveys, test markets, and the panel of experts.

The **buildup method** involves starting at the bottom of an organization and making an overall estimate by adding together estimates from each element. If the buildup method is used for predicting sales, the first step is to have each sales representative estimate sales within his or her territory. These estimates are passed on to the next level in the organization for review and evaluation. Estimates that are too high or too low are discussed with the sales representative so that management can understand the logic that supports the prediction. If the sales representative cannot convince the supervisor, a new prediction based on this discussion is made. The prediction is then passed on to the next level in the organization.

As these subjective judgments are passed up in the organization, they are reviewed and refined until they become, in total, the sales forecast for the organization. It is top management's responsibility to make the final judgment on the forecast's validity. One option is to also make an aggregate forecast using one of the mathematical methods discussed later. Then the aggregate forecast can be compared with the buildup forecast, and the differences between the two can be discussed and reconciled. Once top management has decided on the forecast, it becomes an input used in making capacity, production planning, and other decisions.

In some cases, organizations use surveys to gather information externally. A **survey** is a systematic effort to elicit information from specific groups and is usually conducted via a written questionnaire or phone interview. The target of the survey could be consumers, purchasing agents, economists, etc. A survey may attempt to determine how many consumers would buy a new flavor of toothpaste, estimate the buying activity of purchasing agents in the machine tool business, or gauge the long-term health of the economy. Surveys are used to prepare forecasts when historical data are not available, or when historical data are judged not to be indicative of the future. Surveys can also be used to verify the results of another forecasting technique.

Test marketing is a special kind of survey. In a **test market,** the forecaster arranges for the placement of a new product, or an existing product, that has been modified in cities believed to be representative of the organization's overall market. The analyst then measures the sales behavior in the test market over a period of time. When done for an extended period of time, test marketing can be expensive. However, the results tend to be more accurate than those of a survey of consumers because the consumers actually use the product.

A **panel of experts** is made up of people who are knowledgeable about the subject. This group attempts to make a forecast by building consensus. In an organization, this may involve executives who are trying to predict the level of product technology or plant personnel who are trying to estimate material costs. The panel can be used for a wide variety of forecasts, and with this method, forecasts can often be made very quickly.

The **Delphi Technique** uses a panel of experts and surveys in a particular manner. The members of the panel provide a sequence of forecasts through responses to questionnaires. This sequence of questionnaires is directed at the same item or set of items. After each forecast, results are compiled, and the individuals are informed as to the 50th, or the 75th percentile of the item or items being forecasted. Because response is by questionnaire rather than by group interaction, domination by a few individuals, undue conservatism or optimism, and argumentation are avoided. The Delphi process assumes that as each forecast is conducted and the results disseminated among the panel members, the range of responses diminishes and the median moves to a position representing the "true" consensus of the group.

Analyzing a Time Series

The historical data used in forecasting can be cross-sectional data, time-series data, or a combination of the two. The simplest way to illustrate their differences is with an example. The First National Bank of Oakland wants to project usage of their automated teller service. They have collected data from similar systems in Stockton, San Jose, Santa Cruz, and Berkeley for the past two years. The study has both time-series and cross-sectional elements, as shown in Exhibit 3.2. The time-series part of the data is the two years of data that are available for the banks. The cross-sectional element is represented by the data from more than one bank.

Forecasting sales, costs, and other relevant estimates usually involves time-series data, and the techniques discussed here are useful in predicting such data.

Exhibit 3.2 Time-Series and Cross-Sectional Data

	Jan.	Feb.	Mar.	. . .	Dec.	Jan.	Feb.	Mar.	. . .	Dec.
Stockton										
San Jose										
Santa Cruz										
Berkeley										

Exhibit 3.3 Forecasting Time Line

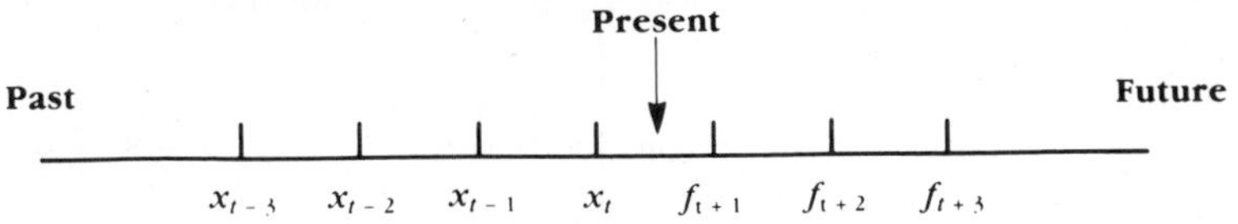

x_t = the actual value of the item to be forecast for the most recent time period t. Prior observations are noted by subtracting 1 from time period t.

f_{t+1} = the forecasted value for the next period. Following periods are designated by adding 1 to time period $t + 1$.

See Exhibit 3.3 for the time line and notation used in forecasting. Each point on the time line has associated with it an actual value, which is represented by x and a subscript. Each point on the line also has a forecasted value, represented by f and a subscript. This is because every period has a forecasted value when it is in the future; as time passes, it will have an actual value.

Simple Moving Average

One approach to forecasting would be to use only the most recent time period to project the next time period. However, this can introduce a significant error into a forecast because any odd occurrence in the previous period will be completely reflected in the prediction. Suppose that in one month a company had a strike that severely restricted the availability of a product and thereby affected sales, or that a temporary price cut caused sales to be significantly greater than normal. If these actions are not repeated in the next month, then using the previous month's sales as the forecast will give a biased prediction.

The purpose of the moving average is to smooth out the peaks and valleys in the data. In the data set shown in Exhibit 3.4, the data fluctuate significantly. Basing a projection on the prior quarter's result could give a significant error. A moving average will smooth these peaks and valleys and give a more reasoned prediction. In the moving average model, the forecast for the next period is equal to the average of the most recent number of time periods.

$$f_{t+1} = \frac{\sum_{i=0}^{n-1} (x_{t-i})}{n}$$

where

f_{t+1} = the forecast for time period $t + 1$; that is, the next time period

x_{t-i} = the observed value for period $t - i$, where t is the last period for which data are available and $i = 0, \ldots, n - 1$.

n = the number of time periods in the average

The longer the time—that is, the greater the n—the more smoothing that will take place. The selection of n is a management decision based on the amount of

Exhibit 3.4 Graph of Imports

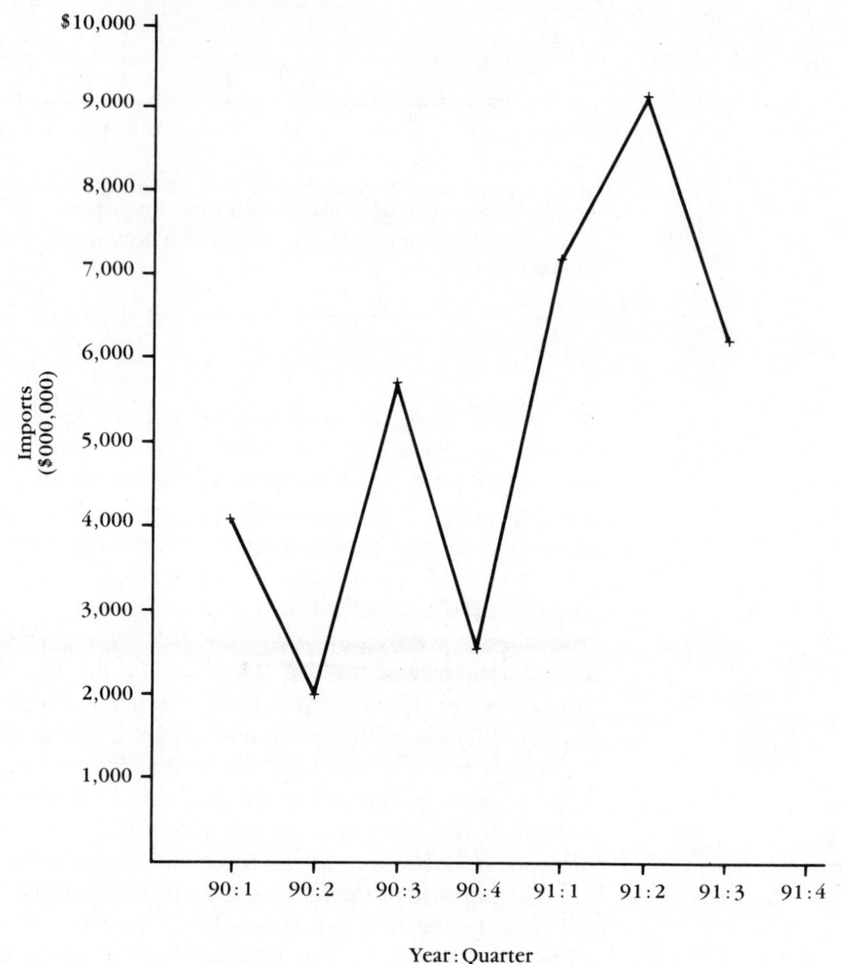

smoothing desired. A small value of n will put more emphasis on recent predictions and will more completely reflect fluctuations in actual sales. In fact, if $n = 1$, then the most recent time period's actual results becomes the next period's forecast.

Example

Following are the data shown in Exhibit 3.4:

Year:Quarter	Imports ($000,000)
1990:1	4,100
1990:2	2,000
1990:3	5,700
1990:4	2,500

Year:Quarter	Imports ($000,000)
1991:1	7,300
1991:2	9,200
1991:3	6,300

To calculate a seven-quarter moving average for imports, sum the most recent seven quarters, and divide by seven. Please observe that the notation year: quarter is used in the subscript here. The fourth quarter of 1991 would be 91:4.

$$f_{91:4} = \frac{(4{,}100 + 2{,}000 + 5{,}700 + 2{,}500 + 7{,}300 + 9{,}200 + 6{,}300)}{7}$$

$$= 5{,}300$$

A three-quarter moving average is calculated as follows:

$$f_{91:4} = \frac{(7{,}300 + 9{,}200 + 6{,}300)}{3}$$

$$= 7{,}600$$

Which estimate is likely to better represent the future? Which prediction should be used? It depends on whether the forecaster feels the last three quarters are a better predictor of what is to come. If so, use the three-month moving average. If the last three months reflect some unusual conditions that are unlikely to recur, then use the seven-month moving average to smooth the high values in the last three quarters. Forecasting models do not give answers to questions. Managerial judgment plays a critical role.

This technique is called a moving average because to forecast the next quarter, the most recent quarter's actual imports are added and the oldest quarter's actual imports are subtracted from the total. In this way, the average continues to be calculated. In a sense, it moves. For the import example, assume the fourth quarter of 1991 had imports totaling \$7,500 million. A three-quarter moving average for the first quarter of 1992 would drop the \$7,300 million, which is the actual value for the first quarter of 1991, and add the most recent quarter. The following illustrates the calculation for the first quarter of 1992:

$$f_{92:1} = \frac{(9{,}200 + 6{,}300 + 7{,}500)}{3}$$

$$= 7{,}667$$

Weighted Moving Average

In a simple moving average, each time period has the same weight. With a weighted moving average, it is possible to assign different weights to each period. The equation for determining weighted moving average is

$$f_{t+1} = \sum_{i=0}^{n-1} (w_{t-i})(x_{t-i})$$

where

w_{t-i} = the weight for period $t - i$, where t is the last period for which data are available and $i = 0, \ldots, n - 1$. The weights for all n periods must sum to 1.0.

Example

In this example, a five-period weighted moving average is calculated for the fourth quarter of 1991.

Year:Quarter	Weight	Imports ($000,000)
1990:1	—	4,100
1990:2	—	2,000
1990:3	.10	5,700
1990:4	.15	2,500
1991:1	.20	7,300
1991:2	.25	9,200
1991:3	.30	6,300

$$f_{t+1} = .1(5{,}700) + .15(2{,}500) + .2(7{,}300) + .25(9{,}200) + .30(6{,}300)$$

$$= 6{,}595$$

If the weights for each period are set at .20, then the weighted moving average and the simple moving average will be equal. Try this for yourself.

The weights for each period need to be selected in some logical way. Usually the most recent periods are weighted more heavily because these periods are thought to be more representative of the future. If there is a trend in the data either up or down, a weighted moving average can adjust more quickly than a simple moving average. Still, this form of the weighted moving average is not as good as regression analysis is in adapting to trends. (Regression analysis will be discussed later in this chapter.)

Exponential Smoothing

Exponential smoothing is really another form of a weighted moving average. It is a procedure for continually revising an estimate in light of more recent data. The method is based on averaging (smoothing) past values. To start a forecast using exponential smoothing, the forecast for the first period, f_{t+1}, would be based on the actual value for the most recent period, x_t. See equation 3.1. The forecast for the second period, f_{t+2}, is equal to the actual value of the previous period, x_{t+1}, times the smoothing constant, A, plus $(1 - A)$ times the prior period's forecast, f_{t+1}. See equation 3.2. Remember, the prior forecast, f_{t+1}, is simply the actual value from period t. The forecast in equation 3.2 is A times the prior period's actual value plus $(1 - A)$ times the prior period's forecast, f_{t+1}.

$$f_{t+1} = x_t \tag{3.1}$$

$$f_{t+2} = A(x_{t+1}) + (1 - A)f_{t+1} \tag{3.2}$$

$$f_{t+3} = A(x_{t+2}) + (1 - A)f_{t+2} \qquad (3.3)$$

$$\vdots$$

$$f_{t+n} = A(x_{t+n-1}) + (1 - A)f_{t+n-1}$$

where

n = some number of periods in the future

$$0 \leq A \leq 1$$

Let's examine one more equation in detail. Equation 3.3 uses the prior period's actual value times the weighting factor, A, plus $(1 - A)$ times the prior period's forecast. Exponential smoothing carries along all the historical actual data in the prior period's forecast.

How should the smoothing constant A be selected before doing an example? First, A must be greater than or equal to zero and less than or equal to one. Within this range, a manager has discretion. What will happen if a manager selects a smoothing constant at an extreme? If $A = 1$, then according to equation 3.2, the forecast will be based solely on the actual value from the prior period. In this case, no smoothing takes place. If the smoothing constant is set to 0, then the prior period's actual value is ignored. Once the forecasting pattern gets started, the forecast is so smooth, it will not change. No actual amounts can enter the equation because $A = 0$. Neither of these alternatives is acceptable.

There are no specific rules about picking the value of A. If the forecaster wants to put more weight on the most recent time period, then A should be set closer to 1. If the manager desires a smoother forecast that will not react violently to short-term change, A should be set closer to 0. Values between .1 and .3 are most commonly used.

Example

Use exponential smoothing to forecast imports from the previous example. To illustrate the impact of the smoothing constant, use $A = .1$ and $A = .6$. To begin, there can be no forecast for the first quarter of available data because no history is available. The forecast for the second quarter is the prior quarter's actual value because no forecast is available for the first quarter. The third quarter's forecast can follow the equations described previously because an actual value and a forecasted value are available for the prior quarter.

For $A = .1$,

$$f_{90:3} = A(x_{90:2}) + (1 - A)f_{90:2}$$

$$= .1(2{,}000) + .9(4{,}100)$$

$$= 3{,}890$$

For $A = .6$,

$$f_{90:3} = .6(2{,}000) + .4(4{,}100)$$

$$= 2{,}840$$

Year:Quarter	Imports ($000,000)	Forecast (1 − A) = .9	Forecast (1 − A) = .4
1990:1	4,100	—	—
1990:2	2,000	4,100	4,100
1990:3	5,700	3,890	2,840
1990:4	2,500	4,071	4,556
1991:1	7,300	3,914	3,322
1991:2	9,200	4,253	5,709
1991:3	6,300	4,748	7,804
1991:4		4,903	6,902

The forecasts are significantly different. The forecast with $A = .1$ does not react to sudden changes. This can be seen graphically in Exhibit 3.5, in which the actual value and the two forecasts are plotted.

Exhibit 3.5 Exponential Smoothing Examples

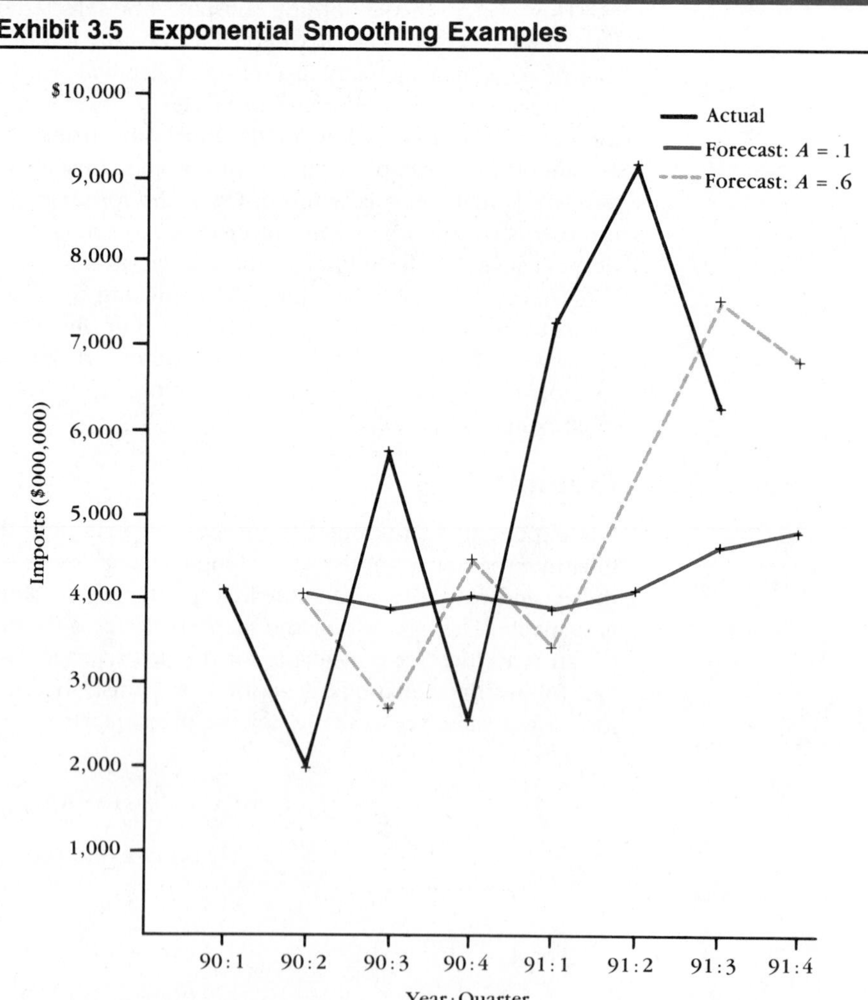

Components of a Time Series

A time series may be influenced by many factors. To this point, we have discussed only one of those components, trend. A significant problem in time-series analysis is to isolate the effects of each component on the item being forecast. These factors are grouped into four categories.

1. Secular trend (T)
2. Seasonal variation (S)
3. Cyclical fluctuations (C)
4. Random fluctuations (R)

Secular trend reflects forces that are responsible for growth or decline over a long period of time. For example, the growth in the 65-plus age group is driving up the demand for vacation homes. **Seasonal variation** reflects forces that act periodically in a fixed period of one year or less. Sales of power boats are much higher in the spring and early summer than in the fall and winter. **Cyclical fluctuations** are changes that occur periodically in a fixed period of more than one year. For example, the health of the economy has an impact on housing starts. Cyclical fluctuations are often referred to as the business-cycle effects. **Random fluctuations** are other types of small variations that may result from many different factors. Time-series analysis generally focuses on estimating the first three factors.

A **stationary time series** is one that does not have a trend component and one whose observations exhibit a constant variance. Exhibit 3.6 illustrates a stationary time series with random fluctuations. A stationary time series may have seasonal variation and cyclical variation, but the overall average does not change.

Exhibit 3.6 Stationary Time Series with Random Fluctuations

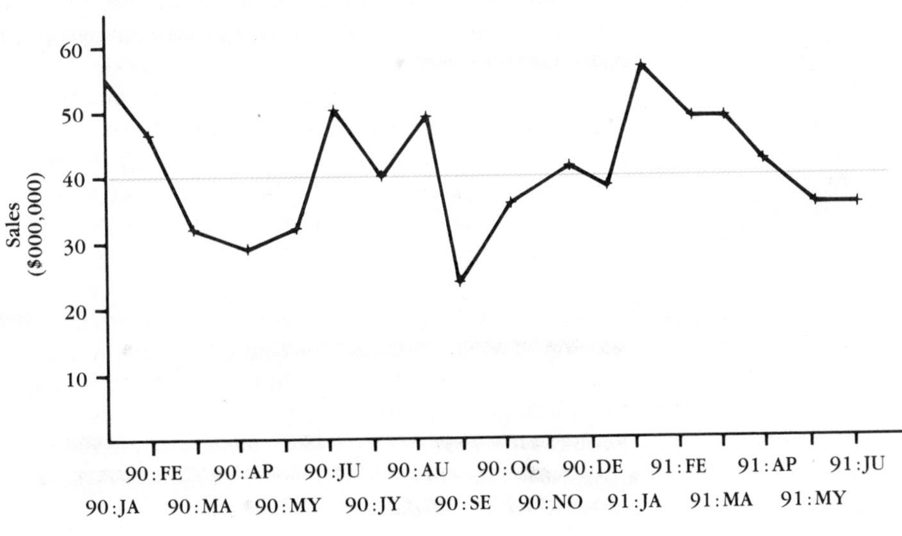

Exhibit 3.7 Stationary Time Series with Seasonal Variation and Random Fluctuations

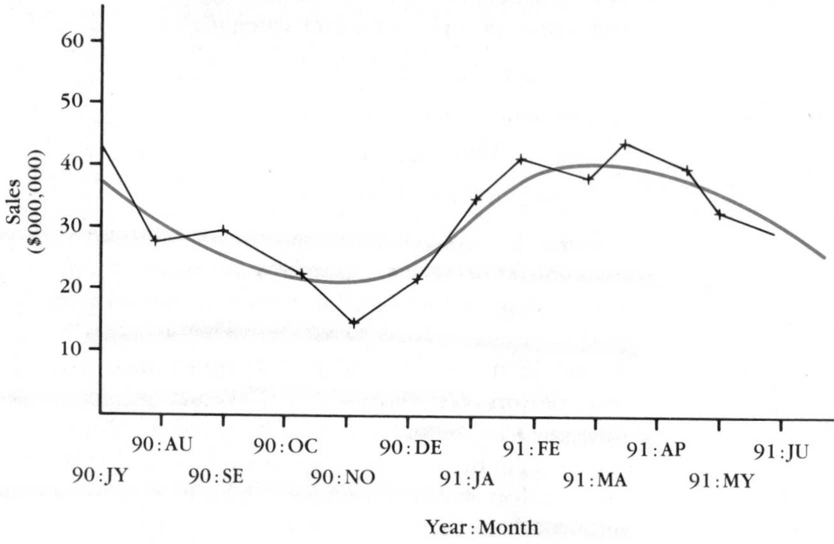

Exhibit 3.7 illustrates a stationary time series with both seasonal variations and random fluctuations.

There are two methods for combining these components in a time series. The **additive model** represents each observation as the sum of the factors: $Y = T + S + C + R$. In this model, each factor is the actual amount, so the trend might be 7,500 units, seasonality might be 300 units, and cyclical fluctuations might be 150 units. The **multiplicative model** combines the factors by multiplying them: $Y = T \times S \times C \times R$. In the multiplicative model, the trend is stated as a number of units, and the remaining factors are percentages, so that seasonality might be 105 percent and cyclical fluctuations might be 80 percent. In other words, seasonality adds 5 percent more to the value of Y during that time period, while the factor that represents the business cycle reduces Y by 20 percent to reflect weakness in the economy. The multiplicative model is more widely used and is discussed here.

Secular Trend. The techniques discussed so far—moving average, weighted moving average, and exponential smoothing—can be used to forecast future values of a time series, but as you recall, these techniques do not directly estimate the amount of trend in a time series. In fact, these forecasting techniques tend to lag behind a time series with a trend component because each of these techniques uses recent history to determine directly the forecast in the next period, rather than to estimate the trend.

Many time series, however, do have a trend component that should be estimated. The graphical method and the method of least squares (regression analysis) are two methods for estimating the trend components. The graphical method is described here, and regression analysis is described later in this chapter. Other techniques can be used and are discussed in the books listed in the Selected Bibliography.

In the **graphical method,** you draw a straight line through the data that describe the underlying, long-term movement in the time series. Exhibit 3.8 shows a time series of a company's fast-food sales that illustrates a trend and random fluctuations. Because of the random fluctuations, some of the actual observations are above the trend line (the blue line), and some are below. The slope of the line, which is drawn by hand using a straightedge, becomes an estimate of the trend in fast-food sales. It is not necessary for the line to intersect the first and last points in the time series as it appears to do in Exhibit 3.8.

From mathematics, the slope/intercept method can be used to get an estimate of the trend. Y, the value of any point on a line, is given by the following equation.

$$Y = a + b(X)$$

Thus, Y is a function of the intersection of the line with the Y-axis (a) plus the slope of the line (b) multiplied by the corresponding point on the X-axis. The intercept (a) is determined by extending the trend line to the Y-axis and reading the intersection point, about \$125 million. The slope or trend is estimated by taking any two points on the line, finding the change in sales (Y-axis), and dividing

Exhibit 3.8 Company Sales of Fast Food

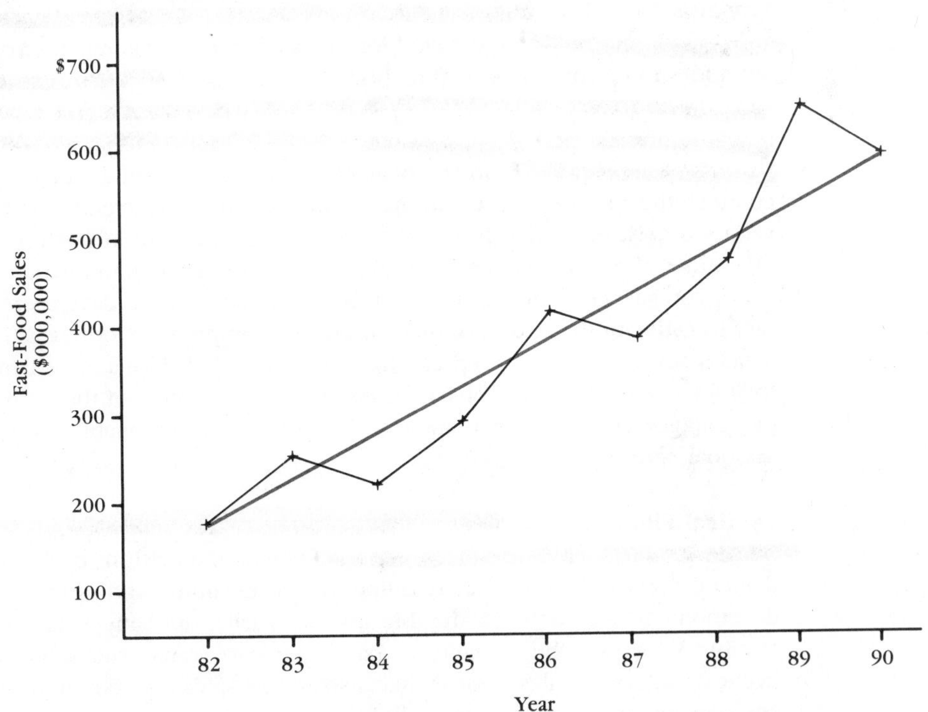

this by the change in time (X-axis). For ease of calculation, we will use the intercept point with the Y-axis which is (1981, \$125) and the point at the opposite end of the blue line. It is important to understand that this is the point on the blue trend line, not the actual sales in 1990. We will estimate that point on the trend line to be about \$600 million.

$$a = \$125 \text{ million}$$

$$b = \frac{\$600 - \$125}{1990 - 1981}$$

$$= \$52.8 \text{ million/year}$$

The trend in fast-food sales as estimated using this model is for sales to increase \$52.8 million dollars per year. To use this estimate of the trend to make future forecasts, it is only necessary to use these parameters in the slope/intercept equation described previously.

$$Y = a + b(X)$$

$$Y = \$125 \text{ million} + (\$52.8 \text{ million/year})(X)$$

In this equation, X is the number of years beyond 1981. For example, to estimate fast-food sales in 1991, X would be 10. For 1992, X would be 11, and so on. The estimated sales for 1992 are

$$Y = \$125 \text{ million} + (\$52.8 \text{ million/year})(11)$$

$$= \$705.8 \text{ million}$$

Seasonal Variation. Seasonal variation is caused by factors that change in force throughout the year. The demand for cross-country skis is much stronger in the fall and winter than it is in the spring and summer. Two simple methods for showing seasonal variation are (1) to graph a year of observations and look for a pattern in the data or (2) to express the value for each month as a percentage of the total for the year. If no seasonal variation exists, then a straight line would connect the monthly observations on the graph. If no trend and no seasonal variation exist each month would represent 8.33 percent of the annual amount. Of course, allowance needs to be made for random fluctuations.

If you suspect that seasonal variation is present in the data, then it is necessary to estimate the extent of that variation. A simple way to do this is to collect data for several years and express the value for each month as a percentage of the total for the year. If these observations are representative of the future, then the percentages given for each month will provide a reasonable estimate of the seasonal pattern.

Cyclical Fluctuations. Cyclical fluctuations are generally thought to be caused by swings in the health of the economy. Cyclical fluctuations can be seen in the demand for such services as retailing, house cleaning, and computer software development and for such durable goods as cars, appliances, and electronics. Exhibit 3.9 shows the demand for passenger cars, vans, trucks, and buses. The cyclical pattern of sales is clear. Because annual sales are shown in the diagram, any seasonal variation in sales is hidden. If the annual sales were broken down into monthly sales, the seasonal variation would be readily apparent. The analysis

Exhibit 3.9 Annual Demand for Passenger Cars, Vans, Trucks, and Buses

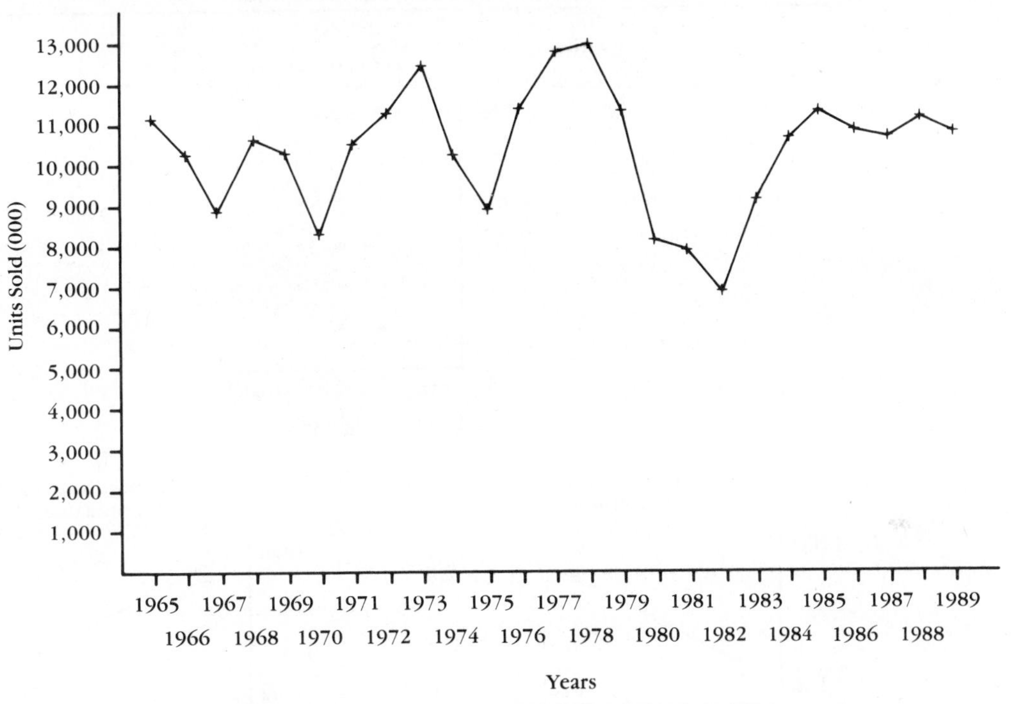

Source: *Survey of Current Business,* United States Department of Commerce Bureau of Economic Analysis, Vol. 45 No. 2—Vol. 70 No. 1.

of cyclical variation is essentially identical to the analysis of seasonal variation where the length of the "season" is the length of the cycle. The difficulty in estimating cyclical variation is that cycles are not regular in length or in amplitude. Further discussion of seasonal and cyclical variations can be found in books listed in the Selected Bibliography.

Regression and Correlation Analysis

Correlation analysis measures the degree of relationship between two variables, and **regression analysis** is a method to predict the value of one variable based on the value of other variables. The **coefficient of correlation** is a measure of the strength of linear relationship between variables. If there is no relationship, then the coefficient of correlation is 0. Perfect positive correlation is 1.0, and perfect negative correlation is −1.0. (See Exhibit 3.10.) Between the limits of perfect positive and perfect negative correlation, there are many levels of strength. Examples are shown in Exhibit 3.11.

Regression analysis can be used to forecast both time-series and cross-sectional data. With time-series data, regression analysis is often used to estimate the slope of a trend line. Regression analysis can be either simple or multiple. **Simple regression** involves the prediction of only one variable (the **dependent**

Exhibit 3.10 Scatter Diagrams Showing Zero, Perfect Positive, and Perfect Negative Correlations

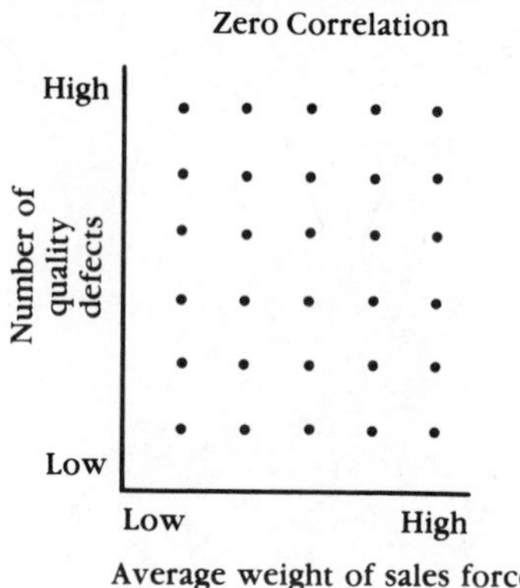

Perfect Positive Correlation

High

Low

Low High

Perfect Negative Correlation

High

Low

Low High

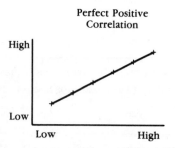

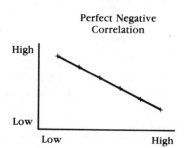

variable) and uses only one variable for prediction (the **independent variable**). **Multiple regression** has only one dependent variable, but can have more than one independent variable.

Simple Regression Model and Correlation

The equation for simple regression follows. Y is the dependent variable, and X is the independent variable. The variable b is the slope of the line, which is estimated by equation 3.4, and variable a is the Y-intercept, which is estimated by equation 3.5. This is like the slope-intercept equation discussed earlier. Here, different methods are used to estimate the slope and the intercept.

$$Y = a + b(X)$$

where

Y = the dependent variable. It depends on the variable X and the model parameters a and b.

X = the independent variable

n = the number of data points in the sample

r = the coefficient of correlation

Exhibit 3.11 Scatter Diagrams Showing Examples of Correlation

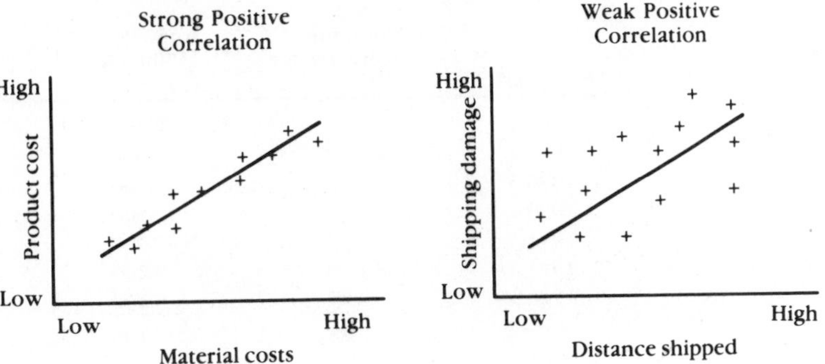

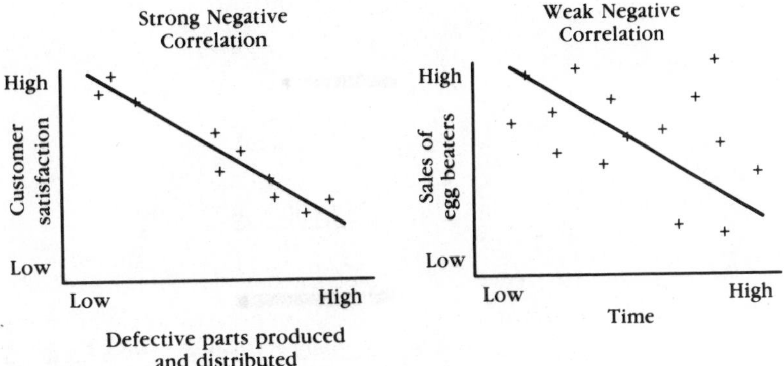

$$b = \frac{n\Sigma XY - \Sigma X \Sigma Y}{n\Sigma X^2 - (\Sigma X)^2} \tag{3.4}$$

$$a = \frac{\Sigma Y}{n} - b\frac{\Sigma X}{n} \tag{3.5}$$

$$r = \frac{n\Sigma XY - \Sigma X \Sigma Y}{\sqrt{[n\Sigma X^2 - (\Sigma X)^2][n\Sigma Y^2 - (\Sigma Y)^2]}} \tag{3.6}$$

Example

When working with time-series data, it is usually easier to convert the time variable from the month/day/year format to simpler numbers. There are many possible ways of coding. Here, the number 1 is used to represent the first time period for which data are available. Following periods will be consecutively numbered. In this example, the assumption is that demand (Y) depends on time

(X), the independent variable. The import data from an earlier example are used for analysis.

Year:Quarter	Coded Value for Year:Quarter (X)	Imports ($000,000) ($Y$)	XY	X^2	Y^2
1990:1	1	4,100	4,100	1	16,810,000
1990:2	2	2,000	4,000	4	4,000,000
1990:3	3	5,700	17,100	9	32,490,000
1990:4	4	2,500	10,000	16	6,250,000
1991:1	5	7,300	36,500	25	53,290,000
1991:2	6	9,200	55,200	36	84,640,000
1991:3	7	6,300	44,100	49	39,690,000
Sum	28	37,100	171,000	140	237,170,000

$$b = \frac{n\Sigma XY - \Sigma X \Sigma Y}{n\Sigma X^2 - (\Sigma X)^2}$$

$$= \frac{7(171{,}000) - 28(37{,}100)}{7(140) - 28^2}$$

$$= \frac{158{,}200}{196}$$

$$= 807.1$$

$$a = \frac{\Sigma Y}{n} - b\frac{\Sigma X}{n}$$

$$= \frac{37{,}100}{7} - \frac{807.1(28)}{7}$$

$$= 2{,}071.6$$

$$r = \frac{n\Sigma XY - \Sigma X \Sigma Y}{\sqrt{[n\Sigma X^2 - (\Sigma X)^2][n\Sigma Y^2 - (\Sigma Y)^2]}}$$

$$= \frac{7(171{,}000) - 28(37{,}100)}{\sqrt{[7(140) - 28^2][7(237{,}170{,}000) - 37{,}100^2]}}$$

$$= \frac{158{,}200}{\sqrt{[196][283{,}780{,}000]}}$$

$$= 0.671$$

Interpreting the results of the model requires an understanding of the original units of the data as well as the slope/intercept method of representing a straight line. The code for the years has been explained. Because the quarters are consecutively numbered, the last quarter of 1991 is coded as 8. The imports are given in millions of dollars. As a result, the imports are projected to increase $807.1 million per quarter. The intercept is $2,072 million, and it represents the point on the regression line for the quarter prior to the first quarter of 1990.

Project the imports for the last quarter of 1991 where the estimated value is represented by Y_e. The predictive model follows.

$$Y_e = 2{,}071.6 + 807.1X$$
$$= 2{,}071.6 + 807.1(8)$$
$$= 8{,}528$$

Thus, the projection for imports is $8,528 million.

Goodness of Fit

How well does the equation determined by regression analysis fit the data? The principles on which simple regression analysis and multiple regression analysis are constructed are similar. The regression model estimates the Y-intercept (a) and the slope of the line (b) that best fits the data. The criterion that is used to determine the "best fit" line minimizes the squared distance from each point to the line. These distances are labeled d_i in Exhibit 3.12, with i equal to 1, . . ., n.

Exhibit 3.12 Regression Line

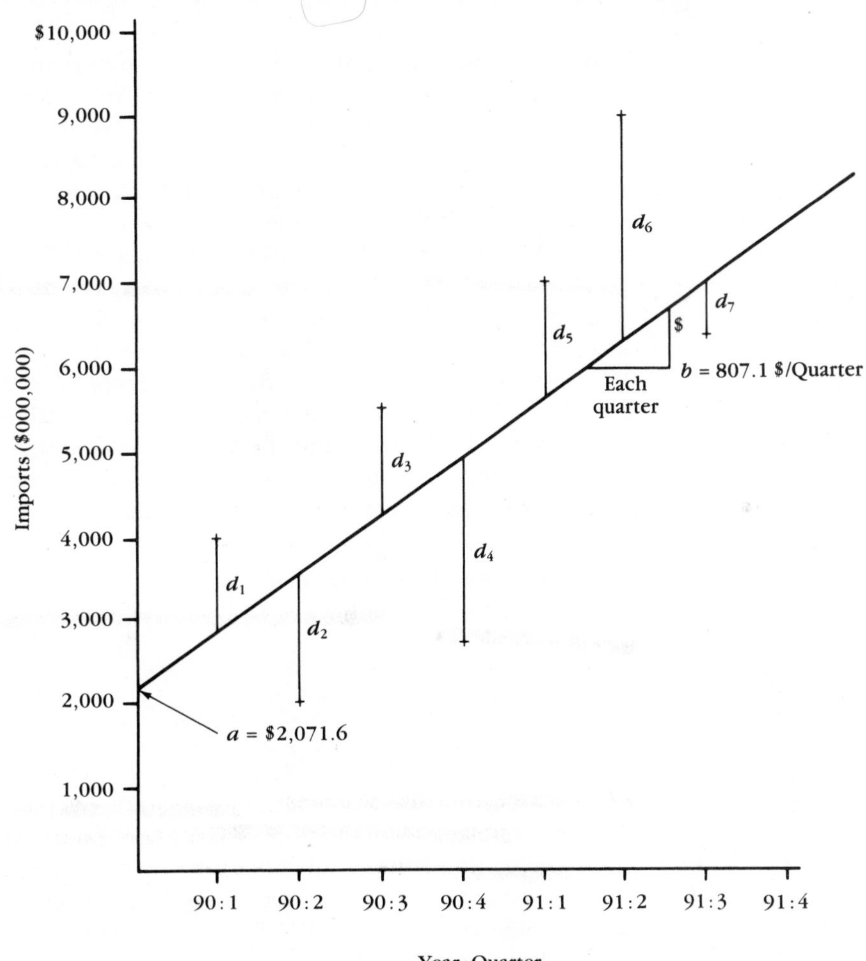

The method used to derive the parameters of the "best fit" line is based on differential calculus and is not covered here. The equations that determine the parameters of the slope (b) and the Y-intercept (a) are 3.4 and 3.5, respectively.

The coefficient of correlation calculated in the prior example ($r = 0.671$) indicates a high degree of relationship between the dependent and independent variables. The higher the coefficient of correlation, the more confident we can be that variation in the dependent variable (imports) is explained by the independent variable (time). This can be observed by looking at the scatter diagram in Exhibit 3.13. A measurement of this variation about the regression line is the **standard error of the estimate,** $s_{y/x}$. It is the difference between each observed value, Y_o, and the estimated value, Y_e. The equation for the standard error of the estimate follows. An alternative formula that is easier to use with a calculator is given in Exhibit 3.13.

$$s_{y/x} = \sqrt{\frac{\Sigma(Y_o - Y_e)^2}{n - 2}}$$

Simple regression models can be constructed for cross-sectional data. The mechanics are similar. The problems at the end of the chapter will help you to sharpen your skills.

Computer Application of Simple Regression Analysis

Many different computer software packages are available for doing both simple and multiple regression analyses. Exhibit 3.14 is the output from STORM, which has a regression analysis module. The coefficients calculated by STORM are the same (with allowances for rounding) as the coefficients calculated by hand. The standard error of the estimate is also the same as the value calculated by hand.

STORM also provides additional information. The **standard error of the coefficients,** 1784.800 and 399.093, are standard deviations for the coefficients. They can be used to test the null hypotheses that the actual values of the coefficients are equal to zero. The **t-values** are the calculated t-statistics for the hypothesis tests. The *two-sided significant probabilities* are the levels that alpha or Type I error would have to be set at in order to fail to reject the null hypothesis. In this example, the trend coefficient would be significant if alpha error is set at 0.1 or higher. On the other hand, the coefficient for the intercept would be significant if alpha error is set at 0.3 or higher.

Multiple Regression Model

Multiple regression has only one dependent variable, but can have many independent variables.

$$Y = a + b_1X_1 + b_2X_2 + \ldots + b_kX_k$$

where

$Y =$ the dependent variable. It depends on the variables X_1 through X_k and the model parameters $a, b_1, b_2, \ldots b_k$, where k is the number of independent variables. (Equations for the parameters are not given here. Rather, you are encouraged to use an available computer package, such as SPSSX(TM), SAS(TM), or MINITAB(TM), or a microcomputer package, to do the necessary calculations.)

Exhibit 3.13 Scatter Diagram and Regression Line for Import Problem

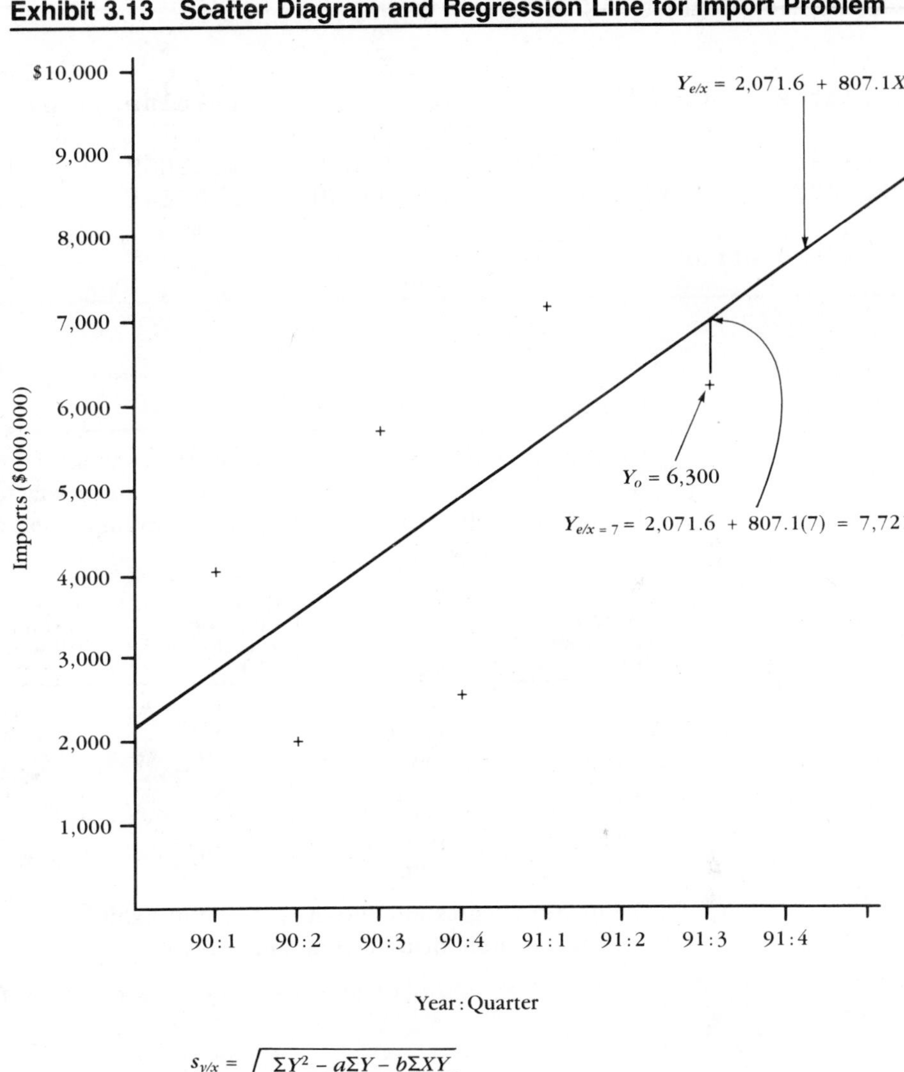

$$s_{y/x} = \sqrt{\frac{\Sigma Y^2 - a\Sigma Y - b\Sigma XY}{n - 2}}$$

$$s_{y/x} = \sqrt{\frac{237,170,000 - 2,071.6(37,100) - 807.1(171,000)}{7 - 2}}$$

$$s_{y/x} = 2111.8$$

X_i = an independent variable, with $i = 1, \ldots, k$. Each independent variable will have n observations or data points.

The concept of minimizing squared distances from each observed point to the "best fit" regression line is still useful. However, because multiple regression requires more than two dimensions, two-dimensional graphs cannot be used. Computerized statistical models are used to make the complex calculations.

Exhibit 3.14 Regression Coefficients for Imports

Variable	Coefficient	Std Error	*t* Value	Two-Sided Sig. Prob.
Constant	2071.42900	1784.80000	1.16059	0.298204
YRS/OUT	807.14290	399.09340	2.02244	0.099061

Standard error of estimate = 2111.804

Example

The prior example uses only one independent variable (time) to predict imports. Most relationships are not that simple because other factors will also affect the dependent variable. To expand the previous example, let's add disposable income and the consumer price index.

Imports ($000,000) ($Y$)	Year:Quarter	Code Value for Year:Quarter (X_1)	Disposable Income (Billions of $) ($X_2$)	Consumer Price Index (X_3)
4,100	1990:1	1	65	110
2,000	1990:2	2	60	111
5,700	1990:3	3	73	113
2,500	1990:4	4	61	113
7,300	1991:1	5	70	117
9,200	1991:2	6	77	118
6,300	1991:3	7	78	117

The multiple regression output is shown in Exhibit 3.15.

The equation for predicting imports is

$$Y_e = -141{,}000 - 1{,}387.6X_1 + 206.35X_2 + 1{,}205.4X_3$$

Exhibit 3.15 Multiple Regression Output

```
THE REGRESSION EQUATION IS
Y= - 141000 - 1388 X1 + 206 X2 + 1205 X3
PREDICTOR        COEF
              -141000
B1            -1387.6
B2             206.35
B3             1205.4
S = 534.6        R-SQ = 97.9%
```

S = Standard error of the estimate
R − SQ = (coefficient of correlation)^2

To predict imports for the fourth quarter of 1991, assume that disposable income is $78 billion and the consumer price index is 118 for the fourth quarter.

$$Y_e = -141{,}000 - 1{,}387.6(8) + 206.35(78) + 1{,}205.4(118)$$
$$= 6{,}232$$

The prediction is $6,232 million worth of imports in the fourth quarter of 1991.

Measuring Forecasting Error

Regardless of which forecasting model is used, it is important to have some means of determining the model's propensity for error. If an organization has been using a particular model to forecast sales for some time, has the model been performing well? How large is the error? One approach is to simply subtract the forecast for one time period from the actual value for the same time period. This can be repeated so that the forecaster has differences for many periods. Some of the differences are positive because the forecast is less than the actual value, and others are negative because the forecast is greater than the actual value. In raw form, these differences tell the forecaster little. A common method used by forecasters to measure forecasting error is to calculate the mean squared error. The **mean squared error (MSE)** is the average of all the squared errors. The differences are squared and added together, and then that total is divided by the number of observations. The following calculations help illustrate the method.

Example

Month	Actual Sales ($) ($x_t$)	Forecasted Sales ($) ($f_t$)	Error ($)	Squared Error
January	419,000	448,000	−29,000	841,000,000
February	480,000	481,000	−1,000	1,000,000
March	601,000	563,000	38,000	1,444,000,000
April	505,000	525,000	−20,000	400,000,000
May	462,000	490,000	−28,000	784,000,000
June	567,000	519,000	48,000	2,304,000,000
				5,774,000,000

$$\text{MSE} = \frac{\sum_{t=1}^{n}(x_t - f_t)^2}{n}$$
$$= \frac{5{,}774{,}000{,}000}{6}$$
$$= 962{,}333{,}333$$

Sometimes the square root of the mean squared error is used to measure the error. This is analogous to the standard error of the estimate which is discussed in the section on regression analysis.

Another often-used approach is the mean absolute deviation. The **mean absolute deviation (MAD)** is the average of the absolute differences between the forecasted values for the variable being forecast, such as sales, and the corresponding actual value. The MAD is similar to the MSE because differences are calculated. However, the MAD is different from the MSE because with MAD the absolute values of the differences are added, while with MSE the differences are squared. In the final step with the MAD, the summed absolute differences are divided by the total number of observations to get the average absolute difference.

$$\text{MAD} = \frac{\sum_{t=1}^{n} |x_t - f_t|}{n}$$

If the previous example is used to demonstrate how to calculate the MAD, the absolute value of the numbers in the error column would be added together. The result is 164,000.

$$\text{MAD} = \frac{\$164{,}000}{6}$$

$$= \$27{,}333$$

The MAD is the average error, and it is measured in the same terms as the original variable in this example, sales dollars. The MAD can be compared to the actual sales to learn how much error to expect. In this example, a MAD of $27,333 only represents about 5 percent of the monthly sales. Practically speaking, the MAD is easier for nonstatisticians to understand than the MSE is because they can understand the concept of average error used to calculate the MAD better than they can the idea of a mean squared error.

Tracking Forecasts and Control Limits for a Forecast

Even if a model fits the historical data perfectly, the relationships on which the model is built can change over time. For example, the demand for microcomputers accelerated rapidly during the middle and latter part of the 1980s. If a forecast for the demand for microcomputers for the decade of the 1990s is based on that rapid period of growth, the forecast might overestimated the demand.

As a result of changing relationships, it is necessary to monitor forecast accuracy. A system to track a forecast can be mathematically sophisticated or very simple. One simple approach is to calculate the difference between the actual demand in a period, x_t, and the forecast for that period, f_t (n is the number of periods).

$$\text{Total forecast error} = \sum_{t=1}^{n} (x_t - f_t)$$

In theory, the total forecast error should be zero or a very small number because if errors are random, then some variations would be positive, and others would be negative. It is only when there are several differences in a row that are positive or negative that the total will become large. This should be a signal to management to review the forecasting model and its assumptions.

Another method of tracking a forecast uses the total forecast error and the MAD. The tracking signal can be calculated as follows:

$$\text{Tracking signal} = \frac{\sum_{t=1}^{n}(x_t - f_t)}{\text{MAD}}$$

The tracking signal calculation takes the result of the forecast error calculation described earlier and divides it by the MAD. Therefore, if the model is an accurate representation of the real-world variable, the tracking signal should theoretically equal zero. If the tracking signal becomes a large positive or negative number, the model may no longer represent the relationships that determine the real variable. The advantage of dividing the total forecast error by the MAD is that managers have a measure of how large the error is. The error could be one MAD, two MADs, or more. The only remaining question is how many MADs there can be before the forecast is bad.

The concept of a confidence interval or control limit can be used. If we can assume that the MAD is a normally distributed random variable, then we can estimate the probability that the MAD will fall within a specific confidence interval. It can be shown that one MAD is equal to .8 standard deviations. As a result, a confidence interval (or control limit) that contains plus or minus one MAD will contain about 58 percent of the area under the normal distribution. In other words, a confidence interval that is plus or minus one MAD will be a 58 percent confidence interval. Other values are shown below.

MAD	**Probability Included by the Confidence Interval**
±1	.581
±2	.890
±3	.984

This means that if the tracking signal is greater than plus three MADs or less than minus three MADs, there is only a 0.016 probability that it came from a forecast that is "on track." When the tracking signal is outside of +3, −3 MAD limits, serious consideration should be given to re-evaluating the forecasting model.

Calculating the tracking signal for the previous example is not difficult. Be careful because the MAD calculation is based on the absolute value of the error, but the numerator of the tracking signal is not the absolute value.

$$\text{Tracking signal} = \frac{\sum_{t=1}^{n}(x_t - f_t)}{\text{MAD}}$$

$$= \frac{\$8{,}000}{\$27{,}333}$$

$$= .293$$

A tracking signal of 0.293 MADs is well within the confidence interval limits. The forecast could be judged to be accurate.

SUMMARY

- A model is an important way of thinking about problems. It is an abstraction from the real problem of the key variables and relationships in order to simplify the problem and improve understanding.
- There are many different types of models, including prototypes used in product design; scale models used in architecture; diagrams and drawings used by scientists, engineers, managers, and others; and mathematical models used in many disciplines.
- Models are used to assist managers and others in answering what-if questions by changing a parameter in the model.
- Forecasting is a type of mathematical model that can be used to predict the future. It is an important part of the planning process in an organization.
- The forecasting process consists of determining the objectives of the forecast, developing and testing a model, applying the model, considering real-world constraints in the application of the model, and revising and evaluating the forecast.
- Forecasting techniques normally use historical data to develop the model that is used to make the projection. If the relationships in the data change over time, the model may no longer predict the future accurately.
- There are qualitative and quantitative methods for developing a forecast.
- Forecasters require a way to measure the amount of forecasting error and a method to track forecasts to see how well the forecast predicts the future.

CAREER PROFILE

Lionel Johnson

Production Planner
Bauer-Landmark Inc.

Bauer-Landmark produces custom-fabricated industrial rubber products. The company carries a complete line of belting, hose, hydraulic hoses, fittings, conveyor idlers, sheet rubber, and ball valves for equipment manufacturers. Bauer-Landmark is primarily a make-to-order manufacturer, which means that production does not begin until an order for the finished product is received. In order to maintain a competitive edge by achieving a short delivery lead time, the company stocks some basic raw materials, such as sheet rubber, high-demand fittings, and various sizes and grades of hose in 1,000-foot rolls.

Responsibilities

Lionel Johnson is responsible for the entire production-planning operation and reports directly to the plant manager. His work includes the preparation of a detailed schedule for production which the plant will use for the next two weeks. A new two-week schedule is produced each week, so the first week of the schedule is regarded as fixed and the second week is considered tentative. The schedule for the second week is the basis for planning. Johnson is also responsible for preparing long-term production plans which become the basis for hiring and layoffs in the work force and for ordering some raw materials that are used in the production process. As part of his job, he takes the aggregate forecast for sales during the next six months and estimates how much and what types of raw materials to order.

Education and Experience

Johnson spent four years in the U.S. Army after high school and then earned his bachelor's degree in business administration in 1979. He began working at Bauer-Landmark after graduation as a special projects coordinator. His first job was to assist the company in moving into its new facility. This provided the company with an opportunity to re-examine the facility layout and the material-handling, material storage, and inventory control policies. After the move was completed, Johnson began working in quality control. He then moved up to material manager before taking the production-planning position.

SOLVED PROBLEMS

The following data are student credit hours for the fall term in the Department of Information Systems and Operations Management (ISOM) at State University. These data will be used in problems 1, 2, and 3.

Year	Student Credit Hours
1983	3,724
1984	5,368
1985	5,968
1986	7,188
1987	7,572
1988	7,576
1989	7,064
1990	4,600

1. Estimate ISOM's enrollment for the academic years beginning in 1990 and 1991, using a five-year moving average.

Solution

$$f_{t+1} = \frac{\sum_{i=0}^{n-1}(x_{t-i})}{n}$$

$$f_{90} = \frac{(5{,}968 + 7{,}188 + 7{,}572 + 7{,}576 + 7{,}064)}{5}$$

$$= 7{,}073.6 \text{ student credit hours}$$

Notice that a projection for the fall quarter of 1990 based on the prior five years would have greatly overestimated actual enrollment. This was caused, in part, by a structural change in the department. It went from teaching four courses that are required of all business majors to three.

$$f_{91} = \frac{(7{,}188 + 7{,}572 + 7{,}576 + 7{,}064 + 4600)}{5}$$

$$= 6{,}800 \text{ student credit hours}$$

2. Use exponential smoothing to calculate 1991 enrollment projections. Begin with the 1983 data, and use a smoothing constant (A) of .3.

Solution

$$f_{t+1} = x_t$$

$$f_{t+2} = A(x_{t+1}) + (1 - A)f_{t+1}$$

$$f_{t+3} = A(x_{t+2}) + (1 - A)f_{t+2}$$

$$\vdots$$

$$f_{t+n} = A(x_{t+n-1}) + (1 - A)f_{t+n-1}$$

Year	Actual Student Credit Hours	Forecast
1983	3,724	
1984	5,368	3,724.0
1985	5,968	4,217.2
1986	7,188	4,742.4
1987	7,572	5,476.1
1988	7,576	6,104.9
1989	7,064	6,546.2
1990	4,600	6,701.5
1991	not available	6,071.1

For 1984, set the forecast equal to the actual value of the prior period. For 1985, calculate the forecast as follows:

$$f_{85} = .3(5{,}368) + (1 - .3)3{,}724$$

$$= 4{,}217.2 \text{ student credit hours}$$

For 1986, the forecast would have been

$$f_{86} = .3(5{,}968) + (1 - .3)4{,}217.2$$

$$= 4{,}742.4 \text{ student credit hours}$$

Skipping to 1991, the forecast is

$$f_{91} = .3(4{,}600) + (1 - .3)6{,}701.5$$

$$= 6{,}071.1 \text{ student credit hours}$$

3. Use regression analysis to project enrollment for 1991.

Solution

$$Y = a + b(X)$$

Year (X)	Student Credit Hours (Y)	Code for Year X	XY	X^2
1983	3,724	1	3,724	1
1984	5,368	2	10,736	4
1985	5,968	3	17,904	9
1986	7,188	4	28,752	16
1987	7,572	5	37,860	25
1988	7,576	6	45,456	36
1989	7,064	7	49,448	49
1990	4,600	8	36,800	64
Sum	49,060	36	230,680	204

Calculate the slope and intercept of the regression line.

$$b = \frac{n\Sigma XY - \Sigma X \Sigma Y}{n\Sigma X^2 - (\Sigma X)^2}$$

$$= \frac{8(230{,}680) - 36(49{,}060)}{8(204) - 36^2}$$

$$= \frac{1{,}845{,}440 - 1{,}766{,}160}{1{,}632 - 1{,}296} = \frac{79{,}280}{336}$$

$$= 236.0 \text{ student credit hours/year}$$

$$a = \frac{\Sigma Y}{n} - b\frac{\Sigma X}{n}$$

$$= \frac{49{,}060}{8} - 236.0\frac{36}{8} = 6{,}132.5 - 1{,}062$$

$$= 5{,}070.5 \text{ student credit hours}$$

Enter the estimates for the regression model parameters a and b. Substitute the code for 1991 (9) into the regression model, and solve for the predicted value, Y_e.

$$Y_e = a + b(X)$$

$$= 5{,}070.5 + 236.0(9)$$

$$= 7{,}194.5 \text{ student credit hours}$$

The prediction for 1991 is 7,194.5 student credit hours. State University should exercise judgment in using any of these models. None of them gives an answer. Each of these forecasts should be tempered with judgment about environmental changes that have fundamentally altered the relationships. In this case, changes in teaching responsibility have significantly altered future student credit hours for ISOM.

QUESTIONS

1. What is model building, and why is model building important for managers?

2. Discuss the different types of models.

3. Describe how models can be used to answer what-if questions.

4. How are models used in business and operations?

5. What is forecasting, and why is it important to an organization?

6. Describe the forecasting process.

7. Discuss the qualitative approaches to forecasting.

8. How does the Delphi Technique work? What are its advantages?

9. What are the components of a time series? Define each component.

10. How is regression analysis different from the moving average, the weighted moving average, and exponential smoothing?

11. What is forecasting error, and why should it be measured?

12. What is meant by tracking a forecast?

PROBLEMS

1. Blast-Away House-Cleaning Service uses powerful water jets to clear loose paint from residential buildings and to clean aluminum siding. The company is trying to arrive at a fast and accurate way of estimating cleaning jobs. The following simple formula is their first attempt. It includes a fixed charge for coming to the job plus time requirements, which are a function of the exterior of the house measured in square feet (sf).

$$\text{Estimated cost} = \$15 + (\$0.06/\text{sf})(\text{sf})$$

a. How much should Blast-Away charge to clean a house that is a rectangle 40 by 28 feet? The distance from the roof line to the bottom of the siding is nine feet.

b. Suppose Blast-Away's labor costs increase and the cost per square foot increases to \$0.064. How much should it charge for the house in part a?

c. What other factors might Blast-Away include in the pricing model to improve the precision of the model?

2. As a service to its customers, Turbo Natural Gas Company will estimate the amount of natural gas required (NGR) in hundreds of cubic feet (CCF) to heat your home. This is done by a mathematical model that considers the square footage on the first floor (sf_1), the square footage on the second floor (sf_2), and the temperature setting on the thermostat. The temperature setting you enter into the model should be the difference between the temperature setting in your home and 65 degrees (*td*). Make sure you keep the minus sign if the setting is less than 65 degrees. The model builder assumed that the homes have eight-foot ceilings, an average amount of good-quality windows, 3.5 inches of insulation in the wall and 6 inches in the attic, and a typical winter.

$$\begin{aligned}\text{NGR} = {} & (0.50\ \text{CCF/sf})(sf_1) + (0.25\ \text{CCF/sf})(sf_2) \\ & + (0.015\ \text{CCF/degree/sf})(td)(sf_1) \\ & + (0.0075\ \text{CCF/degree/sf})(td)(sf_2)\end{aligned}$$

a. How much natural gas will an 1,800-square-foot ranch-style home use if the thermostat is set at 70 degrees?

b. How much natural gas will a two-story home with a total of 2,400 square feet use if the thermostat is set at 63 degrees? There is 1,000 square feet on the second floor.

c. What happens to the natural gas cost in parts a and b if the model is revised and the usage for the first floor increases to 0.60 CCF/sf from 0.50 CCF/sf.

3. It appears that the imports of beef have been increasing about 10 percent annually on the average. Project the 1990 imports using linear regression.

Year	Imports of Beef (Thousands of Tons)
1981	82
1982	101
1983	114
1984	126
1985	137
1986	151
1987	164
1988	182
1989	189

4. Mighty-Maid Home-Cleaning Service has been in operation for eight months, and demand for their product has grown rapidly. The owner/manager of Mighty-Maid is trying to keep pace with demand, which means hiring and training more workers. She believes that demand will continue at the same pace. She needs an estimate of demand so she can recruit and train the work force. The following represents the history of Mighty-Maid:

Time Period	Hours of Service Rendered
December	300
January	750
February	650
March	920
April	1,300
May	1,400
June	1,200
July	1,500

a. Estimate the trend in the data using the graphical method.
b. Estimate the trend in the data using regression analysis.
c. Should there be a difference in these two estimates? What would account for the difference?

5. Use the trend estimated in part b of the Mighty-Maid problem to estimate December through July. Now that both the actual and the forecasted values are available, answer the following questions:

a. What is the MSE for the forecast?
b. What is the MAD for the forecast?
c. What is the value of the tracking signal for the forecast?
d. Is the forecasting model a "good" model?

6. The figures below indicate the number of mergers that took place in the savings and loan industry over a twelve-year period.

Year	Mergers	Year	Mergers
1978	46	1984	83
1979	46	1985	123
1980	62	1986	97
1981	45	1987	186
1982	64	1988	225
1983	61	1989	240

a. Calculate a five-year moving average to forecast the number of mergers for 1990.
b. Determine the amount of measurement error in the forecast. Use the moving average technique to determine the forecast for 1983 to 1989. Then use that seven-year period and the MAD method to calculate measurement error.
c. Calculate a five-year weighted moving average to forecast the number of mergers for 1990. Use weights of .10, .15, .20, .25, and .30, with the most recent year weighted most heavily.
d. Use regression analysis to forecast the number of mergers in 1990.

7. Find the exponentially smoothed series for the series in problem 6, (a) using $A = .1$ and then (b) using $A = .7$, and plot these time series along with the actual data to see the impact of the smoothing constant.

8. The time series below shows the number of firms in an industry over a ten-year period.

Year	Firms	Year	Firms
1980	441	1985	554
1981	468	1986	562
1982	481	1987	577
1983	511	1988	537
1984	551	1989	589

a. Find the five-year moving average for this series.
b. Find the three-year weighted moving average for this series. Use the following scheme to weight the years:

	Weight
Most recent year	.5
Two years back	.3
Three years back	.2

c. Determine the amount of measurement error in the forecast. Use the weighted moving average technique (with the weights from part b) to forecast for 1983 to 1989. Then use that seven-year period to calculate measurement error.
d. Find the exponentially smoothed forecast for this series with $A = .2$.

9. The quarterly data presented here show the number of appliances (in thousands) returned to a particular manufacturer for warranty service over the past five years.

	1st Quarter	2d Quarter	3d Quarter	4th Quarter
5 years ago	1.2	0.8	.6	1.1
4 years ago	1.7	1.2	1.0	1.5
3 years ago	3.1	3.5	3.5	3.2
2 years ago	2.6	2.2	1.9	2.5
1 year ago	2.9	2.5	2.2	3.0

a. Find the equation of the least squares linear trend line that fits this time series. Let $t = 1$ be the first quarter five years ago.
b. What would the trend-line value be for the second quarter of the current year—that is, two periods beyond the end of the actual data?

10. The following are AJV Electric's sales of model EM-5V circuit assemblies over the past sixteen months (in thousands of units):

Month	Sales (Thousands of Units)	Month	Sales (Thousands of Units)
Sept. 1988	55	May 1989	63
Oct. 1988	53	June 1989	53
Nov. 1988	60	July 1989	51
Dec. 1988	49	Aug. 1989	60
Jan. 1989	48	Sept. 1989	58
Feb. 1989	61	Oct. 1989	52
Mar. 1989	61	Nov. 1989	51
Apr. 1989	53	Dec. 1989	63

Use the moving average technique to forecast sales of AJV's model EM-5V for January 1990 (use a three-month base). Does the model appear to be appropriate? Why or why not?

11. Employ the single exponential smoothing technique to forecast sales of AJV's model EM-5V for January 1990 (use $A = .8$). Does the model seem to be appropriate?

12. Utilize the single exponential smoothing technique to forecast sales of AJV's model EM-5V for January 1990 (use $A = .1$). How do the results compare with those in problem 11? Why is one better than another?

13. Using linear regression, forecast the sales of AJV's model EM-5V for January 1990 through June 1990.

14. Thrifty Bank and Trust is trying to forecast on-the-job performance by its employees. The bank administers an aptitude test to new employees. After the normal employee training plus six months on the job, the bank measures on-the-job performance. The following data have been gathered from the last eight people hired:

Employee Number	Score	Transaction per Hour
1	90	36
2	70	29
3	85	40
4	80	32
5	95	42
6	60	23
7	65	29
8	75	33

a. Fit a line to the data using regression analysis. What is the meaning of the parameters that were estimated by the regression analysis model?

b. How well does the model fit the data?

c. How many transactions per hour would you expect from someone who scored 87 on the aptitude test?

d. What is the MAD for the model?

15. The data below were collected during a study of consumer buying patterns.

Observation	X	Y
1	154	743
2	265	830
3	540	984
4	332	801
5	551	964
6	487	955
7	305	839
8	218	478
9	144	720
10	155	782
11	242	853
12	234	878
13	343	940

a. Fit a linear regression line to the data using the least squares method.

b. Calculate the coefficient of correlation and the standard error of the estimate.

c. How could the coefficient of correlation and the standard error of the estimate be used to make a judgment about the model's accuracy?

16. Perfect Lawns, Inc., intends to use sales of lawn fertilizer to predict lawn mower sales. The store manager feels that there is probably a six-week lag between fertilizer sales and mower sales. The pertinent data are shown below.

Period	Fertilizer Sales (Tons)	Number of Mowers Sold (Six-Week Lag)
1	1.7	11
2	1.4	9
3	1.9	11
4	2.1	13
5	2.3	14
6	1.7	10
7	1.6	9
8	2.0	13
9	1.4	9
10	2.2	16
11	1.5	10
12	1.7	10

a. Use the least squares method to obtain a linear regression line for the data.

b. Calculate the coefficient of correlation and the standard error of the estimate.

c. Predict lawn mower sales for the first week in August, given fertilizer sales six weeks earlier of two tons.

Data Sets for Computer Solution

1. Melnack Manufacturing wants to estimate sales of its line of dishwashers for the home. It has collected the following data:

Year	Sales ($000,000)	Advertising ($000)	Housing Starts (Millions of Units)
1977	35	380	1.4
1978	38	390	1.6
1979	46	430	1.7
1980	44	440	1.5
1981	43	450	1.4
1982	47	460	1.3
1983	39	440	1.2
1984	36	470	1.1
1985	35	400	0.8
1986	48	430	0.9
1987	56	410	1.2
1988	67	470	1.5
1989	69	480	1.8

a. Use regression analysis to forecast dishwasher sales for 1990. Assume advertising expenditures will be $500,000 and housing starts will be 1.7 million.

b. Comment on the use of advertising expenditures, housing starts, and trend (time) to predict sales.

2. The U.S. Fabrication Institute is trying to predict manufacturing costs in its members' plants. One executive of the association hypothesized that production costs are a function of the facility's age, the number of middle managers in the plant, and the product volume. The following data were collected from twenty-two plants that make similar products and have approximately the same capacity:

Production Cost ($/Unit)	Facility Age (Years)	Number of Managers	Production Volume (Units/Month) (000)
7.31	7	10	18
8.25	12	14	17
7.07	3	8	20
9.33	6	16	15
8.59	9	12	14
7.75	5	10	21
8.04	5	12	18
8.72	25	10	18
7.14	4	10	19
8.80	11	12	13
8.08	5	18	20
7.52	8	9	19
8.40	11	10	18
7.28	5	8	21
9.11	8	17	14
8.66	10	13	15
7.88	4	9	19
7.64	14	9	17
8.66	24	11	19
7.33	14	9	18
8.45	10	13	16
7.98	8	15	21

a. Develop a model that can be used to predict costs in U.S. Fabrication's member plants.

b. Can the results of this model be used for all plants, or only for plants with characteristics that are similar to those in the sample?

3. Binkelman's Software Services is studying the effects of age, education, and the amount of sick leave taken by an employee on the employee's salary. The company believes that salary increases with age and education, but decreases with the amount of sick leave taken. The following data were collected from nine employees:

Employee Number	Salary ($/Month)	Age (Years)	Education (Years Completed)	Sick Leave (Average Number Days/Year)
1	1,650	36	12	6
2	1,770	23	15	0
3	1,990	22	14	15
4	1,627	27	12	2
5	1,825	33	13	8
6	1,540	41	7	0
7	1,900	25	16	15
8	2,500	33	16	0
9	2,200	35	12	4

a. Use the least squares regression to predict the impact of age, education, and sick leave time on salary.

b. How well does this model predict an employee's salary?

c. If an employee is thirty-eight years old, has earned a master's degree (17 years), and has averaged only two sick days, what would his or her salary be, according to the model?

d. What other factors might have an influence on an employee's salary?

4. The city of Timber Falls depends on the forest products industry for most of its revenue. The city manager believes that revenues are affected by the operating level of the local paper-making plant and the number of board feet of lumber that is cut and shipped to the Midwest. The following data have been collected for the past twelve quarters:

Revenue ($000)	Year:Quarter	Index of Plant Operating Level	Board Feet of Lumber Cut (Millions)
11,000	88:1	70	450
14,500	88:2	90	450
13,300	88:3	85	450
10,900	88:4	65	350
14,800	89:1	70	550
15,000	89:2	70	600
16,000	89:3	75	650
15,500	89:4	75	550
17,000	90:1	80	700
16,700	90:2	90	700
15,800	90:3	85	600
16,400	90:4	85	650

a. Develop a model to predict revenue for Timber Falls, using these data.

b. How well does the model predict revenue?

c. If the Timber Falls plant has a 90 percent operating level, and if the industry cut 700 million board feet of lumber in the first quarter of 1991, what could the city manager expect revenue to be?

MINI-CASES

Blast-Away House-Cleaning Service

As described in problem 1, Blast-Away cleans the exteriors of homes with powerful jets of water. The company has developed a simple model, which is also described in problem 1, that sets the price charged to the customer. After one year of experience, Blast-Away has lost $50,000 on sales of $250,000. At first, the owner, Hadley Powers, could not understand the reasons for his losses. His employees worked hard, and Blast-Away could barely keep up with demand. In fact, Powers was planning to add another crew this year, but if he can not determine the reason for the losses and find a solution, his investors would be reluctant to provide him with additional capital. What caused the loss?

One thing he learned from his accountant is that the model had not included a recovery of his investment in the equipment used on the jobs. Powers had invested $60,000 in equipment at the beginning of the first year and expected it to last three years. His accountant recommended that Powers increase the price charged per job to generate an extra $20,000 to cover equipment costs. Even if Powers were able to do this, his losses would still be $30,000 if all other things remained the same. He had to look further for the problems.

Powers has hired you to carefully examine last year's job tickets, which contain the quoted price; distance from headquarters; size of the house; type of exterior, such as painted wood, aluminum, or brick; and style of the house, such as ranch, two-story, or story-and-a-half. You also have the operator's log book that lists travel time and the time to do each house. As you analyze the job tickets, you notice that a substantial number of the jobs that Blast-Away gets are for small, story-and-a-half or two-story homes located in the suburbs and surrounding rural area. Many of the homes are wood sided, which is the most difficult type to clean to the customer's satisfaction.

1. In addition to the equipment recovery problem, what is causing Blast-Away to lose money?

2. What would you recommend to Powers to correct the problem?

3. What data would you want to collect to verify your recommendations?

Lucy's Lamps-R-Us

Lucy Mertz has opened a specialty lamp shop in a suburban shopping mall. Mertz's shop has an excellent location next to the entrance to the largest and most popular department store in the surrounding five-county area. After a slow beginning, business picked up nicely, and the lamp shop had made a nice profit. To plan for the next year, Mertz decided to use sales for the last eight months to forecast next year's sales. She has asked you to use the following data to project sales. The forecast listed here, which is for last year, was based on judgment. Mertz wants you to use a quantitative approach.

Time Period	Forecasted Sales	Actual Sales
May	$5,000	$ 8,300
June	5,200	10,200
July	5,600	9,900
August	6,200	10,200
September	6,900	9,800
October	7,800	11,400
November	8,500	12,800
December	9,000	14,500

1. How much error existed in the old forecast?

2. Project the sales for January, February, and March of next year.

It is now the end of March, and the actual sales for the first three months are available. The results are disappointing. In January, sales declined because of returns from the Christmas buying season and an increase in bargain hunting. Also, the large department store that anchored Mertz's end of the shopping mall closed at the end of January because of operating losses by the parent company.

Time Period	Actual Sales
January	7,500
February	6,000
March	6,100

3. How would the tracking signal help you to spot a problem?

4. Why did the model give Mertz a poor forecast?

5. What would you recommend to Mertz regarding the forecast for the next three months?

SELECTED BIBLIOGRAPHY

Ashton, David, and Simister, Leslie. *The Role of Forecasting in Corporate Planning*. London: Staples Press, 1970.

Bowerman, Bruce L., and O'Connell, Richard T. *Time Series and Forecasting*. North Scituate, Mass.: Duxbury Press, 1979.

Clark, Charles T., and Jordan, Eleanor W. *Introduction to Business and Economic Statistics*. Cincinnati: South-Western, 1985.

Cryer, Jonathan D. *Time Series Analysis*. Boston: Duxbury Press, 1986.

Eyman, Earl D. *Modeling, Simulation and Control*. St. Paul: West, 1988.

Farnum, Nicholas R., and Stanton, LaVerne W. *Quantitative Forecasting Methods*. Boston: PWS-Kent, 1989.

Granger, C. W. J. *Forecasting in Business and Economics*. New York: Academic Press, 1980.

Gross, Charles W., and Robin, Peterson T. *Business Forecasting*. 2d ed. Boston: Houghton Mifflin, 1983.

Hanke, John E., and Reitsch, Arthur G. *Business Forecasting*. Boston: Allyn and Bacon, 1986.

Johnston, J. *Econometric Methods*. St. Louis: McGraw-Hill, 1972.

Keating, Giles. *The Production and Use of Economic Forecasts*. London: Methuen, 1985.

Maki, Daniel P., and Thompson, Maynard. *Mathematical Models and Applications*. Englewood Cliffs, N. J.: Prentice-Hall, 1973.

Mason, Robert D.; Lind, Douglas A.; and Marchal, William G. *Statistics: An Introduction*. San Diego: Harcourt Brace Jovanovich, 1987.

Padulo, Louis, and Arbib, Michael A. *Systems Theory*. Washington, D.C.: Hemisphere, 1974.

Valentine, Lloyd M., and Dauten, Carl A. *Business Cycles and Forecasting*. Cincinnati: South-Western, 1983.

Wellstead, P. E. *Introduction to Physical System Modelling*. London: Academic Press, 1979.

PART 1
Designing the System

One key to successful operations is an effective system design. An effective design should take into account an organization's products, facilities, and procedures for planning and controlling operations, people requirements, and short- and long-term goals. A system design helps to define a product's cost structure and determines an organization's competitive position for several years. This is true because a design commits the organization to significant capital expenditures for constructing facilities and purchasing equipment.

Finding a design that meets present needs and is flexible enough to meet future needs for new and changing products is essential. Good design does not tie operations to outdated technology. It produces superior products and enhances an organization's ability to compete in today's world markets.

This section contains the following chapters. The ideas in these chapters should help you focus clearly on the key issues and take advantage of the opportunities presented in the design phase of operations.

- CHAPTER 4: New Product Development: A Team Approach
- CHAPTER 5: Capacity Decisions
- CHAPTER 6: Facility Location
- CHAPTER 7: Process Selection
- CHAPTER 8: Facility Layout
- CHAPTER 9: Job Design and Work Measurement

Chapter 4

New Product Development: A Team Approach

CHAPTER OUTLINE

International Aspects of Product Design
Overview of New Product Development
Implementing the Teamwork Approach to New Product Development

The Role of Marketing
Measuring Consumer Needs and Competitive Pressures
The External Environment

Consumer Needs to Product Ideas: The Role of Engineering
Shaping the Product: Product Design
Gaining Strategic Advantage at Federal Express: Product Design Is the Competitive Edge
Product Design for Service Operations
Ethical Issues in Product Design
Engineering for Production: Process Design
Human Engineering

Product Ideas to Product Reality: The Role of Operations

Allies in Product Development: The Role of Suppliers

Capital Formation and Evaluation: The Role of Finance

Information for Decision Making: The Roles of Accounting and Information Systems

Building Product Quality through Product Development
Product Development as a Determinant of Product Quality
Quality Functional Deployment

LEARNING OBJECTIVES

After completing this chapter, you should be able to

- Describe how product development and design determine the product's characteristics, performance, and function.
- Explain that product development is a cooperative effort that requires input from many parts of the organization, including marketing, engineering, operations, finance, and accounting.
- Illustrate how product development can be used to gain a competitive advantage.
- Discuss product design as a determinant of product cost, quality, and customer service.
- List the steps involved in designing and developing new products.
- Explain why product development requires a team effort.
- Describe the role of each member of the design team.
- Explain the relationship between product design and quality.

Ford Motor Company: Applying the Team Approach to New Product Development

A team approach to new product development has produced an American car that is receiving rave reviews from industry experts and consumers. Ford's Taurus and Mercury's Sable are the hottest sellers since the Ford Mustang tantalized consumers in the 1960s. The Taurus and Sable demonstrate that U.S. manufacturers can build a car that excites the average consumer.

How did Ford do it after suffering substantial losses in the early 1980s? To begin, Ford studied customer wants and needs as it never had before and made quality a top priority. Ford put aside its traditional approach to product development and design. Before, product planners developed a general concept and then passed it on to a design team. They, in turn, passed it on to engineering, manufacturing, and finally the company's suppliers. In this highly sequential process, each group worked in isolation, there was little communication, and no one had overall project responsibility.

In contrast, the team approach brings together representatives from each group, and the team takes final responsibility. Because of early involvement by all parts of the design team, problems are resolved before they become crises. With this team approach, manufacturing has been able to make several design suggestions that have resulted in higher productivity or better quality.

Ford forgot the "Detroit knows best" attitude and methodically set out to identify the world's best design features from over fifty different models. Ford launched market studies to determine customer preference. An "ergonomic group" did elaborate testing on seat design, dashboard instruments, and controls. People were timed at pushing buttons, flipping switches, and adjusting dials to find ways to make the car easier to use.

Ford asked assembly-line workers for advice even before the design of the car was complete. Many of the suggestions were used. Simple ideas, such as making all the bolt heads the same size so the worker is not constantly reaching for a new tool, were implemented. More complex suggestions, such as making doors with fewer pieces in order to improve assembly, were also used.

Even suppliers were brought into the design process. They were given long-term contracts and invited to have input on product plans. This allowed Ford to incorporate suggestions that saved money for the supplier as well as Ford, improved quality, and improved productivity.

The results for Ford in the marketplace have been dramatic. Customers are buying, and dealers are happy. Ford has decided to incorporate this new team approach in future product design and development. The team approach allows people with different perspectives to exchange ideas in order to create a better product than would have resulted from their individual efforts.[1]

INTRODUCTION

The purpose of an organization is to bring people together to produce goods or services that the same people could not produce working independently. Insurance companies, banks, and hospitals could not deliver their wide-ranging services without the efforts of many people. Manufacturing automobiles, appliances, and clothing on the scale necessary to meet demand can be accomplished only by people working together in organizations to meet common goals.

The challenges to an organization are to create a product that the market demands, to produce it at a competitive cost, to attain the best level of quality possible, and to deliver it on time. To achieve these objectives in the increasing competitive international marketplace requires a team approach. It is important to remember that an organization is a system, and marketing, engineering, operations, accounting, finance, and the other functional areas should work together.

International Aspects of Product Design

After World War II, developments in air and sea transportation and advances in communications technology made evident the fact that nations could no longer exist as isolated states, ignoring activities outside their borders. Even China shrugged off its isolationist tradition in the 1970s and began to pursue partnerships with foreign countries and companies. Initially, the activities of many companies were limited to international trade—that is, producing products in the home country and shipping a portion of the output to another country. Many companies took the next step, which involved locating production facilities in a foreign country and producing products for that country. As top management's level of sophistication grew in the international arena, it became evident that building a facility in each country or for small groups of countries may not be effective.

Many organizations are designing and developing products that can be produced in different countries and sold in different countries. Timken advertises that its bearings are interchangeable no matter where they are produced. This approach to product design provides Timken with increased flexibility. If there is a problem in one plant, another can easily and quickly take up the slack. Where differences exist between the markets in several countries, it is necessary to accommodate those differences in the product design. For example, electric utilities in the United States and Europe supply different levels of current (voltage). Appliances designed for the U.S. market cannot be used in Europe unless they are modified. In today's environment, managers need to know the world market for their products and potential products.

Overview of New Product Development

Developing new products is a key factor for success because it shapes how the organization competes. Product development offers the opportunity to determine (1) product costs, (2) product quality, and (3) the ability to serve customers. These factors are extremely important in establishing an organization's competitive position.

Product development and the design that results have a direct impact on costs because the design defines (1) how the product will be made, (2) what materials will be needed, and (3) what machines and processes will be used. The procedures and the machines required to make the product affect the labor costs and the investment required. The quantity and type of raw materials specified influence material costs. The organization that can design a product of equal or better quality using methods, machines, and materials that have a total cost lower than that of its competitors will obtain a competitive advantage.

Product quality has become a critical factor for successful competition in the international marketplace. Successfully managing quality includes (1) designing the product to achieve high quality, (2) designing production processes that will transform the design into a quality product, (3) developing sound training programs aimed at improving employee performance, and (4) inspecting the product to determine if steps 1 through 3 have been successful. Organizations produce quality services and goods by designing and building them with care, not merely by inspecting them. Quality management and quality assurance concepts are discussed in Chapter 17.

Customer service can be an important competitive advantage because meeting specific needs and providing rapid, on-time delivery are important to customers. A customer may have specific needs that are different from the needs of an organization's typical customer. Have the products and processes been designed to be flexible enough to adjust to that customer's needs? Can this be accomplished without significant increases in costs? If the answer to both questions is yes, then the system gives the organization an advantage in competing for new customers and markets.

Product development starts by defining markets for new or existing products. Recognizing customer needs raises a series of questions that determine the product's cost, quality, and ability to meet customer needs and ultimately ends with a decision to proceed with the product or not. For an overview of the decision-making process, see Exhibit 4.1.

Initial Assessment Phase

An organization should continually monitor customer preferences to get ideas for new products. However, new product ideas may also come from engineering, operations, top management, or other parts of the organization. For example, an engineering breakthrough may trigger new product ideas, as the microchip did for calculators. A market analysis for an electronic calculator might include the following steps:

1. *Assessment of the market.* What features and performance are desired by customers? How large is the potential market? What are the long-term and short-term opportunities if the organization enters the market?
2. *Appraisal of the competition.* Who are the present competitors in the market? What will their reaction be to a new entry? Who are the other potential entrants to the market? What strengths does the organization possess to gain an edge in this market?
3. *A preliminary market forecast.* How many units can be sold in the first year, second year, and so on? What prices are customers willing to pay?

Many product ideas are discarded after such a market analysis because the expected sales are not sufficient, the estimated market price is too low to make operations profitable, or the competition is too great. Ideas that do meet the criteria are given further consideration.

Engineering and Economic Analysis Phase

A new product idea requires careful analysis and synthesis. **Analysis** is separating a whole into its parts to determine their nature, proportion, function, and relationship. An analysis of an electronic calculator involves breaking it down into its various parts and examining each part, as follows:

1. *Display.* Should the display be electronic, on printed paper, or both? Where should it be located, and how should it be positioned for easy reading? How many significant digits should be included?

Exhibit 4.1 Overview of Product Development

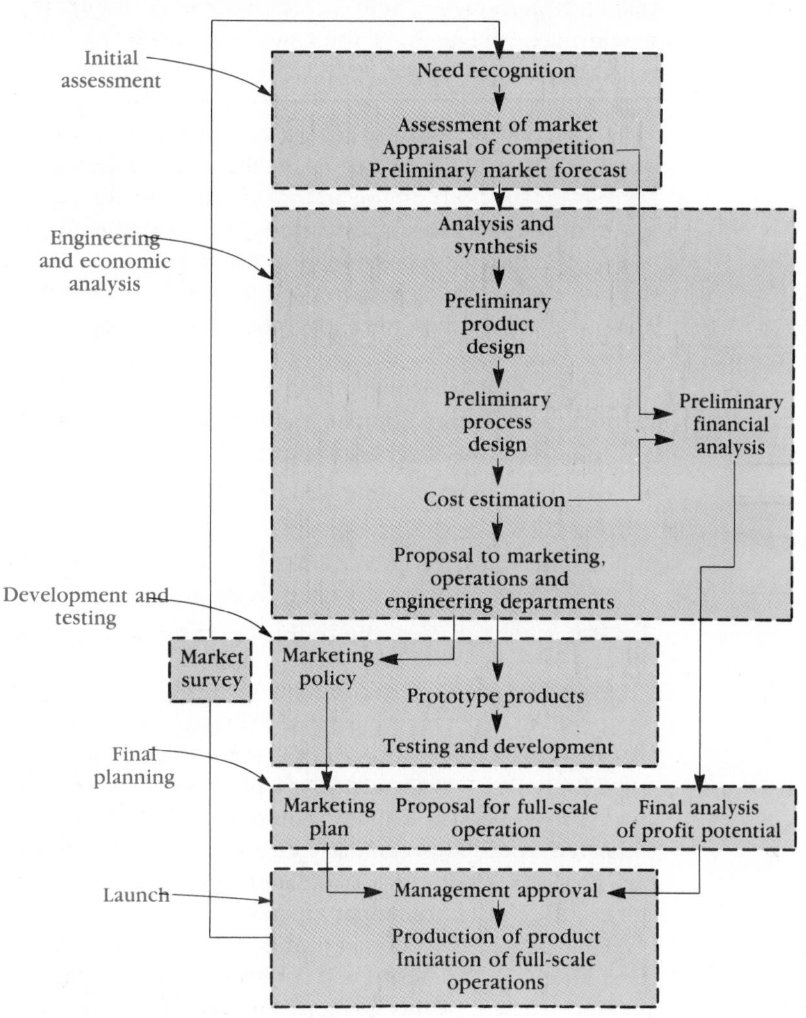

2. *Power supply.* Should the power supply be 120 volt (standard household current), battery powered, or both? Should it have rechargeable batteries?
3. *Keyboard.* What position should each key have? How will the keys be designated?
4. *Processor.* The processor is the electronic circuitry that performs the functions. What functions (such as square roots, logarithms, and present value) should be included in the design? How should these functions be performed? How fast should the response be?

Synthesis is putting the parts or elements together to form a whole. In analysis, each part is examined, and answers to questions are determined. In synthesis, the parts are combined in a way that addresses the interaction between those parts. The concept behind synthesis is to make the best decision for overall performance of the calculator, not to optimize one part. Synthesis is a series of trade-offs. Although a built-in recharger is desirable, the extra weight and size would make the body of the calculator too heavy and too large. Off-the-shelf rechargers are available, so a trade-off is made, and the recharger becomes a separate unit.

Based on the results of analysis and synthesis, a preliminary product design is prepared. The calculator begins to take shape in drawings of the circuits, in stress analysis for the body, in the arrangement of the keys, and so forth. Ideas gathered in the marketing investigation are solidified in the engineering phase.

A production proposal follows the preliminary product design. It addresses the broad problem of how to produce the product—that is, the process design. The following list describes some of the many decisions to consider:

1. *Capacity.* What is the long-term potential demand for the product?
2. *Process.* What equipment, plant layout, and production system are required to support this level of production? How will this equipment be sequenced?
3. *Facility.* Can an existing building be used? If so, what modifications are necessary?
4. *People.* What jobs are required for the new product? What skills are required? What training programs need to be developed?
5. *Materials.* What are the sources of the raw materials? What are the costs?

From the production proposal, cost estimates are prepared. Costs are based on operating data that are available through accounting records. If such records are not available, then experience with similar products can be used to estimate costs. Preliminary financial analysis requires estimates of investment and revenue as well as costs. The capital required to build facilities and buy equipment is estimated from the preliminary engineering design and the preliminary production proposal. Revenue is calculated from estimates of sales volume and selling price made in the preliminary market analysis.

Financial analysts compare the estimated profit (revenue minus cost) with the investment to determine if the product has a sufficient return (profit) for the amount invested. If this financial hurdle is crossed, a proposal for the development of marketing policies, operating plans, and engineering prototypes is prepared.

Development and Testing Phase

Engineering and operations combine to develop a product prototype. **Prototypes** are models of the product. These may be working models, models reduced in scale, or mock-ups of the product. A prototype for the electronic calculator is likely to be a working model made in a laboratory or a small-scale production facility. The model is tested and refined as the engineers strive to eliminate the "bugs" and improve the calculator's performance. Some product ideas are discarded at this point because the prototypes cannot be made to function satisfactorily.

Marketing is charged with formulating policies and developing plans for the advertising, promotion, distribution, and sale of the new product. Plans may be made for advertising campaigns, point-of-sale promotions, and the types of retail and wholesale outlets to be used. Marketing determines where the calculators will be sold—for example, in bookstores, in discount chains, or by mail-order houses.

Final Planning

During development and testing, a proposal for full-scale production is prepared. This proposal is similar to the preliminary production proposal, but includes more details about each of the areas within the business and more accurate estimates of costs. The full-scale proposal obviously includes any changes and new information discovered in the development phase. The marketing plans are finalized, and a final analysis of profit potential is made. The operating and marketing plans and the financial analysis are presented to top management for approval. Many projects never reach the next phase because of poor profit potential.

Launch Phase and Market Surveys

Management approval begins the implementation of the marketing and operating plans. Facilities are constructed, equipment is purchased, people are hired and trained, and materials are acquired. All these actions are aimed at producing the rechargeable electronic pocket calculator, which is the product the organization chose to make in order to achieve its goals.

Market surveys are used to monitor customer satisfaction, detect changing customer needs, and provide this feedback to the organization so the design process can begin again if needed.

Mortality in Product Design

Product design and development do not always or even usually lead to the introduction of a new product. Products can be eliminated at any point in design and development. For example, products can be eliminated for any of the following reasons:

1. Lack of sufficient customer demand
2. Excessive production costs
3. Inability to solve certain technical or engineering problems
4. Insufficient profit potential

The mortality rate of new products is very high, as shown in Exhibit 4.2. Experts vary on how many ideas are required to generate one commercially successful product. The ratio of sixty ideas to one successful product, shown in Exhibit 4.2, is a typical estimate. The key to success in new product development is to eliminate untenable new product ideas as soon as possible in order to bring the best new product to market quickly.

Discarded ideas should be carefully filed for several reasons.

1. When a similar idea is later proposed, the product design questions can quickly be handled by referring to previous attempts.
2. As conditions change in the marketplace, as when demand for the product increases, the design and development activities can be resumed.
3. As technological improvements allow ways to reduce production costs, increase quality, or reduce the needed capital investment, the discarded prod-

Exhibit 4.2 Mortality Rate of New Products

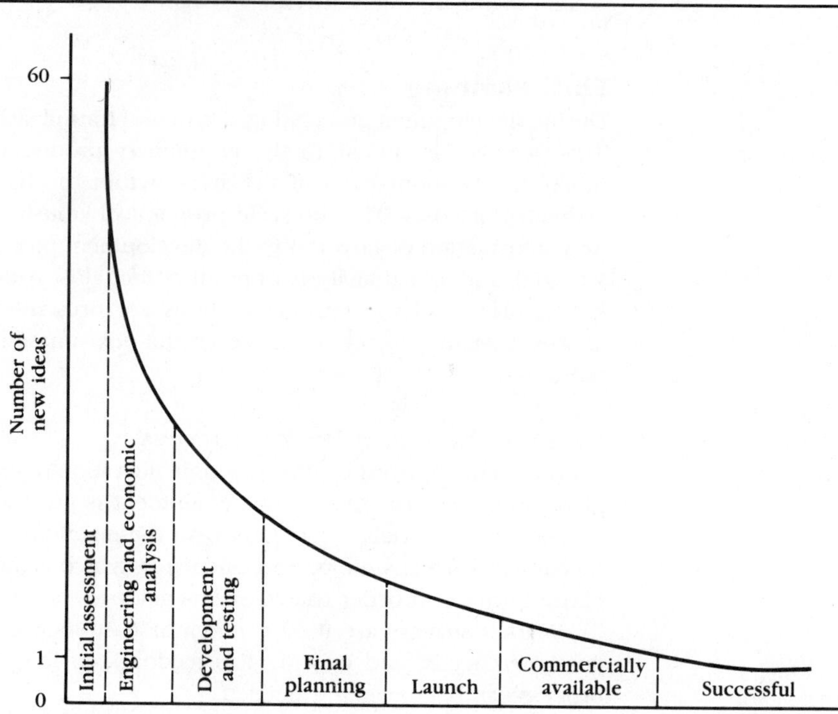

uct idea can be reintroduced. For example, improvements in microelectronics and computer technology have made possible many consumer products, such as compact disc players, that had previously been too expensive to manufacture for home use.

Implementing the Teamwork Approach to New Product Development

The overview of new product development described in Exhibit 4.1 illustrates it as a sequential process beginning with initial assessment and concluding with final planning and product launching. While this is a logical flow for the purpose of providing an overview of new product development, it should not be viewed strictly as a sequential process when applied in a real situation. It should be clear that not all decisions made in the initial assessment phase can or should be made before any decision is made in the engineering and economic analysis phase. Within the engineering phase, not every decision regarding product design can be made before a decision can be made about designing the manufacturing process. A significant amount of overlap between the phases of new product development and a significant amount of information exchange between participants are not only necessary, but also desirable to achieve a high-quality product design that meets customer expectations.

Many organizations are beginning to realize, as Ford Motor Company did when it designed the Taurus, that new product development requires more than the informal exchange of information among participants. Ford needed to quickly develop a new, high-quality, high-performing product to meet the competition. These requirements implied that the company had to design a product that was competitively priced and high in quality by making decisions that met organizational rather than functional area objectives. It also meant that Ford had to shorten the new product development lead time so the product would be available as quickly as possible. Organizations are favoring an approach to product design that involves team building. Rather than establishing teams as needed to deal with special problems, organizations are building teams at the beginning of a new product development effort and giving the team overall responsibility for success. To successfully implement this approach, organizations should:

1. Build teams at the beginning of the new product development efforts that include participants from all areas within the organization and first-tier suppliers.
2. Charge the team with responsibility for the successful completion of the new product development effort.
3. Strive for solutions that meet the objectives of the organization, not for solutions that satisfy the objectives of a functional area. This means that no participant or group of participants can have veto power.
4. Encourage participants to think not only about the task on which the group is presently focused, but also about the impact of the decision on other aspects of product design that the group has considered and will consider. This is the systems approach to new product development.

To better understand the team approach to new product development, examine Exhibit 4.3. It describes the roles of the participants during the various phases of the product development cycle. The roles of the participants are discussed in the rest of the chapter.

THE ROLE OF MARKETING

Marketing's role in product design and development is to research the needs of potential customers. Markets are studied to determine total size, recent and long-term growth rates, competitors, and potential competitors. Measuring consumer needs, estimating competitive pressure, measuring the external environment, and understanding the life of a product are important topics covered in this section.

Measuring Consumer Needs

A primary concern in market research is to evaluate consumer behavior and estimate the level of consumer heed. The market research report describes the features that consumers prefer and provides an estimate of the price difference consumers are willing to pay for each feature. Features on a microwave oven, for

Exhibit 4.3 Relationship Between Product Design and the Functional Areas of an Organization

Phase of Product Development Cycle	*Participant*						
	Marketing	Engineering	Operations	Suppliers	Finance	Accounting	Management Information Systems
Initial Assessment	Market investigation Estimation of volume and price	Interpretation of technical data and participation in technological forecasting	Understanding of production economics and environmental issues		Description of the financial status of the organization		Classification, organization, and tabulation of information at all levels of product development ↓
Engineering and Economic Analysis	Initial formulation of marketing strategy	Analysis of needs Initial product and process design	Preliminary feasibility study for production	Input to the design of product and process	Preliminary financial analysis: return on investment, payback	Data for cost estimation	
Development	Refinement of marketing strategy	Design changes Prototype construction Final product design changes Process selection	Preliminary production plans	Assistance in prototype construction	Continued updating of investment requirements Capital formation	More detailed information on cost and productivity	
Final Planning	Final marketing strategy Development of a distribution system	Machine selection Layout Supervision of equipment installation	Proposal for full-scale production	Planning to acquire resources for full-scale production	Final analysis of return Capital formation	Review of feasibility of final plans	
Launch	Initiation of marketing	Continuing product and process improvements	Initiation of production	Initiation of production	Follow-up evaluation of profit performance	Collection of actual cost data	

example, might include a temperature probe, multiple power levels, and a preprogrammed defrost function. The report also should describe the performance characteristics desired by customers. Should a hair dryer have 1,000 or 1,500 watts of power? Should a health insurance policy cover routine doctor's office visits? Will a car be able to accelerate from zero to fifty miles per hour in eight seconds or less? The research report also contains a preliminary forecast of market size and market price.

Market research thus involves the following considerations:

1. Features
2. Performance characteristics
3. Market size
4. Market price

Marketing uses this information to determine the segment of a market an organization will pursue, to design the distribution system, to select advertising and promotion strategies, to set staffing requirements, and to establish marketing policies. Engineering and operations use this information to shape the product in preliminary design and to investigate the problem of full-scale production. The market research report clearly serves more than one purpose.

In the case where product design and development involve modification of an existing product, the product support group should be included on the team. The product support group is normally involved in working with customers to meet specific needs that a particular customer might have and to solve problems with the product. These people should have many good ideas about what customers want and how the product can be modified to best meet their needs.

Measuring Competitive Pressures

The existence of strong demand for a product does not guarantee its success in the marketplace. Strong consumer demand and the potential high profits that go with that demand attract many competitors. For example, the successful introduction of the first microwave oven brought forth a host of competitors. Understanding the market requires a thorough analysis of existing and potential competitors because as markets begin to grow, new and often powerful competitors will emerge. For example, when microcomputers were introduced in the late 1970s, the market was wide open. Many new firms such as Apple Computer and existing computer firms such as Digital Equipment Corporation (DEC) entered the market.

A careful competitor analysis would have shown that IBM was an important potential competitor. Its eventual entrance into the market forced many of the recently founded companies out of business because IBM had the ability to dominate the computer market. The Osborne computer, once thought to have a bright future in the microcomputer market, was an early casualty. In a short time, IBM has become the leader in microcomputers. The strength of its leadership is demonstrated by the fact that nearly all microcomputer companies offer machines that are IBM compatible. Even DEC has de-emphasized its original microcomputer design in favor of an IBM-compatible version.

Competition in a market can reduce price, increase the demand for better-quality products, and increase the need to provide after-the-sale service. These possibilities should be considered in any complete market analysis. As a result, an organization's plans cannot be static. An organization should be able to anticipate and plan for change. The impact on operations is critical because the road to lower cost, higher quality, and better service winds through operations.

The External Environment

In addition to competitive factors, the market study should take into account environmental factors such as the following:

- The condition of the economy
- The status of technology now and in the future
- The social, political, and legal aspects of the product and its design

Economic Conditions

Present and future economic conditions can significantly alter buying patterns. For example, the sudden interruption of foreign crude-oil supplies during the energy crisis in the 1970s significantly altered the habits of car buyers. As crude-oil and gasoline prices increased, consumers shifted demand away from large cars to smaller, more fuel efficient cars and trucks. In the 1980s, as conservation efforts reduced consumption and crude-oil supplies increased, the price of gasoline dropped, and large cars with bigger engines became more popular.

The Status of Technology

The status of technology is critical to the success of a product because the usefulness of some products is affected by changes in technology. The popularity of component stereo systems has virtually eliminated sales of the one-piece cabinet stereo, and the popularity of color television sets has nearly eliminated sales of black-and-white sets. Front-wheel-drive automobiles have taken a significant share of the car market and will probably take more in the future. All these changes in demand for products were based on technological and engineering improvements. These improvements directly influence operations because they require changes in how the products are produced.

Social, Political, and Legal Considerations

The sales of many products are influenced by social, political, and legal conditions. Some products have suffered dramatically because of legal action. Food products thought to cause cancer have been banned from production. Other products have been affected by the compilation of statistical data that has resulted in a quasi-legal prohibition or warning. Saccharin and cigarettes are examples.

Other products have succumbed to political and legislative pressure brought on by the concern for the environment. A glass company wanted to introduce a beverage container with a plastic base and a glass lining. Technological problems and continued pressure by environmentalists caused the company to reconsider. It is not feasible to ignore concerns that were once thought to be outside the realm of business.

The Product Life Cycle

The **product life cycle** is a series of stages that products pass through. These stages—development, growth, maturity/saturation, and decline—are displayed in Exhibit 4.4.

Development Stage

The development stage includes product testing and development and the introductory period in which sales are very slow. For marketing, it is a time to gain acceptance for the product among wholesale distributors, retailers, and consumers. For operations and engineering, it is a time to work out remaining problems with the production process. For example, the compact disc player is moving from the development into the high-growth phase of the product life cycle, as it displaces sales of audio cassette players.

Growth Stage

The growth stage is characterized by a rapid increase in sales. In this stage, marketing is striving to increase market share by competitive pricing, aggressive promotion, and intensive distribution. Operations is trying to find ways to increase production volumes to keep pace with increasing demand. Large volumes allow operations to apply mass-production techniques that lower costs. Opera-

Exhibit 4.4 Product Life Cycle

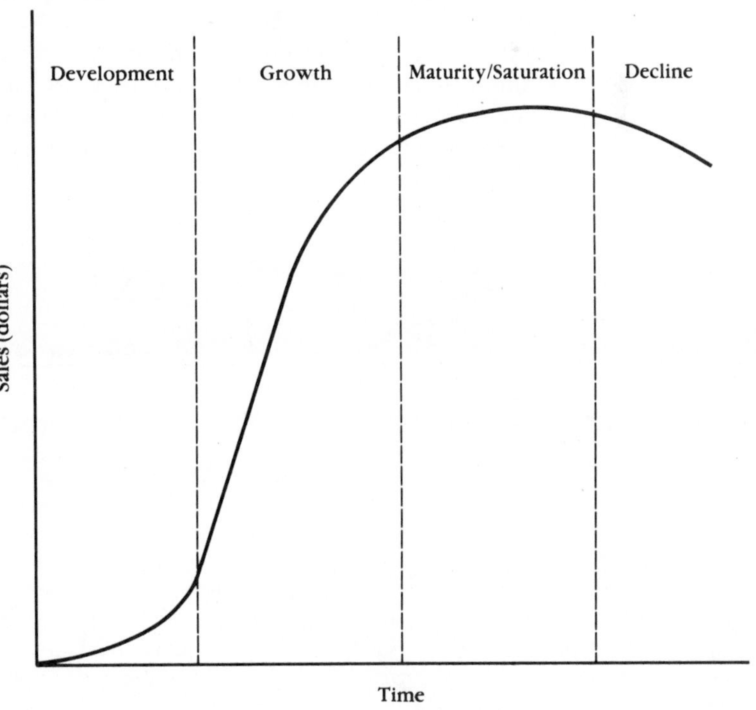

tions is also striving to maintain quality and delivery schedules as the pace of sales quickens. For example, videocassette recorders (VCRs) have recently had a period of very high sales growth and will soon be passing into the maturity stage of the product life cycle.

Maturity/Saturation Stage

Maturity/saturation occurs when sales and distribution have reached their peak. Volume, which reflects the number of customers, the quantity purchased, and the frequency of purchase, is stable. In this stage, price competition can become intense as existing firms try to maintain or increase sales in a market that has little or no growth. Firms begin to specialize (i.e., segment markets) and look for market niches. Pressure continues for further cost reductions. For example, the automobile has had limited growth in sales for many years. The increase in specialty vehicles, such as Jeeps, minivans, small trucks, four-wheel-drive vehicles, vans, and so forth, is the automobile industry's way of segmenting the market. Operations should be able to cope with increasing product variety.

Decline Stage

The decline of mature products is caused by changes in consumer preferences, product technology, competitive activities, and other environmental factors. In this phase, sales decline, and firms take actions ranging from drastic reductions in profit margins to withdrawal from the market. For example, the steel industry is losing market share to plastics in the automotive market and to concrete in construction. These two industries have been major users of steel, and both markets are mature and experiencing limited growth. As a result, sales volume in the steel industry has and will continue to decline. This decline is independent of losses to foreign steel producers.

The length of the product life cycle differs widely among products. For example, it has taken more than seventy years for automobiles to go from development to maturity and saturation. On the other hand, home videocassette recorders, which were introduced a little more than ten years ago, are approaching the end of the growth phase and will soon be a mature product.

INTEGRATING THE SYSTEM

Linking Marketing and Operations Through the Product Life Cycle

A product life cycle is most often viewed as a marketing concept. As seen in our prior discussion, a product life cycle has implications for operations. During the early stages, operations needs to be highly flexible because the product has not taken its final form. Changes will be made through the development phase. As demand increases and the product enters the growth stage, the production system responds with increased investments in facilities to boost production volume and lower costs. As the product enters the maturation/saturation phase and eventually the decline phase, production systems need to be flexible enough to switch to new and growing products. Operations and marketing should work together to ensure coordinated efforts in responding to these changing needs.

FROM CONSUMER NEEDS TO PRODUCT IDEAS: THE ROLE OF ENGINEERING

Engineers transform the ideas generated during the assessment of market needs into a working product. They develop working models, called prototypes, that may eventually be produced in large-scale operations under the direction of the operations manager. It is necessary that the people responsible for design and those responsible for operations work closely together so that designs are feasible in full-scale production.

Design includes two related parts: (1) product design, which shapes the product, and (2) process design, which determines the methods for production. Product design transforms the concept drawn from the market research study into features, characteristics, and performance that differentiate this product from others. The design of an automobile may include reclining front bucket seats, three choices of color, and the ability to brake from fifty to zero miles per hour in under four seconds. These features differentiate that car from other cars in its class. Service operations such as life insurance companies also have important factors to consider in product design. A life insurance company should define the terms of its policy so the benefits to the customer are in line with the premium paid.

Process design describes the methods for making the product. Which machines will be used to bend the metal for a fender, toast the buns for a hamburger, or sort mail in a post office? Process design is the blueprint for production, and it will be discussed in a later section.

Shaping the Product: Product Design

The objective of product design is to create a product with excellent functional utility and sales appeal at an acceptable cost and within a reasonable time. The product should be produced using high-quality, low-cost materials and methods.

Columbus Mutual Life Insurance: Product Design

In product design, engineering encompasses more than physical characteristics such as product strength or dimensional accuracy. Services, like goods, have design problems that need to be addressed. Columbus Mutual sells life insurance policies. In developing new policies, the company will have prototype policies written by lawyers and statisticians to ensure their validity before the policies are marketed widely.

Columbus Mutual will be careful to check the legal limits of its liability so the company charges a fair price for what is covered in the policy. It should check the life expectancy of its potential customers so it charges the proper premium for each age group. Performing these activities well is critical to Columbus Mutual's success. Policies that are too liberal with payouts could lead to financial problems. Policies that do not offer enough coverage for the money will not be competitive.

It should be produced on equipment that is or will be available when production begins. Often a new product will spawn the creation of new equipment. The product should be competitive with or better than similar products on the market in terms of quality, appearance, performance, service life, and price. Product technology is a critical factor in product design.

Product Technology

What has accounted for the dramatic surge in the U.S. standard of living since the end of World War II? Available capital, abundant natural resources, and the world's largest developed market have all contributed to the increase. However, the single largest factor has been developments in science and technology. A Brookings Institute study assigns 44 percent of the increase in productivity to technological innovation. Other economists estimate that during the past two decades, innovation has accounted for 40 percent of the increase in the gross national product (GNP).[2]

Technology can dramatically change the competitiveness of products. The best buggy-whip producers in the world were not able to retain their market size as the automobile replaced the horse and buggy. Technological advances in electronics enabled electronic wristwatches to replace mechanical watches in only a few years. Producers of black-and-white television sets had to adapt to color or face elimination. What will be the impact of microcomputers on the banking industry? Computerized tellers have taken over routine banking functions. New methods of providing services and goods have lowered costs, improved quality, enhanced customer satisfaction, and increased performance. What new technological developments lie just beyond the horizon? The answer to this question will shape the competition for new products and determine which organizations survive.

Technological Forecasting

Organizations have attempted to forecast technology. In product technology, the point is usually not to forecast specific features or to provide a detailed description. The point is to forecast performance. For example, in computers, this could mean forecasting the number of instructions per second that microcomputers will be capable of performing in five or more years. In process technology, there are productivity improvements on the horizon because of advances in computer technology. The potential of microcomputer-controlled robots to reduce costs and improve quality is significant.

Understanding the possibilities of and planning for future technology are often superior to simply waiting and reacting to competitors' movements. Planning for technological change requires the following steps:

1. Monitoring the literature published by research arms of universities, the armed forces, private foundations, and the government, as well as keeping abreast of ideas generated by labor and management. Foreign producers, especially the Japanese, have been successful at improving products and processes through worker-generated ideas.
2. Organizing and classifying breakthroughs and potential breakthroughs into groups for further study.
3. Determining which of these improvements offers an organization potential for improved products or operations. Great care should be taken not to

discard ideas quickly because they do not fit the existing product line or marketing strategy. Also, the people analyzing technology should not be heavily involved with day-to-day operations because their focus on operations may be too narrow and their time demands too great.

4. Reporting the best of these ideas to the marketing research and development engineering groups to see how they might be used.

Design engineers should understand many product and process technologies and determine which are appropriate for the design under consideration.

Product Performance and Characteristics: Goods

So far, the discussion of product design has applied to both services and goods. Because a good is tangible and a service is not, however, there are some differences in the approach to design. To illustrate these differences, this section describes product design for goods, and a later section will describe product design for services.

Producers of goods must be concerned with physical characteristics, but even among goods there are differences. Clearly, an oil refinery and an assembled product, like a standard office stapler, require different approaches to design. An oil refinery is built around a large chemical process, and its products are determined by the laws of chemistry. For example, gasoline results from heating crude oil under pressure. This releases the light and most volatile components, leaving the heavier fuel oils behind. The lighter components are then blended to make gasoline. The performance of gasoline is measured by its rated octane number (RON or octane), which measures volatility. A 92 octane gasoline is more powerful than an 89 octane gasoline.

OPERATIONS IN ACTION

Design for Manufacturability and Assembly: A New Approach to Product Design

A new approach to product design has been developed by two Ph.D.s from England, Geoffrey Boothroyd and Peter Dewhurst. Design for manufacturability and assembly (DFMA) can be a powerful tool to improve product quality and lower manufacturing costs by focusing on manufacturing issues during product design. DFMA is implemented through computer software that points designers toward designs that would be easy to build by focusing on the economic implications of design decisions. This is critical because even though design is a small part of the overall cost of a product, the design decisions fix 80 to 90 percent of the manufacturing costs.

In actual application, DFMA has had some startling successes. With the DFMA software, Texas Instruments reduced assembly time for an infrared sighting mechanism from 129 minutes to 20 minutes. IBM sliced assembly time for it printers from thirty minutes to three minutes. New York Air Brake Co. cut the number of parts in its assemblies by 30 percent and reduced its costs to assemble by 50 percent. Ford Motor Company has been using DFMA for more than five years with great success, and General Motors is aggressively pursuing it. Some firms see DFMA as a way to leap-frog the Japanese with new high-quality, low-cost products.

An office stapler has physical properties. There are problems of stress, reliability, durability, interference, tolerance, product safety, and human engineering. The following list describes some of the important factors in the physical design of goods:

Stress	The stapler should be designed to accept the force of an angry 220-pound clerk who bangs a staple into a twenty-five-page document. Yet the stapler should also respond to the soft touch of a 105-pound manager who wants to staple two pages.
Reliability	The stapler should be able to perform the same task over and over for many years.
Durability	The stapler should be able to handle expected abuses, such as being knocked off the file cabinet or slammed down on the desk, with a low probability of damage.
Interference	The stapler should have dimensional integrity. Key parts should be properly aligned.
Tolerance	The stapler's component parts should be designed and manufactured to a specified level of precision. When reloading a stapler, look at the supports for the replacement staples. The heights of the two bars will not always be exactly the same. If there is too much difference, the staples will jam or will not clinch properly. Tolerance describes how much the bar heights can vary and still be acceptable.
Safety	The stapler's design should make it very difficult to staple a finger to the page or hurt the user in any way.
Human engineering (ergonomics)	The stapler should be designed to be easily handled and loaded.

A series of drawings is made to describe the product and its components in order to address these problems. The drawings are the basis for stress analysis and part compatibility (checking interference and setting tolerances). Models of the product can be constructed to test reliability, durability, product safety features, and the ease of operation (human engineering). The drawings are the maps that describe how the good will ultimately be assembled.

Bill of Materials

A **bill of materials (BOM)** describes the type and quantity of each component part needed to build a good. A BOM is a critical part of the design because it will become the basis for purchasing parts, scheduling production, and managing inventory. A Faber Pencil Company pencil has a simple BOM; yet it tells the manufacturer the component parts needed to make one unit, as shown below.

Part No.	Description	Quantity
16841	Wooden halves that have been hollowed to receive the lead	2 pieces
2824	⅛" diameter lead, 7" long	1 piece
5134	½" long eraser	1 piece
1621	½" long metal band to hold eraser in place	1 piece
7771	Yellow paint	½ ounce
29494	Glue (to attach wooden halves)	¼ ounce

Product Performance and Characteristics: Services

The major difference between design of a good and design of a service is that there are no physical characteristics to consider in service design. Designing a life insurance policy does not require scrutiny of physical properties. It does require detailed study of the legal, statistical, and financial implications of the policy. Lawyers and actuaries replace the traditional design engineer, but the function is still as critical to the organization's success. Designing medical procedures requires the skill and training of a medical doctor, and designing banking services requires skills in financial analysis.

INTEGRATING THE SYSTEM

The Bill of Materials in Design, Planning, and Control

A BOM is one of the results of a product design. It is important for success in several areas in operations. Suppose Faber Pencil Company received an order for 10,000 pencils. How would it plan production? An order for 10,000 pencils alerts the purchasing agent that 10,000 erasers, 70,000 inches of pencil lead (7 inches of lead per pencil; see the BOM), and so on are required. A quick check of on-hand inventory might show that 1,200 erasers and 15,000 inches of pencil lead are available. Purchase orders would be written for the balance.

When the time comes for production, a scheduler could examine the BOM and determine the amount of material required to produce the ordered pencils. These materials could be drawn from stock and transported to the production floor.

A BOM is a critical element in planning and controlling the production of goods. More detailed discussions of these topics are contained in later chapters in the production planning and the managing and controlling sections of this text.

To provide services, it is often necessary to design machines to assist in that process. The design of these machines requires the same attention to physical detail that an automobile, microwave oven, or washing machine requires. A bank that installs electronic tellers to perform routine transactions should be concerned about the machine's reliability, ease of operation, security, and accuracy. The surgeon performing arthroscopic surgery (microsurgery often performed on the knee) should have extremely reliable and accurate equipment.

All service operations have physical characteristics that relate to their facilities. For example, hospitals should consider the layout of patients' rooms and nursing stations, the method of food service, and the design of equipment.

Other organizations that are considered service businesses provide both services and goods. For example, automobile repair and food preparation services have physical properties. In fact, restaurants have Bills-of-Materials call recipes that are used in preparing meals and ordering food. These hybrid operations should consider the physical design of the goods they sell as well as facility and equipment design.

The Role of Computer-Aided Design

Presently, business managers and engineers perceive computer-aided design (CAD) as a tool to assist engineers in designing goods. CAD uses computer technology and a graphic display to represent physical shapes in the same way that engineering drawings have in the past. It is used in the metalworking industry to display component parts, to illustrate size and shape, to show possible relationships to other parts, and to indicate parts deformation under specified loads. After the design has been completed, the engineer can examine many different views or sections of the part and finally send it to a plotter to prepare drawings. This capability greatly reduces engineering time and avoids routine mistakes made in analysis and drawing. It significantly increases productivity and reduces

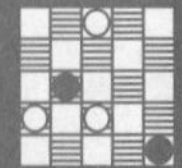

GAINING STRATEGIC ADVANTAGE AT FEDERAL EXPRESS

Product Design Is the Competitive Edge

Air couriers such as Federal Express, United Parcel Service (UPS), Emery Air Freight, and others are going through a shakeout. The steep climb in demand for their package delivery service has lessened, and the industry is faced with serious overcapacity. Competition is ferocious, with many couriers offering discounts to volume customers, and more price cutting is expected. Only two or three major players may survive the shakeout.

Federal Express, the largest of the couriers, has positioned itself strategically for the competition by paying close attention to its product and how it was designed. It has deliberately differentiated itself from other couriers. First, Federal Express has a vast network that can deliver overnight to remote locations like Valdosta, Georgia, and Big Sandy, Montana.

Second, when a Federal operator gets a call to pick up an order, he or she types it into the computer. The order travels to a courier by radio and is displayed on either a hand-held computer terminal or a computer terminal in the truck. Within an hour or two, the package is picked up and shuttled off to the airport. Federal picks up packages as late as 9:00 P.M. Other couriers that cannot respond as quickly stop pickups by 6:00 P.M.

Third, at each step form pickup to delivery, employees log packages into a computer terminal that is linked to the central computer in Memphis. Customers can dial a toll-free number, and an operator will trace the packages using the computer.

Because of the difference in product design, Federal Express is the only company that guarantees delivery by 10:30 the next morning. It is also the only company that guarantees to track down the location of a package for a customer within thirty minutes. Federal Express has gained a strategic advantage through its product design and has positioned itself well for the coming battle.[3]

A courier uses a scanner to read bar codes for transmission into the Federal Express computer system that monitors the location of all packages. *Courtesy: Federal Express Corporation.*

design time, which allows faster delivery. CAD is clearly superior to traditional methods of preparing drawings by hand. Powerful and inexpensive CAD systems are available for use on microcomputers. The dramatic drop in price will accelerate the use of CAD systems in the nineties.

The CAD system has applications in any part of operations in which physical space and relationships are important. If two parts can be visualized, the com-

OPERATIONS IN ACTION

Cincinnati Milacron, Inc.: CAD for Facility Layout

Cincinnati Milacron, Inc., produces robots and machine tools used to shape metal parts in motors, transmissions, and other mechanical devices. As part of its sales and marketing service, the company can help customers design and lay out their facilities. Cincinnati Milacron's technical sales staff uses CAD to represent the factory floor. The model permits testing for clearance and spacing of equipment. For example, when a robot attempts to unload a part from one machine, will it be able to swing past the conveyor without hitting it or having to slow down and make unnecessary movements?

Cincinnati Milacron's technical staff can also use the CAD system to simulate operations by testing running speed and measuring output. This feature provides its customers with estimates of capacity that are useful in decision making. As a result of the analysis, revisions in the design can be made to improve operations. Using CAD to assist customers in the design and layout of their production systems gives Cincinnati Milacron an edge on its competition.

puter graphics systems may be able to display and manipulate them. For example, these systems can analyze the layout of a production system composed of a robot and two machines. The robot can load one machine and then load the other while the first is working the part. The CAD system can model the layout, check on cycle time (the time required to complete one load/unload cycle), and check on potential interference between machines.

Applications of CAD systems are not limited to producing goods. As discussed in the previous sections, service operations have facilities and may have equipment. For example, the service stalls in an automotive center or rooms in a hospital emergency center have physical characteristics that can be represented by the interactive graphics capabilities of a CAD system.

Product Design for Service Operations

As described earlier, manufacturers have to consider physical characteristics in product design. Because services are intangible, service design can be viewed as a series of actions or events that can be performed in sequence. Service design involves deciding which actions belong in the sequence and what order is "best" for the customer. Therefore, developing a flow chart is often one of the first steps in designing a service operation. The flow chart becomes an important tool for analyzing the layout of a facility and understanding the movement of people and information. It is a means for identifying important customer interactions points. Exhibit 4.5 illustrates a flow diagram for a car rental business. Graphical representation of the service design provides a structured way of visualizing what occurs and how each activity relates to the other. The flow chart can also be useful when estimating the capacity of service operations which is discussed in Chapter 5.

Exhibit 4.5 Flow Chart of Car Rental Check-In and Check-Out Process

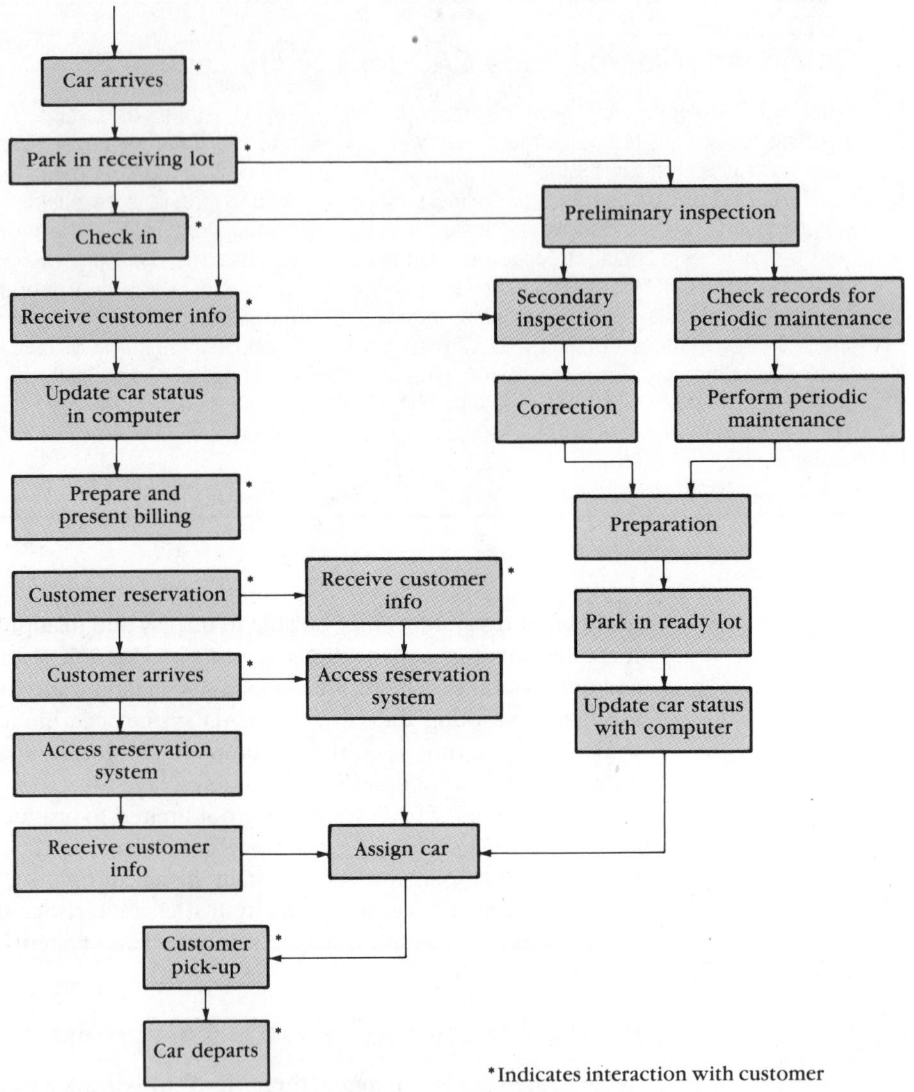

Source: Sasser, W. Earl, Olsen, R. Paul, and Wyckott D. Daryl Management of Service Operations: Text Cases and Readings. Allyn and Bacon Inc.: Boston. 1978. pp. 74.

When designing a service delivery system, management should consider the following:

1. Are the steps arranged in a logical sequence? For example, when a student registers for class, does the student see an advisor before or after selecting his/her classes? Does a credit manager check a customer's credit before or after the contract to deliver the service has been signed?

2. Is the capacity of one operation in the sequence balanced with the others? For example, in a restaurant, are there only fifty spaces in the parking lot, but tables for 200 guests?
3. How much flexibility is available at each step? For example, are the counter workers at a fast-food restaurant trained so they can work at more than one place in the operation?
4. Can steps be combined? Simplifying the process for the customer will often improve customer service and increase operating efficiency.
5. Can steps be done in parallel? Any time steps can be done at the same time, customer throughput time is reduced.
6. Can customers perform the transaction without waiting for someone to do it? Allowing customers to check out of a hotel, check in a rental car, or register for classes on their own will improve customer service. The process needs to be designed so customers can do it easily and accurately.

Ethical Issues in Product Design

What is the responsibility of an organization and its managers to see that the goods and services that they produce do not harm consumers? Consumers who believe they have been damaged by a poorly designed good or service have legal recourse under both civil and criminal statutes. Often, however, only the most serious and obvious offenses are settled in this way. The Ford Pinto is one example. The Pinto had an unprotected gas tank located only 7 inches from the rear bumper, making it susceptible to leakage and fires upon collision. After a number of fiery crashes in which several people died, a California jury awarded $128 million in a lawsuit stemming from an accident involving a Pinto that was struck from the rear. Negative publicity on a nationwide scale caused the market share for the Pinto to drop significantly. It declined 63 percent in just three years, and the Pinto was dropped from Ford's product line. In retrospect, it is easy to say that Ford made a poor decision by not acknowledging the defective design earlier and taking corrective action. The real point is why they did not recognize it when the initial design was made, or, at least, why they did not recognize the problem and correct it when it was called into question.

More difficult ethical issues in product design result when the evidence is not as clear. For example, what responsibilities does a power tool manufacturer have with respect to product safety? Does a power saw manufacturer have the responsibility to design its product so that it is difficult for a child to operate. Suppose a parent is using a power saw and is called away to the telephone for a few minutes. A ten-year-old may wander over, press the trigger and seriously injure himself or herself. A simple and inexpensive lock-out switch that would have to be pressed simultaneously when the trigger is pressed would make it more difficult for that accident to happen. What is the responsibility of the parent? What is the responsibility of the company?

What was the Morton Thiokol company's, the company that designed the O-rings for the space shuttle Challenger, responsibility in the Challenger's tragic accident? Engineers claimed that they warned management of the O-ring problem on the day of the launch. According to the engineers, the O-rings were not designed to work in the unusually cold temperature experienced on launch day.

Unfortunately, there are no equations or rules that can be uniformly applied in all situations. In most cases, business persons are required to weigh the potential costs to the organization and to society for taking actions to correct a problem against the benefits to the organization and to society. The problem is that taking corrective actions leads to costs that occur immediately and can be measured somewhat accurately, while the benefits occur later and are often vague and hard to relate to the organization's bottom line. Correcting the gas tank problem in the Pinto would have meant spending money immediately to relocate, redesign, or cushion the tank. The benefits of taking corrective actions only become clear once the tragedy has occurred. Managers must be able to look beyond the short-term effects on the bottom line to protect customers, as well as stockholders, from the damage caused by producing products that have design flaws.

Engineering for Production: Process Design

Design engineers create the product; production engineers, sometimes called manufacturing engineers, design the process for producing the product. **Process design** is describing how the product will be made. In many cases, a single engineer or team of engineers designs both product and process. The integration of product and process through teams and task forces usually leads to better solutions.

The process design decision has two major components: (1) a technical or engineering component and (2) a scale economy or business component. Technology is discussed in this chapter, and the business or economies-of-scale issues are discussed in Chapter 7. The technical side of process design requires that decisions be made regarding the technology, the sequence of operations, and the methods and procedures to be used for performing the operations.

Process Technology

Process technology varies substantially from industry to industry; therefore, it is difficult to discuss the general characteristics of process design. For example, the production of sheet steel used in cars and appliances requires melting iron ore in a blast furnace, refining it in a basic oxygen furnace, shaping it in a continuous caster, and rolling it on a mill. The process is very different from making microcomputer chips, machining parts for electric motors, or preparing hamburgers.

Design engineers are limited by the existing knowledge and practice regarding process technology. They cannot implement technology that does not exist. It is critical that these engineers be aware of the latest process improvements and that they constantly probe the edge of technology for a "better" method. Designers should insist on a process that is reliable and on systems that are easy to operate. What are the capabilities of new machines? What cost, capacity, or quality advantages do they possess? What levels of skills are required or available in the work force? What new methods are being developed to cast steel, cut plastic, or shape wood? How can the oil-refining process be varied to achieve a greater percentage of gasoline?

Process technology is heavily grounded in engineering issues. These are appropriately discussed in engineering courses, courses offered by community and technical schools, or applied science courses. However, managers should have a framework for understanding and making decisions regarding process

OPERATIONS IN ACTION

McDonald's: Process Design

Designing the process is an area where McDonald's excels. Production engineers describe the grill that cooks the meat, the machine that toasts the buns, and the device that warms the food while it is waiting to be served. They outline the procedures for preparing the food. How long should the meat cook and at what temperature? How long should the buns be toasted? How should the condiments be applied? In many cases, new equipment had to be designed or existing equipment adapted to meet the needs of high volume and fast-paced production (the link between market need and the production system). Consider the simple device for putting french fries into a serving container. This device, which was designed for McDonald's, measures the correct quantity of fries and allows the counter person to put them into the container in less than three seconds.

The production engineer describes the basic flow of materials. The fry cook should be supplied with the patties, buns, and so on, and the counter person should have ample finished product to sell. This material flow becomes the basis for laying out the facility. Where should the grills be in relation to the french fryer, the customer counter, and the beverage dispenser?

The Operations department writes the job descriptions for the fry cook and the counter person. The job descriptions outline the employees' basic responsibilities and the procedures they are to follow. For example, the counter person should use the proper-size bag for a customer's order. On the bottom of each McDonald's bag, there is a letter. Each item sold has a number of points. If three hamburgers, worth one point each, are sold, they are put into a four-count bag. The greater the points, the larger the bag. This prevents workers from fumbling for the correct-size bag and speeds up service.

The job descriptions become the basis for employee training. McDonald's has continued to invest heavily in employee training. Thousands of McDonald's managers have graduated from Hamburger University.

OPERATIONS IN ACTION

National Steel, Inc.: Advances in Process Technology

Changes in process technology are not as easy to understand as changes in product technology because process technology improvements may not change the physical characteristics or performance of the final product. For example, molten steel that emerges from the basic oxygen furnace can be shaped into slabs by continuous casters or can be poured into ingot molds and rolled into slabs in another operation. Regardless of how they are shaped the slabs are heated and rolled into sheet steel used in cars and appliances.

From its appearance on an automobile, it is not possible to determine if the sheet metal was molded in ingots or was cast. The advantages of casting are significant. Cast steel is of higher quality, takes less time to produce, reduces operating costs by 15 to 20 percent over ingot production, and decreases the required capital investment. This important process technology improvement will eventually eliminate the need for molding ingots. National Steel, Inc., has been a leader in the application of continuous-casting technology in this country. National has used this edge in technology to gain an advantage over the other major U.S. steel producers.

This computerized blast furnace produces 8,000 tons of hot metal a day that will be refined into steel by basic oxygen furnaces. ***Courtesy: American Iron and Steel Institute.***

Hot metal is poured into a basic oxygen furnace, where it will be converted into steel. This furnace can convert hot metal into 300 tons of molten steel in about forty minutes. ***Courtesy: American Iron and Steel Institute.***

technologies. Why should process technology be changed? Several reasons are listed below.

1. To increase capacity to meet expected demand. *Example:* supermarkets have installed electronic cash registers to replace old mechanical models. The electronic registers allow fast service, which increases the number of customers who can be served in a time period. Electronic registers also reduce costs and increase accuracy.
2. To reduce the cost of producing the product. *Example:* automobile manufacturers have added robot-controlled spray-painting equipment to their assembly lines to reduce costs and improve painting quality.
3. To increase product quality. *Example:* Burger King flame-broils rather than fries its hamburgers in an effort to improve product quality.
4. To improve customer service. *Example:* the process should be able to deliver the product in a timely fashion. Express mail services have changed the handling of packages by centralizing shipment points and using dependable air service to deliver overnight.
5. To differentiate the product from competitors' products. *Example:* the process should be flexible enough to satisfy customers with different products. The process that produces dishwashers is capable of making several different models on the same line.

To summarize, process technology can be changed to gain or maintain a competitive advantage.

Here, scrap is being charged into a basic oxygen furnace. These furnaces make steel from a combined charge of scrap and hot metal. *Courtesy: American Iron and Steel Institute.*

This multistrand continuous slab caster converts molten steel directly into semifinished shapes ready for further processing. This process results in large savings in labor and energy over traditional casting and primary rolling of ingots. *Courtesy: American Iron and Steel Institute.*

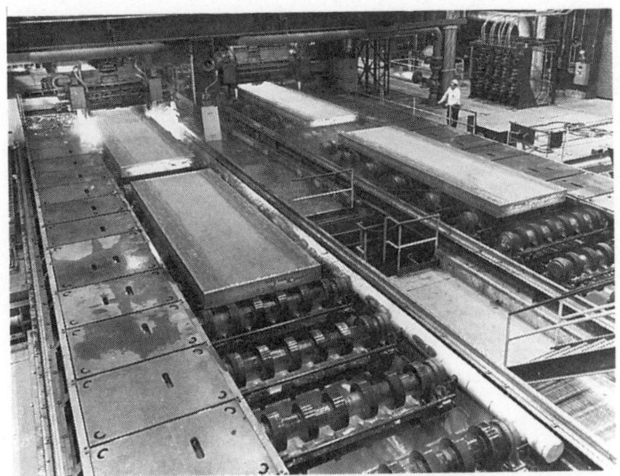

Slabs are being cut to length after emerging from a two-strand continuous caster. *Courtesy: American Iron and Steel Institute.*

The automatic gauge controls roll the plate to the desired length and thickness as it passes back and forth through the finishing stand rolls. Plate can be rolled from slabs produced by a continuous caster. *Courtesy: American Iron and Steel Institute.*

Sequence of Operations: Precedence Diagram

Another part of process design includes determining the sequence of steps required to make a good or provide a service. A **precedence diagram** is a series of nodes representing activities and arcs or lines indicating the sequence of operations. Exhibit 4.6 contains simple examples of precedence relationships. In each example, a letter with a circle around it represents an activity (node) and a line (arc) indicates the sequence. In the first situation, the diagram illustrates that task A must be completed before task B can start. The second diagram shows that task V must be completed before either task Y or task Z can begin, and the third diagram shows that both task M and task N must be completed before task P can begin.

When assembling a complex product such as a typewriter or when servicing a commercial jet engine, the three situations shown in Exhibit 4.6 can be combined to illustrate the operation. For example, the precedence diagram in Exhibit 4.7 represents the steps required to install the engine and transmission in a

Exhibit 4.6 Three Types of Precedence Situations

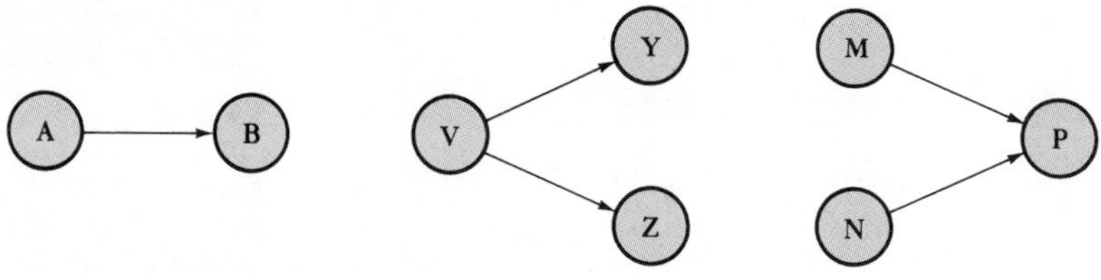

Exhibit 4.7 Engine and Transmission Final Assembly Line

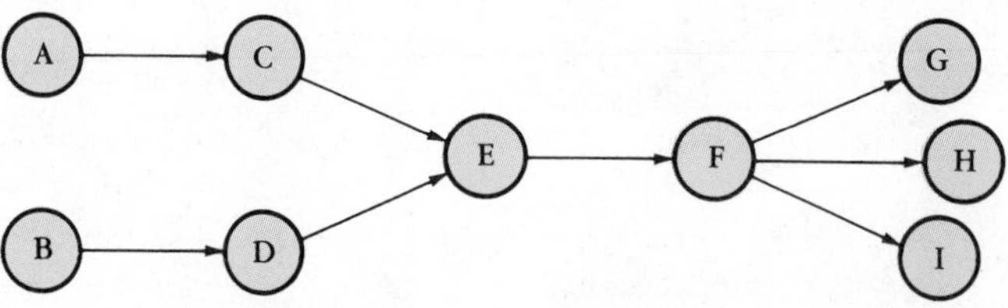

Task	Description	Immediate Predecessors
A	Machine engine parts	—
B	Machine transmission parts	—
C	Assemble engine	A
D	Assemble transmission	B
E	Assemble engine and transmission into one unit	C, D
F	Mount unit in car frame	E
G	Make front-wheel-drive connection to transmission	F
H	Connect fuel lines	F
I	Make electrical connections	F

INTEGRATING THE SYSTEM

Precedence Diagrams Link Design and Production

Precedence diagrams developed in product and process design are very useful in other areas of operations. Understanding precedence diagrams is essential when laying out and scheduling assembly lines. Precedence diagrams provide information regarding the sequence of tasks so a schedule that avoids serious problems can be developed. For example, painting the finish coat on a refrigerator door first and the prime coat second is obviously the wrong sequence. Precedence diagrams can also show preferred sequences. It is easier to put the front seats in a car before the doors are mounted.

Precedence diagrams are useful in construction to avoid structural problems or unnecessary delays and inefficiency. For example, foundation work must precede construction of the first floor. Electric wires should be put in the walls before plaster board or paneling is attached to the wall framing.

front-wheel-drive car. In most front-wheel-drive cars, the engine and transmission are put together first and placed into the car from underneath. This means that mounting the front-wheel-drive mechanism, connecting the fuel tank, and making the electrical connections cannot be done until after the engine and transmission have been installed. Careful examination of the diagram shows that the precedence network contains all three types of precedence relationships. Precedence relationships can also be given in a list format. The precedence list in Exhibit 4.7 communicates the same set of precedences as the diagram does.

The Role of Computer-Aided Manufacturing

Computer-aided manufacturing (CAM) provides computerized control and operation of the production facility through direct or indirect interface with both human and physical resources. Computers are used to monitor and control the production process. Often a feedback loop is provided to automatically correct problems. For example, the thermostat on a furnace is a simple feedback device. It turns the furnace on when the room temperature reaches a certain level and shuts it off when it has increased two to four degrees above that setting.

In paper making, the proper mixture of raw materials should be blended at the correct temperature in order to obtain the required strength. Computer monitoring allows corrections to be made in order to control the process. The paper machine is monitored, and corrections in the process are made automatically. Results of the machine's activities are fed to the plant's computer to give a history of the machine's performance.

Another major area for computer application in production is the microcomputer linked to a robot arm. This intelligent machine can perform some simple functions once performed by people. In this application of CAM technology, robots perform dangerous, dirty, or repetitive tasks once performed by people. These robots can load and unload machines, stock inventory, paint products, weld, and perform many other routine operating jobs. They are adaptable because their microcomputer brains are programmable. The microcomputer's low cost and ease of programming have opened the door for new applications. Future plants may have few direct laborers because microcomputer applications have freed workers from routine machine-tending jobs for more creative tasks. These people will become part of the indirect labor force required to design, program, and maintain these machines.

Service industries use computers to assist in material control, scheduling, and planning. Service businesses also use computers to directly monitor and provide feedback. Supermarkets use optical scanners to read the bar code on products. A computer connected to the scanner through a cash register (computer terminal) checks the price of the item, adds it to the bill, and reduces the inventory balance for that item. Banks use computerized tellers to make transactions. The service industry will continue to increase its use of computers to assist operators in providing better products at lower costs.

Human Engineering

Product design and development should consider the interface between people and the finished product and the interface between people and production equipment. **Human engineering** is the consideration of people in the design of products, facilities, and their environment. The objectives of human engineering, sometimes called **ergonomics,** are (1) to enhance the functional effectiveness of the product and (2) to improve the health, safety, and satisfaction of the user. The approach applies relevant information about human characteristics and behavior to the design of products and processes. Designing a pair of scissors that is easier for left-handed people to use, arranging knobs on a stove so it is easier to determine which knob controls which burner, and designing comfortable automobile seats are all examples of ergonomics.

Product Comfort and Safety

Successful product design should result in a product that is comfortable and easy to use as well as safe to operate. The careful study of the human body has allowed automotive engineers to design seats that are more comfortable and can be adjusted to fit the person. The air conditioner is turned on by turning a switch

INTEGRATING THE SYSTEM

Linking CAD and CAM

A great potential in manufacturing is being realized as computer-aided design (CAD) and computer-aided manufacturing (CAM) are being linked. The parts designed on the CAD computer could be transferred to the CAM computers. The CAD design specifications would be translated into machining instructions. When proper tooling is available, the machining instructions would be downloaded to a computer numerically controlled (CNC) machine.

This linkage would allow a CAD operator to perform both design and manufacturing engineering functions.Products could move quickly and inexpensively from design to manufacturing in as little as a few hours, rather than a few weeks or longer. This linkage would greatly reduce the time and cost required to design and produce a product, thus improving an organization's competitive position by lowering costs, increasing quality, and improving customer service.

clockwise and turned off by turning the switch counterclockwise. It is built that way because users expect it. A more comfortable chair, an easy-to-operate gas grill, or an easy-to-transport portable television offers advantages to customers. These design issues may influence the buying decision as much as style or performance.

Producers are responsible for designing safe products. Safety is not limited to advising consumers how to use the product or to posting labels warning against improper use. The product should be designed to avoid these problems. For example, most earth-moving equipment must have a device that emits a certain sound whenever the equipment is backing up. The equipment is so large that it is difficult for the operator to have a clear view. The sound alerts people to the pending danger. In the successfully designed product, potential problems have been considered, and fail-safe procedures have been developed to avoid serious injuries. For example, today's cars and trucks with manual-shift transmissions have a lock-out switch which will not permit the vehicle to be started unless the clutch is engaged. Prior to this, if the engine was started without engaging the clutch, the vehicle could lerch ahead unexpectedly, injuring anyone standing in front of it. In addition, the product and its safety mechanism are tested to determine if they perform as expected. A product that is safe and reliable will establish a customer base for other products of similar quality.

Human engineering in service operations is also important. Computerized bank tellers are designed to be easy to operate and fail-safe. If a problem occurs, the machine will shut down rather than hand out money. Effective product design implies safety in services as well. People can be injured by improperly repaired appliances, substandard legal services, and faulty medical procedures. Reliability and quality are equally important for services.

Facility Safety

Human engineering is one of the major determinants of plant safety. When machine operators who work with complex equipment are tired, they are prime candidates for accidents. Operators should not have to overextend their reach or muscular capacity. If they do, fatigue will result, and the potential for errors or serious injury will increase.

Gauges and dials should be easy to read and interpret so that operators can take proper action. On gauges that measure factors like heat, pressure, or strength, an increase in these factors will cause the indicator to move from left to right or in a clockwise motion, as shown in Exhibit 4.8. Operators expect this movement and react properly. Simple ideas like this one add little, if any, cost and can greatly increase safety.

Exhibit 4.8 Gauge Example

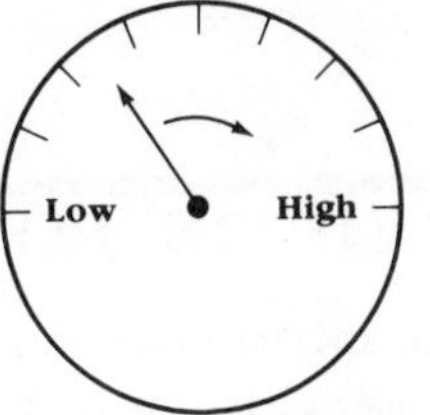

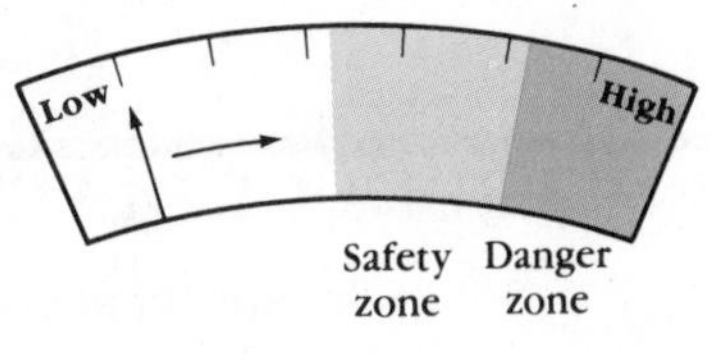

PRODUCT IDEAS TO PRODUCT REALITY: THE ROLE OF OPERATIONS

The operations manager's role is to produce the product as designed, according to the processes selected, and with the available equipment, people, and materials. The production system should function effectively and efficiently day after day, producing far more units of acceptable quality than any small-scale prototype production run might have produced. This is no small task. It requires that operations managers be involved in the product and process design as these take shape. They have insights into what can work on the shop floor and experience with a wide variety of materials, working environments, and people. Their feedback on the product and process designs and the learning that takes place are valuable for all involved.

As the plans for a new product become better defined, the operations manager should begin to anticipate the problems of full-scale production. The questions an operations manager must answer are many and vary widely.

Equipment

Can the machine do what we need to have done?
Which machines are most likely to fail?
Which machines are most critical to obtaining quality parts?
What will my preventive maintenance schedule look like?
What skills are required for machine operators?

Materials

Who are my suppliers?
What are the costs?
How many of each part should be ordered?
When are reorders issued?
Who is responsible for quality?
How are the materials delivered?
Where are the materials stored?

People

Who hires the people?
What are the needed skills?
How much will they be paid?
Who will assign work to these people?
What are the criteria for assigning work?
How will the workers be trained?

Many of these questions do not surface when test products are produced, especially when the engineering staff does most of the work in a small production facility or subcontracts the production to a specialist. These questions address major issues in operations management and will be discussed in the later chapters.

ALLIES IN PRODUCT DEVELOPMENT: THE ROLE OF SUPPLIERS

Why are suppliers playing an increasingly important role in product development? The most important reason for this is the increasing level of outsourcing being practiced today. **Outsourcing** is contracting with another company to do work that was once done by the organization itself. It is common for both manufacturing and service operations to subcontract major components of a job to another company. IBM has established relationships with other companies to provide software support for some of their products. DANA Corp. and Libbey-Owens-Ford are large suppliers to the automotive industry. If suppliers participate in product development, they can:

1. Share design expertise. A supplier such as Libbey-Owens-Ford may have more expertise in manufacturing flat glass than automotive producers do.
2. Change their approach to production to better meet the objectives of the new product development team. A software contractor working on a project for IBM may have to hire and train staff in networking and telecommunications to meet specific requirements of a project.
3. Indicate ways the overall product design can be altered so that the component the supplier is producing can have better quality or cost less. A supplier may suggest moving a mounting bracket that supports a motor that it provides. Shifting the bracket may reduce manufacturing and assembly costs.
4. Suggest additional ways they can participate in the project so that overall objectives of the new product development are met. A supplier may have capabilities or know of other suppliers that have capabilities that will improve the quality of the product.

Waiting until the product design is in place and all the product specifications are set negates the suppliers' ability to help in these areas.

In order for suppliers to be effective in product development and design, they need freedom to make decisions; yet the parts and components that one supplier designs and builds must work well with other parts and components designed by other suppliers. In the final analysis, the finished product, whether a car or a computer, should be the best product possible. This coordination can be achieved via two mechanisms. First, when major suppliers are part of the design team, they have the opportunity to interact with other suppliers. Second, by assigning an entire component to a supplier, such as the accounts receivable package on an information system or the drive assembly on a washing machine, that supplier can approach this component as a module. Modular design provides the freedom for the supplier to make decisions about the component and how the component will function internally, while requiring the supplier to meet certain overall parameters, such as computer language, computer hardware, size, strength, and connecting points. These overall parameters should be set by the product development and design team.

CAPITAL FORMATION AND EVALUATION: THE ROLE OF FINANCE

Finance also has a key role in new product development. New ventures require capital to defray development costs, purchase equipment, build facilities, and cover the cost of starting operations. Before the first product is produced, material and labor costs are incurred. Without capital to invest, product development, design, and prototype construction could not take place.

In addition, staff financial analysts will continually evaluate the new products under consideration. Will these products provide the necessary return on invest-

INTEGRATING THE SYSTEM

Financial Analysis for Justifying New Products and Processes

One concept used by financial managers to analyze investment decisions is the time value of money. Simply stated, a dollar received today is worth more than a dollar received in the future because the dollar received today has earning power. This concept is used to support models like net present value and internal rate of return, which are discussed in finance courses.

Great care should be used in applying these models to analyze investments in new facilities, products, and processes. Many times a substantial portion of the benefits from these types of investments are long term and are difficult to quantify. When operations managers are attempting to justify major long-term investments, they should estimate all of the potential benefits as accurately as possible. During implementation, they should work hard to ensure that those benefits are realized. Without these efforts, management may not be able to justify new opportunities that appear promising.

ment to pay back the original investment plus a reasonable profit? The analyst will use sales forecasts, project price estimates, and production costs to estimate profits. Overhead and investment costs are also estimated. These provide the necessary information to calculate a return on investment.

INFORMATION FOR DECISION MAKING: THE ROLES OF ACCOUNTING AND INFORMATION SYSTEMS

The accounting function involves collecting, organizing, analyzing, and distributing information about performance. Accounting can be very helpful in providing estimates of cost because it has collected cost information on similar products.

The information systems specialist usually works with computer specialists to organize the information for easy access by computer. This information is not limited to the cost data that accountants need. Other examples are listed below.

Area	Information
Marketing	Results of the market survey Information on consumer needs Incoming orders
Engineering	Computer-aided design Computer-aided manufacturing Process control of operations Bill of materials
Operations	Inventory Personnel records Schedule of operations Maintenance records Quality control standards

The need for information systems throughout operations—in fact, throughout the organization—makes the information system a key factor in establishing control.

BUILDING PRODUCT QUALITY THROUGH PRODUCT DEVELOPMENT

As discussed earlier in this chapter, product development is a key factor for organizational success because the product design helps to determine product cost, product quality, and the organization's ability to serve the customer. In today's competitive international marketplace, high quality has become the ticket that gives the organization a chance to compete. This section discusses why product design is so important in determining product quality, describes how quality functional deployment can be used to achieve the quality objective, and describes some of the benefits of improved product quality.

Product Development as a Determinant of Product Quality

The quality of any service or good is determined by (1) how it is designed, (2) the equipment and methods used (process design), and (3) the training and skill of the people doing the work. For example, if several people are interested in starting a hair-styling business, they should be concerned with offering hair styles that are designed to show off the best features of their clients, providing equipment that allows the work force to efficiently achieve the effect desired in the design (i.e., the process design), and train the work force in the skillful and courteous execution of the task. Product quality is determined by actions taken prior to production (product and process design) and by actions taken when the service is being rendered or the good is being produced. Inspection of the finished product provides feedback on product quality.

Product Design

Product design shapes the product's quality. It defines the way in which the good or service will function. Quality has at least two components. First, the product must be designed to function with a high probability of success, or reliability. Reliability is the probability that a product will perform a specific function without failure under given conditions. When product reliability increases, the organization can extend the warrantee on a product without increasing customer claims for repairs or returns. Warrantees for such complex and expensive items as cars and appliances are important decision points for customers. Second, quality is affected by improved operating or performance characteristics, even though reliability may not improve. The goals of product design should be greater performance, greater reliability, and lower total production and operating costs. Quality and costs should not be viewed as trade-offs because improvements in product technology can allow better quality at lower costs.

Process Design

Product quality is an important criterion for selecting the process to produce the goods and services. A thorough system design contemplates the progression of product from assembling resources through final production. The process engineer should be familiar with innovations in process technology that will improve quality. The equipment used in production should be tested to ensure that it meets or exceeds minimal performance standards. The manufacturing engineers should design and plan equipment to monitor the process so that problems can be detected immediately. New equipment should be tested to see if it can meet quality standards. The manufacturing engineer is responsible for following the product specifications and tolerances described in the product design. Improvements in process technology will result in better products at lower costs.

Work Execution

To be successful, the product and process designs must be well executed on the shop floor. At this point, employee training, skill level, and motivation are critical. The people operating the machines, assembling the good, or performing the service should have the necessary skills. They should have training sessions in which the function of the product and process and the roles they are to play are explained. They should feel involved in the production process so they are motivated to suggest improvements and to perform the job according to the design. Unless all relevant information is effectively communicated to the work force, it is unreasonable to expect quality performance.

Inspection

Inspection is the final link in the quality chain. It is the judge of how well the product and process were designed and how well the work force has been educated and motivated. Inspection alone does not improve the quality of any individual product. It merely identifies a substandard item. It is only when the source of the substandard product is identified and corrective action taken that inspection has an impact.

Inspection is useful when the information gathered during the inspection is available to the people doing the product design and process design, as well as the people actually doing the work. This feedback should be as direct as possible so that information is not distorted or lost. Many organizations are having the people who do the work also do the inspection so the feedback is both direct and immediate.

Quality Functional Deployment

We have discussed the determinants of product quality and described why they are important in achieving it. Two things, however, are missing. First, managers need a way to implement what they have learned. Asking people to design a better product does not provide sufficient direction or bring coordinated actions to the task of designing a better product. An approach is needed that focuses the attention of all members of the organization on the quality objective. Second, management must be assured that the product produced by the organization is one that the customer wants.

Quality functional deployment, which originated in Mitsubishi's Kobe shipyard, is being used by some organizations to provide these missing links. **Quality functional deployment** (QFD), sometimes referred to as the "house of quality," is a set of planning and communication routines that focus and coordinate actions and skills within an organization. The foundation of the house of quality is the belief that a product should be designed to reflect customers' desires and tastes. The house of quality is a framework that provides the means for interfunctional planning and communications. People with different problems and responsibilities can discuss various design priorities.

The house of quality begins with the customer, whose requirements are called customer attributes. Similar attributes can be grouped into bundles, and weights can be assigned so that management has an assessment of the importance customers place on each attribute. These attributes are then translated into engineering characteristics. For example, if a customer wants a microcomputer keyboard that is very responsive, engineers may consider the force required to press a key and the distance that key has to be moved before a character registers on the monitor. These engineering characteristics are eventually converted into design elements in the finished product. For example, the engineer will specify the size and strength of the spring that is underneath each key on the microcomputer keyboard. When engineering characteristics affect more than one attribute, trade-offs need to be made. QFD helps managers and engineers focus on customer requirements when developing new products or refining existing products. QFD is discussed in detail in Chapter 17.

Aspects of Improved Quality: The Abilities

In designing high-quality services and goods, organizations must remember that customers value more than product features and performance. Customers value the so-called abilities: durability, reliability, maintainability, and availability. They also value, if only indirectly, a fifth ability: manufacturability.

Manufacturability

Manufacturability refers to the ease with which a product can be produced. Customers tend to prefer products that are easy to manufacture; such products tend to cost less because fewer resources are consumed. Also, a product that is carefully engineered so that it is easy to manufacture will probably be simple to operate. Because the product is easy to manufacture, the work force is likely to make fewer errors, which results in higher product quality.

Durability

Durability implies that the product will continue to function even when it is subjected to hard wear and frequent use. In most cases, durability is an attribute that is used to describe a good rather than a service. A child's wagon should be able to hold up when several children get into it. An automated teller machine should work even when a frustrated customer hits the keys too hard or bangs on the side because the machine did not return the plastic card. Designing a product to be durable requires knowing the extremes of use, rather than the average or normal use.

Reliability

Reliability is the length of time that a product can be used before it fails. Statistically, reliability is the probability that a product will function for a certain period of time without failing under specified operating conditions. For example, a motor in an electronic typewriter might have a 90 percent reliability for 10,000 hours of operation. This means that 10 percent of the motors of similar design would fail before 10,000 hours of operation and 90 percent would last 10,000 or more hours.

The failure rate for many products takes the shape of the curve shown in Exhibit 4.9, which is sometimes referred to as the bathtub curve. The highest

Exhibit 4.9 Product Failure Rate Curve

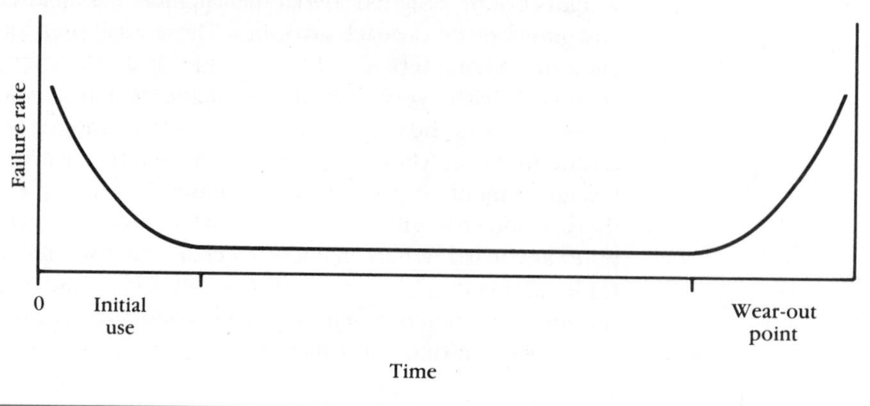

failure rates occur when the product is being "broken in" and when the product is about to wear out. Failures during the break-in period are normally caused by undetected defects in the component parts or the assembly. Why would the information in this curve be useful to a consumer who is deciding whether to purchase an extended warranty on a new television set? The failure rate for a television follows the bathtub curve, so after the short break-in period, which is usually covered by the manufacturer's warranty, the failure rate is very low until the set approaches the point of wearing out.

It is important to recognize that the reliability of a component part and the reliability of the entire product that is made up of many component parts are not the same. Products fail when any critical part fails, so the reliability of the entire product is much less than the reliability of its components. For example, if a microcomputer has 200 critical components, and if each has a reliability of 0.99, the reliability of the entire product is only 0.134. This is calculated as 0.99 raised to the two-hundredth power. High reliability of component parts is critical if an organization desires to achieve highly reliable products.

Maintainability and Availability

Maintainability refers to returning a product to operating condition after it has failed. Customers are concerned that this can be accomplished as quickly as possible and with the expenditure of as few resources as possible. A variety of tactics can be used to achieve these objectives, including designing the product for easy access to critical parts and utilizing modular design and construction that allow entire subassemblies or modules to be easily and quickly replaced.

Preventive maintenance, when done properly, can increase reliability. However, customers will avoid purchasing products with excessive preventive maintenance requirements that drive up costs and reduce up time. For example, the electric motor in a dehumidifier should have sealed and permanently lubricated bearings to avoid the time and expense of maintenance. Customers prefer an automobile that can travel 30,000 miles without a tune-up over one that requires a tune-up every 12,000 miles.

Availability is the amount of time that the system is ready to operate divided by the total time—i.e., the sum of uptime and downtime. Availability is a combination of the system's reliability and maintainability. A system that is highly reliable and has a short repair time will have a high availability. For customer, a product with a high availability is very desireable.

In conclusion, the development and design of a new product has a large impact on the quality of the product. This, in turn, has a large impact on the organization's ability to compete.

SUMMARY

- Product design requires the expertise and decision-making skills of all parts of the organization. Marketing, engineering, operations, finance, accounting, information systems, and personnel all have important roles in the team approach to product design. Exhibits 4.1 and 4.3 summarize these roles.
- Marketing's role is to evaluate consumer needs, determine the potential impact of competitive pressure, and measure the external environment.
- Engineering's role is to shape the product through design, determine the process by which the product will be made, and consider the interface between the product and people (human engineering).
- Operations' role is to ensure that the product that is evolving through marketing and engineering can be manufactured in full-scale production. Furthermore, operations' role is to consider how the product might affect existing operations.
- Finance's role is to develop plans for raising the needed capital to support the product in full-scale production and to assist in the evaluation of the potential profitability of the product.
- Accounting and information systems provide managers with information for decision making.
- Suppliers are playing an increasingly important role in new product development.
- Product development determines the product's characteristics and performance. As a result, product development becomes a competitive weapon for an organization. It is a major determination of the product's costs, quality, and service. If an organization's product is superior, then it can realize a competitive advantage.

CAREER PROFILE

Alan Grier

Manufacturing Systems Manager
DANA Corporation

Alan Grier is responsible for the design and development of a computer-based control system for managing plant operations. The facility uses the latest in manufacturing and computer technology to produce high-quality, low-cost parts. The facility is flexible enough to produce a wide variety of parts with short setup times and minimal work-in-process inventory. Grier's responsibilities include working with engineering to design the facility so that the information system is integrated with the production processes.

The Design

Grier's design of the information system includes the development of systems for all phases of operations, from receiving customer orders to shipping finished parts. The system allows the material manager to assess the needs for materials and to generate orders quickly. The necessary information for scheduling production, controlling tool usage, monitoring preventive maintenance, and determining shipping schedules can be obtained from this computer-based information system. The information system also collects data on actual production, quality performance, and machine failures.

Grier is responsible for updating and improving the system as requests for additional information are received. His ultimate goal is to train the users of computer services so they can develop their own systems.

Education and Experience

Preparation for this responsibility required broad training. Grier had to blend skills in computers and information systems with an understanding of the requirements of managing and controlling a complex operation. He had to understand engineering design concepts in order to communicate effectively with engineering.

Grier's future could include a position as plant manager in this or another plant. It is also possible that with his experience he could advance into a corporate staff position in training and development. If this plant is successful, the company may want to train other managers to lead operations in this direction.

SOLVED PROBLEM

Seth Clock Company assembles alarm clocks from components that it purchases from a variety of suppliers. The following description and list of precedences are given. Draw the precedence diagram.

Task	Description	Immediate Predecessors
A	Make sure all parts are available	—
B	Stain wooden frame that holds the mechanism	A
C	Varnish wooden frame	B
D	Mount electric motor and mechanism onto frame	C
E	Mount decorative ornament on top of clock	C
F	Apply clock face to front of wooden frame	C
G	Mount alarm-set indicator onto clock mechanism	D, F
H	Mount hour hand onto clock mechanism	G
I	Mount minute hand onto clock mechanism	H
J	Mount second hand onto clock mechanism	I
K	Install back plate to secure clock mechanism	D
L	Add trim and cover to clock face to cover the hands	J
M	Pack finished clock	E, K, L

Solution

Start from the top of the precedence list. Try not to allow any of the arcs (lines) to cross. The first three are easy. Task A has no predecessor, task B is preceded by A only, and task C is preceded by B only.

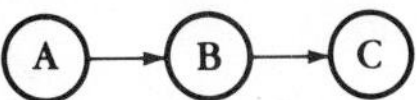

The next three are also easy. Tasks D, E, and F each are preceded by task C only.

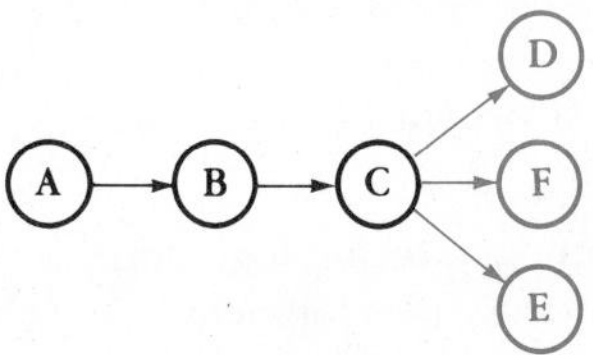

Now we have a problem. Task G is preceded by tasks D and F. If we continue with the diagram as drawn, two or more of the arcs may cross. Therefore, we shift the position of tasks E and F. This has no effect on the accuracy of the diagram because we have not changed relationships. Tasks H, I, and J follow from task G, in order.

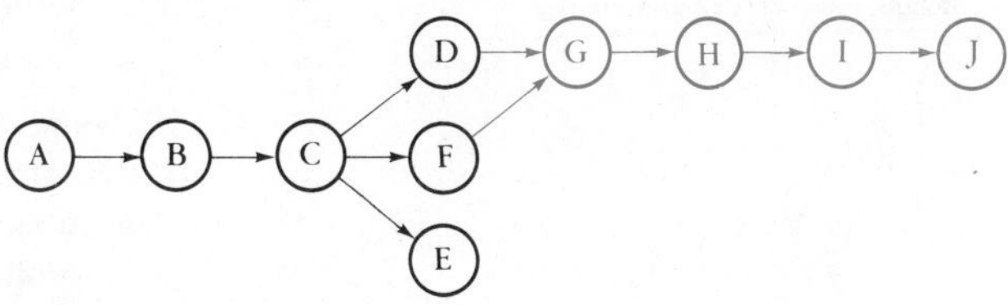

Finally, task K is preceded by task D, task L is preceded by task J, and task M is preceded by tasks E, K, and L.

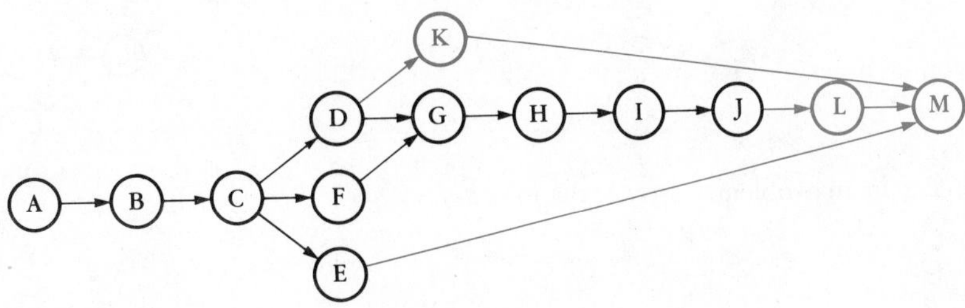

QUESTIONS

1. Explain the following statement: "Product development requires teamwork in order to be successful."

2. Why is product development a critical determinant to the organization's success? Would you consider it to be strategically important?

3. Define marketing's role in product development.

4. Define engineering's role in product development.

5. Define operations' role in product development.

6. Define finance's role in product development.

7. Define accounting's role in product development.

8. Define information systems' role in product development.

9. How does the external environment affect the product development decision?

10. What are the roles of product technology and technological forecasting in product development?

11. What is a bill of materials, and why is it important in operations management? Is it useful in service operations?

12. Explain the differences, if any, between product design for service operations and product design for producers of goods.

13. What is process technology, and why should a company consider changing it?

14. Define human engineering, and describe how it is used to improve product and process design.

15. Comment on the following statement: "Training programs will not be critical in future operations because organizations are continuing to substitute capital for labor."

16. Describe the relationship between product development and quality.

PROBLEMS

1. Given the precedence diagram below, complete the table by filling in the immediate predecessors.

Task	Immediate Predecessors
A	
B	
C	
D	
E	
F	
G	
H	
I	

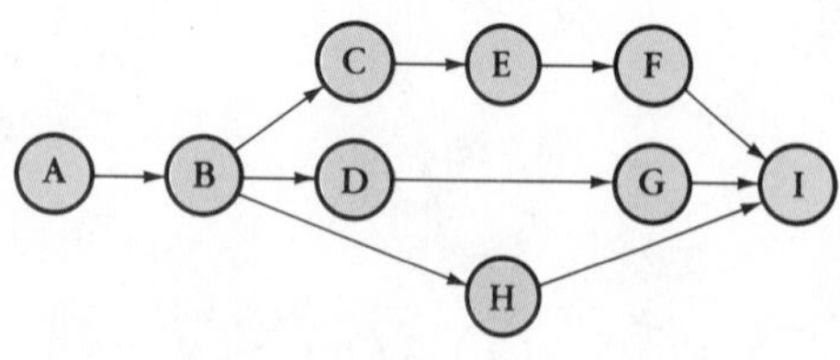

2. Using the diagram in problem 1, answer the following:

a. Which task(s) must be completed before task B can be started?
b. Which task(s) can begin when task E finishes?
c. Which task(s) must be completed before task I can begin?

3. Using the diagram below, answer the following questions:

a. Which task(s) signals the beginning of the project?
b. Which task(s) signals the end of the project?
c. Which task(s) can begin once task C is complete?
d. Which task(s) must be complete before task D can begin?

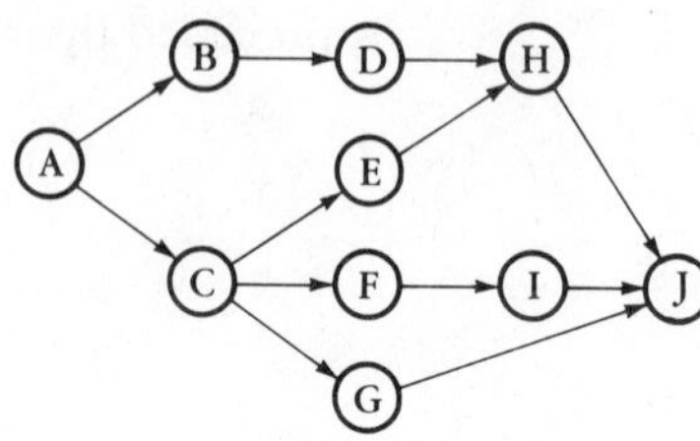

4. Draw the precedence diagram described in the following table:

Task	Immediate Predecessors
A	—
B	A
C	A
D	B, C
E	B
F	—
G	D
H	F
I	G
J	H

5. Pretend you have been visited by an alien life person (ALP). ALP has asked you to explain the ritual that Earth people go through each morning to prepare for work or school. ALP is very good at understanding circles and lines. Develop a set of precedence relationships that describe the activities required to prepare yourself each morning. Also, draw a precedence diagram to represent the relationships. Here are a few hints to get you started. Do not simply list the sequence that you use each morning. For example, you may always brush your teeth before taking a shower. However, there is no preferred sequence, so do not list one as the prerequisite for the other. On the other hand, showering before dressing is preferred by most Earth people. Showering is therefore a predecessor of dressing.

6. Guyer National Research Institute analyzes surveys taken from recent purchasers of new cars. The computer system manager at its computer operations division is charged with installing a new operating system. Following are a list of the tasks and the predecessors among those tasks. Construct a precedence diagram.

Task	Description	Immediate Predecessors
A	Create a virtual machine to hold the files	—
B	Load the information on the tapes to the disks created in task A	A
C	Build a macro library containing any user-created macros	A
D	Build source files	A
E	Generate the nucleus of a new operating system	B, C, D
F	Generate a new command set for the system disk	E
G	Test the new operating system	F
H	Save the shared code for the new operating system if testing is successful	G

7. Finn Construction Company is building a new classroom building for State University. John Finn, the project manager, has laid out the precedence list for construction and has asked you to prepare a precedence diagram. The building is shaped like an H, with north and south wings as well as a ground-level connecting structure.

Task	Description	Immediate Predecessors
A	Clear site and prepare to dig foundations	—
B	Prepare south wing foundation	A
C	Prepare north wing foundation	A
D	Prepare foundation for connecting structure	A
E	Erect first floor of the south wing	B, D
F	Erect second floor of the south wing	E
G	Erect connecting structure	D
H	Erect first floor of the north wing	C, D
I	Erect second floor of the north wing	H
J	Erect third floor of the north wing	I
K	Finish interior	F, G, J

8. Mathews Manufacturing is assembling microcomputers from components the company purchased from suppliers. Following is a list of the tasks and the predecessors among these tasks. Construct a precedence diagram.

Task	Description	Immediate Predecessors
A	Acquire floppy disk drive	—
B	Acquire hard disk	—
C	Acquire mother board	—
D	Acquire power supply	—
E	Acquire mounting frame	—
F	Mount floppy drive to frame	A, E
G	Mount hard disk to frame	B, E
H	Mount mother board to frame	C, E
I	Mount power supply to frame	D, E
J	Make electrical connections	F, G, H, I
K	Test	J
L	Acquire cabinet	—
M	Install frame in cabinet	K, L

Task	Description	Immediate Predecessors
N	Acquire monitor	—
O	Pack and ship	M, N

9. Draw the precedence diagram described in the following table:

Task	Immediate Predecessors
A	—
B	A
C	A
D	A
E	B, C
F	E
G	E
H	F, G
I	F
J	G
K	J
L	I
M	H, K, L
N	M
O	–
P	O
Q	O
R	P, Q
S	R
T	–
U	T
V	T
W	U, V
X	D, N, S, W

MINI-CASES

Vinke Air Freight

Catherine Vinke, president of Vinke Air Freight (VAF), has reached the conclusion that sales of the company's existing product line have reached the saturation stage. Presently, the company offers overnight delivery of large packages anywhere in the continental United States. Although VAF will go anywhere, very few deliveries are made to out-of-the-way places. Vinke believes the company can increase its share of this market, but sees more growth potential in overnight delivery of letters and small packages. She is very interested in pursuing this new venture.

VAF's existing customer base consists of medium-sized and large organizations. Most of its customers ship parts occasionally to meet emergency needs. The parts are usually bulky, so it does not take many customers to fill the planes. Customers generally deliver these parts to a local airport, and VAF takes over. At the arriving airport, VAF has contracted with local carriers to make the delivery. Because the packages are large and there are only a few per plane, this solution has proven to be satisfactory. VAF is headquartered in the heart of the industrial Midwest, Fort Wayne, Indiana.

Vinke has only recently taken over the company from her father, and she is not prepared to undertake this move alone. She has recently hired you to help. To begin, reread the Gaining the Strategic Advantage feature in this chapter, which describes Federal Express and the package delivery industry. Then answer the following questions that Vinke has prepared:

1. What process for new product development should VAF use to determine if small package delivery could be profitable? What are the key questions at each stage of the process?

2. What factors do you feel are important to the customers that use the overnight letter-delivery service? How might they be different form Vinke's present customer base?

3. What are the critical issues involved in designing the service so it can be competitive with others in the industry? In other words, what changes does VAF have to make to be competitive?

4. Considering all the information presently available, would you recommend or discourage adding the new service? Support your choice with specific reasons.

Page Bank and Trust

Ralph Page, the president of Page Bank and Trust in Galapolese, Pennsylvania, has decided to install automatic teller machines (ATMs) at several locations. Galapolese is a rural community, and Page is concerned about customer acceptance of this "high-tech" approach to banking. He has put together a team that includes marketing, financial, and operations experts to design this new service. They will also design the way the service will be provided to the customers.

1. What are the key factors to be considered in gaining customer acceptance? How can Page overcome these problems?

2. How can product design influence the acceptance of these machines by the local population?

3. Following is an example of what a customer might do on a typical visit. Draw a diagram that describes the precedence relationships. Also, describe the reason for each precedence. For example, task B must be preceded by task A because the card cannot be verified until the customer enters it into the ATM.

Task	Description
A	Customer inserts plastic card into ATM
B	Verify that card is recognized by Page
C	Customer enters four-digit code
D	Verify access code
E	Customer requests transfer of funds from savings to checking
F	Verify that funds are available in savings
G	Update savings balance
H	Update checking balance
I	Customer terminates visit
J	ATM prints receipt
K	ATM returns plastic card

SELECTED BIBLIOGRAPHY

Aaker, David A., and Day, George S. *Marketing Research*. New York: Wiley, 1983.

Abernathy, William J., and Utterback, James M. ''Patterns of Industrial Innovation.'' *Technological Review* (June–July 1978): 41–47.

Alting, Leo. *Manufacturing Engineering Processes*. New York: Marcel Dekker, 1982.

Ayres, Robert U. *Technological Forecasting and Long-Range Planning*. New York: McGraw-Hill, 1969.

Basador, Min; Graen, George B.; and Scandura, Terri A. ''Training Effects on Attitudes Toward Divergent Thinking Among Manufacturing Engineers.'' *Journal of Applied Psychology* 71, no. 4 (1986): 612–617.

Buggie, Frederick D., *New Product Development Strategies*. New York: AMACOM, 1981.

Carson, J. W., and Rickards, T. *Industrial New Product Development: A Manual for the 1980's*. New York: Wiley, 1979.

Cetron, Marvin J. *Technological Forecasting: A Practical Approach*. New York: Gordon and Breach, 1969.

De Vera, Dennis; Glennon, Tom; Kenny, Andrew A.; Khan, Mohammad A. H.; and Mayer, Mike. ''An Automotive Case Study.'' *Quality Progress*, June 1988, pp. 35–38.

Fortuna, Ronald M. ''Beyond Quality: Taking SPC Upstream.'' *Quality Progress*, June 1988, pp. 23–28.

Harrigan, Kenneth W. ''Making Quality Job One—A Cultural Revolution.'' *Business Quarterly* (Winter 1984): 68–71.

Hauser John R., and Clausing, Don. ''The House of Quality.'' *Harvard Business Review* 66, no. 3 (May–June 1988): 63–73.

Hayes, Robert H., and Wheelwright, Steven C. ''Linking Manufacturing Process and Product Life Cycles.'' *Harvard Business Review* 57, no. 1 (January–February 1979): 133–140.

Juran, J. M., and Gryna, Frank M., Jr. *Quality Planning and Analysis: From Product Development Through Use*. New York: McGraw-Hill, 1980.

Kantowitz, Barry, and Sorkin, Robert D. *Human Factors: Understanding People-System Relationships*. New York: Wiley, 1983.

Kenny, Andrew A. ''A New Paradigm for Quality Assurance.'' *Quality Progress*, June 1988, pp. 30–32.

McCormick, Ernest J. *Human Factors in Engineering and Design*. New York: McGraw-Hill, 1982.

Moore, Harry D., and Kibbey, Donald R. *Manufacturing Materials and Processes*. Columbus, Ohio: Grid, 1975.

Near, Janet P. ''Whistle-Blowing: Encourage It.'' *Business Horizons* 32, no. 1 (January–February 1989): 2–6.

O'Donnell, Merle, and O'Donnell, Robert J. ''Quality Circles—The Latest Fad or a Real Winner?'' *Business Horizons* (May–June 1984): 48–52.

Ridley, John. *Safety at Work*. London: Butterworths, 1983.

Ross, Phillip J. ''The Role of Taguchi Methods and Design of Experiments in QFD.'' *Quality Progress*, June 1988, pp. 41–47.

Sasser, W. Earl; Olsen, R. Paul; and Wyckoff, D. Daryl. *Management of Service Operations: Text, Cases, and Readings*. Boston: Allyn and Bacon, 1978.

Skinner, Wickham ''The Focused Factory.'' *Harvard Business Review* (May–June 1974): 113–121.

Slautterback, William H. ''Manufacturing in the Year 2000.'' *Manufacturing Engineering*, August 1985, pp. 57–60.

Sullivan, L. P. ''The Seven Stages in Company-Wide Quality Control.'' *Quality Progress*, May 1986, pp. 77–83.

Sullivan, L. P. "Policy Management Through Quality Functional Deployment." *Quality Progress,* June 1988, pp. 18–20.

Utterback, James M. "The Process of Technological Innovation." *Academy of Management Journal* (March 1971): 75–88.

Van De Ven, Andrew H. "Central Problems the Management of Innovation." *Management Science* 32, no. 5 (May 1986): 590–607.

Vollmann, Thomas E.; Berry, William L.; and Whybark, D. Clay. *Manufacturing Planning and Control Systems.* Homewood, Ill.: Irwin, 1988.

Weinberger, Marc G., and Romeo, Jean B. "The Impact of Negative Product News." *Business Horizons* 32, no. 1 (January–February 1989): 44–50.

Wind, Yoram J. *Product Policy: Concepts, Methods, and Strategy.* Reading, Mass.: Addison-Wesley, 1982.

Wind, Yoram; Mahajan, Vijay; and Swire, Donald J. "An Empirical Comparison of Standardized Portfolio Models." *Journal of Marketing* 47 (Spring 1983): 89–99.

Chapter 5

Capacity Decisions

CHAPTER OUTLINE

Introduction
What Is Capacity?
Gaining Strategic Advantage at Ralph's Grocery Company: Bigger Can Be Better
Why Are Capacity Decisions Important?

Estimating Capacity
Changing Product Mix
Adding People
Increasing Motivation
Increasing Machine Production Rate
Improving Quality
Increasing Product Yield
Summary

Determining System Capacity
The Product Layout and System Capacity
The Process Layout and System Capacity
Capacity Decisions and Service Operations
Service Operations and System Capacity

Capacity Decisions for Competitive Advantage
When to Add Capacity
How Much Capacity to Add
Models and Capacity Decision Making
Where to Add Capacity
What Type of Capacity to Add

LEARNING OBJECTIVES

After completing this chapter, you should be able to

- Define capacity as a measure of the organization's ability to provide customers with the requested service or good.
- Explain that capacity estimation is difficult because many management decisions affect capacity.
- Describe how overall capacity of the system is dependent on the capacities of the departments and machines that form the system.
- Determine the bottleneck in a system and demonstrate how that information can be used for managerial decision making.
- Construct models and understand modeling concepts as they apply to capacity-planning decisions.
- Describe the important capacity decisions, such as how much capacity to add, when to add capacity, where to add capacity, and what type (process) of capacity to add.

The Health Care Industry: Coping with Overcapacity

The health care industry is struggling with too many hospitals competing for too few patients. Nearly 40 percent of the hospital beds are empty nationwide. Because a large percentage of a hospital's costs are fixed, a decline in the occupancy rate does not lead to a proportional decline in operating costs. With revenues tied to occupancy rates and a large base of fixed costs, hospital profits are squeezed by overcapacity.

How did the health care industry get into this predicament? After World War II, the baby boom caused substantial growth in the demand for health services. The health care industry, which was dominated by government-owned and private not-for-profit hospitals, expanded to meet this apparently ceaseless increase in demand. However, this expansion was not coordinated, and inefficient hospitals often continued to operate by increasing their subsidy from the government or the private agency that supported them.

Beginning in the 1970s and accelerating in the 1980s, two forces halted the growth in demand for hospital beds and actually caused it to decline. First, dramatic improvements in medical procedures made trips to the hospital unnecessary in some cases and significantly reduced the time of confinement in others. Many medical procedures, such as knee surgery, laser surgery for cataracts, and bunion surgery, are regularly performed on an outpatient basis. For other procedures, such as back surgery, that still involve a hospital stay, the time of confinement has been reduced from weeks to a few days. Second, there has been mounting pressure from insurance providers and the organizations that pay for the insurance policies to reduce the time of confinement.

Uncontrolled growth in the number of hospital beds collided with mounting resistance from health insurance providers and advancing technology to throw health care profits into a tailspin. The solution is clear. Inefficient hospitals will be closed to deal with the problem of overcapacity.

INTRODUCTION

What Is Capacity?

Capacity is a measure of an organization's ability to provide customers with the demanded services or goods in the amount requested and in a timely manner. Capacity is the maximum rate of production. An organization marketing electronic calculators should be able to produce and deliver calculators in sufficient quantities to satisfy consumer demand. This requires the acquisition of physical facilities, the hiring and training of qualified people, and the acquisition of materials to achieve the desired production level. The following important questions about capacity are discussed in detail as major sections in this chapter:

1. How can management estimate capacity?
2. What is system capacity, and why is it important?
3. How can capacity decisions be made to gain a competitive advantage for the organization?

Why Are Capacity Decisions Important?

The importance of capacity-planning decisions is easy to understand because significant capital is usually required to build capacity. Many millions of dollars are required to build a brewery, a hospital, or an assembly plant for washing machines. These expenditures are usually for fixed assets (plant and equipment) that are expensive to maintain and even more expensive to change. Capacity decisions require careful consideration of an organization's long-term objectives and the market demand. They should not be based solely on the principle of minimizing production costs.

To meet future as well as present capacity requirements, facilities should be flexible. Flexible facilities allow managers to

1. Change production volume to respond to customer demand.
2. Produce different products on the same equipment (product mix) to respond to changing customer needs.

GAINING STRATEGIC ADVANTAGE AT FEDERAL EXPRESS

Bigger Can Be Better

The traditional supermarket, with 15,000 items spread over 20,000 square feet, may go the way of the mom-and-pop corner grocery store. Supermarket chains are becoming more competitive as they operate in a market that is not experiencing much growth. In order to maintain or expand profitability, the chains are building larger stores, called superstores, and filling them with more items. Such items as cut flowers, greeting cards, and prescription drugs are becoming a regular part of the shopping experience. This strategy is designed both to sell more items and to draw more customers by providing one-stop shopping.

Ralph's Grocery Company is taking this strategy one step farther. It is opening 14 Ralph's Giant Stores in Southern California. At 100,000 square feet, these hypermarkets are more than twice the size of current superstores and five times the size of traditional supermarkets. These hypermarkets carry about 70,000 items—everything from microcomputers to garden hose—and can generate sales of more than $1,500,000 per week. The average supermarket carries only about 15,000 items and generates approximately $175,000 in sales per week.

Ralph's Giant Stores will display merchandise in shipping containers, as warehouse stores do, but they will also offer full-service delicatessens, bakeries, and fish counters. The stores will also sublease space to independent retailers to sell food items such as soft pretzels and frozen yogurt.

In addition to the advantages of one-stop shopping, Ralph's large-capacity stores offer several operating advantages. The average purchase made by each customer should be higher because of the wide product variety of the stores. Although most traditional grocery items like potatoes, beans, and ground beef have very low profit margins, products like frozen yogurt, costume jewelry, and baked goods have much higher margins and should help to boost both sales and profits.

The large capacity of these stores should allow Ralph's to spread fixed costs over a greater sales volume, thereby reducing costs and increasing profits. Even though the fixed costs of a hypermarket will be greater than those of a superstore or a supermarket, these fixed costs will not rise in proportion to sales. In essence, Ralph's is attempting to take advantage of economies of scale offered by increasing a facility's capacity.[1]

3. Alter product technology and process technology to maintain or improve an organization's competitive position.

The physical facility is a key resource of an organization in its efforts to remain competitive.

ESTIMATING CAPACITY

To estimate capacity, managers must first select a yardstick to measure capacity. In some cases, the choice is obvious—for example, tons per hour of steel or kilowatt hours of electricity. A hospital can use beds as a measure of capacity. Thus, a hospital with 100 beds that are available 365 days per year has a capacity of 36,500 patient-days. Hospitals measure the number of patients admitted and how long each stays so they can calculate patient-days consumed. A comparison of patient-days consumed and patient-days available gives the operating ratio shown below.

$$\text{Hospital's operating ratio} = \frac{24{,}000 \text{ patient-days consumed}}{36{,}500 \text{ patient-days available}} \times 100$$

$$= 65.8\%$$

In general, the operating ratio is calculated according to the following equation:

$$\text{Operating ratio} = \frac{\text{capacity consumed}}{\text{capacity available}} \times 100$$

Finding a yardstick to estimate capacity is more difficult in a restaurant than in a steel making facility or a hospital because there is no uniform product on which the measurement can be based. Capacity could be measured in terms of people served, meals prepared, or the ability to generate sales dollars. It is management's responsibility to select the appropriate measure and apply it.

Once the measure has been selected, estimating capacity appears to be straightforward, involving the following steps. First, determine the maximum rate per hour of the production equipment that is the maximum production rate. Second, determine the number of hours worked in a given time period; and third, multiply those two numbers.

$$\text{Capacity/period} = \text{(maximum production rate/hour)} \times \text{(number of hours worked/period)}$$

$$\text{Production rate} = \frac{\text{(number of units produced)}}{\text{(amount of time)}}$$

Capacity can be changed by changing the number of hours worked in a time period or by changing the production rate. The number of hours worked per time period is affected by several factors, including overtime, multiple shifts, downtime for preventive maintenance, and allowances for unplanned equipment failure.

Example

Given the following information on maximum production rate and hours worked, determine the capacity per week.

Maximum production rate	= 240 units/hour
Number of hours (two shifts)	= 80 hours/week
Overtime	= 10 hours/week
Preventive maintenance (performed on third shift)	= 0
Equipment failure	= 5% of planned hours

$$\text{Capacity/week} = (240 \text{ units/hour})(80 + 10 - 0 \text{ hours/week})(1 - .05)$$
$$= 20{,}520 \text{ units/week}$$

The hours worked per week must be reduced from 100 percent to 95 percent of the available hours because of the 5 percent downtime anticipated for equipment failure.

Management decisions affect capacity. In this example, increases in the amount and quality of preventive maintenance could increase capacity by reducing equipment failure. Other decisions affect capacity by changing the production rate. The following decisions are examined in this chapter:

1. Changing the mix of products produced by the facility
2. Adding people to the production process
3. Increasing the motivation of production employees
4. Increasing the operating rate of a machine
5. Improving the quality of the raw materials and the work in process
6. Increasing product yield

Changing Product Mix

An organization's **product mix** is the percentage of total output devoted to each product. An agency that sells life, house, and automobile insurance might have the following product mix:

Type	Percentage
Life insurance	20
House insurance	30
Automobile insurance	50

How does product mix affect capacity? In the insurance example, it may take more of an agent's time to sell life insurance than automobile insurance. Consequently, a shift in demand toward life insurance policies reduces an agent's capacity. A steel company produces steel of many alloys, shapes, and sizes, and these differences require different production processes and times. For example, the sheet steel that forms the body of an automobile is produced in many widths. A 60-inch piece may be needed for the hood, but a 40-inch piece may be needed for a door panel. The mill that rolls these widths takes about the same amount of time per linear foot regardless of width. Therefore, a mill with a heavy mix of 40-inch pieces will be able to produce fewer tons per hour than will a mill with many 60-inch pieces. What then is the capacity of the processing equipment, and what are the units of capacity? Steel is measured in tons per hour, but those who estimate capacity realize that capacity changes as the mix of steel changes because different products have different production rates. Therefore, product mix must be estimated before capacity can be estimated.

Example

Assume that a company uses steel that is one-eighth of an inch thick and has a density of .2833 pounds per cubic inch. The machines roll steel for 80 hours per week at an average speed of 30 inches per second. The company produces both 40- and 60-inch widths of steel and wants to determine the capacity of each of the product mixes shown below.

Size	Mix 1	Mix 2
40 inches	80%	50%
60 inches	20%	50%

The company's production rate can be calculated as follows:

$$\begin{aligned}\text{Production rate } (PR) &= (\text{production rate for 40-inch})(\text{mix for 40-inch}) \\ &\quad + (\text{production rate for 60-inch})(\text{mix for 60-inch})\end{aligned}$$

The production rate for the 40-inch size (PR_{40}) can be determined as follows:

$$\begin{aligned}PR_{40} &= (\text{width})(\text{thickness})(\text{processing rate inches/hour})(\text{density}) \\ &= (40\text{ in.})(\tfrac{1}{8}\text{ in.})(30\text{ in./sec.})(3{,}600\text{ sec./hr.})(.2833\text{ lbs./cubic in.}) \\ &= 152{,}982\text{ lbs./hr.}\end{aligned}$$

This would be the production rate if only the 40-inch size were produced. Calculate the production rate for the 60-inch size on your own. (Your answer should be 229,473 pounds per hour.)

Now calculate the overall production rate if mix 1 is assumed.

$$\begin{aligned}PR &= (152{,}982\text{ lbs./hr.})(.8) + (229{,}473\text{ lbs./hr.})(.2) \\ &= 122{,}385.6\text{ lbs./hr.} + 45{,}894.6\text{ lbs./hr.} \\ &= 168{,}280.2\text{ lbs./hr.}\end{aligned}$$

Convert this figure to tons per hour.

$$PR = \frac{168{,}280.2\text{ lbs./hr.}}{2{,}000\text{ lbs./ton}} = 84.14\text{ tons/hr.}$$

Next, convert the production rate into an estimate of capacity for a week.

$$\begin{aligned}\text{Capacity for mix 1} &= (PR \text{ of mix 1})(\text{hours worked})\\ &= (84.14 \text{ tons/hr.})(80 \text{ hrs./week})\\ &= 6{,}731.2 \text{ tons/week}\end{aligned}$$

On your own, calculate the capacity if mix 2 is assumed. (Your answer should be 7,649.1 tons per week.) Thus, as the mix shifts away from 40-inch to 60-inch steel, the capacity increases. Capacity is influenced by product mix.

Adding People

Adding people to an operation may increase the maximum production rate. This will occur when the operation is constrained by the amount of labor assigned to it. The capacity of both service operations and manufacturing operations is affected by adding or eliminating people. The Wendy's and Burlington Chair Operations in Action illustrate the flexibility available to an organization in meeting varying levels of demand. Organizations that are successful need to be willing and able to adapt to change. Part of being able to adapt is having flexibility to meet changes in demand volume.

Increasing Motivation

Another way to increase the production rate for an operation with labor constraints is to provide better motivation for employees. Managers should realize that substantial increases in the production rate can be achieved when workers feel they are an important part of the operation. These productivity increases do not require additional labor costs or extra investment in equipment. The people work harder to accomplish more because they have a stake in the organization.

OPERATIONS IN ACTION

Wendy's: Changing Capacity by Changing Staffing Levels

The next time you visit Wendy's, notice the time of day and the number of people working behind the counter. If it is noon, you will see one person working the cash register, a different person getting soft drinks and fries, someone else wrapping and organizing the meals, and yet another person working the grill. But if you enter at 3:00 P.M., a slow period, one person will be working the cash register and getting the drinks and fries, and a second person will be working the grill and preparing the meal. The capacity to prepare food is a function of how many workers are assigned to the task. The operation has a higher capacity when staffed with four people and a lower capacity when staffed with two.

By designing operations with flexibility in staffing, management is able to control labor costs and still provide fast service to the customer. This is important to a fast-food restaurant like Wendy's because labor is a key cost factor that is under direct control of the restaurant manager.

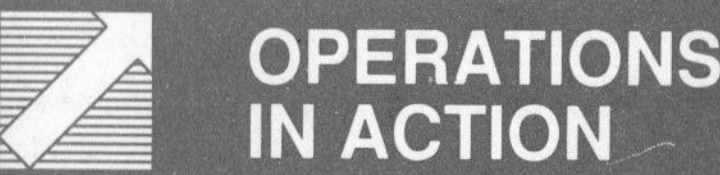

Burlington Chair: Increasing Capacity by Adding Staff

To assemble the frames for twenty-five rocker/recliner chairs at Burlington Chair, each assembler takes his or her work order to the inventory clerk to pick the parts required to make the chairs. This takes about thirty minutes. After returning to the work area, each assembler completes twenty-five chair frames in 3½ hours. To increase the capacity to assemble chair frames, a separate stock picker could be hired to gather inventory for all the assemblers. Then each assembler would be able to increase production by one-seventh because the thirty minutes out of every four hours formerly used to pick stock could be used to assemble chairs. One stock picker could serve eight assemblers.

The capacity improvement is calculated below.

$$\text{Capacity per assembler before stock picker} = (25 \text{ chairs}/4 \text{ hrs.})(8 \text{ hrs./shift})$$
$$= 50 \text{ chairs/shift}$$
$$\text{Capacity per assembler after stock picker} = (25 \text{ chairs}/3.5 \text{ hrs.})(8 \text{ hrs./shift})$$
$$= 57.14 \text{ chairs/shift}$$
$$\text{Capacity increase} = \frac{\text{new capacity} - \text{old capacity}}{\text{old capacity}} \times 100$$
$$= \frac{57.14 - 50}{50} \times 100$$
$$= 14.28\%$$

Traditional approaches for increasing motivation such as increasing pay rates have not been successful. Why have they failed? Employees on an automobile assembly line work on 450 to 500 cars in an eight-hour shift and repeat the same task every fifty to sixty seconds. They may do this five days a week and forty-eight weeks per year for over thirty years. Although the pay is good, it alone does not motivate them because the job has a numbing impact on their minds. In addition, management's traditional view of labor is that assembly-line workers have strong backs and weak minds. In this situation, motivation is impossible and cannot be achieved until the environment is changed.

Improving these conditions requires improvements in automation and a change in management's attitude toward labor. Automation allows management to substitute capital for labor so that firms can use their workers more effectively. Slowly, assembly-line workers will be replaced with automated equipment that can perform the repetitive, boring tasks economically. The work force, which is more intelligent and adaptable, can be used in challenging tasks that better utilize their abilities.

Quality circles (QC) programs are attempts to increase workers' motivation. These programs involve workers in decision making and in determining ways to improve operations. In QC programs, workers are treated as equals with management. Motivated employees will allow an organization to tap talent existing in its work force. People who work faster and more accurately and who use their minds to increase the production rate will improve productivity and make the organization more competitive. Quality circles will be discussed in more detail in Chapter 17.

Increasing Machine Production Rate

In an operation that is machine constrained, adding people will not increase capacity. **Machine constrained** means that the equipment is operating for all the available time at its best speed, while the operators have some idle time. To increase capacity, either new machines should be purchased, or existing machines should be operated more efficiently.

One possibility that was suggested earlier in this chapter is to increase preventive maintenance so that downtime due to machine failure will be reduced or eliminated. Another approach is to develop procedures that more efficiently utilize existing machines. The concept of continuing process improvements states that there is always a way to improve a machine's production rate, and that if production engineers look hard enough, they will find it. Improvements caused by such procedures are not the same as increases in production rates caused by implementing new technology and equipment, but result instead from working smarter. A procedure could be as simple as increasing the heat on the grill to cook the hamburgers faster and without burning them. It could be more complicated, like rolling two pieces of steel simultaneously on a machine that has been designed for only one, as described in the Great Lakes Steel Operations in Action.

OPERATIONS IN ACTION

Great Lakes Steel: Double-Rolling Ingots

An ingot is a large piece of steel that may be 20 inches thick, 50 inches wide, and 12 feet long. As part of the manufacturing process, an ingot's dimensions are changed by rolling the steel on a large mill, much as a thick wad of dough is rolled into a thin piecrust. The ingot described above could become 8 inches thick, 60 inches wide, and 25 feet long. Although the standard procedure for rolling ingots on the mill called for rolling one at a time, plant engineers at Great Lakes Steel developed a method for rolling two ingots at a time. The result was a 17 percent increase in capacity for the rolling mill. This was achieved without significant investment in new technology or equipment. It is clearly an example of working smarter.

This productivity improvement allowed Great Lakes Steel to increase capacity at a time when the company was unable to satisfy customer demand completely. This allowed the company to sell more product, which increased revenue by 17 percent. In addition, the unit labor cost for rolling all ingots was reduced because the same work force is now producing 17 percent more product. This one-two punch—increased availability of product and lower unit costs—gave Great Lakes Steel an edge on its competition.

Improving Quality

Improving quality can often increase the capacity of operations. Simply stated, if an operation produces a product of inferior quality and the product is rejected, the capacity used to produce that product is wasted. Poor quality not only gives the organization's customers a bad impression of its product, but also robs operations of needed capacity.

Increasing Product Yield

In virtually all operations, the quantity of output is less than the quantity of input. **Yield** is the ratio of the quantity of output to the input quantity.

$$\text{Yield} = \frac{\text{quantity of output}}{\text{quantity of input}}$$

The actual yield is a function of the characteristics of the process for producing the product. For example, an oil refinery begins with a barrel of crude oil, but when it is finished, there is less than a barrel of finished products. Small amounts evaporate, are spilled, or are otherwise lost in the process. Some is burned as waste gas. The yield is the percentage of the output that is useful product. A 96 percent yield means ninety-six barrels from every one hundred are made into useful products. If a refinery's engineers find methods to increase the yield by 1 percent, the refinery will have more product to sell, and the effective capacity will be increased.

Summary

Capacity estimation is a necessary prerequisite to capacity planning. Without knowledge of the existing limits on capacity, meaningful capacity planning or production planning cannot take place.

OPERATIONS IN ACTION

Steelcase, Inc.: Better Quality Increases Capacity

Steelcase, Inc., produces four-drawer filing cabinets for office and home use. For simplicity, consider that there are three steps in the operation. First, the flat sheet steel is bent into the various metal parts needed to assemble the cabinet; second, these pieces are assembled; and third, the units are painted.

Suppose that incoming steel is pitted with tiny rust pockets. If the defect is not caught, the metal will be bent, assembled, and painted. It may be rejected at final assembly or, worse yet, rejected by the customer. In either case, some capacity is lost. If the defect is caught by an inspection prior to metal bending, the metal can either be returned or sanded to remove the pitted rust.

Poor quality in metal bending, painting, or assembly can also result in rejected file cabinets. The impact on capacity is negative because resources have been used to make inferior products that must be reworked or scrapped.

Another point to remember is that capacity is not a fixed number within which organizations are forced to live. Capacity is a function of management ingenuity. It can be influenced by good planning, good operating procedures, effective maintenance programs, and other management decisions. The role of operations managers is to investigate the possible methods to increase capacity before investing substantial capital in new facilities.

DETERMINING SYSTEM CAPACITY

Up to this point, our discussion of estimating and improving capacity has focused on only a part of operations. The frame assembly for rocker/recliners and the impact of preventive maintenance on machine capacity are two examples that have been considered. The systems concept, which is an important theme of this text, makes us realize that operations is a combination of different machines/equipment and processes that make finished products. To plan effectively, management must know the capacity of the entire system, not just the individual parts. The term *department* is often used when referring to a portion of the production system.

Before beginning to analyze system capacity, you should know how departments are related. There are two basic arrangements, product layout and process layout. Process selection and layout are discussed in more detail in Chapters 7 and 8, but the discussion here will help you understand different approaches to capacity estimation.

Product Layout. Product-oriented layout is characterized by high demand for the same or similar products. Examples include refining steel, making paper, and processing checks in a bank. In this arrangement, there are few, if any, product variations, and the layout fits the dominant flow of the product—thus, the name *product layout.*

For example, to make paper, wooden logs are ground and chemically treated to produce a watery mixture called pulp. The pulp is pumped to the papermaking machine where excess water is gradually squeezed out, leaving a thin sheet of wet paper. The wet paper passes through a series of dryers that remove the remaining moisture. The dry paper is then rolled into logs that can be 30 feet wide and several feet in diameter. These huge logs are later cut into many different widths. Most types of paper are made using the same process and follow the same flow (see Exhibit 5.1).

Process Layout. The second type of layout is a process-oriented layout. This layout is characterized by low-volume production of any one product and the

Exhibit 5.1 Product-Oriented Layout of Paper Mill

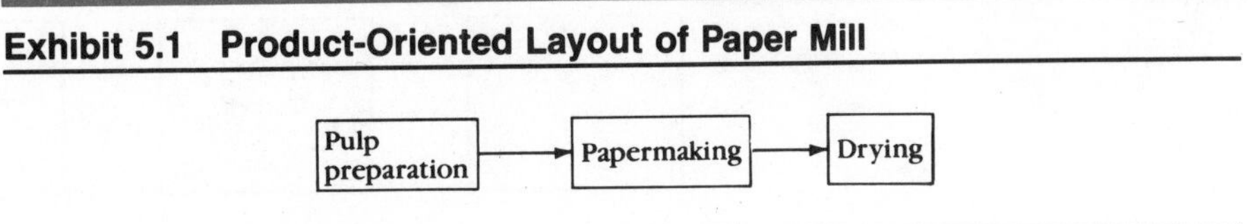

production of many different products with the same equipment. No single product has enough volume to support a dedicated set of machines. Each product has different production requirements that place different demands on the equipment. Examples include a machine shop that produces specialty automotive parts for racing engines and an automotive repair shop that offers a wide variety of service. In this arrangement, the layout is grouped by similar machine types because there is no dominant product flow—thus, the name *process layout.*

An automotive center contains the equipment to analyze a variety of mechanical problems. As seen in the following list, customers desire a variety of services. The facilities are arranged by process because there is no dominant flow (see Exhibit 5.2).

Customer	Services Requested
A	Tires, shock absorbers, wheel alignment
B	Tires, brakes, tune-up
C	Brakes, tune-up, exhaust system
D	Tires, brakes, shock absorbers, muffler
E	Shock absorbers

The capacity of these different systems is determined by analyzing the capacities of the individual departments. Approaches to determining the capacity of both product-oriented and process-oriented layouts are discussed here.

The Product Layout and System Capacity

The capacity of a product-oriented system can be visualized as a series of pipes of varying capacity, with the smallest diameter or capacity holding back the entire system. Exhibit 5.3 illustrates five pipes (departments or machines) with different diameters (capacities). The output from one pipe becomes the input to the next until the finished product exits pipe number five. In Exhibit 5.3, pipe number two cannot handle all the flow that pipe number one can deliver, and therefore it restricts the flow. Because of pipe number two's limited capacity, it starves the downstream pipes. Pipes three, four, and five can work on only what pipe two can deliver. This restriction is called a **bottleneck,** and it determines the system's capacity.

Exhibit 5.2 Process-Oriented Layout of an Automotive Service Center

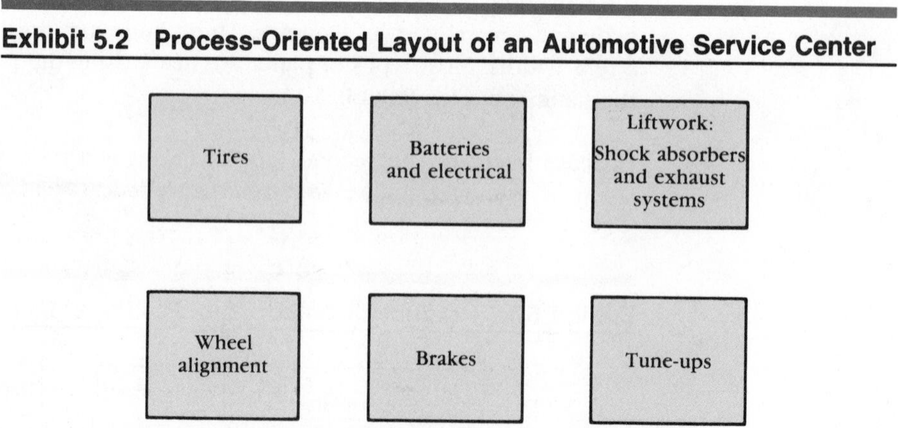

Exhibit 5.3 A Bottleneck in the Product Flow

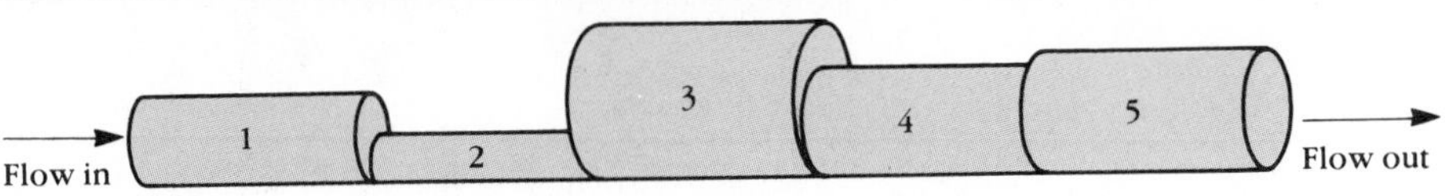

Analysis of System Capacity

In a product-oriented layout, identifying the bottleneck is critical. The importance of this analysis cannot be overstated because the results are used not only in determining capacity, but also in planning and scheduling production, which will be discussed in Section II on planning the system.

The approach to determining the bottleneck is illustrated in Exhibit 5.4. Start at the beginning of the system, and determine the capacity of the first operation or department. This is the system capacity so far. Use this capacity as the input to the next department in the sequence. Can that department take the total input from the previous department and process it completely? If it can, then the system capacity has not changed. If it cannot, then the system capacity is reduced to the capacity of that department. The procedure continues until the end of the process is reached and the system capacity is known.

Consider the example shown in Exhibit 5.5. The basic oxygen furnace has a maximum rate of 4,200 tons per day (tpd), while the continuous caster's rate is 6,000 tpd. Clearly, the capacity of that part of the system is limited by the 4,200 tpd of the slower operation.

Determining the Bottleneck

Now consider the entire system shown in Exhibit 5.6. The capacities are listed below each department. At two points in the steel-making process, outputs from two departments are inputs to a single department. The ratio of each input is listed on the arrow that illustrates the flow. For example, in the blast furnace, 3 pounds of iron ore are mixed with 1 pound of coke. In these cases, the inputs to a department should be combined in the correct proportion until at least one of the inputs is exhausted.

What is the system capacity? Follow along in Exhibit 5.6. Iron ore processing and coke ovens can deliver 3,000 and 1,000 tpd, respectively. (Only 3,000 tons can be used for iron ore processing because of the ratio requirements.) The combined 4,000 tpd is more than sufficient for the blast furnace, which requires only 3,000 tpd total. So far, the blast furnace is holding back production. The blast furnace and scrap handling, in turn, supply 3,000 and 1,500 tpd, which is adequate for the basic oxygen furnace needs of 4,200 tpd. Because the basic oxygen furnace cannot process all available inputs, it is the bottleneck to this point. The basic oxygen furnace cannot deliver sufficient capacity to the remaining departments. Therefore, the basic oxygen furnace is the bottleneck for the system, and the capacity of the system is 4,200 tpd.

To calculate the production rates for each department that allow the system to produce 4,200 tpd, begin at the bottleneck department in Exhibit 5.7. Trace the product flow from the bottleneck to the beginning and the end of the process. In order to achieve 4,200 tpd of basic oxygen furnace input, $(2/3)(4{,}200) = 2{,}800$

Exhibit 5.4 Sequential Approach to Bottleneck Analysis

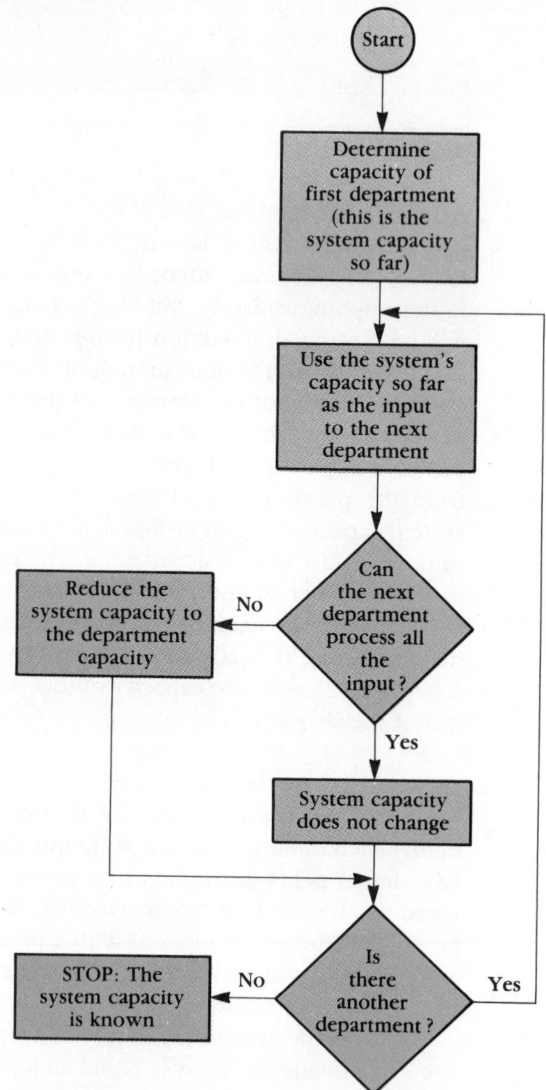

Exhibit 5.5 Simple Steel Production Flow

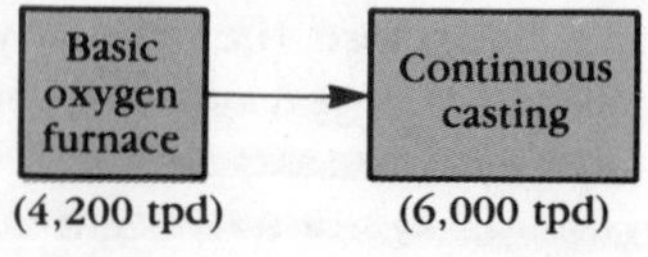

Exhibit 5.6 Steel Production Flow: A Product Layout

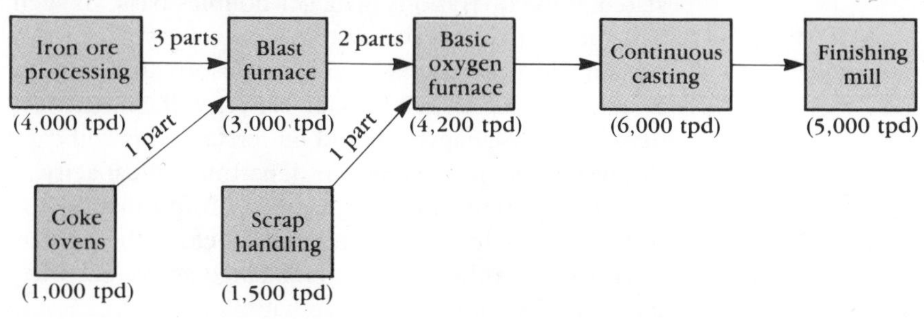

Exhibit 5.7 Determining System Capacity

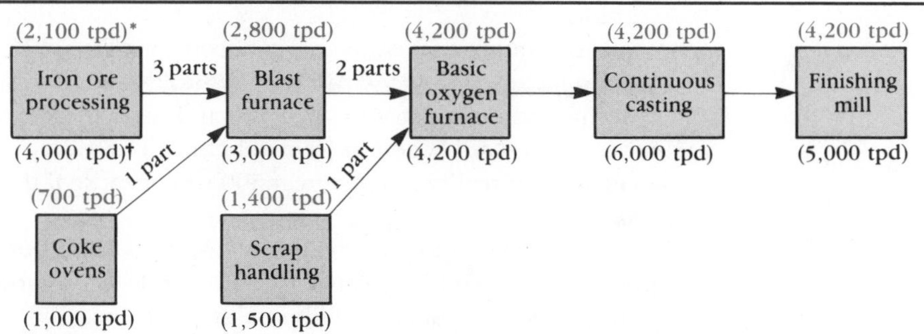

*Numbers above each department indicate the production rate required from that department to achieve a system capacity of 4,200 tpd.

†Numbers below each department indicate the individual department's capacity.

tpd comes from the blast furnace and (⅓)(4,200) = 1,400 tpd comes from scrap. The requirements are listed above each department. The blast furnace requires (¾)(2,800) = 2,100 tpd of iron ore and (¼)(2,800) = 700 tpd of coke. Moving from the basic oxygen furnace to the end of the process is simpler because there are no pairs of departments. The requirement for those departments is 4,200 tpd.

In actual production, each operation in this process would suffer yield loss, which we do not describe here in order to simplify discussion.

Rounding Out System Capacity

It is also important to know which department, machine, or step in the process restricts the system's capacity. An operations manager may be charged with increasing the system's capacity. If he or she tries to do so by increasing blast furnace capacity, there will be no increase in the system's capacity. This organization could spend millions on a new blast furnace and not get one additional ton of steel out of the system because the bottleneck constricts the flow.

The system capacity can be increased by applying resources to the bottleneck department. This approach is called **rounding out capacity** because resources are applied to the bottleneck to bring it into balance with other parts (departments) in the system. Rounding out capacity has a limit, however. Simply stated, if the operations manager doubles basic oxygen furnace capacity because it is the bottleneck, the system's capacity will not double. There is not enough capacity in other departments to absorb that large an increase. As a result of doubling basic oxygen furnace capacity, the bottleneck simply jumps to another department. Managers should understand this and carefully analyze the effect on the system of any increase in departmental capacity.

An important and useful piece of information to determine is how far the system's capacity can be increased before the next bottleneck appears. To answer, examine the requirements listed above each department in Exhibit 5.7. A quick review shows that scrap handling and the blast furnace will be bottlenecks as basic oxygen furnace capacity is increased. With a cushion of 100 tons per day in scrap handling, the capacity of the system could increase by only 300 tpd. (Remember that one part scrap and two parts hot metal from the blast furnace are required.) The scrap handling and blast furnace departments have insufficient capacity to handle an increase of more than 300 tpd in basic oxygen furnace capacity.

If this quick analysis is too confusing, simply set the capacity of the present bottleneck to infinity and rework the problem. The results are shown in Exhibit 5.8. The system's capacity is 4,500 tpd, and there are two bottlenecks: blast furnace and scrap handling. Remember, the basic oxygen furnace capacity was set to infinity. In reality, it must be 4,500 tpd or more if the system capacity is 4,500 tpd.

The analysis of system capacity and associated bottlenecks is extremely important for determining capacity. Rational decisions about capacity can be made only if these concepts are fully understood.

The Process Layout and System Capacity

The process-oriented layout is characterized as a multiple-product facility with low volume per product. The products are different from one another and usually require different methods and procedures in production. There is no dominant

Exhibit 5.8 Rounding Out Capacity

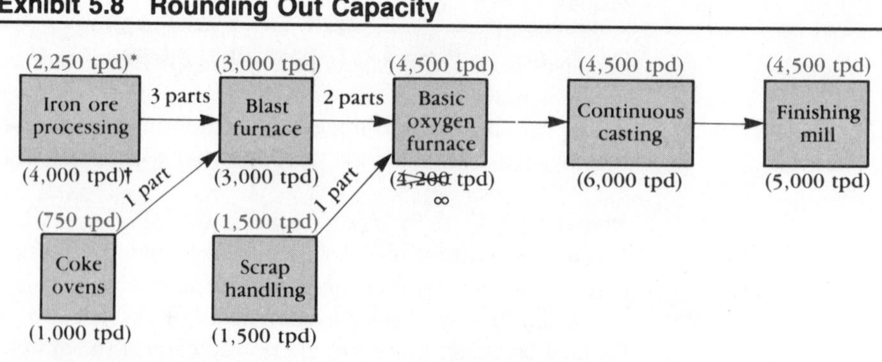

*Numbers above each department indicate the production rate required from that department to achieve a system capacity of 4,500 tpd.

†Numbers below each department indicate the individual department's capacity.

product flow to guide the arrangement of departments as there is in the paper or steel industry, so similar operations are grouped together. The process-oriented layout does not have enough volume in any one product to dedicate specialized production facilities.

A medical center is an example of a process-oriented operation. Patients are screened at the reception desk to determine the nature and seriousness of their injuries and then usually proceed to a waiting room to be called by a nurse or physician. After an initial examination, the method of treatment for each patient is determined. Each treatment could be different and is based on the patient's individual needs. A patient in an automobile accident may be scheduled for X-rays, orthopedic surgery, and application of a cast. The next patient might have heart problems or have taken poison. Each would follow a different path through the medical center. The equipment should be flexible enough to handle a wide range of needs. For example, an X-ray machine should be able to photograph legs, feet, hands, and other areas of the body and should adjust to an infant or an adult.

Analysis of System Capacity

Determining system capacity in a process-oriented layout is more complex than doing so in a product-oriented layout. In the process layout, each product does not follow the same path through the system. The functions and machines are grouped into departments, and different products follow different paths. The layout shown in Exhibit 5.9 has six departments and four different patterns of treatment or products. The departments' capacities are given in patients per week (ppw) and are based on average time per treatment.

The determination of system capacity is not merely a search for the minimum department capacity because there is no dominant flow. The capacity of the system is a function of the jobs presented. For example, if all the patients arriving at the medical center are type A patients (those needing orthopedic care), the capacity of the system will be 250 patients per week. This can be calculated by simply looking at the minimum capacity for departments 1, 2, and 3. If all patients are of type B, then the capacity will be 500 patients per week. For patients of types C and D, the system capacities are 300 and 400 patients per week, respectively. The table at the top of the next page shows the various capacities. The system's capacity is a function of the job types presented.

Exhibit 5.9 A Process Layout of a Medical Center

Departments

Waiting area (1)	(1,000 ppw)
X-ray (2)	(400 ppw)
Orthopedic care (3)	(250 ppw)
Cardiology (4)	(500 ppw)
Neurology (5)	(300 ppw)
Intensive care (6)	(600 ppw)

Patient Type	Department
A	1, 2, 3
B	1, 4, 6
C	1, 2, 5
D	1, 2, 6

Mix	System's Capacity	Bottleneck Department
100% A	250 ppw	Orthopedic care
100% B	500 ppw	Cardiology
100% C	300 ppw	Neurology
100% D	400 ppw	X-ray

Product Mix and Capacity in a Process Layout

If the medical center only processed one type of patient, the system capacity could be easily and accurately estimated, as shown by the prior example. What would the system capacity be if the medical center processed all four types during the same week? To simplify the logic, assume that only type A patients arrive on Monday and Tuesday, type Bs on Wednesday and Thursday, type Cs on Friday and Saturday, and type Ds on Sunday. The system capacity per week for that mix would be calculated as follows:

$$\text{System capacity} = \frac{2}{7}(250\text{ ppw}) + \frac{2}{7}(500\text{ ppw}) + \frac{2}{7}(300\text{ ppw}) + \frac{1}{7}(400\text{ ppw})$$

$$= 357\text{ ppw}$$

The fractions in the preceding equation are the patient mix. A different assumption concerning the number of days per week assigned to each patient type would be a different product mix and would result in a different system capacity.

In reality, not all orthopedic care patients (type A) will arrive on Monday and Tuesday. The method illustrated in the prior calculation is likely to underestimate the system capacity because we have assumed that no patient other than an orthopedic patient arrives on Monday or Tuesday. However, the system does have the capacity to process type B, C, and D patients on Monday and Tuesday in addition to $(2/7)(250\text{ ppw}) = 71.4$ type A patients. How can managers of a medical center get an accurate estimate of system capacity and determine which department is the bottleneck? An often-used technique for estimating capacity in a process layout is simulation. Simulation is a modeling technique that is described in the Supplement to Chapter 13.

In this approach, an estimate of product mix (patient mix) is used to randomly generate arriving patients. A time to service each patient, which is based on historical data, is also randomly generated. The simulation is run for a long period of time, and statistics about the number of patients served and the utilization of each department are kept. (In fact, utilization data should be kept regularly for equipment in a process layout so that bottlenecks can be anticipated and corrective action taken.) Management can change the mix of arriving patients to determine how the system capacity and bottleneck department change. A different mix places different demands on the resources. Managers should plan for the present mix of patients and the associated bottleneck, as well as for the mix possibilities that the future holds.

Capacity Decisions and Service Operations

Most of the concepts discussed in this chapter apply to producers of services as well as to producers of goods. It is important to note, however, that service operations are different from manufacturing operations in some respects. First, services are direct and cannot be inventoried. Whereas the consumption of goods can be delayed, as a general rule services are produced and consumed simultaneously. This means that service organizations must (1) build enough capacity to meet maximum demand, (2) manage demand so that people will use the services at off-peak times (allowing long waiting lines to occur is one way, usually a poor way, to manage demand, and offering monetary incentives to use the service at off-peak times is another way), or (3) choose not to satisfy all the demand.

Each of these options has a cost. Building sufficient capacity to meet maximum demand can mean that a significant portion of the capacity is used infrequently. Having people wait in long lines for service may cause dissatisfaction that will result in a loss of business. For example, a hospital that has long lines in its emergency room is likely to lose business. Choosing to ignore demand means a loss of customers that may have long-term as well as short-term effects.

Second, there is often a high degree of producer-consumer interaction in the production of a service. This frequently introduces a significant amount of uncertainty about processing time, and processing time is a determinant of capacity. For example, a person waiting in line at a bank may have one or many transactions to perform and may be skilled or unskilled at communicating his or her needs. This makes it more difficult to estimate the capacity required to meet uncertain customer demands.

Third, services are not transported to the customer, the customer may come to the service delivery system, as with hair care, or the service delivery system may be brought to the customer, as with carpet cleaning. This has important implications for the location decision, which is discussed in the next chapter. It also means that capacity decisions should result in adequate space for the customer in the service delivery system. For example, many restaurants use a generous bar area to deal with excess demand in the dining area.

Service Operations and System Capacity

The concepts of determining system capacity and finding the bottleneck apply to service as well as manufacturing operations. The principles are the same, but in some cases, the application is different. In the following case, managers of an up-scale restaurant chain are attempting to determine the capacity of their restaurant.

The flow of people through the restaurant follows this sequence. People arrive at the restaurant and park their car. From records that the restaurant keeps, 20 percent of the guests spend time in the bar. The remaining 80 percent of the arrivals go to the dining area. According to standards that management has developed over the years, each dinner served per hour requires about four square feet of kitchen space. Listed below are the resources of the standard restaurant.

Department/Area	Capacity/Size
Parking area	100 spaces
Bar area	80 seats
Dining area	200 seats
Cooking area	600 square feet

On the average, 2.2 people arrive per car, only 80 percent of the seats in the bar are normally available because tables for four are sometimes occupied by two or three people, and only 85 percent of the dining area seats are normally available for the same reason. The average stay is 90 minutes. Everyone in the restaurant orders a meal, and 40 percent of the people in the bar area order a meal. What is the capacity of the system? To begin, the capacity of each area can be calculated in terms of persons served per hour.

Department/Area	Capacity/Size	
Parking area	(100 spaces)(2.2 people/car)/(1.5 hrs.)	= 147 people/hr.
Bar area	(80 seats)(.8)/(1.5 hrs.)	= 43 people/hr.
Dining area	(200 seats)(.85)/(1.5 hrs.)	= 113 people/hr.
Cooking area	(600 sq. ft.)/(4 sq. ft./meal)	= 150 people/hr.

If every customer spent time both in the bar and in the dining area, the system capacity would be easy to determine because each customer would place demands on each area. This would make the restaurant a product layout similar to the steel industry, and the system capacity would be the smallest of the four department's capacities. However, only a portion of the guests use the bar and the dining areas.

To calculate the capacity of the system and determine the bottleneck department in this case, the approach illustrated earlier could be used. However, that method requires tracking two different flows, one involving the dining area and a second following the bar area. Another method will be used here to demonstrate that different approaches are possible. We will start by selecting a level of demand that we are fairly certain the restaurant can satisfy. If it cannot, the demand level is decreased, and another attempt is made. If it can, the demand level is increased. This trial-and-error method can quickly lead to the capacity if care is used in selecting the demand points. (In fact, this trial-and-error approach could be used to solve problems like the steel industry problem described earlier.) By inspecting the department capacities, it is clear that the system's capacity cannot exceed 147 people/hour because that is the capacity of the parking lot and the assumption of this model is that everyone drives. It is also clear that the capacity of the system is at least 100 because all of the department capacities are at least 100, except for the bar area which only serves 20 percent of the customers.

We begin, therefore, by setting the arrival rate (demand) equal to one hundred people per hour. This means that during each hour one hundred people use the parking lot, twenty people use the bar, eighty people use the restaurant, and eighty-eight people order a meal. Everyone in the restaurant orders a meal, and 40 percent of the bar patrons order a meal. None of the individual departments is at capacity, so the analysis continues. The results are shown in the following table:

		Set Demand Equal to			
Department/ Area	***Capacity (People/hr.)***	**100 People/Hr.**	**125 People/Hr.**	**147 People/Hr.**	**113/.8 = 141 People/Hr.**
Parking area	147	100	125	147	141
Bar area	43	20	25	29	28
Dining area	113	80	100	118	113
Cooking area	150	88	110	130	124

Next, we examine what happens if demand is set at 125 people/hour. Once again, none of the departments is at capacity. We now know that the system capacity must be between 125 and 147 people/hour. (Remember that the parking lot can hold no more than 147.) With demand set at 147 people/hour, the parking lot is at capacity, but demand in the dining area exceeds capacity. Bar demand is equal to (147)(.2) = 29. Dining demand is equal to (147)(.8) = 118. Cooking demand is equal to 118 + (29)(.4) = 130. At this point, we are sure that the bottleneck is the dining area, but we are unsure of the system capacity because not everyone uses the dining room. To determine the system capacity, we divide the capacity of the dining area by 0.8, which is the percentage of customers that use the dining area. This calculation yields the system capacity, which is 141 people per hour. If the system capacity is set equal to demand and the department demands are calculated again, the excess capacities in the nonbottleneck departments can be identified. There is considerable excess capacity in the cooking area and in the bar, but the parking lot is near capacity. Expansion plans, if justified by demand, should be aimed at the dining area and the parking lot.

CAPACITY DECISIONS FOR COMPETITIVE ADVANTAGE

Informed capacity decisions can be made only when management (1) knows the ability of their present resources (capacity estimation), (2) knows the bottlenecks and what is causing them (system capacity), and (3) has an estimate of future demand (forecast of customer need). The first two topics have been the major thrust of the chapter to this point. Forecasting is discussed in Chapter 3. Now we can use this information to discuss the capacity decisions listed below.

1. When to add capacity
2. How much capacity to add
3. Where to add capacity
4. What type of capacity to add

When to Add Capacity

Many people argue that determining how much capacity an organization should have is not difficult. The real problem, they would argue, is to obtain an accurate forecast of demand. These managers would state that once an estimate of demand is obtained, it is simply a matter of setting capacity to meet demand. They would also state that the answer to the timing question is easy if an accurate forecast can be obtained. The operations manager determines how long it takes to build additional capacity and adds that lead time to the point where demand exceeds capacity. In Exhibit 5.10, capacity is exceeded two years in the future. If it takes eighteen months to add capacity, then management should begin construction six months from today. In reality, however, the answer to the question is not that simple. To avoid compounding the question of when to add capacity with forecasting error, let's assume, for the moment, that forecasts are guaranteed to be accurate.

Now consider the timing decision in Exhibit 5.10. Should the capacity be added by the end of the second year? The answer is probably no, for several sound reasons. Management could simply choose not to satisfy all the demand during the third year. The forecast shows that the really significant and long-term increase does not take place until the end of year five. It is possible that the

Exhibit 5.10 Capacity versus Demand

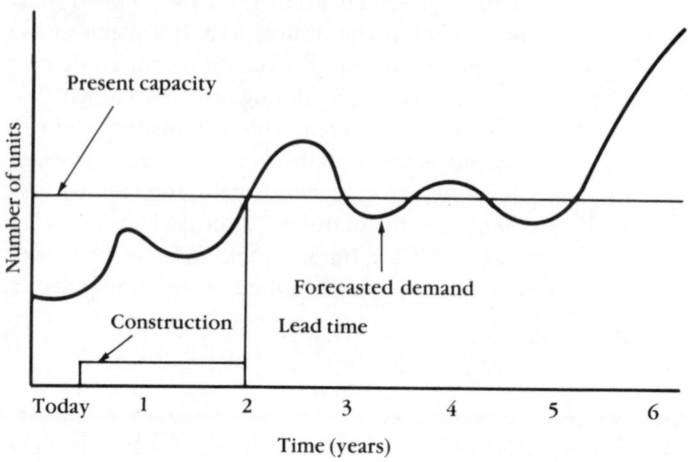

organization has no long-term interest in the market and would choose to allocate resources to other products.

However, failing to fully satisfy demand may not be consistent with a company policy of building market share. If the sales force is told to increase market share, but production cannot deliver the product, then long-term damage to the firm's reputation could result.

If ignoring the excess demand in the third year is not acceptable, then management must find a way to meet that demand. One possibility is to set the production rate higher than demand during the first and second years so that sufficient inventory is created to satisfy demand in the third year. Exhibit 5.11 illustrates this point. Obviously, this solution is limited to goods production because services have no finished-goods inventory.

Other methods of dealing with the capacity shortfall in the third year can be understood by recalling the earlier sections on capacity estimation. From this discussion, you learned that capacity is a variable that is subject to change through management innovation. If the operation runs two shifts five days a week, then overtime or another shift could be considered. Better scheduling, improved operating procedures, or improved quality of raw materials can increase capacity.

Another important concept to remember is system capacity. To increase the capacity of a system, it is necessary to increase the capacity of only the bottleneck operation. It may be possible to buy production capacity to supplement the bottleneck operation and increase overall capacity. This practice of subcontracting work is very common.

How Much Capacity to Add

If additional capacity is built, then how much should be added? Again, assume that the forecasted demand is accurate, and consider the example in Exhibit 5.12. In

Exhibit 5.11 Capacity, Demand, and Production Rate

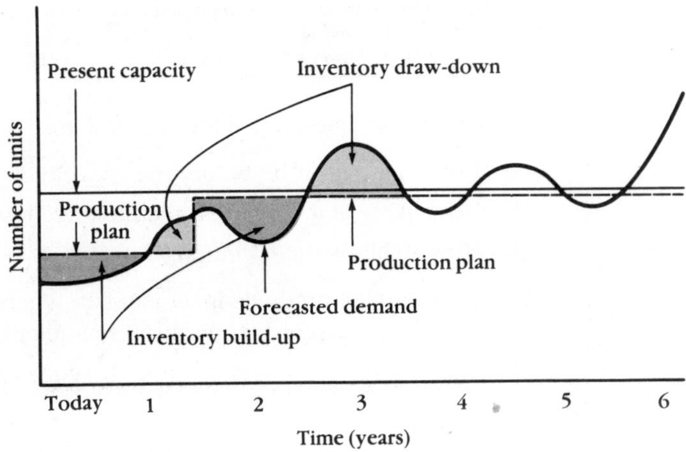

Exhibit 5.12 How Much Capacity to Add?

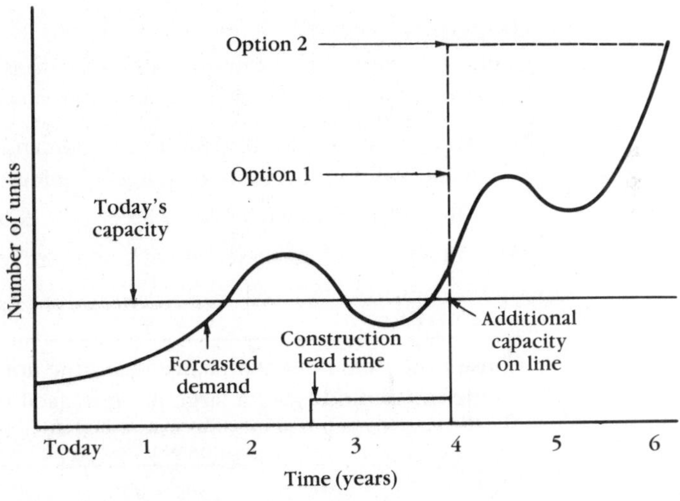

this example, the decision of when to add capacity has been made. Construction will begin in the middle of the third year, and the new capacity will come on line at the end of the fourth year.

Option 1 is to add only enough capacity to handle the demand in the early part of the fifth year. Option 2 is to add enough capacity to handle the increase in the sixth year. The financial versus operating trade-offs of these options are summarized on the next page.

Advantages of Option 1	Advantages of Option 2
1. Limits short-term investment and risk. Changes in technology will not find the organization with as much capital tied up in outdated technology.	1. May reduce long-term investment. Building capacity in one lump instead of two is bound to save total construction costs.
2. Limits unused capacity for which no return on investment is provided.	2. May reduce inflationary effects on construction costs by building now.

The major questions with option 2 are

1. How long will it be before the capacity is needed?
2. How likely is it that the forecasted need will occur?
3. How stable is the technology?

A firm producing products in an industry where the product or process technology is likely to change does not want to build plants that limit its long-term ability to compete.

Models and Capacity Decision Making

What happens if we relax the assumption that our forecast is completely accurate? Because of the uncertainty involved in estimating demand and capacity, statistical techniques such as decision trees can be used to analyze the problems and to answer what-if questions.

Decision Trees

A decision tree is useful in modeling situations that have decisions and probabilities. In capacity decisions, the important variables are

1. An estimate of the distribution of demand—that is, the probability that demand will be any value or range of values,
2. The alternatives available to meet that demand, and
3. The costs and revenues of each alternative.

Example

Consider this example with a five-year time horizon. The organization is trying to decide if it should build a large or small facility to satisfy projected demand.

Units per Year	Probability
200,000	.3
100,000	.5
50,000	.2

The demand from year to year is considered dependent. That is, if demand the first year is 50,000, then demand in years two through five is 50,000, with a 100 percent probability.

The alternatives are as follows:

1. Build a small facility with a capacity of 100,000 units per year. The smaller facility has higher variable costs per unit.
2. Build a facility with a capacity of 200,000 units per year. This facility has lower variable costs per unit.

The operating costs and revenue for each alternative are as follows (X_p is the number of units produced, and X_s is the number of units sold):
Costs for small facility:

$$\text{Costs} = \$3.70/\text{unit } (X_p) + \$400{,}000$$

Costs for large facility:

$$\text{Costs} = \$2.90/\text{unit } (X_p) + \$550{,}000$$

Revenue (all cases):

$$\text{Revenue} = \$10/\text{unit } (X_s)$$

Our analysis of the problem begins with a decision regarding the facility. Either a large facility or a small facility could be built, or nothing could be done. The base case in any decision problem like this is to maintain the status quo. These options are displayed in Exhibit 5.13, extending from the rectangle that represents a decision point. A decision point is controllable by management, and at a decision point, only one option is selected. At the ends of the lines extending from the decision point, the demand distribution is shown by a circle with a line extending from the circle for each possibility in the demand distribution. Management cannot select one of these possibilities because management does not directly control demand. If they did, management would undoubtedly set demand at 200,000 units per year. Demand in units per year is listed above each line extending from the circle, and probability is listed below. Because demand is independent of the facility size, the same demand distribution applies at the end

Exhibit 5.13 Decision Tree for Capacity Decision

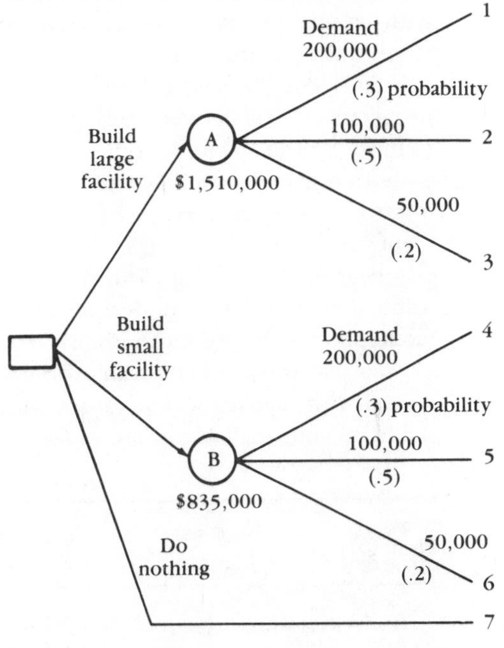

Exhibit 5.14 Calculations for Gross Profit

Endpoint Number	Operating Revenue ($000,000)
1	($10/unit)(200,000 units/yr.)(5 yrs.) = 10
2	($10/unit)(100,000 units/yr.)(5 yrs.) = 5
3	($10/unit)(50,000 units/yr.)(5 yrs.) = 2.5
4	($10/unit)(100,000 units/yr.)(5 yrs.) = 5
5	($10/unit)(100,000 units/yr.)(5 yrs.) = 5
6	($10/unit)(50,000 units/yr.)(5 yrs.) = 2.5
7	= 0

Endpoint Number	Operating Costs ($000,000)	Gross Profit ($000,000)
1	[($2.90/unit)(200,000 units/yr.) + $550,000/yr.](5 yrs.) = 5.65	4.35
2	[($2.90/unit)(100,000 units/yr.) + $550,000/yr.](5 yrs.) = 4.2	.8
3	[($2.90/unit)(50,000 units/yr.) + $550,000/yr.](5 yrs.) = 3.475	(.975)
4	[($3.70/unit)(100,000 units/yr.) + $400,000/yr.](5 yrs.) = 3.85	1.15
5	[($3.70/unit)(100,000 units/yr.) + $400,000/yr.](5 yrs.) = 3.85	1.15
6	[($3.70/unit)(50,000 units/yr.) + $400,000/yr.](5 yrs.) = 2.925	(.425)
7	= 0	0

of each facility option. It is unnecessary to place the demand distribution at the end of the do-nothing option because no matter how many customers demand the product, without a facility to make it, none can be sold.

The endpoints in the decision are numbered one through seven. Exhibit 5.14 has an evaluation of the endpoints. The costs of constructing the facility are included in the annual fixed costs. **Annual fixed costs** are costs that do not vary with volume. These costs are incurred each year and can include supervisory labor, utilities, and support staff.

To begin the analysis, refer to the decision tree in Exhibit 5.13. How do managers choose between alternatives? They need a measuring stick or criterion to make that decision. It could be as simple as taking the largest potential profit without regard for probability. That choice, however, ignores an important piece of information. In most cases, the criterion is to find the alternative with the highest expected profit. The assumption is that a firm makes these types of decisions many times. If the firm chooses the alternative with the greatest expected value, then over a long period of time, it will have made the "best" choices. This tactic implies the ability to absorb the potential losses.

To use the expected-value criterion, the probability distributions are replaced with their expected values. The probability distributions and analysis for the large and small plants are as follows:

Large Plant

Gross Profit ($000,000)	Probability	Expected Value of Gross Profit ($000,000)
4.35	.3	1.305
.8	.5	.4
(.975)	.2	(.195)
		1.51

Large

Thus, $1.51 million is the expected value if the decision to build a large facility is made.

Small Plant

Gross Profit ($000,000)	Probability	Expected Value of Gross Profit ($000,000)
1.15	.3	.345
1.15	.5	.575
(.425)	.2	(.085)
		.835

The expected value of gross profit from building a small facility is $.835 million.

The decision tree model indicates that the large plant has the greater expected value. At this point, the manager may decide to analyze certain what-if questions. Suppose the probability distribution is as follows:

Sales (Units per Year)	Probability
200,000	.1
100,000	.6
50,000	.3

The new expected value for the large facility would be $.6225 million and for the small facility $.6775 million. Try to solve this problem with the new probability distribution for demand. Here, the model is sensitive to small errors in estimating the probability distribution.

The situation described in the example assumes that there are no competitors. What happens if a potential competitor exists? Suppose the probability that a competitor will build a facility is 0.4 if the demand for the product is high (200,000 units per year). Further assume that the probability that a competitor will build a facility is zero if the demand is moderate or low. Because the competitor waits to see what the demand is before making a decision, the earliest the competitor's plant can be operational is the end of the second year. Also, if demand is high and the organization initially built a small facility, it may decide to build another small facility to satisfy demand. This additional facility will be available for production at the end of the second year.

Example

To construct the new decision tree, examine the decision tree for the previous example, which is illustrated in Exhibit 5.13. We can incorporate the changes described here to arrive at a new decision tree, which is illustrated in Exhibit 5.15. First, if the organization described in the previous example builds a large facility, and if demand is 200,000 units per year, then an option must be added at the end of that arc. That option represents the possibility of a competitor building a facility. If a competitor enters the market at the end of the second year, the competitor's market share will be 20 percent in the third year and 35 percent in each of years four and five. Because the organization does not

Exhibit 5.15 Decision Tree for Capacity Decision with Potential Competitor

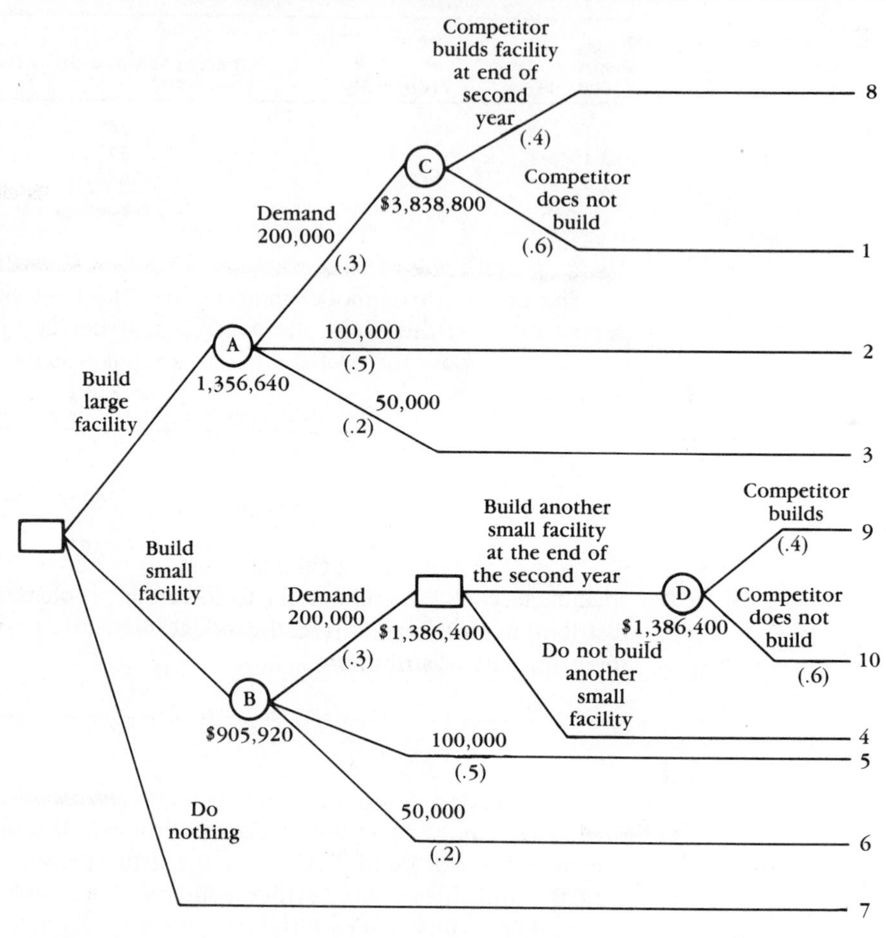

control the competitor's decision, it is an event in the decision tree. Therefore, it is represented by a circle with two outcomes and has a probability associated with each outcome. Because the competitor will take no action if demand is 100,000 or 50,000 units per year, that portion of the decision tree does not change.

If the organization builds a small facility, and if demand is 200,000 units per year, then the organization can decide to build another small facility to satisfy demand. The organization would not want to consider a large facility because the unsatisfied demand is only 100,000 units per year. Once again, the small facility, as well as the facility that a competitor might build, will begin operation at the end of the second year. Because the decision to build another small facility is controlled by the organization, it is represented by a rectangle in Exhibit 5.15 with two options. The competitor's options are shown, once again, as an event with two outcomes.

The competitor's options are not shown at the end of the option for the organization not to build another facility. If demand is 200,000, and if the competitor builds a facility the organization can still sell 100,000 units per year in years three, four, and five.

Endpoints one through seven in Exhibit 5.15 have the same values as endpoints one through seven in Exhibit 5.13. Endpoints eight, nine, and ten are new, and the evaluation of these endpoints is illustrated in Exhibit 5.16.

To use the expected-value criterion once again, the probability distributions are replaced with their expected values. The expected value of the probability distribution represented by node D in Exhibit 5.15 is calculated here.

Gross Profit ($000,000)	Probability	Expected Value of Gross Profit ($000,000)
.706	.4	.2824
1.84	.6	1.104
		1.3864

The expected value of the probability distribution represented by node C in Exhibit 5.15 is calculated on the following page.

Exhibit 5.16 Calculations for Gross Profit with Potential Competitor

Endpoint Number	Operating Revenue	($000,000)
8	Yrs. 1, 2 ($10/unit)(200,000 units/yr.)(2 yrs.)	= 4
	Yr. 3 ($10/unit)(200,000 units/yr.)(.8)	= 1.6
	Yrs. 4, 5 ($10/unit)(200,000 units/yr.)(.65)(2 yrs.)	= 2.6
		8.2
9	Yrs. 1, 2 ($10/unit)(100,000 units/yr.)(2 yrs.)	= 2
	Yr. 3 ($10/unit)(200,000 units/yr.)(.8)	= 1.6
	Yrs. 4, 5 ($10/units)(200,000 units/yr.)(.65)(2 yrs.)	= 2.6
		6.2
10	Yrs. 1, 2 ($10/unit)(100,000 units/yr.)(2 yrs.)	= 2
	Yrs. 3–5 ($10/unit)(200,000 units/yr.)(3 yrs.)	= 6
		8

Endpoint Number	Operating Costs	($000,000)
8	Yrs. 1, 2 [($2.90/unit)(200,000 units/yr.) + $550,000/yr.](2 yrs.)	= 2.26
	Yr. 3 [($2.90/unit)(200,000 units/yr.)(.8) + $550,000/yr.]	= 1.014
	Yrs. 4, 5 [($2.90/unit)(200,000 units/yr.)(.65) + $550,000/yr.](2 yrs.)	= 1.854
		5.128
9	Yrs. 1, 2 [($3.70/unit)(100,000 units/yr.) + $400,000/yr.](2 yrs.)	= 1.54
	Yr. 3 [($3.70/unit)(200,000/yr.)(.8) + $800,000/yr.]	= 1.392
	Yrs. 4, 5 [($3.70/unit)(200,000/yr.)(.65) + $800,000/yr.](2 yrs.)	= 2.562
		5.494
10	Yrs. 1, 2 [($3.70/unit)(100,000 units/yr.) + $400,000/yr.](2 yrs.)	= 1.54
	Yrs. 3–5 [($3.70/unit)(200,000 units/yr.) + $800,000/yr.](3 yrs.)	= 4.62
		6.16

Endpoint Number	Gross Profit ($000,000)
8	3.072
9	0.706
10	1.84

Gross Profit ($000,000)	Probability	Expected Value of Gross Profit ($000,000)
3.072	.4	1.2288
4.35	.6	2.61
		3.8388

Moving backward through the tree, calculate the expected value of node B. To do that, the organization must choose between building another small facility, which has an expected gross profit of $1,386,400, and not building another small facility, which has an expected gross profit of $1,150,000. Because the organization can choose, it selects the build option, which has a higher expected gross profit. The expected gross profit of the selected option is written under the decision box. Now the expected value of node B, which is the small facility option, can be calculated.

Gross Profit ($000,000)	Probability	Expected Value of Gross Profit ($000,000)
1.3864	.3	.41592
1.15	.5	.575
(.425)	.2	(.085)
		.90592

The expected value of node A, which is the large facility option, is calculated here.

Gross Profit ($000,000)	Probability	Expected Value of Gross Profit ($000,000)
3.8388	.3	1.15164
.8	.5	.4
(.975)	.2	(.195)
		1.35664

The model indicates that the large facility option has a higher expected value.

The model described in the extended example above still does not include all conditions. It would be reasonable to assume that more than three demand points or more than two facility sizes are possible. A more sophisticated model could be built with a computer program to consider many more possibilities and could be expanded to include present-value concepts.

Modeling with decision trees is not limited to capacity problems. Decision trees can be applied to any problem that has decisions, outcomes, and probabilities. There are applications in production, marketing, finance, and other areas of business. There are also applications for decision trees in engineering, education, medicine, politics, and a number of other areas.

The Role of Computers in Modeling

Computer packages used in modeling on mainframes have been available for many years. Most companies and universities have such packages available. Recently, reasonably priced packages have also been developed for microcomputers. Their statistical capabilities are quite good, and they can handle large problems because of expanded memory and disk space capabilities.

Where to Add Capacity

The decision of where to add capacity (usually called the location decision) is addressed in Chapter 6. The location decision is complex and involves many factors, which are discussed in that chapter. This decision is strategically important because it commits significant resources to a location. Great care and consideration should be given to the long-term implications of this decision.

What Type of Capacity to Add

In addition to determining how much capacity to add and when to add it, management should consider what type of capacity to add. Type of capacity can be separated into a technological or engineering question and an economies-of-scale or business question. The technological question is process oriented and is discussed in Chapter 4 on new product development.

The economies-of-scale question is a direct link among demand, capacity, and process selection. When demand exists for a product, the capacity will be supplied by one or more firms as long as the price customers are willing to pay is sufficient to cover costs and provide a reasonable profit. In order to have a large demand, a product should be affordable to a large percentage of the potential customers. This, in turn, forces producers to find economical methods of providing those services and goods. The result is a tendency to substitute capital and equipment for people in order to reduce costs and improve quality level.

The choice of mass production, a method involving high fixed costs, should be made whenever technology provides a means of production that brings the price of the product within the price range of many potential customers. It is no longer a matter of choice to produce automobiles by skilled craftspeople working

INTEGRATING THE SYSTEM

Capacity Decisions Influence Production Planning, Marketing, and Finance Decisions

Capacity decisions are key inputs to production planning, marketing, and finance. Capacity decisions determine the amount and type of facilities and equipment that an organization has. Production planning, which is discussed in Section II, examines how an organization uses its facilities and equipment to meet anticipated demand for its products. In production planning, a forecast of demand may indicate that demand is growing, and that present facilities will not be able to satisfy demand in two years. This discovery will trigger consideration of new production facilities and a re-examination of capacity decisions.

When an organization makes a capacity decision, that decision can directly affect marketing performance. Having the proper amount of capacity and the appropriate mix of capacity helps marketing satisfy customer demand. Capacity decisions influence and are influenced by financial decisions. Financial analysis should be performed on the investment to determine if the organization will receive an adequate return on its investment. Also, the organization needs to raise capital to support these investments. Capacity decisions are important to the organization's success.

with hand tools. Without specialized machines to help, the work force cannot produce enough cars or produce them at a price that most people can afford. These and other related concepts are the focus of Chapter 7, which covers process selection.

SUMMARY

- Capacity is a measure of the organization's ability to provide customers with the demanded services and goods in the amount requested and in a timely manner.
- Capacity decisions are critical to the organization's success because they commit significant resources to assets that usually cannot be changed easily or economically. Capacity decisions should be based on the best estimate of the future and should be made so that as much flexibility as possible is retained.
- Capacity should also be obtained in the proper amount. Too much capacity means that money has been invested in resources that are not really needed. Too little means that potential sales and market share are escaping.
- Estimating an organization's capacity is not easy because capacity is affected by management decisions regarding changing the number of hours worked, changing the product mix, adding staff, improving worker motivation, improving machine capabilities, enhancing quality, and increasing product yield.
- Machine and departmental capacities are needed to determine the capacity of a system. A system can go only as fast as its slowest part, which is the bottleneck.
- Increases in system capacity can be achieved by increasing capacity in the bottleneck department. This is called rounding out capacity.
- Capacity decisions include the following: when to add capacity, how much capacity to add, where to add capacity, and what type of capacity to add.

CAREER PROFILE

Mitchell A. Niemiec
General Plant Manager
Capitol Plastics

Capitol Plastics is an injection-molding operation that employs over 300 people. It produces parts twenty-four hours a day, seven days a week. Capitol is a major supplier of plastic parts to Honda of America and Chrysler Corporation. Mitchell Niemiec is responsible for all manufacturing operations for Capitol, including maintenance, purchasing, production control, shipping, receiving, and warehousing.

Meeting Customer Demand

In order to deal with rapidly increasing demand, Niemiec has recently expanded operation from a five-day, three-shift schedule to its present seven-day schedule. The resulting increase in capacity was not enough to meet the increased demand, so more equipment is being purchased and underutilized areas of the plant are being converted to production.

Education and Experience

Niemiec has earned B.B.A. and M.B.A. degrees. While working on his M.B.A., he took courses in operations management. Prior to his position as plant manager, he held positions as a production expediter, foreman, plant superintendent, and production control manager with Capitol.

SOLVED PROBLEMS

1. Wade Chemical Company has a problem with its flow process. Analyze the following diagram and table:

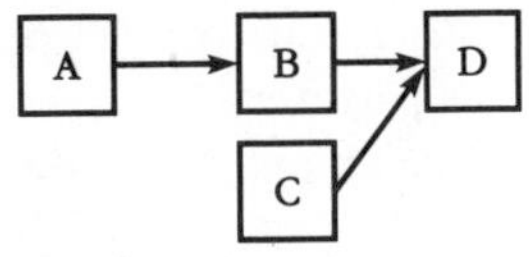

Department	Capacity (Gallons per Hour)
A	100
B	70
C	50
D	120

The ratio for mixing the outputs from departments B and C is two to one. This means that getting three gallons of input to department D requires mixing two gallons of B's output and one gallon of C's output.

a. What is the system's capacity, and which department is the bottleneck?

Solution

Department A can deliver 100 gallons per hour (gph) to department B, which can only use 70 gph, so department A cannot be the bottleneck. Departments B and C combine their inputs to D in a ratio of two to one. If B has only 70 gph to offer, then only 35 gph of C can be used. So far, department B restricts the capacity. To department D will flow 105 gph (70 from B plus 35 from C). Department D has sufficient capacity to process 120 gph. As a result, the system capacity is 105 gph, and department B is the bottleneck.

b. How much slack (unused capacity) is available in the other departments?

Solution

Department	Capacity (gph)	Production Volume to Make 105 gph	Unused Capacity (gph)
A	100	70	30
B	70	70	0
C	50	35	15
D	120	105	15

The production volumes were calculated in part a of this problem. Start at the bottleneck, and work backward to the beginning of the process. How many gph are needed from A to allow B to make 70 gph? Because no other department inputs to B, all 70 gph must come from A. Now work from the bottleneck to the end of the process. Department C must produce 35 gph to get the total gph needed by D. Department D must process 105 gph.

c. How much system capacity can be gained by adding capacity to the bottleneck?

Solution

Allow the capacity of department B to be unlimited, and rework parts a and b of this problem. Now department A can pass on 100 gph. Department B can process all 100 gallons and combine them with Department C's output of 50 gph to deliver a total of 150 gph to department D. Department D can only process 120 gph, so the system capacity is now 120 gph and D is the bottleneck.

Department	Capacity	Production Volume to Make 120 gph	Unused Capacity
A	100	80	20
B	infinite	80	—
C	50	40	10
D	120	120	0

The capacity of department B had to be increased from 70 to 80 gph to achieve the 15 gph increase in system capacity.

2. Bo Schimmer, material manager, is trying to determine if his company should purchase a certain part or produce it in-house. If purchased, it will cost $8 per unit. The company can make it for $5 per unit with a fixed cost of $7,500 on a high-speed machine. Or it can make it using limited automation at a variable cost of $6 per unit with a fixed cost of $4,000. Which alternative should Bo select?

Units Demanded	Probability
7,000	.15
8,000	.45
9,000	.40

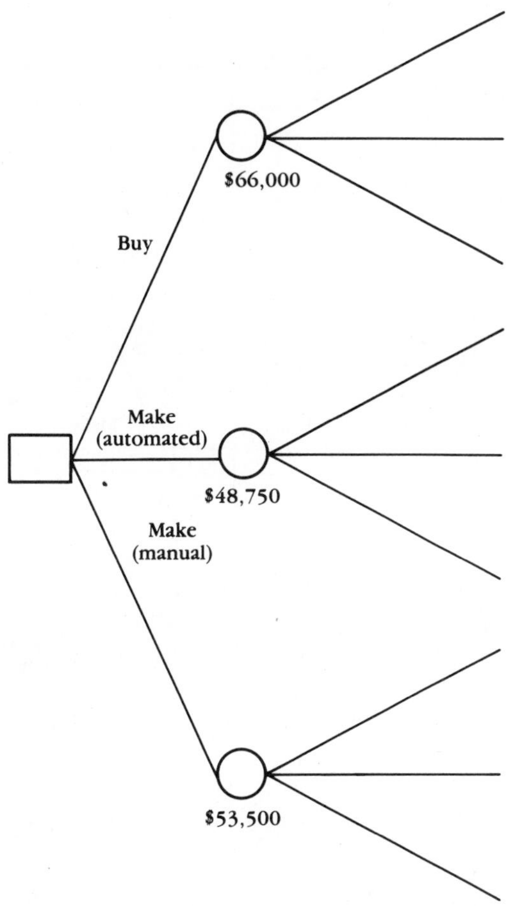

The previous decision tree shows the three alternatives: buy, make using automation, and make with limited automation (manual). For each decision, there are three possible outcomes. The amount required in production and the probability of each outcome are shown in that decision tree.

Sample endpoints are as follows:

Decision	Outcome	Cost Calculation
Buy	Sales = 7,000	\$8/unit × 7,000 units = \$56,000
Make (automated)	Sales = 8,000	(\$5/unit × 8,000 units) + \$7,500 = \$47,500
Make (manual)	Sales = 7,000	(\$6/unit × 7,000 units) + \$4,000 = \$46,000

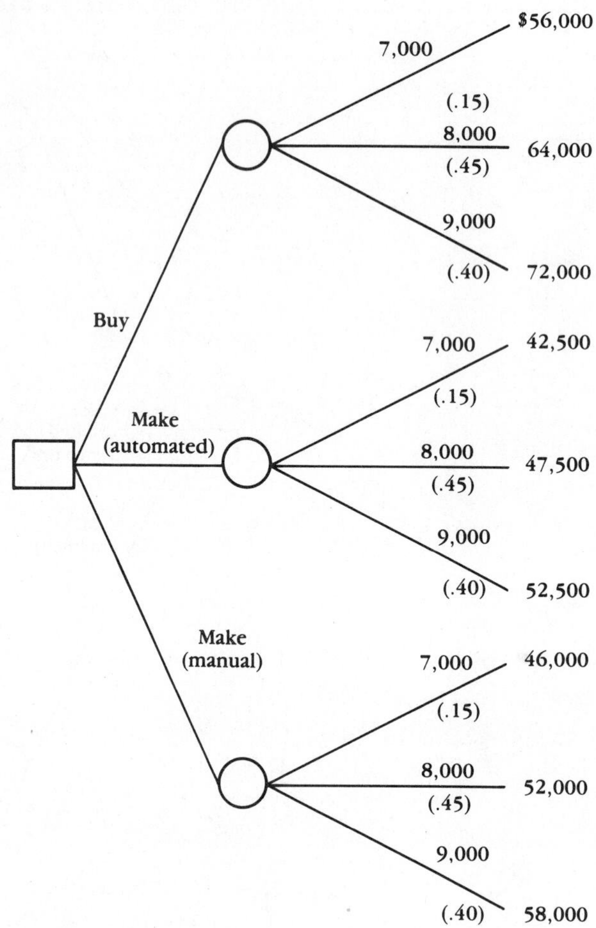

The expected value of the outcomes is calculated for each alternative and shown on the decision tree.

Alternative	Expected Value of Cost
Buy	($56,000 × .15) + ($64,000 × .45) + ($72,000 × .4) = $66,000
Make (automated)	($42,500 × .15) + ($47,500 × .45) + ($52,500 × .4) = $48,750
Make (manual)	($46,000 × .15) + ($52,000 × .45) + ($58,000 × .4) = $53,500

The make with automation alternative has the lowest expected value.

QUESTIONS

1. What is capacity, and why is it important?

2. Why is it difficult to estimate capacity? Isn't capacity a constant?

3. Should an organization always attempt to match its capacity to its estimate of demand? Why or why not?

4. Agree or disagree with the following statement, and support your position: "Capacity decisions are strategically important."

5. What factors influence the capacity of an organization? List any factors you can think of, and explain how they influence capacity.

6. Explain in detail the difference between departmental and system capacity.

7. What are the principles for determining system capacity in the product layout?

8. What are the principles for determining system capacity in the process layout?

9. How does a change in the product mix affect system capacity?

10. What are the important decisions for capacity planners?

11. What are the key factors in determining when to add capacity?

12. What are the key factors in determining how much capacity to add?

PROBLEMS

1. Determine the system capacity and the bottleneck department in the following line flow process. The capacities in pieces per hour for departments A, B, and C are 5,250, 4,650, and 5,300, respectively.

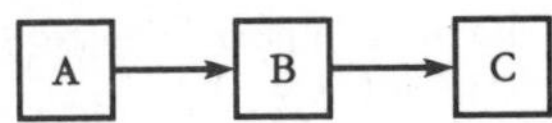

2. Determine the system capacity and the bottleneck department in the following line flow process. The capacities in tons per hour for departments A, B, C, and D are 2,200, 1,100, 1,600, and 2,500, respectively. For each ton of output from department B that is input to department D, two tons from department C must be added.

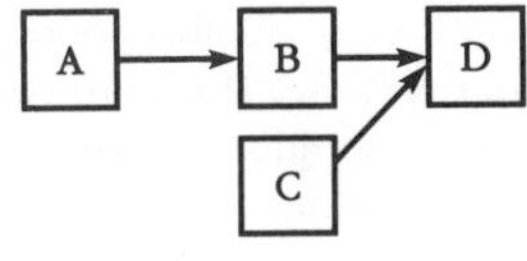

3. Answer the following questions using the information in problem 2:

   a. How much can the system capacity be increased by adding capacity to the bottleneck department?

   b. How much capacity must be added to the bottleneck department to achieve this increase in system capacity?

   c. Which department is the new bottleneck department?

4. Examine the following line flow process:

   a. Determine the system capacity.

   b. Determine which department is the bottleneck.

   c. Determine how much capacity can be gained by adding capacity to the bottleneck.

   d. Explain your answers to a, b, and c.

   e. How would the analysis change if department A achieved an 85 percent yield? Recalculate a, b, and c.

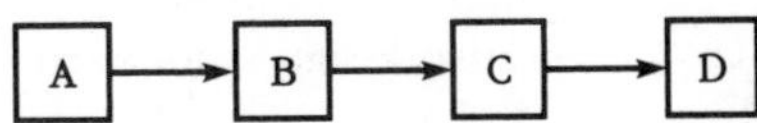

Department	Capacity (Parts/Hour)
A	120
B	110
C	140
D	160

5. Macro Galvanizing coats sheet steel for the appliance industry at its plant in Gary, Indiana. Macro has one production line that can coat steel up to 72 inches

wide. The production line runs 80 hours per week. Regardless of width, the steel is processed at 200 feet per minute. Macro processes only the three widths of steel listed below.

Width (in.)	Product Mix
36	.30
50	.25
60	.45

a. What is the capacity of Macro's production line in square feet of steel coated per week?
b. What is the capacity in square feet per week if the mix changes from .30, .25, and .45 to .40, .40, and .20?
c. What is the capacity in square feet per week if the mix does not change and Macro decides to use 10 percent overtime per week?
d. What is the capacity in square feet per week if the mix does not change, there is no overtime, and Macro experiences 5 percent unplanned downtime?
e. What is the capacity in square feet per week if the mix does not change, there is no overtime, and Macro's engineers find a way to run the line at 220 feet per minute?

6. Allen Bank and Trust processes checks at its Golden, California, Operations Center. The five steps in the process are listed here and must be done in the listed sequence. The listed capacity for each step is the total capacity for all work stations of that type.

Step	Capacity (Checks/Hour)	Number of Work Stations/Step
1	8,000	4
2	6,000	3
3	9,000	1
4	5,000	2
5	7,000	2

a. What is system capacity, and which is the bottleneck step?
b. What is the capacity per work station for each step?
c. How could Allen Bank and Trust increase its capacity to process checks to 6,000 checks per hour?
d. How could Allen Bank and Trust increase its capacity to 10,000 checks per hour?

7. Pacific, Plumber, and Placid Investment Company processes thousands of stock transactions each day at its headquarters in Peoria. Each transaction passes through four steps and must be processed in order. The steps are the same for all transactions except for step 3. In 50 percent of the cases, transactions are processed only by an over-the-counter (OTC) clerk, while the other 50 percent are processed only in the normal manner.

Step	Capacity (Transactions/Hour)	Number of Work Stations/Step
1	10,000	1
2	12,000	2
3	4,000	1
3(OTC)	4,000	1
4	9,000	3

a. What is the system capacity, and which is the bottleneck department?
b. What is the capacity per work station for each step?
c. How could PP&P increase the system capacity to 9,000 transactions, assuming that the OTC requirements remain at 50 percent of the transactions?
d. How could PP&P increase the system capacity to 15,000 transactions, assuming that the OTC requirement shifts to 75 percent of the transactions?

8. Monique Food Processing Company produces light snacks that can be heated in a microwave. The following steps are included in the process:

Steps	Description	Capacity (Units/Hour)
1	Prepare food	200
2	Measure and place in plastic pouch	175
3	Prepare cardboard box	200
4	Insert pouch into box	300
5	Shrink-wrap box	200

a. What is the system capacity, and which is the bottleneck department?
b. How much slack (unused capacity) is available in other departments?
c. How much system capacity can be gained by adding capacity to the bottleneck?

9. Botkins Bicycle Shop manufactures ten-speed bikes. The assembly process requires the components listed below. Botkins can assemble about 350 bicycles per week without overtime. The labor contract allows Botkins' management to add up to 10 percent overtime to assembly operations.

Component	Quantity per Finished Bicycle	Source	Capacity (Units/Week)
Wheels	2	Internal	750
Tires	2	External	900
Frame	1	Internal	400
Brakes	2	External	950

Component	Quantity per Finished Bicycle	Source	Capacity (Units/Week)
Handle bars	1	Internal	600
Pedal and drive sprocket subassembly	1	Internal	500

a. What is the capacity of the facility without using overtime? Which is the bottleneck department(s)?

b. What is the capacity of the facility with overtime? Which is the bottleneck department(s)?

c. What increases in department capacity would be required to increase system capacity to 450 units per week?

10. The Mills Brothers Cereal Company makes a wheat and raisin cereal on one of its production lines. One pound of raisins is required for four pounds of wheat flakes in order to make five pounds of cereal. The following steps are included in the process:

Step	Description	Capacity (Pounds/Hour)
A	Crush wheat	1,400
B	Form flakes	1,200
C	Toast flakes	1,600
D	Coat raisins	250
E	Mix cereal and raisins	1,200
F	Put mixture in box	1,100
G	Place boxes in shipping containers	1,400

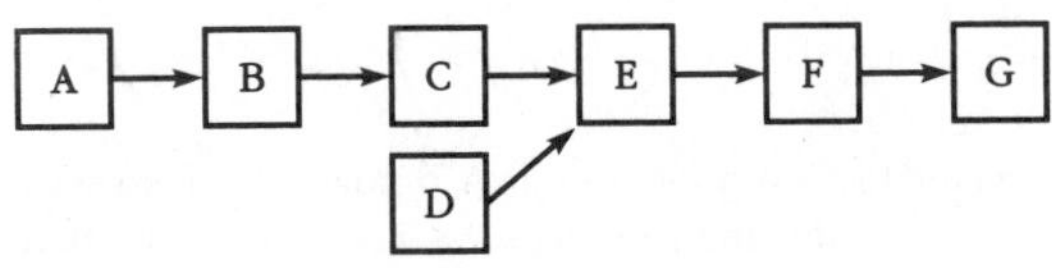

a. What is the system capacity, and which is the bottleneck department?

b. How much slack (unused capacity) is available in other departments?

c. How much system capacity can be gained by adding capacity to the bottleneck?

11. White Chemical has a problem with its operations. Analyze the following flow process:

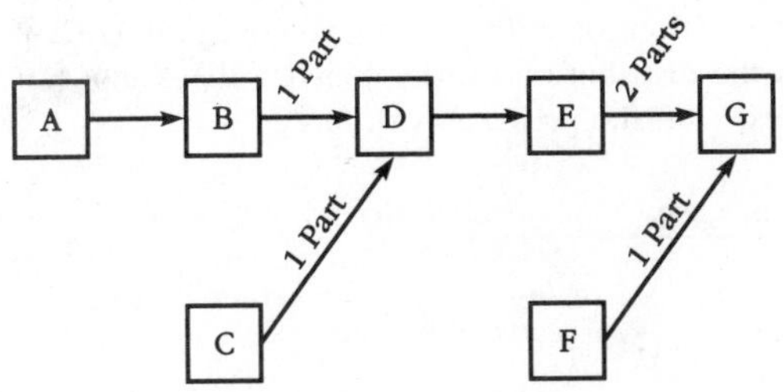

Department	Capacity (Gallons/ Hour)	Department	Capacity (Gallons/ Hour)
A	100	E	100
B	60	F	40
C	50	G	140
D	120		

The ratio for mixing the outputs from departments E and F is two to one. This means that getting three gallons out of G requires mixing two gallons of E's output and one gallon of F's output. The ratio for departments B and C is one to one.

a. What is the system's capacity?

b. Which department(s) is the bottleneck?

c. How much slack (unused capacity) is available in the other departments?

d. How much system capacity can be gained by adding capacity to the bottleneck?

12. Platinum Refining and Chemical Company is examining its pesticide plant. At this time, the company is unable to satisfy customer demand for a new insect spray. You have been asked to spend some time at the facility to determine how output can be increased. Analyze the following line flow process:

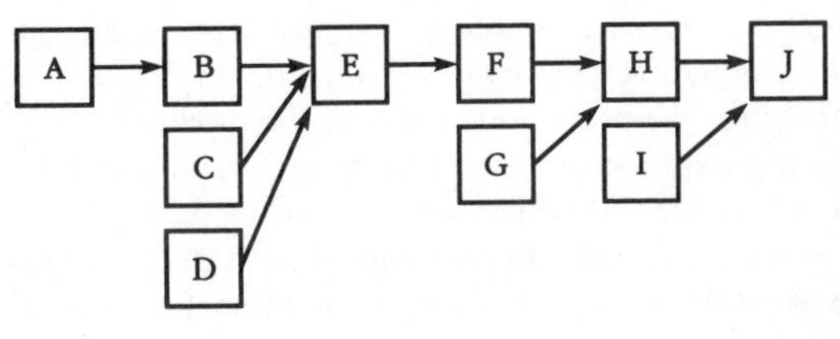

Department	Capacity (Gallons/ Hour)	Department	Capacity (Gallons/ Hour)
A	300	G	600
B	250	H	1,100
C	200	I	300
D	250	J	1,200
E	600		
F	550		

The ratio for mixing the outputs from departments B, C, and D is two to two to one, respectively. This means that getting five gallons out of department E requires mixing two gallons of B's output, two gallons of C's output, and one gallon of D's output. The ratio for departments F and G is one to one. The ratio for departments H and I is four to one.

a. What is the system capacity, and which is the bottleneck department?

b. How much slack (unused capacity) is available in other departments?

c. How much system capacity can be gained by adding capacity to the bottleneck?

13. Brutus Buck, material manager, is trying to determine if his company should purchase a certain part or produce it in-house. If purchased, it will cost $6 per unit. The company can make it for $3.50 per unit with a fixed cost of $9,000 on a high-speed machine. Or it can make it using less automation at a variable cost of $4.50 per unit with a fixed cost of $4,000. Which alternative should Brutus select?

Units Demanded	Probability of Demand
7,000	.30
8,000	.45
9,000	.25

14. O'Hara Software Company is considering expanding its networking portion of the business. Presently, the company has three networking staff members working at corporate headquarters. O'Hara is examining two options. The first would involve adding six new staff members and building a new facility at the present site. The annual cost of this option, including personnel, is $500,000. The second option involves adding twelve new staff members and building a larger facility at a new location. The annual cost of this option, including personnel, is $1,200,000. O'Hara is looking at the profit potential over the next five years. Management estimates that the present staff can handle up to $2,000,000 in sales over the five-year period, that six additional staff positions allow it to handle up to $6,000,000, and that twelve additional staff positions allow it to handle up to $10,000,000. What do you recommend?

Anticipated Demand over Five Years	Probability
2,000,000	.15
4,000,000	.25
6,000,000	.25
8,000,000	.25
10,000,000	.10

15. Markey Merchandising is considering opening a retail store in a mall in Marvee, Minnesota. If Markey builds a store, it will either be a full-line store or a mini-mart. The annual cost for a full-line store is $1,000,000, and the annual cost for a mini-mart is $500,000. Markey does not want to consider sales beyond three years. Gross profit in this case is revenue minus the cost of the merchandise sold. What do you recommend?

Anticipated Gross Profit for Mini-Mart for Three Years	Probability
1,200,000	.2
2,000,000	.4
4,000,000	.4

Anticipated Gross Profit for Full-Line Store for Three Years	Probability
2,000,000	.2
4,000,000	.3
6,000,000	.4
7,500,000	.1

16. Driveway Trucking is planning to increase capacity by purchasing new tractors for its over-the-road fleet. Driveway's management does not know how many tractors to add. Each additional tractor can make three trips per week on the average. Each trip generates $1,500 in revenue and incurs a variable cost of about $700. The annual cost to operate one truck including depreciation is $80,000. Following is the distribution of demand that cannot be satisfied with the existing fleet. How many trucks can Driveway profitably add to the fleet?

Trips per Week	Probability
2	.10
3	.15
4	.20
5	.25
6	.20
7	.10

17. Gandalf Computer Repair Company is faced with greater demand than its present work force can handle. It is considering how to expand service. One proposal would add four new repair persons. This would increase annual fixed operating costs by $100,000 for personnel and other related costs such as equipment. Three new service persons would require an additional $80,000 in annual fixed costs, and two would add $60,000.

The variable operating cost per trip would average $4.50, and the average revenue per trip is $45.00 regardless of adding four, three, or two people. On the average, each worker can make 3.5 trips per day. Base the calculations on 250 working days per year. Following is the distribution of trips per day that cannot be satisfied with the present work force:

Trips per Day	Probability
5	.02
6	.08

Trips per Day	Probability
7	.10
8	.12
9	.20
10	.20
11	.16
12	.10
13	.02
	1.00

a. How many people should be added to the work force to maximize the increase in earnings?

b. What factors should be considered in making the decision?

18. A manufacturer of microcomputers is considering three alternative plant sizes. Demand for its computers depends on the selling price, the manufacturing cost, and the facility size. Following is the distribution of demand:

Annual Demand	Probability Based on Selling Price per Microcomputer		
	$500	**$450**	**$425**
50,000	.6	.5	.3
60,000	.4	.5	.7

Estimates of operating costs for the three facility sizes are as follows:

Level of Plant Operation	Variable Manufacturing Costs per Unit		
Units of Output	**Small Facility**	**Medium Facility**	**Large Facility**
50,000	$ 350	$ 370	$ 400
60,000	—	300	200
(Annual fixed cost)	600,000	820,000	1,000,000

The small facility has a capacity of 50,000 units. The medium and large facilities have capacities that exceed 60,000 units. Which alternative is most attractive on the basis of annual net earnings?

19. Bambino's Bistro and Restaurant has been open for business for nearly three years, and business is better than ever. Management is contemplating another restaurant in a nearby suburb. Their plan is to build a restaurant to serve about 180 people per hour. The restaurant will have a game room, a bar area, and a dining area. From previous experience, management anticipates that 25 percent of the customers will come primarily for the game room, 20 percent for the bar, and 55 percent for dining. The average stay is 75 minutes per customer, and approximately 2.2 people arrive per car. Typically, very few people in the game room order dinner, 30 percent of the people in the bar order dinner, and 100 percent of the people in the dining area order dinner. Each meal prepared per hour requires 4.5 square feet of kitchen area. It is very difficult to push the occupancy for the bar above 90 percent and for the dining area above 90 percent because some parties of two or three are seated at tables for four. The 180 people per hour is the arrival rate.

a. How large should the parking area, bar area, game room, dining area, and kitchen area be to serve 180 people per hour?

b. What would happen to the capacities of the areas if the system capacity is to be increased by 10 percent?

20. Spencerville Products is expanding its operations west of the Mississippi. Its first step is to build a manufacturing facility in Denver to satisfy demand on the West Coast. Spencerville has an option to build either a large facility that has an annual output of 500,000 units per year or a smaller facility with an output of 300,000 units per year. The expected demand for the company's products is shown below.

Annual Demand (Units/Year)	Probability
450,000	.2
300,000	.5
200,000	.3

The company is evaluating the decision on a four-year time horizon. Demand in the first year is expected to hold for the other three years. Revenue per unit is $8.00. The small facility has a variable cost of $2.90/unit and a $350,000 fixed cost. The large facility has a variable cost of $1.80/unit and a $500,000 fixed cost.

a. What size facility should Spencerville Products build?

b. What are some of the assumptions of this model, and how might they change?

21. Suppose Spencerville Products, described in problem 20, has a potential competitor. There is a probability of 0.7 that the competitor will enter the West Coast market if demand is high. Also, if demand is high, and if Spencerville builds only a small facility initially, it may want to consider building another small facility. The competitor and Spencerville Products would not finish construction of the new facilities until the end of the second year. If the competitor builds a new facility, its share of the demand in the third year will be 25 percent, and in the fourth year, it will be 40 percent. What should Spencerville do?

MINI-CASES

Knupp Winery

Tom Knupp, the owner and manager of Knupp Winery, has seen the company grow significantly in the past several years. Demand for the product has continued to be strong, and the present facilities are not sufficient to keep pace with the projected growth. A recent market survey indicates that demand for the product will increase 20 percent next year, with a 0.3 probability. If it does not grow by 20 percent the first year, then the market is projected to grow at 10 and 2 percent with a 0.4 and a 0.3 probability, respectively.

Knupp could expand the facility this year by building a large addition or a small addition to capacity. If he chooses to make a large increase now, the combined first- and second-year profit growth potential would be as follows:

High Sales	Moderate Sales	Low Sales
$120,000	$10,000	$-80,000

If Knupp decides to expand with a small addition, the company would have the following increase in profit potential for the next two years:

High Sales	Moderate Sales	Low Sales
$40,000	$20,000	$-15,000

A simplified description of the process for making wine follows. The grapes are cleaned and prepared for the press operation which squeezes the juice from the grapes. The juice is strained to remove impurities and placed into large vats to ferment. After the appropriate time for aging has past, the wine is bottled and shipped to distributors.

1. Analyze the alternative for expanding Knupp Winery. (Hint: use a decision tree or table.)

2. Before Knupp makes a final decision to expand, he should consider other possibilities. What are some other ways to increase capacity? How might these be used?

3. Make a recommendation to Knupp, and support it.

Beck Manufacturing

Al Beck, president of Beck Manufacturing, wants to determine the capacity of his facility, which produces steering gears for auto manufacturers. He has asked you to sort through the data and determine the capacity of the system and how that capacity might be increased. The operation is a product layout that produces large numbers of nearly identical products. The process includes milling, grinding, boring, drilling, and assembling, in that order. Each finished product requires one operation on each type of machine. For example, each finished part is processed on one of the five milling machines, one of the seven grinding machines, etc.

The facility runs two eight-hour shifts per day, with a third shift for maintenance. The industrial engineering department has provided you with the following data on present operations. In addition, you have been told that assembly operations, while not unlimited, can be easily changed to meet the need.

Operation	Number of Machines	Run Time per Piece	Reject Rate
Milling	5	2 min.	3%
Grinding	7	3	5
Boring	3	1	2
Drilling	6	2.5	7

1. Calculate the capacity of each machine center and the capacity of the system.

2. If Beck wants to expand capacity, where should he focus the company's efforts? How much extra capacity can he get without causing another operation to become the bottleneck?

3. How might Mr. Beck expand capacity without purchasing new equipment? Be specific.

SELECTED BIBLIOGRAPHY

Freidenfelds, John. *Capacity Expansion: Analysis of Simple Models with Applications*. New York: Elsevier North-Holland, 1981.

Griffin, James M. *Capacity Measurement in Petroleum Refining*. Lexington, Mass.: Heath Lexington Books, 1971.

Morris, William T. *The Capacity Decision System*. Homewood, Ill.: Irwin, 1967.

Sasser, W. Earl; Olsen, R. Paul; and Wyckoff, D. Daryl. *Management of Service Operations: Text, Cases, and Readings*. Boston: Allyn and Bacon, 1978.

Skinner, Wickham. ''The Focused Factory.'' *Harvard Business Review*, 62, no. 3 (May–June 1974): 113–121.

Tompkins, James A., and White, John A. *Facility Planning*. New York: Wiley, 1988.

Vollmann, Thomas E.; Berry, William L.; and Whybark, D. Clay. *Manufacturing Planning and Control Systems*. Homewood, Ill. Irwin, 1988.

Wemmerlov, Urban. ''A Note on Capacity Planning.'' *Production and Inventory Management*. 3rd Quarter, (1980): 85–89.

Chapter 6

Facility Location

CHAPTER OUTLINE

LEARNING OBJECTIVES

After completing this chapter, you should be able to

- Discuss location as a strategic decision.
- Discuss the quantitative and qualitative factors influencing the location decision.
- Integrate the qualitative factors with the quantitative factors in order to make effective location decisions.
- Analyze the spatial relationships involved in the location decision, using the load-distance method.
- Analyze transportation costs with the transportation problem.
- Describe how the location decision influences other operating decisions.
- Explain the international ramifications of the location decision.
- Discuss special implications of the location decision for service operations.

OPERATIONS IN ACTION

The Automotive Industry: Japanese Transplants Keep Growing

In 1982, in Marysville, Ohio, Honda Motor Company opened the doors to the first Japanese-owned facility to manufacture automobiles in the United States. (Honda also produces motorcycles in an adjacent facility.) Since that time, there have been two major additions to the facility, capacity has grown to 510,000 units per year, and Honda exports cars from Marysville to Tokyo. Honda's move to the United States was quickly followed by transplants from Nissan, Toyota, Mazda, Mitsubishi, Fuji and Isuzu, and Suzuki, bringing the total to ten such plants by 1990 with a total capacity of nearly 2.5 million units per year. What caused the Japanese to locate that much capacity in North America?

Initially, the Japanese were responding to pressure from U.S. auto makers and the UAW to build cars in North America, rather than relying 100 percent on imported cars. American auto makers felt that if the Japanese manufacturers were forced to pay UAW wages and accept work practices in the union contracts, a level playing field would be created, and U.S. producers could compete. American auto makers felt that poor quality and high absenteeism were part of doing business in this country. Seven of the ten transplants have avoided union contracts by locating in rural or semirural areas of the Midwest and by hiring first-generation factory workers. As a result, they have enjoyed lower health care costs, less costly pension benefits, and lower wage rates. These seven facilities have also avoided work rules that restrict productivity and increase the number of labor hours required to build a car.

The other three transplants are joint ventures with the Big Three U.S. auto makers and must accept the UAW as part of doing business. In each case, the joint venture has been very successful. The Japanese have been very particular about whom they select from the UAW work force, and they have negotiated much more flexible work rules with the UAW. With these advantages and with better management, transplants enjoy a $700 per vehicle cost advantage over the Big Three. In addition to this cost advantage, the transplants have better quality records than the Big Three's plants do. The Japanese are no longer being encouraged to locate here by U.S. manufacturers.

Why have the Japanese continued to locate facilities in North America, and why do they have plans to locate even more facilities here? One reason is the favorable dollar-yen exchange rate. With the yen buying more U.S. dollars, investments in this country are much cheaper than they were in the early 1980s. Locating facilities in the Midwest gave the Japanese credibility with the car-buying population in the Midwest. This is an area where the Japanese have not been as successful in attracting first-time buyers as they have been on the West or East Coast. It is much easier to explain that the Honda you purchased was made in Marysville or that the Camry you drive was produced in Georgetown, Kentucky. Also having facilities located in the United States allows the Japanese to be more responsive to customer needs and to reduce transportation costs. Finally, it certainly helps in the political arena.[1]

INTRODUCTION

Facility location is the placement of a facility with respect to customers, suppliers, and other facilities with which it interacts. Many of the principles and techniques used in locating a facility are the same whether an organization is selling fried chicken or groceries, is providing fire protection or health services, is storing electronic parts or food, or is making computer chips or paper. The managers locating a facility should consider the costs of operating at a location, including costs to acquire the land and build the facility, as well as costs for labor, taxes, and utilities. They should consider the convenience of a particular location for customers, as well as the cost to transport materials to the facility and move finished product from the facility. They should also consider access to banking, educational, and other activities that are important to the success of their organization. Many factors, both quantitative and qualitative, influence the location decision.

What often differs from one industry to another are the weights assigned to these various factors. The size of the weight assigned to a factor indicates its importance. By assigning different weights to different factors, the importance of one factor can be differentiated from that of another. For example, a primary factor in locating a fire station is its response time to the buildings in that fire district. Thus, response time should be assigned a large weight. In locating a restaurant, easy access by customers is more important than the cost to transport raw material to the facility. An organization producing solar cells may feel that it is very important to locate in an area close to a university or research park that specializes in silica science. Organizations that produce plywood, dimensional lumber, or paper need a readily available supply of wood, so they usually locate near timber resources. Managers of labor-intensive operations may feel that low labor cost is the critical factor that determines the location of their facility.

The location decision usually involves commitment of large capital investment that normally cannot be moved from one location to another. As a result, it should be viewed as a long-term, strategic decision because it has a major impact on the organization's ability to compete. The location decision should not be based solely on marketing issues, production factors, or transportation costs. Successful managers integrate the relevant factors and weigh them appropriately in order to make the best long-term decision for the organization.

This chapter also discusses the factors that affect the location decision, including quantitative and qualitative factors, and how these factors can be integrated. Over the past two decades, the breaking down of barriers between countries has greatly accelerated the investment in new facilities by foreign competitors. The implications of international competition for the location decision are discussed. Special consideration is given to the location decision for service operations.

LOCATION AS A STRATEGIC DECISION

In addition to the quantitative and qualitative factors that affect the location decision, an organization must recognize that location is a long-term commitment of resources. This long-term commitment should fit with the organization's overall strategy, which should be linked to the organization's existing and potential customer base. How should an organization respond as population shifts from the Northeast and the Great Lakes areas to the West and the South? What new opportunities are created by the expansion of the population base in the warmer climates? More air conditioners and swimming pools are obvious answers, and many others exist. As population shifts across the United States, the center of any market is likely to shift. Should an organization have a strategy that moves facilities to deal with long-term population shift?

OPERATIONS IN ACTION

Wal-Mart: Location Is a Key to Success

Samuel Walton, the founder of Wal-Mart, has built a very successful department-store chain that boasts more than 950 stores. Wal-Marts, for the most part, do not compete head to head with the large discount chain stores in major metropolitan areas. The Wal-Mart strategy is to locate stores offering high-quality products at discount prices in small towns. Here, its primary competitors are small independent stores; older, less-efficient chains like Western Auto and Gambles; and mail-order chains. Wal-Mart beats the small independents on price; the older, less-efficient chains on price, quality, and service; and the mail-order chains on immediate availability of merchandise. The location decision is an important part of the Wal-Mart strategy because it greatly reduces direct competition with the big-volume national discount stores and it forces direct competition with stores that are not prepared for Wal-Mart's larger and more efficiently run operations. The location decision is a key to success at Wal-Mart.

Looking to the future, Wal-Mart will expand by locating stores in regions that the company has not previously explored. It may also expand by placing stores in small cities. Walton may feel that his organization now has the experience and size to go head to head with the large discount chains.

Sometimes organizations develop marketing and operating strategies that have an impact on the location decision. We will discuss the regional facility strategy and the product facility strategy. The **regional facility strategy** means that each facility is assigned a market area and each facility produces a complete line of products for that area. This is often done when customer convenience and access are important, or when outbound transportation costs are very high. Fast-food restaurants, instant oil change operations, and branch banks are examples of operations located so as to provide maximum customer convenience and access. In fact, many customer-oriented service operations are located in this way. Bottle making, corrugated box production, and aluminum can making operations are examples of facilities that would be located by region to hold down outbound transportation costs. These products have high shipping costs because the finished products occupy a lot of space.

The **product facility strategy** means that one facility is responsible for producing one product or product line and shipping that product all over the country and around the world. This approach is popular when there are advantages to specialization and economies of scale, and when transportation costs are not prohibitive. The production of spark plugs and igniters for aircraft engines would be an example of a product facility strategy.

FACTORS AFFECTING THE LOCATION DECISION

Many factors affect the location decision. To discuss these in an organized manner, the factors are grouped into four subsections. The first subsection describes managing the quantitative factors, including the impact of location on cost, the rising importance of government incentives, the impact of location on revenue, and a way to analyze cost and revenue. The second subsection describes the quantitative factors and illustrates how these can be analyzed and then integrated with the qualitative factors. The third subsection explains ways to analyze the spatial relationships in the location decision. The last subsection discusses the effects of the location decision on other operating factors.

Managing the Quantitative Factors

Quantitative factors include the costs associated with facility construction, production, overhead, and transportation to and from the facility. Recently, state and local governments have offered incentives to attract and retain businesses and jobs. Such incentives include tax abatement, low-interest loans, help in cutting through red tape, low business taxes, and low rates for unemployment insurance and worker's compensation. Finally, the location can affect sales volume and selling price. The announcement of a new facility may initiate price cutting or other costly product promotion activities by existing competitors in the area.

OPERATIONS IN ACTION

Fort Wayne, Indiana: Making Itself an Attractive Location for Organizations

Fort Wayne, Indiana, has become increasingly attractive to organizations. For Fort Wayne, it has been a long road back from its low point in 1982, when declines in its manufacturing base pushed unemployment to 14.5 percent. Companies, led by International Harvester, closed facilities and eliminated thousands of high-paying jobs.

By 1986, Fort Wayne had an unemployment rate of 5.7 percent, which was 1.3 percent below the national average. A nearby truck assembly plant built by General Motors brought 3,500 additional jobs. General Electric and Magnavox have been convinced to expand, rather than cutting back operations and employment.

How has Fort Wayne been able to attract outsiders and convince existing companies to expand operations? The city possesses many features that make it a desirable location. It contains a pool of highly skilled and trained employees who have faced unemployment once and understand the need for companies to remain competitive. The city is located on Interstate 69 within a half-day's truck drive of much of the industrial United States. Because General Motors wanted to accommodate just-in-time deliveries from parts suppliers, Fort Wayne's location was one of several advantages that attracted it to the city.

In addition, the city has become an attractive place to work. A $4 million campaign for a new art museum was recently completed, and a $7 million campaign for the city's Fine Arts Foundation is under way. The city has a botanical garden, as well as a performing arts center designed by the late Louis Kahn. Furthermore, the city has a well-run government, parks full of flowers, a peaceful atmosphere, and attractive, reasonably priced housing.

Fort Wayne offers low-interest financing, tax abatement, grants, and job training. Indiana has generous tax abatement, minimal red tape, and a government that seeks out new business. Indiana also has the lowest insurance rates for worker's compensation and the lowest unemployment insurance taxes in the United States. Fort Wayne has put together a package that is very attractive to organizations considering the location decision.[2]

The Impact of Location on Costs

The location decision plays an important role in shaping the cost function. The total-cost equation is

$$TC = (VC)X + FC$$

where

TC = total cost

VC = variable cost per unit

X = the number of units produced

FC = fixed costs

Variable costs are affected by prevailing wage rates, material costs, utility rates, and transportation costs for incoming materials and outgoing finished products. Fixed costs are affected by construction and land costs and the cost of administration, all of which are likely to be lower in rural areas. There also may be tax incentives or other special considerations for a site.

To prepare cost estimates for a site, data are collected and analyzed. To illustrate, Exhibit 6.1 contains data for a site in Indianapolis, Indiana, for a facility

Exhibit 6.1 Data for Site in Indianapolis, Indiana

Variable Production Costs

	Type	Rate	Projected Usage
Labor	Welding Electrical General assembly	\$10.00/hr. \$12.00/hr. \$ 9.00/hr.	0.5 hrs./unit 0.3 hrs./unit 1.1 hrs./unit
Material	Sheet metal Threaded fasteners Electrical wire	\$.40/lb. \$2.00/100 \$.06/lineal ft.	100 lbs./unit 20/unit 70 lineal ft./unit
Utilities	Natural gas Electricity	\$4.00/1,000 cu. ft. \$.06/kilowatt hr.	500 cu. ft./unit 200 kilowatt hrs./unit
Transportation	In rail Motor carrier Motor carrier Out motor carrier	\$.03/lb. (sheet metal)* \$.04/lb. (fasteners) \$.04/lb. (wire) \$20/unit (finished)	100 lbs./unit 5 lbs./unit 4 lbs./unit 4 lbs./unit 1
Facility Overhead			\$2,100,000
Initial Investment	Land acquisition costs Building construction Plant start-up costs Initial employee training		\$175,000,000
Special Considerations	Tax abatement Low-interest loans Supplementary training expenses		\$25,000,000

*Rates are given from a specific origin to a specific destination, so distance has been accounted for.

to build computer control panels. These data can be used to prepare a pro forma operating budget.

Exhibit 6.1 contains projected labor, material, and utility usage in addition to the rates. Labor usage can be estimated with techniques that are described in Chapter 9, which discusses job design and work measurement. Projected material usage is derived from the bill of materials described in Chapter 4, which discusses product design. Utilities may have both fixed and variable components. Some utility costs are variable and directly linked to producing a product, such as the power required to run a drill press. In other cases, utility costs cannot be linked to a product. An example is the energy needed to heat a building. The amount of heat required is not related to the number of units produced. Exhibit 6.1 shows variable utility costs. The fixed component of utilities is included in overhead expense.

Transportation costs are a function of the quantity of materials shipped, the distance traveled, and the type of carrier used. Price quotes are usually easy to obtain.

Exhibit 6.1 also lists as a lump sum an estimate of facility overhead expenses, such as supervisors, material handling, and plant management staff. The value of the investments in the facility and the value of any special considerations are also listed as lump sums. The special considerations figure is shown as a savings that should be deducted from the initial investment.

Exhibit 6.2 shows a pro forma operating budget based on producing 45,000 units/year for the site described in Exhibit 6.1. An operating budget usually does not include capital costs for facilities.

Exhibit 6.2 Pro Forma Operating Budget for One Year (Based on Estimated Sales of 45,000 Units)

Labor		
Welding	($10.00/hr.)(.5 hrs./unit)(45,000 units)	$225,000
Electric	($12.00/hr.)(.3 hrs./unit)(45,000 units)	162,000
Assembly	($9.00/hr.)(1.1 hrs./unit)(45,000 units)	445,500
Total labor costs		$832,500
Material		
Sheet metal	($.40/lb.)(100 lbs./unit)(45,000 units)	$1,800,000
Fasteners	($2.00/100)(20/unit)(45,000 units)	18,000
Wire	($.06/lin.ft.)(70 lin.ft.)(45,000 units)	189,000
Total material costs		$2,007,000
Utilities		
Natural gas	($4.00/1,000 cu./ft.)(500 cu./ft./unit)(45,000 units)	$ 90,000
Electricity	($.06/kwh)(200 kwh/unit)(45,000 units)	540,000
Total utility costs		$630,000
Transportation		
Sheet metal	($.03/lb.)(100 lb./unit)(45,000 units)	$135,000
Fasteners	($.04/lb.)(5 lb./unit)(45,000 units)	9,000
Wire	($.04/lb.)(4 lb./unit)(45,000 units)	7,200
Finished product	($20.00/unit)(45,000 units)	900,000
Total transportation costs		$1,051,200
Variable costs		$4,520,700
Facility overhead*		2,100,000
Grand total		$6,620,700

*Some overhead costs can be variable, but to simplify the discussion in this case, we will assume all overhead costs are fixed.

The costs of making products at this facility can now be estimated. Considering only the variable costs, we can calculate the unit variable cost as follows:

$$\text{Unit variable cost} = \frac{\$4,520,700}{45,000 \text{ units}}$$
$$= \$100.46/\text{unit}$$

The cost including a share of the annual facility overhead is

$$\text{Cost with overhead} = \frac{\$6,620,700}{45,000 \text{ units}}$$
$$= \$147.13/\text{unit}$$

The Rising Importance of Government Incentives

As discussed in the Operations in Action earlier in this chapter, the city of Fort Wayne and the state of Indiana have offered substantial incentives to entice businesses to locate there. These efforts are not limited to Indiana and Fort Wayne. Many states have been very aggressive in their efforts to attract new businesses.

One incentive offered by state and local governments is a significant reduction in property taxes. They have also offered low-interest loans, provided paid free training to work forces, and subsidized wages for some period of time. In addition, many states and cities have established agencies that can help private industry slice through governmental red tape. In some cases, they have put together parcels of land by using their powers of eminent domain. Simply stated, eminent domain means that an owner can be forced to sell property to the government at fair market value if it will be used for the good of all. Once obtained, properties are sold to private industry for development.

Governments can acquire property more quickly and less expensively than private industry can. As soon as word leaks out that private industry is interested in developing an area, the land prices are sure to increase significantly. With the power of eminent domain, the government can avoid being held up by owners of key parcels.

In some cases, businesses that have been in the state for years are grumbling about the preferred treatment given to newcomers, and some states are beginning to wonder if the jobs created are worth the costs of the incentives. Even so, the bidding wars among the states for the jobs these new developments bring are likely to continue. The pressure on elected officials to create jobs in the short term seems to mask the long-term impact that this treatment might have on future revenues and expenses of the state.

The Impact of Location on Revenue

It is possible that a plant's location will influence the sales volume, as well as the selling price per unit of a product. The revenue function is

$$TR = (SP)X$$

where

TR = total revenue

SP = selling price per unit

X = the number of units sold

Any influence that location has on marketing efforts can affect sales volume. For example, if a location is selected that has a higher cost, then a higher selling price may be needed. This can affect the volume sold. A location that is convenient for customers can increase sales volume.

Suppose an organization announces plans to locate a facility in a region where a competitor already has a facility making the same product. The competitor may feel threatened by the move. Increased competition, leading to vigorous price cutting, may result. The foreign invasion into the U.S. car market has led to renewed efforts to improve quality and to lower prices. This threat has been amplified as foreign firms have located more and more automobile assembly plants in this country.

An Approach for Integrating Cost, Revenue, and Time

To make effective location decisions, management must organize the potential costs and revenues for each site in a way that allows them to be easily compared. The discussion here can only begin to define the important factors to consider in developing such a model. Let's begin by examining the cost data for the Indianapolis site, which is detailed in Exhibits 6.1 and 6.2, and for an alternative site in Lexington, Kentucky. The new facility is scheduled to produce 45,000 units per year. The costs and revenues for both sites are listed below. (The incentives are to be subtracted from the initial investment.)

	Indianapolis	Lexington
Variable costs	\$ 100.46/unit	\$ 95.77/unit
Annual overhead	\$ 2,100,000/year	\$ 1,900,000/year
Initial investment	\$175,000,000	\$168,000,000
Incentives	\$ 25,000,000	\$ 10,500,000

Comparing Costs Using the Same Time Period. We make several assumptions in this comparison: (1) revenue is not affected by either choice, (2) sales

INTEGRATING THE SYSTEM

The Location Decision Affects Marketing Performance

Serving the customer should be a primary concern in locating facilities. In some cases, the customer is best served if an organization takes advantage of low production costs or low transportation costs. In other cases, convenience is more important. In the location of service operations, such as food preparation and banking, customer convenience is a principal concern. A desirable location is usually a key to success in the fast-food business, and customers demand conveniently located branch banks.

The customer-convenience aspect of location is usually not as strong in the production of goods. Even so, for many years, producers of bottles and cans have located close to large breweries to add to their customers' convenience and to reduce transportation costs. Convenience and timely deliveries are becoming more important to industrial customers, as is clearly shown by the increased application of just-in-time. The trend may be to locate close to customers in order to increase the reliability of that link. The case of GM and its Fort Wayne plant is certainly one example.

volume per year, selling price, unit variable costs, and fixed costs do not change over the period in question, and (3) the time value of money is ignored. After this simple model is constructed, each of these assumptions will be relaxed to determine their effect on the model.

Example

We can compare the costs of the Indianapolis and Lexington sites over a five-year period, using the total-cost equation. (The subscript I stands for Indianapolis and the subscript L for Lexington.)

$$TC = (VC)X + FC$$

$$\begin{aligned} TC_I &= (\$100.46/\text{unit})(45{,}000\ \text{units/year})(5\ \text{years}) + \\ &\quad (\$2{,}100{,}000/\text{year})(5\ \text{years}) + \$175{,}000{,}000 - \$25{,}000{,}000 \\ &= \$22{,}603{,}500 + \$10{,}500{,}000 + \$150{,}000{,}000 \\ &= \$183{,}103{,}500 \end{aligned}$$

$$\begin{aligned} TC_L &= (\$95.77/\text{unit})(45{,}000\ \text{units/year})(5\ \text{years}) + \\ &\quad (\$1{,}900{,}000/\text{year})(5\ \text{years}) + \$168{,}000{,}000 - \$10{,}500{,}000 \end{aligned}$$

$$TC_L = \$21{,}548{,}250 + \$9{,}500{,}000 + \$157{,}500{,}000$$

$$TC_L = \$188{,}548{,}250$$

Over a five-year period, Indianapolis has a lower total cost.

At what point in time will the costs of these two sites be equal? In this case, X will represent the number of years until costs are equal. This may be a very useful piece of information for managers in choosing between the alternatives.

$$TC_I = TC_L$$

$$\begin{aligned} &(100.46)(45{,}000)X + 2{,}100{,}000X + 175{,}000{,}000 - 25{,}000{,}000 \\ &= (95.77)(45{,}000)X + 1{,}900{,}000X + 168{,}000{,}000 - 10{,}500{,}000 \end{aligned}$$

$$\begin{aligned} &\$4{,}520{,}700X + \$2{,}100{,}000X + \$150{,}000{,}000 \\ &= \$4{,}309{,}650X + \$1{,}900{,}000X + \$157{,}500{,}000 \end{aligned}$$

$$\$6{,}620{,}700X - \$6{,}209{,}650X = \$157{,}500{,}000 - \$150{,}000{,}000$$

$$\$411{,}050X = \$7{,}500{,}000$$

$$X = 18.25\ \text{years}$$

Check the answer by substituting the time X into the cost equations for Indianapolis and Lexington and seeing if the costs are equal.

If we allow the amount sold per year to vary, the point of equal costs could be viewed in a different way. In the model, the number of years could be a constant, and the number of units sold per year could become a variable. If we assume that the time period is set at five years, how many units must be sold each year if costs are equal? Here, the variable X represents the number of units sold each year.

$$TC_I = TC_L$$

$$(100.46)(X)5 + (2{,}100{,}000)5 + 175{,}000{,}000 - 25{,}000{,}000 = (95.77)(X)5$$
$$= (1{,}900{,}000)5 + 168{,}000{,}000 - 10{,}500{,}000$$

$$X = 277{,}186 \text{ units/year}$$

Allowing Revenue to Be a Variable. What happens if revenue is affected by the choice of a site? This means that the sales volume and/or the selling price could be different. In order to include these possible changes, the model must compare profits rather than costs. In addition to varying the number of units sold per year and the number of years, management can vary the selling price to see the impact that it has on profits. Because of the added complexity of the model, computers are useful. Managers could write a computer program that allows them to calculate profits under a variety of circumstances, or they could use one of the popular spreadsheet programs to lay out several alternatives quickly. Probabilities could be assigned to alternatives, and expected values could be calculated.

Applying the Time-Value-of-Money Concept. Enhancing the model to include the time value of money forces managers to separate costs and revenue by period. Then they must apply the appropriate discount factors to make current and future expenses and revenue comparable in terms of today's dollars. To accomplish this, a computer program or a spreadsheet program is needed.

We will not explain the details of discounting expenses and revenues here. However, a word of caution is appropriate. In many cases, the simple approaches described in this chapter may be all that is necessary. It is possible that differences in revenue are not significant or that one site is clearly superior to another. There are significant costs in developing and testing a sophisticated model, so you should be sure there is something to gain by doing it.

Including the Qualitative Factors

Qualitative factors are also affected by the location decision. Although their direct impact on profits is usually not measurable, these factors need to be carefully considered and integrated into the decision by management. The appendix at the end of the chapter contains a list of many of the qualitative factors that could be considered.

To integrate qualitative factors into the location decision, managers should

1. Decide which factors are relevant to the problem.
2. Weight each of the factors—several factors may be relevant, but some might be far more important than others.
3. Evaluate each site so that rational comparisons can be made.

Unless a manager makes a judgment about the importance of each factor, all the factors are assumed to have equal weights. These weights are usually selected prior to determining the rankings or raw scores so that the weights are not biased by the scores. The weights are multiplied by the scores to determine the weighted scores. Then the weighted scores are added to determine total scores.

Example

Let us continue the Indianapolis and Lexington example. A committee has determined that the following factors are relevant to the decision. Indianapolis and Lexington are ranked on a scale of 1 to 10, with 10 being most desirable. The rankings are subjective estimates of some of the factors contained in the appendix at the end of this chapter.

	Weight	*Indianapolis* Raw Score	*Lexington* Raw Score
Recreational activities	20	8	7
University research facilities	40	8	8
Union activity	40	4	7
Banking services	80	7	6
Available labor pool	60	7	5

So the rankings can eventually be added, 10 must be considered "good" in all cases. For example, a 10 in university research activities is desirable and indicates high levels of research; a 10 in union activity is also desirable, but may indicate low levels of union activity.

Multiply the weight by the raw score for both Indianapolis and Lexington.

		Indianapolis		*Lexington*	
	Weight	Raw Score	Weighted Score	Raw Score	Weighted Score
Recreational activities	20	8	160	7	140
University research facilities	40	8	320	8	320
Union activities	40	4	160	7	280
Banking services	80	7	560	6	480
Available labor pool	60	7	420	5	300
Total			1,620		1,520

As long as the same weights are applied to each location, the weighted scores are comparable. The absolute value of each score does not have meaning, but comparing total scores is useful.

If Indianapolis is superior in terms of profits and investment, then the choice between the two is easy because Indianapolis also has a slight qualitative edge. If Indianapolis is not superior in profits and investment, then management should judge the impact of these qualitative factors on the long-term success of the organization. Even though a mathematical model can be used to analyze the data, the results still must be interpreted and a decision made.

Analyzing Spatial Relationships

In locating some facilities, convenient access by the customer or the ability to transport large quantities of material easily and quickly may be very important. For example, if an urgent care medical center is to be successful, it should be easily accessible by its customers. If a warehouse is to make daily deliveries to supermarkets in its region, it should be located so that deliveries are consistently on time and economical to make. In cases like these, management may want to analyze directly the distances that customers and materials move. We will investigate the load-distance method and the transportation problem.

The Load-Distance Method of Facility Location

The **load-distance method,** sometimes called the **center-of-gravity method,** can be used to measure the proximity of a proposed facility to its customers, suppliers, and other facilities with which it interacts. In the load-distance method, the locations of these customers, suppliers, and others are known. This makes it possible to calculate the distance part of the load-distance method. It is also reasonable to assume that the loads from the customers, suppliers, and others being served to the proposed facility are known. This is the load portion of the load-distance method. For example, if a city council is attempting to locate a new fire station, they would know the location of the buildings to be served and would attempt to locate the new fire station so that response time is minimized.

An effective way to measure distance is to use grid coordinates on a map or other to-scale drawing. Exhibit 6.3 illustrates the distance from a facility to a customer, d_i. The subscript i denotes the ith customer, and i varies from 1 to n where n is the total number of customers. That distance can be found by applying the Pythagorean theorem. The line d_i is the hypotenuse of a right triangle.

$$d_i^2 = \Delta x_i^2 + \Delta y_i^2 \tag{6.1}$$

$$d_i = \sqrt{(15 \text{ miles} - 3 \text{ miles})^2 + (9 \text{ miles} - 5 \text{ miles})^2}$$

$$= 12.65 \text{ miles}$$

Exhibit 6.3 Distance from Facility to Customer

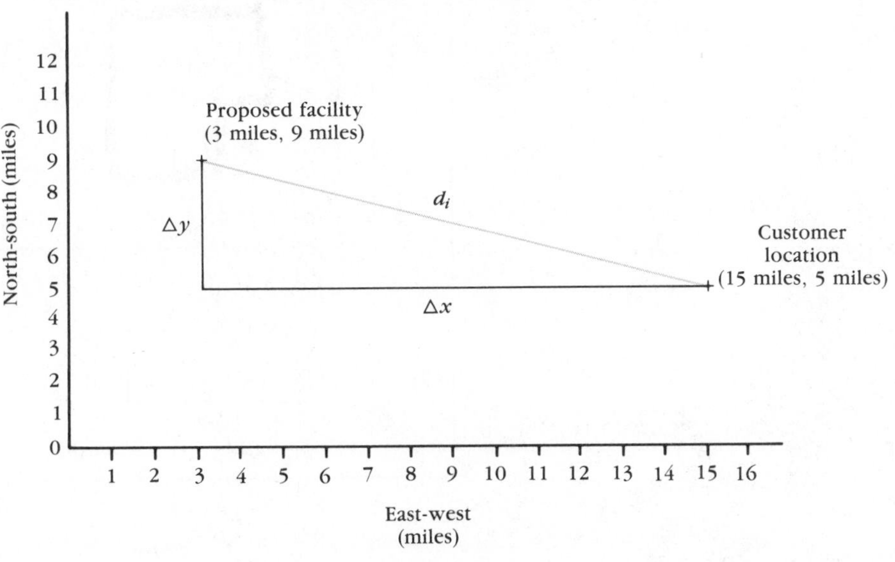

It is not necessary that these be the actual distances. It is only necessary that the distances be to scale. For example, if a map of the United States is used for this analysis, a ruler could be used to measure the distances in inches, or a grid could be marked off and the number of grid lines between two locations counted.

The activity or load between the two locations shown in Exhibit 6.3 would have to be estimated. For example, how many grocery items will be required at a particular supermarket, or how many potential patients for a new medical center are located in a particular suburb?

A new facility is likely to have many potential customers, and each customer has a distance and an activity level. To find an appropriate location for the facility, we will attempt to find a central location that will minimize the distance traveled by all customers of the new facility. This central location can be thought of as the center of gravity.

Example

City government is trying to locate a new health care unit to serve the needs of its residents. Exhibit 6.4 shows the zip code areas and the location of the center of each zip code area in the city on a north-south and east-west grid. These center points were determined visually. The distance between the blue grid lines is actually 0.5 mile, but we can use the grid numbers to estimate distance because

Exhibit 6.4 Health Care Unit Location Problem

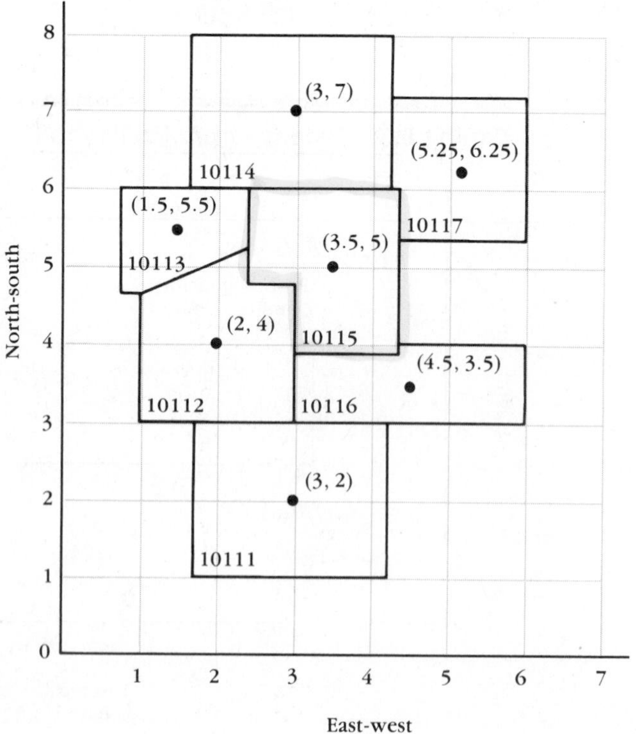

the map we are using is to scale. City planners have collected estimates of the population by zip code. The following table contains the population and coordinate information:

Zip Code	Population a_i	Coordinates x_i	y_i	$(a_i)(x_i)$	$(a_i)(y_i)$
10111	30,000	3	2	90,000	60,000
10112	25,000	2	4	50,000	100,000
10113	11,000	1.5	5.5	16,500	60,500
10114	8,000	3	7	24,000	56,000
10115	18,000	3.5	5	63,000	90,000
10116	24,000	4.5	3.5	108,000	84,000
10117	12,000	5.25	6.25	63,000	75,000
Total	128,000			414,500	525,500

To determine the location of the new facility, the coordinates are multiplied by the population. These multiplication products are then totaled. By doing the calculations in this way, we are assuming that the new facility is located at the origin. In the next step, we calculate an offset from the origin to take into account the population in each zip code.

The coordinates of the new facility location are determined by the following equations. This mathematical process has allowed us to calculate the center of the population—in other words, the center of gravity.

$$xf = \frac{\sum_{i=1}^{n} (a_i)(x_i)}{\sum_{i=1}^{n} (a_i)}$$

$$yf = \frac{\sum_{i=1}^{n} (a_i)(y_i)}{\sum_{i=1}^{n} (a_i)}$$

where

xf = distance along the x axis from the origin to the center of gravity

yf = distance along the y axis from the origin to the center of gravity

a_i = the activity level (load) from the ith location to the proposed facility

x_i = the coordinate on the x axis for the ith customer location

y_i = the coordinate on the y axis for the ith customer location

The coordinates of the center of gravity are

$$xf = \frac{414{,}500}{128{,}000} = 3.24 \qquad yf = \frac{525{,}500}{128{,}000} = 4.11$$

To locate the new facility in Exhibit 6.4 so that the load-distance is minimized, the new facility should be 3.24 grid lines west of the origin (the positive direction on the x axis) and 4.11 grid lines north of the origin (the positive direction on the y axis). This would place it in the southeast corner of zip code 10115.

The results of the load-distance method do not provide management with the answer to the location decision. The model provides additional information. Suppose that the location we just calculated is in a very expensive section of the city, and that locating the new health care unit one grid line to the east (one half of a mile) would significantly lower the cost of acquiring the land. Management should carefully weigh the benefits of moving the new health care unit from the "center of the population" against the extra cost for the land. The obvious considerations are how much less the land costs and how much customer inconvenience is caused if the unit is moved one grid line to the east. The difference in land cost can be obtained from a real estate agent. The level of inconvenience can be estimated with the following equation:

$$LD = \sum_{i=1}^{n} (a_i)(d_i)$$

where

LD = the total load-distance for any proposed location

d_i = the distance from a proposed location to the ith location being served, as determined by equation 6.1

The total load-distance can be calculated for the location that is the "center of the population." The load-distance can also be calculated for the location that is one grid line to the east. The difference between these two totals is an estimate of how much inconvenience is caused by moving the health care unit to the east.

The principles of the load-distance method can be applied to any problem where the decision involves locating a single facility with respect to two or more customers, suppliers, or other facilities. This concept is widely applicable to service and manufacturing operations. In fact, some of the ideas discussed here are applicable to the job shop layout question, which is discussed in Chapter 8.

The Transportation Problem

The transportation problem is concerned with the distribution of goods or services from sources to destinations. For example, an organization producing bicycle parts may have two manufacturing plants that ship parts to four regional warehouses or distribution centers. These centers, in turn, supply retail outlets. Analyzing the transportation problem helps management decide which plant should ship finished bicycle parts to which warehouse in order to minimize transportation costs. If the company is considering adding another production facility or warehouse, the transportation problem could be used to select among alternative locations.

Getting Started. To solve the transportation problem, managers need to know the capacity of the sources and the destinations, which in the bicycle example are plants and warehouses, respectively. They also need an estimate of the transportation cost between each source and destination. Once these data are available, a low-cost solution could be found using several techniques. Vogel's Approximation Method is described here because it can quickly generate good, feasible solutions. In many cases, these solutions may be optimal, but there is no guarantee that a solution is optimal. To be feasible, the total capacity of all the sources cannot be exceeded by the capacity of the destinations. The reverse is also true.

To get started, consider the following problem. Proton Consulting Service provides engineering advice to nuclear power plants that are under construction. The company has offices in San Francisco, Chicago, and St. Louis. The nuclear power plants that have contracts with Proton are located in Denver, Cleveland, Louisville, and Baltimore. Following are the annual capacities of the company offices and the needs of the power plants measured in person-days.

Proton Offices	Capacity (Person-Days)	Power Plant	Needs (Person-Days)
San Francisco	1,000	Denver	450
Chicago	750	Cleveland	600
St. Louis	500	Louisville	300
Total capacity	2,250	Baltimore	650
		Total needs	2,000

The average travel cost for each possible assignment is listed in the upper right-hand corner of each box in the transportation matrix shown in Exhibit 6.5. Because the total capacity of the sources is greater than the needs of the power plants, a dummy destination is added to absorb the excess capacity. The capacity of the dummy destination is equal to the difference between the capacities of the sources and the needs of the destinations. The transportation costs for the dummy destination are all set to zero.

Vogel's Approximation Method. Vogel's Approximation Method works by evaluating the differences in transportation costs. The modeler examines each row and column of the transportation matrix in Exhibit 6.4 and calculates the difference between the lowest cost cell in a particular row or column and the second lowest cost cell in the same row or column. For example, in the Denver column, the lowest is $90 per day, and the second lowest is $95 per day, for a difference of $5. This would be repeated for all rows and columns; the results are displayed in Exhibit 6.6.

Exhibit 6.5 Transportation Matrix for Proton Consulting Service

	Destination					
Source	Denver	Cleveland	Louisville	Baltimore	Dummy	Capacity
San Francisco	95	150	195	160	0	1,000
Chicago	90	85	100	145	0	750
St. Louis	115	100	80	130	0	500
Demand	450	600	300	650	250	2,250

Exhibit 6.6 First Assignment for Proton Consulting Service

	Destination						
Source	Denver	Cleveland	Louisville	Baltimore	Dummy	Capacity	Row penalty
San Francisco	95	150	195	160	0 250	1,000	95
Chicago	90	85	100	145	0	750	85
St. Louis	115	100	80	130	0	500	80
Demand	450	600	300	650	250	2,250	
Column Penalty	5	15	20	15	0		

A row or column with a large difference would be a high priority assignment because if the lowest cost cell in that row or column is not taken, then a much higher cost cell will have to be selected. On the other hand, a row or column with a small difference would be a low priority assignment because if the low cost cell is not taken, there is another cell with close to the same cost. In Exhibit 6.6, the largest penalty is for the San Francisco row, so we assign as much as possible to the cell in that row with the lowest cost. Because the dummy destination only needs 250 person-days and San Francisco can supply 1,000 person days, we can only allocate 250. Allocating more would violate the demand constraint and would unbalance capacity and demand.

Now that 250 person-days have been assigned to the dummy destination, that column can be eliminated from further consideration. As a result, Exhibit 6.7 has a dotted blue line through the dummy destination column. Changes between the transportation matrix in Exhibit 6.6 and the one in Exhibit 6.7 are highlighted in color. The capacity of San Francisco and the dummy demand have been reduced by 250 person-days. To ensure that this is done accurately, the new capacities and the new demands are added to see if they are still equal. The total, shown at the intersection of the capacity column and the demand row, is 2,000. Whenever a column is eliminated, the row penalties must be recalculated, and whenever a row is eliminated, the column penalties must be recalculated. Exhibit 6.7 shows the transportation matrix with the dummy column eliminated and the new row penalties. The largest penalty cost is still in the San Francisco row. The lowest cost cell in that row is San Francisco to Denver, so we allocate as much as possible to that cell, which is 450 person-days. We cannot exceed 450 person-days, or Denver will be over supplied.

We can now proceed to the next assignment, which is shown is Exhibit 6.8. The Denver column has been eliminated, and the row penalties have been recalculated. In this case, only two of the penalties changed. The capacity demand balance has been checked, and the remaining amount to be assigned is 1,550 person-days. When the row and column penalties are examined, there is a tie for the largest row or column penalty. The St. Louis row and the Louisville column

Exhibit 6.7 Second Assignment for Proton Consulting Service

Destination

Source	Denver	Cleveland	Louisville	Baltimore	Dummy	Capacity	Row penalty
San Francisco	[95] 450	[150]	[195]	[160]	[0] 250	750 ~~1,000~~	55 ~~95~~
Chicago	[90]	[85]	[100]	[145]	[0]	750	5 ~~85~~
St. Louis	[115]	[100]	[80]	[130]	[0]	500	20 ~~80~~
Demand	450	600	300	650	0 ~~250~~	2,000 ~~2,250~~	
Column Penalty	5	15	20	15	~~0~~		

Exhibit 6.8 Third Assignment for Proton Consulting Service

Destination

Source	Denver	Cleveland	Louisville	Baltimore	Dummy	Capacity	Row penalty
San Francisco	[95] 450	[150]	[195]	[160]	[0] 250	300 ~~750~~	10 ~~55~~
Chicago	[90]	[85]	[100]	[145]	[0]	750	15 ~~5~~
St. Louis	[115]	[100]	[80] 300	[130]	[0]	500	20
Demand	0 ~~450~~	600	300	650	0	1,550 ~~2,000~~	
Column Penalty	~~5~~	15	20	15			

both have 20. In the case of a tie, the modeler can pick one at random. We will use the Louisville column. The lowest cell in that column is St. Louis to Louisville, so we allocate as much as possible, which is 300 person-days. (In this particular case, we would have gotten the same result if we had selected the St. Louis row.)

The remaining assignments are listed here.

Assignment Number	Row by Column	Person-Days Assigned
4	Chicago to Cleveland	600
5	San Francisco to Baltimore	300
6	Chicago to Baltimore	150
7	St. Louis to Baltimore	200

Exhibit 6.9 Final Transportation Matrix for Proton Consulting Service

	Destination					
Source	Denver	Cleveland	Louisville	Baltimore	Dummy	Capacity
San Francisco	450 [95]	[150]	[195]	300 [160]	250 [0]	1,000
Chicago	[90]	600 [85]	[100]	150 [145]	[0]	750
St. Louis	[115]	[100]	300 [80]	200 [130]	[0]	500
Demand	450	600	300	650	250	2,250

The final transportation matrix is shown is Exhibit 6.9. The cost of the solution is \$213,500 and can be found by multiplying the assignment in each cell of the matrix by the corresponding transportation cost. Please note that the capacities and demands balance, and that there will be 250 person-days of idle capacity in San Francisco. Also, the solution generated by Vogel's Approximation Method is not necessarily an optimal solution.

The transportation problem can be formulated and solved as a linear programming problem to get an optimal solution. Other methods for finding optimal solutions are available. These can be found in management science books listed in the Selected Bibliography.

Analyzing New Facility Locations with the Transportation Problem. Any organization that is planning to add a new facility into its present operations can use the solution procedure described here to analyze the impact of the change on transportation costs. Suppose that Proton wanted to eliminate the San Francisco office and open a new office in Atlanta. To evaluate the impact of the new facility on transportation cost, management could do the following:

1. Evaluate the solution with San Francisco as an active office. That would be the problem that we just completed. The value of the solution can be obtained by multiplying the amount allocated to each cell by the transportation cost of that cell. It would be (450 person-days)(\$95/day) + (300)(160) + (250)(0) + (600)(85) + (150)(145) + (300)(80) + (200)(130) = \$213,500.
2. Remove San Francisco from the problem, and insert Atlanta with its capacity and transportation costs.
3. Solve the new problem using Vogel's Approximation Method, and evaluate the new solution.
4. Compare the solution with Atlanta in the problem to the solution with San-Francisco in the problem. This provides an estimate of the difference in transportation costs.

Role of the Computer in Analyzing Spatial Relationships

The problems that we have discussed in the text have been made small deliberately so that computations can be kept to a minimum. In many cases, location decisions involve many alternatives which would make calculation by hand tedious. There are ways that computers can be used to help with the analysis in both the load-distance method and the transportation problem.

In the load-distance method, a spreadsheet can be developed using Lotus 1–2–3 or similar package. The spreadsheet model would allow the user to multiply the population (load) by the coordinates for each location. These products could then be totaled and the center of the population calculated. Review the example problem in the load-distance section to see how this could help the modeler.

Many commercially available packages exist for solving the transportation problem. These packages use a variety of techniques to find a solution that minimizes transportation costs. The most common method used is the MODI (modified distribution) method. The MODI method is used in the STORM software to find a solution that minimizes transportation costs.

The Location Decision's Effect on Other Operating Factors

The location decision can have a significant impact on an organization's ability to compete. It can influence costs, selling price, demand, educational opportunities for employees and their families, and access to financial services. How can the location decision affect other factors in production?

Assume that demand for an organization's product exceeds present capacity. An organization can consider two options to increase capacity: the on-site option is to build additions to the existing plant, and the off-site option is to design and build a new plant. On-site expansion is more popular because it usually involves less capital investment. Many services, such as shipping, receiving, and administration, may not have to be expanded. Only the critical operations—that is, the bottlenecks—require capacity increases.

On the other hand, on-site expansion can create many problems, especially if it is a repeated practice. As more production space is added, material handling and storage become more difficult because inventory space is often converted to production. As new product variations are added, the once-simple product flow becomes complicated by twists, turns, and backtracking because plant additions often occur over many years and no long-term planning for future additions is made. When on-site expansion is used to add capacity, intraplant transportation and communication can become strained.

Staying at the same site often postpones the introduction of new product and process technologies. Old equipment and old production methods are used longer than they should be. Future product innovation, productivity increases, quality improvements, and cost reductions can be negatively affected. On-site expansion can mean a growing number of workers, products, and processes that need to be managed. Such layering of expanded responsibilities creates real complexities for managers at all levels.[3]

INTERNATIONAL DIMENSIONS OF THE LOCATION DECISION

In the past twenty years, the international dimensions of business and business operations have grown dramatically. Facility location is one of the most obvious results. As mentioned in the Operations in Action at the beginning of this chapter, ten Japanese automobile assembly plants were built in this country during the decade of the 1980s. A host of foreign suppliers has located manufacturing facilities in the United States. The British, the West Germans, the French, and the Japanese have invested heavily in this country. Organizations headquartered in the United States have major production facilities in other countries. This section discusses some of the reasons for locating facilities in foreign countries and ethical considerations in the locating of facilities in foreign countries.

Why Locate in a Foreign Country?

There appear to be several reasons why organizations decide to locate facilities in foreign countries. An organization may seek

1. Comparative advantage in the quantitative aspects of producing goods or services.
2. Closeness to a market that it serves.
3. Improved political relationships.
4. Resources that are scarce in the home country.

Comparative advantage appears to be one of the major advantages to locating facilities in foreign countries. Some countries have lower labor, utility, transportation, or material costs than others do. These advantages are sometimes short-term advantages that disappear after several companies have made major expenditures for new facilities. The law of supply and demand works in all countries, not just the United States. There may also be good reasons for the differential in costs. If labor costs are low in a particular country, perhaps the labor force is not very skilled, or perhaps the country has other disadvantages that offset the cost savings. In some industries, labor costs are less than 10 percent of total costs.

Organizations may locate in other countries to be close to their market. When a country exports a substantial amount of product to a particular country, locating a facility there may be appropriate. This allows the company to tailor products to the needs of customers in that country and to deliver products to customers quickly. It can also dramatically reduce the logistical problems and costs of moving products around the world.

There may be political advantages to locating a production facility in a country that accepts many imports from an organization. Job creation and contribution to the tax base are powerful political tools. This decision may also lower any trade deficit that exists between the two countries.

In some cases, countries actually have a shortage of labor or other resources in the home country. One possible solution is to import labor; the other is to build facilities in other countries. For example, one advantage that East Germany brings to the eventual reunification of East and West Germany is surplus labor.

Ethical Considerations in the Location Decision

Ethics should be a part of all business decision making. The decision to locate operations in another country brings special ethical problems. For example, in the United States, paying government officials "extra" money, a bribe, to speed up the processing of applications or to obtain favorable ruling is not only unethical, but also a criminal offense. In other countries, it is sometimes considered a

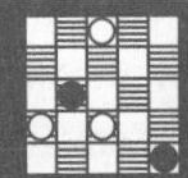

GAINING STRATEGIC ADVANTAGE WITH LOCATION

Is "Made in America" Back in Style?

In the 1970s and 1980s, many organizations in a wide variety of industries sought the low labor cost advantage of manufacturing in other countries from Mexico to the Far East and many places in between. This migration occurs now and is likely to continue. However, there are increasing signs that some organizations making location decisions are choosing the United States, and others that have moved operations offshore are bringing some of them home.

After years of relying on cheap labor in the Far East, clothing manufacturers are beginning to recognize the advantage of fast turnaround and delivery they can achieve by locating operations that serve the U.S. market in the United States. With at least three months between order and delivery when facilities are located in the Far East, apparel manufacturers require a large inventory. Sometimes this inventory becomes obsolete because of the changing nature of U.S. fashion. The lower value of the U.S. dollar versus other currencies makes U.S. wages lower and foreign wages higher in the world marketplace. Organizations are moving production to the United States to escape rising costs, avoid U.S. import quotas and tariffs, and get closer to their customers. Kurt Salmon Associates Inc., a prominent consultant to the apparel industry, states that reducing lead times is an important strategy for the 1990s.

The apparel industry is not the only one that has returned operations to the United States. When Lionel Trains shifted production of its model electric trains to Mexico in 1983, the company's idea was to capitalize on the country's low wage rate. Problems with the work force and delays in production kept Lionel from meeting customer demand. It gave up retail shelf space to its competition. In 1985, it reopened its plant in Mt. Clemens, Michigan.

In 1980, Tandy Corporation decided to manufacture its new line of color computers in South Korea. In the fall of 1987, Tandy moved production to its Ft. Worth facility. The reasons for the switch were rising shipping costs, a reluctance to tie up inventory on the long overseas trip, a change in currency valuation, and a redesign of the product to reduce the manual labor requirements in assembly. By making the switch, the company realized a cost savings of 7.5 percent.

These examples may not be enough to turn the tide on our balance of payments, but they do indicate that locating in the United States can be an attractive alternative.[4]

normal part of doing business. In the late 1970s, the United States passed laws designed to cope with what this country viewed as the unethical practice of bribery. However, these laws are not very clear. In response, some companies have decided to eliminate all "questionable payments," legal or illegal. Some of the companies have been surprised to find that their business has not fallen off as they expected. Their actions have been reinforced by a number of foreign governments that have passed stricter laws or have begun to enforce laws that are already on the books.

LOCATION ANALYSIS FOR SERVICE OPERATIONS

Location analysis for service operations has some differences from location analysis for manufacturing operations. In manufacturing, the decision process includes an analysis of distribution costs, using, for example, the transportation problem, and service delivery times, for which the load-distance approach can be used. In many service operations, on the other hand, product does not move to customers; customers move to the product. Thus, the location of service stations, restaurants, supermarkets, and retail outlets depends on concentrations of demand and the location of competition. The load-distance method discussed earlier may be useful in analyzing the location of service operations with respect to the potential client base.

To determine the potential client base that might use a proposed retail service facility, a manager may examine population, average income, number of competitors, traffic counts, and other information by census tract, zip code, or other classification. Public service facilities, such as post offices, schools, and welfare offices, should be located so as to be convenient to their client base. While public service organizations do not have the bottom-line, profit-driven motivation for providing convenient service, they should seek to provide the maximum benefit to the group they serve. Many times, cost-benefit analysis is used to make the location decision and other decisions for public institutions.

The location of emergency units, such as fire protection and ambulance service, is determined by minimizing response time, providing minimum coverage, and operating from a mobile location. Response time, the time from a request for service to the delivery of that service, is important when time is a critical factor. The objective is to locate a facility so that the maximum response time to any point served by the unit is minimized.

Minimum coverage implies that all customers have a minimum level of coverage. For example, no house in the city will be more than one mile from a fire station or an ambulance service. The number and placement of facilities required to provide minimum coverage can be determined by grouping customers into appropriate population centers and examining candidate facility locations to see if the minimum coverage is provided. This can be accomplished by listing the population centers in the columns of a table and listing the potential facility locations in the rows of the same table. Then each potential facility can be judged to determine if the minimum coverage is achieved. In many cases, more than one candidate facility may be required to provide that coverage.

With mobile locations, some units might be directed from place to place without returning to base. One good example of this is dispatching police cars. To deal with this problem, mobile units may be assigned a travel area. Simulation, which is discussed later in the text, is one tool that can be used to analyze this type of problem.

SUMMARY

- The facility location decision should not be based entirely on production factors and transportation. It is a long-term strategic decision that can have a major impact on the organization's ability to compete.
- Locating a facility can have strategic implications. Some organizations employ a regional facility approach where one facility is responsible for producing all the products for that area of the country. Others employ the product facility

strategy where one plant produces one product or product line and ships it all over the country.

- Both quantitative and qualitative factors influence the location decision. These factors should be integrated if the decision-making process is to work effectively.
- In locating some facilities, convenient access by the customer or the ability to transport large quantities of materials may be very important. The load-distance method and the transportation problem are two models that can be used to analyze spatial relationships.
- The location decision can have a significant impact on an organization's ability to compete. It can influence costs, selling price, demand, and access to financial services.
- Locating facilities in foreign countries has increased dramatically. Many of these organizations are attempting to gain some comparative advantages that one country may have or to be closer to their market. Others are relocating for political reasons or to remedy resource scarcity in the home country.
- Some service operations have to look at special considerations in making the location decision. The location of emergency units such as fire stations depends on response time, minimum coverage, and mobile location.

CAREER PROFILE

William Winkler

Deputy Fire Chief
Staffing and Operations

William Winkler is a deputy fire chief for staffing and operations and reports directly to the fire chief. The fire department for which he works is responsible for providing fire protection and prevention services for a rapidly growing metropolitan area.

Responsibilities

Winkler is responsible for planning the placement of new fire stations, closing obsolete stations, establishing the overall schedule for the work force, and hiring and training new firefighters. Winkler and his staff prepare an annual staffing plan that matches department needs with available firefighters. From this, he is able to determine if new recruits are needed, and he is able to budget for overtime, if necessary, to cope with the growing demand for fire protection. Each month, detailed schedules are developed.

As the metropolitan area grows, Winkler meets with his staff to plan the location of new fire stations. As the population migrates from the center to the outer edges of the city, existing fire stations that are less efficient may be closed. To maintain the city's good fire rating, response times to fires must be kept low. Insurance companies use these ratings to set the rates for fire insurance in the city.

Experience and Education

Before joining the fire department, he studied science for two years at the college level. Prior to holding the position of deputy fire chief, Winkler advanced through the ranks of the fire department. As he progressed through, he saw the need to finish his college education. He complete his liberal arts degree with a minor in business administration in 1978. He has attended many training courses in fire prevention, firefighting techniques, and administration. Winkler believes that continuing education is important for advancement in any field.

SOLVED PROBLEMS

1. Cappelli Venture Capital is planning a joint venture with Cervati Insurance to establish a clearinghouse for a new nationwide credit card. One of the necessary decisions is where to locate the facility. Information on two possible locations is listed below.

	Galveston, Texas	Boston, Massachusetts
Variable cost	\$.245/transaction	\$.270/transaction
Annual fixed costs	\$4,000,000	\$4,100,000
Initial investment	\$16,000,000	\$13,500,000

a. At a volume of 20 million units per year for a five-year period, which facility has the lower cost?

Solution

$$TC_G = (\$.245 \text{ trans.})(20{,}000{,}000 \text{ trans./yr.})(5 \text{ yrs.}) + (\$4{,}000{,}000/\text{yr.})(5 \text{ yrs.}) + \$16{,}000{,}000 = \$60{,}500{,}000$$

$$TC_B = (\$.270 \text{ trans.})(20{,}000{,}000 \text{ trans./yr.})(5 \text{ yrs.}) + (\$4{,}100{,}000/\text{yr.})(5 \text{ yrs.}) + \$13{,}500{,}000 = \$61{,}000{,}000$$

Galveston has the lower cost over a five-year period.

b. At what annual volume do these facilities have equal costs?

Solution

$$(\$.245/\text{trs})(X \text{ trans./yr.})(5 \text{ yrs.}) + (\$4{,}000{,}000/\text{yr.})(5 \text{ yrs.}) + \$16{,}000{,}000 = (\$.270/\text{trans.})(X \text{ trans./yr.})(5 \text{ yrs.}) + (\$4{,}100{,}000/\text{yr.})(5 \text{ yrs.}) + \$13{,}500{,}000$$

$$\$1.225X + \$36{,}000{,}000 = \$1.35X + \$34{,}000{,}000$$

$$(\$1.35 - \$1.225)X = \$2{,}000{,}000$$

$$X = 16{,}000{,}000 \text{ trans./yr.}$$

c. Graph the results of part b.

Solution

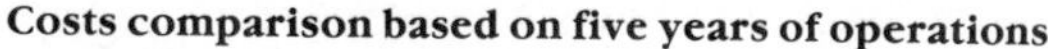

Costs comparison based on five years of operations

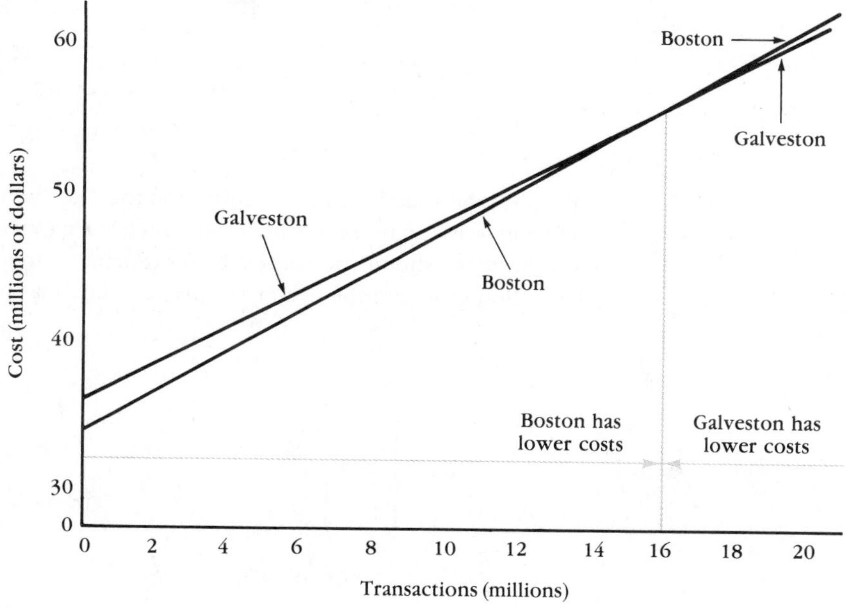

2. Ole Chug and Glug Brewing and Distributing Corporation is planning to build a brewery and distribution system for the northwestern portion of the United States and Canada. It has decided to have major distribution centers in Sacramento, California; Salt Lake City, Utah; Helena, Montana; Vancouver, Canada; and Portland, Oregon. The owner of Ole C and G has asked you to recommend the site for the new brewery.

Solution

First, examine an atlas and trace the part of the United States and Canada shown in the following exhibit. Then add the x and y axes and the grid lines. With this information and estimates of the demand for Ole C and G's product at each distribution center, the following table can be constructed. The coordinates on the grid are measured to the closest 0.25.

	Demand (Barrels/Month)	Coordinates			
	a_i	x_i	y_i	$(a_i)(x_i)$	$(a_i)(y_i)$
Sacramento	30,000	.75	4.0	22,500	120,000
Salt Lake City	20,000	3.75	4.5	75,000	90,000
Helena	35,000	4.0	6.75	140,000	236,250
Vancouver	40,000	1.5	8.25	60,000	330,000
Portland	50,000	1.25	6.75	62,500	337,500
	175,000			360,000	1,113,750

Next, the coordinates are multiplied by the demand, and these values are totaled so the center of the demand can be found.

$$xf = \frac{\sum_{i=1}^{n} (a_i)(x_i)}{\sum_{i=1}^{n} (a_i)} \qquad yf = \frac{\sum_{i=1}^{n} (a_i)(y_i)}{\sum_{i=1}^{n} (a_i)}$$

$$= \frac{360{,}000}{175{,}000} \qquad = \frac{1{,}113{,}750}{175{,}000}$$

$$= 2.06 \qquad = 6.36$$

Finally, when the location is plotted on the map, you discover that this would put the brewery in the northeast corner of Oregon. Management decides that the brewery should be shifted to the Portland area because of better transportation connections, water supply, and labor availability.

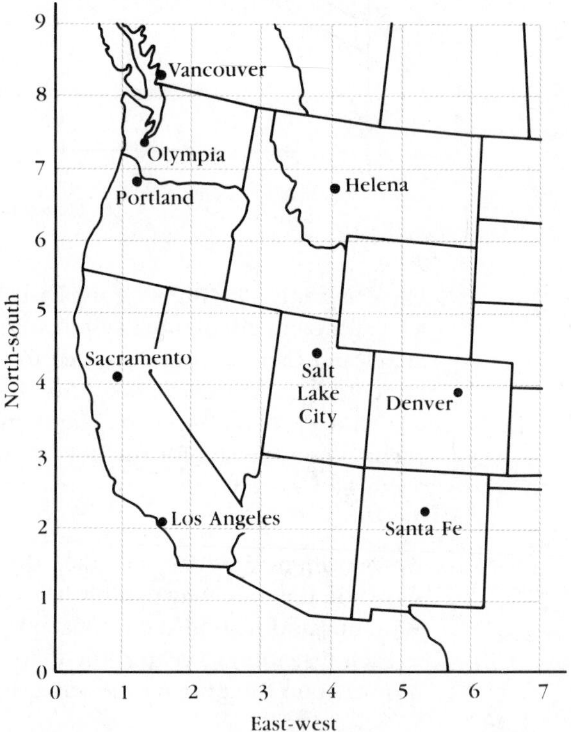

3. International Microcomputer Corporation has assembly operations in Chicago, Illinois; San Francisco, California; and Milan, Italy. These assembly operations receive disk drives from plants in Seoul, South Korea; San Diego, California; and Taipei, Taiwan. The disk drive operations cannot keep up with demand, so a fourth plant will be opened. One of the locations being considered is Monterrey, Mexico. The transportation cost per unit is given in the upper right-hand corner of each cell, and the demand and capacity are given in units per month. What will the transportation cost be if the Monterrey

location is added? Note that a dummy destination had to be added because the capacity of the sources exceeded the requirements of the destinations.

Destinations

Sources	Chicago	San Francisco	Milan	Dummy	Capacity	Row Penalties
Seoul	9	6	15	0	5,000	6
San Diego	3	2	12	0	3,000	2
Taipei	12	7	9	0	10,000	7
Moneterrey	5	3	14	0	5,000	3
Demand	7,000	8,500	5,500	2,000	23,000	
Column Penalties	2	1	3	0		

First, calculate the row and column penalties by subtracting the lowest cost in particular row or column from the second lowest cost in the same row or column. Second, pick the row or column with the largest penalty and allocate the maximum amount possible to the cell in that row or column that has lowest shipping cost. In this way, the penalty of taking the next highest cell in that row or column is avoided. Third, make the allocation, recalculate the penalties, and adjust the demand and capacity as shown in the next matrix.

Destinations

Sources	Chicago	San Francisco	Milan	Dummy	Capacity	Row Penalties
Seoul	9	6	15	0	5,000	3
San Diego	3	2	12	0	3,000	1
Taipei	10	7	9	0 2,000	8,000	2
Moneterrey	5	3	14	0	5,000	2
Demand	7,000	8,500	5,500	0	21,000	
Column Penalties	2	1	3			

Repeat the previous step; that is, find the highest penalty row or column, allocate to the lowest cost cell, recalculate the penalties, and adjust the demand and capacity to reflect the allocation. There is a tie, so the Milan column is selected at random. The results of the second allocation are shown in the next matrix.

	Destinations					
Sources	Chicago	San Francisco	Milan	Dummy	Capacity	Row Penalties
Seoul	9	6	15	0	5,000	3
San Diego	3	2	12	0	3,000	1
Taipei	10	7	5,500 9	2,000 0	2,500	3
Moneterrey	5	3	14	0	5,000	2
Demand	7,000	8,500	0	0	15,500	
Column Penalties	2	1				

The remaining allocations are shown in the following table. There are some ties in the solution, so you might have a slightly different answer.

Remaining Allocation	Amount (Number of Units)
Seoul to San Francisco	5,000
Taipei to San Francisco	2,500
San Diego to Chicago	3,000
Monterrey to San Francisco	1,000
Monterrey to Chicago	4,000

QUESTIONS

1. Why is the facility location decision important to an organization?

2. What factors are affected by the choice of locations? Which of these factors can be measured in dollars, and which cannot?

3. How can qualitative and quantitative factors be integrated to make a sound and logical location decision?

4. What hidden factors are influenced by on-site location, and how are they influenced?

5. Why are spatial relationships important in the location decision?

6. What are the principles that support the development of the load-distance method of facility location?

7. How can the facility location decision be analyzed using the transportation problem method of solution?

8. Why is location a strategic decision?

9. What are the international dimensions of the location decision?

10. What role does ethics play in locating new facilities in foreign countries?

11. What special problems are faced by service operations in locating new facilities?

PROBLEMS

1. Derwall Developers specializes in analyzing facility location decisions. Presently, the company is looking at two locations, Orlando, Florida, and Olympia, Washington, for which it has determined the following cost information:

	Orlando	Olympia
Variable costs	\$14.70/unit	\$16.45/unit
Annual fixed costs	\$12,000,000	\$11,000,000
Initial investment	\$166,000,000	\$145,000,000

a. At a volume of 800,000 units per year for a ten-year period, which facility has the lower cost?

b. At what annual volume do these facilities have equal costs? Once again, assume a ten-year period.

c. Graph the results of part b.

2. Marvin Manufacturing is considering three locations for its new plant: Tucson, San Diego, and Newark.

	Tucson	San Diego	Newark
Variable costs	\$1.60/unit	\$1.45/unit	\$1.50/unit
Annual fixed costs	\$1,800,000	\$2,000,000	\$1,900,000
Initial investment	\$14,000,000	\$16,000,000	\$15,000,000

a. At a volume of 2 million units per year for a five-year period, which facility has the lowest cost?

b. At what annual volume do these facilities have equal costs? Once again, assume a five-year period. (Hint: It is helpful to graph each of the cost equations before solving for the point where the costs are equal.)

3. Intensive Technologies, Inc., does consulting for the aerospace industry. Corporate headquarters are located in Washington, D.C., but the organization is planning to relocate on the West Coast. It is considering three sites: Seattle, Portland, and Oakland. The full costs of operating at each site, which include initial investment, annual fixed costs, and variable costs, are approximately equal. A management team from Intensive Technologies has visited each city and has evaluated each site, using the criteria below. The evaluation uses a one-to-ten scale, with one being the best score. The criteria and the weight assigned to each criteria were selected by top management.

	Weight	Oakland Score	Portland Score	Seattle Score
University research specializing in aerospace	50	4	2	2
Available pool of skilled engineers	50	4	3	2
Opportunity for advanced management education	40	2	3	3
Cultural activities	20	1	2	3
Recreational activities	20	2	4	3

a. What is the weighted score for each city?

b. Which city has the advantage in terms of the qualitative factors? Is this advantage significant?

c. What is your recommendation to top management?

4. Barrel City Health Care System is looking for a new location for its corporate headquarters. It is considering Atlanta, Georgia, and Danville, Illinois. The cities are rated from one to ten on each of the following factors, with ten the best score.

	Weight	Atlanta Score	Danville Score
Cultural activities	40	8	6
University research facilities	80	8	8
Union activities	60	8	4
Banking services	60	6	8
Available labor pool	20	6	8

a. Determine the weighted scores for both cities.

b. How can these scores be integrated with cost differences?

c. Suppose the following costs apply:

	Atlanta	Danville
Operating costs	$1,400,000/year	$1,300,000/year
Initial investment	$22,000,000	$20,000,000

Over a ten-year period, Danville has a $3,000,000 advantage. To determine that, take the difference in operating costs per year, and multiply it by ten years. Then add the difference in initial investment. Under what circumstances might the company still choose Atlanta? How much would Barrel have to value each point of Atlanta's qualitative advantage to make it the new headquarters?

5. Shaker Transportation, Inc., moves merchandise from regional warehouses to distribution centers for a small chain of department stores that operates in the Southwest. Capacity and demand are given in truckloads per month. The costs that are listed in each cell in the matrix are dollars per truckload.

Destination (Distribution Center)

Source (Warehouse)	Oklahoma City	San Antonio	Santa Fe	Tucson	Capacity
Lubbock	250	280	220	390	1,180
Phoenix	370	450	280	140	1,440
Demand	740	625	690	565	

a. Assign shipments from regional warehouses to distribution centers so that transportation costs are minimized.

b. What happens to this assignment if the transportation costs from Phoenix to Santa Fe decline from $280 per truckload to $200 per truckload?

c. Is an organization always interested in making the decision so that costs are minimized?

6. Hazlet Manufacturing ships air compressor tanks from plants located in Milan, Michigan, and Lexington, Kentucky, to customers in Bismarck, North Dakota; Baton Rouge, Louisiana; Youngstown, Ohio; and Tampa, Florida. Hazlet's customers use these air compressors as one component of commercial spray-painting equipment. Hazlet is having trouble keeping up with demand for the air compressors and is considering building another manufacturing facility. The company is presently negotiating with a new and potentially large customer in Lincoln, Nebraska. For the new facility, Hazlet is considering Montgomery, Alabama, and Des Moines, Iowa. Because shipping costs are a major expense, the plant manager has asked you to investigate transportation costs in each case. Capacity and demand are given in units per month, and transportation costs are dollars per unit.

Destination (Customer's Plant)

Source (Plant)	Baton Rouge	Bismarck	Tampa	Youngstown	Capacity
Lexington	14	18	16	12	12,420
Milan	17	15	17	9	9,380
Demand	6,740	8,400	5,050	5,670	

The new facility will initially have a capacity of 5,000 units per month and is designed to easily accommodate an additional 5,000 units per month. Working from left to right across the table, the transportation costs per unit for Des Moines are 17, 11, 19, and 14. The transportation costs per unit for Montgomery are 9, 19, 12, and 15.

a. Which new facility would allow Hazlet to minimize transportation costs?

b. Are there other factors that affect that decision? What happens if Hazlet is able to sign the new customer in Lincoln to a long-term contract?

c. Is an organization always interested in making the decision so that costs are minimized?

7. Le Havre Manufacturing, Inc., which is located in Le Havre, France, is planning to expand operations into Germany. Initially, Le Havre's management is planning to build one consolidation warehouse which will ship products to customers throughout Germany. If Le Havre is successful, it will locate production facilities in Germany. The expected demand for Le-Havre's products is given here.

Customer Location	Demand (Units/Year)
Hamburg	42,000
Cologne	22,000
Stuttgart	37,000
Munich	66,000
Dresden	45,000
Berlin	113,000

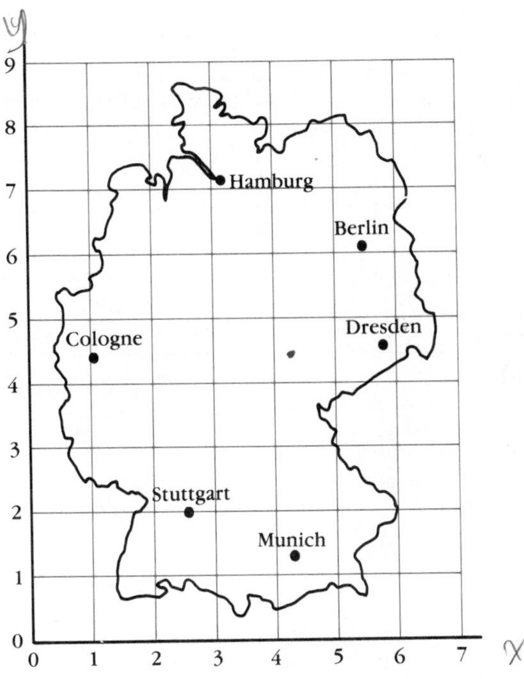

a. Where should the consolidation warehouse be built so it is centrally located? Estimate the coordinates for the customers to the nearest 0.25 of a grid line.

b. What other factors should be considered in locating the facility?

8. Tipton Bearing, Inc., is planning for the worldwide distribution of its ball bearings. As part of its strategy, Tipton is planning to build a manufacturing facility to serve Asia. It plans to have consolidation warehouses in the following cities: Hiroshima, Japan; Seoul, South Korea; Beijing, China; Hong Kong; Calcutta, India; and Karachi, Pakistan. The new manufacturing facility will serve these warehouses. The expected demand from these warehouses is given below. Estimate the coordinates for the customer to the nearest .25 of a grid line.

Customer Location	Demand (000,000 Units/Year)
Hiroshima	860
Seoul	390
Beijing	340
Hong Kong	490
Calcutta	240
Karachi	410

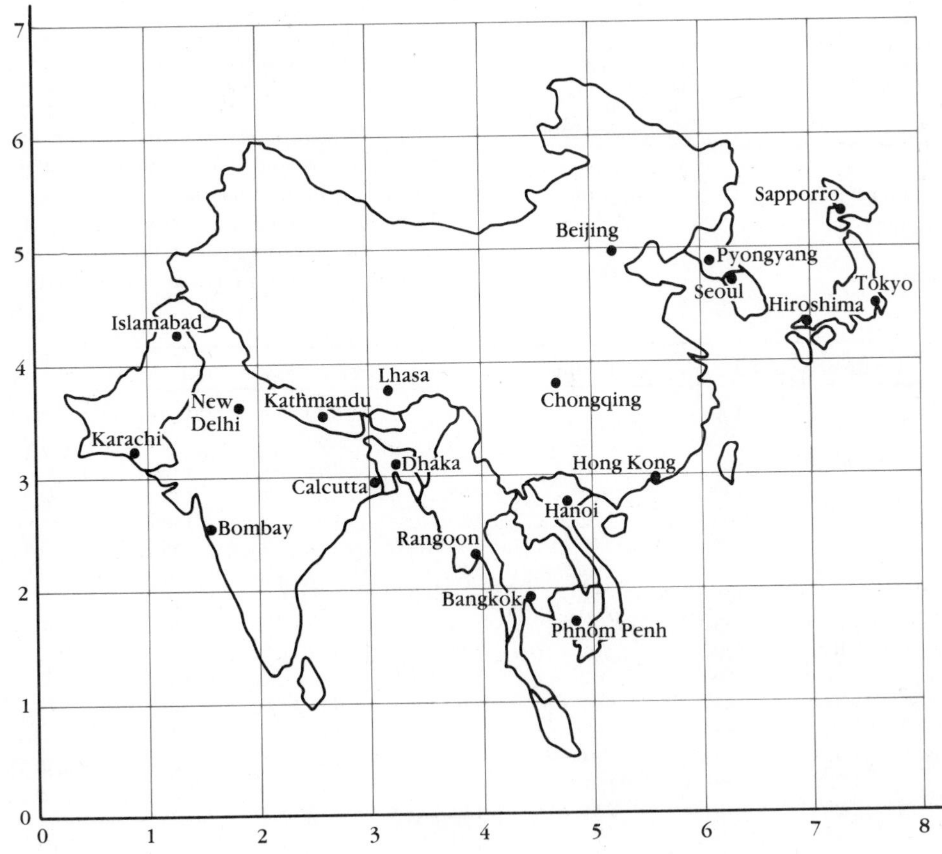

a. Where should the manufacturing facility be located if it is to be placed at the "center of gravity" based on demand?

b. Is this a good choice for this situation? Provide justification for your answer.

c. If it is not a good choice, what other location should you consider?

DATA SET FOR COMPUTER SOLUTION

1. J.C. Roebuck, Inc., is a nationwide chain of department stores that carry a full line of merchandise. With increasing competition from discount department stores, the company has undertaken a program that will improve customer service and reduce costs. One of the areas where costs will be reduced is the transportation of merchandise from the six regional warehouses and twenty distribution centers. Merchandise is shipped in standardized containers. The capacities of the regional warehouses and the forecasted demands of the distribution centers are given below.

Regional Warehouse	Capacity (000,000 Containers/Week)
Albany, New York	1,500
Atlanta, Georgia	1,900
Columbus, Ohio	2,200
Denver, Colorado	1,400
Sacramento, California	1,800
St. Louis, Missouri	1,200

Distribution Center	Forecasted Demand (000,000 Containers/Week)
Akron, Ohio	670
Baltimore, Maryland	545
Boston, Massachusetts	620
Buffalo, New York	395
Detroit, Michigan	505
Harrisburg, Pennsylvania	420
Helena, Montana	340
Indianapolis, Indiana	535
Jackson, Mississippi	390
Los Angeles, California	890
Memphis, Tennessee	400
Milwaukee, Wisconsin	300
Minneapolis, Minnesota	415
Oklahoma City, Oklahoma	445
Phoenix, Arizona	380
Portland, Oregon	625
Raleigh, North Carolina	450
San Jose, California	310
Syracuse, New York	520
Tallahassee, Florida	630

The following table contains the various transportation costs to ship one hundred containers from the source to the destination:

Management has asked you to allocate the capacity of the regional warehouses to the distribution centers so that transportation costs are minimized.

	Source					
Destination	**Albany**	**Atlanta**	**Columbus**	**Denver**	**Sacramento**	**St. Louis**
Akron	50	100	25	140	180	120
Baltimore	75	90	75	150	190	130
Boston	80	120	100	165	195	130
Buffalo	25	105	20	145	190	125
Detroit	65	105	30	130	175	130
Harrisburg	55	95	45	135	180	135
Helena	190	210	170	95	110	120
Indianapolis	70	100	55	100	145	65
Jackson	135	55	90	125	150	70
Los Angeles	220	190	210	120	85	145
Memphis	110	70	80	100	130	30
Milwaukee	90	125	60	110	145	60
Minneapolis	105	135	75	105	115	70
Oklahoma City	150	90	110	70	105	60
Phoenix	175	120	160	80	90	110
Portland	220	240	190	120	80	140
Raleigh	90	50	95	140	210	110

	Source					
Destination	**Albany**	**Atlanta**	**Columbus**	**Denver**	**Sacramento**	**St. Louis**
San Jose	225	210	180	110	15	125
Syracuse	25	90	35	115	180	135
Tallahassee	125	45	90	130	200	140

MINI-CASES

Bunraku Beverage, Ltd.

For several years, Bunraku Beverage, Ltd., of Japan has considered ways to successfully enter the U.S. market. European brewers have entered the market by exporting products from facilities located in their home country. This helps them to maintain their "high quality" image for which the European brewers can command a high price. The extra transportation costs incurred with this approach are small compared to the price premiums that they receive. Besides, if they located a brewery in the United States, they might tarnish their image.

Bunraku Beverage, on the other hand, does not have a long history in the brewing business that the company can easily transform into a premium brand image at a premium price. Its strategy is to produce a high-quality product and charge rock-bottom price. In order to be successful, Bunraku must cut cost in all areas that do not affect product quality. To do this, the company is planning to build operations in the United States. The first brewery and distribution system will be west of the Mississippi River. If operations are successful, another brewery and distribution system will be opened in the East. The distribution centers will be located in Santa Fe, New Mexico; Helena, Montana; Olympia, Washington; Los Angeles, California; and Denver, Colorado. The forecasted demand in barrels per year is listed below.

Distribution Center	Annual Demand (Barrels/Year)
Santa Fe	100,000
Helena	120,000
Olympia	220,000
Los Angeles	200,000
Denver	140,000

1. Where should the brewery be located?

2. Mr. Yamamoto, company president, believes strongly that the brewery should be located in the Los Angeles area. Does your analysis support this?

3. What would you recommend to Mr. Yamamoto? Justify your recommendations.

4. What other information ought to be collected?

5. Write a report that describes how such a study might be done.

Walldot Greeting Cards, Inc.

Walldot, Inc., presently produces greeting cards in Harrisburg, Pennsylvania, and St. Louis, Missouri. It has regional distribution centers in Las Vegas, Austin, St. Louis, Atlanta, and Albany. The capacities of the production facilities and the demand from the distribution centers are listed here.

Production Facility	Capacity (100,000 Cards/Year)	Distribution Center	Forecasted Demand (100,000 Cards/Year)
Harrisburg	400	Las Vegas	200
St. Louis	370	Austin	150
Total		St. Louis	240
capacity	770	Atlanta	160
		Albany	210
		Total demand	960

The figures for the production facilities represent capacity without overtime. During the past two years, Walldot used substantial overtime to keep up with growing demand. Demand is expected to increase next year. Walldot is planning to build a new production facility next year that will produce 200 million cards per year and that can be expanded eventually to 400 million. The company is considering a location in Charlotte, North Carolina, and another in Salt Lake City, Utah. The cost data for the two locations follow.

Proposed Facility	Initial Investment	Annual Fixed Costs	Variable Costs Excluding Transportation ($/1,000 cards)
Salt Lake City	$2,000,000	$350,000	$82.00
Charlotte	2,500,000	290,000	80.00

Management has asked you to analyze the costs for doing business in these two facilities for the next five years. To simplify the analysis, they have suggested that you assume no growth over the next five years and use the following transportation costs. Transportation costs are given per 100,000 cards.

Source	Destination				
	Las Vegas	Austin	St. Louis	Atlanta	Albany
Harrisburg	500	400	250	300	150

Source	Destination				
	Las Vegas	Austin	St. Louis	Atlanta	Albany
St. Louis	300	350	100	350	250
Salt Lake City	200	500	300	650	500
Charlotte	600	400	450	150	300

Write a recommendation to Walldot's management based on the information provided in the case.

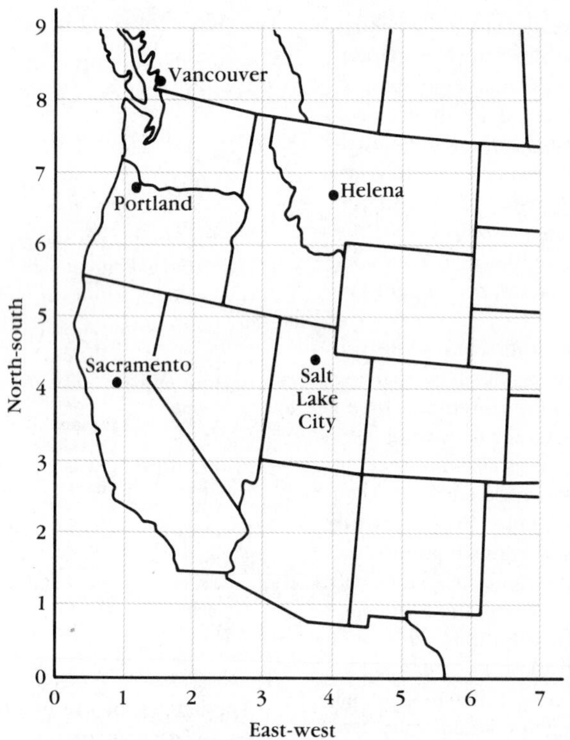

SELECTED BIBLIOGRAPHY

Albrecht, Karl. *At America's Service*. Homewood, Ill.: Dow Jones–Irwin, 1988.

Anderson, David R.; Sweeney, Dennis J.; and Williams, Thomas A. *Quantitative Methods for Business*. St. Paul: West, 1989.

Ball, Donald A., and McCulloch, William H., Jr. International Business. Plano Tex.: Business Publications, 1985.

Francis, R. L., and White, J. A. *Facilities Layout and Location: An Analytical Approach*. Englewood Cliffs, N.J.: Prentice-Hall, 1987.

Hillier, Frederick S., and Lieberman, Gerald J. *Introduction to Operations Research*. New York: McGraw-Hill, 1990.

Robinson, Richard D. *Internationalization of Business: An Introduction*. Chicago: Dryden, 1984.

Schilling, David A. "Dynamic Location Modeling for Public-Sector Facilities: A Multi-Criteria Approach." *Decision Sciences* 11, no. 4 (October 1980): 714–724.

Schmenner, Roger W. "Looking Beyond the Obvious in Plant Location." *Harvard Business Review,* 57, no. 1 (January–February 1979): 126–132.

Schmenner, Roger W. "Multiple Manufacturing Strategies Among the Fortune 500." *Journal of Operations Management* 2, no. 2 (February 1982): 77–86.

Stevenson, William J. *Introduction to Management Science*. Homewood, Ill.: Irwin, 1989.

Tompkins, James A., and White, John A. *Facilities Planning*. New York: Wiley, 1984.

Chapter 6 Appendix

Qualitative Factor in Location Analysis

Many factors that cannot be measured in dollars should be considered in the location decision. The factors in the following list are often important.

LOCATION

Country ______

Distance in miles from:

Chicago ______
Dallas ______
Denver ______
Kansas City ______
Los Angeles ______
Memphis ______
New York ______
Omaha ______
St. Louis ______

POPULATION

	1990	1980	1970
City	______	______	______
County	______	______	______

MUNICIPAL SERVICES

Type of local government: ______
Comprehensive city plan: Date completed ______
Under way ______ Under consideration ______
City zoning ordinance in effect: Yes ______ No ______
County zoning ordinance in effect: Yes ______ No ______
Subdivision ordinance with design standards in effect: ______
Number of full-time fire department personnel: ______
Number of volunteer fire department personnel: ______
Fire insurance class: In city ______ Outside city ______
Number of full-time city police officers: ______
City engineer employed: Yes ______ No ______
Garbage service provided: Yes ______ No ______
Public library in city: Yes ______ No ______

EDUCATIONAL FACILITIES

Type	Number	Teachers	Enrollment	Grades
Elementary school	______	______	______	______
Junior high school	______	______	______	______
High school	______	______	______	______
Trade and technical school	______	______	______	______
Junior college	______	______	______	______
University	______	______	______	______

University Research Activity ______

______

______

COMMERCIAL SERVICES

Machine shop in city: Yes ________ No ________ Number ________
Tool-and-die service in city: Yes ________ No ________
Electric motor repair service in city: Yes ________ No ________
Type of newspaper in city: Daily ________ Weekly ________
Radio station(s): Yes ________ No ________ Number ________

BANKING SERVICE

Number of banks in city ________
Assets of largest $ ________

TRANSPORTATION SERVICES

Train

Community served by railroad(s): Yes ________ No ________
Distance to nearest loading point: ________ miles
Number of freight train trips per day: ________
Reciprocal switching available: Yes ________ No ________
Piggyback ramp available: Yes ________ No ________
Distance to nearest piggyback service: ________ miles
Name(s) of railroad(s): ________

Motor carrier

Highway bus service available: Yes ________ No ________
Number of highways serving city: Federal ________ State ________
Distance to nearest interstate interchange: ________ miles
Number of motor freight carriers serving community: ________

Barge

City adjoins navigable river: Yes ________ No ________
Barge dock available: Yes ________ No ________
Channel depth: ________ ft. Length of season: ________ mi.

Airplane

Distance to nearest public airport: ________ mo.
Length of longest runway: ________ feet
Runway lighted: Yes ________ No ________
Private aircraft storage available: Yes ________ No ________
Private aircraft maintenance available: Yes ________ No ________
Distance to nearest commercial air transportation: ________ miles
Name(s) of airline(s) serving point: ________

____

____

Length of time goods in transit to: ________

City	Days by Railroad	Days by Motor Freight
Atlanta	________	________
Chicago	________	________

Cleveland ______ ______
Dallas ______ ______
Denver ______ ______
Kansas City ______ ______
Los Angeles ______ ______
Memphis ______ ______
Minneapolis ______ ______
New Orleans ______ ______
New York ______ ______
St. Louis ______ ______

UTILITIES

Water

Water supplied by: Municipal ______ Private ______
Name of supplier: ______
Address: ______
For rate information, contact: ______

Source of city water: river(s) ______ Well(s) ______ Lake(s) or reservoir(s) ______
Supply of river water available: ______ cu. ft./sec.
Supply of lake or reservoir water: ______ gals.
Water supply approved by State Board of Health: Yes ______ No ______
Capacity of water plant: ______ gals./min.
Capacity of water plant: ______ gals./day
Average consumption: ______ gals./day
Peak consumption: ______ gals./day

Sanitation

Type of sewage treatment plant: ______
Treatment plant certified by the State Board of Water Pollution: Yes ______ No ______
Characteristics of waste treatment plant:

Measurement	Capacity	Present Load
Gallons per day	______	______
Population equivalent	______	______

Natural Gas

Natural gas service available: Yes ______ No ______
Name: ______
Address: ______
For rate information, contact: ______

Electricity

Suppliers Municipal ______ Private ______ Co-op ______
Name(s): ______
Address(s): ______
For rate information, contact: ______

LOCAL MANUFACTURING CHARACTERISTICS

Number of manufacturing plants in community: ______
Number of manufacturing plants with unions: ______
Number of manufacturing employees in community: ______
Strikes within last five years affecting 5 percent or more of the labor force: ______
Major manufacturers or other large employers in community: ______
Name of firm: ______
Employment: ______
Product(s) manufactured: ______

Labor Market Analysis: ______

Date of last labor market survey: ______
Results of survey: ______

Estimated Labor Force Available: Total ______
This estimate can be documented: Yes ______ No ______

County Labor Data: ______ County

Civilian work force (annual average): ______
Unemployed: ______
Unemployed as a percentage of work force: ______
Total employment: ______
Agricultural employment: ______
Nonagricultural employment: ______
Manufacturing employment: ______
Nonmanufacturing employment: ______

HEALTH FACILITIES

Number of hospitals in community: ______ Number of beds: ______
If no hospitals, distance to nearest facility: ______ miles
Clinic in community: Yes ______ No ______
Medical personnel: MD(s) ______ DO(s) ______
Nurses: Registered ______ Practical ______

RECREATIONAL FACILITIES

Type of recreational facilities available in city or within ten miles:

Public golf courses(s) ______ Public park(s) ______
Public tennis court(s) ______ Public swimming pool(s) ______
Country clubs available: Yes ______ No ______
Nearest public access to lake or river: ______ miles
Activities allowed: Swimming ______ Fishing ______
Water skiing ______ Motor boating ______

LOCAL INDUSTRIAL DEVELOPMENT ORGANIZATION

Name of group: ______
Person to contact: ______
Address: ______

Phone number: Home: ______
Business: ______ Area Code: ______

Chapter 7

Process Selection

CHAPTER OUTLINE

LEARNING OBJECTIVES

After completing this chapter, you should be able to

- Describe the process selection decision and how it is influenced by the volume of product demanded.
- Construct a cost-volume-profit model of a firm and understand how the model can be used to evaluate risk in operations and to calculate the break-even point for both single- and multiple-product cases.
- Explain why mass production does not necessarily mean products with inferior quality or shoddy workmanship.
- Define the different process types: line flow, batch flow, flexible manufacturing system, manufacturing cell, job shop, and project.

OPERATIONS IN ACTION

Digital Equipment Corporation: Changing the Production Process as the Organization Grows

Digital Equipment Corporation (DEC) filled a need in the computer market that IBM did not foresee, and as a result, it grew to be IBM's most serious challenger. Before DEC brought out its product, all computers were big mainframes housed in special centers, pampered by experts, and used to process large batches of data efficiently. DEC's specialty became the design and manufacture of smaller, less-expensive machines, called minicomputers, that required less special attention. Because of their characteristics, these reliable machines could be economically applied to a variety of business and scientific tasks. DEC's computers could be moved out of the computer center and placed under the control of department managers, giving rise to new and innovative applications. As a result, the demand for DEC's computers grew rapidly.

This rapid growth required DEC to evolve over time from a small job shop producer to a large integrated producer of computer hardware. In the late 1950s, DEC began by producing a few computers. Sales did not reach the million-dollar level until 1960. At that time, DEC's production process was small and geared to produce only a few computers each year, using large amounts of hand labor. There were few managers in the organization, and decision making was a simple process. As the company grew (sales reached $500 million in 1975), the number of different products increased, and the volume of each product increased. To cope with this demand, DEC added more automated production equipment.

The current production process and the organization that supports it are substantially different from the 1960s version. In the early 1960s, DEC founder Ken Olsen and a few close associates did the marketing, engineering, manufacturing, and financial planning. As the company grew, an organizational structure evolved in which DEC moved to a product-line organization with strong product managers and eventually to an organization built around functional areas, such as accounting, marketing, and manufacturing.

As the organization has grown, operations have evolved as well. The production equipment has become more sophisticated, and the production processes have become more automated to reduce labor and material costs and keep pace with rapidly increasing demand. To be successful in the future, DEC must continue to change and improve its production process.[1]

INTRODUCTION

Thus far in the Designing the System section of the book, we have discussed (1) the teamwork approach for developing new products to meet customer needs, Chapter 4; (2) methods for estimating the organization's capacity, Chapter 5; (3) important capacity decisions, such as how much capacity to add and when to add it, Chapter 5; and (4) how to determine where new capacity should be located, Chapter 6. This chapter focuses on the process selection decision and attempts to show the relationship between process selection and the topics listed above. **Process** describes the way in which the product is made. **Process selection** is a series of decisions that include technical or engineering issues and volume or scale issues.

The technical issues include the basic technology used to produce a service or good. For example, deciding to use electronic analysis to diagnose engine malfunctions is a technical decision for an automotive repair service. Deciding whether your automotive repair service should be large enough to serve two cars per hour or twenty cars per hour is a volume or scale issue. The technical or engineering aspects of process design are discussed in Chapter 4 and will not be repeated here. This chapter focuses on the volume or scale aspects of process selection.

The volume or scale decision involves applying the proper amount of mechanization to leverage the organization's work force. In this case, **leverage** means to make the work force more productive through the use of better tools. For example, one person working alone with a few simple tools may be able to build an automobile, but he or she cannot build it at a cost that will allow that person to compete with organizations that employ sophisticated tools for producing automobiles. That person and others like him or her cannot build enough to satisfy demand without significant automation and an organization to leverage their time and skills. More sophisticated tools allow the work force to produce more with the same commitment of time and effort. This productivity increase lowers the unit cost of the product and raises the capacity of the work force.

In general, as more sophisticated tools are provided to the work force, productivity gains will be achieved, and greater costs will be incurred to buy the tools. This presents an interesting trade-off between efficiency and costs in the process selection decision. As more sophisticated tools are applied to the production process, productivity and capacity increase, and labor cost per unit declines. On the other hand, as tools become more sophisticated, the cost of acquiring them tends to increase, which translates into increased fixed costs. The analysis of these trade-offs should consider the volume demanded by the customer.

To better understand the process selection decision, this chapter (1) describes how process selection is related to product design and capacity decisions, (2) discusses the cost-volume-profit model of the firm, and (3) describes a series of process alternatives that consider cost and volume.

PROCESS SELECTION RELATES TO PRODUCT DESIGN AND CAPACITY

Because the organization of a textbook is sequential, you might think that product design, capacity, and process selection are sequential decisions. In fact, these decisions need to be considered simultaneously. The way the product is designed affects how many people will buy it, which affects the amount of capacity the producer will seek to attain, which affects the process and the costs to produce the product, which affects how many people can afford to buy it. This logic can be represented as a circle with customers at the center, as illustrated in Exhibit 7.1. Because a circle has no beginning or end, it should be considered as a whole. If these decisions are not viewed as a whole, a decision in product design that might offer the best technical solution could cause the product to fail because it makes the product less attractive to the customer or increases the cost of the product beyond the reach of most consumers. Process selection should be integrated with decisions about product design and capacity. This reinforces a major theme of the book: that operations and an organization are parts of a system and decisions made in one area have a significant impact on other areas.

Exhibit 7.1 Product Design, Process Selection, and Capacity Decisions Are Closely Related

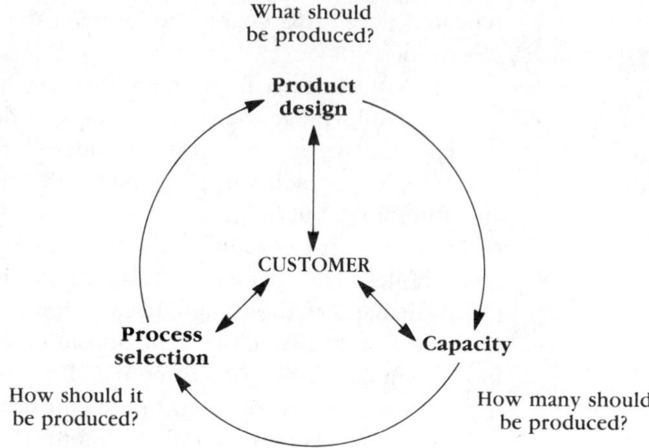

Relating Process Design to Product Design

Decisions made in designing the product clearly have an impact on the process. For example, if a fast-food sandwich is described as flame-broiled, the process should include equipment for flame-broiling, rather than grills for frying. If a bed is described as brass, there is no need for woodworking equipment. Process selection, in turn, influences the product design. Product design should be undertaken in an environment that is defined by the available process technologies. The digital watch and the electronic typewriter are examples of situations in which improvements in technology greatly altered the product. Product design and process design are interdependent decisions.

Relating process and product design goes beyond the examples listed in the preceding paragraph. The teamwork concept first discussed in the chapter on new product development is quickly changing how organizations approach product and process design. The automotive industry, aircraft builders, computer manufacturers, and others are combining design engineers with process engineers (sometimes called manufacturing engineers) to create design teams. These teams are charged with doing what is best for the customer, rather than finding the best product design or the best process design. Because the design engineers and the process engineers work together, the lead time required to bring a new product from an idea to a reality is reduced significantly. This effort, called simultaneous engineering, enables the organization to participate in time-base competition. By doing what is best for the customer, the organization hopes to be rewarded with increased demand for its products and high profit margins. These teams also improve communication between these two important groups, which decreases the number of engineering change orders, avoids unnecessary delays and gets the product to market more quickly, and avoids mistakes so as to reduce costs. The Northrop Operations in Action offers further illustration of the benefits.

OPERATIONS IN ACTION

Northrop: Combining Product and Process Design

The automotive industry calls it simultaneous engineering; others call it design and build, Northrop calls its version of combining product and process design "parallel release." At Northrop, this involves getting the manufacturing people who build a product to work side by side with the designers, literally moving desks and people. This commitment to change involved more than simply moving furniture; it began at the top and moved through the corporation.

Traditionally, the designers did not concern themselves with how manufacturing would make a part. The design engineers worked in their own building and had little reason or opportunity to confer with the manufacturing engineers. With the new joint design and manufacturing team, designers have become more aware of manufacturing practices and capabilities. This team approach allows the designers to take advantage of these manufacturing practices and capabilities in their designs. In this environment, manufacturing engineers better understand designers' problem and can often provide innovative solutions.

The benefits from this new practice are coming quickly. The team is well on its way to achieving a 70 percent reduction in engineering change orders. Each change order requires special handling, which disrupts manufacturing and increases the frustration level of the work force. Labor cost is expected to be reduced 30 to 50 percent, while delivery times are expected to be cut dramatically. Northrop's management believes this approach will make the company more competitive and significantly increase its chance of landing a multibillion dollar contract for the fighter plane of the 1990s.[2]

Process Selection and Capacity

Process selection is also related to the volume demanded in the marketplace. If the market for the product is estimated at only 1,000 units per year, it may be difficult to justify an expensive specialized machine that produces 100 units per hour. A machine like this would be required to operate only ten hours each year. It is unlikely that the cost of the machine could be supported by the 1,000 units demanded unless a very high price is charged for each unit.

Example

A machine shop needs to drill four holes in a three- by five-inch plate that is one-quarter inch thick. Management could purchase a manual drill press or an automatic drill press that can run with only periodic operator attention. The following data are available for analysis. Note that material costs can be ignored in making this comparison because material requirements are the same regardless of the machine used.

Machine	Annual Fixed Costs	Variable Labor Costs	Production Rate
Manual	\$1,000	\$18.00/hour	10 units/hour
Automatic	\$9,000	\$2.00/hour	100 units/hour

The total-cost equation is as follows:

$$TC = FC + (VC)(X_p)$$

where

TC = total cost

FC = fixed costs

VC = variable cost per unit

X_p = number of units produced

Comparing Costs. What is the cost to produce 1,000 units per year on each machine? From the following calculations, it is clear that the manual machine has lower costs. Dividing the total cost by the volume produced gives a unit cost that includes the variable cost and a share of the fixed costs.

Manual:

$$TC = \$1{,}000 + \frac{\$18.00/\text{hr.}}{10 \text{ units/hr.}}(1{,}000 \text{ units})$$
$$= \$2{,}800$$
$$\text{Unit cost} = \frac{\$2{,}800}{1{,}000}$$
$$= \$2.80 \text{ per unit at a volume of } 1{,}000$$

Automatic:

$$TC = \$9{,}000 + \frac{\$2.00/\text{hr.}}{100 \text{ units/hr.}}(1{,}000 \text{ units})$$
$$= \$9{,}020$$
$$\text{Unit cost} = \frac{\$9{,}020}{1{,}000}$$
$$= \$9.02 \text{ per unit at a volume of } 1{,}000$$

What happens if 10,000 plates are needed? The marginal cost of drilling each additional plate on the automatic machine is only \$.02 because the labor cost is \$2.00 per hour and the output is 100 units per hour. On the manual machine, the marginal cost of drilling a plate is \$1.80.

Manual:

$$TC = 1{,}000 + \frac{18.00}{10}(10{,}000)$$
$$= \$19{,}000$$
$$\text{Unit cost} = \frac{\$19{,}000}{10{,}000}$$
$$= \$1.90 \text{ per unit at a volume of } 10{,}000$$

Automatic:

$$TC = 9{,}000 + \frac{2.00}{100}(10{,}000)$$
$$= \$9{,}200$$

$$\text{Unit cost} = \frac{\$9{,}200}{10{,}000}$$

$$= \$.92 \text{ per unit at a volume of } 10{,}000$$

For 10,000 plates, the unit cost for the automatic operation is significantly lower. As demand for the part increases, the automatic process becomes more and more attractive.

The Indifference Point. At what production volume are the costs of the manual and the automatic machines equal? The variable X represents the volume produced. To check the accuracy of the following calculations, substitute the computed value of X into the total-cost equation for each machine to see if the two total costs are equal. Except for differences caused by rounding, they should be.

$$\text{Total cost manual} = \text{Total cost automatic}$$

$$(\$1{,}000) + \frac{\$18.00}{10 \text{ units}}(X) = (\$9{,}000) + \frac{\$2.00}{100 \text{ units}}(X)$$

$$(1{,}000) + (1.80)(X) = (9{,}000) + (.02)(X)$$

Solve for X:

$$(1.80 - .02)(X) = 9{,}000 - 1{,}000$$

$$X = \frac{8{,}000}{1.78}$$

$$X = 4{,}494 \text{ units}$$

The Power of Volume to Reduce Costs. This problem illustrates how unit costs can be decreased by purchasing high-speed equipment and producing large numbers of parts. The following table lists the unit costs for various volumes. Verify the unit cost for 100,000 parts as an exercise.

Volume	Manual	Automatic
1,000	$2.80	$9.02
10,000	1.90	.92
100,000	1.81	.11

The example above makes many simplifying assumptions, such as unlimited capacity, no increase in maintenance costs, and no increase in the failure rate of the machine as volume increases. These and other relevant factors could be estimated and considered in the analysis. In any case, the impact of volume on unit cost is very clear.

UNDERSTANDING THE SCALE FACTOR

In business and economics, the concept of economies of scale has long been important. The **economies-of-scale** doctrine states that there is a most efficient size for a facility and a most efficient size for the firm. In practice, the doctrine has been used both to justify building larger facilities for the production of goods and services and to justify purchasing more automated equipment to speed production and lower costs.

An organization can use both or either of these approaches to leverage the time and talents of the people who create the large volume of services and goods demanded by its customers. If organizations and society are to progress, investments in equipment and facilities (fixed costs) must be made to increase the productivity of labor and management.

Modeling the Scale Factor: Cost-Volume-Profit Model

To understand scale or volume issues, it is helpful to construct a simple model of the organization. As defined in Chapter 3, a model is an abstraction of the key variables and relationships in a real problem and is used to simplify the problem and increase understanding. The **cost-volume-profit (C-V-P) model,** a simple model of an organization, uses estimates of costs, revenues, volume sold, and volume produced in order to estimate profit.

C-V-P Model Formulation

The C-V-P model is formulated by determining total revenue and costs, as shown in the following equations:

$$TR = (SP)(X_s)$$

where

TR = total revenue

SP = selling price per unit

X_s = number of units sold

$$TC = FC + (VC)(X_p)$$

where

TC = total cost

FC = fixed cost

VC = variable cost per unit

X_p = number of units produced

The profit (P) equation is

$$P = TR - TC$$

By substituting the TR and TC equations into the equation for profit, the following mathematical model can be used to calculate profits, given sales and production volumes. This is the cost-volume-profit model.

$$P = SP(X_s) - [FC + VC(X_p)]$$

This model can also be manipulated to determine the volume required to earn some targeted value for profit. In order to do this, we assume that the number of units sold equals the number of units produced.

If $X = X_s = X_p$, then

$$P = SP(X) - [FC + VC(X)]$$

$$P = SP(X) - VC(X) - FC$$

$$P + FC = (SP - VC)(X)$$

Solve for X as follows:

$$X = \frac{(P + FC)}{(SP - VC)}$$

If C is defined as contribution per unit, then $C = (SP - VC)$. Thus, the equation becomes

$$X = \frac{(P + FC)}{C} \quad (7.1)$$

The **profit point** is the number of units (X) that must be produced and sold at the contribution (C) in order to cover the fixed costs (FC) and profit (P). Exhibit 7.2 represents the model graphically and illustrates the profit point. If the profit is set to zero, equation 7.1 is recognizable as the so-called break-even formula. The **break-even point (BEP)** is the volume that must be produced and sold so that profit is zero.

Exhibit 7.2 Cost-Volume-Profit Model

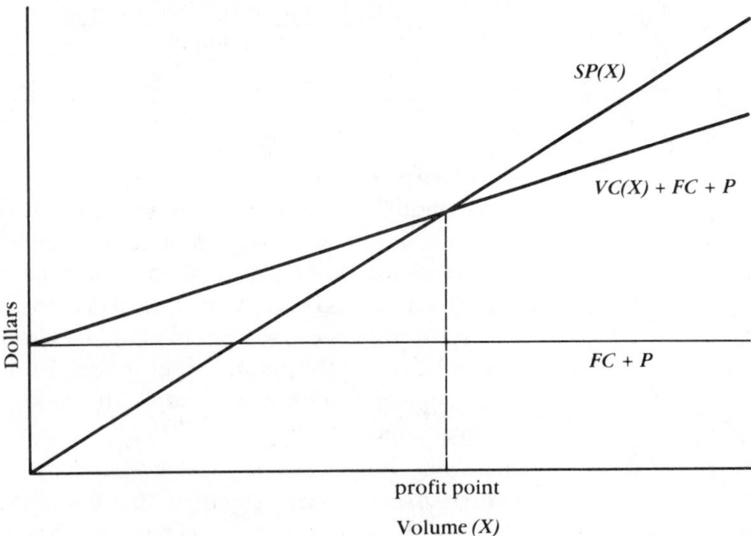

If profit (P) is set equal to zero, then the profit point is equal to the break-even point.

Example

The mechanics of applying the C-V-P model are relatively simple. To calculate the profit point, you must know the selling price, variable costs, and fixed costs. Management can determine the projected level of profit to be used in the model. In this example, the fixed cost and profit are for a one-month period.

$$SP = \$8.00/\text{unit}$$

$$VC = \$4.50/\text{unit}$$

$$C = \$3.50/\text{unit}$$

$$FC = \$25{,}000/\text{month}$$

$$P = \$8{,}000/\text{month}$$

In this case, the number of units that must be produced and sold to make \$8,000 profit in a month is 9,429 units; that is the profit point.

$$X = \frac{FC + P}{C}$$

$$= \frac{\$25{,}000/\text{month} + \$8{,}000/\text{month}}{\$3.50/\text{unit}} = 9{,}429 \text{ units/month}$$

Managers can use this number in many ways. Here are two examples. First, if the organization has a capacity of only 5,600 units per month, then achieving an \$8,000 profit is not possible. Second, if the sales forecast is for 9,000 units, then that profit level cannot be achieved because not enough units will be sold.

Changes can be made to the model for the purpose of doing sensitivity analysis and answering what-if questions. For example, what if the variable costs increased from \$4.50 to \$5.00 per unit? Under these circumstances, the profit point becomes 11,000 units per month.

$$X = \frac{\$25{,}000/\text{month} + \$8{,}000/\text{month}}{\$3.00/\text{unit}} = 11{,}000 \text{ units/month}$$

C-V-P Assumptions

The C-V-P model, like any other model, makes several assumptions. The assumption that sales volume equals production volume has already been mentioned. The model also assumes that total cost and total revenue are linear functions of volume. The model is based on historical data for costs and revenue. Any changes in these relationships caused by changes in technology, demand, or strategy may invalidate the use of this or any other model. Users of models should understand these assumptions, or they may apply the model ineffectively and thus obtain misleading results.

The Multiple-Product Case of the C-V-P Model

Our discussion of the C-V-P model has considered only single-product firms. But many organizations produce more than one product, using the same set of fixed costs. How can this firm be modeled? In this case, another set of variables, product mix, is added to the revenue and cost relationships.

To solve the problem, a weighted contribution based on the mix of each product is calculated. Consider the following example.

Example

A company produces shovels, axes, and hoes. The table below gives the selling price, variable cost, and contribution for each product. The product mix and profit target are also listed. The fixed costs are shared by all three products.

	Shovels	Axes	Hoes
Product mix	45%	20%	35%
Selling price/unit	$12	$16	$9
Variable cost/unit	$ 6	$ 7	$4
Contribution/unit	$ 6	$ 9	$5

Profit target = $20,000/yr.
Fixed costs = $30,000/yr.

The mix is the number of each product produced and sold divided by the total sold. The weighted contribution is calculated as

$$WC = \sum_{i=1}^{n} M_i(SP_i - VC_i)$$

where

WC = weighted contribution per unit

M_i = product mix as a percentage of total sales for product i, where $i = 1, \ldots, n$ for n different products or product lines

SP_i = selling price for product i

VC_i = variable cost for product i

Thus, the weighted contribution for the product mix shown above is

$$\begin{aligned} WC &= .45(\$12/\text{unit} - \$6/\text{unit}) + .2(\$16/\text{unit} - \$7/\text{unit}) + \\ &\qquad .35(\$9/\text{unit} - \$4/\text{unit}) \\ &= \$6.25/\text{unit} \end{aligned}$$

In the multiple-product case, the weighted contribution per unit substitutes for the contribution per unit in equation 7.1.

$$X = \frac{P + FC}{WC} \tag{7.2}$$

$$= \frac{\$20{,}000 + \$30{,}000}{\$6.25/\text{unit}}$$

$$= 8{,}000 \text{ units}$$

Interpreting the Results. The variable X is measured as a composite unit—that is, a unit consisting of 45 percent shovel, 20 percent ax, and 35 percent hoe.

One composite unit

.45 Shovel
.20 Axe
.35 Hoe

Weighted contribution = $6.25

The number of units, 8,000, represents the total number of shovels, axes, and hoes that must be produced and sold to make a $20,000 profit. The number of shovels required is (.45)(8,000 units), or 3,600 units.

Product	Mix	No. Required
Shovel	.45	3,600 units
Ax	.20	1,600
Hoe	.35	2,800
		8,000 units

What Happens to the Profit Point If the Mix Changes? In this model, the mix affects the profit point. If the estimated mix is different from the actual mix, then the profit point will change. Assume the mix changes to 50 percent shovels, 10 percent axes, and 40 percent hoes, and the total number of units produced and sold remains 8,000. How is profit affected?

	Shovels	Axes	Hoes
Product mix	50%	10%	40%
Selling price/unit	$12	$16	$9
Variable cost/unit	$ 6	$ 7	$4
Contribution/unit	$ 6	$ 9	$5

Profit target (P) = unknown
Fixed costs = $30,000/yr.

Equation 7.2 can be restated and used to calculate profit.

$$X = \frac{P + FC}{WC}$$

$$WC(X) = P + FC$$

$$P = WC(X) - FC$$

We know the fixed costs are $30,000, and the volume is given as 8,000 units. First, we have to calculate the weighted contribution based on the new mix.

$$WC = \sum_{i=1}^{n} M_i(SP_i - VC_i)$$

$$= .5(\$12/\text{unit} - \$6/\text{unit}) + .1(\$16/\text{unit} - \$7/\text{unit}) + .4(\$9/\text{unit} - \$4/\text{unit})$$

$$= \$5.90\text{ unit}$$

Now profit can be calculated.

$$P = \$5.90(8{,}000 \text{ units}) - \$30{,}000$$
$$= \$17{,}200$$

The profit is only $17,200 dollars because demand shifted away from axes, which have a higher contribution per unit, to the lower-contribution shovels and hoes. Profit is not only a function of the volume produced and sold, but also a function of the product mix.

The C-V-P Model and Operating Leverage

The C-V-P model has uses in addition to calculating profit points. It also illustrates a fundamental concept in process selection. The volume of product demanded by customers and the organization's share of that market determine the organization's cost structure. To have large demands, a product must be priced so that large numbers of people can afford to buy it. If food processors sold for $250, the market would be much smaller than it would be if they sold for $50.

A small unit price forces the development of automated production systems in order to reduce total costs. How is this achieved? Capital in the form of equipment is substituted for labor to improve labor productivity and to utilize materials more efficiently. (Recall the example with the automated versus the manual drill press.) Larger volumes will support the engineering time necessary to make changes in product design and material specifications, thus, reducing costs and improving performance. Volume is a key to the process selection decision.

Low-Volume Option. When demand for a product is low, whatever the reason, it is difficult to support expensive specialized equipment for production. In such cases, more hand labor is used, and labor costs per unit of production are generally greater. Also, material costs are not as carefully scrutinized. A dollar of material savings on each unit cannot command much engineering and management time when only a few units, say 200, are required. This low-volume producer has a cost structure like the one shown in Exhibit 7.3.

High-Volume Option. The case for more specialization is much stronger if 2 million units are required. As volume grows, management is forced to change their operating philosophy because competitive pressure on price forces cost reductions. Cost reductions are achieved by shifting to an operation with high fixed costs and low unit variable costs, as shown in Exhibit 7.4. The variable names are subscripted with an M to indicate mass production. The products tend to be more uniform and are priced for the mass market.

Moving from Low Volume to High Volume. The change in operating position from low to high fixed costs brings greater risk and greater reward. This trade-off is referred to as **operating leverage.** The greater risk is evident in Exhibit 7.5, which shows the low-fixed-cost alternative in black and the high-fixed-cost alternative in blue.

Exhibit 7.3 Cost Structure of Low-Volume Producer (Low Fixed Costs and High Unit Variable Costs)

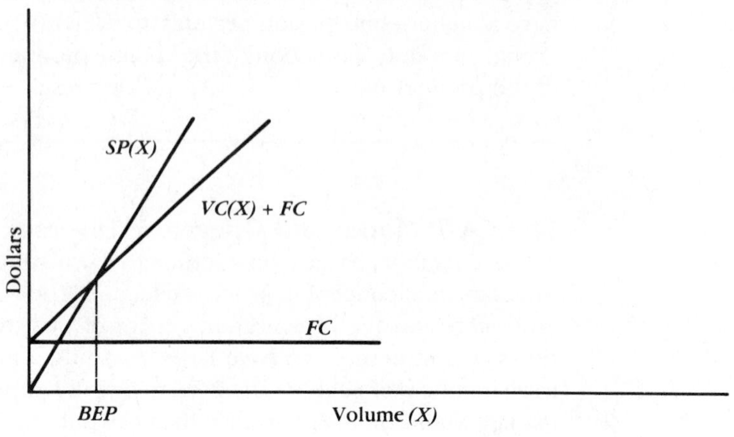

Exhibit 7.4 Cost Structure of High-Volume Producer (High Fixed Costs and Low Unit Variable Costs)

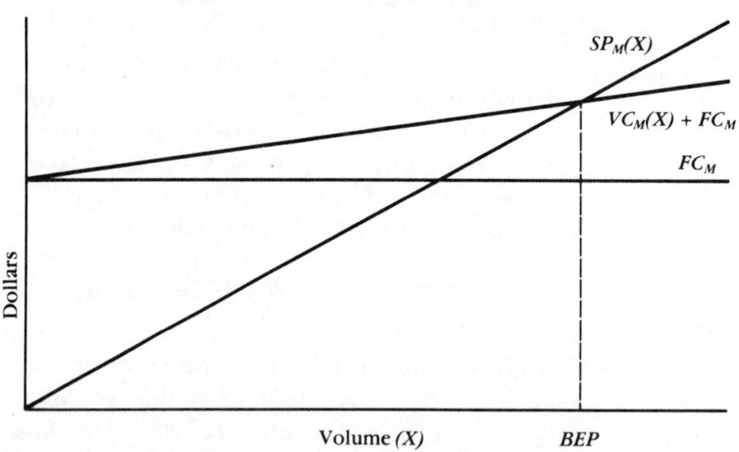

The low-fixed-cost operation has a substantially lower break-even point, and variable costs can be reduced significantly as volume drops below the break-even point. The losses incurred can be small. The opposite is true for mass production. As volume drops below the zero profit point, the losses mount rapidly because most of the costs are fixed.

An increase in volume favors the mass producer because greater volume adds only small unit variable costs. The fixed costs do not change. This rapid increase in profits is stopped only by the capacity limits of the existing asset base. That is

Exhibit 7.5 Operating Leverage

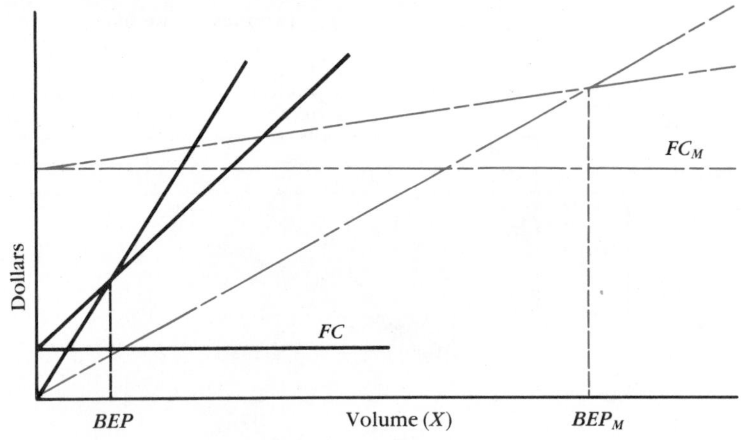

why mass producers prefer to operate at their capacity. This high operating ratio leads to high profits in the well-managed organization. The mass-producer is leveraging operations by adding fixed costs in the form of specialized equipment. The reward for this risk is greater profit potential.

Process Selection and Economies of Scale

From the perspective of economies of scale, process selection focuses on the volume of product demanded in the market. Organizations can influence that volume by increasing advertising, providing better service, and producing higher-quality products. Regardless of how that volume is generated, an organization needs to respond to higher demand with an appropriate process.

When does an organization have sufficient volume to justify specialized, high-speed equipment? Is a demand of 50,000 units per year sufficient? It is not possible to give specific answers to these questions because the answers depend on what the organization produces. For example, if it produces space shuttles, then an annual demand of 50,000 would certainly be large enough to support specialized facilities, and even 5,000 would be considered a large volume. However, if the organization is processing checks for a bank, 50,000 a year is a very small number, and even 1 million per year is not a large number.

In process selection, Hayes and Wheelwright (1979, p. 133) have suggested that product and process can be viewed through two sides of a matrix. Exhibit 7.6 displays a series of process alternatives that can be matched with identifiable product characteristics so that efficient operations can be achieved. High-volume operations are usually referred to as **line flow processes.** One type of line flow is the continuous flow process. A **continuous flow** does not usually identify individual units; rather, the product is mixed and flows together in a continuous stream. Oil refining is a good example of a continuous flow process. The term **assembly line** is used to describe the high-volume assembly of discrete prod-

Exhibit 7.6 Matching Process Alternatives with Product Characteristics

Product Characteristics

High volume, commodity products | High volume, some product variety | Moderate volume, multiple products | Low volume, many products | One-of-a-kind products

Low unit costs ←→ High unit costs

Process Alternatives

Continuous flow

Assembly line

Batch flow

Job shop

Project

Low product variety ↕ High product variety

Oil refining

Assembling washing machines

Producing mufflers for the replacement market

Operating a hospital emergency room

Designing and implementing a customized information system

No match of process alternatives with product characteristics

No match of process alternatives with product characteristics

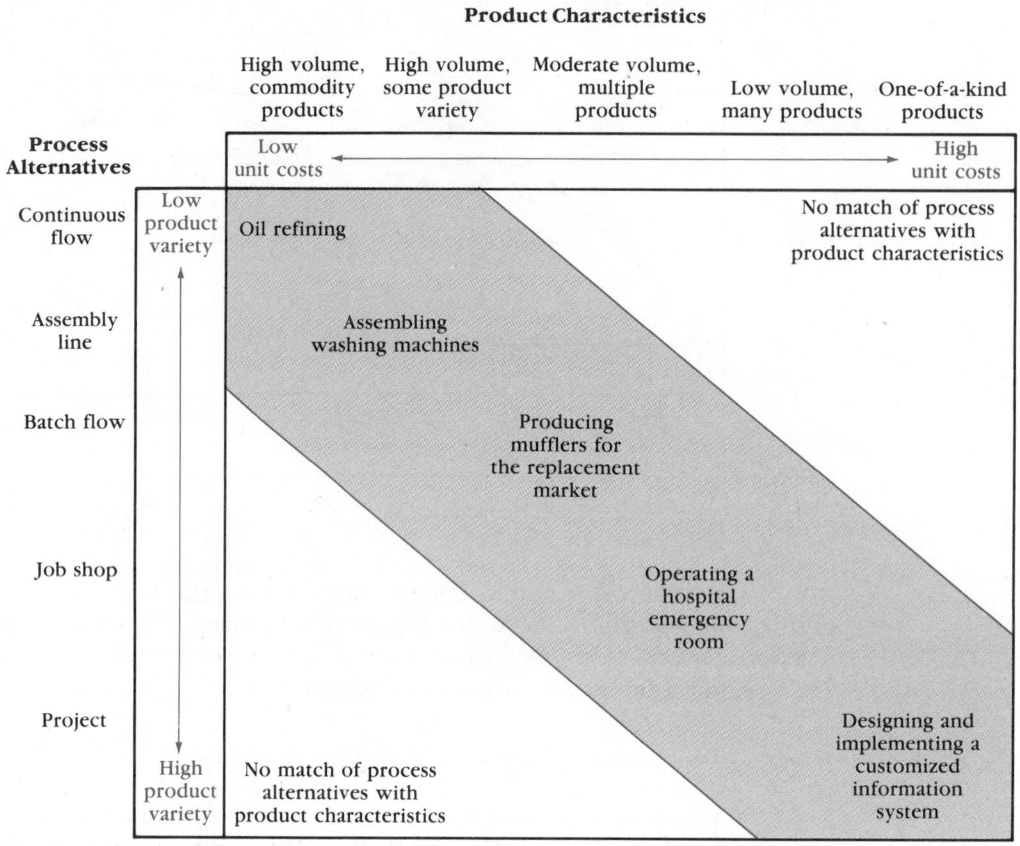

Adapted from Robert H. Hayes and Steven C. Wheelwright, "Linking Manufacturing Process and Product Life Cycles,"

ucts. A washing machine is a good example of an assembly-line product. Continuous flow and assembly lines are usually dedicated facilities that produce large volumes with little if any difference in the products.

Batch is a term used to describe a production process that does not have sufficient volume from a single product to fully use the facility. In this case, the facility produces several products to build sufficient volume. When this resource sharing exists, a transition time (**changeover time**) is usually required to change the facility from being able to make one product to being able to make the next.

As an example of a batch producer, consider a company that supplies the local muffler shop with parts. Although mufflers on various cars have different shapes and sizes, many are produced on the same equipment because the replacement market is usually not large enough to support equipment dedicated to making one replacement muffler. Production of the different shapes and sizes requires the equipment to be adjusted (changed over) between production runs for different mufflers. These changes take time and cost money, but are necessary to maintain enough volume to support the large investment in equipment.

As product volume declines, batching operations may no longer be possible. Here, only a few units of a product are required, and there may be no assurance that the order will be repeated. The differences between products can be significant. In this situation, usually called **job shop** production, the facility is general and flexible enough to meet a variety of needs. To achieve this flexibility, job shops generally have a much higher unit cost than line flow or batch processes for the same product. Fancy restaurants and hospital emergency rooms are examples of job shops. Both types of organizations offer great product variety and cater to individual customer demands.

At the bottom of the volume scale are **projects,** which are usually one-of-a-kind operations. Each job is different from the rest. Most large construction jobs are projects, and many service operations can be categorized as projects. Installing new computer hardware, adding major new computer software, and implementing a new management planning and control system all could qualify as projects.

The relationship between product and process illustrated in Exhibit 7.6 indicates that there is a one-to-one relationship between product volume and the type of process. For example, Exhibit 7.6 indicates that one-of-a-kind products cannot be produced on an assembly line or in a continuous flow shop. In essence, Exhibit 7.6 implies that an organization's options are limited to product and process matches on the diagonal. The diagram implies that if an organization wants to achieve the low cost obtained in continuous flow or assembly-line operations, it must significantly limit product variety. An organization that wants to achieve the product variety obtained in a job shop or projects must incur high unit costs.

With the advances in information and manufacturing technologies described in Chapter 2, organizations have new process alternatives, manufacturing cells and flexible manufacturing systems, that may allow them to achieve high product variety and low costs simultaneously. These technological advances expand the feasible product/process matches in Exhibit 7.6. We may not be ready to build nuclear power plants on an assembly line, but we can create appliances, automobiles, and other services and goods with increasing variety, while maintaining or reducing the unit cost. As information and manufacturing technologies continue to expand, the shaded blue diagonal that represents the feasible product/process matches will continue to expand.

The following sections describe the traditional process alternatives: continuous flow, assembly line, batch, job shop, and project, as well as manufacturing cells and flexible manufacturing systems.

Line Flow Processes

Continuous flow operations and assembly lines have some differences; yet both are high-volume, mass-production operations characterized by a standardized product with interchangeable parts. Because of this, the process is the same for each unit, and the product has a dominant product flow through the facility. Because there is little or no product variation, there is no reason to have more than one path through the facility. Furthermore, the equipment that processes the products should be arranged "around" the product so that material-handling and transportation costs are not excessive. This approach is called a **product layout.**

In terms of the cost structure, a continuous flow process or an assembly line has relatively high fixed costs and relatively low variable costs. The high fixed costs are, in part, a result of the substantial investment in specialized equipment.

There are some differences between a continuous flow process and an assembly line. In a continuous flow process, the product is often a commodity in

Fiberglass insulation flows off the end of this production line. Later, it will be packaged and shipped to customers. *Courtesy: Owens Corning Fiberglass, Inc.*

Engines for front-wheel-drive luxury cars are assembled to transmissions and other components to become a complete power train in a section of the General Motors–Orion plant. After final inspection, the units are carried by a conveyor to a marriage point with the unitized body. *Courtesy: General Motors.*

which one unit is not distinguishable from another. In this case, the producer makes no attempt to track each unit separately. For example, in refining gasoline from crude oil, one gallon of unleaded regular gasoline is like another. The production of fiberglass insulation is high volume and fast-paced. It is not feasible to track and identify each piece produced. The emphasis is on measuring inputs and comparing them to outputs.

The traditional assembly-line process allows some variations among units. Options are usually selected from a list of possibilities, and the minor adjustments needed can be made by workers on the production line. Adding power steering to a car or a temperature probe to a microwave oven is relatively easy to do. Customizing mass-assembled products generally take place in a separate facility or in the aftermarket. For example, many customers buy vans from mass-producers and have small shops customize them.

The mass-assembled product is often tracked by some product identification code or serial number. This can require considerable clerical time and expense. The continuous flow and assembly-line characteristics are summarized in Exhibit 7.7, along with the other process types.

Mass Production and Quality

Mass production of goods and services does not necessarily imply inferior quality. A Rolls Royce could be made at the same quality level in quantities of five thousand or five million. The reasons that five million Rolls are not produced are

OPERATIONS IN ACTION

UTM Credit Union: Responding to Demands

Operators enter check amounts as check processing machines read encoded information on each document in order to verify accuracy. *Source: Society Bank and Trust Corporation.*

In service operations as in manufacturing, volume plays a key role in determining how an organization responds to demand. UTM Credit Union serves several hundred employees with such services as traditional checking and savings accounts, automobile and other small consumer loans, and automated teller service. UTM cannot offer the wide variety of service usually available at banks with thousands of customers. In fact, their automated teller service is possible only because of an affiliation with a large bank.

UTM's methods for processing transactions are significantly different from those used in larger banks. UTM's transaction volume cannot support the sophisticated computer-aided processing of transactions and high-speed check-clearing equipment found in many banks. More hand labor is used to process transactions because the volume is not sufficient to support large investments in specialized, high-speed equipment. Volume is a key determinant in process selection.

Exhibit 7.7 Characteristics of the Process Alternatives

Process	Volume	Product variety	Product flow	Facility layout	Fixed costs	Variable costs	Equipment
	Characteristics						
Continuous flow	High	Standard	Dominant	Product	High	Low	Special purpose
Assembly line		Standard with minor modification	Dominant	Product	High	Low	Special purpose
Batch		Some variation	Dominant	Product	Moderate to high	Low	Some flexibility
Flexible manufacturing system		Moderate variety	Dominant	Product	High	Low	Flexible
Manufacturing cell		Moderate variety	Dominant	Product	Moderate	Low to moderate	Flexible
Job shop	Low	Major differences	Random	Process	Low	High	Flexible
Project	One	One-of-a-kind	Not applicable	Fixed position	Low to moderate	High	Flexible

(1) the market could not purchase that volume at the usual price and (2) the product would lose its prestige image if it were regularly seen on the highway.

It is the pressure on price that forces cost to be reduced. This pressure forces the substitution of less-expensive materials and less-expensive methods of production. The organization that can find ways to make these substitutions and raise product quality at the same time will be rewarded by increasing sales and profits. It should not be an excuse for inferior design or shoddy workmanship.

Evidence that high-quality products can be mass-produced can be seen in many of the products we use every day. Automobiles, televisions, stereos, and dishwashers are a few examples. The old adage "They don't make 'em like they used to" is certainly true. Today's products are better.

Batch Flow

When quantities are not sufficient to support dedicated production facilities, several groups or batches are produced using the same facility. These products are usually similar in design and have similar processing requirements. For example, glass containers come in a variety of sizes, but are designed and built similarly. A key to understanding if the differences among products are meaningful can be found when the equipment is shut down to change from one product to another. If the time for these changes is not significant and the sequence of operations is similar, then it is like a line flow process. On the other hand, if the changeover time is significant, then these products should be built in batches.

OPERATIONS IN ACTION

The Automotive Industry: Substituting Plastic for Metal Parts

In an effort to reduce costs and improve fuel economy, automotive engineers have replaced hundreds of pounds of steel auto parts with plastic. Initially, many plastic parts were inferior because they lacked the strength and durability of metal. Today, however, better resins make these parts more durable and flexible, and they don't rust. The result is a better product that costs less.

Efforts will continue to replace metal parts with plastic. Plastic parts are being considered for such exterior body parts as hoods and fenders. Exterior body parts made of plastic will not rust like steel does, will resist nicks and dings that often show on a metal exterior, and will require less energy in shaping and forming than metal parts. General Motors Corporation's new minivan uses plastic body panels that are glued to a lightweight metal frame. The technique is much stronger than engineers expected and should yield significant weight saving in future models.

OPERATIONS IN ACTION

Sun Microsystems, Inc.: Automated Assembly Lines

Sun Microsystems builds computer work stations (personal computers, network servers, etc.) for a variety of applications including computer-aided design. The company was founded in 1982 and went from $8.6 million in sales in 1983 to $537 million in 1987. Operations had outgrown the existing facility and was restricting sales because of late delivery.

In designing their new facility, Sun management decided to build three major products on the same assembly line. Each of these products had many options, so material handling and coordination became very important. The computers are built in random sequence, so that a small desktop computer with four megabytes of memory could be followed by a much larger desk-side computer with 2.3 gigabytes of memory, which could be followed by cabinet-size network server.

To make the system work, Sun uses a specially built roller-conveyor system that delivers kitted subassemblies to the assembly area. The routing is handled by a computer system that shows worker availability and the status of each job. An automated material-handling system coordinates the ordering and preparation of materials for assembly.

With the new system in place, Sun was able to increase capacity, which allowed revenue to increase by 150 percent, tripling net income. On-time shipments increased dramatically. With the flexible assembly system, Sun has the capability to respond to changing customer needs.[3]

Some organizations are attempting to build assembly lines that not only are automated, but also have increased flexibility. To meet customer demand for greater product variety, organizations like Sun Microsystems, Inc., are building different products on the same assembly line. Because organizations can build several different products on the same production equipment, they avoid the extra expense of building and operating multiple assembly lines. They enjoy the benefits of economies of scale even when the volume of individual products is low.

Because of the similar processing requirements in batch operations, one or a few product flows dominate. For example, appliance manufacturers may produce several different models of refrigerators on the same assembly line. In cases where changeover time is significant, manufacturers may produce a batch—say, one week's production of a particular model—and then switch to another model. Although the models show some differences from batch to batch, these differences are not significant enough to change the product-oriented layout of the facility. If a producer is able to design the product and the process so that different models can be produced one after the other with zero or near zero changeover time, then the process is similar to an assembly line that is producing a standard product. (You may want to review the Operations in Action on Sun Microsystems, Inc.) The disadvantages of batch production are that (1) changeover time is nonproductive and (2) extra inventory must be maintained to satisfy demand for the products that are not being produced.

Firms that use batch processing will tend to incur higher unit costs than mass-producers will because of equipment downtime for changeover, larger amounts of inventory, and increased labor costs due to the changeovers. The greater the time devoted to changing facilities, the greater the cost differential suffered by batch operations. The key to moving to lower-cost production is to eliminate or at least greatly reduce the changeover time. One way to do this is to eliminate product variety. Henry Ford did this in the early days of automobile production when he said that customers could have cars of any color as long as it was black. The approach of standardizing products does not work for all products and no longer works as well in the automotive industry as it did in Henry Ford's day.

Management problems become more difficult when production becomes less of a line flow process and more of a batch process. The following questions arise when batch processes are used:

1. How are products to be sequenced in the facility?
2. How many units of one product should be made before production is switched to another?
3. How much inventory should be kept of the products that are not being produced?

These scheduling and lot-sizing issues are discussed in Chapters 13 and 16.

Manufacturing Cells and Flexible Manufacturing Systems

Manufacturing cells, sometimes called cellular manufacturing, and flexible manufacturing systems (FMS) are process options that offer the potential to produce low-cost products that meet varying customer requirements. Manufacturing cells are discussed in Chapter 2. (You may find it helpful to review that part of the chapter.) Manufacturing cells rely on group technology to build a family of parts with similar design and processing characteristics. In this way, a product-oriented layout (cell) can be designed that will reduce material-handling costs, increase machine utilization, and cut production lead times. Because the processing is similar, less time is required to change from one product within the family to another. See Exhibit 7.7.

An FMS is similar to a manufacturing cell because it relies on group technology to build families of parts. Also like a manufacturing cell, an FMS produces low-cost products with high variety. The major differences are that an FMS tends

OPERATIONS IN ACTION

Badger Meter, Inc.: From Job Shop to Manufacturing Cells to FMS

Badger Meters, Inc., is located in Milwaukee and makes flow meters that range in size from household water meters to large water mains. The company produces 110 different meter housings in quantities that vary from 1 to 1,000 per year. The industry is very competitive and is plagued with overcapacity and price cutting. Many of the valves are purchased by public utilities through competitive bidding. An order can be lost for a few cents per meter.

Badger's first step was to take existing production equipment from the process-oriented job shop layout and rearrange it into a manufacturing cell. In one case, one person was able to operate three machines and produce a finished casting in six minutes. With the old system, the time, including delays for material handling and scheduling, was measured in days. The manufacturing cells reduced material-handling requirements, cut production time, and lowered costs.

Today, Badger uses an FMS built by Kearney & Trecker Corporation to produce the meter housings. To implement the system, Badger constructed a model of the new facility and held a series of meetings with employees. The meetings were used to explain the new operations and to obtain ideas and suggestions from employees. The workers also visited Kearney & Trecker's facilities to learn how the FMS operates and what maintenance procedures to follow. The FMS has been very successful.[4]

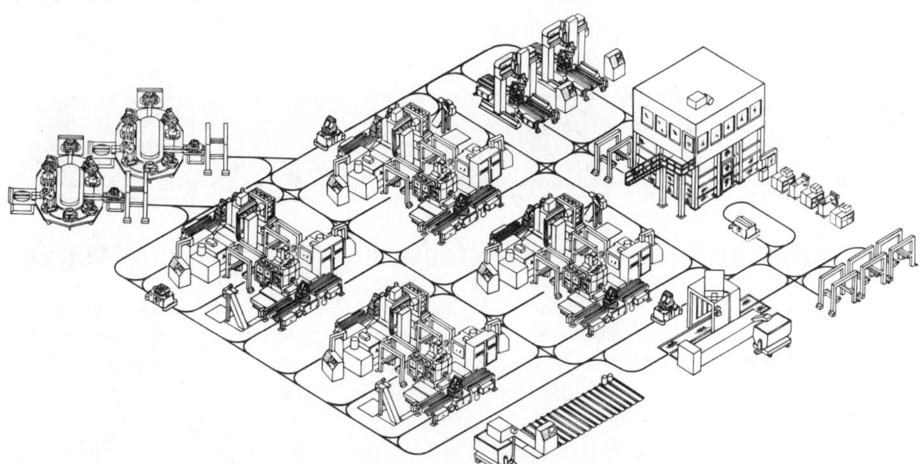

This schematic layout of an FMS illustrates how several manufacturing centers are linked by automated guided vehicles that travel on particular paths. Each center contains automated material-handling devices, automated machine tools, and computers to coordinate the activities generated within each center and between centers. *Courtesy: Cincinnati Milacron, Inc.*

to have more automation, robots, and computer control than a manufacturing cell does and that it usually operates without people tending the machines.

FMSs grew from the need to cope with demand for increasing product variations. With an FMS, an organization can capture new markets by accumulating production requirements from several low-volume products. Higher-volume op-

OPERATIONS IN ACTION

Ford Motor Company: Moving from Hard Automation to Flexible Manufacturing

The automotive industry required millions of eight-cylinder engines per year in the 1960s and early 1970s. To produce these economically, automotive engineers designed a sophisticated set of machining stations called **transfer lines.** The transfer line could produce a machined engine block without operator intervention.

This approach seemed ideally suited for mass production because it produced low-cost, high-quality engines. After the oil embargo of 1973, demand for large engines dropped dramatically. Faced with changing government fuel economy requirements, tough worldwide competition, and shifting customer taste, the automotive industry found that transfer lines did not have enough flexibility to adapt to other engine sizes. Changeover was costly. The term **hard automation** is used to describe processes that have limited flexibility.

In Romeo, Michigan, Ford is constructing a new flexible manufacturing system (FMS) to build a family of modular engines for the 1990s. Ford is designing new V-8 and V-6 engines for fuel efficiency and ease of manufacturing. The FMS at Romeo will be capable of producing more than a dozen engine sizes and configurations on one production line. To increase the likelihood of the project's success, Ford has put design engineers and manufacturing engineers on the same team. The FMS is a big gamble for Ford, which has already spent $1 billion on the project. However, Ford feels it is a necessary one if the company is to be competitive in the 1990s.[5]

INTEGRATING THE SYSTEM

Computer-Integrated Manufacturing for Improving Marketing Efforts

Computer-integrated manufacturing (CIM) can be important for improving an organization's position in the market. Not only can it be used to design and produce a wide variety of products to satisfy diverse customer needs, but also it can produce them at low cost. These production capabilities can be turned into marketing advantages by offering customers high-quality specialized products at low costs.

Most competitors can achieve low costs by using mass-production approaches for a single product. Others can give product variety, but only by using higher-cost job shop production. With CIM's design and flexible manufacturing capabilities, an organization can gain an advantage over the mass-producers by offering variety at a cost that approaches that of the mass-producer. The organization can gain an advantage over the job shop by offering lower-cost products that approach the variety that can be achieved in a job shop. These enhanced production capabilities allow the firm to gain an advantage on the competition through new approaches to the market.

erations allow the arrangement of a set of machines in one layout to produce all the different products. However, the products must be similar enough to have the same or a similar sequence of operations, and the machines must be flexible enough to handle the differences. This is feasible with computer technology and robotics that can quickly be adapted to new products. Manufacturing cells and FMSs enable organizations to increase the volume of product moving across a group of machines and thereby reduce operating costs.

The differences among the hard automation that is often found in mass production; the flexible manufacturing systems that are now being applied; and the general-purpose equipment that is usually found in job shops are important to understand. These process alternatives affect several basic issues involved in production. The level of automation affects capital investment, unit costs, flexibility, and capacity. As FMSs become even more flexible, low-volume jobs will be grouped for production on them. As FMS technology becomes better understood and lower in cost, large homogeneous markets can be segmented because the FMS will provide customers with product variety and low costs. As shown in Exhibit 7.8, the area of application for FMSs will continue to increase as technology improves.

Job Shop

A job shop does not produce large quantities of the same or even similar products, but is dominated by a large number of different products produced in small volumes. Because the products are different, they do not follow the same path through the facility. In fact, the movement of products between work centers is

Exhibit 7.8 Automation Systems

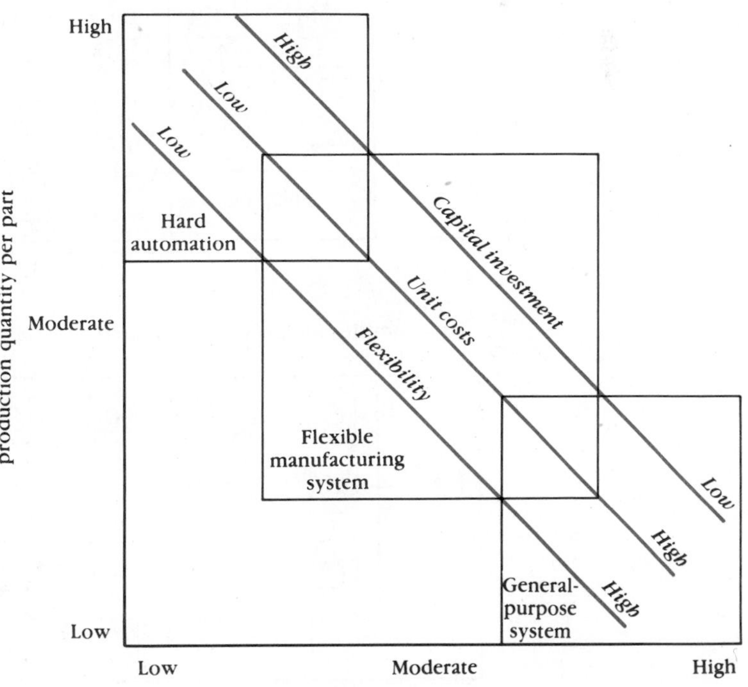

best characterized as random. As a result, it is not possible to organize machines by product flow as in the line flow processes or even in batch operations. It is necessary to group machines by process or type of operation because one work center is equally as likely to require work as any of the remaining centers. The job shop is one of the process alternatives shown in Exhibit 7.7.

Because the products are very different, specialized equipment cannot be justified. Job shops use flexible equipment to meet the needs of the diverse product group. A job shop produces different products on general-purpose machines using skilled labor. The cost structure has low fixed costs and high unit variable costs.

Gains in manufacturing, computer, and information technologies will permit more flexibility and thus allow products now made in job shops to be produced in families, as shown in Exhibit 7.9. In addition, as FMSs and the information systems that control them become capable of producing a wider variety of parts, the products once produced in job shops will become less expensive. These products will move up the volume scale seen in Exhibit 7.7 without losing their

Exhibit 7.9 Process Flows Before and After Applying Group Technology to Achieve Manufacturing Cells

Job Shop: Jumbled Flow

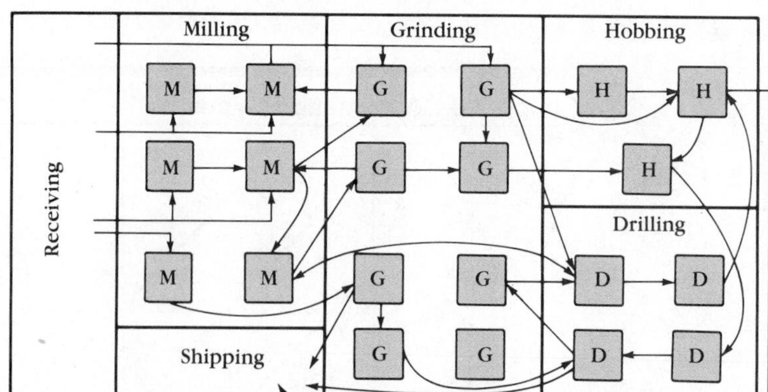

Families of Parts and Manufacturing Cells: Organized Flow

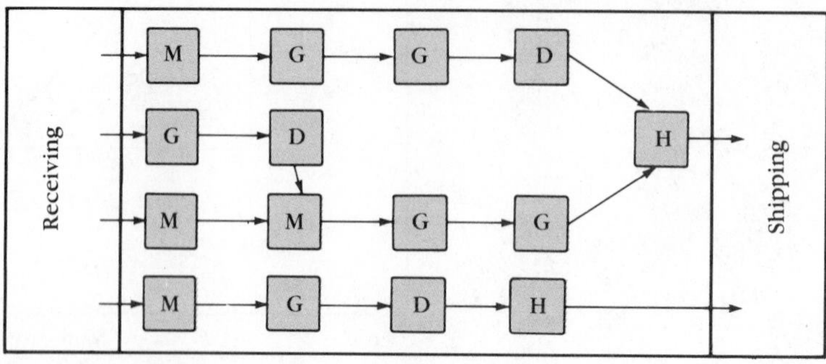

appeal to the market. Such a move can provide an organization with a competitive edge—low price, high quality, and product variety.

Project

Projects usually involve a one-of-a-kind product. Typical examples are found in the construction industry and include the construction of large ships, plants, and office buildings. In a project, cost structure is not the same as in other processes because there is only a single unit. In one sense, the cost for the project is all variable. Fixed costs in the form of overhead begin to make sense when a firm is engaged in more than one project and can spread certain major equipment costs and overhead costs over several different projects.

Product flow is not meaningful in projects because the end product of most construction projects is designed to remain stationary. The usual term that describes the layout is *fixed position*. A project-oriented operation is very flexible, allowing extensive customizing of the finished products.

Projects are common in service operations as well. Consider a manufacturer of electric motors that is building a new assembly plant. The consulting firm hired to design and install the computer system and the communication network for the plant will approach this as a project. This consulting firm is obviously providing a service and is using a project management approach to successfully complete the work.

Process Selection Summary

As with any classification scheme, an organization may not fit neatly into any of the process categories of continuous flow, assembly line, flexible manufacturing system, manufacturing cell, batch, job shop, or project. In some organizations,

OPERATIONS IN ACTION

Westinghouse: Developing and Installing Manufacturing Information Systems

Westinghouse's consulting group develops and installs software systems for controlling "factories of the future." These software systems can track each part through the facility, maintain information on product quality and machine failures, assist in scheduling jobs through the facility, and track inventory of materials and supplies.

Systems have been installed in facilities in Lima, Ohio, and Columbia, South Carolina. Each system has been tailored to the needs of the facility. Both installations are going through the start-up stage, so hard data are not yet available. The plant in South Carolina expects a unit cost of less than $20, compared with a unit cost of nearly $40 in traditional plants. Response to customer needs is expected to be faster because the facility is flexible enough to quickly change from one part to the next.

To design these individualized systems, Westinghouse draws the needed talent from a pool of experts and forms a project team. Because each system is different, different groups may be used to develop each system. This approach allows Westinghouse to pull together resources to meet specific customer needs. Flexibility in assigning personnel is a key factor for success.

production is a combination of different process types. For example, Ford Motor Company uses continuous flow, assembly lines, batch processing, and job shops. We discussed each type for several purposes: (1) to show the differences and similarities among these processes, (2) to illustrate that different approaches are necessary to successfully manage them, and (3) to provide a basis for analyzing a firm's operation in order to better understand how it functions. We have already seen that the layout and the cost structure for an assembly line and a job shop are fundamentally different. A review of Exhibit 7.7 may help to summarize the differences.

Consider the process selection decision from another perspective. Would it be possible for all firms to choose labor-intensive approaches, such as job shops and projects, for production? The immediate response should be no because there are simply not enough labor hours available to produce the millions of dishwashers, hair dryers, automobiles, banking transactions, hamburgers, consulting reports, and so on that are demanded. Without specialized tools to improve productivity, people in this country and abroad would not be able to maintain their present living standard. The mass-production alternatives, line flow processes and large batch production, are essential to maintain the flow of products. Further improvements in living standards will be achieved by the following means:

1. Improving these mass-production approaches with better technology, including computer application.
2. Moving as many products as possible from job shops to large-scale production, thereby freeing people for creating new products and processes.

THE FOCUSED FACTORY

The previous sections of this chapter have illustrated how investing in specialized equipment to attain high volume can reduce unit costs. For many years it was accepted procedure for operations to produce more and more units in order to lower costs. This created two problems. First, facilities grew larger and larger as more capacity was added. More levels of management had to be added to cope with the increasing numbers of people. Facilities with 3,000 or 4,000 employees were common, and in some cases, facilities had 10,000 or more employees and covered many acres. Buildings with more than a million square feet (about 24 acres) were common, and more than one building could be at a location. The sheer size of these facilities made them difficult to manage. Coordination and communication of activities became major problems. Second, faced with rapid market changes and shorter product life cycles, facility managers added the production of different products to facilities that were designed to have limited flexibility in order to keep volume high and costs low. The results were increased downtime for equipment changeover and overloads on information systems that were designed to manage homogeneous products and processes.

In many cases, management's response was to add staff personnel and indirect labor to handle these problems. This created a "hidden factory" of overhead costs. In some cases, the costs of handling materials, maintaining equipment, and coordinating operations exceeded the cost savings from increasing volume. The revolution in manufacturing taking place today is the reaction of business to make manufacturing more responsive to customer needs, while increasing productivity and reducing costs.

One approach to dealing with the increasing complexity caused by divergent customer needs is to build smaller focused factories, as advocated by Wickham Skinner (1974, p. 114). These smaller facilities often have less than 500 employees and concentrate on making a few products. These simplifed factories not only limit the number of different products made, but also limit the scope of operations to include only a few process technologies. Focused factories do not attempt to produce several different quality levels; they strive for the highest quality at all times. What the focused factory may give up because it does not fully take advantage of economies of scale, it makes up by simplicity in management and control. Manufacturing cells and flexible manufacturing systems, with their families of parts, could be considered a logical extension of the focused factory.

THE ROLE OF COMPUTERS IN THE PRODUCTION PROCESS

The application of computer and information systems to the production process is on the verge of revolutionizing the way in which services and goods are produced. The application of information technology to service operations is already evident in airline reservation systems, overnight express package delivery, moneymarket checking accounts, and others. Soon to be coming to the mass market are banking, ordering groceries, and accessing library reference services from home via a microcomputer and a modem.

The impact of computer and information systems on the manufacturing process for goods may be even greater. Robots have been around for several years,

INTEGRATING THE SYSTEM

Product Design, Capacity, and Process Selection

Before moving to the next chapter, we should briefly review the strong relationships among product design, capacity, and process selection. A market study shapes the product's features and performance characteristics and defines a group of people who may be willing to purchase the product at a certain price. The design describes the product and its characteristics, both physical and nonphysical. The capacity is based on obtaining a reasonable share of the estimated market, and process selection is driven by the volume demanded and by cost and quality considerations.

These interrelationships are not one-directional. The firm's ability or lack of ability to produce the product may alter the product design, the capacity, or even the market segment willing to purchase the product. Performance characteristics of the product, which are described in the market study and designed into the product, may be unobtainable in full-scale production. This causes the market analysis and product design to be re-examined.

Changes in the design may occur as the manufacturing engineer lays out the process. A subtle change in design can often reduce costs, improve quality, or increase performance. All parts of the management team working to bring the product into being should be willing to listen and learn from other members.

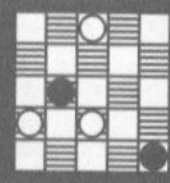

GAINING STRATEGIC ADVANTAGE AT IBM

Smart Automation Provides Low-Cost Products and Flexible Manufacturing Capabilities

IBM builds Proprinters in Lexington, Kentucky, in only a few minutes with eight-station, robotized assembly lines. The plant builds more than 1 million Proprinters and Selectric typewriters per year and can deliver finished product in three to fifteen days. As a result of its automation efforts and improved organization, IBM continues to dominate the U.S. market for full-sized typewriters, with a 44 percent share. Its Proprinter holds a strong position with its reputation for high quality and 10 percent annual gains in productivity. Integrating manufacturing operations with the organization's strategy has enabled IBM to gain a competitive advantage.

IBM is also attempting to gain a larger share of the laptop (portable) microcomputer market with its state-of-the-art, fully automated factory in Austin, Texas. The IBM laptop is the first computer produced completely using robots. The new computer is assembled, tested, packed, and shipped without anyone lifting a finger. Increased productivity from this automated, robot-operated assembly line and a newly developed computer chip could cut the laptop's cost by 50 percent.

IBM hopes its new production process and lower price will boost sales and increase customer acceptance of portables. IBM's strategy seems to be to increase sales in this growing market with a low-cost, high-quality product. This strategy could propel IBM past Hewlett-Packard in market share. As a result, IBM's manufacturing costs per unit could drop even farther as their production facility, which has high fixed and low variable costs, produces more and more units.

In addition to low costs, IBM's laptop facility has been built to provide the company with flexible manufacturing capabilities. The assembly line is designed to produce cost-effectively any electronic product that is 24 × 24 × 14 inches or smaller. According to IBM automation specialist Clark Preston, "We can build printers, other PCs or toasters." With its Austin facility, IBM is in a position to respond with unprecedented speed to rapid and unexpected shifts in the computer market. Low-cost operations and manufacturing flexibility give IBM strategic alternatives in defending its PC business from foreign and domestic clones.[6]

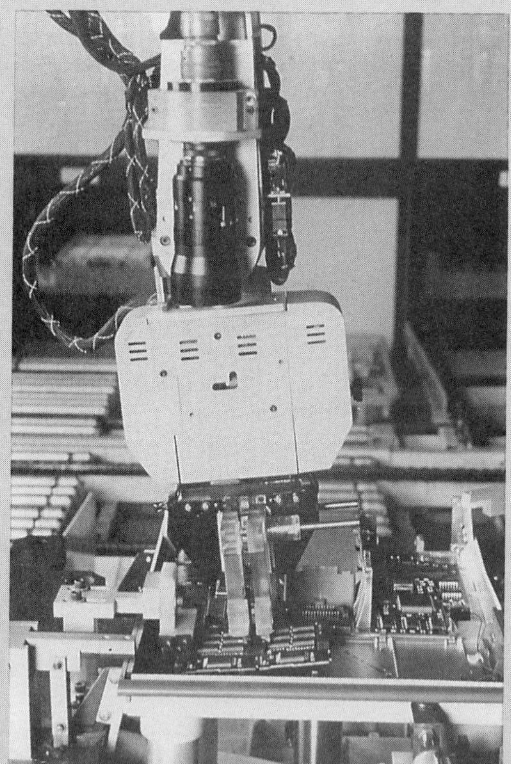

A robot inserts circuit boards into a laptop computer in IBM's Austin, Texas, facility. ***Courtesy: IBM.***

but managers are just beginning to understand how to use them effectively. A robot is a key part of a flexible manufacturing system (FMS). Computer-aided design (CAD) and computer-aided manufacturing (CAM) are being combined with information systems to create new factories.

Detailed decision making can be done via computer links to data bases. This approach can remove the details of controlling minute-by-minute production and free managers for planning and improving the system. Information about the process is collected, summarized, and stored on computers for later access by management, enabling better decision making. In this facility, people play a lesser role in terms of hands-on manufacturing, but a greater role in managing and controlling operations.

SUMMARY

- Process defines the way that the product should be produced. Does the product have sufficient volume to justify large investments in plant and equipment to leverage the worker output? If not, then much highly skilled, high-cost labor must be used.
- Process selection is closely related to the product design and capacity decisions. Products with widespread appeal to the consumer will require a process that can deliver these products at competitive prices and in large volume.
- The cost-volume-profit model of the firm is one way of viewing the processing options. This model allows the organization to examine the risks associated with selecting the "right" processing option. Mass-production alternatives involve greater risk, but have the potential for greater return.
- Process selection is a function of volume demanded. The different process types include line flow, which includes continuous flow and assembly line, batch, job shop, and project, as well as manufacturing cells and flexible manufacturing systems. Each of these process types is summarized in Exhibit 7.7.
- In the future, flexibility in the production process will play an increasingly important role. Changing consumer demand and specialized designs will give a competitive edge to producers who have flexibility.

CAREER PROFILE

Carol Larkins

Production Scheduler
North Star Steel Company

Carol Larkins is a production scheduler for North Star Steel Company, which produces bar and rod steel. Its bar stock might be used as a stabilizer bar to prevent excessive sway in the rear of a car as it takes a hard corner. North Star uses an electric furnace to melt steel, which is then cast and rolled into shape.

Responsibilities

Larkins is responsible for developing production schedules for the entire line of the company's products. This includes scheduling all processes from the electric furnaces through final finishing. She allocates steel production to incoming customer orders so that the due dates are satisfied and the equipment highly utilized. High equipment utilization is important to Larkins and to North Star because of the company's large investment in equipment, which creates a high fixed-cost base. (North Star is a line flow process.) Larkins' scheduling practices are important in making the operations run smoothly.

Experience and Education

Larkins has attended numerous workshops and seminars, has had much on-the-job training, and is now extending her education through college courses in business and operations management. Her career opportunities include becoming a first-line supervisor or department head.

SOLVED PROBLEMS

1. Big Beaver Security Analyst, Inc., has decided to offer financial services via a computer-based electronic network. Customers with a microcomputer and a modem can place an order for a transaction at any time. Big Beaver is planning to lease the needed equipment at an annual cost of $15,000. Each transaction costs Big Beaver $.56. The company plans to charge customers $.75 for each transaction using the network regardless of the size of the purchase. This $.75 is in addition to the normal commissions charged to customers.
   a. If Big Beaver's goal is to break even on the electronic network and make money through the commissions, how many customers must access the system?

Solution

The equation for the cost-volume-profit model is

$$X = \frac{(P + FC)}{C} \tag{7.1}$$

where

X = the number of units produced and sold

P = planned profit

FC = fixed costs

C = the contribution, which is the selling price per unit minus variable costs per unit

$$X = \frac{(0 + \$15{,}000)}{(\$.75 - \$.56)}$$

$$= 78{,}947 \text{ transactions}$$

b. Big Beaver's marketing staff believes that just as many people will use the system if the transaction charge is raised to \$1.00. At what volume will Big Beaver break even if it raises the charge to \$1.00?

Solution

$$X = \frac{0 + \$15{,}000}{(\$1.00 - \$.56)}$$

$$= 34{,}091 \text{ transactions}$$

c. Big Beaver's financial staff believes that it is poor policy to offer services without expecting a profit. What happens to the profit point in parts a and b if profit is set at 15 percent of the annual lease costs?

Solution

$$X = \frac{\$2{,}250 + \$15{,}000}{(\$.75 - \$.56)}$$

$$= 90{,}789 \text{ transactions}$$

Transactions will have to increase from 78,947 to 90,789 if a \$.75 transaction fee is charged.

$$X = \frac{\$2{,}250 + \$15{,}000}{(\$1.00 - \$.56)}$$

$$= 39{,}205 \text{ transactions}$$

Transactions will have to increase from 34,091 to 39,205 if \$1.00 is charged for each transaction.

2. Elaine Foundry, Inc., forges metal heads for hammers and hatchets at its Lake Cayuga plant. Information on its costs and product mix is shown in the following table:

	Hammer Head	Hatchet Head
Product mix	.85	.15
Selling price/unit	\$1.80	\$3.40
Variable cost/unit	\$1.50	\$1.65

Annual fixed costs are estimated at \$350,000.

a. At what volume will Elaine cover its costs, given the present mix?

Solution

The weighted contribution is calculated as

$$WC = \sum_{i=1}^{n} M_i(SP_i - VC_i)$$

The profit point is calculated as

$$X = \frac{(P + FC)}{WC} \qquad (7.2)$$

The weighted contribution is determined as follows:

$$WC = .85(\$1.80 - \$1.50) + .15(\$3.40 - \$1.65)$$
$$= \$.5175 \text{ per composite unit}$$

The profit point for zero profit is

$$X = \frac{(0 + \$350{,}000)}{\$.5175}$$
$$= 676{,}329 \text{ composite units}$$

The volume of hammer and hatchet heads required to cover costs is

$$\text{Hammers} = .85(676{,}329) = 574{,}880$$
$$\text{Hatchets} = .15(676{,}329) = 101{,}449$$

b. At what volume will Elaine Foundry report a $100,000 profit, given the present mix?

Solution

The profit point for a $100,000 profit is

$$X = \frac{(\$100{,}000 + \$350{,}000)}{\$.5175}$$
$$= 869{,}565 \text{ composite units}$$

The volume of hammer and hatchet heads required to achieve a profit of $100,000 is

$$\text{Hammers} = .85(869{,}565) = 739{,}130$$
$$\text{Hatchets} = .15(869{,}565) = 130{,}435$$

c. If the product mix is changed to .8 for hammer heads and .2 for hatchet heads, at what volume of hammer and hatchet heads will Elaine achieve a $100,000 profit?

Solution

Weighted contribution:

$$WC = .80(\$1.80 - \$1.50) + .20(\$3.40 - \$1.65)$$
$$= \$.59 \text{ per composite unit}$$

The profit point for $100,000 profit is

$$X = \frac{(\$100{,}000 + \$350{,}000)}{\$.59}$$
$$= 762{,}712 \text{ composite units}$$

The volume of hammer and hatchet heads required to achieve a profit of $100,000 is

$$\text{Hammers} = .80(762{,}712) = 610{,}170$$
$$\text{Hatchets} = .20(762{,}712) = 152{,}542$$

d. With this new mix, what happens to the volume required to make a \$100,000 profit if the selling price of a hammer head is raised \$.05?

Solution

Weighted contribution:

$$WC = .80(\$1.85 - \$1.50) + .20(\$3.40 - \$1.65)$$
$$= \$.63 \text{ per composite unit}$$

The profit point for \$100,000 profit is

$$X = \frac{(\$100{,}000 + \$350{,}000)}{\$.63}$$
$$= 714{,}286 \text{ composite units}$$

The volume of hammer and hatchet heads required to achieve a profit of \$100,000 is

$$\text{Hammers} = .80(714{,}286) = 571{,}429$$
$$\text{Hatchets} = .20(714{,}286) = 142{,}857$$

QUESTIONS

1. What is process selection, and how can the organization use it to gain competitive advantage?

2. How is process selection related to product design and capacity determination? What are some examples?

3. Explain how the cost-volume-profit model of the firm is derived. How is it useful to operations managers in making the process selection decision?

4. What is operating leverage, and how does it help to explain risk in the organization?

5. Support or refute this statement: "The quality of mass-produced goods and services must be inferior."

6. What are line flow processes, and what characteristics help to define them? Give examples.

7. What is batch flow, and what characteristics help to define it? Give examples.

8. What is a job shop, and what characteristics help to define it? Give examples.

9. What is a project, and what characteristics help to define it? Give examples.

10. How will flexibility help an organization achieve a competitive advantage?

11. How can computers be used in the production process, and how will their role change?

12. What is a focused factory?

13. How are manufacturing cells and flexible manufacturing systems affecting the process selection decision.

PROBLEMS

1. Nelson, Neddel, and Nickersen Stock Brokers are planning to invest in automated equipment that will process stock transactions. The equipment requires a $12 million annual investment. The operating costs are $120.00 per hour. The equipment can generate 5,000 transactions per hour.

a. What is the unit cost of a transaction if 1 million are required?
b. What is the unit cost if 10 million are required?
c. What is the unit cost if 100 million are required?
d. Why would NNN want to keep the level of transactions high?

2. George's Mold Shop is planning to bid on a plastic part for one of the Big Three auto makers. If George's gets the bid, the manager is planning to buy a new semiautomatic machine to speed up the process. The annual fixed cost of the machine is $45,000. The machine requires only part-time supervision, and the labor cost is estimated at $1.50 per hour. This has been calculated as 0.08 hour of labor at $18.75 per hour. On the average, the machine can produce 140 pieces per hour and is expected to operate for 2,000 hours per year.

a. What is the unit cost of a plastic part if 10,000 are required?
b. What is the unit cost if 100,000 are required?
c. What is the unit cost if 200,000 are required?
d. What is the unit cost if the machine operates at capacity for the entire year?

3. Slimline Manufacturing makes briefcases. It is considering the purchase of new stitching machines for its final assembly. Following are the data for analysis:

System	Annualized Fixed Costs	Variable Costs
Spurance	$3,500	$1.25/unit
Yamamoto	$8,000	$0.85/unit

a. If Slimline's demand is for 8,300 briefcases per year, which system should the company use?
b. If Slimline needs to stitch 19,800 cases per year, which system has the lower cost?
c. At what volume do the two alternatives have equal costs?

4. Finn Bank and Trust is comparing a manual system for processing checks with a highly automated system. Presently, the bank processes about 10,000 checks each workday, and it operates 250 days per year. In the near future, it is planning to sell check-processing services to other small rural banks in the area. The bank's management has collected the following data:

System	Annualized Fixed Costs	Variable Labor Costs
Manual	$ 50,000	$0.045/check
Automatic	$350,000	$0.005/check

a. At its present volume of checks, which system should Finn use?

b. If Finn can process checks for other banks and boost its volume to 100,000 checks per day, which system has the lower cost?

c. At what volume do the two alternatives have equal costs?

5. The X-ray machine at Marchal Medical Center was purchased and installed nearly four decades ago. Medically, the machine functions very effectively, but requires excessive time to adjust for each patient. A new X-ray machine is available that will reduce the time required to serve a patient.

System	Annualized Fixed Costs	Variable Labor Costs
Old X-ray	$ 40,000	$4.00/X-ray
New X-ray	$120,000	$1.00/X-ray

a. Which system would give lower cost if the annual patient demand is 15,000?

b. If volume could be boosted to 20,000 patients per year, which system would give the lower cost?

c. At what patient volume do these alternatives have equal costs?

6. Quill Pen Company sells pens that are often purchased as graduation presents. The pens sell for $5.50 each and cost $1.50 per unit to produce. Fixed costs total $40,000 per year.

a. How many pens must Quill sell to cover fixed costs?

b. How many units must Quill sell to make $50,000 profit per year?

c. If fixed costs increase $10,000 per year, then what are the answers to a and b?

7. Brockman Visiting Nurse Service has determined that it costs about $20 each time one of its nurses visits a sick person at home. The charge is $30, part of which is paid by the patient and part by insurance. Overhead expenses are $7,000 per month.

a. How many calls does the service have to make to cover overhead expenses?

b. How many calls must it make to ensure a $3,000 profit per month?

8. A. J. Electronics produces monitors for microcomputers. It has a one-shift operation with fixed costs of $25,000 per month. The cost of purchased parts is $20 per unit, and the standard labor cost is $15 per unit. The company sells the monitors for $55 each to customers who sell them under their brand names.

a. How many monitors does A. J. have to produce and sell each month to cover costs?

b. How many monitors must be produced and sold to meet a $5,000 target profit?

9. Presently, A. J. has the capacity to produce 1,600 monitors each month if it maintains a one-shift operation. The A. J. sales staff is negotiating a deal with a major seller of microcomputers that will increase units sold per month from approximately 1,400 to 3,000. If the deal is successful, the operations manager plans to add a second shift. Adding a second shift will increase fixed costs by $10,000 per month and increase production labor costs to $16 per unit for those units produced on the second shift. This increase is due entirely to paying a premium (shift differential) for second-shift labor. The unit price for purchased parts will drop by $.50 for units produced on both shifts because of discounts for buying larger quantities. The addition of a second shift will add 1,600 units per month to capacity.

a. Graph A. J.'s cost-volume-profit relationship for one shift only.

b. Graph A. J.'s cost-volume-profit relationship for two shifts.

c. How many units must A. J. produce and sell to cover its costs when the second shift is in place?

d. At what volume does A. J. make a $24,000 profit per month?

e. What happens to the company's profit if the selling price of monitors drops by $5 per unit? Be specific, using calculations to support your answers.

10. Carder Kitchen Utensil Production makes steak knives and salad forks in the same facility.

	Steak Knives	Salad Forks
Product mix	.7	.3
Selling price/unit	$.80	$.40
Variable cost/unit	$.50	$.25

Annual fixed costs are estimated at $250,000.

a. At what volume will Carder cover its costs, given the present mix?

b. At what volume will Carder report a $150,000 annual profit, given the present mix?

c. If the mix changes to .6 for steak knives and .4 for salad forks, recalculate the answers to parts a and b.

d. If the price of a steak knife is raised $.05, what is the impact of this new mix on the volume required to make a $150,000 profit?

11. Junge Hardware Products makes nuts, bolts, and washers in the same facility.

	Nuts	Bolts	Washers
Product mix	.4	.4	.2
Selling price/unit	$.07	$.09	$.03
Variable cost/unit	$.03	$.06	$.001

Annual fixed costs are estimated at $2,500,000.

a. At what volume will Junge cover its costs, given the present mix?

b. At what volume will it report a $1,500,000 annual profit, given the present mix?

c. If the price of a bolt is raised $.01, what happens to the volume required to make a $1,500,000 profit?

12. Winken, Blinken, and Knod, Inc., is considering three different machines to grind contact lenses. The annual costs and operating costs are listed below.

System	Annualized Fixed Costs	Variable Operating Costs
Manual grinder	$ 9,000	$5.00/lens
Automatic grinder	$30,000	$2.50/lens
Computer-controlled automatic grinder	$50,000	$0.75/lens

a. If 10,000 lenses are needed, which option has the lowest cost?

b. If 20,000 lens are needed, which option has the lowest cost?

c. At what volume(s) of lens production do the alternatives have equal costs?

d. How would you explain these options to management?

MINI CASES

Tilley Video Disc, Inc.

William ("Call Me Billy") Tilley, founder, president, and chairman of the board of Tilley Video Disc, Inc., has a very pleasant problem. The market for video discs is expanding rapidly, and he has accepted an attractive offer for his controlling interest in Tilley Video Disc. He will retain his current management responsibilities. The deal is contingent on Billy's development of a plan to expand production from 10,000 to 50,000 units and to lower production costs. Evers, Inc., the company making the offer, feels the growth in sales will be dramatic if costs can be significantly reduced.

Presently, production of the video discs takes place in one plant in Rimer, Oregon. The plant was formerly a slaughterhouse and meat-packing facility. Billy has quickly come to the conclusion that production could be maintained at this facility, but that significant on-site expansion is not sound. The equipment in the facility was purchased from a bankrupt company and has been used for several years. It can best be characterized as slow, general-purpose equipment. Following are data on the existing plant for the last twelve months:

Selling price	$6.50/unit
Variable cost	$3.20/unit
Total production	9,824/year
Rejects	644/year
Sales	9,180/year
Estimated capacity	10,000/year
Annual fixed costs	$20,000

Evers' vice-president for marketing thinks that the selling price should be reduced to about $5.00 in order to achieve the needed sales growth and to grab market share in the highly competitive consumer market. As a consultant to Billy Tilley, you are charged with developing a plan that will allow the company to increase capacity by 400 percent and reduce variable costs by 20 percent. You should use the cost-volume-profit model in building your plan. Use a target annual profit of $80,000. Provide a written report that addresses the following questions:

1. Is it a good idea to keep the existing facility?

2. What benefits might be derived from the new technology?

3. Should one facility be built, or should the plan have several small facilities similar to the present facility?

4. Why and how will the cost structure of the new facility differ from that of the existing one? Be specific. Use the C-V-P model to help describe the differences.

Dailey Computer Service

Kathy Dailey, president of Dailey Computer Service, has called you into her office to help plan the company's future. Profits have been declining even though sales have increased. During this time, selling price and costs have not changed. The company sells three services—a payroll package, data entry services, and computer forms. The following table shows the revenue and costs of these services:

	Payroll Package	Data Entry (per 1,000)	Computer Forms (per 100)
Selling price	$3,500	$25	$35
Variable cost	$ 800	$16	$30

Fixed costs average $40,000 per month.

Sales data for the last two months are listed below.

	Two Months Ago		Last Month	
	Units	Sales	Units	Sales
Payroll (packages)	7	$ 24,500	5	$ 17,500
Data entry (1,000)	2,500	62,500	2,200	55,000
Forms (100)	1,400	49,000	2,000	70,000
Total sales		$136,000		$142,500

1. How did the firm manage to increase sales, hold the line on price and costs, and make less money? Be specific—Dailey wants numbers to back up your answer.

2. If Dailey Computer Service maintains the same sales mix as last month, how can it achieve a profit of $10,000 next month? Once again, be specific.

3. From what you have discovered in this analysis, answer the following questions:

a. How should Dailey Computer Service approach marketing?

b. Should price changes be considered?

SELECTED BIBLIOGRAPHY

Abernathy, William J. "Production Process Structure and Technological Change." *Decision Sciences* 7, no. 4 (October 1976):607–619.

Botta, Elwood. *Meeting the Competitive Challenge.* Homewood, Ill.: Richard D. Irwin, 1984.

Droy, John B. "It's Time to 'Cell' Your Factory." *Production Engineering,* December 1984, pp. 50–52.

Chang, T. C., and Wysk, R. A. *An Introduction to Automated Process Planning Systems.* Englewood Cliffs, N.J.: Prentice-Hall, 1985.

Gerwin, D. "Control and Evaluation in the Innovation Process: The Case of Flexible Manufacturing Systems." *IEEE Transactions on Engineering Management* EM-28, no. 3 (August 1981):62–70.

Gerwin, D., and Tarondeau, J. C. "Case Studies of Computer Integrated Manufacturing Systems: A View of Uncertainty and Innovation Process." *Journal of Operations Management* 2, no. 2 (February 1982):87–89.

"Manufacturing Cells: Blueprint for Versatility." *Production,* December 1984, pp. 38–40.

Hayes, Robert H., and Wheelwright, Steven C. "Link Manufacturing Process and Product Life Cycles." *Harvard Business Review* 57, no. 1 (January–February 1979):133–140.

Miller, Jeffrey G., and Vollmann, Thomas E., "The Hidden Factory," *Harvard Business Review* 63, no. 5 (September–October 1985):142–150.

Schmenner, Roger. "Before You Build a Big Factory." *Harvard Business Review* 54, no. 4 (July–August 1976):71–81.

Skinner, Wickham. "The Focused Factory." *Harvard Business Review* 52, no. 3 (May–June 1974):114–121.

Vonderembse, Mark A., and Wobser, Gregory S. "Steps for Implementing a Flexible Manufacturing System." *Industrial Engineering* 19, no. 4 (April 1987):38–48.

Williams, Vearl A. "FMS in Action." *Production* (January 1985):41–43.

Chapter 8

Facility Layout

CHAPTER OUTLINE

LEARNING OBJECTIVES

After completing this chapter, you should be able to

- Illustrate the objectives of the layout decision for a continuous flow process, an assembly line, a batch process, a manufacturing cell, a flexible manufacturing system, and a job shop.
- Explain the layout for a continuous flow process and why it is dominated by precedence relationships.
- Describe the need to balance workloads on an assembly line.
- Explain the important issues in laying out an assembly line.
- Describe the relationship between the capacity of an assembly line and its cycle time.
- Balance a simple assembly line and understand the role of computers in assembly-line balancing.
- Explain the problems of motivating assembly-line workers and describe some possibilities for improving motivation.
- Discuss the important differences between batch processes and continuous flow and assembly-line processes.
- Describe techniques for building families of parts used in manufacturing cells and flexible manufacturing systems.
- Construct a model of the job shop layout problem and apply techniques for developing a layout.
- Explain the role of computers in determining a job shop layout.

Honda of America, Inc.: A Well-Designed Facility Makes a Difference

The Honda plant in Marysville, Ohio, produces 875 cars per day with about 2,400 workers. The Jeep plant in Toledo, Ohio, produces 750 cars with about 5,400 workers. Many factors, including restrictive work rules, poor management decisions, lack of employee motivation, and poor employee-management relationships, contribute to this productivity difference. But a large part of the difference can be seen by examining the facilities.

The ten-year-old Honda facility is located in a rural setting about 30 miles northwest of Columbus. The Jeep facility is located 100 miles north in Toledo, the center of the industrial Midwest. This large, inner-city factory built around the turn of the century produced thousands of Jeeps during World War II.

Moving inside, the Honda facility, which is all on one floor, produces its cars with 1.7 million square feet of neatly arranged floor space, while the Jeep facility fills more than 5 million square feet. At Honda, cars move in an orderly way from the beginning to the end of the assembly line. The Jeep line winds up and down through several levels and through most of the facility's more than sixty interconnected buildings. The production lines are broken at several points, and partially assembled bodies must be dragged to the next point on the line. This slows production and requires more employees.

Further, the Jeep facility inhibits the use of just-in-time because it takes a day or two for parts delivered to the plant to move through the maze of buildings to the assembly line. This complex arrangement has evolved over time as management added capacity to this facility. At Honda, parts are often delivered only a few hours before they are needed and quickly move to the assembly line.

The Jeep plant is an example of what can happen to the layout of an existing facility when many additions and modifications are made over a long period of time. Honda's smooth product flow was not interrupted in 1986 when the facility's capacity was doubled with the addition of a second assembly line. This addition was planned before the facility was built, and provisions were made in the original facility design and layout to accommodate the increase.

Managers should be wary of "safe" expansion plans that add capacity to existing facilities. Many times, these convenient and less expensive additions are "good" in the short run because they require a smaller investment. However, making several of these short-term decisions without considering the long-term implications can lead to jumbled product flows and inefficient operations. Without careful planning and consideration of the long-term effects of adding capacity to existing facilities, managers may be growing monsters that eventually become impossible to manage.[1]

INTRODUCTION

In this chapter, we discuss facility layout questions for the continuous flow, assembly-line, batch, manufacturing cell, flexible manufacturing, and job shop processes. **Facility layout** is the arrangement of the work space. Broadly defined, it can involve questions at a minimum of three levels of detail.

1. At the highest level, how should the departments or work groups be arranged? Which departments or groups should be adjacent, and which can be placed farther apart? For example, in a hospital, how close should the pediatrics department be to the X-ray department?

2. Next, within the departments or work groups, how should people, equipment, and storage be arranged? How large should the department be? Within an X-ray department, how much equipment should there be, and how should it be arranged? There may be more than one machine, space for viewing X rays, and storage.
3. Finally, how can the arrangement of each work space within a department be designed so that assigned tasks can be efficiently and effectively carried out? How should the work station where the technician operates the machine be arranged? How should the space for viewing X rays be designed for easy use by doctors and technicians? These and other issues are discussed in Chapter 9.

These layout issues are all related. For example, the size of the facility is dependent on the size of each department, which, in turn, is dependent on the number of people, the amount of equipment, and the amount of storage space. The amount of space each person needs is a function of how well the individual's work space has been designed.

This chapter will focus on the first issue, arranging departments. The same concepts used for arranging departments can be applied to layout within a department. For example, within a department the proximity of two pieces of equipment implies the same approach to managing spatial relations as the positioning of two departments.

The objectives of facility layout are similar, regardless of whether the layout is for an office building, a steel mill, a hospital, or a ship. One objective is to provide convenient access between two groups or departments that interact heavily. It costs money to move people, information, and materials around a facility. Management would like to minimize that cost without reducing the organization's overall effectiveness.

In some cases, departments that depend on the same resource may have to be located physically close together even though they interact very little. For example, both shipping and receiving may require use of an overhead crane to load and unload heavy parts to railcars. Because both departments require access to the crane and the railcars, they are likely to be located close together even if they interact very little.

In other cases, departments or functions that are potentially detrimental to one another should be separated to the extent possible. A sanding operation and a painting operation are not compatible because the grit from sanding may travel through the air and land on the fresh paint. These operations are likely to be physically separated unless special booths are built for painting.

CONTINUOUS FLOW PROCESSES

The layout for a continuous flow operation builds directly on the concept of minimizing the distance that people, information, and material move. An activity matrix for a continuous flow process is shown in Exhibit 8.1. An **activity matrix** organizes and displays the movement of people, parts, or other things between departments. The zeros in Exhibit 8.1 indicate no movements between those pairs of departments. The number ten represents ten items moving from one

Exhibit 8.1 Activity Matrix for Continuous Flow Process

From Department	To Department 1	2	3	4	5
1		10	0	0	0
2	0		10	0	0
3	0	0		10	0
4	0	0	0		10
5	0	0	0	0	

department to another. The items could be pieces of wood used to make furniture, stock purchase transactions, or even people moving from one point to another.

The matrix does not consider movements from department 1 to department 1, 2 to 2, and so on. These intradepartment moves should be considered separately. As shown in the matrix in Exhibit 8.1, product movement follows the same sequence through the departments: 1–2–3–4–5. The flows between any other pair of departments or in any other sequence are zero. As a result, the layout that minimizes the costs of moving between departments is simple—it follows the product's sequence of operations. This is why a continuous flow process and assembly lines are said to have a product-oriented layout.

Even in cases where other minor product movement exists, the dominant flow will govern the layout. It is only when these other flows become significant that the process is no longer a continuous flow or an assembly line. When many different paths or sequences occur, the process takes on characteristics typical of a job shop.

Because the layout for continuous flow processes follows the product's sequence of operations, the technical aspects of the process selection ultimately dictate the layout. Consider the following note on oil refining as an example of a layout for a continuous flow process.

Oil-Refining Process Note

Crude oil is composed of a complex mixture of hydrocarbons. The composition varies according to the source of the crude. The refining process converts the crude oil into usable products such as gasoline, diesel fuel, kerosene, and heating oil. The process can be divided into three steps: distillation, alteration of molecular structure, and purification.

Distillation works because different end products, such as gasoline and kerosene, have different boiling points. The crude oil is pumped through tubes in a furnace heated to 700° F. A mixture of vapor and unvaporized oil passes from the furnace into a fractionating column that contains perforated trays. The vapor condenses at various trays, which means that different products come out from the column at different levels. Gasoline is lighter than heating oil and therefore condenses at a different level. Exhibit 8.2 shows a fractionating column.

Exhibit 8.2 Fractionating Column

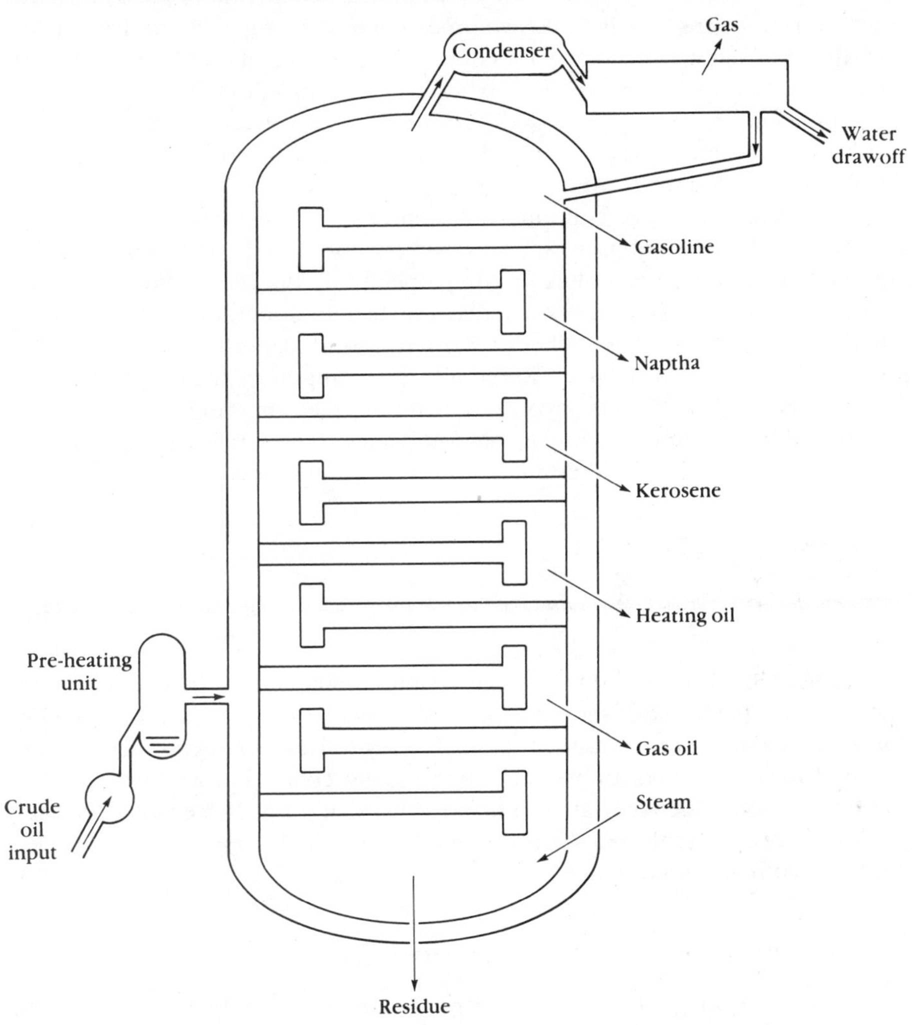

The process cannot end at this point because too much of the crude ends up as heavy oils for which there is little demand and therefore a low selling price. Altering the molecular structure of these oils will change their chemical structure and render hydrocarbons for which there is greater demand. Various processes are used to alter chemical structure, including thermal cracking and reforming, catalytic cracking, catalytic reforming, polymerization, and alkylation.

Purification processes are used to remove impurities such as sulfur compounds, gums, and waxes. The processes include absorption and stripping, solvent extraction, and thermal diffusion.

We do not expect you to memorize or gain an in-depth understanding of the chemistry in the oil-refining process. The purpose of the note is to illustrate that the technology of a process has a major impact on business performance and that the layout for continuous flow process is determined by following the product flow.

Continuous Flow Processes and Service Industries

Many continuous flow operations are found in the production of goods because many service operations lack the volume required to support the large fixed investment in facilities necessary for continuous flow operations. There are some notable exceptions, however. The U.S. Postal Service handles billions of pieces of correspondence with thousands of expensive and sophisticated sorting machines and handling systems. It is very clearly a flow shop, with many facilities spread throughout the country.

Large banks also have continuous flow processes. Most customers see only the small branch operations, which tend to be tailored to the individual customer's needs and thus are more like job shop operations. But the central processing area is a continuous flow operation that can handle hundreds of thousands of transactions each day. Here, checks written against deposits in the bank are processed and the information entered into the computer system.

The approach to facility layout for handling mail or processing checks is similar to the approach to facility layout for making steel or refining oil. Once the sequence of operations is determined, the layout will follow.

ASSEMBLY LINES

An assembly line is designed to arrange various components into a final product that conforms to standards set in the product design. The purpose of an assembly line is to divide complex tasks into small, easy-to-learn segments that can be repeated over and over. An assembly line usually consists of a series of **work stations** or **work centers** at which individuals perform these tasks on each product. Most assembly lines are designed to produce large volumes of one product that has limited options.

Instrument Panel Assembly Process Note

Knoxville Auto Equipment is a major producer of automotive speedometers, tachometers, fuel gauges, and the instrument panels that hold these items. About 75 percent of its business comes from contracts with the auto makers for the assembled instrument panels. Exhibit 8.3 lists the task descriptions and the estimated times for completion, and Exhibit 8.4 shows the precedence diagram.

Knoxville has an order for 50,000 of these units for next year. The company usually works a standard forty-hour week for fifty weeks per year. During those fifty weeks, there are ten paid holidays. How should the line be laid out? How should the tasks be assigned? These questions will be addressed in the following sections.

Determining the Layout

Like the continuous flow process, the assembly line has a product structure or precedence relationships that describe each task to be performed. In the Knoxville example, the light bulbs in the instrument panel (tasks 11–15) must be installed before the case can be put over the speedometer (task 16). How long

Exhibit 8.3 Task Descriptions and Times for Instrument Panel Assembly

Task	Description*	Time (Min.)	Task	Description*	Time (Min.)
1	Case to line	.08	22	Turn filter	.05
2	Neck gasket to speedometer	.07	23	Hi beam filter	.05
3	Clip to speedometer	.08	24	Spring to slider to case	.25
4	Printed circuit to case	.08	25	Fasten seat belt filter	.06
5	Label to case	.08	26	Temperature gauge	.10
6	Clip to case	.09	27	Cable	.22
7	Clip to case	.09	28	Pointer	.10
8	Clip to case	.09	29	Battery charge and fuel gauges	.12
9	Clip to case	.09	30	Screw	.07
10	Clip to case	.09	31	Screw	.07
11	Bulb to case	.07	32	Screw	.07
12	Bulb to case	.07	33	Tachometer	.10
13	Bulb to case	.07	34	Screw	.07
14	Bulb to case	.07	35	Screw	.07
15	Bulb to case	.07	36	Screw	.07
16	Case over speedometer	.08	37	Screw	.07
17	Grommet screw	.08	38	Screw	.07
18	Grommet screw	.07	39	Screw	.07
19	Case up	.07	40	Retainer	.09
20	Brake and oil filter	.06	41	Lens	.20
21	Turn filter	.05	42	Inspect	.50

*Tasks cannot be further split due to the spatial arrangement of equipment and inventory.

Instrument panels are built up in a subassembly line at the GM–Orion assembly plant. Each is then connected to a computer for a total check of all of its functions before the panel is sent by overhead conveyor to the point where it is installed in a GM full-size luxury car. *Courtesy: General Motors.*

Exhibit 8.4 Precedence Diagram for Instrument Panel Assembly

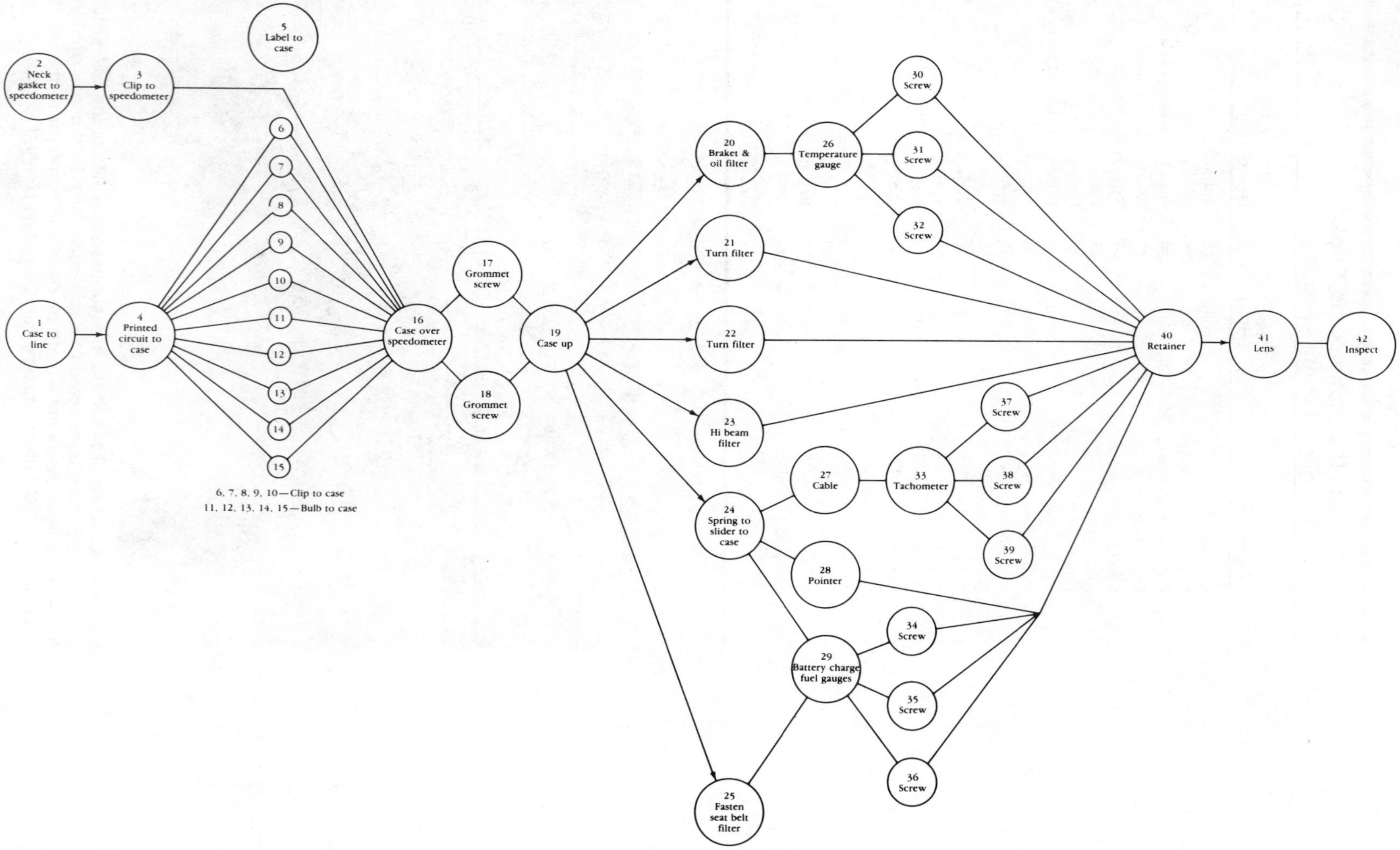

6, 7, 8, 9, 10—Clip to case
11, 12, 13, 14, 15—Bulb to case

will each of these tasks take? It is necessary to have an estimate of the time required to perform each task so that reasonable estimates of production rate and capacity can be made.

Objectives

There are two major objectives in laying out an assembly-line process. First, to lower material-handling costs, the line should be positioned for a continuous flow of assembled products. This can be achieved by following the precedence diagram and positioning work stations so that distance traveled is reduced to the lowest level compatible with efficient operations. This is similar to the continuous flow process, which also has a dominant flow.

Second, the assembly line should have balance in the same way that the continuous flow process has balance. That is, each work center or work station should be assigned an equal amount of work. If this is not done, then the stations that have less work to do and thus are faster will wait for the stations that have more to do (the bottlenecks). An imbalance in the work assigned reduces capacity and increases costs.

Once the tasks are assigned to work stations by observing all precedence relationships, the first objective can be achieved by sequencing work stations to minimize material movement. The second objective, assigning an equal amount of work to each station, requires further discussion. Consider the following mailing service problem.

Example

An organization uses computers and automation to process large amounts of mail that are often used in marketing campaigns to sell insurance or to raise money for charity. The time for completing each task, the precedence relationships, and the number of work stations are given. Assume that one person is assigned to each station. The times listed here are based on processing 1,000 pieces of mail contained in one packet.

This example demonstrates the impact on capacity and costs when an assembly line is improperly balanced.

Assembly-Line Work Stations **Precedence Diagram**

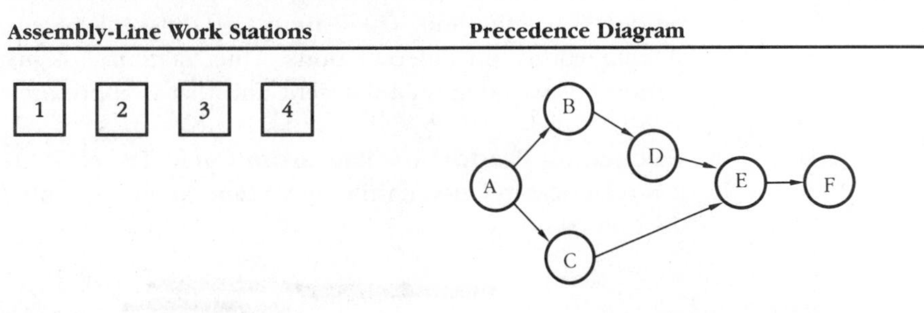

Task	Description	Estimated Time (Seconds)
A	Prepare for next packet	60
B	Prepare address labels	30
C	Sort material for stuffing	90
D	Apply address labels	45
E	Stuff envelopes	45
F	Seal envelopes and place in mailer	90
	Total time required	360

To illustrate the impact of an unbalanced assembly line, we have deliberately assigned tasks to the stations so that the workload is uneven. Techniques for assigning tasks to work stations are discussed later in this section.

	Work Station 1	Work Station 2	Work Station 3	Work Station 4
Tasks	A	B, C	D, E	F
Time	60	120	90	90

Results of the Assignment. How many seconds of work are required to assemble each packet? The sum of the estimated task times is 360 seconds. How much time is there between completed packets exiting the line? This time is determined by the station with the most task time assigned to it—in this case, work station 2. After the line has produced the first packet, it will take 120 seconds for the next packet to exit the line because station 2 acts as a bottleneck, starving downstream stations and restricting flow from upstream stations. The 120-second time between completed packets will continue for each packet thereafter even though the last station takes only 90 seconds. The only way a packet can get to work station 4 is to pass through station 2, and it takes 120 seconds to do all the tasks assigned at that station.

Cycle time is the amount of time required to produce a unit (i.e., minutes per piece or seconds per piece). Cycle time is the reciprocal of the production rate. When viewed independently, each work station has its own cycle time. Because station 2 has the longest station cycle time, its cycle time becomes the **system cycle time** for the entire assembly line. The system cycle time for the assembly line is the time between the nth unit (any unit) and the $n + 1$ unit (next unit) exiting the line when the bottleneck station is working to capacity. (When the term *cycle time* is used in reference to an assembly line, the authors are referring to *system cycle time.*)

The difference between the sum of the task times for the entire job (360 seconds) and the cycle time (120 seconds) is sometimes difficult to understand. Visualize the difference in this way. The sum of the task times would be like following a product from the beginning of the first station to the end of the last station. Cycle time is like standing at the end of the line and watching consecutive products exit the line. These times are different because stations are working simultaneously on different units. Thus, station 1 is just starting a unit while station 3 is working on a different unit that is approximately half complete.

Calculating Production Rate from Cycle Time. There is a direct mathematical relationship between the cycle time in an assembly line and the line's production rate.

$$\text{Production rate} = \frac{1}{\text{cycle time}}$$

$$= \left(\frac{1}{120 \text{ sec./unit}}\right) 3{,}600 \text{ sec./hr.}$$

$$= 30 \text{ units/hr}$$

Calculating Idle Time. It is important to know how much idle time there is at each work station. This is time for which an organization is paying, but receiving no output. The sum of the idle times at each station is the idle time in the system.

In this system, there is a total of 120 seconds of idle time for each unit produced. Station 1 has only sixty seconds of work, and therefore the person at this station must wait another sixty seconds (idle time) before beginning work on the next unit. If the person continued to work without waiting, station 1's output would be sixty units per hour. This is twice the rate that the bottleneck station, station 2, can achieve. The unused thirty units per hour would accumulate as inventory. But this inventory buildup would not be acceptable because the bottleneck station could not catch up during normal operating time.

The bottleneck station, station 2, has no idle time. It allows only thirty units per hour to pass to stations 3 and 4. This allows 120 seconds at each of these stations to complete ninety seconds' worth of work. Therefore, stations 3 and 4 each have thirty seconds of idle time.

Calculating Unit Labor Cost. What is the unit labor cost if each person at the station receives $20 per hour including fringe benefits for eight hours' work? The total labor cost for eight hours is (8 hours/shift)(4 workers/shift)($20/hour), or $640/shift. The total number of units produced is (30 units/hour)(8 hours/shift), or 240 units/shift. The unit cost is ($640/shift)(240 units/shift), or $2.67/unit.

A Balanced Assembly Line. We will now assign tasks so that the line is "perfectly" balanced—that is, so that each station has exactly the same task time. This is accomplished by shifting task B from station 2 to station 1. Note that the precedence relationships are not violated. (Techniques for balancing an assembly line are discussed later in this chapter.)

	Work Station 1	Work Station 2	Work Station 3	Work Station 4
Tasks	A, B	C	D, E	F
Time	90	90	90	90

The table below lists the total task time, cycle time, production rate, idle time, and unit cost for the unbalanced line and the balanced line.

	Unbalanced Line	Balanced Line
Total task time	360 seconds	360 seconds
Cycle Time	120 seconds	90 seconds
Production rate	30 units/hr.	40 units/hr.
Idle time	120 seconds/unit	0
Unit cost	$2.67/unit	$2.00/unit

You can see that the balanced layout increases the system's capacity and reduces the idle time and the unit cost. It is far more efficient than the initial unbalanced layout.

Introduction to Balancing the Line

The importance of the line balance is described in the preceding sections, but how is the balance achieved? There are many possibilities for achieving a balance, including some that are mathematically sophisticated. We will limit our discussion to a few possibilities that can easily be applied to even large line-balancing problems.

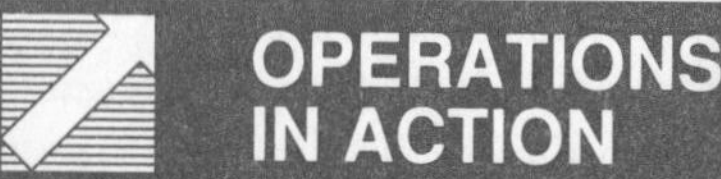

OPERATIONS IN ACTION

Whirlpool Corporation: Designing for Automated Assembly

Whirlpool Corporation, Benton Harbor, Michigan, sells more than $4 billion annually in appliances and operates eighteen U.S. plants plus seven plants in foreign countries. It found early in the 1980s that its washing machines were becoming overpriced. The major problems were that the basic washer design had not been changed since the 1950s and that manual assembly was slow and costly.

Whirlpool's basic model was a high-quality product that was well received in the marketplace, but the top-loading outside cabinet was a major structural part on which other parts were hung. So the cabinet went in place at the beginning of the assembly line, and workers had to reach down through the openings to attach parts. This was slow and costly and did not lend itself to automated assembly.

Now, several years and $162 million later, its 1.5-million-square-foot Clyde, Ohio, plant is the largest washer-producing plant in the world. The lower cost and better quality that automation made possible, plus Whirlpool's good name and modern marketing, have raised the company's share of the market. The plant has increased output by 80 percent, while increasing employment from 2,400 to 3,700.

Whirlpool redesigned the washer for automated assembly. It has a frame inside to which most parts are attached. It is put together from the bottom up and is accessible from all sides. The cabinet goes on last and is held in place by only a few screws. This helps to hold down repair and warranty costs.

Remember that the objective of balancing is to assign tasks to work stations so that each station has a balanced load. For these discussions, we will assume that each work station has only one person assigned to it. If a balanced workload is achieved, then the idle time at each work station will be zero. The elements of the balancing equation are as follows:

C = cycle time for the balance

t_i = task time for element i, where $i = 1, \ldots, n$ tasks

$\sum_{i=1}^{n} t_i$ = total task time required to assemble one unit

N = theoretical minimum number of work stations

m = actual number of stations in the balance

There must be a target or goal in order to measure the efficiency of the balance. The theoretical minimum number of work stations (N) allows the person doing the balancing to have a gross measure of performance. It is the total task time divided by the cycle time, rounded up to the nearest whole number.

$$N = \frac{\sum_{i=1}^{n} t_i}{C}$$

Think of N as the minimum number of equal-sized time blocks required to cover the sum of the task time. The size of these blocks is the cycle time. Given a cycle time (C), a balance that achieves the minimum number of stations is the best solution in terms of minimizing worker idle time.

Selecting a Cycle Time Determines System Capacity

Balancing the line is a key factor in managing an assembly operation. The balance not only affects the plant layout and determines the unit labor cost, but also determines the capacity of the system. Remember that the cycle time chosen for the balance is the reciprocal of the production rate. For an assembly line, this production rate is the maximum rate, and the maximum rate of production is the definition of capacity.

Cycle time and capacity are linked by the relationship illustrated in Exhibit 8.5. Capacity should be a function of the estimated customer demand. It is not necessary to set capacity exactly equal to demand. For example, in a fast-growing business, management may want to set capacity at a level higher than present demand to allow room for growth.

Are there theoretical or practical limits to the cycle time, or can any number that results from the calculations described in Exhibit 8.5 be used? Theoretically, the cycle time must be equal to or less than the sum of all the task times (Σt_i). If the cycle time equals Σt_i, then the solution to balancing the assembly line is trivial. All tasks are assigned to a single work station; that is, one person does the entire assembly. The cycle time should be equal to or greater than the maximum of the individual task times (t_i). To achieve a cycle time that is less than the maximum of t_i, the longest task would have to be divided between two or more stations, or other special arrangements would have to be made. The following statement helps to define the theoretical limits on cycle time:

$$\text{Max.}(t_i) \leq \text{Cycle time} \leq \Sigma t_i$$

Practically speaking, when assembly lines are not automated, a cycle time of a few seconds or less is generally too short. Usually, too much time is lost when a worker has to start, stop, and move a unit to the next station every few seconds.

In some cases, it may be necessary or desirable to have more than one assembly line. The number of hours each assembly line operates per week is another important piece of information. By combining these two pieces of infor-

Exhibit 8.5 Relation of Capacity to Cycle Time

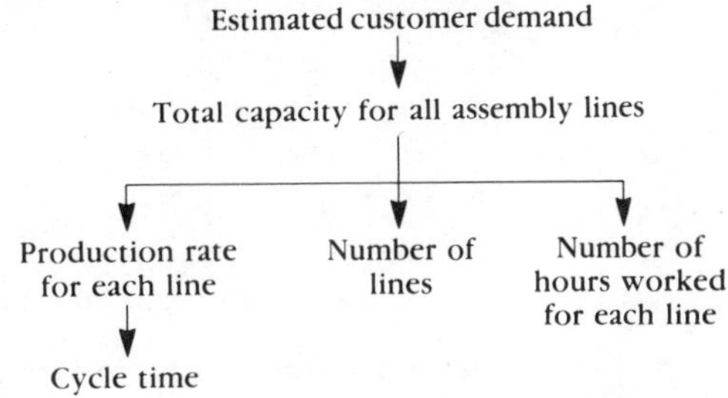

mation with the desired capacity, it is possible to calculate the production rates for the assembly lines. Once the production rate is known, the cycle time can easily be calculated, as described in the previous section.

When there is only one assembly line, the following formulas can be used to calculate capacity. If hours worked per year is used in the formula, then annual capacity is calculated. In the equation, *PR* is the production rate, and *H* is the hours worked for the line.

$$\text{Capacity} = (PR)H$$

When cycle time (C) is substituted for *PR*, the equation becomes

$$\text{Capacity} = \frac{H}{C}$$

For situations with more than one assembly line, the capacity of the individual lines can be totaled.

If the required capacity and the available hours (H) are known, then the product rate can be calculated as follows:

$$PR = \frac{\text{capacity}}{H}$$

Example

Farmall produces irrigation systems for vegetable growers, distributing these systems primarily in the West and Southwest. Its Clarkson plant assembles a modulator to control water flow. This unit, which is used on most of Farmall's irrigation systems, has a forecasted demand of 15,000 units per month. Even though demand is highly seasonal, Farmall has decided to balance its assembly line to produce 400 units during a forty-hour week.

Periods of higher demand will be satisfied through overtime and from inventory built during nonpeak periods. Periods of lower demand will call for shorter workweeks and will allow for the annual two-week vacation and for a modest buildup of inventory. The required cycle time is calculated as follows:

$$PR = \frac{\text{capacity}}{H}$$

$$= \frac{(400 \text{ units/wk.})}{(40 \text{ hrs./wk.})}$$

$$= 10 \text{ units/hr.}$$

Next, production rate is converted to cycle time as follows:

$$C = \frac{1}{PR}$$

$$= \left(\frac{1}{10 \text{ units/hr.}}\right) 60 \text{ min./hr.}$$

$$= 6 \text{ min./unit}$$

Now, let us assume that Farmall anticipates rapid growth and projects a need to produce 700 units per week. It is considering building another assembly line.

What would the production rate per hour and the cycle time have to be if each line worked forty hours per week?

$$PR = \frac{\text{capacity}}{H}$$

$$= \frac{700 \text{ units/wk.}}{40 \text{ hr./wk.} + 40 \text{ hr./wk.}}$$

$$= 8.75 \text{ units/hr.}$$

Next, convert production rate to cycle time.

$$C = \frac{1}{PR}$$

$$= \left(\frac{1}{8.75 \text{ units/hr.}}\right) 60 \text{ min./hr.}$$

$$= 6.86 \text{ min./unit}$$

This cycle time would be applied to each assembly line.

Technique for Assembly-Line Balancing

How are tasks assigned to work stations to achieve a balanced load? Which tasks are available to be assigned at the first station? Consider the tasks involved in assembling a briefcase. The precedence diagram in Exhibit 8.6 shows which task or tasks are available. In the example, two tasks, A and B, have no preceding task and would be put in the list of tasks available for assigning to a work station.

How is the task selected from this list? Although one option would be to select a task at random by flipping a coin or rolling dice, this method would not

INTEGRATING THE SYSTEM

Close Ties Between Assembly-Line Balance and Scheduling

Layout, unit costs, and system capacity are all directly affected by the assembly-line balance. In addition, the balance provides the framework for scheduling production. After the assembly line has been balanced, the direct labor requirements will be known. Because these requirements must be met when the line is running, a scheduler knows how many people are needed and which jobs must be filled. In addition, the production rate is known if the line is running, and this in turn sets the units produced per hour. The bill of materials, from the product design, lists the quantity of each component part needed in the assembly. If the facility assembles forty microwaves per hour and each microwave has twelve push buttons, then the material manager should provide 480 buttons for each hour scheduled.

This view of planning and scheduling materials is the basis for material requirements planning (MRP) and just-in-time (JIT). Once again, the importance of viewing operations as a system with interrelated decisions and actions should be clear. These topics will be discussed in greater detail in Section II.

Exhibit 8.6 Briefcase Sample Problem

Task	Description	Estimated Time (Seconds)	Preceding Task
A	Cut leather	80	—
B	Assemble frame	100	—
C	Sew left side to frame	40	A, B
D	Sew right side to frame	40	A, B
E	Sew bottom to frame	70	C, D
F	Attach closure and handle	100	E
		430	

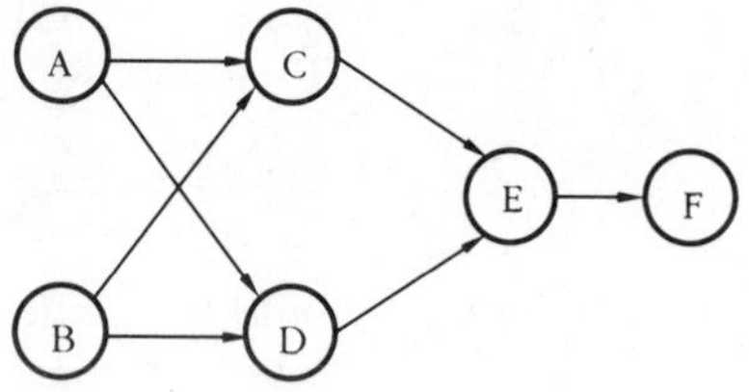

necessarily lead us toward a good solution. What is needed is a systematic way of selecting a task that will move us closer to a good solution. Many articles and books discuss various decision rules. Automobile and appliance manufacturers spend millions of dollars investigating different methods of balancing their huge assembly lines. A few of the simplest choice rules are listed here.

- *Longest task time*—select the task with the greatest task time that will fit in the remaining station time.
- *First in the list*—select the task that has been in the list of tasks available for assignment for the longest time. This requires keeping track of when each task had all of its precedences assigned and entered the task-available list.
- *Most following tasks*—select the task with the most tasks following. This is determined by counting those tasks on the precedence diagram.

Because it is possible for two tasks to tie based on any of these criteria, a tie-breaking method should be determined. For example, if the choice rule is longest task time first, another rule such as first in the list could be used when two tasks have the same time. If there is still a tie, then the modeler could use another choice rule or select a task at random.

Do these rules produce good results? There is no guarantee that any of these rules will reveal the best answer or even a good answer. Research has been done on these and other rules, and the longest task time rule often performs well.

Example

Let's find a balance for the briefcase example in Exhibit 8.6. The plant manager has been directed to balance this single-line operation with one forty-hour shift. The line should produce 1,200 units per week.

$$PR = \frac{\text{capacity}}{H}$$

$$= \frac{1{,}200 \text{ units/wk.}}{40 \text{ hrs./wk.}}$$

$$= 30 \text{ units/hr.}$$

$$C = \frac{1}{PR}$$

$$= \frac{1}{30 \text{ units/hr.}}$$

$$= \left(\frac{1}{30 \text{ units/hr.}}\right) 3{,}600 \text{ sec./hr.}$$

$$= 120 \text{ sec./unit}$$

$$N = \frac{\sum_{i=1}^{n} t_i}{C}$$

$$= \frac{430 \text{ sec.}}{120 \text{ sec./station}}$$

$$= 3.58 \text{ or } 4.0 \text{ stations}$$

The preliminary calculations indicate that the cycle time needed to produce 1,200 units per week is 120 seconds for each unit. Given the problem constraints, the best balance will have four stations. Even if that can be achieved, the total system will have (4.0 − 3.58) stations, or .42 stations, that are idle. This best balance will have (.42 stations) (120 sec./station), or 50 seconds, of idle time for each unit produced. The only way to reduce this idle time is to reduce the sum of the task times (the numerator of N) or to change the cycle time (the denominator of N).

The balancing procedure is relatively simple, once the fundamentals of an assembly line are understood and the preliminary calculations have been made. Exhibit 8.7 shows a form that can be used to balance a line. The starting point is the list of tasks available to be scheduled. The longest-task-time rule is used to

Exhibit 8.7 Balanced Line for the Briefcase Problem

Task Available to Be Scheduled	Task Selected	Assigned to Station	Time Remaining at the Station (Seconds)
A, B	B	1	20
A	A	2	
C, D	D	2	0
C	C	3	
E	E	3	10
F	F	4	20

stays idle

50

Total 4 work stations

choose between these tasks because it is easy to use and often gives good results. In case of a tie, the first-in-the-list rule will be used to break it. If there still is a tie, a random choice will be made.

Tasks A and B are the only possible first choices because of precedence. Task B is longer and will be assigned to the first station. The station time remaining is 120 seconds − 100 seconds, or 20 seconds. Once B has been assigned, other tasks may be available. Examination of the precedence diagram in Exhibit 8.6 shows that no further tasks are available because all other tasks follow task A. Because no other options exist, task A is assigned next.

Task A requires 80 seconds and will not fit at station 1, so it is assigned to the next station. There are now 40 seconds remaining at station 2. The assignment of A puts both C and D into the available list. The longest-task-time rule results in a tie, as does the first-in-the-list rule. We thus pick a task randomly, and task D is selected. Task D uses the remaining forty seconds at station 2. The process continues in a similar manner.

The resulting balance has four stations and a total of fifty seconds of idle time. The balance delay or percent idle time is calculated as follows:

$$\begin{aligned}\begin{matrix}\text{Balance delay}\\ \text{(percent idle time)}\end{matrix} &= \frac{\text{idle time}}{\text{time available in the line}}(100)\\ &= \frac{(m)(C) - \sum_{i=1}^{n} t_i}{(m)(C)}(100)\\ &= \frac{(4\text{ stations})(120\text{ sec./stations}) - 430\text{ sec.}}{(4\text{ stations})(120\text{ sec./station})}(100)\\ &= 10.4\%\end{aligned}$$

Because the balance has the theoretical minimum number of work stations, achieving a better balance would require a change in the cycle time or the total task time. A change in the task time would involve engineering changes in the assembly procedure. A change in the cycle time would change the production rate, which would affect the balance between capacity and demand.

The Role of Computers in Balancing the Line

Balancing assembly lines by hand can be a long and tedious process when large problems are encountered. Consider the instrument panel example described earlier in this chapter. Although the process is simpler than the assembly of an air conditioner or a tractor, the number of tasks would make manual balancing difficult. Computer models have been developed that can perform assembly-line balancing. These models can keep track of all the details in the procedure and can be run quickly with a variety of cycle times and selection methods. In fact, one of the biggest advantages of computerized line balancing is being able to use more complicated procedures for selecting tasks from the available list.

The Computer Method of Sequencing Operations for Assembly Lines (COMSOAL) rapidly generates large numbers of feasible solutions that can quickly be evaluated to determine which one gives the best balance. Other computer-based solution procedures have been developed by industry to assist in the line-balancing process.

Material Handling

The delivery system for materials is also included in facility design and layout. Such a system may be as simple as using carts or hand trucks to deliver materials. At the other extreme, it may include sophisticated, computerized, automated procedures that require no operator. Automated guided vehicle (AGV) systems and automated storage and retrieval systems (AS/RS) are widely used in new facilities and in the modernization of existing ones.

An AGV can deliver large numbers of products over a variable path. The vehicle, which resembles a fork-lift truck, is directed by computer to a pickup and delivery point. Wires embedded in the floor or lines painted on the floor with special paint guide the vehicle.

AS/RS are used to store small amounts of work-in-process inventory so it can be quickly identified, located, and moved to the assembly area. Often an AGV can be teamed with an AS/RS to hold and deliver parts without being touched by people. Fixed-path conveyor systems are still used in assembly operations when the repeatability of the task is high and the sequence of operations, once set, does not vary.

Motivation

Our discussion of assembly lines would not be complete without considering motivational problems. The repetitive nature of assembly lines often makes them boring places to work. The skills required to work on the line can easily be mastered, and any mental challenges to the job are quickly overcome. Motivational problems often surface as high absenteeism, excessive use of drugs and alcohol, sabotage, and theft.

Issues and Possible Solutions

Solutions to motivational problems are not simple. How can a person be motivated to repeat the same task 350 to 400 times per shift for five days a week and for fifty weeks a year? (The Honda and Jeep plants both operate at about that rate.) Money is not an important motivator in the Honda and the Jeep cases. Automotive workers are well paid and have good fringe benefits. The Jeep workers make more than the Honda employees, and yet the Honda employees are more productive and have greater motivation. Clean, safe, comfortable plants are not the answer because they already exist.

Two possible answers play a role in improving the situation. First, the substitution of equipment for people will continue. Computer-controlled machines should perform repetitive manufacturing tasks. Much welding and spray painting are already done by robots. The development of robots with vision capability will allow greater use of this tool in assembly.

The second solution, which is harder to achieve, is for organizations to use their employees' intelligence. Employees should be encouraged to think about ways to solve problems related to their job and to improve plant operations. They

GAINING STRATEGIC ADVANTAGE AT VOLVO

A New Approach to an Automotive Assembly Line

At Volvo's new plant in Uddevalla, Sweden, a radical approach to building cars has been in full operation since the beginning of 1989. Rather than the traditional assembly line with many work stations and one-minute cycle times, the Volvo plant employs teams of seven to ten workers. Each team works in one area and assembles four cars per shift. Members of the team are trained to handle all of the jobs. Typically, a worker will repeat a job about every three hours. Uddevalla is divided into six assembly plants, and each plant has eight teams. The teams do their own scheduling, quality control, hiring, and other duties normally performed by supervisors.

One of the major advantages of Uddevalla's design is that workers have a greater sense of satisfaction, which leads to improved attention to detail, low absenteeism, and high quality. From the humanistic and motivational perspectives, Uddevalla is a ringing success. Quality and workmanship levels at Uddevalla are higher than at Volvo's other plants, but what about efficiency? After all, the reason that Henry Ford shifted production to the assembly line was to improve productivity, and he was enormously successful. Volvo claims that Uddevalla is already producing cars with fewer labor hours than its other three Swedish plants are.

For Volvo, workmanship and quality are extremely important. Part of Volvo's strategy is to produce a luxury car aimed at the top end of the car-buying market. Volvo is likely to give this new team concept the go-ahead even if the efficiency at Uddevalla does not exceed that of its other facilities. The quality and workmanship improvements derived from this team approach to manufacturing will probably be sufficient to offset lower productivity. If the Uddevalla plant is successful, its approach will probably spread to other Volvo facilities, including its Kalmar plant which uses teams of fifteen to twenty employees and a work cycle of thirty minutes.[2]

should be asked to consider how quality and productivity can be improved and if there might be better methods of production.

Improved Labor and Management Relations

Labor-management relationships are a key to effective use of employees in problem solving. At the Honda facility described earlier in this chapter, labor relations, worker motivation, and employee involvement are good, and productivity is high. Workers willingly contribute to improving the product, the manufacturing process, and efficiency of operations. The Honda plant uses U.S. workers who are led, for the most part, by U.S. managers. Management treats the work force with respect and expects the workers to contribute to improving operations.

Employees should understand that better quality and improved productivity lead to long-term job security. Quality circles can be an important part of employee involvement. When implemented, however, many of these programs have failed. The most common mistake during implementation is to assume that these programs will build better relations between labor and management. But these programs require good relations to work effectively. Where good relations do not exist, these programs are almost certainly doomed to failure. Quality circles will be discussed in more detail in Chapter 17.

BATCH PROCESSING

To operate economically, continuous flow and assembly lines, which are both line flow processes, require large volumes of the same or closely related products. However, many products do not have enough volume to support such mass production. To maintain low costs at lower volumes, products with some variations are produced on the same set of equipment. This requires equipment that is flexible enough to deal with the increased variations.

For example, Composite Container Corporation produces containers for frozen orange juice and lemonade concentrate. These containers, holding 6, 12, or 18 ounces, are constructed from two ends punched from sheet metal and a cardboard tube. All three tube sizes are made on the same machine. The machine must be shut down for several hours when sizes are changed.

Composite Container's major advantage in using the same machine for all three sizes is to increase equipment utilization and to reduce product costs so the organization can remain competitive as a supplier to the frozen concentrate industry.

What principles guide the layout in batch operations? Efforts should be directed at (1) combining products with similar processing requirements (those that use the same equipment in approximately the same way) and (2) using the same or a similar sequence of operations. Capturing the same sequence and building on it is such a strong idea because material-handling costs can quickly get out of hand when materials are delivered all around the facility. The keys to layout in batch processing are to find as much similarity among the products as possible and to increase the facility's flexibility to handle product variation so that variation in material movement is reduced.

USING GROUP TECHNOLOGY TO ORGANIZE MANUFACTURING CELLS AND FLEXIBLE MANUFACTURING SYSTEMS

Group technology (GT) is an approach to manufacturing that is based on the idea of grouping similar parts into families, which leads to economies in the manufacturing cycle. In design, it enables firms to organize existing designs so they can be easily retrieved, and it encourages standardization of designs. In process planning, it enables firms to simplify product flow and to organize equipment. In production, it enables firms to achieve mass-production efficiency where production variety exists. How does group technology establish the families of parts needed to organize manufacturing cells and flexible manufacturing systems? Many different methods exist. We will discuss visual inspection, product flow analysis, and coding and classification.

Visual inspection, sometimes called **tacit judgment,** involves the visual review of design drawings and specifications for similarities. This fairly simple process can result in good families of parts if relatively few parts are involved.

Product flow analysis (PFA) uses process plans to form families of parts. From the process routing for a part, a list of machine codes is determined. The process routing is a description of how the part is to be processed and on which machine the processing will take place. For example, a part could be processed on machines 01, 03, and 05. The numbers merely designate particular machines or types of machine. Parts with identical machine codes are grouped into "packs" for further analysis. A pack might contain many different parts, but all the parts are processed on the same machines. All the parts in a pack will be in the same family of parts. However, a family of parts may include several packs that have similar, but not identical process routings.

The following example illustrates a facility with five different types of machines. The process routings for the company's parts have been analyzed, and the parts have been grouped into six different packs. A number 1 at the intersection of a particular row and column indicates that the pack is processed on the machine. For example, all parts in pack D are processed on machines 01, 02, and 03.

Machine Code	*Packs* A	B	C	D	E	F
01	1	—	1	1	—	—
02	1	1	—	1	—	1
03	—	1	1	1	1	—
04	—	—	—	—	1	1
05	—	1	—	—	1	1

The idea is to group packs with similar machining requirements together. This is usually done by shifting rows and columns so that the ones are as close as possible to a diagonal line that runs from the upper left-hand corner of the matrix to the lower right-hand corner. The following matrix shows one possible solution. Sophisticated computer programs have been written to do this with the large problems that are often encountered in real companies.

Machine Code	*Packs* D	A	C	B	F	E
01	1	1	1	—	—	—
02	1	1	—	1	1	—
03	1	—	1	1	—	1
04	—	—	—	—	1	1
05	—	—	—	1	1	1

One family of parts could include packs D, A, and C and would be processed in a manufacturing cell or flexible manufacturing system that includes machines 01, 02, and 03. The other family of parts could include packs B, F, and E and would be processed in a manufacturing cell or flexible manufacturing system that includes machines 02, 03, 04, and 05. In machining operations, a company may have more than one machine of each machine code or type. If this organization does not have two of the same machines coded 02 and 03, then it will have to purchase additional equipment or share existing equipment.

Another method for determining families of parts is **coding and classification.** In a coding and classification scheme, each part is given a code, which can be twenty digits or more. The code defines size, shape, metal type, machining requirements, and other factors. These codes can then be quickly scanned by a computer to determine which parts are similar. There are many commercially available coding and classification schemes on the market, including Opitz, Brisch, MICLASS, and CODE developed in West Germany, the United Kingdom, the Netherlands, and the United States, respectively. Specialty codes have emerged to deal with unique problems in some organizations.

Once the families of parts are organized, the facility layout can be determined by following the dominant sequence of the family. In this way, material handling is simplified, and costs are reduced. See the Operations in Action on the next page.

JOB SHOPS

Use of job shops should be limited to cases where the volumes are so low and the differences between products are so great that line flow processes and batching are not feasible. The techniques discussed here apply equally well to laying out a hospital clinic, government offices, an automotive repair facility, and a manufacturing plant.

The first step in approaching the job shop layout problem is to understand the fundamental difference between the job shop and the line flow processes. In a line flow, the movement of product is clearly defined. Exhibit 8.10 on page 312 illustrates the point by showing an activity matrix for the line flow. In this case, 100 units of product are produced and move methodically through the work stations (departments). As discussed earlier, the layout follows this dominant flow.

Now, consider the case at the other extreme. Here, the flow is random. This means that the chance (probability) of a unit in one department moving to any other department is equal for all possible departments. If the activity matrix for a facility is random, like the one displayed in the lower half of Exhibit 8.10, then it makes little difference what the layout is. All departments interact equally, so one layout seems to be as good as another.

Fortunately, in most real job shop problems, the product flow is not completely random. Typically, the activity matrix would look like the one shown in Exhibit 8.11 on page 313 for the offices and laboratories of the Rieselinger Research Institute. Although a dominant pattern is not as apparent as it would be in a line flow process, a pattern can be found. Finding this hidden pattern and using it to determine the layout should give a better solution than simply guessing at the layout.

Finding the Pattern and Determining the Layout

To model the layout question in a job shop and find the hidden pattern, the objective of the layout should be well defined. If significant amounts of supplies, materials, people, and information are transferred between two departments, then it is logical to conclude that they should be adjacent, provided other factors are equal. The amount of activity between two departments can be measured and considered directly in the layout. The distance between any two operations can be measured and the cost per unit distance determined.

Objectives

Now it is possible to evaluate any layout by multiplying the activity level by the distance by the cost per unit distance. The objective is to minimize the cost of movement between departments. The following model uses all department pairs except for $i = j$. Such movements would be within a department.

OPERATIONS IN ACTION

Quadrum Corporation: Applying GT to Improve Operations

Quadrum Corporation manufactures parts for transmissions used in medium- and heavy-duty trucks. One of the parts it produces is a power input shaft for the transmission.

This piece is the major component for taking the power from the engine and distributing it through the truck's transmission.

Exhibit 8.8 Quadrum Corporation's Existing Job Shop Layout

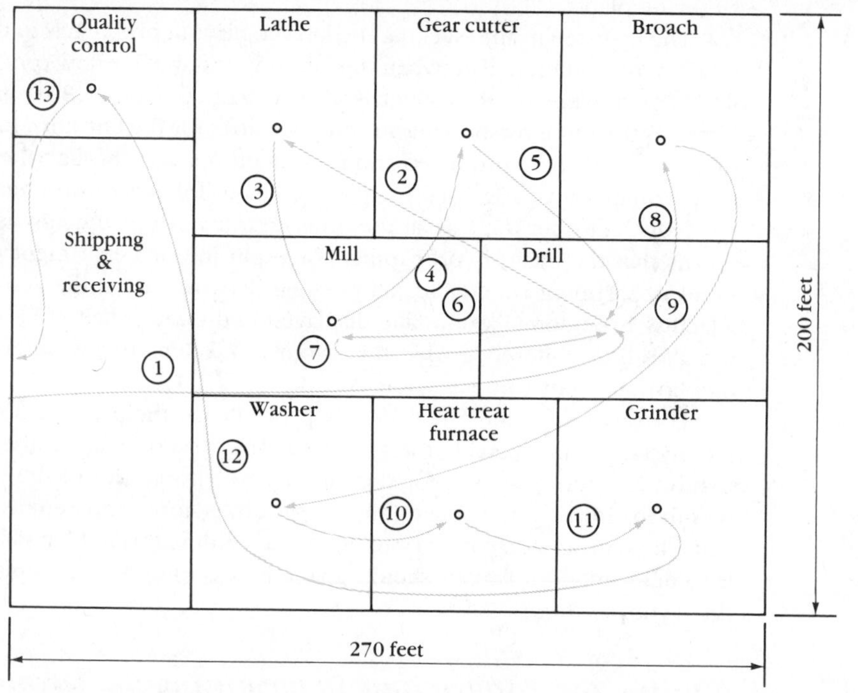

$$\text{Objective function} = \text{minimize} \sum_{i=1}^{n} \sum_{j=1}^{n} A_{ij} D_{ij} C_{ij} \text{ for all } i \neq j \tag{8.1}$$

A_{ij} = the activity level from department i to department j; $i = 1, \ldots, n$, and $j = 1, \ldots, n$, where n is the number of departments

D_{ij} = the distance from department i to department j

C_{ij} = the cost per unit distance from department i to department j

Exhibit 8.9 Quadrum Corporation's Proposed Layout for Transmission Parts

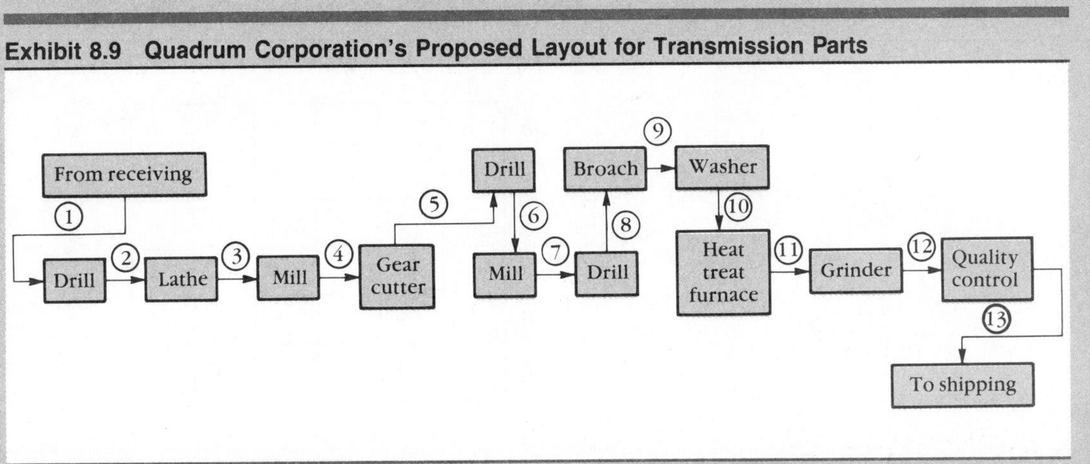

The market for these trucks is not large, there are many models and options to choose from, and Quadrum is not the only supplier. As a result, the demand for any one input shaft is not large enough to support production in a line flow process. In fact, demand for the part is spread over ninety different part numbers. Presently, production takes place in a job shop that produces other transmission parts. Parts travel from department to department, and significant work-in-process inventory clogs the facility. Exhibit 8.8 shows the existing job shop layout. The facility has approximately 54,000 square feet.

Quadrum has applied group technology (GT) to the production problem and has consolidated the ninety parts into ten families. It is planning to pull equipment from the job shop and dedicate it to the production of these families. The proposed layout, shown in Exhibit 8.9, is greatly simplified and will enhance productivity. This new layout will require only 8,000 square feet, and the total distance that work in process will travel is only 550 feet, including the return trip to receiving. This is clearly superior to the present job shop arrangement.

The purpose of applying the model is to minimize the cost of moving people, product, and information among departments or work centers. Before using this model, the following information must be collected:

1. Activity data.
   - If this is an existing facility, records of past jobs and the movements between departments should be available.
   - If records do not exist, the present set of jobs and future jobs can be used to build the activity matrix.

Exhibit 8.10 Activity Matrices for a Dominant and a Random Product Flow

Dominant Product Flow for Line Flow Process

From Department \ To Department	A	B	C	D	E	F
A		100	0	0	0	0
B	0		100	0	0	0
C	0	0		100	0	0
D	0	0	0		100	0
E	0	0	0	0		100
F	0	0	0	0	0	

Random Flow for Job Shop

From Department \ To Department	A	B	C	D	E	F
A		20	20	20	20	20
B	20		20	20	20	20
C	20	20		20	20	20
D	20	20	20		20	20
E	20	20	20	20		20
F	20	20	20	20	20	

The number in each cell of the matrices represents the number of units moved from one department to another.

- If it is a new facility, estimates of the activity levels can be generated from the types of jobs expected in the facility.
- What-if analysis can be done by changing the activity levels to reflect a different mix of jobs.

2. Estimates of the distance between all departments. To achieve these measurements, an initial layout of the facility is determined by the model builder.
   - If an existing building is to be used, the analyst should work with a drawing that is to scale.
   - If a new building is to be constructed, the analyst can work without boundaries to determine the building's shape. Still, working to scale is important.
3. Estimates of the costs per unit distance traveled.
   - Estimates of transportation costs can usually be made from data available in accounting records.

Exhibit 8.11 Activity Matrix for the Rieselinger Research Institute

To Department

From Department	A	B	C	D	E	F
A		15	35	20	40	50
B	10		20	20	50	10
C	15	0		40	40	20
D	10	15	30		10	10
E	30	0	40	10		10
F	50	20	0	0	30	

(trips measured in average number per day)

A	Executive offices	**D**	Research report writing offices
B	Stress laboratory	**E**	Marketing offices
C	Group dynamics laboratory	**F**	Word processing and mail room

- If they cannot be, there are at least two options for the analyst. First, information from other similar operations can be used to estimate costs. Second, the cost per unit distance can be assumed to be equal for all trips between departments. This is a very reasonable assumption if no other information is available.

Technique for Determining the Layout

The previous section defined the objective that management is trying to achieve in a job shop layout. How can the objectives of minimizing handling and transportation costs be achieved? One approach would be to evaluate every possible layout and pick the best one. However, like the assembly-line balancing problem, there are usually too many possible layouts to make this approach feasible for a large problem, even with the fastest computers. Instead, management's efforts are usually aimed at finding a "good" solution.

The following outlines the steps of such a procedure. These steps will be discussed in the next several sections.

Step 1. Determine a feasible initial solution.

Step 2. Evaluate the new solution(s), and keep the best one. Is the solution satisfactory? If so, stop; otherwise, continue with step 3.

Step 3. Change the present solution in an effort to find an improved solution. Return to step 2.

Our analysis will be based on the problem described in Exhibit 8.11.

Finding an Initial Layout. Finding an initial layout is a very important and difficult step. It is important because the small amount of time spent finding a "good" initial solution can greatly reduce the amount of work necessary in later steps. It is difficult because of the large number of options that should be considered. What happens if the departments are different sizes? How could the departments be shaped? A 1,000-square-foot department could be approximately 31.5 by 31.5 feet, 50 by 20 feet, 40 by 25 feet, or oddly shaped (see Exhibit 8.12).

The designer of a new building must consider many different building shapes. What about multiple stories? Because the layout question is complex and full coverage cannot be given in an introductory course, we will make some simplifying assumptions. (Remember that models are used to simplify a complex problem, while retaining the key variables and relationships.) We will assume that an organization has a new facility with departments of equal size and shape. This gives us the freedom to arrange the departments in a wide variety of ways and to switch any department pair without affecting the positioning of the other departments. Exhibit 8.13 displays the layout for the problem described in Exhibit 8.11.

To complete the initial solution, one department is assigned to each of the six spaces. If the "goodness" of the initial solution is not important, the departments can be assigned in any way. Let's investigate a quick way of finding a good initial solution.

The Adjacent-Department Method. The adjacent-department method assumes that the cost per unit distance is equal for all trips, so that cost is not a factor. It also assumes that departments can be categorized as adjacent, one department

Exhibit 8.12 Department Shape

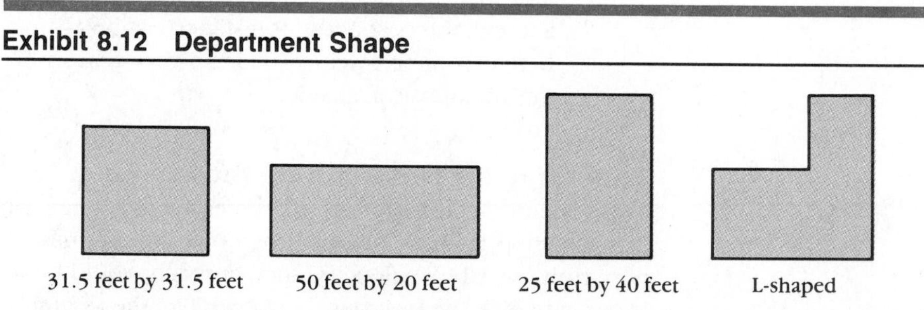

Exhibit 8.13 Facility Layout for Equally Sized Departments

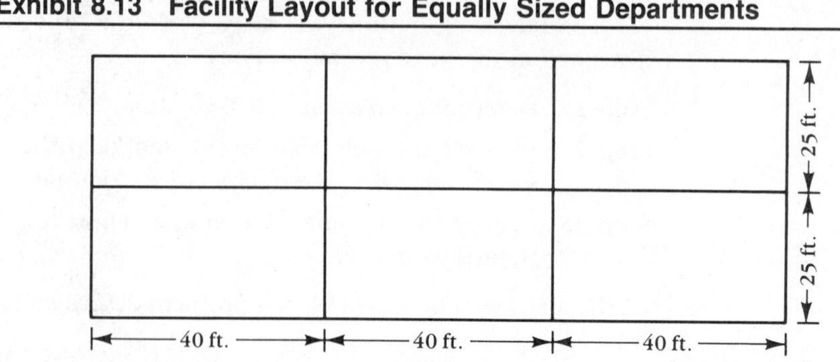

away, two departments away, and so on. Thus, the distance between departments can be assigned as 0, 1, 2, and so on. This simplifying assumption permits the user to make quick judgments about the positioning of departments and to make relatively few calculations. This method is not as precise as the model described by equation 8.1, but it should give us a good initial solution.

To begin, add the return trips together so that the trips from A to B and B to A total 25, the trips from A to C and C to A total 50, and so on. This will simplify the calculations by cutting the number of cells in half. We can do this because the cost per unit distance has been assumed to be equal for all trips. Exhibit 8.14 contains the recalculated activity levels for the problem in Exhibit 8.11.

Now we can begin to assign the departments to positions in the layout. The ranked activity levels shown in Exhibit 8.15 indicate that departments D and F have the least interaction and should be placed far apart, and that A and F have the highest interaction level. Exhibit 8.16 shows the layout to this point. Department

Exhibit 8.14 Job Shop Activity Matrix Representing Trips Between Departments Restated from Exhibit 8.11

From Department \ To Department	A	B	C	D	E	F
A		25	50	30	70	100
B			20	35	50	30
C				70	80	20
D					20	10
E						40
F						

Exhibit 8.15 Ranked Activity Levels

Department Pair	Activity Level
A–F	100
C–E	80
A–E	70
C–D	70
A–C	50
B–E	50
E–F	40
B–D	35
A–D	30
B–F	30
A–B	25
B–C	20
C–F	20
D–E	20
D–F	10

Exhibit 8.16 Partial Layout

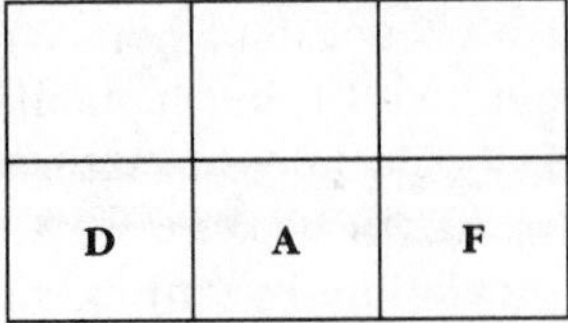

A could have been located above F rather than to the left of F. Try the problem using this choice, and see if you achieve a better initial solution.

We can see from the ranked activity levels in Exhibit 8.15 that departments D and E also have limited interaction and should not be adjacent. Departments C and E have the second highest level of interaction. Consequently, we add departments C and E to the layout. This leaves the position of department B set by default. The resulting layout is shown in Exhibit 8.17.

How good is this solution? According to the method of assigning distances as 0, 1, 2, and so on, adjacent departments are given a 0 distance. Departments that are separated by another department are assigned a distance of 1. The value of the solution measured in trips between nonadjacent departments is 110, as shown in Exhibit 8.18. The smaller the number of trips between nonadjacent departments,

Exhibit 8.17 Layout

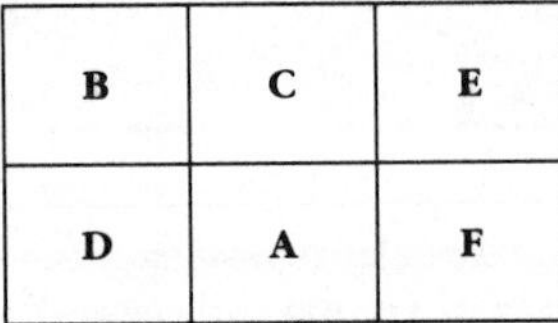

Exhibit 8.18 Evaluation

Department Pair	Activity Level (A_{ij})	Distance (D_{ij})	(A)(D)
B–E	50	1	50
B–F	30	1	30
D–E	20	1	20
D–F	10	1	10
			110

the better the solution. All other department pairs are considered adjacent and thus have a distance factor of 0. This analysis treats such department pairs as A–C and C–F as adjacent. Although this simplifying assumption does make the model easier to work with, it may reduce its accuracy. For small problems like the one used in this example, this procedure will often yield a good final solution.

We could continue with the adjacent-department method to improve the initial solution. Instead, let's take the solution we have found so far and consider distances and costs.

Evaluating the Solution. How good is the solution if actual distance and cost information is used? Using the initial solution displayed in Exhibit 8.17, it is possible to obtain distances from the center of each department to the center of all other departments. Exhibit 8.19 shows the layout with the center of each department plotted. The distances displayed in Exhibit 8.20 can be determined in two ways. First, if the departments and department centers are drawn to scale, the distances can be measured directly from the drawing. Second, because the departments are equally sized and organized into rows and columns, they can be easily calculated. For example, the distance from department B to department C is 40 feet because the center of each department must be 20 feet from the boundary. The distance from department A to department B can be found by applying the Pythagorean theorem. The line from A to B is the hypotenuse of a right triangle defined by the points A, B, and D.

$$(\text{Distance A to B})^2 = (\text{distance B to D})^2 + (\text{distance A to D})^2$$

$$\text{Distance A to B} = \sqrt{25^2 + 40^2}$$

$$= 47.2$$

Other schemes can be used for measuring distance if they more accurately represent reality or are easier to work with. This scheme is used because it is typical of the method used by computer-based procedures.

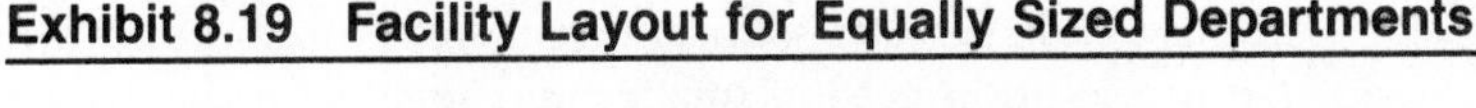

Exhibit 8.19 Facility Layout for Equally Sized Departments

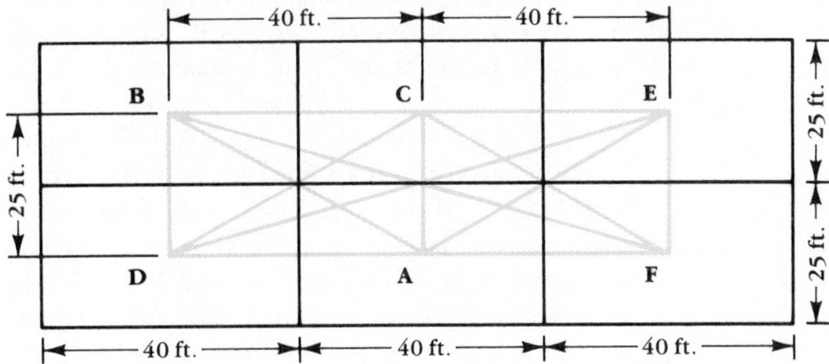

Exhibit 8.20 Value of Layout

Department Pair	Activity Level (A_{ij})	Cost (C_{ij})	(A)(C)	Distance (D_{ij})	(A)(C)(D)
A–B	25	1 $/ft.	25	47.2	1,180
A–C	50	1	50	25	1,250
A–D	30	1.5	45	40	1,800
A–E	70	1	70	47.2	3,304
A–F	100	1	100	40	4,000
B–C	20	2	40	40	1,600
B–D	35	1	35	25	875
B–E	50	2	100	80	8,000
B–F	30	1	30	83.8	2,514
C–D	70	1	70	47.2	3,304
C–E	80	1	80	40	3,200
C–F	20	1.5	30	47.2	1,416
D–E	20	2	40	83.8	3,352
D–F	10	1	10	80	800
E–F	40	1	40	25	1,000
					37,595

Exhibit 8.20 lists the cost per unit distance for each department along with the activity level and the distance. In the case where cost per unit distance is the same for all departments, the cost column can be bypassed by setting all values equal to 1. The activity level is multiplied by the cost per unit distance and then by the distance for each department. These values are summed to give the result for equation 8.1. Each new solution will be evaluated in this way, and the lowest value will indicate which solution is the "best." The absolute value of the number is not important, but how it compares with other solutions is important.

Stopping Rules. Stopping rules are more difficult to discuss in an introductory text because much theoretical work is required before full understanding can be achieved. The problem is to determine how good the present solution is when compared with the optimal solution. It is difficult to know when the solution is getting close to the optimal. In manually solved problems, there are two questions to ask. Have a significant number of attempts been made? Are improvements in the solution getting smaller and smaller? If the answer to both of these questions is yes, then consider stopping. Stopping rules for computer-based solutions are easier to define and will be discussed in a later section.

Generating a Better Solution. An initial solution and the value of that initial solution have been determined. The next task is to find a way to improve on the 37,595 figure shown in Exhibit 8.20. If we had unlimited time and patience, we could make many changes in the departments' locations and evaluate all the solutions, using a computer. To find a better solution when solving the problem by hand, we can examine the $(A)(C)(D)[(\text{Activity})(\text{Cost})(\text{Distance})]$ column in Exhibit 8.20. We can try to find a large $(A)(C)(D)$ value for a department pair, and see if a switch can be made that will significantly reduce this value.

In this problem, the largest $(A)(C)(D)$ value is 8,000 units. This is caused by one of the largest $(A)(C)$s, 100, moving nearly the greatest distance, 80 feet. To find a better solution, we switch departments C and E, as shown in Exhibit 8.21. The recalculated $(A)(C)(D)$ values are shown in Exhibit 8.22. The new value is 36,071, which is lower than the initial solution. This process is continued until the solution is satisfactory.

Modeling Layouts with Departments of Unequal Size

The mechanics of modeling layouts are largely unaffected by the size and shape of the departments. The only substantial change lies in how to arrive at an initial

Exhibit 8.21 Revised Facility Layout for Equally Sized Departments

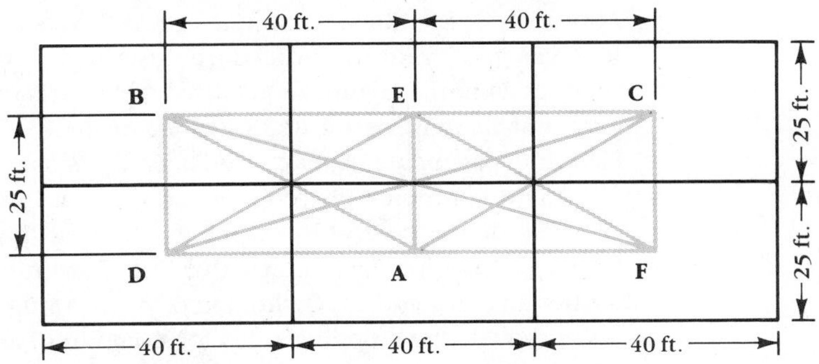

Exhibit 8.22 Value of Revised Layout

Department Pair	Activity Level (A_{ij})	Cost (C_{ij})	(A)(C)	Distance (D_{ij})	(A)(C)(D)
A–B	25	1 $/ft.	25	47.2	1,180
A–C	50	1	50	47.2	2,360
A–D	30	1.5	45	40	1,800
A–E	70	1	70	25	1,750
A–F	100	1	100	40	4,000
B–C	20	2	40	80	3,200
B–D	35	1	35	25	875
B–E	50	2	100	40	4,000
B–F	30	1	30	83.8	2,514
C–D	70	1	70	83.8	5,866
C–E	80	1	80	40	3,200
C–F	20	1.5	30	25	750
D–E	20	2	40	47.2	1,888
D–F	10	1	10	80	800
E–F	40	1	40	47.2	1,888
					36,071

layout and then to revise this layout once a switch has been made. Two approaches are possible. The first is to draw the layouts to scale and then measure distances from center to center, using a ruler. The scale does not matter because the absolute value of $(A)(C)(D)$ is not important. Only the relative values are important, so in this case it makes no difference whether the measurements are in feet or in inches. The second approach is to cut pieces of paper to scale and quickly and easily move them around to make new layouts. Even if the edges of two departments overlap somewhat, this approach gives an accurate enough layout. Once the departments are in place, a ruler can again be used to measure distance between departments.

The Role of Computers in Job Shop Layout

Solving the job shop layout problem can be time-consuming and tedious. Several computer procedures exist for assisting with the layout. Computerized Relative Allocation of Facilities Technique (CRAFT) was developed by Buffa and Armour. It works much like the procedure described in the previous section. The user supplies an initial layout, an activity level matrix, and cost information. If certain departments must be located together to share a key resource, this can be specified. If departments cannot be adjacent, this can also be specified.

These computer procedures can calculate many alternatives very quickly. CRAFT reduces the cost by switching all department pairs and calculating values for $(A)(C)(D)$ for each alternative. The lowest-cost alternative is selected for further analysis, and the switching of pairs continues.

Although the stopping rules for computer-based procedures are still somewhat arbitrary, they are easier to implement than those for a manual procedure. The brute power and speed of the computer allow it to investigate quickly far more alternatives than can be reasonably done by hand. The following approaches can be considered:

1. Specify a certain amount of computer time, and use the best solution found.
2. Allow the model to perform the switching of pairs only a certain number of times.
3. Specify an increment of improvement to be achieved with each evaluation. If this is not achieved, the procedure will end. For example, one could specify that at least a 2 percent reduction from the last solution must be achieved or the search ends.
4. Combine some of these rules. For example, the procedure can stop after a certain amount of time or after a specified number of switches, whichever is lower.

Other computer-based procedures, such as Computerized Facility Design (COFAD), Plant Layout Analysis and Evaluation Technique (PLANET), Computerized Relationship Layout Planning (CORELAP), and Automated Layout Design Programs (ALDEP), are also available. These procedures attempt to maximize nearness ratings. However, solutions generated by computer models are not guaranteed to be optimal.

Systematic Layout Planning

In some cases, managers may want to summarize nearness on a subjective scale with factors other than activity levels and costs. **Systematic layout planning (SLP)** involves using the codes and matrix shown in Exhibit 8.23 to arrive at an appropriate layout.

We begin the solution procedure by positioning department pairs that are categorized as absolutely necessary and those that are categorized as undesirable. Once these pairs are positioned, it is possible to work on the very important, important, and somewhat important categories to locate the remaining departments in the layout. Exhibit 8.24 displays the layout using this approach. Departments R and F are positioned first. Then A and T are positioned. Because T and D are undesirable, they are put at opposite ends of the facility. This gives the location of department W by default.

We can use a simple evaluation procedure to judge the effectiveness of this solution. First, we count the number of times each code appears in the matrix in

Exhibit 8.23 Information for Systematic Layout Planning for a Machine Shop

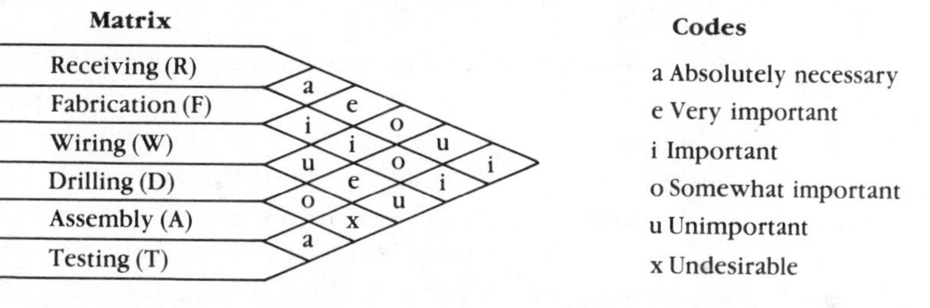

Exhibit 8.24 Solution and Evaluation of Machine Shop Layout

A	R	F
T	W	D

Evaluation Codes	Number of Appearances in Matrix	Number of Times Satisfied in Layout	Percentage Satisfied
a	2	2	100%
e	2	2	100
i	4	3	75
o	3	1	33
u	3	3	100
x	1	1	100

Exhibit 8.23. Next, we count the number of times each condition is satisfied. For codes a, e, i, and o to be satisfied, the departments must be adjacent, as departments A and R are, or diagonally opposite, as A and W are. Any location satisfies code u because the relative location of that pair of departments is unimportant. Separation by one or more departments satisfies code x. The percentage satisfied column in Exhibit 8.24 indicates that the proposed solution is effective at meeting the nearness codes. This approach works well on problems with relatively few departments.

USING LAYOUT FOR COMPETITIVE ADVANTAGE

The impact of a good layout on an organization's performance may not be as obvious as good product design skills or superior capacity planning. The effects of layout are subtle, yet important. Recall the discussion of the Honda and Jeep facilities earlier in this chapter. Although the companies produce about the same number of cars, their respective inputs (costs) are very different.

The evolution of the layout at the Jeep facility without careful planning or direction resulted in a very inefficient layout. This layout prevents Jeep from fully exploiting its market advantage because of the cost penalty it incurs in manufacturing.

Efficient layouts reduce unnecessary material handling. Good layouts help to maintain low costs, which is a critical part of building and maintaining market share. Good layouts also keep product flowing through the facility, which is important for providing good customer service. A facility choked with inventory is more likely to damage products and lose customers' orders.

Layout decisions should be made only after consideration of the long-term impact on the overall facility. Managers should ask themselves how the organization's performance will be affected by a proposed change in layout. How will costs, as well as quality and delivery time to the customers, be affected? For example, an inefficient layout with many material movements may cause delays in processing because the transport system is overloaded. This can cause unnecessary idle time for equipment as departments wait for the next batch of products. It could also delay customer shipments.

If a change is made in layout, how will future options be affected? Will this change increase opportunities for making layout improvements, or will some opportunities be lost? Individual layout decisions may not seem important, but when added together over time, these decisions can be powerful determinants of an organization's success.

SUMMARY

- Facility layout is based on easy access between departments or groups of people that interact heavily.
- Layouts for continuous flow processes are determined by the dominant product flow. The primary goal is to reduce material handling.
- Assembly-line layouts also attempt to reduce material handling. The assembly-line balancing procedure attempts to equalize the work assigned

to each work station, determines staffing levels, and sets the capacity of the line.

- Batch processing requires building parts in families with similar characteristics. This is necessary because the volume of a single product is not sufficient to support a dedicated system.
- Group technology involves building volume by combining parts with similar processing requirements. It is the basis for establishing manufacturing cells and flexible manufacturing systems.
- In a job shop, processes are usually grouped by departments because no product or group of products has sufficient volume to justify a layout with a single dominant product flow. Finding an effective layout requires working with activity levels between departments.

CAREER PROFILE

George B. Taylor

Distribution Manager
U.S. Postal Service

George Taylor manages mail distribution at a main post office that is a hub for smaller area post offices. As the distribution manager, he oversees the collection of mail from hundreds of drop points throughout the city, supervises the sorting and processing of tens of thousands of letters and packages each day, and ensures that these sorted letters and packages reach their destination. He is faced with a very large and complex material-handling problem.

Responsibilities

Taylor is responsible for the work performed by more than 500 craft employees and 40 managers. He has helped to implement new automation and mechanization programs that have increased productivity and reduced costs in mail processing. These installations use sophisticated computer-controlled equipment to sort mail. The efficient movement of mail from start to finish within the post office was an important criterion in determining the facility's layout. The management issues that Taylor faces, including designing, planning, and controlling operations, are similar to those faced by his counterparts in manufacturing operations.

Experience and Education

Prior to becoming manager of distribution, Taylor held the following positions: clerk, foreman, letter-sorting machine supervisor, general supervisor, superintendent, quality control specialist, officer in charge, and postmaster. A possible career move is to become the director of mail processing (equivalent to a plant manager) at a large post office. He could become a postal career executive, a position equivalent to an organization's corporate staff.

Taylor's broad experience has prepared him for his present position. In addition, he has taken correspondence courses, attended classes at the Postal Management Academy, and taken the Quality Control Course and the Postmaster Training Course. Taylor is planning to take additional courses in operations management.

SOLVED PROBLEMS

1. Waddel Machine Tool Company has a small shop with six departments of approximately the same size. The company makes specialty gears for equipment manufacturers. Its present layout and an activity matrix showing trips per week between department pairs follow. Find an improved layout by trying to minimize the activity level times distance. Cost per unit distance is assumed to be equal for all department pairs.

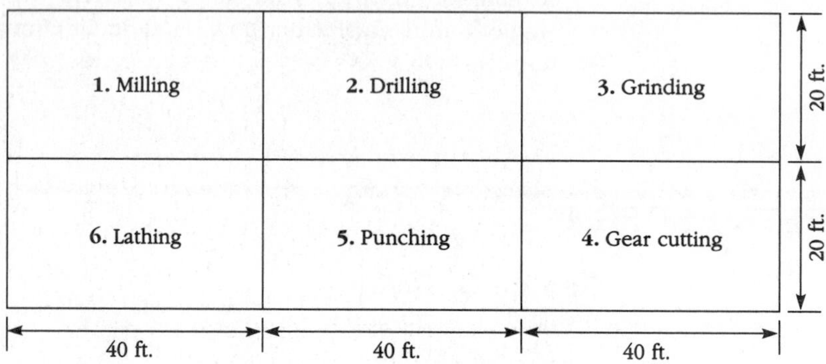

From Department	To Department 1	2	3	4	5	6
1	—	30	40	100	60	—
2	15	—	30	20	10	15
3	20	40	—	10	30	—
4	15	10	20	—	10	15
5	—	20	60	30	—	15
6	30	—	80	10	10	—

Solution

First, add the trips from department 2 to department 1 to the trips from department 1 to department 2. This should be done for each trip and return trip because the costs per unit distance for all department pairs are equal. The revised activity matrix is shown below.

From Department	To Department 1	2	3	4	5	6
1	—	45	60	115	60	30
2	—	—	70	30	30	15
3	—	—	—	30	90	80
4	—	—	—	—	40	25
5	—	—	—	—	—	25
6	—	—	—	—	—	—

Second, evaluate the present layout.

$$\text{Objective function} = \text{minimize} \sum_{i=1}^{n}\sum_{j=1}^{n} A_{ij}D_{ij}C_{ij} \text{ for all } i \neq j \qquad (8.1)$$

Distances will be measured from center of department to center of department. The activity level times distance column sums to 40,605, as shown below. The new layout will try to improve on this sum.

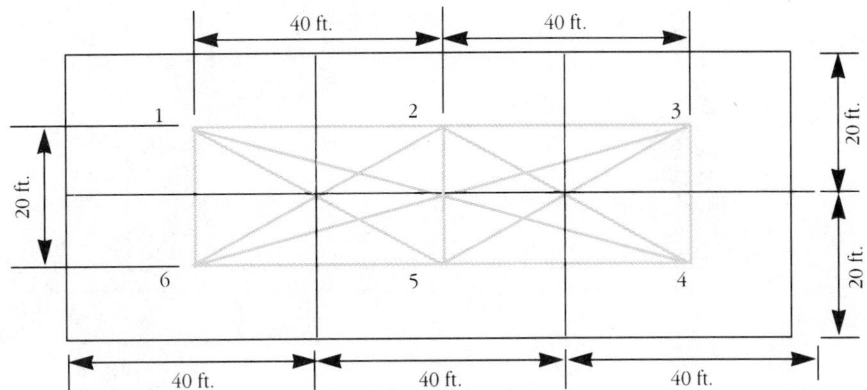

Path	Activity Level (A_{ij})	Distance (D_{ij})	(A)(D)
1–2	45	40	1,800
1–3	60	80	4,800
1–4	115	82.5	9,488
1–5	60	44.7	2,682
1–6	30	20	600
2–3	70	40	2,800
2–4	30	44.7	1,341
2–5	30	20	600
2–6	15	44.7	671
3–4	30	20	600
3–5	90	44.7	4,023
3–6	80	82.5	6,600
4–5	40	40	1,600
4–6	25	80	2,000
5–6	25	40	1,000
			40,605

Third, find a better solution. If this problem were being solved using a computer, the procedure for finding a better solution would be to switch every pair of departments and evaluate each new layout. This is not practical for manual solutions, so we must make an intelligent judgment.

- Scan the $(A)(D)$ column to see which pair contributes the most toward the 40,605.
- If that is caused by a large number of activities moving a long distance, then there is potential for improving the solution by bringing that pair closer together.
- If that does not yield an improvement, try another pair with a high $(A)(D)$.

As a result of doing this, it is determined that pair 1–4 has the highest $(A)(D)$. To bring them closer together, departments 4 and 6 are switched, giving the following layout. The new layout has a value of 32,167, which is significantly better than the original solution.

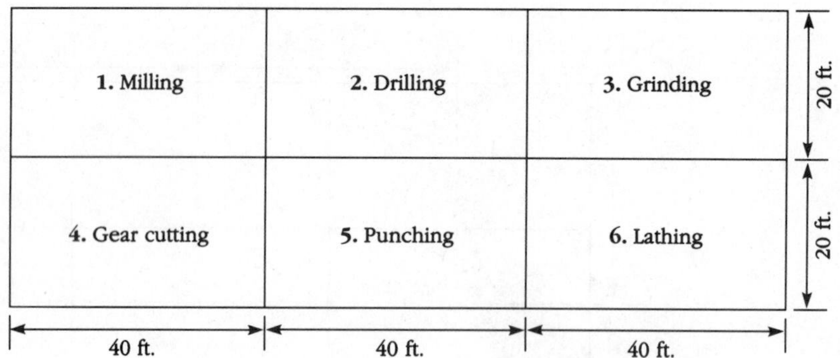

Path	Activity Level (A_{ij})	Distance (D_{ij})	(A)(D)
1–2	45	40	1,800
1–3	60	80	4,800
1–4	115	20	2,300
1–5	60	44.7	2,682
1–6	30	82.5	2,475
2–3	70	40	2,800
2–4	30	44.7	1,341
2–5	30	20	600
2–6	15	44.7	671
3–4	30	82.5	2,475
3–5	90	44.7	4,023
3–6	80	20	1,600
4–5	40	40	1,600
4–6	25	80	2,000
5–6	25	40	1,000
			32,167

2. Flick Fabrication Company assembles kitchen units that are shipped to recreational vehicle manufacturers for installation. Following is a list of tasks and precedence relationships for its deluxe kitchen unit:

Task	Time (Minutes)	Immediate Predecessors
A	4.5	—
B	1.4	A
C	2.6	A
D	6.0	—
E	3.3	B, C
F	2.4	C, D
G	5.5	B
H	1.0	G, E
I	2.9	F
J	4.8	H, I

a. Calculate the theoretical minimum number of work stations for a six-minute cycle time.

Solution

$$N = \frac{\sum_{i=1}^{n} t_i}{C}$$

$$= \frac{34.4 \text{ min.}}{6 \text{ min./station}}$$

$$= 5.73 \text{ or } 6 \text{ stations}$$

b. Balance the line using a six-minute cycle time and the longest-task-time rule.

Solution

Initially, tasks A and D are available. Task D is selected to be assigned at the first station because it takes longer to complete. When the task time for D, six minutes, is subtracted from the cycle time, six minutes, there is zero time remaining at the first station.

For the next assignment, only task A is available. Task A is assigned to station 2, and there is 6 − 4.5 or 1.5 minutes remaining at station 2.

Next, tasks B and C become available because task A has been assigned. Task C is longer than B, but cannot be assigned in the station time remaining. The next longest task, B (in this case, the only other task available), is assigned because it can fit at the station. If task B could not fit in the time remaining at station 2, then task C would have been assigned to the third station. The station time remaining is 0.1 minutes (station time remaining before task B is assigned, 1.5 minutes, minus the task time for B, 1.4 minutes).

See if you can follow the rest on your own.

Tasks Available to Be Scheduled	Task Selected	Station Assigned	Time Remaining at the Station
A, D	D	1	0
A	A	2	
B, C	B	2	.1
C, G	G	3	.5
C	C	4	
E, F	E	4	.1
F, H	F	5	
H, I	I	5	.7
H	H	6	
J	J	6	.2

c. What is the percentage of idle time for this balance?

Solution

The most efficient balance has been achieved because it requires only the theoretical minimum number of work stations. The idle time, which is 4.44 percent, is the best we can achieve, given the problem's constraints. Often, well-balanced lines can achieve idle-time percentages of 2 percent or less.

$$\begin{aligned}\text{Balance delay (percent idle time)} &= \frac{m(C) - \sum_{i=1}^{n} t_i}{m(C)}(100) \\ &= \frac{6(6) - 34.4}{6(6)}(100) \\ &= 4.44 \text{ percent}\end{aligned}$$

d. How many units can Flick produce if the line runs eighty hours per week?

Solution

$$\begin{aligned}\text{Capacity} &= \frac{H}{C} \\ &= \frac{(80 \text{ hrs./wk.})(60 \text{ min./hr.})}{6 \text{ min./unit produced}} \\ &= 800 \text{ units/wk.}\end{aligned}$$

QUESTIONS

1. What is facility layout? What objectives does an organization try to achieve with facility layout?

2. Discuss the differences and similarities in the objectives of the layout for a continuous flow process, an assembly line, a batch process, and a job shop.

3. Briefly describe how to determine the layout for a continuous flow process.

4. Explain the significance of precedence relationships in determining an assembly-line layout.

5. What are the objectives of balancing an assembly line?

6. How does the cycle time used in balancing the line determine the capacity of the line?

7. What role do computers play in assembly-line balancing?

8. Motivation of assembly-line workers has been and will continue to be a problem. Describe some ways to address this issue.

9. Batch processing depends on combining several similar products that require the same or similar processing. How does this help management determine the facility layout?

10. Flexible manufacturing systems are an effort to produce products with greater variability on the same set of equipment with minimal changeover time. How can group technology help in this process?

11. Describe job shop layout. How is it different from the approach to assembly-line balancing?

12. Describe the solution procedure for job shop layout.

13. What role do computers play in job shop layout?

PROBLEMS

1. Managers at Simpson Steel Machine Shop have analyzed all the parts the company produces for the purpose of building a manufacturing cell. Given the information below, recommend groupings for families of parts.

Machine Codes	*Packs* A	B	C	D	E
21	1	—	1	—	—
22	—	1	—	—	1
23	—	1	—	1	—
24	1	—	—	—	—

2. For each of the following, determine whether the layout would be a product, a process, or a fixed-position layout:

a. The location of departments within a college or university
b. A hospital emergency room
c. A self-service cafeteria
d. Building a custom-designed home
e. A prefabricated factory-built home

3. Firmtech has a projected customer demand that averages 480 items per working day. Firmtech's production has the following task times assigned to each station:

Station 1 (40 seconds)	Station 2 (25 seconds)	Station 3 (30 seconds)	Station 4 (30 seconds)

a. What is the cycle time? What is the production rate per hour?
b. What should the cycle time be to produce the 480 units per day demanded by customers if the production line works 7.5 hours per day?
c. If management chooses to run the line for 7.5 hours per day using a cycle time of forty seconds, what are the results?
d. How would you propose that management solve this problem?

4. Benskee Brokerage House has organized its stock transaction processing system into a line flow process with the following work assignments. To complete a transaction, steps A through F must be completed. The times listed are to process one transaction.

Work Station	Task Assigned	Task Times (Seconds)
1	A, B	40, 90
2	C	120
3	D	100
4	E, F	40, 40

a. Assuming that one person is assigned to each work station, which is the bottleneck operation?

b. What is the hourly production rate for this operation?

c. If each clerical worker makes $11.00 per hour, what is the labor cost per transaction?

5. The following precedence diagram and times are given for the assembly of the pump on a washing machine. The times in seconds are listed by each activity.

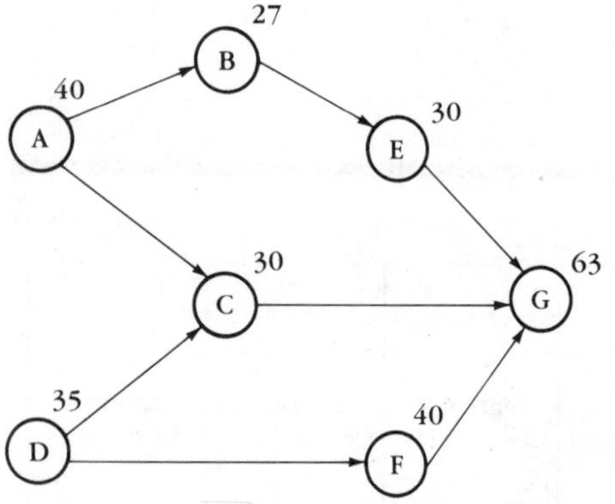

a. Assuming a cycle time of seventy seconds, balance the assembly line, using the longest-task-time rule. Break any ties using the first-in-the-list rule. Ties at the second level will be broken by picking at random.

b. What is the balance delay for the pump?

c. How many pumps can be built if the line is producing 7.25 hours per day?

6. Pietro's Sandwich Shop has signed a contract to deliver a minimum of 2,000 and a maximum of 4,000 sandwiches to each home game of a major league baseball team. Even 2,000 is more than double its best sales day. The sandwiches need to be made each day. Pietro's does not want any holdovers. To make this many sandwiches, it will have to use an assembly line. Following are the precedence relationships and estimates of the time required for each step:

Task	Description	Time (Seconds)	Immediate Predecessors
A	Spread both buns with mayonnaise	15	—
B	Add green pepper	10	A
C	Add lettuce	5	A
D	Add meat	7	A
E	Add cheese	6	A
F	Add tomato	5	A
G	Wrap finished sandwich	10	B, C, D, E, F

Because most of the workers will be college students, the number of hours the assembly line can work is a variable. However, due to delivery-time constraints, management figures that nine hours of actual production time is all they can expect after allowing for breaks.

a. What cycle time is required for Pietro's to make delivery of 4,000 sandwiches, using the full nine hours for production?

b. Devise a plan that would allow Pietro's to build 4,000 sandwiches. Include in this plan the cycle time, the number of assembly lines, and the hours worked. Keep in mind that on some days it may only have to build 2,000 sandwiches.

c. Balance the line, using the cycle time determined in part b.

7. Delphos Division has balanced its production line as shown below.

Work Station	Tasks Assigned	Tasks Times (Seconds)
1	A, B	40, 30
2	C	80
3	D, E	40, 40
4	F	60
5	G	50

a. Which is the bottleneck operation, assuming that one person is assigned to each station?

b. Assuming an eight-hour workday, what is the maximum daily output? What is the balance delay of the present balance?

c. If each production worker makes $13 per hour, what is the labor cost per unit produced?

d. If Delphos Division management assigned two people to stations 2 and 3, what would the maximum daily output become? What would happen to the unit cost of a product?

8. Garfinkle Bank and Trust needs to balance its check-processing line. Following are the tasks required to completely process a check:

Task	Time (Seconds)	Immediate Predecessors
A	6	—
B	2	A
C	6	—
D	2	A
E	4	B, D
F	2	E
G	2	—
H	6	G
I	8	F, H

a. If these tasks cannot be further divided, what is the minimum cycle time?

b. Balance the line, using the longest-task-time rule and the cycle time determined in part a.

c. Determine the percentage of idle time for the balance.

9. Cable Manufacturing's assembly line has the following requirements:

Task	Time (Seconds)	Immediate Predecessors
A	30	—
B	60	—
C	20	A, B
D	40	A
E	50	D
F	20	C
G	30	E, F
H	50	G

a. What is the maximum daily output of the assembly line if it operates eight hours per day?

b. Using the cycle time determined in part a, balance the assembly line, using the longest-task-time rule. What is the percentage of idle time for the line?

c. Assuming the cycle time can be changed, how can the idle time percentage be reduced?

d. Find a balance that is better than the one found in part b.

10. A small manufacturer has four departments. The following loads are transported between departments:

From	To: A	B	C	D
A	—	40	25	70
B	10	—	40	20
C	45	80	—	15
D	30	10	45	—

Assume that all departments are the same size and shape. Also, assume that material-handling costs per unit distance are the same for all trips. Calculate the distance between departments as described in the chapter. Use the following building layout:

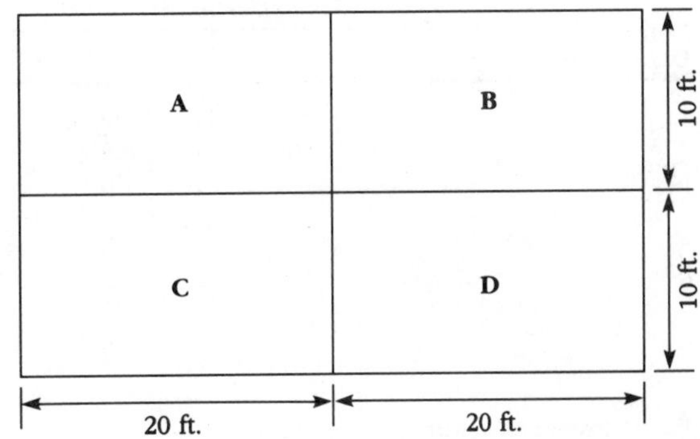

a. Evaluate the initial solution, using the model described in equation 8.1.

b. Try to find a better solution by switching department pairs. Evaluate the solution to see if it is better than the initial solution.

11. Quik-Grow Flower Shop is moving into new headquarters. The following information about the activity levels between departments has been collected over the past few months. This represents trips per day between departments.

From	To: A	B	C	D	E	F
A	—	0	100	40	20	10
B	—	—	0	70	10	0
C	—	—	—	140	50	60
D	—	—	—	—	80	10
E	—	—	—	—	—	20
F	—	—	—	—	—	—

New Building Design

a. Using the adjacent-department method, find a good solution to the layout problem.

b. How do you know it is a good solution?

12. Nashua Medical Center is considering a new location for department 4, Pediatrics. The center would like to switch it with department 5, Neurology. Activity levels are measured in movement of staff between departments.

From Department	To Department 1	2	3	4	5	6
1	—	35	50	100	20	0
2	—	—	30	20	10	15
3	—	—	—	10	30	0
4	—	—	—	—	10	15
5	—	—	—	—	—	15
6	—	—	—	—	—	—

Present Layout

4	2	3
6	5	1

a. Given the layout and other information, what is the impact of this change? Use the adjacent-department criteria discussed in the text.

b. Can any further improvements be made? If so, what are they? If not, why not?

13. Seeman Satellite Dish Company has a small manufacturing facility in Wyoming. Its present layout and an activity matrix showing trips per week between department pairs follow. The company wants to find an improved layout by trying to minimize activity level times distance. Cost per unit distance is assumed to be equal for all department pairs.

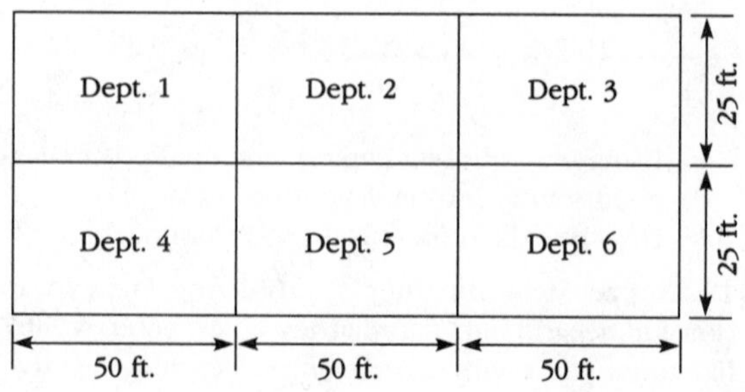

From Department	To Department 1	2	3	4	5	6
1	—	70	60	—	40	100
2	85	—	70	80	90	85
3	80	60	—	90	70	100
4	85	90	80	—	90	85
5	—	80	40	70	—	85
6	70	90	20	100	90	—

Improve on the present layout using the adjacent-department method.

14. Conway Cablevision Company is attempting to organize its new offices and has asked you to develop a new layout plan. The departments and the proposed building design are shown below.

a. Develop the layout for Conway.

b. Evaluate the layout plan.

Matrix

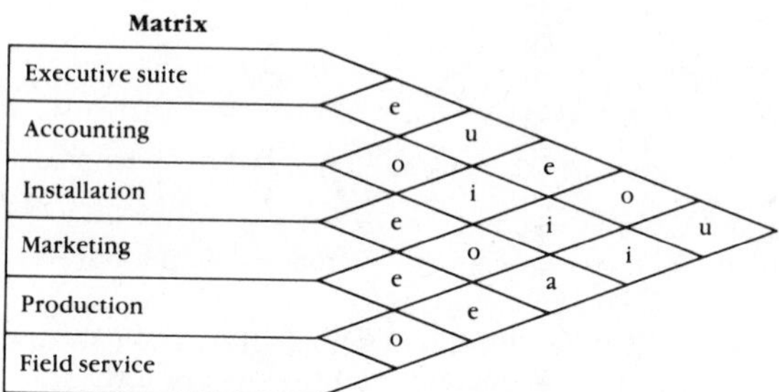

Code

a Absolutely necessary
e Very important
i Important
o Somewhat important
u Unimportant
x Undesirable

New Building Design

15. Medwich Urgent Care is building new facilities and has asked you to develop the layout. The departments and the proposed building design are shown below.

a. Develop a layout for Medwich.
b. Evaluate the layout.

Matrix

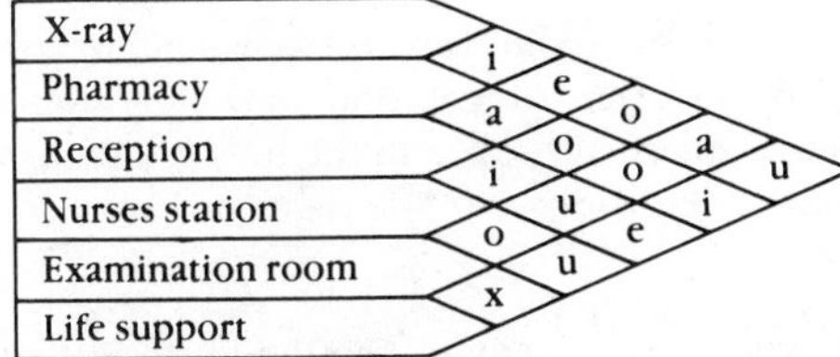

Building Design

Code
a Absolutely necessary
e Very important
i Important
o Somewhat important
u Unimportant
x Undesirable

16. Webster's Metal Working is attempting to organize its parts into families for production using a flexible manufacturing system. It has obtained the following information:

Machine Code	*Packs* A	B	C	D	E	F	G	H	I
101	1	—	1	—	—	—	—	1	1
102	—	1	—	1	—	1	—	—	—
103	—	1	—	1	—	—	—	—	—
104	1	—	1	—	1	—	1	1	—
105	—	1	—	—	—	1	—	—	—
106	—	—	—	1	1	1	1	—	—
107	1	—	—	—	1	—	1	—	—

a. How should Webster organize its families of parts?
b. What are the advantages of organizing parts into families?

17. Huss Drive Gear Company is preparing to balance its production lines located in Luckey, Ohio; Warwick, North Dakota; and Breckenridge, Texas. Each line is to be balanced in the same way, and each has a 300-second cycle time.

Task	Time (Seconds)	Immediate Predecessors
A	300	—
B	125	A
C	100	A
D	200	B, F
E	250	C
F	50	—
G	225	D
H	125	A
I	175	H
J	150	E, G, I
K	225	I
L	75	H
M	100	K, L
N	175	M
O	150	M
P	125	N, O
Q	75	B

a. Draw a precedence diagram for the tasks.
b. What is the theoretical minimum number of work stations? How many units can Huss produce if each line works forty hours per week?
c. Balance the line using a 300-second cycle time and the longest-task-time rule.
d. What is the percentage of idle time for this balance?
e. Rebalance the line with a 360-second cycle time. What effect does this have on Huss's capacity and the percentage of idle time of the balance? Use the longest-task-time rule.

18. Gatsbee Electronics assembles microcomputers from top-quality components and sells them to students at about 60 percent of the price of a comparable computer purchased through a retail outlet. The following steps are required to assemble each microcomputer. The workers will be paid $9.00 per hour.

Task	Time (Minutes)	Immediate Predecessors
A	3	—
B	8	A
C	4	A
D	9	B,C
E	12	A
F	4	D,E
G	4	F
H	8	F
I	9	G,H
J	7	H
K	2	J
L	6	J
M	5	J
N	9	K,L
O	11	M
P	3	O

a. If the assembly line is expected to produce forty microcomputers per eight-hour day, what should the cycle time be?

b. Balance the assembly line with that cycle time.

c. What is the balance delay for that balance?

d. Is the assembly line efficient? If not, what would you do to correct the problem? Be specific. Rebalance the line, if necessary.

19. The International Institute for the Preservation of Goldfinches (IIPG) is moving from the 59th to the 69th floor of the Sears Tower. This gives it an opportunity to shift office space and reduce travel time between departments. The present activity matrix giving movements per month and the layout are shown below.

	To				
From	**B**	**D**	**E**	**G**	**H**
A	400	300	100	200	—
C	300	—	700	100	100
F	—	—	200	—	300
I	100	200	600	—	100

Present Layout

A	**B**	**C**	**D**
E	**F**	**G**	**H**
I	**J**	**K**	**L**

a. Assume that transportation costs per unit distance are equal for all trips. Evaluate the present solution, using the adjacent-department method described in the chapter. Assume that diagonal departments such as A and F in the present layout have 0 distance. Departments situated as A and C are a distance of 1, departments situated as A and G are a distance of 1, and so on. If you are unsure about a distance, like that between A and L, look at the distance assigned to other pairs, and make a reasonable assumption. Remember, you are the model builder.

b. Suppose that department F is the executive suite, and that the cost per unit distance for any trip starting or ending in department F is four times the cost per unit distance of any other trip. With these new conditions, solve the problem as described in part a.

20. Able Print Shop is moving to a new building that is 120 by 165 feet. Department heads have submitted the following requests for space in the new building, and these have been approved. The requested sizes are as follows:

Department	**Length (Feet)**	**Width (Feet)**
Art (A)	60	60
Binding (B)	60	60
Cutting (C)	60	30
Layout (L)	30	30
Packing and shipping (PS)	30	30
Printing (P)	75	60
Storage (S)	60	45
Receiving (R)	60	30

The annual numbers of loads among departments are shown below.

	To							
From	**A**	**B**	**C**	**L**	**PS**	**P**	**S**	**R**
A	—	100	100	800	100	100	100	—
B	—	—	100	—	300	—	—	—
C	—	400	—	—	100	—	—	—
L	400	100	—	—	—	900	100	—
PS	—	—	—	—	—	—	—	—
P	—	400	500	—	200	—	100	—
S	200	600	—	100	300	10	—	—
R	50	100	—	100	200	50	1,400	—

What is your layout recommendation? The objective is to minimize activity level times distance.

21. The State University College of Business Administration is moving into a new building. The dean has asked you to suggest a layout. The square-footage requirements for each area are given, along with the number of trips made from one area to another in one month.

Department or Area	**Space Requirement (Net Square Feet)**
Dean's Area (D)	900
Graduate Studies (GS)	600
Undergraduate Studies (UG)	900
Business Research Center (BR)	600
Graduate Assistant's Area (GA)	1,200
Accounting (A)	2,400
Finance (F)	1,800

Department or Area	Space Requirement (Net Square Feet)
Information Systems and Operations Management (I)	3,000
Management (MG)	3,600
Marketing (MK)	3,000

From	*To* D	GS	UG	BR	GA	A	F	I	MG	MK
D	—	20	5	40	0	100	120	200	150	180
GS	40	—	20	150	300	50	50	70	60	40
UG	10	30	—	0	0	100	40	200	120	80
BR	150	200	0	—	100	200	140	400	300	200
GA	0	150	0	300	—	70	40	100	40	50
A	50	80	10	50	10	—	200	300	80	40
F	40	100	5	40	5	150	—	100	60	30
I	100	200	10	50	5	250	120	—	600	100
MG	80	100	5	30	10	100	40	400	—	140
MK	50	50	10	20	10	60	50	120	120	—

a. Assume that the average graduate assistant is paid 20 percent of the salary of the average faculty member or administrator. What layout would you recommend? The objective is to minimize activity level times distance times cost for all trips.

b. What would you recommend if the building being designed has two stories of equal size?

Data Sets for Computer Solution

1. Scott Medical, Inc., is planning to open a new clinic on the West Coast. The clinic will be patterned after similar facilities in the South and on the East Coast. The estimated activity levels are shown below. Patient movements among the departments have been estimated from statistical analysis of other facilities. All departments are approximately the same size, 1,200 square feet.

Department	Code
Cardiology	C
Laboratory	L
Waiting area	W
Ob./gyn.	O
Pathology	Pa
Pediatrics	Pe
Pharmacy	Ph
X-ray	X

From	*To* C	L	W	O	Pa	Pe	Ph	X
C	—	100	50	—	50	—	200	—
L	—	—	—	200	200	400	—	—
W	—	—	—	200	100	500	—	300
O	—	—	—	—	—	—	100	20
Pa	—	—	—	—	—	—	50	—
Pe	—	—	—	—	—	—	250	300
Ph	—	—	—	—	—	—	—	—
X	—	—	—	—	—	—	—	—

Determine the layout for the new facility. The building has not yet been designed, so it is possible to build nearly any configuration, just so all departments are on one floor. What relative department locations do you recommend for minimizing patient flows (walking distances)?

2. Gerrard Manufacturing produces small appliances for use in the home. One of its lines assembles hand mixers according to the following list of requirements:

Task	Time (Seconds)	Immediate Predecessors
A	64	—
B	28	A
C	37	A
D	37	A
E	23	A
F	43	A
G	54	—
H	25	B,C
I	15	G
J	36	E,F
K	52	H,D
L	25	F
M	63	L
N	42	—
O	43	N
P	54	O
Q	29	P
R	27	J,M
S	37	I
T	25	S
U	40	T
V	44	K,R
W	20	U,V
X	52	Q,W

a. Construct a precedence diagram from this list of precedences.

b. Use a computer-based assembly-line balancing program to balance the line. These balances will provide the basis for determining the information in the following matrix. The choice rule to use is left to your discretion.

c. The information in this table would be used to help management decide which balance to use. Which choice would you make? Support your answer.

Cycle times (Seconds)	80	90	100	110	120
Production rate (Pieces/hr.)					
Percentage idle time					
Actual number of stations					
Theoretical minimum number of stations					

MINI-CASES

Colorado Ski Corporation

Colorado Ski Corporation produces bindings for downhill skis. Skiers are a notoriously fickle group and change buying habits often. The bindings are sold primarily in the United States, although there is some foreign distribution. Colorado Ski expects that foreign demand will enjoy substantial growth, while U.S. demand will increase only slightly. Presently, binding sales are about 150,000 per year, with anticipated sales growth of 12 percent next year and the year after. For the three years following, projections are for 8 percent growth each year.

Demand is highly seasonal, and 60 percent of the annual demand is projected to be sold in October, November, and December. Bindings are relatively easy to store. Therefore, management has decided to smooth production somewhat. Production in August, September, October, and November is set at 12 percent of projected demand. Production for January, February, and March is set at 4 percent and for the other months at 8 percent.

Colorado Ski has asked you to balance the binding assembly line to satisfy next year's production. For planning purposes, assume that each month has twenty-one working days. Assume that a shift has 7.5 hours of actual production time. As the assembly-line balancer, you may choose the number of assembly lines, the number of shifts, and the cycle time. Set the production rate so that demand for the peak months can be met. This will mean that extra capacity is available during the nonpeak months. The precedence list and estimated task times are as follows:

Task	Estimated Time (Seconds)	Immediate Predecessors
A	43	—
B	32	—
C	45	A
D	26	A
E	54	A,B
F	8	C
G	44	D,E
H	12	—
I	30	F,H
J	13	G
K	28	I

1. Balance the assembly line to satisfy the production plan for next year (with a percentage of demand produced each month) as described in the case.

2. Prepare a plan for meeting the projected demand increases for each of the next five years. Assume the production plan does not change.

3. Describe the impact on the present solution if Colorado Ski decided to produce the same amount each month—that is, to level production. What extra costs would be incurred? What would the risks be? What are the potential advantages?

Barstowe Research Laboratory

Barstowe Research Laboratory has been a pioneer in biological engineering. The company wants to move from its cramped quarters to a new facility on a piece of property it owns in the suburbs. Barstowe is planning to build a one-story research laboratory and administrative offices.

As the facility planner, you have worked with the department heads to estimate the square-footage requirements for the new facility.

Department		Square Feet Required
A	Accounting	600
M	Marketing	900
RD	Research director	300
GM	General management	1,200
AL	Animal laboratory	2,000
G	Genetics	1,200
B	Biochemistry	1,800
P	Physiology	1,200
CB	Cell biology	1,600
DNA	DNA research	1,600

The table at the end of this mini-case lists the activity level between each department pair. These levels are measured in trips per month by employees. Because the cost per unit distance traveled is the same, all trips are shown in the top right of the activity table even if the trip went from B to A rather than from A to B.

1. Determine the layout for the new facility.

2. How can the model be used to address what-if questions?

3. What if DNA research becomes more important in the future and its activity level with cell biology increases? How will this affect the solution?

4. Other than trying to minimize the time to move people from one point to another, is there some other important factor that ought to be considered when arranging groups of scientists?

	To									
From	**A**	**M**	**RD**	**GM**	**AL**	**G**	**B**	**P**	**CB**	**DNA**
A	—	220	40	260	20	0	0	0	0	0
M	—	—	120	240	0	40	80	30	110	60
RD	—	—	—	100	200	180	150	150	220	140
GM	—	—	—	—	40	120	100	140	120	150
AL	—	—	—	—	—	300	40	120	240	100
G	—	—	—	—	—	—	120	80	100	40
B	—	—	—	—	—	—	—	120	200	100
P	—	—	—	—	—	—	—	—	120	80
CB	—	—	—	—	—	—	—	—	—	240
DNA	—	—	—	—	—	—	—	—	—	—

SELECTED BIBLIOGRAPHY

Apple, James M. *Plant Layout and Material Handling*. New York: Wiley, 1977.

Arn, E. A. *Group Technology*. West Berlin: Springer-Verlag, 1975.

Buffa, Elwood S., and Miller, Jeffrey G. *Production-Inventory Systems: Planning and Control*. Homewood, Ill.: Irwin, 1979.

Byrett, Donald L.; Ozden, Mufit H.; and Patton, Jon M. "Integrating Flexible Manufacturing Systems with Traditional Manufacturing, Planning, and Control." *Production and Inventory Management Journal*, Third Quarter, (1988): 15–21.

Flynn, Barbara B., and Jacobs, F. Robert. "An Experimental Comparison of Cellular (Group Technology) Layout with Process Layout." *Decision Sciences* 18 (1987): 562–581.

Guerrero, Hector H. "Group Technology: I. The Essential Concepts." *Production and Inventory Management*, First Quarter, (1987): 62–70.

Han, Min-Hong, and McGinnis, Leon F. "Throughput Rate Maximization in Flexible Manufacturing Cells." *IIE Transactions* 20, no. 4 (December 1988): 409–417.

Hartley, John. *FMS at Work*. Bedford, UK: IFS (Publications), 1984.

Hyer, Nancy L. *Group Technology at Work*. Dearborn, Mich.: Society of Manufacturing Engineers, 1984.

Kinney, Hugh D., and McGinnis, Leon F. "Design and Control of Manufacturing Cells." *Industrial Engineering*, October 1987, pp. 28–38.

Knight, Donald O., and Wall, Michael L. "Using Group Technology for Improving Communication and Coordination Among Teams of Workers in Manufacturing Cells." *Industrial Engineering,* January 1989, pp. 32–34.

Kusiak, Andrew. "An Expert System for Group Technology." *Industrial Engineering,* October 1987, pp. 56–61.

Lin, Li, and Bedworth, David D. "A Semi-Generative Approach to Computer-Aided Process Planning Using Group Technology." Computers and Industrial Engineering. 14, no. 2 (1988): 127–137.

Mecklenburg, J. C. *Plant Layout: A Guide to the Layout of Process Plants and Sites.* New York: Wiley, 1973.

Mital, Anil; Kromodihardjo, Sudiyono; and Channaveeraiah, Chetan. "Quantification of Subjective Descriptors of Part Geometry with an Aim to Increase the Sensitivity of Group Technology." Computers and Industrial Engineering. 14, no. 2 (1988): 211–218.

Muller, T. *Automated Guided Vehicles.* Bedford, UK: IFS (Publications), 1983.

Muther, Richard, and McPherson, K. "Four Approaches to Computerized Layout." *Industrial Engineering,* 2, no. 2 (February 1970): 39–42.

Reed, Ruddell. *Plant Layout: Factors, Principles, and Techniques.* Homewood, Ill.: Irwin, 1966.

Runcie, John F. "By Days I Make the Cars." *Harvard Business Review* 58, no. 3 (May–June 1980): 106–115.

Salomon, Daniel P., and Biegel, John E. "Assessing Economic Attractiveness of FMS Applications in Small Batch Manufacturing." *Industrial Engineering,* June 1984, pp. 88–96.

Shtub, Avraham. "Estimating the Effect of Conversion to a Group Technology Layout on the Cost of Material Handling." *Engineering Costs and Production Economics* 16 (1989): 103–109.

Stanfel, Larry E. "Machine Clustering for Economic Production." *Engineering Costs and Production Economics* 9 (1985): 73–81.

Suresh, Nallan C., and Meredith, Jack R. "Achieving Factory Automation Through Group Technology Principles." *Journal of Operations Management* 5, no. 3 (February 1985): 151–167.

Vakharia, Asoo J. "Methods of Cell Formation in Group Technology: A Framework for Evaluation." *Journal of Operations Management* 6, no. 3 (May 1986): 257–267.

Vonderembse, Mark A., and Wobser, Gregory S. "Steps for Implementing a Flexible Manufacturing System." *Industrial Engineering,* April 1987, pp. 38–48.

Zisk, Burton I. "Flexibility Is Key to Automated Material Transport System for Manufacturing Cells." *Industrial Engineering* 15, no. 11 (November 1983): 58–64.

Chapter 9

Job Design and Work Measurement

LEARNING OBJECTIVES

After completing this chapter, you should be able to

- Discuss the four areas encompassed by job design.
- Define specialization, job rotation, job enlargement, and job enrichment.
- Utilize the techniques of methods analysis.
- Discuss some factors to consider in work place layout.
- Summarize ethical concerns of job designs.
- Explain the importance of time standards.
- List the steps of a stopwatch time study.
- Calculate standard time based on information from a stopwatch time study.
- Describe the use of predetermined time standards.
- Explain how work sampling is performed.
- Use learning curves to calculate time per unit.
- Determine the learning factor based on historical data.
- Calculate average time per unit for a learning curve.
- Calculate wages under piece-rate and bonus plans.
- Discuss how employee compensation plans may vary among countries.

New United Motor Manufacturing, Inc.: Increasing Productivity Through Job Design

New United Motor Manufacturing, Inc. (NUMMI), is a joint venture that brings together the world's largest auto maker, General Motors, with one of its primary competitors, Toyota. This organization, which is half owned by each company, occupies an assembly plant in Fremont, California, that had previously been closed by General Motors. The company produces the Geo Prizm and the Toyota Corolla. The product and process designs were developed by Toyota, and the final products are marketed by General Motors and Toyota. All direct labor employees in the plant are members of the United Auto Workers (UAW) union.

NUMMI's operations are quite different from those of most companies. Workers are organized into teams, each with a team leader who acts as a player-coach. Each team is responsible for all activities related to its job, including quality, cost, safety, and productivity. Each team also has its own room within the plant. These rooms are designed as comfortable places where team members can congregate during lunch periods or breaks. One group even has a large tree in the middle of its room.

Although NUMMI's labor organization is nonstandard, there is a great deal of emphasis on standardized work. Each task has been organized in the correct sequence for maximum efficiency. A standardized work chart is developed for each task and visually shows the actions that make up that task. Efforts are continually made to eliminate wasted time spent on such activities as waiting or walking.

The standardization of tasks also helps greatly in planning. Since the required time is known for each activity, it is possible to plan for the work force needed to perform a given task within a required period of time. For example, if material must be unloaded from a truck within thirty minutes and the standard time for that task is sixty minutes per worker, then two workers must be scheduled. This standardization also allows for problems to be spotted easily when deviations occur from the standard.

When General Motors operated the plant, it experienced about 25 percent absenteeism, and there were roughly four thousand unsettled grievances between labor and management when the plant was closed. Today, although most employees are drawn from the same group that had previously worked at the plant, attendance is 97 percent, and there are no grievances.

While the environment at NUMMI may seem very unusual, it actually represents a current trend in the organization of production and operations activities. As you read this chapter, you will learn about some of the theories behind the organization of workers into teams. You will also find out how work activities can be improved and about the role that time standards play in helping to bring about that improvement.

INTRODUCTION

In the preceding chapters, you have learned about such technological innovations as computer-integrated manufacturing (CIM), computerized material requirements planning (MRP), and robotics, all of which are revolutionizing the field of production/operations management. But with all this emphasis on technology, it's very easy to forget about the single most important aspect of any production operation—*people*. It is people who design, build, and operate the computerized and automated systems that you have read about in previous chapters. In fact, even though much has been published lately about the use of robots and other types of automation, most production and operations processes are basically done by people. This is especially true in service industries. Even highly automated companies still require people to oversee and direct the operations of their automated systems.

This chapter describes some methods for designing the jobs that people do and explains how the work performed in those jobs can be measured. As you will see, job design is a critical factor in the development of products, as well as processes; the way a person does his or her job will have a major impact on the quality of the product produced and the ability of the production process to function as designed.

In any job, there are alternative ways various tasks can be performed. For instance, one job design might specify that, when putting washers on a bolt, the employee hold the bolt in one hand and drop the washers on with the other hand (see Exhibit 9.1). An alternative job design might utilize a **fixture**—a device for holding parts—so both the worker's hands could be used to put on washers. Which design is best? One way to answer that question is by determining which method takes the lesser amount of time and produces better quality. That's where work measurement comes in.

Work measurement is a tool used to determine the amount of time a work activity, or task, should take under ordinary conditions. Most companies use work measurement for production planning purposes or, as described above, to compare alternative job designs. But many other companies also tie their employees' wages directly to output. Such piece-rate or incentive systems are based on time standards determined from a work measurement study. Even without such

Exhibit 9.1 Alternative Methods for Putting Washers on Bolts

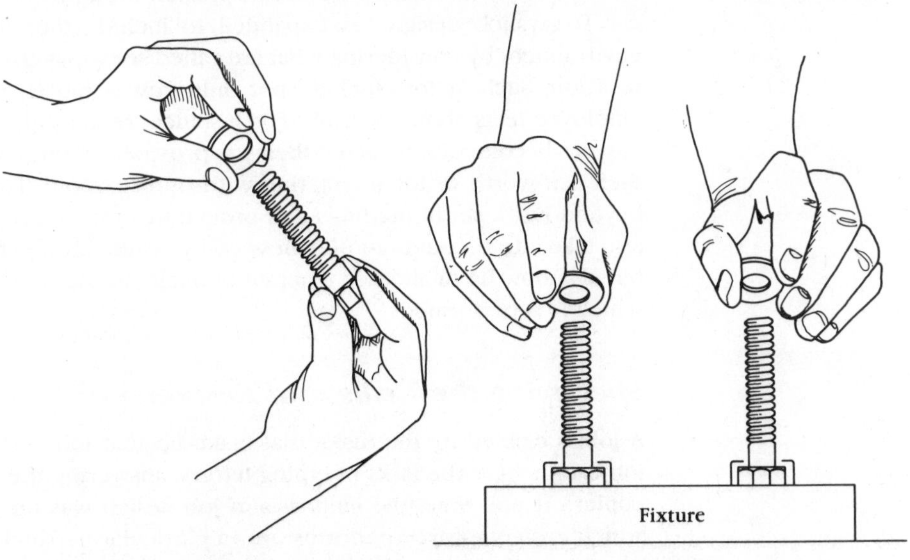

Fixture

Design A

Design B

output-based pay systems, any company must have some idea of the time it will take to perform a given task so that operations and capacity planning can be performed.

JOB DESIGN

Job design actually encompasses four different areas of concern:

1. Specifying the *tasks and responsibilities* the job encompasses
2. Defining the *methods* to be used in performing the job
3. Laying out the *physical environment* in which the job will be performed
4. Identifying the *social and psychological environment* in which the person will be working

Traditionally, job design was concerned with specifying the tasks to be performed by a worker and the way in which those tasks were to be done. For example, a person responsible for "ringing up" customers' purchases in a grocery store often has no other tasks to perform. Specific details about opening and closing the register and how each purchase is to be entered are all specified. Additionally, the exact way that a checkout person is to perform the job may be documented. Such documentation might indicate the procedure for approving customers' checks or for verifying the price of an item so that those tasks can be done as quickly as possible and with the least amount of effort.

For many years, job design has also been involved with the physical environment of a job. Although this often means specifying the allowable levels of noise, dirt, temperature, and so forth, it can also be concerned with the layout of facilities. For example, the checkout area in a grocery store is designed so the person ringing up purchases has everything in easy reach and can operate efficiently with minimum effort and no wasted motion.

Today, job design has expanded to include the social and psychological environment by considering what are called **sociopsychological factors** related to a job. Such factors include not only how a job is done, but also how the employee feels about that job. For instance, research has shown that most employees become dissatisfied if their job provides no opportunities for recognizing their self-worth or for interacting with other people. Thus, job design goes far beyond just a set of methods and procedures that specify a set of tasks. It must also take into account not only how easily or quickly a person may perform a job, but also how he or she will react emotionally to that job and the environment in which it is performed.

Specifying the Tasks and Responsibilities of a Job

A job is defined by the **tasks** that make up that job. For example, a secretary's job can include the tasks of typing letters, answering the telephone, and making copies. At one time, the emphasis in job design was on **job specialization,** in which each employee performs only a particular narrowly defined task. You can see this philosophy applied in company typing pools in which employees are concerned only with typing, not with answering the telephone or making copies. Job specialization has both advantages and disadvantages. On the one hand, job specialization can lead to increased efficiency and productivity. For instance, most individuals in professional sports specialize in a particular sport or even a particular position, such as shortstop or quarterback. This allows those individuals to use their unique talents and abilities to the greatest advantage and to concentrate specifically on improving their performance in one set of tasks. Through specialization, individuals can become expert at a given activity.

On the other hand, too much specialization can lead to boredom and job dissatisfaction. One of the best examples of this occurs in assembly lines, where, for example, a particular worker may be responsible only for fastening a certain bolt. In this case, the worker can quickly become expert with little effort. The result is a lack of challenge and job dissatisfaction.

To overcome the disadvantages of specialization, while still enjoying some of its benefits, many companies have used **job enlargement, job rotation,** and **job enrichment**. Job enlargement and job rotation are strategies that give workers an increased number or variety of tasks to perform. The rationale is that if workers are allowed to perform more than one task, the boredom and dissatisfaction that result from overspecialization will not occur.

The approach taken in job rotation is periodically to shift workers from one job to another. In this way, workers can learn new skills and face new challenges as they change jobs.

With job enlargement, an employee's job is expanded to include several tasks. The idea here is to allow a person to see that he or she is making a meaningful contribution to an entire product—not just putting a bolt into a hole. Another purpose of job enlargement is to avoid boredom by providing new challenges in much the same way as job rotation.

A common criticism of job enlargement and job rotation is that giving a person two boring tasks to perform instead of one will not lead to job satisfaction. Job enlargement and job rotation focus only on the **horizontal expansion** of work by giving a person more tasks or more jobs to perform, as shown in Exhibit 9.2. Instead, many experts argue that job satisfaction depends on a **vertical expansion** of the job description.

This vertical expansion, or **vertical loading,** emphasizes giving workers responsibility for planning many of their own activities and, to some extent, allowing them to make decisions related to the job they are performing.

Methods Analysis

The tasks that make up a job can be done in many different ways, as indicated in Exhibit 9.1, which shows two ways to put a washer on a bolt. In most cases, certain work methods will be more productive than others. Thus, the second area of concern in job design is to identify those methods that are most efficient.

Several techniques can be used to identify the most efficient way of performing a specific task. In general, such techniques are often grouped under the headings of **methods improvement, methods analysis,** or **work improvement**. These techniques are concerned only with the physiological aspects of a task—how easy the task is to do or how quickly the person can work.

Flow Process Charts

The **flow process chart** is used for analyzing the movements of a worker or the flow of materials through a process. In general, the flow process chart will be specified by the product and process designs, which were discussed in Chapters

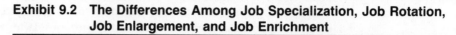

Exhibit 9.2 The Differences Among Job Specialization, Job Rotation, Job Enlargement, and Job Enrichment

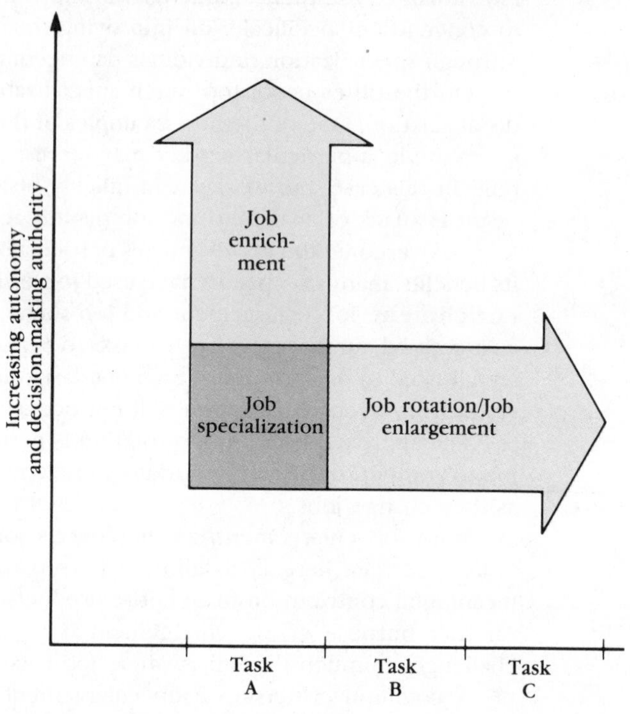

4 and 7. The flow process chart is especially useful in identifying ways of improving the process by eliminating unnecessary idle time, minimizing the distances things must be moved, or rearranging tasks for greater efficiency.

Five symbols are used to describe the actions of a worker or the processing of a part or product, as shown in Exhibit 9.3.

1. *Circle*—indicates that some operation is being performed, either by the worker or on the part
2. *Arrow*—represents either transportation of material or movement of the employee from one location to another
3. *Square*—represents an inspection operation
4. *Capital D*—indicates a delay or wait
5. *Triangle*—indicates storage of material, parts, etc.

The flow process chart can be used to design a new task or to improve an existing one. In the first case, the flow process chart will help to identify possible problems that may occur or indicate ways that performance of the task can be improved. For an existing task, the first step is usually to chart the task as it is

Exhibit 9.3 Flow Process Chart for Fast-Food Restaurant Counter

Present Method ☒ **PROCESS CHART**
Proposed Method ☐

SUBJECT CHARTED Counter Employee at Fast-Food Restaurant DATE ____
CHART BY ____
CHART NO. ____
DEPARTMENT ____ SHEET NO. __ OF __

DIST IN FEET	TIME IN MINS	CHART SYMBOLS	PROCESS DESCRIPTION
		Operation	Take order and receive money
10		Transportation	Walk to bag storage area
		Operation	Get proper size bag for order
5		Transportation	Walk to hamburger chute
		Operation	Place hamburger in bag
3		Transportation	Return to counter
		Inspection	Check order for next item
10		Transportation	Walk to fry vat
		Operation	Scoop fries into serving container
		Operation	Place serving container in bag
10		Transportation	Return to counter
		Inspection	Check order for next item
5		Transportation	Walk to drink dispenser
		Operation	Obtain proper size cup
		Operation	Start cup filling
	.25	Delay	Wait for cup to fill
5		Transportation	Walk to counter
		Operation	Hand order to customer
48	.25		Total

SUMMARY

	PRESENT METHOD	PROPOSED METHOD	DIFFERENCE
Operations ○			
Transportations ⇨			
Inspections □			
Delays D			
Distance Traveled in Feet			

performed now. After that, the flow process chart is examined to identify possible areas for improvement. The following questions provide some guidelines:

- Is there any unnecessary idle time? If necessary idle time exists, could it be used to perform another activity?
- Can distances be shortened to decrease or eliminate time for movement of the worker or materials?
- Can efficiency be improved by rearranging activities?
- Can the work area be rearranged to improve efficiency?
- Is it possible to reduce the number of times a part or product must be handled?

Exhibit 9.3 is the flow process chart for an existing job. As you can see, each of the symbols has been used to indicate the activity a worker is performing at each step of the process. The time for each delay is indicated, as is the distance that the person must travel in performing the task. Can you see any possible improvements in the process shown in Exhibit 9.3?

One possible way of improving the process would be to use a drink dispenser that shuts off automatically when the cup is full and have the employee get the french fries while the drink dispenser is filling the cup. In this way, the .25 minutes previously spent waiting can be used to perform another activity. The process chart for this revised method is shown in Exhibit 9.4. Notice that this one slight change has saved 10 feet of walking distance and eliminated the .25-minute delay. The process can be improved in several other ways; you should be able to spot at least a few.

Left-hand/Right-hand Charts

Another type of chart useful in job design is known as the **left-hand/right-hand chart** or the **two-hand operation chart**. The purpose of this chart is to achieve the same end as a flow process chart, but at a more detailed level. Instead of simply examining the actions of an employee, the left-hand/right-hand chart lists precisely what each hand is doing at all times during the performance of a task.

The philosophy behind this chart is that both hands should be kept equally busy—much like a pair of employees. If one is idle much of the time and the other does most of the work, then there is an imbalance that can be improved.

This chart uses the same symbols as flow process charts. However, the triangle symbol, which represents storage in flow process charts, is now used to designate times when a hand must hold something. Exhibit 9.5 shows a left-hand/right-hand chart for the existing operation used to assemble part of a faucet. Note that the left hand is used primarily for holding, while the right hand does most of the work.

Instead of using the hand to hold this part, it might make more sense to develop some kind of a fixture that could hold the part, much as was shown in Exhibit 9.1. Such a fixture would free the left hand to perform more work. In addition, a power screwdriver would save the right hand and arm from the continual exertion of tightening screws. This power screwdriver could be hung so it is out of the way, but still within easy reach to pull down for use. With the holding fixture and power screwdriver, the operation chart would appear as shown in Exhibit 9.6. Note the much more even use of both hands in performing work under the revised design.

Exhibit 9.4 Revised Flow Process Chart for Fast-Food Restaurant Counter

Present Method ☐
Proposed Method ☒

PROCESS CHART

SUBJECT CHARTED Counter Employee at Fast-Food Restaurant DATE ____
CHART BY ____
CHART NO. ____
DEPARTMENT ____ SHEET NO. __ OF __

DIST IN FEET	TIME IN MINS	CHART SYMBOLS	PROCESS DESCRIPTION
		Operation	Take order and receive money
10		Transportation	Walk to bag storage area
		Operation	Get proper size bag for order
5		Transportation	Walk to hamburger chute
		Operation	Place hamburger in bag
3		Transportation	Return to counter
		Inspection	Check order for next item
5		Transportation	Walk to drink dispenser
		Operation	Obtain proper size cup
		Operation	Start cup filling
5		Transportation	Walk to fry vat
		Operation	Scoop fries into serving container
		Operation	Place serving container in bag
5		Transportation	Return to drink dispenser
5		Transportation	Walk to counter
		Operation	Hand order to customer
38	.0		Total

SUMMARY

	PRESENT METHOD	PROPOSED METHOD	DIFFERENCE
Operations ○	8	8	0
Transportations ⇨	7	7	0
Inspections ☐	2	1	1
Delays D	1	0	1
Distance Traveled in Feet	48	38	10

Exhibit 9.5 Left-hand/Right-hand Chart

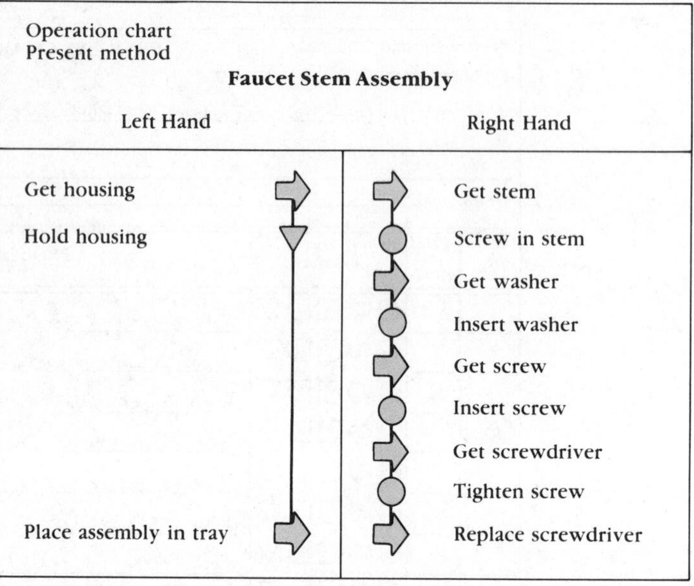

Reprinted by permission from page 466 of *Applied Production and Operations Management,* 3/e by Evans et al.;

Exhibit 9.6 Revised Procedure

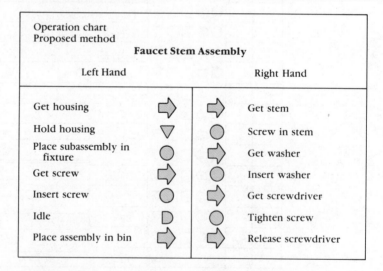

Operation chart
Proposed method

Faucet Stem Assembly

Left Hand	Right Hand
Get housing	Get stem
Hold housing	Screw in stem
Place subassembly in fixture	Get washer
Get screw	Insert washer
Insert screw	Get screwdriver
Idle	Tighten screw
Place assembly in bin	Release screwdriver

Reprinted by permission from page 468 of *Applied Production and Operations Management,* 3/e by Evans et al.;

Operator-Machine Chart

The tools for job design described thus far have concentrated primarily on improving human operations. However, the way that an operator interacts with one or more machines can also have a major impact on how well the person can do that job, the amount of idle time (either operator or machine) that will occur, and how fatiguing the job will be for the operator. To record such interactions, an **operator-machine chart** is used.

Once again, the objective of using such a chart is to identify possible areas for improvement. In the case of an operator and one or more machines, the objective is usually to minimize the idle time of the operator *and* the machines. However, with extremely expensive or critical equipment, it may actually be less costly overall to have some operator idle time as long as the machines are kept operating.

Exhibit 9.7 shows an operator-machine chart for two numerically controlled lathes (lathes that are operated by a program). Although such machines may require considerable setup time, they can run without direct operator involve-

Exhibit 9.7 Operator-Machine Chart for Two Machines

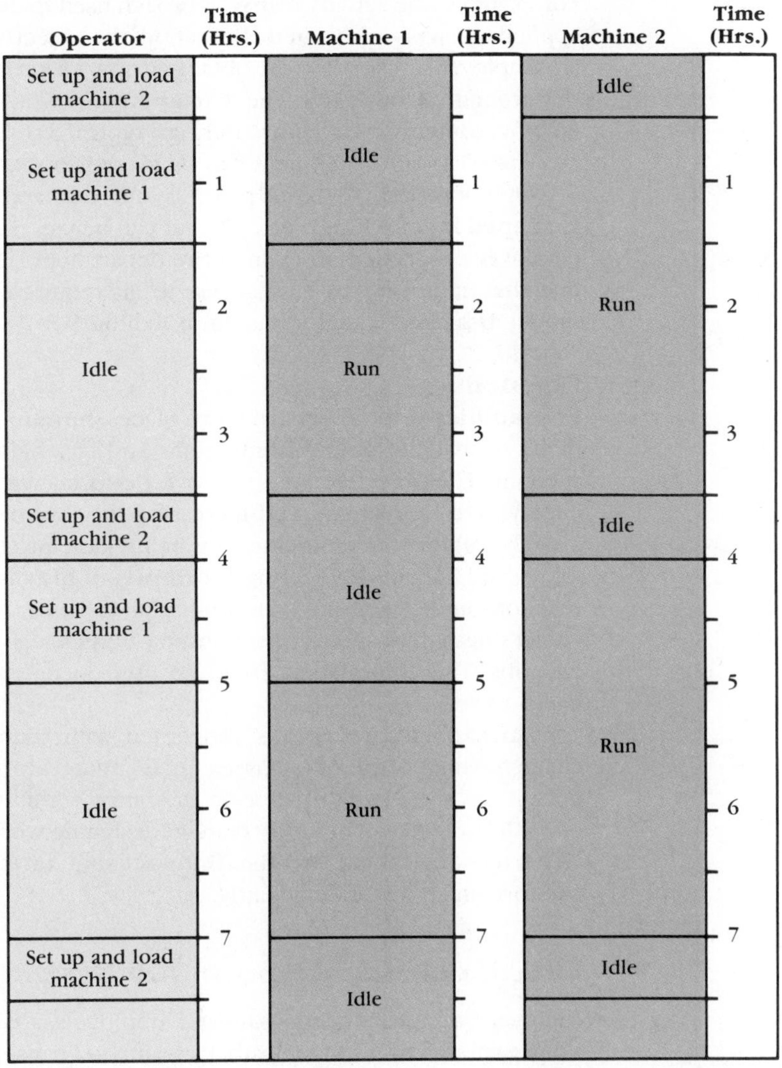

Operator	Time (Hrs.)	Machine 1	Time (Hrs.)	Machine 2	Time (Hrs.)
Set up and load machine 2		Idle		Idle	
Set up and load machine 1	1		1	Run	1
Idle	2	Run	2		2
	3		3		3
Set up and load machine 2		Idle		Idle	
Set up and load machine 1	4		4	Run	4
Idle	5	Run	5		5
	6		6		6
Set up and load machine 2	7	Idle	7	Idle	7

ment. Thus, one operator may run two such machines, being idle while either machine is running, but working when a machine is loaded and set up to run.

As you can see in Exhibit 9.7, considerable idle time results when one machine has finished running, but the other is still being set up and loaded. Can you see how these operations might be done differently to decrease machine idle time?

Designing the Physical Environment

Work Place Layout

Chapter 8 discussed techniques and concepts that can be applied to the layout of an entire production facility. On a more detailed level, companies are also concerned with designing the layout of individual work places within a facility so that they are consistent with the overall facility layout, enabling workers to do their jobs efficiently.

Some of the methods for facility layout can also be used for work place layout. For example, the activity matrix approach used to design a job shop layout can be applied to a work place. In this situation, the objective is to minimize the distance an employee must move in obtaining raw materials, operating equipment, or performing various tasks. The activity matrix would show the total distance an employee might have to move during a typical day. Through careful arrangement, raw materials and equipment can be placed so that distance is minimized.

One approach to work place layout that appears especially useful is the **U-shaped layout**. This type of layout can be used to design everything from one employee's work station to an entire department. The advantage of this layout is that the employee has easy access to all required materials and equipment. A sample U-shaped layout is shown in Exhibit 9.8.

Ergonomics

Ergonomics is the design of work places, furniture, machines, tools, and other items so that the physical limitations and capabilities of people are taken into account. The objective is to improve performance by increasing speed and accuracy, reducing fatigue, and increasing the ease of use by the worker.

The subject of ergonomics can be divided into two components: work physiology and human engineering. **Work physiology** is the study of people's bodily reactions under working conditions. For instance, we can monitor how an individual's heart rate and oxygen consumption change as he or she performs different jobs. This information could be used in determining how often someone needs to rest.

Human engineering is concerned with taking into account the physical characteristics of people. For example, there are certain limits on how far a person can reach with ease or on the range within which information displayed on a CRT screen can be easily read. In designing work stations, all of these human characteristics should be taken into account to ensure that workers will feel comfortable and work efficiently.

Ethical Considerations in Job Design

Each year, hundreds of thousands of employees are injured on the job, some seriously enough to result in death. Unfortunately, many of these deaths and injuries could have been prevented. Although all work involves some degree of risk,

Exhibit 9.8 U-Shaped Layout

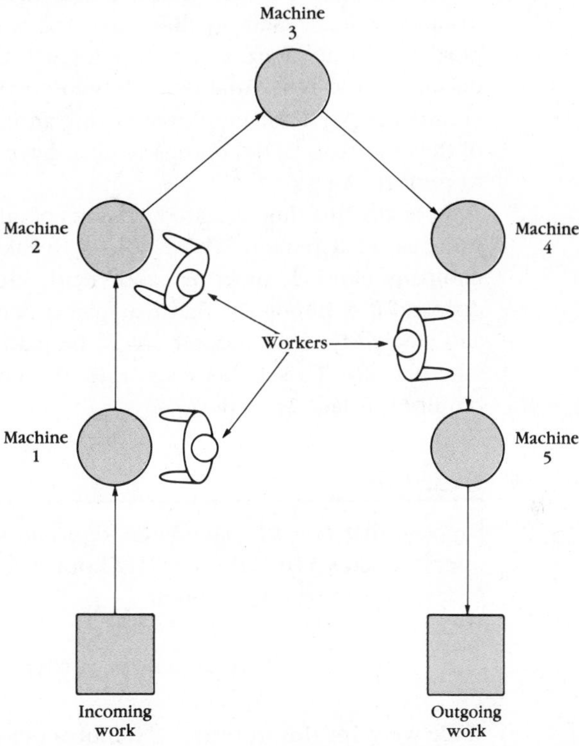

much of that risk can be reduced by specifying proper work methods and laying out facilities so that employees are not placed in highly dangerous situations.

In the past, many companies have not paid enough attention to the safety of their employees. As a consequence, state and federal governments have stepped in with various regulations. Of these, the best known is the Occupational Safety and Health Act (OSHA), which set up a federal agency to oversee safety standards for all types of work. OSHA standards relate to everything from allowable noise levels to design of equipment, and federal inspectors can fine companies for noncompliance.

However, well-run companies realize they have an ethical obligation to provide safe and healthful working conditions for their employees regardless of government regulations. As we said before, employees are a company's most valuable asset, and it is smart business for a company to protect and preserve those assets.

WORK MEASUREMENT

One important aspect of any job is the time it normally takes to perform a certain task. In some jobs, all that matters may be to have a rough idea of the time needed for each task. For example, knowing roughly how long it takes to have a letter typed can help a manager plan ahead so that letters get sent out on time. In this case, an exact time estimate is not needed.

In other situations, accurate measures of task time may be essential. For instance, when assembly-line balancing was discussed in Chapter 8, it was important that accurate times be known for each task so that the line could be balanced. Another situation in which accurate task times are essential is when companies pay their employees using an incentive or piece-rate system. In both of these situations, the company must have an accurate idea of the time required to perform a task.

Usually this time is stated in terms of minutes per unit. For example, consider the case of a person whose job is to take telephone orders for a mail-order company like L. L. Bean or Land's End. Such companies receive many calls per day, and it is important that the mail-order operators handle these calls quickly and efficiently. Thus, people might be paid based on the number of orders they take per day. To set this wage rate, the company must know the average time required to take an order.

Example

Suppose that records have been kept and we know that the average mail-order operator takes 510 calls in a forty-hour week. To determine the average time per order, we can use the formula

$$\text{Average time per order} = \frac{\text{total time}}{\text{number of orders}}$$

Since we want this in terms of minutes per order, we must divide the number of minutes in a week by the average number of calls handled per week.

$$\frac{40 \text{ hours}}{\text{week}} \times \frac{60 \text{ minutes}}{\text{hour}} = 2{,}400 \text{ minutes per week}$$

$$\text{Average time per order} = \frac{2{,}400 \text{ minutes}}{510 \text{ orders}}$$

$$= 4.7 \text{ minutes per order}$$

The time calculated above is called the **standard time** and is usually expressed in terms of time per unit (e.g., 3.75 minutes per part) or units per time period (e.g., sixteen parts per hour). This represents the time it should take to perform a task under ordinary conditions, allowing for rest periods, fatigue, and other unavoidable delays. There are several different ways in which this standard time can be obtained other than the one demonstrated above.

Historical Data

One of the easiest ways to develop a time standard is by using **historical data,** as was done in the preceding example. However, the main disadvantage of historical data is that they include past inefficiencies. Therefore, historical data can be used as a starting point and as a basis for comparison, but other methods may be better for identifying possible improvements.

Time Studies

The most common way of developing the standard time for a task is through a time study, usually done with a stopwatch. During a time study, an experienced worker performs the task repeatedly. Each repetition of the task is termed a **work cycle**. The stopwatch time recorded for each cycle is used to develop a standard time that represents how long it should take an average worker to perform that same activity.

The stopwatch time study is usually performed in a series of steps, beginning with evaluation of the task and proceeding through a series of calculations until the standard time is obtained. We will briefly summarize those steps here so that you can be aware of the basic procedure. But first, we need to introduce some new terminology.

We have already discussed the distinction between a job and the tasks that make up that job. However, tasks may be further broken down into **elements.** Each element is a segment of a task. For example, the task of typing a letter might be broken down into the following elements:

- Obtain paper from drawer.
- Insert paper in typewriter.
- Type letter.
- Remove paper from typewriter.

The reason for this further breakdown is twofold. First, it is often easier for the time-study operator to time each element separately. Second, ways of improving a job can often be identified by looking at each individual element.

One further stage of refinement will also be of concern to us here. That is, each element may be divided into individual **movements**. For instance, the element described above of obtaining paper from a drawer might be further divided into the following movements:

- Reach a distance of one foot to drawer.
- Pull drawer open six inches.
- Reach three inches to paper.
- Grasp paper.
- Move paper two feet from drawer to typewriter.

While this extreme level of detail might seem unnecessary, it is actually the stuff of which methods improvement is made. By analyzing each movement, we can identify ways of improving efficiency. For example, to improve the element of obtaining paper, one might place the paper in an open bin on the desk—eliminating several time-consuming steps. These individual movements will also be useful for another type of work measurement procedure to be discussed later. For now, we go on to describe the steps of a time study.[1]

Step 1. Make sure that all procedures specified in the company's labor agreement are followed. This often requires that the supervisor and the worker—and sometimes the union representative—be informed before the time study begins.

Step 2. Observe the task, and make any improvements in the operator's performance of the task.

Step 3. Record information about the task and how it is being performed for future reference in case the standard is questioned.

Step 4. Break the task into elements such that each has unique starting and ending points but is long enough to be timed easily. Starting and ending points can be when a part is picked up or put down or when a machine is started or stopped.

Step 5. Time enough work cycles to be assured of a reasonable sample. It is possible to determine sample size statistically, but most companies are more concerned with the cost of performing a time study. Usually, between five and fifteen cycles are timed.

Step 6. Average the observed times. The result is usually called the **cycle time** or **selected time**. This represents the average time it took the worker being observed to perform the task.

Step 7. Adjust the cycle time for the efficiency and speed of the worker who was observed. The person performing the time study must estimate, based on past experience, how fast or slow that worker performed the task in relation to an average worker. This produces a **rating factor**. A worker who performed the task 25 percent faster than average would be assigned a rating factor of 125 percent. Using this rating factor and the cycle time, a **normal time** is calculated.

$$\text{Normal time } (NT) = \text{cycle time } (CT) \times \text{rating factor}$$

Step 8. Make further adjustments. It is not reasonable to expect employees to work continuously without time for rest. Delays may also occur when the worker must wait for more material. These factors must also be entered into the calculation through an **allowance**. The standard time, which includes allowance for personal time, rest, and delays is calculated as follows.

$$\text{Standard time } (ST) = \text{Normal time } (NT) \times \text{allowance}$$

The allowance is calculated as 1.00 plus the percentage of normal time allocated for allowances.

Example

Suppose that Apple Computer Corporation wants to determine the standard time for an operation that involves soldering connections on a circuit board. They set up a time study, obtain the following information, and perform the calculations shown below.

1. Ten work cycles are timed and the information shown below obtained.

Cycle no.	1	2	3	4	5	6	7	8	9	10
Time (sec.)	9.8	10.2	9.3	9.8	10.1	10.2	9.6	9.9	9.5	10.0

By averaging these times, we obtain an average cycle time.

$$CT = 98.4/10 = 9.84 \text{ seconds per unit}$$

2. The time-study operator has determined that the worker being timed was working 10 percent faster than average, so a 110 percent rating factor is used, and normal time is calculated as

$$NT = CT \times \text{rating factor}$$
$$= 9.84 \times 1.10 = 10.82 \text{ seconds per unit}$$

3. Allowances for this job equal 20 percent of normal time. Thus, after adjusting for allowances, the standard time will be

$$ST = NT \times \text{allowance}$$
$$= 10.82 \times 1.20 = 12.98 \text{ seconds per unit}$$

This is the standard time that would be used in production planning and in employee compensation, if relevant.

Predetermined Time Standards

In analyzing any kind of manual task, it is possible to break that task into a series of movements, such as reaching, grasping, and carrying, among others. Researchers have been able to develop standard times for each of these basic movements. By breaking any task into the appropriate basic movements, it is possible to develop a standard time for the entire task by adding up the standard times for each individual movement.

This approach is especially useful in developing time standards for a new job that has not yet been implemented. Because predetermined time standards are based on thousands of observations made under controlled conditions, individual workers are not being timed, and there is less room for disagreement about the

OPERATIONS IN ACTION

Federal Express: Cutting Cycle Time to Improve Service

Federal Express has a commitment that packages for next-day delivery will reach their intended destination by 10:30 A.M. But in a place like Boston, that means up to 4,000 packages arriving from FedEx's hub in Memphis must be trucked from Boston's Logan Airport to a ground station, sorted, and loaded into delivery vans by 8:35 A.M.

In the past, meeting that schedule was difficult. However, no one was quite sure where to start in shortening the cycle time. To find out, the ground station crew performed a work study of its sorting operation, carefully keeping track of any idle time in the process.

As a result of that study, a new system was developed and implemented. Now delivery vans are on the road at least fifteen minutes earlier than before, and Federal Express's operation in Boston boasts a 99 percent service level.[2]

results. For these reasons quite a few companies use predetermined standards, although the stopwatch time study approach is still more common.

Methods-Time Measurement (MTM)

One of the best-known predetermined time systems is **methods-time measurement (MTM),** which was developed by H. B. Maynard. In this system, each movement has been determined to take a certain number of **time measurement units (TMUs).** Each TMU is equal to .00001 hour, or .036 second. For example, the standard time to reach a distance of one foot to an object in a fixed location is 9.6 TMUs—about .35 second.

Maynard Operation Sequence Technique (MOST)

A recent simplification of MTM is called **MOST®,**[3] which stands for Maynard Operation Sequence Technique. MOST is based on MTM, but is much faster and easier to use. It was found after studying extensive MTM data that nearly all operations involved the same set of basic motions performed in the same sequence. As a result, three fundamental sequence models were developed: the General Move Sequence, the Controlled Move Sequence, and the Tool Use/Equipment Use Sequence.

For example, a General Move involves moving objects manually from one location to another. The General Move Sequence consists of the following subactivities:

- A Action distance (mainly horizontal motion)
- B Body motion (mainly vertical)
- G Gain control
- P Place

Putting these subactivities in the order they are usually performed, the General Move Sequence is

A B G A B P A

Based on the distance an object must be moved, its weight, and other factors, an **index** may be assigned to each subactivity. Exhibit 9.9 shows the index values for the General Move Sequence. When an activity is studied, the index number corresponding to each subactivity is written as a subscript to that activity, as shown below.

$$A_1 \quad B_0 \quad G_1 \quad A_{16} \quad B_6 \quad P_1 \quad A_{16}$$

Each index number corresponds to ten TMUs. Thus, the time in TMUs for the above activity would be

$$(1 + 0 + 1 + 16 + 6 + 1 + 16) \times 10 = 410 \text{ TMUs}$$

Since each TMU is .0006 minute, this corresponds to a time of

$$410 \text{ TMU} \times .0006 \text{ minute/TMU} = .246 \text{ minute}$$

It should be noted that the times calculated based on the index values will be *normal* times. They must be adjusted for allowances to obtain standard times.

Exhibit 9.10 shows the MOST calculations for an electronics assembly operation. The method has also been applied to many different types of operations, including clerical jobs.

Exhibit 9.9 Index Values for MOST General Move Sequence

m▷	ABGABPA		General Move		
INDEX	A	B	G	P	INDEX
	ACTION DISTANT	BODY MOTION	GAIN CONTROL	PLACE	
0	≤ 2 IN ≤ 5 CM			HOLD TOSS	0
1	WITHIN REACH		LIGHT OBJECT LIGHT OBJECT SIMO	LAY ASIDE LOOSE FIT	1
3	1–2 STEPS	BEND AND ARISE 50% occ	NON SIMO HEAVY OR BULKY BLIND OR OBSTRUCTED DISENGAGE INTERLOCKED COLLECT	ADJUSTMENTS LIGHT PRESSURE DOUBLE	3
6	3–4 STEPS	BEND AND ARISE		CARE OR PRECISION HEAVY PRESSURE BLIND OR OBSTRUCTED INTERMEDIATE MOVES	6
10	5–7 STEPS	SIT OR STAND			10
16	8–10 STEPS	THROUGH DOOR CLIMB ON OR OFF			16

Reprinted from Kjell B. Zandin, *MOST Work Measurement Systems* (New York: Marcel Dekker, 1980), p. 19, by courtesy of Marcel Dekker, Inc.

Recently, a computerized version of MOST has begun to gain wide acceptance in industry. A dedicated minicomputer is used to store information about the work-center layout and methods to perform various jobs. This information can be easily retrieved to calculate the standard time for a given task based on the stored information and data collected from the work center. This computerized procedure greatly reduces the time required to develop a time standard.

Work Sampling

Many jobs involve activities that are not repetitive. For example, secretaries may spend part of their time typing letters, answering the telephone, or greeting visitors. Police officers also perform many different and varied activities, each of which is not done repetitively and does not always take the same amount of time. In these cases, it is not reasonable to perform the type of time study discussed previously. Instead, the job designer usually wants to develop an estimate of the percentage of each workday spent on different activities.

Work sampling is used in developing an estimate of the percentages of time a worker spends on different activities. The idea behind work sampling is to observe a worker at random times throughout the work period, recording what

Exhibit 9.10 MOST Calculations for Electronic Assembly Operation

MOST-calculation

ELECTRONIC ASSEMBLY

Code

Date 7/29/87

Sign. A.A.

Page 1/1

Activity INSTALL CONNECTOR ON PC-BOARD

Conditions EDGE CONNECTORS ONLY

No.	Method
1	POSITION EDGE CONNECTOR TO BOARD
2	ALIGN CONNECTOR TO ACCURATE LOCATION
3	PLACE SCREW TO HOLE IN CONNECTOR F2
4	MOVE WASHER TO SCREW ON BOARD F4
5	FASTEN NUT 2 SPINS USING FINGERS F2
6	FASTEN 2 SCREWS 5 SPINS USING SCREW-DRIVER
7	PLACE BOARD TO RACK

No.	Sequence Model	Fr	TMU
1	$A_1 B_0 G_1 A_1 B_0 P_6 A_0$		90
3	$A_1 B_0 G_1 A_1 B_0 P_3 A_0$	2	120
4	$A_1 B_0 G_1 A_1 B_0 P_1 A_0$	4	160
7	$A_1 B_0 G_1 A_1 B_0 P_3 A_0$		60
	A B G A B P A		
	A B G A B P A		
	A B G A B P A		
	A B G A B P A		
	A B G A B P A		
	A B G A B P A		
	A B G A B P A		
	A B G A B P A		
	A B G A B P A		
	A B G A B P A		
	A B G A B P A		
	A B G A B P A		
	A B G A B P A		
	A B G A B P A		
2	$A_0 B_0 G_0 M_3 X_0 I_{16} A_0$		190
	A B G M X I A		
	A B G M X I A		
	A B G M X I A		
	A B G M X I A		
	A B G M X I A		
	A B G M X I A		
	A B G M X I A		
5	$A_1 B_0 G_1 A_1 B_0 P_1 F_3 A_0 B_0 P_0 A_0$	2	140
6	$A_1 B_0 G_1 A_1 B_0 P (3 A_1, F_{10}) A_1 B_0 P_1 A_0$	(2)	330
	A B G A B P A B P A		
	A B G A B P A B P A		
	A B G A B P A B P A		
	A B G A B P A B P A		
	A B G A B P A B P A		
	A B G A B P A B P A		
	A B G A B P A B P A		
	A B G A B P A B P A		
	A B G A B P A B P A		
	A B G A B P A B P A		
	A B G A B P A B P A		
	A B G A B P A B P A		

TIME = .65 minutes (min.) 1090

the worker is doing each time. For example, a work sampling study of a secretarial job would involve the random selection of times when the secretary will be observed. At each observation, a record is kept of what the secretary was doing at that particular moment in time. Over a long enough period of time, a profile of activities performed and their relative frequency can be developed. That profile might look like this:

Activity	Percentage of Time Observed
Typing	50%
Answering telephone	20
Greeting visitors	15
Stocking supplies	5
Taking dictation	5
Personal time	3
Idle	2

While work sampling's primary advantage is in studying nonrepetitive activities, it can also be used to develop time standards for repetitive, cyclical jobs. However, in such cases, several hundred observations are often required to achieve acceptable accuracy. Also, it is not possible to develop the detailed elemental information through work sampling that is available from a stopwatch time study.

LEARNING CURVES

As we have discussed, time standards can be an extremely useful management tool. However, there are situations in which time standards have little meaning because task times are changing. This occurs most often when a new product or new technology is introduced. At first, employees may be unfamiliar with their tasks, parts may not fit together properly, or other problems may arise. Gradually, many of these problems are sorted out, and workers become able to perform their tasks in less time. As time goes by, better methods will be developed so that task times can be reduced even further. The end result is that the time it takes to make each unit of the product will decrease as the cumulative number of units produced increases, as shown in Exhibit 9.11.

The curve shown in Exhibit 9.11 is called a **learning curve** and indicates how the time required per unit of product decreases as the cumulative number of units produced increases. This curve is based on the formula

$$Y_n = Y_1 n^b$$

where

Y_n = the time it will take to produce the nth unit

Y_1 = the time it took to produce the first unit

n = number of units

r = learning factor

$$b = \frac{\log r}{\log 2}$$

Exhibit 9.11 75 Percent Learning Curve

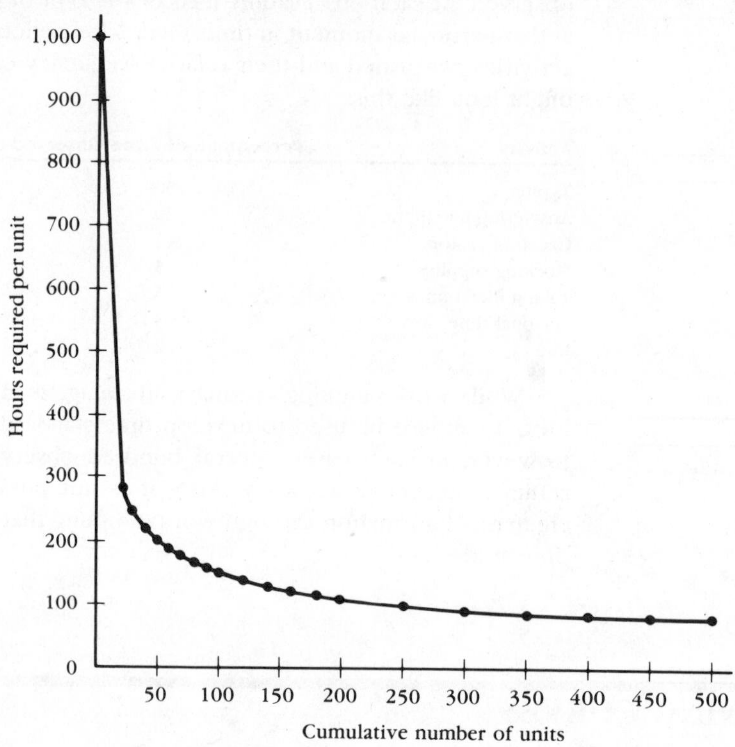

Although this formula may look formidable, what it actually indicates is that the time per unit will decrease by a constant factor every time the cumulative number of units produced doubles. The **learning factor** indicates the relation between these two times.

Example

A learning factor of .8, which is usually referred to as an 80 percent learning curve, would mean that the time it takes to produce the second unit is only 80 percent of the time it took to produce the first unit. Then the time it takes to produce the fourth unit will be 80 percent of the time it took to produce the second, and so on. For a job that required ten hours to produce the first unit, the time for each successive unit with an 80 percent learning curve would be

Unit Number (n)	Time per Unit (Hours)
1	10
2	.8(10) = 8
4	.8(8) = 6.4
8	.8(6.4) = 5.12
16	.8(5.12) = 4.096

Unfortunately, the approach used above to determine the time per unit when the cumulative number of units doubles cannot be used to determine how long it should take to produce the third unit, the fifth unit, and so on. In those situations, we must resort to the learning-curve formula.

Example

An aircraft company is producing a new commercial jet. Based on past experience, the learning factor is .7, and it is expected that the first unit will require 1,000 hours to produce. How long should the fifth unit take?

$$b = \frac{\log .7}{\log 2}$$

$$= \frac{-.1549}{.3010}$$

$$= -.5146$$

$$Y_n = Y_1 n^b$$

$$= 1{,}000(5)^{-.5146}$$

$$= 436.8 \text{ hours}$$

Thus, the fifth unit should take 436.8 hours to produce.

These calculations can become rather tedious if they must be performed a large number of times. Fortunately, tables exist that eliminate the need for the detailed calculation shown above. Such a table is shown in Exhibit 9.12.

Using a Learning-Curve Chart

Referring to Exhibit 9.12, you can see that the time shown across the first row, corresponding to unit number 1, is 1.000 for all learning factors. Now looking down the Unit Time column for an 80% learning curve, you can see the unit time for unit number 2 will be .800 and the unit time for unit number 4 will be .640. Thus, the numbers given all show the time required to produce each unit as a *proportion* of the time it took for the first unit. If the first unit required ten hours and a learning factor of .8 is in effect, the time required for unit number 5 will be

$$.596 \times 10 \text{ hours} = 5.96 \text{ hours}$$

The column labeled Total Time indicates the cumulative time it will take to produce the corresponding unit number *and all preceding units*. Thus, the total time to produce the first through fifth units with an 80 percent learning curve and ten hours required for the first unit will be:

$$3.738 \times 10 \text{ hours} = 37.38 \text{ hours}$$

Exhibit 9.12 Learning-Curve Chart

	75% ($b = -.415$)		80% ($b = -.322$)		85% ($b = -.234$)		90% ($b = -.152$)	
Unit No.	Unit Time	Total Time	Unit Time	Total Time	Unit Time	Total Time	Unit Time	Total Time
1	1.000	1.000	1.000	1.000	1.000	1.000	1.000	1.000
2	.750	1.750	.800	1.800	.850	1.850	.900	1.900
3	.634	2.384	.702	2.502	.773	2.623	.846	2.746
4	.562	2.946	.640	3.142	.723	3.345	.810	3.556
5	.513	3.459	.596	3.738	.686	4.031	.783	4.339
6	.475	3.934	.562	4.229	.657	4.688	.762	5.101
7	.446	4.380	.534	4.834	.634	5.322	.744	5.845
8	.422	4.802	.512	5.346	.614	5.936	.729	6.574
9	.402	5.204	.493	5.839	.597	6.533	.716	7.290
10	.385	5.589	.477	6.315	.583	7.116	.705	7.994
11	.370	5.958	.462	6.777	.570	7.686	.695	8.689
12	.357	6.315	.449	7.227	.558	8.244	.685	9.374
13	.345	6.660	.438	7.665	.548	8.792	.677	10.05
14	.334	6.994	.428	8.092	.539	9.331	.670	10.72
15	.325	7.319	.418	8.511	.530	9.861	.663	11.38
16	.316	7.635	.410	8.920	.522	10.38	.656	12.04
17	.309	7.944	.402	9.322	.515	10.90	.650	12.69
18	.301	8.245	.394	9.716	.508	11.41	.644	13.33
19	.295	8.540	.387	10.10	.501	11.91	.639	13.97
20	.288	8.828	.381	10.49	.495	12.40	.634	14.61
21	.283	9.111	.375	10.86	.490	12.89	.630	15.24
22	.277	9.388	.370	11.23	.484	13.38	.625	15.86
23	.272	9.660	.364	11.59	.479	13.86	.621	16.48
24	.267	9.928	.359	11.95	.475	14.33	.617	17.10
25	.263	10.19	.355	12.31	.470	14.80	.613	17.71
30	.244	11.45	.335	14.02	.450	17.09	.596	20.73
35	.229	12.62	.318	15.64	.434	19.29	.583	23.67
40	.216	13.72	.305	17.19	.421	21.43	.571	26.54
45	.206	14.77	.294	18.68	.410	23.50	.561	29.37

Exhibit 9.12 can be used to calculate the time required to produce each unit, up to unit number 3,000 for common learning factors. Further, the table will tell you the *total* time required to produce that number of units.

Estimating the Learning Factor

One problem faced in using the learning-curve chart is determining which learning curve rate to use. In many organizations, industrial engineers are trained to select learning factors based on those commonly used in a particular industry or for certain operations. For example, aircraft assembly operations have been found to follow an 80 percent learning curve.

If historical data are available, they can also be used to estimate the learning factor by rearranging the learning curve formula to

$$n^b = \frac{Y_n}{Y_1}$$

Exhibit 9.12 *continuing*

	75% ($b = -.415$)		80% ($b = -.322$)		85% ($b = -.234$)		90% ($b = -.152$)	
Unit No.	**Unit Time**	**Total Time**	**Unit Time**	**Total Time**	**Unit Time**	**Total Time**	**Unit Time**	**Total Time**
50	.197	15.78	.284	20.12	.400	25.51	.552	32.14
60	.183	17.67	.268	22.89	.383	29.41	.537	37.57
70	.172	19.43	.255	25.47	.369	33.17	.524	42.87
80	.162	21.09	.244	27.96	.358	36.80	.514	48.05
90	.155	22.67	.235	30.35	.348	40.32	.505	53.14
100	.148	24.18	.227	32.65	.340	43.75	.497	58.14
120	.137	27.02	.214	37.05	.326	50.39	.483	67.93
140	.129	29.67	.204	41.22	.314	56.78	.472	77.46
160	.122	32.17	.195	45.20	.304	62.95	.462	86.80
180	.116	34.54	.188	49.03	.296	68.95	.454	95.96
200	.111	36.80	.182	52.72	.289	74.79	.447	105.0
250	.101	42.08	.169	61.47	.274	88.83	.432	126.9
300	.094	46.94	.159	69.66	.263	102.2	.420	148.2
350	.088	51.48	.152	77.43	.253	115.1	.411	169.0
400	.083	55.75	.145	84.85	.245	127.6	.402	189.3
450	.079	59.80	.140	91.97	.239	139.7	.395	209.2
500	.076	63.68	.135	98.85	.233	151.5	.389	228.8
600	.070	70.97	.128	112.0	.223	174.2	.378	267.1
700	.066	77.77	.121	124.4	.215	196.1	.369	304.5
800	.062	84.18	.116	136.3	.209	217.3	.362	341.0
900	.059	90.26	.112	147.7	.203	237.9	.356	376.9
1,000	.057	96.07	.108	158.7	.198	257.9	.350	412.2
1,200	.053	107.0	.102	179.7	.190	296.6	.340	481.2
1,400	.050	117.2	.097	199.6	.183	333.9	.333	548.4
1,600	.047	126.8	.093	218.6	.177	369.9	.326	614.2
1,800	.045	135.9	.090	236.8	.173	404.9	.320	678.8
2,000	.043	144.7	.087	254.4	.168	438.9	.315	742.3
2,500	.039	165.0	.081	296.1	.160	520.8	.304	897.0
3,000	.036	183.7	.076	335.2	.153	598.9	.296	1,047

Taking logs of both sides, we obtain

$$b \log n = \log\left[\frac{Y_n}{Y_1}\right]$$

and can then solve for b as follows:

$$b = \frac{\log(Y_n/Y_1)}{\log n}$$

The definition of b can then be used to determine its value.

$$b = \frac{\log r}{\log 2}$$

$$\log r = b \log 2$$

$$r = 10^{(b \log 2)}$$

Example

An electronics manufacturer has found that the time needed to produce a certain circuit board has been decreasing. While it took 4.8 hours to produce the first board, the 125th one required only .95 hour. What learning factor is in effect?

$$b = \frac{\log(Y_n/Y_1)}{\log n}$$

$$= \frac{\log(.95/4.8)}{\log(125)}$$

$$= \frac{-.703518}{2.09691}$$

$$= -.3355$$

$$r = 10^{(b \log 2)}$$

$$= 10^{(-.3355 \log 2)}$$

$$= 10^{(-.101)}$$

$$= .79$$

Thus, a learning curve rate of 79 percent is in effect.

Pricing Under the Learning-Curve Effect

When the learning curve is in effect, a company can find it difficult to determine its labor costs because the labor time required per unit will be decreasing. However, the values for total time in the learning-curve chart can be used to determine *average* labor time per unit.

Example

The company of Forges et Ateliers is a French metalworking shop located in the city of Clermont-Ferrand. It recently received an order to produce 100 units of a new type of forging. Based on past experience, the company expects an 85 percent learning curve to be in effect. If the first unit required 2.4 direct labor hours and employees are paid at the rate of FF (French francs) 70 per hour, what will be the average direct labor cost on the entire order?

Using the learning-curve chart, the total time for 100 units will be

$$2.4(43.75) = 105 \text{ hours}$$

The total cost for this number of hours will be

$$\text{FF } 70(105) = \text{FF } 7{,}350$$

The average direct labor cost per unit will be total cost divided by number of units, or

$$\frac{\text{FF } 7{,}350}{100} = \text{FF } 73.5 \text{ per unit}$$

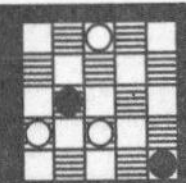

GAINING STRATEGIC ADVANTAGE AT TEXAS INSTRUMENTS

Using Preemptive Pricing to Increase Market Share

Exhibit 9.13 Preemptive Pricing Strategy on a Learning Curve

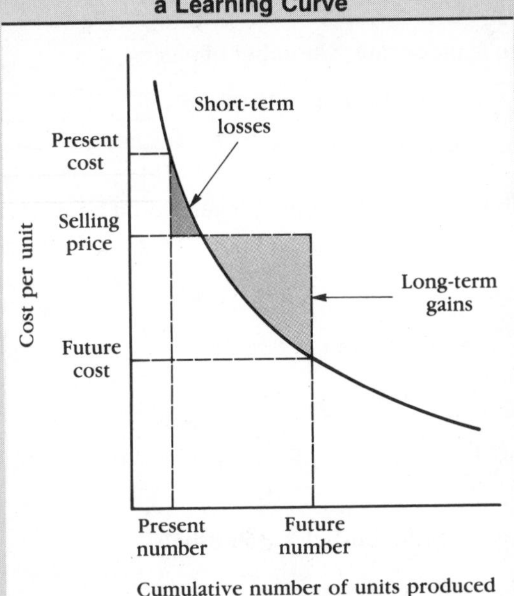

Learning curves are a useful management tool that can be used to estimate costs based on the time required to produce each unit. The aircraft industry has found them especially useful when calculating the costs of producing a new type of airplane. Learning curves have also been used extensively by Texas Instruments Company as part of its **preemptive pricing** strategy for calculators. TI determines its location on the curve and then sets a market price that provides only a slim profit margin, if any. This lower price helps to increase TI's market share. Such preemptive pricing can even be used to set a market price that is below the cost of production. Even though the company loses money in the short run, as it moves down the experience curve and increases its market share, these short-term losses will be more than offset by long-term gains, as shown in Exhibit 9.13.

PIECE-RATE AND BONUS PLANS

Another common use for standard times is in determining wage rates. The philosophy in this case is to tie an employee's earnings to his or her output. To do this, a standard against which to measure performance is needed, and that standard is usually the standard time for performing an activity or job.

This approach is usually called a **wage incentive plan**. There are many different types of wage incentive plans in use today. In this section, we will try to describe some of the more common ones.

Piece-Rate Plans

Employees working under **piece-rate plans** are paid a certain amount per unit of production. For instance, a farmhand might be paid a set amount per bushel of produce picked. The advantage of this system is its simplicity. The employee can easily calculate how much he or she has earned at any given point in time, and to a large extent, the employee has control over his or her own earnings.

The piece-rate system was much more popular before minimum-wage laws went into effect. Today, either the piece rate must be set so that it enables employees to earn at least the minimum wage, or there must be a base pay rate that is earned if the piece rate would place the employee below minimum wage.

Example

The minimum wage rate is $4.25 in 1991, which is also the base rate for apple picking at the Lipe Orchards. The piece rate is $1.00 per bushel. The first day on the job, a new apple picker picks only twenty bushels in an eight-hour day. The piece-rate wage would be

$$\begin{aligned} \text{Piece-rate wage} &= \text{piece rate} \times \text{number of pieces} \\ &= \$1.00/\text{bushel} \times 20 \text{ bushels} \\ &= \$20.00 \end{aligned}$$

Because this is below the minimum wage, the apple picker would be paid at the base rate

$$\begin{aligned} \text{Base-rate wage} &= \text{base rate} \times \text{hours worked} \\ &= \$4.25/\text{hour} \times 8 \text{ hours} \\ &= \$34.00 \end{aligned}$$

Suppose that the second day this same apple picker picks thirty-five bushels. The piece-rate wage would be

$$\begin{aligned} \text{Piece-rate wage} &= \$1.00/\text{bushel} \times 35 \text{ bushels} \\ &= \$35.00 \end{aligned}$$

Because this exceeds the base rate, the apple picker would be paid on a piece-rate basis for the second day's work.

Standard-Hour Plans

The **standard-hour system** is another incentive plan that is used much more frequently today than the piece-rate system. Under the standard-hour system, each job has a standard time assigned to it. An employee performing that job is paid based on the standard time—regardless of how long it actually took to do the job. For instance, a plumber might be paid on the basis of one standard hour to fix a leaky faucet. Even if it actually takes only thirty minutes to complete the job, the plumber is still paid for one hour's work. As with the piece-rate system, a base determines the minimum pay a person will receive, usually based on the hours actually worked.

Example

Steve Chervany just began work as a machinist for the Essex Tool and Die Company. Steve's pay rate is $12 per hour. During his first day, Steve worked on a job with a standard time of .12 hours per unit and produced fifty units during the eight-hour day. Steve's earnings under the standard hour system would be

$$\text{Standard-hour wage} = \text{standard time} \times \text{wage rate} \times \text{units produced}$$
$$= .12 \text{ hrs./unit} \times \$12\text{/hr.} \times 50 \text{ units}$$
$$= \$72$$

Because this standard-hour wage is less than Steve would have received based simply on hours worked, Steve would be paid his base wage instead.

$$\text{Base wage} = \text{hours worked} \times \text{wage rate}$$
$$= 8 \text{ hrs.} \times \$12\text{/hr.}$$
$$= \$96$$

During his second day on the job, Steve produces forty units of a part that has a standard time of .25 hours per unit. His earnings using the standard-hour system would be

$$\text{Standard-hour wage} = .25 \text{ hrs./unit} \times \$12\text{/hr.} \times 40 \text{ units}$$
$$= \$120$$

Since this exceeds the base wage, Steve's pay for his second day on the job would be based on the standard-hour rate.

An example of a standard-hour system with which you may be familiar is the flat-rate system used by auto mechanics. Under this system, any repair job is given a standard time. Usually the customer is charged, and the employee paid, based on that standard time regardless of how long the job actually took.

Group Incentive Systems

The incentive systems described thus far have been aimed at rewarding individuals for individual effort. But in most work situations, an individual's performance is often influenced by a group. For example, one worker on an assembly line cannot speed up without speeding up all workers on the line. For this reason, group incentive plans have often been very successful.

One of the best-known group incentive plans is the **Scanlon plan**. Named after Joseph Scanlon, a union president at the Lapointe Machine Tool Company, the Scanlon plan is an example of what can be accomplished when union, labor, and management all work together toward a common goal.

The Scanlon plan attempts to forge labor and management into a team whose objective is to increase productivity. Production committees review suggested methods to improve operations. If a particular suggestion does not involve another department and requires no capital expenditure, then the committee can approve implementation. For suggestions that cannot be approved by a production committee, a screening committee of company employees and top management makes the implementation decision.

OPERATIONS IN ACTION

Lincoln Electric: An Incentive System Raises Productivity—for Fifty-Six Years!

Lincoln Electric has had an incentive system in effect since 1934. The results of that system are astounding, as workers' bonuses average 97.6 percent of regular earnings. The company has also benefited by operating for fifty-six years without a losing quarter and has not had to lay off employees for forty-two years. This is because Lincoln Electric's employees are about three times more productive than employees in comparable industries are. Lincoln, which is the world's largest manufacturer of welding equipment, has been able to capture over 40 percent of the U.S. market. Turnover, except for retirements, is nonexistent, and the company's market share is holding steady.

The 3,000 factory employees at Lincoln are paid on a piece-rate basis for each acceptable unit produced. Further, a bonus is awarded each year. That bonus is based on supervisors' twice-yearly evaluations of an employee's dependability, ideas and cooperation, quality, and output. Bonuses usually equal annual wages.

According to one survey, 87 percent of the companies studied have some form of incentive program. Among them are Alcoa, Caterpillar, Deere, DuPont, Ford, General Motors, and many others. Based on the success of Lincoln's program, many others are showing an increased interest.[4]

Under a Scanlon plan, employees are rewarded for their cost-reduction efforts. Any reduction in the labor cost per unit of output is reflected in an employee bonus, which is based on a ratio of total labor costs to the value of output. This ratio must be renegotiated from time to time due to changes in other costs, such as materials and overhead.

Example

The public accounting firm of Hardwick and Mitchell pays bonuses to its tax accountants based on a Scanlon plan, using total value of billings as a measure of output. For the base period, total labor costs were $120,000 on billings of $240,000. Thus, the profit-sharing ratio is

$$\begin{aligned}\text{Profit-sharing ratio} &= \text{base period labor costs/value of output}\\ &= \$120{,}000/\$240{,}000\\ &= .50\end{aligned}$$

In a recent year, labor costs were $150,000 for billings of $320,000. Using the profit-sharing ratio, the allowed payroll would be

$$\begin{aligned}\text{Allowed payroll} &= \text{profit-sharing ratio} \times \text{value of output}\\ &= .50 \times \$320{,}000\\ &= \$160{,}000\end{aligned}$$

Since actual labor costs were below the allowed payroll, the difference is distributed as a bonus.

$$\begin{aligned}\text{Bonus} &= \text{allowed payroll} - \text{labor costs}\\ &= \$160{,}000 - \$150{,}000\\ &= \$10{,}000\end{aligned}$$

International Aspects of Employee Compensation

Many companies in the United States use piece-rate and bonus plans to reward individual employees for high productivity. However, the culture in other countries often is more oriented toward groups, downplaying the importance of an individual. For example, in Japan, the norm is that a group is always more important than an individual.

Because of this sort of cultural difference, employee compensation in countries such as Japan often focuses on group performance, rather than on individual performance. Thus, group compensation plans such as the Scanlon plan may be more appropriate.

A further difference may relate to nonwage forms of compensation. While many companies in the United States provide health insurance and retirement plans for their employees, companies in Japan often provide housing, food, recreation, and even a company hospital. For example, Toyota City is a company town for Toyota employees. Within this town, Toyota provides inexpensive housing, a high school, and a hospital for its employees and even makes low-cost loans to employees so they can purchase houses through the company's Toyota Home subsidiary.

SUMMARY

- Job design encompasses the areas of tasks and responsibilities, methods, physical environment, and social and psychological environment.
- In job specialization, employees are given a narrow set of tasks to perform; in job rotation, they are regularly moved from one narrowly defined job to another. With job enlargement, the number of tasks is increased, while job enrichment gives employees more responsibility for planning and decision making.
- A flow process chart can be used to analyze either the motions of a worker or the flow of materials and is used to improve a process.
- The left-hand/right-hand chart is used for a more detailed analysis of the activities of a worker. The objective is to find ways to use both hands to the fullest extent possible.
- An operator-machine chart is used to record the interactions between workers and equipment. This type of chart can be helpful in reducing the idle time of workers and machines.
- In work place layout, we are concerned with minimizing travel distance, reducing fatigue, and making equipment and facilities easy for workers to use.
- Job design must be concerned with work methods and design of the working environment that stress the safety and health of employees.

- Time standards are used for production planning and scheduling, facility layout, and cost estimation, as well as for determining employee compensation.
- The result of a stopwatch time study will be a cycle time. This must be adjusted by a rating factor to achieve normal time. The normal time is then adjusted for allowances to obtain a standard time for the activity.
- It is also possible to calculate standard times from predetermined time standards. This requires breaking a task into small units, such as reach, grasp, or carry. Two of the most common predetermined time standard methods are MTM and MOST.
- Work sampling uses random observations to estimate the percentages of time spent on various activities.
- According to the learning-curve formula, the time required to produce one unit of a product decreases by a constant percentage each time the cumulative number of units produced is doubled.
- By rearranging the learning-curve formula, historical data can be used to estimate the learning factor.
- Piece-rate and bonus plans compare actual production to a standard and reward employees for performance above that standard.
- Outside the United States, there may be increased emphasis on group performance, so that group compensation may be most appropriate. Foreign companies may even provide recreational facilities or housing for their employees.

CAREER PROFILE

Thomas E. Freedman
Plant Manager
Frito-Lay, Inc.

Education and Experience

Tom Freedman studied industrial engineering and operations research at Cornell University under an Air Force ROTC scholarship. Before spending a short time in the Air Force Reserves, Freedman completed his studies in the University of Pittsburgh MBA program, majoring in operations management.

Freedman began work after graduation as a team manager, a first-line supervisory position, for Procter and Gamble. In that position, he was responsible for sixteen technicians and four converting lines that produced over 1.5 million Pampers diapers each *day*. He then went on to become a departmental industrial engineer and moved his department from a $600,000 loss to a $200,000 profit during just one year. After that, he became operating department manager, responsible for five managers, eighty technicians, and a $40 million annual budget. Freedman's last position with Procter and Gamble was as a cost reduction/systems manager, a role in which he developed projects that resulted in annual savings to the company of over $2 million.

Freedman moved to Frito-Lay as a senior industrial engineer and started six productivity improvement programs, one of which was a methods improvement program that produced annual savings in excess of $32 million. He was then promoted to programs manager and, two years later, to group manager, Operations Field Support. In that position, he was in charge of nine industrial engineers and two specialists developing projects and processes that facilitate productivity improvement programs within the Frito-Lay manufacturing organization.

Current Duties and Responsibilities

From his job as group manager for Frito-Lay, Freedman was promoted to production manager and then operations manager of the company's plant in Killingly, Connecticut. That plant is one of the largest snack-food plants in the world.

In his current role, Freedman is in charge of the Frito-Lay plant in Wooster, Ohio. That plant is responsible for over $80 million in sales each year. Although it was a very traditional plant when he became its manager, Freedman has worked to change the relationships between workers and management. Much of that change involves increased technical training of employees and a shift to employee involvement through bottom-up management.

SOLVED PROBLEMS

1. A time study of an airline reservations clerk determined that the cycle time was 1.35 minutes, with a performance rating of 105 percent. The allowance factor is 20 percent of normal time. Determine the standard time for this task.

Solution

a. $NT = CT \times \text{rating factor}$
$= 1.35 \text{ minutes} \times 1.05$
$= 1.42 \text{ minutes}$

b. $ST = NT \times \text{allowance}$
$= 1.42 \text{ minutes} \times 1.20$
$= 1.70 \text{ minutes}$

2. A company has estimated that a learning curve of 80 percent applies to its operations. The first unit required four hours. Using the learning-curve formula, determine how long the second and third units will take to produce. Using the learning-curve chart in Exhibit 9.12, determine how long it will take to produce the first 100 units.

Solution

a. The second unit should take only 80 percent as long to make as the first unit if an 80 percent learning factor is in effect.

$$\text{Time for second unit} = .80 \times \text{time for first unit}$$
$$= .80 \times 4 \text{ hours}$$
$$= 3.20 \text{ hours}$$

b. Time for the third unit will be calculated using the formula

$$Y_n = Y_1 n^b$$

$$b = \frac{\log r}{\log 2} = \frac{\log .8}{\log 2}$$

$$= \frac{-.0969}{.3010}$$

$$= -.3219$$

$$Y_n = Y_1 n^b$$

$$= 4(3)^{-.3219}$$

$$= 2.81 \text{ hours}$$

c. In Exhibit 9.12, we go to the 80 percent column and follow down Total Time to the row for unit number 100. The value there is 32.65. This is then multiplied by the time it took for the first unit.

$$32.65 \times 4 \text{ hours} = 130.6 \text{ hours to make the first 100 units}$$

3. An engineering consulting firm has begun using a new computer graphics program to design bridge trusses. The company has noticed a learning curve in effect, as its first truss required ten hours to design, but the twenty-eighth one took only six hours.
   a. What learning factor is in effect?
   b. Determine the *average* time per unit for the first fifty bridge trusses designed, based on the learning-curve rate.

Solution

a.

$$Y_1 = 10, Y_n = 6, n = 28$$

$$b = \frac{\log(Y_n/Y_1)}{\log n}$$

$$= \frac{\log(6/10)}{\log 28}$$

$$= \frac{-.22185}{1.447158}$$

$$= -.1533$$

$$r = 10^{(b \log 2)}$$

$$= 10^{(-.1533 \log 2)}$$

$$= 10^{(-.046)}$$

$$= .90$$

b. Based on a learning-curve rate of 90 percent, the learning-curve chart indicates that the total time for the first fifty units will be

$$10(32.14) = 321.4 \text{ hours}$$

The *average* time per unit will be

$$\frac{321.4 \text{ hours}}{50 \text{ units}} = 6.428 \text{ hours}$$

QUESTIONS

1. Examine Exhibit 9.3 and indicate some ways you would change the process to make it more efficient. Think not only about the worker's activities, but also about equipment that could reduce the time for this job.

2. Differentiate between job design and work measurement. How are they related?

3. What is ergonomics, and how does it relate to job design?

4. Describe some situations in which poor design of the physical environment leads to low productivity, worker dissatisfaction, or other undesirable outcomes.

5. Differentiate among a job, a task, and an element.

6. Describe the purpose of a flow process chart and how it is used to improve efficiency.

7. Exhibit 9.7 shows an operator-machine chart for an operator who sets up and runs two machines. Suggest ways that the operation could be improved to reduce idle time.

8. What is the philosophy behind using a left-hand/right-hand chart?

9. What are the differences among ergonomics, work physiology, and human engineering?

10. In other courses, you have probably studied Maslow's Hierarchy or other sociopsychological models. Use those, or your own ideas, to explain why workers are usually happier working in teams than working individually.

11. What are the advantages of using a U-shaped layout?

12. Differentiate among job specialization, job enlargement, and job enrichment.

13. Why does breaking a task into individual movements often lead to improvements in efficiency?

14. What are the disadvantages of using work sampling to develop time standards for standard, repetitive operations?

15. Define the following terms:
   a. Cycle time
   b. Normal time
   c. Standard time
   d. Allowances

16. Why are time standards important in managing operations?

17. Why would preemptive pricing be advantageous for established companies in an industry, but not for new companies in that same industry?

18. Explain how work sampling differs from time study. In what type of situation is each most appropriate?

19. What are the advantages and disadvantages of methods such as MOST and MTM?

20. List the steps you would follow in setting a time standard for data entry clerks in an insurance company.

21. Select a country other than the United States, and explain whether its employees are rewarded on the basis of individual or group output and whether nonwage compensation is used.

PROBLEMS

1. Make a flow process chart for your school's course registration system based on the student's viewpoint.
   a. Identify ways the system could be changed to reduce the time you spend waiting in line and walking from one location to another.
   b. Suppose the school wants to minimize idle time for its registration employees, but is not concerned about waiting or traveling time for students. How would you change the system?

2. Select some activity you perform with your hands, such as eating or washing your car, and draw a left-hand/right-hand chart for the activity.

3. Suppose you are editor of the monthly newsletter for a student organization. It is your job to assemble the three pages of this newsletter, put on a cover page, staple those pages together, fold the newsletter in half and staple the halves together, and then attach an address label and a stamp.
   a. Develop a left-hand/right-hand chart showing how you might perform this activity.
   b. Suppose you must have 100 newsletters ready to mail by tomorrow morning and must also study for a test. How might you alter the process to maximize your efficiency?

4. In a stopwatch time study, it is found that the cycle time for a certain task is 4.30 minutes. The rating factor is evaluated as 90 percent, and allowances are equal to 10 percent of normal time. Determine the standard time.

5. A job has been studied and found to have the following times for each cycle:

Cycle	1	2	3	4	5	6
Time (mins.)	4.71	4.54	4.89	4.76	4.83	4.61

The time-study operator estimates that the rating factor is 95 percent. Allowances for this job account for 15 percent of normal time. Determine the standard time.

6. Operators in the check-processing department of a large bank must manually enter the amount of each check. Based on time studies, the standard time is .03 minute per check. During a typical eight-hour day, operators experience thirty minutes of unavoidable delays and require twenty minutes for personal time. Each operator is allowed three fifteen-minute coffee breaks per day.

a. How many checks would be processed per day by an operator working at 90 percent of standard?

b. How many checks would be processed per day by an operator working at 110 percent of standard?

7. A certain task has been broken into elements and each element timed. The performance rating for each element is shown below, and the allowance factor is 20 percent for this job. Combine these element times to calculate a standard time for the entire task.

		Observation				
Element	**Rating**	**1**	**2**	**3**	**4**	**5**
Obtain part	95%	.25	.32	.28	.26	.32
Position	110%	.45	.48	.42	.48	.43
Drill	90%	.73	.82	.86	.72	.76
Remove part	105%	.12	.10	.15	.13	.14

8. A certain task involves walking six steps, bending down to pick up a lightweight piece of metal, returning six steps, and carefully inserting the piece of metal into a holding fixture. Use the General Move Sequence of MOST to determine the normal time for this task in minutes.

9. A certain operation requires the operator to grasp a part that is within reach, disengage the part from a holding fixture, move the part to a subassembly that is also within reach, and then carefully insert the part into that subassembly. Allowances for this task are 15 percent of normal time. Determine the standard time, using the MOST General Move Sequence.

10. The business college dean at a large state university complains that she spends too much time dealing with student complaints. Over a one-week period, the dean is observed at random times, and the following data recorded:

Day	**Times Observed**	**Times Handling Student Complaints**
Monday	14	6
Tuesday	12	7
Wednesday	18	7
Thursday	15	6
Friday	14	9

a. What work measurement method is this?

b. Based on this limited sample, what percentage of the dean's time is spent handling student complaints?

c. Suggest ways to reduce the time the dean spends on student complaints.

11. A company has determined from past experience that its learning-curve percentage is 85 percent. If it takes 1,000 hours to produce the first unit, how long should the second, fourth, and eighth units each take?

12. The Nicholas Tool Company has just introduced a new line of CNC lathes. Based on past experience, the company expects a 90 percent learning curve to apply to the manufacturing time for these lathes. The first unit required 400 hours to produce. Nicholas estimates that each hour of production time costs an average of $30. Based on this, how long will it take to produce the company's first three units, and what will be the total production cost of these machines?

13. The Qewb Brothers provide tax assistance services. Each year they hire a new group of employees and train them in preparing tax returns. Based on past experience, the time it takes one of these employees to prepare a standard tax return follows a 75 percent learning curve. However, Herbie Qewb, one of the brothers, has designed a new training program to lower this to 70 percent. If the first tax return takes an average of two hours to prepare and these employees are paid $10 per hour, what would be the cost savings per employee on the first four returns if the new training program is adopted?

14. Arlene Crouch has become interested in building radio-controlled (R/C) airplanes. Her first plane took 100 hours to build. However, Arlene became more proficient and found that her tenth plane required only 53.85 hours. What is Arlene's learning factor for building R/C airplanes?

15. Steve Tasks has just started up a new computer company that manufactures the "LaST" computer. Steve found the first "LaST" computer assembled in his new plant required thirty-eight direct labor hours to produce. Based on past experience, Steve expects an 80 percent learning curve to apply. If direct labor costs $12 per hour, what will be the average cost of direct labor on Steve's first fifty "LaST" computers?

16. The Computer Company, a computer sales and service operation, has just contracted with a regional insurance company to install a local area network (LAN) involving ten computers in the insurance company's headquarters office. Part of the network installation involves installing a network board and software in each of the ten computers. Employees of the Computer Company have no previous experience with this particular installation. It is estimated that the first unit will require thirty minutes of installation time.

- **a.** Draw graphs of the installation time required for each of the ten computers, using 75 percent and 85 percent learning curves.
- **b.** Determine the total cumulative installation time for each learning-curve rate.

17. Memory Associates has just developed a new supercomputer. However, the supercomputer business has become extremely competitive, and Memory Associates wants to introduce its new product at a price that will undercut the competition. The first unit produced required $1 million for materials and 200,000 hours of direct labor at $15 per hour. If Memory Associates prices its new supercomputer at $2 million per unit, how many units must be produced and sold before the selling price will cover the direct labor and material costs if an 80 percent learning curve is in effect?

18. Nadrina Spencer has just started a new job assembling electrical circuit boards. She is paid on a piece-rate basis of $.50 per board and has a base wage rate of $5.00 per hour. During her first two eight-hour days on the job, Nadrina assembles 75 boards and 100 boards, respectively. Calculate Nadrina's pay each day.

19. John Whitehead works for a company that makes men's shirts. The pay rate is based on a standard-hour system that uses .05 hour as the standard time to cut out the pieces of a shirt. John's base pay rate is $5.75 per hour. Yesterday, John cut out 200 shirts in eight hours, but today he cut out only 150 in the same time. Calculate John's pay for both days.

20. The Herkimer Oscilloscope Company uses a Scanlon plan. During the base period, the company's total labor costs were $4.3 million on sales of $50 million. During this past year, the company reduced its labor costs to $4.0 million on sales of $55 million. What would be the employee bonus for this past year?

MINI-CASES

Elco Industries

Elco Industries manufactures soundproofing material for use in automobiles. This material, which usually is not seen by the average car owner, goes under the carpet, inside the doors, or even inside the wheel wells to insulate passengers from engine and road noises. Elco's customers are the Big Three auto makers—Chrysler, Ford, and General Motors.

Elco's employees have traditionally been paid on a straight wage basis—so much salary per hour. Therefore, there had never been any interest in the past in developing time standards. Recently, however, the companies Elco supplies have been demanding delivery of orders within a specified narrow time range. This has caused problems for Elco in that orders are often not ready by the required shipping date. The result has been extensive use of expediting and air freight, or even air-charter shipments to get orders to the customers on time.

Elco has been considering the implementation of time standards in order to help it plan operations better and meet its customers' delivery schedules. However, the union representing Elco's employees, the UAW, has not been receptive to this idea. The union sees it as a way to push employees for more output or even as an excuse to eliminate some jobs.

1. Describe how time standards could be used to help Elco deal with its on-time delivery problems.

2. How would you deal with union concerns that time studies will lead to higher output demands being placed on the workers?

3. Could time standards actually benefit the employees?

4. What other benefits could such time studies have for both the company and the employees?

5. How would you proceed in performing the time studies that would be needed to set standards?

Nerco Machining Co.

The Nerco Machining Company is a job shop operation that does custom machining work. Recently, the company has developed a contract for specialty machining work with a new customer. It is anticipated that if Nerco's work is satisfactory to this new customer, a long-term relationship will be developed. Such a relationship would be very beneficial to Nerco, probably resulting in at least a million dollars worth of work each year.

This contract calls for some machining of a special molybdenum alloy. Nerco has previously worked with similar materials, although not this precise alloy. In addition, the particular machining operations involved are slightly more complex than the usual work that Nerco does for its customers. However, in developing the bid for this job, Nerco had used data it collected from similar jobs and estimated a labor cost of $22.50 per piece.

Nerco's employees are skilled machinists who are paid on a standard-hour basis. Their base wage rate is $18 per hour, and each machinist works a forty-hour week. Overtime work is paid at time and a half. Due to this high cost, overtime is extremely rare and has been used in the past only when an important job would be late without the use of overtime.

For the new contract, Nerco has set the standard time as 1.25 hours per piece, which was based on past experience with similar jobs. However, the company's machinists have been complaining that the standard time is too low. They argue that this job is much more complex and the material more difficult to work with than that used for previous jobs. In fact, the first part produced took 1.85 hours of actual machining time, and the second part required 1.5 hours to machine.

For the third part, Brock Thurston, the shop foreman, requested that a time study be conducted. The cycle time for this third part was found to be 1.3 hours, and the time-study expert estimated operator efficiency at 90 percent. However, he noted that the machinist appeared to be having some trouble with machining the part and thought that performance would improve as more experience was gained with the job. The allowance factor for this job is 20 percent.

Brock Thurston is still unsure. Even though the times are dropping for this job, they are still above the standard. He wonders whether the standard should be reset due to the uniqueness of the work required under the new contract. He is also worried because the first ten pieces of this order must be completed within another 7.5 regular time hours—a time that seems unreasonable based on how long it took to finish the first three. A late delivery could jeopardize any future orders from this customer. Brock wonders if he should plan to schedule overtime to get the job done.

Silicon Valley Semiconductor

Silicon Valley Semiconductor (SVS) manufactures microprocessor chips used in personal computers. Due to the many manufacturers in the United States and overseas, pricing for these chips has become cutthroat, with the industry experiencing a 25 percent decrease in chip prices each year.

Brenda Thornton, vice-president of finance for SVS, has become increasingly concerned about whether her company can continue to compete effectively in this market. SVS is a relatively small producer and is having trouble generating a reasonable profit, given existing costs and market prices.

As operations manager, you have been asked to respond to Brenda's concern. You know that SVS began producing chips about a year ago and has produced 100,000 chips since then. Based on the past year's results, SVS is operating on an 80 percent learning curve. You also know that materials account for roughly 50 percent of the cost of a chip, with direct labor accounting for the other half.

As vice-president of finance, Thornton is also aware of the 80 percent learning rate for SVS. One question she has raised is whether SVS can follow the industry's 25 percent price reduction when it operates on an 80 percent learning curve. Further, she has pointed out that this learning factor applies only to the direct labor cost, which accounts for only half of product cost. It is not expected that material costs will change appreciably.

1. Explain how an 80 percent learning curve could produce a cost decrease of 25 percent per year.

2. Determine what increase in volume would have to be produced each year to generate such a cost decrease.

3. Based on the fact that direct labor accounts for 50 percent of product cost, how many units must SVS produce each year for the next three years to maintain a 25 percent decrease in product cost each year?

SELECTED BIBLIOGRAPHY

Alexander, D. C. "A Business Approach to Ergonomics." *Industrial Engineering* 17, no. 7 (July 1985): 32–39.

Barnes, Ralph M. *Motion and Time Study: Design and Measurement of Work*. 8th ed. New York: Wiley, 1980.

Carlisle, Brian. "Job Design Implications for Operations Managers." *International Journal of Operations and Production Management 3,* no. 3 (1983): 40–48.

Hutchingson, R. D. *New Horizons for Human Factors in Job Design*. New York: McGraw-Hill, 1981.

Konz, Stephan. *Work Design: Industrial Ergonomics*. 2d ed. New York: Wiley, 1983.

Landel, Robert D. *Managing Productivity Through People: An Operations Perspective*. Englewood Cliffs, N.J.: Reston, Prentice-Hall, 1986.

Muramatsu, R.; Miyazaki, H.; and Ishii, K. "A Successful Application of Job Enlargement/Enrichment at Toyota." *IIE Transactions* 19, no. 4 (1987): 451–459.

Ritzman, Larry P.; King, Barry E.; and Krajewski, Lee J. "Manufacturing Performance—Pulling the Right Levers." *Harvard Business Review* 62, no. 2 (March–April 1984): 143–152.

Sanders, Mark A., and McCormick, Ernest J. *Human Factors in Engineering and Design*. 6th ed. New York: McGraw-Hill, 1987.

Wygant, Robert M. "Improving Productivity with Financial Incentives." *Engineering Management International* 4 (1987): 87–93.

Yelle, Y. E. "The Learning Curve: Historical Review and Comprehensive Survey." *Decision Sciences* 10, no. 2 (April 1979): 302–328.

Zandin, Kjell. *MOST Work Measurement Systems*. New York: Marcel Dekker, 1980.

PART II
Planning the System

The second chapter of this text dealt with the important role operations plays in successfully implementing an organization's competitive strategy. In that chapter, eight steps were presented for linking strategy and operations. The last three of those steps were designing systems for operations, planning for operations, and managing and controlling operations.

The chapters of Part I have addressed the first step just listed by describing how an operations system can be designed to support a company's competitive strategy. Now, in this section, we go on to address the second step—planning for operations.

The chapters of this section continue our top-down approach, beginning with an emphasis on organizational strategic planning and continuing to the detailed minute-by-minute planning of schedules for employees and equipment. Further, you will learn about many concepts and techniques, such as distribution requirements planning and just-in-time operations, that are completely revolutionizing the way many businesses operate today. Those topics are organized into the following chapters:

- CHAPTER 10: Transforming Strategic Plans into Business and Operations Plans
- CHAPTER 11: Planning for Material and Resource Requirements
- CHAPTER 12: Just-in-Time and Synchronous Operations
- CHAPTER 13: Scheduling
- CHAPTER 14: Project Planning and Scheduling

Chapter 10

Transforming Strategic Plans into Business and Operations Plans

CHAPTER OUTLINE

LEARNING OBJECTIVES

After completing this chapter, you should be able to

- Describe how organizational objectives become operations objectives.
- Explain the role of a business plan.
- Define the term aggregation in production planning.
- Explain how the process decision will constrain aggregate planning decisions.
- Discuss the differences between make-to-order and make-to-stock companies.
- Define order-winning criteria and list the most common ones.
- Explain how order-winning criteria will influence the aggregate plan.
- List the cost considerations relevant to aggregate planning.
- List the most common reactive aggregate planning strategies.
- Develop aggregate plans using the three pure strategies and mixed strategies.
- Calculate the costs of an aggregate plan.
- Use the graphical procedure to develop an aggregate plan.
- Use the tabular procedure to develop an aggregate plan.
- Discuss international aspects of aggregate planning.
- List proactive strategies for demand management.
- Explain differences between aggregate plans for service organizations and those for manufacturers.

OPERATIONS IN ACTION

Ford Motor Company: Facing the Highs and Lows of Meeting Customer Demand

During the early 1980s Ford Motor Company was in a life-threatening situation. With capacity far exceeding demand, the company had shut down many of its automobile plants, some of them permanently. Seeing an increasing level of cut throat competition in the automobile industry, Ford decided to adopt the strategy of downsizing its capacity in order to survive, thus avoiding the problems of excess capacity.

But by late 1988, this strategy caused other problems, as Ford was having trouble meeting extremely strong customer demand for its products. For example, early in 1988 Georgia-Pacific Corporation had ordered fifty Ford pickup trucks for its fleet operations, expecting them to be delivered in a few weeks. However, after several months had passed and the trucks were still not available, Georgia-Pacific cancelled its order with Ford and bought trucks from GMC, Chevrolet, and Dodge.

In an attempt to meet demand during 1988, Ford had scheduled all its plants to operate at full capacity, using overtime work to meet demand. Unfortunately, that plan produced an unwanted side effect, as quality suffered. For instance, Ford's Wixom, Michigan, plant found that defects jumped by 75 percent on the Lincoln Town Car it produces.

In 1990, the picture changed again as U.S. auto makers were in a slump. Squeezed by such drastic changes in a few years, Ford has become extremely cautious. Although sales in January of 1990 jumped for other auto makers, Ford's sales were down 5.3 percent from a year earlier. However, Ford says its sales were hurt because plant shutdowns had delayed shipment of fleet orders. Industry sources predict U.S. auto makers will build a total of 1,471,209 cars during the first quarter of 1990, down 22.5 percent from a year earlier. Dealer inventories have been reduced from the normal eighty-seven-day supply to sixty-five days' worth.

In efforts to increase customer demand, Ford has been offering rebates of $1,000 on some models and 6.9 percent financing. However, if demand increases too much, Ford may not be able to respond to meet it.[1]

INTRODUCTION

Planning is probably one of the most important, yet least understood, jobs that a manager performs. Poor planning can mean a company's inability to handle unexpected occurrences. But good planning can place a company in an extremely strong competitive position, one from which the organization is prepared to deal with any event. However, all parts of the organization—marketing, operations, finance, and so on—must work together in the planning process to ensure that they are moving in harmony with one another.

Probably the most important planning activity is concerned with developing a competitive strategy. In today's extremely competitive global marketplace, organizations can ill afford to go forth without a well-planned strategy, which must include the operations function as well as every other part of the organization. As Chapter 2 stressed, operations can be an extremely valuable competitive weapon. The rise of such Japanese companies as Toyota, Mitsubishi, and Sanyo has been tied largely to their effective development and execution of competitive strategies—and the integration of operations activities into those strategies. As more companies enter the world market, each one tries to capture its own share of that market. The ability of a company to do so will depend heavily on how well it has done its homework in developing a strategic plan and in using the operations function as a tool for implementing that plan.

Planning in an organization must begin at the top with strategic planning. The strategic plan is then converted into a business plan—a blueprint for actually implementing the strategic plan. Based on the business plan, each part of an organization must then develop its own plans that describe how the various parts will work to implement the business and strategic plans. This series of planning stages is shown in Exhibit 10.1. In this chapter, we discuss how operations develops its plan to meet corporate objectives and to serve the customer.

THE LINKS FROM STRATEGIC PLANNING TO OPERATIONS PLANNING

An organization's strategic plan is usually stated in broad, general terms that most often apply to the entire organization, instead of to individual functional areas. However, for that strategic plan to be implemented, it must be "operationalized." **Operationalizing the strategic plan** means converting it into detailed plans for each functional area. The purpose of this section is to describe briefly how that process is accomplished. Later, we will deal with the development of plans that are specific to the operations function.

Transforming Organizational Objectives into Sales and Operations Objectives

The organizational objectives and strategy developed by top management provide a frame of reference for all activities within an organization. However, those companywide objectives and strategies must be converted into specific plans at the lower organizational levels. For example, consider the company objectives listed at the top oi Exhibit 10.2. Obviously, before those objectives can be achieved, they will have to be converted into specific objectives for sales and operations. Some possible objectives for those levels are also shown in Exhibit 10.2, although many others are possible.

Exhibit 10.1 Stages of Organizational Planning

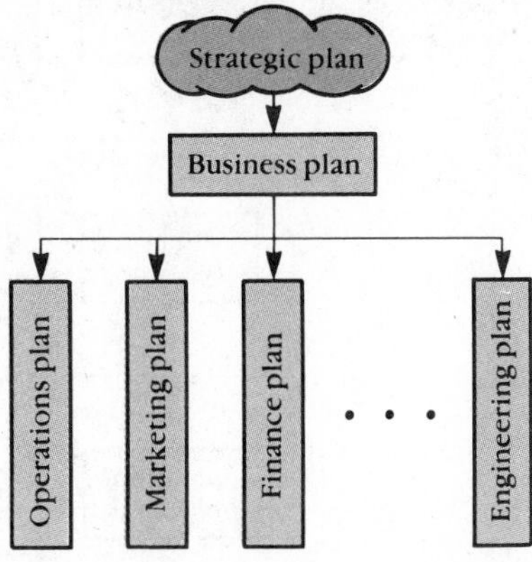

Exactly how an organization's objectives get converted into sales and operations objectives is up to the individual organization's management. In other chapters, we have already discussed ways that process design, facility location, and other operations decisions can be used as competitive weapons in achieving the organization's objectives. The problem in converting organizational objectives into objectives for sales and operations lies in being sure that all are consistent. Exhibit 10.3 depicts one possible approach.

The process depicted in Exhibit 10.3 consists of the following steps:

Step 1: **State strategy and objectives.** As we have been stressing, the process must begin with a statement of the organization's objectives and its strategy for achieving those objectives.

Step 2: **Forecast demand for products and/or services.** As discussed previously in Chapter 3, several methods of forecasting may be used, depending on the relevant planning horizon. Any forecast that is developed must contain both statistical and judgmental forecast components in estimating future demand.

Step 3: **Develop sales objectives.** The forecast developed in step 2 should indicate whether or not the company's objectives for sales will be met. If not, the marketing area must develop its own set of objectives to meet the corporate objectives.

Step 4: **Develop objectives for the operations function.** The sales objectives developed in step 3 will indicate the demands that will be placed on operations. Organization strategy and objectives, combined with the sales objectives, will help determine operations objectives.

Once these specific functional area objectives have been developed, the next step is to frame them in terms of a business plan.

The Business Plan

The strategic plan describes organizational objectives and presents a general blueprint for achieving those objectives. From those organizational objectives,

Exhibit 10.2 A Hierarchy of Objectives

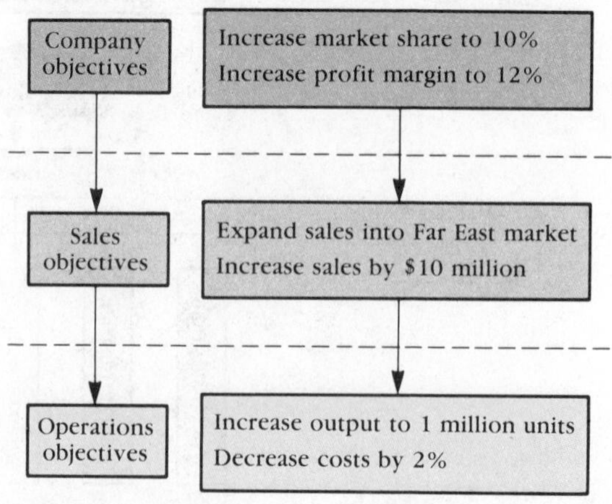

Exhibit 10.3 Converting Organization Objectives into Operations Objectives

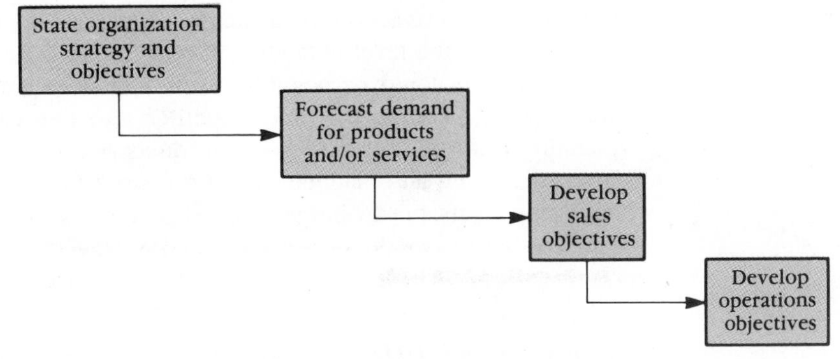

the company develops objectives for other functional areas of the organization. When those functional area objectives are put into concrete terms, the business plan is generated. The **business plan** is a medium-range statement of planned sales, production, and inventory levels, usually stated in terms of dollars, on a monthly basis. Thus, the business plan is generally more concrete and specific than the strategic plan is. The business plan states exactly what is expected of the sales and operations areas, although not how those results will be achieved. The business plan is a direct input to the company's operations planning activities.

MEDIUM-RANGE OPERATIONS PLANNING

Medium-range planning is concerned with a time horizon that is generally from six to eighteen months in the future. While long-range operations planning deals with facilities and resources, medium-range operations planning develops ways to utilize those resources.

The decisions that are usually made as part of medium-range operations planning include the following:

- Work-force size
- Operating hours of the facilities
- Levels of inventory that will be maintained
- Output rates for the processes
- Quantities of raw materials that will be required

While these decisions are much more specific to particular products than facility or resource decisions, medium-range operations planning is still quite general in nature. Aggregated groups of product type are usually considered, instead of specific product models.

Aggregation in Medium-Range Operations Planning

Aggregation refers to the combining of products into groups or families for planning purposes. For instance, an appliance manufacturer might begin medium-range planning by determining output rates for the broad product families of refrigerators, stoves, and dishwashers. Later on, as part of short-range planning, the appliance company would begin to break those output rates down into specific models, such as side-by-side, frost-free, or energy-efficient refrigerators. While this grouping by product seems logical, it is not uncommon for companies to group end items according to similar processing operations or production time needed, or by the level of labor skill required to make the product (see Exhibit 10.4). Thus, it could be possible for an appliance manufacturer to group dishwashers and washing machines together into one category for medium-range planning purposes because both products use the same production facilities. Inventory levels and planned size of the work force are also considered only in aggregate terms, not by individual end product or by particular job descriptions. For this reason, medium-range operations planning is also often referred to as **aggregate planning**, a term that we will also use in this book.

The Organizational Context of Aggregate Planning

Aggregate planning is a first rough-cut approximation at determining how existing resources of people and facilities should be used to meet projected demand for an organization's goods or services. For example, consider the demand forecast for a product group shown in Exhibit 10.5. In aggregate planning, a company must determine what work-force levels, overtime production, inventory, and so forth it will use to meet that demand. Although such decisions may seem innocuous, they can actually have a major impact on an organization's ability to compete successfully. Consequently, aggregate planning decisions must be made with reference to the organization's competitive strategy. At the same time, however, earlier process selection decisions will limit the options available.

Planning Constraints Caused by Type of Process

Chapter 7 has already discussed the process selection decision and how it relates to organizational strategy. Further, the process alternatives, ranging from continuous flow and assembly line to job shop and project, were discussed. By the time a company approaches the aggregate planning problem, it will already have selected the type of process to be used.

Unfortunately, each type of process has major implications for changes in output level, as shown in Exhibit 10.6. For instance, continuous flow processes are represented by steel mills or oil refineries. The ability to change the output levels of such processes is extremely limited and usually requires a new facility.

Exhibit 10.4 Aggregation in Planning

Group I			Group II			Group III		
Grouped by product category			Grouped by processing operations			Grouped by labor requirements		
Item 1	Item 2	Item 3	Item 4	Item 5	Item 6	Item 7	Item 8	Item 9

Exhibit 10.5 A Twelve-Month Forecast Showing Varying Demand for a Product Group

Month	Forecasted Demand
January	12,000
February	11,000
March	13,000
April	11,000
May	12,000
June	15,000
July	10,000
August	13,000
September	11,000
October	13,000
November	9,000
December	10,000

Exhibit 10.6 Options for Changing Output by Process Type

Process Type	Level of Output Change	Methods to Vary Output
Project	Incremental	Change working hours Change work-force size
Job shop	Incremental	Change working hours Change work-force size
Batch	Incremental to stepped	Change working hours Change work-force size Add or subtract shifts Shut down facility
Assembly line	Stepped	Add or subtract shifts Shut down facility
Continuous flow	Facility	Shut down facility Build new facility

On the other hand, job shops are usually quite flexible, and output levels may be changed by hiring additional employees, scheduling more work hours, or utilizing alternative equipment. In developing aggregate plans, an organization must take into account the possible changes that can be made in the output levels of the processes being used.

Make-to-Order Versus Make-to-Stock

A second area of concern in aggregate planning is whether the organization can produce to build up inventory and then use that inventory later to meet demand. Service organizations, since they provide a service, cannot inventory that service and must meet demand as it occurs. Likewise, job shops produce custom products to customer order and usually cannot produce for inventory. However, companies in the process industries, such as oil refining, make a standard product that can be kept in inventory to meet future demand.

Reflecting Order-Winning Criteria in the Plan

Any company, to stay in business, must win orders from its customers. Any time you select a certain restaurant at which to eat, a particular car to buy, or a certain movie to see, the company providing that good or service has won your order, and its competitors have not.

Your ordering decisions will be based on certain criteria that you use, whether consciously or subconsciously. For example, your choice of a restaurant might be based on the price, quality of food, range of items on the menu, or speed of service. In fact, the decision you make about which car to buy could include many of the same criteria. These are called **order-winning criteria.**[2]

Order-winning criteria include, but are not limited to, the following:

- Price
- Quality
- Delivery speed
- Delivery reliability
- Range of products provided
- Ability to meet customer specifications

The order-winning criteria with which a company decides to compete must also be taken into account in the aggregate plan. For example, a company stressing delivery speed must ensure either that it has inventory on hand to meet customer demand or that sufficient capacity is always available. In contrast, a company emphasizing price as an order winner will strive to keep costs low, which may mean minimizing work-force and inventory levels.

Cost Considerations

A final factor to be considered in aggregate planning, but one that is often easiest to determine, is cost. The following are the major costs that must be included. However, it is important to keep in mind that the aggregate plan that minimizes cost may not necessarily be the best. The other organizational factors already mentioned will often take priority over cost.

- *Payroll Costs.* These are the costs associated with having a certain number of employees on the payroll. They usually include wages, health insurance, social security, retirement contributions, and vacation pay.
- *Hiring Costs.* Costs associated with hiring include those for advertising, interviewing and training and those for productivity losses and scrap until the new employee becomes proficient at the job.
- *Layoff Costs.* These include severance pay, state-mandated payments into an unemployment fund, and productivity losses due to "bumping" by senior union employees.
- *Overtime Costs.* Overtime is usually paid at a rate equal to 150 percent of the regular hourly rate. Further, productivity and quality may drop for employees who have already worked a full day. All these factors should be considered in overtime cost.
- *Inventory Holding Costs.* These will include the cost of capital tied up in inventory, as well as the variable costs of insurance, taxes, obsolescence, theft, and spoilage. It is usually calculated based on average inventory.

- *Subcontracting Costs.* When a company cannot meet demand with its own resources, it will subcontract with another to provide the good or service. Whatever cost the company pays its subcontractor must be included.
- *Back Orders, Stockouts, and Lost Sales.* If demand cannot be met when it occurs, it may be possible to convince the customer to accept later delivery through a back order. In this case, additional paperwork cost is incurred, and customer good will suffers. In other cases, the sale may be lost, meaning lost income and lost good will.

Strategies for Meeting Demand

Reactive Strategies

One approach to aggregate planning is to treat the demand forecasts as given and to focus on ways of meeting that demand, whether through inventory or changes in work-force levels or both. The following are some of these **reactive strategies:**

- Vary the number of employees through hiring or layoffs.
- Schedule overtime work or allow employees to slack off.
- Add or eliminate second or third shifts.
- Schedule vacations or plant shutdowns.
- Build up or draw down finished-goods inventory.
- Subcontract work to outside suppliers.
- Build up order backlogs during peak periods.
- Back-order items not available or incur lost sales.

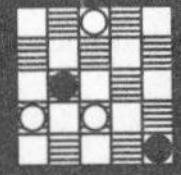

GAINING STRATEGIC ADVANTAGE AT THOMASVILLE FURNITURE

Combining Corporate and Manufacturing Strategies to Focus on Order-Winning Criteria

Although it has been in business since 1904, Thomasville Furniture was in trouble in the early 1980s. A recession, combined with increased foreign competition in 1982, had cut sales enough that Thomasville was operating at only 51 percent of capacity and had operating income of just $1 million on sales of $187 million. To reverse this trend, Thomasville developed an overall corporate strategy and then tied that strategy together with a manufacturing strategy.

To begin, the company identified the order-winning criteria of its customers. Primary among those were quality, value, and delivery speed.

To serve these order winners, Thomasville revised its manufacturing strategy by focusing on quality and delivery. For example, to shorten delivery time, the company shifted its focus from make-to-order to make-to-stock. As a result, 85 percent of orders are shipped within thirty days of receipt, instead of the three to six months that is more common in the furniture industry.

The result is that Thomasville's sales have increased dramatically. Further, the company is recognized as a leader in the furniture industry and is able to compete successfully with foreign manufacturers.[3]

There are many different ways to combine these various reactive strategies. However, three general "pure strategies" are often identified. In demonstrating each, we will use the twelve-month demand forecast presented earlier in Exhibit 10.5. However, we will also indicate how each pure strategy would be most appropriate for different types of processes and organizational competitive strategies.

Strategy 1: Vary the Work-Force Size. The basic idea of this strategy is to vary production to meet demand. If demand rises and falls, then production will have to rise and fall. But under this particular strategy, the variations in production are achieved by varying the number of employees.

Usually this strategy means hiring more employees when demand is high and then laying off employees when demand drops. For example, retail outlets usually handle the Christmas rush by hiring additional salespeople on a temporary basis for the peak-demand periods. Afterward, the sales force returns to its normal size. Companies that provide a service, since they cannot inventory that service, most often follow this strategy. However, manufacturing companies may also follow the same approach because it minimizes the level of finished-goods inventories. It is not uncommon for auto manufacturers to utilize a variation of this strategy by completely shutting down several assembly plants for a week or more when production exceeds sales.

Example

Hickory Hill packages and sells gift boxes of fruit by mail. The company cannot carry any inventory of finished products due to spoilage. Further, the packaging operation is rather simple, and new employees can be trained quickly. The company is located near a large metropolitan area, and new employees are readily available. On the average, each employee can produce 1,000 gift boxes of fruit per month. Payroll costs, including wages and fringe benefits, average $1,730 per employee per month. It usually costs about $200 to hire a new employee and $300 to lay one off. The twelve-month aggregate plan used by Hickory Hill and its associated costs are shown in Exhibit 10.7.

Strategy 2: Hold Work-Force Size Constant, But Vary Its Utilization. In some cases, it will be undesirable to vary the work-force size due to labor agreements or hiring costs, or for labor-relations reasons. Under such conditions, the work-force size may be held constant, but its utilization varied through the use of overtime or a shortened work week. In this situation, the hiring and layoff costs associated with strategy 1 are avoided, but they are generally replaced by higher payroll and overtime costs. In addition, employees who must work overtime are generally less productive and more accident-prone due to fatigue. Second and third shifts are also usually less productive than first shifts are because workers on the later shifts are usually newer, are less skilled, and sometimes are working another job during daytime hours.

A variation of this strategy involves **subcontracting,** or **outsourcing,** which is buying parts or subassemblies from outside suppliers whenever a company's capacity is insufficient to meet its needs from internal production. In this situa-

Exhibit 10.7 Varying Work-Force Production Strategy for Aggregate Planning

Month	Forecasted Demand	Planned Production	Required Employees	Employees Hired	Employees Laid Off
January	12,000	12,000	12	—	—
February	11,000	11,000	11	—	1
March	13,000	13,000	13	2	—
April	11,000	11,000	11	—	2
May	12,000	12,000	12	1	—
June	15,000	15,000	15	3	—
July	10,000	10,000	10	—	5
August	13,000	13,000	13	3	—
September	11,000	11,000	11	—	2
October	13,000	13,000	13	2	—
November	9,000	9,000	9	—	4
December	10,000	10,000	10	1	—
		Totals	140	12	14

Costs:

Payroll:	140 employee-months at $1,730/month	=	$242,200
Hiring:	12 employees at $200/hiring	=	2,400
Layoffs:	14 employees at $300/layoff	=	4,200
			$248,800

tion, a company would subcontract with an outside supplier instead of using overtime to meet production requirements. Instead of overtime costs, the company incurs the added cost of paying another company to make the parts.

Example

Stemple-Hartley sells personalized stemware that has the customer's initials engraved in each piece. The company has ten highly skilled craftsmen who would be hard to replace. Further, because of the custom nature of its product, Stemple-Hartley does not maintain a finished-goods inventory. On the average, each employee can engrave 1,000 pieces per month. By union contract, overtime work is limited to 200 pieces per employee per month. However, a subcontractor is available to engrave up to 5,000 pieces per month.

Each employee is paid an average of $1,730 per month in wages and fringe benefits. Overtime work costs $2.60 per unit, and the subcontractor charges $3.00 per unit. The aggregate plan developed by Stemple-Hartley and its costs are shown in Exhibit 10.8.

Strategy 3: Produce a Constant Amount and Use Inventory to Absorb Fluctuations. Under this last strategy, a company will try to keep production constant, but meet demand fluctuations through inventory variations. In this case, inventory will build up during periods of low demand when the production rate exceeds demand. Then when demand exceeds the company's ability to produce,

Exhibit 10.8 Aggregate Production Plan Using Overtime and Subcontracting

Month	Forecasted Demand	Employment Level	Regular-Time Planned Production	Overtime Planned Production	Units Subcontracted
January	12,000	10	10,000	2,000	—
February	11,000	10	10,000	1,000	—
March	13,000	10	10,000	2,000	1,000
April	11,000	10	10,000	1,000	—
May	12,000	10	10,000	2,000	—
June	15,000	10	10,000	2,000	3,000
July	10,000	10	10,000	—	—
August	13,000	10	10,000	2,000	1,000
September	11,000	10	10,000	1,000	—
October	13,000	10	10,000	2,000	1,000
November	9,000	10	9,000*	—	—
December	10,000	10	10,000	—	—
	Totals	120	119,000	15,000	6,000

Costs:

Payroll:	120 employee-months at $1,730/month	=	$207,600
Overtime:	15,000 units at $2.60/unit	=	39,000
Subcontracting:	6,000 units at $3.00/unit	=	18,000
			$264,600

*Production rate is cut back, underutilizing ten employees who produce only 9,000 units.

this inventory will be drawn down to meet demand. Companies that produce products with seasonal demand, such as air conditioners or snow blowers, often follow this strategy. Its major disadvantage is that storage space and money will be tied up in maintaining the inventory. However, the positive side is that work-force size and hours worked remain constant.

Of course, this last strategy is not usually feasible for service organizations because their product cannot be stored as inventory. For example, an airline must be able to meet the demand that exists for its airplane seats whenever that demand occurs. Thus, service organizations are usually concerned only with strategies that involve varying either the work-force size or its utilization.

Example

EMC, Inc., manufactures power supplies for personal computers. Because computer owners expect to replace their power supply quickly, EMC always maintains an inventory of finished products. On the other hand, its employees are highly trained and difficult to replace. For these reasons, EMC prefers to maintain a constant work force and build up inventory. Each employee can produce an average of 1,000 power supplies per month. Wages and fringe benefits average $1,730 per employee. Further, it costs $.17 to hold one power supply in inventory for one month. The aggregate plan EMC would use and its costs are shown in Exhibit 10.9.

Exhibit 10.9 Aggregate Plan with Varying Inventory

Month	Forecasted Demand	Planned Production	Required Employees	Beginning Inventory	Ending Inventory
January	12,000	12,000	12	2,000	2,000
February	11,000	12,000	12	2,000	3,000
March	13,000	12,000	12	3,000	2,000
April	11,000	12,000	12	2,000	3,000
May	12,000	12,000	12	3,000	3,000
June	15,000	12,000	12	3,000	0
July	10,000	12,000	12	0	2,000
August	13,000	12,000	12	2,000	1,000
September	11,000	12,000	12	1,000	2,000
October	13,000	12,000	12	2,000	1,000
November	9,000	12,000	12	1,000	4,000
December	10,000	12,000	12	4,000	6,000
		Totals	144	25,000	29,000

Costs:

Payroll: 144 employee-months at \$1,730/month = \$249,120

Inventory: $\frac{25{,}000 + 29{,}000}{2(12)} = 2{,}250$ units per month

Annual inventory cost: 2,250 (12) at \$.17/unit/month = 4,590

\$253,710

Mixed Strategies

As you review the preceding aggregate plans, you should notice that in each case, we used exactly the same demand and cost figures. However, each company used a different approach based on its unique circumstances and competitive strategy.

In actual practice, companies usually combine several of the preceding pure strategies to meet their own unique requirements. For example, Exhibit 10.10 shows a mixed strategy that combines hiring and layoffs with overtime and inventory. In this case, the company might have limited finished-goods storage space, but also wants to keep its work-force size fairly constant. Of course, many other mixed strategies could be developed.

Because of the complexity of aggregate planning by trial and error, several systematic methods have been developed. Two of them are described next.

The Graphical Approach. The most common approach to medium-range, or aggregate, operations planning is a graphical one. This **graphical approach** indicates cumulative demand for the product versus cumulative production and can be very useful in developing a mixed strategy, using the following series of steps:

1. Develop a graph that shows numbers of units on the vertical axis and time throughout the planning horizon on the horizontal axis.
2. Graph *cumulative* expected demand from the beginning of the planning horizon to its end.
3. Develop a production plan, and use the graph developed in the preceding steps to graph *cumulative* production throughout the planning horizon.
4. Compare cumulative demand to cumulative production. Areas where cumulative production exceeds cumulative demand indicate an inventory buildup.

Exhibit 10.10 A Mixed Aggregate Planning Strategy

Month	Fore-casted Demand	Employ-ment Level	Regular Time Pro-duction	Over-time Pro-duction	Employ-ees Hired	Employ-ees Laid Off	Begin-ning Inven-tory	Ending Inventory
January	12,000	10	10,000	2,000	—	—	0	0
February	11,000	10	10,000	1,000	—	—	0	0
March	13,000	12	12,000	1,000	2	—	0	0
April	11,000	12	12,000	—	—	—	0	1,000
May	12,000	12	12,000	—	—	—	1,000	1,000
June	15,000	12	12,000	2,000	—	—	1,000	0
July	10,000	12	12,000	—	—	—	0	2,000
August	13,000	12	12,000	—	—	—	2,000	1,000
September	11,000	12	12,000	—	—	—	1,000	2,000
October	13,000	10	10,000	1,000	—	2	2,000	0
November	9,000	10	10,000	—	—	—	0	1,000
December	10,000	10	10,000	—	—	—	1,000	1,000
	Totals	134	134,000	7,000	2	2	8,000	9,000

Costs:

Payroll:	134 employee-months at \$1,730/month	= \$231,820
Overtime:	7,000 units at \$2.60/unit	= 18,200
Hiring:	2 employees at \$200/hiring	= 400
Layoffs:	2 employees at \$300/layoff	= 600
Inventory:	$\frac{8{,}000 + 9{,}000}{2(12)} = 708.33$ units per month	
Annual inventory cost:	708.33(12) at \$.17/unit/month	= 1,445
		\$252,465

Whenever cumulative demand exceeds cumulative production, demand will not be met at that time.

5. Perform the above steps until a satisfactory production plan is developed.

Example

The Regal Toy Company has fifty employees who make and assemble various plastic toys. The aggregate plan for Regal is stated in terms of planned toy production each month, in number of toys, based on the following sales forecast:

Month	Jan.	Feb.	Mar.	Apr.	May	June
Sales forecast	12,000	16,000	14,000	18,000	16,000	16,000
Cumulative	12,000	28,000	42,000	60,000	76,000	92,000

On regular time, the company can produce an average of 15,000 toys per month, as indicated below.

Month	Jan.	Feb.	Mar.	Apr.	May	June
Production	15,000	15,000	15,000	15,000	15,000	15,000
Cumulative	15,000	30,000	45,000	60,000	75,000	90,000

Exhibit 10.11 shows a graph comparing total cumulative demand (dashed line) with total cumulative regular-time production (solid line). The inventory level at any time is the amount by which cumulative production exceeds cumulative demand. As Exhibit 10.11 indicates, inventory will reach zero at the end of

Exhibit 10.11 Graphical Aggregate Planning

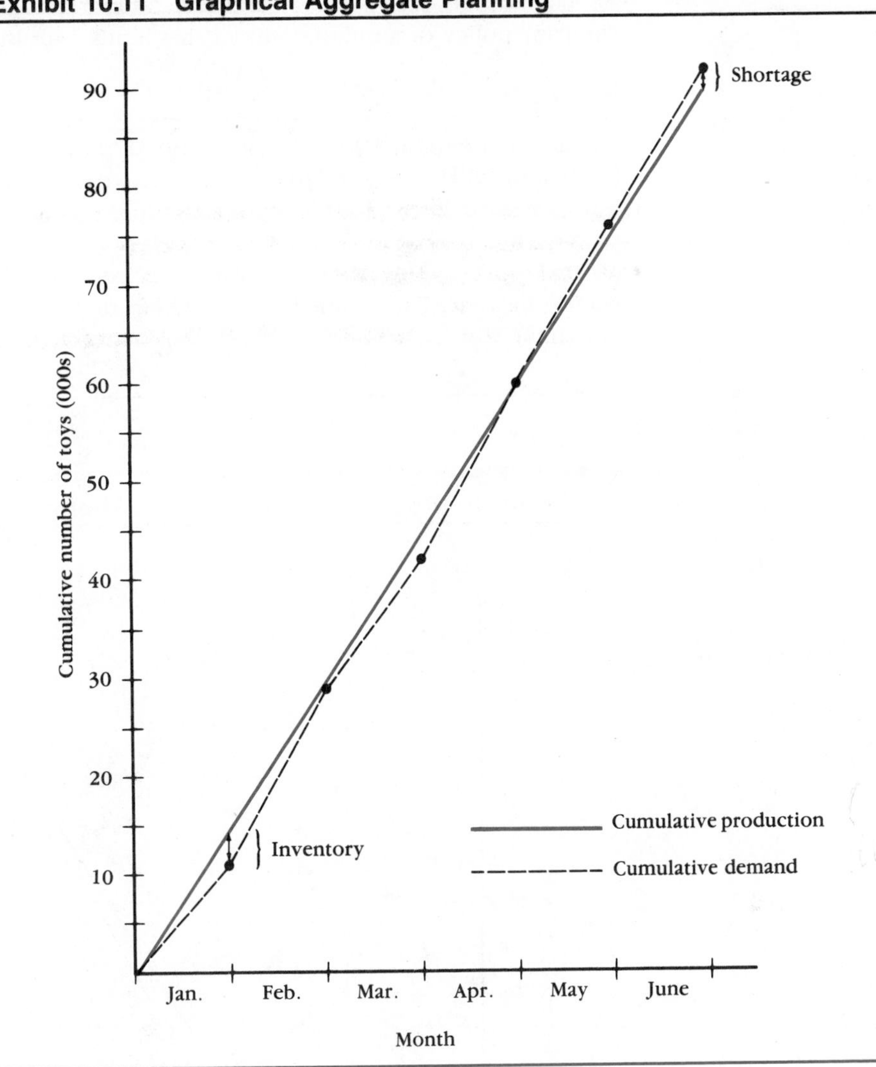

April. After that, production is insufficient to meet demand by an amount equal to 1,000 units per month.

Regal Toy might decide to schedule overtime in May and June so an extra 1,000 units could be produced each month. Under that mixed strategy, cumulative production and cumulative demand would coincide from the end of April through the end of June.

This graphical approach is best used for determining what the inventory level will be at any given time and whether demand can be satisfied from available inventory and planned production. If demand exceeds available supply, then the planner must decide whether production will be increased through assigning overtime, through hiring, or possibly by subcontracting with an outside supplier.

The determination of which approach to follow is usually based on the costs associated with each strategy and any other relevant considerations, such as company policy or a union contract that limits overtime or hiring.

Example

The graph of Exhibit 10.11 can also be used to determine what constant level of production will be required to meet cumulative demand. Note that if a straight line is drawn from the origin of the graph out to the cumulative demand point that is farthest above the cumulative production, this line indicates a constant-production plan that will meet demand. Cumulative demand is farthest above cumulative production for June. Thus, a line is connected from the origin to that point, as shown in Exhibit 10.12. This line corresponds to monthly production of 15,334 units.

Exhibit 10.12 Aggregate Plan to Avoid Shortages

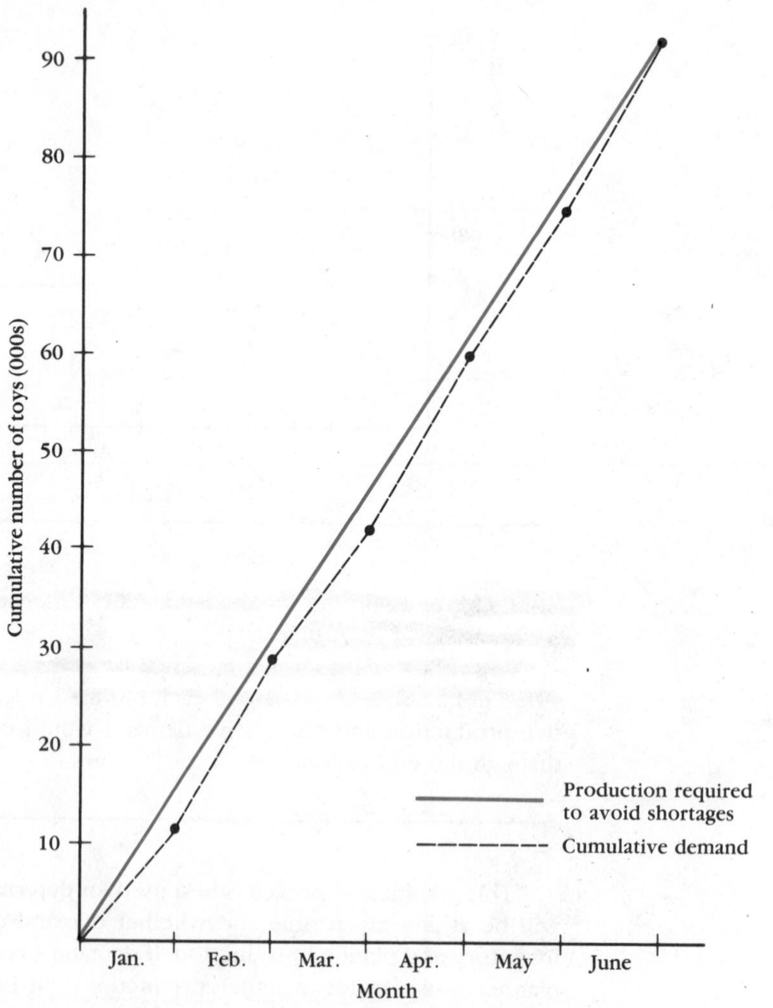

A Tabular Method. A second method that attempts to simplify the aggregate planning problem uses a transportation problem tableau, as shown in Exhibit 10.13. Rows of this tableau represent possible product *sources,* such as regular time, overtime, and subcontracting, for each month. Columns of the tableau correspond to *demand* each month. The last two columns to the right indicate capacity not used and available capacity from each source. The last row indicates demand requirements in each month.

Notice that production in January (the first three rows) may be used to meet demand for January. However, by carrying inventory from one month to the next, it can also be used to meet demand in successive months. In contrast, production in later months cannot be used to meet demand for January unless back orders or backlogs are allowed. In this example, we assume they are not.

In the upper right-hand corner of the cells are unit-cost figures, using the following symbols:

R = cost per unit of regular-time production

T = cost per unit of overtime production

Exhibit 10.13 Tableau for Solving Aggregate Planning Problems

		January	February	March	April	Unused Capacity	Capacity Available
January	Regular time	R	$R+H$	$R+2H$	$R+3H$		
	Overtime	T	$T+H$	$T+2H$	$T+3H$		
	Subcontract	S	$S+H$	$S+2H$	$S+3H$		
February	Regular time		R	$R+H$	$R+2H$		
	Overtime		T	$T+H$	$T+2H$		
	Subcontract		S	$S+H$	$S+2H$		
March	Regular time			R	$R+H$		
	Overtime			T	$T+H$		
	Subcontract			S	$S+H$		
April	Regular time				R		
	Overtime				T		
	Subcontract				S		
	Demand						

S = cost per unit of subcontracting

H = cost per unit to hold inventory for one month

Thus, a unit produced on regular time in January and sold that same month will cost the producer R. However, a unit produced in January on regular time and not sold until April will cost $R + 3H$ because it must be carried as inventory for three months.

To develop an aggregate plan using this tableau, use the following steps:

1. Copy all figures from the Capacity Available column into the Unused Capacity column.
2. Find the cell with lowest cost in the first month's column, and put the *minimum* of either unused capacity for that row or demand for that column into the cell. Adjust unused capacity accordingly.
3. Repeat the preceding step until all demand for the month is satisfied.
4. Proceed to the next month (column), and repeat steps 2 and 3.

When the process is completed, all entries across a row, including unused capacity, must add up to the capacity available. Likewise, all entries in a column must add up to the demand for that column. The solution obtained by this method is shown in Exhibit 10.14.

When back orders are allowed, we can modify the tableau so demand in a given month can be satisfied by production in a later month. The associated cost will represent production cost plus back-order cost.

Computer Solution as a Transportation Problem. The tabular technique just described actually uses the transportation method, which was described in Chapter 6. While small problems can be solved manually, larger problems are best done on the computer. For instance, Exhibit 10.15 shows output from the STORM computer software for the problem just described.

Aggregate Planning in an International Context

Chapter 6 discussed reasons for a company to locate its facilities in a foreign country. Among those reasons was an increased ability to serve foreign markets. However, there is often a tendency then to develop product designs that are unique to each market. While customization of products to particular markets can be desirable as a competitive strategy, it often makes aggregate planning more difficult.

For example, suppose a company operates production facilities for a given product in two different countries. If those two products are the same, then excess capacity at one facility can be used to meet demand that the other facility may not be able to serve due to capacity limitations. On the other hand, if the products produced are not the same, then excess capacity will go unused at one facility, and some demand will be unmet in the market served by the other facility.

To avoid this second scenario, many companies develop product designs that can be used in several different markets. As a result, aggregate planning can be done by the organization on a global basis, rather than on a facility-by-facility basis.

Exhibit 10.14 Tableau Solution to Aggregate Planning Problem

		January	February	March	April	Unused Capacity	Capacity Available
January	Regular time	1.73 10,000	1.90	2.07	2.24	~~10,000~~ 0	10,000
	Over-time	2.60 2,000	2.77	2.94	3.11	~~2,000~~ 0	2,000
	Sub-contract	3.00	3.17	3.34	3.51	5,000	5,000
February	Regular time		1.73 10,000	1.90	2.07	~~10,000~~ 0	10,000
	Over-time		2.60 1,000	2.77 1,000	2.94	~~2,000~~ ~~1,000~~ 0	2,000
	Sub-contract		3.00	3.17	3.34	5,000	5,000
March	Regular time			1.73 10,000	1.90	~~10,000~~ 0	10,000
	Over-time			2.60 2,000	2.77	~~2,000~~ 0	2,000
	Sub-contract			3.00	3.17	5,000	5,000
April	Regular time				1.73 10,000	~~10,000~~ 0	10,000
	Over-time				2.60 1,000	~~2,000~~ 1,000	2,000
	Sub-contract				3.00	5,000	5,000
	Demand	12,000	11,000	13,000	11,000		

Proactive Strategies

Rather than reacting to variations in customer demand, many companies use **proactive strategies** in an attempt to alter that demand. Such strategies are aimed at smoothing demand and bringing it into line with available capacity. Some possible approaches follow.

Produce Products That Are Seasonal Complements

The idea behind this strategy is to find products with alternating demand patterns so that demand for one is high when demand for the other is low. For example, companies that manufacture both snow blowers and lawnmowers take advantage of complementary products. The same approach is used by state highway departments, which operate largely as service organizations. In northern climates, the same crews used for snow plowing during the winter do the mowing during the summer.

Offer Discounts and Promotions

The objective here is to increase demand during low periods through incentives to buy. Conversely, prices can be raised during high-demand periods. Hotels

Exhibit 10.15 Computer Output of STORM Software Package for an Aggregate Planning Problem

```
                    Aggregate Planning

      TRANSPORTATION - OPTIMAL SOLUTION - SUMMARY REPORT

------- Cell ------                         Unit        Cell
Row              Column     Amount          Cost        Cost

JAN R.T.         JANUARY     10000        1.7300  17300.0000
JAN R.T. Subtotal = 17300.0000

JAN O.T.         JANUARY      2000        2.6000   5200.0000
JAN O.T. Subtotal = 5200.0000

JAN SUB.           Dummy      5000        0.0000      0.0000
JAN SUB. Subtotal = 0.0000

FEB R.T.        FEBRUARY      9000        1.7300  15570.0000
FEB R.T.           MARCH      1000        1.9000   1900.0000
FEB R.T. Subtotal = 17470.0000

FEB O.T.        FEBRUARY      2000        2.6000   5200.0000
FEB O.T. Subtotal = 5200.0000

FEB SUB.           Dummy      5000        0.0000      0.0000
FEB SUB. Subtotal = 0.0000

MAR R.T.           MARCH     10000        1.7300  17300.0000
MAR R.T. Subtotal = 17300.0000

MAR O.T.           MARCH      2000        2.6000   5200.0000
MAR O.T. Subtotal = 5200.0000

MAR SUB.           Dummy      5000        0.0000      0.0000
MAR SUB. Subtotal = 0.0000

APR R.T.           APRIL     10000        1.7300  17300.0000
APR R.T. Subtotal = 17300.0000

APR O.T.           APRIL      1000        2.6000   2600.0000
APR O.T.           Dummy      1000        0.0000      0.0000
APR O.T. Subtotal = 2600.0000

APR SUB.           Dummy      5000        0.0000      0.0000
APR SUB. Subtotal = 0.0000

Total Cost = 87570.0000

Number of iterations = 12
```

located in summer vacation spots often do this by cutting prices in the winter and raising them in the summer. The telephone company also does this with late-night and weekend telephone rates.

Increase Advertising in Slack Periods

Advertising can obviously have a great impact on demand. During periods when demand is ordinarily low, increased advertising can generate increased demand. Conversely, significant amounts of money can be saved by reducing advertising if demand is already sufficient to use available capacity.

Aggregate Planning for Service Organizations

As we have already mentioned, service operations generally are unable to hold their product in inventory and must provide the service when it is demanded. For example, unoccupied hotel rooms cannot be saved up from periods of low demand to satisfy peak-period demands. Thus, in general, services are limited to proactive strategies and to those reactive aggregate planning strategies that do not involve inventory. However, services are often better able to use order backlogs as one way to meet peak demand.

Planning with Order Backlogs

There are now many service outlets that will change the oil and oil filter in your car on demand. Such facilities are designed to provide immediate service. However, if you want major repair work done on your car, you will probably have to schedule that for some time in the future, not necessarily when you want the work done. The reason is that major repair shops have limited capacity. When that capacity limit is reached, orders are backlogged by making appointments for

OPERATIONS IN ACTION

Gillette's Sensor and Coors' Keystone: What to Do When Demand Exceeds Supply

Gillette Company's Sensor razor and Adolph Coors Company's Keystone beer are two new products that encountered phenomenal success. In fact, both products far exceeded original sales projections. Keystone, for example, sold 60 percent more than projected. Stores selling the Sensor razor have been unable to keep it on their shelves and say that new shipments are running late.

In both cases, the companies involved have no more capacity immediately available. Coors has a total brewing capacity estimated at about 19 or 20 million barrels per year, a limit it is very close to right now. Similarly, Gillette currently has limited capacity available, although more has been scheduled to come up in 1991.

For both companies, plans for acquiring more capacity have been speeded up, with Coors considering an acquisition of the Detroit-based Stroh brewery. However, Gillette is also attempting to shift demand to the latter part of 1990 when it will have additional capacity. To do this, the company has scaled back advertising planned for early 1990 and instead has moved that budget into ads for the later part of the year.[4]

future dates. The major cost of this strategy comes from lost sales when the customer goes elsewhere for service.

Example

Midwest Diesel Service operates a rebuilding service for the diesel engines in large trucks. Each employee of Midwest Diesel can rebuild an average of ten engines per month. Payroll costs average $2,500 per month per employee, and the company currently has twelve employees and cannot hire more due to space limitations. Further, the company does not want to lay off any employees due to the difficulty of replacing them. Based on past experience, each order backlogged from one month to the next will cost $300 in lost sales and lost customer good will. Overtime work is limited to one-fifth of regular time each month, and employees are paid a 50 percent premium for overtime work. Exhibit 10.16 indicates the aggregate plan Midwest Diesel has developed for the next six months.

Proactive Strategies

Although limited somewhat in reactive strategies, service organizations quite often have more options for shifting demand than do manufacturers. In addition to those proactive strategies described earlier, service organizations can also take advantage of the following.

Fixed Service Schedules. Many service organizations, such as airlines, buses, and railroads, maintain a fixed schedule. This fixes capacity, which customers then use up when they purchase tickets. Ticket purchases also offer some opportunity for adding capacity, as railroads can put on additional cars or bus lines can schedule more than one bus if demand justifies doing so.

Exhibit 10.16 An Aggregate Plan for Services with Backlogs

Month	Demand Forecast	Regular-Time Production	Overtime Production	Beginning Backlog	Ending Backlog
January	100	100	—	—	—
February	110	110	—	—	—
March	130	120	10	—	—
April	150	120	24	0	6
May	130	120	16	6	0
June	120	120	—	—	—
		Totals	50	6	6

Costs:

Payroll:	12 employees × 6 months = 72 employee-months at $2,500/month	$180,000
Overtime:	$50 \times \frac{\$2{,}500}{10}(1.50)$	= 18,750
Back orders:	6 at $300 each	= 1,800
		$200,550

OPERATIONS IN ACTION

The Restaurant Industry: Focusing on Speed, Convenience, and Price to Increase Customer Demand

The restaurant industry is facing difficult times as sales growth has been decreasing. To increase that demand, companies have been using a variety of proactive strategies. For example, Taco Bell recently lowered its prices on tacos to $.59 from $.79.

Other restaurants have focused on speed. Rally's, Inc., a fast-food company that emphasizes hamburgers, offers no inside seating. Instead, each of the company's restaurants has two drive-through windows. Customers at Rally's can have their order in less than a minute, while Burger King or McDonald's requires two or three minutes.

Convenience has also become important. For instance, Red Lobster restaurants found customers often complained about long waits to get a table on weekends. To overcome that problem, the company's restaurants in Atlanta are currently testing "Call-Ahead Seating." Instead of being required to be at the restaurant in person to get on the waiting list, customers may call up in advance and then arrive when their table is ready.

Carrying convenience one step farther, a company named Restaurant Express now offers to pick up meals from restaurants that do not have their own delivery service and deliver those meals to customers' homes.[5]

Appointments for Service Times. Physicians and dentists use appointments to smooth out demand for their services. Customers know in advance when they will obtain service, rather than just showing up and having to wait for service. Appointments also help to eliminate slack time for the service facility.

Customer Involvement. Self-serve gas stations, salad bars, and automatic teller machines all get the customer involved in the service process. To a large extent, this option enables the system to respond to its own demand.

SUMMARY

- Manufacturing objectives are developed from corporate objectives and marketing objectives.
- The business plan is a financial statement of the company's medium-range objectives.
- Medium-range operations planning is concerned with decisions regarding work force, output, and inventory for six to eighteen months into the future.
- Aggregation in planning combines products into groups.
- Processes will place constraints on output changes.
- Make-to-order companies cannot produce for inventory.
- Order-winning criteria—how companies win customers—include price, quality, delivery speed and reliability, range of products, and ability to meet customer specifications.

- Costs considered in aggregate planning include payroll, hiring, layoffs, overtime, inventory, subcontracting, and back orders or lost sales.
- Three "pure strategies" for reacting to demand include varying the work force, using overtime or subcontracting, and varying the inventory.
- In aggregate planning, a company can take a global viewpoint if facilities in different countries produce products that are alike.
- Proactive strategies attempt to smooth demand.
- Service organizations cannot carry inventory, but they can often use order backlogs or schedule orders.

CAREER PROFILE

John R. E. Ruhl

Vice-President and General Manager
Steelcase Inc./Stow and Davis Wood Division

Steelcase, Inc., is the world's largest manufacturer of office furniture and is a company that has always led the way in utilizing innovative methods for production and operations management. Steelcase was one of the first companies to adopt MRP and is still recognized as an outstanding example of its successful use.

Educational Background and Career Steps

John Ruhl earned his bachelor's degree in business administration at Miami University in Oxford, Ohio. Envisioning a career in teaching, he was awarded a teaching fellowship to pursue the master's degree in accounting at the University of Illinois. A short time after graduation, Ruhl passed the CPA exam and was lured away from teaching by a job with the audit staff of Arthur Andersen in the company's Chicago office. After four years in auditing, he decided that accounting was not for him and started looking around for other careers. It was then that Steelcase offered John the job of assistant to the plant manager of its Grand Rapids, Michigan, plant. Ruhl took the job and has been happy with his decision ever since.

For the first several years with Steelcase, Ruhl's duties involved what he calls being a "go-fer." He was responsible for expediting materials, finding out why a certain customer order was late, or doing any one of several other activities to keep things running smoothly. But in 1969, he was assigned as project manager for a project that eventually evolved into one of the very first MRP implementations.

Experience with MRP

As part of the MRP project, Ruhl worked with the late Oliver Wight, a world-recognized consultant on MRP implementation, and members of Wight's consulting group. As Ruhl says, "They showed me, more than anyone else, what better planning can do in operating manufacturing units." He also found that product quality is closely linked to planning: "If you don't have a well-planned and controlled manufacturing operation, it's unlikely that you could expect good conformance to quality requirements."

Position Today

In 1976, Ruhl was asked to become general manager of Steelcase's plant in Fletcher, North Carolina. In that position, he is responsible for 850 employees and some $120 million in shipments each year, in addition to coordinating all the activities involved with managing a plant of that size.

According to Ruhl, the company's emphasis today is on simplification and more employee involvement. As a make-to-order company with 100,000 possible product variations, the Stow and Davis Wood Division must be able to respond quickly. However, it found the MRP system alone could not provide that quick response. By also using JIT, employee involvement, and Quality Circles, the company has been able to reduce the manufacturing cycle time from thirty-three days to just ten. Under Ruhl's direction, the company is constantly working to improve its performance as a "world class" manufacturer.

The Future

Ruhl is a person happy with his manufacturing management responsibilities. In fact, he turned down a possible advancement into finance because he wanted to stay in manufacturing. Ruhl feels one of the best things he can do is to encourage good people to enter the manufacturing field, especially with companies like Steelcase where the "teamwork ethic" brings out the best in people as they work together to solve problems. He also believes one of the best entry-level jobs in manufacturing is the position of first-line supervisor because it entails so much direct involvement with people and operations.

SOLVED PROBLEMS

1. Company A operates a fast-food restaurant. It is able to hire high school and college students very easily on a short-term basis so that any variations in demand are met by changes in the work-force size. If Company A needs one employee for every 1,000 customers per month, determine the planned work-force size each month, given the following demand forecast. Determine costs if each employee earns an average of $350 per month, and if it costs $50 to hire an employee and $100 to lay one off.

Month	Jan.	Feb.	Mar.	Apr.	May	June	July	Aug.
Expected Customers	10,000	9,000	8,000	9,000	11,000	12,000	13,000	12,000

Solution

For each month, divide the expected number of customers (demand) by the number of customers each employee can serve per month (1,000). The result is as follows:

Month	Expected Customers	Employees Required	Employees Hired	Employees Laid Off
Jan.	10,000	10	—	—
Feb.	9,000	9	—	1
Mar.	8,000	8	—	1
Apr.	9,000	9	1	—
May	11,000	11	2	—

Month	Expected Customers	Employees Required	Employees Hired	Employees Laid Off
June	12,000	12	1	—
July	13,000	13	1	—
Aug.	12,000	12	—	1
Totals		84	5	3

Costs:

Payroll:	84 employee-months at $350/month	=	$29,400
Hiring:	5 employees at $50/hiring	=	$ 250
Layoff:	3 employees at $100/layoff	=	300
			$29,950

2. Company B runs a printing and duplicating service. Its staff is highly skilled, and replacements are difficult to find. The company uses overtime to add capacity. During slack-demand periods, Company B still provides its employees with a full forty-hour workweek, although at times they may have nothing to do. Determine overtime requirements each month, based on the following information if each job takes an average of four hours to complete. Regular-time wages average $8.50 per hour, and overtime earns a 50 percent premium.

Month	Jan.	Feb.	Mar.	Apr.	May	June
Expected Number of Jobs	40	50	35	40	50	50
Regular-Time Hours Available	173	156	185	171	167	183

Solution

a. Calculate the total hours required each month by multiplying the expected number of jobs by 4.

b. Subtract the regular-time hours available from the hours required for each month. If this figure is negative, then excess capacity is available. Otherwise, overtime is needed as shown below.

Month	Jan.	Feb.	Mar.	Apr.	May	June	Total
Expected Number of Jobs	40	50	35	40	50	50	265
Hours Required	160	200	140	160	200	200	1,060
Regular-Time Hours Available	173	156	185	171	167	183	1,035
Overtime Hours Required	0	44	0	0	33	17	94

Costs:

Regular Time:	1,035 hours at $8.50/hour	=	$8,797.50
Overtime:	94 hours at [($8.50)(1.50)]/hour	=	1,198.50
			$9,996.00

3. Company C manufactures precision electrical equipment. Like Company B, it wants to maintain a constant work-force size. However, overtime is very expensive, so Company C prefers to let finished-goods inventory fluctuate. The company currently produces at the rate of 5,000 finished units per month, but forecasted demand is as shown below. What is the ending

finished-goods inventory expected to be each month if 3,000 units are expected to be in stock at the beginning of January? Calculate inventory holding costs if each unit costs $.50 to store for one month.

Month	Jan.	Feb.	Mar.	Apr.	May	June	July	Aug.	Sept.
Forecasted Demand	4,000	3,000	6,000	7,000	5,000	6,000	7,000	5,000	4,000

Solution

a. Start with the beginning inventory for the first month.
b. Subtract forecasted demand from production, and add that to beginning inventory. This will give ending inventory.
c. Take ending inventory from the month just completed, and make that beginning inventory for the next month.
d. Repeat steps b and c until all months are calculated.

Month	**Production**	−	**Forecasted Demand**	=	**Excess (Shortage)**	+	**Beginning Inventory**	=	**Ending Inventory**
Jan.	5,000		4,000		1,000		3,000		4,000
Feb.	5,000		3,000		2,000		4,000		6,000
Mar.	5,000		6,000		(1,000)		6,000		5,000
Apr.	5,000		7,000		(2,000)		5,000		3,000
May	5,000		5,000		0		3,000		3,000
June	5,000		6,000		(1,000)		3,000		2,000
July	5,000		7,000		(2,000)		2,000		0
Aug.	5,000		5,000		0		0		0
Sept.	5,000		4,000		1,000		0		1,000
					Totals		26,000		24,000

$$\text{Average monthly inventory} = \frac{26{,}000 + 24{,}000}{2(9)} = 2{,}778$$

Inventory holding costs:

2,778 units × 9 months at $.50/unit/month = $12,500

QUESTIONS

1. What are the steps in converting organizational objectives into operations objectives?

2. What is the role of a business plan in the planning process?

3. What changes in output level are possible for each type of process?

4. How will the aggregate plan differ in a make-to-stock company compared to a make-to-order company?

5. List and define the costs that are relevant to aggregate planning.

6. Develop a list of possible reactive strategies and a list of possible proactive strategies for meeting demand.

7. What reactive and proactive strategies are available to both service organizations and manufacturers? Which are available to only one or the other?

8. For automobile manufacturers today, what would you say are the major order winners?

9. Consider Wendy's and McDonald's. In what ways might their competitive strategies differ? How might the aggregate planning for each reflect those differences?

10. Suppose a company identifies quality as an order winner. Would this company want to have an aggregate plan with large work-force variations? Why or why not?

11. Find some recent articles that indicate various ways companies vary output to meet demand. Write a report summarizing those articles.

12. Black and Decker makes many different power tools and household products. Describe some possible ways these products might be aggregated for planning purposes.

13. Select an actual service operation, and describe some reactive and proactive strategies it uses to meet demand.

14. The XYZ Company produces a very standardized product and emphasizes immediate delivery. Its work force is highly skilled. What reactive aggregate planning strategies would probably be used?

15. Describe some ways, reactive and proactive, in which colleges and universities meet demand.

16. What change would be made in the tableau method for aggregate planning to allow back orders?

PROBLEMS

1. Given the following forecasted demand, develop a production plan that uses a varying work force if each employee can produce 2,000 units per month.

Month	Forecasted Demand (Units)	Month	Forecasted Demand (Units)
Jan.	80,000	May	80,000
Feb.	90,000	June	70,000
Mar.	90,000	July	60,000
Apr.	80,000	Aug.	50,000

2. For the situation in problem 1, determine the total cost of hirings and layoffs if it costs $500 to hire an employee and $1,000 to lay off an employee. There are forty employees at the beginning of January.

3. A fast-food restaurant performs its planning in terms of sales dollars. In the past, the restaurant has needed one employee per $10,000 of sales. Temporary help is readily available so that work-force size may be varied easily and inexpensively. How many employees should the restaurant plan to have working each month?

Month	Forecasted Sales	Month	Forecasted Sales
May	$100,000	Aug.	$120,000
June	120,000	Sept.	120,000
July	130,000	Oct.	100,000

4. A commercial laundry does its planning in terms of tons of laundry per month. The laundry's equipment has a maximum capacity of 3 tons of laundry per hour. Given the following forecast of demand, determine overtime hours that will be required each month:

Month	Forecasted Demand (Tons)	Regular-Time Hours Available
Aug.	500	184
Sept.	500	168
Oct.	550	192
Nov.	600	176
Dec.	650	184
Jan.	600	192
Feb.	500	160
Mar.	600	192

5. An electronics manufacturer maintains a constant work force of forty employees. Each employee can produce ten units of the company's product per hour. Regular-time work is eight hours per day. Given the following demand forecast and working days, determine the number of overtime hours that will be needed each month:

Month	Demand Forecast (Units)	Working Days
Jan.	70,000	24
Feb.	60,000	18
Mar.	75,000	25
Apr.	70,000	21
May	80,000	24
June	80,000	20

6. Refer to problem 5. Employees earn an average wage of $12 per hour on regular time and a 50 percent premium for overtime work. Calculate the regular payroll cost and overtime cost for each month.

7. The Lee Key Boat Company manufacturers power boats. Obviously, spring and summer are its high-demand seasons. During fall and winter, the company builds up inventory in anticipation of the spring-summer peak. If Lee Key produces an average of 2,000 boats per month, determine the company's expected ending inventory each month, based on the following sales forecast. The company expects to have 3,000 boats left in inventory at the end of August.

Month	Forecasted Sales (Units)	Month	Forecasted Sales (Units)
Aug.	3,000	Feb.	800
Sept.	1,500	Mar.	1,500
Oct.	1,000	Apr.	2,000
Nov.	1,000	May	4,000
Dec.	1,000	June	6,000
Jan.	1,000	July	4,000

8. For the Lee Key Boat Company, of problem 7, determine the total inventory carrying cost for the year if it costs $30 per month to store each boat in inventory.

9. Referring to problem 7, the Lee Key Boat Company, develop a graph that shows cumulative production and cumulative sales. (Be sure to include beginning inventory for August as the starting point for cumulative production.)

10. The Sunshine Dairy plans its production in gallons of product per month. A maximum of 1,000 gallons may be carried over from one month to the next; otherwise, spoilage occurs. If demand cannot be met in a given month, the company loses sales. Inventory carrying cost is $.10 per gallon per month, and the cost of a lost sale is $.30 per gallon. Sunshine's maximum production rate is 20,000 gallons per month. Using the following demand forecast, determine monthly production to minimize inventory and lost sales costs without exceeding the inventory limit.

Month	Forecasted Sales (Gallons)	Month	Forecasted Sales (Gallons)
June	15,000	Sept.	19,000
July	22,000	Oct.	18,000
Aug.	20,000	Nov.	22,000

11. Diamond Electronics is developing an aggregate plan for the first six months of the next year. The company expects to have capacity on regular time to produce 5,000 units per month at a labor cost of $3 per unit. Each month 1,000 units can be produced on overtime at a cost of $4.50 per unit. Back orders are not allowed, but the company is willing to carry inventory from one month to the next at $.50 per unit. Use the tableau method to develop an aggregate plan that will meet the following demand forecast for lowest total cost:

Month	Jan.	Feb.	Mar.	Apr.	May	June
Forecasted Demand	3,000	3,000	6,000	7,000	6,000	4,000

12. Suppose in problem 11 that back orders are allowed at a cost of $1 per unit. Again, use the tableau method to develop an aggregate plan.

13. Norge Company manufactures washers and dryers. For aggregate planning purposes, each product is treated separately, although both require many of the same production facilities. The forecasted demand, in units, is shown below.

Month	Forecast for Washers	Forecast for Dryers
Aug.	100,000	80,000
Sept.	120,000	90,000
Oct.	100,000	90,000
Nov.	150,000	100,000
Dec.	170,000	110,000
Jan.	140,000	100,000
Feb.	100,000	80,000

The parts for each washer and dryer are machined on the same equipment, but there are separate washer and dryer assembly lines. Each washer requires .3 hour of machining time and .1 hour of assembly time. Each dryer requires .2 hour of machining time and .15 hour of assembly time. Calculate the total machining and assembly requirements for each month.

14. Referring to problem 13, suppose that Norge has available 50,000 hours of machining time each month

on regular time. An additional 20,000 hours is available on overtime. After that, a second shift must be added. Calculate overtime hours required each month, and indicate which months will require a second shift for machining.

15. Referring to problems 13 and 14, suppose that regular-time pay is $10.00 per hour, overtime pay is $15.00 per hour, and second-shift pay is $10.50 per hour. Reevaluate your solution for problem 14 to determine when it is less expensive to add a second shift instead of using overtime. The second shift must be paid for a minimum of 20,000 hours each month even if that much time is not needed.

16. Using the data from problem 13, graph the total assembly requirements and the total machining requirements for each month.

17. The Branchville office of Eastern Bell Telephone Company is planning its requirements for telephone installers. Based on past experience, the following forecast of installation hours required each month has been developed:

Month	Forecast of Installation Hours	Month	Forecast of Installation Hours
Apr.	1,800	Aug.	3,500
May	2,000	Sept.	3,000
June	2,800	Oct.	2,200
July	3,500		

The company currently has fifteen installers who each work an average of 175 hours per month.

a. Draw a graph of cumulative installation hours available versus cumulative installation hours forecast.
b. In the past, Eastern Bell has had a policy of maintaining a sufficient number of installers to meet peak-period demand. If enough additional installers were hired before April to meet peak demand, graph cumulative installation hours available versus cumulative hours forecast.

18. In addition to the data given in problem 17, suppose each installer is paid $7.50 per hour.

a. Calculate total payroll costs if enough additional installers are hired before April to meet peak demand over the planning horizon.
b. Eastern Bell is considering subcontracting work to an independent electrical contractor for periods when demand exceeds existing installation capacity. Determine how many installation hours would need to be subcontracted each month if the existing work force of fifteen is maintained.
c. If the subcontractor charges $15 per hour, compare the costs of subcontracting with the costs of maintaining the peak-period work force over the planning horizon. Which minimizes total costs?

19. The Itty Bitty Machine Company has just entered the pocket computer market. Although the company is starting with modest sales, it expects sales to grow before leveling off at 6,000 units per month, as shown in the following twelve-month forecast:

Month	Sales Forecast	Month	Sales Forecast	Month	Sales Forecast
Jan.	4,000	May	4,700	Sept.	5,700
Feb.	4,200	June	4,800	Oct.	6,000
Mar.	4,300	July	4,900	Nov.	6,000
Apr.	4,500	Aug.	5,300	Dec.	6,000

The company currently has fifty employees on its payroll, each of whom can assemble 100 computers per month. It costs $500 to hire a new employee and $1,000 to lay an employee off. Employees each earn $1,500 per month, but overtime work earns a premium of 50 percent above regular pay. It costs $10 per month to store one unit in inventory for one month. There are 400 units currently on hand for the beginning of January.

a. Calculate production plans for the twelve-months, using each of the three pure strategies.
b. Calculate the total costs associated with each of your production plans developed in part a.

20. Referring to problem 19, suppose that the Itty Bitty Machine Company does not want to lay off employees. Develop a production plan, using any pure strategy (without layoffs) or a mixed strategy, to minimize total cost over the planning horizon.

21. FyreGlow is a manufacturer of gas barbecue grills. As you might expect, demand for its product is highest during the warm months of the year and lowest during the cold months. The following indicates expected demand during the next year:

Month	Sales Forecast	Month	Sales Forecast	Month	Sales Forecast
Jan.	3,000	May	4,800	Sept.	4,000
Feb.	3,500	June	5,000	Oct.	3,500
Mar.	4,000	July	5,200	Nov.	3,000
Apr.	4,500	Aug.	4,500	Dec.	3,000

In the past, FyreGlow has produced a constant 4,000 units per month by maintaining a work force of twenty employees, with each employee producing 200 units per month. As a result, the company has incurred large inventory carrying costs at $2 per unit per month. Now, however, FyreGlow is considering offering discounts during the cold months to level out demand. How much discount per unit would FyreGlow be willing to offer to offset its current inventory carrying costs?

22. Suppose the FyreGlow Company in problem 21 has decided it wants to consider producing a complementary seasonal product during the cold months and

chooses to make fireplace inserts. It is expected that each employee will be able to produce fifty fireplace inserts per month.

a. How many employees will be needed to meet demand for barbecue grills without stockpiling?

b. Based on the answer from part a, what is the number of fireplace inserts that can be produced each month?

Data Sets for Computer Solution

1. The North Pole Snow Shovel Company makes only one product, aluminum snow shovels. The company is currently developing a production plan for the next six months and has the following demand forecast:

Month	July	Aug.	Sept.	Oct.	Nov.	Dec.
Demand Forecast	1,000	5,000	20,000	40,000	50,000	50,000

Each snow shovel requires one hour of production time to make. Each hour of regular-time production costs $8, and each overtime hour costs $12. The following indicates the hours of production time that are expected to be available each month:

Month	July	Aug.	Sept.	Oct.	Nov.	Dec.
Regular	5,000	5,000	40,000	40,000	40,000	40,000
Overtime	2,000	2,000	20,000	20,000	20,000	20,000

It costs $1 per month to store a snow shovel in inventory. The company wants to satisfy demand in each month and will not tolerate back orders or lost sales. What production plan will minimize total costs over the planning horizon?

2. The Batestown Furniture Company manufactures two products, sofas and chairs. Each sofa requires twenty-five hours of production time, and each chair requires fifteen hours. Regular-time production costs $10 per hour, and overtime costs $15 per hour. The demand forecast of each item for the next five months is shown below.

Month	Jan.	Feb.	Mar.	Apr.	May
Sofas	200	250	300	200	150
Chairs	450	500	700	500	400

The company expects to have the following production time (hours) available each month:

Month	Jan.	Feb.	Mar.	Apr.	May
Regular	15,000	15,000	15,000	12,000	12,000
Overtime	7,000	7,000	7,000	5,000	5,000

It costs $50 to store a sofa and $25 to store a chair in inventory each month. All expected demand must be satisfied. How many of each product should be produced each month to minimize total costs?

MINI-CASES

Dylex, Ltd.

Dylex, Ltd., is a Toronto-based operator of apparel chain stores. Like other apparel merchandisers, Dylex has begun to realize that fashion changes quickly, and that word about it spreads much faster than it did before cable television was available. While it used to take a year for word of New York fashions to reach the Midwest, people in Des Moines, Iowa, know what's hot in New York and Paris right now—and they want the same thing. To stay competitive, Dylex must react to fashion changes quickly. It must also know what customers want.

At the same time, Dylex has to be careful about what it carries in stock. Too many of a slow-moving item can mean disaster. Although the company used to pay 6 percent interest on borrowed money, it is now getting a break to pay 11 or 12 percent. Every item carried in stock for an extra month costs money.

On the other hand, keeping track of inventory has become a time-consuming and expensive task. With 1,000 stores and 80,000 different products, Dylex has found it hard to keep track of what is selling and what isn't. By the time it can react, competitors might have already reduced their prices on items that aren't moving.

1. What is the organization's apparent competitive strategy?

2. What would you say are some order-winning criteria for Dylex?

3. In developing its aggregate plan, what would be important criteria for Dylex to consider?

4. In developing its aggregate plan, Dylex must consider that although it is a service organization, it can carry inventory. Thus, staffing of stores and inventory are not directly related. How would this affect the aggregate plan?

5. What are some proactive strategies Dylex could use to shift demand?

Farquhar Industries, Inc.

Farquhar Industries, Inc., is a medium-size producer of custom metal products. The company recently got a contract to make the chassis for a well-known microcomputer. This part will be produced using dedicated, highly automated equipment. But the company frequently gets contracts to make special orders of custom products. These are usually produced on general-purpose equipment and involve a high degree of skilled labor. For medium-range planning purposes, the company divides its products according to the type of process required—job shop or line flow. Further, demand requirements for the job shop are stated in terms of hours because of the large number of different products produced, each requiring various amounts of processing time. On the other hand, the line-flow product demand is stated in terms of units because the production rate is relatively constant for these items. The forecasted demand in each area for the coming year is shown below.

Month	Manual Operation Demand Forecast (Hours)	Automatic Operation Demand Forecast (Units)
January	1,800	6,000
February	1,500	4,000
March	1,900	5,000
April	1,600	6,000
May	2,000	5,000
June	2,200	6,000
July	2,000	7,000
August	1,800	6,000
September	1,700	5,000
October	1,800	6,000
November	2,000	8,000
December	1,500	6,000

Normally, both operations work eight hours per day, five days per week. The automatic operation produces at an average rate of forty units per hour. Any time that the process is operating, five employees who earn $12.50 per hour must be present. Work on products requiring manual operations is a little different. Each employee there earns an average of $16.00 per hour, and there are currently ten employees. Extra employees can be hired in that area, but the cost of advertising, interviewing, and so on is about $500 per employee hired. Any employees laid off receive one month's pay as compensation. Overtime work is paid at a 50 percent premium and is limited to two hours per day on weekdays and four hours on Saturday.

Bill Dixon is production manager for Farquhar. He is working on developing an aggregate plan for the coming year and has two major concerns. First, the company's relations with its employees have been good, but there is some talk of unionizing. Too many layoffs could lead to more than talk. Second, the cost of carrying inventory has been increasing. Custom-made products are not inventoried, but high-volume products are inventoried at an average cost of $1.50 per unit per month. Carrying cost is a major concern with 2,000 units now in stock.

Suppose you are Bill Dixon. Develop an aggregate plan that meets Farquhar's company objectives, and determine the total costs associated with that plan.

SELECTED BIBLIOGRAPHY

Burch, Earl E.; Oliff, Michael D.; and Sumichrast, Robert T. "Linking Level Requirements in Production Planning and Scheduling." *Production and Inventory Management* 28, no. 2 (1987): 123–131.

Connell, Bertrum, C.; Adam, Everett, E., Jr.; and Moore, Aimee N. "Aggregate Planning in a Health Care Foodservice System with Varying Technologies." *Journal of Operations Management* 5, no. 1 (1984): 41–55.

Hayes, Robert H., and Wheelwright, Steven C. *Restoring Our Competitive Edge: Competing Through Manufacturing*. New York: Wiley, 1984.

Hill, Terry. *Manufacturing Strategy: Text and Cases*. Homewood, Ill.: Irwin, 1989.

Judson, Arnold S. "Productivity Strategy and Business Strategy: Two Sides of the Same Coin." *Interfaces* 14, no. 1 (January–February 1984): 103–115.

Mangiameli, P., and Krajewski, L. "The Effects of Workforce Strategies on Manufacturing Operations." *Journal of Operations Management* 3, no. 4 (August 1983): 183–196.

Skinner, Wickham. "Operations Technology: Blind Spot in Strategic Management." *Interfaces,* 14, no. 1 January–February 1984): 116–125.

Vollmann, Thomas E.; Berry, William L.; and Whybark, D. Clay. *Manufacturing Planning and Control Systems.* 2d ed. Homewood, Ill.: Dow Jones–Irwin, 1987.

Wheelwright, Steven C. "Reflecting Corporate Strategy in Manufacturing Decisions." *Business Horizons,* February 1978: 57–66.

Wheelwright, Steven C., and Hayes, Robert H. "Competing Through Manufacturing." *Harvard Business Review* 63, no. 1 (January–February 1985): 99–109.

Chapter 10 Supplement

Linear Programming

SUPPLEMENT OUTLINE

Introduction

Formulating the Problem Mathematically

Solving the Mathematical Problem
Graphical Solution Procedure
Applications of Computer Procedures

Limitations and Extensions of Linear Programming

LEARNING OBJECTIVES

After completing this supplement, you should be able to

- Formulate a resource allocation problem mathematically.
- Solve a linear programming problem with two variables, using the graphical method.
- Use a computer program to solve problems with two or more variables.
- Interpret the output from a computer program for linear programming.

INTRODUCTION

The techniques and ideas discussed in Chapter 10 give us ways of planning for resource requirements. However, they do not necessarily tell us how to allocate resources to competing activities. For example, a company may not have sufficient capacity to produce all the end items it would like. Which items should be produced? Or suppose that additional capacity can be added through overtime, an additional shift, or subcontracting. Which of those alternatives should be used, or should they be combined in some way? In both of those questions, the problem is to determine how best to allocate scarce resources.

One management-science technique that can be used to solve resource allocation problems is linear programming. **Linear programming** is a mathematical technique that can solve any resource allocation problem as long as that problem can be stated in terms of linear functions—that is, functions of the form $ax = b$. In solving resource allocation problems, a series of steps must be followed. These steps are listed below and will be described further in the following sections.

1. Formulate the problem mathematically.
2. Solve the mathematical problem.
3. Translate the mathematical solution into real terms.

FORMULATING THE PROBLEM MATHEMATICALLY

To formulate a linear programming problem mathematically, it is necessary to convert the problem statement into a particular mathematical form. A linear programming problem formulation always includes variables, an objective function, and constraints. **Variables,** such as X_1 and X_2, are used to represent things we want to determine—such as number of units to produce or overtime hours to be worked. The **objective function** is a linear function that includes the variables and indicates what is to be achieved. The **constraints** are linear functions, also stated in terms of the variables, that limit our actions.

Example

A company produces two types of racquetball racquets, fiberglass and graphite, using the same equipment for both. Each racquet requires two operations: forming and stringing. During the next month, there will be only 240 hours of forming time and 300 hours of stringing time available. Each fiberglass racquet requires .3 hour of forming time and .6 hour of stringing time. Each graphite racquet takes .4 hour to form and .4 hour to string. If the company earns a profit of \$10 per fiberglass racquet and \$12 per graphite racquet, how many of each should be produced to maximize profit, assuming the company can sell whatever it produces?

Let X_1 = the number of fiberglass racquets to produce, and

X_2 = the number of graphite racquets to produce.

The objective is to maximize profit (Z), which can be stated as

$$\text{Maximize } Z = 10X_1 + 12X_2 \qquad \text{(objective function)}$$

The constraints will be stated in terms of hours available for forming and stringing. Each type of racquet will use a certain amount of this time, which cannot be exceeded. So the constraints will be

$$.3X_1 + .4X_2 \leq 240 \qquad \text{(forming time constraint)}$$

$$.6X_1 + .4X_2 \leq 300 \qquad \text{(stringing time constraint)}$$

In addition, it would not make sense to produce a negative number of racquets, so we must also state that

$$X_1 \geq 0, X_2 \geq 0 \qquad \text{(non-negativity restrictions)}$$

SOLVING THE MATHEMATICAL PROBLEM

Graphical Solution Procedure

Because the mathematical formulation of a linear programming problem is stated in terms of linear functions—that is, functions that do not include powers of variables (e.g., X^2 or X^3) or variables multiplied together (e.g., X_1X_2)—it is possible to graph these functions as straight lines on a graph of X_2 and X_1. This graph may then be used to solve the problem by following these steps:

1. Set up the graph so X_1 is on the horizontal axis and X_2 on the vertical axis.
2. Graph each constraint.
   - **a.** Write the constraint as an equation.
   - **b.** Set X_1 equal to zero, and solve for X_2. Plot this point.
   - **c.** Set X_2 equal to zero, and solve for X_1. Plot this point.
   - **d.** Connect the two points with a straight line.
   - **e.** Set both X_1 and X_2 equal to zero, and determine which side of the line satisfies the inequality condition.
3. Find the optimal point.
   - **a.** Determine the feasible region where all constraints are satisfied.
   - **b.** Choose an arbitrary objective function value.
   - **c.** Graph the objective function equation as in step 2.
   - **d.** Move the objective function line parallel to itself to increase (maximization) or decrease (minimization) until a corner point of the feasible region is reached. That corner point will be the optimal point.

Example

Suppose we wish to solve the racquetball racquet problem formulated in the previous example. That formulation was

Maximize $Z = 10X_1 + 12X_2$ (objective function)

subject to

$.3X_1 + .4X_2 \leq 240$ (forming time constraint)

$.6X_1 + .4X_2 \leq 300$ (stringing time constraint)

$X_1 \geq 0, X_2 \geq 0$ (non-negativity restrictions)

Step 1: Set up the graph. We label the horizontal axis X_1 and the vertical axis X_2.

Step 2: Graph each constraint.

a. For the first constraint (forming time), we write this as the equation $.3X_1 + .4X_2 = 240$.

b. Setting X_1 equal to zero, we have $.4X_2 = 240$. Dividing both sides of the equation by .4, this becomes $X_2 = 600$. This point is plotted on the vertical (X_2) axis of the graph.

c. Setting X_2 equal to zero, we have $.3X_1 = 240$. Dividing both sides of the equation by .3, this becomes $X_1 = 800$, which is plotted on the X_1 axis.

d. The two points are connected by a straight line.

e. If we set X_1 and X_2 each equal to zero, then the first constraint becomes $0 + 0 \leq 240$. Since this condition is true, then any point on the line or on the same side of it as the origin (the point where $X_1 = 0$ and $X_2 = 0$) will satisfy the constraint. The result is shown in Exhibit 10.17.

The other constraint may be graphed in a similar manner. The non-negativity restrictions are satisfied by points on the axes or to the right of the X_2 axis and above the X_1 axis.

Exhibit 10.17 Graphing Constraints

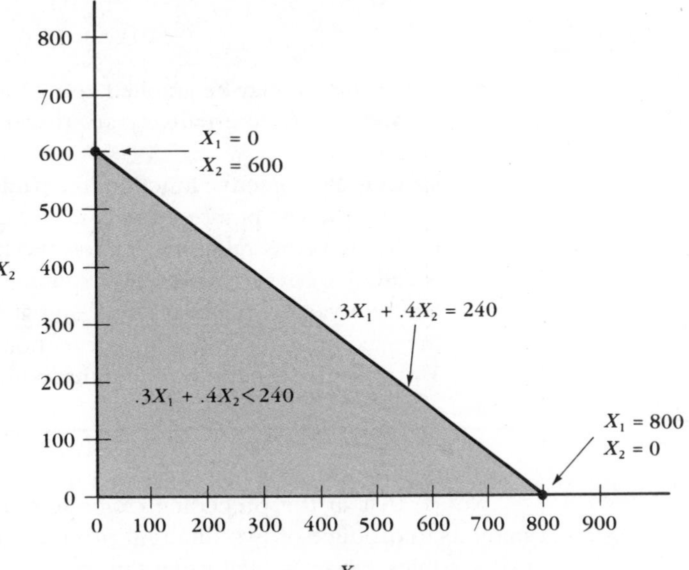

Exhibit 10.18 Finding the Optimal Point

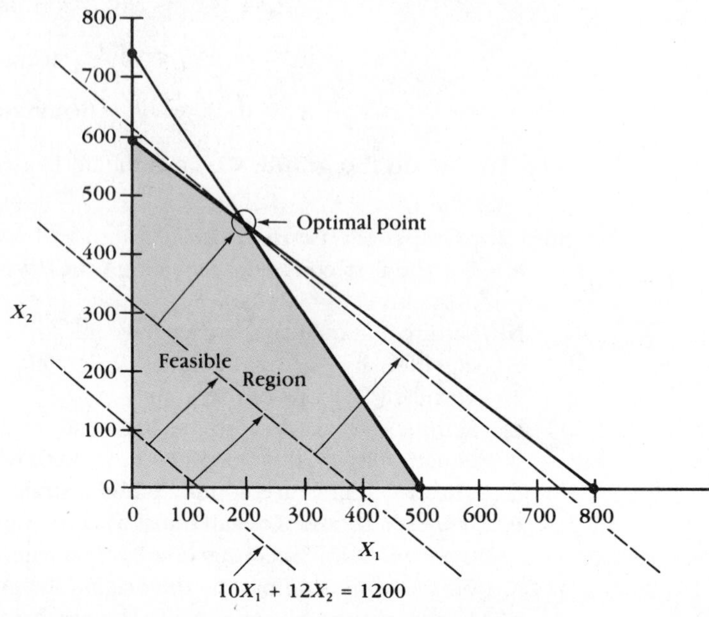

Step 3: Find the optimal point.

a. The **feasible region** is the area that satisfies all constraints. This area is highlighted in Exhibit 10.18.

b. Suppose we arbitrarily decide to let the objective function equal 1,200. Thus, the objective function equation will become

$$10X_1 + 12X_2 = 1{,}200$$

c. This equation may be graphed, using the procedure from step 2 in which X_1 and X_2 are alternatively set to zero. This line is shown in Exhibit 10.18.

d. Moving the objective function line parallel to itself away from the origin, we find the last point of the feasible region that the line touches occurs where two constraint lines intersect. This intersection of constraint lines is called a **corner point** or **extreme point.** The maximum objective function value will always be found at a corner point. For this problem, the maximum is found at the corner point where $X_1 = 200$ and $X_2 = 450$. The objective function value at that point is $10(200) + 12(450) = 7{,}400$.

Notice that in the preceding example our concern was with determining amounts to produce of two different products. However, any problem involving two variables can be solved using this graphical procedure.

Applications of Computer Procedures

The graphical procedure just described works fine for two variables. But to solve problems of more than two variables, a mathematical procedure called the simplex method must be used. While it is possible to perform the simplex calculations by hand, numerous computer programs are available to do the grunt work for you. Therefore, we will not discuss the details of the simplex algorithm in this book. However, we will show the input and output formats for one popular computer package that includes linear programming.

Input to Linear Programming Software

Most available computer software for linear programming allows you to enter the problem just as you formulated it. In some cases, you need to enter only the coefficients of each variable and the right-hand side values. For example, Exhibit 10.19 shows the data input format for the STORM linear programming module. The data used in this example are those from the racquetball racquet production planning problem we just solved graphically.

Notice that after specifying the number of variables and constraints, and after indicating whether the objective is to be maximized or minimized, we have to enter only objective function and constraint coefficients and right-hand-side values. Notice also that we did not have to enter the non-negativity restrictions because all computer software for linear programming takes these into account automatically. However, STORM also allows us to override this restriction in the row labeled VARBL TYPE. In this problem, the non-negativity restrictions remain in effect, as indicated by POS.

Exhibit 10.19 STORM Computer Program Input for Linear Programming Problem

```
                STORM DATA SET LISTING
         LINEAR & INTEGER PROGRAMMING DATA SET

Problem Description Parameters
Title : Racquetball Racquet Production Problem
Number of variables        :          2
Number of constraints      :          2
Starting solution given    :         NO
Objective type (MAX/MIN)   :        MAX

ROW LABEL FIBERGLASS   GRAPHITE CONST TYPE      R H S      RANGE
OBJ COEFF        10.        12.       XXXX       XXXX       XXXX
FORMING          0.3        0.4         <=       240.          .
STRINGING        0.6        0.4         <=       300.          .
VARBL TYPE       POS        POS       XXXX       XXXX       XXXX
LOWR BOUND         .          .       XXXX       XXXX       XXXX
UPPR BOUND         .          .       XXXX       XXXX       XXXX
INIT SOLN         0.         0.       XXXX       XXXX       XXXX
```

Exhibit 10.20 STORM Computer Program Output for Linear Programming Problem

```
          Racquetball Racquet Production Problem
            OPTIMAL SOLUTION - DETAILED REPORT
      Variable          Value          Cost     Red. cost    Status
1   FIBERGLASS       200.0000       10.0000      0.0000       Basic
2     GRAPHITE       450.0000       12.0000      0.0000       Basic

Slack Variables
3      FORMING         0.0000        0.0000     -26.6667 Lower bound
4    STRINGING         0.0000        0.0000      -3.3333 Lower bound

    Constraint  Type         RHS            Slack    Shadow price
1      FORMING   <=       240.0000         0.0000         26.6667
2    STRINGING   <=       300.0000         0.0000          3.3333

Objective Function Value = 7400
```

Interpreting the Computer Output

Exhibit 10.20 shows the output provided by STORM for the racquet production problem. As indicated by the column labeled Value, the optimal solution is to produce 200 fiberglass racquets and 450 graphite racquets. However, this output provides additional information not obtained from the graphical solution.

Slack Variables. These indicate how much unused capacity is available in the ≤ constraints. As can be seen in Exhibit 10.20, all available time for forming and stringing is being fully utilized.

Reduced Cost. Values in this column indicate how much the objective function would change if a variable with a value currently equal to zero had its value increased by one unit. Thus, if one hour of slack time were left available for forming, the objective function value would *decrease* by $26.6667.

Shadow Price. This indicates how much the objective function would increase if the right-hand side of a constraint were increased by one unit. In this problem, the objective function will increase by $3.3333 if we add another hour of stringing time.

LIMITATIONS AND EXTENSIONS OF LINEAR PROGRAMMING

The idea of using linear programming for resource allocation problems is fine, but it has two primary disadvantages. First, linear programming requires that all functions be linear. This can be a problem because in many real situations, the costs are nonlinear. For example, the costs dealt with in aggregate planning often are not linear. In hiring a skilled machinist, a company may have to spend X dollars. But finding ten skilled machinists may be much more difficult and cost much more than $10X$ dollars. Likewise, the unit cost of holding inventory may increase greatly due to greater space limitations and more possibilities for damage as the total quantity of inventory increases.

Second, linear programming requires that there be one objective, and that this objective be stated as a linear mathematical function. Many times, companies will have several objectives. For example, a company might want to minimize variations in work-force size, but also keep inventory below a certain level. Other possible objectives, such as limiting overtime work to no more than five days in a row, can be even more difficult to handle with linear programming. In other instances, there may be objectives, such as improving customer relations or presenting a good corporate image, that are often difficult to quantify.

The best approach is probably to use linear programming as one input to the aggregate planning process. But the manager, not the technique, must make the final decision. The manager should evaluate how important cost minimization is or how restrictive the use of linear functions would be in determining the importance that should be placed on the linear programming solution.

Further, various extensions of linear programming are available, although we will not explain them in this text. For example, *goal programming* can be used when more than one objective exists. Problems involving a nonlinear objective function or nonlinear constraints can also be solved using the techniques of *nonlinear programming.* Many excellent textbooks that explain and demonstrate these techniques are available in the fields of management science and operations research.

SUMMARY

- Linear programming can be used to solve resource allocation problems that can be stated as linear functions.
- A linear programming problem has one objective function that is to be either maximized or minimized and a set of constraints that may be equations or inequalities.
- For problems of two variables, each axis of a graph corresponds to one of the variables.
- After graphing the constraints, a feasible region is identified as satisfying all constraints.
- The optimal solution is found at a corner of the feasible region.
- Problems with more than two variables may be solved using the simplex method, which is usually programmed on a computer.
- The value of a slack variable in computer output indicates how much unused capacity is available for its associated constraint.
- Reduced cost shows how much the objective function would change if a variable with a value of zero had its value increased by one.
- Shadow price indicates how much the objective function would increase if the right-hand side of a constraint were increased by one unit.

SOLVED PROBLEM

The Lee Key Boat Company can make two different types of wooden boats: dinghies and skiffs. Each dinghy it makes can be sold for a profit of $30 and each skiff for a profit of $50. Both types of boat must go through three operations. The following table lists the processing time at each operation and the total time available during the planning period:

	Processing Time (Hrs./Unit)		
Operation	**Dinghies**	**Skiffs**	***Total Time Available (Hrs.)***
Cutting	1	2	40
Assembly	2.5	1	50
Painting	1	1	25

Use linear programming to determine how many of each boat should be made to maximize profit.

Solution

Step 1: Formulate the problem mathematically:

$$\text{Let } X_1 = \text{the number of dinghies to produce, and}$$

$$X_2 = \text{the number of skiffs to produce.}$$

The mathematical formulation is

$$\text{Maximize } 30X_1 + 50X_2 \quad \text{(objective to maximize profit)}$$

subject to

$$1X_1 + 2X_2 \leq 40 \quad \text{(constraint on cutting time)}$$

$$2.5X_1 + 1X_2 \leq 50 \quad \text{(constraint on assembly time)}$$

$$1X_1 + 1X_2 \leq 25 \quad \text{(constraint on painting time)}$$

$$X_1, X_2 \geq\geqslant 0 \quad \text{(non-negativity restrictions)}$$

Step 2: Solve the mathematical problem. Since this involves two variables, it can be solved graphically, as shown in the graph below.

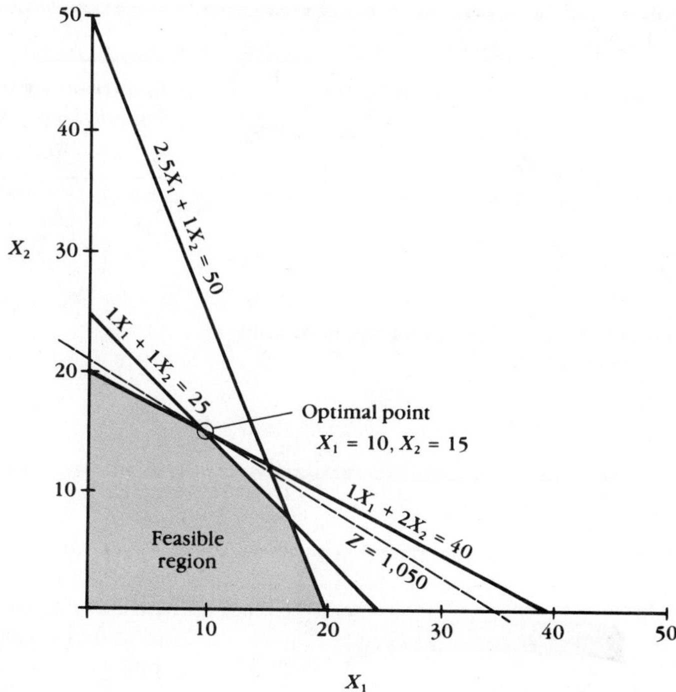

Step 3: Translate the mathematical solution into real terms. The graphical solution indicates that the optimal point is $X_1 = 10, X_2 = 15$. This means Lee Key should produce ten dinghies and fifteen skiffs. Such a plan will use up all cutting and paint but will leave ten hours available in assembly. Total profit will be \$1,050.

QUESTIONS

1. Explain what is meant by a linear function.

2. Why can't linear programming problems of four variables be solved graphically?

3. Define the following terms:

a. Corner point
b. Extreme point
c. Feasible region

4. Why can linear programming problems have only one objective function?

5. Explain some advantages and disadvantages of using linear programming for aggregate planning.

6. Define the following terms:

a. Slack variable
b. Reduced cost
c. Shadow price

PROBLEMS

1. Solve the following linear programming problem graphically:

$$\text{Maximize } 3X_1 + 5X_2$$

subject to

$$1X_1 + 2X_2 \leqslant 40$$

$$2X_1 + 1X_2 \leqslant 50$$

$$X_1, X_2 \geqslant 0$$

2. Solve the following linear programming problem graphically:

$$\text{Minimize } 5X_1 + 4X_2$$

subject to

$$4X_1 + 6X_2 \geqslant 12$$

$$12X_1 + 6X_2 \geqslant 24$$

$$3X_1 + 4X_2 \leqslant 24$$

$$X_1, X_2 \geqslant 0$$

3. The Bunch-a-Burgers Restaurant uses its french fryer for making both french fries and onion rings. Each batch of onion rings takes three minutes, and each batch of french fries take five minutes. The restaurant earns a profit of $5 for every batch of french fries and $7 for every batch of onion rings. In order to satisfy customers, Bunch-a-Burgers must make at least eight batches of french fries and five batches of onion rings each lunch hour. Assuming that whatever quantity they make can be sold, how many batches of each should be made to maximize the lunch-hour profit?

4. A company that manufactures printing equipment makes three different parts that can each be machined on either of two machines, A and B. Machine A is older and takes longer to process each part, but costs less to operate. It costs $70 per hour to run machine A and $100 per hour to run machine B. The processing time for each part on each machine is shown below.

	Processing Time (Hours/Unit)	
Part	**Machine A**	**Machine B**
1073	.3	.2
432	.5	.4
1598	.2	.1
Time available	40 hours	40 hours

The company must make at least 80 of part 1073, 40 of part 432, and 100 of part 1598. Formulate this as a linear programming problem to determine how many of each part should be produced on each machine to minimize total cost, while meeting production requirements. (Hint: Use variable X_{ij} to represent the number of units of part i produced on machine j.)

5. A company produces three products—A, B, and C—and can sell as much of each as it can produce. The contribution margin of each product is, respectively, $35, $42, and $53. The three products must be processed through four different departments, although each product does not go through all departments. The processing time required for each product in each department and the departmental capacities are as follows:

	Processing Requirement (Hours)			
Department	**A**	**B**	**C**	***Hours Available***
100	3		4	225
200	2	1	4	250

Department	Processing Requirement (Hours) A	B	C	Hours Available
300		2	2	150
400	3	2		175

Formulate as a linear programming problem to maximize the contribution margin with available capacity.

6. The Doggone Good Pet Food Company wants to develop a blend of dog food that will meet certain nutritional requirements at the lowest cost. The company has three ingredients to blend together: X, Y, and Z. Each pound of ingredient X costs $.75, each pound of ingredient Y costs $.62, and each pound of ingredient Z costs $.44.

In a five-pound bag of dog food, the company wants at least 2,000 grams of protein, at least 1,000 grams of fiber, and no more than 500 grams of fat. Each ingredient provides the following:

	Ingredient X	Y	Z
Grams of protein per pound	700	500	400
Grams of fiber per pound	300	400	400
Grams of fat per pound	75	100	125

Formulate the problem to determine how many pounds of each ingredient should be added to make a total of five pounds, while meeting the nutritional requirements at minimum cost.

7. An advertising agency is developing an ad campaign for one of its clients. This campaign will involve advertisements in newspapers, on radio, and on television. Each dollar spent on newspaper ads produces three exposure units, each dollar spent on radio ads produces five exposure units, and each dollar spent on television produces six exposure units. The client has specified that only $50,000 is available for the ad campaign, and that at least 200,000 exposure units must be generated. Further, no more than twice as much can be spent on television as on newspaper ads, and at least $10,000 must be spent on radio. Formulate this as a linear programming problem to maximize exposure units within the available budget.

Data Sets for Computer Solution

1. Solve the linear programming formulation of problem 4.

2. Solve problem 3, and determine the value of an extra minute of cooking time on the french fryer.

3. In the solution of problem 4,

   a. How much capacity is unused?

   b. What is the value of additional time on each machine?

4. Solve the formulation of problem 5, and determine the value of an extra hour available in department 200.

5. Solve problem 6, and determine how much the cost of making a five-pound bag of dog food will increase if at least one pound of ingredient Y must be included.

SELECTED BIBLIOGRAPHY

Anderson, David R.; Sweeney, Dennis J.; and Williams, Thomas A. *An Introduction to Management Science: Quantitative Approaches to Decision Making*. 5th ed. St. Paul, Minn.: West, 1988.

Eppen, Gary D.; Gould, J. F.; and Schmidt, C. P. *Introductory Management Science*. 2d ed. Englewood Cliffs, N.J.: Prentice-Hall, 1987.

Hooker, J. N. "Karmarkar's Linear Programming Algorithm." *Interfaces* 16, no. 4 (July–August 1986): 75–90.

Leff, H. Stephen; Dada, Maqbool; and Graves, Stephen C. "An LP Planning Model for a Mental Health Community Support System." *Management Science* 32, no. 2 (February 1986): 139–155.

Oliff, Michael, and Burch, Earl. "Multiproduct Production Scheduling at Owens-Corning Fiberglass." *Interfaces* 15, no. 5 (September–October 1985): 25–34.

Chapter 11

Planning for Material and Resource Requirements

CHAPTER OUTLINE

LEARNING OBJECTIVES

After completing this chapter, you should be able to

- Describe the relationships among aggregate planning, master scheduling, MRP, and capacity planning.
- Show how a master schedule is developed from an aggregate plan.
- Calculate projected on-hand inventory and available-to-promise quantities.
- Determine when to schedule a master schedule quantity.
- Explain some characteristics of master scheduling in practice.
- Use the method of overall factors to estimate capacity requirements based on a master schedule.
- Describe several ways to adjust for insufficient capacity.
- Explain how the bill of materials is adapted to MRP.
- Use MRP to develop planned order releases for items at all levels of the bill of materials.
- Develop a load report and load profile based on MRP output, routings, and labor standards.
- Explain how closed-loop MRP improves plan validity.
- Describe the characteristics of MRP II.
- Discuss how MRP can be used for service organizations.
- Use distribution requirements planning to plan orders from warehouses and distribution centers.
- Discuss the ethical aspects of MRP and capacity planning.

OPERATIONS IN ACTION

Boeing: Planning for Capacity and Material Requirements

Boeing is the company that manufactured the first jet passenger plane, the Boeing 707, in 1958. Since then, the company has maintained its lead in the aircraft industry against such competitors as McDonnell Douglas, Lockheed, and the European consortium Airbus Industrie. But, today, Boeing faces the problem of meeting huge demand for its highly successful 747.

In the early 1980s, Boeing faced uncertain demand for its planes. A world oil crisis, recession, and the uncertain future of airline deregulation forced it to lay off 20,000 experienced employees. Today, Boeing is experiencing extremely strong demand for its products, especially the 747 jumbo jet. However, this demand has caused problems due to Boeing's smaller work force with a large number of new, inexperienced employees.

When airlines order new aircraft, they usually order them in bunches, waiting several years or more until placing another order. Fortunately—or unfortunately—for Boeing, right now a lot of airlines are ordering a lot of planes. While this high demand creates a rosy picture, it also produces major headaches for production in meeting that demand.

For example, Boeing buys the lavatories for its 747s from Jamco, a Japanese manufacturer. Deliveries from Jamco have been behind schedule, meaning that completion of the planes is held up because lavatories are unavailable when needed.

In this chapter, you will learn about techniques that companies today are using to plan for capacity and material requirements. While such techniques may not avoid all the problems Boeing faces, they can help a company identify ways of dealing with those problems.[1]

INTRODUCTION

The preceding chapter dealt with how a company moves from its strategic plan to a medium-range operations plan, or aggregate plan. The aggregate plan indicates how the organization intends to meet demand for the good or service it provides. Thus, the aggregate plan is a statement of planned output, inventory, and/or staffing levels, usually by product groups on a monthly basis.

Because of its broad, general nature, the aggregate plan cannot be implemented directly. Instead, another, more detailed plan must usually be developed based on the aggregate plan. This latter plan is called a master production schedule.

In meeting the demand for its goods or services, an organization will need to use various resources and materials. However, if sufficient quantities of those resources and materials are not available when needed, customer service will suffer. Therefore, when developing a master production schedule, a company must ensure that the schedule is realistic in terms of its resource and material requirements.

In this chapter, we explain how to develop a master production schedule. Further, we indicate how an organization can determine the resource and material requirements of that schedule and then plan to have the appropriate quantity of materials and resources available at the right time.

MASTER PRODUCTION SCHEDULING

The master schedule—or master production schedule (MPS)—is based on the medium-range operations plan, or aggregate plan, discussed in Chapter 10. While that plan was "aggregated" in terms of product groups, the master schedule is "disaggregated." The **master schedule** is a specific statement of exactly what, usually stated in terms of individual end items or product models, will be produced in each time period. Usually these time periods are weeks, although they may be days or even hours. The master schedule is thus a detailed extension of the medium-range operations plan, or aggregate plan.

Developing the MPS

Because the master schedule is a statement of exactly what will be produced, the company must be sure of two things:

1. The master schedule must satisfy the needs of marketing.
2. The master schedule must be "doable" by operations.

Developing a master schedule that is close to the aggregate plan, yet that still satisfies marketing and operations, is no easy task. The aggregate plan was developed based on a strategy that maintained acceptable inventory and work-force levels. The master schedule should still be based on that strategy, but must now do so for individual end items. In addition, the master schedule must not place more capacity demands on any machine or work center than can reasonably be met by existing capacity.

Due to the difficulties involved in developing a good master production schedule, the job is usually done by experienced individuals called **master schedulers.** But because it is likely you will someday have contact with a master schedule, we will show you how they are developed under two different situations. Following the approach taken by real companies, we will begin with the aggregate plan.

We will use the Maine Woods Company, which produces wooden toys, as an example. The company's production process is quite labor intensive and relies heavily on skilled woodworkers who use such equipment as saws, lathes, routers, and jointers to make most of the parts that go into the company's finished products.

The company's medium-range, or aggregate, production plan is developed on a monthly basis for one year into the future. For planning purposes, the company's forty-eight different products are grouped by product characteristics into three product families: wheel goods, blocks, and baby toys. It is these families that are reflected in the aggregate plan. Exhibit 11.1 shows that plan for the wheel-goods products only.

As you can see, the company has developed an aggregate plan that emphasizes maintaining a constant work force. Due to the high skill level required of its employees, Maine Woods does not want to use hiring and layoffs. Instead, inventory is built up in anticipation of high demand during late summer and fall when the retail stores that sell Maine Woods' toys order in preparation for Christmas. Overtime has been planned only as a necessity in October and November when no inventory will be available to draw on.

Exhibit 11.1 Maine Woods Co. Aggregate Plan, Wheel-Goods Product Group

Month	Demand Forecast	Regular-Time Production	Overtime Production	Beginning Inventory	Ending Inventory
January	1,800	2,000		0	200
February	1,700	2,000		200	500
March	1,800	2,000		500	700
April	1,500	2,000		700	1,200
May	1,800	2,000		1,200	1,400
June	1,900	2,000		1,400	1,500
July	2,000	2,000		1,500	1,500
August	2,500	2,000		1,500	1,000
September	2,500	2,000		1,000	500
October	2,900	2,000	400	500	0
November	2,400	2,000	400	0	0
December	2,000	2,000		0	0

Matching the Master Schedule to the Aggregate Plan

Referring again to the Maine Woods aggregate plan shown in Exhibit 11.1, you can see that during the early part of the year, production exceeds demand, thus building up inventory. During that time period, the company's objectives for the master production schedule will be to

- Produce quantities that will match the aggregate plan.
- Produce each individual product in proportion to its expected demand.
- Schedule production so available capacity is not exceeded.

The wheel-goods product group consists of three products: tricycles, toy wagons, and scooters. Past experience indicates that orders for these will be divided so that about half are for tricycles and the remaining orders are equally divided between wagons and scooters. Thus, in January, the planned production of 2,000 units should be divided so 1,000 tricycles, 500 toy wagons, and 500 scooters are produced. The same should also be done for February and March.

Exhibit 11.2 shows one possible master schedule that satisfies the preceding requirements. Notice that the total production of all three products in each month matches the aggregate plan for that month. Further, production of each individual product is spread out evenly so the production facilities will not be overloaded in some weeks and underloaded in others.

The master schedule shown in Exhibit 11.2 could be extended across the first nine months of the year because planned production in each of those months is the same. However, in October, planned production increases to 2,400 units. To meet this increase, we can simply spread the difference evenly across that month, keeping each product's proportion of the total the same as before. Exhibit 11.3 shows the master schedule with increased output for October.

Taking Customer Orders into Account

The master schedules just developed were based strictly on the aggregate plan and historical information about demand for each product. However, customer

Exhibit 11.2 Maine Woods Co. Master Production Schedule, Wheel-Goods Product Group: Constant Planned Production

	Month	January				February				March			
	Week	1	2	3	4	5	6	7	8	9	10	11	12
Product	Tricycle	250	250	250	250	250	250	250	250	250	250	250	250
	Toy wagon	250		250		250		250		250		250	
	Scooter		250		250		250		250		250		250
	Totals	2,000				2,000				2,000			

Exhibit 11.3 Maine Woods Co. Master Production Schedule, Wheel-Goods Product Group

	Month	September				October			
	Week	37	38	39	40	41	42	43	44
Product	Tricycle	250	250	250	250	300	300	300	300
	Toy wagon	250		250		300		300	
	Scooter		250		250		300		300
	Totals	2,000				2,400			

orders must enter into the process. Otherwise, we may be producing based on a plan that is no longer valid because actual demand has changed.

To show how a master schedule can be developed that takes demand into account, let's remove inventory buildup from the picture by concentrating on the company during November and December when no inventory is available and demand must be met from current production. We will also concentrate on just one product—the toy wagon.

Suppose we are in the last week of October, and our forecasts still indicate that 600 toy wagons (one-fourth of 2,400) will be ordered during November and another 500 (one-fourth of 2,000) during December. We can enter this information in Exhibit 11.4 in the Forecast demand row. However, actual customer orders may differ from the forecast. Therefore, the next row in Exhibit 11.4 indicates actual orders booked. Notice how the actual orders received decrease as we go farther into the future. As those time periods draw closer to the present, we will expect orders to increase, coming closer to the forecast.

Calculating Projected On-Hand Inventory. Because Maine Woods produces toy wagons only every other week, a key to meeting customer orders will be

Exhibit 11.4 Maine Woods Co. Master Production Schedule Based on Demand Forecast and Booked Customer Orders for Toy Wagons

On-hand inventory at end of October = 100

Month	November				December			
Week	45	46	47	48	49	50	51	52
Forecast demand	150	150	150	150	125	125	125	125
Customer orders booked	170	165	140	120	85	45	20	0
Projected on-hand inventory	230	65	−85					
Master schedule	300							

inventory on hand. For example, notice that the company has 100 toy wagons in on-hand inventory at the end of October. However, customer orders for the first week of November are 170. Therefore, unless more wagons are produced, demand cannot be met. To avoid this problem, Maine Woods has already scheduled another batch of 300 wagons for production during the first week of November, as shown in Exhibit 11.4.

To plan additional production of toy wagons, which will be scheduled in the Master schedule row of Exhibit 11.4, it will be necessary to calculate the projected on-hand inventory. We refer to this as "projected" because it is based on information currently available. As new customer orders arrive, the actual on-hand inventory each week may change.

To determine projected inventory on hand for a specific week, perform the following calculations:

1. Add either actual inventory on hand from the preceding week or projected on-hand inventory from the preceding week to any quantity shown in the Master schedule row for the week being calculated.
2. Determine the *larger* of forecast demand or customer orders booked.
3. Subtract the amount determined in step 2 from the amount in step 1. The result becomes projected on-hand inventory for the week in question.

Example

Refer to Exhibit 11.4 for Maine Woods. The projected on-hand inventory for weeks 45, 46, and 47 is calculated as follows:

Week 45:

1. Actual on-hand inventory from the preceding week (last week of October) is 100 units.
2. The master schedule amount in week 45 is 300.

3. Customer orders booked in week 45 are 170, which is larger than the forecast for that week (150).

$$\text{Projected on-hand inventory} = 100 + 300 - 170 = 230$$

Week 46:

1. Projected on-hand inventory from the preceding week (week 45) is 230 units.
2. The master schedule amount in week 46 is 0.
3. Customer orders booked in week 46 are 165, which is larger than the forecast for that week (150).

$$\text{Projected on-hand inventory} = 230 + 0 - 165 = 65$$

Week 47:

1. Projected on-hand inventory from the preceding week (week 46) is 65 units.
2. The master schedule amount in week 47 is 0.
3. Forecast demand in week 47 is 150, which is larger than the customer orders booked for that week (140).

$$\text{Projected on-hand inventory} = 65 + 0 - 150 = -85$$

Entering a Master Schedule Quantity. Whenever projected on-hand inventory becomes negative, as it has in week 47, the need for more production is indicated. Thus, a master schedule quantity must be entered for week 47.

The exact quantity to schedule will be determined on the basis of production capacity available, expected demand, and desired batch sizes. Following its procedure of producing toy wagons every other week, Maine Woods would plan to produce enough to meet demand for the next two weeks, which would be 300, based on the demand forecast shown in Exhibit 11.5. Notice that the projected on-hand inventory balance for week 47 has been recalculated, based on the new master schedule quantity.

Determining the Amount Available to Promise

We have just dealt with the problem of scheduling production to meet projected demand. However, you should keep in mind that customer orders will constantly be coming in with requests for completion of each order in a desired week. For example, suppose a customer has just contacted Maine Woods and requested fifty toy wagons to be shipped in week 46. Will the company have enough toy wagons available to meet this new order plus the existing orders for 335 already entered in weeks 45 and 46?

To determine whether new orders can be accepted within a given time period, companies calculate an available-to-promise quantity. This represents the number of units that can be promised for completion any time before the next master schedule quantity.

The available-to-promise quantity is calculated as follows:

1. In the first time period of the planning horizon, add actual on-hand inventory from the preceding time period to any master schedule quantity and then

Exhibit 11.5 Calculation of Available-to-Promise for November and December for Maine Woods Co.

On-hand inventory at end of October = 100

Month	November				December			
Week	45	46	47	48	49	50	51	52
Forecast demand	150	150	150	150	125	125	125	125
Customer orders booked	170	165	140	120	85	45	20	0
Projected on-hand inventory	230	65	215	65	190	65	190	65
Master schedule	300		300		250		250	
Available-to-promise	65		40		120		230	

subtract the sum of customer orders booked before the next master schedule quantity.

2. For subsequent weeks, calculate available-to-promise only for those weeks when a master schedule quantity is indicated. Subtract the sum of customer orders booked before the next master schedule quantity from the master schedule amount for the given week. *Do not* include projected on-hand inventory, as that amount could be used in preceding weeks if more orders are booked.

Example

Referring to the Maine Woods example shown in Exhibit 11.5, we will determine available-to-promise quantities for November.

Week 45:

Actual on-hand inventory from the preceding week (end of October) = 100. The master schedule quantity for week 45 = 300. The sum of customer orders booked before the next master schedule quantity (week 47) = 170 + 165. The available-to-promise quantity = (100 + 300) − (170 + 165) = 65

Week 46:

There is no master schedule quantity in this week, so it is skipped.

Week 47:

The master schedule amount = 300. The sum of customer orders booked before the next master schedule quantity (week 49) = 140 + 120. The available-to-promise quantity = 300 − (140 + 120) = 40

This indicates that Maine Woods can promise another sixty-five units to its customers for completion in week 45 or 46. However, based on current information, only forty more units may be promised for week 47 or 48.

Master Scheduling in Practice

Our discussion of master production scheduling thus far has been designed to give you the basics. In actual practice, the job is much more difficult and involved. In this section, we will briefly survey a few key points of which you should also be aware.

An Iterative Process

The steps we followed in the preceding section would generally lead to a "trial" MPS, not necessarily the final one. As Exhibit 11.6 indicates, after this trial master schedule is developed, a determination must be made as to whether sufficient capacity is available. Although the aggregate plan was developed to ensure that adequate overall capacity would be available, the specific mix of products and timing of production can mean that there will not be sufficient capacity in every week. This check is performed using rough-cut capacity planning, which will be discussed in the next section of this chapter.

Next, marketing must approve the master schedule. Marketing may have special promotions or other plans that must be reflected in the master schedule.

Exhibit 11.6 Iterative Process for Developing a Master Production Schedule

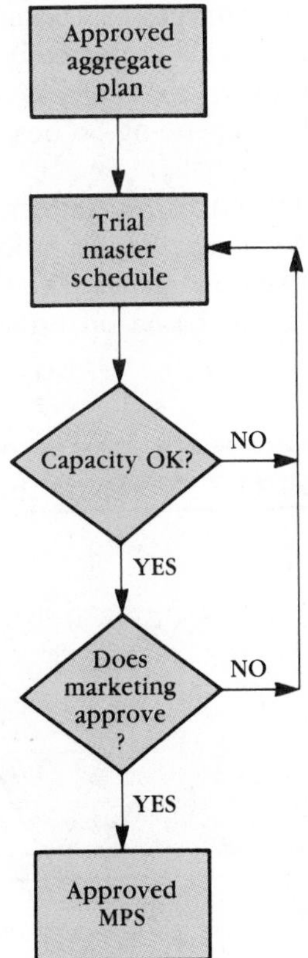

If the trial MPS does not satisfy marketing's requirements, then it must be redone. Meeting the various internal and external demands with available resources is what makes master scheduling so difficult.

Freezing the Master Schedule

An important point that must be stressed is that the plans we have been discussing are not something a company can do once a year and then put away in a drawer. Planning is a continuous process that can be thought of somewhat like rolling out a scroll. As time passes, the scroll keeps getting rolled up on the end closest to us and unrolled at the other end, so that new material is always coming into view. This idea has been referred to as "rolling through time."[2]

Obviously, forecasts far into the future will be less accurate than nearer-term forecasts. Thus, it may be necessary to make changes in planned production as the planning horizon draws nearer. For instance, a company might find that demand for one of its products is far exceeding the company's forecasts. This organization would be foolish not to alter its production plans to meet the increased demand. Thus, both the aggregate plan and the master schedule will change as time passes.

But too much change can be disruptive. For example, a company might have already hired employees and bought materials to meet its production plan. Altering that plan could mean idle employees or inventories of unused materials. To avoid such problems, many companies "freeze" their master schedule for a certain time into the future. **Freezing the master schedule** means that no further changes can be made after a certain point in time. For instance, a company may indicate that the master schedule will be frozen for one month into the future. Thus, no changes may be made once a plan gets within one month of its execution date. This is depicted in Exhibit 11.7. The master schedule is commonly frozen over several weeks or a month, although longer and shorter periods are possible depending on how easily a company can change its plans.

The Demand Management Process

In developing a master production schedule for the Maine Woods Company, we took two approaches. The first was based on producing to inventory, while the second was based on producing to customer orders. In actual practice, both

Exhibit 11.7 Freezing the Master Schedule

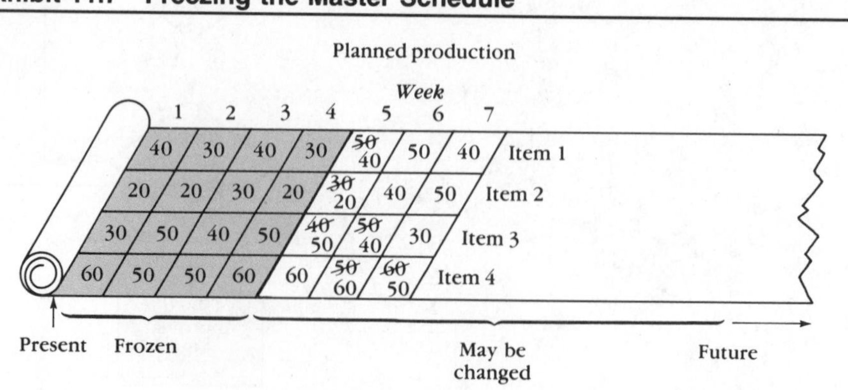

sources of demand must be considered. However, there are also other sources of demand. For example, companies that operate multiple plants often have one plant producing parts for another plant. Such orders would be identified as **interplant orders.** Further, many companies produce replacement parts for their products, such as starter motors for automobiles or blades for lawnmowers. These **service parts** requirements must also be considered. **Demand management** is the process of recognizing all such sources of demand and reflecting them in the master schedule. Such a process is depicted in Exhibit 11.8.

Planning Horizons

The aggregate plan is generally developed for a year or more into the future. However, the master schedule usually does not need to go that far, especially since it becomes more difficult to manage as the number of time periods increases. As a general rule, many companies use six months for their master schedule. However, the most important rule is that the master scheduling horizon must be at least equal to the longest cumulative lead time of any product and its component parts. In other words, enough time must be allowed from the time a master schedule quantity is entered for all parts and raw materials to be ordered from suppliers, component parts to be manufactured, and the final product to be assembled and shipped. Otherwise, the master schedule will be difficult to meet for those products with long cumulative lead times.

The Master Schedule for Custom Products

A company that produces a relatively small number of end items has a hard enough job of master scheduling. But consider a firm producing custom products that are made to order. Each product group may have numerous possible options. A good example of this situation would be a fast-food restaurant like Burger King.

Burger King says you can "have it your way." That means that you can get a Whopper with or without onion, with or without cheese, with or without a pickle, and so on. If Burger King tried to develop a master schedule for all the

Exhibit 11.8 Recognizing All Sources of Demand Through Demand Management

	Week					
	1	2	3	4	5	6
Customer demand	100	125	75	150	200	100
Interplant orders	25		50			75
Service parts	5		10		5	
Branch warehouse orders	50	50	50	50	50	50
Research & development orders		5			5	
Marketing samples	15		20		15	
Total demand	195	180	205	200	275	225

possible combinations of Whoppers, it would have a horrendous master scheduling problem. In fact, it would probably be almost impossible to forecast how many customers would want each combination.

Instead, companies that must produce highly customized products on a made-to-order basis must develop a master schedule that is based on modules, or options, instead of specific end products. A company such as Burger King would probably develop a master schedule for Whoppers and then just figure that a certain percentage of those will require a pickle, another percentage will want onion, and so forth. An automobile manufacturer would develop a master schedule for each engine type, each transmission type, and each body style and then worry about how those would be combined at the final assembly stage, as shown in Exhibit 11.9. A detail such as paint color could be dealt with the way Burger King might order pickles. A certain amount of each color would be ordered based on past experience and then used as needed. The actual combinations of options would be specified later when the final assembly schedule is developed.

ROUGH-CUT CAPACITY PLANNING

The aggregate plan is a first step in ensuring that sufficient labor, capital, and machine time will be available to meet customer demand. However, the aggregate plan only looks at those resources in aggregate terms. The technique of rough-cut capacity planning is a means of determining whether sufficient capacity exists at specific work centers to execute the master schedule.

Exhibit 11.9 Master Schedule for Custom Products

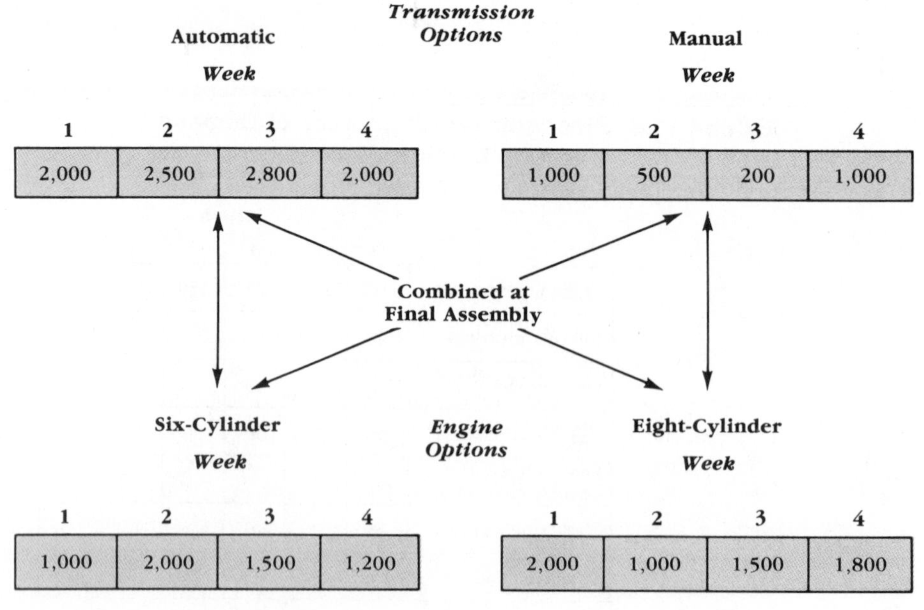

Calculating Requirements by Overall Factors

The purpose of rough-cut capacity planning is to determine whether approximately enough capacity will be available to meet the master production schedule. Thus, we will not be concerned with developing an exact figure. One method many companies use because of its simplicity and ease of calculation is the **method of overall factors.** This method relies primarily on historical accounting information to determine how many standard hours are required per unit of each product. By multiplying this figure by the number of units planned for production each week, an overall capacity requirement can be determined. This requirement can then be broken down by individual work centers, again based on historical data.

Example

Let's return to the production plan for Maine Woods' wheel goods. According to Exhibit 11.1, an aggregate production of 2,000 units has been planned for January. In developing the master schedule of Exhibit 11.2, Maine Woods has converted that planned production into the detailed schedule for its three wheel-goods products, toy wagons, tricycles, and scooters, shown in Exhibit 11.2.

Based on historical accounting information, each tricycle required .6 standard hour to produce, each toy wagon required .3 standard hour, and each scooter required .2 standard hour. This information can be used, as shown in Exhibit 11.10, to calculate capacity requirements for each product. By summing the weekly capacity requirements across all products, the total capacity requirements can be determined, as shown at the bottom of Exhibit 11.10.

Suppose Maine Woods is concerned about the high usage of its cutting and drilling operations. Again, based on historical accounting information, 40 percent of all standard hours are spent on cutting and 35 percent on drilling. The other 25 percent of standard hours is used for noncritical operations that are not of concern.

This historical information can be used to estimate capacity requirements at each operation. For example, in week 1, a total of 225 standard hours is required. Of this, we would expect 90 hours (40 percent) to be required for cutting and 78.75 hours (35 percent) to be required for drilling. Exhibit 11.11 shows the estimated capacity requirements for each work center each week.

Handling Insufficient Capacity

Once a company has estimated capacity requirements at each work station or operation, those figures can be compared to capacity available. In some cases, excess capacity may be available, which would indicate the opportunity to either book more orders or decrease working hours. In other cases, however, requirements may exceed capacity available.

If insufficient capacity is available to meet the master schedule, the easiest approaches are for a company to try to either shift some scheduled production into an *earlier* time period that has excess capacity or to schedule overtime, if possible. If neither of those approaches is possible, more major changes may have to be made in the master schedule.

Exhibit 11.10 Calculation of Total Capacity Requirements for a Master Schedule

Tricycles

January

Week	1	2	3	4
Master schedule	250	250	250	250
Capacity required	150	150	150	150

.6 standard hour per tricycle

Toy wagon

January

Week	1	2	3	4
Master schedule	250		250	
Capacity required	75		75	

.3 standard hour per toy wagon

Scooter

January

Week	1	2	3	4
Master schedule		250		250
Capacity required		50		50

.2 standard hour per scooter

Total capacity required (standard hours)	225	200	225	200

Exhibit 11.11 Calculation of Estimated Capacity Requirements for Individual Work Stations

	Week 1	2	3	4
Total capacity required (standard hours)	225	200	225	200
Cutting—40% (standard hours)	90	80	90	80
Drilling—35% (standard hours)	78.75	70	78.75	70

Example

Maine Woods has 100 hours of cutting time available each week and 80 hours of drilling time. Thus, based on Exhibit 11.11, sufficient capacity is available to meet the master schedule. In fact, weeks 2 and 4 have considerable excess.

However, an important customer has just asked whether an order for seventy-five tricycles could be completed in week 3. Although week 3 falls within the master schedule's frozen time period, the vice-president of manufacturing has approved an override if capacity is available.

Seventy-five tricycles would require an additional forty-five standard hours (75 × .6) in week 3. Of these additional hours, we would expect 18 (40 percent) to be for cutting and 15.75 (35 percent) to be for drilling. Exhibit 11.12 indicates the capacity requirements for cutting and drilling if this new order is accommodated. Unfortunately, with only 100 hours of cutting time and 80 hours of drilling time, sufficient capacity will not be available.

Maine Woods has several options, including turning down the order for week 3. One option is to schedule overtime as necessary in week 3 for cutting and drilling. The customer might be charged a higher price to cover the added cost.

Another option is shown in Exhibit 11.13. In this case, the seventy-five tricycles have been spread among weeks 2, 3, and 4 (thirty-five in week 2, five in week 3, thirty-five in week 4) to utilize available regular-time capacity. In this case, all of the customer's order could not be completed in week 3, but perhaps enough could be finished to satisfy the customer.

MATERIAL REQUIREMENTS PLANNING

The medium-range (aggregate) plan and master schedule can be used to generate rough estimates of the labor and equipment that will be needed. But another important resource, materials, is not really accounted for. One approach that has been used in the past for material planning is to be sure that enough of everything the company uses is always in inventory. This meant that huge inventories had to be maintained, resulting in extensive warehouse space and a large amount of

Exhibit 11.12 Proposed Master Schedule Requiring Overtime in Week 3

	Week 1	2	3	4
Tricycles	250	250	325	250
Toy wagons	250		250	
Scooters		250		250
Cutting capacity required (standard hours)	90	80	90+18= 108	80
Drilling capacity required (standard hours)	78.75	70	78.75+15.75= 94.5	70

Exhibit 11.13 Proposed Master Schedule with Changes to Avoid Overtime

	Week 1	2	3	4
Tricycles	250	(250+35) 285	(250+5) 255	(250+35) 285
Toy wagons	250		250	
Scooters		250		250
Cutting capacity required (standard hours)	90	88.4	91.2	88.4
Drilling capacity required (standard hours)	78.75	77.35	79.80	77.35

money tied up in that inventory. Even then, many companies found that certain crucial items used in many of their products always seemed to run out at the wrong time. No matter how much inventory was kept, a large demand for certain parts could deplete the supply of those parts rather quickly.

For example, suppose a company makes barbecue grills. Each grill has wheels on it, and the various models of grills all use the same wheels. Although the company's requirements for wheels are rather high, they are constant. However, if the company runs out of wheels, then everything must stop until more wheels become available. This company also makes gas barbecue grills that require a propane cylinder. Demand for gas grills is low enough that these are produced only intermittently. Thus, demand for the propane cylinders will be zero at those times when other grills are being produced, but will increase greatly when gas grills are being made. This type of demand pattern, called **lumpy demand,** occurs in lumps or batches. For both the wheels and the propane cylinders, the company might consider maintaining large inventories. But for the wheels, such a policy would result in unnecessarily large inventories since the relatively constant demand rate means the company could plan ahead and order just enough for, say, one week at a time—or even less. Likewise, for the propane cylinders, why bother having cylinders sitting around when gas grills are not being produced? Instead, the company could order the cylinders to arrive just shortly before gas barbecue production is scheduled to begin. The approach that could be used in both of these cases is called material requirements planning. **Material requirements planning (MRP)** is a process that uses bills of materials, inventory records, and the master schedule to determine when orders must be released to replenish inventories of parts or raw materials.

The idea behind MRP is simple; you probably do it yourself in planning a special meal. A few days ahead of time, you figure out what you want to have, check the ingredients you need, and then go out and buy whatever you don't have enough of. The same approach is used in operations management as follows.

The master schedule is what corresponds to your menu. Recall that the master schedule indicates precisely what end items, and in what quantities, the company plans to produce over some time horizon. By using the bills of materials, a company can determine what parts and materials, and how many of each, it needs to meet the master schedule. Inventory records will show how much is on hand. From this, it can be determined which parts or materials will come up short and how much more is needed of each.

The Data Files Used by MRP

For companies today, MRP is a computerized information system. As such, it requires data to provide the information needed for decision making. We have already mentioned the three most important data requirements of MRP—master production schedules, bills of materials, and inventory records. Generally each of these is kept in a separate computer data file.

Master Schedule File

We have already discussed in great detail the master production schedule. For MRP purposes, the master schedule is what "drives" the system and generates material requirements. As mentioned earlier, this master schedule may be at the finished-products level for companies like Maine Woods that manufacture standard products. However, for companies making customized products, the master schedule may be at the level of components or subassemblies.

Bills of Materials File

Chapter 4 has already briefly discussed bills of materials. However, because MRP is a computerized system, some modifications are made to the bills of materials, as described below.

Indicating Product Structure. The bill of materials serves two purposes. First, it lists all the components of a product. Second, it shows the relationships among those components. For example, Exhibit 11.14 shows an exploded view of the tricycle produced by Maine Woods. One possible bill of materials would simply list all these component parts.

However, in manufacturing this tricycle, the front wheel, its supports, the axle, and the steering column are subassembled before the entire tricycle is put together. Likewise, the seat and rear axle supports are subassembled before final assembly.

One way to indicate these subassemblies is through a product structure tree diagram, as shown in Exhibit 11.15. Notice that all the parts brought together at final assembly are listed together on level 1. Any parts that are components of subassemblies are listed on level 2. Connecting lines indicate which parts go into which subassembly.

Indented Bills of Materials The tree diagram is useful for showing us relationships among components. However, it cannot be read directly by the computer. Instead, an indented bill of materials is used by MRP to provide information about product structure. Each item is identified with a level, as shown in Exhibit 11.15. In an indented bill of materials, each level is indented from the one above it. Exhibit 11.16 is the indented bill of materials for Maine Woods' tricycle.

Low-Level Coding. Notice in Exhibit 11.16 that the same wheels are used on the front and back of the tricycle. However, the wheels at the rear are on level 1 because they are not part of a subassembly, while the front wheel is a level 2 item. In a situation like this, there is the possibility of placing separate orders for the same part. To avoid this possibility, any part is always assigned the *lowest* level

Exhibit 11.14 Exploded View of Maine Woods' Tricycle

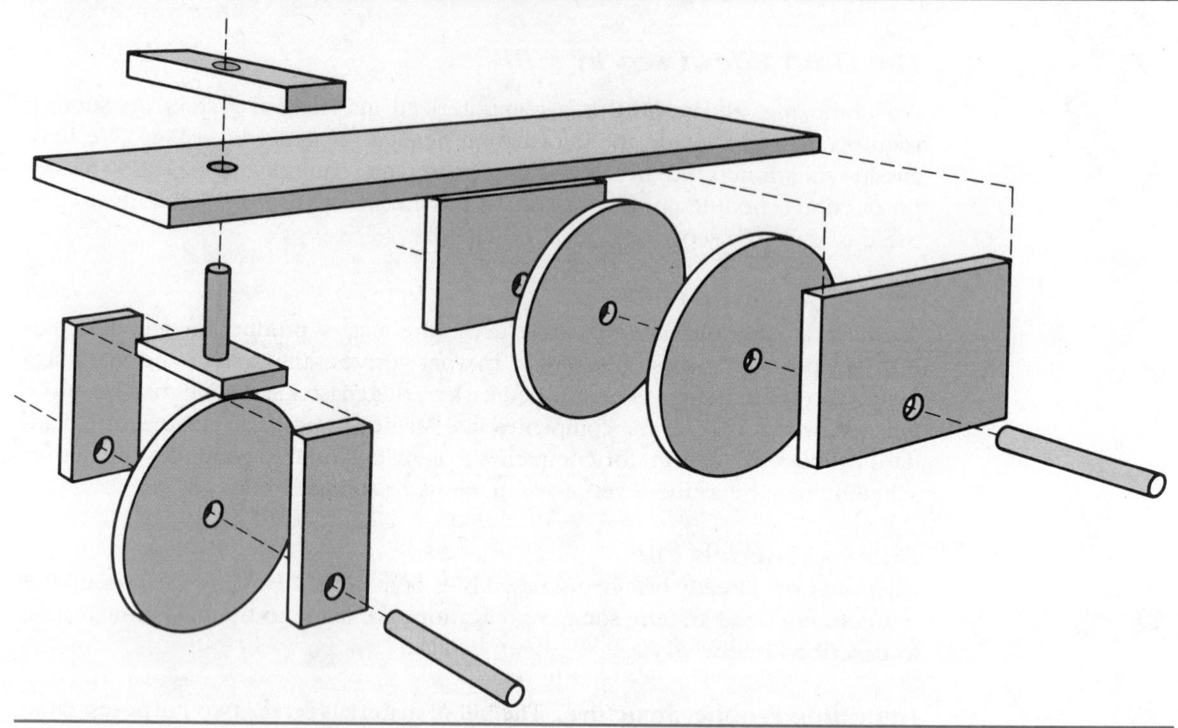

Exhibit 11.15 Product Structure Tree Diagram for Maine Woods' Tricycle

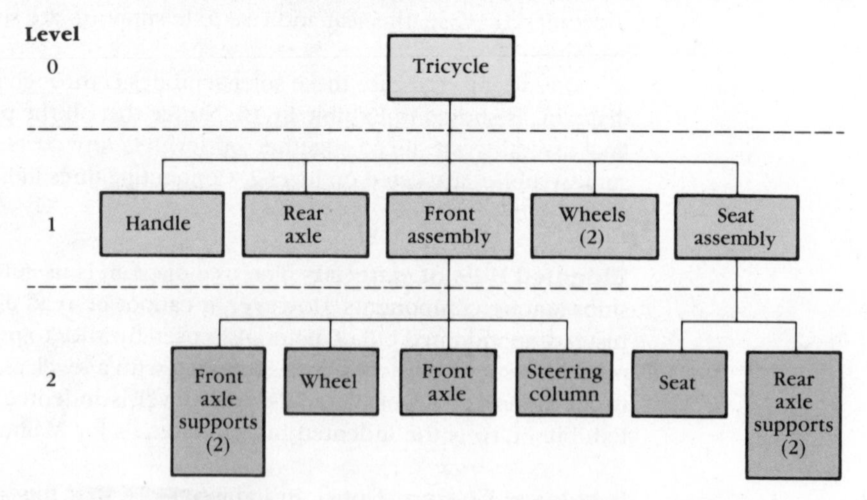

Exhibit 11.16 Indented Bill of Materials for Maine Woods' Tricycle

Level	Part No.	Quantity	Description
0	127	1	Tricycle
1	3417	1	Handle
1	2973	1	Rear axle
1	463	1	Front assembly
2	3987	2	Axle support (front)
2	5917	1	Wheel
2	2673	1	Front axle
2	3875	1	Steering column
1	5917	2	Wheel
1	587	1	Seat assembly
2	4673	1	Seat
2	3965	2	Axle support (rear)

(highest level number) at which it appears. Thus, the wheels should always appear as a level 2 item. This is called **low-level coding.**

The Inventory File

In order for MRP to work, accurate inventory records must be kept. For most companies, this means continually updating inventory records as items are withdrawn or added. To automate this function, many are using **bar codes,** which are similar to the universal product codes (UPCs) you see on items at the grocery store. Even then, mistakes can be made.

Cycle Counting. To reconcile inventory records and correct errors, many companies using MRP also employ what is called cycle counting. Using this method, a physical count of each part is made at least once during its replenishment cycle, which is the period between orders to replenish inventory.

Determining Planned Order Releases for Level 1 Items

Displaying MRP Information

The information obtained from bills of materials, inventory records, and the master schedule can all be brought together in the diagram of Exhibit 11.17, which is the table commonly used to calculate and display MRP information.

You should notice that there are time periods across the top of the table. These represent time periods for planning purposes, or **time buckets.** The time buckets correspond to the master schedule, which, as we said previously, is usually drawn up in terms of weeks. The purpose of using these time periods is to state requirements for component parts and materials in terms of the total quantity needed during each time bucket. This process of stating requirements by time bucket is often called **time phasing.**

The first row in Exhibit 11.17 is labeled Gross requirements. **Gross requirements** represent the total quantity needed of a particular item in each time bucket, based on the master schedule and the bill of materials regardless of current inventory of that item. The second row, **Scheduled receipts,** shows whether any orders for that item have been placed previously, but not yet re-

Exhibit 11.17 Table for MRP

		Time Period						
		1	2	3	4	5	6	7
Gross requirements								
Scheduled receipts								
Projected ending inventory								
Net requirements								
Planned receipts								
Planned order releases								

ceived. Entries in this row indicate when that order should come in and how many units should be in it. **Projected ending inventory** shows the planned number of units that should be available at the *end* of each time bucket. If the number of units available is not sufficient to cover gross requirements, then the row labeled **Net requirements** indicates the number of units the company is short. An entry in Net requirements indicates that a replenishment order will need to be placed. Thus, the last two rows show Planned receipts and Planned order releases. The **Planned receipts** row shows when orders must arrive in order to avoid a shortage of necessary parts or materials, as indicated by the Net requirements row. The **Planned order releases** row indicates the time periods in which those orders must be released (or placed) to arrive at the correct time. The difference between *scheduled* receipts and *planned* receipts is that scheduled receipts correspond to orders that have actually been placed some time in the past, but not yet received. Planned receipts correspond to orders planned for release, but not yet released. Both scheduled receipts and planned receipts are included as units available in the MRP record.

MRP Logic

The information in Exhibit 11.17 may be completed for each part or raw material as follows:

1. Obtain the bill of materials for the appropriate end product.
2. Begin with a level 1 item from the bill of materials.
3. Multiply the number of units of the level 1 item needed per unit of finished product (from the bill of materials) by the master schedule quantity for each time bucket. Insert this as gross requirements for the appropriate time bucket.
4. Enter any scheduled receipts of the item, based on lead time and orders previously released, in the appropriate time buckets.
5. Determine how many units should be in inventory at the start of the first time bucket. Enter this in the square to the left of that first time bucket.
6. Perform the following steps for each time bucket, beginning with the first, until the end of the planning horizon is reached. Add projected ending in-

ventory from the preceding time bucket to scheduled receipts for the present period. If this total equals or exceeds gross requirements for the present period, go to step a. Otherwise, go to step b.

a. If gross requirements in the time bucket being planned are *less than or equal to* the projected ending inventory from the preceding time bucket plus scheduled receipts for the current period, enter the difference as projected ending inventory in the present period. Leave net requirements blank, and repeat this step for the next time bucket.

b. If gross requirements are *greater than* projected ending inventory from the preceding time period plus scheduled receipts for the time bucket being planned, enter the difference as net requirements. Leave projected ending inventory blank for the present time period until the following substeps have been performed:

(1) For any period in which net requirements appear, plan an order release and corresponding receipt to cover the net requirements.

(2) Subtract net requirements from planned receipts, and enter the total as projected ending inventory for the current time bucket. Proceed to step a for the next time bucket.

Example

Let's return to the Maine Woods Company. The bill of materials for tricycles, shown in Exhibit 11.16, indicates the front assembly (part #463) is a level 1 item. The inventory file for this item shows 100 units are expected to be in inventory at the end of December. Production *lead time,* the time it takes to receive front assemblies after more are ordered into production, is two weeks. An order for 500 front assemblies was released earlier and is scheduled for receipt during week 1 of January. Using the master schedule for tricycles of Exhibit 11.13, determine planned order releases for front assemblies.

Step 1. The bill of materials (Exhibit 11.16) indicates one front assembly is needed for each tricycle.

Step 2. Front assemblies are a level 1 item, so you may begin planning with them.

Step 3. The master schedule for weeks 1 through 6 is shown at the top of Exhibit 11.18. Because one front assembly is needed for each tricycle, the gross requirements for front assemblies in each week will be the same as the master schedule quantities of tricycles.

Step 4. The scheduled receipt of 500 units is entered for week 1.

Step 5. The 100 front assemblies projected to be in inventory at the end of December are entered in the Projected ending inventory box to the left of week 1.

Step 6.

Week 1: Gross requirements in week 1 are *less than* projected ending inventory from the previous week plus scheduled receipts for week 1. The difference,

$$(100 + 500) - 250 = 350,$$

is entered as projected ending inventory for week 1, as shown in Exhibit 11.18.

Exhibit 11.18 MRP for Front Assemblies

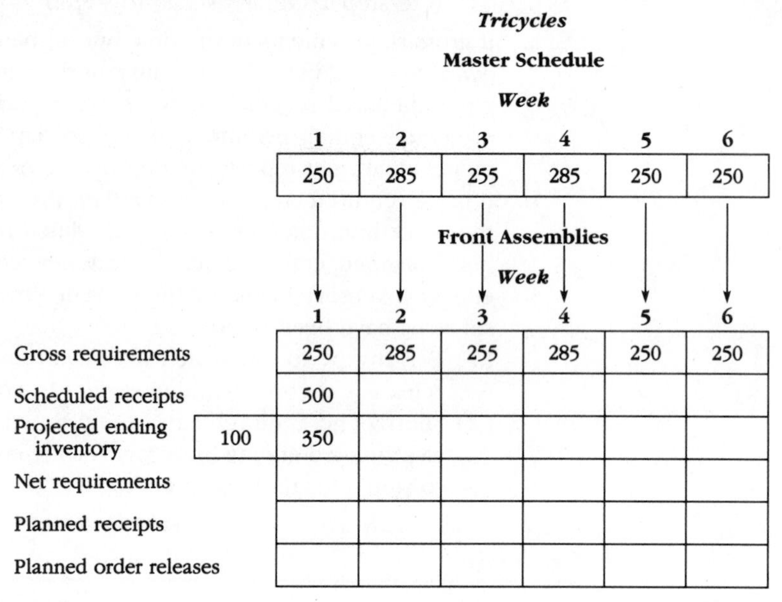

Tricycles
Master Schedule
Week

1	2	3	4	5	6
250	285	255	285	250	250

Front Assemblies
Week

		1	2	3	4	5	6
Gross requirements		250	285	255	285	250	250
Scheduled receipts		500					
Projected ending inventory	100	350					
Net requirements							
Planned receipts							
Planned order releases							

Week 2: Gross requirements in week 2 are *less than* projected ending inventory from week 1. Projected ending inventory for week 2 is

$$350 - 285 = 65$$

as shown in Exhibit 11.19.

Week 3: Gross requirements in week 3 are *greater than* projected ending inventory from week 2 by 190 units. This difference is entered as net requirements for week 3.

Exhibit 11.19 Partially Completed MRP: Front Assemblies

Week

		1	2	3	4	5	6
Gross requirements		250	285	255	285	250	250
Scheduled receipts		500					
Projected ending inventory	100	350	65	0			
Net requirements				190			
Planned receipts				190			
Planned order releases		190					

Exhibit 11.20 Completed MRP: Front Assemblies

		Week 1	2	3	4	5	6
Gross requirements		250	285	255	285	250	250
Scheduled receipts		500					
Projected ending inventory	100	350	65	0	0	0	0
Net requirements				190	285	250	250
Planned receipts				190	285	250	250
Planned order releases		190	285	250	250		

(1) An order for week 3 net requirements must be planned for receipt in week 3. Because the lead time is two weeks, the order must be planned for release in week 1 (week 3 − 2 weeks lead time = week 1).

(2) The planned receipts for week 3 are 190 units, and net requirements are 190 units. Therefore, the projected ending inventory for week 3 will be zero.

Weeks 4 through 6 are completed in the same way, producing the results shown in Exhibit 11.20.

Determining Planned Order Releases for Lower-Level Items

In the preceding example, we determine planned order releases for front assemblies, which are a level 1 item. The gross requirements for all level 1 items will be determined from the master schedule. But items that are level 2 in the bill of materials will be used in making level 1 items. Thus, their gross requirements will be determined from *planned order releases for level 1 items,* not from the master schedule.

Example

The front assemblies that were just planned using MRP are a level 1 item. However, the front axle supports used in that assembly are level 2. Therefore, the gross requirements for front axle supports will be determined by the *planned order releases for front assemblies,* as shown in Exhibit 11.21.

Combining Requirements

Many times, one particular part or subassembly will be used in more than one product. In such cases, the gross requirements for that part must take into account all planned production of products or subassemblies that use that part.

Exhibit 11.21 MRP for a Level 2 Item: Front Axle Supports

Front Assemblies

			1	2	3	4	5	6
Level 1	Planned order releases		190	285	250	250		

Front Axle Supports*

			1	2	3	4	5	6
Level 2	Gross requirements		380	570	500	500		
	Scheduled receipts		500					
	Projected ending inventory	40	160	0	0	0		
	Net requirements			410	500	500		
	Planned receipts			410	500	500		
	Planned order releases		410	500	500			

*2 axle supports per front assembly
Lead time = 1 week

Example

The front wheel in the Maine Woods tricycle is exactly the same as the two rear wheels. However, the front wheel is part of a subassembly, while the rear wheels are not. Furthermore, the wheels on Maine Woods' scooter are also the same as the wheels used on its tricycle. Therefore, gross requirements for wheels (part #5917) will be the sum of planned order releases for tricycle front assemblies (Exhibit 11.20) plus the master schedule quantities for tricycles (Exhibit 11.13), multiplied by two, and scooters (Exhibit 11.13), also multiplied by two, as shown in Exhibit 11.22.

In this instance, you should note that *low-level coding* has been used, as the wheels are treated as a level 2 item even though the tricycle's rear wheels and both the scooter's wheels would ordinarily be level 1 items. By using low-level coding, we are able to combine all requirements for these wheels and plan all order releases at one time.

CAPACITY REQUIREMENTS PLANNING

As was mentioned previously, the master schedule is developed, or disaggregated, from the aggregate plan. Thus, the master schedule can provide much more exact measures of the capacity requirements than the aggregate plan can. As the master schedule is developed, rough-cut capacity planning is used to check capacity requirements against capacity availability. But rough-cut capacity planning does not take into account **lead-time offsetting**, or the amount ahead of time component parts must be made to meet the master schedule for end items.

Exhibit 11.22 Combining Demand from Multiple Sources and Levels

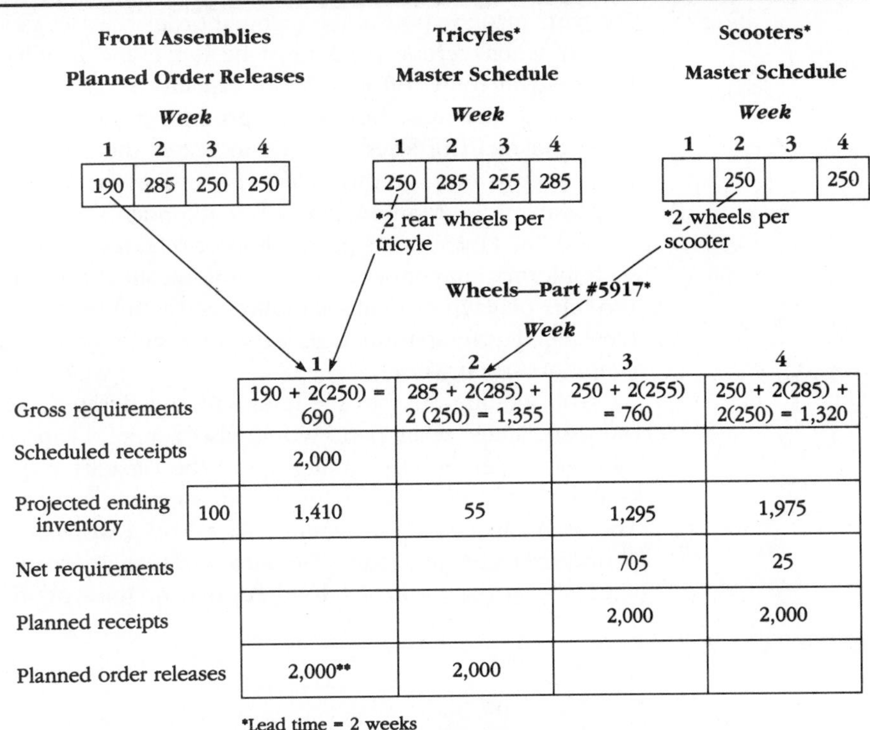

Front Assemblies — Planned Order Releases

Week	1	2	3	4
	190	285	250	250

Tricyles* — Master Schedule

Week	1	2	3	4
	250	285	255	285

*2 rear wheels per tricyle

Scooters* — Master Schedule

Week	1	2	3	4
		250		250

*2 wheels per scooter

Wheels—Part #5917*

Week		1	2	3	4
Gross requirements		190 + 2(250) = 690	285 + 2(285) + 2 (250) = 1,355	250 + 2(255) = 760	250 + 2(285) + 2(250) = 1,320
Scheduled receipts		2,000			
Projected ending inventory	100	1,410	55	1,295	1,975
Net requirements				705	25
Planned receipts				2,000	2,000
Planned order releases		2,000**	2,000		

*Lead time = 2 weeks
**Minimum order quantity = 2,000

INTEGRATING THE SYSTEM

MRP Coordinates Purchasing and Operations

The output from MRP is a schedule of planned order releases. If those are for component parts or subassemblies made by the company itself, then a **shop order**—an order that authorizes production to make certain component parts or subassemblies—will be released. If the planned order release is for a part or raw material that is purchased from an outside vendor, then a **purchase order**—an authorization for a vendor to supply parts or materials—will be released.

The operations part of a company is usually the area responsibile for running MRP. Thus, operations is aware that the release of a shop order means that a certain part or component should be started into production because a need will exist for it some time in the future. Since operations generated the shop order release, it will usually be aware that it is a valid order and should be produced in the quantity indicated.

However, purchase orders are usually handled by a purchasing or procurement department. If the order releases generated by MRP are to be carried out, then the purchasing department must be aware of what the MRP system is doing and trust in the output it generates. This requires close coordination between the operations part of an organization and its purchasing arm.

Because MRP performs lead-time offsetting when it generates planned order releases, MRP can form the basis for much more detailed capacity calculations. For parts made in-house, the planned order releases generated by MRP indicate exactly when certain parts must be made and in what quantity. Those order releases will touch off a series of capacity requirements on the machines and equipment that must be used in producing those parts and subassemblies. By using the **routing sheet,** which indicates the sequence of machines or work centers a part must go through during processing and the labor standards, it will be possible to determine capacity requirements at each operation.

Exhibit 11.23 shows planned order releases for tricycle axle supports, along with information contained in the routing sheet for that part. In each week, the run time on each machine is multiplied by the order quantity for that week and then added to setup time to get capacity requirements. This is done for each work center and each week.

You should note that the information generated in Exhibit 11.23 is only for one part. Many other parts would also generate capacity requirements on the same work centers. By adding up all the capacity requirements for each work center in each week, a total figure for capacity requirements will be generated. The total capacity requirements placed on a work center during a given time period are called the **load.** The output of capacity requirements planning (CRP) is usually in the form of a **load report,** or **load profile,** which is a graphical

Exhibit 11.23 Capacity Requirements Planning for Tricycle Axle Supports

Tricycle Axle Supports

	Week 1	2	3	4
Planned order releases	410	500	500	

Routing Sheet and Labor Standards

Process	Setup Time	Run Time per Unit
Cut	.2 hr.	.1 hr.
Drill	.1 hr.	.02 hr.

Capacity Requirements (Standard Hours)

	Week 1	2	3	4
Cut	.2 + .1(410) = 41.2	.2 + .1(500) = 50.2	50.2	
Drill	.1+ .02(410) = 8.3	.1+ .02(500) = 10.1	10.1	

Exhibit 11.24 Drill Work-center Load Report

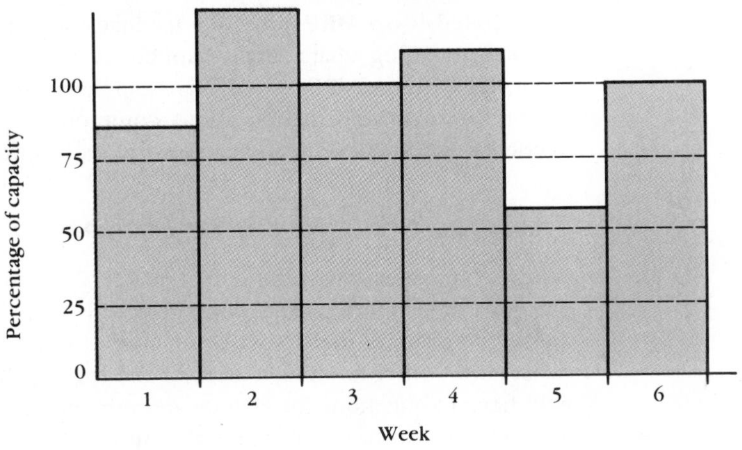

representation of the load on each work center by time period. An example of a load report is shown in Exhibit 11.24.

The Ethics of MRP

An important aspect of the relationship between a company and its customers is delivery reliability. For make-to-order companies especially, customers depend on the delivery due dates agreed on. Before the development of MRP, a company had to use rough estimates to determine when it thought a customer order could be shipped. Unfortunately, this left a lot of room for unethical behavior. For example, a company might agree to a certain shipping date to win a customer order, knowing from past experience that it might not be able to meet that date.

With MRP and capacity planning, a company is able to determine within a reasonable level of doubt when it will be able to ship an order. Thus, a great deal of uncertainty is eliminated from the order-promising process. Further, MRP provides the visibility necessary to determine whether unforeseen events, such as machine breakdowns or late deliveries from suppliers, will delay a customer order. If so, a company can then notify the customer involved so that the customer can plan accordingly. Such capability can greatly increase the level of trust between a company and its customers.

EXTENSIONS OF MRP

Closed-Loop MRP

Capacity requirements planning is of significant benefit in ensuring that a company's plans are realistic and can be implemented. However, MRP, as we have discussed it so far, can only project what will happen. In reality, machines may break down, deliveries from suppliers may be delayed, or some other calamity may occur. If these events are not reflected back in the MRP plan, then that plan will be invalid.

Closed-loop MRP provides feedback about the *execution* of production plans. By tracking what actually happens on the shop floor and then reflecting that information in the MRP record, plans can be kept valid. Instead of just "launching" orders with no information about completion, closed-loop MRP provides the feedback loop necessary to keep information up to date.

Manufacturing Resource Planning

Many companies have found that material requirements planning can greatly improve their operations through better planning. MRP also forces companies to better coordinate the activities of operations, marketing, and purchasing. But what about other functional areas of an organization? Surely the master schedule will have implications for finance and personnel in terms of work-force requirements and purchases of materials. And how can a company be sure that its operations plan fits in appropriately with the business plan?

You should recall that in the preceding chapter we described how the business plan of an organization ties together all parts of that organization. But if that business plan is to be implemented, then all functional areas must base their activities on the plan. To do that, an extension of MRP has been developed called manufacturing resource planning.

Manufacturing resource planning, or **MRP II,** as it is commonly called, is a way of tying all parts of an organization together with the operations activity to build on the business plan. As we discussed in Chapter 10, the business plan is an overall blueprint that specifies the company's objectives and how it plans to reach them. The operations function will develop its own goals and plans to help achieve the corporate objective, as will marketing, finance, and all other parts of the organization. However, the actions of one functional area will have an impact on the other areas. For instance, if marketing plans a promotional effort that will greatly increase sales, then operations must be ready and able to turn out enough product to meet that increased demand. This might mean hiring more employees or buying additional equipment, which will in turn have a major impact on the financial area. Because the operations activity is such an integral part of any organization, it can be especially vulnerable to the actions taken by other departments, while operations in turn can have a major influence on other areas of the company through its actions.

Cost Control

The planned orders that MRP produces can also provide information about expected expenditures. Planned purchase order releases can be used to estimate future payments to suppliers. Shop order releases will generate needs for machine time and labor, so they can also be used to estimate future expenses. Before the development of MRP II, companies used cost accounting primarily as a means of keeping score after the fact. It was a way to find out what it had cost to do what was already done.

But MRP II can change the way companies operate. By generating cost projections, it is possible to plan for production costs ahead of time and then compare actual costs to these projections. Any major deviations can be spotted and investigated. A related advantage with MRP II is that it can be used to answer what-if kinds of questions. As we have said before, things may not always go according to plan. But one good way to be ready when Murphy's law strikes is by trying out various possibilities. Using MRP II, a company can estimate the effect of a supplier cost increase and develop strategies to deal with it, instead of trying to react after the fact. Exhibit 11.25 shows how MRP II ties together all parts of the organization.

Simulation

Simulation is the use of some model of reality to predict the impact of certain changes. With MRP II, simulation can be used to answer the what-if kinds of questions mentioned above. Because MRP II generates cost figures, a company can immediately see how any projected changes will affect the organization's financial health. For instance, marketing might want to know what would happen if sales were increased by 10 percent. MRP II could be used to see how such a change would influence capacity utilization, labor costs, and cash flow. Or the operations area might want to know how a change in the production plan might influence its material costs. In each of these situations, MRP II could be used in "simulation mode" to project the impact of proposed changes.

MRP in Service Organizations

Although MRP was originally developed for manufacturing companies, it can also be applied to service organizations. Instead of the master schedule's representing goods to be produced, it can represent services to be provided.

Exhibit 11.25 MRP II

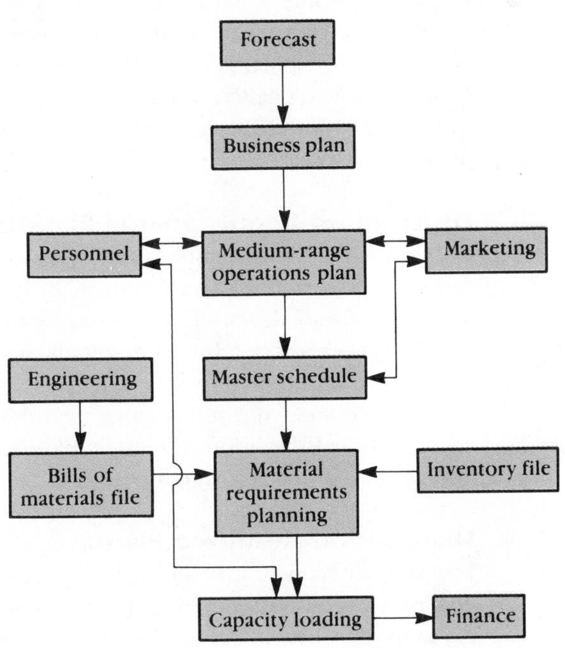

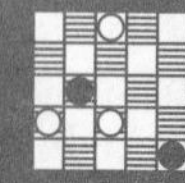

GAINING STRATEGIC ADVANTAGE AT BEN & JERRY'S

An MRP II System Provides Important Strategic Information

If you are an ice cream connoisseur, you have probably run across Ben & Jerry's by now, especially if you live on the East Coast. From a small ice cream shop in 1978, Ben & Jerry's Homemade, Inc., has become a company that sells over $30 million of product per year and employs over 200 people.

Due to such phenomenal growth, Ben & Jerry's found it was having trouble managing the inventory and production of its thirty-six flavors. Further, the company was not able to gather timely information about sales and costs.

To solve these multiple problems, Ben & Jerry's purchased an MRP II package named IMPCON, marketed by Computer Systems Development, which is one of many commercially available MRP II packages on the market.

For Ben & Jerry's, the first job of the MRP II system was not related to manufacturing. Instead, the company badly needed to collect information about sales trends and profitability. Thanks to this system, the company now knows that 50 percent of its sales come from New York and New England, 80 percent of what it sells is in the form of pints, and its top three flavors are Heath Bar Crunch, New York Super Fudge Chunk, and Cherry Garcia.

Today, Ben & Jerry's is using its MRP II system to manage the whole operation, from raw materials to finished-product inventories, including order processing, capacity planning, and production scheduling. The information that system provides helps the company develop a smart competitive strategy.[3]

For example, an airline's master schedule could be the number of flights from different cities each week. In this case, the materials required to provide that service would be fuel for the airplanes, meals for the passengers, and so forth. Likewise, hospitals can develop a master schedule of the number of different types of surgeries each week. Materials required would be various surgical supplies.

In one particular setting, the MRP approach has been applied so widely that a variant of MRP, called distribution requirements planning, has been developed. In that case, the MRP planning logic is applied to requirements for retail outlets or warehouses.

Distribution Requirements Planning

Distribution networks often consist of local outlets or service centers that are supplied from regional warehouses. In turn, these regional warehouses may be fed by a national distribution center. By thinking of each level in the distribution network as a level in a bill of materials, it is possible to see that orders placed by the service centers will generate gross requirements at the regional warehouses. Likewise, orders from the regional warehouses will produce gross requirements at the national distribution center. Exhibit 11.26 shows an example of distribution requirements planning (DRP).

Distribution Resource Planning

Just as manufacturing resource planning (MRP II) expands the role of MRP to generating requirements for personnel, capital, and so forth, distribution resource planning expands the role of DRP. Distribution resource planning generates requirements for warehouse space, workers, vehicles, and capital.

Exhibit 11.26 Distribution Requirements Planning

Dallas Service Center

		Week 31	32	33	34
Forecast demand		600	300	400	400
Scheduled receipts			1,000		
Projected ending inventory	650	50	750	350	950
Planned receipts					1,000
Planned order releases			1,000		

Phoenix Service Center

		Week 31	32	33	34
Forecast demand		250	300	350	450
Scheduled receipts		500			
Projected ending inventory	300	550	250	400	450
Planned receipts				500	500
Planned order releases		500	500		

Southwest Regional Warehouse

		Week 31	32	33	34
Gross requirements		500	1,500		
Scheduled receipts		900			
Projected ending inventory	100	500	0		
Planned receipts			1,000		
Planned order releases		1,000			

Contel: Distribution Requirements Planning on a Microcomputer

Contel is a $3 billion telecommunications company, providing telephone service to over 2 million customers in thirty states. To provide that service, Contel must use a wide range of equipment and supplies, including telephones, fiber-optic cable, and fax machines, that are purchased from over 400 manufacturers.

To purchase and distribute all these materials, Contel operates a subsidiary, Contel Material Management Company. This subsidiary stocks over 4,700 major items in four primary distribution centers across the country. From these distribution centers, products are shipped to warehouses operated by other divisions of Contel.

Because of constant developments in the telecommunications industry, inventory can quickly become obsolete. Further, it is important that a nationwide company such as Contel have the right items in the right place at the right time. Having beige phones in supply in New Jersey won't help if a customer in California has just ordered beige phones and the Los Angeles distribution center is out of them. Faced with these problems of having too much inventory of the wrong items in the wrong places, Contel decided to implement a DRP system.

Although most DRP systems run on minicomputers or mainframes, the system chosen by Contel was based on microcomputers because of their lower cost and greater flexibility. Since implementation, the company has observed that 88 percent of its orders can be supplied off the shelf, up from 82 percent previously. Further, inventory turnover has improved 12 percent. Due to the planning capabilities of DRP, Contel now is also able to negotiate better prices and reduced lead times with its suppliers.[4]

SUMMARY

- The production planning process leads from an aggregate plan to a master schedule to MRP.
- The master schedule is a more detailed version of the aggregate plan, usually by end products and weeks.
- The master schedule must produce quantities that will match the aggregate plan, be in proportion to demand, and not exceed available capacity.
- Master schedule quantities are planned to meet the larger of forecast demand or customer orders booked.
- Available-to-promise indicates how many units are planned for production, but not yet committed to customer orders during a time period.
- For custom products, the master schedule is usually prepared in terms of options or modules.
- The method of overall factors uses historical information about capacity requirements to make a rough-cut capacity requirements estimate from the master schedule.
- When insufficient capacity exists, overtime may be scheduled or demand shifted to time periods with slack.
- Material requirements planning (MRP) uses the master schedule, bills of materials, and inventory records to plan orders for subassemblies and parts.
- An indented bill of materials is used in MRP to indicate product structure.
- Capacity requirements planning uses routing sheets and labor standards to develop time-phased estimates of capacity requirements based on planned order releases.
- Closed-loop MRP provides feedback about execution of the MRP plan.
- Manufacturing resource planning (MRP II) provides simulation capabilities and cost information for other functional areas of the business.
- Distribution requirements planning (DRP) is used to determine planned orders in a distribution network.
- Service organizations can use MRP to plan requirements for supplies and materials based on planned service usage.
- Master scheduling and capacity planning enable companies to determine whether they can actually meet customer delivery dates.

CAREER PROFILE

Barry Blood

Manager of Manufacturing
Honeywell Space and Strategic Avionics Division

Honeywell Space and Strategic Avionics Division is a part of Honeywell Corporation. The division is responsible for making controls for rockets and spacecraft—everything from the NASA space shuttle and space probes to ballistic missiles. Ninety-nine percent of the division's business is from the U.S. Department of Defense or from NASA.

Educational Background and Career Steps

Barry Blood began his studies in a field relatively far removed from the factory floor. That field was horology (watchmaking), which he studied at Bradley University. After graduation, Blood went to work in a jewelry store and became its manager. However, he left that job after two years and used his watchmaking skills as an instrument technician for Honeywell. After taking some business courses at a junior college, Blood became a production supervisor and later moved into production control, where frequent work with contracts led him to pursue a law degree by mail through LaSalle University's Extension Program. From that point, he worked up the ladder to manager of production control.

Current Position

Today, Barry Blood is manager of manufacturing for Honeywell's Space and Strategic Avionics Division. In that position, he is responsible for 350 employees, ranging from manufacturing engineers and quality engineers to machinists and tool-and-die makers. Each year, Blood's department has a budget of $16 million and is responsible for performing work on seventy to eighty contracts.

In his position, Blood is involved with the division's MRP system—a hybrid that closely resembles MRP II. This system is used to generate requirements based on contracts the company has signed. Under Blood's direction, techniques have been developed that use output from the MRP program to control work on the shop floor. In fact, these techniques have been so successful that his company is currently converting them to computer software and Blood is doing a lot of outside consulting to show other companies how to apply his ideas.

Blood also is actively involved with the local American Production and Inventory Control Society (APICS) chapter, an organization that he feels is the best source of information about new trends and techniques in the production/operations management field. He is a frequent speaker and lecturer on such subjects as asset management, just-in-time production, and MRP, and he recently presented a paper entitled "Shop Floor Control? Who Are You Kidding!" at a national APICS conference.

SOLVED PROBLEMS

1. Southern Electronics manufactures disk drive controller cards for personal computers. To meet demand, the company's aggregate production plan calls for 4,000 cards to be manufactured during January and 5,000 during February. In the past, 20-megabyte (Mb) controller cards have made up 40 percent of the total demand for controller cards. Demand for these cards is expected to be uniform throughout each month.

a. If 500 of the 20-Mb controller cards are in inventory at the end of December and customer orders booked are as shown below, determine the master schedule and the available-to-promise quantities for each month. Southern prefers to produce 20-Mb controller cards in batches of 1,000.

	January				February			
	1	2	3	4	5	6	7	8
Customer Orders booked	500	350	400	350	300	300	250	200

b. Based on historical accounting data, each 20-Mb card requires 4.2 standard hours to produce. Thirty percent of all standard hours are used by the wave soldering machine. Based on the master schedule established in part a, estimate capacity requirements for wave soldering each week to produce the 20-Mb controller cards.

Solution

a. If 40 percent of controller card demand is for 20-Mb cards, then 1,600 will be demanded during January and 2,000 during February. Assuming uniform demand, 400 will be demanded each week in January and 500 each week in February. The table of Exhibit 11.27 may be completed.

b. Each 20-Mb card requires 4.2 standard hours, and if 30 percent is used by the wave soldering machine, then requirements for each board will be .30(4.2) = 1.26 standard hours. Based on the master schedule, the requirements for wave soldering of 20-Mb cards will be

	Week							
	1	2	3	4	5	6	7	8
Standard hours	0	1,260	0	1,260	0	1,260	0	1,260

2. The Arctic Snow Shovel Company manufactures aluminum snow shovels that have the following bill of materials:

Level	Item	Quantity Required
0	Aluminum snow shovel	1
1	Blade assembly	1
2	Blade	1
3	Aluminum sheet	1.5 ft.

Exhibit 11.27 Master Schedule for 20-Mb Controller Cards

On-hand inventory at end of December = 500

Month	January				Febuary			
Week	1	2	3	4	5	6	7	8
Forecast demand	400	400	400	400	500	500	500	500
Customer orders booked	500	350	400	350	300	300	250	200
Projected on-hand inventory	0	600	200	800	300	800	300	800
Master schedule		1,000		1,000		1,000		1,000
Available-to-promise	0	250		350		450		800

Level	Item	Quantity Required
2	Blade plate	1
2	Rivets	10
2	Handle connector	1
1	Handle assembly	1
2	1.5″ diameter wooden shaft	3 ft.
2	Plastic handle	1
2	1″ flat-head wood screws	4

Arctic currently has no blade assemblies on hand. The production lead time for making blade assemblies is one week, and they may be produced in any quantity. There are 100 blades in stock and another 1,000 in production due to be completed next week. Lead time is also one week for blades, which are produced in batches of 1,000. The aluminum sheet for these blades is ordered in quantities of 10,000 feet, and there are currently 2,000 feet in stock. The lead time for ordering aluminum sheet is two weeks.

Based on the preceding information and the following master schedule for snow shovels during the next six weeks (it is currently week 27), determine planned orders for aluminum sheet:

Master Schedule—Aluminum Snow Shovels

Week					
28	**29**	**30**	**31**	**32**	**33**
500	400	600	600	400	400

Solution

Because aluminum sheet is a component of blades, which are in turn a component of blade assemblies, we must perform MRP for all three items, as shown in Exhibit 11.28, illustrating the MRP for aluminum snow shovels.

3. The Discount Club, a retailer located in Atlanta, operates wholesale warehouse stores throughout the Southeast. The company maintains a distribution center in Atlanta and warehouses in Norfolk and Tallahassee. One item the company sells is motor oil, which is bought in bulk barrel quantities through the Atlanta distribution center. Given the information in Exhibit 11.29, calculate planned order releases from the Atlanta distribution center if shipments to the warehouses are in 500-barrel quantities and shipments to the distribution center are in 2,000-barrel quantities. The lead time for shipments to the warehouses is one week and for shipments to the distribution center is two weeks.

Solution

The results are shown in Exhibit 11.30.

Exhibit 11.28 MRP for Arctic Snow Shovels

	Week 28	29	30	31	32	33
	500	400	600	600	400	400

Blade Assembly

		28	29	30	31	32	33
Gross requirements		500	400	600	600	400	400
Scheduled receipts		500					
Projected ending inventory	0	0	0	0	0	0	0
Net requirements			400	600	600	400	400
Planned receipts			400	600	600	400	400
Planned order releases		400	600	600	400	400	

Blade

		28	29	30	31	32	33
Gross requirements		400	600	600	400	400	
Scheduled receipts		1,000					
Projected ending inventory	100	700	100	500	100	700	
Net requirements				500		300	
Planned receipts				1,000		1,000	
Planned order releases			1,000		1,000		

Aluminum Sheet

		28	29	30	31	32	33
Gross requirements			1,500		1,500		
Scheduled receipts							
Projected ending inventory	2,000	2,000	500	500	9,000		
Net requirements					1,000		
Planned receipts					10,000		
Planned order releases			10,000				

Exhibit 11.29 Information for Discount Club Distribution Requirements Planning

Norfolk

		Week 37	38	39	40
Gross requirements		200	150	175	200
Scheduled receipts		500			
Projected ending inventory	50				
Planned receipts					
Planned order releases					

Tallahassee

		Week 37	38	39	34
Gross requirements		150	200	200	150
Scheduled receipts					
Projected ending inventory	220				
Planned receipts					
Planned order releases					

Atlanta

		Week 37	38	39	40
Gross requirements					
Scheduled receipts					
Projected ending inventory	700				
Planned receipts					
Planned order releases					

Exhibit 11.30 Planned Order Releases for Discount Club Motor Oil

Norfolk

		Week 37	38	39	40
Gross requirements		200	150	175	200
Scheduled receipts		500			
Projected ending inventory	50	350	200	25	325
Planned receipts					500
Planned order releases				500	

Tallahassee

		Week 37	38	39	34
Gross requirements		150	200	200	150
Scheduled receipts					
Projected ending inventory	220	70	370	170	20
Planned receipts			500		
Planned order releases		500			

Atlanta

		Week 37	38	39	40
Gross requirements		500	0	500	0
Scheduled receipts					
Projected ending inventory	700	200	200	1,700	1,700
Planned receipts				2,000	
Planned order releases		2,000			

QUESTIONS

1. Define the following terms:

a. Rough-cut capacity planning
b. Time bucket
c. Lead-time offsetting
d. Freezing the master schedule
e. Available-to-promise

2. Explain how a restaurant could use MRP. In what ways would its use in a restaurant differ from its use in a manufacturing organization?

3. Describe the information generated by MRP II and how it could be used by the following departments in a company:

a. Personnel
b. Finance
c. Marketing
d. Engineering

4. Explain how MRP can decrease a company's inventory while improving its customer service level.

5. Discuss the relationship between MRP and MRP II.

6. Why is it important for an organization to plan and allocate resources?

7. Define the following terms:

a. Bill of materials
b. Net requirements
c. Gross requirements
d. Scheduled receipts
e. Planned receipts

8. Why are there separate lines for planned receipts and scheduled receipts in the MRP table?

9. Describe how capacity requirements planning differs from rough-cut capacity planning.

10. What information is needed for capacity requirements planning, and how is that information obtained?

11. The time you have available for studying is a limited resource. For the next week, develop a load profile that compares the time you have available (capacity) with time you *should* devote to studying for all your courses. What are your options if capacity is exceeded?

12. In what units might the capacity of a hotel be expressed, and what options are available if it is expected that capacity will be exceeded?

13. What are some things a company can do when rough-cut capacity planning indicates insufficient capacity to meet the master schedule?

14. How is the master production schedule modified for computerized MRP?

15. How does closed-loop MRP maintain the validity of a production plan?

16. How does MRP improve a company's ability to behave ethically toward its customers?

PROBLEMS

1. The aggregate plan for Brookline Clothing Company indicates 3,750 men's pants are to be produced during March. Of these, 20 percent are style 493. Assuming there are five weeks of production in March, develop a master schedule for style 493 men's pants if they are produced in batches of 250 at a time.

2. A certain company has forecast demand during the first nine weeks of the year as 350 units per week for product A. Projected inventory of product A at the end of December is 800 units. If product A is produced in batches of 1,000, determine the master schedule and the available-to-promise quantities, based on the following customer orders booked:

				Week				
1	2	3	4	5	6	7	8	9
300	400	375	325	300	280	300	250	200

3. The Evans Sporting Goods Company has developed an aggregate plan that calls for producing 5,000 units of its wood-products group during April. Baseball bats make up 80 percent of this product group, based on past sales. At the end of March, the company expects to have 800 bats available in inventory. Customer orders booked in the five weeks of April are as follows:

		April		
		Week		
1	2	3	4	5
900	875	850	745	720

If bats are produced in batches of 2,000, develop a master schedule, assuming forecast demand was expected to be uniformly distributed throughout the month.

4. A company has the following master schedules for two of its products:

Product A

Week							
1	2	3	4	5	6	7	8
240	300	350	350	400	300	300	400

Product B

Week							
1	2	3	4	5	6	7	8
500	450	400	400	300	350	500	500

Both products must be processed on the same critical machine. Product A requires .2 hour of time on this machine per unit, and product B requires .1 hour per unit. The machine is available 120 hours per week. Use rough-cut capacity planning to determine whether sufficient capacity will be available on the machine. Suggest possible ways that any capacity shortage might be solved.

5. The Ernie and Winnie Public Accounting Company has just two employees (Ernie and Winnie). Ernie is available thirty hours per week for auditing and twenty hours per week for tax preparation. Winnie is available ten hours per week for auditing and thirty hours per week for tax preparation. Each audit takes five hours, and each tax preparation takes two hours. The company has received requests to perform the following audits and tax preparations each week during the next month.

	Week 1	2	3	4
Number of audits requested	5	8	10	9
Number of tax preparations requested	10	8	9	7

Identify possible problems that might occur if each employee's auditing and tax preparation times are fixed. What if excess time for one activity can be used for the other activity?

6. Referring to your answer in problem 3, historical information shows that two standard hours are required to produce each baseball bat. Further, 60 percent of all standard hours for wood products have been for lathe time and 40 percent for finishing. Estimate the standard hours required in each operation to produce the bats scheduled in problem 3.

7. Referring to problem 6, suppose 2,000 standard hours of lathe time and 1,500 standard hours of finishing time are available each week. Determine whether sufficient capacity will be available each week. If not, suggest ways to meet demand with available capacity.

8. Central Eye Hospital has scheduled the following numbers of cataract surgeries during each of the next four weeks. Each cataract surgery requires the use of five pairs of surgical gloves. These gloves are ordered from a supplier in quantities of 1,000 pairs at a time. Ordering lead time is two weeks. Inventory records indicate that there will be 200 pairs of gloves in inventory at the start of week 1. An order for 1,000 more is expected to arrive during week 1.

	Week 1	2	3	4
Surgeries scheduled	30	60	55	60

Use MRP to schedule planned order releases for gloves.

9. A company that manufactures furniture produces a particular type of coffee table. As you might guess, each coffee table has four legs. The production lead time for these legs is two weeks. Inventory records show that 2,500 of these legs will be available as on-hand inventory at the beginning of week 32. An order for 2,500 legs has already been released and is scheduled to arrive in week 33. These legs may be produced in any quantity. Use MRP to schedule planned order releases.

Master Schedule—Coffee Tables

Week					
32	33	34	35	36	37
500	400	450	300	450	400

10. A company that makes canned soups has developed the following master schedule for its 12-ounce cans of vegetable beef soup:

Master Schedule—12-Oz. Vegetable Beef Soup

Week					
12	13	14	15	16	17
1200	1500	600	900	2000	1500

Each 12-ounce can of vegetable beef soup requires 7 ounces of beef broth. The company currently has 9,000 ounces of beef broth that will be available in week 12. Production lead time for beef broth is one week. Each ounce of beef broth requires 3 ounces of beef bones. These bones are ordered from a supplier in multiples of 32,000 ounces (2,000 pounds) and have a lead time of two weeks. There will be 30,000 ounces on hand at the beginning of week 12, and another

32,000 ounces are scheduled for receipt during week 13. Develop planned order releases for beef bones.

11. Referring to Problem 10, suppose that the supplier of beef bones has just called and indicated that the delivery of 32,000 ounces for week 13 has been delayed until week 14. How would you have to alter the master schedule for production of vegetable beef soup to compensate for this change if it is uneconomical to produce less than 100 cans of soup at a time?

12. An electronics manufacturer makes a product designated as S400. Each S400 is assembled from one of each of two subassemblies, A38 and B493.

Subassembly A38 requires two of part 1438 and two of component 1297. Component 1297 in turn is made from one of part 6438 and five fasteners numbered 4217.

Subassembly B493 consists only of two units of part 1395 and four fasteners numbered 4217.

- **a.** Draw a tree diagram indicating the structure of product S400.
- **b.** Using low-level coding, at what level would fastener 4217 be coded in the BOM?
- **c.** Develop an indented bill of materials for product S400.

13. Referring to problem 12, the master schedule for product S400 is as shown below.

Master Schedule—S400

Week 43	44	45	46	47
2,000	2,400	3,000	2,300	2,700

- **a.** Determine gross requirements for A38 and B493 in each week.
- **b.** Suppose that, in addition to the information provided, the MRP system's item master file indicates the following lead times, and the inventory data file indicates the current amounts on hand and the scheduled receipts shown below.

Item	*Lead Time (Weeks)*	*On-Hand Week 42*	*Scheduled Receipts* Quantity	Week
A38	2	3,000	3,000	44
B493	1	3,000		
1438	1	3,000		
1297	1	4,500		
1395	3	4,000	10,000	44
4217	2	60,000		
6438	1	5,000		

Develop planned order releases for parts 1438 and 1395.

- **c.** Using the preceding information, develop planned order releases for all parts and fasteners.

14. Referring to problem 9, suppose the master schedule for coffee tables is altered, so 500 tables are planned for production in week 33. Change the planned order releases for table legs accordingly.

15. The Skillful Machining Company makes two different parts that both require milling. The planned order releases for these parts are shown below, along with the mill time required by each. If the milling machine is available sixty hours per week, develop a load profile for the milling machine in each week.

	Week 1	2	3	4	5	6
Planned order releases—part A	100		50	300	50	100
Planned order releases—part B	200	200	100	200	100	

	Setup (Hrs./Batch)	Run (Hrs./Unit)
Part A	1	.3
Part B	2	.2

16. The Davis Auto Center has scheduled the following numbers of transmission repairs on each day for the coming week. Each transmission repair requires two hours of transmission specialist time and four hours of general mechanic time. The company has one transmission specialist who works eight hours per day and two general mechanics who each work eight hours per day. Develop load profiles for the transmission specialist and the general mechanics.

Transmission Repairs Scheduled

Mon.	Tues.	Wed.	Thurs.	Fri.
1	3	2	2	3

17. A furniture manufacturer operates two regional warehouses, both of which are supplied from the company's main factory distribution center. Shipping time from the factory to each warehouse is one week. A particular model of sofa is shipped in standard quantities of fifty units, and production lead time is two weeks.

Given the following information, use DRP to determine planned order releases for each warehouse and for the factory.

Chicago Warehouse

	Week 31	32	33	34	35
Forecast demand		30	30	40	40
Scheduled receipts		50			
Projected ending inventory	10				

New Orleans Warehouse

	31	32	33	34	35
Forecast demand		20	30	30	40
Scheduled receipts					
Projected ending inventory	40				

Factory Distribution Center

	31	32	33	34	35
Scheduled receipts		100			
Projected ending inventory	20				

Data Sets for Computer Solution

1. A company makes an end product, A, which consists of subassembly B and component parts C and D, as shown in the following tree diagram. Each level of the diagram shows the items, and the number of those items, needed for the next higher level. The company's inventory records indicate that 50 of subassembly B and 1,000 of part C will be on hand at the beginning of week 1. Production lead time for subassembly B is one week, and 100 are scheduled to arrive in week 1. Part C is ordered from a supplier in lots of 1,000 and has a two-week lead time. Develop planned order releases for part C, based on the master schedule below.

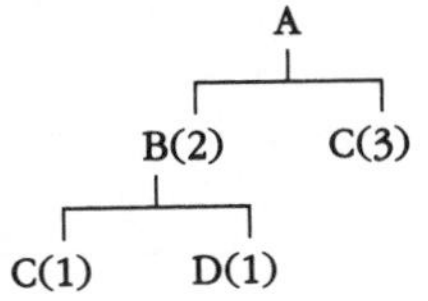

Master Shedule—A

1	2	3	4	5	6
50	75	25	60	75	80

2. The Chesapeake Company manufactures two pieces of computer furniture: a computer table and an ergonomically designed computer chair. The company has just finished developing its master schedule for each item over the next eight weeks, as shown below.

Computer Table

1	2	3	4	5	6	7	8
200	300	250	250	300	300	350	350

Chair

1	2	3	4	5	6	7	8
300	300	250	250	300	300	200	200

Each of these products has the bill of materials indicated below.

Level	Part No.	Description
0		Computer table
1	2075	Wood top
1	2702	Wood shelf
1	2876	Wood sides (2)
2	124	Casters (2)
1	29	Screws (16)
0		Ergonomic chair
1	452	Seat assembly
2	2703	Wood backing
2	6359	Fabric (1 sq. ft.)
2	6390	Padding (.8 sq. ft.)
1	2877	Wood sides (2)
2	124	Casters (2)
1	453	Knee pad assembly
2	2704	Wood backing
2	6359	Fabric (.8 sq. ft.)
2	6390	Padding (.5 sq. ft.)
1	29	Screws (16)

All wooden parts are ordered from an outside supplier and have a lead time of two weeks. They may be ordered in any quantity desired. Both casters and screws are ordered from a hardware manufacturer who ships only in multiples of 10,000 units, with a lead time of four weeks. Fabric and padding must be ordered in multiples of 5,000 square feet and have a three-week lead time. Each seat assembly requires .2 hour of upholstery labor, and each knee pad assembly requires .1 hour of upholstery labor. The planned lead time for each is one week. The finished products are shipped unassembled, but .1 hour of packaging time is required for each one. The company currently has the following inventory levels of each item, and an order with 10,000 casters and 40,000 screws is due to arrive in week 2.

Part No.	Inventory Level
2075	500
6359	8000 sq. ft.
2702	600
2876	1300
124	5000
29	10,000

Part No.	Inventory Level
452	300
2703	600
6390	8000 sq. ft.
2877	1400
453	500
2704	400

Use this to develop planned order releases for each component. If there will be eighty hours of labor time available for making seats and knee pads and sixty hours available for packaging each week, develop a load profile for these two operations.

3. A French company distributes and sells bottled water in the United States. From its bottling plant in the Loire Valley, the company ships to two distribution centers in the United States—one on the East Coast and one on the West. Each of these distribution centers then serves three warehouses, which ship to such customers as grocery stores, restaurants, and specialty shops. The following table indicates order quantities in cases and lead time in weeks for each facility to receive its orders.

	Order Quantity (Cases)	Lead Time (Weeks)
Warehouse A	100	1
Warehouse B	100	1
Warehouse C	150	2
Warehouse D	50	1
Warehouse E	100	1
Warehouse F	100	2
West Coast dist. center	2,000	5
East Coast dist. center	1,000	3

Based on this information, determine gross requirements at the bottling plant if warehouses A, B, and C are served by the West Coast distribution center and warehouses D, E, and F are served from the East Coast.

Warehouse A

	Week 9	10	11	12	13	14	15	16
Forecast demand		30	20	40	30	40	40	30
Scheduled receipts		100						
Projected ending inventory	10							

Warehouse B

	Week 9	10	11	12	13	14	15	16
Forecast demand		40	30	20	10	10	40	20
Scheduled receipts								
Projected ending inventory	40							

Warehouse C

	Week 9	10	11	12	13	14	15	16
Forecast demand		20	50	30	20	50	40	30
Scheduled receipts		150						
Projected ending inventory	30							

Warehouse D

	Week 9	10	11	12	13	14	15	16
Forecast demand		30	40	10	10	30	40	20
Scheduled receipts								
Projected ending inventory	40							

Warehouse E

	Week 9	10	11	12	13	14	15	16
Forecast demand		50	50	30	10	40	50	30
Scheduled receipts		100						
Projected ending inventory	20							

Warehouse F

	Week 9	10	11	12	13	14	15	16
Forecast demand		30	20	20	10	20	10	30
Scheduled receipts								
Projected ending inventory	60							

West Coast Distribution Center

	Week 9	10	11	12	13	14	15	16
Scheduled receipts								
Projected ending inventory	500							

East Coast Distribution Center

	Week 9	10	11	12	13	14	15	16
Scheduled Receipts								
Projected ending inventory	350							

MINI-CASES:

Able Electronics Company

Mike Lanier, production manager for the Able Electronics Company, has just sat through another frustrating meeting with the company's marketing manager, Pam Brandt. Pam has been getting complaints from customers that their orders are not being delivered on time. Mike had to admit that the company's on-time delivery record of 53 percent was not very good. But Mike felt that it was partly the fault of Able's salespeople. In their efforts to make a sale, the company's salespeople often promised delivery within a period of time that they knew would be difficult, if not impossible, for production to meet. Many times, these orders were for special, customized products that required different parts or different processes than Able used on its standard products.

Able Electronics produces printed circuit boards and other electronic components that are sold to companies that use them to make a range of products from computer hardware to televisions and radios. In the past, the company has produced some 2,000 fairly standard products. However, the competitive electronics business has increasingly required that Able be willing to customize its products to customer needs as foreign competition has picked up the business in standardized products by offering much lower prices than Able. Able now makes a total of about 3,600 different products, although only about 300 different components are used.

To meet this increased demand for customized products, Able has started increasing its levels of component-parts inventory. This has helped somewhat, but, on the other hand, the company's inventory investment has increased dramatically from $824,000 to $1,243,000 during the past year. This has also been partly due to efforts to increase the finished-goods inventory for standard products. The rationale behind that move was that it would allow the company to meet standard orders from inventory, freeing up more time to make special orders. Unfortunately, that has not worked. In fact, the on-time record for special orders has worsened.

At one time, the company had considered using MRP, but that idea was abandoned because Able thought that with the large number of different products it made, developing a master schedule would be next to impossible. Now Mike Lanier wonders if he shouldn't reconsider.

1. How might MRP help Able deal with some of its problems?

2. What approach could Able use to overcome the problem of master scheduling for customized products?

3. How would master scheduling improve the salespeople's ability to give customers more realistic delivery dates?

4. What aspects of MRP would be most useful to Able?

Space Age Furniture Company

The Space Age Furniture Company manufactures tables and cabinets to hold microwave ovens and portable televisions. These products are made in various sizes and with various features, but all follow basically the same production and assembly operations. However, two of these products—the Saturn microwave stand and the Gemini TV stand—have a part (no. 3079) that requires machining on a special lathe used only for making that part. At present, the machine is run by Ed Szewczak, a machinist who also operates other machines in Space Age's shop. Once set up and started, the lathe can run essentially unattended. However, the machinist must be present, even if not actually attending the machine, any time one of the machines, including the lathe, is in operation. At present, Ed works a regular forty-hour week. However, due to the workload for producing part 3079, it has been necessary to schedule frequent overtime for him in order to get the necessary parts finished in time.

Coral Snodgrass, operations manager for Space Age, has just heard from Ed's foreman that Ed is becoming unhappy about so much overtime. As Coral knows, Ed has been with the company a long time and is an excellent, reliable employee. Skilled machinists with Ed's experience and employment record are extremely difficult to find. Coral wonders what can be done to alleviate this problem.

Recently, Space Age began using an MRP system that has helped reduce inventories greatly and improve on-time deliveries. In fact, Space Age carries no finished-goods inventory. Instead, everything in the master schedule is being produced for customer orders, so it all gets shipped out the door almost immediately. Previously, Space Age had estimated that it cost $1.25 per week to store each Gemini and $1.50 per week to store each Saturn that wasn't shipped immediately. The master schedule for these two items for the next six weeks is shown below.

Master Schedule

	Week 1	2	3	4	5	6
Gemini	600	400	700	500	400	600
Saturn	300	400	400	600	300	300

The part in question, 3079, is used in two different subassemblies: no. 435, which is used in the Gemini TV stand, and no. 257, which is used in the Saturn microwave stand. One of part 3079 is used in each subassembly, and one of each subassembly is used in each of the final products.

Part 3079 may be produced in essentially any quantity since the lathe that makes it is used for nothing else. However, both of the subassemblies are produced using the same equipment. To minimize changeover time, Space Age has decided that these subassemblies should be made in minimum quantities of 1,000 at a time, although there is no problem with capacity on the equipment that makes them. In fact, an order for 1,000 of subassembly 435 is due to be received in week 1, as is an order for 1,000 of subassembly 257. Lead time for both these subassemblies is one week, and there is no inventory of either expected to be on hand for the beginning of week 1. There is also no on-hand inventory of part 3079, and no orders are in process.

Ed Szewczak earns $22 per hour and gets a 50 percent premium for any overtime work. Whenever part 3079 is run, there is no setup time, but processing takes .03 hour per unit. It costs $.25 per week to hold any of these parts over from one week to the next. The cost of holding each subassembly in inventory is $.75 per unit per week.

1. What options are open to Coral in dealing with this problem?

2. How would reducing the minimum quantity of subassemblies help?

3. What are the costs of carrying excess items in inventory at each stage?

4. What is the trade-off between overtime costs and inventory costs?

Disk-O-Tech, Inc.

Disk-O-Tech, a manufacturer of fixed disk drives (hard disks) for personal computers, is located in the "Silicon Valley" south of San Francisco. The company manufactures only two sizes of fixed disks, 20 megabyte (Mb) and 40 megabyte. Both products require essentially the same manufacturing processes, except that the 40-Mb drive has more surface area for storing data.

Demand for these fixed disks comes from two sources: distributors of computer equipment and personal computer manufacturers. Demand from the latter is usually known well in advance due to long-term contracts. However, orders from distributors are coming in all the time, and demand may fluctuate. For example, the following information is now known at the beginning of December:

Forecast of Demand from Distributors

	Month Jan.	Feb.	Mar.	Apr.	May	June
20 Mb	5,000	4,000	4,000	4,500	5,000	5,000
40 Mb	2,000	1,500	2,000	2,000	3,000	3,000

Original Equipment Manufacturer (OEM) Contracts

1. 3,000 20-Mb drives per month, January through September.
2. 1,000 40-Mb drives per month, January through December.
3. 2,000 of each, April through November.

For medium-range production planning purposes, Disk-O-Tech assumes that 1.6 labor hours are required per unit regardless of size and lumps both disk drives together in its production plan. At present, the company has 100 direct labor employees who each work eight hours per day. Those employees earn an average of $8.00 per hour. Overtime is limited to two hours per day and is paid at a 50 percent premium. Employees work five days per week, with national holidays as paid vacations. It currently costs Disk-O-Tech $500 to hire a new employee and $1,000 to lay one off.

Disk-O-Tech expects to have 1,000 20-Mb and 500 40-Mb drives in stock at the beginning of January. It costs $.30 to store a disk drive for a month, and inventory cost is based on end-of-month inventory.

1. Based on the preceding information, develop a medium-range (aggregate) production plan for the coming year (use actual calendar working days) that minimizes cost over the six-month planning horizon.

2. For master scheduling purposes, Disk-O-Tech calls the first week of January week 1 and numbers each week sequentially throughout the year. Within each month, the OEM orders are divided among weeks as uniformly as possible. The following table shows weekly forecasted distributor demand for the first nine weeks of the year and actual orders received as of the beginning of December.

Distributor Orders

	20 Mb		*40 Mb*	
Week	**Forecast**	**Received**	**Forecast**	**Received**
1	1,000	800	400	500
2	1,000	1,100	400	500
3	1,000	1,200	400	300
4	1,000	900	400	400
5	1,000	900	400	300
6	1,000	700	400	200
7	1,000	500	400	200
8	1,000	300	400	100
9	1,000	200	400	0

For rough-cut capacity purposes, Disk-O-Tech checks its MPS requirements for final assembly against availability. Each 20-Mb drive requires .2 hour of assembly time, and each 40-Mb drive requires .3 hour. There are presently fifteen employees in the assembly department.

Based on your medium-range plan and the preceding information, develop a master schedule for the first nine weeks of next year (again, use a calendar to determine actual working days). Develop a load profile that compares load to capacity for final assembly each week.

3. The 20-Mb drive has one read/write head, and the 40-Mb drive has two. However, these heads are the same for both products. Lead time for manufacturing heads is two weeks, and on-hand inventory of heads is expected to be 10,000 two weeks before the end of December.

Each read/write head must be manufactured on a special machine, of which Disk-O-Tech has only one. Each head requires .01 hour of manufacturing time on this machine. Using your MPS and the preceding information, develop a schedule of planned order releases for heads, and determine capacity requirements each week for the machine that makes them.

SELECTED BIBLIOGRAPHY

American Production and Inventory Control Society. *Capacity Planning and Control*. Falls Church, Va.: American Production and Inventory Control Society, 1979.

Anderson, John C.; Schroeder, Roger G.; Tupy, Sharon E.; and White, Edna M. "Material Requirements Planning Systems: The State of the Art." *Production and Inventory Management* 23, no. 4 (1982): 51–67.

Bahl, H. C., and Ritzman, Larry P. "An Empirical Investigation of Different Strategies for Material Requirements Planning." *Journal of Operations Management* 3, no. 2 (1983): 67–77.

Berry, William L.; Vollmann, Thomas E.; and Whybark, D. Clay. *Master Production Scheduling*. Falls Church, Va.: American Production and Inventory Control Society, 1979.

Chung, C. H., and Krajewski, Lee. "Planning Horizons for Master Production Scheduling." *Journal of Operations Management* 4, no. 4 (August 1984).

Khumawala, Basheer M.; Hison, Charles; and Law, Japhet S. "MRP II in the Service Industries." *Production and Inventory Management* 27, no. 3 (1986): 57–63.

Krupp, James A. G. "Why MRP Systems Fail: Traps to Avoid." *Production and Inventory Management* 25, no. 3 (1984): 48–53.

Martin, Andre J. *DRP: Distribution Resource Planning*. Englewood Cliffs, N.J.: Prentice-Hall, 1983.

Mehra, Satish, and Reid, M. J. "MRP Implementation Using an Action Plan." *Interfaces* 12, no. 1 (February 1982): 69–73.

Orlicky, Joseph. *Material Requirements Planning*. New York: McGraw-Hill, 1975.

Schroeder, Roger G.; Anderson, John C.; Tupy, Sharon E.; and White, Edna M. "A Study of MRP Benefits and Costs." *Journal of Operations Management* 2, no. 1 (October 1981): 1–9.

Steinberg, Earle E.; Lee, William B.; and Khumawala, Basheer. "Requirements Planning Systems in the Health Care Environment." *Journal of Operations Management* 2, no. 4 (August 1982): 251–259.

White, Edna M; Anderson, John C.; Schroeder, Roger G.; and Tupy, Sharon E. "A Study of the MRP Implementation Process." *Journal of Operations Management* 2, no. 3 (May 1982): 145–153.

Wight, Oliver W. *Production and Inventory Management in the Computer Age*. Boston: CBI Publishing, 1974.

Wight, Oliver W. *MRP II: Unlocking America's Productivity Potential*. Williston, Vt.: Oliver Wight Limited Publications, 1981.

Chapter 12

Just-in-Time and Synchronous Operations

CHAPTER OUTLINE

LEARNING OBJECTIVES

After completing this chapter, you should be able to

- Explain the basic concepts of just-in-time (JIT).
- Describe what is meant by the "pull" system.
- Explain the use of C-kanban and P-kanban.
- Calculate the number of kanban cards needed for a part.
- Discuss some ways to simplify the production process.
- Explain why quality control is important to JIT.
- List the main components of total preventive maintenance (TPM).
- Explain how JIT is applied to services.
- Discuss the planning process under JIT.
- Determine a mixed-model assembly sequence.
- Calculate cycle times.
- Explain the similarities and differences between MRP and JIT.
- Discuss the cultural aspects of JIT.
- Identify bottlenecks and capacity-constrained resources.
- Explain the difference between a process batch and a transfer batch.
- Show how to set up a drum-buffer-rope system.
- Explain how MRP, JIT, and synchronous manufacturing are similar and different.

OPERATIONS IN ACTION

Harley-Davidson: Using JIT to Win Back Market Share

The assembly line at Harley-Davidson. Courtesy: *Harley-Davidson Motor, Co., Inc.*

Who hasn't seen a gleaming Harley-Davidson motorcycle cruising easily down the highway and been awed by the machine's sleek lines and powerful rumble? For many years, Harley-Davidson held a preeminent position as the only motorcycle company in the United States. But with the arrival of all the new Honda, Kawasaki, and Yamaha motorcycles from Japan, Harley was hit hard during the 1970s. Somehow, those Japanese companies were able to offer state-of-the-art cycles of higher quality at a lower price than comparable Harleys. In fact, in 1978 Harley-Davidson's motorcycle business was in big trouble when the company tried, but failed, to prove that Japanese companies were dumping motorcycles on the U.S. market at prices below manufacturing costs. The precariousness of Harley's position in the marketplace came to light when it was shown in court that operating costs of those Japanese manufacturers were a full 30 percent below Harley's costs. One of the primary reasons for those lower costs was the Japanese use of just-in-time (JIT) manufacturing. In 1982, Harley-Davidson decided that it too would have to use JIT if it was to survive.

Harley-Davidson already had a bad reputation among its suppliers for changing production schedules at the last minute and then making frantic calls to suppliers for needed parts. When Harley announced that it was going to a just-in-time system, most suppliers were skeptical, eventhough they knew little about JIT. Their past experiences with Harley made them doubt that the company would have the dedication to follow through with such a system.

In spite of some initial problems in getting suppliers to go along, Harley stuck by its plans for JIT, developing its own system called MAN (Material As Needed). To get recalcitrant suppliers interested, the company sent out teams of buyers and engineers. These teams went to suppliers' plants and showed how machines could be modified to reduce the setup times between jobs and improve the quality of parts. They even taught courses in statistics to help the suppliers' employees use statistical quality control. Vendors were also invited to visit Harley's plant in York, Pennsylvania, where they could see the benefits of JIT. Many of those vendors asked for help in applying the methods to their own facilities.

The results for Harley have been dramatic. Today, the company is recognized as one of the outstanding U.S. users of JIT. The motorcycle business is profitable again, largely due to decreases in manufacturing costs. For instance, the company has been able to reduce the cost of warranty work, scrap, and rework by 60 percent. Overall, setup time on machines has been reduced by 75 percent. The number of suppliers has also been reduced, enabling Harley to work out better contracts and reduce the distances from suppliers to its plant. This has meant a more reliable supply network and less need for large inventories of parts.

For Harley-Davidson, JIT has been a way to eliminate many problem areas in its production operations. Costs have been reduced, leading to greater profitability. A higher-quality product also has meant more satisfied customers.[1]

INTRODUCTION

Within the past twenty years, worldwide competition has increased substantially, and successful companies have been forced to constantly improve their operations. During the 1970s, many companies turned to MRP as a way of getting a leg up on their competition and were successful. But, today, companies are finding that MRP is not enough. Two new approaches to operations are now gaining increasing favor—just-in-time (JIT) and synchronous manufacturing. In this chapter, we describe both and compare them to MRP and to each other.

JUST-IN-TIME

Originally pioneered by the Japanese auto maker Toyota, just-in-time (JIT) is now being used by many organizations throughout the world, including General Motors, Apple Computer, and IBM. Although many companies are just beginning to use JIT, the idea has been around for quite some time. In fact, Toyota has been using JIT for about twenty years and claims that the original concept of JIT was put forth by none other than Henry Ford.[2]

When the success of Japanese companies first brought attention to JIT, many people outside of Japan immediately classified it as an inventory control system. In fact, it is often referred to under other names, including stockless production and zero inventories. Although it is true that the low level of inventory carried by companies operating under JIT is one apparent aspect of the system, JIT is actually much more than just another system for controlling inventory. Companies successfully using JIT find it really amounts to a totally different philosophy of how a company should operate. Thus, we will define **just-in-time (JIT)** as a philosophy of operation that seeks to maximize efficiency and eliminate waste in any form, influencing all parts of a company, including purchasing, engineering, marketing, personnel, and quality control, and even determining the relationships among the company, its suppliers, and its customers. As you will learn, the benefits of JIT go far beyond cost savings due to reduced inventories, even extending into a company's strategic planning.

Fundamental Concepts of JIT

Flow Manufacturing

If you think back to the discussion of aggregate planning in Chapter 10, you will recall that inventory represents a huge capital investment that ties up money a company could put to other uses. For instance, without large inventory investments, a company could buy better equipment, develop new product lines, or even give its employees raises. Thus, any unnecessary inventory is actually robbing a company of other, more beneficial ways to use the money.

Material requirements planning (MRP) was identified in Chapter 11 as one possible way to cut down inventories. During the discussion of MRP, we had introduced the thought that it did not make much sense to have parts and materials sitting around in inventory "just in case" they would be needed. By using MRP, a company can convert the master schedule into requirements for component parts and raw materials, allowing the company to determine exactly what is needed and when it is needed. In this way, unnecessary inventories can be reduced.

But MRP does not cut inventory to the minimum possible. Using MRP, companies usually group their requirements together for a week, or more, at a time. Thus, orders are generally placed to cover at least a week's worth of production and are planned to arrive at the beginning of the week in which they are first needed. Some excess inventory—at least for short periods of time—is therefore inevitable in an MRP system. Suppose, though, that we modify the MRP idea by refusing to look several weeks into the future. Instead, we will look only at what is being produced now and order just what we need for current production.

For an automobile manufacturer, this might mean that no inventory of tires would be kept in stock. Instead, the four tires for a car would arrive just at the moment they must be mounted on the rims just before being put on the car as it rolls down the assembly line. The result would be absolutely no inventory of tires. Carrying this idea further, there would be no inventory of the other parts that go on a car either. Instead, parts would be delivered from suppliers or from the manufacturing operation for those parts just when they were needed to be put on a car and only in the quantity needed for that car. Throughout the entire operation, there would be no unnecessary inventory—only work-in-process inventory destined for immediate use at the next processing operation.

Think of how this would work. A worker finishes a carburetor part and immediately hands it to another worker, who combines that part with others to produce an assembled carburetor. As soon as the carburetor is finished, it gets handed to another worker, who puts it on an automobile rolling down the assembly line. All along the way, the same thing happens as parts and subassemblies are produced only when needed and only in the quantities needed for immediate use.

Thinking back to Chapter 7, you might begin to realize that an objective of JIT is to make materials flow as they would in a continuous flow process, such as an oil refinery. In a refinery, work-in-process inventories are kept to a minimum, and material flows smoothly from one processing step to the next. The difference is that a company's objective with JIT is to make this smooth, uninterrupted flow run all the way from suppliers to final customers.

Exhibit 12.1 presents a useful analogy. Think of parts, materials, subassemblies, and final products as water. If there are many pools in which this water can collect as inventory, then the flow will not be smooth and swift, but will be like a series of quiet, stagnant ponds, as shown at the top of Exhibit 12.1. An objective of JIT is to eliminate these ponds and produce a smooth, rapid flow—like the mountain stream shown at the bottom of that exhibit.

Simplified Production Process

Eliminating inventory is often much more difficult than it might seem. For example, what if a certain machine takes five hours to readjust (setup time) whenever the company switches from making one part to making another? Obviously, if only one unit is made at a time, the machine will probably spend more time being readjusted than it will making parts. The answer to this problem is to simplify—either by buying a more general-purpose machine that can easily be

Exhibit 12.1 Water Analogy of JIT

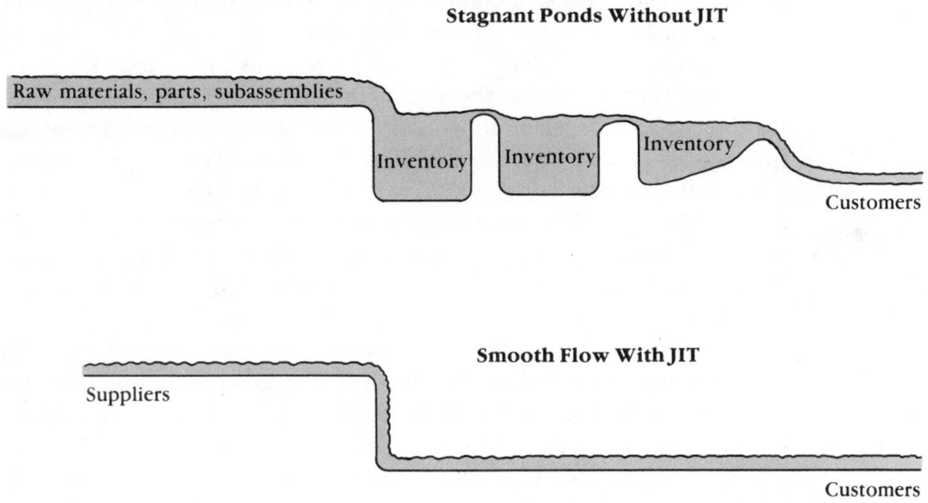

Stagnant Ponds Without JIT

Raw materials, parts, subassemblies

Inventory

Inventory

Inventory

Customers

Smooth Flow With JIT

Suppliers

Customers

changed from making one part to making another or by simplifying the readjustment process in some way. Companies that use JIT often have many general-purpose machines and have developed simple ways of switching them from making one part to making another. Often this setup time can be reduced to less than a minute. In fact, some companies have eliminated setup time altogether by using one simple machine for each part, instead of trying to do all parts on one complex, multipurpose machine.

Another problem encountered in using JIT has to do with the movement of materials. In the preceding section, we described how one worker might hand a carburetor part to another worker, who assembles the finished carburetor. But what if those workers are on opposite sides of the plant and an elaborate automated handling system has been used to move those parts in large batches? Once again, the answer is to simplify by getting rid of the automated handling system and moving the workers so they are in close proximity. Many companies implementing JIT have thrown out complex material-handling systems and rearranged the plant so workers could simply move parts by hand from one operation to the next.

Most companies using traditional purchasing methods will buy large quantities from their suppliers once every month or every couple of months. These transactions usually involve much paperwork, such as purchase requisitions, packing slips, bills of lading, and invoices, for each order. A company using JIT, which sometimes places orders with suppliers several times per day, would be deluged in paperwork under this traditional approach to purchasing. To avoid such a problem, many companies have used **blanket purchase requisitions,** which authorize a vendor to supply a certain total quantity spread out over a certain time. Individual orders may be initiated by phone calls or by some other method.

Uncovering Problems Buried by Inventory

While inventory reduction is the most obvious aspect of JIT, its most valuable benefit is that it forces a company to uncover problems and inefficiencies in its operations. To see why, consider the electric power supplied to your home. The actual flow of electricity occurs only in response to a need for power, such as when you turn on a light. There is no inventory of electricity anywhere between your home and the generating plant. In essence, your electricity is supplied *just in time.* Now suppose that something occurs between the generating plant and your home—maybe a wire goes down or a transformer burns out. No matter what the problem, you'll be aware that something is wrong when you have no electricity. If this happens to enough other people, the electric company will be deluged with calls; a crew will be dispatched immediately to find the problem and remedy it.

The situation is very similar for a company operating under JIT. With little or no inventory, any problem that disrupts the flow of work will become immediately obvious to everyone as work centers must shut down for lack of materials. Attention will immediately focus on the problem, and all effort will be devoted to solving that problem. However, because it is realized that production will again be disrupted if the problem reoccurs, effort will be devoted to a long-term problem solution, not just a quick fix.

An Emphasis on Quality Control

One problem that can be especially disruptive in a JIT system has to do with quality. Think again of the carburetor assembly operation in an automobile factory. Suppose the worker making carburetor parts turns out a defective one. When the next worker tries to assemble that part on the carburetor, it won't fit. This immediately causes a problem because there will now be no assembled carburetor to put on the next car. Everything will come to a halt because of that one bad part. And all eyes will be turned on the worker who made that bad part. You can probably bet that person will take steps to ensure that the same thing does not happen again.

But what if these parts were produced in large batches? The worker assembling carburetors could just toss the bad part onto a pile with other bad parts and reach into the batch for a good part. There would be no incentive to change anything or to improve, especially on behalf of the worker making parts—who probably doesn't even know a bad part was made. By producing in batches, with large inventories, a company could chug along like this and never realize a problem existed—and also not realize how much better and more efficiently it could be operating.

The water analogy used in Exhibit 12.1 also illustrates this point. As before, parts and materials are represented by water. But this time, we can think of problems as rocks below the water, as shown in Exhibit 12.2. Some of these rocks may be just visible from the surface of the water, but may be difficult to remove due, at least in part, to the water. Other rocks may be totally obscured by the water. These rocks may represent quality problems, machine-breakdown problems, or any other problems that can disrupt production. When the water level is lowered, the rocks can be clearly identified and removed.

To achieve the level of quality required, JIT companies are adopting **total quality control (TQC).** TQC will be discussed more in Chapter 17, but briefly it is an approach to quality that emphasizes "quality at the source" by placing responsibility on all parts of the organization to build quality into the product.

Exhibit 12.2 Problems Hidden by Inventory

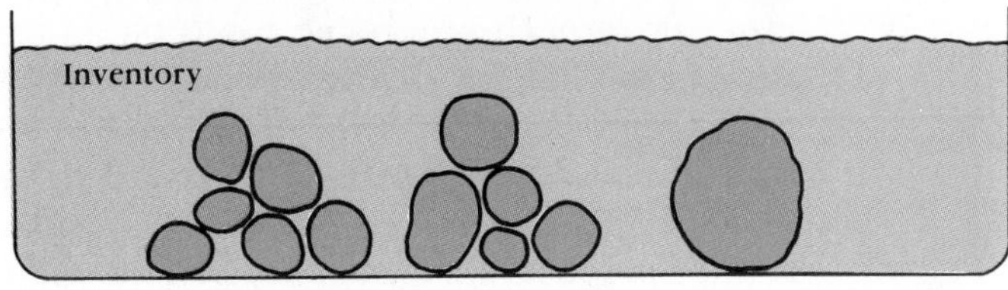

Rocks can be seen and removed when the water level is lowered

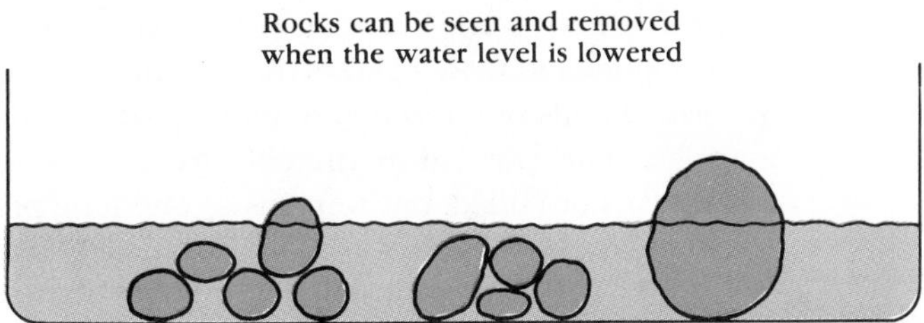

Constant Improvement as an Organizational Philosophy

The objective of eliminating waste in any form is difficult to achieve. Even such companies as Toyota, which has been using JIT for many years, still have not reached that goal. But it remains a goal toward which they are constantly striving. A company operating under JIT is constantly working to improve efficiency, reduce waste, and smooth the flow of materials. In working toward those ends, the company uncovers many problems and finds better ways to do practically everything.

Even companies that have been extremely successful with JIT have not stopped trying to improve. Such companies as Toyota, once their own systems have been put in place, extend some aspects of JIT to their suppliers—and even to their customers. For example, Toyota has worked to get their suppliers to use JIT and to tie into Toyota's JIT system. At the other end, efforts have been undertaken to keep demand at the constant, uniform rate that is needed for a smooth flow from supplier to customer.

The JIT "Pull" System

Although the differences and similarities between MRP and JIT will be discussed in detail later, we will briefly describe one very important difference here. Most traditional production systems, including MRP, use what is called a "push" system to move materials through the system. A **push system** is based on the idea that materials get *pushed* through the processing operations based on a schedule. Under this system, an order to produce a part or product gets "launched" into the system at a scheduled time and is pushed from one work center to another according to that schedule.

MRP is a slightly improved push system in the sense that each order release is based on requirements generated by the master schedule. Thus, materials are pushed through the system in an effort to meet that schedule. Everything is based on what has been planned to happen at some time in the future.

JIT uses a "pull" system to move parts and materials. Instead of pushing materials through processing based on a preplanned schedule, a **pull system** moves materials based on actual needs at successive work centers. Thus, if work center A provides parts to work center B, A will produce only in response to an actual need for more parts at B. This pull system concept actually starts with customer demand, which pulls finished products from the company. As those finished products are made, they pull the appropriate materials through processing. Materials and parts are also pulled from vendors and suppliers.

One way of comparing a push system and a pull system is based on the idea of a rope. Suppose we think of material moving through the various production processes as a rope. Under MRP, coils of rope (batches) are created at various machines and work centers throughout the plant. The MRP logic is used to ensure that all coils of the rope are moved forward through the processes at the appropriate time, preventing the coils from building up at any one spot. With JIT, the rope is not coiled, but remains as one long piece running through all processes. To move the rope forward, one has to simply pull on the end; there is no need to coordinate movement of coils because there are no coils, as shown in Exhibit 12.3.

The key element of a pull system is some means for communicating backward through the production process whenever more parts or materials are needed at "downstream" work centers. In some instances, workers can determine visually

Exhibit 12.3 Push System Versus Pull System

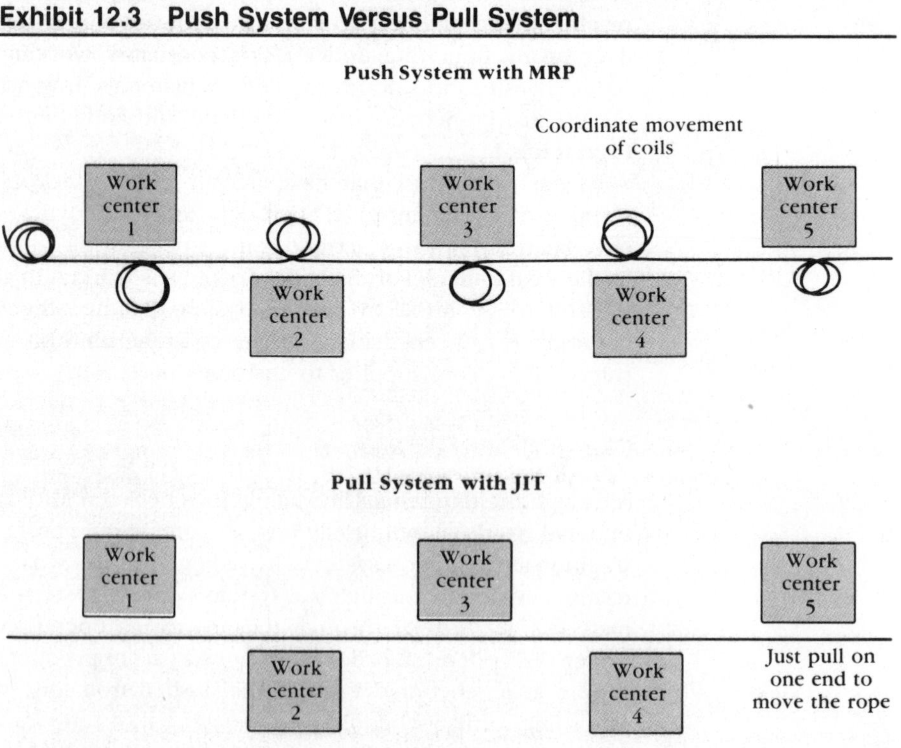

when the next work center needs to be supplied. However, work centers are often too far apart physically for direct visual communication, and visual communication will not work with suppliers whose plants are at least several miles away.

Kanban Systems

Within a JIT system, there are several ways that pull signals can be communicated, but one of the best known is a method developed by Toyota based on cards, or kanban (con-bon), as they are called in Japan. **Kanban** is a Japanese word that can refer to a sign or a marker and literally means "visible record." However, in the operations context, the word ***kanban*** refers strictly to a card that is used to signal the need for more materials, parts, or subassemblies at downstream operations (see Exhibit 12.4).

Standard Containers of Parts. Theoretically, the ideal situation with JIT would be to produce one unit at a time. However, this usually is not possible. For instance, the travel time to and from a supplier may be much longer than the time between requirements for the part from that supplier, or there may be an imbalance in the production rate between a particular work center and the preceding work center that supplies it. In these and other cases, it is necessary to move containers of parts rather than single units. A kanban is most often associated either with the movement of a container of parts or with the production of parts to fill an empty container. Accordingly, two types of kanban are generally used, the conveyance kanban and the production kanban.

Conveyance Kanban. The **conveyance kanban,** or **C-kanban,** is an authorization to move a container of parts or materials. Without it, nothing can be moved. The way a C-kanban works is depicted in Exhibit 12.5. As the exhibit

Exhibit 12.4 Example of a Kanban Card

M.A.N. SHIPPING AUTHORIZATION

PART NUMBER DESCRIPTION DELIVERY TO
17389-83A ROCKER ARM 903

CONTAINER PALLETAINER QUANTITY 800

Ship To:
HARLEY-DAVIDSON MOTOR CO. INC.
11700 W. Capitol Drive
Milwaukee, WI 53201

Card Seq. 3

Exhibit 12.5 Single Kanban System

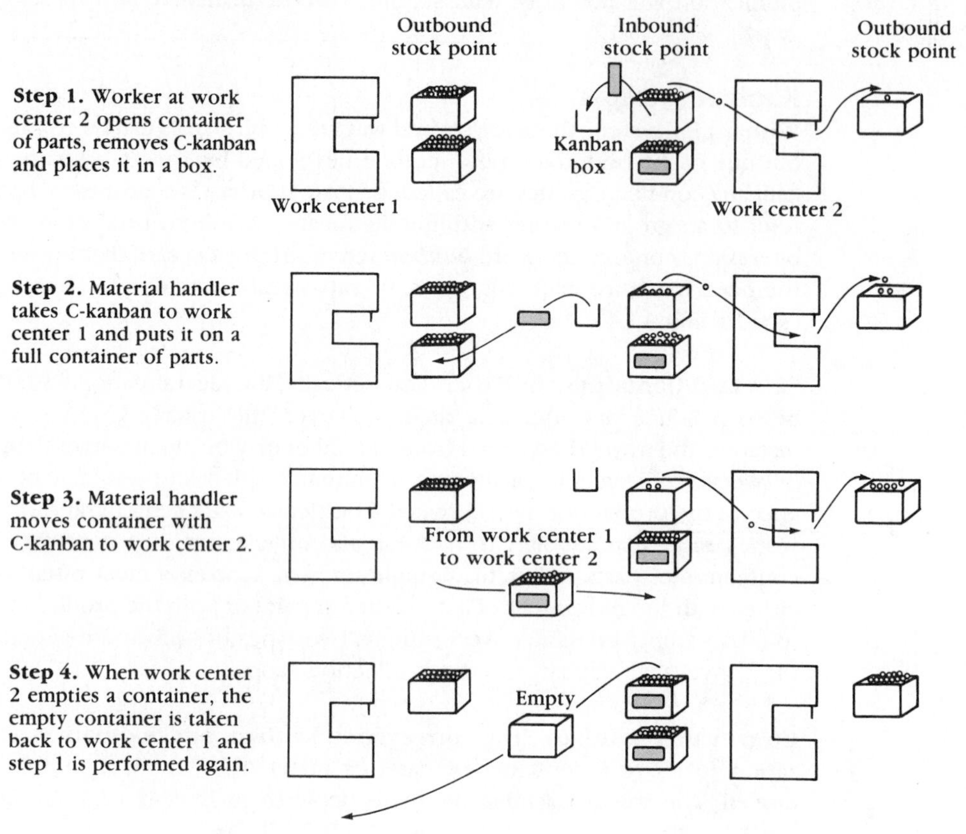
Outbound stock point
Inbound stock point
Outbound stock point
Step 1. Worker at work center 2 opens container of parts, removes C-kanban and places it in a box.
Kanban box
Work center 1
Work center 2
Step 2. Material handler takes C-kanban to work center 1 and puts it on a full container of parts.
Step 3. Material handler moves container with C-kanban to work center 2.
From work center 1 to work center 2
Step 4. When work center 2 empties a container, the empty container is taken back to work center 1 and step 1 is performed again.
Empty

shows, any container with parts in it cannot be moved without the C-kanban attached.

Many companies, notably Kawasaki in the United States, use only the C-kanban. This single-card kanban system is still an effective means of controlling inventory. The number of full containers is limited by the number of C-kanban, and inventory at the using work center (work center 2 in Exhibit 12.5) can be replenished only when a container is emptied. Thus, that work center cannot possibly horde extra parts. The feeding work center (work center 1) usually produces to some sort of schedule, which may be generated through MRP. This schedule is generally based on the expected day's requirements for work center 2. However, limited storage space at work center 1 is generally used to shut off production at that work center if parts are not being used up at the expected rate (for instance, if work center 2 is shut down for some reason). In order for the single-card kanban system to work, the following rules must be observed:

1. Containers holding parts can be moved only when a card is attached.
2. Standard containers must always be used.
3. Each standard container can be filled only with the standard number of units.

Production Kanban. Some companies, primarily Toyota in Japan, use a two-kanban system that combines the conveyance kanban with a production kanban. The **production kanban,** or **P-kanban,** is used to authorize the production of parts or subassemblies. The two-kanban system, which combines the C-kanban and the P-kanban, is known as a **dual-card kanban system.** Its major advantage over single-card kanban is that it allows greater control over production as well as over inventory.

The dual-card system operates as shown in Exhibit 12.6. Note that in this case, work center 1 does not produce to a schedule, but only when it is authorized to do so by a P-kanban.

Exhibit 12.6 Dual-Card Kanban System

Step 1. Worker at work center 2 opens a container of parts and places the C-kanban in a box.

Step 2. Material handler takes C-kanban and an empty container to work center 1.

Step 3. The material handler removes the P-kanban from a full container of parts and places it in the box.

Step 4. The C-kanban is placed on the full container.

Step 5. Full container (with C-kanban) is taken to work center 2.

Step 6. P-kanban at work center 1 is authorization to make more parts. P-kanban is placed on container when full. Start again with step 1.

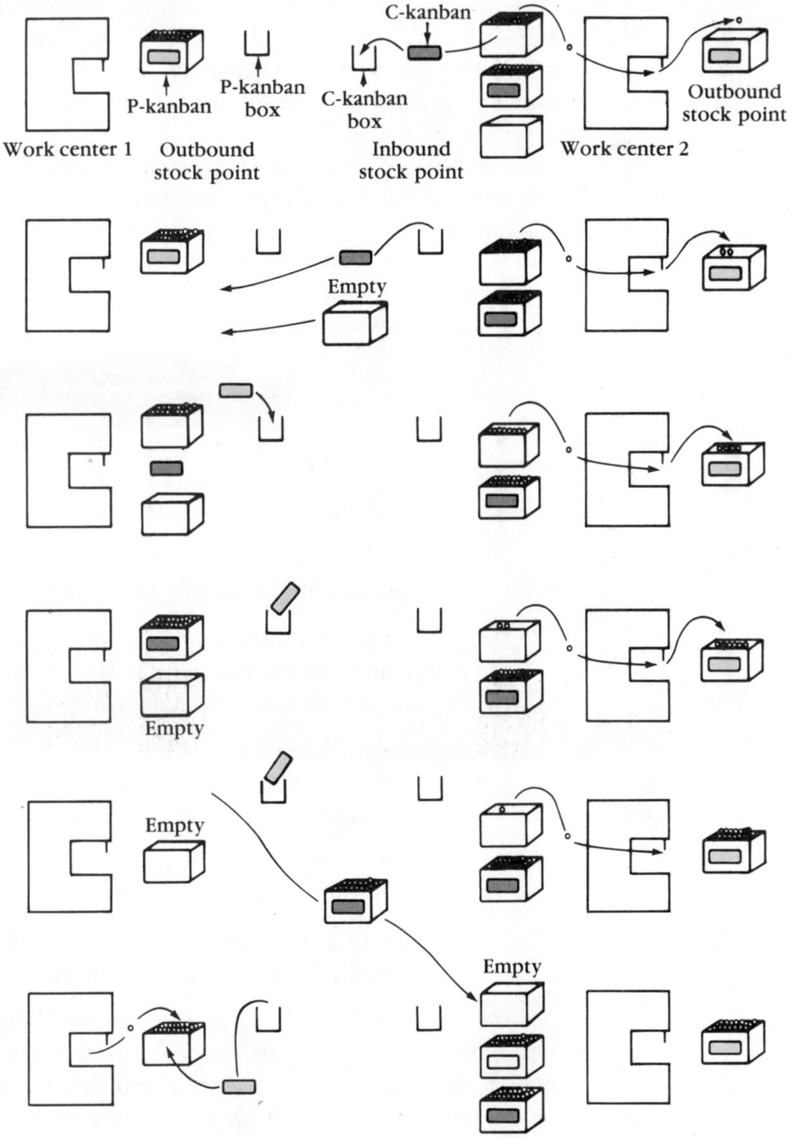

Although the rules for the dual-card system are similar to those for a single-card system, there are enough slight differences that it is worth listing the dual-card rules here.

1. Either a C-kanban or P-kanban must be attached to all containers of parts, except the one currently being used.
2. A container of parts can never be moved without a C-kanban.
3. Standard containers must always be used.
4. Each standard container can be filled only with the standard number of units.
5. A standard container of parts can be produced only when an unattached P-kanban authorizes it.
6. A P-kanban is attached to a container once it has been filled.

Determining the Number of Kanban. As you can see, the dual-card kanban system very easily restricts inventory. Work center 2 cannot replenish its inventory without an available C-kanban, and work center 1 cannot produce more without an available P-kanban. Thus, the maximum inventory level in the system will always be the total number of kanban (P-kanban and C-kanban) multiplied by the number of units per standard container. For example, if each container holds fifty units and there are three kanban, total inventory will be limited to a maximum of $3 \times 50 = 150$ units.

One question that must be answered in using the kanban system is "How many cards should there be?" Robert Hall, a well-known author and expert on JIT, suggests the following formula:[3]

$$y = \frac{D(T_w + T_p)(1 + X)}{a}$$

where

y = total number of kanban cards (conveyance plus production) for a given part

D = planned usage rate for the part (units/day)

T_w = average waiting time for replenishment of parts—the time that elapses between when a C-kanban is removed from a container of parts until it is returned on a new container of parts (fraction of a day)

T_p = average production time for a container of parts—the time that elapses after a P-kanban is placed in the box until it can be placed back on a completed container of parts (fraction of a day)

X = a policy variable set by management corresponding to possible inefficiency in the system

a = capacity of a standard container, in units (should usually be less than 10 percent of daily usage for that part)

If the value of X is set to zero, then the preceding formula provides just enough inventory ($y \times a$) to cover the time required to produce and move a container of parts. In other words, it will be the minimum necessary to avoid stopping the process to wait for more parts. When X is increased above zero, it represents the excess, as a proportion of the minimum possible, that is being introduced to accommodate possible inefficiencies.

Example

A certain part is used at the rate of 500 per day, and the standard container holds twenty-five units. The average time that elapses after a P-kanban is put in the P-kanban box until it is placed on a full container of parts is .23 day. The average time for a C-kanban to make a complete circuit is .02 day. Management has set X at .2.

$$y = \frac{500(.02 + .23)(1 + .2)}{25} = 6$$

Therefore, a total of six kanban cards should be available for this part. However, five would be the minimum with no inefficiency ($X = 0$).

The JIT philosophy of always seeking improvement will lead companies to try to decrease inventory. This is easily done by reducing the number of cards available. The way this usually works is that companies get everything running smoothly with a given number of cards. They then remove one card and wait to see what problems surface as inventory decreases. These problems are then attacked until the system can run smoothly again with the decreased number of cards. Then another card is removed, and the problem-solving process starts again. It is a never-ending quest for improvement.

Simplifying the Production Process

Earlier we used several analogies involving water to describe JIT. Such analogies have been used by many others before us, but they provide a useful way of thinking about JIT. Remember that the objective of JIT is to eliminate the pools of inventory and obtain a smooth, steady flow of materials all the way from supplier to customer.

Within a plant, we can think of that flow much like the creeks and rivulets that converge into streams—with those streams eventually converging into rivers. In this analogy, streams could be made up of processing operations for individual parts. Those parts flow together into subassemblies, which are then eventually joined together as finished products. The objective of JIT is to keep all those rivers and tributaries flowing smoothly without any pools of inventory. The following material describes some ways to achieve that objective.

Plant Layout

Notice, at the top of Exhibit 12.7, that each part must move from one machine area to another. This requires a lot of material handling and also encourages the production of each part in large batches. But when the machines are rearranged, as shown at the bottom of Exhibit 12.7, each part can flow directly from one processing step to the next. This type of layout also allows the production of small batches since each group of machines is dedicated to just one part. Also, there will not be interference between two parts that must both be processed on the

Exhibit 12.7 Rearranging Machine Layout for Smoother Flow

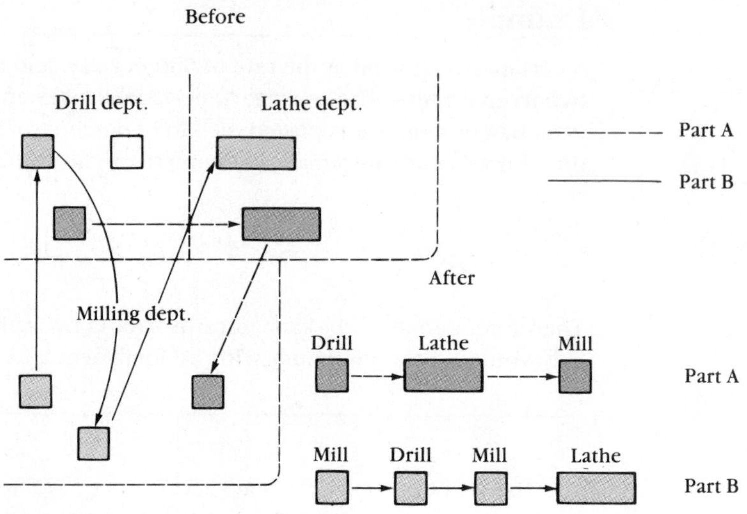

Before

Drill dept.
Lathe dept.
Milling dept.

After

Drill Lathe Mill
Part A

Mill Drill Mill Lathe
Part B

------ Part A
—— Part B

same machine. It is this type of interference that leads to long queues of parts to be processed.

Group Technology. One disadvantage with the preceding layout, in which machines are rearranged for each part, is that a large number of parts could mean a large number of these machine groupings. Group technology, a concept discussed in Chapter 8, is one way of avoiding this problem. Recall that **group technology (GT)** is the grouping together into "families" of parts that require the same—or a very similar—sequence of processing operations. For example, many different parts might all follow the sequence lathe-mill-grind. These parts could all be grouped together as a family. The processing operation, which would include a lathe, a mill, and a grinder, would be known as a group technology (GT) cell, or a group of machines that have been brought together to process a particular family of parts.

Group technology is very important in JIT because it allows companies to maintain a smooth flow of materials by grouping machines together for sequential processing. At the same time, group technology can reduce the number of different processing cells required.

U-Shaped Layout. Remember that one of the primary objectives of JIT is efficiency. Group technology and GT cells can help increase efficiency by improving material flow, reducing material handling, and increasing machine utilization. However, people must usually operate those machines. Using those people efficiently means that the minimum possible number of people should be used and that they must be able to communicate effectively. To achieve this end, a U-shaped layout usually works best.

INTEGRATING THE SYSTEM

Group Technology Ties Together Product Design and Facility Layout

Group technology also plays an important role in product design. To see why, consider again the two parts presented in Exhibit 12.7. Part A required the sequence of operations drill-lathe-mill; part B required the sequence mill-drill-mill-lathe. Suppose we could redesign part B so that both milling operations could be done last in the sequence. In that case, both parts A and B could go into the same family and be processed by the same GT cell. This type of approach not only saves on equipment and floor space for that equipment, but also can lead to better equipment utilization as more parts are made on the same machines. Achieving such results requires close coordination between engineering, which designs the parts, and operations, which must lay out the facilities to produce those parts.

In a **U-shaped layout,** the machines are arranged as shown in the photograph on page 490. Materials will flow in at one end, go around the U, and come out as finished parts at the opposite side of the same end where they started.

Reducing Setup Time

Setup time is the time it takes to readjust a machine or group of machines after making one particular part or product until acceptable units of another part or product are produced. Setup time may involve changing the tooling, adjusting the equipment, checking to be sure that the new part or product is being made to specifications, and then readjusting the equipment if it is not.

Setup time is an important consideration in JIT because it disrupts the smooth flow of materials. For example, a GT cell may be used to make several different parts. Although each of those parts follows the same essential processing sequence, each may require different tooling in the machines or a different machine setting. If excessive time is taken for setup in changing from one part to another, then the flow of materials will be momentarily stopped—causing downstream processing operations to pause until the flow resumes. If "upstream" operations continue unchecked, unnecessary inventory will build up in the system, much as water builds up when a dam is placed across a river.

Thus, another objective in a JIT system is to reduce setup time as much as possible. The activities that can help reduce setup time are as follows:

- Closely examine each setup to determine steps that can be eliminated or better ways of doing things.
- Prepare as much ahead of time as possible. All tools and equipment should be readily available in predetermined locations.
- Try to do as much setup as possible with the machine running. Stop the machine only when absolutely necessary.
- Use special equipment to shorten downtime whenever possible.
- Practice and refine the setup procedures.

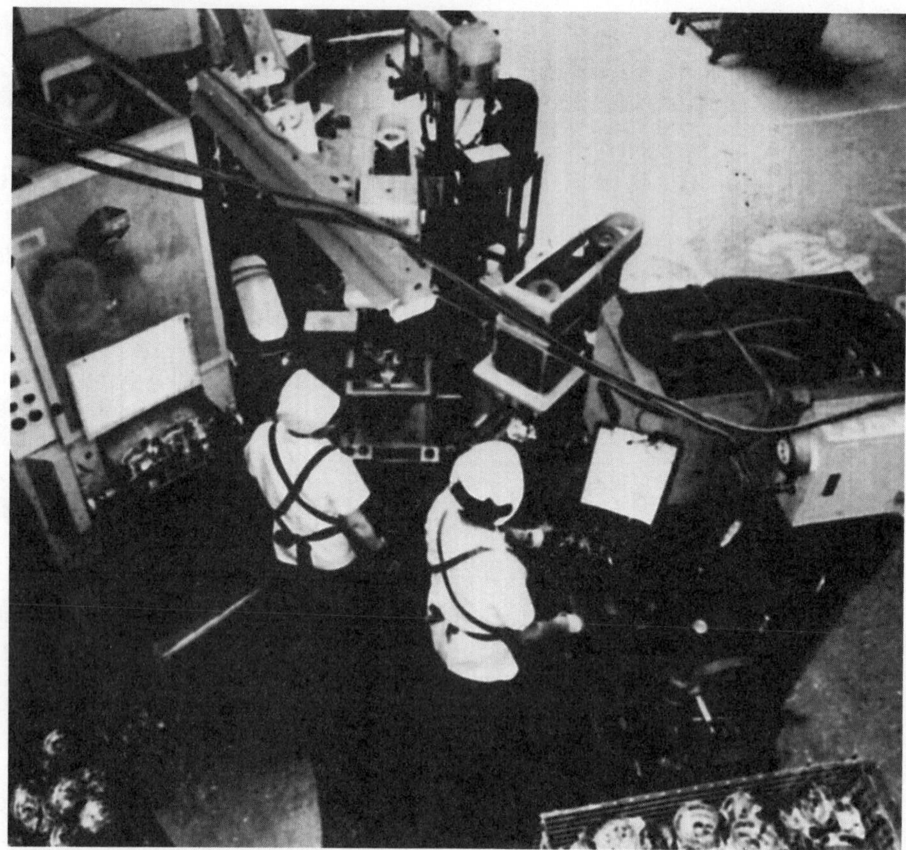

A typical U-shaped Layout. Reprinted by permission from page 126 of *JIT Factory Revolution* by Hirano and Black, Copyright © 1988 by Productivity Press. All rights reserved.

Exhibit 12.8 indicates the setup time reductions that several companies have been able to achieve by using the procedures described above. As you can see, these changes did not occur overnight. In fact, companies often think it is not possible to reduce setup times on certain equipment. But Exhibit 12.8 shows what can be achieved with hard work and dedication.

One question you might ask at this point is "How small must setup time be?" The answer is that it depends. Some operations may have enough slack that the existing setup time is not disrupting material flow. In those cases, nothing needs to be done. But other operations may cause problems. As we discussed before, the idea is to remove inventory from the system and see what problems surface. If those problems involve setup time on a machine, then that setup time should be reduced. In general, if setup time is less than or equal to cycle time, then disruptions will be minimal. Recall that cycle time is the time it takes to perform a specified activity. In this instance, cycle time is the processing time required for each unit of a given part on a given machine. Thus, if setup time does not exceed cycle time, the disruption of flow will be limited to only one unit. This effect can be further minimized if it is arranged so that each machine performs its setup just

Exhibit 12.8 Setup Time Reductions

Company	Machine	Date	Original Setup Time	Date	Reduced Setup Time
Toyota	1,000-ton press	1945	4 hrs.	1971	3 min.
Toyo Kogyo	Ring-gear cutter	1975	6+ hrs.	1980	10 min.
Hitachi	Die-casting machine	1976	1.25 hrs.	1983	3 min.
Omark Industries	Punch press	1982	2+ hrs.	1983	3 min.
General Electric	45-ton press	1982	50 min.	1983	2 min.
Black & Decker	Punch press	1982	1 hr.	1984	1 min.

Source: Mehran Sepehri, *Just-in-Time, Not Just In Japan* (Falls Church, Va.: American Production and Inventory Control Society, 1986). pp. 4–11.

ahead of a new part as that part flows from one machine to another. For example, if a company switches from making one product to making another, then each successive operation can perform its setup as the new parts flow through the system, causing the entire system to skip just one cycle.

Total Preventive Maintenance

Machine breakdowns are another possible source of disruptions to the smooth flow in a JIT system. However, machines that are not properly lubricated or maintained can produce defective parts without actually breaking down. To prevent either of these results from occurring, companies have adopted what is referred to as **total preventive maintenance** (TPM), also called total *productive* maintenance.

TPM involves three main components:

1. An emphasis on *preventive* maintenance. Efforts are undertaken to avoid equipment breakdowns by frequent inspection, lubrication, and the use of proper operating techniques.
2. The allocation of time each day for maintenance. Companies sometimes allow one entire shift for maintenance or set aside specific time during each shift.
3. Operator responsibility for maintenance. Instead of assigning this responsibility to a maintenance department, operators are trained to perform all but the most complicated maintenance on the machines they operate.

Planning in JIT Systems

You may have the feeling that JIT is a complete departure from all the planning concepts we discussed in the two preceding chapters. Actually, this is not true. Companies that use JIT successfully still follow most of the planning steps that we mentioned previously, from strategic planning to master scheduling. In fact, as you will see, it is even possible to combine JIT and MRP. However, some changes must be made in the planning and scheduling process under JIT. Basically, those changes make the process easier.

Operations Planning and Master Scheduling

The reason why planning and scheduling are so much easier with JIT is basically that requirements for parts and materials can be tied directly to each unit of the end item. If fifty units of the end item will be made during a given day, then enough parts and subassemblies must be ordered for that day to make the fifty units. Since JIT is based on the idea of having just what is needed when it is needed, parts are usually not ordered in large batches. Instead, a steady stream of material in small batches is maintained at a rate that will match the production of end items.

The Aggregate Plan. The aggregate production plan for a company using JIT is basically the same as that for any other company, except that the JIT planning horizon may be somewhat shorter. Production is generally planned by product families on a monthly basis for about one year into the future. This plan is used for determining general work-force requirements and overall capacity needs and for ordering any parts or materials that have extremely long lead times.

The Master Schedule. In terms of its level of detail, the master schedule for a company using JIT will be the same as that for most other companies that follow a master schedule. That is, planning is usually done in weekly time buckets and by individual end items or product options. However, the master schedule is usually developed with a two- to three-month planning horizon instead of the six- to twelve-month horizon used for MRP. The master schedule is also frozen for about one month into the future under MRP, whereas this time fence may be less with JIT due to the shorter lead times.

In an MRP environment, the master schedule is usually what drives the MRP derivation of planned order releases. However, in JIT the pull system often eliminates this need for order release planning because parts and materials will be produced only in response to a downstream signal. The master schedule is used only when items with long lead times must be ordered. Thus, in a JIT system, the master schedule is primarily an intermediate step in reaching the final assembly schedule.

The Final Assembly Schedule

The final assembly schedule is an exact statement of the final products that are to be assembled. The final assembly schedule is stated on a daily basis, but most often goes only about a week into the future. Because lead times are usually so short in a JIT environment, it is the final assembly schedule that indicates which component parts, and their quantities, will be made each day.

The JIT philosophy of eliminating unnecessary inventory has a major impact on the final assembly schedule. So far, we have talked about eliminating work-in-process inventory. But it is important that any unnecessary finished-goods inventory also be eliminated. However, this is hard to do when a company makes more than one finished product.

The approach that has been followed in traditional manufacturing systems is to make a large number of one product before switching over to another. This means that the inventory of each finished product will build up when that item

Exhibit 12.9 Finished-Goods Inventory with Long Production Runs

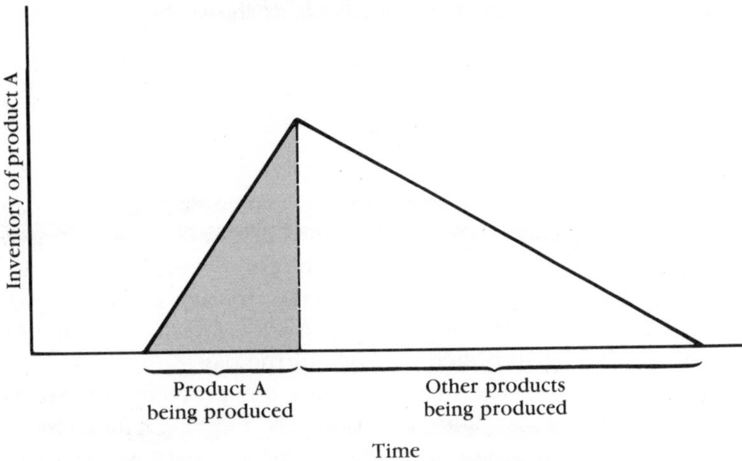

is being produced, but then drop back down when other products are being made, as shown in Exhibit 12.9.

This approach is inefficient because it leads to large levels of finished-goods inventory at some times and very low levels—with the possibility of being unable to satisfy customer demand—at other times. A better approach is to "level" the final assembly schedule. A **level assembly schedule** means simply that the number of units of each end product produced at a time is as small as possible, and that total daily production of each matches average daily demand during the scheduling horizon. In other words, if the scheduling horizon is twenty working days and demand during that period is expected to be 300 units, a level schedule would mean producing 15 units (300/20) each day.

The idea of a level assembly schedule is that the smallest reasonable number of units of each end product should be produced at a time. Thus, even if fifteen units of a product are to be made during a given day, those fifteen units should be spread throughout the day. This even spread is achieved through mixed-model sequencing.

Mixed-Model Sequencing. Mixed-model sequencing is a procedure for maintaining the uniform production required by a level assembly schedule. If a company makes several different end items (different products or different models of the same product), it is desirable to spread the production of each evenly throughout each day. However, in order to keep the system running as smoothly as possible, there should be some continuity in the sequencing of those end items. For example, if four different products (A, B, C, and D) are produced, then the ideal schedule would be to produce them in some sequence such as A-B-C-D and to repeat that same sequence throughout the day for each day in the planning horizon. But sometimes demand for one product will be greater than for others. In that case, the sequence may have to be varied somewhat.

Example

A company produces three products. Expected demand for each during the next twenty working days is as shown below.

Product	Expected Demand	Daily Requirements
A	420	420/20 = 21
B	280	280/20 = 14
C	140	140/20 = 7

The daily requirements are obtained by dividing expected demand over the planning horizon by the number of working days in the time horizon. To maintain a level schedule, the company needs to plan so that each product's daily requirements will be produced every day, evenly spread throughout the day if possible. It is also desirable that a set sequence of products be made, and that this sequence be repeated throughout the day.

The trick in solving this problem is to find the largest integer that divides evenly into each product's daily requirements. In this case, the number is 7. Thus, the company should develop a sequence that will be repeated seven times each working day.

Product	Daily Requirements/7
A	21/7 = 3
B	14/7 = 2
C	7/7 = 1

The result of dividing the daily requirements for each product by the largest integer that divides into each evenly is the number of times each product must be repeated in the sequence. Thus, product A should appear three times, product B twice, and product C once. Developing the sequence takes some trial and error, but the following is one possibility that would satisfy the company's objectives:

A–B–A–B–A–C

This sequence would be repeated seven times each day to produce the required twenty-one units of product A, fourteen units of B, and seven units of C, while still leveling the assembly schedule.

It should be noted in the above example that the mixed-model sequence produced is not the only one possible. Such a sequence would smooth out the production, but could also cause problems due to excessive changeovers. When the cycle time is short, it may be desirable to produce more than one unit of each end product at a time. Thus, the following sequence would also be acceptable for short cycle times:

A–A–A–B–B–C

In fact, there might be restrictions that would justify producing even more units of each product at a time. For example, these products might be packed ten per carton for final shipping. In such a case, it could make more sense to produce thirty of A, twenty of B, and ten of C at a time, instead of letting partially filled shipping cartons sit around. Regardless, the objective is to smooth out production by producing each item in the smallest quantities that are reasonable, given existing constraints.

Calculating Cycle Times. The purpose of obtaining a level assembly schedule is to smooth out the production of each end item so that it will closely match demand. However, a level schedule also smooths out the requirements for component parts that go into each finished product. This makes the pull system work better because demand for each part will be fairly uniform throughout the day, instead of occurring in batches, as it would if each finished product were made in large batches.[4]

However, the flow of component parts must be adjusted to match the rate at which finished products will be produced. For example, if we make one product C every hour, it will do us no good to have a machine that makes parts for product C turning out one every two hours—or even one every half hour. What we would like is to match the production rate of all components to the final assembly schedule. This is done through cycle times.

Cycle time, as you learned in Chapter 7, is a measure of how often a particular product is made. For example, automobile assembly lines usually have a cycle time of about one minute. In other words, a new car rolls off the line every minute. The cycle time of any product can be calculated as follows:

Cycle time = working time per day/units required per day

Example

For the preceding example, the cycle time is calculated by using the formula given above. Suppose the plant is in production for seven hours (420 minutes) each day, and it must produce a total of forty-two units each day (twenty-one of A, fourteen of B, and seven of C) to match daily demand. Then the cycle time will be

420 minutes/42 units = 10 minutes/unit

This calculation can be extended to each of the individual products in order to determine how often each of these would be produced, based on a mixed-model sequence.

Product	Daily Requirements	Cycle Time
A	21	420/21 = 20 minutes
B	14	420/14 = 30 minutes
C	7	420/7 = 60 minutes

This means that one product A will be produced every twenty minutes, on the average, throughout the day by using the completely level sequence developed in the preceding example. In order to make this possible, the people and machines that supply parts and subassemblies for product A must also be balanced to produce with a cycle time of twenty minutes. Likewise, the entire system must be coordinated to produce one product—either A, B, or C—every ten minutes. In some cases, this may mean that ways must be found to reduce setup times, or that more machines must be added. However, it can also mean that some machines will not produce at their capacity. It is much more desirable in a JIT system to have machines sitting idle than to have them producing inventory that is not needed. Ideally, though, *all* resources should be used as efficiently as possible. This may mean finding ways to use the same machine to make several different parts so it can be used efficiently without making excess inventory.

JIT in Service Operations

Our discussion thus far has emphasized the application of JIT to manufacturing because that is where it was developed and has been applied most frequently. However, manufacturing and service organizations both produce a product, whether that product is a good or a service. Thus, many of the production ideas of JIT can be applied to service operations. In fact, service organizations may have somewhat of a head start because of their lack of work-in-process and finished-goods inventories.

The JIT ideas that are probably most immediately relevant to services are that waste in any form should be eliminated, and that efforts should be made to constantly improve. Specifically, we can focus on the following areas.

Simplified Production Process

Service operations often differ from manufacturing in that customers are more directly involved, and are often active participants, in the production process. For example, automated teller machines allow customers to enter transaction information formerly entered by bank tellers. Because most customers are not trained employees, the process must be as simple and obvious as possible.

Uncovering Problems Buried by Inventory

Even though services often have no finished-goods inventory, they still may have inventories of supplies or even work-in-process, as with loan applications in a bank. Those inventories can hide problems just as easily as inventory in a factory can. In fact, recent studies have shown that speed is becoming an important order winner for service operations. By uncovering problems through reduced inventory, service organizations can work toward providing the service when the customer wants it.

An Emphasis on Quality Control

Due to the direct contact between customers and service organizations, quality problems will be much more obvious to the customer. Further, the definition of quality is often broadened in service organizations to include the helpfulness and friendliness of salespeople or even the pleasantness of the decor in a facility. For these reasons, service organizations must especially emphasize quality throughout their entire operation.

Strategic Planning and JIT

We have already discussed strategic planning and its importance in Chapter 10. Any company must develop an organizational strategy based on its strengths and weaknesses, the competitive and economic environment, and the type of product it produces. However, JIT offers some very special competitive opportunities to the company that uses it. The following are those opportunities that have been listed by Robert Hall.[5]

Quality and Reliability

Total quality control is something that can have several payoffs. In a JIT system, the goal of TQC is to eliminate all defects. This means lower costs because scrap is virtually eliminated. At the same time, customers will be happier since they will be getting higher-quality products that are likely to last longer. This also means fewer returned items and fewer warranty repairs, which also will result in reduced costs. The goal of constant improvement will eventually lead to production of a product that gives the customer greater value at a lower price.

Product Flexibility

JIT production gives a company considerable flexibility in several ways. For one, producing to a level schedule means that each product is produced each day. Changes in customer demand can usually be accommodated rather quickly because the system is already designed to change from making one product to making another quite easily. Such is often not the case with companies that make long production runs of each product.

Low work-in-process inventories also provide added flexibility. With minimal inventories in the pipeline, companies can quickly switch to making different parts. There is less motivation to keep on producing a given product—even though demand has dropped—just to use up parts inventories.

Volume Flexibility

It may seem contrary to the goal of using a level assembly schedule to smooth production to argue that companies using JIT have more flexibility to change their volume. But the results indicate that successful JIT implementation leads companies to a position in which they have greater capability to respond to sudden surges or drops in demand.

Part of this flexibility is related to low inventories. A company with very little work-in-process inventory can quickly cut off its production in response to a drop in demand. The ability to respond when demand increases is a result of the smooth material flows in a JIT system. Smooth flows generally mean that machines and people are being employed at a steady, uniform pace. When it is necessary to increase output, the ability is there to quicken that pace. It is like the difference between a marathon runner and a sprinter. Like the marathon runner, a JIT system is not going flat out all the time, so it has some extra capacity to sprint when necessary. A sprinter, on the other hand, is running flat out and has nothing left when a quick burst of speed is needed.

Delivery Dependability

All of the strategic aspects of JIT discussed so far help contribute to delivery dependability. Improved quality will mean that shipments to customers are not held up because of quality problems in the product or because of delays caused by defective parts. Product and volume flexibility means that the company is better able to respond when customers suddenly change the size or product mix of their orders.

Asset Utilization

We have mentioned several times that part of the JIT philosophy is to use all resources efficiently. This extends to capital assets, such as plant and equipment. Because JIT requires less inventory, much less floor space is required. Plants using

JIT often require less than half the space of traditional plants making the same product.

To obtain quick setups, many companies have found that buying simple, general-purpose equipment is better than buying more sophisticated, specialized equipment. Since general-purpose equipment usually costs less, the total investment in machinery will be less. In addition, this equipment is usually used more uniformly. The special-purpose machinery may sit idle until the one part it is designed to make is needed. General-purpose machinery can be kept busy making many different parts.

Maintenance is also an important aspect of JIT. To maintain the smooth flow of materials, it is essential that machine breakdowns be avoided. Companies using JIT concentrate heavily on strong preventive maintenance programs and on operating machines well below their rated maximum capacities. This means that equipment will last much longer, giving the companies a greater return on investment.

People Utilization

Companies using JIT depend heavily on their employees to solve problems. However, utilization of people extends even further than this. For instance, maintaining the smooth flow of materials often means that one employee may have to operate several different machines. This cross-training leads to greater worker utilization. Likewise, companies using JIT tend to examine closely any areas where waste might be present. One such area in many companies is the office staff. Efforts are usually undertaken to find ways that managerial jobs can be combined or even eliminated—something few companies have done in the past.

Cost Minimization

The JIT philosophy of avoiding waste leads logically to cost minimization. Although the cost savings associated with inventory reduction have often received the most notice, other savings may be more substantial. For instance, total quality control can both cut material costs substantially and save on the labor costs that might have gone into making defective products. A level schedule avoids costly overtime by evenly loading the plant. Likewise, extensive machine maintenance will mean that downtime will be eliminated, repair costs will be lower, and equipment will last longer. Overall, companies using JIT have been able to achieve much lower costs than their competitors have.

Comparing MRP and JIT

MRP and JIT are similar in some ways, but different in others. Both seek to have parts and materials available only when needed and in exactly the right quantities. However, MRP is very much computer based, while JIT generally uses the computer very little. The following sections discuss some more of the most notable differences between MRP and JIT.

Production Planning

Planning with JIT is much simpler than with MRP. In MRP, the bill of materials is exploded to generate requirements for component parts. However, these re-

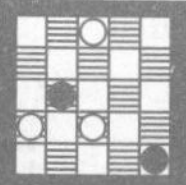

GAINING STRATEGIC ADVANTAGE AT IBM

Using JIT to Achieve Manufacturing Excellence

JIT has played an important role in achieving manufacturing excellence. Previously, IBM had produced only to customer order, which resulted in considerable problems for manufacturing. For example, at its Raleigh, North Carolina, plant IBM makes some 250 different product types from over 60,000 parts. Keeping track of all these items and controlling production required the development of complex computerized systems. At the same time, many products had been designed with little concern for the difficulties encountered in making them. As a result, many of the manufacturing processes were overly difficult. Production to customer order resulted in unstable production schedules and many wide swings in the production rate.

To overcome these problems, IBM adopted many of the basic concepts of JIT. For instance, each product was standardized to eliminate the large number of possible different configurations. Features that customers frequently requested were included as part of the standard product. In order to level the production schedule, IBM stopped making to customer order and began producing to a production plan developed jointly by marketing and manufacturing. This production plan levels the schedule for up to three months, resulting in stable production rates for manufacturing and steady demand for parts from suppliers.

IBM has also concentrated on cutting its work-in-process inventories to achieve a continuous flow of materials. However, the approach taken to achieve this end is somewhat different from the one taken in traditional kanban. Material is moved from one work station to another by robot. When a work station's work input gets low, an electronic signal causes the robot to get another container of parts from the feeding work station. There has also been considerable emphasis on quality. A great deal of this emphasis has been concentrated in engineering on designing products that are easy to make with high quality designed in. However, manufacturing has also altered its procedures so that parts are stress-tested as early as possible before being assembled into the final product.

This coordination of JIT operations with other parts of the business has resulted in decreased manufacturing costs, lower inventories, greater product reliability, and a shorter time between new product design and customer availability. For IBM, these results have produced a considerable competitive advantage.[6]

quirements must be offset by the lead time. With JIT, lead-time offsetting is not usually necessary because parts are produced as needed and lead times are short.

Likewise, the planning horizon for JIT is usually much shorter than for MRP. Companies using MRP generally develop an aggregate plan that looks twelve to eighteen months into the future and a master schedule that has a six-month horizon. These time periods are shortened with JIT, so the aggregate plan may be twelve months or less. The master schedule generally has a two- to three-month horizon.

Capacity Planning

Rough-cut capacity planning in an MRP system attempts to estimate the resource requirements of the aggregate plan and master schedule. However, this may not be accurate because lead-time offsetting does not take place at that point. It is not until after the MRP calculations have been performed that a more accurate calculation can be performed, using capacity requirements planning. At this point, capacity problems are usually handled by scheduling overtime, offloading, or changing the planned order releases or master schedule.

Because JIT has such short lead times, even rough-cut capacity planning can be relatively accurate. Also, the level assembly schedule tends to avoid periods when a particular machine or work center would be overloaded. If capacity problems are going to occur, they can be identified at early stages of the planning process. The emphasis in JIT on maintaining a smooth production flow also helps eliminate the need for capacity requirements planning by keeping machines operating below their capacities.

Inventory Control

The emphasis with MRP is on maintaining accurate inventory records. Thus, physical counts of the on-hand inventory must be taken at regular intervals to rectify any errors. Although the objective of MRP is to have materials available only when needed and in the right quantities, the focus of MRP on batches guarantees that there will be some excess inventory at various times—and the chance of running out at other times.

The JIT pull system eliminates any need for record keeping as long as the system is followed religiously. If standard containers are used, then it is a simple matter to determine inventory by counting the number of containers. Likewise, the kanban cards (or whatever signaling device is used) will limit overall inventory levels. When inventory reaches its maximum, the flow is automatically stopped, and when inventory gets low, more material is automatically pulled through the system.

International Dimensions of JIT

Because it was the Japanese who first successfully implemented JIT, much has been written about whether its success there is at least partially a function of the culture. Some authors have written that the Japanese management system is much more participatory than are those of other countries, including the United States. Further, they have emphasized that employees in Japan are much more dedicated to the company—partly because of the tradition of lifetime employment—than are employees in other countries. As a result, the question has been raised whether JIT can succeed outside Japan.

At this time, there appear to be enough companies using JIT in other countries to argue that it can work outside Japan. For example, many U.S. companies, such as Harley-Davidson, have been successful with JIT. In addition, quite a few Japanese companies, such as Toyota, Nissan, and Kawasaki, now use JIT methods to operate plants very successfully in the United States.

Obviously, some changes must be made to accommodate cultural differences. For example, much has been said about Japanese workers who do calisthenics and sing the company song before work each day. In the United States, such programs have not been successful. On the other hand, U.S. workers have developed their own unique ways to show company pride, such as T-shirts and hats with company slogans. Thus, the basic principles of JIT appear to be applicable anywhere even though particular details may need modification based on cultural differences.

OPERATIONS IN ACTION

Graybill: From JIC to JIT to Synchronous Manufacturing

Graybill, Inc., has been manufacturing industrial switches for over forty years and operates two plants near Chicago and one in Taiwan. All component parts are purchased from suppliers and then assembled by Graybill into finished products.

The company has been a major competitor in the industry and, until recently, followed the usual "just in case" (JIC) approach of maintaining large inventories and producing in large batch sizes. Following this system, inventories were huge, rejects were high, delivery lead times were long, and customer service was poor. But until the mid 1980s, this type of performance was competitive in the industry.

About five years ago, Graybill noticed that its competition was improving, cutting into Graybill's profits. To counter this, the company decided to implement JIT. When it did, significant improvements became obvious within months. Work-in-process inventories dropped from a high of 60,000 parts per department to 15,000 or less, and manufacturing lead time dropped to two weeks.

By 1988, however, the company noticed no further improvement with JIT, and customer demand still exceeded the company's production capacity by 30 percent! At that point, a decision was made to use synchronous manufacturing.

To begin, Graybill sought to find the bottlenecks in its operation. Each process was allowed to run at full capacity, and some processes shortly had huge inventories built up in front of them. Those were the bottlenecks. After identifying them, the company proceeded to set up a drum-buffer-rope system.

Under the new synchronous manufacturing system, work-in-process has declined further to between 3,000 and 6,000 parts per department. Throughput has increased by more than 30 percent, and manufacturing lead time is now one to five days.[7]

SYNCHRONOUS MANUFACTURING

In the first edition of this book, we included a section about an interesting new software package called OPT® (Optimized Production Technology), which had been used by about 100 large companies to schedule production. However, aside from a set of OPT® Rules, not much was known about the inner workings of that software. Since then, the developer of OPT®, Dr. Eliyahu Goldratt, has expanded his OPT® Rules into what he calls the General Theory of Constraints. This theory leads to an overall operating philosophy that is similar in some respects to JIT. When applied to a manufacturing operation, the result is referred to as **synchronized** or **synchronous manufacturing.**

While synchronous manufacturing is similar in some ways to JIT, it is also different. Goldratt claims the results for synchronous manufacturing can be better and take less time to achieve. Instead of focusing on reducing all batch sizes, synchronous manufacturing begins by finding the bottlenecks.

Bottlenecks and Capacity-Constrained Resources

Chapter 5 defined a bottleneck as any department, work station, or operation that restricts the flow of product through the production system. Thus, a bottleneck is any resource that has capacity equal to or less than the demand placed on it. A nonbottleneck resource, on the other hand, is one that has capacity greater than the demand placed on it. A capacity-constrained resource (CCR) is a nonbottleneck that is being utilized close to its capacity, and that may become a bottleneck if not utilized carefully.

The reason synchronous manufacturing focuses on bottlenecks is that these determine output for the entire production process. For example, if machine A produces parts at the rate of fifty per hour and feeds them to machine B, which runs only ten per hour, the final output through these two machines will be only ten per hour. In this example, machine B is the bottleneck, and machine A is a nonbottleneck. Analysis of this example leads to the following two principles:

1. An hour of production time lost at a bottleneck subtracts one hour of output from the entire production system.
2. An hour of time saved at a nonbottleneck only adds an hour to its idle time.

These two principles have major implications for scheduling production of each type of resource, as you will see.

Process Batches and Transfer Batches

In discussing JIT, we mentioned that one objective is to eliminate any excess inventory. To do this, companies would ideally produce just one unit of each part or subassembly at a time. By reducing these batch sizes, it is possible to move toward the smooth, continuous flow that we mentioned earlier. However, it is possible to argue that reducing all batch sizes may produce undesirable results.

For example, consider the two situations shown in Exhibit 12.10. In the first case, batch sizes have been kept small, so that frequent setups are required between batches. Approximately half of the available time is used unproductively

Exhibit 12.10 Effect of Increasing Size of Process Batch

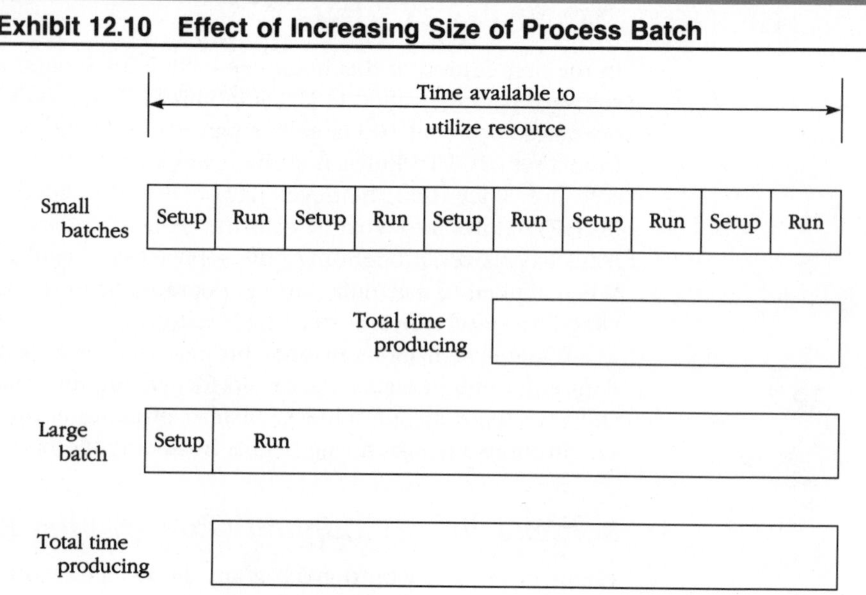

for setups. In the second case, however, batch sizes are larger, and less time is spent for setups. Therefore, more time is available to be producing.

For a bottleneck or CCR, any time spent in setups will be lost production. Therefore, it is desirable to give bottlenecks and CCRs large batch sizes to process, minimizing their nonproductive setup time.

For nonbottlenecks, however, the situation is different. Excess capacity is available at nonbottleneck resources, so more time can be spent on setups without detrimental effects. Further, suppose a nonbottleneck work center must process parts and then feed them to a bottleneck. If the nonbottleneck produces in large batches, the bottleneck may be kept idle, waiting for that large batch to finish processing. Small batch sizes at the nonbottleneck work center, on the other hand, will tend to provide a continuous flow of materials for the bottleneck.

But suppose the nonbottleneck work center must process large batches. Is there any way to avoid delaying the bottleneck? The answer is that we must differentiate between the quantity processed and the quantity moved.

Process Batch Versus Transfer Batch

Most companies have tended to operate under the philosophy that a batch being processed on one machine did not get moved to the next machine until the entire batch was completed. For example, if machine A is making a batch of 100 parts, the parts do not get moved to the next operation, machine B, until all 100 have been completed on A. But what if machine B is a bottleneck resource that must sit idle, waiting for parts from machine A? Surely it would be better to keep feeding parts to machine B as they are finished on A.

This is the idea of a transfer batch. While large batch sizes may be desirable for processing to reduce setups, they can also lead to idle time at operations farther along in the product flow. Thus, the transfer batch, the amount transferred from one operation to another, may not be the same as the process batch, which is the amount processed at one time on a machine. Exhibit 12.11 shows how a smaller transfer batch can reduce idle time and increase output.

Drum, Buffer, Rope

In synchronous manufacturing, three elements are of key importance. They are referred to as the drum, the buffer, and the rope.

The Drum

The drum is what determines the rate of production. In MRP, JIT, and synchronous manufacturing, that rate corresponds to the master production schedule (MPS). However, in MRP and JIT, the master schedule is determined primarily from market demand. For MRP, capacity requirements planning can determine when there will be insufficient capacity to meet the master schedule. However, adjustments must then be made to the master schedule on an ad hoc basis.

With synchronous manufacturing, on the other hand, the bottleneck resources are used to develop the schedule, ensuring that bottleneck capacity is not exceeded. Other nonbottleneck resources are scheduled to serve the bottleneck by varying process batch and transfer batch sizes. Thus, the bottleneck resource is the drum; it sets the rate of all other operations to match its own, which becomes the "drum beat" for the entire process.

Exhibit 12.11 Effect of Decreasing Size of Transfer Batch

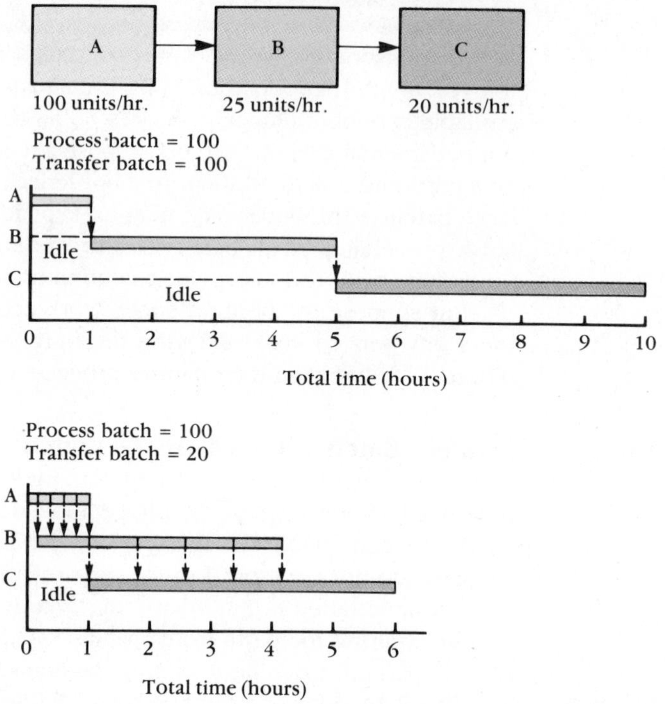

The Buffer

In spite of the carefully developed MPS, deviations will occur due to unforeseen events. In order to prevent such events from disrupting output of finished goods, buffers are placed at carefully selected locations. These buffers may be of two types—a stock buffer or a time buffer. Although both are actually inventory buffers, the amount in a time buffer is determined by the amount of output the system could produce during the period of time it takes to correct a disruption. This is often set as one-half the total manufacturing lead time.

In general, the key location for time buffers will be before bottlenecks. That way, the bottlenecks can keep working even if the flow of material to them is disrupted.

The other prime location for buffer inventories will be at locations where parts from the bottleneck are combined with parts from other processes. This is to prevent those assembly or subassembly processes from having to shut down due to problems at nonbottleneck resources. If they did shut down, then the bottleneck process would also have to be stopped, losing production for the whole system, or excess inventory would be built up.

Stock buffers are inventories of finished goods held in anticipation of market demand. Their size is usually determined by forecasts of possible demand increases. The placement of both time buffers and stock buffers is shown in Exhibit 12.12.

Exhibit 12.12 Network Flow Diagram with One Bottleneck

The Rope

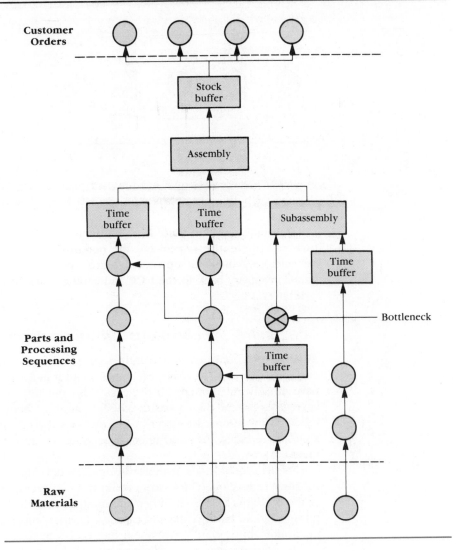

In Exhibit 12.3, we used a rope analogy to show how materials are *pulled* through a JIT system. That analogy is also useful for synchronous manufacturing because it shows how the rate at which processes operate must be linked together. We have already explained that a bottleneck operation will set the "drum beat" or production rate for the entire operation. For processes that come after the bottleneck, their rate of operation will be paced by what is produced from the bottleneck. However, operations before the bottleneck have the potential of producing too fast for the bottleneck, thus creating excess inventory.

To prevent the buildup of excess inventory, there must be a linkage between a bottleneck and the processes that feed it. This linkage is referred to as the rope.

Exhibit 12.13 Use of Ropes with a Capacity-Constrained Resource

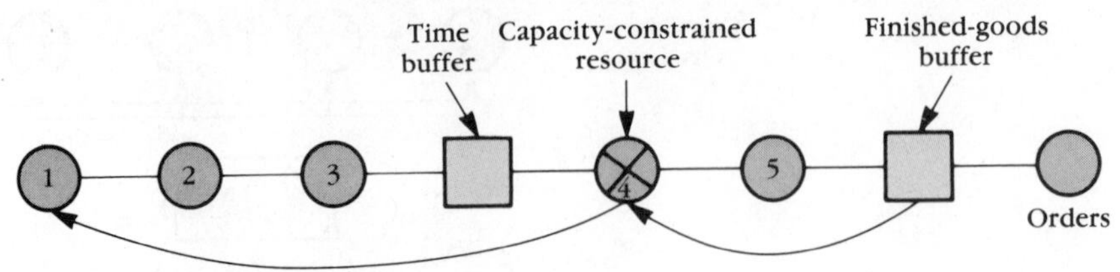

The rope can be a formal schedule of planned production or informal daily discussions between employees at the bottleneck and employees at other work stations.

In some situations, there is no bottleneck. However, there may be a CCR. In that case, the entire system has the potential of producing more than market demand. To avoid such a problem, there must be two ropes: one from finished-goods inventory back to the CCR and another back from the CCR, as shown in Exhibit 12.13.

Comparing Synchronous Manufacturing, MRP, and JIT

All three techniques are aimed at the same goal—ensuring that production meets customer demand. However, each goes about it in a slightly different way. As we have already mentioned, MRP works from the top down, beginning with an aggregate plan and then a master schedule, altering them as needed to stay within capacity limitations. However, MRP does not directly provide guidance about appropriate batch sizes and offers little guidance in terms of scheduling equipment.

While synchronous manufacturing also develops a master schedule, that schedule is developed more from the bottom up, working from available capacity at the bottleneck or CCR. When the master schedule is developed, there is no question about having sufficient capacity. Further, information can be obtained to determine appropriate process and transfer batch sizes.

JIT takes the approach of eliminating all forms of waste. Thus, buffer inventories would be eliminated, and both process and transfer batches would be as small as possible. If these changes cause problems, then ways are found of eliminating the problems, instead of working around them, as is done with synchronous manufacturing.

SUMMARY

- JIT is a philosophy of constant effort to eliminate waste.
- The focus of JIT is to reduce inventories and uncover problems hidden by that inventory.
- Total quality control (TQC) is a companywide effort that focuses on quality at the source.

- JIT is classified as a "pull" system because materials are pulled through processing operations as they are needed.
- A C-kanban is an authorization to move parts or material.
- A P-kanban is an authorization to produce more parts.
- The level of inventory can be controlled by varying the number of kanban in use for each part.
- Total preventive maintenance (TPM) seeks to avoid disruptions by means of regularly scheduled maintenance and operator responsibility for maintenance.
- JIT concepts of simplifying, using TQC, and uncovering problems are especially applicable to services.
- Setup time is reduced by conducting careful studies, performing as much work as possible while the machine is running, modifying tools and fixtures for quick setup, keeping tools handy, and practicing the setup operation.
- MRP and JIT both seek to have necessary parts available in the right quantities. However, MRP emphasizes computerized planning, while JIT stresses a smooth, steady flow of materials.
- A bottleneck is a process with capacity less than or equal to demand. A capacity-constrained resource (CCR) has the potential to be a bottleneck.
- A process batch is the quantity processed between setups. A transfer batch is the quantity moved between processes.
- Synchronous manufacturing focuses on bottlenecks and schedules based on them. Buffers are used to maintain flow, and ropes are used to communicate.

CAREER PROFILE

Doug Sutton

Plant Manager
Kawasaki Motors Manufacturing

Education and Work Background

After earning a B.S. degree in business administration from the University of Nebraska, Doug Sutton went to work as production planner for an electronics company that makes resistors. After two years, he moved on to another position as production planner with a company that was using MRP. It was this MRP experience that initially led Kawasaki to hire Sutton as a production planner in its Lincoln, Nebraska, plant.

When Kawasaki first built the Lincoln plant, MRP was to be used for production planning and control. It was in this MRP environment that Sutton worked his way up from production planner to supervisor of production control and then to manager of production control. When the Kawasaki plant in Lincoln became one of the first U.S. organizations to switch from MRP to JIT, Doug Sutton was heavily involved in the JIT implementation.

According to Sutton, his MRP experience helped somewhat in converting to JIT. For example, he was able to conceptualize JIT planning in terms of a two-level bill of materials—final assemblies and component parts. At the same time, he concentrated on the idea that to reduce batch sizes economically, setup costs would also have to be reduced. In fact, some of the changes involved in implementing JIT were actually steps backward in terms of technology. Previously, the company had been using conveyors to move material around the plant. But it found these too inflexible for JIT and ended up replacing the conveyors with hand carts.

Sutton's last position in Lincoln was planning manager, a position in which he oversaw production control, receiving and stores, the finished-goods warehouse, and all activities related to the Lincoln plant's Foreign Trade Zone status. In many companies, each of these areas might have its own manager. However, part of the JIT philosophy is to maximize efficiency—and this includes eliminating unnecessary managerial titles.

Current Duties

In his current position as plant manager of the Kawasaki plant in Maryville, Missouri, Sutton has been responsible for all start-up activities of that plant, which began operation in June 1989. The Maryville plant produces small industrial engines that are used in such products as lawnmowers. Although the product has changed, Sutton is still applying the JIT ideas he learned at Kawasaki's Lincoln, Nebraska, plant. However, the situation now is somewhat different as the customers of Sutton's plant are original equipment manufacturers (OEMs) who demand just-in-time delivery of the engines that go into their products.

SOLVED PROBLEMS

1. A certain part's inventory level is controlled by kanban. The time that elapses between when a C-kanban is removed from a container of parts and when it is returned on another container averages .05 day. Production time for a container of parts after a P-kanban is placed in the box is .15 day. Daily production is scheduled at 200 units, and a standard container holds 20 units. Management has set an allowance of 10 percent for inefficiency in the system. How many kanban cards should be used?

Solution

$$T_w = .05, T_p = .15, D = 200, a = 20, X = .10$$

$$y = \frac{D(T_w + T_p)(1 + X)}{a}$$

$$= \frac{200(.05 + .15)(1 + .1)}{20}$$

$$= 2.2$$

Thus, the company must decide whether to use two or three kanban cards. It might start with three (corresponding to an X of .5) and then try pulling one out and operating with just two (corresponding to an X of 0).

2. A company produces four models (A, B, C, and D) of its product. Monthly demand is expected to be 400 units for models A and B, 200 units for C, and 100 for D. There will be twenty working days in the month and eight hours

of work each day. Develop a mixed-model sequence that produces only one unit of each product at a time. Calculate the cycle time per unit and the average cycle time for each model.

Solution

Model	Monthly Demand	Daily Demand
A	400	400/20 = 20
B	400	400/20 = 20
C	200	200/20 = 10
D	100	100/20 = 5

The largest integer that divides evenly into each daily demand is 5. Thus, a sequence will be developed that must be repeated five times each day. In that sequence, models A and B will each appear four times (20/5), C will appear twice (10/5), and D will appear once. One possible sequence is

A–B–C–A–B–C–A–B–D–A–B

A total of fifty-five units must be produced during the 480 minutes each day. Thus,

$$\text{Cycle time} = 480 \text{ minutes}/55 \text{ units} = 8.73 \text{ minutes}$$

The average cycle time for each model is calculated by dividing daily demand into the number of minutes worked per day (480 in this case).

Model	Daily Demand	Cycle Time
A	20	480/20 = 24 min.
B	20	480/20 = 24 min.
C	10	480/10 = 48 min.
D	5	480/5 = 96 min.

3. The operations shown in Exhibit 12.14 are each available 480 minutes per day. Market demand is thirty units per day. Based on this information, determine

Exhibit 12.14 Network Flow Diagram for Solved Problem 3

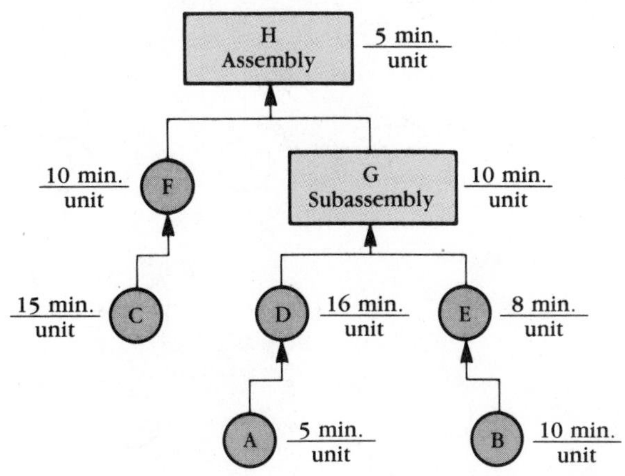

a. Which resources are bottlenecks, capacity-constrained resources, and nonbottlenecks.

b. Where time buffers and stock buffers should be placed.

c. What the recommended size of the time buffers would be, in units, if manufacturing lead time is two days.

Solution

a. Based on operating 480 minutes per day, the maximum output from each process will be

Process	Maximum Output (Units/Day)
A	480/5 = 96
B	480/10 = 48
C	480/15 = 32
D	480/16 = 30

Exhibit 12.15 Solution to Solved Problem 3

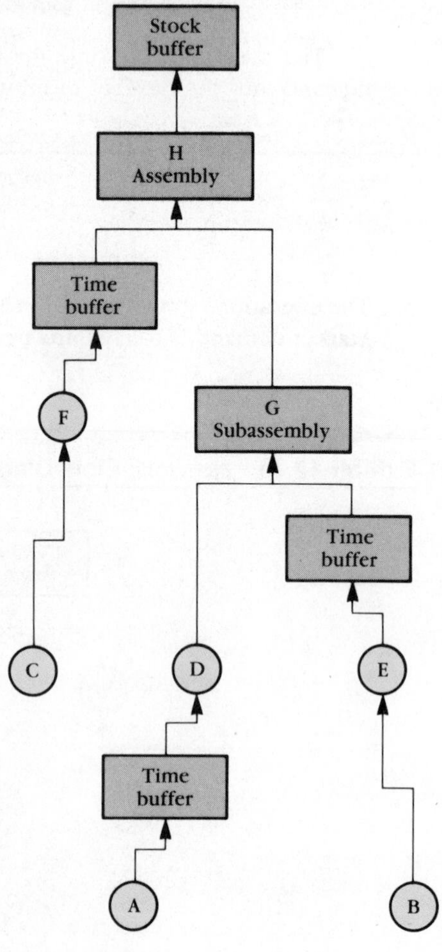

Process	Maximum Output (Units/Day)
E	480/8 = 60
F	480/10 = 48
G	480/10 = 48
H	480/5 = 96

Because the maximum output of process D equals market demand, it is a bottleneck. Further, process C is close, so it is a capacity-constrained resource. The others can produce well above market demand.

b. Time buffers should be placed before the bottleneck and between the bottleneck and other processes fed by the bottleneck. The stock buffer should be in finished-goods inventory. These buffers are shown in Exhibit 12.15.

c. If the manufacturing lead time is two days, this corresponds to production of sixty units. One-half of the lead time (the recommended amount) would then be thirty units.

QUESTIONS

1. List the aspects of JIT that result from elimination of excess inventory.

2. Which aspects of a fast-food restaurant are done just-in-time? Which are more similar to batch production?

3. In general, would you say that service organizations operate in a just-in-time mode? Why or why not?

4. Define what is meant by a pull system and a push system.

5. "The drumbeat of production" is a term frequently used to describe the coordinated movement of materials through a production process. What generates a "drumbeat" in an MRP system? In a JIT system? In synchronous manufacturing?

6. Explain why it is important to level the assembly schedule in JIT. Why isn't this so important with MRP?

7. Develop a list of companies or industries that might best benefit from the results that JIT produces.

8. Are there any companies or industries for which JIT would be totally inappropriate? Why?

9. Draw a chart that indicates the JIT planning process. How does this compare with a planning chart used in an MRP system?

10. Define the following terms:

a. Drum
b. Buffer
c. Rope

11. In an MRP system, what might be thought of as serving the function of a rope?

12. Suppose you have a factory that is not using JIT, MRP, or synchronous manufacturing. How might you identify the bottlenecks?

13. Explain the use of the C-kanban in a single-card system and the use of the C-kanban and the P-kanban in a dual-card system.

14. What are some ways a production process can be simplified? Explain each.

15. Describe at least two ways that quality control is important in JIT.

16. Find an article about a company using JIT outside Japan, and determine whether any modifications have been made to fit local culture or business practices.

17. What is the difference between a process batch and a transfer batch? When are they most likely to be the same?

18. What are the similarities and differences among MRP, JIT, and synchronous manufacturing?

PROBLEMS

1. General Radio Company produces different models of radios using JIT. Circuit boards for these radios are pulled through processing by a dual-card kanban system. Four hundred units of a particular board are used per day, and a standard container holds twenty boards. The time between removal of a C-kanban from a container and its return on a new container of boards is .01 day. Elapsed time between placing a P-kanban in the box and completion of a container of boards is .14 day. Management wants to allow for an inefficiency factor of .33. How many kanban cards should be authorized for this circuit board?

2. The Ota Toy Company makes toy wagons using JIT. Axles for these wagons are pulled through production using a dual-card kanban system. Daily usage of these axles is 600, and each standard container holds fifty axles. Cycle time for a C-kanban is .02 day and for a P-kanban is .10 day. Management has decided that it does not want to allow for inefficiency in the system. How many kanban cards should be authorized for axles?

3. A manufacturer of televisions produces three different models—X, Y, and Z. Demand over the next month is expected to be 400 units for model X, 200 units for model Y, and 100 for model Z. There will be twenty working days in the month. Develop a mixed-model sequence.

4. An automobile manufacturer makes two-door sedans, four-door sedans, convertibles, and station wagons. Customer demand for the next 25 production days is expected to be 400 two-door sedans, 300 four-door sedans, 300 convertibles, and 200 station wagons. Develop a mixed-model sequence that will level the assembly schedule and satisfy daily demand?

5. Refer to problem 3. Suppose that the company has eight working hours each day. Calculate cycle times for the three different television models.

6. Refer to problem 4. If the automobile manufacturer runs the plant seven hours each day, calculate cycle time for each type of car.

7. A company currently uses a job shop arrangement of equipment to make four parts that are used in its final products. The routings for these parts are shown below. Suggest how GT cells could be arranged to produce these parts.

Part #	Routing Sequence
3072	Lathe, mill, grind, drill
274	Shear, punch press, grind, deburr
2987	Mill, drill, grind
1075	Shear, punch press, punch press, deburr

8. The five parts listed below are all produced using a process layout consisting of a drill department with three drills, a lathe department with two lathes, one milling machine, and a heat treating department. Given the following routings, suggest some ways that machines could be rearranged to produce a smoother flow of parts. Unfortunately, heat treating must remain as one department.

Part #	Routing Sequence
1973	Lathe, mill, heat treat, drill
2075	Lathe, drill, heat treat
398	Lathe, drill
4098	Mill, heat treat, drill
298	Mill, drill, lathe

9. A company is trying to use JIT to make several different products. One of those products is assembled from the three parts listed below. Cycle time for that product is twenty-five minutes. Based on the following information, suggest some changes that must be made for JIT to work smoothly. (Note: Each part is made on different machines.)

Part #	*Operation 1* Setup	*Operation 1* Run	*Operation 2* Setup	*Operation 2* Run
298	5	2	10	6
1073	20	5	15	10
2987	60	10	15	2

Part #	*Operation 3* Setup	*Operation 3* Run	*Operation 4* Setup	*Operation 4* Run
298	30	10		
1073	20	5	24	1
2987	20	10	25	5

10. Product P1 is produced by processing material through operations A, B, C, and D, in that sequence. There are 480 minutes of processing time available per day, and each unit of product P1 requires fifteen minutes at A, thirty minutes at B, ten minutes at C, and twenty-three minutes at D. Market demand is twenty units per day. Categorize each operation as a nonbottleneck, bottleneck, or capacity-constrained resource.

11. The process shown below produces a product with daily demand of fifty units and operates 480 minutes per day. Indicate which process should be the drum, where the buffers should go, and where the ropes should be.

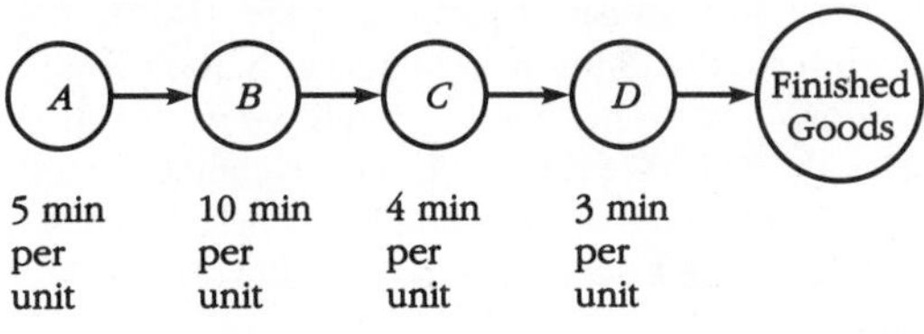

12. Referring to the preceding problem, suppose market demand drops to forty-five units per day. Now which process should be the drum, where should the buffers be located, and where should the ropes be?

13. Process A feeds process B, which in turn feeds process C. A particular part requires ten minutes per unit on A, twenty-five minutes per unit on B, and thirty minutes per unit on C.

a. Indicate how long it would take to process a batch of 300 units if process batch and transfer batch are the same.

b. Let process batch be 300 units and transfer batch be 50. Now how long would it take to process the entire batch through all three operations?

MINI-CASES

Southern Gear Company

The Southern Gear Company manufactures transmissions and speed reducers used in various farm machinery and industrial equipment. The company has been working on implementing MRP for the past three years, but has not achieved the success for which it had hoped. It is now Monday morning as we join the company's executive committee during its weekly meeting.

Barry Renter (vice-president of manufacturing): Look, I know we haven't achieved the results with

MRP that we had expected. But I think that's because we haven't been able to bring inventory under control. We still don't have more than 90 percent accuracy in our inventory records, and that's meant that we've run out of parts when the MRP said we should have had enough. That's why I think JIT can help us. It's a way to eliminate the need to maintain accurate inventory records.

Dave Ashley (vice-president of marketing): But, Barry, how can we possibly go to JIT when our customer orders jump all over the place? You know as well as I do that one problem we've had in implementing MRP is freezing the master schedule. Our customers just expect us to meet their every whim, and they expect to be able to change their orders at the last minute. I just don't think we can achieve the level schedule that I understand JIT requires.

Al Simone (president and CEO): Dave's got a point, Barry. I think one of our strong points has been that we're willing to try to respond quickly to customer demand even though we haven't always been able to do so because of parts shortages. But in any case, with twenty different products and 200 possible variations of those products, I think we're forced to stick with MRP. We're getting some significant offshore competition that's offering lower prices than we are. I'm not sure I want to scrap a million-dollar MRP system to try JIT.

Barry: I don't think we have to scrap MRP. All I'm suggesting is that we continue using MRP for planning, but implement some aspects of JIT such as the kanban system. I also think we could benefit from going to group technology. I've been looking at the bills of materials and routings. Even though we produce 200 different possible end items, we make those from only fifty different main parts, and many of those parts follow the same processing sequence. Part of our problem in controlling inventory has been tracking it through those long queues in the job shop. Group technology could simplify things for us.

1. Based on the information given, would JIT be appropriate for Southern Gear?

2. Could JIT help to alleviate the problem of not being able to satisfy customer orders on short notice?

3. Is Barry Renter right in suggesting that MRP can be used in conjunction with JIT? If so, what would be the function of MRP?

4. What additional information would you like to have before making a decision?

5. What step should Southern Gear undertake first if it decides to use JIT?

Steel Office Products—JIT

Steel Office Products make four different types of steel filing cabinets: a three-drawer letter size, a five-drawer letter size, a three-drawer legal size, and a five-drawer legal size. The company currently uses the layout shown in the top right illustration to make these products. However, plans are under way to switch to JIT production.

Each filing cabinet is assembled from three basic parts: the cabinet, the drawers, and the guides the drawers slide on, as shown in the bottom right illustration. All cabinets use the same guides. Both letter-size cabinets use the same drawers, as do both legal-size cabinets. However, each product has its own cabinet.

Plant Layout for Steel Office Products

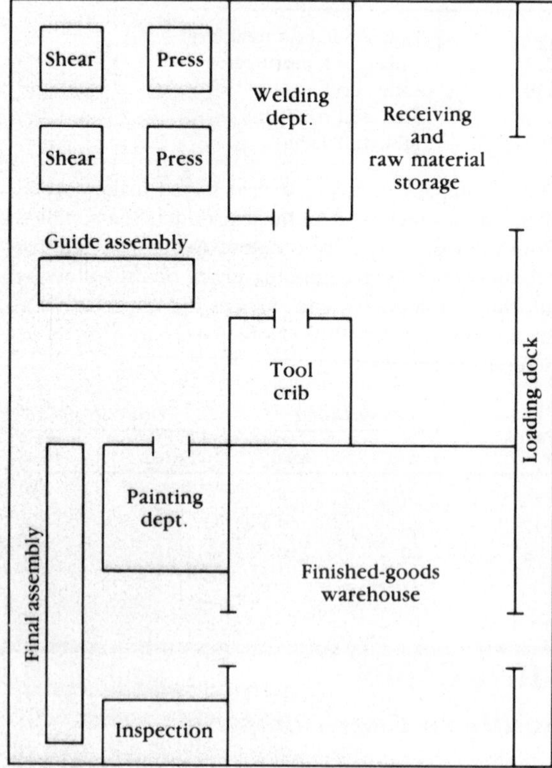

Basic Parts for Filing Cabinet

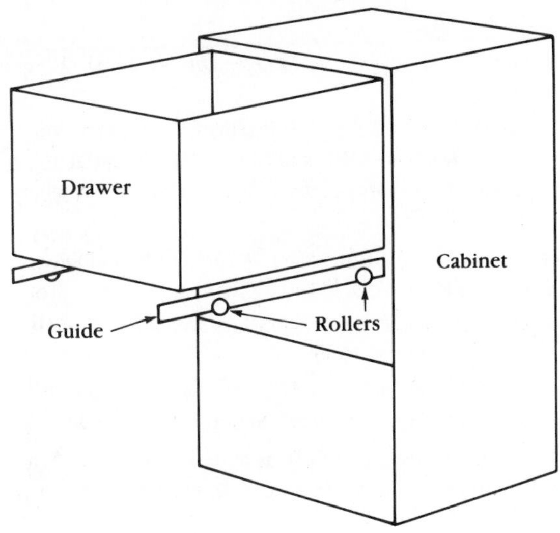

The guides (two per drawer) have rollers (two per guide) for the drawers to slide on. These rollers are purchased from an outside supplier, but all other component parts are made internally, using sheet steel that is bought from a supplier. The sequence of processing operations for each part is listed below. There is no difference in times between legal-size and letter-size or between three-drawer and five-drawer cabinets, but a setup must be performed each time they switch from one to the other. The following tables show the operation sequence and the processing time for each part in minutes per unit.

Cabinet

Operation	Setup	Run
Shear	5	.5
Press	60	1
Weld	20	3
Paint	45	3

Drawer

Operation	Setup	Run
Shear	3	.4
Press	50	.8
Weld	10	2
Paint	45	1

Guides

Operation	Setup	Run
Shear	2	.3
Press	20	.5
Assemble	5	2

The plant operates five days per week, eight hours per day, and expects to continue doing so. Weekly demand for the four products is fairly constant at an average rate of eighty five-drawer letter-size units, fifty three-drawer letter-size units, forty five-drawer legal-size units, and thirty three-drawer legal-size units.

1. What mixed-model sequence should be used?

2. What would the cycle time be for each product?

3. Based on these cycle times, will there be any problems with the processing times shown above? If so, what changes must be made?

4. Suggest a possible rearrangement of the plant to facilitate flow.

5. Can you identify any other changes that should be made to help implement JIT?

Steel Office Products—Synchronous Manufacturing

The data for Steel Office Products have been presented in the preceding mini-case. However, suppose the company decides that instead of implementing JIT, it will use synchronous manufacturing.

1. Draw a diagram depicting the manufacturing process for the filing cabinets in a manner similar to Exhibit 12.12. (Hint: The diagram will have three "legs," one for each component.) Be sure to show the subassembly operation for the guides.

2. Based on information about demand, the number of drawers and guides needed for each product, and processing times, determine whether any process or processes are bottlenecks or CCRs.

3. If you were to include buffers, where would you locate them?

SELECTED BIBLIOGRAPHY

Burnham, John M. ''Some Conclusions About JIT Manufacturing.'' *Production and Inventory Management* 28, no. 3 (1987): 7–11.

Goldratt, Eliyahu E. ''Computerized Shop Floor Scheduling.'' *International Journal of Production Research* 26, no. 3 (1988): 443–455.

Goldratt, Eliyahu, and Cox, Jeff. *The Goal*. Croton-on-Hudson, N.Y.: North River Press, 1984.

Hall, Robert W. *Attaining Manufacturing Excellence*. Homewood, Ill.: Dow Jones–Irwin, 1987.

Hiroyuki, Hirano, and Black, J. T. *JIT Factory Revolution*. Cambridge, Mass., Productivity Press, 1988.

Jacobs, F. Robert. ''The OPT Scheduling System: A Review of a New Production Scheduling System.'' *Production and Inventory Management* 24, no. 3 (1983): 47–51.

Krajewski, L. J.; King, B.; Ritzman, L. P.; and Wong, D. S. ''Kanban, MRP and Shaping the Manufacturing Environment.'' *Management Science* 33, no. 1 (January 1987): 39–57.

Nakajima, Seiichi. *Introduction to TPM*. Cambridge, Mass.: Productivity Press, 1988.

Schonberger, Richard J. *World Class Manufacturing*. New York: Free Press, 1986.

Umble, M. Michael, and Srikanth, M. L. *Synchronous Manufacturing*. Cincinnati: South-Western, 1990.

Vollmann, Thomas E. ''OPT as an Enhancement to MRP II.'' *Production and Inventory Management* 27, no. 2 (1986): 38–47.

Chapter 13

Scheduling

CHAPTER OUTLINE

LEARNING OBJECTIVES

After completing this chapter, you should be able to

- Summarize the data needed for scheduling.
- Explain the difference between sequencing and dispatching.
- List the six possible criteria for scheduling and discuss the trade-offs involved with each.
- Explain why the scheduling of a continuous flow process is usually concerned only with run length.
- Discuss issues of concern in scheduling an assembly line.
- Explain how a batch process is scheduled and calculate the run-out time of a product.
- Discuss the impact of flexible manufacturing systems on the scheduling problem.
- Use dispatching rules to schedule jobs and discuss each rule.
- Sequence jobs on one machine to minimize flow time or minimize changeover time.
- Sequence jobs on two machines using Johnson's Rule.
- Discuss how priorities are determined in MRP systems.
- Use backward or forward loading with finite or infinite loading.
- Develop a Gantt load chart.
- Explain the use of input/output control.
- Discuss how simulation helps in developing schedules.
- Describe how scheduling for services differs from manufacturing.
- Discuss some of the ethical issues related to scheduling.

Essochem: Using a Microcomputer for Production Scheduling

Essochem Europe, Inc., manufactures lube-oil additives through a two-stage process. The first stage is a reaction operation in which various raw materials are combined chemically to produce intermediate products. During the second stage, these intermediate reactor products are blended into finished goods. The plant can select from among twenty different raw materials to produce twelve possible reactor products. These reactor products can be mixed with twenty-five blend components to produce sixty different finished products.

The scheduling problem for Essochem involves determining which finished products will be produced on each of eight blenders. However, this problem is made more complex because the reactor products and blend components needed for a particular product must be available. Reactor products must also be scheduled for production on three possible reactor lines. In addition, no finished-goods inventory is maintained; all finished products are produced to customer order. Also, the blender must be cleaned out after producing some products.

To help solve this complex scheduling problem, Essochem has developed a microcomputer system called PRISMS (Production Reporting and Information System for MRP and Scheduling). PRISMS generates daily and weekly production schedules, as well as monthly production plans. To do this, it requires bills of materials, inventory records, and details about blenders and reactors. The system also tracks individual customer orders and maintains inventory records. Because the PRISMS system has been implemented on a microcomputer, its costs are low, and it is relatively easy to use.[1]

INTRODUCTION

Scheduling is the last step in the planning process that began with strategic planning and proceeded through increasingly detailed planning activities. Recall that each successive stage of the planning process built on its preceding stage. In this chapter, we will describe how to schedule people, equipment, and facilities so that earlier steps in the planning process can be executed. For example, we will be concerned with such activities as sequencing different parts on a machine so that the production schedule can be met.

In discussing scheduling, we are getting into one of the most challenging areas of production/operations management (P/OM). Scheduling presents many day-to-day problems for operations managers because of changes in customer orders, equipment breakdowns, late deliveries from suppliers, and a myriad of other disruptions. At the same time, scheduling is one aspect of production planning for which few, if any, really satisfactory techniques have been developed due to the complexity of most scheduling problems. But scheduling is currently receiving considerable attention. In this chapter, we will discuss scheduling problems in various processes and present some methods for solving these problems.

Let us frame our discussion of scheduling by supposing that a company's master schedule calls for the production of two different products during a given time period. Using material requirements planning (MRP), it has been determined that certain parts for each of those finished products must be started into production during week 20, as shown by the circled figures in Exhibit 13.1.

The routings for these two parts are shown in Exhibit 13.2. Capacity requirements planning (CRP) has been used to determine that insufficient capacity will exist in week 20 on the lathe, which is the "gateway," or first work center, for both parts. Management investigated both short-run and long-run solutions to this capacity problem, but has decided that they will follow a short-run strategy and schedule overtime to alleviate the capacity problem in the lathe department.

In this situation, two scheduling problems have been indicated. One has to do with scheduling employees and the other with scheduling the two parts. Since overtime will be used in the lathe department, it will be necessary to schedule an employee or employees to work during that overtime. The second scheduling

Exhibit 13.1 Production Plan for Two Products

Master Schedule—Product A

Week	19	20	21	22	23	24
	500	200	300	400	200	300

Part # 103–B

		19	20	21	22	23	24
Gross requirements		500	200	300	400	200	300
Scheduled receipts							
Projected ending inventory	740	240	40	0	0	0	0
Net requirements				260	400	200	300
Planned receipts				260	400	200	300
Planned order releases			(260)	400	200	300	

Master Schedule—Product B

Week	19	20	21	22	23	24
	100	400	300	450	200	300

Part # 2065

		19	20	21	22	23	24
Gross requirements		200	800	600	900	400	600
Scheduled receipts			1,400				
Projected ending inventory	200	0	600	0	0	0	0
Net requirements					900	400	600
Planned receipts					900	400	600
Planned order releases			(900)	400	600		

Exhibit 13.2 Routings for Two Parts

Part # 103-B

Operation Number	Description of Operation
1	Lathe
2	Drill
3	Deburr
4	Mill
5	Grind

Part # 2065

Operation Number	Description of Operation
1	Lathe
2	Drill
3	Heat treat

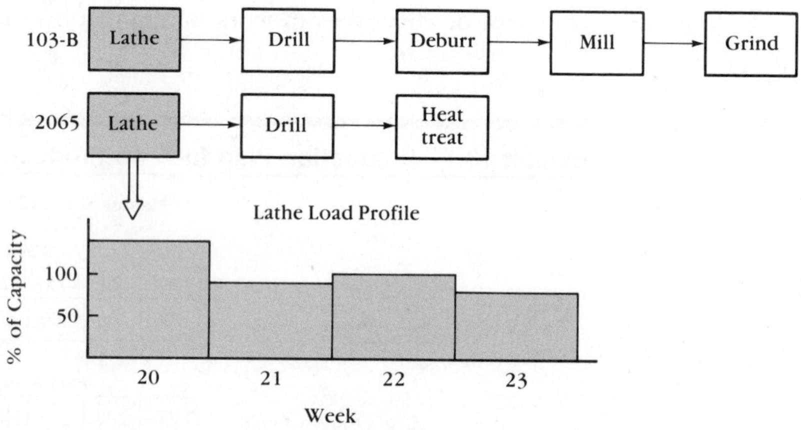

problem, scheduling the parts, occurs because both parts will be released to the lathe department at the same time. This second scheduling problem is one of **sequencing**—determining which part to produce first.

OVERVIEW OF THE SCHEDULING PROCESS

Data Collection

Obviously, before scheduling can take place, there must be something to schedule. However, more important, sufficient information about the jobs, activities, employees, equipment, or facilities that are to be scheduled is needed. Depending on the scheduling situation, various types of data must be collected, as shown below.

1. Jobs
   - **a.** Due dates
   - **b.** Routings, with standard setup and processing times
   - **c.** Material requirements
   - **d.** Flexibility of due dates
   - **e.** Importance of being completed by due date

2. Activities
   a. Expected duration
   b. Precedence relationships
   c. Desired time of completion
3. Employees
   a. Availability
   b. Job capabilities
   c. Efficiency at various jobs
   d. Wage rates
4. Equipment
   a. Machine or work center capacities
   b. Machine or work center capabilities
   c. Cost of operation
   d. Availability
5. Facilities
   a. Capacities
   b. Possible uses
   c. Cost of use
   d. Availability

Much of this information will be known and available within the organization. Other information must be gathered. However, in most instances, a great deal of important information must come from customers themselves. That information is obtained when orders are entered, a process we discuss next.

Order Entry

The first step in obtaining information about orders involves entry of the order into a company's information system. For a **make-to-order company,** one that produces only to customer orders or that provides services, this could occur when a customer places an order. Given existing production schedules, capacity available, and the customer's desired due date, this particular order can be scheduled. This order scheduling will be a rough estimate based on capacity requirements to produce the customer's order. Actually producing that order will require further scheduling of the individual parts and components for a product or the employees and facilities for a service.

In a **make-to-stock company,** one that produces for inventory and meets customer orders from inventory, production orders will be entered by the company itself based on the inventory level of each item in its stock and the expected future demand of that item. In general, a make-to-stock company has a somewhat easier job of scheduling since it has some control over which products will be made. A make-to-order company usually must produce whatever is demanded by the customers.

In an MRP environment, the MRP system will generate planned order releases based on the master schedule. This is another form of order entry—in this case, for individual parts or subassemblies. Again, the process is similar except that the master schedule generates requirements for materials and parts.

Orders Released for Production

As you learned in Chapter 10, the planning process involves a continual movement from strategic plans for the distant future toward more detailed plans for the less-distant future. As time gets closer to the present, plans become more precise and detailed until the time comes when each order is released for production. At that point, the schedule is implemented.

Because scheduling is the last step in production planning, it deals with the very near future. Plans are made to schedule a particular job, activity, or employee, but those plans are not converted into a detailed schedule until the last possible moment. The earlier planning stages dealt with determining what level of resources would be needed to meet the production plan. Scheduling allocates those resources.

When dealing with minute details, such as individual machines, parts, or employees, it is always possible that changes will occur. An employee may become ill or quit; a machine may break down; the raw materials for a part may not arrive on time. Because of these possibilities, scheduling must usually wait until the existing conditions are known with relative certainty. Even then, last-minute changes must often be made. But this is what makes scheduling so challenging—and so difficult.

As time moves forward and the scheduled starting time for a job or order is reached, that job or order is released for production. That step starts it on its way through the processing operations. But that is not the last step.

Sequencing and Dispatching

The final steps in scheduling are the actual sequencing of activities, jobs, or parts in the order they should flow through processing, then dispatching of those jobs. For our purposes, we will define **dispatching** as the assignment of priorities and the selection of jobs for processing at a work center or facility. For example, a customer order for a made-to-order product will have to be sequenced in with other orders. When the time comes for work to begin on that order, it will be dispatched at the first work center according to its priority at that time. In the following discussion of scheduling, we will concentrate primarily on ways of sequencing—whether of parts, orders, jobs, activities, or employees.

Managerial Considerations in Scheduling

Scheduling in P/OM is an attempt to allocate scarce resources. For example, machine time is a scarce resource that is allocated to different jobs, employee time is allocated to different activities, and facilities are scheduled for a given activity at a particular time period. In all of these scheduling problems, different criteria may be used in deciding which of several schedules is best. Those criteria may relate to the amount of time equipment might sit idle, the importance of a certain order or a certain customer, or the level at which a resource is utilized.

The problem of scheduling can be quite complex; what appears to be an optimal schedule from one viewpoint may be far from optimal from another. For example, a certain schedule may utilize one machine very efficiently, but may mean idle time for machines farther along in the processing operations. Another schedule might mean that an important customer's order will not be delivered on time. In general, there are six criteria that may be used in evaluating different possible schedules.

1. Providing the good or service when the customer wants it
2. Minimizing the length of time it takes to produce that good or service (called **flow time**)
3. Minimizing the level of work-in-process (WIP) inventories
4. Minimizing the amount of time that equipment is idle
5. Minimizing the amount of time that employees are idle
6. Minimizing costs

Which of these criteria are most relevant will often depend on the product or service being produced, the particular industry a company is in, and especially the organization's competitive strategy. Different production processes will also incur different problems, and certain criteria will thus be more important. To make matters more difficult, it is usually impossible to satisfy all of the six criteria listed above at one time. Instead, management must choose among the various trade-offs described below.

- *Providing the good or service when the customer wants it.* Requires flexibility. Can lead to large inventories and excess capacity during periods of low demand.
- *Minimizing flow time.* Requires flexibility, short setup times, and fast production rates. Can require having excess capacity available.
- *Minimizing WIP inventories.* May require excess capacity or the use of a pull system. Can lead to high machine or employee idle time.
- *Minimizing machine idle time.* Often means keeping capacity low or accepting any customer orders. Can result in high inventories, the overloading of equipment, and late orders.
- *Minimizing employee idle time.* Often means keeping work-force size low or accepting any orders. Can result in employee discontent, late orders, and high inventories.
- *Minimizing costs.* Often requires compromises on the preceding criteria. The problem is to properly define and measure all relevant costs. Can result in poor customer service—a cost that is difficult to measure.

In determining which criteria to use, a company must carefully consider its corporate objectives, competitive strategy, and capabilities. The company's scheduling decisions will have a great impact on facility design, the type of equipment used, and the work-force requirements.

TECHNIQUES FOR SCHEDULING LINE-FLOW AND BATCH PROCESSES

In scheduling, we will be dealing primarily with two questions:

1. When should a given job, order, or product be processed?
2. How many units should be processed at a time?

The answers to these questions can have a great impact on the way a processing operation is run. For instance, a company that makes ice cream must decide which flavors should be made when. If chocolate is made before vanilla, there may be extensive time spent cleaning the equipment between runs. On the other hand, producing vanilla before vanilla-fudge marble may mean no cleanup between runs. In addition, the company must decide how many gallons of one flavor to make before it starts making another. The company does not want to produce so much of a given flavor that the ice cream deteriorates before it is sold. By the same token, producing small quantities at a time will mean excessive time spent cleaning and refilling the equipment between runs.

In this section, we will look at various techniques for scheduling. Because the scheduling problem is different for different types of processes, we will discuss the rules that are appropriate for each of the major process types—line flow, batch, and job shop.

Scheduling Continuous Flow Processes

A **continuous flow process** is one in which materials flow in a continuous, or nearly continuous, stream from beginning to end. A good example of a continuous flow process is an oil refinery. Such production processes are generally characterized by few different finished products, only a few possible routings, and low work-in-process inventories.

Under such conditions, the relevant scheduling criteria become rather limited. For example, flow time is determined by the production process, rather than by a schedule. Work-in-process inventory is also not a major problem because it is generally quite low for continuous flow processes. Thus, the scheduling problem in a continuous flow process boils down to determining when to change over from making one product to making another. The relevant criterion is usually to minimize cost, although minimizing the time the facility is idle during changeover could also be important.

Scheduling an Assembly Line

An **assembly-line process** is similar to continuous flow, but instead of the products being continuous items, such as a stream of gasoline or a roll of paper, the products are discrete, individual items, such as automobiles.

One of the best examples of an assembly-line process is the automobile assembly line. In this example, the product follows a fixed path. Like the continuous flow process, an assembly-line process usually produces a limited number of products, and the routings are usually the same. Work-in-process inventory is also usually small. Thus, the same basic ideas used for scheduling in continuous flow can also be used for assembly-line process scheduling. However, there are two particular problems unique to assembly-line scheduling that we will discuss here.

Line Balancing

Chapter 8 presented assembly-line balancing in the context of facility layout. The emphasis there was on determining how many work stations would be needed to achieve a desired cycle time and which tasks should be assigned to each station to minimize "balance delay." Assembly-line balancing also provides the framework for scheduling. By assigning tasks to work stations, the material flow and job assignments have been specified by the line balance.

Keep in mind, however, that assembly-line balancing is not a perfect science. In actual practice, people with different abilities will be assigned to those stations. The result may be that even though a perfect balance was achieved theoretically, the result in practice will not be perfect. Some employees will often be able to complete their tasks in less than the average time. Others will take longer. The end result is that a line balanced in theory may be unbalanced in practice.

Scheduling is one approach to overcoming this problem. A skillful supervisor will know which employees can work faster and will assign those to the stations with more work. On a dynamic basis, tasks may even be shifted from one work station to another as trouble spots appear. Thus, scheduling, in the sense of assigning employees to work stations or tasks to employees, is an integral part of fine-tuning the balance of a line.

This fine-tuning is especially important in JIT. The emphasis on always trying to eliminate waste leads companies using JIT to try to reduce the number of work stations to an absolute minimum. To do this, company management will balance a line and then gradually try to take tasks away from one work station, rebalancing the line, if necessary, each time. If one of the work stations has its tasks reduced enough, that station will be eliminated and the line operated with the remaining stations. At that point, attempts will be made to eliminate another station. This process requires constant rebalancing and reassignment of employees to work stations.

Sequencing

Earlier we mentioned that sequencing was the problem of determining the order in which parts or products should be processed. That particular problem is relevant to an assembly-line process. Take, for example, an automobile assembly line. That line may be balanced for producing a particular make and model of car. But it will be out of balance for a different make or model. For instance, the work stations that install seats and interior padding will probably require a longer period to do a station wagon than they will a two-door sedan. If too many station wagons are sequenced in a row, those work stations will be **overcycled.** In other words, the amount of work to do will consistently exceed the cycle time.

The importance of mixed-model sequencing was discussed in Chapter 12. In that case, the objective was to obtain a level schedule that would smooth out the requirements for parts and subassemblies. This approach helps to eliminate many of the problems associated with machine scheduling because it eliminates many of the conflicts between different parts that must be processed on the same machine.

Scheduling Batch Processes

In batch processes, the number of possible products is greater than in line-flow processes. Further, the production volume of each product is usually less than in a line-flow process. As a result, the same resources are used to produce at least several different products, producing a batch of each product at a time.

Because of this batch production, how many units to produce in a batch and which product to produce become important questions. In answering them, the criterion of cost minimization is usually used to determine production quantity.

Because each product is produced only intermittently, it must be produced often enough to avoid running out of inventory. Thus, the sequencing of products is often determined on the basis of which one is likely to run out of inventory first.

Economic Order Quantity

One approach to determining production quantities for batch processes is to use what is called the **economic order quantity (EOQ)** to balance the costs of changeover with the costs of storing the finished product. Exhibit 13.3 depicts this trade-off. Basically, the more of a given product produced at one time, the higher the storage costs. But producing less means more frequent changeovers and a higher annual cost of changeovers. The EOQ point minimizes total annual costs. This idea will be discussed more in Chapter 16. For now, you need only realize that some order quantity, or lot size, will minimize costs, as shown in Exhibit 13.3. This quantity will usually tell us how much of each product to make at one time in a continuous flow process.

Run-Out Time

One problem with using EOQ is that it considers only how much of each product to produce at one time; EOQ does not indicate which product should be produced next. One method that can be used to answer this second question is called **run-out time.** This is simply a calculation of how long it will be before the company will *run out* of each product at current usage rates and is determined as follows:

$$\text{Run-out time} = \frac{\text{current inventory}}{\text{usage rate}}$$

Exhibit 13.3 Economic Order Quantity

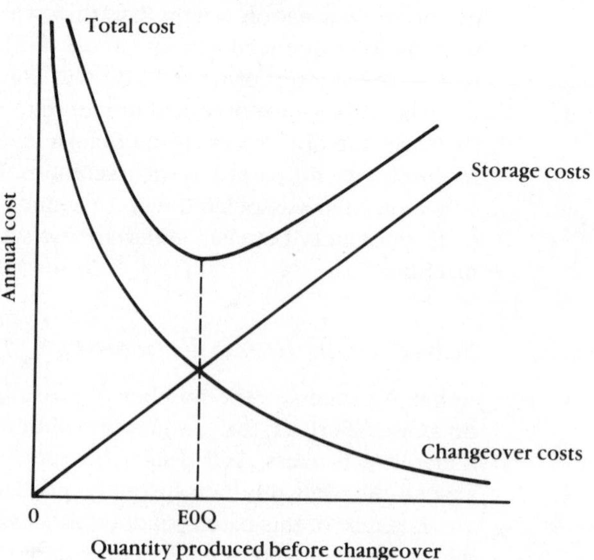

Example

Exhibit 13.4 indicates current inventory and demand rates for five different products made by a continuous flow process. Run-out time calculations are shown for each of the five different products. Based on those calculations, product E should be produced next since it will run out first, in two weeks.

Exhibit 13.4 Run-Out Time Calculations

Product	Current Inventory	Demand Rate (Units per Week)	Run-Out Time (Weeks)
A	1,000	200	1,000/200 = 5
B	500	150	500/150 = 3.3
C	2,000	500	2,000/500 = 4
D	2,500	500	2,500/500 = 5
E	600	300	600/300 = 2

In actual practice, the order quantity and order sequence questions must be answered simultaneously. However, a discussion of that procedure is beyond the scope of this text.

Flexible Manufacturing Systems

It was mentioned before in discussing the use of the EOQ for production scheduling that the basic trade-off was between product changeover costs and inventory carrying costs. But when the cost of changeover becomes extremely small, the question of how many to produce at a time is less important.

Flexible manufacturing systems (FMSs) have been able to reduce changeover costs to the point that it is economical to produce just one product or part at a time. The question then becomes one of sequencing to keep this changeover time—and consequently the cost—low enough.

Group technology, which has been discussed in previous chapters, is an important aspect of any FMS. By grouping similar products into families, a GT cell within an FMS has to deal only with products that have similar characteristics. This tends to reduce the sequencing problem. Because computerized control is an important part of an FMS, the computer can be used to evaluate different possible sequences and determine the best one for each cell.

JOB SHOP SCHEDULING

One type of production process for which very few satisfactory scheduling techniques have been developed is the job shop. Unlike continuous flow or assembly-line processes, a job shop has many different and intersecting routings. Different

OPERATIONS IN ACTION

BMW: Providing Customers with a Wide Choice of Options by Combining Assembly-Line and Batch Scheduling

Most assembly lines are not designed for great flexibility. However, BMW's competitive strategy involves offering customers numerous options in terms of color and door style, and even variations for different countries. As a result, the BMW plant at Regensburg, West Germany, produces two completely identical cars only about once in four months.

To allow for all these variations, the assembly operation has been designed for flexibility, allowing different cars to follow different paths through processing. However, the painting operation cannot operate efficiently if colors are varied to exactly meet the assembly sequence.

To handle this problem, painting is scheduled in batches of one color. The sequence of batches for each day's color requirements is planned ahead of time to maximize efficiency. The painted car bodies, which may not be scheduled in assembly until later that day, are stored on shelves and then removed when needed.[2]

jobs will be vying for time on the same machines. The decision about which job to process first on a given machine can have a major impact on what happens at other machines or work centers—possibly overloading some, while leaving others idle.

Sequencing Using Dispatching Rules

One of the earliest approaches to job shop scheduling was to focus on the criteria for scheduling that were mentioned earlier in this chapter. Those criteria could be used to generate dispatching rules to be used at an individual machine or work center. The five most common dispatching rules are described below.

Earliest Due Date

This earliest-due-date rule focuses on the criterion of providing the product when the customer wants it. The rationale is that whichever job is due first should be started first. The advantage of this approach is that some jobs may meet their due dates. This rule is popular with companies that are sensitive to due-date changes. However, finishing one job on time may make many more late. The method also does not consider how long it will take to process the job—which led to the next rule.

Shortest Processing Time

The rationale for the shortest-processing-time rule is to get the most work done as quickly as possible in order to minimize the level of WIP inventory. Unfortunately, jobs with long processing times may be made quite late as they wait for shorter jobs to be finished. Otherwise, this rule usually tends to work best on most measures.

Longest Processing Time

The longest-processing-time rule uses a different strategy—to get the jobs that will take longest done first, leaving time at the end to do the short-processing-time jobs. The rationale behind this rule is that jobs with long processing times may be more likely to miss their due dates than are jobs with short processing times. However, the great disadvantage of this approach is that many short jobs may also miss their due dates because of one long job. This rule also tends to result in an increase in WIP inventory. It may be used when a critical job has a long lead time.

First Come, First Served

This rule is often used in service facilities because it is usually seen as the fairest one by customers. However, it totally ignores due date or processing time, so it does not perform well on such measures.

Critical Ratio

The critical-ratio rule is an attempt to combine the preceding rules into one that considers both due date and processing time. It is based on calculating the critical ratio (*CR*), which is

$$CR = \frac{\text{time until due date}}{\text{processing time remaining}}$$

This rule, which appears to be used quite often in practice, is implemented by scheduling those jobs first that have the lowest critical ratio. Values of *CR* below one mean the job will be past due. A negative value means it is already past due. This rule has the advantage of scheduling those jobs first that have the greatest chance of missing their due dates.

It should be noted that this rule differs from the others in that it is *dynamic.* That is, a job's critical ratio will change over time as the number of days until the due date changes and the processing time remaining changes. Thus, the critical ratio must be constantly updated.

Example

The Hillside Machine Corporation has four jobs waiting to be run on its lathe. Exhibit 13.5 shows the days until due date and the processing time remaining for each job. Hillside wants to see what sequences will be generated by using each of the five dispatching rules. Exhibit 13.5 shows these sequences. It is interesting to note that in this example, the longest-processing-time and critical-ratio rules happen to produce the same sequence of jobs—although such will not always be the case.

Sequencing Jobs on One Machine

Minimizing Average Flow Time. As we have mentioned, flow time is the amount of time it takes to produce a product. If the product spends a large amount of time waiting to be processed, then its flow time will be long. By processing as many jobs as possible during a given period of time, average flow time will be minimized. The way to achieve this result is by using the shortest-processing-time rule, which has been proven to always minimize average flow time.

Exhibit 13.5 Comparison of Dispatching Rules

Job (Order Arrived)	Days Until Due Date	Processing Time Remaining
A	10	5 days
B	20	3 days
C	15	10 days
D	40	2 days

Earliest due date: A–C–B–D

Shortest processing time: D–B–A–C

Longest processing time: C–A–B–D

First come, first-served: A–B–C–D

Critical ratio:

Job	A	B	C	D
CR	10/5 = 2	20/3 = 6.67	15/10 = 1.5	40/2 = 20

C–A–B–D

Example

Refer to the Hillside Machine Corporation data in the previous example. Suppose we keep track of how many days each job takes until it is done, using the critical-ratio and shortest-processing-time rules. As the results in Exhibit 13.6 indicate, all four jobs are finished within twenty days regardless of which rule is used. However, with the critical-ratio rule, the average time each job spends before completion is 15.75 days. With the shortest-processing-time rule, the average time is only 9.25 days.

Minimizing Changeover Times. One factor we have not considered is the setup time between jobs. In some cases, the setup time or cost will depend on the processing sequence, as we indicated earlier with the different flavors of ice cream. In those cases, a procedure that provides a good solution, although not necessarily the best, is as follows:

1. Select the lowest setup time or cost among all possibilities. Schedule the associated jobs first and second.
2. Now find the next job that will minimize setup time or cost after the current last job, excluding any jobs already scheduled.
3. Repeat step 2 until all jobs are sequenced.

Exhibit 13.6 Comparison of Average Flow Times for Two Sequencing Rules

Critical-Ratio Rule			*Shortest-Processing-Time Rule*		
Job	**Start**	**End**	**Job**	**Start**	**End**
C	0	10	D	0	2
A	10	15	B	2	5
B	15	18	A	5	10
D	18	20	C	10	20
	Total	63		Total	37

Average flow time
= 63/4 = 15.75 days

Average flow time
= 37/4 = 9.25 days

Example

Five jobs are to be processed on a single machine. All jobs will meet their due dates, so the objective is to minimize total setup cost. The setup costs are as follows:

		Follower Job				
		A	B	C	D	E
	A	—	$30	$20	$25	$35
	B	$40	—	20	30	30
Predecessor Job	C	25	40	—	25	35
	D	30	15	28	—	47
	E	32	45	39	23	—

The lowest-cost sequence is D–B with $15, so these jobs are scheduled first and second, respectively. After B, the lowest setup cost is incurred if job C is scheduled. Following C, the lowest setup cost is obtained by scheduling job A. Finally, job E is scheduled, giving the sequence D–B–C–A–E, with a total setup cost of $15 + $20 + $25 + $35 = $95.

Sequencing Jobs Using Johnson's Rule

When there are two successive machines or work centers through which a group of jobs must all be sequenced, Johnson's Rule can be used to minimize total processing time for the group of jobs, which is called the **makespan** time. The method utilizes the following steps:

1. List the jobs and the time each requires at each work center.
2. From the list, select the job with shortest time at either work center (break ties arbitrarily). If the time is for the first work center, proceed to step 2a. If it is for the second work center, proceed to step 2b.

   a. Place the job as close to the beginning of the sequence as possible without replacing other jobs. Go to step 3.
   b. Place the job as close to the end of the sequence as possible without replacing other jobs. Go to step 3.

3. Eliminate the job just scheduled from your list. Return to step 2.

You should notice that this rule requires all jobs to follow the same sequence through both work centers. The sequence cannot change at the second work center.

Example

University Data Services has five computer payroll jobs waiting to be processed before Friday afternoon. Each job requires computing and then printing, in that order. Based on past experience, the company estimates each job will take the following time:

	Processing Time (Hours)	
Job	**Computing**	**Printing**
A	1.5	1.0
B	1.0	.75
C	.5	1.25
D	2.0	1.5
E	.75	.5

Using Johnson's Rule, we proceed as follows. Two jobs, C and E, have shortest processing time of .5 hours. We arbitrarily select C. Because its shortest time is for the first operation, we schedule job C at the beginning of the sequence.

C	_	_	_	_
1	2	3	4	5

We eliminate job C from further consideration and return to step 2. Now job E has shortest processing time. Because that time is for the second operation (printing), we schedule job E at the end of the sequence.

C	_	_	_	E
1	2	3	4	5

Job E is now eliminated from the list. Therefore, job B has the shortest processing time, which is for the second operation. Job B is scheduled as close to the end of the sequence as possible.

C	_	_	B	E
1	2	3	4	5

After eliminating job B, of the remaining two jobs, A has the shortest processing time. Because that time is for the second process, we schedule A as close to the end as possible, which turns out to be the third position.

C	_	A	B	E
1	2	3	4	5

Exhibit 13.7 Processing of Computer Jobs Based on Sequencing by Johnson's Rule

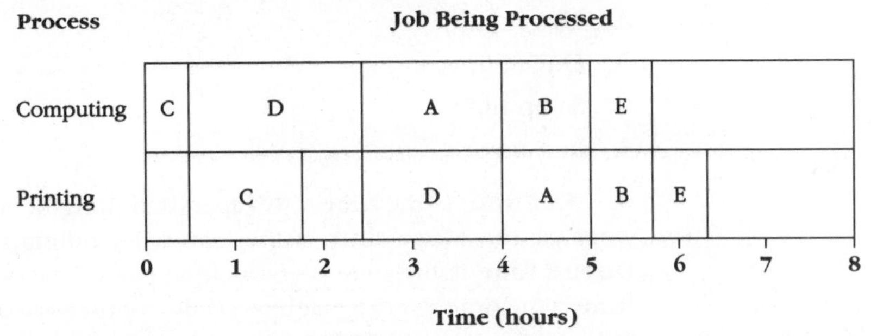

The last remaining job is placed in the remaining slot in the schedule, producing the following sequence.

$$\frac{C}{1} \quad \frac{D}{2} \quad \frac{A}{3} \quad \frac{B}{4} \quad \frac{E}{5}$$

This sequence of jobs produces the processing sequence for each operation shown in Exhibit 13.7. As you can see, this method completes all jobs within 6.25 hours and leaves only .5 hour of idle time for the printer at the beginning of the sequence and .75 hour between jobs C and D.

DISPATCHING IN MRP

The rules just mentioned are limited in the sense that they only consider the conditions that exist for a given point in time and a given work center. By and large, they ignore the fact that a given part may be part of a subassembly that must be made before the final product can be assembled. Critical ratio is the only rule mentioned that comes close to considering the complexity of successive lead times.

But MRP takes those lead times into account. As long as the planning lead times used in MRP are valid, then the priority of each item should be based on the MRP lead times. Therefore, in an MRP system, priorities are determined by referring to the planned order releases and lead times. Thus, the dispatching rules are irrelevant to MRP systems. Instead, MRP works from the order due dates, scheduling order releases far enough ahead of time that these due dates should be met. Unfortunately, there may still be conflicts at machines and work centers. We now discuss ways of scheduling to avoid such conflicts.

Machine Loading

The dispatching rules previously described attempt to determine a schedule based on simply looking at the attributes, such as due date or processing time, of each job. However, the time it takes for a job to actually get processed consists of the following five components:

1. Wait time
2. Move time
3. Queue time
4. Setup time
5. Run time

Wait time is the time a job spends waiting before being moved to the next work center. **Move time** is the material-handling time between work centers. **Queue time** is the time spent waiting to be processed at a work center. **Setup time** is the time to get a machine ready to process that job, and **run time** is actual processing time.

In general, all of these components—except queue time—will be fairly fixed. Queue time really depends to a large extent on the workload that has been scheduled for each work center. If a machine's capacity is being used extensively, then it is more likely that many jobs will be waiting for processing at that machine. When the capacity of a work center is exceeded, it is a certainty that lines of work (queues) will build up in front of that work center.

Loading is an approach to scheduling that tries to take capacity utilization into account. There are several different approaches to loading. However, loading begins with scheduling.

Forward Scheduling

Suppose we start from the present time and begin scheduling each job to start at the earliest possible moment. That is **forward scheduling.** As jobs progress through work centers, each work center will have a certain workload placed on it from the jobs that must be processed. Exhibit 13.8 indicates the schedule that would be generated by forward scheduling for four jobs (A, B, C, and D) and three work centers (lathe, mill, and drill), based on the following information and assuming six hours for wait/move time between machines.

	Work Center Sequence and Processing Time (Setup and Run Times in Hours)					
Job	**Operation 1**		**Operation 2**		**Operation 3**	
A	Lathe	3	Drill	2	Mill	4
B	Mill	4	Drill	3		
C	Lathe	2	Mill	3	Drill	4
D	Drill	5	Lathe	4		

You should notice that in Exhibit 13.8, we begin each job as close to time zero as possible and schedule it through each of the successive operations, allowing six hours for wait/move time between machines. However, some jobs have been delayed (queue time) on certain work centers because another job had already started on that work center. For example, job C had to wait three hours before it could start on the lathe because job A was still being processed on that machine. This approach of making one job wait if another has been scheduled on the same machine is called **finite loading** because it takes into consideration the limited capacity on each machine. Another approach uses **infinite loading,** which does not take capacity considerations into account. To demonstrate the other type of scheduling, we will use infinite loading.

Exhibit 13.8 Forward Schedule for Four Jobs with Finite Loading

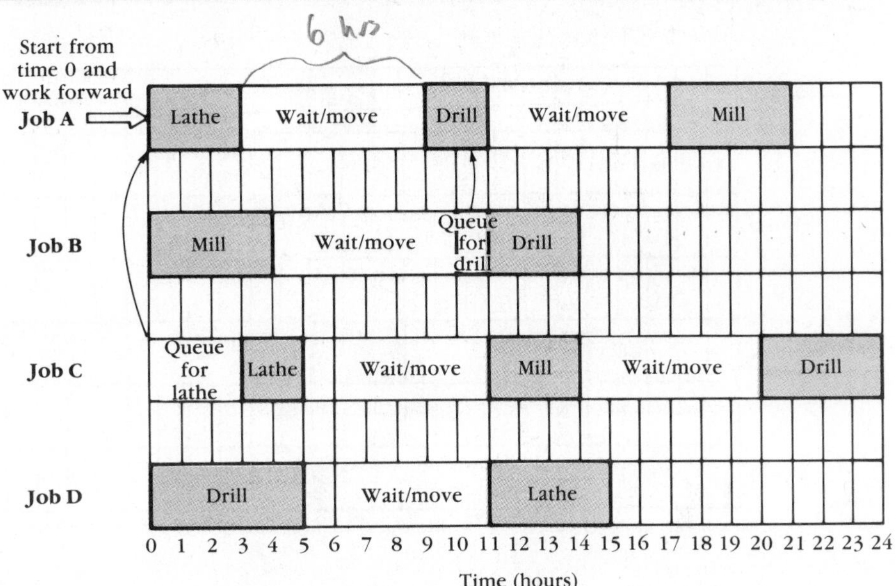

Backward Scheduling

The idea with **backward scheduling** is to start from a desired due date and work backward. We will use the information for the four jobs and three work centers presented previously, but add the following due dates:

Job	Due Date
A	Hour 24
B	Hour 16
C	Hour 24
D	Hour 16

In this case, we will use *infinite loading*, ignoring the problem of having more than one job at the same work center at the same time. The resulting schedule is shown in Exhibit 13.9.

Notice that in this case we began by scheduling the last operation for each job so that it would end at the time due, working backward through each operation. You should also notice that certain work centers have been scheduled to do more than one job at a time. This may not be a problem if more than one machine is available, or if sufficient slack capacity is available to get each job finished by its due date.

Actually, either finite or infinite loading can be used with either forward or backward scheduling. However, it is probably most common that forward scheduling uses finite loading and backward scheduling uses infinite loading.

Either of the preceding schedules can also be used to generate a load profile for each work center. A **load profile,** as you should recall from our discussion in Chapter 11, indicates the workload being placed on that work center. Exhibit 13.10 shows the load profiles for the backward schedule of Exhibit 13.9 on an

Exhibit 13.9 Backward Schedule for Four Jobs with Infinite Loading

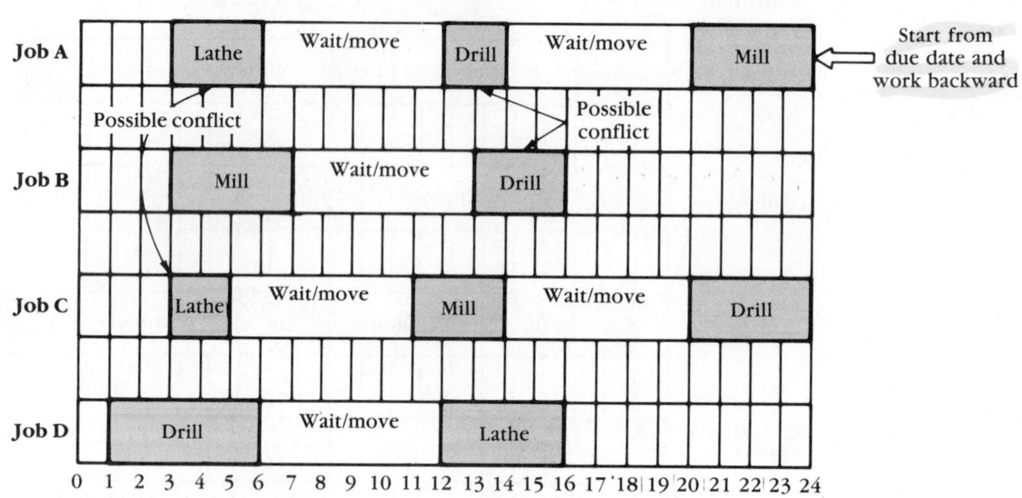

Exhibit 13.10 Load Profiles for Backward Schedule

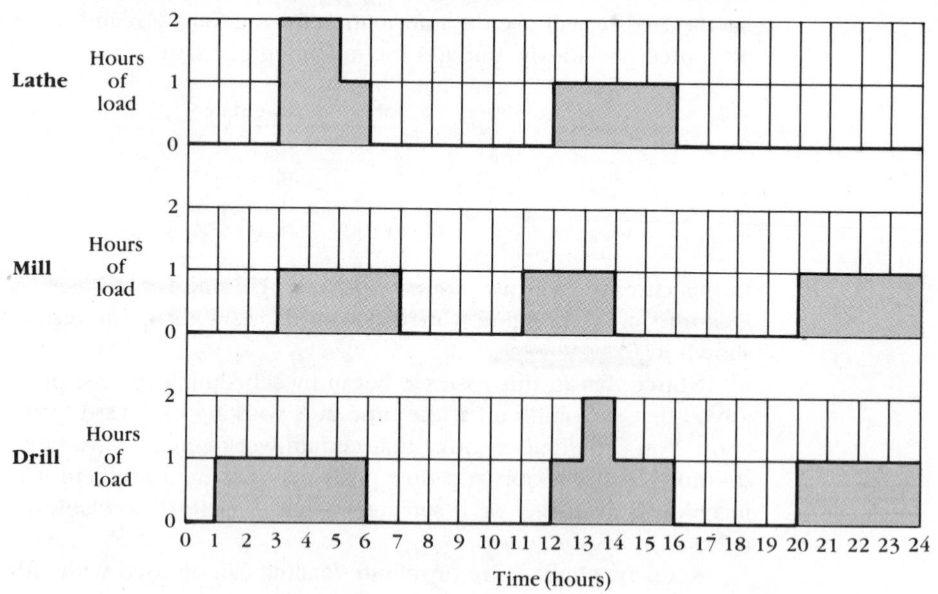

hourly basis. Those were obtained by adding up the number of jobs scheduled during each hour for each machine. Notice that any hour in which more than one hour of machine time is scheduled could present a problem if only one of each machine is available.

The reason we have discussed both forward and backward scheduling is that each is widely used—and many companies use both. Forward scheduling is useful for jobs that need to start right away. Backward scheduling works well when a desired due date is specified. We also discussed both finite and infinite loading. The problem with finite loading is that it requires much more effort for companies to keep track of which jobs are scheduled for which machines at what time. Unforeseen problems, variations in processing time, and many other factors usually combine to make this a wasted effort. Therefore, most companies use infinite loading and then worry about how to deal with overloaded work centers after they have worked up the load profile.

This helps to point up the importance of capacity requirements planning and its tie-in with both the medium-range production plan and the master schedule. While capacity requirements planning is only a rough estimation, it still helps to ensure that sufficient capacity will be available. If the master schedule is realistic from a capacity viewpoint, then infinite loading usually does not produce too many problems.

Sequencing

In presenting the forward schedule with finite loading, we did not allow two jobs to be in the same work center at the same time. Thus, if job 1 had been started at work center A, job 3 had to wait. But would it have been better to start job 3 on work center A first and make job 1 wait? To answer that question, we can use a device that allows us to schedule each work center—the Gantt load chart. The **Gantt load chart** is a device that has been around for many years. Although it has not been widely used recently, this sequencing tool is getting more current use as companies realize the importance of their sequencing activities.

Each work center can be indicated by a bar of the Gantt load chart. The job being processed at each work center and its processing time can also be indicated. Exhibit 13.11 shows the Gantt load chart that corresponds to the forward finite load schedule of Exhibit 13.8.

The Gantt load chart is very useful for finite scheduling because it allows only one job to be run on each machine or work center at a time. Any conflicts will immediately become apparent. However, developing these charts for a large number of machines and many jobs can become tedious.

Input/Output Control

Input/output control is a method of managing work flow and queue lengths. The idea is simple. If work is put into a work center faster than it comes out, a queue will build up. If work is put in at a slower rate than it comes out, the work center may run out of work.

Exhibit 13.12 shows the input/output report for a work center. Notice that cumulative deviation of actual input from planned input and cumulative deviation of actual output from planned output are recorded each week. Further, the cumulative change in backlog is determined each week by comparing actual input

Exhibit 13.11 Gantt Load Chart for Forward Schedule

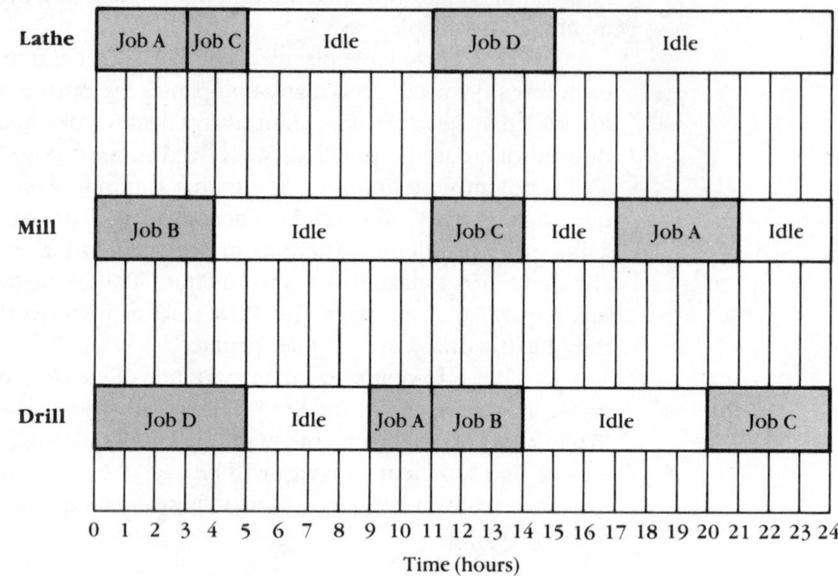

Exhibit 13.12 Input/Output Report in Standard Hours

	Week					
	43	**44**	**45**	**46**	**47**	**48**
Planned input	400	380	410	370	375	360
Actual input	350	390	400	370	365	380
Cumulative deviation	–50	–40	–50	–50	–60	–40

	Week					
	43	**44**	**45**	**46**	**47**	**48**
Planned output	410	400	400	370	380	390
Actual output	380	400	380	400	380	370
Cumulative deviation	–30	–30	–50	–20	–20	–40

Backlog (hours)	80	50	40	60	30	15	25

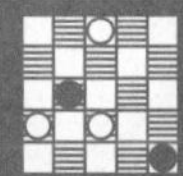

GAINING STRATEGIC ADVANTAGE AT AMERICAN AIRLINES

Scheduling Helps the Airline Compete with On-Time Performance

The on-time performance of airlines has become a major order winner, with each airline trying to be at the top of each month's ratings. But on-time performance depends to a large extent on the schedule an airline puts together. For instance, American was having trouble with a certain flight that was always late leaving Chicago's O'Hare Airport because it got blocked by another plane leaving at the same time.

To avoid such problems, American must carefully schedule its 420 airplanes for 2,140 daily flights to 150 different airports. However, the problem is further complicated by various federal regulations and noise restrictions. As an example, the pilots' labor contract requires a rest of 11.5 hours between flights. Thus, a crew that flies into a city at night may not be able to fly out early the next morning. Further, certain noisier (stage 2) aircraft are not allowed to use certain airports.

One approach to solving such problems is to chart all takeoff and landing times. For example, to help ensure that its flights will not be delayed at Chicago, American's schedulers develop charts of all airlines' takeoff and landing schedules at O'Hare. Any open spot during the day can be used by American to schedule its flights without fear of being delayed by another airline's flight.[3]

to actual output. For example, in week 43, actual output exceeds actual input by thirty hours. Therefore, the cumulative backlog decreases by that amount. In week 45 actual input exceeds actual output by twenty hours, so backlog increases by twenty hours.

Simulation in Developing Schedules

By now, you should realize that scheduling and sequencing can be rather difficult in some situations. This is especially true in job shops where many different end products require different operations. Unfortunately, trying to develop schedules manually in such situations can be extremely time-consuming and difficult. There are just too many combinations to consider.

To help deal with this difficulty, computers have been employed. Using simulation techniques, it is possible to develop a trial schedule on the computer and then test that schedule without actually processing the jobs. Through this simulation, potential problems can be identified and an improved schedule developed. Today, more companies are developing computer simulation programs to help solve their scheduling problems. We will not discuss the details here, but some basic simulation concepts are presented in the supplement to this chapter.

SPECIAL PROBLEMS IN SCHEDULING SERVICES

Thus far we have been discussing scheduling in the context of producing goods. In that context, inventory was an important consideration, whether it was work-in-process inventory or finished-goods inventory. However, scheduling for services requires a different approach, and we will spend some time discussing a few aspects of that area.

No Finished-Goods Inventory

One major difference between scheduling the production of goods and scheduling the production of services is that a service cannot be inventoried. For example, a company that manufactures air conditioners can build up its inventory during the winter months in preparation for peak summer demand. But a hospital cannot build up an inventory of emergency-room services in advance. Unlike goods, services can be produced only at the time of demand. This means that the strategies for meeting that demand are more limited for services than for goods.

In scheduling services, we are not so concerned with the question of sequencing as we were previously. The scheduling problems in service industries usually have to do with determining what level of capacity should be made available at different times. For example, a hospital emergency room needs to know how many employees to schedule for weekends versus weekday mornings; a fast-food restaurant needs to determine how many employees it should schedule for lunch hour and how many for late evening.

Scheduling Strategies

Schedule for Peak Demand

A possible approach to scheduling for services is to schedule for peak demand. That means that sufficient capacity will be available at any time to meet the peak expected demand. The advantage of this approach is that it allows for demand to be met at all times under normal conditions. However, its greatest disadvantage is that a large portion of capacity may be idle a great percentage of the time.

Chase Demand

In discussing strategies for medium-range operations planning, we mentioned two strategies by which a company adjusts its production rate to match demand—varying the work force and using overtime. Either of these strategies can be very useful for service companies if they can estimate expected demand with reasonable accuracy. For example, Burger King restaurants maintain extensive records of historical demand during various days of the week and hours of the day. This information is used by each restaurant to determine how many employees it should schedule during each hour.

This strategy works best if the employees are willing to work on a part-time basis. Fast-food restaurants are one industry that is able to schedule its employees in this way. The primary advantage of this strategy is that it costs less than scheduling for peak demand, while still enabling the organization to meet its anticipated demand. The disadvantages are that it requires an extremely flexible work force and that demand forecasts must be fairly accurate.

Other Strategies

Some other possible strategies involve scheduling appointments or reservations for service, increasing consumer participation, creating adjustable capacity, sharing capacity, and cross-training employees.

The reservation strategy is commonly used by restaurants, hotels, and airlines. Reservations allow an organization to determine the advance demand for its service, while also limiting access to that service. Airlines, in particular, have used reservations to control access to their lowest fares. Those travelers who are willing to book their flights far in advance and satisfy certain length-of-stay criteria get the best fares; those who book only hours before the flight, when space may be limited, must pay the highest fares.

Fast-food restaurants have successfully used consumer participation, such as having customers serve themselves from the salad bar or draw their own drinks, as a way of reducing staffing requirements. This reduces the work-force scheduling problems considerably because fewer people are needed. Self-service gas stations also use this principle. One employee who takes the customers' money can usually handle any level of demand because the most labor-intensive part—pumping the gas—is done by the customers themselves. In fact, some gas stations have eliminated the employee altogether and replaced that person with a device to accept credit cards!

Adjustable capacity involves the ability to use only part of the facilities or available employees at any given time. For example, restaurants can close off sections when demand is low. The waiters and waitresses who would serve those sections can fill salt shakers and perform other activities in preparation for peak demand. As the demand increases, those waiters and waitresses can be moved to waiting on tables as sections are opened. Cross-training employees also provides similar advantages. If employees are trained to perform more than one activity, then they can be shifted from one to another as demand changes.

Sharing capacity is a way that different organizations, or even different parts of the same organization, with different demand patterns can use the same facilities, and possibly the same employees. For example, many churches have found that their Sunday school facilities, which are normally idle during the week, can be put to good use for day-care centers. On the weekend, when day care is not in session, the church will use those facilities. Airlines have also been able to share gates, check-in facilities, and even ground crews.

Ethical Issues in Scheduling

In the preceding chapter, we have already discussed how master scheduling and MRP can help a company make due-date commitments to its customers with a high degree of certainty. However, scheduling plays an important role in ensuring that those due-date commitments are met. If jobs are scheduled without considering due dates, then many of the due dates may not be met.

To avoid that occurrence, companies must set scheduling priorities to meet customer due dates. One dispatching rule we have already discussed, the critical ratio, takes due dates into account and compares them to remaining processing time. By using such a procedure that sets priorities based on due dates, companies can be sure the due-date commitments they have made are kept visible throughout all operations.

However, in service operations, there may be other considerations. For example, waiting lines at service facilities almost always operate on a first come, first served basis, especially in the United States where everyone wants to feel he or she is being treated equally. However, some service facilities may use other scheduling rules.

For example, hospital emergency rooms usually treat the most critical cases first. Thus, someone with a broken arm may have to wait while a heart-attack victim receives treatment. Likewise, an airplane running low on fuel may be given priority over other planes in landing at a busy airport.

Obviously, some scheduling situations may involve more ethical considerations than others. However, all scheduling must take into account the organization's objectives, while treating customers in an ethical manner.

SUMMARY

- Scheduling requires information about jobs, activities, employees, equipment, and facilities.
- Sequencing is the determination, ahead of time, of the order in which work is to be done. Dispatching involves setting priorities and starting jobs at a work center based on those priorities.
- Criteria for scheduling include due date, flow time, WIP inventory, idle time, and costs. Doing well on some criteria can mean performing poorly on others.
- Continuous flow processes produce only a limited number of products, and flow time and work-in-process are determined by the process itself. Thus, the scheduling decision usually involves how much of each product to make at one time.
- The sequencing of products on an assembly line and line balancing are two issues of concern in scheduling.
- A batch process is scheduled by determining the number of units to produce and which product to make next.
- A flexible manufacturing system makes scheduling easier by reducing changeover time and using group technology.
- Dispatching rules include the earliest due date; shortest processing time; longest processing time; first come, first served; and critical ratio.
- The shortest-processing-time rule will minimize average flow time for jobs on one machine.
- Johnson's Rule minimizes makespan time when jobs must be processed on two machines in the same sequence.
- Priorities are set in an MRP system by considering due dates and lead times of jobs.
- Finite loading treats capacity as a limited resource, while infinite loading does not.
- Forward scheduling starts from the present and schedules forward. Backward scheduling starts from due dates and schedules backward.
- Input/output control manages work flow and queue length by balancing the input to a work center with its output.
- Computer simulation allows companies to quickly develop alternative schedules and test those schedules before jobs are actually released.
- In scheduling for services, we usually have no finished-goods inventory, so we must schedule capacity to meet demand.
- In scheduling manufacturing, we must ensure that due-date promises are kept. In services, first come, first served is usually the rule unless other factors are more important than fairness.

CAREER PROFILE

Mark Drusch

Director of Schedule Analysis
Continental Airlines

Educational Background and Career Steps

Mark Drusch's higher education began at Northwestern University, where he studied political science and international relations. Upon graduating, he took a job with First City Bank of Houston, Texas, in its South American lending department. As part of that job, Drusch was involved with airlines doing business in South America and developed contacts with people from Continental Airlines.

About six years ago, Drusch decided to leave the bank and take a job with Continental as a senior analyst for schedule planning. In that job, he was directly responsible for developing schedules for aircraft, routes, and crews. From there he advanced to manager of market development and then to manager of airline planning.

As manager of airline planning, Drusch was responsible for all route planning and development, fleet planning, aircraft selection, competitive and strategic planning, and legal issues. For example, when Continental was considering the addition of some cities in Oregon and California to its routes, Drusch's job was to analyze the competition and the market to determine whether sufficient traffic would be available for Continental. Another problem Drusch had to deal with was adding more flights to existing routes. For instance, Continental had two flights daily from New York's LaGuardia Airport to New Orleans. Questions Drusch had to answer included "Is there enough traffic to justify a third flight?" and "If so, what impact could that have on other existing routes?"

Airport-noise legislation enacted by such cities as Denver, Colorado, and Bakersfield, California, made Drusch's job even trickier. In planning additional routes, the company must determine whether it has sufficient low-noise (stage 3) aircraft to serve those routes. With its five-year planning horizon, Continental must continually forecast any other changes that might affect its operations.

Current Position and Duties

In his current position as director of schedule analysis for Continental, Drusch is responsible for looking at markets and aircraft flows. Compared to his earlier jobs, Drusch indicates the latest one involves more fine-tuning to maximize the company's revenue potential, while also minimizing costs.

SOLVED PROBLEMS

1. A company has five jobs waiting to be processed. The data on these jobs are shown below, in the order they arrived for processing.

Job	Days Until Due	Processing Time Remaining (Days)
A	30	35
B	20	15
C	25	25
D	10	12
E	15	10

Job	Days Until Due	Processing Time Remaining (Days)
D	10	12
E	15	10

In what sequence would the jobs be done for each dispatching rule?

Solution

a. *Earliest due date:* Sequence in order starting with the job having the fewest days until the due date.

D (10 days)–E (15 days)–B (20 days)–C (25 days)–A (30 days)

b. *Shortest processing time:* Sequence starting with the job having the shortest processing time.

E (10 days)–D (12 days)–B (15days)–C (25 days)–A (35 days)

c. *Longest processing time:* Start with the job having the longest time, and work backward (reverse the sequence for the shortest-processing-time rule).

A (35 days)–C (25 days)–B (15 days)–D (12 days)–E (10 days)

d. *Critical ratio: CR* = (days until due)/(processing time remaining). Jobs with the lowest critical ratios are scheduled first.

D (10/12)–A (30/35)–C (25/25)–B (20/15)–E (15/10)

e. *First come, first served:* Use order of arrival. A–B–C–D–E

2. The following jobs must be processed on two machines. Use Johnson's Rule to develop a sequence.

	Processing Time (Hours)	
Job	Machine A	Machine B
P	2.4	3.2
Q	3.0	2.8
R	5.2	4.0
S	4.7	3.4
T	3.0	3.2

Solution

a. Identifying the shortest processing time, we select job P. Because this is on machine A, we schedule job P first.

b. The next shortest processing time is for job Q. Because this is on machine B, job Q is scheduled last.

c. Job T now has the shortest processing time. Because that time is on machine A, job T comes after P.

d. Job S now has the shortest processing time, which is for machine B. Therefore, S gets scheduled before Q.

e. Job R fills in the middle slot to produce the following sequence:

P	T	R	S	Q
1	2	3	4	5

QUESTIONS

1. In describing JIT, the analogy of a stream is often used to represent material flow. Explain how this analogy could also be used when simulating material flow in a job shop.

2. Discuss the ways in which flexible manufacturing systems may alter the activities of production scheduling.

3. Allen-Bradley has developed a CIM system that is designed to produce the orders received in one day by the end of the next day. Would scheduling be easier or more difficult for Allen-Bradley, as compared with a company that has a one-month backlog of orders?

4. List the six criteria that can be used for scheduling.

5. Which scheduling criterion do you think is most relevant for a fast-food restaurant? For a physician's office? For a hospital emergency room?

6. Which of the dispatching rules do you use when deciding which homework assignment to do first?

7. Explain why scheduling a continuous flow production process involves different methods from those used for scheduling a job shop process.

8. What service operations might use the scheduling methods traditionally used for job shops?

9. For each of the dispatching rules, indicate which scheduling criteria will be satisfied and what the advantages and disadvantages of that rule would be.

10. List the data needed for scheduling, and indicate the usual sources.

11. How does dispatching differ from sequencing?

12. How are priorities set for jobs in an MRP system?

13. Explain the purpose of using input/output control.

14. How can computer simulation be used for scheduling?

PROBLEMS

1. A company produces four types of paper in batches. Based on the following information, which product should be produced next according to the run-out time criterion?

Product	Demand Rate (1,000 Ft. per Month)	Current Inventory (1,000 Ft.)
Kraft paper	30,000	80,000
Duplicator bond	20,000	40,000
Regular bond	60,000	150,000
Carbon tissue	10,000	40,000

2. The David Harleyston Bicycle Company produces its two models of bicycles, the Avenger and the Hawk in batches. Based on the following, which model should be produced next?

Model	EOQ	Current Inventory	Monthly Sales
Avenger	2,000	10,000	30,000
Hawk	5,000	6,000	20,000

3. A consultant must complete four reports. She estimates that report A will take four hours, report B will take three hours, report C will take six hours, and report D will take two hours. In what sequence would she do the reports, using the shortest-processing-time rule?

4. A job shop has four jobs waiting to be processed on its computer numerically controlled (CNC) lathe. Determine the sequence of these jobs by using each of the five dispatching rules. Assume today is day 107, jobs arrived for processing in the order listed, and the following information is given:

Job	Due (Day)	Processing Time on CNC Lathe (Hours)	Total Processing Time Remaining (Days)
A	120	4	12
B	113	8	5
C	125	2	7
D	115	10	10

5. Late Wednesday afternoon, Data Processing Associates had four jobs waiting to be processed the next day. Each of these jobs requires keyboarding the data and then processing them on the company's minicomputer. The keyboarding is done by DPA's data entry clerks who work from 8:00 A.M. to 5:00 P.M., with an hour for lunch at noon. The computer will be available continuously beginning at 9:00 A.M. on Thursday. Jobs may be either processed immediately after keyboarding or held for processing later.

Job	Keyboarding Time (Hours)	Processing Time (Hours)	Time Due
A	1	1	3:00 P.M.
B	1	2	12:00 NOON
C	2	.5	2:00 P.M.
D	2	2	5:00 P.M.

a. Develop schedules using the shortest-processing-time, longest-processing-time, and earliest-due-date rules, and draw Gantt load charts for keyboarding and processing, based on each rule.

b. Evaluate each of the schedules in part a with respect to customer service by calculating average past due hours per job for each scheduling rule.

6. Bill Berry, the heat treating department's second shift foreman at Ace Machine Tool Company, is bucking to become foreman on the first shift. To look good, Bill wants to keep queues in his department to a minimum, so he has been using the shortest-processing-time rule to schedule work. However, the assembly department, which usually receives jobs after they have been processed in Berry's department, is complaining they often do not get jobs early enough to meet the due dates.

a. The following jobs are currently in queue at the heat treating department and must all be processed through the heat treating department and then through the assembly department. Develop a schedule based on the shortest processing time, and draw a Gantt chart for each department.

	Processing Time (Days)		
Job	Heat Treating	Assembly	Days Until Due
317	3	1	12
318	1	3	4
324	2	3	10
326	4	2	8

b. Determine whether there is a schedule that can meet all the due dates.

c. Comment on the implications of allowing each machine or work center to schedule its own work.

7. Dr. Houseworth, an orthopedic surgeon, likes to be kept busy during his office hours. All patients scheduled must first have X-rays before they see the doctor. On a certain Monday morning, Dr. Houseworth arrives at his office, and the following three patients are waiting to be X-rayed and to see him. Determine the sequence in which the patients should be X-rayed to minimize the time Dr. Houseworth is idle.

Patient	Time to X-Ray (Min.)	Time with Doctor (Min.)
Mrs. Green	5	10
Mr. White	15	20
Miss Gray	10	20

8. The following jobs are waiting to be processed on one machine. Determine the sequence that will minimize average flow time.

Job	Processing Time (Days)
A	4
B	2
C	6
D	3
E	5

9. Four jobs must be processed on one machine. The company wants to minimize total changeover time between jobs. What sequence should be used?

		Changeover Time (Minutes)			
		Follower Job			
		W	X	Y	Z
Predecessor Job	W	—	35	42	65
	X	28	—	47	52
	Y	36	24	—	48
	Z	32	37	59	—

10. An automobile paint shop has six cars to paint. The time that will be required to clean out the equipment and so forth between jobs is indicated. In what order should the jobs be done to minimize total changeover time?

		Changeover Time (Minutes)					
		Follower Job					
		A	B	C	D	E	F
Predecessor Job	A	—	5	16	10	20	8
	B	10	—	13	20	14	6
	C	15	9	—	15	18	9
	D	23	4	14	—	20	5
	E	13	6	10	15	—	7
	F	15	5	12	18	17	—

11. The following jobs are waiting to be processed through two work centers.

a. Use Johnson's Rule to determine a sequence.

b. Draw a Gantt load chart for each work center.

	Processing Time (Hours)	
Job	Work Center 1	Work Center 2
A	3	2
B	2.4	3.2
C	1.8	4
D	2.2	3.5

12. A printer has six printing jobs to be done. Each job requires typesetting and printing.

a. Use Johnson's rule to sequence the jobs based on the following expected processing times.

b. Draw Gantt load charts for printing and typesetting.

	Processing Time (Hours)	
Job	**Typesetting**	**Printing**
1	2	3
2	3	4
3	2.5	1.75
4	1.25	2
5	3.5	2.5
6	2.25	3

13. A city government requires that all new construction projects be reviewed by an architect, a city planner, and an environmental engineer (in that order). Four different construction projects are waiting to be reviewed, and the review time of each has been estimated as shown below.

Project	Architect	City Planner	Environmental Engineer
A	3 hrs.	2 hrs.	4 hrs.
B	2 hrs.	3 hrs.	2 hrs.
C	4 hrs.	1 hr.	3 hrs.
D	2 hrs.	1 hr.	3 hrs.

If the four projects must be processed in the order A, B, C, D by each person, use forward schedulingwith finite loading to develop a Gantt load chart for each person.

14. Five parts must be processed through the following operations, and each has the due date shown. The following table shows the time required for each processing operation:

Part A	Part B	Part C
Lathe (2 days)	Lathe (1 day)	Mill (1 day)
Mill (3 days)	Grind (1 day)	Drill (1 day)
Drill (1 day)	Mill (2 days)	Due at end of day 5
Due at end of day 8	Drill (1 day)	
	Due at end of day 6	

Part D	Part E
Mill (3 days)	Drill (1 day)
Grind (1 day)	Mill (3 days)
Lathe (2 days)	Grind (1 day)
Drill (1 day)	Drill (1 day)
Due at end of day 10	Due at end of day 6

Use backward scheduling with infinite loading to develop a schedule for each part.

15. Develop a load profile for the city planner in problem 13.

16. Develop a load profile for the mill in problem 14.

MINI-CASES

The Carbondale Clinic

The Carbondale Clinic, located in Carbondale, Illinois, is a large group practice of about thirty physicians. The clinic employs about 100 people and serves a regional population of about 100,000. Specialties ranging from pediatrics to psychiatry are offered by the clinic, which also operates its own lab, X-ray room, and outpatient surgical center.

For some years, the clinic has been receiving complaints from its patients that appointment times are not being met. For instance, a patient with an appointment for two o'clock might not get in to see the physician until four o'clock. However, the clinic has felt that such delays are unavoidable due to the uncertainty involved in the time it takes to adequately examine each patient and the possibility of emergency cases that must be inserted into the schedule.

Several criteria are used for scheduling. For instance, many patients are scheduled for annual physical exams. These are usually scheduled at least several weeks in advance because they require coordination of lab facilities and the physician's time. However, some physicians will begin examining a patient and decide that the patient needs a physical immediately. The physicians feel this does not really cause problems because they can send the patient down to the lab while they continue to see other patients.

Some patients also phone the clinic for an appointment when they have nonemergency, routine problems such as a mild fever or a sore throat. Such patients are scheduled into available time slots as soon as possible—usually a day or two from the time they call. The objective here is to fit such patients in as quickly as possible without overloading the schedule with more patients than can reasonably be examined in a time period. Usually the plan is to schedule four patients per hour.

However, each day various emergencies occur. These can range from a splinter in the eye to a heart attack, and these cases cannot wait. For an emergency that is not life threatening, the approach is to try to squeeze the person into a time slot that is not too heavily scheduled. However, a case of life or death—such as a heart attack—means that the schedule must be disrupted and the patient attended to immediately.

Currently, all scheduling of appointments is done centrally. However, this frequently causes problems because the people making appointments often do not know how long it should take to examine a patient with a particular complaint. On the other hand, the nurses in each department are usually too busy to do the scheduling themselves. Generally, if there is a doubt about whether a patient can be fitted into a time slot, the preference is to go ahead and schedule the patient. This is because the physicians prefer not to have any empty times in their schedules. At times, if it looks as if there might be an available opening, the clinic even calls patients that were originally scheduled for a later time and asks them to come in earlier.

It has been suggested that waiting-line theory be used to conduct a study of the clinic, but that has not yet been done. However, the clinic has remodeled its waiting room to make it more attractive during the long waits.

1. What alternatives do you see for solving the problem of long waits, while still being able to handle emergencies?

2. Should the practice of centralized scheduling be continued? Why or why not?

3. Could waiting-line theory be used to help solve this problem? Why or why not?

4. Are there other ways besides remodeling that could make excessive waiting time less burdensome to the patients?

Central Electronics Company

The Central Electronics Company makes electronic chassis that are used to hold the components of such things as televisions and microcomputers. Central has just received an order from a large microcomputer manufacturer with whom Central would like to develop a long-term relationship. If this order can be completed by the due date, such a relationship is almost assured. However, the chances of meeting that due date do not look good.

Each chassis in this order consists of four parts. Each part has the routing and the run times given below. In addition, there is a one-hour setup time on each machine whenever it is changed from making one part to another or even from performing one operation to another on the same part. The following table shows the run time in minutes per unit for each part.

Rail	**Bracket A**
Press—2 mins.	Shear—1 min.
Drill—1 min.	Press—1 min.
Press—2 mins.	Press—3 mins.
Shear—1 min.	Drill—5 mins.

Bracket B	**Shield**
Shear—1 min.	Shear—6 mins.
Press—2 mins.	Press—1 min.
Drill—1 min.	Drill—1 min.
	Drill—4 mins.
	Shear—2 mins.

Central has only one press, one drill, and one shear, and they are available only eight hours per day. The order for 150 units must be completed within five days. Each machine must be set up at the start of processing and again whenever a different operation or part is processed on it. There is no assembly time, as the individual parts are shipped to the customer, which assembles them. However, 150 of each part must be completed within five days for the order to be filled.

1. If the parts are made in batches of 150, will it be possible to meet the deadline? (Hint: Develop a Gantt load chart for each machine.)

2. Can you identify one machine that has the heaviest load (the bottleneck machine)?

3. What should your strategies be for scheduling production on that bottleneck machine?

4. How can you schedule other machines to be sure that the bottleneck is not idle?

The Glenn Wilson Machining Company

The Glenn Wilson Machining Company is a job shop that does custom machining work for its industrial customers. At present, the company has ten jobs that must all be processed on the same five machines (100, 200, 300, 400, and 500). Further, each job must be processed in the sequence 100–200–300–400–500, although some jobs do not need processing on every machine. However, as long as each job follows the correct sequence of processing operations, it does not matter in what order the jobs are processed on a given machine.

The company works a five-day week with Saturday available for overtime. Each machine is operated by one employee who earns $120 per day during the week, regardless of whether the machine is busy or not, and $180 for overtime work on Saturday. The contracts for these ten jobs awaiting processing each contain a penalty clause that assesses the Glenn Wilson

Machining Company $100 per day when the job goes past its due date.

The following information is available:

	Job									
	Z	**Y**	**X**	**W**	**V**	**U**	**T**	**S**	**R**	**Q**
Due by end of week	2	3	3	4	4	5	6	6	7	7
Machine	**Processing Time (Days)**									
100	—	—	—	—	—	—	8	9	4	2
200	—	—	—	5	4	7	—	7	1	2
300	—	—	6	7	—	2	6	9	4	3
400	—	7	2	—	8	5	6	—	2	3
500	8	6	1	2	3	5	4	1	8	—

In the preceding table, dashes indicate operations that have already been completed (job Z on machine 100) or ones that are not part of the processing sequence (machine 400 for job W).

It is currently the end (Saturday) of week 0. Develop a production schedule that will minimize total payroll and late costs for the Glenn Wilson Machining Company.

SELECTED BIBLIOGRAPHY

Baker, Kenneth R. *Introduction to Sequencing and Scheduling*. New York: Wiley, 1984.

Browne, J. "Production Activity Control—A Key Aspect of Production Control." *International Journal of Production Research* 26, no. 3 (1988): 415–427.

Greene, James H., ed. *Production and Inventory Control Handbook*. 2d ed. New York: McGraw-Hill, 1987.

Hill, Arthur D.; Naumann, J. D.; and Chervany, Norman L. "SCAT and SPAT: Large-Scale Computer-Based Optimization Systems for the Personnel Assignment Problem." *Decision Sciences* 14, no. 2 (April 1983): 207–220.

Kanet, John K., and Hayya, Jack C. "Priority Dispatching with Operation Due Dates in a Job Shop." *Journal of Operations Management* 2, no. 3 (May 1982): 167–175.

Vollmann, Thomas E.; Berry, William L.; and Whybark, D. Clay. *Manufacturing Planning and Control*. 2d ed. Homewood, Ill.: Irwin, 1988.

Chapter 13 Supplement

Management-Science Tools and Scheduling

SUPPLEMENT OUTLINE

LEARNING OBJECTIVES

After completing this supplement, you should be able to

- Calculate the steady-state conditions for single- and multiserver queues.
- Discuss how simulation is used for scheduling.
- Manually simulate a simple system.

APPLICATIONS OF WAITING-LINE MODELS TO SCHEDULING

Almost any operation that provides a good or service will involve waiting lines. Those waiting lines are often painfully obvious to us when we are waiting to cash a check at the bank or standing in line at a fast-food restaurant. In discussing job shop scheduling, we mentioned that queue time (or waiting-line time) is a major component of the time a job spends in processing.

Because waiting lines, or queues as they are often called, are so prevalent, they are worthy of further discussion. In fact, some general mathematical formulas have been developed that can provide useful information about waiting-line characteristics. In this section, we will discuss a few of the more general formulas.

Objectives

Most waiting-line situations involve a trade-off between two costs—the cost of capacity and the cost of waiting time. For instance, a bank may find that long lines of customers have been building up at certain times of the day. The capacity of the bank to serve customers could be increased by adding more equipment and employees. This would probably reduce the waiting lines, but at additional cost. On the other hand, there are several costs associated with having customers waiting to be served. In the case of a bank, these costs would be mostly subjective, such as the cost of lost good will when customers feel they must wait too long for service. However, in other situations, the costs are rather obvious. For instance, the cost of keeping ships waiting for dock space to unload their cargoes can run into tens of thousands of dollars per day.

In general, our objective will be to find some reasonable balance between the costs of capacity and the costs of waiting. If those costs are easily determined, then we can try to minimize total cost. In other cases, it may be necessary to make a managerial decision. For example, in determining required staff for an emergency room, a manager must decide how long patients can be kept waiting because the cost of a human life is not easy to calculate.

Classification Scheme

There are several different types of waiting lines. For example, the characteristics of a waiting line of jobs that will be processed on only one machine are different from those of a line of customers waiting to be served by any one of a dozen bank tellers.

To differentiate between different possible waiting-line situations, a classification scheme has been developed that specifies three parameters:

$$A/B/C$$

where

A = the probability distribution for number of arrivals per unit of time
B = the probability distribution for service time
C = the number of servers

*M/M/*1 Model

The most common waiting-line model is the one in which the number of arrivals per unit of time follows the Poisson probability distribution (represented by *M*), service time is exponentially distributed (also represented by *M*), and there is just one server. This is called the single-server queuing model.

Even for this general case, there are several variations. However, we will concentrate on the most common of those by assuming that there are no limits on the length of the waiting line and that arrivals to the waiting line will not depart, no matter how long the line might be.

For this particular model, two variables must be specified in advance. They are

$$\lambda \text{ (lambda)} = \text{average arrival rate}$$

$$\mu \text{ (mu)} = \text{average service rate}$$

In general, these variables are specified in terms of number per time period. For example, customers might arrive at a drive-up window at the average rate of twenty per hour and be served at the average rate of thirty per hour.

Using these variables and the probability distributions that have been specified for number of arrivals per unit of time and service time, it is possible to develop some formulas that describe certain characteristics of the waiting line in question. We will not derive these formulas, but instead present them as tools that can be useful in evaluating waiting-line situations. These formulas apply only to what are called **steady-state conditions**—that is, the conditions that prevail after any start-up variations have disappeared.

Utilization Factor. One of the easiest, and most useful, characteristics to calculate is the **utilization factor,** which indicates the percentage of time the machine or person providing service will be occupied. This is simply

$$\rho \text{ (rho)} = \lambda/\mu$$

Probability of Being Idle. If ρ is the probability of the server's being busy, then the probability of its being idle, or the percentage of time it will be idle, is

$$P(0) = 1 - \frac{\lambda}{\mu}$$

Average Number of Units Waiting. The two preceding characteristics provide information about the facility. However, the other aspect of waiting lines has to do with the things or people that are waiting. The average number that will be waiting in the queue at any one time is designated as

$$L_q = \frac{\lambda^2}{\mu(\mu - \lambda)}$$

Average Time Spent Waiting. We may be concerned not only about how many customers or jobs must wait, but also about how much time each must spend waiting. The average time that is spent waiting in the queue can be calculated as

$$W_q = \frac{\lambda}{\mu(\mu - \lambda)}$$

M/M/s Model

The other model that is most relevant to P/OM is known as the multiserver model and is designated as *M/M/s.* This means once again that the number of arrivals per unit of time follows a Poisson probability distribution and that service time is exponentially distributed. However, there is now more than one server even though there is still just one waiting line. This situation is similar to that adopted by many banks and airlines in which all customers wait in one line and then proceed to the first available counter. Again, we present the formulas without derivation.

Utilization Factor. The variable s represents the number of servers. If we assume that the service rate, μ, is the same for each server, then the percentage of time each server is utilized will be

$$\rho = \frac{\lambda}{s\mu}$$

Probability of Being Idle. Unfortunately, in this model, we cannot calculate the probability of the facility's being idle by simply subtracting the utilization factor from one. This is because there is now more than one server. The calculation is now somewhat more complex, as shown below.

$$P(0) = \frac{1}{\sum_{n=0}^{s-1} \frac{(\lambda/\mu)^n}{n!} + \frac{(\lambda/\mu)^s}{s!(1 - \lambda/\mu s)}}$$

However, Exhibit 13.21 provides $P(0)$ values for common λ/μ and s values.

Average Number of Units Waiting for Service. The average number of units waiting for service, which depends first on the calculation of $P(0)$, is

$$L_q = \frac{P(0)(\lambda/\mu)^s\rho}{s!(1 - \rho)^2}$$

Average Time Spent Waiting. Finally, the average time spent waiting can be calculated easily if L_q has been calculated first.

$$W_q = \frac{L_q}{\lambda}$$

Machine Scheduling for Goods

To demonstrate the use of these formulas, suppose that a company has one lathe and that jobs arrive to be processed by this lathe at the average rate of twenty per week. On the average, the lathe can process twenty-five jobs each week. Suppose we want to determine the average number of jobs waiting and the average time each job spends in the queue. This information can be extremely useful for estimating the time it will take to complete each job and the total amount of work-in-process inventory.

Based on the above information, we have an *M/M/*1 system with $\lambda = 20$ per week and $\mu = 25$ per week. The average time each job spends waiting will be

$$W_q = \frac{20}{25(25 - 20)} = .16 \text{ week}$$

The average number of jobs waiting will be

$$L_q = \frac{20^2}{25(25 - 20)} = 3.2 \text{ jobs}$$

One other useful bit of information is the percentage of time the lathe will be occupied processing jobs. This will be the utilization factor, which is

$$\rho = \frac{20}{25} = .8 \text{ or 80 percent of the time}$$

Scheduling for Services

All of us have felt the frustration of having to choose among several waiting lines when there was more than one server—only to find out later that we picked the wrong line. Facilities that have gone to just one waiting line save us from this dilemma. But is that the only reason that many banks, airlines, and other service facilities have started using one line with multiple servers? To answer that question, let's look at the characteristics of each system.

For the sake of argument, suppose that a bank has five tellers and that each teller can serve customers at an average rate of fifteen per hour. Customers arrive at the bank at an average rate of one every minute. If we assume that each customer randomly chooses a line to wait in and then does not switch lines afterward, we can think of each teller and each waiting line as a single-server waiting line with $\mu = 15$ per hour and $\lambda = 60/5 = 12$ per hour.

In this instance, the average time each customer must wait will be

$$W_q = \frac{12}{15(15 - 12)} = .266 \text{ hour or 16 minutes}$$

The average length of *each* waiting line will be

$$L_q = \frac{12^2}{15(15 - 12)} = 3.2 \text{ customers}$$

Since there will be five waiting lines, we can expect about sixteen customers waiting at any one time.

Now suppose the bank decides to institute just one waiting line. The customer at the head of that line will move to whichever teller becomes available first. This is now an *M/M/s* model with five servers.

First, it is necessary to calculate the probability of no one in the system, $P(0)$. Recall that, for this case, there is just one waiting line, the arrival rate is sixty per hour, and the service rate per teller is fifteen per hour. Thus, $\lambda/\mu = 60/15 = 4$.

$$P(0) = \frac{1}{\frac{(4)^0}{0!} + \frac{(4)^1}{1!} + \frac{(4)^2}{2!} + \frac{(4)^3}{3!} + \frac{(4)^4}{4!} + \frac{(4)^5}{5!(1 - 60/75)}}$$

$$= .012987$$

The second calculation will be the average number in the waiting line.

$$L_q = \frac{.012987(4)^5(60/75)}{5!(1 - 60/75)^2}$$

$$= 2.22$$

Now the average time a customer spends waiting can be calculated as

$$W_q = 2.2/60 = .0367 \text{ hour or 2.2 minutes}$$

As you can see, the reduction in the average number of customers waiting and the average waiting time is dramatic. It is no wonder that many service organizations have adopted this type of waiting line.

SIMULATION AS A SCHEDULING TOOL

The queuing formulas presented above can be extremely useful in providing information about waiting-line characteristics. However, it should be remembered that those figures are only *averages.* If the average waiting-line length is twenty, that could mean that at some times there is no one in the line, while at other times there are fifty people. Those queuing formulas do not give us any information about the dynamics of the system.

There are other situations in P/OM where we would like to know how a particular process will behave over time. One way to gather that information is through simulation.

Incrementing Time

One thing a simulation must do is to proceed through time. Basically, there are two approaches to doing this, event-oriented and time-oriented. **Event-oriented simulations** move from one event to another and increment the time accordingly. For example, the simulation of jobs on a machine might begin when a certain job starts processing, then increment to the finish of that job, and then go from there to the start of the next job. In this way, that simulation can skip over large periods of time during which a job is being processed and go instead to the events of primary interest.

Time-oriented simulation increments the time by a constant amount. Unlike event-oriented simulation, which may skip over large blocks of time, time-oriented simulation accounts for every moment of time, making events occur at the appropriate moments in time.

Deterministic Simulation

One approach to simulation is based on the idea that everything is fixed, or **deterministic.** Under this approach, we would assume that the time it will take to process a particular job on a machine is known and fixed, or that the total number of jobs to be done is known and will not change. Using this approach, we would develop a computer program that would step each job through its processing operations, following the routings and processing times that are given.

This type of simulation can be extremely useful for identifying possible problems that could occur. Through a computer simulation, it is possible to model, in a matter of seconds, some process that might actually take days or even weeks in reality. The computer simulation is useful for identifying problems, trying different options, or testing out ideas before putting them into practice.

Deterministic Simulation of a Job Shop

Deterministic simulation is gaining in popularity as a means of scheduling production. The advantage is that a company can try out different schedules and sequences to see how they will work before actually dispatching jobs to the shop. To see how this works, consider the four jobs shown in Exhibit 13.13. We can simulate using the shortest-processing-time rule to sequence these jobs on the three machines.

Exhibit 13.13 Four Jobs on Three Machines

Job	Processing Sequence and Times
A	Lathe (2 hrs.), mill (1 hr.), drill (2 hrs.), mill (2 hrs.)
B	Drill (3 hrs.), lathe (1 hr.), mill (1 hr.)
C	Mill (1 hr.), lathe (4 hrs.)
D	Mill (2 hrs.), lathe (1 hr.), mill (1 hr.), drill (3 hrs.)

The status of each machine and job can be indicated, as shown in Exhibit 13.14. Starting at time zero, we will begin job A on the lathe and job B on the drill. Jobs C and D are both waiting for the mill; we start job C first because it has the shortest processing time, but show that job D is waiting in the queue.

Because the time required to process each job is in terms of hours, we can use time-oriented simulation, but increase the time in increments of one hour. Exhibit 13.14 shows five hours of simulated time.

Exhibit 13.14 Deterministic Simulation of Four Jobs on Three Machines

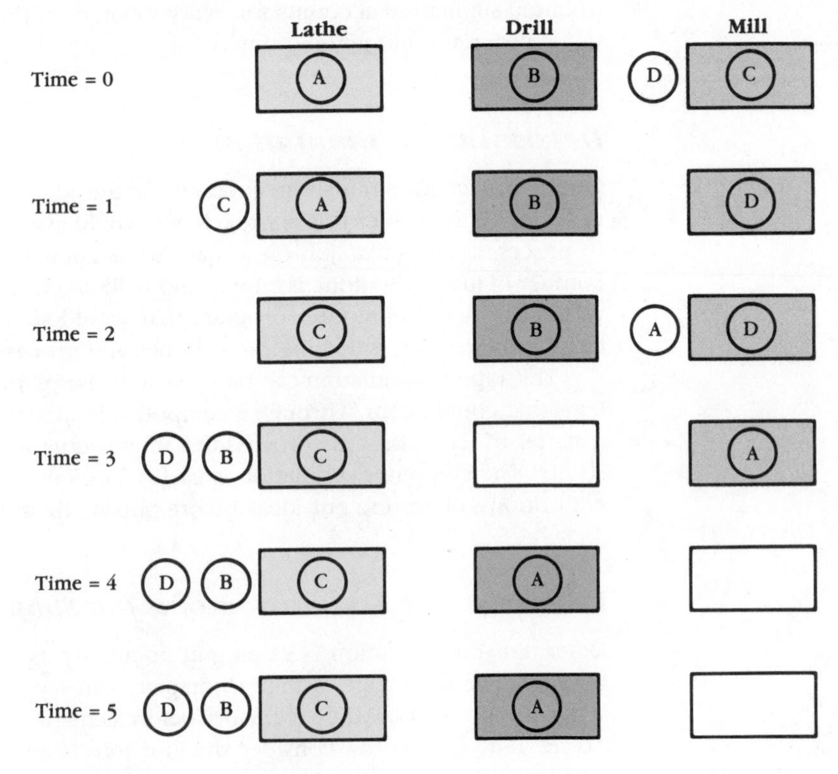

Probability-Based Simulation

Another widely used approach to simulation takes a somewhat different approach. **Probability-based,** or **Monte Carlo simulation,** as it is often called, takes into account the fact that things can change. Instead of treating processing time as fixed, the Monte Carlo approach assumes that it will vary between certain values according to some predetermined probability distribution.

Generating Probabilistic Events

The other important aspect of simulation applies only to probabilistic simulations. That is, there must be some way of generating events that occur probabilistically. For instance, if processing time will vary, we must have a way of generating processing times according to an appropriate probability distribution. This is done with a process generator.

A **process generator** is simply a method of generating numbers that follow a given probability distribution. A couple of simple process generators are dice and a roulette wheel. However, for simulation, we usually want to have a computer do all the work, including generating the numbers. To do this, we can take advantage of computer programs that generate random numbers. (For example, Exhibit 13.22 at the end of this supplement lists some random numbers.)

To demonstrate how a process generator can produce numbers that will be useful for simulation, we will go through two simple demonstrations.

Simulating Machine Failure

One area of concern in P/OM is machine failure. A machine failure can mean shutting down an operation, an assembly line, or even an entire plant. Suppose we know that a certain machine fails from time to time. We have kept track of the time between failures and the frequency of those times, as shown in Exhibit 13.15. Thus, Exhibit 13.15 indicates that we observed one instance in which the time between machine failures was between zero and ten hours, there were five times when it was eleven to fifteen hours between failures, and so on.

Suppose we are considering a new maintenance procedure for dealing with these failures and want to test it out, through simulation, before actually putting the new procedure into practice. To do this, we need to simulate the machine failures so that our simulation resembles the observed failures shown in Exhibit 13.15.

Exhibit 13.15 Frequency of Time Between Failures

Time Between Failures (Hours)	Frequency of Time Between Failures
0–10	1
11–15	5
16–20	7
21–25	6
26–30	4
31–35	2

This is done by developing a process generator that equates certain random numbers to times between failures. To begin, we must simplify things by taking the observed time ranges and referring only to the midpoint of each. Thus, a time between failures that would fall in the 0–10 range will be treated as five hours between failures.

The second step is to convert observed frequencies for each time between failures to percentages (or probabilities). This is done by dividing each observed frequency by the total number of observations (25). The last step then requires us to equate a range of random numbers with each time so that the probability of a random number's falling in that range will be the same as the probability of the corresponding time between failures.

Suppose we use two-digit random numbers (00–99). Since there are 100 possible numbers in that range, and each has a probability of .01 of being picked, we can combine groups of numbers to give us any probability to two decimal places. For example, there are four numbers in the range from 00 to 03 (00, 01, 02, 03). If each has a probability of .01 of being picked out of the table, then the probability of picking any one of the four numbers (00, 01, 02, 03) will be $4 \times .01 = .04$, which corresponds to the probability of approximately five hours between failures.

Exhibit 13.16 shows the random numbers that have been selected to correspond with each time between failures. Notice that we have given each random number a unique time interval with which it corresponds. This is our process generator. To generate times between failures, all we need do is to randomly pick numbers from Exhibit 13.22 and relate them to a time between failures. To ensure that the numbers are selected randomly, one approach is to number slips of paper so that each slip has one row number on it. For Exhibit 13.22, there would be forty slips of paper for the forty rows. These are all placed in a jar and mixed up. Another set of slips is numbered for the columns (ten slips for the ten columns of Exhibit 13.22) and placed in a *different* jar. One slip of paper is selected from each jar, designating the row and column from which the random number is to be obtained. The slips are replaced and mixed before the next selection. This scheme avoids any unconscious tendency to select only numbers from a certain part of the table or to follow any pattern that might produce nonrandom results.

The results for ten simulated failures are shown in Exhibit 13.17. Notice that we let time = 0 represent the time when the first failure occurred. We then

Exhibit 13.16 Process Generator

Observed Time	Midpoint	Frequency	(%)	Random Numbers
0–10	5	1	(4)	00–03
11–15	13	5	(20)	04–23
16–20	18	7	(28)	24–51
21–25	23	6	(24)	52–75
26–30	28	4	(16)	76–91
31–35	33	2	(8)	92–99
		25	100	

Exhibit 13.17 Simulation Results

Failure Number	Time (Hrs.)	Random Number	Time Between Failures (Hrs.)
1	0	12	13
2	13	64	23
3	36	79	28
4	64	18	13
5	77	73	23
6	100	00	5
7	105	20	13
8	118	89	28
9	146	18	13
10	159		

generated a random number and corresponding time between failures to determine when the next failure would occur. This process continued for each successive simulated failure.

Example

Simulating a Single-Server Queue The same approach can be used to simulate a queuing system. Suppose that we have a single-server system, and that the times between arrivals and service times listed in Exhibit 13.18 have been observed. This time it will be necessary to develop a process generator for times between arrivals, as well as for service times. But the procedure is the same as for the machine-failure simulation discussed previously. The process generators are shown in Exhibit 13.19.

To simulate this single-server queuing system now requires slightly more bookkeeping than does the machine-failure simulation. In this case, we must generate time between arrivals. But for each arrival, we must also generate a service time. In some cases, the person being served may not leave until after several others arrive. Therefore, we must keep track of arrival and departure times, and also the number waiting. The results for this simulation are shown in Exhibit 13.20.

Exhibit 13.18 Single-Server Queue

Time Between Arrivals (Mins.)	Observed Frequency	Service Time (Mins.)	Observed Frequency
0–2	3	0–2	5
3–5	8	3–5	9
6–8	16	6–8	20
9–11	12	9–11	10
12–14	9	12–14	4
15–17	2	15–17	2

Exhibit 13.19 Queuing Simulation Process Generators

Time Between Arrivals (Mins.)	Midpoint	Observed Frequency	(%)	Random Numbers
0–2	1	3	(6)	00–05
3–5	4	8	(16)	06–21
6–8	7	16	(32)	22–53
9–11	10	12	(24)	54–77
12–14	13	9	(18)	78–95
15–17	16	2	(4)	96–99

Service Time (Mins.)	Midpoint	Observed Frequency	(%)	Random Numbers
0–2	1	5	(10)	00–09
3–5	4	9	(18)	10–27
6–8	7	20	(40)	28–67
9–11	10	10	(20)	68–87
12–14	13	4	(8)	88–95
15–17	16	2	(4)	96–99

Exhibit 13.20 Simulation of Single-Server Queue

Arrival Number	Arrival Time	Enter Service	Random Number	Service Time	Leave Service	Random Number	Time Until Next Arrival	Number Waiting
1	0:00	0:00	21	:04	0:04	84	:13	0
2	0:13	0:13	91	:13	0:26	00	:01	0
3	0:14	0:26	74	:10	0:36	67	:10	1
4	0:24	0:36	12	:04	0:40	00	:01	2
5	0:25	0:40	52	:07	0:47	49	:07	3
6	0:32	0:47	36	:07	0:54	75	:10	4
7	0:42	0:54	18	:04	0:58	84	:10	3
8	0:52	0:58	45	:07	1:05	73	:10	3
9	1:02	1:05	89	:13	1:18	03	:01	1
10	1:03	1:18	30	:07	1:25			2

Exhibit 13.21 P(0) Values for Multiserver Queuing Systems

	Number of Servers (s)			
Ratio (λ/μ)	2	3	4	5
0.15	0.8605	0.8607	0.8607	0.8607
0.20	0.8182	0.8187	0.8187	0.8187
0.25	0.7778	0.7788	0.7788	0.7788
0.30	0.7391	0.7407	0.7408	0.7408
0.35	0.7021	0.7046	0.7047	0.7047
0.40	0.6667	0.6701	0.6703	0.6703
0.45	0.6327	0.6373	0.6376	0.6376
0.50	0.6000	0.6061	0.6065	0.6065
0.55	0.5686	0.5763	0.5769	0.5769
0.60	0.5385	0.5479	0.5487	0.5488
0.65	0.5094	0.5209	0.5219	0.5220
0.70	0.4815	0.4952	0.4965	0.4966
0.75	0.4545	0.4706	0.4722	0.4724
0.80	0.4286	0.4472	0.4491	0.4493
0.85	0.4035	0.4248	0.4271	0.4274
0.90	0.3793	0.4035	0.4062	0.4065
0.95	0.3559	0.3831	0.3863	0.3867
1.00	0.3333	0.3636	0.3673	0.3678
1.20	0.2500	0.2941	0.3002	0.3011
1.40	0.1765	0.2360	0.2449	0.2463
1.60	0.1111	0.1872	0.1993	0.2014
1.80	0.0526	0.1460	0.1616	0.1646
2.00		0.1111	0.1304	0.1343
2.20		0.0815	0.1046	0.1094
2.40		0.0562	0.0831	0.0889
2.60		0.0345	0.0651	0.0721
2.80		0.0160	0.0521	0.0581
3.00			0.0377	0.0466
3.20			0.0273	0.0372
3.40			0.0186	0.0293
3.60			0.0113	0.0228
3.80			0.0051	0.0174
4.00				0.0130
4.20				0.0093
4.40				0.0063
4.60				0.0038
4.80				0.0017

Exhibit 13.22 Random Number Chart

15	71	59	63	79	51	93	13	80	58
08	95	09	88	28	79	63	08	01	20
19	83	57	55	15	09	26	60	66	40
45	44	87	46	22	67	16	13	84	21
76	34	07	55	03	15	21	68	67	12
42	49	92	69	16	58	26	40	30	87
38	88	29	13	08	04	70	40	81	89
47	56	28	17	10	78	55	27	18	92
82	05	64	36	54	30	72	23	29	69
37	39	36	81	99	56	89	64	02	98
49	75	48	84	45	75	49	36	74	03
43	12	11	63	30	75	64	56	26	41
37	03	53	70	06	05	91	25	57	48
11	59	24	06	27	49	02	88	66	94
45	29	55	20	96	70	52	18	78	31
55	77	70	41	38	25	69	74	73	83
89	76	36	72	91	26	29	75	33	95
09	57	40	37	46	10	96	29	89	41
67	15	52	53	69	46	95	80	77	57
84	53	58	90	04	16	84	25	53	67
51	37	96	32	06	64	61	05	37	40
67	46	64	62	29	72	09	64	20	49
14	85	28	10	77	50	06	71	15	64
10	24	46	91	97	15	00	83	98	75
52	53	98	13	50	79	63	74	63	10
03	72	83	73	85	22	90	00	61	88
02	48	25	66	45	51	63	95	91	09
09	29	41	84	14	01	63	76	51	43
13	94	26	48	42	47	26	82	38	33
42	97	96	54	83	88	56	40	38	36
61	10	33	14	60	58	24	58	21	42
59	02	23	78	21	43	67	30	71	05
04	39	02	67	94	54	63	38	92	26
83	68	57	58	42	73	55	84	08	04
24	50	28	97	74	01	34	73	19	52
65	69	16	04	38	30	06	85	09	71
57	30	56	94	03	02	41	60	70	54
91	66	15	71	54	26	79	39	70	02
00	79	05	32	91	09	73	53	88	17
02	25	33	62	75	21	06	10	75	66

SUMMARY

- The characteristics of waiting lines (queues) can be calculated using steady-state formulas.
- Queuing systems are classified according to the probability distributions for arrivals and service time and the number of servers.
- Deterministic simulation assumes all factors are constant and will not change.
- In probabilistic simulation, a process generator is used to represent a probability distribution for the values of variables.

SOLVED PROBLEM

An airline has three clerks at its ticket counter, and each clerk takes an average of five minutes to serve each customer. Customers form a single line and proceed to whichever clerk is available next. Arrivals to this line occur at an average rate of twenty-five per hour, Poisson distributed. Service times are exponentially distributed. Determine the average length of the waiting line and the average time a customer must wait.

Solution

a. Convert both arrival rate and service rate to number per time period. Thus, the arrival rate, λ, is 25/hour. Service rate is

$\mu = 1$ customer/5 minutes $\times$ 60 minutes/hour $= 12$ customers/hour

b. Use the values of λ and μ calculated above to calculate

$$P(0) = \frac{1}{\displaystyle\sum_{n=0}^{s-1} \frac{(\lambda/\mu)^n}{n!} + \frac{(\lambda/\mu)^s}{s!(1 - \lambda/s\mu)}}$$

$$= \frac{1}{\dfrac{(25/12)^0}{0!} + \dfrac{(25/12)^1}{1!} + \dfrac{(25/12)^2}{2!} + \dfrac{(25/12)^3}{3!(1 - 25/36)}}$$

$$= .098$$

c. The average number of customers in the queue is

$$L_q = \frac{P(0)(\lambda/\mu)^s \rho}{s!(1 - \rho)^2}$$

$$= [.098(25/12)^3(25/36)]/3!(1 - 25/36)^2$$

$$= 1.1$$

d. The average waiting time is

$$W_q = \frac{L_q}{\lambda}$$

$$= \frac{1.1}{25} = .044 \text{ hour or } 2.64 \text{ minutes}$$

QUESTIONS

1. Describe the classification scheme for queuing models.

2. Explain what is meant by steady state conditions.

3. What meaning does the utilization factor have in single-server and multiserver models?

4. Why have many service organizations gone to a single line with multiple servers?

5. What is the difference between deterministic and probability-based simulation?

6. Explain the two procedures for incrementing time in a simulation.

7. What are some advantages of simulation?

8. How might simulation be used in each type of process?

9. Which types of processes would queuing theory be most relevant to?

10. What are the two costs for which trade-offs must be considered in queuing systems?

PROBLEMS

1. The Davis Auto Center has one person who performs tire services, such as putting on new tires, rotating tires, and fixing flats. Cars arrive for tire service at the rate of two per hour. On the average, each car is serviced in fifteen minutes. Assuming that arrivals follow the Poisson probability distribution, and that service time follows the exponential distribution, calculate the steady state conditions.

2. The student recreation center at a large midwestern university has a computerized stationary bicycle. During peak periods, students arrive to use that bicycle at the average rate of three per hour, Poisson distributed. Each person rides for an average of fifteen minutes, but riding times are exponentially distributed.

- **a.** How many students would you expect to see waiting for the bicycle, assuming all who arrive wait.
- **b.** What percentage of time is the bicycle being used?
- **c.** What is the probability that no one is using the bicycle?
- **d.** What is the average time a student will spend waiting?

3. The heat treating machine at the Forbes Foundry Company processes jobs at an average rate of one per hour, exponentially distributed. Jobs arrive at the rate of one every 1.2 hours, Poisson distributed. What is the utilization rate of the heat treating operation, and how long must the average job wait for heat treating?

4. Complete the deterministic simulation of Exhibit 13.14.

- **a.** How long is each machine idle?
- **b.** How long must each job spend waiting for processing?

5. A shoe repair shop has found that the times between customer arrivals follow the pattern shown.

Time (Minutes)	Probability
5	.10
10	.20
15	.30
20	.15
25	.10
30	.10
35	.05

Develop a process generator for this distribution, using two-digit random numbers.

6. Air Chicago's ticket counter at O'Hare Airport has been experiencing some backlogs. A study indicates that customers arrive at an average rate of ninety per hour and that arrivals are Poisson distributed. There are currently three ticket agents, and customers seem to choose among the three lines randomly, but remain in one line once they choose. Each ticket agent can serve an average of forty customers per hour. The agents' service times are exponentially distributed.

Calculate the steady-state conditions for the current system. What would these conditions be if Air Chicago went to just one line that would feed all three ticket agents?

7. The automatic teller machine (ATM) at a bank can serve just one customer at a time. Data have been collected concerning the time between successive customer arrivals at the ATM for service and the service time. Use the following information and a random-number table to simulate ten customer arrivals:

Time Between Arrivals (Min.)	Frequency	Service Time (Min.)	Frequency
1	30	1	70
2	50	2	20
3	10	3	10
4	10		

SELECTED BIBLIOGRAPHY

Banks, Jerry, and Carson, John S., II. *Discrete-Event System Simulation*. Englewood Cliffs, N.J.: Prentice-Hall, 1984.

Christy, David P., and Watson, Hugh J. ''The Application of Simulation: A Survey of Industry Practice.'' *Interfaces* 13, no. 5 (October 1983): 47–52.

Newell, Gordon F. *Applications of Queuing Theory*. New York: Chapman & Hall, 1982.

Solomon, Susan L. *Simulation of Waiting Lines*. Englewood Cliffs, N.J.: Prentice-Hall, 1983.

Vinrod, B., and Altiok, T. ''Approximating Unreliable Queuing Networks Under the Assumption of Exponentiality.'' *Journal of the Operational Research Society* (March 1986): 309–316.

Watson, Hugh J. *Computer Simulation in Business*. New York: Wiley, 1981.

Chapter 14

Project Planning and Scheduling

CHAPTER OUTLINE

LEARNING OBJECTIVES

After completing this chapter, you should be able to

- List the planning steps for a project.
- Draw a project network, using either activity-on-arc or activity-on-node representation.
- Calculate the earliest start, earliest finish, latest start, and latest finish times for a project.
- Determine which activities are on the critical path.
- Use PERT to calculate expected times and variances for activities.
- Calculate the probability of completing a project within a given time period.
- Explain how resource requirements may be leveled.
- Use time/cost trade-offs to reduce project duration.
- Discuss the role of computers in project planning and control.

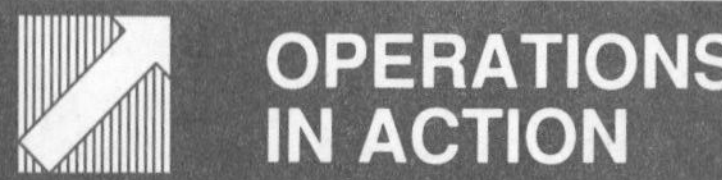

British Airways: Project Scheduling Helps Change the Corporate Image

British Airways owns 167 aircraft and employs 20,000 people. When the company decided to change its corporate image through a complete change in aircraft colors and interiors and new designs for employee uniforms, a public promotion of this new image was planned.

To go with this promotional effort, BA wanted to have a completely refitted Boeing 747 ready, along with new employee uniforms. However, no one was sure whether either could be ready in time for the promotion.

To answer that question, the company used a computer program called PertMaster that was run on a microcomputer. BA's planners entered all relevant information about ordering, procuring, and applying the new paint; buying new upholstery and carpets; the time needed to remove the old airplane interiors and replace them with new; and the time needed to design and sew the new uniforms. Based on the project schedule, it was determined that the uniforms would not be ready in time and that only the exterior paint on the 747 could be ready.

However, the company also determined that sufficient time remained to prepare a Boeing 737—a smaller plane. This was done, and the promotion went off with a newly outfitted 737 as the star of the show. The 747 with new exterior paint was available as a backdrop.

Without the availability of a project-scheduling computer program, British Airways could never have accounted for all the activities that were part of this project. Without scheduling this project, it might have planned for a promotion with new uniforms and a 747 when neither could have been ready in time.[1]

INTRODUCTION

In the preceding chapter, we discussed methods for scheduling different types of processes, from line flow to job shop. However, one type of process we did not mention was the project. That is because the procedures for planning and controlling projects are considerably different from those for the other types of processes and deserve an entire chapter unto themselves.

Projects such as installing new equipment or building a new facility represent another scheduling problem, although one that is often easier to deal with than job shop scheduling. The problem in project scheduling is to determine when each activity must begin or end so that the entire project can be completed on time. For example, in building a new facility, ground must be broken before the foundation can be poured, which must be done before the walls can be put up.

Projects need not involve building activities. For example, many service organizations deal with projects on a regular basis. The development of an advertising campaign and the installation of a new management information system are examples of nonbuilding projects.

Managing projects involves the usual managerial functions of *planning, scheduling,* and *controlling.* In order to ensure successful completion of the project, each of these must be performed. We will briefly describe the planning process first and then go on to discuss in more detail some common tools for carrying out the functions of scheduling and controlling.

PLANNING FOR PROJECTS

Before starting a project, the following steps must be carried out:

1. Develop a **statement of work,** describing the objectives to be achieved and the work to be done.
2. Proceed to a **work breakdown structure** that defines the individual activities or tasks that must be performed as part of the project and the precedence relationships among them.
3. List the resources, including money, personnel, equipment, and material—both internal and external—needed to complete the project.
4. Estimate the time required to perform each activity, and tie the resource requirements to that time frame.

NETWORK REPRESENTATION OF A PROJECT

As the saying goes, one picture is worth a thousand words. In managing a project, there are important relationships among various activities that are often better presented visually. For example, certain activities may not be able to begin until others are completed. Still other activities may be able to proceed simultaneously. One excellent way that has been found to visually represent a project is through a network. Two forms of project networks are discussed below.

Activities on Nodes

Because projects consist of activities that have certain precedence relationships, we can utilize the precedence diagrams from Chapters 4 and 8. In those chapters, the tasks were represented by circles (called **nodes**) and the relationships were indicated by arrows (called **arcs** or **branches**).

For example, suppose the College of Business at Middle Illinois State University is planning to install a computerized information system to maintain information about its students. Exhibit 14.1 is a list of the activities that have been

Exhibit 14.1 Work Breakdown Structure, Most Likely Durations, and Precedence Relationships for Information System Project

Activity	Most Likely Duration (Weeks)	Immediate Predecessor(s)
A. Select computer software	3	—
B. Install software	5	A
C. Install office network	7	A
D. Test software	6	B
E. Develop data base	8	B
F. Train employees	3	C, D
G. Implement system	2	E, F

identified for that project, the most likely duration of each activity, and the precedence relationships.

These relationships among activities are represented graphically in Exhibit 14.2. Notice that each node corresponds to an activity, indicating the letter designation of that activity and its duration. Arrows indicate the precedence relationships. For example, activity A (software selection) must be completed before activity B (software installation) can begin.

This type of network representation is referred to as **activity-on-node (AON) representation** because a node corresponds to each activity. However, an alternative representation in which activities are represented by arcs is also used frequently.

Activities on Arcs

We can also think of each activity as having a specific beginning and ending point. For example, activity A in the building project will have a point in time when it begins and a point in time when it ends. These beginning and ending points can be thought of as **events,** and nodes can be used to represent such events.

Following this line of reasoning, if nodes represent the events that begin and end an activity, then the arrow connecting these two nodes can represent that activity, as shown in Exhibit 14.3. In fact, Exhibit 14.3 is the **activity-on-arc (AOA)** network diagram that corresponds to the information system project of Exhibit 14.2. In this case, notice that we have now assigned numbers to the nodes, designating them as events. Thus, each activity may be designated not only by the arc that represents it, but also by the events that begin and end it. For example, activity A can also be designated as 1–2, its beginning and ending nodes.

Dummy Activities

One additional requirement results from the fact that arcs are used in an AOA network to represent activities *and* precedence. In some cases, we may need to indicate precedence when no activity exists. In those cases, we use a **dummy activity,** represented by a dashed arrow. Dummy activities have a duration of zero and are used only to show precedence. Exhibit 14.4 shows two AON networks and the corresponding AOA networks that require dummy activities.

Exhibit 14.2 Activity-on-Node Network Representation of Information System Project

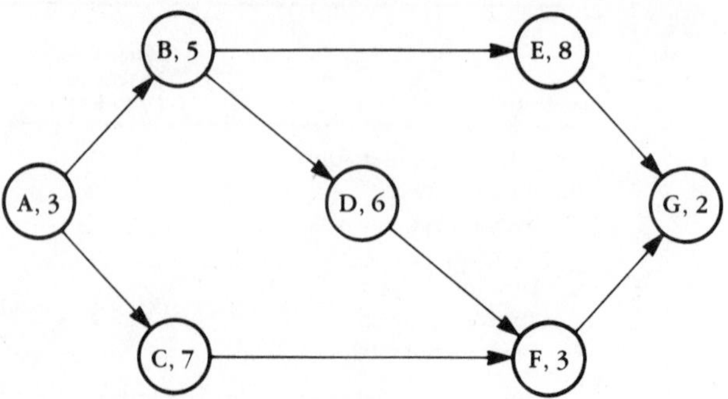

Exhibit 14.3 Activity-on-Arc Representation of Information System Project

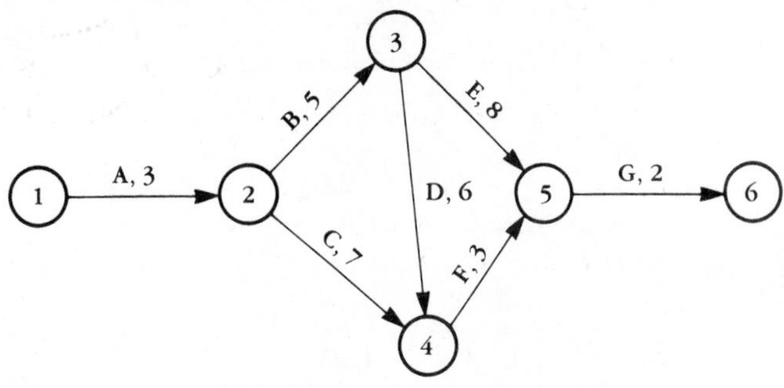

Exhibit 14.4 Comparison of Networks Requiring Dummy Activities for Activity-on-Arc Representation

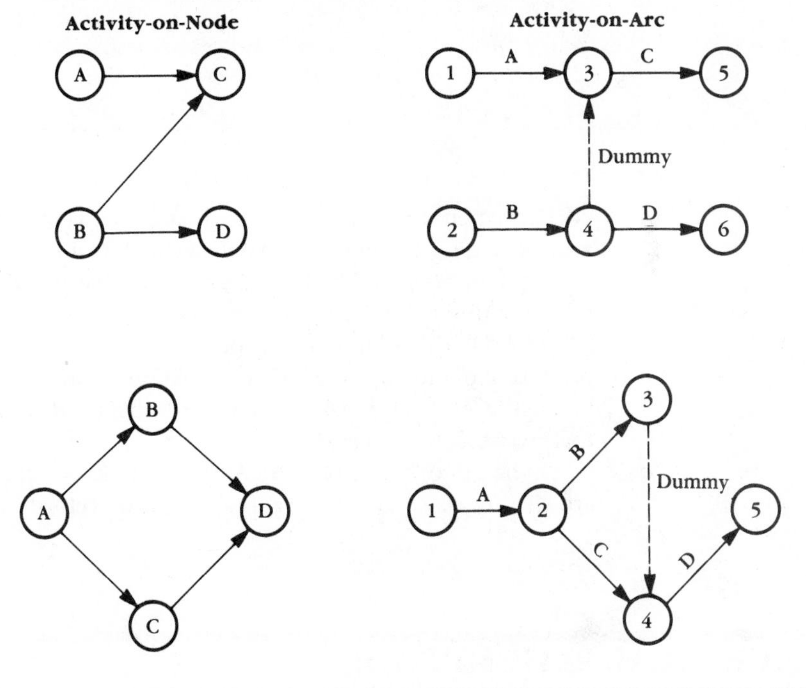

In the top pair of networks in Exhibit 14.4, activity C is preceded by both A and B, but activity D is preceded only by B. Using the AOA network representation, a dummy activity is needed; otherwise, the diagram would imply D is also preceded by both A and B.

A second situation in which a dummy activity is useful is when each activity must have a unique pair of beginning and ending events. This is especially im-

OPERATIONS IN ACTION

The U.S. Navy, du Pont, and Remington-Rand Develop PERT/CPM

During the 1950s, three different organizations were faced with project management problems that were not easily solved by using techniques that existed at that time. Previously, projects had been managed using Gantt charts. However, such charts did not easily show precedence relationships and quickly became unwieldy for large projects.

The problem faced by the U.S. Navy involved the Polaris missile project and coordination of some 3,000 contractors and suppliers involved in that project. Making matters worse, many activities that made up that project had never been done before, and estimates of the time they would take were uncertain.

At the same time, du Pont faced a different problem. It had to shut down its chemical processing plants on a regular basis to perform routine maintenance. Because the activities had been done before, excellent time estimates were available. However, the company wanted to determine the shortest possible time to complete the maintenance and to identify the activities that were critical to that shortest completion time. For help in developing a method, the company hired Remington-Rand.

The method developed by the Navy was called the **program evaluation and review technique (PERT)** and allowed uncertain time estimates to be used. On the other hand, du Pont and Remington-Rand developed a technique that does not use probabilities and called it the **critical path method (CPM).** Today, both techniques are referred to jointly as PERT/CPM, and the distinctions between them are minor. Both techniques can accommodate uncertain time estimates, and both can use either AOA or AON network representation.

portant when using computer programs that represent activities by their associated beginning and ending events. In the bottom pair of networks in Exhibit 14.4, activity D is preceded by both B and C. So that B and C can have different ending events, a dummy activity must be included.

In both cases shown, the dummy activity has been used strictly to show precedence and to clarify that precedence relation. Dummy activities are not needed in AON networks because arcs are used only to indicate precedence in that network representation.

In practice, both AON and AOA networks are used. However, AON networks are slightly easier to work with and will therefore be used in this chapter.

THE CRITICAL PATH METHOD

The information provided by Exhibit 14.2 is useful in understanding relationships among activities. However, it is possible to obtain much more information by using the **critical path method (CPM).** CPM provides a way for us to determine the earliest time each activity could start, based on expected durations and precedence relationships. Further, we can determine when the entire project is expected to be completed.

By working backward from a desired completion date for the project, it will also be possible to determine the latest time each activity could start and finish without delaying the entire project. Finally, we can calculate what is called the critical path, which will consist of those activities that determine how long it will take to complete the entire project.

Calculating Start and Finish Times

Earliest Times

If we let time zero represent the starting time for this project, then activities A and B can begin immediately at time zero. Their expected finish times can be found by adding the expected duration to the starting time of zero. We will designate these starting and finish times as the **earliest start (ES)** and **earliest finish (EF)** since they are the earliest times the activities can start and finish, based on the starting time of zero and expected durations.

If the earliest finish time for activity A is 3 (0 + 3), then that also is the earliest time that C can start since activity C must be preceded by A. For any activity, its earliest start time will be the time at which all of its predecessor activities are completed. The earliest finish time for C can also be determined using the general rule

$$EF = ES + \text{activity duration}$$

The earliest start and earliest finish times for all activities in the project can be calculated the same way and are shown in Exhibit 14.5 by adding the earliest start and earliest finish information to the CPM diagram.

Exhibit 14.5 Calculation of Earliest Start and Finish Times

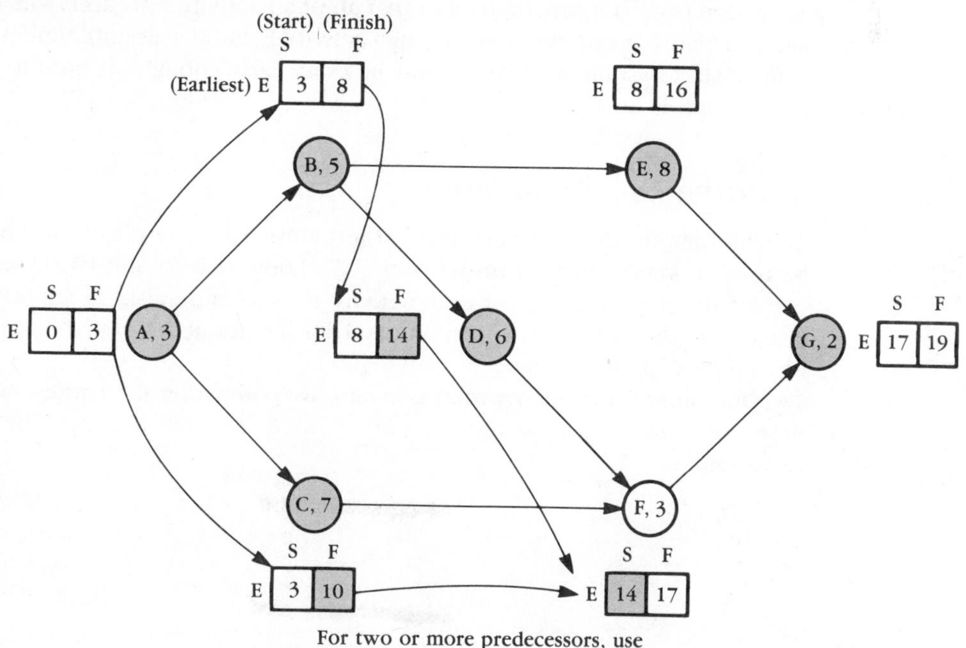

You should note that if an activity, such as F, has more than one predecessor, its earliest start time will be the *latest* of the predecessor earliest finish times. This may sound a bit like double talk, but all it means is that no activity can start until *all* of its predecessors are finished.

Exhibit 14.5 indicates that we should expect the entire project to take 19 weeks. We can also see the *earliest* time that each activity is expected to start. But one other question we might like to answer is how late each activity can be in order to meet a desired completion date.

Latest Times

Suppose the project must be completed within 19 weeks. That represents the *latest* time that activity G (the last activity of the project) can finish without making the project late. The latest time that G can *start* will just be its duration, 2, subtracted from 19. Using this approach, we have determined the **latest finish (LF)**and **latest start (LS)** for activity G. At each node, the latest start time can be calculated using the general rule

$$LS = LF - \text{duration}$$

We can keep working *backward* from the desired completion date to determine latest finish and latest start times by realizing that all of an activity's predecessors must be completed by its latest start time. For instance, if G cannot wait past time 17 (19 − 2) to start, then the latest finish time for F will be 17. These latest start and latest finish times can be included on the CPM diagram, as shown in Exhibit 14.6.

Again, you should notice that a choice must be made when one activity, such as B, is a predecessor to more than one other activity. In this case, B precedes both D and E. In such instances, the latest finish time of an activity will be the *earliest* of the latest start times of its predecessors. If this sounds like double talk again, don't worry—just remember that all of an activity's predecessors must be finished before it can start. Even though activity E could wait until time 9 to start, D must start by time 8. Thus, B must be done early enough for both to start on time, which is time 8.

Avoiding Late Completion

The information about earliest start, earliest finish, latest start, and latest finish can be used to keep a project on schedule. We know that *ES* and *EF* represent the earliest times we can expect each activity to start and finish. *LS* and *LF* are the latest times that each activity can start and finish without delaying the project past its desired completion date.

One more bit of information is useful. By comparing the earliest and latest times, we can determine the amount of *slack* for each activity. The slack is calculated as

$$\text{Slack} = LF - EF$$

or

$$\text{Slack} = LS - ES$$

Exhibit 14.7 indicates the slack for each activity in the project described above.

Exhibit 14.6 Calculation of Latest Start and Finish Times

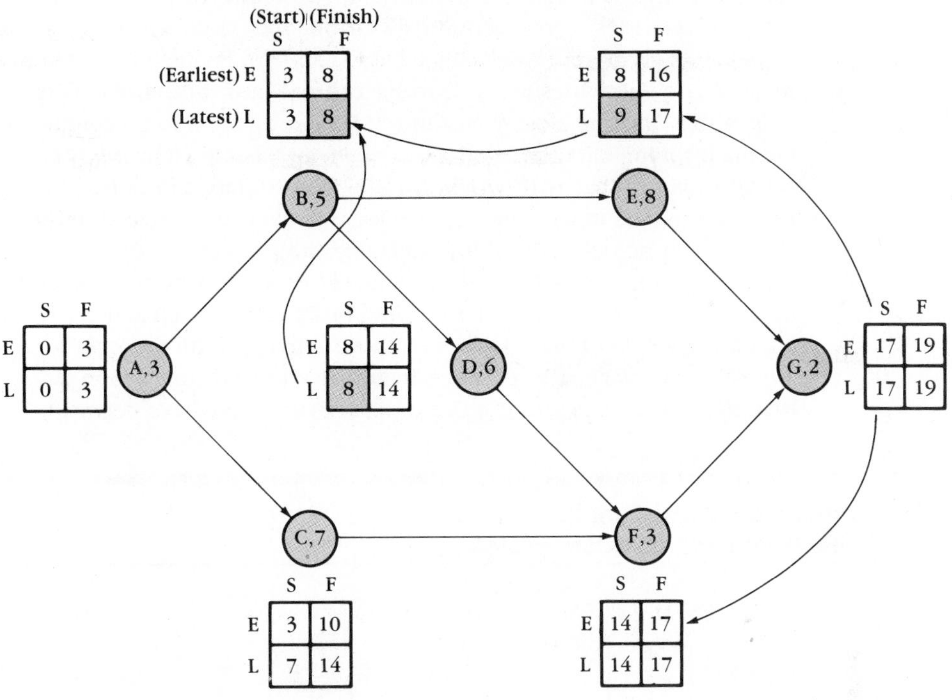

Exhibit 14.7 Calculation of Slack and Determination of Critical-Path Activities

Activity	Duration	*Start* Earliest	*Start* Latest	*Finish* Earliest	*Finish* Latest	*Slack*	*Critical Path?*
A	3	0	0	3	3	0	Yes
B	5	3	3	8	8	0	Yes
C	7	3	7	10	14	4	No
D	6	8	8	14	14	0	Yes
E	8	8	9	16	17	1	No
F	3	14	14	17	17	0	Yes
G	2	17	17	19	19	0	Yes

The **slack time,** or **slack,** represents how much leeway each activity has in its starting time and duration. For instance, activity C has slack of four weeks. This means that C can wait four weeks beyond its earliest start time, or it can take four weeks longer than the expected duration—without delaying the project.

The Critical Path

Note that some activities have more slack than others. If we look at all the slack times, we will see that there is one lowest time that is common to several different activities. Those activities with the least slack will form a path through the CPM diagram from beginning to end. This path is called the **critical path,** and its associated activities are said to be **critical-path activities.** They are the activities that must be closely monitored if the project is to be completed on time. On the diagram in Exhibit 14.8, the critical path has been highlighted because the activities along that path (A, B, D, F, G) must start and finish on time, or the project will take longer than 19 weeks. However, we can also tell that activities C and E can be delayed without delaying the project.

You should note that the least amount of slack does not necessarily have to be zero. For a desired completion time of 22 weeks, each activity would have at least three weeks of slack. However, those activities with the least amount of slack are still the critical-path activities. In fact, if a desired completion date is specified that is less than the earliest finish time, activities may have *negative* slack. In this

Exhibit 14.8 Highlighted Critical Path in AON Network Diagram for the Information System Project

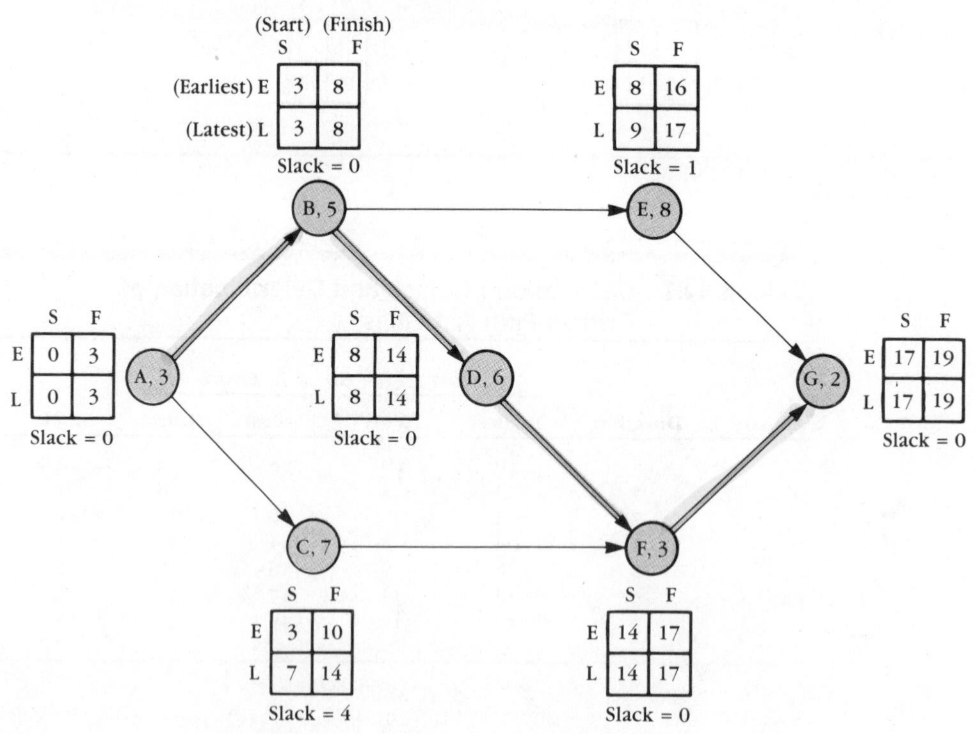

case, activity times must be shortened, a topic we will discuss later in this chapter. Regardless, the activities with the least amount of slack will still constitute the critical path.

INTRODUCING PROBABILITY WITH PERT

In our discussion of CPM, we used a duration for each activity that represented how much time the activity would be most likely to take. However, many factors may cause that time to vary. To deal with that possible variation, the **program evaluation and review technique (PERT)** uses the beta probability distribution.

The beta distribution was chosen because its most likely value can fall anywhere between its end points. Unlike the normal probability distribution, which is symmetrical and must have the most likely value exactly in the middle, the beta distribution allows the most likely time estimate to be close to the pessimistic time, close to the optimistic time—or anywhere in between.

By obtaining three time estimates, instead of just one, for each activity, it is possible to calculate the expected duration of each activity and the standard deviation of that duration. Those values can then be used to determine an expected completion time for the project, as well as the probability of completing the project within a given time period.

Estimating Activity Time

The three time estimates used to calculate expected activity time are these:

1. **Optimistic time (a):** the shortest time the activity will reasonably take
2. **Most likely time (m):** the time this activity would take *most* of the time
3. **Pessimistic time (b):** the longest time the activity would be expected to take

Using these three values, it is possible to calculate the *expected* duration of an activity. You should note this expected time may not be the same as the most likely time (m). Expected time represents an *average* time, while most likely time is the amount of time it takes *most often.* The formula for the **expected time** is

$$t_e = \frac{a + 4m + b}{6}$$

The variance of activity duration is

$$\sigma^2 = \left(\frac{b - a}{6}\right)^2$$

Example

In the information system example of Exhibit 14.1, we used only one duration for each activity, the most likely time. However, suppose we want to take probabilities into account by including the optimistic and pessimistic times. Exhibit 14.9 shows those three time estimates for each activity.

Exhibit 14.9 Expected Times and Variances for Activities in the Information System Project

Activity	Optimistic Time (a)	Most Likely Time (m)	Pessimistic Time (b)	Expected Time (t_e)	Variance σ^2
A	2	3	4	3	0.11
B	5	5	5	5	0.00
C	4	7	16	8	4.00
D	4	6	20	8	7.11
E	6	8	10	8	0.44
F	3	3	3	3	0.00
G	2	2	2	2	0.00

Notice in some cases that all three time estimates are the same. Those are activities that will always take a set amount of time, without any variation.

The expected time for each activity is calculated, using the formula introduced previously. For example, the expected time for activity C will be

$$t_e = \frac{a + 4m + b}{6}$$

$$= \frac{4 + 4(7) + 16}{6} = 8 \text{ weeks}$$

The variance in that completion time will be

$$\sigma^2 = \left(\frac{b - a}{6}\right)^2$$

$$= \left(\frac{16 - 4}{6}\right)^2 = 4.00$$

Probability of Completion by a Given Time

The expected activity times and variances obtained from PERT allow us to estimate the probability of completing a project within a specified period of time. To do this, we must determine a variance for the critical path. This variance will be calculated by assuming that the durations of activities along the critical path are independent of one another. Thus, the variance of the critical-path time will be the sum of variances of activities on the path.

To determine the probability of completing the critical-path activities within a certain time, we will assume the completion time is normally distributed. Although we had used the beta distribution for each activity's duration, we may now use the normal distribution for the sum of those durations based on the central limit theorem of statistics, which states that the sum of independent activity times follows a normal distribution as the number of activities becomes large. Although a large number of activities may not be on the critical path, the normal distribution is still a good approximation.

To determine the probability of completion by a given time, we use the z transformation formula:

$$z = \frac{T' - T}{\sqrt{\Sigma \sigma_{cp}^2}}$$

where

T' = desired completion date

T = sum of t_e for critical path activities

$\Sigma \sigma_{cp}^2$ = sum of variances for critical path activities

The probability of completion by T' may be determined then by using the normal probability table in the appendix at the end of this chapter.

Example

Suppose we want to know the probability of completing the information system project within twenty three weeks. Using the expected activity times from Exhibit 14.9 and the precedence network from Exhibit 14.8, we can determine that the critical path consists of activities A, B, D, F, and G, which give an expected project completion time of twenty one weeks. The sum of variances for activities on the critical path will be

$$\Sigma \sigma_{cp}^2 = 0.11 + 0 + 7.11 + 0 + 0 = 7.22$$

Then the z value will be

$$z = \frac{T' - T}{\sqrt{\Sigma \sigma_{cp}^2}}$$

$$= \frac{23 - 21}{\sqrt{7.22}} = .74$$

Referring to the normal probability distribution in the appendix at the end of this chapter, the probability corresponding to a z value of .74 is .7704 or 77 percent.

Joint Probabilities and Multiple Critical Paths

The procedure we have just described assumes only one critical path. However, there may be more than one. Further, a path that is not critical may have greater variance than the critical path does, making it possible for that path to end up being critical before the project is completed.

In such situations, the safest approach is to calculate the probability of completion for each path and then multiply those probabilities together to obtain a joint probability of completing all paths by the desired time.

OTHER RESOURCE CONSIDERATIONS

Up to this point, we have been concerned only with time. However, projects invariably involve other resources, such as people, equipment, and money. In scheduling a project, it is important to consider the usage of these resources. Further, there will be some trade-offs among the resources. In some instances, it will be possible to trade time for the other resources.

Balancing Resource Requirements

It should be remembered that time is not the only resource being scheduled for a project. Each activity of the project will also require certain other resources, such as people and equipment, for its completion. By scheduling activities, we are also scheduling those other resources. Based on the resource requirements associated with each activity, a diagram similar to the load profile discussed earlier can be developed. For example, Exhibit 14.10 indicates the work-force level that will be required corresponding to each activity that makes up a project. The top part of Exhibit 14.10 shows the expected start and finish times for each activity and the number of people needed for that activity. These requirements have been combined to develop the diagram at the bottom of Exhibit 14.10.

Exhibit 14.10 Resource Requirements

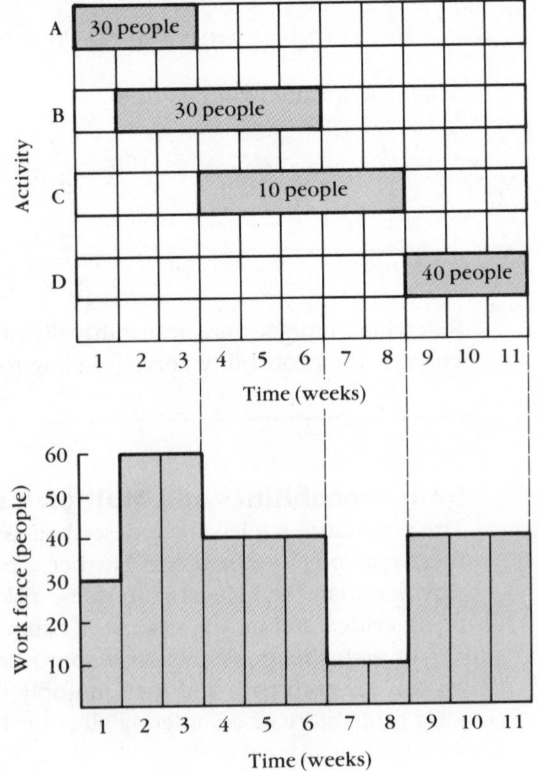

As you can see in Exhibit 14.10, the resource requirements will rise and fall as activities begin and end. Some activities may require more resources than others. A problem in scheduling any project is to smooth out these resource requirements to the extent possible. For example, it would usually be undesirable to have the large work-force drop shown in weeks 7 and 8 of Exhibit 14.10 because this could mean having to lay off a large number of workers—an expensive proposition due to unemployment compensation and an action that could create poor labor-management relations.

Many times, resource requirements can be smoothed by shifting the start or finish of activities. If slack exists, then it can be put to use in this way. Other times, it may be necessary to delay the project finish or even replan the project in order to avoid large fluctuations in resource requirements. For the project indicated in Exhibit 14.10, activity B, which has large work-force requirements, can be delayed two weeks, resulting in a smoother work-force level, as shown in Exhibit 14.11.

Crashing the Critical Path: Time/Cost Trade-Offs

In some instances, it may be necessary to shorten the time for a project. This can often be done, but at the cost of incurring higher expenses. For example, activity times may be shortened by hiring more employees, scheduling overtime, or adding an extra shift. All of these strategies will shorten the overall activity

Exhibit 14.11 Smoothed Work-Force Requirements

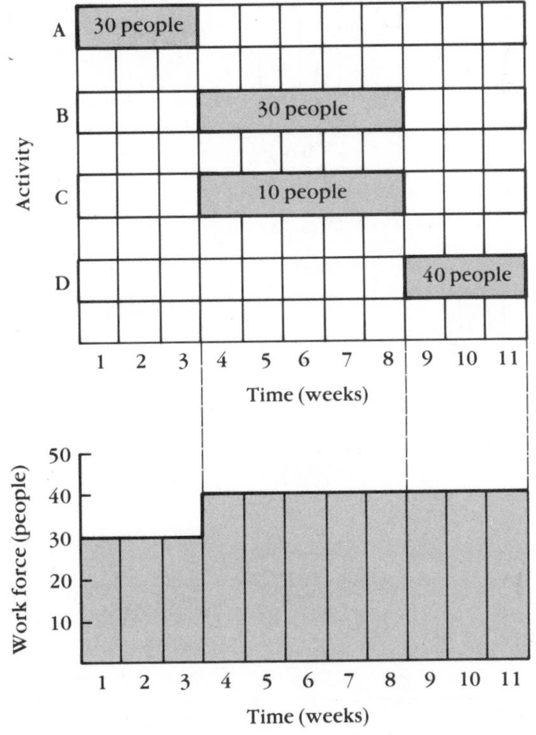

time—but will also mean higher labor costs. In cases where a project's duration must be shortened, the question becomes one of determining how to do so for the least additional cost.

Consider the project depicted in Exhibit 14.12. The earliest expected completion time for this project is nineteen weeks. Suppose that the completion time must be shortened by reducing the time for certain activities.

The activity times indicated in Exhibit 14.12 are usually called *normal times.* The **normal time** represents the time an activity will take under normal conditions. However, it may be possible to shorten the time for some activities. The shortest possible time an activity can be completed in is called its **crash time.** The cost associated with doing an activity in its normal time is called **normal cost,** and the cost incurred when an activity's duration is shortened to the crash time is called **crash cost.** The normal time and cost and the crash time and cost for the project of Exhibit 14.12 are listed in Exhibit 14.13.

It is usually assumed that the cost increase per time reduction will be proportional. For example, activity E can be shortened by two weeks for an additional cost of $1,800. If we wanted to reduce the time for E by only one week, we will assume that would cost us an extra $900. The additional cost incurred per week of time reduction is shown as the last column in Exhibit 14.13. Note that

Exhibit 14.12 CPM Diagram for a Project

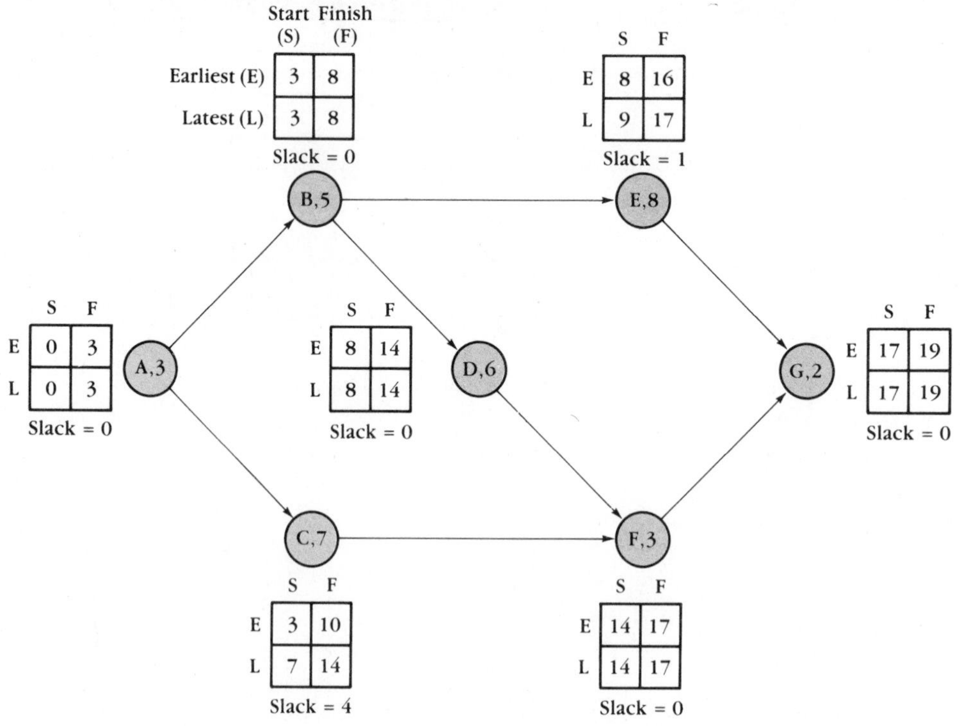

Exhibit 14.13 Normal Times and Costs and Crash Times and Costs

	Normal		Crash		
Activity	Time	Cost	Time	Cost	*Cost/Week*
A	3	$1,000	2	$2,000	$1,000/1 = $1,000
B	5	2,000	5	2,000	—
C	7	1,500	4	1,800	$300/3 = $100
D	6	5,000	4	6,000	$1,000/2 = $500
E	8	3,000	6	4,800	$1,800/2 = $900
F	3	1,200	3	1,200	—
G	2	500	2	500	—

some activities, such as B, cannot be shortened. We indicate that with a dash in the Cost/Week column.

Determining Which Activities to Crash

Suppose we want to complete the project of Exhibit 14.12 in eighteen weeks instead of the nineteen it would normally take. Which activity or activities should be shortened? To answer that question, first consider which activities influence the project duration. Can you tell which activities are the ones that determine how long the project will take?

Recall from our earlier discussion that slack time indicates how much leeway a certain activity has in its starting and finishing times. Some activities have more slack than others, but those that have the lowest slack values are called *critical-path activities.* Those activities on the critical path are the ones that will determine a project's duration. In this case, the critical path consists of activities with zero slack—namely, A, B, D, F, and G. At least one of those activities must be shortened before the project can be completed in less time.

To determine which of the critical-path activities to shorten, we refer to the Cost/Week column of Exhibit 14.13. Shortening the duration of any critical-path activity will shorten the project duration. But since it costs more to shorten some activities than others, it makes sense to pick the critical-path activity with the lowest cost/time value. That would be activity D. Thus, we choose to shorten activity D by one week for an additional cost of $500. The entire project will now take only eighteen weeks, as shown in Exhibit 14.14.

More Than One Critical Path

Suppose we want to reduce the project duration even further to seventeen weeks. Once again, the key is to reduce the duration of at least one activity on the critical path. But the problem now is that there is more than one critical path (you can easily verify this for yourself by looking at the slack values in Exhibit 14.14). There are three paths through the diagram of Exhibit 14.14, from beginning to end. They, and the sums of their activity times, are listed below.

A–B–E–G	18 weeks
A–B–D–F–G	18 weeks
A–C–F–G	15 weeks

Exhibit 14.14 CPM Diagram for Project with Reduced Time

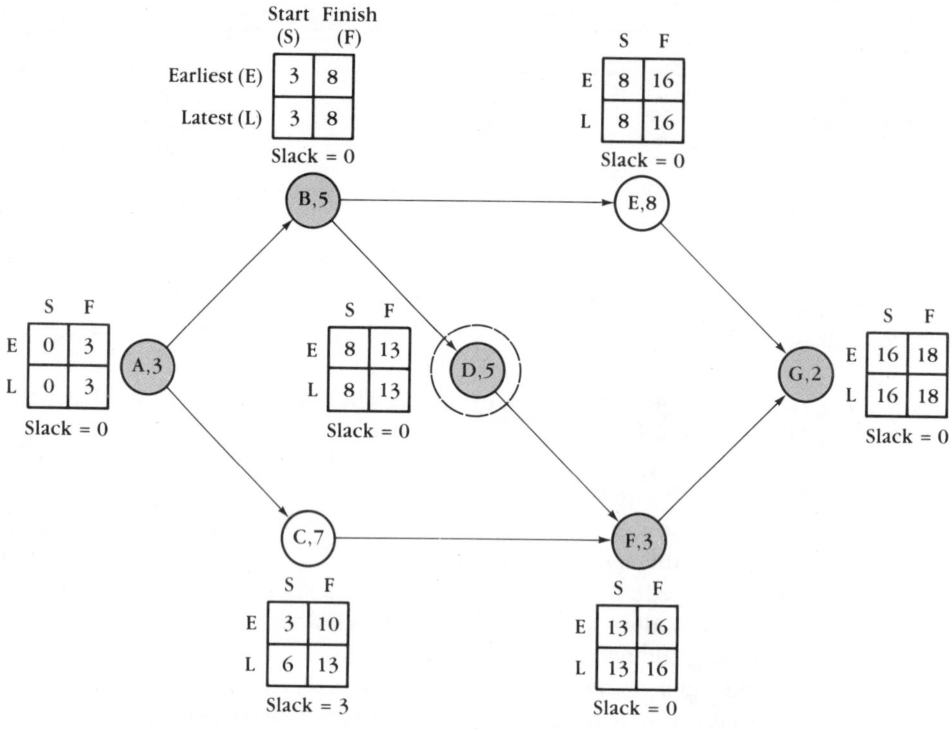

Before activity D was shortened, the path A–B–D–F–G took nineteen weeks and was the only critical path. But now two paths are critical—A–B–D–F–G and A–B–E–G. The problem here is that if an activity on only one critical path is shortened, then those activities on the other critical path will not take any less time, and the project duration will not be shortened. This means that activities on both critical paths must be reduced before the project duration will decrease.

There are several options here. First, one activity on each critical path could be selected. Again, we would select the lowest cost/time activity. On path A–B–E–G, that would be activity E, while the lowest cost/time activity on path A–B–D–F–G would be activity D, which would be shortened an additional week from five to four. The total cost of this option would be:

Reduce activity E by 1 week	$ 900
Reduce activity D by 1 week	500
Total additional cost	$1,400

The second option involves shortening the duration of an activity common to both paths. The common activities are A, B, and G. That is, those activities lie on both critical paths. Of those, only A can be reduced, at a cost of $1,000 per week. Since reducing activity A's duration will shorten both critical paths—and for less

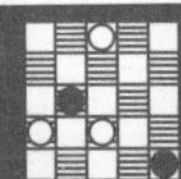

GAINING STRATEGIC ADVANTAGE AT GENERAL ELECTRIC

Using Speed to Compete Effectively

General Electric used to take three weeks to deliver an order for a custom-made industrial circuit breaker box; now it takes three days. To bring about such a time reduction, the company assembled a project team that focused on overhauling the manufacturing process. This team was made up of people not just from manufacturing, but also from design and marketing.

Part of the reason orders took so long was that engineers had to custom-design each box, taking about a week. Now, however, a computer is used to make designs from a limited number of interchangeable parts.

Another bottleneck that was identified involved decision making on the factory floor. To shorten that time period, the company put a lot of decisions in the hands of its employees. Now the workers on the floor schedule their own vacations and even determine their own production rate based on required production each day.

By focusing on the activities required to get a job done and by finding ways to shorten those activity times, GE has been able to speed up its operations. Today, productivity is up 20 percent, and costs have dropped 30 percent. Moreover, the company is gaining market share in a competitive business.[2]

cost than reducing an activity on each critical path—this second option is the one we will choose.

To summarize, when shortening the duration of a project, it is important to check for multiple critical paths. If more than one exists, then either an activity on each critical path or an activity common to the critical paths must be reduced. Whichever option produces the least total cost is the one to choose.

COMPUTERIZED PERT/CPM

Our discussion up to this point has treated the project activities as fixed entities. However, in a real project, things are constantly changing. Some activities may be found to be unnecessary, and other activities that had not been planned may come up as the project progresses. Further, the relationships among activities may change.

Thus, the project plan is not something that can be done once and then forgotten. Instead, it must be constantly updated and revisited. On a major project, doing so requires considerable effort and is difficult to do manually. For that reason, a number of computerized versions of PERT/CPM are available to run on microcomputers. One of those was mentioned in the British Airways example at the beginning of this chapter. Exhibit 14.15 shows the computer output for the problem discussed in this chapter when run on the STORM software package.

Exhibit 14.15 Sample of Output from STORM Computer Program's PERT/CPM Module

Student Information System Project
ACTIVITIES IN THE ORDER AS ENTERED

Activity Name	Symb	Mean Time /Std Dev	Earliest Start/Fin	Latest Start/Fin	Slack
SELECT SOF	A	3.0000	0.0000	0.0000	0.0000 c
		0.3333	3.0000	3.0000	
INSTALL SO	B	5.0000	3.0000	3.0000	0.0000 c
		0.0000	8.0000	8.0000	
INSTALL NE	C	8.0000	3.0000	8.0000	5.0000
		2.0000	11.0000	16.0000	
TEST SOFTW	D	8.0000	8.0000	8.0000	0.0000 c
		2.6667	16.0000	16.0000	
DEVELOP DA	E	8.0000	8.0000	11.0000	3.0000
		0.6667	16.0000	19.0000	
TRAIN EMPL	F	3.0000	16.0000	16.0000	0.0000 c
		0.0000	19.0000	19.0000	
IMPLEMENT	G	2.0000	19.0000	19.0000	0.0000 c
		0.0000	21.0000	21.0000	

The computations were based on 7 activities
Expected project completion time = 21.0000

Activity std dev = (pessimistic - optimistic) / 6.0
Std dev of project completion time = 2.6874

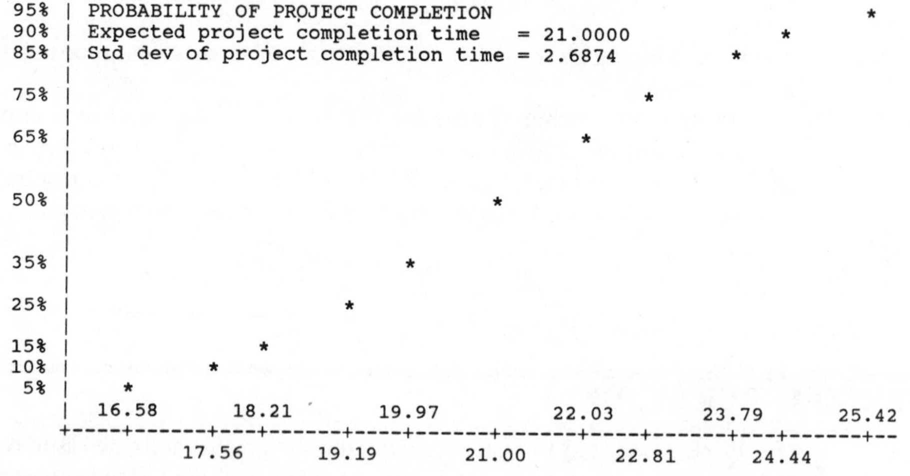

SUMMARY

- The planning steps for a project are these: develop a statement of work, define the work breakdown structure, list the resources, and estimate activity times.
- The activity-on-node (AON) network diagram is similar to a precedence diagram.
- Dummy activities are used in activity-on-arc (AOA) diagrams to show precedence only.
- The earliest start and finish times for activities are calculated by working forward based on precedence relationships.
- The latest start and finish times are calculated by working backward from a desired completion date.
- Slack is the difference between latest start and earliest start or between latest finish and earliest finish.
- The critical path consists of those activities with the least slack.
- PERT uses an optimistic time, a most likely time, and a pessimistic time to calculate expected time for each activity.
- The probability of completing a project within a given time is calculated using the normal distribution and the sum of the variances of critical-path activities.
- Resource requirements may be leveled by shifting activities with slack time.
- Project duration is shortened with the least cost by crashing those activities on the critical path that have the lowest cost per time ratios.
- Computers are used for updating and replanning projects.

CAREER PROFILE

Jean Thompson
Supervising Consultant
Coopers & Lybrand

Education and Work Experience

As an undergraduate student, Jean Thompson majored in management with a concentration in decision support systems at Southern Illinois University at Carbondale. After earning the B.S. degree, she went on for an M.B.A. with a concentration in accounting and took enough accounting courses to pass the CPA exam.

With her educational background, Thompson knew she wanted to enter management consulting services and recruited for that type of position with Coopers & Lybrand. At that time, the company did not put new hires into consulting, but was willing to work something out. Therefore, Thompson went to work in the company's audit department for three months and then was moved to the consulting department.

Current Duties and Responsibilities

Thompson works in the Information Technology Group, which is responsible for all aspects of implementing an information system for a client—from initial sale to final delivery. She currently spends most of her time with implementation activities: systems requirement analysis, solution definition, designing and building, and testing and transition.

In her supervisory role, Thompson manages the project activities: planning the implementation, tracking progress against the plan, and revising the schedule as appropriate. In this job, she utilizes many software productivity tools, including computer programs for project management and control. Further, she must balance many variables in order to provide service to the client and profitability to her firm. Acting as a liaison among systems developers, users, and upper management, Thompson finds that communication is also a key aspect of her job.

Future Positions

The next career steps for Thompson within Coopers & Lybrand would be to manager and then to partner, but both require further development of her sales abilities. One thing Thompson likes about her work is its diversity. So far, she has worked with companies in telecommunications, education, retailing, and utilities, among others. If she ever decides to change jobs, Thompson knows a lot about what other fields are like.

SOLVED PROBLEMS

1. A project consists of the following activities. Draw the AON diagram, and determine the earliest start, earliest finish, latest start, and latest finish times for each activity, based on a desired completion date as early as possible. Indicate the critical path.

Activity	Duration (Days)	Immediate Predecessor(s)
A	10	—
B	8	A
C	15	A
D	12	B, C
E	11	B
F	5	D, E

Solution

a. The AON diagram is drawn first, based on the precedence relationships given (see Exhibit 14.16).

b. Start with activity A and set *ES* equal to 0; then calculate *EF* = *ES* + duration.

c. The *ES* of each other activity is the *latest EF* of its predecessors. Calculate *EF* as in step b.

d. When the last activity is reached, set its *LF* to the desired completion date, and then calculate *LS* = *LF* − duration.

e. The *LF* of each other activity is the *earliest LS* of the activities it must precede. Calculate *LS* as in step d.

f. Slack = *LF* − *EF* or *LS* − *ES*. The critical path is comprised of those activities with the lowest slack value, as indicated by the double lines in Exhibit 14.16.

2. A project consists of the following activities, with the estimated times and precedence relationships shown. Using this information, draw an AOA net-

Exhibit 14.16 AON Diagram for Solved Problem 1

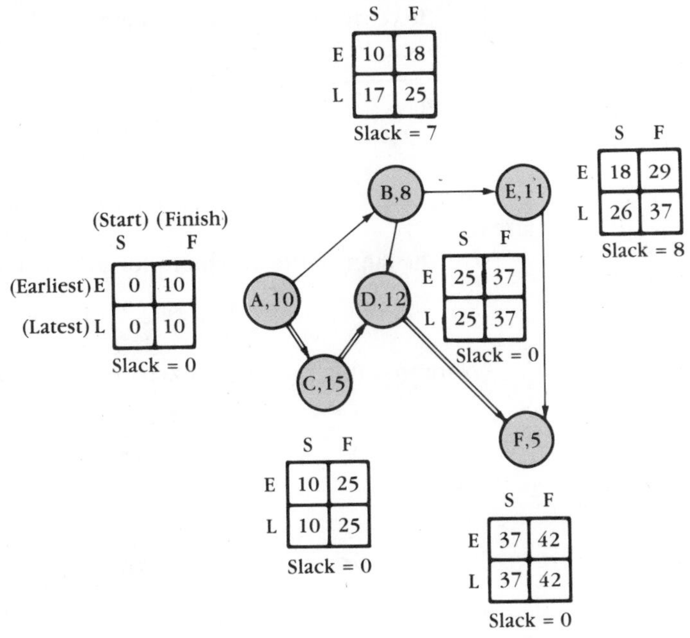

work diagram, determine the expected time and variance for each activity, and estimate the probability of completing the project within sixty days.

Activity	Optimistic Time (a)	Most Likely Time (m)	Pessimistic Time (b)	Immediate Predecessor(s)
A	5	6	7	—
B	10	13	28	—
C	1	2	15	A
D	8	9	16	B
E	25	36	41	B, C
F	6	9	18	D

Solution

a. The expected time and variance for each activity are calculated using these formulas:

$$t_e = \frac{a + 4m + b}{6} \qquad \sigma^2 = \left(\frac{b - a}{6}\right)^2$$

Activity	Expected Time (t_e)	Variance (σ^2)
A	6	0.11
B	15	9.00
C	4	5.44
D	10	1.78
E	35	7.11
F	10	4.00

b. The project AOA diagram is shown in Exhibit 14.17. Notice that a dummy activity has been used to indicate that E is preceded by B and C, although D is preceded only by B.

c. There are three possible paths in this network. Each has the total expected time shown.

A–C–E	45 days
B–dummy–E	50 days
B–D–F	35 days

Thus, the path B–dummy–E is the critical path, with an expected duration of fifty days.

d. The sum of the variances for critical-path activities will be

$$\sum \sigma_{cp}^2 = 9.00 + 0 + 7.11 = 16.11$$

(Note that the dummy has zero variance because it takes zero time.)

$$z = \frac{T' - T}{\sqrt{\sum \sigma_{cp}^2}}$$

$$= \frac{60 - 50}{\sqrt{16.11}} = 2.49$$

The probability associated with a z value of 2.49 is 99.36 percent. Thus, this is the probability of completing the project within sixty days.

3. The project shown in Exhibit 14.18 has the normal costs and crash costs indicated below. Determine how much each activity should be shortened to complete the project within twenty-six days.

	Normal		*Crash*	
Activity	**Time**	**Cost**	**Time**	**Cost**
A	5	$2,000	4	$6,000
B	8	3,000	6	6,000
C	2	1,000	2	1,000
D	3	4,000	2	6,000
E	9	5,000	6	8,000
F	7	4,500	5	6,000
G	4	2,000	2	5,000

Exhibit 14.17 AOA Diagram for Solved Problem 2

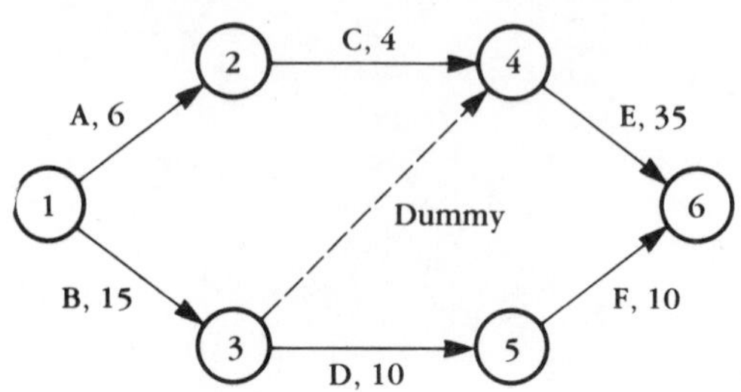

Exhibit 14.18 Network Diagram for Solved Problem 3

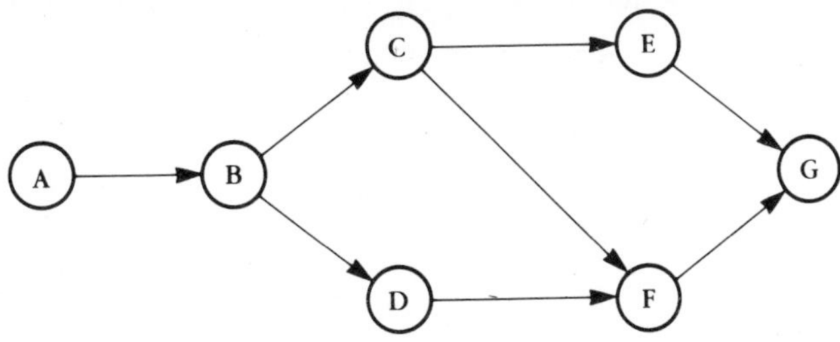

Solution

a. The cost per day for shortening each activity is

Activity	Normal Time − Crash Time	Crash Cost − Normal Cost	Cost per Day
A	1	$4,000	$4,000
B	2	3,000	1,500
C	0	0	—
D	1	2,000	2,000
E	3	3,000	1,000
F	2	1,500	750
G	2	3,000	1,500

b. The paths through this network and their associated normal times are

A–B–C–E–G: 5 + 8 + 2 + 9 + 4 = 28
A–B–C–F–G: 5 + 8 + 2 + 7 + 4 = 26
A–B–D–F–G: 5 + 8 + 3 + 7 + 4 = 27

Thus, A–B–C–E–G is the present critical path. The activity on this path with lowest cost per day is E. Therefore, activity E will be shortened by one day. Now the time for each path is

A–B–C–E–G: 5 + 8 + 2 + 8 + 4 = 27
A–B–C–F–G: 5 + 8 + 2 + 7 + 4 = 26
A–B–D–F–G: 5 + 8 + 3 + 7 + 4 = 27

At this point, two critical paths exist, and either one activity on each path or one activity common to both must be shortened to reduce the project time.

The common activities are

Activity	Cost per Day
A	$4,000
B	1,500
G	1,500

The activities unique to each path are

Combination	Combined Cost per Day
C and D	Not possible due to C
C and F	Not possible due to C
E and D	$1,000 + $2,000 = $3,000
E and F	$1,000 + $750 = $1,750

The lowest cost alternative is to reduce either B or G at a cost of $1,500.

QUESTIONS

1. What are the planning steps for a project?
2. What is the purpose of a statement of work?
3. What is a work breakdown structure?
4. Explain the difference between an activity-on-node diagram and an activity-on-arc diagram.
5. Why are dummy activities used?
6. Define the critical path.
7. What probability distribution is used for PERT?
8. Which activities are examined first in reducing the duration of a project?
9. Explain how resource usage can be leveled for a project.
10. Discuss some ways in which PERT/CPM is similar to MRP.
11. How could a Gantt load chart be used for project scheduling?
12. What is the role of computers in project planning and control?

PROBLEMS

1. A project has the following activities, activity durations, and predecessors. Draw the AON diagram, and calculate the earliest start and earliest finish times. Assume the project must be completed within twenty days. Calculate the latest start and latest finish times and the slack for each activity.

Activity	Duration (Days)	Predecessor(s)
A	5	—
B	8	A
C	4	A
D	3	B
E	5	C
F	3	D, E

2. For problem 1, draw the AOA network.

3. The AON diagram for a project is shown below. Using the precedence relationships and task times given, do the following:
   a. List all paths through the network and indicate the time for each path.
   b. Indicate which path is the critical path.
   c. Calculate the earliest start, earliest finish, latest start, latest finish, and slack times for each activity.

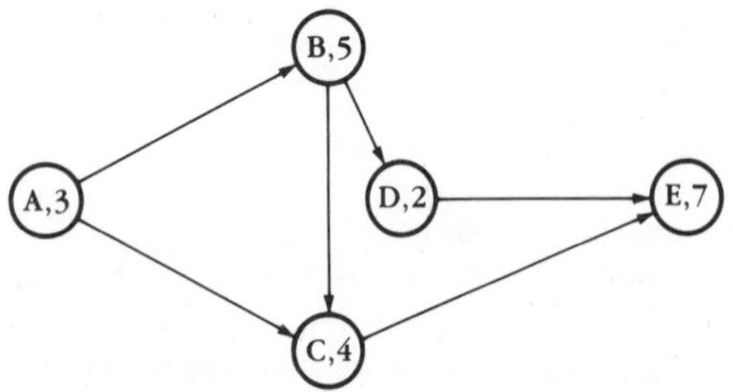

4. The AON diagram for a project is shown below. Determine the earliest start, latest start, earliest finish, latest finish, and slack times for each activity, based on a desired completion time of twenty-eight days. Find the critical path.

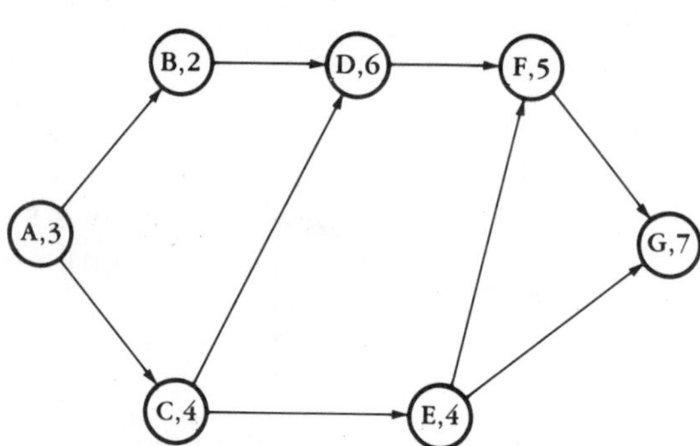

5. MadAve Advertising Agency is developing a magazine advertising campaign for a new client. The following activities have been identified as necessary in order to complete the project:

Activity	Duration (Weeks)	Immediate Predecessor(s)
A. Develop ad concept	2	—
B. Plan photo layout	1	A
C. Hire models	1	B
D. Take photographs	1	C
E. Write ad copy	3	A
F. Develop camera-ready copy	1	D, E
G. Select publications for ad	2	A
H. Send ad to publications	1	F, G

a. Draw an AON diagram for this project.
b. Calculate the earliest start, earliest finish, latest start, latest finish, and slack times for each activity.
c. Identify the critical path.

6. Associated Technologies Company has been working on a new product—a laser oven—through its well-known division that already markets microwave ovens. Unfortunately, the company has just learned that an overseas competitor is also developing a laser oven and plans to bring it to market in six months. If Associated Technologies is to capture a large share of the market first, its product must be out within ninety days.

Fortunately, Associated has been taking an integrated approach to new-product development, and most pieces are already in place. After considering every possible reduction in time, the company came up with the following activities that must be completed and their respective times:

Activity	Duration (Days)	Immediate Predecessor(s)
A. Finalize distribution channels	30	—
B. Complete prototype testing	15	—
C. Finalize product design	30	B
D. Complete BOM files	15	C
E. Finalize production process	10	C
F. Complete employee training	14	E
G. Distribute sales literature	7	A, C
H. Produce and distribute product	14	D, F, G

a. Draw an AON diagram for this project.
b. Calculate the earliest start and earliest finish times for each activity.
c. Based on the desired completion time of ninety days, determine the latest start, latest finish, and slack times for each activity.
d. Identify the critical path.

7. The Compu-Form Company provides computer services to business and industry. The company is planning to replace one of its computers and has identified the following activities that will make up that project:

Activity	Duration (Hours)	Immediate Predecessor(s)
A. Shut down old machine	1	—
B. Disconnect wiring from computer	1	A
C. Remove old computer	3	B
D. Remove old wiring	2	B
E. Connect new wiring to peripherals	2	D
F. Test wiring connections	1	E
G. Move in new computer	3	C
H. Connect wiring to computer	2	E, F, G
I. Install operating system	1	H
J. Check memory	1	I
K. Check operating system	1	I
L. Check peripherals	1	J, K

Determine the shortest time it will take to complete this project and which activities are on the critical path.

8. A project consists of the following activities. Determine the expected time and the variance for each activity.

Activity	Optimistic Time	Most Likely Time	Pessimistic Time
A	4	6	10
B	3	3	3
C	8	11	14
D	3	15	17
E	3	5	12

9. A project is made up of the following activities. Determine the expected time and the variance for each one.

Activity	Optimistic Time	Most Likely Time	Pessimistic Time
A	2	6	12
B	3	7	9
C	8	14	16
D	3	10	18
E	3	10	12
F	10	12	20
G	12	19	27
H	9	10	15

10. Referring to the network diagram of problem 3, use the following information to determine the probability of completing the project by time 22:

Activity	Optimistic Time	Most Likely Time	Pessimistic Time
A	2	3	6
B	1	5	7
C	3	4	9
D	2	2	2
E	2	7	9

11. Referring to the network diagram of problem 4, determine the probability of completing the project by time 26, based on the following information:

Activity	Optimistic Time	Most Likely Time	Pessimistic Time
A	1	3	5
B	2	2	2
C	2	4	6
D	2	6	8
E	3	4	9
F	2	5	12
G	3	7	8

12. A project has been planned with the following activities, expected start and finish dates, and cash expenditures. Develop a load profile that will indicate cash requirements during the project.

Activity	Start	Finish	Cash Expenditure
A	0	3	$6,000
B	0	5	2,000
C	3	8	4,000
D	2	8	5,000
E	5	6	2,000

13. A project consists of the following activities, with the normal times and crash times listed. Based on the cost information, determine how much additional money must be spent to reduce the project duration by one day from its normal time and which activity should be shortened.

	Normal		
Activity	**Time (Days)**	**Cost**	***Immediate Predecessor(s)***
A	5	$ 500	—
B	3	600	A
C	8	1,000	A
D	8	400	B
E	6	700	C
F	3	600	D, E

	Crash	
Activity	**Time (Days)**	**Cost**
A	3	$ 800
B	2	700
C	5	1,600
D	8	400
E	5	800
F	1	900

14. The Able Construction Company must complete the following activities as part of a building project. It is desired that this project be completed in the shortest time possible. Determine what that time is, which activities should be shortened, and the total project cost.

	Normal		
Activity	**Time (Days)**	**Cost**	***Immediate Predecessor(s)***
A	6	$1,000	—
B	10	1,200	A
C	9	600	A
D	9	800	B, C
E	8	1,500	C
F	5	500	D, E

	Crash	
Activity	**Time (Days)**	**Cost**
A	5	$1,300
B	9	1,300
C	8	1,200
D	7	1,200
E	6	2,000
F	5	500

Data Sets for Computer Solution

1. The Acme-Worldwide Construction Company has contracted to build an apartment building on the site of several existing structures. The company has determined that the following activities will need to be performed, with the expected durations shown below.

Activity	Duration (Days)	Immediate Predecessor(s)
A. Demolish existing structures	10	—
B. Excavate and grade site	12	A
C. Pour foundation	20	B
D. Install in-ground plumbing	15	B
E. Install sewer connections	12	B
F. Install underground electrical	17	B
G. Install anchor bolts	6	C
H. Pour concrete substructure	14	C, D, E, F, G
I. Erect steel skeleton	25	H
J. Install cross-bracing	27	I
K. Install plumbing	39	J
L. Install electrical	24	J
M. Pour concrete floors	10	K, L
N. Install walls and ceilings	33	M
O. Install windows	14	N
P. Move in fixtures and appliances	7	N

Activity	Duration (Days)	Immediate Predecessor(s)
Q. Connect fixtures and appliances	14	N
R. Paint walls and ceilings	27	O
S. Install carpeting	33	R
T. Remove construction materials	5	O
U. Touch up and clean	15	T

Determine how long it should take to complete this project and which activities will form the critical path.

2. Data Processing Associates has a contract to install an information system for one of its clients. The project has been broken down into the following activities with associated precedence relationships and time estimates. Determine the expected time and variance for each activity and probabilities for completing the project within various times.

Activity	Optimistic Time	Most Likely Time	Pessimistic Time	Immediate Prede-cessor(s)
A	2	4	7	—
B	1	5	8	A
C	2	8	10	A
D	9	9	9	B
E	2	6	8	C, D
F	8	12	20	E
G	3	5	9	F
H	2	4	7	F
I	1	3	9	G
J	8	9	12	H, I
K	3	4	9	J
L	4	6	10	K
M	8	9	10	L, N
N	3	8	9	K
O	4	6	7	M

MINI-CASES

Donna Davin & Associates, CPA

After graduating from college and passing the CPA exam, Donna Davin went into accounting practice. Today, her practice has grown to include five other accountants and an office staff of eight. Much of her company's business has come from doing tax returns.

Being a small operation, her company has not been heavily computerized. However, it was recently decided that productivity could be improved by beginning to use some tax-related software and by taking advantage of the IRS electronic system for filing returns.

One of Donna's employees has developed a list of activities and estimated times, in weeks, to implement the computerized system.

Activity	Immediate Predecessor(s)
A. Select software	—
B. Select equipment	A
C. Obtain software	A
D. Obtain equipment	B
E. Install equipment	D
F. Hold classroom training	C
G. Test equipment	E
H. Install software	C, G
I. Test software	H
J. Give hands-on training	F, I
K. Implement pilot	J
L. Implement full system	K

Activity	Optimistic Time	Most Likely Time	Pessimistic Time
A	1	3	4
B	2	3	4
C	4	8	15
D	3	4	5
E	1.2	1.5	2
F	1	1	1
G	0.2	0.5	1
H	0.5	0.7	1
I	0.3	1	3
J	2	3	4
K	2	3	5
L	3	4	5

Donna is concerned because she would like to have the new system ready by the end of the year, which is six months away. As she looks at these times, she notices that the time to obtain software could vary considerably. This is because one software package they are considering is not yet on the market in final form. Depending on how long that takes, the whole implementation might be delayed. Donna wonders whether it would be safer to go with another software package that could definitely be obtained within four weeks. However, that package does not have as many features as the new one.

Custom Metal Products Company

Custom Metal Products Company is a job shop specializing in a full range of services from design to fabrication. Recently the company accepted an order to design and manufacture the prototype of a new high-performance clutch. The activities that must be performed are shown, along with the normal and crash times (in days) and the costs.

Activity	Immediate Predecessor(s)
A. Design prototype	—
B. Develop BOM	A
C. Develop routing	A
D. Develop tooling	A
E. Obtain materials	B
F. Produce tooling	D
G. Make prototype	C, E, F

	Normal		*Crash*	
Activity	**Time**	**Cost**	**Time**	**Cost**
A	12	$3,000	8	$8,000
B	4	1,000	2	2,000
C	5	2,000	3	3,500
D	9	5,000	6	9,000
E	10	—	10	—
F	4	2,000	2	3,000
G	5	6,000	3	9,000

According to the company's contract, the prototype is to be delivered within twenty-eight days, or a penalty of $1,000 per day will be incurred. Custom Metal Products would like to minimize its costs on this project.

SELECTED BIBLIOGRAPHY

Cleland, David I., and King, William R. *Project Management Handbook.* New York: Van Nostrand Reinhold, 1983.

Kerzner, Harold. *Project Management for Executives.* New York: Van Nostrand Reinhold, 1984.

Mantel, Samuel J., and Meredith, Jack R. "IEs Are Best Suited to Challenging Role of Project Manager." *Industrial Engineering* 18, no. 4 (1986): 54–60.

Moder, J.; Davis, E. W.; and Phillips, C. *Project Management with CPM and PERT.* 3d ed. New York: Van-Nostrand Reinhold, 1983.

O'Neal, Kim. "Project Management Computer Software Buyer's Guide." *Industrial Engineering* 19, no. 1 (January 1987): 53–63.

Smith, Larry A., and Gupta, Sushil. "Project Management Software in P&IM." *P&IM Review* 5, no. 6 (June 1985): 66–68.

Smith, Larry A., and Mills, Joan. "Project Management Network Programs." *Project Management Quarterly* (June 1982): 18–29.

Chapter 14 Appendix

Areas Under the Standardized Normal Curve from $-\infty$ to $+z$

z	.00	.01	.02	.03	.04	.05	.06	.07	.08	.09
.0	.5000	.5040	.5080	.5120	.5160	.5199	.5239	.5279	.5319	.5359
.1	.5398	.5438	.5478	.5517	.5557	.5596	.5636	.5675	.5714	.5753
.2	.5793	.5832	.5871	.5910	.5948	.5987	.6026	.6064	.6103	.6141
.3	.6179	.6217	.6255	.6293	.6331	.6368	.6406	.6443	.6480	.6517
.4	.6554	.6591	.6628	.6664	.6700	.6736	.6772	.6808	.6844	.6879
.5	.6915	.6950	.6985	.7019	.7054	.7088	.7123	.7157	.7190	.7224
.6	.7257	.7291	.7324	.7357	.7389	.7422	.7454	.7486	.7517	.7549
.7	.7580	.7611	.7642	.7673	.7704	.7734	.7764	.7794	.7823	.7852
.8	.7881	.7910	.7939	.7967	.7995	.8023	.8051	.8078	.8106	.8133
.9	.8159	.8186	.8212	.8238	.8264	.8289	.8315	.8340	.8365	.8389
1.0	.8413	.8438	.8461	.8485	.8508	.8531	.8554	.8577	.8599	.8621
1.1	.8643	.8665	.8686	.8708	.8729	.8749	.8770	.8790	.8810	.8830
1.2	.8849	.8869	.8888	.8907	.8925	.8944	.8962	.8980	.8997	.9015
1.3	.9032	.9049	.9066	.9082	.9099	.9115	.9131	.9147	.9162	.9177
1.4	.9192	.9207	.9222	.9236	.9251	.9265	.9279	.9292	.9306	.9319
1.5	.9332	.9345	.9357	.9370	.9382	.9394	.9406	.9418	.9429	.9441
1.6	.9452	.9463	.9474	.9484	.9495	.9505	.9515	.9525	.9535	.9545
1.7	.9554	.9564	.9573	.9582	.9591	.9599	.9608	.9616	.9625	.9633
1.8	.9641	.9649	.9656	.9664	.9671	.9678	.9686	.9693	.9699	.9706
1.9	.9713	.9719	.9726	.9732	.9738	.9744	.9750	.9756	.9761	.9767
2.0	.9772	.9778	.9783	.9788	.9793	.9798	.9803	.9808	.9812	.9817
2.1	.9821	.9826	.9830	.9834	.9838	.9842	.9846	.9850	.9854	.9857
2.2	.9861	.9864	.9868	.9871	.9875	.9878	.9881	.9884	.9887	.9890
2.3	.9893	.9896	.9898	.9901	.9904	.9906	.9909	.9911	.9913	.9916
2.4	.9918	.9920	.9922	.9925	.9927	.9929	.9931	.9932	.9934	.9936
2.5	.9938	.9940	.9941	.9943	.9945	.9946	.9948	.9949	.9951	.9952
2.6	.9953	.9955	.9956	.9957	.9959	.9960	.9961	.9962	.9963	.9964
2.7	.9965	.9966	.9967	.9968	.9969	.9970	.9971	.9972	.9973	.9974
2.8	.9974	.9975	.9976	.9977	.9977	.9978	.9979	.9979	.9980	.9981
2.9	.9981	.9982	.9982	.9983	.9984	.9984	.9985	.9985	.9986	.9986
3.0	.9987	.9987	.9987	.9988	.9988	.9989	.9989	.9989	.9990	.9990

PART III
Management and Control of Operations

The first section of this text discussed the design of the operations system, and the second section discussed planning and the preparation of plans and schedules to meet organizational goals. The design and planning phases take place before services or goods are actually produced. Two sets of issues remain to be resolved. First, the production process needs to be managed so that actual production is directed toward the goals outlined in the planning phase. Second, information about performance needs to be collected and fed back to evaluate (1) the effectiveness of management in guiding the actual production phase, (2) the reasonableness of the plans and schedules, and (3) the appropriateness of the design of the production system. **Control** is gathering information in order to evaluate the system, provide feedback, and take corrective action. Control systems are an important part of the management function.

This section is organized around key topics that should be carefully managed and controlled so that the performance of operations meets the organization's expectations. The first two chapters in this section discuss material management and inventory control using lot-sizing models. In manufacturing firms, the cost of materials often exceeds 55 percent of the total cost to produce a product. The third chapter describes concepts and techniques for managing and controlling quality. The fourth chapter discusses the role of people in the organization and the importance they have in determining organizational success. The fifth chapter explains that information is an essential part of managing and controlling operations because information is the basis for decision making. The final chapter provides some future direction for operations management. The material is organized into the following chapters:

- CHAPTER 15: Material Management
- CHAPTER 16: Lot-Sizing Models
- CHAPTER 17: Quality Management
- CHAPTER 18: Technology and Human Resources
- CHAPTER 19: Creating Information Systems to Manage and Control Operations
- CHAPTER 20: Future Directions for Operations Management

Chapter 15

Material Management

CHAPTER OUTLINE

LEARNING OBJECTIVES

After completing this chapter, you should be able to

- Explain the important parts of material management, including purchasing, inventory control, material handling, storage, and distribution.
- Describe the physical flow of materials through the organization, from receiving through shipping and delivery.
- Explain why it is important that these physical flows be monitored and controlled by information flows.
- Define the important issues in developing a system for purchasing the services and goods needed by an organization.
- Construct a model for analyzing the make-versus-buy decision.
- Contrast just-in-time purchasing practices with traditional purchasing practices.
- Discuss international sourcing of materials.
- Describe the important issues in inventory control.
- Explain why firms maintain inventory and describe the cost trade-offs that determine how much inventory to keep on hand.
- Describe how service operations react to questions involving inventory.
- Define the important aspects of material handling and storage, including receiving, shipping, material-handling devices, storage devices, and intelligent warehousing.
- Illustrate the importance of distribution systems and describe how they can be used to tie various organizations into a production chain.

OPERATIONS IN ACTION

The Automotive Industry: Buying from a Single Source Has Caught On

For many years, purchasing agents would not dream of buying a critical part from only one vendor. What if that vendor went out of business? What if that vendor's facility burned down? What if that vendor's quality deteriorated? What if that vendor took advantage of the single-source relationship by offering slow deliveries or trying to increase the price? These reasons and others like them often motivated purchasing agents to maintain two or three sources for each part ordered. The primary vendor might get 60 percent of all the orders for a specific part. A secondary vendor might get 30 percent, and a third vendor might get the remainder. With this arrangement, the customer could play one vendor off against another so that price could be kept as low as possible.

Today, organizations and their purchasing agents are embracing the concept of a single source for a part. The pressures of competition in a global marketplace are putting a premium on closer ties and greater trust between vendors and customers. To be competitive, an organization must rely on its supplier base to produce the highest possible quality and to achieve continuing productivity improvements. This can be accomplished only when customers and suppliers share information and expertise. When organizations involve vendors in product design, the vendors can make suggestions that allow them to achieve lower cost in their production process. These savings can benefit both the vendor and the customer. If the customers merely pass on their needs via design drawing and specifications, the vendors may be severely limited in what they can accomplish.

In the automotive industry, sole sourcing is widely practiced. At both General Motors and Ford Motor, purchasing executives note that 98 percent of their automotive parts made by outside suppliers are single-sourced. Automotive industry executives note that single sourcing reduces the need for communication because their companies deal with fewer vendors. The vendors that they deal with are more cooperative so the effectiveness of their communications actually improves. Because there is no fallback supplier, the automobile companies pick their vendors more carefully and monitor their performance more closely. From the automotive industry perspective, single sourcing is here to stay.[1]

INTRODUCTION

Materials are the physical items consumed in producing goods and services. As discussed in Chapter 1, materials are one of the major inputs to the production process. For producers of goods, materials include the parts purchased for use in manufacturing, the gasoline purchased for delivery trucks, and the lubricants used in preventive maintenance. For service operations, materials include the bed linens used in hospitals, the food purchased by restaurants, and the forms required by banks for processing checks and sending monthly statements.

Material management includes decisions regarding the procurement, control, handling, storage, and distribution of materials. This chapter, which is organized around these decisions, includes major sections on the following topics:

- Purchasing
- Inventory control

- Material handling and storage
- Distribution systems

Purchasing is the activity of acquiring services and goods for the organization. It includes all the activities necessary for filling the organization's long- and short-term needs for materials.

Inventory is material that is stored in anticipation of some future use. Inventory can be used as an alternative to future production. It is created when production (or procurement, in the case of purchased parts) exceeds consumption. Inventory can be classified as follows:

- Raw materials
- Work-in-process
- Finished goods
- Supplies

Raw-material inventories are goods purchased and stored for later use in the production process. **Work-in-process inventories** are products that the organization has partially completed. **Finished-goods inventories** are final products awaiting customer acceptance and delivery. **Supply inventories** are materials that are not part of the finished product, but are consumed in production. Examples of supply inventories include lubricants used in machine maintenance, paper for the copying machine, and fuel for equipment.

Material handling includes systems for moving materials within the facility. It implies a physical component (equipment to perform the task) and an informational component (decisions about when and how much should be moved).

A **distribution system** is a system for material handling between suppliers and customers. It involves moving materials between facilities and has a physical and an informational component. Distribution systems link customers and suppliers in a chain in which basic materials like iron ore, crude oil, and lumber are transformed into consumer products like powerboats, toasters, and furniture.

To be successful at managing and controlling materials, management should understand how decisions made within the material management function affect other parts of the organization and vice versa. For example, when production planning decides to schedule a part for production, the materials must be procured, received, and handled before the act of producing the part begins. It is also important that these actions be done efficiently and effectively so that costs can be kept low and customers' due dates can be satisfied.

It is also important that an organization have an integrated view of the elements within material management. Are the policies and procedures used in purchasing consistent with those used in inventory control? Are the proper material-handling and -control devices available for the type and quantity of material ordered and for the way the material is packaged? These are basic questions that many readers believe would be effectively dealt with by all or at least most organizations. This is not the case, however, because many organizations do not have an integrated material management function. The manager of purchasing, the manager of inventory control, the manager of material handling, and the manager of the distribution system may all report to different supervisors. This makes the coordination of policies and procedures and the integration of decisions much more difficult. Successful organizations are devising innovative ways to integrate the elements of material management.

MATERIAL FLOW AND THE ORGANIZATION

In this section, we give an overview of material flow and also describe the information flows needed to direct and coordinate the physical flows. Throughout this section, we note the differences in approach between a traditional view of material management and newer ideas that center around just-in-time (JIT).

Physical Flows

In a traditional approach, material flow begins as products arrive from suppliers and move through a centralized receiving area. These materials are counted and quality-tested to verify supplier performance. In the JIT approach to material handling, materials flow directly to the work stations without spending time in a holding area. JIT puts the burden of counting and delivering quality parts on the supplier. Contracts with suppliers that fail to meet these tough standards are not renewed.

Once purchased and received from the supplier, the materials are either processed or stored as inventory. Material that is initially stored will later be retrieved for processing.

After materials have entered production, they are usually categorized as work-in-process, or WIP (pronounced "whip"), inventory. It is possible that before a product is complete, it could make several trips between WIP storage and production. Management should strive to make these trips as infrequent as possible because of the excessive material-handling costs that can be incurred and the possibility of damage. One objective of just-in-time is to reduce WIP inventory to only those batches that are presently being worked on and to eliminate extra handling, storage, and waste.

After final processing, the product can be shipped. Products produced to satisfy a future order or to fill a forecasted order that did not materialize are placed in finished-goods inventory. Warehousing and distribution systems should be developed to deliver these products to customers effectively and efficiently.

Exhibit 15.1 shows a schematic drawing of material flow for toy locomotives made by Lima Locomotive Works. The component parts consist primarily of wood, paint, and fasteners, and the processes include wood forming, painting, and assembly. The exhibit illustrates the possibility of material movement in the production system. The necessary material flows are shown in blue.

The flows shown in black in Exhibit 15.1 should be minimized because they add nothing to the value or quality of the product, only to the cost. With an advanced JIT system, the wood, paint, and fasteners would bypass the centralized receiving area and flow directly to the point on the production line where they are applied to the product.

Information Flows

Whether an organization produces services or goods, management needs to synchronize the physical flow of material with information flows. The physical flow must be managed so that products move efficiently from point to point within the facility. As a part of directing these flows, information from the production plan

Exhibit 15.1 Material Flow for Toy Locomotive

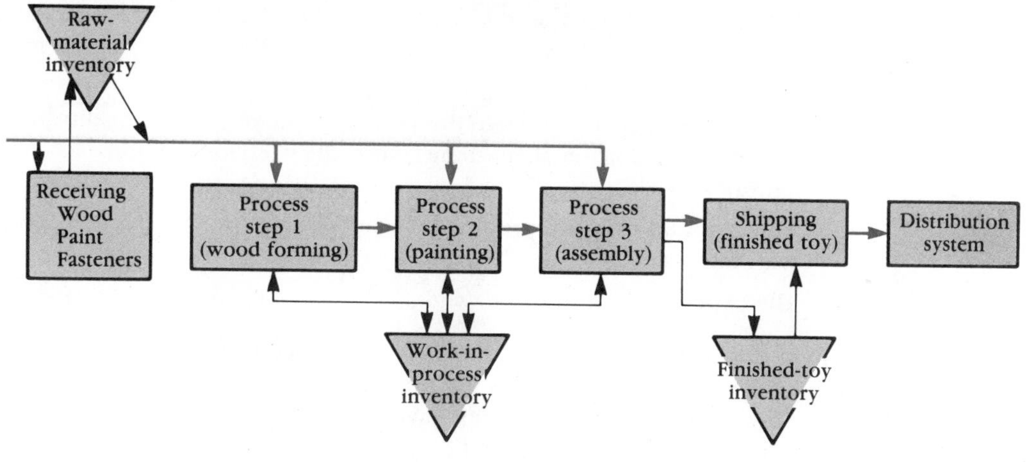

is transmitted to the material movers (people, robots, etc.). It is also necessary to track the material as it moves through the facility. Thus, reports (information) on material movement should be available.

Managing the physical flow illustrated in Exhibit 15.1 requires a flow of information from production planning to the production floor, as well as a flow of information from the production floor to production planning. The following information should be transferred from production planning to the production floor:

1. The products to be produced and the quantity of each
2. The required steps and the sequence of these steps to make the product
3. The materials required to make the product
4. The date when the products are needed for delivery to the customer

INTEGRATING THE SYSTEM

Facility Design and Material Flow

Chapter 8 discussed facility layout for the different process types, including continuous flow processes, assembly lines, and job shops. Layout decisions are based on the material movements required in the facility. Certain layouts make those movements easier and less costly.

An organization that can successfully implement JIT can substantially reduce the size of its facility because receiving, in-process inventory storage, and shipping areas can be reduced. The product can flow through the facility more quickly and with lower handling costs.

The following information should be transferred from the production floor back to production planning:

1. The status of all jobs presently being worked on. This should include customer identification, work completed, material consumed, needs for additional tooling, and so on.
2. The problems encountered to this point. This might include quality problems with purchased material, machine failure, the need for additional information, and so on.
3. A description of actual production. This description will then be compared with the plan.
4. The expected completion date.

These information flows play a critical role in successfully managing and controlling operations. We will discuss information flows in more detail in Chapter 19.

These information flows do not have to be computer based. For example, the JIT system described in Chapter 12 uses cards (kanbans) or other visual signals to transmit critical information within the organization.

PURCHASING

Purchasing is the activity of acquiring goods and services for an organization. We use the terms **customer** and **supplier** throughout this section of the text to refer to the buyer and the seller. Another word in common use is **vendor,** which is another term for supplier.

The costs of materials, which are purchased from other companies or are transferred between divisions of the same company, represent about 55 percent of the cost of the finished product. That figure is typical of manufacturing firms. Labor constitutes about 10 percent, with the remainder being overhead expenses. Because of the significant expense of purchased parts, purchasing is critical to an organization's success.

Example

For Air Projects Company, the cost of purchased materials is about 58 percent of each sales dollar. Labor represents about 12 percent and profit 7 percent. Sales last year totaled $127 million. Management has been instructed to cut production costs by 10 percent, but can reduce material and labor costs only. In which area is management most likely to find the savings desired? The firm's present cost structure and profit are shown below.

Description	As a Percentage of Sales	Millions of Dollars
Material costs	58	73.66
Labor costs	12	15.24
Other costs (including overhead)	23	29.21
Profit	7	8.89
Total	100	127.00

A 10 percent reduction in production costs would be .10(73.66 + 15.24) or $8.89 million. What if the savings are taken entirely from material costs?

Entire 10 Percent Taken from Material Costs

Description	As a Percentage of Sales	Millions of Dollars
Material costs	51	64.77
Labor costs	12	15.24
Other costs (including overhead)	23	29.21
Profit	14	17.78
Total	100	127.00

What if the savings are taken entirely from labor costs?

Entire 10 Percent Taken from Labor Costs

Description	As a Percentage of Sales	Millions of Dollars
Material costs	58	73.66
Labor costs	5	6.35
Other costs (including overhead)	23	29.21
Profit	14	17.78
Total	100	127.00

It is very unlikely that the full 10 percent savings could come from reductions in the direct-labor work force because labor represents a small part of the company's cost. In this case, labor costs would have to go from $15.24 million to $6.35 million, a drop of over 50 percent. Cost containment programs in purchasing can help Air Projects achieve its goal.

Purchasing has a major impact on an organization's ability to compete because it has a significant impact on the cost of a product. The rapid and on-time delivery of materials and services allows the production system to continue to run smoothly and to deliver products in a timely manner. To explain purchasing in more detail, we will examine the following areas of responsibility for a purchasing manager:

1. Defining specifications for the purchased good or service
2. Obtaining price quotations
3. Developing criteria for supplier selection
4. Classifying suppliers according to performance
5. Evaluating the make-or-buy decision
6. Awarding the contract
7. Expediting
8. Gathering information for follow-up and evaluation

Defining Specifications

Determining specifications begins with the design of the product. For goods, the physical dimensions of the part are set, along with the specifications that will allow the part to fit with other parts (tolerances). The strength and durability necessary to carry the load placed on the part are determined by the type of material specified and its size and shape. Performance levels the parts must meet are also set. For example, an electronic component must accept a specified voltage or offer a specified resistance in order to function properly.

Different factors are important in determining specifications for purchased services. A contract to provide computer software services would specify that the supplier meet the organization's standards for internally developed software. These could include standards for file and data base design, the programming languages used, and even the way certain programming statements are used.

While these functions begin in design, purchasing should carry through to acquire the services or goods that will do the job. What is the purchasing department's role in product design? Input from the purchasing department can be useful in the early stages of product design for the following purposes:

1. To determine the availability of certain parts and material.
2. To provide up-to-date cost data that can be used to project the cost of producing the product in-house. This information is necessary for carrying out financial analysis regarding the product's profit potential.
3. To judge whether the specifications can be met from the current list of suppliers. In some cases, designers may specify tolerances that cannot be met or that can be met only with a significant increase in purchase price. The purchaser may have firsthand knowledge about possible alternatives that will cost less.
4. To ensure that the specifications are consistent with accepted commercial standards, the drawings and tolerances are clearly understood and not sub-

OPERATIONS IN ACTION

Saint Francis College: Purchasing Janitorial Service

For many years Saint Francis College has used its own building and grounds department to provide janitorial service. The president of Saint Francis believes the college can save money by contracting for this service from local providers, of which there are many. Sister Thomas, who is responsible for purchasing, has developed the following procedure to address the problem:

1. Work with the buildings and grounds supervisor to determine the present scope and level of service.
2. Survey users of the existing service to determine if they are satisfied with the present service and how it might be improved.
3. Work with the buildings and ground supervisor to develop a new set of cleaning specifications for each area to be cleaned.
4. Obtain preliminary price quotations to determine if the service desired can be provided at a cost the college can afford.

Saint Francis College would proceed to supplier selection and the other purchasing activities following basically the same procedures as a manufacturer buying component parts for electric motor assembly.

ject to different interpretations, and the material satisfies the purposes intended.

Once the product is designed, it is the purchasing manager's responsibility to select material and sources that will be the most advantageous to the company. The purchasing manager may develop single or multiple sources for each required part.

In buying services, the process is very similar. The only major difference is that physical units are not exchanged between supplier and customer.

Obtaining Price Quotations

One of the most important areas in purchasing is controlling costs. The real cost of a purchased product is not the unit price, but is what purchasing agents call **lowest final cost,** which is the lowest total cost to the buying firm. Included in the total cost would be such things as the purchase price, shipping and receiving costs, costs to rework defective products, and costs for special processing that would not be necessary if another supplier were used. The lowest-final-cost objective relies on the system view of the firm. Following are a few examples of the factors that influence the final cost:

1. Low-cost parts that are out of tolerance may be difficult to fit and require more time in processing. This could delay production and increase labor costs.
2. Parts that are designed for easy assembly will increase productivity, will decrease labor costs, and may lead to better quality in the finished product. Paying more for that part can easily be justified.
3. Substandard material or performance of a service may lead to excessive scrap and rework.

There are four primary methods of determining the purchase price of materials: price lists, competitive bidding, two-step bidding, and negotiation.

Published Price Lists and Market Data

Price lists are often imposed by suppliers and are generally found with standard products such as transportation services, gasoline, and sheet metal screws. Information found in price lists should not be viewed as fixed, however, because an organization may have enough influence in the marketplace to negotiate a better deal. Also, discounts on the published prices are often given if customers order more than a specified quantity. Purchasers should keep in mind that market demand for a product may be soft and lower prices may lie ahead.

Competitive Bidding

Although competitive bidding can be used for standard products, it is essential for specialized products where price lists are not available. The obvious purpose of a competitive bid is to provide competition among suppliers. This process is initiated by sending suppliers a **request for quotation.** The request should include all the information needed to prepare a quotation, including detailed specifications, plans, and drawings. Once again, great care should be used to ensure that the specifications are not subject to different interpretations. If they are, then bids may not be comparable because different assumptions have been made.

Two-Step Bidding

Two-step bidding is a blend of competitive bidding and negotiation. It is useful when the supplier is not fully knowledgeable about the design and building of the final product. The first step involves obtaining initial bids from suppliers along with preliminary designs and plans for further development of the product. In the second step, the supplier presenting the best technical design and an acceptable price is approached to establish a final detailed design and a negotiated price.

Negotiations

Negotiations are usually carried out with only one supplier because of the large amount of time and expense required to prepare for and conduct them. A negotiated price is usually applied to specialized products, and the negotiated price is valid only for the job being considered.

Developing Criteria for Supplier Selection

An organization should meet certain standards before it can be considered as a supplier. A major factor in judging a supplier is whether the supplier has a well-developed quality control program. Such a quality control program assures the customer that consistent, high-quality products will be delivered.

Suppliers also need to make timely delivery of services and goods. The difference between the time the order is placed and the time the product is delivered is called **lead time.** A delivery is timely if the lead time is short and the order is delivered when promised. Late deliveries should not be tolerated, whether an organization is using JIT, MRP, or some form of lot sizing to control inventory. Furthermore, early deliveries should be accepted only when there is some compelling reason for doing so. Extra inventory causes storage problems and incurs storage costs.

Suppliers should be willing to work with customers to meet their needs. Cooperation and assistance in problem solving are the mark of a successful supplier. In summary, the major criteria for judging suppliers are

1. Quality goods and services,
2. Timely deliveries,
3. Cooperation and assistance in meeting customer needs, and
4. Price.

Many organizations design formal programs to certify suppliers. With **supplier certification,** a supplier must be able to meet specific criteria. In many cases, a supplier has to receive certification before it can ship the first part. This often involves visits to the plants by the certifying organization to ensure that all of the criteria have been met. Suppliers that achieve certification are also subject to continuing review and evaluation, as described in the following section on supplier performance.

Certification programs can be established under a variety of circumstances. They most certainly apply to situations where a supplier is the sole source for the part. Under these circumstances, which are becoming more common with JIT systems, no other suppliers provide a portion of the demand. Here, a close and cooperative working relationship needs to exist between the customer and its sole supplier for that part.

Classifying Suppliers According to Performance

Whether an organization has a certification program or not, a supplier's performance should be monitored so that a performance review can be held with the supplier. Such a review, which may be carried out annually, should be supplemented by notification to a supplier every time there is a violation of the criteria. This does not mean that a supplier should be suspended from the certified list for a single violation. But it does mean that a supplier should be informed of mistakes so that corrective action can be taken. There is a further reason for informing suppliers about mistakes. If a supplier sends out defective products or misses a delivery date and does not hear from the customer, the supplier will get the mistaken impression that these items are not important.

Evaluating the Make-or-Buy Decision

At some point in the process of acquiring resources, management must decide if the organization should make the good or service or if the organization should buy it from suppliers. Whether a service or good is provided inside the organization or is purchased from suppliers, management must ask the following questions:

1. Who has the technical capabilities to provide the good or service?
2. Can they deliver a quality product?
3. Can they make timely deliveries?
4. What costs are associated with each alternative?

Management should consider internal sources for services or goods with the same thorough analysis used to evaluate an external source. Internal sources should perform at the same high level expected from other suppliers.

Cost Analysis

Analysis of the make-or-buy decision requires that some assumptions be made about the organization's present capabilities. Initially, assume the following:

1. The organization has the technical capabilities to produce the service or good.
2. The organization can produce a high-quality service or good and deliver it in a timely manner.
3. The organization will have to purchase the equipment and hire and train the people to provide this new product.

In the following discussion, we will use the example of Johns Manufacturing Company to clarify the cost analysis procedure. We will relax each of the assumptions above to examine its impact on the make-or-buy decision.

Example

The purchasing agent for Johns Manufacturing Company, which produces computer modems, is trying to determine whether the company should buy or make the metal case that holds the electronic components. If Johns buys the case, no further processing would be required until assembly. If Johns makes it, the company would have to buy a small press to bend the metal, small machine tools to drill and grind the stamped part, and some painting equipment. Johns has gathered the following cost estimates for making the case:

Description	Variable Costs per Unit
Sheet metal	$ .22
Paint	.10
Press labor	.28
Machinist labor	.30
Paint labor	.24
Indirect labor	.66
	$1.80

Annual fixed costs: $15,000

The sheet metal and paint costs were obtained by contacting suppliers and are based on the grades of steel and paint requested and the quantity purchased. The press, machinist, and paint labor estimates are based on job design and work-measurement studies, which are discussed in Chapter 9. These studies give managers a standard time per piece, which can be multiplied by the pay rate from the labor contract to give a unit cost. Indirect labor includes costs for material handlers, supervisors, and maintenance personnel who are not directly associated with production. The figure for annual fixed costs is an accounting estimate of the annual cost of the equipment, including a share of the purchase price. For this example, assume that the equipment costs $75,000 and has a five-year life.

Johns has also sought estimates for buying the case and has received a price quotation from a supplier of $4.27 per metal case delivered to the plant. How can Johns evaluate the trade-offs between making and buying the case? The company will use one year as the initial time frame for evaluation. In the equations below, X represents the number of cases required per year.

$$\text{Cost to buy per year} = (\text{purchase price})X \tag{15.1}$$

$$\text{Cost to make per year} = (\text{variable costs/unit})X + \text{annual fixed costs} \tag{15.2}$$

$$\text{Cost to buy per year} = (\$4.27/\text{unit})X$$

$$\text{Cost to make per year} = (\$1.80/\text{unit})X + \$15{,}000$$

Next, Johns set the cost to make equal to the cost to buy in order to find the number of units (X) for which the two costs will be equal.

$$\text{Cost to buy} = \text{cost to make}$$

$$4.27X = 1.80X + 15{,}000$$

$$2.47X = 15{,}000$$

$$X = 6{,}073 \text{ units/year}$$

The value of X in this mathematical model tells Johns the point where the cost to buy and the cost to make are equal. For values of X less than 6,073, the cost of buying is lower. For values of X greater than 6,073, the cost of making is lower.

If the logic of this conclusion is not clear to you, consider the case where only a single unit is required. According to equation 15.1, the cost to buy a single unit would be \$4.27. According to equation 15.2, the cost to make a single unit each year would be \$15,001.80. (Actually, the cost to make the first unit is \$75,001.80, based on cash flow, because the money for the equipment is spent before the first unit is produced.) Clearly, buying is preferred if only one unit is required.

As demand increases from one to two units, the cost of buying increases by \$4.27, but the cost of making increases only \$1.80. As the number of units increases, the cost of buying will eventually be equal to and then greater than the cost of making. This can be visualized in Exhibit 15.2 by following the two cost functions to the point of intersection and beyond. Johns is earning the difference between \$4.27 and \$1.80 (\$2.47) for each unit it makes rather than buys after the first unit.

Treating the Make-or-Buy Decision as an Investment Decision

It is a mistake to think that the model tells managers what to do in this situation. In this case, the model implies that the organization should buy if it needs less than 6,073 units per year for five years and should make if it needs more than 6,073. If Johns follows that logic, it could make a very serious error. To understand this potential error, work through the following example.

Exhibit 15.2 Make and Buy Costs for Johns Manufacturing Company

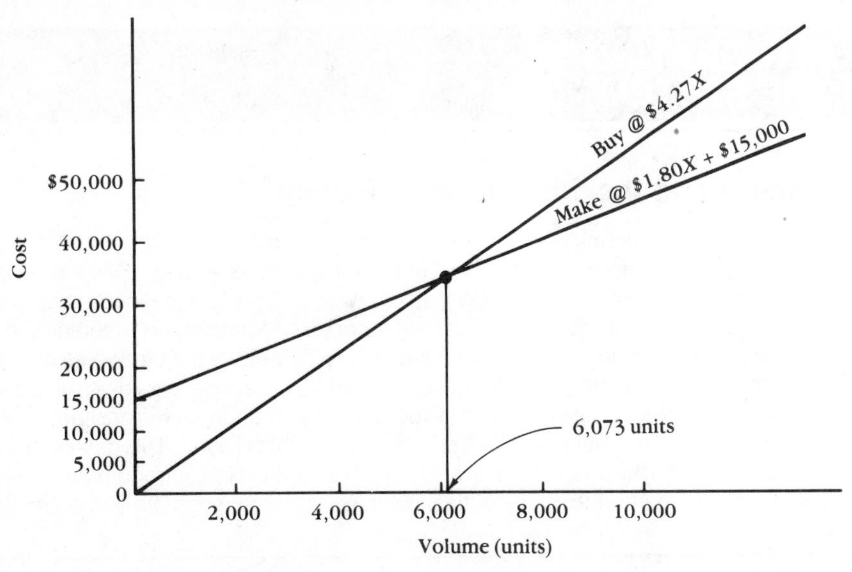

Example

Assume that Johns projects a demand for 6,074 parts per year. The model shows that it costs less to make the part for this amount of demand. The difference between making and buying the part for a volume of 6,074 units can be calculated as follows:

Cost to make	= $1.80(6,074) + $15,000	= $25,933.20/year
Cost to buy	= $4.27(6,074)	= $25,935.98/year
Difference		$2.78/year

The savings is $2.78 because the break-even point is rounded from 6,072.8745 to 6,073 units/year. If the savings is calculated for 6,075 units, the savings will increase by $2.47 to $5.25/year. We leave the verification of this calculation to you.

The more important question is whether Johns Manufacturing should make the part if the demand for the product is 6,074 units per year. Let's continue the assumption that Johns has the technical expertise to deliver a high-quality product in a timely manner. To find the answer, look at the cash outlays for the part. If the part is purchased, Johns would expend ($4.27/unit)(6,074 units) = $25,935.98 over the year. If demand for the product is uniform over the year, then the company's outlays can also be uniform. Assume that Johns orders once each month. The cash outflow would be $25,935.98/12, or $2,161.33 in each month.

If Johns decides to make the part, it must pay out a large amount of cash ($75,000) to buy equipment for production. The annual fixed cost represents that cost spread over several years. But in terms of cash flow, the $75,000 goes out before the first part is made. Even though the total cash flow over a five-year period will be approximately the same for buying and making (different by $2.78 per year, or $13.90 over five years), the timing of those flows is significantly different, as shown in Exhibit 15.3.

INTEGRATING THE SYSTEM

Finance and the Time Value of Money

A fair question for Johns management to ask is, How large should the return be to justify the difference in cash flows? This question leads to two important sets of other questions. First, as an organization, what return would Johns like to receive on invested capital? What return is required to keep stockholders satisfied and to recapture the principal and maintain payment on the organization's debt? The answers to this first set of questions require in-depth study of financial principles that should be the primary subject of another course. Second, once these broad guidelines are defined, what models can be used to reconcile the difference in cash flows? The concept of the time value of money and the technique of present valuing of future cash flows provide managers with insights that help them make these decisions. The details of these models are given in most introductory finance textbooks. Tax effects should also be considered.

Exhibit 15.3 Cash Flows for Johns Manufacturing

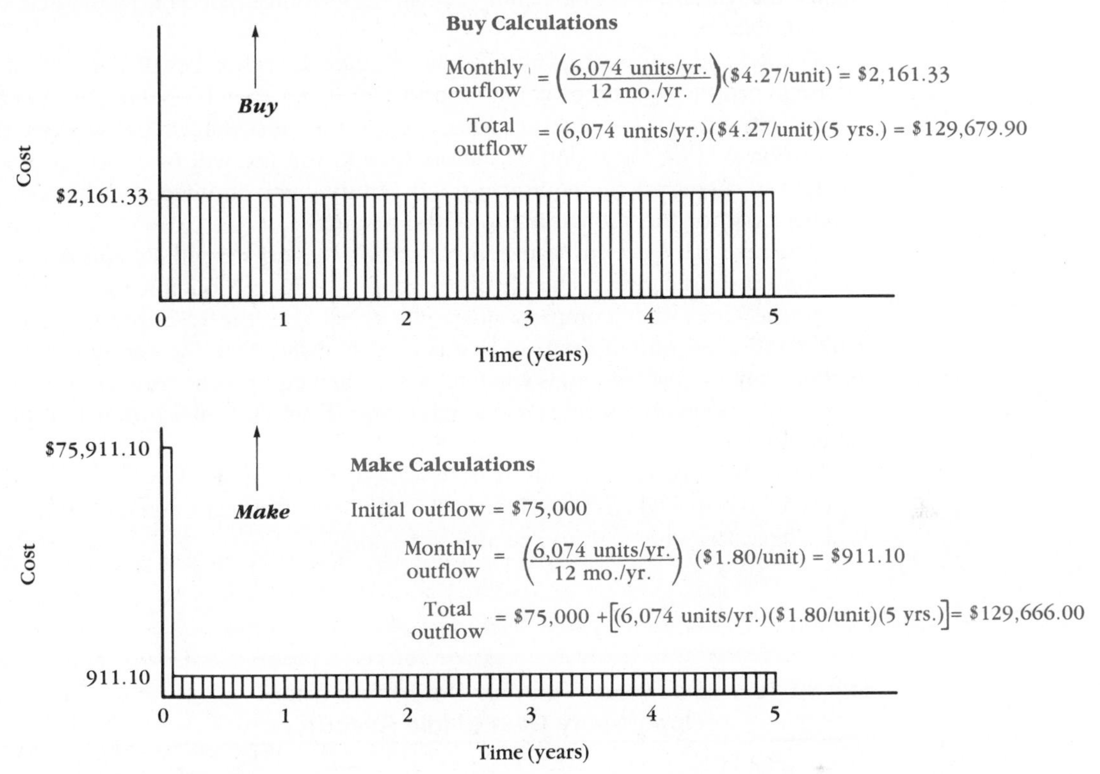

Johns should anticipate a significant return if it makes an initial outlay of $75,000. An annual return of $2.78 on a $75,000 investment is not large enough to justify the investment in making the part.

Assume That Johns Manufacturing Has Idle Capacity

What happens to the analysis if Johns has idle capacity? Let's assume that Johns has existing floor space for which it has no future plans. Also, all of the equipment required to start processing is available in-house. In this case, the company would not have to make an initial investment of $75,000 for equipment. Let's assume that the equipment Johns will use to make the part is utilized 50 percent of the time. Further, assume that processing the parts for the modem will increase the equipment utilization to only 60 percent.

Because all the equipment and the floor space are available, is it fair to assume that the investment (initial outlay) is zero? To determine whether this is so, Johns must first ask if there are alternative uses for the floor space and the equipment. If the answer is yes, then there is an opportunity cost for using those resources. The cost of these resources is the value the resources have if applied to an alternate use. For example, could the stamping machine be used to subcontract work from an office equipment manufacturer? If the answer is no, there is a chance that the resources may not have an opportunity cost. Follow the decision chain in Exhibit 15.4.

The next question Johns must ask is whether the resources that are intended for use in production can be sold. If the answer is yes, then the selling price is the opportunity cost. If the answer is no, then Johns must determine whether this application will be for a long or a short time. If the use will be short-term, it is possible to disregard the equipment and facility costs because no other opportunities exist for the profitable use of the resource.

If the use is long-term, management should be very careful. First, it is hard to imagine a resource for which only one organization has a profitable long-term use. As soon as one other company determines that use, the resource will have a market value. Second, if the resource is used without charging enough to cover its replacement cost (which is what happens when equipment costs are ignored), the organization will not receive enough money from customer orders to replace the equipment.

Once the investment value is determined, it can be used in calculating the annual fixed costs, which are substituted into the cost-to-make equation, equation 15.2. Thereafter, the analysis remains the same.

Exhibit 15.4 Decision Chain for Determining the Opportunity Cost of Idle Resources

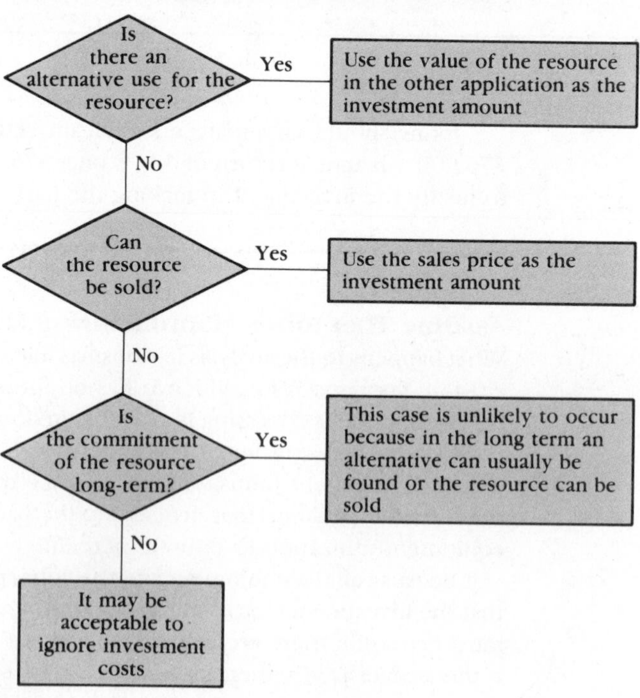

Technology, Quality, and Timely Delivery

Any make-or-buy decision should take into account factors other than the economic factors discussed above. Does the organization possess the technical expertise to produce the good or service? Johns may possess great technical expertise in the electronics of modem design, but can it stamp metal as well as a company that does so full time? Acquiring expertise costs money, and those costs should be included as part of the investment.

Quality products and timely deliveries can work for or against a supplier. In some cases, outside suppliers have better quality and more reliable deliveries. In other cases, inside suppliers are superior. Such qualitative factors need to be integrated with the economic analysis when deciding whether to make or to buy. How much lower does the cost of a supplier have to be before an organization will accept a poor delivery performance? Some people would argue that meeting delivery is a minimum requirement for the job. These decisions require judgment and careful analysis.

Considering a Volume Discount

Many times suppliers are willing to give discounts if customers agree to purchase a minimum number of units over the life of the contract. The discount may or may not be linked to a minimum order size.

Example

Suppose that one of Johns Manufacturing's suppliers has proposed a discount if the firm will agree to purchase 10,000 or more units each year. The make-or-buy data in this situation are listed below.

To Make

Description	Variable Costs per Unit
Sheet metal	\$.22
Paint	.10
Press labor	.28
Machinist labor	.30
Paint labor	.24
Indirect labor	.66
	\$1.80

Annual fixed costs: \$15,000

To Buy

Amount	Unit Cost
Less than 10,000 each year	\$4.27
10,000 or more each year	\$3.00

How does this situation change the model? A graph of the make alternative and the two purchase alternatives will provide the needed insight (see Exhibit 15.5). For the make alternative and the initial purchase alternative of \$4.27 per unit, the cost of making and the cost of buying are equal at 6,073 units. The new purchase option is graphed as a broken line until it reaches 10,000 units, signifying that the option does not become effective until Johns commits to buy 10,000 or more units each year.

Exhibit 15.5 Make and Buy Cost for Johns Manufacturing with Price Discount

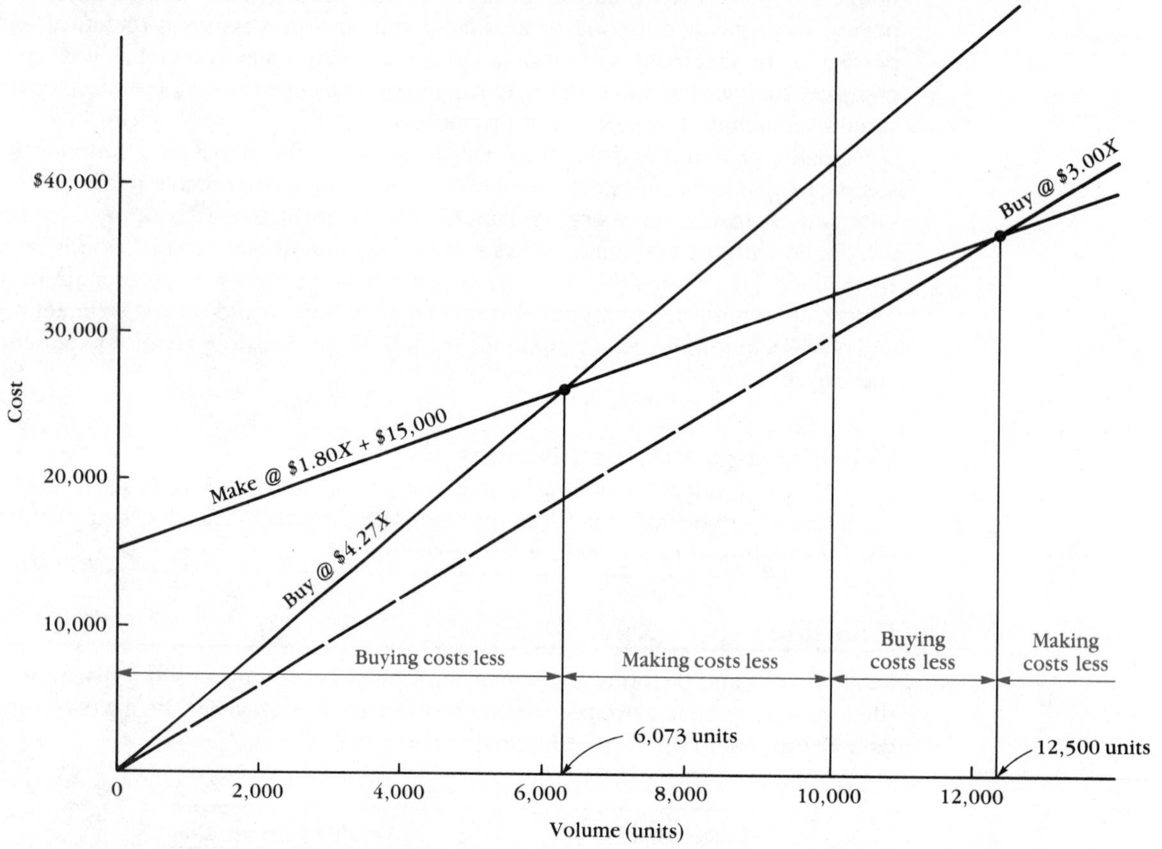

$40,000
30,000
Cost
20,000
10,000
Make @ $1.80X + $15,000
Buy @ $4.27X
Buy @ $3.00X
Buying costs less
Making costs less
Buying costs less
Making costs less
6,073 units
12,500 units
0 2,000 4,000 6,000 8,000 10,000 12,000
Volume (units)

With the discount, it appears that the cost of making is lower from 6,073 units until you reach 10,000 units per year. After 10,000 units, it costs less to take advantage of the discount and buy up to 12,500 units per year. After 12,500 units, it costs less to make than to buy:

$$\$3.00X = \$1.80X + 15{,}000$$

$$1.20X = 15{,}000$$

$$X = 12{,}500 \text{ units/year}$$

Exhibit 15.5 indicates the points where making costs less and where buying costs less. But management must still consider availability of capital for the investment, differences in cash flows, technical expertise, product quality, and timely delivery.

The model has one error as presently formulated: it indicates that the cost of making 9,999 units is lower than the cost of buying. But with one approach, it would cost less to buy at that volume, with no changes in the model's costs or assumptions. (Hint: Think about ordering 10,000 units even though only 9,999 units are needed.)

When would this tactic cease to be effective? This tactic would be effective as long as the cost to purchase 10,000 units per year at \$3.00 per unit is less than or equal to the cost of making X units at \$1.80 per unit plus \$15,000 in annual fixed costs. The cost to purchase 10,000 units equals the cost to make when demand is 8333.33 units. So management could order and pay for 10,000 units and take delivery of only 8,334 units and have a lower total cost than if the company makes 8,334 units per year. We leave the calculations to you.

Awarding the Contract

One difficult aspect of the purchasing function is deciding which supplier should receive the contract. Making this decision requires consideration of all the factors related to performance. It requires managers to compare suppliers with low price and slow delivery with suppliers with higher prices and better delivery records. Two cautions should be mentioned:

1. Quality has become a critical factor in determining an organization's success. Many organizations do not accept inferior quality regardless of the price offered.
2. Do not be satisfied with poor performance, whether the supplier is internal or external. Other suppliers may offer better performance. An organization and its suppliers should strive for continued improvement.

Expediting

Expediting is the monitoring of supplier deliveries of materials that in some way have become critical for the customer. For example, production schedulers may have forgotten to order floppy disk drives, and now they are needed quickly. Inventory records may overstate the number of threaded fasteners (nuts) available. The supplier may not have met the delivery date for some reason. Expediters phone suppliers to talk about the importance of an order. They plead with and threaten suppliers to get their order moved up in line for fast delivery.

Expediting is usually caused by a failure of the organization or its suppliers. Efforts should be made to solve the problem by eliminating the source of the problem, rather than by relying on expediting. Eliminating the source of the problem involves better supplier selection and improved control of purchasing functions. A well-run purchasing operation should strive to eliminate expediting by making suppliers responsive to the organization's needs.

Gathering Information for Follow-Up and Evaluation

As part of an organization's supplier certification program, the purchasing department should collect and maintain information about each supplier. This information should be used to evaluate performance and to determine the future acceptability of all suppliers. In addition, both positive and negative information should be given as feedback to all suppliers. Suppliers who are doing a good job should be positively reinforced. Suppliers who are not performing well may not fully understand the importance of their performance to the customer's organization.

These poorly performing suppliers may not even be aware of the extent of their shortcomings. Clear and immediate feedback may help them improve.

Just-in-Time Purchasing Versus Traditional Purchasing

JIT purchasing concepts have received an increasing amount of attention from academic researchers and practicing managers, and it is becoming an important element in an overall JIT program. JIT purchasing is effective at helping companies control their inventory system, reduce inventory buffers, reduce space needs, reduce material handling, and reduce waste. JIT purchasing differs from traditional purchasing practices in the following ways:

Activity	Traditional Purchasing	JIT Purchasing
Supplier selection	Single criterion, usually price via competitive bidding; in most cases, a 2 or 3 percent reject rate is acceptable	Multiple criteria, including price, delivery, and service with high quality; a low (near zero) percentage reject rate is essential
Supplier characteristics	Multiple sources of supply for most parts; distance from customer not important	Single sources of supply for most parts; shorter distance between customer and supplier
Supplier/customer relationships	Adversarial relationship	Partnership, with both groups working toward common objectives
Product specifications	"Tight" specifications, which inhibit the supplier from suggesting changes that may improve overall product performance; the buyer relies more on the design specifications than on product performance	"Loose" specifications, which allow the supplier latitude in designing the product and encourage innovation
Purchase lot size	Purchases are made in large batch sizes with less frequent delivery	Purchases are made in small lots with frequent delivery
Receiving inspection	Buyers are responsible for receiving, counting, and inspecting all incoming parts	Counting and inspection by the customer are eliminated; the supplier is responsible
Negotiation and bidding	Primary objective is to achieve the lowest possible price	Objectives are to achieve high product quality through long-term contracts and a fair price
Determining mode of transportation	Concern for outbound freight and lower outbound costs	Concern for inbound and outbound freight, as well as on-time delivery

JIT purchasing practices require customers and suppliers to rethink many activities related to purchasing. If customers purchase and take delivery of small quantities of parts, how can transportation be managed so costs are not excessive? If a customer demands daily rather than weekly shipments, can the supplier continue with the same paperwork system, or will the mountain of paperwork bury them? If customers and suppliers are to work together, how will their relationships be affected?

Managing Transportation with JIT

Prior to the implementation of JIT, the size of the shipment was normally governed by the amount of material that would fit into a railroad car or a trailer on a tractor-trailer. Shipping less than truck load (LTL) or less than car load was usually avoided because it costs significantly more per 100 pounds shipped than a full truck or car load. With frequent shipment in a JIT system, the shipment size is often less than a full truck or car load.

To respond, some shipments that traveled by rail are now moving by truck because a truck is smaller than a rail car (usually less than half the size). Also, trucking is more flexible and usually more reliable than rail deliveries. In other cases, shipments are being combined. If a supplier makes several different parts for the same customer, it may be possible to combine smaller quantities of different parts in one shipment, instead of shipping each part separately in larger batches. In this way, smaller quantities of each part can still be shipped economically.

This same idea can also apply to suppliers who ship only a few parts. For example, several different suppliers located in the same geographical area can all ship small quantities to one central warehouse. These shipments can then be combined for final shipment to the customer.

Another similar idea is to have the trucks from a supplier follow a daily route that takes them to several different factories, unloading a small shipment at each. This approach usually works best for different plants of the same customer, although the idea may also be applied to different customers' plants.

Managing Paperwork with JIT

Shipping in small quantities could create a paperwork nightmare if each shipment had to use the same paper trail as is commonly used for larger shipments. To get around this problem, companies using JIT usually develop a long-term contract with suppliers that calls for shipments amounting to a certain total over a given time period. The bulk of the paperwork is associated with this blanket purchase order, and only a system of checks and balances is used to keep track of actual shipments. Often daily releases are transmitted electronically.

Fewer Suppliers, Better Relationships

The traditional approach to purchasing has been to buy parts and materials from many suppliers. This allowed a company to play its suppliers off against each other in efforts to get the lowest price and best delivery terms. However, the result has often been an adversarial relationship between suppliers and customers that was not conducive to the JIT philosophy of improvement.

Instead, companies using JIT tend to have fewer suppliers, but view each of them as a copartner in the production process. By having fewer suppliers, a company concentrates on developing lasting relationships and long-term agreements, instead of short-term price advantages. The suppliers are assured of getting more business from that particular customer, and they increase their chance of attaining a long-term contract.

Tiering of the Supplier Base

In some industries, such as the automotive and appliance industries, the organization doing the final assembly is attempting to reduce the number of suppliers with which it will deal directly. These select few represent the first tier of the supplier base for the organization that does the final assembly. This group interacts closely with its customer. It is also responsible for coordinating the second tier of suppliers that provide the first tier with components that ultimately find their way to the assembly line. In the past, many of these second-tier suppliers dealt directly with the organization doing the final assembly.

Helping Suppliers Improve Quality

The copartner relationship between supplier and customer leads the customer to help its suppliers improve their quality. It is not unusual for a company using JIT to conduct training sessions for its suppliers on methods of quality control. This philosophy is often extended to include frequent visits by representatives of the customer to inspect its vendor's facilities. These visits include close inspection of quality-control procedures, inspection records, and testing devices. At the conclusion of each visit, the customer's representatives usually make suggestions for improvement of the vendor's operations.

Ford Motor Company has instituted an award for its suppliers who pass a set of stringent quality criteria. This award, the Q1 award, is nationally recognized as an indication of a company's exceptional quality record and its continuing commitment to quality. Ford regularly takes out a full-page ad in the *Wall Street Journal* to list those suppliers who have received its Q1 award. Such recognition helps the suppliers in the marketplace and also helps guarantee Ford a continued stream of high-quality parts.

Ethical Issues in Purchasing

Purchasing agents are often very important individuals within the organization. Not only do they control the acquisition of materials, which account for more than 50 percent of the costs of a typical manufactured good, but also they have much information about the cost of competitors' products and bids. It is unethical for a purchasing agent to decide to purchase services or goods from one supplier that does not fully meet the criteria when another supplier does. This decision is not in the best interest of the company that pays his or her salary. If this behavior is motivated by payoffs from the supplier that receives the preferential treatment, the actions of the purchasing agent may be illegal, as well as unethical.

In addition, a purchasing agent may possess "insider" information about the cost structure of a supplier or a specific bid a supplier has made. Passing along this "insider" information to a competitor of the supplier could provide that competitor with an unfair advantage. These actions would also be considered unethical and, if done in exchange for money, could be illegal.

INTERNATIONAL SOURCING OF MATERIALS

International sourcing of materials can be accomplished by buying services and goods from suppliers from another country or by deciding to produce services or goods in one country for use in another. Clearly, the purchasing decision is subject to most of the considerations discussed earlier in this chapter, whether the supplier is in the home country or in another country. In addition to those factors, a new set of variables is introduced when services and goods are purchased from another country. These could include the following:

- **Absolute quotas** limit the entry of a service or good into a country for a period of time.
- **Tariffs** are extra charges placed on goods or services that are imported into the home country. Special tariffs may be levied if trade agreements are violated.
- **Tariff rate quotas** are tariffs that increase with the volume that is imported.
- **Trade embargoes** may eliminate trade between two countries for a period of time. Trade could be eliminated entirely or in a specific product or product line.
- **Voluntary import quotas** are agreements between governments that limit the import of services and goods.

Manufacturing products in a foreign country for import to the home country can lead to an additional set of variables. If an organization is attracted to a country by its low hourly wage rate, it should consider carefully the other labor costs. In some countries, the cost of legally imposed fringe benefits may be significantly higher than those to which the organization is accustomed. Also, the true cost of labor should include training and the impact on training costs if the turnover rate is high. Assuming that the productivity of the work force in the foreign country is equal to the productivity of the work force in the home country can be a mistake. Labor laws in some countries may make it difficult to fire ineffective workers or to lay off workers.

Materials purchased in the country may not be of consistently high quality; energy availability and quality may also be a problem. Many things that can be done easily in the home country may be difficult to do in the other country, and the reverse could certainly be true. Sourcing materials from other countries should be considered carefully.

INVENTORY CONTROL

Inventory control is the effort to maintain inventory levels and costs within acceptable limits. It includes models that determine how much inventory to order and when to order it as well as systems for monitoring inventory levels for management evaluation and decision making. Chapter 16 will discuss inventory control in depth.

What Is Inventory?

Inventory is an alternative to future production or procurement. This is true for raw-material, work-in-process, finished-goods, and supply inventories. In a wholesale or retail business or in a production facility, inventory is recognizable as boxes of parts or as racks of clothes. Material becomes inventory after it is purchased and delivered to the facility and placed in a storage or holding area. Because materials represent such a large part of the finished product's cost (55 percent is the average in manufacturing firms), an organization's investment in inventory can become excessive unless properly controlled. If an organization's investment in inventory is large, it should receive substantial benefits for holding it.

Why Maintain Inventory?

Why do people store food at home? Supermarkets have adequate storage, and people could go to the store every time they are hungry. But people can avoid the expense and time loss of too many trips to the supermarket by storing food in refrigerators. People are willing to purchase and operate refrigerators (the costs) in order to avoid excessive procurement costs (the benefits). Also, when a food item has an especially low price, consumers may stock up to cut costs.

The costs of holding a stock of food at home include the initial cost of the refrigerator, the operating costs (electricity) of the refrigerator, and the interest costs on capital tied up in the food stored in the refrigerator. If you purchased a side of beef for $300.00, for example, you could not place the money in a bank account and earn a return. The interest that you could have earned by investing the money is the opportunity cost of capital.

We can draw several general conclusions from this example:

1. There is a cost associated with procuring inventory. In the refrigerator example, the cost is the time and expense of going to the store each time you want something to eat.
2. There is a cost associated with holding inventory. The cost of electricity for the refrigerator and the opportunity cost of capital are two examples.
3. These costs work in opposite directions. Smaller inventories mean more frequent trips and greater procurement costs. Larger inventories mean fewer trips and larger holding costs.
4. Part of any inventory control procedure is to find the right balance between procurement and holding cost.
5. Focusing on the trade-off in point four should not shift management's attention away from finding ways of cutting procurement costs (finding ways to reduce the cost of each trip to the store) or cutting inventory holding costs (finding ways to reduce electricity consumption).

More details regarding the costs and benefits of holding inventory will be described in Chapter 16.

Because the costs of holding inventory are significant, organizations should do so only when there are significant advantages. Inventory allows an organization to

1. Separate production of a good from consumption.
2. Smooth work flows within the production system.
3. Take advantage of an unusually low price for a product.
4. Stock up in anticipation of a cutoff in supply.

Separating Production from Demand

Finished-goods inventory is used to buffer the demand for products from the operations that produce them. The amount of finished-goods inventory required to fill that need varies widely. In a project, where the product is unique and built to meet a specific need, there should be no finished-goods inventory. In a job shop, where most jobs will be different and limited repetition of orders may occur, there may be only small amounts of finished-goods inventory.

In batch operations and line-flow processes, the need for finished-goods inventory becomes greater. Typically, in these types of operations, customers choose from a list of models and features. Customization can occur, but is often held within well-defined limits. For example, the cabinet color and the features on a new dishwasher must be selected from a predetermined list.

Advantages of holding some finished-goods inventory for both customers and suppliers are listed below.

1. Some finished-goods inventory is required in the link between customer and supplier to smooth the transition. For example, Libbey-Owens-Ford (LOF) supplies glass to auto makers. Even if operated on a just-in-time basis, there will be some finished glass in transit. A small amount of finished glass, one or two days, may be kept at the auto maker's plant and at LOF's plant. The cost of transportation dictates a shipment quantity greater than one windshield. The amount of inventory actually needed is presently a hot topic for debate. The answer lies in a careful analysis of the trade-offs between the costs of ordering, including transportation costs, and the costs of holding inventory.
2. Some finished-goods inventory is kept to smooth the unevenness of demand. Sears is more likely to sell refrigerators in the evening and on weekends. However, most of its refrigerators are made on first shift (typically 7:00 A.M. to 3:00 P.M.) Monday–Friday. To cope with this timing difference, Sears keeps an inventory of refrigerators to insulate production from customer demand. Car batteries are another good example. The demand for replacement car batteries is highly seasonal, and Sears and its battery suppliers should be prepared to deal with this uneven demand.
3. Some finished-goods inventory is needed to deal with the uncertainty in demand. Consider car batteries once more. Sears sells more batteries in the winter than in the spring. But the big sales splurge begins as temperatures drop below freezing and really takes off when temperatures hover around zero degrees Fahrenheit. When will this occur? It is difficult to predict the weather, so Sears increases its inventory of batteries in the northern states as autumn turns to winter.

In summary, every effort should be made to keep finished-goods inventory as low as possible. But in some cases, it may not be possible to eliminate it.

Smoothing the Flow of Product Through the Facility

The primary purpose for holding raw-material and work-in-process inventory is to maintain a smooth work flow through the production facility. Imagine an assembly-line or a continuous flow process without WIP inventory. These processes have been developed to improve efficiency by having products at various stages of completion. Raw material is a buffer between the customer and the supplier in the production chain. In fact, the windshield that is finished goods to Libbey-Owens-Ford is raw material (purchased parts) to the auto maker.

With JIT, smaller production lot sizes are recommended to minimize WIP inventory. Even if an organization can achieve the goal of a production lot size of one, it will still have some WIP inventory.

Speculation

An organization may stock more raw-material inventory than normal because it anticipates that stocks may be unavailable in the future. This is a regular occurrence when a strike is anticipated. Most electric utility companies that burn coal will buy extra when the United Mine Workers contract is about to expire. Electric utilities cannot afford to be without coal, so they may stock a three-month supply, or more, before a strike. An organization may also buy extra quantities when prices are temporarily depressed or when prices are expected to increase.

Inventory in Service Operations

Because a service is not tangible, service industries cannot maintain finished-goods inventory. The problems that service industries face because they cannot have finished-goods inventory can be understood by reviewing the reasons that producers of goods keep inventory. A service operation cannot separate the pattern of demand from production. If everyone wants to do his or her banking on Friday afternoon, the bank must provide the service at that time or face the possibility of losing customers. The bank cannot store transactions ahead of time. Service operations have two options: beefing up capacity to manage the peak loads, or trying to shift customer demand to nonpeak times by offering incentives.

Service operations can inventory the resources that provide the service. Extra people and facilities—that is, capacity—can be maintained to deal with unexpected increases in demand. In this way, service industries trade off the costs of extra capacity against the costs of a dissatisfied customer. Resource inventory is the service industry's option.

By offering reduced prices and other incentives, service operations can attempt to shift demand from peak to nonpeak periods. Many local transit authorities offer reduced rates to travelers during off-peak times. Phone companies offer discounts for long-distance calls after normal business hours and on the weekends. The logic behind these decisions is that the organization will incur most of the costs whether or not there is an additional rider or an additional caller. The bus is operated, and the driver is paid whether the bus is full or empty. Because most of the costs are incurred anyway, the revenue generated is almost entirely profit.

Managers of service operations need to determine whether it is better for their organizations to inventory resources or to offer incentives to deal with demand at peak periods. For many organizations, a combination of these approaches may be most effective.

In spite of the lack of finished-goods inventory, most services have significant inventory and inventory-related problems. First, many services are hybrids that sell goods in addition to a service. Retail stores, restaurants, and repair shops all sell goods, as well as services. The inventory they are required to maintain can be as significant to them as the inventory required for manufacturing.

In a service operation like a hospital or bank, the primary product is a "pure" service. But these organizations still require inventory in the form of supplies. Supplies are materials that are consumed in the process of production, but are not sold directly to the customer. Supplies needed by hospitals include bed linens and gowns. Supplies needed by banks include paper, pencils, and forms.

The Role of Computers in Inventory Control

Computers play an important role in monitoring and controlling inventory. In MRP II, computers project material needs, store information on existing inventory levels, and monitor the production process.

OPERATIONS IN ACTION

Chrysler Corporation: Mandating Electronic Transfer for Suppliers

Chrysler has mandated that its suppliers be able to receive releases (orders) for parts electronically. It has also required that suppliers transmit shipping notices to Chrysler electronically. A typical release will be sent directly from Chrysler's mainframe computer via telephone lines and a communications device (modem) to the supplier's computer, which could be a mainframe, a minicomputer, or a microcomputer.

Electronic transfer gives the supplier accurate, up-to-date information on which to base decisions. In many cases, this has allowed suppliers to reduce lead times by up to one week. Chrysler has coupled electronic transfer with just-in-time delivery to further reduce its work-in-process inventory by giving suppliers information that will make them more responsive. The other auto makers are also implementing electronic transfers. The advantages are simply too great to allow Chrysler to get too far ahead.

More and more manufacturers are being required to place bar-coded labels on all their products. These bar codes can be printed from inventory information contained in the computer. When customers receive these products into their plants, the bar codes can be scanned and the information entered directly into the computer. Customers and suppliers also transfer information about the ordering and shipment of parts via electronic transfer. In **electronic transfer,** phone lines function as data circuits to move information between two computers. In many cases, bar codes and electronic transfer eliminate the need for rekeying data, which is time-consuming and prone to error.

For service operations, the point-of-sale collection of data for inventory control is growing rapidly. Many traditional cash registers have been replaced with computer terminals that gather information about the products sold via optical scanning or keypad input. Daily records of products sold help managers control inventory.

MATERIAL HANDLING AND STORAGE

Material handling and storage are important parts of managing materials. In this section, we describe receiving and shipping, material-handling devices, storage devices, and intelligent warehouse systems.

Receiving and Shipping

When properly performed, receiving permits the rapid flow of material into a facility. Ideally, the material would move directly to the production line without making an intermediate stop in a warehouse or other storage area. However, if the material cannot be used immediately, it will be placed in storage, and information regarding its location will be filed in the facility's information system. For planning and controlling operations, accurate information regarding materials must be available.

Shipping is the beginning of the delivery system that sends the customer the product ordered in a timely and efficient manner. Ideally, the material shipped would come directly from the production line and be loaded on a truck or railway car headed for the customer's plant. Shipments are sometimes made from finished-goods inventory. Information about what to ship, where to ship it, and how to ship it are critical. Managers cannot get away from the need for accurate information and the transmission of that information.

Material-Handling Devices

How will the material be moved? Physically moving material requires equipment of various kinds, depending on the type and amount of material to be moved. Listed below are a few material-handling devices and a summary of when they might be used.

1. *Overhead cranes.* Overhead cranes are used to move very heavy objects through a plant. They come in a variety of sizes, and many are able to lift 25 tons or more. Moving steel slabs is an example of an overhead crane application. Overhead cranes are efficient at moving small parts only if the parts can be put together in a large batch and moved in one trip.

An overhead crane places a full ladel of molten steel on a continuous caster turret. After the ladel in use on the right is empty, the turret will swing around and position the full ladel over the continuous caster. The overhead crane will remove the empty ladel and return it to the basic oxygen furnace for a refill of steel. *Courtesy: American Iron and Steel Institute.*

A conveyor belt transports fiberglass insulation to the next stop in the production process. ***Courtesy: Owens Corning Fiberglass.***

A forklift is used to move palletized containers of orangeade. ***Courtesy: Clarklift of Northwest Ohio, Inc.***

This automated guided vehicle is capable of moving parts over a variety of paths. *Courtesy: Cincinnati Milacron.*

A drive-through pallet rack allows an operator easy access to pallets as well as the space to stack them on four levels. *Courtesy: Renco Products, Inc.* Here, the operator of a pallet truck is able to drive into the rack to access inventory stacked in the rear.

2. *Conveyors.* Conveyors are used to move large numbers of items along a fixed path. Some conveyors have belts that can move parts or granular material; others have a series of hooks that can move parts through a paint system.
3. *Forklifts.* Forklifts are used to move parts through varying paths. Because they have drivers, these vehicles are very flexible. Forklifts generally do not move large volumes of parts along the same path.
4. *Automated guided vehicles (AGVs).* AGVs are used to move parts through a variety of paths. AGVs are flexible in that they can be directed to follow more than one path.

Storage Devices

The number of different storage devices is almost as large as the number of different materials. One key to selecting a storage device is the accessibility of the material. Another key relates to its ability to utilize vertical and horizontal space efficiently.

The following storage devices are common:

1. Large bins with chutes that can easily feed materials to a process are often used for bulk storage of products. Other bulk products may be stored in 55-gallon drums or other large containers. Products stored in bulk are usually commodity items that do not have an individual part identity. Some examples

are sand for glassmaking, stone for paving roads and parking lots, limestone for making steel, and chemicals for making paper.

2. Pallet racks are devices that can stack pallets on top of one another. A **pallet** is a storage platform, usually made of wood, that a forklift can easily pick up. Pallets facilitate quick movement of groups of parts from one point in a facility to another.
3. Drive-in racks allow forklifts to drive between the racks, which are in vertical columns. Forklifts can drive in and pull material from any point in the rack and drive out again to deliver it. Drive-in racks are the basis for intelligent warehouse systems, which will be discussed in the next section. In intelligent warehouse systems, computer controls guide driverless vehicles to the proper rack.
4. Flow-through racks tend to be used for smaller products that move in and out of inventory quickly. In a flow-through rack, the shelves are tilted in one direction and are themselves rollers. Materials are added at the back of the shelves and roll down to the front, where they are removed.
5. Bin racks are used for storing smaller parts. Bins may have special dividers, spacers, or containers for keeping parts from mixing together.

Intelligent Warehouse Systems

Warehousing has taken on new meaning with the advent of just-in-time. Traditionally, warehouses full of raw-material, work-in-process, and finished-goods inventory were considered necessary. Today, inventory is viewed as a necessary evil, and many strong JIT advocates would drop the word *necessary.* In any case, much less inventory is needed to keep a plant running smoothly than was previously thought.

Intelligent warehouse systems have been applied for many years. Such a device, often called an automated storage and retrieval system (AS/RS), consists of a series of racks and storage locations. An AS/RS includes one or more vehicles that move through this set of racks to store and retrieve parts. An AS/RS also includes a computer, which tracks the parts as they enter and leave storage.

An AS/RS has the following capabilities:

1. Placing a part or parts at the proper location within the storage unit. Data entered into the AS/RS computer signal the vehicle to move to the correct location in the storage unit. The vehicle, as mentioned before, is guided via computer control. The process can also be used to remove parts.
2. Tracking inventory levels, remembering the location of all items, and integrating its information with other parts of the manufacturing system.
3. Linking with automated guided vehicles to provide a material-handling system that is controlled entirely by computer.

DISTRIBUTION SYSTEMS

The distribution system is the physical link between suppliers and customers. In a complex production environment, which is typical of most developed countries, distribution systems link a series of suppliers and customers into a production chain.

Building a Production Chain

A **production chain** includes the entire series of processes by which basic materials—such as trees, crude oil, iron ore, and sand—are converted into finished products—such as houses, automobiles, and microcomputers. A microcomputer, for example, has parts that are (1) molded from plastic, which is derived from crude oil; (2) shaped from steel, which comes from iron ore; and (3) made of glass, which is made from sand.

Consider the process of making paper. The production chain for this process is illustrated in Exhibit 15.6. The process begins with the logging of trees. The trees are converted into wood chips, and the chips are processed into large rolls of paper called logs, to which special coatings or other treatments may be added. The logs, which may be 300 inches long, are slit to the required length, and these smaller rolls are cut into sheets of the desired dimensions.

Distribution of materials at the various stages of production ties these separate operations into the production chain. A company that performs all the steps in the production chain is said to be completely vertically integrated. In many cases, several companies participate in building a complex product before it is delivered to the customer.

The Levels in a Distribution System

A distribution system links suppliers and customers, and it can have several distinct levels. Inventory may be maintained for distribution to customers in any of the following locations:

Exhibit 15.6 Production Chain for Paper

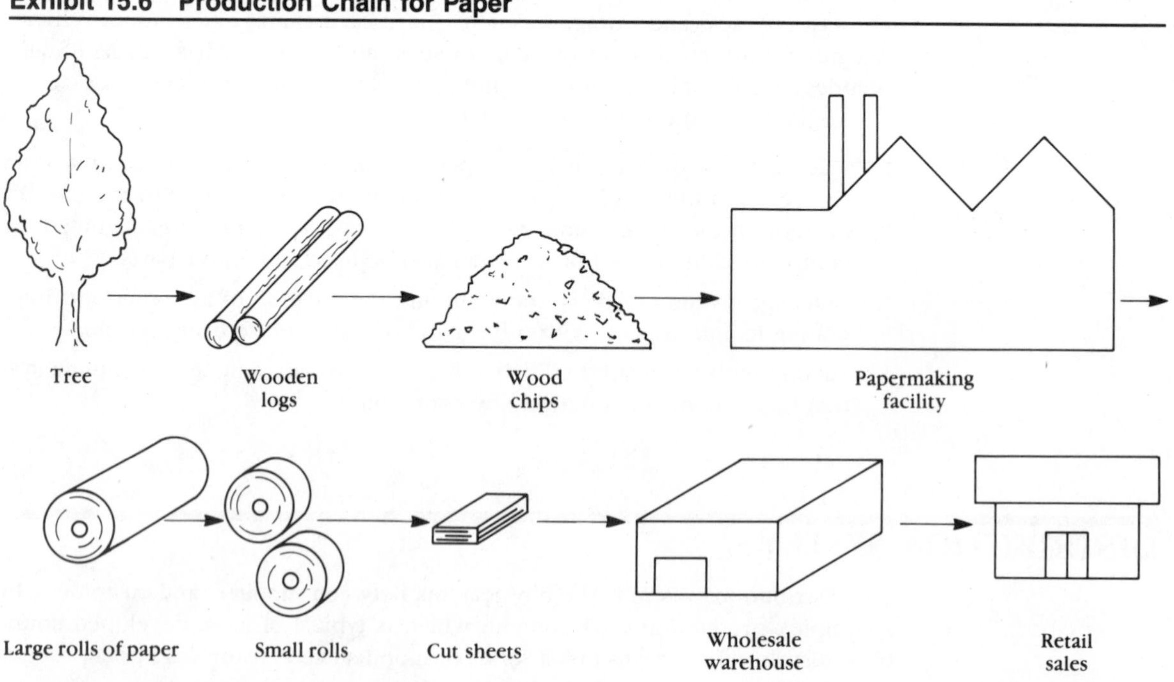

1. The supplier's facility
2. In transit
3. A regional warehouse
4. A distribution center
5. The customer's facility

Products stored at the supplier's facility and in transit have been described previously and require no further discussion. Exhibit 15.7 shows a distribution system for a facility operating out of Buffalo, New York. Each distribution center serves a large number of customers. The distribution centers act as order-taking and order-processing centers. Each center maintains a limited inventory of high-demand items, which are frequently replenished from larger stocks at the regional warehouse.

Large orders received by a distribution center may be shipped directly from the regional warehouse or the supplier's facility to the customer's facility. Small orders may be shipped to the distribution center, along with items ordered by other customers. These shipments will be broken down at the distribution center and shipped with orders for other customers.

Regional warehouses often hold the bulk of the inventory in the distribution system because small inventories in several distribution centers would be more

Exhibit 15.7 Distribution System for One Supplier Facility Serving Many Customers

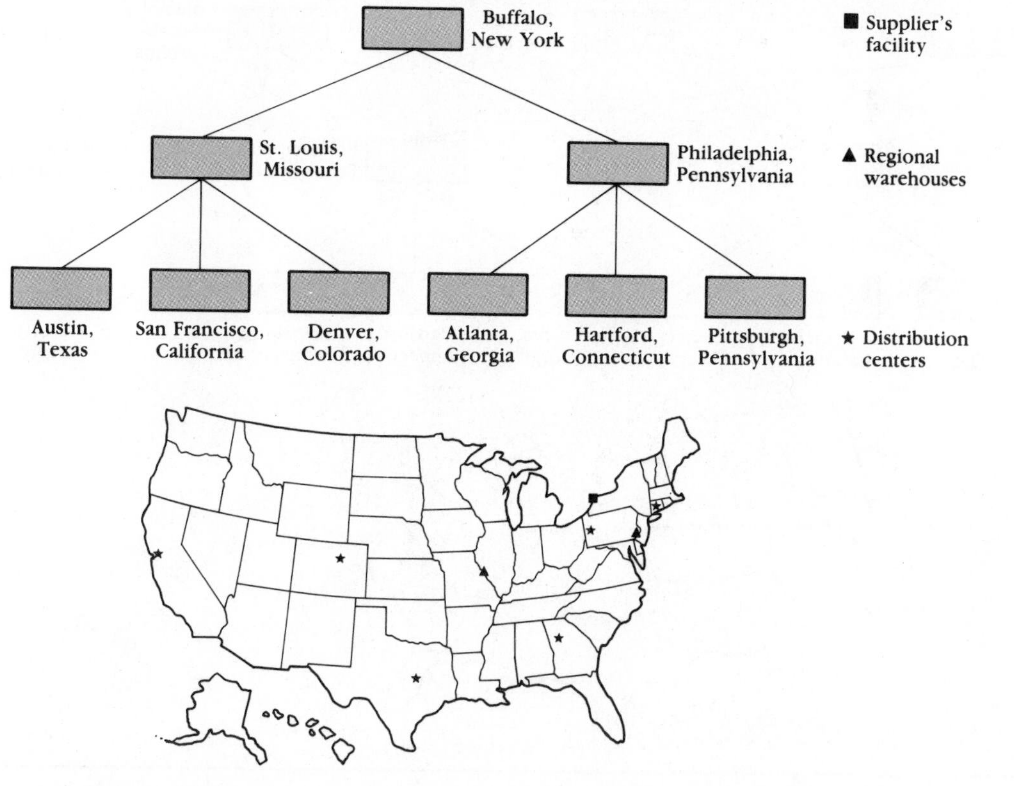

difficult to control and replenish. In addition, the sum of the inventory required at many distribution centers would be significantly greater than the inventory required at fewer regional warehouses.

Now, consider the case where many facilities feed a wide variety of products into the same regional warehouse. The regional warehouse can receive shipments of different products from several plants and organize them for shipment to the distribution centers. In fact, the regional warehouse could be run by a separate organization, and the suppliers could be from many different organizations. Such an arrangement is common when smaller organizations with limited resources require broad distribution of their products. Warehousing companies act as middlemen to distribute products of more than one company. Exhibit 15.8 illustrates the flow of materials in a distribution system with multiple supplier facilities.

Distribution Requirements Planning

Like production systems, distribution systems cannot operate efficiently and effectively without planning. **Distribution requirements planning (DRP)** uses forecasts of customers' orders to estimate the quantity of materials to have available at the distribution centers. Demands at the distribution centers, in turn, are aggregated to determine requirements at regional warehouses, which in turn

Exhibit 15.8 Distribution System for Multiple Supplier Facilities Serving Many Customers

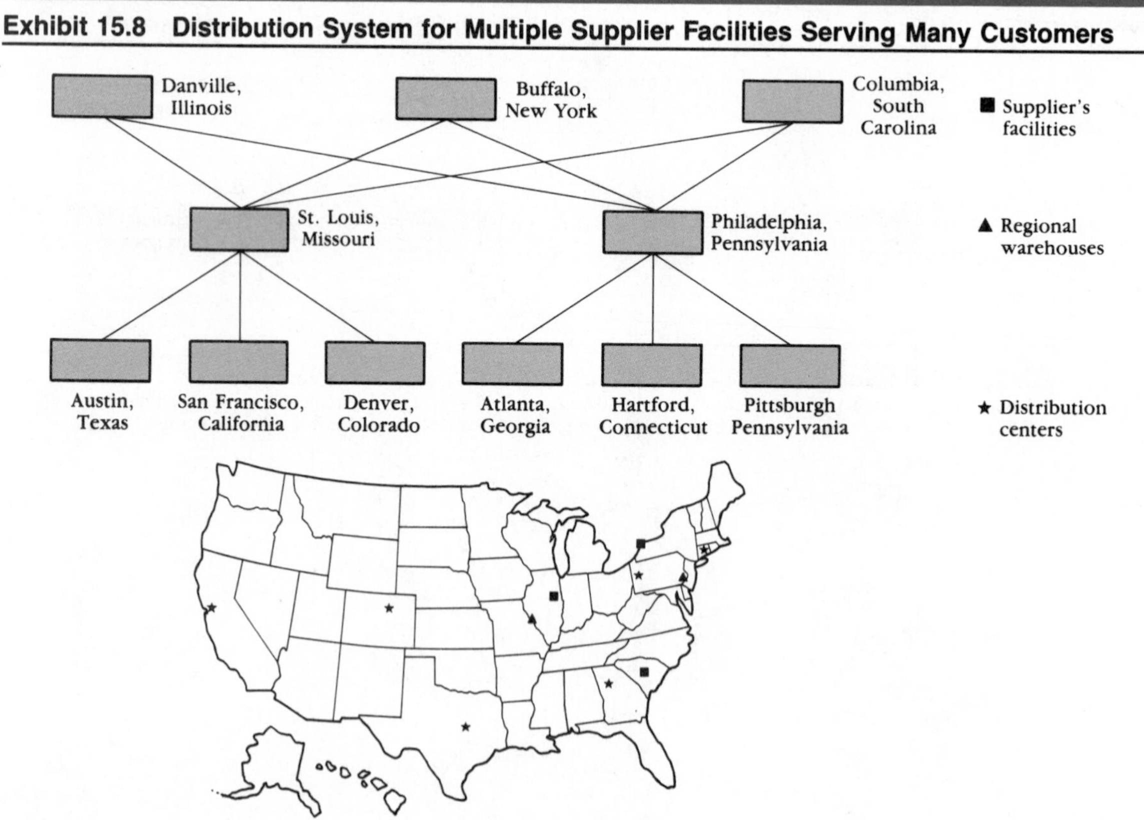

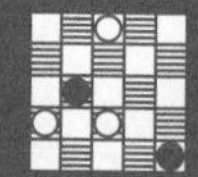

GAINING STRATEGIC ADVANTAGE AT HECHINGER'S

Using Advantages in Distribution to Improve Performance

Hechinger's is based in Landover, Maryland, and has nearly seventy stores in eight eastern and midwestern states. The company sells about 40,000 items—from hammers to hoses and from saws to sinks. To avoid declining sales during an economic slowdown, Hechinger targets the do-it-yourselfer, rather than the professional home builder. In tough times, when people buy fewer homes, they fix up their present homes. When housing sales rush ahead, buyers go to work on their newly acquired homes.

Hechinger's uses its inventory control and distribution system to improve its operating position and gain an advantage on the competition. To maintain its profit margins, Hechinger's management pays careful attention to inventory in its stores and in the distribution system. In the stores, each item is tracked to determine how quickly it is moving. Adjustments are made for items that are not paying for their shelf space. In the distribution system, rapid response to orders placed by a store is necessary to avoid stock-outs. Keeping close track of inventory turnover allows the company to have higher than average profits.

Hechinger's also plans to use its distribution system to expand operations economically. The company is proposing to add about twelve new stores a year. This amount of expansion can be expensive, but Hechinger's management plans to take the sting out of these expenses by taking advantage of the company's centralized distribution system. New stores will be located within the present coverage area (the East and the Midwest). Effective management of operations can improve performance and enhance an organization's competitive position.[2]

influence requirements at supplying facilities. Exhibit 15.8 illustrates the levels in distribution planning.

DRP is an effort to link customers to suppliers through an integrative planning system. Like MRP, DRP assumes that demand is dependent and lumpy. DRP uses the logic of MRP to schedule orders in advance at a supplying facility. To begin, the gross requirements for a distribution center are the forecasts of customer demand for the week. This projected demand is measured against on-hand inventory at a distribution center. When on-hand inventory drops below a certain level (the trigger point), the distribution center schedules a shipment of products from a regional warehouse. The regional warehouse uses the scheduled shipments to the distribution centers as its demand forecast. In turn, the regional warehouse makes decisions about on-hand inventory and decides whether to schedule a shipment from the supplier's facility. The schedules of shipments received from the regional warehouse become the incoming orders for production planning at the supplier's facility. This is only a brief description of DRP; further information can be found in the references listed in the Selected Bibliography.

Several advantages can be achieved with properly implemented DRP systems:

1. Improved customer service, which means that a higher percentage of deliveries are made on time
2. Lower distribution costs
3. Reduced inventory
4. Less obsolete inventory

Changes in Distribution Systems

In the recent past, distribution systems have often been used to store large amounts of materials for rapid delivery to a customer. In a sense, these stacks of inventory were used to buffer inflexible production systems that were incapable of making the swift adjustments required to keep pace with rapidly changing customer needs.

In the future, distribution systems should be able to adjust to the requirements of just-in-time delivery from factories that are capable of making small production lots. Inventory buffers in the system will be greatly reduced. More frequent deliveries of smaller loads may be required. As a result of just-in-time, DRP time horizons will become shorter than one week, and the trigger points that generate a shipment from the next higher level in the distribution system will decrease.

INTEGRATING THE SYSTEM

The Distribution System Completes the Loop

The distribution system is an important part of an organization. It is the interface between marketing and operations. An organization starts by estimating market reaction; product and process design follow. Resources are acquired, and production begins. When the product is delivered through the distribution system, the organization starts again with the market's reaction and adapts the product to meet customer needs. Exhibit 15.9 shows that distribution completes the loop back to the customer.

Exhibit 15.9 The Marketing and Operations Interface

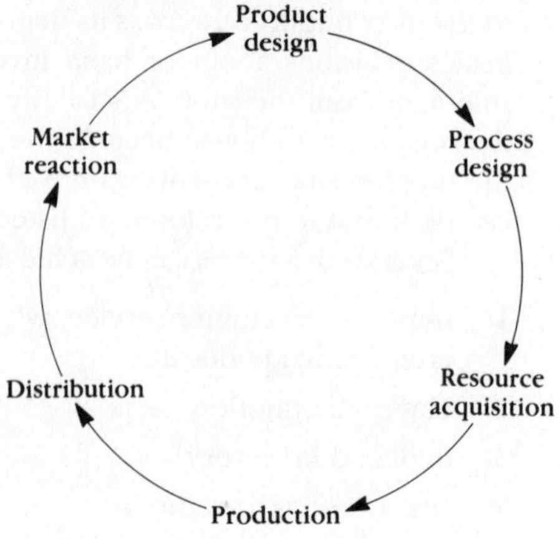

SUMMARY

- Material management includes decisions about the procurement, control, handling, storage, and distribution of materials.
- Material flow within an organization has both a physical component and an informational component. The information flowing from planning and scheduling to the work area provides direction for the physical flow. The information coming back from the work area provides feedback on actual production.
- Purchasing includes defining product specifications, obtaining price quotations, developing criteria for supplier selection, classifying suppliers according to performance, evaluating the make-or-buy decision, awarding contracts, expediting, and evaluating performance. Ethical behavior by purchasing agents is essential.
- International sourcing of materials is becoming more and more common.
- In making the pricing decision, purchasing managers should look at the lowest total cost. This includes the selling price, freight, receiving costs, and any special processing that is not required of comparable products.
- When evaluating the make-or-buy decision, an organization should consider technical expertise, product quality, and reliable and timely delivery, in addition to the price charged.
- JIT influences the purchasing decision because lot size is reduced, supplier selection is more carefully examined, product specifications are loosened, and receiving inspection is eliminated.
- Inventory is an alternative to future production. Significant costs and definable benefits are associated with holding inventory. An organization needs to evaluate these costs and benefits to make an appropriate decision about how much inventory to hold.
- Material handling and storage are important parts of effective material management.
- An organization maintains inventory to separate production from consumption, ensure smooth work flows within the production system, take advantage of short-term price fluctuations, and offset temporary disruptions in supply.
- Intelligent warehouse systems are computer-controlled storage and retrieval systems that can operate without people.
- A distribution system is the physical link between supplier and customer. Distribution systems can link several sets of customers and suppliers together to form a production chain. A production chain involves all the processes by which raw materials, such as iron ore, are converted into finished products, such as toasters.

CAREER PROFILE

Terry L. Bowman
Material Manager
The Aro Corporation

Terry Bowman is the material manager for the Aro Corporation, which manufactures parts for the automobile industry. He is directly responsible for purchasing, warehousing, receiving, shipping, and material handling. In addition, Bowman is responsible for production control, which involves preparing short-term production plans and schedules, and for shop floor control, which involves monitoring and controlling the actual production process.

Special Projects

In addition to these "routine" duties, Bowman is involved in a number of special projects. In an effort to expand its customer base, Aro Corporation has developed a model program that emphasizes immediate delivery of the firm's most popular products. Bowman is also involved in implementing JIT. In conjunction with this effort, he is responsible for developing a layout that incorporates manufacturing cells and line-flow processes to smooth material flows through the plant. He is also responsible for coordinating purchasing and manufacturing efforts on new products.

Education and Experience

To prepare himself for these responsibilities, Bowman earned a B.S. in business administration and has participated in conferences and seminars sponsored by the company and professional organizations. Before assuming his present position, Bowman was a bank auditor and a buyer for Style Line Products. Within Aro Corporation, he has held positions in planning and has been a production line supervisor. In the future, he could become the plant manager, the director of materials, the director of manufacturing, and eventually the vice-president of manufacturing.

SOLVED PROBLEMS

1. Clark Computing sells software through the mail. The company includes a computer manual with each piece of software. Clark is trying to decide if it should contract with an outside supplier to prepare the manuals or hire in-house staff to prepare them. Following are cost estimates for the two options:

Buy	Make
$.75 per manual	Variable cost = $.45 Annual fixed costs = $10,000

a. Which alternative has the lower total cost if annual demand is 22,000 units?

Solution

$$\text{Cost to buy} = (\$.75/\text{unit})(22{,}000 \text{ units}) = \$16{,}500$$

$$\text{Cost to make} = (\$.45/\text{unit})(22{,}000 \text{ units}) + \$10{,}000 = \$19{,}900$$

At 22,000 units, buying has the lower total cost.

b. At what annual volume do these alternatives have the same cost?

Solution

$$\text{Cost to buy} = \text{cost to make}$$

$$(\$.75/\text{unit})(X\text{ units}) = (\$.45/\text{unit})(X\text{ units}) + \$10{,}000$$

$$(\$.30/\text{unit})(X\text{ units}) = \$10{,}000$$

$$X = 33{,}333\text{ units}$$

c. Graph the alternative described in part b. The solution is shown at the top of page 642.

2. If Clark Computing agrees to order at least 50,000 units per year, the supplier will reduce the price to $.61 per unit. The graph for this alternative is shown at the bottom of page 642.

a. At what point are the cost of making and the cost of buying at $.61 (committing to 50,000 or more units per year) equal?

Solution

$$\text{Cost to buy} = \text{cost to make}$$

$$(\$.61/\text{unit})(X\text{ units}) = (\$.45/\text{unit})(X\text{ units}) + \$10{,}000$$

$$(\$.16/\text{unit})(X\text{ units}) = \$10{,}000$$

$$X = 62{,}500\text{ units}$$

b. Determine when the cost of making is equal to the cost of buying 50,000 units. (Note: Remember from the discussion in the text that it is possible to commit to and pay for 50,000 units even if Clark needs fewer units.)

Solution

$$\text{Cost to buy} = \text{cost to make}$$

$$(\$.61/\text{unit})(50{,}000\text{ units}) = (\$.45/\text{unit})(X\text{ units}) + \$10{,}000$$

$$(\$.45/\text{unit})(X\text{ units}) = \$30{,}500 - \$10{,}000$$

$$X = 45{,}556\text{ units}$$

When Clark's needs are 45,556 to 49,999 units, the company will have lower costs if it commits to and pays for 50,000 units per year.

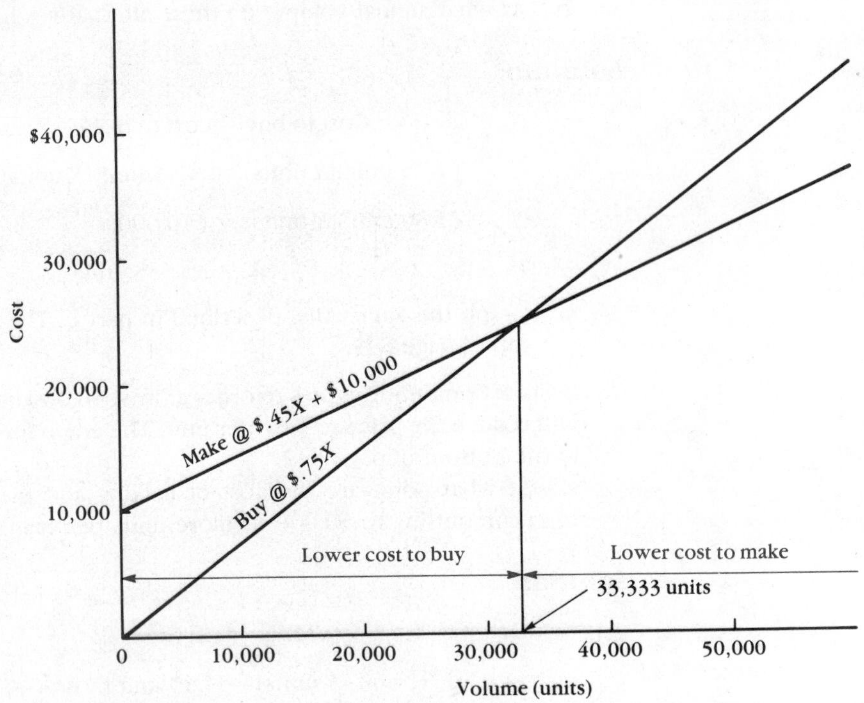

40,000
30,000
20,000
10,000
Cost
Make @ $.45X + $10,000
Buy @ $.75X
Buy @ $.61X
Lower cost to buy
Lower cost to make
Lower cost to buy
Lower cost to make
33,333 units
62,500 units
0
10,000
20,000
30,000
40,000
50,000
60,000
70,000
80,000
Volume (units)

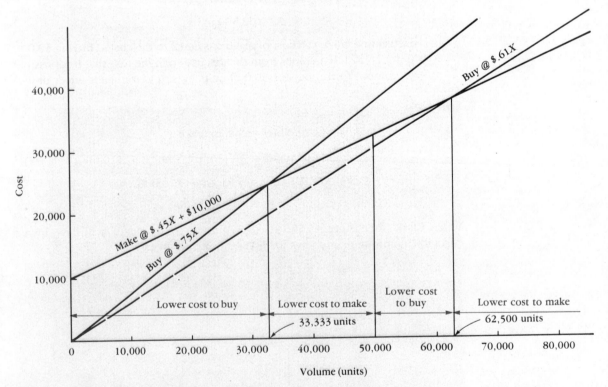

QUESTIONS

1. What are the major issues in material management? Define each of them.

2. Provide an overview of material flow in the organization, and explain how the application of JIT can affect that flow.

3. Describe the relationship between facility design and material flow.

4. List and define the important issues in purchasing.

5. Why is the purchasing function so important to an organization?

6. What are the critical issues in determining whether to buy or to make a product?

7. How does JIT influence the purchasing function?

8. Describe the cost trade-offs in deciding how much inventory to hold.

9. Given the high costs of holding inventory, what are the major reasons for organizations to hold inventory?

10. In responding to questions involving inventory, how do service operations differ from producers of goods?

11. What are the advantages of an intelligent warehouse system?

12. Describe a production chain, and illustrate how it is used to bring complex products to the consumer.

13. How is the facility location decision related to decisions regarding the design of a distribution system?

14. Explain the following statement: "Distribution completes the loop back to the customer."

PROBLEMS

1. The local Blue Crab restaurant chain has twenty restaurants in the Gotham City area. Presently, the restaurants have a contract with a local cleaner to wash all of their tablecloths. Blue Crab is responsible for pickup and delivery of the tablecloths. Blue Crab's management is contemplating buying laundry equipment and cleaning its own tablecloths. The local cleaner is charging $.50 per tablecloth. Blue Crab estimates that after an annual investment of $20,000, the cost to launder the tablecloths in-house will be only $.30.

- **a.** Which alternative has a lower cost if each restaurant averages 110 dirty tablecloths per week?
- **b.** At what annual volume of tablecloths per restaurant will the cost of doing the laundry in-house equal the cost to continue the present service?
- **c.** What other factors should be considered in making the decision?

2. Wazlick Manufacturing is considering machining a cast part that it has purchased ready for assembly in the past. The cost estimates are as follows:

Buy	Make	
$4.25/unit	Purchase price of raw casting	= $1.30/unit
	Labor	= $1.80/unit
	Annual fixed costs	= $48,000

- **a.** Which alternative has the lower total cost if annual demand is 38,000 units?
- **b.** At what volume are the cost of making and the cost of buying equal?
- **c.** Graph the alternative described in part b.
- **d.** What other factors should be considered in making this decision?

3. Suppose the supplier in problem 2 offers to reduce the unit price to $3.90 if Wazlick agrees to order at least 50,000 units per year.

- **a.** Graph this new alternative.
- **b.** Prepare a table that shows which alternative has the lower cost for any volume.

Volume	Lower Cost
1 to X units	
$X + 1$ to Y units	
$Y + 1$ to Z units	
and so on	

- **c.** The annual fixed cost of $48,000 represents the initial investment annualized over a five-year period. Wazlick's actual investment to start machining parts is $240,000. Should Wazlick's management make this decision by picking the alternative with the lower total cost or by considering it as an investment decision? Explain why.

4. Barnside's Manufacturing Division is examining its present operations to determine how it can better utilize its present asset base. One of the company's metal-stamping presses is used only 25 percent of the time. A company salesperson has discovered an opportunity to stamp out metal disks for another division in the company. The disks will be used by the other division to make campaign buttons for a special election. Barnside's accountant has determined that the fixed costs per week to operate the press for this job are \$12,000. The press does not have any other uses at this time, and the proposed job will take only about 10 percent of the capacity for the next four weeks. If Barnside's other division buys the disks from an outside source, the cost per 1,000 will be \$20.00. If the Manufacturing Division makes the disks, the variable cost per 1,000 will be \$15.50.

a. If the demand is for 10 million disks, which option has the lower cost?
b. At what volume are the cost of buying and the cost of making equal?
c. What would you recommend in this case?

5. Springfield Manufacturing is negotiating a purchase contract for metal stampings. The contract calls for an annual fixed payment of \$12,000 plus \$1.20 for each stamping. As an alternative, the company could purchase stamping presses and make the parts. The annual fixed cost would be \$40,000, and the variable cost would be \$.40 per unit.

a. At a volume of 40,000 units per year, which alternative has the lower cost?
b. At what volume is the cost of making equal to the cost of buying?
c. If the company has idle capacity on existing stamping machines, what effect would this have on the decision? Describe how Springfield should value the idle capacity.

6. Bismark Medical Clinic uses large quantities of tongue depressors. Presently, the clinic buys disposable depressors made of wood for \$6.50 per 100. Management is looking for ways to save money and is considering reusable depressors made of stainless steel. These depressors would have to be sterilized after each use. It is estimated that Bismark would have to buy eighty metal depressors at \$9.50 each, but that they would last indefinitely. Bismark's management estimates that the annual fixed costs for metal depressors, including replacement of lost depressors, would be about \$700. The variable cost for cleaning the depressors is \$.02 each.

a. If Bismark uses 20,000 tongue depressors each year, which alternative has the lower cost?
b. At what point are the cost of using metal depressors and the cost of buying disposable depressors equal?
c. Even if the cost to purchase metal depressors is lower and there is a good return on the investment, why might Bismark choose to keep using disposable depressors?

7. For Allen Products, Inc., the cost of purchased materials is about 55 percent of each sales dollar. Labor represents about 15 percent and profit 7 percent. Sales last year totaled \$140 million. Management must cut production costs (material and labor costs) by 8 percent and can reduce only material and labor costs. In which area is management more likely to find the 8 percent savings? Allen's present cost and profit structure is shown below.

Description	**As a Percentage of Sales**	**Millions of Dollars**
Material costs	55	77.0
Labor costs	15	21.0
Other costs (including overhead)	23	32.2
Profit	7	9.8
Total	100	140.00

a. Assume that management can take the 8 percent reduction only from material costs. Determine its new cost structure.
b. Assume that management can take the reduction only from labor costs. Determine this new cost structure.
c. Where should the management of Allen Products first look for savings?

8. State University is opening a branch campus at Chagrin Falls. The school is planning to lease one building with 120,000 square feet. The lease is for five years with an option for another five. State's administration has only committed to the Board of Regents to operate the campus for five years. Operating beyond that point is based on enrollment. State's director of buildings and grounds is trying to determine whether she should purchase the necessary janitorial equipment and hire staff to maintain the building or whether she should contract with a local service to clean and maintain the building. The initial cost for the equipment is \$70,000, and the cost per square foot to clean and maintain the building is \$1.50 per year. The cost to purchase the service is \$1.90 per square foot per year.

a. Which alternative has the lower total cost over a five-year period?
b. The local janitorial service is very anxious to get the contract. What square-foot price should it quote to get the job?
c. What would you recommend, and why?

MINI-CASES

The city of Barnwell, Georgia, presently does all of its own repair work on city vehicles. The annual fixed cost of the repair facility is $100,000. The average repair has a variable cost of $86. Mechanics are paid $12 per hour, which includes fringe benefits. Barnwell keeps records on both actual and standard labor hours. The actual labor figures are taken from the job tickets given to the mechanics. These tickets are punched into a time clock at the beginning and the end of a job. Standard times are taken from manuals that list national standard repair times for all types of services. Last year, the actual labor hours totaled 21,200 and the standard hours 18,500. Also, the city had to pay for 1,500 hours of nonproductive idle time.

Acme Service Center has carefully examined Barnwell's records and has offered to do all repairs for a fixed fee of $40,000 per year plus $17 per hour. Acme will guarantee its work and do rework without an additional labor charge. Acme further agrees to charge only for standard labor hours. If a job takes more than the standard hours, Acme will take the loss. On the other hand, if a job takes fewer hours, Acme will still be paid for the standard hours. Acme has also agreed to buy parts and shop materials from the source the city is presently using and to have that source bill the city directly. Acme does not get to mark up the parts. Acme plans to use nonunion labor and to pay wages of $10.50 per hour, including fringe benefits. Acme wants the city to commit to a ten-year contract.

Put yourself in the city manager's position.

1. How do the economics of this decision look if next year's repairs are about the same as last year's?

2. What factors other than the cost of the service should be considered?

3. What advantages are there to the city if it makes the contract with Acme?

4. What is your recommendation to the city?

Davis Company

Davis Company is a long-established producer of mechanical cash registers. When electronic cash registers took over the market several years ago, the company was forced to invest in the new technology to maintain its existing business. Eventually, Davis mastered the technology well enough to attract new business. On the heels of the electronic cash register came more sophisticated computer terminals that could be linked together to form an information network. Davis also mastered that technology and has developed successful manufacturing as well as design capabilities. At the present time, the organization has some unused time in product design.

Davis Company is looking for new business and is proposing to design and build mobile phones. It is closely examining one of the major electrical components to determine if it should make the part or buy it. Actually, the decision is far more complex than a simple make-or-buy calculation because Davis has four options to consider, as shown in the table below.

1. Graph these different alternatives.

2. Develop a table showing the low-cost alternative for any volume of production per year.

3. What factors other than costs need to be considered?

4. Make a recommendation to management on which option to pursue.

Unit Cost

Option	Stage 1	Stage 2	Stage 3	Annual Fixed Costs
Process all the way	$ .90	$1.10	$1.30	$100,000
Buy complete at stage 1 and process through stages 2 and 3	1.30	1.10	1.30	70,000
Buy complete at stage 2 and process through stage 3	—	3.10	1.30	20,000
Buy complete at stage 3	—	—	5.00	0

SELECTED BIBLIOGRAPHY

Back, Herbert. "Decentralized Integration—Advantage or Disadvantage of Logistics and JIT—Concepts." *Computers in Industry* (The Netherlands) 6, no. 6 (December 1985): 529–541.

Bagchhi, Prabir K.; Raghunathan, T. S.; and Bardi, Edward J. "The Implication of Just-in-Time Inventory Policy on Carrier Selection." *Logistics and Transportation Review* (Canada) 23, no. 4 (December 1987): 373–384.

Barket, D. E., and Farrington, B. *The Basic Arts of Buying*. London: Business Books Limited, 1976.

Bornemann, Alfred H. *Essentials of Purchasing*. Columbus, Ohio: Grid, 1974.

Bowersox, Donald J.; Closs, David J.; and Helferich, Omar K. *Logistical Management*. New York: Macmillan, 1986.

Cavinato, Joseph L. *Purchasing and Materials Management*. St. Paul: West, 1984.

Combs, Paul H. *Handbook of International Purchasing*. Boston: Cahners, 1976.

Coyle, John J., and Bardi, Edward J. *The Management of Business Logistics*. St. Paul: West, 1988.

Gupta, Yash P., and Bagchi, Prabir. "Inbound Freight Consolidation Under Just-in-Time Procurement: Application of Clearing Models." *Journal of Business Logistics* 8, no. 2 (1987): 74–94.

Hall, R. W. *Zero Inventories*. Homewood, Ill.: Dow Jones–Irwin, 1983.

Heinritz, Stuart F.; Farrell, Paul V.; and Smith, Clifton L. *Purchasing Principles and Applications*. Englewood Cliffs, N.J.: Prentice-Hall, 1986.

Martin, Andre J. *Distribution Resource Planning*. Englewood Cliffs, N.J.: Prentice-Hall; Essex Junction, Vt.: Oliver Wight Limited, 1983.

Messner, William A. *Profitable Purchasing Management*. New York: AMACOM, 1982.

Muller, T. *Automated Guided Vehicles*. Bedford, U.K.: IFS Publications, 1983.

Quinn, Francis J. "No Room for Error." *Traffic Management* (September 1984): 28–34.

Storhagen, Nils G., and Hellberg, Roland. "Just-in-Time from a Business Logistics Perspective." *Engineering Cost and Production Economics* (The Netherlands) 12, no. 1–4 (July 1987): 117–121.

Tompkins, James A., and White, John A. *Facilities Planning*. New York: Wiley, 1984.

Voss, C. A., ed. *Just-in-Time Manufacturing*. United Kingdom: IFS Ltd.; Berlin: Springer-Verlag, n.d.

Weatherston, David. "Transportation Makes the JIT Connection." *Industrial Management* (April 1986): 40–44.

Chapter 16

Lot-Sizing Models

CHAPTER OUTLINE

LEARNING OBJECTIVES

After completing this chapter, you should be able to

- List the variable costs that make up ordering and holding costs.
- Explain why only variable costs are considered in inventory-control models.
- Describe the three assumptions underlying the EOQ model.
- Use the EOQ model to calculate a lot size.
- Explain how the finite replenishment rate model differs from the EOQ model.
- Calculate a lot size using the EPQ formula.
- Calculate economic order quantities under quantity discounts.
- Determine the reorder point.
- Calculate required safety stock to achieve a desired service level.
- Classify items using ABC analysis.
- Explain the differences between continuous and periodic review control systems.
- Explain how a base stock system works.
- Calculate the order-up-to level for a periodic review system.
- Describe the differences between dependent and independent demand.
- Calculate MRP lot sizes, using either the period order quantity model or the Silver-Meal heuristic.

OPERATIONS IN ACTION

Weyerhaeuser Company: Controlling Wood-Chip Inventories

Weyerhaeuser Company produces paper products. An important part of its operations involves the conversion of wood chips into pulp—the first step in making paper. To perform this conversion process, Weyerhaeuser operates many pulp mills throughout the country. Each pulp mill takes in raw wood chips and, after several chemical reactions, produces paper pulp. Some of this pulp is used by Weyerhaeuser's own paper plants, but much of it is sold to other paper companies.

The pulp-making operation is basically a continuous flow process; there is very little work-in-process inventory—and then due only to the time needed for chemical reactions to take place. Thus, any interruption in the input of wood chips will mean that the entire process must be stopped.

Part of Weyerhaeuser's wood chip inventory for making paper pulp. *Courtesy of Weyerhaeuser Company.*

Shutting down a pulp mill is an expensive proposition. It means that all processes must be stopped and equipment cleaned out before being restarted. During the pulp mill downtime, employees will usually be laid off. The disruption in output also means that many customer orders will not be delivered as requested. Thus, it makes sense for Weyerhaeuser to maintain sufficient inventories of wood chips so that the pulp mill will not shut down.

On the other hand, wood-chip inventories can be expensive. A ton of chips costs about $50. A typical inventory of 100,000 tons means a $5million investment. Due to the nature of wood chips, such an inventory is subject to natural degradation. This degradation can mean inventory losses or extra costs required to produce acceptable pulp from degraded wood chips. The problem is to balance these inventory costs against the costs of a possible mill shutdown.

To solve this problem, Weyerhaeuser has developed a computerized system called SPRINT. This system estimates the probability that wood-chip inventory will be depleted based on expected deliveries of wood chips and projected orders for paper pulp. The system determines an inventory level that produces an acceptable risk of having to shut down the pulp mill.

The SPRINT model is currently in use at half a dozen Weyerhaeuser pulp mills to manage a total current inventory of 200,000 tons of wood chips. The results with SPRINT have been impressive. Inventory has been decreased by 190,000 tons over three years, and annual inventory costs have been decreased by $2 million since the model was implemented.[1]

INTRODUCTION

In this chapter, we will deal with the issue of lot sizing. **Lot sizing** is the process of determining how much of a raw material, part, or product should be ordered or produced at a time. As you read through this chapter, you should keep in mind that the techniques presented here are best applied in situations either where there is uncertainty or where batches must be used. If a company is able to control its environment sufficiently to effectively utilize MRP or JIT, then the techniques of lot sizing become less relevant. However, as you will see, some of the ideas discussed here can still be used for determining planned order releases in MRP or even for controlling setup time reduction with JIT.

CONCEPTS OF LOT SIZING

In previous chapters, we talked about the huge amounts of money that can be tied up in inventory. However, there are also various ongoing costs that are incurred whenever inventory is stored or replenished. These include the costs of ordering and holding inventory.

Cost of Ordering

One major component of cost associated with inventory is the cost of replenishing it, usually called **ordering cost.** If a part or raw material is ordered from outside suppliers, then this really is an ordering cost. On the other hand, parts, subassemblies, or finished products may be produced in-house. In this case, ordering cost is actually represented by the costs associated with changing over equipment from producing one item to producing another. This is usually referred to as **setup cost.** To simplify things, we will refer to both ordering costs and setup costs as *ordering costs.*

Ordering costs may include many different items. Some of these will be relatively fixed, and others may vary. For our purposes it will be important to differentiate between those ordering costs that do not change much and those that are incurred each time an order is placed. For example, suppose a company currently places orders for a given part with its supplier five times per year. If, instead, the company ordered six times per year, which costs would probably change (variable costs), and which would probably not (fixed costs)? The general breakdown between fixed and variable ordering costs is as follows:

Fixed Costs	**Variable Costs**
Staffing costs (payroll, benefits, etc.)	Shipping costs
Office, furniture, and equipment	Cost of placing an order (phone, postage, order forms)
	Cost of lost production during setup
	Cost of materials used during start after setup
	Receiving and inspection costs

Cost of Holding Inventory

Although it costs money to replenish inventory, it also, unfortunately, costs money to hold that inventory. Such **inventory holding costs,** also called **carrying costs,** may include costs paid for storage space, interest paid on borrowed money to finance the inventory, and any losses incurred due to damage or obsolescence.

Once again, we must differentiate between fixed and variable costs of holding inventory. Suppose we maintain a certain inventory level of a finished product. What if that inventory level is increased by one unit? Which costs would not change (fixed costs), and which would change (variable costs)? The general breakdown for inventory holding costs is as shown below.

Fixed Costs	Variable Costs
Capital costs of warehouse	Cost of capital in inventory
Taxes on warehouse and property	Insurance on inventory value
Costs of operating warehouse	Losses due to obsolescence, theft, spoilage
Personnel costs	Taxes on inventory value
	Cost of renting warehouse space

In the next section, we will discuss the most basic approach to determining lot sizes—the **economic order quantity (EOQ) model.** In developing the EOQ model, we will attempt to minimize total annual costs by varying the order quantity, or lot size. Because, over the short run, lot-size variations affect only variable costs, those are the only costs that we will consider. Before starting that section, you should be sure you understand the differences between the fixed and variable costs that are listed above. Also, you should realize that the division between fixed and variable costs may change depending on the context. If additional personnel must be hired, staffing costs may be considered variable.

THE ECONOMIC ORDER QUANTITY MODEL

Ordering cost and holding cost can be thought of something like two children on a seesaw. When one goes up, the other goes down, and vice versa.

This trade-off appears to present somewhat of a quandary: if we attempt to decrease total annual variable holding costs, total annual variable ordering costs will increase—and vice versa. The way out of this dilemma is to combine the two costs as total annual variable costs and worry only about minimizing that cost. As Exhibit 16.1 indicates, there is just one point where total costs are minimized. The order quantity associated with that point is called the economic order quantity (EOQ).

While Exhibit 16.1 indicates, conceptually, where the economic order quantity point is, we need more information to calculate that point mathematically. First, however, we need to discuss four assumptions underlying our discussion.

Assumptions of the EOQ Model

Constant Known Demand

The first assumption we make in developing the EOQ model is that demand is fairly stable, or constant, and that we know reasonably well what that demand will be. Recall that in discussing MRP, we indicated demand for component parts or raw materials would often occur in bunches or lumps. That situation was referred to as **dependent** or **lumpy demand.** Such highly variable demand is not adaptable to the EOQ model. Instead, demand must be smooth and constant—what is called **independent demand.**

Exhibit 16.1 Total Annual Variable Costs

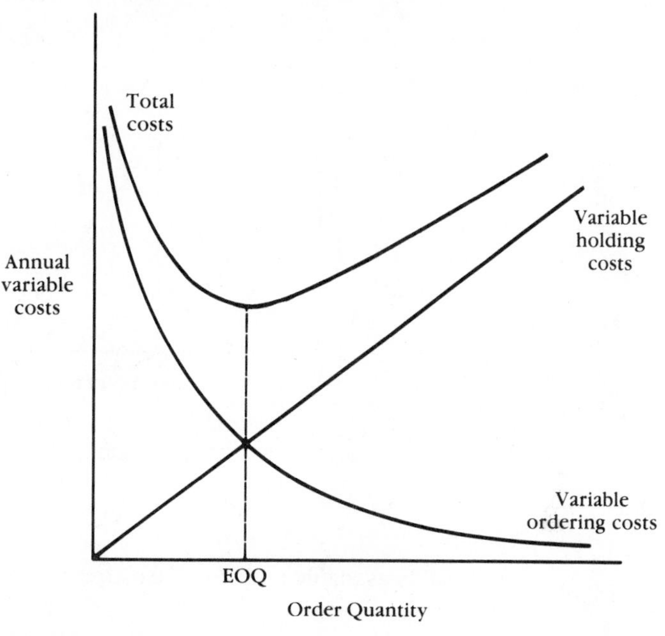

Cost per Unit Not Dependent on Order Quantity

Most things can be purchased at a lower cost per unit if they are bought in larger quantities. For instance, large sizes of laundry detergent usually cost less per ounce than smaller sizes do. However, that situation makes purchase cost a variable cost—something the EOQ model does not account for. Thus, we will also assume that purchase cost per unit remains the same, regardless of whether we are buying one, one hundred, or one thousand units each time.

Entire Order Delivered at One Time

This assumption relates to how inventory is replenished. One possibility would be to build inventory up gradually, as would happen in a clothing factory. As a particular model of jacket is produced, the inventory of that jacket builds up gradually. However, another possibility is for all units in an order to arrive at one time. This is what happens when a clothing store orders from a factory. The factory ships an entire order of the jacket at one time; the store's inventory is replenished all at once. It is this latter, **instantaneous replenishment,** that we will assume occurs. This assumption, combined with the assumption of constant demand, results in the inventory pattern depicted in Exhibit 16.2.

Ordering and Carrying Costs Known and Independent

The final assumption is that we can determine the variable costs of ordering and carrying inventory. In many cases, such costs can be determined from company records or from the accounting department. However, such costs are sometimes

Exhibit 16.2 Basic EOQ Inventory Pattern

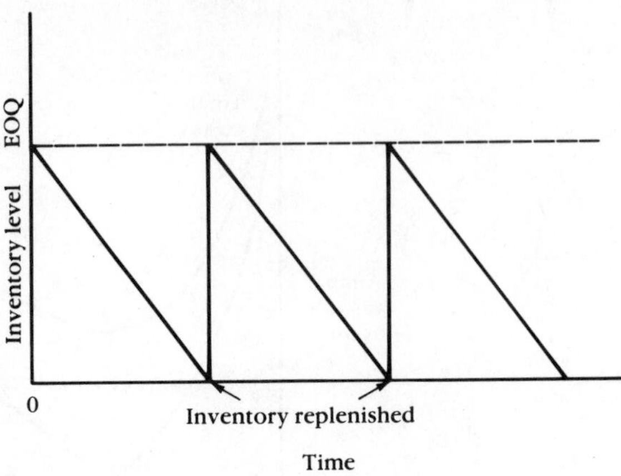

not readily available and must be estimated. We also assume the two costs are not related in any way.

These assumptions may seem restrictive, and possibly unrealistic. However, recall that the EOQ model is the basic starting point. We will show that this particular model may be altered to relax some of these assumptions—and more closely match reality. But we must begin with the basics.

Mathematical Statement of the Model

Variables to Be Used

Stating the EOQ formula in mathematical terms will require that we use variables to represent the important problem parameters. The variables of concern are as follows:

$$D = \text{annual demand rate (units/year)}$$

$$Q = \text{order quantity or lot size (units)}$$

$$C_o = \text{variable ordering cost (\$/order)}$$

$$C_h = \text{variable holding cost (\$/unit/year)}$$

Once again, you should note that we are concerned only with variable costs. In this case, the variable ordering costs will represent any additional costs incurred when another order is placed, and are stated as cost per order. Holding costs also include only the variable costs associated with keeping one more unit in inventory. Since we are concerned with annual costs, this is stated as cost per unit per year.

One other way of stating inventory holding costs is to break C_h into two components. If you think a minute about the variable holding costs, you will realize that they will depend on the number of units in inventory and the value of each unit.

In most instances, it is possible to state inventory holding cost, C_h, as a percentage of unit cost per year (\$/\$/year). The greatest part of this percentage is accounted for by capital tied up in the inventory. Since cost of capital is usually stated as a percentage, this makes it especially convenient to state holding cost in this form. To do so, we use the following variables.

$$v = \text{cost or value of item (\$/unit)}$$

$$r = \text{holding-cost percentage of unit value (\$/\$/year)}$$

Then $C_h = vr$.

Annual Variable Ordering Costs

Regardless of how many units are ordered at a time, we can always determine how many orders must be placed by dividing annual demand, D, by the order quantity, Q. Thus,

$$\text{Orders placed per year} = \frac{D}{Q}$$

Since the cost per order is C_o, annual variable ordering costs can be easily calculated as follows:

$$\text{Annual variable ordering costs} = \frac{D}{Q}C_o$$

Annual Variable Holding Costs

Notice in Exhibit 16.2 that our theoretical inventory pattern fluctuates between the EOQ and zero when lot sizes equal to the EOQ are ordered each time. Suppose, instead, that we let the variable Q represent the quantity ordered each time. In that case, the maximum inventory level would be Q, assuming inventory is replenished just as it reaches zero. Minimum inventory would still be zero.

This fluctuation in inventory level makes the calculation of annual holding costs somewhat difficult because we will have a different number of units in inventory at any one time. To make matters worse, each unit will be in inventory for a different length of time—some for a very short period, others longer. This means the calculation of annual holding costs requires the use of integral calculus. However, there is an easier, but equivalent way to determine annual holding costs.

The method we will use to determine annual holding costs is based on average inventory level. Because inventory follows a uniform pattern, with a maximum of Q and a minimum of zero, the average level will be halfway between the maximum and minimum values, or $Q/2$. In terms of the number of units in inventory, and the time each unit spends there, our fluctuating system is actually equivalent to maintaining $Q/2$ units at all times, as shown in Exhibit 16.3. This simplifies the calculation of annual variable holding costs to

$$\text{Annual variable holding costs} = \frac{Q}{2}C_h$$

Exhibit 16.3 Average Inventory

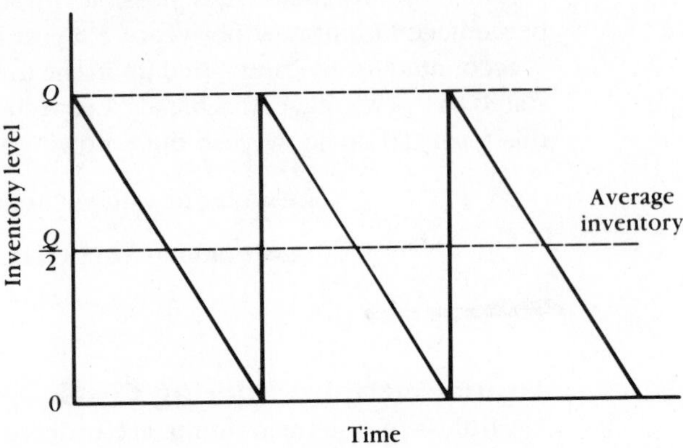

Economic Order Quantity Formula

Total annual variable costs will be the sum of holding costs and ordering costs. Using the formulas developed above, this will be

$$\text{Total annual variable costs} = \frac{Q}{2}C_h + \frac{D}{Q}C_o$$

The economic order quantity will be the point at which this total cost function is minimized. An easy way to find this point is by realizing that the EOQ occurs where annual holding costs and annual ordering costs are equal, as shown in Exhibit 16.1. In mathematical terms, this is

$$\frac{Q^*}{2}C_h = \frac{D}{Q^*}C_o$$

Note that we have used Q^* to designate the optimal value of Q, which is the economic order quantity. Solving the above equation for Q^*, we obtain

$$(Q^*)^2 = \frac{2DC_o}{C_h}$$

and by taking the square root of each side,

$$Q^* = \sqrt{\frac{2DC_o}{C_h}}$$

Example

Bill Green, inventory control manager for the Plymouth Metal Products Company, is responsible for developing inventory policies regarding all items the company stocks. One item that falls under his control is the machining oil that must be used for lubrication in many machining operations. This oil costs $5 per gallon. Variable costs of storing it in inventory amount to 25 percent of unit cost per year. Paperwork and shipping costs for placing an order are \$10 per order. Each year the company uses an average of 500 gallons, a rate that is not expected to change. How many gallons should be ordered each time to minimize total annual variable costs?

D = 500 gallons per year, C_o = \$10 per order, v = \$5 per unit, and r = \$.25 per \$ per year.

$$C_h = 5(.25) = \$1.25 \text{ per unit/year}$$

$$EOQ = \sqrt{\frac{2DC_o}{C_h}} = \sqrt{\frac{2(500)(10)}{1.25}}$$

$$= 89.44 \text{ gallons}$$

Since an order must be placed for whole gallons, Bill would probably round this off to 89 gallons per order.

Sensitivity of the EOQ Value

The EOQ in the preceding example did not come out to an even value. In fact, rounding off to the nearest whole number still gave a result that was somewhat unusual. It would be far more likely that Bill Green could order 90 gallons at a time than 89. But suppose this oil comes in 55-gallon drums. In that case, the closest order quantity would be two drums, or 110 gallons. What impact will this have on total annual variable costs if Plymouth Metal Products must order 110 gallons of machine oil at a time?

As it turns out, the total annual variable cost function is rather "flat" around the EOQ, as shown in Exhibit 16.4. In other words, order quantities can be varied considerably from the EOQ, especially above it, without greatly increasing costs.

Exhibit 16.4 Total Annual Cost Curve Near the EOQ

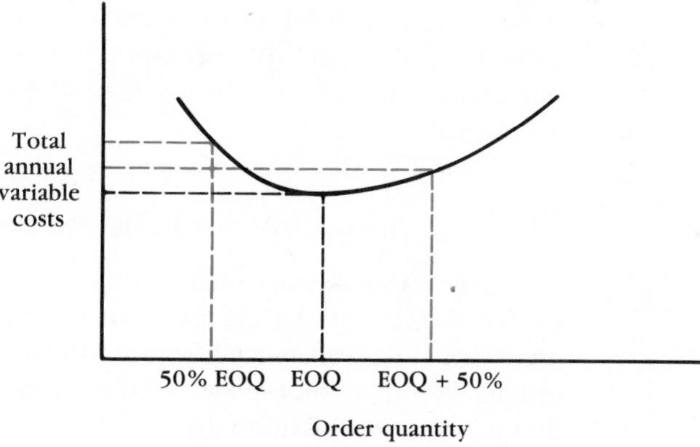

Example

Suppose Plymouth Metal Products wants to determine how much higher costs will be if it orders in lots of 110 gallons instead of the 89.44 gallons determined by the EOQ formula.

The total annual variable costs for the EOQ of the preceding example will be

$$\begin{aligned}\text{Total annual variable costs} &= \frac{Q}{2}C_h + \frac{D}{Q}C_o \\ &= \frac{89.44}{2}(\$1.25) + \frac{500}{89.44}(\$10) \\ &= \$55.90 + \$55.90 = \$111.80\end{aligned}$$

However, by changing Q to 110, the total annual variable costs will become

$$\begin{aligned}\frac{Q}{2}C_h + \frac{D}{Q}C_o &= \frac{110}{2}(\$1.25) + \frac{500}{110}(\$10) \\ &= \$68.75 + \$45.45 \\ &= \$114.20\end{aligned}$$

Thus, the cost increase incurred by ordering in quantities of 110 gallons at a time is only $2.40, or 2.15 percent more than the total annual variable costs of ordering EOQ quantities.

As this example indicates, the cost consequences of varying from the EOQ are not very great. The EOQ value should be thought of only as a ballpark figure that indicates approximate minimum-cost order quantities, not as a value that must be used exactly.

VARIATIONS ON THE EOQ MODEL

Starting from the basic EOQ model, it is possible to develop other models that either have less restrictive assumptions or are appropriate for other situations. In this section, we discuss only a few of the many possibilities that have been developed.

Finite Replenishment Rate Model

One basic EOQ assumption was that all units in a replenishment order are delivered at one time. This is usually true for retail outlets, warehouses, or distributors that order from a manufacturer. However, a company that manufactures the product it sells cannot instantaneously produce all units in an order. This situation is depicted in Exhibit 16.5.

This finite replenishment rate has an important impact on the EOQ calculation. Under the EOQ assumption of instantaneous replenishment, inventory

Exhibit 16.5 Quantity Produced During Replenishment Period Versus Maximum Inventory

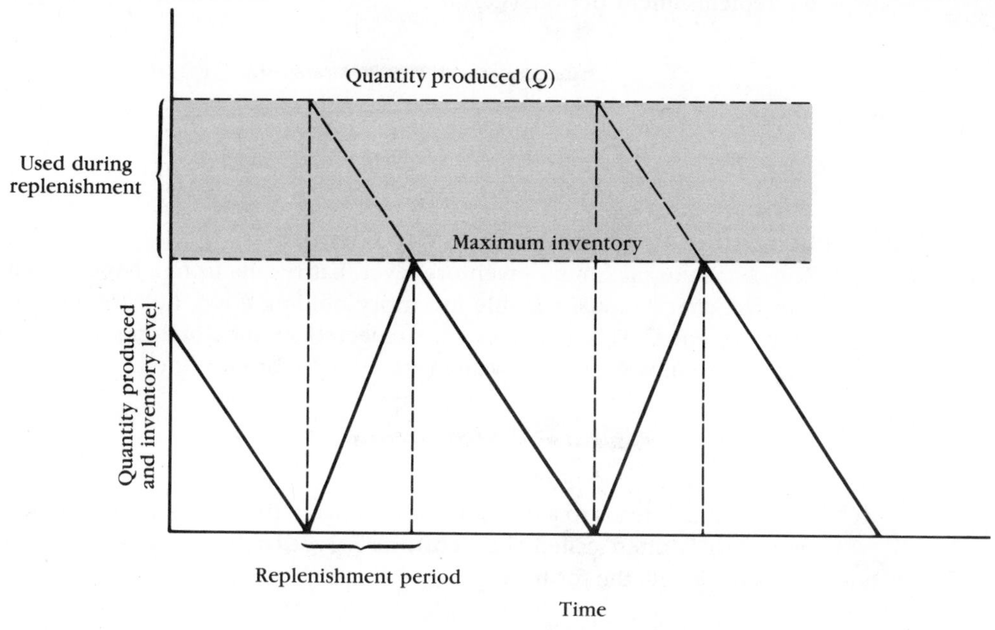

jumped up to the order quantity level whenever a replenishment occurred. However, with a finite replenishment rate, this does not occur because some items are being removed from inventory at the same time that others are being added. The net result is that maximum inventory will never reach the quantity ordered. Thus, the calculation of average inventory and, consequently, holding costs will change.

The finite replenishment rate model includes a period of time for producing the quantity ordered. This time period is shown in Exhibit 16.5. Mathematically, it can be calculated based on the replenishment rate where

$$p = \text{replenishment rate (units/day)}$$

If Q is the quantity ordered, or lot size, then the time to produce Q will be

$$\text{Replenishment period} = \frac{Q}{p} \text{ (days)}$$

During that same period, units are being withdrawn from inventory. We already know the annual demand rate, D. However, we must also use the daily demand rate,

$$d = \text{daily demand rate (units/day)}$$

Thus, the number of units used during the replenishment period will be the length of the replenishment period (Q/p) multiplied by the daily demand rate, or

$$\text{Usage during replenishment period} = \frac{Q}{p}d \text{ (units)}$$

The maximum inventory level is simply the lot size that was produced, Q, minus the number of those units that were used, or taken out of inventory, during the replenishment period, $(Q/p)d$.

$$\text{Maximum inventory level} = Q - \left(\frac{Q}{p}\right)d$$
$$= Q\left(1 - \frac{d}{p}\right)$$

Economic Production Quantity Formula

The change in maximum inventory level that results from a finite replenishment rate will affect annual variable inventory holding costs, but not annual variable ordering costs. This effect can be reflected in the total annual variable cost formula by substituting the value $Q(1 - d/p)$ for Q in the holding cost term.

$$\text{Total annual variable costs} = \frac{Q}{2}(1 - d/p)C_h + \frac{D}{Q}C_o$$

The result leads to a new lot-size formula in the case of a finite replenishment rate. This is often called the **economic production quantity (EPQ).** Stated mathematically, the formula is

$$\text{Economic production quantity} = \sqrt{\frac{2DC_o}{C_h(1 - d/p)}}$$

Example

One of the items made by the Plymouth Metal Products Company is a metal printer stand for microcomputers. By coincidence, the annual demand rate, ordering cost, and holding cost for this finished product are the same as for the machining oil described in the previous example. Demand is fairly uniform and is not expected to change over the next year. The production rate is fifty units per day.

Because this product is manufactured over a period of time, we must use the economic production quantity formula. This requires that daily demand rate also be determined. Suppose the company operates 250 days per year. Dividing annual demand by 250 provides daily demand of two units per day.

$D = 500$ units/year, $C_o = \$10$ per order,

$C_h = \$1.25$ per unit/year, $p = 50$ units/day, and $d = 2$ units/day.

$$\text{EPQ} = \sqrt{\frac{2DC_o}{C_h(1 - d/p)}} = \sqrt{\frac{2(500)(10)}{1.25(1 - 2/50)}}$$
$$= 91.29.$$

Total annual variable costs

$$= \frac{Q}{2}\left(1 - \frac{d}{p}\right)C_h + \frac{D}{Q}C_o$$

$$= \frac{91.29}{2}\left(1 - \frac{2}{50}\right)(\$1.25) + \frac{500}{91.29}(\$10)$$

$$= \$54.77 + \$54.77 = \$109.54$$

Once again, because an integer number of units must be produced, we could round this off to 91, or even to 90 or 100, without incurring excessive additional costs. You should also notice that even though all the costs and the demand rates were the same for this product and for the machining oil of the previous example, the quantity calculated here is higher, and the annual costs are lower. If the production rate were closer to demand rate, then the difference would be even greater due to the number of units withdrawn from inventory during the production period.

Quantity Discounts

Another assumption in the basic EOQ model was that purchase price remained the same regardless of how many units were purchased. In reality, this is usually not true. For example, things usually cost less, per unit, when purchased by the case rather than individually. An entire truckload generally will cost even less per unit. Therefore, the order quantity directly influences the purchase price of an item.

Incorporating quantity discounts into the order quantity calculations requires that we modify the total-cost calculation to include purchase cost—which had not been included previously because it was a fixed cost. Now, however, the total annual cost of purchasing an item may vary due to quantity discounts.

Unfortunately, this also means that we can no longer simply substitute numbers into a formula and get the correct answer, as we did for the EOQ and the EPQ. This occurs because quantity discounts occur in a stepwise manner, as shown in Exhibit 16.6. When this pattern of purchase costs is used to calculate total annual purchase cost and then combined with ordering and holding costs, the total-cost curve appears as shown in Exhibit 16.6. An iterative procedure is required to determine the order quantity that generates lowest total annual costs.

Procedure for Calculating Lot Size with Quantity Discounts

The procedure for calculating lot sizes with quantity discounts is based on using the unit cost, v, and holding-cost percentage, r, to calculate holding cost. In other words,

$$C_h = vr$$

Notice that as the unit purchase cost varies, so does the holding cost.

Step 1. Start with the lowest unit price. Calculate the holding cost, C_h, for this price, and then determine the EOQ. If this EOQ is "feasible"—in other words, if it falls in the range of order quantities required for that unit price—then this is the optimal order quantity. Stop here.

If the EOQ is not feasible, determine the *minimum* order quantity required for that unit price, and calculate the total annual variable costs (holding cost, ordering cost, *and purchase cost*) associated with that minimum order quantity. Proceed to step 2.

Exhibit 16.6 Total Annual Cost with Quantity Discounts

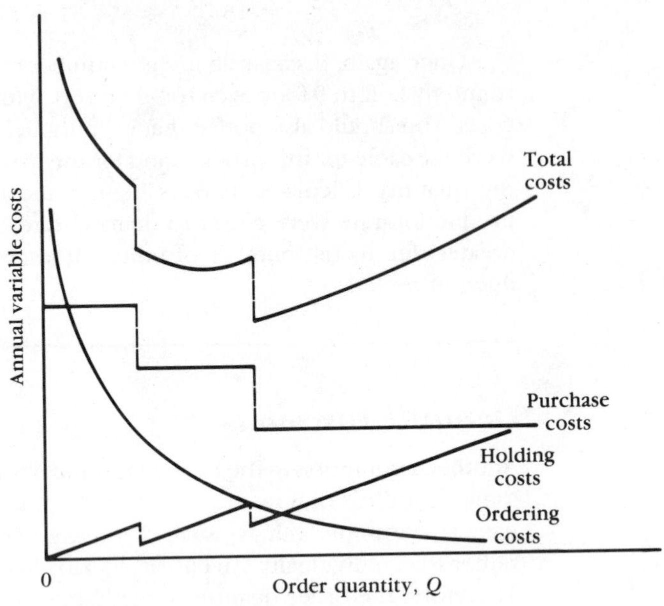

Step 2. For the next higher unit price, calculate holding cost, and determine EOQ. If the EOQ is feasible, then calculate its total annual variable costs, and compare this with the total annual variable costs for order quantities calculated previously. That order quantity with the lowest total annual variable costs will be optimal. Stop here.

If the EOQ is not feasible, repeat this step until a feasible EOQ is found; then calculate its associated total annual costs, and compare these costs with all total annual costs previously calculated. The order quantity with the lowest associated total annual variable costs will be optimal.

Example

Bill Green, of Plymouth Metal Products, has learned that the supplier of machining oil will begin offering quantity discounts according to the following schedule:

Gallons Ordered	Unit Price
54 or less	\$5.00
55–274	4.80
275–549	4.60
550 or more	4.50

Bill wonders whether he should change his lot size for ordering machining oil.

To answer his question, we will proceed through the steps described above.

Step 1. Calculate the holding cost and EOQ corresponding to the lowest unit price. This unit price will be \$4.50, and its associated holding cost is (.25)(\$4.50) = \$1.125/gallon/year.

$$\text{EOQ} = \sqrt{\frac{2(500)(10)}{1.125}}$$

$$= 94 \text{ gallons (rounding to the nearest whole number)}$$

However, this is not feasible because at least 550 gallons must be ordered each time to obtain the \$4.50 unit price. Thus, we calculate the total annual variable costs, including purchase cost (Dv), associated with ordering 550 gallons each time.

$$\text{Total annual variable costs} = \frac{Q}{2}C_h + \frac{D}{Q}C_o + Dv$$

$$= \frac{550}{2}\$1.125 + \frac{500}{550}\$10 + 500(\$4.50)$$

$$= \$309.38 + \$9.09 + \$2{,}250.00$$

$$= \$2{,}568.47$$

Step 2. For the next higher unit price, calculate holding cost, and determine EOQ. This next higher unit price will be \$4.60, obtained by ordering between 275 and 549 gallons each time. Holding cost will be (.25)(\$4.60) = \$1.15/gallon/year and

$$\text{EOQ} = \sqrt{\frac{2(500)(10)}{1.15}}$$

$$= 93 \text{ gallons}$$

This also is not feasible since 93 is not in the range of 275 to 549 gallons required for the \$4.60 unit price. Thus, taking the minimum value in that range of 275, we calculate associated total annual variable costs.

$$\text{Total annual variable costs} = \frac{Q}{2}C_h + \frac{D}{Q}C_o + Dv$$

$$= \frac{275}{2}\$1.15 + \frac{500}{275}\$10 + 500(\$4.60)$$

$$= \$158.13 + \$18.18 + \$2{,}300.00$$

$$= \$2{,}476.31$$

Since the EOQ for this unit price was not feasible, we proceed to the next higher price of \$4.80 per gallon. Its holding cost will be \$1.20/gallon/year, and the EOQ is 91 gallons.

This EOQ is feasible, so we calculate its total annual variable costs.

$$\text{Total annual variable costs} = \frac{Q}{2}C_h + \frac{D}{Q}C_o + Dv$$

$$= \frac{91}{2}\$1.20 + \frac{500}{91}\$10 + 500(\$4.80)$$

$$= \$54.60 + \$54.95 + \$2{,}400.00$$

$$= \$2{,}509.55$$

We then compare all the total annual variable costs calculated so far, as shown in the following table:

Order Quantity (gallons)	Total Annual Variable Costs
550	$2,568.47
275	2,476.31
91	2,509.55

Thus, the lowest-cost order quantity will be 275 gallons, and Plymouth Metal Products should change its lot size for machining oil.

STOCK-OUTS AND SAFETY STOCK

Order-Point Determination

In all of our calculations thus far, we have made the important assumption that inventory would somehow be replenished just as it hit zero. Thus, the minimum inventory level was treated as zero. In most situations, the replenishment of inventory requires some advance notice. For example, a company that orders materials from a supplier must account for the time it takes that order to reach the supplier's offices, the time to fill the order, and then the shipping time. This is called **lead time.**

Failing to account for lead time, or allowing an inadequate amount of lead time, can cause an organization to run out of inventory. This situation is known as a **stock-out.** Any time a stock-out occurs, the result is likely to be a disruption in production, idle employees, and unhappy customers. Most companies try to avoid stock-outs if at all possible.

Doing so requires that inventory replenishment lead time be taken into account. Probably the easiest way to account for lead time is to use what is called an **order point.** An order point is simply a level of inventory at which an order should be placed, accounting for lead time and safety stock, so that the order will come in before a stock-out occurs. Exhibit 16.7 shows how the order point is determined.

The concept depicted in Exhibit 16.7 is that the order point should be a level of inventory that will be sufficient to last throughout the lead time, with inventory

Exhibit 16.7 Order-Point Determination

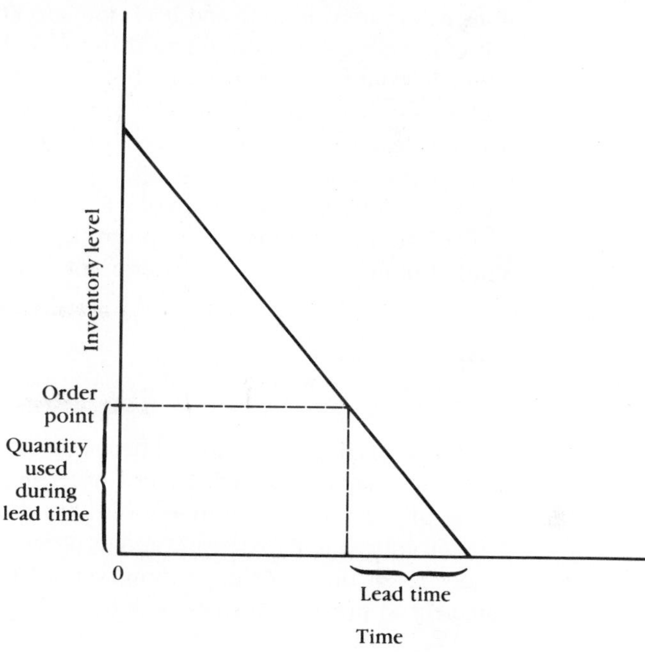

reaching zero just as the order arrives. Mathematically, the order point can be determined as follows. We will use the following symbols:

$$d = \text{daily demand rate (units/day)}$$
$$m = \text{lead time (days)}$$

Then the order point, r, can be determined by using the formula given below.

$$r = dm$$

Example

Suppose that Plymouth Metal Products wants to determine the order point for its machining oil. We have already determined that daily demand would be 2 gallons per day (500 gallons per year/250 working days per year). Suppose we also learn that lead time for ordering the machining oil is ten working days. The order point is

$$\begin{aligned} r &= dm \\ &= 2(10) \\ &= 20 \text{ gallons} \end{aligned}$$

So, when only twenty gallons are left in inventory, an order for more should be placed. That order should arrive just as inventory reaches zero.

Safety Stocks

The explanation of order-point determination given above works well in situations where demand rate and lead time are known and invariant. Unfortunately, it is much more common to find that demand and lead time are both variable. If either lead time or demand, or both, is less than expected, there will be no problem—when the order arrives, some inventory will be left. But if either demand or lead time, or both, exceeds our expected values, then a stock-out will occur because inventory will hit zero before the order arrives, as shown in Exhibit 16.8; there is no margin of safety in the preceding order-point calculation.

To avoid stock-outs, most companies add a **safety stock,** which is an extra amount of inventory, to the order-point calculation so that

$$r = dm + s$$

where

$$s = \text{safety stock}$$

What this does is to add a buffer of inventory that can be expected to remain when an order is received. Instead of letting inventory hit zero when an order comes in, we only let it drop to *s,* the amount of safety stock, as shown in Exhibit 16.9. Of course, due to demand and lead-time variability, more or less may remain at any given time. We hope, however, that this buffer of safety stock will be sufficient to prevent most stock-outs.

Service Level

No matter how much safety stock a company carries, there is always some chance that a stock-out will occur due to unusually high demand or an extremely long lead time. It usually is just not possible for a company to avoid stock-outs alto-

Exhibit 16.8 Stock-Out Occurrence

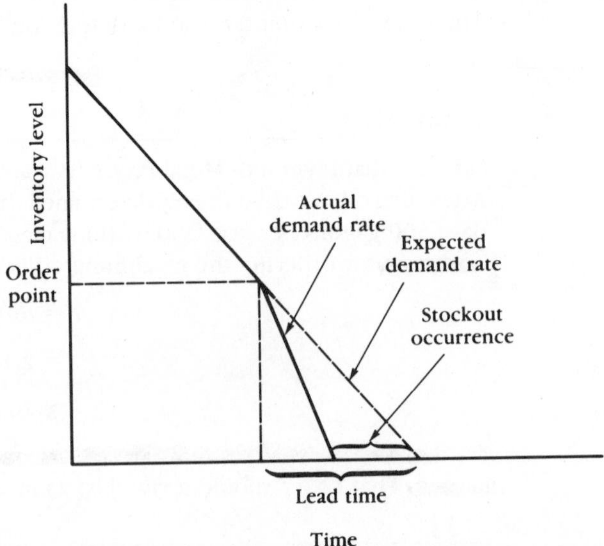

Exhibit 16.9 Inventory Level with Safety Stock

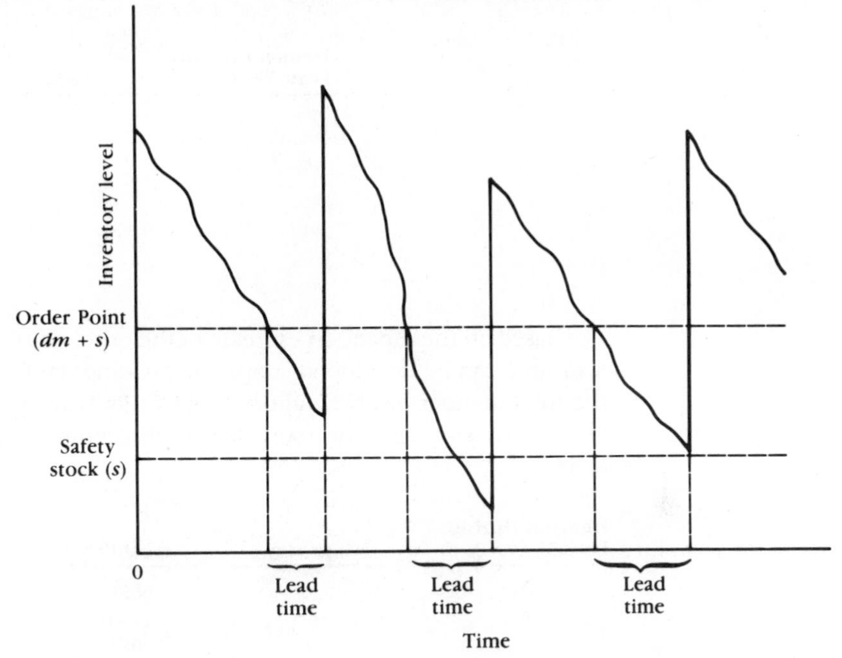

gether. Instead, companies can select a level of stock-outs that they are willing to accept.

Several measures can be associated with stock-outs, ranging from determining the expected **time between stock-outs (TBS)** to minimizing total cost, including the cost of stock-outs. However, the most common measure, and the one we will use here, is service level.

Service level, for our purposes, is the percentage of times a replenishment order is received before a stock-out occurs. For instance, a 95 percent service level would indicate that 95 percent of all orders placed to replenish inventory are received before a stock-out occurs. But in 5 percent of the cases, inventory will hit zero before the order is received.

Determination of service level is a managerial decision that must be based on many factors. A company that competes on the basis of service may choose a service level of 99 percent or higher. Another company may be in an industry where meeting customer demand from inventory is not important. For the latter, a service level of 80 percent, or even lower, may be acceptable.

Once the service level has been determined, a company may proceed to calculate its safety stock. We now discuss that procedure for two different situations.

Discrete Probability Distribution

A discrete probability distribution is used when a variable may have only certain discrete values. For instance, lead-time demand is often stated in terms of whole units (not fractions).

If a company has kept records of its lead-time demand, a frequency distribution can be developed, based on that data. For example, suppose the following information has been found:

Demand During Lead Time	Frequency
5	3
6	6
7	10
8	12
9	9
10	5
11	3

Based on these data, an estimate of the probability of each demand during the lead time can be developed simply by dividing the frequency of occurrences by the total number of observations (48). Cumulative probabilities can also be developed by summing the individual probabilities associated with each demand level.

Demand During Lead Time	Frequency	Probability	Cumulative Probability
5	3	.0625	.0625
6	6	.1250	.1875
7	10	.2083	.3958
8	12	.2500	.6458
9	9	.1875	.8333
10	5	.1042	.9375
11	3	.0625	1.0000

The cumulative probabilities represent the probability, based on past data, that demand during the lead time will be less than or equal to the corresponding value. For instance, based on past experience, there is a 64.58 percent probability that demand will be eight units or less during the lead time.

Suppose that the firm wants a 90 percent service level. To achieve that, it must be able to satisfy demand before inventory runs out at least 90 percent of the time. What order point is required? To find out, look at the cumulative probabilities calculated previously, and determine which is greater than or equal to 90 percent. For our data, that would be 93.75 percent, corresponding to a demand of ten units. Thus, to have a service level of 90 percent, the organization must place an order when its available inventory reaches ten units.

Continuous Probability Distribution

In some cases, it may be reasonable for a company to use the discrete probability distribution approach described above. However, other times there may not be sufficient data to calculate probabilities with any reasonable certainty. Or, as for liquids, certain items may have an infinite number of possible values of demand during the lead time. In those cases, it can make more sense to utilize a continuous probability distribution that approximates actual demand. The most commonly used is the normal probability distribution.

The normal probability distribution is described by a mean and a standard deviation. For our purposes, these values are

$\bar{D}_L$ = average demand during lead time

σ_L = standard deviation of demand during lead time

The safety stock necessary to obtain a desired service level can be calculated as

$$\text{Safety stock} = z\sigma_L$$

where

z = number of standard deviations from the mean required to obtain desired service level

The reorder point is then

$$r = \bar{D}_L + \text{safety stock}$$

$$= \bar{D}_L + z\sigma_L$$

As Exhibit 16.10 indicates, the service level—or probability of no stock-out—will be equal to the area under the normal curve up to $\bar{D}_L + z\sigma_L$. Thus, the value of z is determined on the basis of the desired service level.

Example

A company has average demand during the reordering lead time that is normally distributed with a mean of thirty-five and a standard deviation of six. What safety stock and reorder point are necessary to obtain a 90 percent service level?

Referring to the normal distribution table in the Chapter 14 Appendix, we see that the probability closest to .90 is .8997, which is in the 1.2 row and .08 column. Thus, a z value of 1.28 is needed to obtain a 90 percent service level.

Exhibit 16.10 Normal Probability Distribution

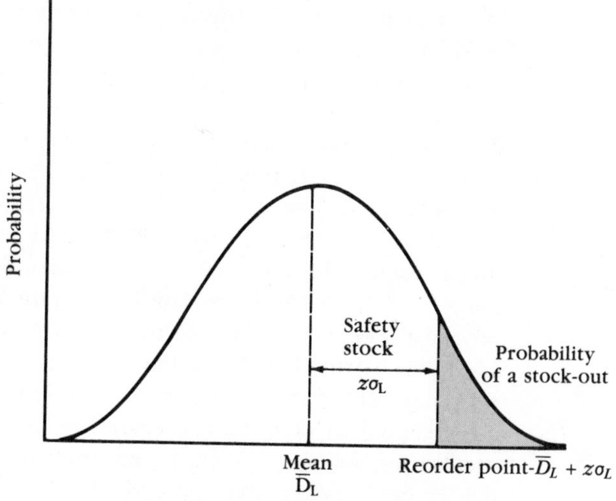

$$\text{Safety stock} = z\sigma_L$$
$$= 1.28(6)$$
$$= 7.692 \text{ or } 8$$
$$\text{Reorder point} = \bar{D}_L + \text{safety stock}$$
$$= 35 + 8$$
$$= 43$$

INVENTORY CONTROL SYSTEMS

In the discussion up to this point, we have assumed that a company would know exactly how many units it had left in inventory at any given time. While that may not seem unreasonable, just consider the average supermarket. How can the supermarket manager possibly keep track of the inventory level of each of several thousand, or even several hundred, different items when customers are continually removing those items from the shelves for purchase? The problem of maintaining an accurate inventory count may be even worse for a manufacturing company, which might inventory over ten thousand separate parts and raw materials. Even trying to keep track of a small percentage of those items can be an overwhelming task.

Several different approaches have been developed to handle that problem. The more common, general ones will be discussed here. However, there are many variations on these, and you should keep in mind that each company or organization will have its own system for controlling and tracking inventory.

ABC Classification

As it turns out, companies often need not keep extremely accurate track of all inventory items. For instance, certain parts may have a relatively low value and be used infrequently; those items can often be monitored very loosely. On the other hand, high-value, high-usage items must be tracked carefully and continuously.

To determine which inventory items should receive the highest level of control, a scheme has been developed called **ABC analysis.** The idea behind this scheme is that if we multiply the dollar value of each item by its annual usage, we will obtain a **dollar usage** value. As it turns out, dollar usage follows the *Pareto Principle,* and only 20 percent of all the items account for 80 percent of the total dollar usage, while the remaining 80 percent of the items account for only 20 percent of the dollar usage. This leads to the ABC classification, based on the idea of focusing our efforts where the payoff is highest.

After calculating the dollar usage for each inventory item, the items are ranked by dollar usage, from highest to lowest. The first 20 percent of the items are assigned to class A. These are the items that warrant closest control and monitoring. Accurate inventory records are important, and there is a high potential for cutting costs through careful buying and close scrutiny of safety stocks.

The next 30 percent of the items are classified as B items. These deserve less attention than A items. Finally, the last 50 percent of items are C items. These have the lowest dollar usage and can be monitored loosely, with larger safety stocks maintained to avoid stock-outs.

Continuous Review Systems

One extreme example of possible methods for maintaining inventory records is to continuously review the inventory level. In actuality, companies do not usually monitor their inventory on a continuous basis. Instead, records are kept and changes made only when a replenishment or withdrawal occurs. There are several ways of handling this.

Transaction Recording

Probably the most common system, transaction recording, uses some way of recording inventory level and then changing this when a replenishment is received or a withdrawal made. The simplest way to do this is based on keeping a file card for each inventory item. When changes in inventory occur, they are noted on the appropriate card. Several commercial systems, such as Kardex or VISI-Record, are based on this approach.

However, many companies have moved to computerization of their record-keeping function. As inventory changes occur, they can be entered into the computer file.

The most recent approach to transaction recording utilizes bar codes. By placing a bar code on each item that indicates a code number associated with that item, companies can enter transaction data directly into the computer by simply passing a wand or scanner over the bar code. This eliminates the possibility of clerical errors during data entry and allows for immediate updating of inventory records.

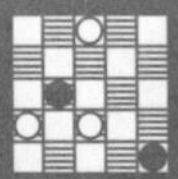

GAINING STRATEGIC ADVANTAGE AT TOYS "R" US

Using Inventory Information to Provide Customer Service

Toys "R" Us currently has over 300 stores in the United States and almost 40 overseas. Each one of those stores has about 46,000 square feet of floor space and carries 18,000 items. Just keeping track of all that inventory could be a horrendous job in itself.

However, Toys "R" Us must not only track its inventory. To stay competitive the company must know which items are selling and which are not. Running out of a hot item can mean lost sales, while having too much of something passé means wasted space and excess costs.

Every day the thousands of cash registers at Toys "R" Us stores transmit sale information back to the company headquarters in Rochelle Park, New Jersey. Computers collect information so store managers can know exactly how many of each item were sold the day before, how many have been sold in the year to date, and how many were sold last year.

Computers also handle the reordering automatically. Thus, when Toys "R" Us tried stocking scooters, the computers picked up the fact that the initial order of 10,000 sold out in two days and immediately ordered larger quantities. As a result, Toys "R" Us sold over a million scooters that year. Computers also picked up the end of the Trivial Pursuit game fad and stopped ordering more.[2]

Point-of-Sale Systems

This same bar-code technology has been utilized by grocery stores to update their inventory records immediately whenever an item is purchased. As that item passes over the scanner at the checkout counter, the bar code is read, and the store's inventory level of that item is reduced by one. Such systems are called point-of-sale systems.

Retail outlets utilize a similar approach with character-recognition devices. Again, the purpose is to allow immediate recording of the inventory withdrawal that occurs when an item is purchased.

Periodic Review Systems

For many organizations, the time and effort of maintaining continuous inventory records may not be worth it. Even within an organization, it may be desirable to use a continuous review system only for class A items and to control B and C items by other means. A commonly used system that is generally less expensive and requires less record keeping is the periodic review system.

Under periodic review, the inventory level of an item is checked only at regular intervals, such as every week or every month. This approach is convenient for organizations such as grocery stores or discount stores that order on such a schedule. However, one problem with this approach is that an order point may be passed before an inventory review is conducted.

The EOQ order-point approach described earlier is most applicable under a continuous review system because an order can be triggered as soon as inventory drops to the order point. With the periodic review system, a different approach to ordering and lot-size determination must be taken.

Review Interval

Think for a minute back to the EOQ model and Exhibit 16.2. The time that elapses between replenishments really depends on the order quantity, or lot size. We used this idea to determine the number of replenishment orders placed per year. In a periodic review system, the opposite will occur. That is, the time between reviews, or the **review interval (R),** will determine average order quantity because the annual demand must be met during a year. If orders are placed frequently, then each order will be smaller. Infrequent ordering means large lot sizes.

Recall, though, that we still have the classic trade-off between variable ordering costs and variable inventory holding costs. Thus, the review interval that is chosen can directly affect total annual variable costs.

Fortunately, you have already learned most of what is needed to calculate that optimal interval, R, when you learned how to calculate EOQ. The reason why is that the relationship between order size and order interval means that an economic order quantity will also produce an economic order interval. In other words, the optimal review interval is simply the interval that would result in ordering an EOQ quantity each time. This order interval will be the EOQ divided by demand rate, D.

$$\text{Optimal review interval, } R = \frac{\text{EOQ}}{D}$$

Example

The Hunziker Hardware Store carries many different items, ranging from nails and screws to appliances and hot-water heaters. It doesn't make sense for them to maintain a continuous review system for the many small hardware items they carry. Instead, they would like to determine a review interval at which all items ordered from one regular supplier can be checked and ordered at one time.

One such group consists of brass items, such as screws, hinges, and cupboard handles. Because all such items are basically similar in terms of cost and demand level, they have been grouped together. Annual demand rate for these items is 10,000 units per year. Ordering cost is $25 per order, and holding cost is $.02 per unit per year. Using the above data, we can determine the EOQ as follows:

$$EOQ = \sqrt{\frac{2(10{,}000)(25)}{.02}}$$

$$= 5{,}000 \text{ units}$$

Based on this, the review interval is

$$R = \frac{\text{EOQ}}{D}$$

$$= 5{,}000/10{,}000$$

$$= \frac{1}{2} \text{ year}$$

Thus, the Hunziker Hardware Store should review its inventory levels of these small hardware items twice per year and order the required quantity of each.

Order-Up-to Level

The next question to be answered in a periodic review system is how much to order. Under continuous review, a replenishment order was always placed when inventory reached the order point. However, in a periodic review system, the inventory level at the time of review will vary, as depicted in Exhibit 16.11.

If a constant amount were ordered each time, it would be very difficult to recover from a low inventory level. Instead, the quantity ordered must bring inventory back up to a level sufficient to cover anticipated demand before the next order is received. This is called the **order-up-to level,** or *S.* A diagram of an order-up-to level is shown in Exhibit 16.11.

Another difference between continuous and periodic review systems relates to the period of time that must be covered by an order. Under continuous review, inventory level is monitored continuously and an order placed whenever that inventory reaches the order point. However, under a periodic review system, once an order has been placed, the inventory will not be checked again until the next review period. Thus, the amount ordered each time must be sufficient to cover expected demand during the review interval *plus* demand during the lead time, as shown in Exhibit 16.12, or a stock-out will occur. If the review interval, *R,* and the lead time, *M,* are stated in terms of a year, then the order-up-to level to cover demand during the review interval plus the lead time must be

$$S = D(R + M).$$

Exhibit 16.11 Order-Up-to Level in a Periodic Review System

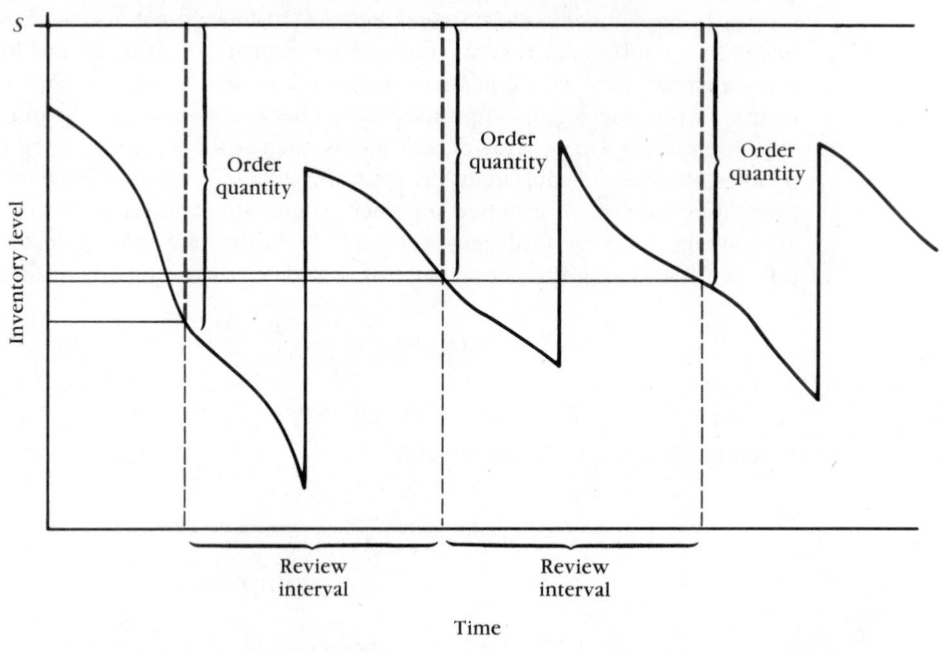

Exhibit 16.12 Period of Time an Order Must Cover

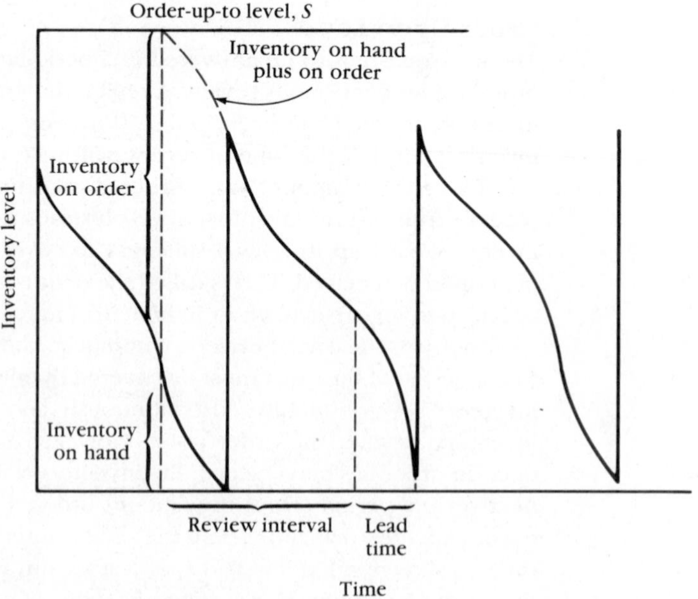

Example

It was determined in the previous example that the review interval for the common group of brass hardware items will be ½ year for all items in that group. One of the hardware items in that group is a brass gate hinge that has a demand of 1,000 units per year. Lead time is ⅒ year. What should the order-up-to level be for this hardware item? We can use the preceding formula to calculate this level as follows:

$$
\begin{aligned}
S &= D(R + M) \\
&= 1{,}000(.5 + .1) \\
&= 600 \text{ units}
\end{aligned}
$$

This means that whenever the hardware store reviews inventory of this group of items, it should order enough of the brass gate hinges to bring on-hand plus on-order inventory up to 600 units. For example, suppose that during the semiannual inventory review, it is found that 100 brass gate hinges are in inventory. In that case, 500 brass gate hinges (600 − 100) should be ordered.

Safety Stock

The order-up-to level developed above can be thought of in some ways as the order point in a continuous review system. As with the basic order-point calculation, the preceding order-up-to formula does not include safety stock. Because of the nature of periodic review systems, safety stock is probably more important and necessary for them than for continuous review systems. It will also be larger, as you will see.

Under a continuous review system, the lead time following an order was the period of time when a stock-out could occur. Therefore, we calculated safety stock using the standard deviation of demand during the lead time. However, with a periodic review system, a stock-out could theoretically occur at any time between review periods and during the lead time. Thus, safety stock for a periodic review system must be calculated based on the standard deviation of demand during the review interval plus the lead time. Except for this modification, the calculation is the same as for a continuous review system; safety stock will now be added to the order-up-to level.

Example

The brass gate hinge discussed in the previous example had an order-up-to level of 600 with no safety stock. Suppose that demand during the review interval plus the lead time has a standard deviation of 100 units. What must the order-up-to level be set at to obtain a 95 percent service level if we assume demand is normally distributed?

From the normal probability tables (Chapter 14 Appendix), a probability of 95 percent corresponds to a z value of 1.645. Therefore, the safety stock will be

$$\text{Safety stock} = z\sigma_{I+L}$$
$$= 1.645(100)$$
$$= 164.5 \text{ or } 165 \text{ hinges}$$

Adding this to the expected demand during the review interval plus the lead time (the S calculated in the preceding example), the new order-up-to level becomes

$$S = D(R + M) + \text{safety stock}$$
$$= 1{,}000\,(.5 + .1) + 165$$
$$= 765$$

Base Stock Systems

A very simple inventory control system often used by retailers and warehouses is called the base stock system. In its simplest form, the **base stock system** is a periodic review system with the order-up-to level, S, equal to average demand during the lead time plus safety stock. Thus, inventory level is minimized. However, a replenishment order must be placed whenever a withdrawal is made, making this approach most appropriate for low-volume, high-cost items.

However, many variations of this system exist. For example, warehouses and distribution centers often replenish their inventory on a regular basis, such as every week. Thus, instead of placing a replenishment order every time there is a withdrawal, orders will be accumulated until the end of each week. Weekly shipments will simply equal the total withdrawals during the preceding week.

Aggregate Performance Measures

You should recall that, as discussed in Chapters 11 and 12, inventory represents a tremendous capital investment. In general, the companies that can operate with less inventory are the ones that operate more efficiently. Several aggregate performance measures can be used to judge how well a company is utilizing its inventory resources.

Average Inventory Investment

One of the most common measures and one that is easy to interpret, **average inventory investment,** is just the dollar value of a company's average level of inventory. This information is usually quite easy to obtain from a company's accounting data.

The primary disadvantage of this measure is that it makes comparisons of companies difficult. For example, larger companies will generally have more inventory than smaller companies will. Thus, a large multinational company might have a larger average inventory investment than a small business, but could still be using its inventory more efficiently.

McKesson Corporation: Service Merchandising—A New Concept in Retailing

Grocery stores must operate on notoriously thin profit margins. However, some items they stock can offer high margins. Those items are the so-called nongrocery items that range from health and beauty aids to antifreeze. But if those items are not managed correctly, they can become unprofitable.

A further headache is that such items must often be ordered from different vendors. That's where McKesson comes in. The company's service merchandising operation distributes 26,000 different nongrocery items. But more than that, McKesson even keeps track of inventory and restock shelves for the 18,000 supermarkets that are its customers.

With hand-held bar code scanners, store clerks can automatically record information about inventories on the shelves. Using information stored in the scanner, McKesson restocks the shelves within 48 hours and also identifies slow-moving items.

By contracting with McKesson for service merchandising, grocery stores can restock their shelves with nongrocery items more often and more quickly than they could otherwise. In addition, they have to deal with only one vendor who analyzes sales trends for them.[3]

Inventory Turnover Ratio

Inventory turnover ratio is a measure that allows for better comparison among companies. This ratio is calculated by comparing a company's sales to its average inventory investment, as follows:

$$\text{Inventory turnover} = \frac{\text{annual cost of goods sold}}{\text{average inventory investment}}$$

The **inventory turnover ratio** indicates how many times during a year the inventory turns over, or is sold. Because it is a relative measure, companies of different sizes can be more easily compared. Thus, in general, a company with a higher turnover ratio will be using its inventory more efficiently. For example, automobile companies using JIT often have inventory turnover ratios of 60 or 70, while those not using JIT may be in the range of 6 to 25.

However, one disadvantage of this ratio is that figures among industries may not be comparable. For example, grocery stores must carry much larger inventories than automobile manufacturers do.

Days of Inventory

A measure closely related to inventory turnover is days of inventory. The calculation procedure is as follows:

$$\text{Days of inventory} = \frac{\text{average inventory investment}}{\text{annual cost of goods sold}} \times \text{days per year}$$

The **days of inventory** indicate approximately how many days of sales can be supplied solely from inventory. Thus, the lower this value is, the more efficiently inventory is being used. In general, inventory turnover can be converted to days of inventory by using the following calculation:

$$\text{Days of inventory} = \frac{\text{annual working days}}{\text{inventory turnover ratio}}$$

LOT SIZING FOR MRP SYSTEMS

The models and systems described so far in this chapter are appropriate for independent demand, such as the demand for supplies or finished products. For dependent-demand items, such as component parts, subassemblies, or raw materials, MRP is the most appropriate system because the demand for such items depends on the master schedule—and is therefore known in advance.

The planned order releases in MRP were determined by starting with a master schedule and then applying the MRP logic through bills of materials and inventory records. Those planned order releases represent the quantity that must be ordered during each time bucket in order to satisfy planned production requirements.

For example, Wheel Products Corporation makes skateboards. The company buys wheels for its skateboards from a supplier. Planned production of skateboards over a future period of eight weeks is indicated by the following master schedule:

Master Production Schedule—Skateboards

Week							
1	**2**	**3**	**4**	**5**	**6**	**7**	**8**
800	800	500	500	1,000	900	900	600

Since each skateboard requires four wheels, it will be simple to determine projected gross requirements. Planned inventory on hand at the start of that period is 4,000 wheels, and replenishment lead time is one week. Based on this, the planned order releases can be determined as indicated in Exhibit 16.13.

Exhibit 16.13 Planned Order Releases for Skateboard Wheels

		Week							
		1	**2**	**3**	**4**	**5**	**6**	**7**	**8**
Projected gross requirements		3,200	3,200	2,000	2,000	4,000	3,600	3,600	2,400
Scheduled receipts									
Projected ending inventory	4,000	800	0	0	0	0	0	0	0
Net requirements			2,400	2,000	2,000	4,000	3,600	3,600	2,400
Planned receipts			2,400	2,000	2,000	4,000	3,600	3,600	2,400
Planned order releases		2,400	2,000	2,000	4,000	3,600	3,600	2,400	

These planned order releases use what is called **lot-for-lot lot sizing.** In other words, each planned order (or lot) is simply based on a corresponding time bucket's net requirements. Under this system, an order is placed once each time period (each week in this case) to meet a future period's net requirements.

Since each order will be used up during a week, inventory holding costs will be low. On the other hand, weekly orders can make annual ordering costs high. Even though many firms that have MRP systems use lot-for-lot ordering, it may be possible to reduce annual costs by combining orders. That is, instead of placing an order for 2,400 wheels in week 1 and another order for 2,000 wheels in week 2, Wheel Products might release an order for 4,400 wheels in week 1 and order nothing in week 2. This means one less order—and the associated savings in ordering costs. Of course, the trade-off will be higher inventory holding costs.

Just as there were a number of lot-sizing procedures for independent demand items, we will find various ways of lot sizing in MRP systems. In this section, we will describe what seem to be the more common methods.

Costs

The same variable costs of ordering and holding inventory that were applied in the independent-demand situations will be used here. Each time an order is placed, the variable ordering cost will be incurred. However, we will make several simplifying assumptions about the holding-cost calculation.

We will assume, first, that any order will be received at the beginning of a week. Further, any quantity used during a week will not incur a holding cost. The holding cost will be calculated only for quantities carried over from one week to the next. This will simplify our calculations, while having no appreciable effect on the outcome.

Period Order Quantity

Recall that when we discussed the periodic review system, we converted the EOQ into an equivalent time period. That was how the optimal review interval was determined. The same approach can be used in MRP, except that since demand is known, the interval becomes a time period over which net requirements are batched together in one planned order release. The order quantity that results, which will vary as net requirements vary, is called the **period order quantity,** or **POQ.** The interval over which net requirements are combined will be called the **order period.**

If the annual demand rate is represented by D, then the POQ order period can be expressed as a fraction of a year by the formula

$$\text{Order period} = \frac{\text{EOQ}}{D}$$

Example

For the Wheel Products Company, total planned production over the eight-week master schedule period is 6,000 skateboards. This means that over that same eight-week period, 24,000 wheels will be needed. This figure can be converted to an estimated annual demand for wheels as follows:

$$24{,}000 \text{ wheels/8 weeks} \times 52 \text{ weeks/year} = 156{,}000 \text{ wheels/year}$$

The cost of placing an order for wheels is $25, and the inventory holding cost is $.25 per wheel per year. This means that

$$\text{EOQ} = \sqrt{\frac{2(25)(156{,}000)}{.25}}$$

$$= 5{,}586$$

Then,

$$\text{Order period} = \frac{\text{EOQ}}{D}$$

$$= \frac{5{,}586}{156{,}000}$$

$$= .0358 \text{ year}$$

Converting this to weeks, we have

$$\text{Order period} = .0358 \text{ year} \times 52 \text{ weeks/year}$$

$$= 1.86 \text{ weeks}$$

which we would round up to 2.

This means that planned orders would be set for every two weeks by combining the net requirements for each two-week period, as shown below.

	Week							
	1	2	3	4	5	6	7	8
Net requirements	0	2,400	2,000	2,000	4,000	3,600	3,600	2,400
Planned receipts	0	4,400	0	6,000	0	7,200	0	2,400
Planned order releases	4,400	0	6,000	0	7,200	0	2,400	0

Note that because our time horizon ends at week 8, the planned receipt for week 8 reflects only that week's net requirements. As the time horizon is moved farther into the future, the planned receipt for week 8 would include net requirements for weeks 8 and 9.

Will using this lot-sizing strategy produce lower costs than using lot-for-lot will? To find out, we must calculate the total costs of each method over the eight-week period.

Using lot-for-lot sizing, there will be no holding costs since each lot will be used during the week it is received. Therefore, the total cost will be based wholly on ordering cost.

Total cost using lot-for-lot: 8 orders × $25/order = $200

With the POQ strategy, we must calculate both ordering cost and holding cost. Remember that holding cost will be incurred only on quantities that are carried over from one week to another. Any amount used up within a week incurs no cost. For example, out of the first week's order for 4,400 wheels, 2,400 will be used in week 2 when the order is received. The remaining 2,000 must be carried over to week 3 and will incur a holding cost.

To calculate that cost, we must convert holding cost per wheel into a weekly figure:

Holding cost: (\$.25 per wheel/yr.)/(52 wks./yr.) = \$.0048 per wheel/wk.

Based on this, total cost of the POQ strategy will be

Ordering cost: 4 orders × \$25/order	=	\$100.00
Holding cost: \$.0048(2,000 + 4,000 + 3,600)	=	46.08
Total cost	=	\$146.08

Thus, it is less expensive to order by the POQ strategy.

The Silver-Meal Heuristic

One other method that works extremely well, especially when the demand pattern varies considerably, is called the **Silver-Meal heuristic.**[4] The idea behind this method is to minimize the total cost per unit of time for each order. For example, if a particular order will satisfy demand for *n* time periods, then the total cost per unit of time will be

$$\frac{\text{Ordering cost} + \text{total holding costs to end of period } n}{n}$$

Example

Suppose we apply the Silver-Meal heuristic to the Wheel Products Company situation. We begin with the first week for which there are nonzero net requirements, week 2, and determine cost per week of ordering for that week only, which will include only ordering cost.

Week 2 only: \$25/1 week = \$25/week

Next, we consider planning a receipt in week 2 to cover net requirements of weeks 2 and 3. There will now be holding costs for the week 3 quantity:

Weeks 2 and 3: (\$25 + .0048 × 2,000)/2 weeks = \$17.30/week

Thus, it is less expensive, on a per-week basis, to order enough for weeks 2 and 3. What about placing one order for weeks 2, 3, and 4? You should be sure to notice that now the quantity needed for week 4 will arrive in week 2 and must be carried over for two weeks before it is used up.

Weeks 2, 3, and 4: [\$25 + \$.0048(2,000 + 2(2,000))]/3 weeks = \$17.93/week

Since this is a higher cost per week than combining only weeks 2 and 3, we will not combine the net requirements from weeks 2, 3, and 4 in one planned order. We proceed now by considering the cost of not combining any other orders with the order for week 4 net requirements.

Week 4 only: \$25/1 week = \$25/ week

Now, what if we combine the week 5 net requirements with those for week 4 and plan to receive 6,000 units in week 4? This will mean carrying 4,000 units over one week, and the cost per unit time will be

$$\text{Weeks 4 and 5: } (\$25 + \$.0048 \times 4{,}000)/2 \text{ weeks} = \$22.10/\text{week}$$

Since this produces a lower cost per week than not combining orders, we continue and consider combining the orders for weeks 4, 5, and 6.

$$\text{Weeks 4, 5, and 6: } [\$25 + \$.0048(4{,}000 + 2(3{,}600))]/3 \text{ weeks} = \$26.25/\text{week}$$

Once again, this cost increase means we have gone too far, and these orders should not be combined. Therefore, we combine orders for weeks 4 and 5 only.

The Silver-Meal heuristic continues in this way until we reach the last week for which a planned order exists. The final planned order releases using this method turn out to be the same as for the POQ lot-sizing method.

SUMMARY

- Variable costs of ordering inventory include telephone, postage, shipping, and setup costs.
- Variable costs of holding inventory include cost of capital, insurance and taxes on inventory value, obsolescence, pilferage, and spoilage.
- Only variable costs are considered in inventory models because those are the only costs influenced by lot-size variations.
- The economic order quantity model is based on the assumptions that demand is constant and known with some certainty, cost per unit does not depend on order quantity, and an entire order is delivered at one time.
- The finite replenishment rate model is a variation of the EOQ model in which inventory usage during the replenishment period must be considered.
- Quantity discounts mean that the total-cost curve is discontinuous, requiring an iterative procedure to find the minimum cost point.
- The order point is determined from expected demand during the lead time.
- If demand during the lead time is variable, then a safety stock may be added to the order point, based on a probability distribution.
- In ABC analysis, the 20 percent of the items with highest dollar usage are class A, the next 30 percent are class B, and the last 50 percent are class C. Class A items get the tightest control and C items the loosest.
- In a continuous review inventory system, inventory level is constantly monitored, and orders are placed whenever necessary.
- In a periodic review system, inventory is checked at regular intervals, and enough is ordered to bring inventory up to a desired level.
- A base stock system is a variation of periodic review.
- Aggregate inventory investment, inventory turnover ratio, and days of inventory are three aggregate inventory performance measures.
- In an MRP system, planned order releases may be combined to minimize total cost.

- The period order quantity model converts EOQ into an equivalent order period.
- The Silver-Meal heuristic seeks to combine planned orders so that total cost per time period is minimized.

CAREER PROFILE

Sarah Wenzel

Production and Inventory Control Manager
Exide Electronics

Educational Background and Career Steps

Sarah Wenzel began her studies as a general business major at Bowling Green State University in Ohio. Working in the dean's office in the business college, she noticed which business majors were most actively sought by company recruiters. These observations, combined with a lack of interest in either accounting or marketing, led her to finish the B.S. degree in business administration with an area of specialization in procurement and materials management, an area she has found challenging and rewarding.

After graduation, Wenzel went to work for Eaton Corporation in its materials internship program. For two years, she worked in various divisions of Eaton, performing functions ranging from purchasing to production planning. At the end of the internship period, Wenzel took a job as production planner at Eaton's Air Controls Division in Roxboro, North Carolina.

Wenzel had intended to stay with Eaton, but through the local APICS chapter, she met someone from Raychem Company, a San Francisco–based company specializing in materials management sciences. Raychem was building a new plant for its telecommunications division near Raleigh and asked Wenzel to start up the production and inventory control area—a job that would mean designing and implementing systems, procedures, policies, and departments. She jumped at the challenge.

After the excitement and challenge of bringing a new plant on line, Wenzel found the routine of day-to-day operations too confining. She also faced limited advancement possibilities with Raychem since the next career step would have meant a move to California—a move she preferred not to make.

Once again, her contacts with other production and inventory control professionals through the local APICS chapter paid off. Northern Telecom was looking for someone to fill the job of production control manager in the company's DMS-10 Division and contacted Wenzel. She interviewed for, was offered, and accepted that job. Northern Telecom, at that time, had some 6,500 people working in the Raleigh area.

Current Position and Duties

After working with Northern Telecom for several years, Wenzel began to feel the company was too large and impersonal. When a personal tragedy caused her to re-examine her life, she decided to leave Northern Telecom and take six months off to travel around Europe on a Eurailpass. When she returned to the United States, Wenzel looked for a job with a smaller company and found one with Exide Electronics.

Exide employs 1,200 people and manufactures uninterruptable power supplies for all sizes of computers, from personal computers to large systems. Because it is much smaller than Northern Telecom, Wenzel believes Exide offers greater opportunities for her to have a personal impact on its direction. For example, she has been a proponent of employee involvement and is thus very pleased with Exide's strong employee involvement program, which offers everyone in the company eighty hours of training per year.

Although her title is production and inventory control manager, Wenzel is responsible for managing the company's receiving, shop floor scheduling, traffic, and distribution functions. Working with Exide, Wenzel has continued her involvement with APICS and now serves as a member of the JIT Certification Examination Committee.

SOLVED PROBLEMS

1. *Basic EOQ Model.* The Home-Like Motel supplies complimentary bars of soap to its guests. Usage of this soap is fairly constant at the rate of 2,000 cases per year. It costs the motel \$10 to place an order for more soap regardless of how many cases are ordered. About 5 percent of the soap is lost each year due to pilferage by employees and spoilage from damp storage conditions. In addition, the motel estimates that its cost of capital tied up in inventory is 15 percent. If each case of soap costs \$5, determine how many cases of soap should be ordered each time.

Solution

Inventory holding cost, $C_h = (.05 + .15) \times \$5 = \$1\text{/case/year}$

Ordering cost, $C_o = \$10\text{/order}$

Annual demand, $D = 2{,}000\text{ cases/year}$

$$\text{EOQ} = \sqrt{\frac{2DC_o}{C_h}} = \sqrt{\frac{2(2{,}000)(10)}{1}} = 200 \text{ cases per order}$$

2. *Finite Replenishment Rate.* A company that makes kitchen faucets has found that demand for its model #8501 faucet is fairly constant at the rate of 100,000 units per year. Each different faucet is made using the same equipment, and it costs \$100 in lost production and scrap every time a change is made from producing one model of faucet to another. The cost of materials and labor in each #8501 faucet is \$40, and the inventory holding cost is 25 percent of this per unit per year. If #8501 faucets are produced at the rate of 1,000 per day, how many should be produced in each production run based on 250 working days per year?

Solution

$$\text{Inventory holding cost, } C_h = .25(40) = \$10/\text{year}$$

$$\text{Ordering (setup) cost, } C_o = \$100$$

$$\text{Annual demand, } D = 100{,}000 \text{ units/year}$$

$$\text{Daily demand rate, d} = 100{,}000/250 = 400 \text{ units/day}$$

$$\text{Daily production rate, p} = 1{,}000 \text{ units/day}$$

$$\text{EPQ} = \sqrt{\frac{2DC_o}{C_h(1 - d/p)}} = \sqrt{\frac{2(100{,}000)(100)}{10(1 - 400/1{,}000)}}$$

$$= 1825.74 \text{ units}$$

This could be rounded to 1,826 units, or even to 2,000 units, per production run without incurring excessive additional costs.

3. *Quantity Discounts.* The I-40 Truck Stop Restaurant has just been informed by its supplier of potatoes that quantity discounts will be given as follows:

Pounds per Order	Price per Pound
1–299	\$.20
300–499	.15
500 or more	.10

The restaurant currently uses 5,000 pounds of potatoes per year, but has been ordering only about a week's worth (100 lbs.) at a time. It costs \$.25 (the cost of a phone call) to place an order for potatoes regardless of the order size, and the inventory holding cost is estimated as 20 percent of average inventory value per year. How many pounds should be ordered each time to minimize total annual variable costs? Assume that potatoes can be kept without spoilage for a long period of time.

Solution

$$\text{Inventory holding cost, } C_h = .20 \times \text{price per pound}$$

$$\text{Inventory ordering cost, } C_o = \$.25/\text{order}$$

$$\text{Demand, } D = 5{,}000 \text{ pounds/year}$$

Step 1. The lowest price per unit is \$.10/pound, which gives a holding cost, C_h, of .20(.10) = \$.02/pound/year.

$$\text{EOQ} = \sqrt{\frac{2DC_o}{C_h}} = \sqrt{\frac{2(5{,}000)(.25)}{.02}} = 353.55 \text{ or } 354 \text{ pounds}$$

This EOQ is not feasible since at least 500 pounds must be ordered to obtain the \$.10 unit price. Therefore, we calculate the total annual variable costs associated with ordering 500 pounds each time.

$$\text{Total annual variable costs} = \frac{Q}{2}C_h + \frac{D}{Q}C_o + Dv$$

$$= \frac{500}{2}(.02) + \frac{5{,}000}{500}(.25) + 5{,}000(.10)$$

$$= \$507.50$$

Step 2. Proceed to the next higher unit price, \$.15 per pound. The holding cost, C_h, is .20(.15) = \$.03/pound/year

$$\text{EOQ} = \sqrt{\frac{2(5{,}000)(.25)}{.03}} = 288.68 \text{ or } 289 \text{ pounds}$$

This EOQ is also infeasible for its unit price, so we calculate the total annual variable costs of ordering 300 pounds.

$$\text{Total annual variable costs} = \frac{Q}{2}C_o + \frac{D}{Q}C_h + Dv$$

$$= 300/2(.03) + 5{,}000/300(.25) + 5{,}000(.15)$$

$$= \$758.67$$

We now proceed to the next higher unit price of \$.20 per pound. The holding cost will be .20(.20) = \$.04/pound/year.

$$\text{EOQ} = \sqrt{\frac{2(5{,}000)(.25)}{.04}} = 250 \text{ pounds}$$

This EOQ is feasible, so we stop here and calculate its total annual variable costs.

$$\text{Total annual variable costs} = \frac{250}{2}(.04) + \frac{5{,}000}{250}(.25) + 5{,}000(.20)$$

$$= \$1{,}010.00$$

Next, we compare the order quantities and costs, which are listed below.

Order Quantity	Total Annual Variable Costs
500	\$ 507.50
300	758.67
250	1,010.00

Our comparison reveals that the lowest price strategy is to order 500 pounds of potatoes each time.

4. *Reorder Point and Safety Stock for a Continuous Review System.* The Kleenway Supermarket maintains a continuous review inventory system and reorders based on an order-point calculation. The company has found that demand for canned tomatoes averages fifty cases per week and has calculated an EOQ of 200 cases. The lead time for these tomatoes averages one week, with a standard deviation of ten cases during the lead time. If Kleenway wants to maintain a service level of at least 95 percent, what reorder point should be used for canned tomatoes?

Solution

The z value corresponding to a 95 percent probability is 1.645.

$$\sigma_L = 10$$

$$\text{Expected demand during lead time} = 50 \text{ cases}$$

$$\text{Safety stock} = z\sigma_L = 1.645(10)$$

$$= 16.45 \text{ or } 17 \text{ (rounding up)}$$

$$\text{Reorder point, } r = \text{expected demand during lead time} + \text{safety stock}$$

$$= 50 + 17 = 67 \text{ cases}$$

5. *Order-Up-to Level and Safety Stock for a Periodic Review System.* Easy-Mart is a discount store that uses a periodic review inventory control system. One item has an average annual demand of 12,000 units. Inventory holding cost for the item is $2.40 per unit per year, and ordering cost is $25 per order. Ordering lead time averages one-half month, and the standard deviation of monthly demand is 200 units. What should the order-up-to level be for this item if Easy-Mart wants a 90 percent service level?

Solution

For a service level of 90 percent, $z = 1.28$.

$$\text{Inventory holding cost, } C_h = \$2.40/\text{unit/year}$$

$$\text{Inventory ordering cost} = \$25/\text{order}$$

$$\text{Annual demand, } D = 12{,}000 \text{ units/year}$$

$$\text{EOQ} = \sqrt{\frac{2DC_o}{C_h}} = \sqrt{\frac{2(12{,}000)(25)}{2.40}} = 500 \text{ units}$$

$$\text{Optimal review interval, } R = \frac{EOQ}{D}$$

$$= 500/12{,}000 = 1/24 \text{ year or } 1/2 \text{ month}$$

Thus, review interval (1/2 month) + lead time (1/2 month) = 1 month, and expected demand during the review interval plus the lead time = 12,000/12 = 1000.

$$\text{Safety stock, } s = z\sigma_{I+L} = 1.28(200) = 256 \text{ units}$$

$$\text{Order-up-to level} = \text{expected demand during review interval and lead time} + \text{safety stock}$$

$$= 1{,}000 + 256 = 1{,}256 \text{ units}$$

6. *Lot Sizing for MRP Systems.* The Ace Computer Company uses MRP to plan the production of its circuit boards. One of those circuit boards has a lead time of two weeks, and the following net requirements have been determined. It costs $50 to set up for a production run and $.20 per week to store

each board in inventory. Use the Silver-Meal heuristic to determine planned order releases.

	Week					
	1	2	3	4	5	6
Net requirements	0	0	100	50	25	100

Solution

Ordering for week 3 only, ordering cost = \$50, holding cost = 0.

Cost per week = \$50/1 = \$50

Ordering for weeks 3 and 4, ordering cost = (\$50, holding cost = 50(\$.20) = \$10.

Cost per week = (\$50 + \$10)/2 = \$30

Ordering for weeks 3, 4, and 5, ordering cost = \$50, holding cost = [50 + 2(25)](\$.20) = \$20.

Cost per week = (\$50 + \$20)/3 = \$23.33

Ordering for weeks 3, 4, 5, and 6, ordering cost = \$50, holding cost = [50 + 2(25) + 3(100)](\$.20) = \$80.

Cost per week = (\$50 + \$80)/4 = \$32.50

Since the cost per week increased, we order for weeks 3, 4, and 5 together and for week 6 separately, as shown below.

	Week					
	1	2	3	4	5	6
Net requirements	0	0	100	50	25	100
Planned receipts			175	0	0	100
Planned order releases	175	0	0	100		

QUESTIONS

1. Using the EOQ total-cost curve, explain why even those companies not using JIT would find it beneficial to reduce setup times.

2. List the fixed and variable costs that constitute inventory ordering cost.

3. List the fixed and variable costs that constitute inventory holding cost.

4. One approach sometimes suggested for calculating ordering cost is to take the purchasing department's annual operating budget and divide by the number of orders placed per year. Explain the potential errors that could be made by doing this.

5. Explain what you think might happen if a manufacturing company attempted to use the EOQ formula with a reorder point to control inventories of component parts instead of planning order releases through MRP. Use a diagram of dependent-demand inventory to support your answer.

6. Your neighborhood grocery store probably maintains continuous inventory records if it has scanners at the checkout counters. Yet orders for most items are delivered on a weekly basis. Describe how you think this continuous review system is combined with a periodic delivery system.

7. Define the following terms:

a. Average inventory investment
b. Inventory turnover ratio
c. Days of inventory

8. The Silver-Meal heuristic attempts to minimize total relevant cost per unit time. Explain how a similar procedure could be used that would minimize total cost *per unit ordered.*

9. Why is it that companies might calculate the EOQ for an item even when that item must be ordered in standard quantities, such as multiples of 100?

10. How does the finite replenishment rate inventory model differ from the EOQ model with instantaneous replenishment?

11. List the assumptions underlying the EOQ model.

12. Define the following terms:

a. Service level
b. Time between stock-outs
c. Safety stock

13. Why must a different approach be used when determining the EOQ under quantity discounts?

14. Why is more safety stock required for the same service level under a periodic review system than under a continuous review system?

15. Explain why the EOQ formula could not be used directly for lot sizing in a MRP system.

16. Suppose a certain part is placed in class C, using ABC analysis. However, this is a critical part, and a stock-out could stop the whole factory. What should you do about safety stock for this item?

PROBLEMS

1. Fast-Mart is a discount retailer that uses a point-of-sale system to maintain continuous inventory records. A particular item has an average annual demand of 40,000 units. It costs \$25 to replenish inventory of that item, which has a value of \$10 per unit. If inventory carrying cost is 20 percent of unit value, how many should be ordered each time to minimize total annual variable costs?

2. Suppose Fast-Mart has found that the item described in problem 1 has a lead time of two working days. If the company operates 250 days per year, determine the reorder point for that item.

3. The Fill-er-Up gas station has found that demand for its unleaded gasoline is fairly constant and uniform at the rate of 100,000 gallons per year. Fill-er-Up must pay \$100 for shipping per order of gasoline, which it currently buys for \$.75 per gallon. Inventory carrying cost is 10 percent of unit cost per year. How many gallons should be ordered at a time?

4. Suppose that in problem 3, Fill-er-Up's underground storage tanks can only hold 10,000 gallons of unleaded gasoline. What is the extra cost incurred by ordering this quantity each time instead of the EOQ?

5. A company has annual demand of 5,000 units for one of its products. The value of this product is \$100 per unit, and the inventory carrying cost is 20 percent of unit value. The setup cost is \$200 per production run. This product can be produced at the rate of 20,000 per year. How many should be produced at one time to minimize total annual costs?

6. Suppose the company described in problem 5 wants to maintain a safety stock for the product described. Standard deviation of the demand during lead time is 500 units, and it has been decided that service level should be at least 95 percent. What safety stock level is necessary?

7. The Slick Oil Company buys crude oil from a supplier that has recently offered the following quantity discounts:

Barrels Ordered	Price per Barrel
1–999	$20.00
1,000–2,999	18.00
3,000 or more	17.50

If inventory holding cost is 25 percent of the unit price and it costs $100 for each order, regardless of order size, how many barrels should Slick order each time to satisfy its annual demand of 10,000 barrels?

8. Burger-Farm is a fast-food restaurant that buys hamburger buns from a local bakery. Those buns are used at the rate of 50,000 per year. The baker has just offered Burger-Farm the following quantity discounts:

Buns Ordered	Price per Bun
1–999	$.030
1,000–1,999	.028
2,000 or more	.027

If it costs Burger-Farm $1 for each order placed and the inventory holding cost is 25 percent of unit cost, determine how much should be ordered each time to minimize total annual variable costs.

9. Referring to problem 8, suppose Burger-Farm is limited to ordering only one week's worth of buns at a time due to storage space limitations and spoilage problems. What impact will this have on total annual variable cost?

10. The Young Professionelle Shoppe is a boutique for professional women. A periodic review system is used to control inventory. Suppose that a certain blazer has an average annual demand of 1,000 units. The ordering cost is $5, and the inventory carrying cost is $10 per unit per year. What should the review interval be for this blazer?

11. Suppose that the Young Professionelle Shoppe of problem 10 prefers to review its inventory weekly. Estimate the effect on total annual variable costs of following this procedure.

12. A discount retail store uses a periodic review inventory system under which each item's inventory level is reviewed twice monthly. Suppose it has been determined that a particular item has an average annual demand of 6,000 units, with a standard deviation of 100 units per month. If lead time is one-half month and the store wants a service level of 85 percent, determine the order-up-to level for this item.

13. The Goodstone Tire Store has been using a periodic review system to control its inventory. For one tire model, the annual demand averages 5,000 units. In the past, inventory was reviewed on a basis so that review interval plus lead time was one month. Standard deviation of demand during this period was fifty units. The company is now planning to use a continuous review system. Suppose lead time is one week and the standard deviation of demand during lead time is ten units. For a 90 percent service level, compare the safety stock necessary under periodic review with what would be necessary for continuous review.

14. Joe's Newspaper Stand carries *Barron's*. Joe has noticed that demand for this weekly newspaper follows the pattern below.

Demand	Frequency
10	4
11	6
12	7
13	8
14	4
15	2

Joe has never sold less than ten copies or more than fifteen. If Joe wants a service level of 90 percent, how many copies of *Barron's* should he order each week?

15. Mary Costagliano, production planner for the Good-Health Pharmaceutical Company, has determined the following net requirements for one of the raw materials used in making pharmaceuticals:

	Week						
	34	35	36	37	38	39	40
Net requirements (lbs.)	150	50	100	125	200	100	75

It costs $25 every time an order for this material is placed, and the inventory holding cost is $6/lb./year. If annual demand is 5,000 lbs., use the POQ strategy to develop planned orders for a lead time of one week.

16. For the data of problem 15, suppose inventory holding cost is $.12/lb./week. Use the Silver-Meal heuristic to calculate planned order releases.

17. The Ajax Machine Company has used MRP to develop the following net requirements for component part B-529. The setup cost is $100, and the inventory holding cost is $.25/unit/week. Use the Silver-Meal heuristic to determine lot sizes that will minimize cost per time period.

Week							
5	6	7	8	9	10	11	12
50	100	300	80	40	100	50	75

18. The Quickie Calculator Company uses MRP to plan orders for the component parts of its calculators. One component has an ordering cost of $10, an inventory holding cost of $.10/unit/week ($5.20/unit/year), and average annual demand of 1,000 units. Use both POQ and the Silver-Meal heuristic to calculate planned order releases for the following net requirements if lead time is one week. Compare the total cost of both methods.

	Week					
	1	2	3	4	5	6
Net requirements	0	50	20	0	30	80

19. Use lot-for-lot, POQ, and Silver-Meal to plan order releases for the following net requirements, using a two-week lead time. It costs $60 to place an order, and the inventory holding cost is $.50/unit/week ($25/unit/year). Annual demand averages 3,000 units. Compare the total costs of each strategy over the planning horizon.

	Week						
	28	29	30	31	32	33	34
Net requirements	100	20	10	80	40	10	120

20. A company that recently read about JIT wants to reduce its inventory level by decreasing lot sizes. Several of the company's products are made on the same assembly line. The line must be changed over each time a different product is made. The company has used the EPQ model to determine lot sizes. Suppose the company arbitrarily decides to cut the lot size for each product in half. What reduction in changeover cost (setup cost) must occur if these new lot sizes are to still be optimal for the EPQ model?

21. An inventory clerk at the Fargo Machine Tool Company has just calculated the EOQ for one of the steel alloys used by this company as 500 pounds. However, the lead time for ordering this steel is four months, and the company uses 150 pounds per month, giving an order point of 600 pounds—which is greater than the EOQ! Can you help this inventory clerk figure out how to handle this case, in which order point exceeds the EOQ?

22. West Coast Furniture Distributors is a company that buys furniture in large quantities at low prices from manufacturers and then sells to the public at prices below what most furniture stores charge. To minimize costs, West Coast Furniture uses EOQ for ordering.

For one particular model of sofa, the manufacturer has now agreed to cover part of the shipping costs, reducing the ordering cost from $50 per order to $40. At the same time, West Coast Furniture has been ableto obtain lower interest rates on borrowed money, reducing its inventory carrying cost from 25 percent of unit cost to 20 percent.

The company expects to sell 1,225 of these sofas per year and pays $100 to purchase each one.

a. What effect will the preceding changes have on the EOQ?

b. What effect will the preceding changes have on the total annual costs of ordering and carrying inventory?

23. Referring to problem 22, how many days' worth of demand will be covered by each order of sofas?

24. The student advisement office at Central State University has a student worker who copies and assembles a handbook for students whenever the supply of these runs low. Past observation indicates that these handbooks are given out at the rate of four per day. The student worker can copy and assemble 100 per eight-hour day. The student worker is paid $3.75 per hour, and it takes .5 hour to prepare everything to produce a batch of handbooks. The cost of carrying inventory is related to handbooks that are damaged or become obsolete due to changes in degree requirements. On average, 10 percent of all handbooks become unusable, and each one costs $1.00 in materials, labor, and copying costs.

a. If the office is open 250 days per year, how many handbooks should the student worker produce at a time?

b. How many days of demand will be supported by this order quantity?

25. Referring to problem 24,

a. What will be the maximum handbook inventory, assuming the minimum is zero?

b. What is the average inventory of handbooks?

26. Northwest Tool and Die Co. has been using economic production quantity to determine lot sizes for a standard product it manufactures. This product has been sold at the rate of 1,500 per year, costs $5 per unit, has a 25 percent carrying cost, and costs $500 for each setup. NTDC operates 250 days per year, and the part under consideration can be produced at the rate of 100 per day.

Recently, however, NTDC has undertaken a setup reduction program, and the cost of setting up to make this product has been reduced from $500 to $100.

a. What impact will this have on the production lot size?

b. What impact will this change have on the total annual cost of setting up and producing this product?

27. A company maintains inventories of the following nine items. Based on this information, determine which are A items, B items, and C items.

Item #	Value	Annual Usage
209	$14.76	2,000
4914	5.98	15,000
37	1.15	297,000
387	6.48	6,000
3290	2.17	6,000
235	75.00	300
48	23.95	7,000
576	4.32	5,000
14	932.00	1,000

Data Sets for Computer Solution

1. Dog's Life Enterprises manufactures dog collars and leashes, which it sells to pet stores, discount stores, and even supermarkets that carry pet supplies. The company buys all the components for its products from suppliers and then assembles the products itself. There are three products: a standard dog collar, a diamond-studded collar, and a leash. All three are made by taking very strong nylon webbing material, cutting it to the correct length and sewing the ends, and then adding the appropriate hardware items. The company produces these finished products to stock and uses a continuous review inventory system to monitor the finished-goods inventory. Based on past experience, the following information is available:

Product	Annual Demand	Unit Value	Lead Time
Standard collar	10,000	$ 2.00	1 wk.
Diamond collar	2,000	15.00	2 wks.
Leash	20,000	3.00	1 wk.

Product	Std. Dev. of Lead Time Demand	Production Rate
Standard collar	100	500/wk.
Diamond collar	25	100/wk.
Leash	150	2,000/wk.

The company uses a simple MRP system to plan its orders for the hardware items. However, nylon webbing and thread are used at a fairly constant, uniform rate, so these are ordered by EOQ. In addition, the company uses the same system to order such supplies as sewing machine needles and oil. The information is given below.

Item	Annual Usage	Unit Value	Lead Time
Nylon webbing	120,000 ft.	$ .05/ft.	4 wks.
Thread	200,000 ft.	.001/ft.	3 wks.
Needles	1,000	.25	1 wk.
Oil	20 gal.	12.00	2 wks.

Item	Std. Dev. of Lead Time Demand	Package Quantity
Nylon webbing	1,000	20,000 ft.
Thread	1,200	50,000 ft.
Needles	10	100
Oil	1	5 gals.

The cost of setup for one of the products is $50, and the company wants to maintain a 95 percent service level. The cost of ordering materials and supplies is $5. The carrying cost for all items is 25 percent of unit value. Determine the EOQ, order point, and safety stock for each of the above.

2. Refer to the Chesapeake Company, problem 2 in the Data Sets for Computer Solution section of Chapter 11. Compare the period order quantity and Silver-Meal heuristic with lot-for-lot ordering for the wooden parts and the seat and knee-pad assemblies. Which produces the lowest cost, based on the following information?

Part #	Description	Unit Value
2075	Wood top	$20.00
2702	Wood shelf	15.00
2876	Wood side	30.00
2703	Wood backing	3.00
2877	Wood side	10.00
2704	Wood backing	2.00
452	Seat assembly	8.00
453	Knee-pad assembly	6.00

It costs $20 for each order placed for wooden parts. Setup costs for making the seat assembly or knee-pad assembly are $50, and the inventory carrying cost is 23 percent of unit value.

MINI-CASES

Fast-Foto, Inc.

Fast-Foto manufactures "mini-labs" for developing photographs within several hours. These mini-labs are sold to photo stores, drugstores, and even gas stations. In addition, Fast-Foto sells the chemicals and supplies used by these machines and offers repair and parts services for the mini-labs it sells.

Fast-Foto has undergone tremendous growth within the past several years, and the company is starting to feel the pinch. Demand for the company's product has increased to the point that 200 units must be produced each month. Producing this number is not so bad, except that it is sometimes difficult to ensure that all parts will always be available in sufficient supply. This problem has been made worse by demand for repair parts. As the number of units sold has increased, so have the requirements for replacement parts. There have often been conflicts between the need to take parts for repair orders and requirements for those same parts in assembling new units.

Jan Byrnes is inventory control manager of Fast-Foto. Jan's primary concern has been with implementing an MRP system that can be used to control the ordering and production of parts and components for the company's product. However, the problems associated with spare parts have been increasingly disruptive to the MRP system since the assembly operation and repair operation both draw their needed parts from the same parts inventory. Jan has found it extremely frustrating to develop a master schedule for assembly of new units and then use MRP to schedule planned orders, only to find later that the master schedule could not be met because of parts being withdrawn for repairs of previously sold units.

The question of controlling inventory of supplies such as photographic paper and chemicals has also come up. In the past, a periodic review system had been used for these items. But now, the question has been raised as to whether a continuous review system would work better, even though the periodic review method has not caused problems.

As Jan thinks about these problems, she begins to wonder whether there is some way the spare-parts requirements could be included in MRP or whether a safety stock quantity should just be added to the MRP calculations. Jan has even started to think that maybe the spare-parts operations should just be run the way photographic supplies are now. But that would cause problems in terms of separate orders for the same parts. Jan isn't sure what to do.

Elco Industries

Elco Industries manufactures soundproofing material for automobiles. This material, which is usually found under the carpet, behind the back seat, or inside the doors, is manufactured from ground-up fabric, called "shoddy." This shoddy is combined with various resins that hold the material together, and then this mixture is formed to the desired thickness in an Air-Lay machine. The material that comes out of the Air-Lay is then cut into several standard rectangular sizes, called blankets. These blankets are then cut to the appropriate shape, depending on the model of car and the location in which they will be used. The blanket is then formed into the desired contour—for example, so that it will conform to the transmission tunnel—and molded under heat and moderate pressure. The process is basically a simple one.

Elco Industries' customers are the Big Three auto makers: GM, Ford, and Chrysler. In the past, Elco has produced blankets in several standard sizes, based on EOQ quantities, and then used these as needed to meet specific customer orders, which were usually received monthly and came in about one month ahead of the required shipping date. However, this approach has sometimes resulted in problems, as there might not be enough blankets of the appropriate size to meet a particular order. The inventory of these blankets has also been maintained somewhat haphazardly, resulting in occasional production of more blankets of a given size when there were already plenty in inventory.

Recently, two changes have occurred. First, Elco has begun to implement an MRP system to plan its production. Second, Elco's customers have all begun switching to JIT. This second change has meant that orders are received each month and indicate quantities and shipping dates *by week* for the next month. It also means that orders *must* be shipped on time or one of the customer's auto assembly plants will be shut down. If this happens, Elco could lose a big part of its business when that auto maker decides to switch to Elco's competitor.

Doug Smith, production manager for Elco, is trying to decide how to handle the production of blankets from the Air-Lay machine. Any time the machine is switched from one size or thickness of blanket to another, a downtime of one day is incurred. This has been estimated as a cost in terms of lost production of $300, although that figure is based only on the cost of shoddy and resin that go into a day's production. Actually, the Air-Lay machine has excess capacity compared with other processes in the plant.

Doug has decided to take the following month's orders for one particular product, the Ford Probe "package tray," and try several alternatives:

- Continue to use EOQ for blankets
- Plan blanket production by MRP and
  - use lot-for-lot ordering for blankets
  - use the POQ strategy
  - use the Silver-Meal heuristic

The required shipments for the Probe package trays are as follows:

	Week			
	1	2	3	4
Required shipments (cases)	20	30	20	25

The particular blanket used for this package tray is not used in any other product. The average annual demand is 1,300 cases, and the inventory holding cost for these blankets is estimated as $1/case/week ($52/case/year). Production lead time is one week.

Of course, another idea that has been suggested to Doug is to carry a safety stock of either blankets or finished package trays (which are worth about four times as much as the blankets, due to added labor and materials). But this idea has not been very appealing since Elco actually knows what its demand will be next month because of the customer orders. The real problem, it seems to Doug, is to figure out the best way of meeting those orders on time for minimum cost.

SELECTED BIBLIOGRAPHY

Adkins, A. C., Jr. ''EOQ in the Real World.'' *Production and Inventory Management* 25, no. 4 (1984): 50–54.

Brown, Robert G. *Materials Management Systems*. New York: Wiley, 1977.

Fordyce, James M., and Webster, Francis M. ''The Wagner-Whitin Algorithm Made Simple.'' *Production and Inventory Management* 25, no. 2 (1984): 21–30.

Gaither, Norman. ''A Near Optimal Lot-Sizing Model for MRP Environments.'' *Production and Inventory Management* 22, no. 4 (1981): 75–90.

Peterson, Rein, and Silver, Edward A. *Decision Systems for Inventory Management and Production Planning*. 2d ed. New York: Wiley, 1984.

Plossl, George W., and Welch, W. Evert. *The Role of Top Management in the Control of Inventory*. Reston, Va.: Reston, 1979.

Ronen, David. ''Inventory Service Measures—A Comparison of Measures.'' *International Journal of Operations and Production Management* 3, no. 2 (1983): 37–45.

Schonberger, Richard J., and Schniederjans, Marc J. ''Reinventing Inventory Control.'' *Interfaces* 14, no. 3 (May–June 1984): 76–83.

Chapter 17

Quality Management

CHAPTER OUTLINE

Introduction

Quality Assurance Programs
Foundations of Quality Assurance
Costs of Quality
The Ethics of Quality
Quality Audits

Statistical Quality Control
Acceptance Sampling
Statistical Process Control

Companywide Quality Control
Total Quality Control
Quality Circles
Taguchi Methods
Quality Function Deployment
Managing the Quality of Services
Gaining Strategic Advantage at American Express: Managing for Delivery of Quality

LEARNING OBJECTIVES

After completing this chapter, you should be able to

- Define the word *quality* from an organizational viewpoint.
- Summarize the steps to quality management proposed by Philip Crosby and W. Edwards Deming.
- Explain how to measure the cost of quality.
- Summarize the activities of a quality audit.
- Use MIL-STD-105D to determine sample size and accept/reject numbers.
- Develop and use an *X*-bar chart.
- Develop and use an *R* chart.
- Develop and use attribute charts.
- Describe the components of total quality control.
- Explain the concept of quality circles.
- Describe how a fishbone diagram is used.
- Explain the use of Pareto analysis.
- Explain the Taguchi loss function.
- Describe how Taguchi methods are used to reduce deviation from target values.
- Explain how the voice of the customer is deployed.
- Discuss quality management in service organizations.

OPERATIONS IN ACTION

Florida Power and Light: Keeping the Vultures Out of the Electricity

When most of us think of quality, we think of it as one way of differentiating between products. For that reason, the idea of an electric utility company focusing on quality may seem a bit absurd. After all, how do you differentiate one type of electricity from another?

But electric utilities actually provide a service. And to Florida Power and Light's customers, an important aspect of that service is receiving electricity without interruption. That's why the company found its number one customer complaint was power outages, which averaged seventy minutes per month.

To eliminate those outages, Florida Power and Light set out to identify the primary causes. In an area that averages eighty days a year with thunderstorms, lightning turned out to be number one. Therefore, FP&L worked with its suppliers to develop advanced surge protectors that could protect transformers from lightning damage.

The second most common cause of power outages turned out to be vultures. The birds apparently like to perch on the company's towers, and their droppings were shorting out insulators. To eliminate that cause, plywood shields were put up, and structures taller than the electric towers were built to attract birds away from the power lines.

FP&L was able to reduce the average length of power outages to sixty minutes per month and as a result entered the competition for Japan's prestigious W. Edwards Deming prize for quality. On November 14, 1989, Florida Power & Light became the first non-Japanese company to win that award. However, the company has not stopped there in its quest for improvement. It is also analyzing weather data so repair crews can be placed where storms are most likely to strike, further reducing the length of power outages.[1]

INTRODUCTION

Quality is a term that we all use rather loosely. Most of us think of quality in terms of the best there is—such as a Rolls Royce automobile or a five-star French restaurant. But this definition of quality is quite different from the one used by quality experts.

For example, a Rolls Royce automobile would meet the authors' needs very nicely. Unfortunately, neither of us can afford one just yet. Instead, we must be content with automobiles that still meet our basic needs (reliable transportation to and from work, satisfaction of our self-images as successful professors, appropriateness for our families, etc.)—but at a reasonable cost. Thus, we will use the following definition of quality, which has been developed by John Groocock, vice-president for quality at TRW.

> The quality of a product is the degree of conformance of all of the relevant features and characteristics of the product to all of the aspects of a customer's need, limited by the price and delivery that he or she will accept.[2]

You should be sure to realize that the word *product*, as it is used in this definition, could refer to either a good or a service. Thus, we can talk about the quality of a good, such as an automobile, or we can just as easily talk about the quality of a service, such as health care or transportation. In either case, the key will be to determine the needs of customers and provide a "product" that meets those needs at a price and availability the customer will accept.

One reason we like this definition is that it appears to include all the dimensions of quality that have been identified by David Garvin, a professor at Harvard University and an expert on quality. Those dimensions are

- Performance
- Features
- Reliability
- Conformance
- Durability
- Serviceability
- Aesthetics
- Perceived quality

In this chapter, we will explore ways of assuring and maintaining quality. Although our emphasis will be primarily on the operations activity, you should keep in mind that quality is a companywide responsibility. We think the above definition conveys that importance through its requirements that customer needs be met at a price and delivery the customer will accept. We proceed now to discuss ways that companies are making sure that this happens.

QUALITY ASSURANCE PROGRAMS

Quality assurance differs from quality control. Quality control includes methods and procedures for testing and maintaining the level of quality that is desired. **Quality assurance**, on the other hand, is much broader and includes any activities related to making sure that quality is maintained at the desired level. These activities can range from design to installation. Quality assurance involves not only setting up standards, but also documenting those standards and the procedures for achieving them and then implementing a program to assure that quality is achieved.

Many companies have quality assurance programs, but those programs can differ greatly from one company to another. For that reason, we will not discuss the details of any one company's quality assurance program. Instead, we list some specific points of programs promoted by two of today's quality experts.

Foundations of Quality Assurance

Philip Crosby

Philip Crosby has developed a set of fourteen *steps* for achieving zero defects—that is, no defective parts, or 100 percent quality.[3] Those steps, in the order they should be performed, are as follows:

1. Obtain management's commitment to quality.
2. Establish a quality improvement team.

3. Take measurements of the existing quality.
4. Estimate the cost of quality.
5. Spread quality awareness throughout the company.
6. Encourage actions to correct quality problems.
7. Establish a zero defects program committee.
8. Train supervisors concerning the zero defects program.
9. Have a day when all employees will be educated about zero defects and commit themselves to producing zero defects.
10. Have individual employees or groups set goals for improving their work.
11. Remove the causes of errors.
12. Recognize the achievements of employees.
13. Establish a companywide quality council.
14. Go back and do it all again so that the commitment to quality is renewed on a regular basis.

W. Edwards Deming

A slightly different set of fourteen points has been proposed by W. Edwards Deming, another recognized consultant and former chief statistician for the U.S. Bureau of Standards.[4] Deming is widely credited with being the one person who turned the Japanese from producers of low-quality merchandise into a nation that can boast some of the world's highest-quality products. It is interesting to compare Deming's fourteen points with Crosby's. Both Deming and Crosby stress the importance of employee involvement and management commitment. However, Crosby tends to stress slogans and programs, while Deming argues that such approaches are not enough, and that employees must be trained to use statistical tools as a means of measuring and improving quality. Deming's steps are as follows:

1. Establish a constant objective of improvement.
2. Adopt a new philosophy of quality control.
3. Don't rely on mass inspections. Use statistical methods to prove quality is built in.
4. Reduce the number of vendors, and don't buy on the basis of price.
5. Use statistical methods to find problem areas.
6. Train employees effectively on the job.
7. Improve supervision.
8. Drive out fear so employees will feel free to ask questions and make suggestions.
9. Promote communication among departments, suppliers, and customers.
10. Eliminate slogans. Show employees how to solve problems.
11. Use work standards carefully. They may have a detrimental effect on quality and limit production.
12. Give workers the tools to evaluate their own work and to take pride in it.

13. Use a training program to keep employees up to date and teach them new skills.
14. Put everyone to work in teams to accomplish the transformation.

One thing that is apparent from both Crosby's and Deming's lists is that the development of a quality assurance program is a long, arduous process. It cannot be just window dressing if it is to achieve results. Any quality assurance program must extend through the organization—from top management on down. It must also develop a constant awareness and interest in improvement on the part of employees.

Costs of Quality

One aspect of any quality assurance program is the measurement of costs associated with quality. Recently, a group of experts, including Philip Crosby, has argued that such costs should include only those associated with producing defective goods or services. However, not all quality control experts agree. A more general, and more widely accepted, approach is to divide **quality costs** into three general categories: costs of preventing defects, costs of appraising quality, and costs associated with the production of defects. Each of these categories is shown in Exhibit 17.1.

Optimal Cost Level

The traditional view of quality costs has been that there is some optimal number of defects that will minimize total costs, as shown in Exhibit 17.2. The idea presented by this graph is that costs of inspection and prevention decrease as the number of defects allowed increases. At the same time, the costs associated with such defects increase. The optimal number of defects occurs at some middle level.

However, current thinking differs significantly from this traditional viewpoint. The current view is shown in Exhibit 17.3. The idea here is basically that inspection and prevention costs do not have to be increased in order to have fewer defects. Thus, there is no trade-off between costs of defects and costs of avoiding defects. The optimal level occurs at the zero defects point. Although not

Exhibit 17.1 Costs Associated with Quality

Prevention Costs	Appraisal Costs	Costs of Defects	
		Internal Costs	External Costs
Planning	Testing	Scrap	Returns
Developing procedures	Inspection	Rework	Adjustments
Training	Audits	Retest	Warranty work
Designing systems		Downtime	Allowances
Reporting		Yield Losses	Good will loss
		Evaluation of defects	Lost sales

Exhibit 17.2 Traditional View of Quality Costs

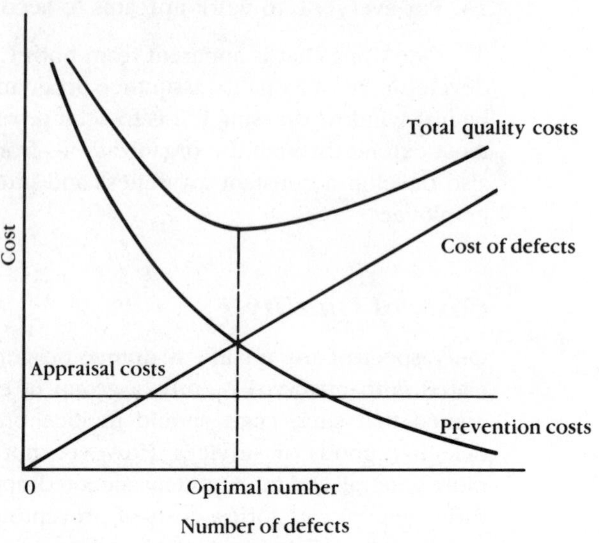

Exhibit 17.3 Current View of Quality Costs

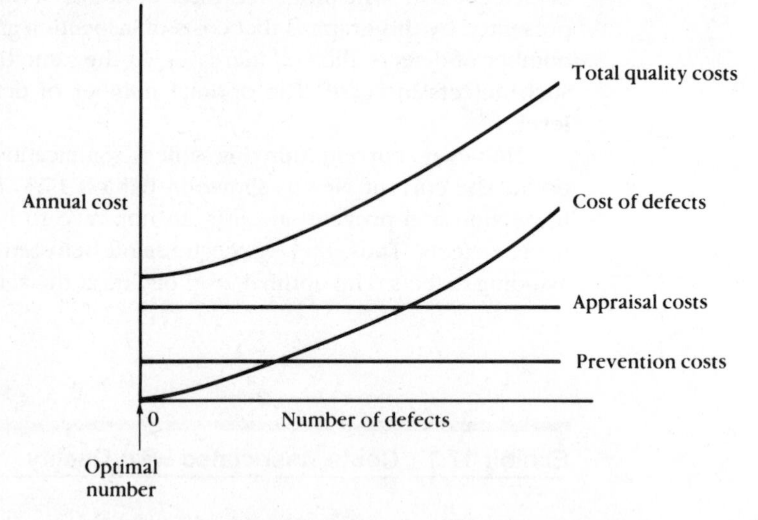

all companies would agree with this view, most probably realize that today so much emphasis is placed on quality that it is in their own best interests to work toward zero defects. Even if inspection and prevention costs do increase, these are more than offset by savings in other areas and by improved relations with their customers.

The Ethics of Quality

The cost trade-off view of quality that has traditionally applied can lead companies to place a cost on deaths and injuries that may result from their products. For instance, it was alleged that Ford at one time had compared the cost of redesigning the gas tank on its Pinto against the expected costs of lawsuits from deaths and injuries that would result if it did not.

Fortunately, the trade-off attitude is changing, and many companies, including Ford, are placing a very high value on quality. Companies realize that taking shortcuts on quality may increase profits in the short run, but can ruin a company in the long run. In fact, later in this chapter, we will discuss an approach to quality that considers all of the relevant costs to society.

However, in meeting the needs of customers, companies may still face ethical dilemmas. For example, most automobile buyers have indicated they will not pay extra for air bags even though such devices can reduce deaths and injuries. Should automobile manufacturers then make air bags standard equipment even if doing so means increasing the price of an automobile? In answering such questions, companies may need to take a proactive role in protecting the customer's health and safety.

Quality Audits

An important aspect of any quality management program involves determining the existing quality of a product. One way of measuring that quality is through a **quality audit**. However, a good audit actually determines whether specific standards have been set, whether procedures have been developed and documented, and whether the processes are capable of achieving those standards. It also determines whether quality is being maintained and examines the product's quality compared to that of competitors.

John Groocock, of TRW, whose definition of *quality* we quoted earlier in this chapter, has presented the following steps used in TRW's internal quality audits:

1. *Quality to the customer*. Is conformance of the product to established quality standards measured? Is quality of the organization's product compared with that of competitors' products?
2. *Quality costs*. Have the costs of quality been measured, and have areas for possible cost savings been identified?
3. *Design review*. Do procedures exist to review designs for quality? Are these procedures being carried out?
4. *Product qualification*. Have procedures been established and followed to qualify new products before any deliveries to customers?
5. *Product liability*. Has each product been scrutinized regarding safety, and are appropriate records kept? Does a written plan exist for dealing with a major product liability problem?
6. *Process capability*. Has the capability of all processes been measured, and is that information used in product design and development?

7. *Incoming inspection*. Are incoming lots inspected in an efficient manner, and are appropriate records kept?
8. *Supplier quality*. Are suppliers made aware of their quality responsibilities? Are records kept on nonconformance?
9. *Process control*. Has the company developed policies for controlling processes? Have employees been trained to follow those policies?
10. *Inspection and test planning*. Do inspection and test plans exist for all products, and are records maintained on the results? Is all test equipment calibrated regularly?
11. *Quality performance indicators*. Are quality performance indicators regularly published throughout the organization and made available to employees?
12. *Employee involvement program*. Are employees involved in quality improvement through some process such as quality circles?
13. *Multifunctional quality improvement team*. Has a quality improvement team covering all functional areas been established to monitor quality and to work to improve it?
14. *Quality business plan*. Has quality been integrated into the organization's business plan—and from there into the overall strategic plan?[5]

STATISTICAL QUALITY CONTROL

So far, we have discussed the general concepts and behavioral techniques of quality management. However, **statistical quality control (SQC)** plays an extremely important role in monitoring and maintaining quality. It is through statistical methods that processes can be examined to determine whether their **capabilities** match design requirements. For example, if a part must be produced so that its diameter is within .00001 inch of a specified value, then one must determine whether the equipment used to produce that part is capable of maintaining such accuracy. Statistics can be used to make that determination.

Also, it is important to monitor the quality of certain processes so that problems can be detected early. For instance, a bank would want to measure the number of errors made by its tellers. If the number of errors increased by a statistically significant amount, then the bank would have to determine the cause and correct it. Even a significant decrease in the number of errors would be cause for further investigation to determine what factors had produced the decrease. Once identified, those factors could be built into the bank's procedures in an effort to permanently decrease the number of teller errors.

Acceptance Sampling

One of the earliest uses of statistical methods in quality control was for **acceptance sampling**. The idea behind acceptance sampling is to take a relatively small sample from a batch of parts or material, to inspect only the sample, and then to make inferences about the entire batch based on results obtained from the sample. For example, an automobile manufacturer might have a policy that at least 98 percent of the headlights it purchases from a supplier must meet certain specifications concerning brightness, beam width, and average life. Rather than test every headlight it receives, the automobile manufacturer could take a sample of headlights from each batch it receives, test the sample, and then determine whether or not to accept the hypothesis that the entire batch satisfies its specifications.

The same approach can also be used within a company for monitoring and controlling production processes. For example, a company that manufactures pharmaceuticals could take a sample from each batch it produced, test that sample, and then use the results to determine whether the entire batch is acceptable or whether the entire batch should be examined more closely and some adjustments made in the production process.

Possible Sampling Errors

Acceptance sampling, like any statistical hypothesis testing based on a sample, is always open to errors. For instance, the percentage of defectives in a sample may be either much larger or much smaller than in the entire batch. Thus, it is always possible to end up concluding that a batch is unacceptable when it is actually acceptable or, what may be worse, to accept a batch that is actually unacceptable.

The possibility that either of these undesirable outcomes will occur can be reduced through the selection of sample size. Obviously, the larger a sample, the more closely it will resemble the batch. However, there is a trade-off between the cost of sampling and the cost of errors. Therefore, acceptable probabilities of coming to an incorrect conclusion are usually determined first, and then the sample size and the number of defectives allowed in that sample are calculated, based on those probability values.

The probability of not accepting a lot that is actually acceptable (a **type I error**) is designated as α (**alpha**). This probability is often called **producer's risk**. The other possible error is to accept a lot that is actually unacceptable (a **type II error**). The probability that this error will occur is designated as β (**beta**), which is often called **consumer's risk**.

It is common practice to set the value of α (producer's risk) at 5 percent and β (consumer's risk) at 10 percent. However, other values are possible. By determining the desired values of α, β, and several other parameters, it is possible to calculate the required sample size. The other parameters needed to do this are the percentage of defectives in a batch that would be acceptable, termed the **acceptable quality level (AQL)**, and the percentage of defectives in a batch that would be definitely unacceptable, called the **lot tolerance percent defective (LTPD)**.

OC Curves

The AQL is a percentage of defectives that would be acceptable in the entire batch. LTPD specifies a percentage of defectives that is definitely unacceptable. These two values can be related to the producer's risk and the consumer's risk through an **operating characteristic curve**, or **OC curve**.

The OC curve is a graph that shows probabilities, using the hypergeometric probability distribution, for a certain sample size, of accepting a lot, given the actual percentage of defectives (which is not known) in that lot. For example,

Exhibit 17.4 is an OC curve for samples of size ten drawn from a lot of 1,000 units where the lot is accepted if no more than one defective is found in the sample. As can be seen, if the lot actually contains 10 percent defectives, the OC curve indicates there is approximately a 65 percent probability of accepting the lot, based on a sample of size ten.

It is possible, through trial and error and extensive calculations, to select a sample size that will provide the desired values of α and β for given AQLs and LTPDs. This is done by varying the sample size and the number of defectives allowed until the probability of accepting a lot with the percentage of defectives equal to the LTPD becomes β at the same time the probability of rejecting a lot with the percentage of defectives equal to the AQL becomes α. This relationship is shown in Exhibit 17.5 for $\alpha = .05$, $\beta = .10$, AQL = .03, and LTPD = .20. Notice that in Exhibit 17.5 the probability of accepting a lot with the percentage of defectives equal to the LTPD (a bad lot) is exactly β, while the probability of *not* accepting (1 − the probability of accepting) a lot with the percentage of defectives equal to the AQL (a good lot) is α.

MIL-STD-105D

It is possible to manually calculate the sample size necessary to produce a desired OC curve. However, tables are available to do the tedious job for you. Probably the most widely used set of tables has been developed by the U.S. government and is known as MIL-STD-105D. The MIL-STD-105D tables are based on predetermined OC curves. Thus, the user needs to know only the batch size, the AQL, and the desired level of inspection (usually level II) to easily determine the required sample size and the number of defectives specified for accepting or rejecting the lot. The various levels of inspection correspond to different sample sizes relative

Exhibit 17.4 OC Curve for Sample of Size Ten from a Lot of 1,000*

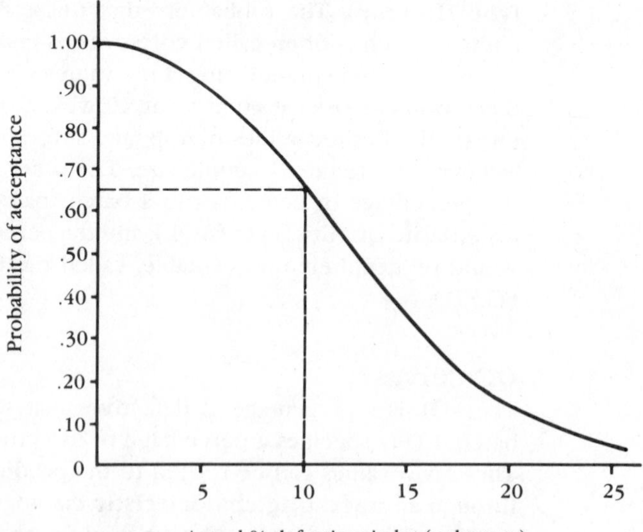

*Lot is accepted if no more than one defective is found in the sample.

Exhibit 17.5 OC Curve for Specified AQL and LTPD

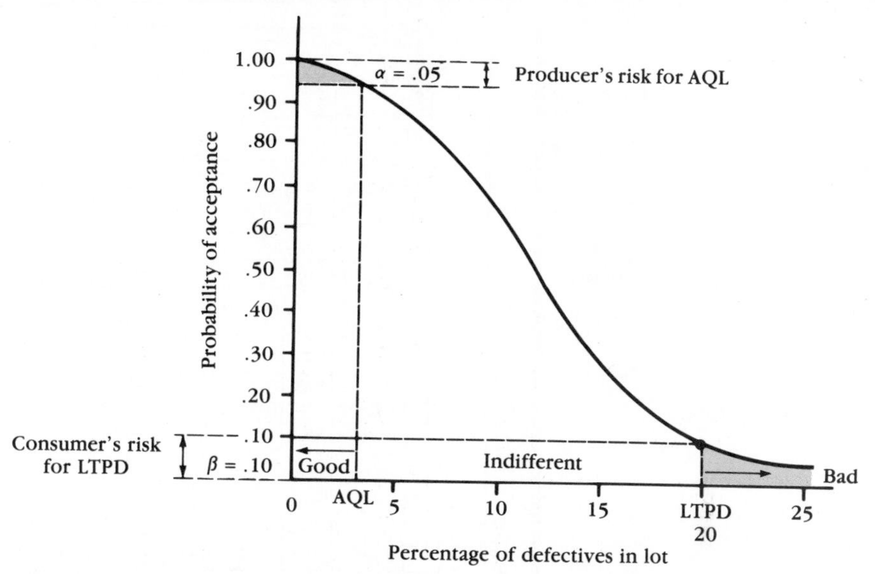

Exhibit 17.6 Sample-Size Code Letters for MIL-STD-105D

Lot or Batch Size	*Special Inspection Levels*				*General Inspection Levels*		
	S-1	**S-2**	**S-3**	**S-4**	**I**	**II**	**III**
2-8	A	A	A	A	A	A	B
9-15	A	A	A	A	A	B	C
16-25	A	A	B	B	B	C	D
26-50	A	B	B	C	C	D	E
51-90	B	B	C	C	C	E	F
91-150	B	B	C	D	D	F	G
151-280	B	C	D	E	E	G	H
281-500	B	C	D	E	F	H	J
501-1,200	C	C	E	F	G	J	K
1,201-3,200	C	D	E	G	H	K	L
3,201-10,000	C	D	F	G	J	L	M
10,001-35,000	C	D	F	H	K	M	N
35,001-150,000	D	E	G	J	L	N	P
150,001-500,000	D	E	G	J	M	P	Q
500,001 and over	D	E	H	K	N	Q	R

to the batch size. Portions of the MIL-STD-105D tables are shown in Exhibits 17.6 and 17.7. The first step in using them is to look up the lot size and then follow across that row to the desired inspection level in Exhibit 17.6. The letter in that row and column is then used in Exhibit 17.7 to determine sample size. One then follows across to the desired acceptable quality level (AQL) column. The number

Exhibit 17.7 Master Table for Single-Sampling Plans (Normal Inspection), MIL-STD-105D

Acceptable Quality Levels (normal inspection), Ac Re for each level:

Sample size code letter	Sample size	0.010	0.015	0.025	0.040	0.065	0.10	0.15	0.25	0.40	0.65	1.0
		Ac Re	Ac Re	Ac Re	Ac Re	Ac Re	Ac Re	Ac Re	Ac Re	Ac Re	Ac Re	Ac Re
A	2	↓	↓	↓	↓	↓	↓	↓	↓	↓	↓	↓
B	3	↓	↓	↓	↓	↓	↓	↓	↓	↓	↓	↓
C	5	↓	↓	↓	↓	↓	↓	↓	↓	↓	↓	↓
D	8	↓	↓	↓	↓	↓	↓	↓	↓	↓	↓	↓
E	13	↓	↓	↓	↓	↓	↓	↓	↓	↓	↓	0 1
F	20	↓	↓	↓	↓	↓	↓	↓	↓	↓	0 1	↑
G	32	↓	↓	↓	↓	↓	↓	↓	↓	0 1	↑	↓
H	50	↓	↓	↓	↓	↓	↓	↓	0 1	↑	↓	1 2
J	80	↓	↓	↓	↓	↓	↓	0 1	↑	↓	1 2	2 3
K	125	↓	↓	↓	↓	↓	0 1	↑	↓	1 2	2 3	3 4
L	200	↓	↓	↓	↓	0 1	↑	↓	1 2	2 3	3 4	5 6
M	315	↓	↓	↓	0 1	↑	↓	1 2	2 3	3 4	5 6	7 8
N	500	↓	↓	0 1	↑	↓	1 2	2 3	3 4	5 6	7 8	10 11
P	800	↓	0 1	↑	↓	1 2	2 3	3 4	5 6	7 8	10 11	14 15
Q	1250	0 1	↑	↓	1 2	2 3	3 4	5 6	7 8	10 11	14 15	21 22
R	2000	↑	↑	1 2	2 3	3 4	5 6	7 8	10 11	14 15	21 22	↑

Sample size code letter	Sample size	1.5	2.5	4.0	6.5	10	15	25	40	65	100	150	250	400	650	1000
		Ac Re	Ac Re	Ac Re	Ac Re	Ac Re	Ac Re	Ac Re	Ac Re	Ac Re	Ac Re	Ac Re	Ac Re	Ac Re	Ac Re	Ac Re
A	2	↓	↓	↓	0 1	↓	↓	1 2	2 3	3 4	5 6	7 8	10 11	14 15	21 22	30 31
B	3	↓	↓	0 1	↑	↓	1 2	2 3	3 4	5 6	7 8	10 11	14 15	21 22	30 31	44 45
C	5	↓	0 1	↑	↓	1 2	2 3	3 4	5 6	7 8	10 11	14 15	21 22	30 31	44 45	↑
D	8	0 1	↑	↓	1 2	2 3	3 4	5 6	7 8	10 11	14 15	21 22	30 31	44 45	↑	↑
E	13	↑	↓	1 2	2 3	3 4	5 6	7 8	10 11	14 15	21 22	30 31	44 45	↑	↑	↑
F	20	↓	1 2	2 3	3 4	5 6	7 8	10 11	14 15	21 22	↑	↑	↑	↑	↑	↑
G	32	1 2	2 3	3 4	5 6	7 8	10 11	14 15	21 22	↑	↑	↑	↑	↑	↑	↑
H	50	2 3	3 4	5 6	7 8	10 11	14 15	21 22	↑	↑	↑	↑	↑	↑	↑	↑
J	80	3 4	5 6	7 8	10 11	14 15	21 22	↑	↑	↑	↑	↑	↑	↑	↑	↑
K	125	5 6	7 8	10 11	14 15	21 22	↑	↑	↑	↑	↑	↑	↑	↑	↑	↑
L	200	7 8	10 11	14 15	21 22	↑	↑	↑	↑	↑	↑	↑	↑	↑	↑	↑
M	315	10 11	14 15	21 22	↑	↑	↑	↑	↑	↑	↑	↑	↑	↑	↑	↑
N	500	14 15	21 22	↑	↑	↑	↑	↑	↑	↑	↑	↑	↑	↑	↑	↑
P	800	21 22	↑	↑	↑	↑	↑	↑	↑	↑	↑	↑	↑	↑	↑	↑
Q	1250	↑	↑	↑	↑	↑	↑	↑	↑	↑	↑	↑	↑	↑	↑	↑
R	2000	↑	↑	↑	↑	↑	↑	↑	↑	↑	↑	↑	↑	↑	↑	↑

↓ = Use first sampling plan below arrow. If sample size equals, or exceeds, lot or batch size, do 100 percent inspection.
↑ = Use first sampling plan above arrow.
Ac = Acceptance number.
Re = Rejection number.

Source: U.S. Department of Defense. MIL-STD-105D, Sampling Procedures and Tables for Inspection for Attributes. Washington, D.C.: U.S. Government Printing Office, 1957.

in the Ac column (the **acceptance number**) indicates the maximum number of defectives allowed in the sample for acceptance of the lot. The number in the Re column (the **rejection number**) is the minimum number of defectives in the sample that are required for rejection of the lot.

Example

The Yates Software Company purchases blank computer diskettes from a supplier. Yates has determined that it wants an acceptable quality level of 1 percent and that it will use general inspection level II. Diskettes come in lots of 2,000.

In Exhibit 17.6, the code letter for a lot size of 2,000 and general inspection level II is *K*. In Exhibit 17.7, code letter *K* indicates a sample size of 125. The column in that row that corresponds to an acceptable quality level of 1.0 shows that the acceptance number (Ac) is 3 and the rejection number (Re) is 4. Thus, Yates would take samples of 125 diskettes from each lot of 2,000. If three or fewer diskettes in each sample are defective, the lot will be accepted. If four or more are defective, the lot will be rejected.

Thus far, we have talked of either accepting or rejecting a lot. However rejecting a lot does not always mean throwing it out or sending it back to the supplier; there are several other alternatives. For one, if it is possible to test each individual item in the batch (100 percent inspection) without destroying these items, we may wish to do so and thus separate the acceptable units from the ones that are unacceptable. This is especially common if the items are needed in production and there is not sufficient time to return them to the supplier for corrective action. Likewise, a batch of portland cement that was rejected because it did not contain enough sand would not be thrown out—instead, we would just add more sand. The purpose of acceptance sampling is not to identify lots that should be thrown out, but to avoid unnecessarily incurring the costs associated with 100 percent inspection or of taking actions to salvage unacceptable materials. The following section discusses one other possible way of gaining as much information as possible while keeping inspection costs down.

Multiple Sampling Plans

The preceding discussion treated acceptance sampling as an approach in which the accept/reject decision is made based on a single sample from each batch. Another approach to acceptance sampling relies on **multiple samples**. In this case, the initial sample is smaller than under a **single-sample plan**. The results from that first small sample may indicate acceptance or rejection of the lot, or they may also indicate the need for an additional sample. Several successive samples may be taken until the lot is finally either accepted or rejected.

The advantage of multiple sampling is that fewer items may need to be tested. This is especially true if the lot is either obviously good or bad. When destructive testing is used, this can be a great advantage and a good justification for the possible additional time and effort involved in multiple sampling.

Exhibit 17.8 shows a multiple sampling table for sample size code letter *K*. The table may be used for a single sample, for two samples (**double sampling**), or for a series of samples (**multiple sampling**). Notice that the size of each sample for the double and multiple plans is considerably less than for the single-

Exhibit 17.8 Sampling Plan for Sample-Size Code Letter: K

Type of sampling plan	Cumulative sample size	Less than 0.10	0.10	0.15	×	0.25	0.40	0.65	1.0	1.5	2.5	×	4.0	×	6.5	×	10	Higher than 10	Cumulative sample size
		Acceptable quality levels (normal inspection)																	
		Ac Re	Ac Re	Ac Re	Ac Re	Ac Re	Ac Re	Ac Re	Ac Re	Ac Re	Ac Re	Ac Re	Ac Re	Ac Re	Ac Re	Ac Re	Ac Re	Ac Re	
Single	125	▽	0 1	Use letter J	Use letter M	Use letter L	1 2	2 3	3 4	5 6	7 8	8 9	10 11	12 13	14 15	18 19	21 22	△	125
Double	80	▽	•				0 2	0 3	1 4	2 5	3 7	3 7	5 9	6 10	7 11	9 14	11 16	△	80
	160						1 2	3 4	4 5	6 7	8 9	11 12	12 13	15 16	18 19	23 24	26 27		160
Multiple	32	▽	•				# 2	# 2	# 3	# 4	0 4	0 4	0 5	0 6	1 7	1 8	2 9	△	32
	64						# 2	0 3	0 3	1 5	1 6	2 7	3 8	3 9	4 10	6 12	7 14		64
	96						0 2	0 3	1 4	2 6	3 8	4 9	6 10	7 12	8 13	11 17	13 19		96
	128						0 3	1 4	2 5	3 7	5 10	6 11	8 13	10 15	12 17	16 22	19 25		128
	160						1 3	2 4	3 6	5 8	7 11	9 12	11 15	14 17	17 20	22 25	25 29		160
	192						1 3	3 5	4 6	7 9	10 12	12 14	14 17	18 20	21 23	27 29	31 33		192
	224						2 3	4 5	6 7	9 10	13 14	14 15	18 19	21 22	25 26	32 33	37 38		224
		Less than 0.15	0.15	×	0.25	0.40	0.65	1.0	1.5	2.5	×	4.0	×	6.5	×	10	×	Higher than 10	
		Acceptable quality levels (tightened inspection)																	

△ = Use next preceding sample-size code letter for which acceptance and rejection numbers are available.
▽ = Use next subsequent sample-size code letter for which acceptance and rejection numbers are available.
Ac = Acceptance number
Re = Rejection number
• = Use single-sampling plan above (or alternatively use letter N).
= Acceptance not permitted at this sample size.

Source: U.S. Department of Defense. MIL-STD-105D, Sampling Procedures and Tables for Inspection for Attributes. Washington, D.C.: U.S. Government Printing Office, 1957.

sampling plan. There is also a range of values that fall between the acceptance and rejection numbers for all but the final sample.

Here's how the multiple sampling plans work. After the first sample is taken, if the number of defectives in the sample is equal to or less than the acceptance number, the lot may be accepted without further sampling. Likewise, if the number of defectives is greater than or equal to the rejection number, the lot may be rejected. However, if a sample's number of defectives is between accept and reject, then successive samples are taken until a definite accept/reject decision is made.

Example

Yates Software has decided to use a double sampling plan, but to keep all other factors the same as in the previous example. Exhibit 17.8 shows that the first sample size for double sampling is 80. In the column for an acceptable quality level of 1.0, the acceptance number is 1, and rejection number is 4. Thus, if one or fewer defective diskettes are found in the sample, the lot is accepted. On the other hand, if four or more defectives are found, then the lot is rejected. However, any number of defectives between these two values will require a second sample of size 80 (for a cumulative sample size of 160). If the *cumulative* number of defectives from both samples is four or less, the lot is accepted. If the cumulative number of defectives is five or more, the lot is rejected.

Statistical Process Control

The acceptance sampling approach described above is most commonly used either when a company receives parts or materials from a supplier or when it is preparing to deliver its product to a customer. In general, acceptance sampling is not done during intermediate processing steps. A more proactive approach to quality control is to ensure that parts and components meet specifications as they are being produced—not after a batch has already been made. This type of quality control is called **process control**. Although its basic philosophy differs from that of acceptance sampling, process control still lies in the area of sampling. With process control, though, we will take samples as items are being produced.

The Concept of Statistical Control

There will always be some variation in any production process due to changes in materials, temperature, humidity, level of operator attention, and many other factors. Much of this variation is due to **chance causes** or **common causes** that occur randomly and cannot be predicted. These may include fluctuations in line voltage, changes in temperature, changes in moisture content of materials, and so forth.

However, some variation is due to **assignable causes,** such as tool wear, miscalibration of equipment, or material purchased from different suppliers. Assignable causes do not occur randomly and usually can be identified and corrected.

When a process is operating so that its output is affected only by chance causes, then the process is in a state of **statistical control** or "**in control**."

Exhibit 17.9 Factors for Control Limits

Sample of Size n	A_2	D_3	D_4	n
2	1.880	0	3.268	2
3	1.023	0	2.574	3
4	0.729	0	2.282	4
5	0.577	0	2.114	5
6	0.483	0	2.004	6
7	0.419	0.076	1.924	7
8	0.373	0.136	1.864	8
9	0.337	0.184	1.816	9
10	0.308	0.223	1.777	10

However, if assignable causes are affecting output, then the process is said to be "**out of control**."

Because the only way to tell if assignable causes are affecting output is by checking that output, we will need to use some method for identifying when a process that was in control has gone out of control. Statistical process control (SPC) is that method.

X-Bar and *R* Charts

The mean of a sample is designated as $\bar{X}$ (*X*-bar) and its range—the difference between the largest and smallest values in the sample—is designated as *R*. When a process is in control, these values should ordinarily stay within certain limits, designated as **control limits,** on a **control chart**.

To construct a control chart, take successive samples over time, usually at least ten samples of size five. Based on the means of these samples and their ranges, a **grand mean** $\bar{\bar{X}}$ (*X*-double bar), or mean of the means, and a mean range $\bar{R}$ can be calculated. As long as the process stays in control, there is a very low probability that any sample mean or range will go above an **upper control limit (UCL)** or fall below a **lower control limit (LCL)**. These upper and lower control limits, which are three standard deviations from the mean, are calculated as follows:

$$UCL_{\bar{x}} = \bar{\bar{X}} + A_2\bar{R}$$

$$LCL_{\bar{x}} = \bar{\bar{X}} - A_2\bar{R}$$

$$UCL_R = D_4\bar{R}$$

$$LCL_R = D_3\bar{R}$$

The values of A_2, D_3, and D_4 for various sample sizes (n) are shown in Exhibit 17.9.

Example

A fast-food restaurant wants to ensure that the machine filling 10-ounce soft drinks remains in control. During a time when the machine is believed to be

Exhibit 17.10 Samples from Soft-Drink Machine

Sample	*Observations (Ounces in cup)* 1	2	3	4	5	$\bar{X}$	*R*
1	9	9.7	10.1	9.2	9.5	9.5	1.1
2	9.7	10.1	10.5	10.2	10.5	10.2	.8
3	10.2	10.1	9.8	9.6	9.8	9.9	.6
4	10.1	9.2	9.5	9.2	9.0	9.4	1.1
5	9.6	10.1	9.9	9.7	9.7	9.8	.5
6	10.1	9.1	9.2	9.6	9.5	9.5	1.0
7	9.7	10.1	10.1	9.8	10.3	10.0	.6
8	10.2	9.3	9.5	9.9	9.1	9.6	1.1
9	9.9	10.2	10.1	9.7	10.1	10.0	.5
10	10.0	9.8	10.2	10.3	10.2	10.1	.5
						$\bar{\bar{X}} = 9.8$	$\bar{R} = .78$

operating in control, samples of size five are taken, as shown in Exhibit 17.10. These samples were taken at one-hour intervals over a nine-hour period.

Based on this information, the control limits are

$$UCL_{\bar{X}} = \bar{\bar{X}} + A_2\bar{R}$$
$$= 9.8 + .577(.78)$$
$$= 10.25$$
$$LCL_{\bar{X}} = \bar{\bar{X}} - A_2\bar{R}$$
$$= 9.8 - .577(.78)$$
$$= 9.35$$
$$UCL_R = D_4\bar{R}$$
$$= 2.114(.78)$$
$$= 1.65$$
$$LCL_R = D_3\bar{R}$$
$$= 0(.78)$$
$$= 0$$

Exhibit 17.11 shows the *X*-bar and *R* charts for these ten samples. Notice that we have indicated the upper and lower control limits for each with dashed lines. Further, the mean and range of each sample have been plotted.

Because all points are within the control limits and there do not appear to be any unusual trends or deviations, the company's assumption that the process is in control is probably valid. These charts can now be used to control the process by extending the control limits into the future and continuing to plot sample means and ranges.

Exhibit 17.11 $\bar{X}$ and R Charts for 10-Ounce Soft Drinks

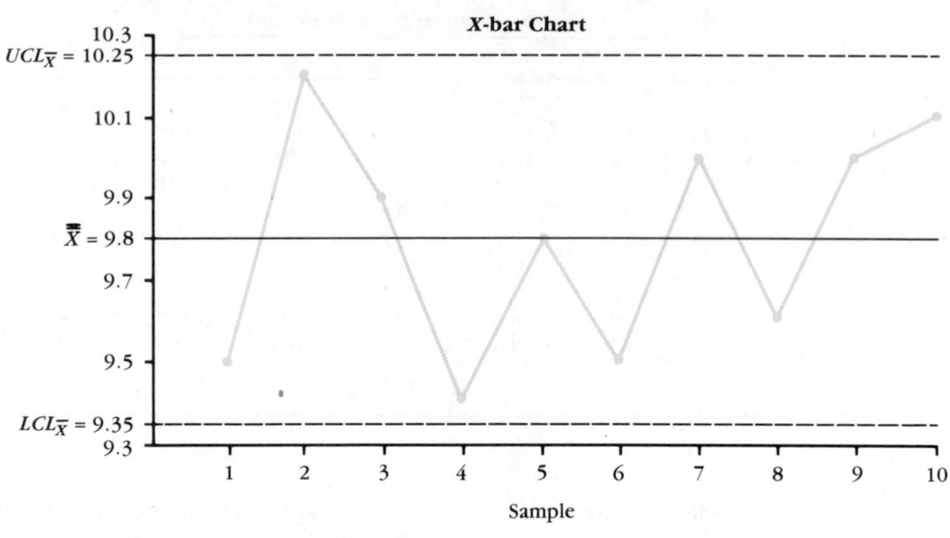

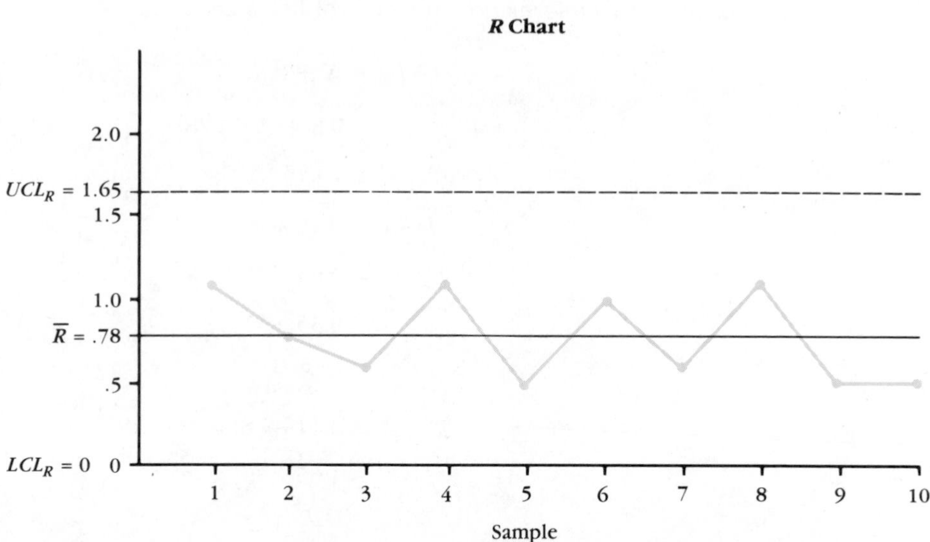

Identifying Out-of-Control Conditions

The primary indication that the process may be out of control—in other words, that assignable causes are affecting the output—is that one or more points will be outside of the control limits for either $\bar{X}$ or R. However, the following are also causes for concern and justify investigation to determine their cause:

- Two successive points near either control limit
- Run of five points above or below mean
- Trend in either direction
- Erratic behavior or sudden changes in level

Example

After developing its control charts, the fast-food restaurant from the previous example has continued taking samples of size five from its soft drink machines every hour. The most recent five samples produced the following results:

Sample	$\bar{X}$	R
1	10.1	1.2
2	9.5	1.2
3	10.2	1.3
4	9.4	1.4
5	9.4	1.5

When graphed on the control charts, these samples appear as shown in Exhibit 17.12. Although no points are outside the control limits, there is still

Exhibit 17.12 Control Charts with Out-of-Control Warnings

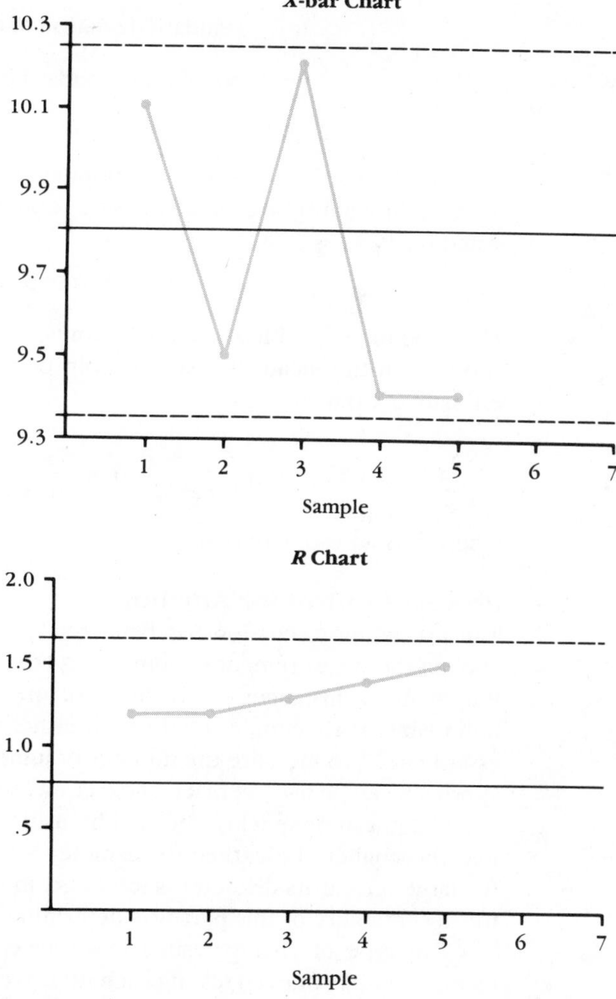

cause for investigation for the following reasons, any of which by itself would prompt us to check for assignable causes of variation:

- There is erratic behavior of $\overline{X}$.
- The last five R values are all above the mean.
- There is an upward trend in the R values toward the upper control limit.
- The last two $\overline{X}$ values are both near the lower control limit.

Process Mean and Standard Deviation

The theoretical foundation of control charts is the **central limit theorem,** which states that the means of samples from a population will be normally distributed with the mean equal to the population mean, μ, and standard deviation

$$\sigma_{\overline{X}} = \frac{\sigma}{\sqrt{n}}$$

where

$$\sigma_{\overline{X}} = \text{standard deviation of the sample means}$$

$$\sigma = \text{population standard deviation}$$

$$n = \text{sample size}$$

Usually we do not know the population mean and the standard deviation. Instead, these must be estimated, using $\overline{\overline{X}}$ in place of μ. The relationship between $\overline{R}$ and $\sigma_{\overline{X}}$ is

$$A_2\overline{R} \approx 3\sigma_{\overline{X}}$$

Thus, the upper and lower control limits we have used are three standard deviations from the mean. The relationship between $\overline{R}$ and $\sigma_{\overline{X}}$ may also be used to estimate σ from $\overline{R}$

$$\hat{\sigma} = \frac{A_2\overline{R}\sqrt{n}}{3}$$

where $\hat{\sigma}$ is an estimate of σ.

Process Control for Attributes

The preceding discussion has been related to process control in situations involving the measurement of something (e.g., height, weight, diameter, voltage). But in many instances, such detail of measurement is either unnecessary or impossible. For example, a light bulb either works, or it doesn't—we don't necessarily need to measure the number of lumens given off. Some times a go/no-go approach can be used in place of exact measurements. For example, the diameter of a piston can be quickly checked by using two cut-out circles. If the piston fits into the smaller circle, then its diameter is below tolerances. If it doesn't fit into the larger circle, its diameter is too large. In this case, nothing was measured, but the acceptability of this part was determined.

This type of testing results in an accept/reject decision for each part. By taking a sample, or even testing each item, we can develop a record of the number of defective parts versus the number that were acceptable. This information can

INTEGRATING THE SYSTEM

Product Design Must Be Tied to Process Capability

The concepts of process mean and process standard deviation are very important in process design and capability. For example, many products are designed with dimensions that have **tolerance limits**. The number of ounces in a 16-ounce soft-drink bottle does not have to be exactly 16, but can vary from that by some tolerance limit. This tolerance might be ± .5 ounce. The dimension for a ball bearing might be .375 inch ± .00005 inch. This means an acceptable ball bearing could be as small as .37495 inch or as large as .37505 inch. These are the tolerance limits.

However, such tolerances are meaningless if the process cannot maintain them. For example, a soft-drink container that must be filled to 16 ounces ± .5 ounce requires a process with the capability to fill all bottles within the tolerance limits when the process is operating correctly. If the process standard deviation is .45 ounce, then a fair number of bottles could be filled to unacceptable levels just because of random variation, meaning the process is not capable of staying within the tolerance limits. This situation is depicted in Exhibit 17.13, where the shaded area indicates the probability that a "16-ounce" bottle will be filled with an amount that is either above or below the tolerance limits, based on a process mean of 16 and a process standard deviation of .45 ounce.

This situation is unacceptable, however, and the process must be designed so that it can maintain the specified tolerances. This becomes especially important under conditions where each successive operation can have its own variation. The sum of these variations can lead to an unacceptable variation in the final product.

Exhibit 17.13 Process Standard Deviation and Tolerance Limits

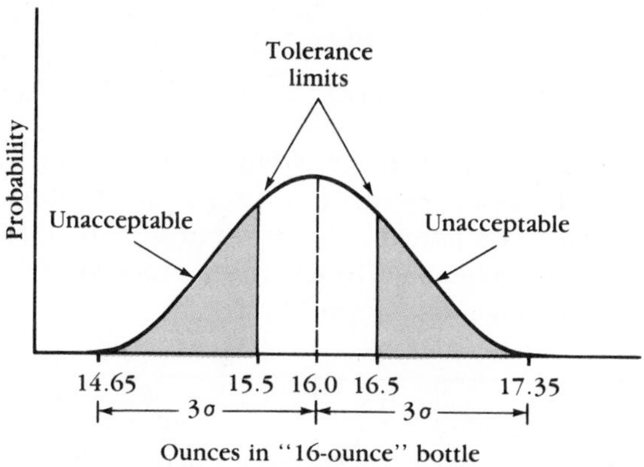

be plotted, using an approach similar to the X-bar chart already described. If the percentage of defectives in each sample is plotted, then this is called a ***p* chart**. The p chart shows the percentage of defectives in each sample.

Upper and lower control limits can be calculated for p charts. In fact, these limits are a little easier to calculate than for an X-bar chart because the standard deviation of p can be determined directly from the process mean.

If the proportion of items defective is being measured for a process in control, then $\overline{p}$ (p bar) will be the average proportion of units defective for a group of samples taken from that process. Based on this value, the standard deviation of the mean proportion of defectives in samples of size n can be calculated as

$$\sigma_p = \sqrt{\frac{\overline{p}(1 - \overline{p})}{n}}$$

The upper and lower control limits for the p chart are then calculated as

$$UCL_p = \overline{p} + 3\sigma_p$$

$$LCL_p = \overline{p} - 3\sigma_p$$

Example

First-Rate Air Express Company guarantees delivery of packages within twelve hours or less, or the customer pays nothing. The company keeps track of the percentage of packages not delivered within twelve hours for every 1,000 packages the company handles. For a recent period of time when the delivery process was in control, that percentage averaged 2 percent. The company can determine upper and lower control limits for a p chart by calculating

$$\sigma_p = \sqrt{\frac{\overline{p}(1 - \overline{p})}{n}}$$

$$= \sqrt{\frac{.02(.98)}{1000}} = .0044$$

Then,

$$UCL_p = .02 + 3(.0044) = .0332$$

$$LCL_p = .02 - 3(.0044) = .0068$$

Thus, if the percentage of late deliveries per 1,000 packages exceeds 3.32 percent, the company should consider investigating. Likewise, if the percentage drops below .68 percent, it may mean that some procedures are being used to help ensure on-time deliveries. Those procedures should be determined so they can be continued on a formal basis.

In some cases, we can keep track of only the number of defects found, not the number of nondefects. Thus, we will not be able to record percentage of defects. For example, we can count the number of defects per 1,000 feet of electrical cable, but the number of nondefects cannot be counted. In this instance, we must use a ***c* chart** to monitor the number of defects.

When the number of defects is counted, then $\overline{c}$ (c bar) will be the average number of defects over a group of samples. Again, the standard deviation of the mean number of defects is calculated based on this value

$$\sigma_c = \sqrt{\overline{c}}$$

and

$$UCL_c = \bar{c} + 3\sigma_c$$

$$LCL_c = \bar{c} - 3\sigma_c$$

Example

The Jackson County Bank keeps track of the number of errors made per 100 customer transactions. This number has been averaging five while the process has been in control. The bank would like to set up a control chart to monitor the number of errors.

$$\sigma_c = \sqrt{\bar{c}} = \sqrt{5} = 2.24$$

$$UCL_c = \bar{c} + 3\sigma_c = 5 + 3(2.24) = 11.72$$

$$LCL_c = \bar{c} - 3\sigma_c = 5 - 3(2.24) = -1.72$$

Because the value calculated for the LCL_c is negative and a negative number of errors cannot occur, we instead use zero for the lower control limit. In this case, the bank will take action only if the number of errors per 100 transactions exceeds 11.72.

Overall Measures of Quality

The measures described above usually apply to either a particular variable or an attribute of a part. However, companies today are beginning to use a more general, overall measure of quality that is expressed in terms of **defective parts per million (ppm)**. Before the advent of a strong emphasis on quality management and zero defects programs, companies commonly measured the number of defects produced in terms of percentages (defective parts or products per hundred produced). However, today it is not uncommon to hear companies discuss production processes that turn out as few defects as 100 ppm (100 defective parts or products for every million produced). In fact, it is not uncommon to see figures around 10 ppm (.001 percent defectives). Such small numbers of defective parts or products mean a company is truly approaching the goal of zero defects.

Locating Inspection Operations

As we mentioned previously, the traditional approach to inspection and testing has been to check parts and materials when they arrive from suppliers and to check finished products before they are shipped to customers. In general, companies have not followed formal inspection and test procedures at intermediate processing operations. However, this approach can be costly because the cost of scrapping or reworking a defective part is much less than scrapping or rebuilding a finished product that does not work because of one defective part.

The current philosophy is that inspection or testing should be carried out on important characteristics as early as possible. For example, critical dimensions of a part should be checked soon after that part is made; transactions performed by tellers at a bank should be checked as soon as possible after those transactions have occurred.

A second part of the current philosophy is that inspection should be as simple and automatic as possible, while still being accurate. Thus, the checking of a part's dimensions could be done by simple **go/no-go gages** that the part must pass through on its way to the next operation. Or, as is now done in automobile assembly plants, automatic measurements can be made by low-power laser beams as parts and materials move through processing. Within the bank, transactions might be given a preliminary check by the computer to ensure that they are reasonable.

In general, inspection should occur

- When material is received from suppliers.
- After operations with high scrap rates.
- Before high-cost operations.
- Before parts are joined irreversibly to other parts.
- Before shipment to customers.

COMPANYWIDE QUALITY CONTROL

It has already been mentioned in Chapter 12 that quality control is extremely important to JIT. As a result, companies using JIT have applied extensively the methods and concepts described earlier in this chapter. However, some of those companies have gone on to develop certain philosophies and techniques that extend well beyond the quality control procedures used by most other organizations. In this section, we briefly describe a few of the more important quality control aspects of **companywide quality control (CWQC)**.

Total Quality Control

Total quality control (TQC) is a term that has become associated with JIT systems, although it was originally coined by an American quality control expert, Armand V. Feigenbaum.[6] Many of the concepts and methods we have discussed above are part of TQC. However, the basic philosophy behind TQC is much broader and actually consists of five categories:

1. Organization
2. Goals
3. Basic principles
4. Facilitating concepts
5. Techniques and aids

Organization

The most important underlying philosophy of TQC is that the individual worker is the one responsible for quality, not a quality control department. This means that employees must be adequately trained and indoctrinated with quality control principles so they can ensure that good products are being produced. A separate quality control department, not directly responsible for production, cannot do the job.

Goals

As with JIT in general, the goals of TQC are constant improvement and perfection. Just as the JIT goal is to eliminate all waste, TQC works toward the production of zero defects. In seeking this goal, companies must continually strive to improve the way they do things.

Basic Principles

The basic principles of TQC include several topics we have already discussed. One of these is statistical process control, which is used by individual workers at each work station to control quality throughout the entire process.

A second basic concept of TQC is the extensive display of charts, graphs, tools, and procedures related to quality control. Some of these displays may include the X-bar and other charts we discussed earlier. However, other types of displays may be simple bar graphs or line charts, indicating a company's progress toward its goal of zero defects.

Other basic principles of TQC include the responsibility of workers to correct their own errors, 100 percent inspection, line-stop authority if problems occur, and improvement projects.

Facilitating Concepts

Implementation of the TQC basics can actually help facilitate further improvement. For example, once process control has reached the point that few, if any, defects are produced, the need for frequent inspections is eliminated. In fact, some companies inspect only the first and last units of a batch just to be sure the process has not drifted; process capabilities are so good that if the first and last units of a batch are acceptable, then intermediate units will be, too. This same approach can be used to eliminate incoming inspection of parts and materials from suppliers once the supplier's quality control record has been established.

Some other facilitating concepts in TQC are much less glamorous, but also possibly more important. One of these is housekeeping. Plants that use JIT emphasize a neat layout and clear aisles. TQC also emphasizes keeping the work area and equipment clean and in good repair. As with the basic responsibility for quality control, the responsibility for housekeeping usually falls on the workers.

Small lot sizes and the operation of machines below their rated capacity are important components of JIT. They are also included as facilitating concepts in TQC, although for different reasons. With small lot sizes, it is more likely that quality problems are caught early before a large batch of defective parts is produced. Likewise, by running machines well below capacity, it is less likely that breakdowns or excessive wear will occur.

Techniques and Aids

We have already discussed some of the techniques and aids that are part of TQC earlier in this chapter. Another aid in TQC is the development of foolproof processes, referred to by the Japanese as *poka-yoke*. For example, if a device that automatically monitors tool wear can be attached to a machine, then that device can shut off the machine when wear has reached a point where defectives might be produced. Other, similar ideas can be used to make it extremely difficult to produce defective products.

Quality Circles

Quality circles—also known as quality control circles, QC circles, or even QCCs—are an approach to participatory problem solving that has worked well in Japan and is achieving moderate success in the United States. In essence, a quality circle is a group of employees who meet on a regular basis, usually once per week, to solve problems that relate to their job activities.

It is interesting to note that quality circles first originated in Japan as reading groups. In 1960, the Japanese Union of Scientists and Engineers (JUSE), an organization largely concerned with quality control in Japan, began attempts to familiarize supervisors and workers with the concepts and techniques of quality control. First, a textbook was published, and then a periodical began publication in 1962. JUSE suggested that groups be formed to read and discuss the material, and these groups were called QC circles.

Today, quality circles are well established in Japan. According to one estimate, 77 percent of all Japanese companies with more than 10,000 employees have something akin to quality circles.[7] Even in the United States, where overall results are somewhat mixed, many companies have been extremely successful with this approach. Research to date seems to indicate that those companies where quality circles have flourished are ones that have made a definite commitment to making them work. Others, where the concept has failed, have too often seen QC circles as a fad or "quick fix" for underlying problems. In this section, we will present some techniques used by QC circles to identify problem causes.

Cause-Effect Diagrams

One useful approach that has been developed and used successfully to analyze a problem is the cause-effect diagram, also known as the Ishikawa or fishbone diagram. The purpose of this diagram is to identify possible problem causes and then explore each of these in detail until the cause or causes have been determined.

In general, the fishbone diagram is a useful method by which quality circles identify problem causes. The usual approach begins with four possible problem areas, as shown in Exhibit 17.14. These are methods, materials, equipment, and personnel. The effect, or problem, constitutes the "head" of the fish.

Exhibit 17.14 Beginning of Fishbone Diagram

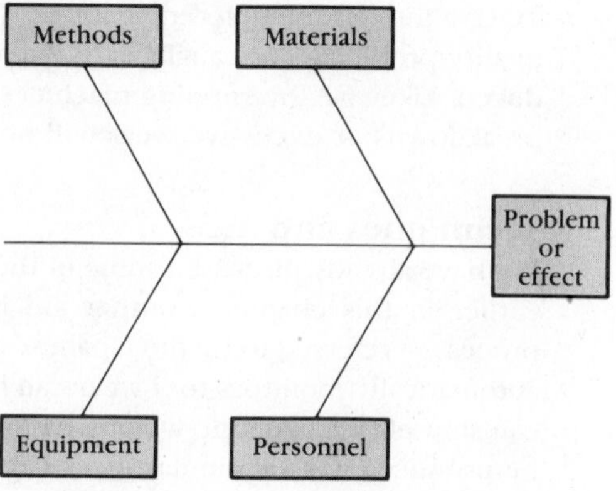

Under each possible cause, possible subcauses are identified and investigated. These subcauses are factors that may or may not be producing the effect. Information is gathered about the problem and used to fill in the fishbone diagram. Gradually, some possible subcauses are eliminated until eventually the true problem cause is identified. A completed fishbone diagram is shown in Exhibit 17.15 for the problem of complaints of cold food from customers at a fast-food restaurant. You should notice that in Exhibit 17.15 the possible subcauses are listed as assumptions. Each of these must be examined to determine whether it is true. Any assumptions that are not met must be examined further.

Pareto Analysis

Another useful problem identification and problem-solving tool that is often used by quality circles is known as **Pareto analysis**. The idea is to separate the "important few" from the "trivial many" and is based on the concept that 20 percent of the items in a group will account for 80 percent of the cost, value, problems, or whatever is being measured. This idea was introduced in Chapter 16 as ABC analysis, and is useful in quality control because it allows us to focus on the "important few" causes of defects and to ignore, at least in the beginning, the "trivial many."

Usually Pareto analysis is based on organizing the data into a diagram so that the major problems or problem causes can be identified. Often this diagram can be a simple bar chart. For example, the chart shown in Exhibit 17.16 indicates the number of defects of each type found in circuit boards. As is obvious, a great majority of problems were caused by soldering defects. Armed with this information, a quality circle can then use Pareto analysis to specify the problem cause

Exhibit 17.15 Fishbone Diagram for Fast-Food Restaurant

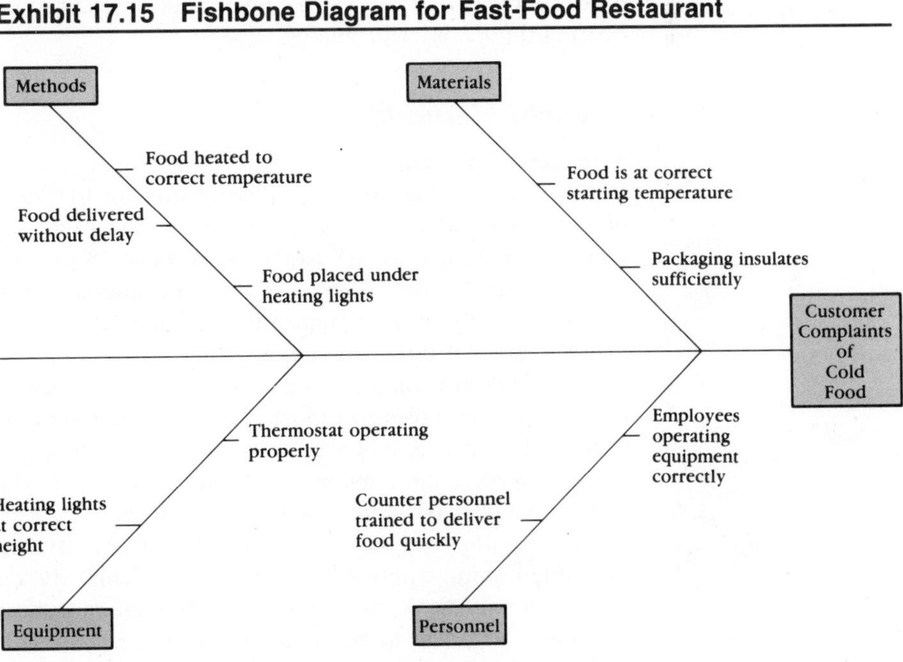

Exhibit 17.16 Pareto Analysis of Circuit Board Defects

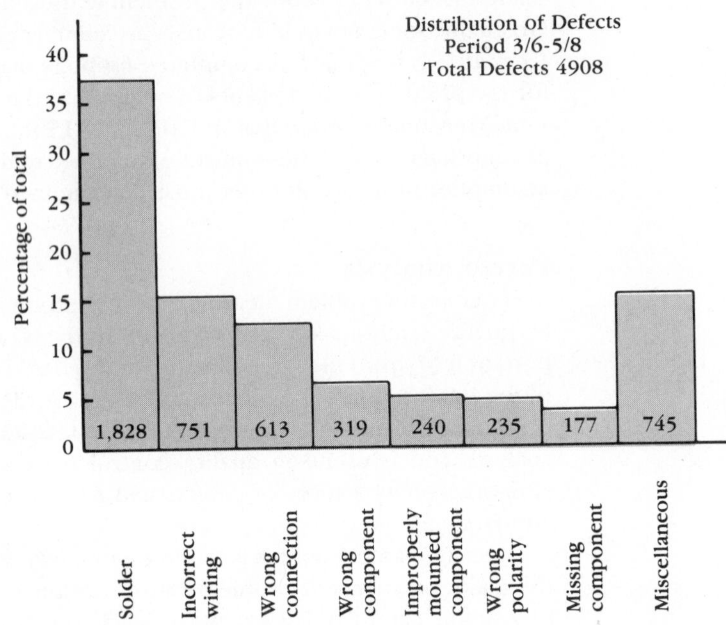

Source: Joseph M. Juram, Leonard A. Seder, and Frank M. Gryna, Jr., *Quality Control Handbook*, 2d ed. (New York: McGraw-Hill, 1962), p. 26–11.

more succinctly or can use a cause-effect diagram to determine exactly what is causing these solder problems.

Taguchi Methods

The Loss Function

Genichi Taguchi has proposed a **loss function** that measures the loss to society of producing parts or products that deviate from a "target value." For example, consider the case of Ford,[8] which owns about 25 percent of Mazda. Several years ago, Ford and Mazda both produced transmissions for use in a car Ford was marketing in the United States. Both companies used identical specifications to manufacture these transmissions.

However, it turned out the transmissions produced by Ford generated much higher warranty costs and more numerous customer complaints than did those produced by Mazda. When the transmissions were disassembled, it was found that all parts were within specified tolerances, but only those produced by Mazda were all exactly on target—with no variation.

The random variation in parts produced by Ford meant that when parts were assembled, some combinations caused problems. The cost to society turned out to include warranty and repair costs, as well as lost time and productivity for customers who had to get their cars repaired.

OPERATIONS IN ACTION

Westinghouse: Improving Quality by Focusing on Processes

A number of years ago, Westinghouse set up a unit, called the Productivity Center, to help the company raise its productivity. However, within months, Westinghouse realized that productivity was a function of quality and immediately renamed that unit the Productivity and Quality Center. Today, it is usually referred to as the Quality Center.

In fact, the company has found that the best way to satisfy customers is by focusing on quality rather than productivity. Further, instead of concentrating just on the quality of the product, Westinghouse pays attention to the entire process—from engineering and plant maintenance to customer billing.

This link with the customer has become extremely important. For example, one customer thought it could reduce its ordering costs by tying into Westinghouse's computerized ordering system. But Westinghouse provided even more. After having its Quality Center analyze the customer's purchasing operations, the cost of placing an order for that customer dropped from $86 to $12.

The results of these efforts can be seen throughout the company. For example, the company's Thermo King plant in Galway, Ireland, had 300 employees and 48 quality teams. In fact, Westinghouse's Nuclear Fuel Division won the 1988 Malcolm Baldrige Award, the U.S. equivalent of Japan's Deming Award for quality.[9]

Thus, according to Taguchi, the process distribution for process A, shown at the left of Exhibit 17.17, is preferable to process B, shown at the right. This is because the loss function for process A will be much less, even though it is not centered at the target, because there is less overall variation. Further, it may be possible to center process A at the target through a simple adjustment.

However, process B's wide variation may be caused by hundreds of different factors, all of which must be investigated. When assembled with other parts, those from process B may also produce unacceptable combinations.

Exhibit 17.17 Frequency Distribution of Sample Means from Two Different Processes

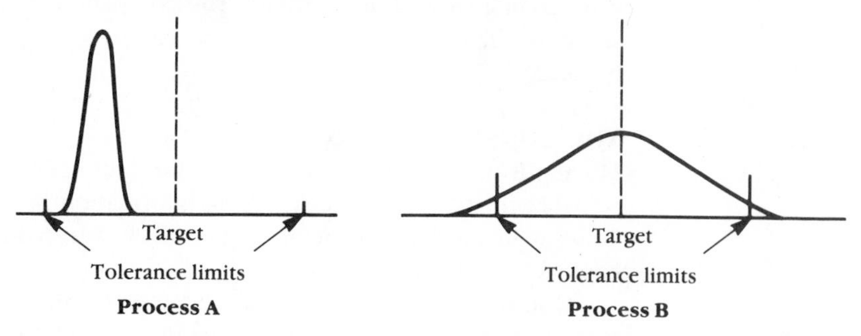

Using Experimental Design

In order to minimize Taguchi's loss function, deviation from the process target value must be minimized. However, many different factors, ranging from materials used to operator training, can affect process deviation. To identify those that are most relevant, the statistical methods of experimental design are used.

By using experimental design, several factors can be changed simultaneously, keeping track of the value of each factor and the resulting process output. Statistical analysis is then used to determine which factor or factors are most significant.

For example, ITT produces automotive wiring harnesses for Ford.[10] At certain points, those wiring harnesses must be welded together. However, the welds sometimes fail. Using an experimental design, it took five days for engineers to find a way of reducing process deviation from the target value. Results of that experiment were communicated to other wiring harness suppliers for Ford, resulting in a cost saving of $1 million per year.

Quality Function Deployment

Taguchi methods provide ways of minimizing process deviation from the target value. But one question to be answered is what that target value should be in the first place. To answer that question, we must return to the needs of the customer. However, a problem arises here because customers usually state their needs in broad general terms. On the other hand, process targets must be stated in very specific terms, such as thickness, weight, or time.

Quality function deployment provides a means by which companies take the "voice of the customer" and convert it into target values throughout the entire organization.

The Voice of the Customer

Customers, especially if they are final consumers, will state their requirements in phrases, called **customer attributes**. Customer attributes usually describe product characteristics, such as "easy to use," "reliable," and "inexpensive to operate." However, customers may also include other manufacturers, retailers, or government agencies. Their customer attributes may be quite specific or even more general, such as "easy to inventory" or "safe to use."

These customer attributes can be collected through market surveys or consumer sampling or even by comparison to competitors' products. Often the company may have to fill in the blanks. For example, customers may say they want a car that is "fun to drive." The company may have to develop secondary attributes from this, such as "fast response," "good mileage," and "quick handling."

The House of Quality

Moving from customer attributes to product specifications requires a series of steps. Each step will require taking information from the previous one and refining it further. The process begins with converting customer attributes into engineering characteristics.

One tool for doing this is the **house of quality**. The house of quality is a diagram that resembles a house, as shown in Exhibit 17.18. Customer attributes

Exhibit 17.18 House of Quality for "Fun to Drive" Customer Attribute

	Engineering characteristics	Engine performance				steering		
		Acceleration 0-60 mph	Passing time	Fuel economy	•••	Turning radius	•••	Customer importance
Customer attributes: Fun to drive	Fast response	+	+	−				9
	Good mileage	−	−	+				7
	Good handling					+		8
	•••							
Objective measures	Our car	10 sec.	12 sec.	30 mpg.		20 ft.		
	Competitor A	8.5 sec.	9 sec.	25 mpg.		25 ft.		
	Competitor B	9 sec.	10 sec.	27 mpg.		28 ft.		
	Target	8 sec.	8 sec.	30 mpg.		20 ft.		

are placed along the left side of the house and are related to engineering characteristics across the top. Positive relationships are shown with plus signs and negative ones with minus signs. For instance, the time necessary to accelerate from zero to sixty miles per hour is related to responsiveness, but may have a negative relationship to mileage.

The roof of the house indicates positive and negative relationships among engineering characteristics. For example, the time necessary to accelerate from zero to sixty miles per hour will have a positive relationship with passing time. However, both of these have a negative relationship with fuel economy.

Objective measures for each engineering characteristic, comparing the company's product to those of competitors, are shown in the basement of the house, along with target values for our product. Notice in this case that our current values of fuel economy and turning radius are acceptable and thus become the target values. However, acceleration must be improved.

In some cases, there may be trade-offs, as between acceleration and fuel economy. In making a choice between one or the other, the importance of each customer attribute can be considered. Those importance ratings are shown along the right-hand side of the house.

Moving from One House to Another

This first house of quality translates the "voice of the customer" into engineering characteristics. However, engineering characteristics by themselves will not tell us how to make a car. Those characteristics must be translated into parts characteristics, as shown in Exhibit 17.19. Parts characteristics define how the engineering characteristics will be achieved.

But the parts characteristics cannot be achieved unless the process is planned to do so. Thus, another chart is required to convert the parts characteristics into process details, describing how the parts are to be produced with the required characteristics. Finally, production requirements are developed that specify inspection details, measuring methods, operator training, and so forth.

Using the four steps shown in Exhibit 17.19, the voice of the customer has been deployed throughout the entire organization. Further, all parts of the organization have had to work together to achieve that deployment.

Managing the Quality of Services

The primary difficulty with measuring the quality of service operations is that much is based on intangibles. Because there is so much customer contact in services, the customer's perception of quality is extremely important. Such factors as friendliness of personnel, decor of the facility, and even the type of music being played can influence customer perceptions.

However, many factors can be measured and controlled, using the procedures we have just discussed. For example, banks routinely monitor the accuracy

Exhibit 17.19 Successive Houses of Quality Deploy the Voice of the Customer Throughout the Organization

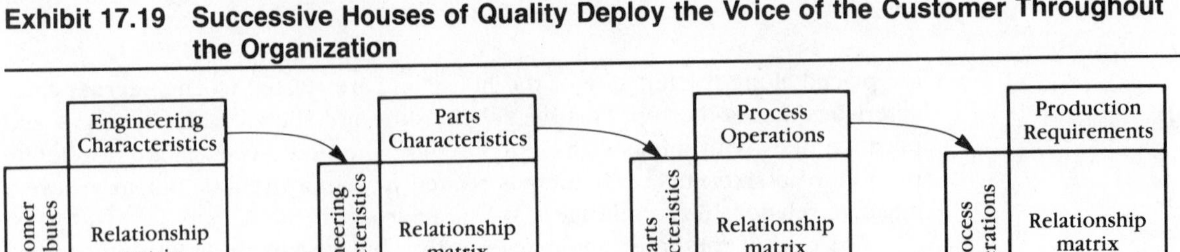

GAINING STRATEGIC ADVANTAGE AT AMERICAN EXPRESS

Managing for Delivery of Quality

The credit card business is one service industry in which quality is extremely important. And one credit card company that knows that best is American Express. While manufacturing companies can patent their product, there is no patent on service. As the CEO of American Express, James Robinson, is quoted as saying, "Quality is the only patent protection we've got."

From Robinson on down, American Express focuses on delivering the highest quality of service possible. For example, the company's Travel Related Services Division uses a measure of quality as the basis of its self-assessment. Some components of that measure are the time it takes operators in service centers to answer a customer call (seven seconds) and the time it takes for customers reporting lost cards to receive replacements (forty-eight hours).

However, the company also devotes considerable effort to measuring intangibles through extensive customer surveys. The information from those surveys is used to focus the company's marketing efforts, providing car-rental insurance for customers who want it and twenty-four-hour phones for customers who want that service.

The recent experiences of one traveler show how well the company is doing.[11] While traveling in the south of France, he lost all his traveler's checks and credit cards. He found out that replacement of his MasterCard would require going to Paris, a round trip of 1,000 miles. It also turned out the only place to replace his stolen Bank of America traveler's checks was a hotel closed for renovation.

Finally, the traveler remembered he had applied for an American Express card before leaving the United States. After walking *four blocks* to the local AmEx office, he was able to get a replacement card and $600 in cash and traveler's checks by that afternoon. Now *that's* service.[12]

of their transactions and account records. Further, the average waiting time for service can be tracked. Airlines routinely keep track of their on-time performance and use this as a marketing tool.

Even intangibles can be measured through customer surveys. For example, Ford Motor Company sends out questionnaires to its customers a few months after purchase. Those questionnaires seek to assess customer satisfaction not only with the automobile, but also with the services provided by the dealership. Each dealership is then assigned a numerical rating in the four areas of sales, vehicle preparation, service, and overall customer satisfaction.

SUMMARY

- Quality is defined as "the degree of conformance of all the relevant features and characteristics of the product to all of the aspects of a customer's need, limited by the price and delivery he or she will accept."
- Quality assurance differs from quality control in that assurance involves creating a companywide environment that promotes high quality.

- Philip Crosby and W. Edwards Deming have each proposed fourteen steps, from top-management involvement to employee involvement to quality control.
- The costs of quality include prevention, appraisal, and failure costs.
- Quality circles are groups of workers who work together to solve problems that affect their jobs.
- The fishbone diagram is one tool used by quality circles to identify problem causes.
- The current emphasis in statistical quality control is to spot potential problem areas before defects are produced.
- Acceptance sampling uses statistical information gained from a sample to determine whether an entire batch should be accepted or rejected.
- Process control uses statistical methods to identify when a process may have gone out of control and should be investigated.
- Total quality control includes organization, goals, basic principles, facilitating concepts, and techniques and aids.
- The Taguchi loss function measures loss to society when process output deviates from a target value.
- Taguchi methods use experimental design to identify major factors affecting a process.
- Quality function deployment is a way to carry the voice of the customer throughout an organization's activities.
- The house of quality is used to convert customer attributes to engineering characteristics and then finally to production methods.

CAREER PROFILE

Dennis Hecker

Director of Quality Assurance
Wendy's International

Everyone is familiar with Wendy's in its role as a major competitor with McDonald's and Burger King in the fast-food business. Wendy's currently operates some 4,000 restaurants worldwide and opens a new one every 24 hours. Although customers of other fast-food franchises may ask, "Where's the beef?" Dennis Hecker, Wendy's director of quality assurance, is one person who can answer that question and also give you a long list of specifications that must be met by the beef used in Wendy's hamburgers.

Educational Background and Work Experience

Originally from Mineral Ridge, Ohio, Hecker earned a B.S. in microbiology from Ohio State University and went to work as a quality assurance inspector for Borden. In that role, he inspected a large variety of food-processing operations throughout the United States and Canada. Then, in 1980, he started working for Wendy's as a quality assurance specialist, one of only three people who were responsible for maintaining quality within the 1,500 Wendy's restaurants that existed at that time. In 1983, Hecker was promoted to supervisor of quality assurance, responsible for overseeing the quality assurance laboratory and one quality assurance specialist.

It was six months later that Wendy's decided to make quality assurance an even more important part of its organizational strategy, and Hecker became the manager of quality assurance. In that role, he put together plant auditing and supplier sampling programs and developed a very structured, organized approach to corporatewide quality assurance.

Current Position and Duties

Hecker was named director of quality assurance for Wendy's in 1984. He is currently responsible for overseeing a staff of ten and for maintaining all aspects of quality associated with Wendy's in four different areas: store inspection, plant audits, production audits, and laboratory sampling and testing.

Wendy's quality assurance involves an extensive amount of activity. For example, french fries are evaluated on twelve different attributes and must achieve total compliance with specifications. Each year Hecker's staff performs over 300 sanitation audits of supplier plants. Each plant must score at least 70 points out of a possible 100 during these audits. If any defects are not corrected with thirty days, the supplier is dropped as a source for Wendy's. One company that had been providing 100,000 pounds of ground beef per week was recently dropped for not meeting Wendy's specifications for ground beef.

The company also inspects its restaurants on a regular basis, using a sampling plan. Out of the sixty Wendy's restaurants in Atlanta, twenty-five might be examined unannounced at any one time. The most common deficiencies found are reported to the area restaurant supervisor for correction.

Just in case some unacceptable food should slip through the inspection program, Wendy's also has a sophisticated recall program. Notices can be directed to any or all of Wendy's restaurants by computer within a few hours so that any problems can be caught before they ever reach the customer.

SOLVED PROBLEMS

1. The following data have been collected from a process that makes capacitors for electrical circuit boards. The process was operating in control, and twenty samples of size four were taken. The capacitance (in microfarads) of each capacitor was measured and the sample mean calculated. The process standard deviation, σ, has not been calculated, but information was collected about the range of each sample. Use this information to develop an *X*-bar chart and an *R* chart.

Sample	Capacitance (mfd) of Each Unit in Sample				$\bar{X}$	R
1	1.25	1.32	1.24	1.29	1.275	.08
2	1.31	1.28	1.26	1.32	1.2925	.06
3	1.28	1.24	1.22	1.26	1.25	.06
4	1.32	1.27	1.29	1.30	1.295	.05
5	1.25	1.25	1.27	1.31	1.27	.06
6	1.28	1.31	1.29	1.27	1.2875	.04
7	1.26	1.33	1.27	1.27	1.2825	.07

Sample	Capacitance (mfd) of Each Unit in Sample				$\bar{X}$	R
8	1.28	1.30	1.31	1.29	1.295	.03
9	1.26	1.28	1.29	1.26	1.2725	.03
10	1.31	1.30	1.32	1.28	1.3025	.04
11	1.28	1.29	1.24	1.31	1.28	.07
12	1.31	1.30	1.26	1.24	1.2725	.07
13	1.26	1.31	1.32	1.29	1.295	.06
14	1.28	1.27	1.27	1.29	1.2775	.02
15	1.29	1.23	1.28	1.27	1.2675	.06
16	1.30	1.31	1.32	1.29	1.305	.03
17	1.27	1.26	1.29	1.28	1.275	.03
18	1.26	1.31	1.27	1.30	1.285	.05
19	1.27	1.32	1.25	1.28	1.28	.07
20	1.26	1.29	1.32	1.30	1.2925	.06
					25.6575	1.04

Solution

$$\bar{\bar{X}} = \text{sum of sample means/number of samples}$$
$$= 25.6575/20 = 1.282875 \text{ microfarads}$$
$$\bar{R} = \text{sum of sample ranges/number of samples}$$
$$= 1.04/20 = .052 \text{ microfarads}$$

Referring to Exhibit 17.9, we find that the value of A_2 for a sample of size four is .73. Thus,

$$UCL_{\bar{X}} = \bar{\bar{X}} + A_2\bar{R}$$
$$= 1.282875 + .73(.052)$$
$$= 1.320835 \text{ microfarads}$$

and

$$LCL_{\bar{X}} = \bar{\bar{X}} - A_2\bar{R}$$
$$= 1.282875 - .73(.052)$$
$$= 1.244915 \text{ microfarads}$$

Again referring to Exhibit 17.9, we see that the value of D_3 for samples of size four is 0 and D_4 is 2.28. Thus,

$$UCL_R = D_4\bar{R}$$
$$= 2.28(.052)$$
$$= .11856 \text{ microfarads}$$
$$LCL_R = D_3\bar{R}$$
$$= 0(.052)$$
$$= 0 \text{ microfarads}$$

The *X*-bar and *R* charts are shown below.

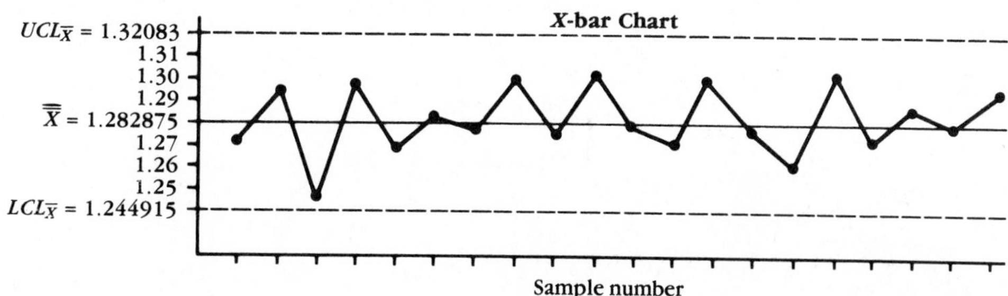

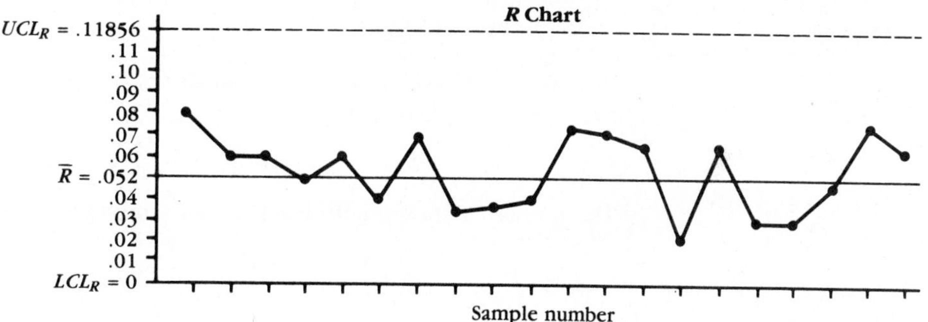

2. A company has kept track of the number of defectives found in twenty-five samples of size 100 taken from a process making Christmas tree lights. Use this information to develop a *p* chart for the process.

Sample	Defectives	Sample	Defectives	Sample	Defectives
1	4	9	5	17	4
2	2	10	6	18	6
3	6	11	9	19	7
4	3	12	4	20	4
5	7	13	6	21	5
6	8	14	3	22	9
7	2	15	2	23	2
8	4	16	1	24	3
				25	5

Total defectives = 117

Solution

$$\begin{aligned}\overline{p} &= \text{total defectives/(number of samples} \times \text{sample size)}\\ &= 117/(25 \times 100)\\ &= .0468\end{aligned}$$

$$\sigma_p = \sqrt{\frac{\bar{p}(1-\bar{p})}{n}}$$
$$= \sqrt{.0468(.9532)/100}$$
$$= .021$$
$$UCL_p = \bar{p} + 3\sigma_p$$
$$= .0468 + 3(.021)$$
$$= .1098$$
$$LCL_p = \bar{p} - 3\sigma_p$$
$$= .0468 - 3(.021)$$
$$= -.0162$$

Because *LCL* is less than zero, we must set it to zero since it is not possible to have a negative percentage.

$$LCL_p = 0$$

The *p* chart is shown with the first ten samples plotted.

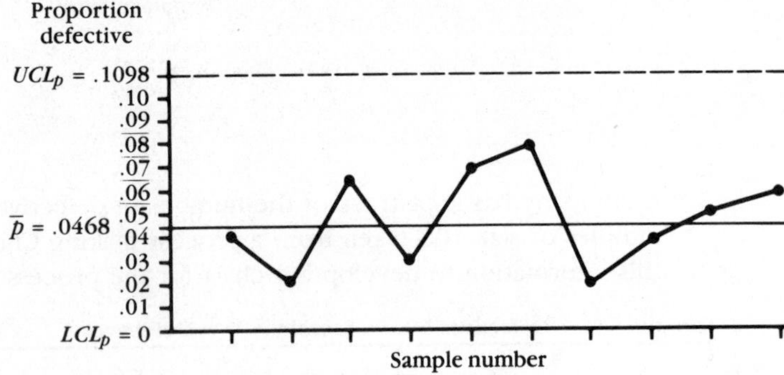

3. The numbers of near misses recorded for twenty months at a large airport are shown below. Use this information to develop a *c* chart.

Month	Near Misses	Month	Near Misses
1	2	11	4
2	1	12	1
3	0	13	2
4	3	14	0
5	4	15	0
6	0	16	4
7	2	17	2
8	4	18	1
9	1	19	4
10	3	20	2

Solution

$$\begin{aligned}
\bar{c} &= \text{Total number/number of samples} \\
&= 40/20 = 2.0 \text{ near misses} \\
\sigma_c &= \sqrt{\bar{c}} \\
&= \sqrt{2.0} \\
&= 1.414 \\
UCL_c &= \bar{c} + 3\sigma_c \\
&= 2.0 + 3(1.414) \\
&= 6.242 \text{ near misses} \\
LCL_c &= \bar{c} - 3\sigma_c \\
&= 2.0 - 3(1.414) \\
&= -2.242 \text{ near misses}
\end{aligned}$$

Because *LCL* is negative and there cannot be a negative number of near misses, we set it to zero.

$$LCL_c = 0$$

The *c* chart is shown below, with the first ten points plotted.

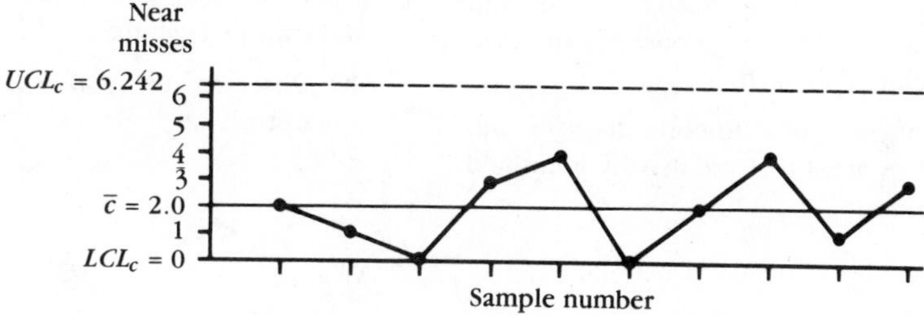

The organization should explore why some months had no near misses to see if procedures can be improved.

QUESTIONS

1. List some costs to society that might be included in the Taguchi loss function for automobiles.

2. List some customer attributes associated with stereo equipment, and group these together by categories. Suggest some possible engineering characteristics that could measure achievement of these attributes.

3. One "quality myth" is that increased quality means increased costs. Use your own personal knowledge or information provided in the Operations in Action vignettes to show this may not be true.

4. One argument against quality circles says that they will not work in the United States because the culture is different from that in Japan. Discuss this in terms of your knowledge about the Japanese management system.

5. Explain, from a quality control viewpoint, why companies that use JIT are very conscientious about maintaining their equipment in good condition.

6. List the three categories of quality costs, and briefly define each.

7. Explain the difference between acceptance sampling and process control.

8. List the categories of total quality control and briefly describe a few of the ideas, concepts, or techniques that are included in each.

9. Describe the purpose of a fishbone diagram, and list the four problem areas that are usually identified on such a diagram.

10. Discuss how Pareto analysis is used in quality control.

11. Describe how a hotel might apply the techniques discussed in this chapter, including statistical quality control methods.

12. Define the following terms:

a. AQL

b. LTPD

c. α risk

d. β risk

13. What are some of the differences between single and multiple sampling plans?

14. Explain the purpose of an OC curve.

15. Describe what is meant by process capability.

16. Discuss the relationship between process capability and tolerances.

17. How do tolerances differ from control limits?

18. Explain how the idea of quality function deployment might be applied to a service organization that is not providing a tangible good as its product.

19. How do the fourteen steps to zero defects proposed by Philip Crosby differ from the philosophy of W. Edwards Deming?

20. Describe how quality assurance differs from quality control.

PROBLEMS

1. A certain process has been sampled using samples of size four while the process was in control, and it was determined that the grand mean, $\bar{\bar{X}}$, is 3.56. The mean of sample ranges, $\bar{R}$, is .41.

a. Set up a control chart for this process with *UCL* and *LCL* three standard deviations from the mean.

b. The following sample means have been determined from samples just taken: 3.25, 3.68, 3.75, and 4.03. Should any corrective action be taken?

2. A fast-food restaurant advertises that customers will receive their orders in two minutes or less. A set of ten samples of size five was taken recently, and it was determined that the grand mean of those samples was 1.86 minutes. The mean of sample ranges is .46 minute. Is the restaurant's claim reasonable?

3. The Federal Reserve Bank of St. Louis uses acceptance sampling procedures to assess the quality of paper currency that it puts into circulation. The bank uses an AQL of .25 percent. If paper currency is packed in batches of 20,000 bills, what should the sample size and accept/reject numbers be, using MIL-STD-105D at general inspection level II?

4. The Charge-o-Ray Battery Company performs lot sampling of its finished batteries before shipping them to customers. One of those customers, the federal government, requires the use of MIL-STD-105D at general inspection level II. If batteries are shipped in batches of 75, indicate the inspection plan that should be used for an AQL of .15 percent.

5. A company has decided to use double sampling for batches of sheet steel that are received from a supplier. The company has decided to use MIL-STD-105D at general inspection level II. If incoming batches contain 1,500 sheets of steel, what should be the sample sizes and accept/reject numbers for an AQL of 2.5 percent?

6. The PeeWee Cuisine Company manufactures gourmet food for babies. They receive turnips in batches of 600 and use MIL-STD-105D at general inspection level III. Recently, the company used double sampling. In its first sample, there were three unacceptable turnips. In the second sample from that same batch, there were three more unacceptable ones. If PeeWee Cuisine uses an AQL of 1 percent, what decision would it make regarding that batch of turnips?

7. A hotel has determined that its policy will state that it should take no more than ten minutes from when a guest enters the hotel until that guest is checked in and has been shown to his or her room. A study took random samples of six guests at a time and determined that mean time for check-in and showing to the room was six minutes, with an average range of two minutes. Will there be problems in maintaining the hotel policy?

8. Suppose you are given the following information that has been taken from samples of soft drinks filled by an automatic machine in a fast-food restaurant. When the process is in control, the machine fills each cup so that the grand mean, $\bar{\bar{X}}$, is 12 ounces and the mean range for samples of size five will be .3 ounce.

- **a.** Develop *X*-bar and *R* charts for the soft-drink machine.
- **b.** What is your initial interpretation of the following data, taken from a recent series of samples, when plotted on the *X*-bar and *R* charts?

Sample	Ounces per Cup				
1	11.8	11.7	12.0	11.9	11.8
2	12.2	12.0	12.1	12.1	12.0
3	11.9	12.1	11.8	11.7	12.1
4	12.0	11.7	12.3	11.8	12.3

9. A company has decided to take samples of size six from one of its milling machines. A particular dimension has been measured, and the results are shown below.

Sample	Individual Measurements (Diameter in Inches)					
1	1.25	1.27	1.24	1.28	1.29	1.23
2	1.23	1.22	1.23	1.25	1.27	1.26
3	1.26	1.27	1.23	1.23	1.24	1.23
4	1.23	1.25	1.25	1.27	1.28	1.29
5	1.24	1.28	1.29	1.23	1.29	1.28
6	1.23	1.25	1.28	1.23	1.28	1.27
7	1.27	1.24	1.25	1.25	1.27	1.27
8	1.29	1.27	1.23	1.26	1.27	1.26
9	1.23	1.24	1.23	1.25	1.26	1.24
10	1.27	1.27	1.26	1.23	1.29	1.28

This particular measurement is supposed to be 1.25 inches ± .05 inch. Based on these data, comment on the process capability with regard to tolerances.

10. The Kleen City Police Department has been collecting information regarding the number of crimes per 1,000 residents for various parts of the city, and that number has stayed around four for several years. The following data have been collected based on a recent month:

Precinct	Crimes per 1,000 residents
1	2
2	4
3	3
4	6
5	5
6	11
7	9
8	3
9	2
10	4

Based on statistical analysis using a *c* chart, is there any reason to believe any of the precincts are out of line in terms of number of crimes?

11. The Kentucky Cable Company randomly inspects samples from the cable it produces. When the process is in control, it averages three defects per 10,000 feet of cable. The following numbers of defects were found in samples taken recently. Plot this information on a *c* chart. What can you say about the process that is producing this cable?

Sample	Defects per 10,000 feet
1	3
2	2
3	4
4	3
5	6
6	4
7	4
8	5
9	7
10	8

12. The Central Data Processing Company recently took random samples of 100 entries to determine the number of entries made incorrectly by its data entry personnel. The following information was gathered:

Sample	Errors per 100 Entries	Sample	Errors per 100 Entries
1	3	11	4
2	6	12	5
3	5	13	3
4	6	14	4
5	2	15	4
6	5	16	2
7	4	17	7
8	3	18	4
9	4	19	5
10	3	20	5

Use this information to develop a p chart with UCL and LCL $3\sigma_p$ from the mean.

13. A pharmaceutical company that markets an EPT (early pregnancy test) kit has conducted extensive testing to determine that the kit should produce an average of 40 false positives (test indicates the person is pregnant when she is not) per 1,000 tests. The company has been following a policy of contacting random samples of customers who bought the kit each month to determine how many "false positives" customers have been receiving. These data are shown below. If the sample size is 1,000, use this information to develop a p chart and make some statements about the test kits.

Month	False Positives
January	56
February	43
March	54
April	47
May	45
June	60
July	55
August	64
September	72

14. Patients at the Shady Rest Nursing Home have been complaining a lot recently. The nursing home's administrator has kept track of these complaints and categorized them as shown below. Use Pareto analyis to identify the area(s) the administrator should be most concerned about.

Complaint Type	Number
Poor food	14
Lack of care by staff	37
Incorrect medicine given	29
Dirty conditions	97
Lack of things to do	23

15. Referring to problem 1, suppose the process standard deviation is known to be .2. Recompute the control limits, and compare them with those calculated using the mean range.

16. A particular part is specified to have a diameter of 3.00 inches with a tolerance of +/− .05 inch. The process making that part is operating in statistical control with a process mean of 3.00 inches and a standard deviation of .02 inch.

a. Use the normal probability distribution table in the Chapter 14 Appendix to determine what percentage of parts produced will not be within tolerance due to random variation if the process stays in control.

b. Suppose the process mean drifts to 3.01 inches. Now what percentage of parts will not be within tolerance?

17. A pharmaceutical manufacturer must ensure that a particular capsule contains 5 grams of medicine. To do so, the company establishes an SPC program that specifies that samples of size five will be taken at random from the output and their contents weighed. The process filling these capsules is in statistical control and has a process mean of 5 grams with a process standard deviation of .05.

a. Develop upper and lower control limits for an X-bar chart.

b. If the process remains in control, what is the probability a sample mean will be outside the control limits?

c. Suppose the process mean drifts to 4.99 grams. What is the probability a sample mean will be outside the control limits?

18. A certain casino in Las Vegas advertises that its slot machines pay off an average of 50 percent of the time. Recently, one gambler observed that in ten tries he received a payoff from the casino's slot machines only once. Does the gambler have a reason to claim false advertising?

19. In problem 18, what sample size would be necessary to claim the casino's advertising is false if the gambler finds the slot machines pay off only 40 percent of the time in the sample?

20. As part of its quality control effort, management of the Greenwich Restaurant randomly selects a sample of nine diners each evening and asks them whether they were satisfied with the food and the service. On average, only one of the individuals sampled is not totally satisfied. However, on a recent night three people in the sample were not totally satisfied. Is this cause for concern?

21. Taste-Rite Foods manufactures apple toaster pastries in batches of 1,000. Each pastry is weighed and must weigh 8 ounces with a .5 ounce tolerance limit. Any pastry not within these tolerance limits is rejected. On average, ten pastries are rejected from each batch. Using this information, the process has been controlled with a p chart.

However, it is also known the process that produces these pastries has a mean of 8 ounces and a process standard deviation of .3 ounce. It has been suggested that samples of size four be taken during production of the pastries and that the process be controlled using X-bar and R charts. Comment on the suggested change.

Data Sets for Computer Solution

1. A certain process is running in control, and the following measurements are taken of a critical dimension. Use this information to calculate the process mean and standard deviation.

.2497	.2497	.2503	.2499	.2501
.2502	.2500	.2498	.2503	.2500
.2504	.2501	.2498	.2499	.2502
.2500	.2501	.2500	.2498	.2499
.2499	.2500	.2497	.2499	.2503
.2501	.2502	.2502	.2499	.2500
.2496	.2499	.2497	.2502	.2499
.2501	.2502	.2500	.2498	.2497
.2497	.2501	.2497	.2500	.2503
.2499	.2498	.2502	.2500	.2497

2. The process examined in problem 1 has been modified slightly through the use of a different material. The following samples were taken. Use this information and the results of problem 1 to determine whether this has changed the process mean.

Sample					
1	.2505	.2499	.2502	.2507	.2502
2	.2501	.2505	.2506	.2503	.2504
3	.2501	.2506	.2505	.2507	.2504
4	.2506	.2507	.2502	.2499	.2507
5	.2503	.2506	.2508	.2502	.2506
6	.2505	.2507	.2499	.2506	.2503
7	.2506	.2507	.2505	.2505	.2502
8	.2501	.2505	.2503	.2508	.2505
9	.2503	.2505	.2502	.2507	.2501
10	.2505	.2504	.2506	.2501	.2508

MINI-CASES

Memorial Hospital

Memorial Hospital is a privately owned 600-bed facility located in Cincinnati, Ohio. The hospital provides a broad range of health care services, including complete laboratory and X-ray facilities, an emergency room, an intensive care unit, a cardiac care unit, and a psychiatric ward. Most of these services are provided by several other hospitals in the Cincinnati metropolitan area. In fact, Memorial has purposely avoided getting involved in any specialized fields of medicine or obtaining very specialized diagnostic equipment because it was felt that such services would not be cost-effective. The Cincinnati General Hospital, located only a few miles away, is affiliated with the University of Cincinnati School of Medicine and offers up-to-date services in those specialized areas. Instead of trying to compete with Cincinnati General on the basis of special services, Memorial Hospital has concentrated on offering high-quality general health care at an affordable price. Compared with the much larger Cincinnati General, Memorial stresses close personal attention to each patient from a nursing staff that cares about its work. In fact, the hospital has begun placing ads in newspapers and on television, stressing its patient-oriented care.

However, the hospital's administrator, Janice Fry, is concerned about whether the hospital can really deliver on its promises and worries that failure to provide the level of health care patients expect could end up driving patients away. Janice met recently with the hospital's managerial personnel to discuss her concerns. The meeting raised some questions about how the hospital's quality of health care could be assured. Jessica Morton, director of nursing, raised the question, "How do we measure the quality of health care? Do we give patients a questionnaire when they leave, asking whether they were happy here? That doesn't seem to get at the question since we could make a patient happy, but really give them lousy health care." Several other questions came up concerning the hospital's efforts to keep costs down. Some people were concerned that an emphasis on costs would be detrimental to quality. They argued that when a person's life is at stake, costs should not be of concern.

After the meeting, Janice began thinking about these questions. She remembered reading recently that total quality control (TQC) is being used by some companies to improve their quality. She thought that had a nice ring to it—if only the idea could be used in a hospital.

1. Discuss some ways that a hospital might measure quality.

2. Go through the steps presented earlier for a quality audit, and discuss how each might be modified in Memorial's case.

3. What would be the costs of quality for Memorial Hospital? How could the value of a human life be included?

4. Are there any ideas or techniques from TQC that could be used by Janice to help Memorial focus on providing quality health care?

5. What measures could Memorial use to assess the quality of health care it is providing?

Manoogian Metal Products

John Manoogian started Manoogian Metal Products as a way of avoiding boredom after his retirement from Lockheed Corporation. John had worked for Lockheed for thirty years, starting as a laborer and working up to become a skilled machinist, and then eventually machine shop foreman. Upon his retirement at age fifty-five, John still felt the need to be involved in something productive, so he and two friends pooled their resources and used John's metalworking experience to open a small machine shop in a rented building. The techniques John had learned at Lockheed for working with exotic metal alloys turned out to be useful, and Manoogian was able to develop contracts with several aerospace companies to provide specialty machining services.

Manoogian Metal Products started out with some used equipment bought at auction from a company that had gone bankrupt. The equipment was not really modern, but was still in good condition and came at a very reasonable price. As Manoogian's business grew, the company gradually replaced some of the equipment that was wearing out, although much of the old equipment still remained. Manoogian recently built a new facility and has had to forgo some new equipment purchases until its financial position improves as business grows.

But now John is worried that some equipment may have to be replaced sooner due to defects that are showing up in some of the parts. Two of these parts are #1057 and #1058, shown in the illustration at the top of page 757. Part #1057 has a groove cut in its top, whereas part #1058 has a ledge on it. The ledge of part #1058 must fit into the groove on part #1057 so that the holes in each part line up for a shaft to go through. Dimension *A* is .375" ± .0001", dimension *B* is 1.25" ± .0001", and dimension *C* is .625" ± .0001". The hole diameter is .5" ± .00002". Based on these tolerances, the two holes can have a maximum misalignment of .0002". Any more than that and the shaft will not fit.

Manoogian Metal Products Part Specifications

Part #1057

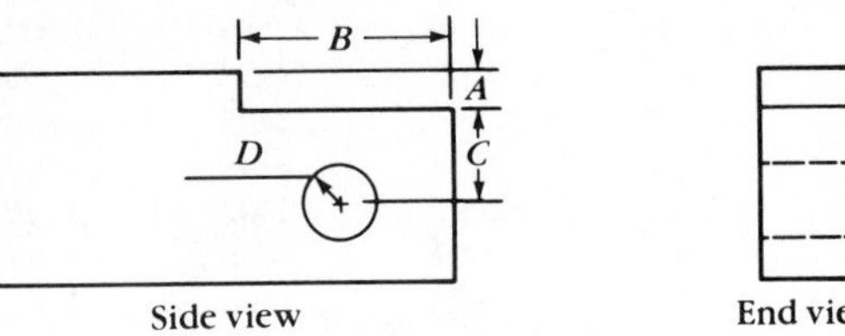

Side view   End view

Part #1058

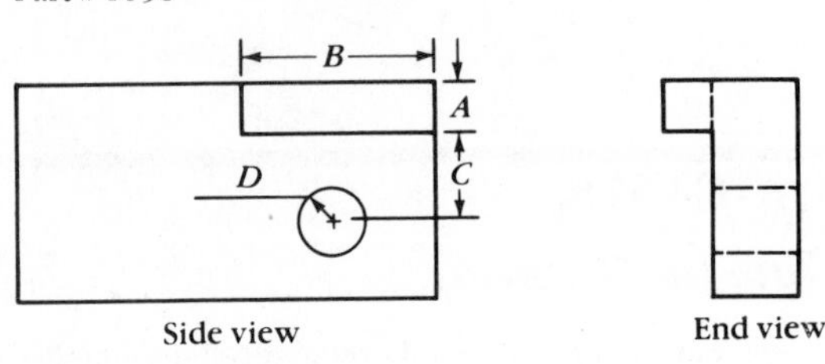

Side view   End view

However, the following defects have been found after machining the two parts in a batch of 1,000 units:

Problem	Number
Hole in #1057 out of spec.	34
Hole in #1058 out of spec.	45
Misalignment of holes	127
Other	23

To try to identify the cause of this problem, the following data were collected regarding each of the dimensions by taking samples of size five every hour:

	A		B	
Sample	$\bar{X}$	R	$\bar{X}$	R
1	.37502	.00023	1.25002	.00003
2	.37510	.00018	1.25003	.00005
3	.37505	.00021	1.24997	.00002
4	.37498	.00015	1.24999	.00001
5	.37507	.00015	1.25001	.00004
6	.37499	.00020	1.24995	.00005
7	.37496	.00017	1.24998	.00003

	A		B	
Sample	$\bar{X}$	R	$\bar{X}$	R
8	.37503	.00023	1.25001	.00002
9	.37501	.00012	1.25000	.00007
10	.37496	.00017	1.25004	.00004

	C		D	
Sample	$\bar{X}$	R	$\bar{X}$	R
1	.62504	.00013	.50001	.00003
2	.62499	.00008	.49998	.00002
3	.62497	.00012	.50003	.00003
4	.62505	.00010	.50000	.00002
5	.62509	.00020	.50001	.00001
6	.62499	.00009	.50000	.00004
7	.62491	.00013	.50001	.00003
8	.62498	.00018	.49999	.00002

	C		D	
Sample	$\bar{X}$	R	$\bar{X}$	R
9	.62507	.00002	.50000	.00001
10	.62501	.00009	.49999	.00003

1. According to this information, where is the problem occurring?

2. Does it appear that the process capabilities are sufficient to meet the specifications?

3. What procedure might Manoogian Metals take in the short run to alleviate this problem?

4. How could this problem have been detected earlier? Should the company's procedures be changed?

5. Can you suggest a change in machining practices that might help avoid the problem?

SELECTED BIBLIOGRAPHY

Besterfield, Dale H. *Quality Control*. 3d ed. Englewood Cliffs, N.J.: Prentice-Hall, 1990.

DelMar, Donald, and Sheldon, George. *Introduction to Quality Control*. St. Paul, Minn.: West, 1988.

Deming, W. Edwards. *Out of the Crisis*. Cambridge, Mass.: MIT Center for Advanced Engineering Study, 1986.

Ealey, Lance A. *Quality by Design: Taguchi Methods and U.S. Industry*. Dearborn, Mich.: ASI Press, 1988.

Evans, James R., and Lindsay, William M. *The Management and Control of Quality*. St. Paul, Minn.: West, 1989.

Feigenbaum, Armand V. *Total Quality Control*. 3d ed. New York: McGraw-Hill, 1986.

Garvin, David A. *Managing Quality*. New York: Free Press, 1988.

Sullivan, Lawrence P. "Quality Function Deployment." *Quality Progress* 19, no. 6 (June 1986): 39–50.

Chapter 18

Technology and Human Resources

CHAPTER OUTLINE

Technology's Impact on the Organization

Gaining Strategic Advantage at Parkland Hospital: Applying Computer Technology for Improved Decision Making

Sociotechnical Systems

Management Discovers the Human Side of Automation

Summarizing the Impacts

The Changing Roles of People in Operations

The Impact of Computer-Aided Design and Computer-Aided Manufacturing

The Impact of Expert Systems

The Impact of Robots

The Impact of Computer-Based Information Systems

People Build Competitive Advantage

Training and Development

Leadership

Communication

Motivation

LEARNING OBJECTIVES

After completing this chapter, you should be able to

- Discuss the impact that computers and technology have on an organization and its performance.
- Explain why technological advances and computer-based automation require highly skilled and trained people.
- Discuss how future jobs will require people to perform a wide variety of tasks, work in teams, apply participative management, and possess integrative skills. Labor and management should be capable of judging the impact of their actions on other parts (subsystems) within the organization.
- Describe why future organizations will be smaller, more flexible, and more responsive to change.
- Define the impact of computer-aided design, computer-aided manufacturing, and expert systems on operations.
- Discuss the situations in which robots have advantages over people and in which people hold the edge.
- Explain why people are an organization's most precious resource and why their talents should be used to the fullest extent.
- Explain why training and development, leadership skills, communication, and motivation are important to gain the full benefit of technological advances.

OPERATIONS IN ACTION

DANA Corporation: Factory with a Future

DANA Corporation's plant in Columbia, South Carolina, produces constant-velocity joints for front-wheel-drive cars. This device gives each front wheel the flexibility to accept power from the engine and transmission, whether turning a corner, going over a bump, or moving straight ahead.

One of the concepts behind the plant's design is to effectively utilize human resources by building on people's strengths. This means giving people the tools to become more productive. Starting in the office, information technology has been applied to increase the effectiveness and efficiency of the managers and engineers. These people will have access to current customer-order status, production reports, machine reliability, quality levels, and inventory via real-time computer links to the production floor. Clerical and low-level management positions have also been reduced.

Out on the factory floor, robots, automated guided vehicles, and other automated material-handling devices are being installed to replace people at routine and repetitive tasks. Computer-based control systems are being installed to manage the routine decisions that are frequently made during production. When should the groove grinder start the next part? How much inventory is ahead of the drill? When should drill bits be replaced?

The workers at this plant are not mere machine tenders. They are trained to take advantage of their ability to think and react to unexpected problems. They perform maintenance, deal with machine failures, handle problems related to quality, and watch for other problems. They are also trained and encouraged to look for ways to improve quality, lower costs, increase productivity, and enhance customer service. DANA understands the value of people and is trying in this and in other facilities to use the whole person for the betterment of the company and the individual.

TECHNOLOGY'S IMPACT ON THE ORGANIZATION

A quick look back at the last ninety years shows the tremendous impact that technology can have. Ninety years ago, the few automobiles that existed were owned only by the very wealthy. There were no airplanes, televisions, dishwashers, or household refrigerators. Electricity and the telephone were still in their infancy. Traveling across the country took several days by train. Today, the products mentioned above have reached the maturity/saturation phase of the product life cycle, and hundreds of new services and goods have become essential parts of the economic system.

Forty-five years ago, the first big, slow, expensive computers emerged from laboratories to start a new era of technological improvements. Because of continuing advances in technology, today we can buy a personal computer with 100 times more capability for less than one-thousandth the cost of one of the first computers. The impact of computer technology has been tremendous, and the future holds even more promise.

Computer, information, and manufacturing technology will have a significant impact on shaping the future of organizations. Not only will operations be influenced by this evolutionary change, but also the entire organization will change in

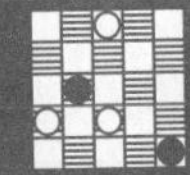

GAINING STRATEGIC ADVANTAGE AT PARKLAND HOSPITAL

Applying Computer Technology for Improved Decision Making

The performance of any organization is determined to a large extent by the quality of its people and the decisions they make. To make effective decisions, people in organizations need meaningful, accurate, and up-to-date information. An organization that develops ways to understand and to implement computer technology to improve information processing and decision making will gain an important advantage over its competition.

On the horizon are many breakthroughs in computer technology that could improve information processing. One such breakthrough, optical data storage, uses laser beams to read data on plastic platters, similar in concept to the compact disc player. This technology allows an organization to store and retrieve large amounts of information economically, thus making way for many new applications.

In the future, a doctor at Parkland Hospital will be able to sit at a computer and in a few moments search several years' worth of medical journal publications for every occurrence of the word *emphysema.* Parkland's doctors will be able to quickly reference the most recent information in treating medical problems. Hospital efficiency will be improved because doctors will have access to information that will allow them to reduce unnecessary tests and treatments, as well as to increase the likelihood of proper treatment and recovery.

The area in which Parkland operates, which is typical of many areas in this country, has too much capacity. Because of the excess supply, Parkland faces stiff competition. As this competition increases, the quality and costs of treatment will become important strategic factors in determining long-term success.

Optical data storage technology can put a vast amount of information at the fingertips of future physicians and of managers as well. This will allow any organization to streamline operations. As the Parkland Hospital example shows, an organization that can master this technology and apply it effectively can gain an advantage over competitors by making better decisions with fewer, better-trained people.

response to the new capabilities presented by these technologies. Regardless of the significance of these advances, their full impact will not be felt unless people in organizations can use them effectively. People make technology work.

Sociotechnical Systems

The integration of people and technology requires knowledge of the way people and groups behave and the way machines and technical systems behave. Organizational objectives are best met not by optimizing the technical system (equipment) and adapting the social system (people) to it, but by jointly optimizing the technical and the social aspects in the system. Organizations that blend social and technical aspects are called **sociotechnical systems.**

An approach to designing an organization that fully considers both social and technical aspects requires an interdisciplinary design team. To be effective, the team would require a constant interchange among engineers, operations managers, social scientists, financial controllers, personnel specialists, and so on. To guide this process of designing a sociotechnical system, Albert Cherns offers the following checklist from his book *Sociotechnics.*

1. *Compatibility.* The process of designing the sociotechnical system should be compatible with its objective. To achieve systems that give workers more freedom to make decisions and to apply their knowledge (i.e., participative management), the process of designing the system should also be participative.
2. *Minimizing critical specifications.* No more should be specified in a job design than is necessary. While it may be necessary to be quite specific about what is to be done, it is rarely necessary to be specific about how a job is to be done. Careful observation of people at work demonstrates that people work to get things done in spite of the rules. As the railway workers in Britain have shown, the whole system can be brought to a grinding halt by "working to the rules."
3. *Controlling variance.* A variance is an unprogrammed event. Variances that cannot be eliminated should be controlled as near to the point of origin as possible. The origin might be a quality defect or an equipment failure. Workers need the freedom to act on and learn from problems that arise. In the quality control example, the worker that makes the part should inspect it so that he or she can learn quickly from the problem. Creating a separate inspection function merely lengthens the process of control and feedback to the worker.
4. *Adaptive ability.* An organization should be responsive to changes in the environment. People with freedom in decision making can adjust if not constrained by rigid work rules.
5. *Effective boundary location.* In any organization, departmental boundaries have to be drawn somewhere. These boundaries should be drawn in such a way that interaction within a department is high and required interaction between departments is lower. This is one of the principles of group technology and manufacturing cells. By grouping similar products together for production, less time and fewer resources are needed to transport materials between departments.
6. *Information flows where needed.* Systems should be designed to provide information to those who must take action on it. In most cases, information that is really useful only at lower levels is supplied to upper management. This acts as an incitement to management to intervene in operations for which their subordinates are and should be responsible.
7. *Feedback that is consistent with the objectives.* The system that supports and rewards behavior should be designed to elicit appropriate behavior. For example, if an organization is designed on the basis of group or team operations with team responsibility, the incentive system should be aimed at the group, not the individual.
8. *Design as an iterative process.* No system can be perfect. Even if it could, the environmental assumptions on which it is based would change. The multifunctional, multilevel, multidisciplinary team required for design is also needed for its evaluation and review.

Examples of sociotechnical systems and how the effective design of these systems can lead to improved performance are discussed in the following *Business Week* article, "Management Discovers the Human Side of Automation."

*Management Discovers the Human Side of Automation**

Companies Are Finding That Workers Are the Key to Making Technology Pay Off

Like thousands of companies . . . , Shenandoah Life Insurance Co. marched eagerly into the world of high technology. It installed a $2 million system to computerize processing and claims operations at its Roanoke (Va.) headquarters. But the results were disappointing. It still took 27 working days—and handling by 32 clerks in three departments—to process a typical application for a policy conversion.

Shenandoah's problem stemmed from its bureaucratic maze, not from defects in the technology. Only by radically reorganizing its work system could it reap the benefits of automation. The company grouped the clerks in "semiautonomous" teams of five to seven members. Each team now performs all the functions that once were spread over three departments. Team members learned new skills, bringing them greater job satisfaction—and better pay. As a result, the typical case-handling time dropped to two days, and service complaints were practically eliminated. By 1986, Shenandoah was processing 50% more applications and queries with 10% fewer employees than it did in 1980.

The productivity gains at Shenandoah Life are part of a powerful synergism taking root in the U.S.—the pairing of people with automation. American managers are finally learning what the Japanese discovered years ago: The solution to fading competitive ability, sluggish productivity growth, and poor quality cannot be found in the mythical black box of a miraculous technology. To realize the full potential of automation, leading-edge companies are integrating workers and technology in "sociotechnical" systems that revolutionize the way work is organized and managed.

This is an immensely important trend, one that is producing a new model of job design and work relations that will shape the workplace well into the 21st century. Nevertheless, the changeover isn't occurring fast enough. The great wave of automation that has swept through offices and factories since 1980 is losing momentum, largely because not enough companies are adopting the innovative work practices that get the most out of automation. Many managers are reluctant to "run the kind of social revolution at work that is needed to make technology pay for itself," says productivity expert George H. Kuper, who heads the Manufacturing Studies Board, a research arm of the National Academy of Sciences.

People Problems

With or without work reforms, computer-based technology is having an enormous impact on workers. In one way or another, it has changed the jobs of 40 million to 50 million people, almost half of the U.S. work force. It has made some jobs more challenging and "de-skilled" others. It has caused severe dislocations at specific work sites by eliminating jobs, raising a fundamental question of whether government and business are investing enough money and expertise in

*Reprinted from September 29, 1986 issue of *Business Week* by special permission, © 1986 by McGraw-Hill, Inc., by John Hoerr in New York and Michael A. Pollock in Washington, with David E. Whiteside in Detroit and bureau reports.

retraining displaced workers. For the entire nonfarm economy, however, technological change helped produce a 10.4 million increase in jobs between 1979 and 1986.

But contrary to the engineers' vision of factories run by robots, the high-tech workplace depends more than ever on people. "There will be fewer of them, but the ones who are there will be critical," says Gerald I. Susman, an expert on work and technology at Pennsylvania State University. Mistakes by poorly trained, poorly motivated workers can cause enormous damage, as demonstrated by the nuclear accidents at Three Mile Island and Chernobyl. Says Lyman D. Ketchum, a pioneering consultant on teamwork: "We're moving increasingly into dangerous, unforgiving technologies that can't be operated safely with uncommitted people."

Most important, it is becoming evident that advanced computer technology calls for a radical change in traditional work practices. The old "scientific management" method of dividing work into discrete tasks that require little skill or training becomes obsolete in a computerized workplace where many functions—including materials handling, assembly, inventory control, and testing—are integrated by computer. "The integration no longer makes it possible to define jobs individually or measure individual performance," says Richard E. Walton of Harvard University. "It requires a collection of people to manage a segment of technology and perform as a team."

Global Competition

For these reasons, more companies are installing work systems that emphasize broader-based jobs, teamwork, participative managers, and multiskilled workers. The innovations include a range of other labor policies aimed at developing "committed" workers, including enhanced job security, continuous training programs, and compensation schemes that reward group performance [Exhibit 18.1]. Industries such as autos, steel, and communications have been moving slowly in this direction with the cooperation of their unions since the beginning of the "quality-of-work-life" [QWL] movement in the 1970s.

But the new innovations go far beyond QWL reforms that involve workers in problem-solving groups or otherwise aim at making jobs more satisfying. Now the movement is being fueled by global competition and the need for a high rate of product innovation. The average life cycle of an electronics product, for example, is only three to five years. Experts say that while the U.S. may not be able to compete with countries that turn out standardized products and parts at low wages, it can create new market niches for customized products. But manufacturers must be able to switch quickly from one product line to another, and flexible work systems—when combined with computer-based technology—give them that ability.

The new "paradigm," as organizational behavior specialists call it, will gradually replace the old system characterized by authoritarian management and an extreme division of labor epitomized by the assembly line. The new approach often entails sociotechnical planning—that is, integrating the psychological and social needs of workers with technological requirements in designing a new plant or redesigning an old one. Harvard's Walton contrasts the old "control" paradigm with the new model of "commitment."

The payoff can be significant. Many plants that were designed with sociotechnical methods and use the most radical innovation, semiautonomous teams,

Exhibit 18.1 The Changing Approach to Organizing Work

What Management Assumes About Workers

OLD WAY Worker wants nothing from the job except pay, avoids responsibility, and must be controlled and coerced.	NEW WAY Worker desires challenging job and will seek responsibility and autonomy if management permits.

How the Job Is Designed

OLD WAY Work is fragmented and deskilled. Worker is confined to narrow job. Doing and thinking are separated.	NEW WAY Work is multiskilled and performed by teamwork where possible. Worker can upgrade whole system. Doing and thinking are combined.

Management's Organization and Style

OLD WAY Top-down military command with worker at bottom of many supervisory layers; worker is expected to obey orders and has no power.	NEW WAY Relatively flat structure with few layers; worker makes suggestions and has power to implement changes.

Job Training and Security

OLD WAY Worker is regarded as a replaceable part and is given little initial training or retraining for new jobs. Layoffs are routine when business declines.	NEW WAY Worker is considered a valuable resource and is constantly retrained in new skills. Layoffs are avoided if possible in a downturn.

How Wages Are Determined

OLD WAY Pay is geared to the job, not the person, and is determined by evaluation and job classification systems.	NEW WAY Pay is linked to skills acquired. Group incentive and profit-sharing plans are used to enhance commitment.

Labor Relations

OLD WAY Labor and management interests are considered incompatible. Conflict arises on the shop floor and in bargaining.	NEW WAY Mutual interests are emphasized. Management shares information about the business. Labor shares responsibility for making it succeed.

Data: Richard E. Walton, Harvard University; BW

are 30% to 50% more productive than their conventional counterparts. In most plants, these teams manage themselves without first-line supervisors, determine their own work pace within parameters set by management, schedule their own vacations, and have a voice in hiring and firing team members and deciding when they qualify for raises. This is a relatively new creature on the U.S. industrial scene, and both managers and workers give it high praise.

In 1976 fewer than two dozen manufacturing plants in the U.S. organized work on a team basis. By 1986 teamwork was used in several hundred offices and factories, especially new, highly automated plants with small work forces of 25 to 500 people. One example is a diesel engine plant jointly owned by Cummins Engine Co. and J. I. Case Co. in Whittakers, N.C. Teamwork, says plant manager John C. Read, brings out "an entrepreneurial cowboy spirit" in American workers. "When this spirit gets wrapped into team efforts to figure out why a machine went down—and if management gets out of the way—it's a tremendously powerful tool."

Many workers like teamwork for its greater variety of tasks, compared with repetitive jobs on a conventional assembly line. That's true of Randy Gilbert, 10-year veteran of General Motors Corp., who now is an elected team coordinator in Buick City, GM's showcase plant that combines high technology and Japanese management methods. "Once in a while I get bored and switch jobs with someone just to relieve the tedium," he says. That wasn't possible before.

Not Fast Enough?

But technology experts say teamwork and other innovative practices are not spreading fast enough. Although the sociotechnical revolution is here to stay, plants that use teamwork still constitute only a small minority of U.S. workplaces.

If teamwork produces such good results, why haven't more companies tried it? For one thing, it requires a drastic change in management style and methods. The old idea that a manager's main function is to control workers is replaced with the concept that a manager should encourage employees to use initiative. This goes against the grain of everything managers have been taught since the early years of the century, says Lyman Ketchum, who helped design one of the first sociotechnical plants in the U.S., a Gaines Foods, Inc. plant that opened in Topeka, Kan., in 1971. To accept the commitment model of work, he says, managers have to go through a "personal paradigm shift, which is a deep psychological process."

John B. Myers, vice-president for human resources at Shenandoah Life, adds that most managers are comfortable with old-style bureaucracies in which orders are passed from top to bottom. "Bureaucratic organizations become habit-forming, just like cigarettes," he says. "That's why they don't change."

The slowness to change may have implications for productivity growth. The rise in output per man-hour in the U.S. has lagged behind that of Japan and European nations for more than a decade. Bureau of Labor Statistics economists estimate that productivity will increase at an average annual rate of 1.7% through the mid-1990s, about double the rate of the mid-seventies to mid-eighties, largely because of new technology.

This projection, however, is based on a continuing high rate of technological innovation that may not happen. The 1980s started with glowing predictions of pushbutton factories linked to executive suites in vast computer networks. And the "paperless" electronic office was said to be just around the corner.

But the unmanned factory has not arrived. Computer-integrated manufacturing (CIM), in which shop-floor machines are operated by a central computer, is a reality in only a few plants. And many offices are still struggling with . . . computer networks.

Pulling Back

Investment in new technology is not increasing nearly as fast as was predicted in the early 1980s. In early September 1986, Dataquest, Inc., a San Jose (Calif.) market research firm, lowered its projection of industrial automation sales in 1990 by 13%, to $34 billion. Robot sales are also slowing down. "I'm very discouraged," says Richard M. Cyert, president of Carnegie-Mellon University. "For the future of manufacturing in this country, we have to find a way to move automation ahead at a faster pace."

Many companies are pulling back from overambitious automation projects. In its blueprint to convert seven plants to produce a new midsize car, GM had intended to install more than 1,000 robots and replace conventional car assembly lines with the automatic guided vehicle (AGV), a moving "island" of car parts. Now, however, only three plants will be converted. In addition to financial and marketing reasons, GM has had problems integrating technology with its management systems, observers say.

The complexities involved in making CIM work are stymieing automation efforts at many companies. Few have managed to tie the major management functions of engineering, production, and marketing into a single, computerized information system. This kind of linking is necessary for companies to gain one of the larger benefits of computer technology—eliminating layers of middle managers and technicians who now do this work. In addition, computerizing new techniques such as just-in-time inventory control may have as much impact in cutting production costs as eliminating direct labor and managers, says Penn State's Susman. "But reducing inventory tightens the couplings between parts of an organization," he adds, "and this requires workers who know what they're doing."

GM is going ahead with other projects, including a highly automated front-axle plant in Saginaw, Mich. When this plant reaches full production . . . it will be run entirely by robots part of each working day. This plant illustrates the new U.S. emphasis on human skills. It will be operated by 38 hourly employees, all members of the United Auto Workers, who survived a stringent selection process. They are now being schooled in electronic, mechanical, and problem-solving skills and will have more than a year of training before the plant begins making axles.

This amount of training is new in the U.S., although the Japanese have routinely engaged in such comprehensive programs for years. It is one of the ways Japan invests in human resources so that automation will "make people more productive," says Thomas J. Gallogly, a metalworking expert in the Commerce Dept.'s International Trade Administration. The Japanese also enlist workers in "quality circles" to solve production and quality problems. Lifetime job security is emphasized in Japan as well, although for limited numbers of workers in the larger companies.

Wider Scope

When American managers began touring Japanese plants in the mid-1970s, the Japanese stressed the importance of these human factors, recalls Kuper of the Manufacturing Studies Board, who led some of those tours. "Our managers kept looking for the technological solution to the growing Japanese success," he says. "The Japanese were trying to be honest with us, but we were too stupid to listen."

Now, U.S. employers are belatedly turning to the human side of technology, partly by borrowing the Japanese techniques but also by using other methods. For example, Japanese companies do not emphasize a fundamental redesign of jobs to make them more appealing to workers. Furthermore, when the Japanese use production teams, they usually keep them under the control of first-line foremen.

Indeed, the semiautonomous team idea originated in experiments at British coal mines in the late 1940s. Behavioral scientists at London's Tavistock Institute of Human Relations, led by Eric Trist—now professor emeritus at the Wharton School—concluded that industry needed a new paradigm of work organization. By stressing autonomous work groups, jobs of wider scope, and worker involvement in decision-making, Trist and his colleagues said, companies could adjust much more easily to fast-changing market and political conditions.

Trist and others developed the "sociotechnical systems" [STS] concept of work design. STS calls for involving workers whenever possible in planning a new or redesigned plant, as auto workers have been involved in GM's Saturn project. Usually, the technical design came first, and work flow and the placement of work stations followed. In designing an auto plant, for example, engineers would specify a conventional assembly line that allows only one social system: Workers must stay at fixed stations along the line, performing the same task every 30 seconds or so.

"Traditionally, jobs were designed with no capacity for people to initiate anything," says Harvey F. Kolodny, a professor at the University of Toronto. "If things went wrong, you'd get an inflexible response. We should design jobs so that workers can be more than a pair of hands behaving in a mechanical way."

To give workers a greater variety of duties, a sociotechnical auto-plant design would call for teams to assemble entire subunits of a car from parts moved through the plant on AGVs. Team members would be free to move around, rotate jobs, pace themselves within a much longer work cycle of perhaps five minutes or more, and have more control over product quality. Studies show that group assembly not only makes workers feel better but also produces higher quality.

The STS concept moved from Britain to Norway and Sweden, where Volvo used it in designing its plant at Kalmar, Sweden, which opened in 1974. Kalmar's work force is divided into about 20 production teams; each assembles a major unit of a car in an average of 20 minutes to 40 minutes. Production costs at Kalmar are 25% lower than at Volvo's conventional plants, and the company has built a new plant at Uddevalla based on the Kalmar experience.

Teamwork also began to appear in the U.S. in the 1960s. But for years it was confined to a handful of pioneering companies, including Procter & Gamble, Cummins Engine, Gaines Foods, Sherwin-Williams, the Packard Electric Div. of GM, Hewlett-Packard, TRW, and Best Food, a unit of CPC International.

In the past few years, scores of companies that traditionally set the patterns in industrial relations have adopted the concept. Among them are General Electric, Ford, most GM divisions, and Westinghouse, as well as Xerox, Honeywell, Digital Equipment, and other high-tech companies. Shell Canada Ltd. runs four chemical and refinery plants with sociotechnical principles. Even the financial services industry is picking up the concept. In addition to Shenandoah Life, Lincoln National Life and American Transtech have reorganized their paper-processing operations into teams, and one giant insurance company, Aetna, is on the verge of doing so.

For the most part, the teamwork movement has been a quiet revolution. Many of the leading companies have not trumpeted their findings, partly because they believed their innovations provided a competitive edge. Now some of the pioneers are opening up a bit, and their evidence of superior performance in teamwork is impressive.

Procter & Gamble Co., which established its first team-based plants in the 1960s and now has 18 such sites, has always refused to comment publicly on the matter. However, it confirms remarks made in late 1984 by Senior Vice-President David Swanson in a closed meeting at Harvard. Swanson said P&G's teamwork plants were "30% to 40% more productive than their traditional counterparts and significantly more able to adapt quickly to the changing needs of the business."

Person to Person

Cummins Engine has three teamwork plants, including the North Carolina site, and has used elements of the team approach at its older plants in Columbus, Ind. Cummins also has been reticent about the new-style plants. But in a recent interview with *Business Week,* Vice-President Ted L. Marsten said that Cummins is convinced that "this is the most cost-effective way to run plants. In traditional plants, work was broken down to the lowest common denominator, and there was not a lot of flexibility. We created teams to get the work to flow in the most productive way. The people felt a lot better about the work they did, and we got a much higher-quality product."

In Oregon, Tektronix, Inc. converted a few years ago from assembly-line manufacturing in its metals group to teams. Each "cell" of 6 to 12 workers turns out a product that can be manufactured in relatively few steps. One particular cell now turns out as many defect-free products in three days as an entire assembly line did in 14 days with twice as many people. Xerox Corp. began using teams in some of its operations a few years ago and has found them to be "at least 30% more productive" than conventionally organized operations, says Dominick R. Argona, manager of employee involvement.

The Gaines Foods plant in Topeka, which received heavy publicity in the early 1970s for its new style of management, has proved that teamwork there was not a passing fad. Over fifteen years after it started production, the plant still uses teamwork—both in the office and on the shop floor. Plant manager Herman R. Simon says Topeka produces the same pet foods as a sister plant in Kankakee, Ill., at 7% lower labor costs. Once a unit of General Foods Corp., Gaines is now a wholly owned subsidiary of Anderson, Clayton & Co.

Shenandoah Life's decision to embrace teamwork is a classic illustration of why technology can't solve all problems. Even after installing an automated system, the company found that processing clerks were still, in effect, "passing papers from person to person electronically," says Myers. "It made no sense to have a new technology and yet operate the old social system."

Since experimenting with one clerical team in 1983, Shenandoah has formed nine teams of employees who before worked in separate departments. Former first-line supervisors belong to a team that "advises" the processing groups. Shenandoah has never laid off employees, but the team system has enabled it to reduce the work force by 14%, down to 229, over the past year and a half.

"Turf Issues"

The team approach also can help shape the kinds of goods and services a company produces. Shenandoah's disability income team—which includes an actuary, an underwriter, and a marketing specialist—took only six months to develop and market a policy amendment designed to attract new business. If all the skills needed to design a new product are contained in one team, Myers says, product development doesn't get hung up on the "turf issues" that arise when several departments are involved in planning a new product.

Because of the difficulty in changing the culture and management style in existing plants, most teamwork plants are "greenfield" sites, and most are non-union. Indeed, the sociotechnical trend can present a problem for unions. Where employees have been allowed a strong voice in decision-making and largely manage themselves in teams, organizers have had a tough time presenting a case for unionization.

A number of unions, however, have worked jointly with management to convert existing plants to the team concept. These include the Auto Workers, Electronic Workers, Clothing & Textile Workers, and Steelworkers. One successful example involves the Aluminum Workers and a Rohm & Haas Co. plexiglass plant in Knoxville, Tenn. Within four years after the plant began changing to team organization, productivity—measured as square feet of plexiglass produced per worker-hour—had risen some 60%.

But resistance to the concept remains fairly strong in these and other unions because it requires changes in many traditional union-management relations. Instead of multiple job classifications, for example, a teamwork plant usually has only one or two. Production and maintenance work, traditionally separated under the scientific management organization of work, tend to merge into one fluid work system.

High Anxiety

For all its productiveness, teamwork is very difficult to implement and keep working successfully. Changes in plant and corporate management, from participative to old-style managers, have doomed many a promising teamwork experiment. Personality conflicts in teams also cause problems. Indeed, says Cummins' John Read, tension levels in sociotechnical plants tend to be higher than in conventional workplaces. "It's wrong to think of teamwork plants as merely happy places," he says. "But the tensions tend to be constructive, and they produce high performance."

High performance is what U.S. industry needs if it is to make the most of computer-based automation, say technology experts. While the U.S. is still behind Japan in matching workers and new manufacturing techniques, it is trying to catch up. "We need work environments that produce continuous innovation in a highly competitive global economy," says Eric Trist. The new model of work relations is not yet the dominant one, he adds, but "I'd be sad if we weren't getting close to that point by the end of the century."

Summarizing the Impacts

Several key points are made in the *Business Week* report. An organization should not move ahead with automation until its people understand technology and, more importantly, how it can be used to improve performance and gain an advantage over the competition. In the future, organizations will be smaller, more flexible, and more responsive to change.

Smaller Organizations

As a result of automation efforts and fuller utilization of people's skills, organizations will become smaller. Organizations like General Motors, Owens Corning Fiberglas, and General Electric are cutting back on production workers and managers without proportional cuts in responsibility or output. The people who remain become more productive by establishing a teamwork approach, employing improved technology, and being able to perform many jobs.

Although large organizations will continue to exist, they will be subdivided into smaller, more responsive groups or divisions. They will have greater profit-and-loss responsibility and will be leaner and more flexible.

More Flexible Organizations

Organizations will become more flexible in dealing with people and opportunities. The people within the organization will also become flexible. This provides an opportunity for individuals to see the organization as a whole, to see how the parts interact, and to devise plans and strategies that move the entire organization ahead—not just one part. The idea that an organization is a system with complicated interactions will be understood more readily and implemented more frequently.

More Responsive Organizations

As a result of understanding and implementing sociotechnical systems, the new organization will have the human skills to use technology to respond rapidly to the organization's changing environment. Firms will have the capabilities to rapidly design new products through the use of computer-aided design and the flexible manufacturing capabilities to quote short production lead times. They will have computer-supported production planning and control systems to guide the orders through the production facility quickly.

As organizations make efforts to become more responsive, people's roles in the organization will expand, and training for both management and labor will become more important. Computer-assisted instruction may be employed to improve training effectiveness and reduce costs. **Computer-assisted instruction (CAI)** is self-paced, computer-guided learning, and it can help organizations upgrade people's skills quickly and economically. The organization should possess the capabilities to process information and manage the complex organization with fewer, better-trained people.

THE CHANGING ROLES OF PEOPLE IN OPERATIONS

In operations, the individual's role has changed and will continue to change significantly. The following subjects will be discussed in the next several sections:

1. Computer-aided design (CAD) and computer-aided manufacturing (CAM) allow an organization to leverage the time of design engineers and production personnel. This leveraging occurs because the computer helps to organize and manage routine functions, freeing more of the engineers' time for designing the product and the process. The result is more high-quality designs in less time.
2. Using expert systems to make routine operating decisions can change the way people spend their time. Expert systems may replace some management jobs the way that robots have taken over some direct labor jobs. For example, using expert systems for scheduling production is feasible with today's technology.
3. Robots and other computer-controlled devices can be used to replace some production jobs and upgrade others. The implication is more brainwork and less brawnwork in today's well-managed organization.
4. Computer-based information systems can be implemented to reduce paper handling and increase productivity. This implies more computer training for

managers to the point that managers with these skills will become the rule rather than the exception.

The Impact of Computer-Aided Design and Computer-Aided Manufacturing

Properly implemented CAD systems allow engineers to produce better designs in less time. They will have more time for problem solving and creativity in their designs. As a result, fewer people can produce more high-quality designs. The organization can build a competitive advantage by offering shorter lead times and high-quality designs. Technical education for draftspersons will become less important in the future, and technical training for CAD operators will be in greater demand.

CAM systems allow manufacturing engineers to take a design and quickly make a finished part. The computer instructions that define the part inside the CAD computer can be transferred to computer numerically controlled (CNC) machines. Manufacturing engineers can handle a greater variety of parts with less work and a smaller technical staff. It also allows them to get involved in a wider variety of tasks so they become familiar with the operations as a system. People can be organized into work teams that are flexible enough to manage a wide variety of tasks.

Even greater advantages can be achieved if the organization is successful at linking CAD and CAM. This link would allow one engineer to follow a product from product design through process design and finally to actual production. This will help to break down traditional barriers among design engineers, process engineers, and operations managers. Questions of invading another department's turf will no longer be valid as these responsibilities blend together over time and these separate departments disappear.

The Impact of Expert Systems

An **expert system (ES)** is a computer program that uses knowledge and inference procedures to solve problems requiring significant human expertise. The knowledge and the inference procedures are attempts to create a model of the best practitioners in the field. The builders of ESs are generally referred to as **knowledge engineers.**

ESs are often built by interviewing experts in a field and attempting to capture their expertise. Knowledge engineers determine which facts and rules of thumb an expert uses in decision making. From this, the knowledge engineer determines the inference strategy that the expert uses in problem solving. The knowledge engineer develops a system, most often a computer-based system that attempts to simulate the expert's behavior.

For example, the grilling time for steak depends on the heat of the coals, the thickness of the meat, the amount of fat in the steak, and the desired result (rare or well done). The cook may judge the heat by waving a hand across the coals, look at the size of the steak, and use a rule of thumb to estimate the cooking time for a rare steak. The cook will examine the steak periodically as it cooks and may adjust the original estimate.

An ES attempts to capture these rules of thumb. To use the ES, the heat, thickness, fat content, and desired result are input into the system. Also, moni-

General Electric: Using Expert Systems to Eliminate Delays and Boost the Productivity of Maintenance

General Electric builds diesel locomotive engines and maintains field service engineers who travel around the country advising repair shops on difficult problems. The traditional approach to training new field service engineers was to pair an experienced engineer and a novice for several months or years. As the older engineers retired, the younger engineers had learned enough to work on their own. The problem with this training method is that it is expensive and the newly trained field service engineers could take their skills to another company.

GE decided to build an expert system that would capture the expertise of the senior engineers. The designers and builders of the expert system spent several months interviewing the senior engineers and collecting as much knowledge as possible. A prototype of the expert system was built, and testing took place over a three-year period. During this time, the information and the number of decision rules in the expert system increased. The expert system enables a novice engineer or technician to uncover a problem and to learn its solution by working with the expert system. Because the expert system explains the logic of the advice given, it can be an important part of a training program. The system is currently installed at every railroad repair shop served by GE. The expert system eliminates delays, boosts productivity at the repair shops, and reduces the amount of time and travel for field service engineers. Best of all, the expert system cannot quit and take its knowledge elsewhere. GE recognizes the need to continuously update the expert system so that its knowledge is current.

toring devices may be necessary to control the cooking process. It is likely that the heat of the coals will increase as the fat drips into the fire, and adjustments to the cooking time may be necessary.

If a computer program is to function like an expert human, it should be able to do the things that humans commonly do. Experts consult with others to help solve problems. Expert systems can ask questions, explain their reasoning, and justify their conclusions. They can also function with incomplete or uncertain information. These systems usually have access to large data bases filled with facts related to the subject.

The impact of expert systems on people in operations will be significant. Many low-level management and clerical functions will be replaced with expert systems that can handle 95 percent of the decisions. Human intervention will occur when a decision cannot be made. The expert system will be more reliable and will not fall into a pattern of poor performance. As expert systems become more sophisticated, they will be able to make more complex decisions. Thus, to continue to be productive, remaining managers will require better training and higher skill levels than they do today.

People's roles will change in many ways as these systems are implemented. Skilled people will be required to build and to maintain these systems. Engineers and managers will have to be trained in their use. This training goes beyond simple tasks, such as training people how to sign onto the system, which commands to enter, and how to interpret the results. People will require training for more complex tasks, such as being able to recognize when an expert system may provide improved decision making, how to properly implement a system, and how expert systems can be linked together to improve operations. Use of expert systems will increase productivity for labor and management and allow organizations to run more smoothly with fewer people.

The Impact of Robots

Many people have uncertain feelings about robots and their role because they possess some humanlike qualities. They can be taught (programmed) to do a variety of tasks and can react to different situations using built-in logic. Newer versions have been equipped with vision systems to recognize different shapes, locate parts on a moving conveyor, and determine how parts should fit together in an assembled product.

One key to integrating robots and people and reducing uncertainty is to understand the strengths and weaknesses of robots and the strengths and weaknesses of people. Once understood, this can help managers identify appropriate applications.

When Are Robots Better?

According to Isaac Asimov, the strength of a robot is its ability to do simple and repetitive jobs more steadily, more reliably, and with fewer complaints than a human being could—or should. Does a robot displace a human being? Certainly, but the displacement occurs in a job that is beneath the dignity of a human being, simply because a robot can do it. It can occur in a job that is mindless and boring, physically exhausting, or dangerous. A better job can be found for a person. Steady advances in robotics will allow robots to shoulder more of the drudgery of the world's work so that people have more and more time to take care of its creative and joyous aspects.

There are several broad areas of application for robots, and the list will expand as new technology is developed. Several current applications are listed below.

Applications	Examples
Material handling	Placing and removing parts from pallets, parts handling, and transportation
Machine loading and tool changes	CNC metal-cutting machines (shaping pistons for an engine) Presses for stamping sheet metal (filing-cabinet construction) Casting operations (transmission shells)
Coatings and applications	Resin and other coatings Adhesives (bonding metal to glass) Sealants (watertight seals in cars)
Welding	Spot welding sheet metal Arc welding steel pipe or plate
Assembly	Fitting two or more parts together (windshield to car body) Tightening fasteners (nuts to bolts or plastic clips) Inserting electronic components (microcomputer assembly)
Inspection	Tolerances (checking machined parts for cracks or defects in form)

Most applications could be improved with a reliable vision system. Presently, a part must be in the same position each time a robot applies paint, loads a machine, or welds a part. If a part or a machine is out of position, the attempt

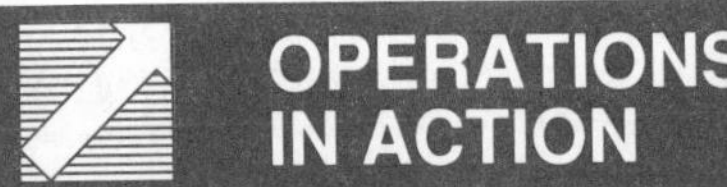

New Applications for Robots

Robots are breaking out of Detroit and the automotive business. They are becoming lighter, faster, more intelligent, and less expensive. These more sophisticated robots are being purchased by candy makers, pharmaceutical houses, underwear manufacturers, and plastic molders. Some are used in custom upholstery factories to deal with the different patterns required for each chair. One slices carpet to fit inside customized vans. A novelty company uses a robot to stretch balloons flat so they can be painted with festive slogans. Another holds class rings in place while they are engraved using lasers. Robot applications will continue to increase as new capabilities are developed.

A major current research area is improved vision systems. Assembly and inspection are two areas in which vision systems can have the largest impact. Positioning parts for assembly and visual inspection of parts offers opportunities for new applications.[1]

usually fails. Unless some type of sensing device is available, a robot will even continue to work without a part to process. We have seen more than one spray-painting robot apply paint to thin air because parts were not placed on the paint line.

When Are People Better?

Even the most sophisticated robot falls far short of humans in terms of overall capability. We do not know of a single job that a robot can do faster than a person. When an executive of Unimation, which was the first company to commercially produce robots, was asked why this is so, he responded that the robot's creator does not have as much experience as the person's creator. Robot performance will improve, but it will have to come a long, long way to match the speed and flexibility of a person.

People can create and think, whereas robots can deal only with situations for which they have been programmed. The robot's advantage comes from its endurance and high degree of repeatability. A person will start faster and may be able to maintain that rate for one or two hours before tiring. At that time, the rate may drop, and the number of errors will increase. The robot can continue to work at the same steady pace, and over an eight-hour shift, the robot may produce as much as or more than a person.

People can manage tasks that robots find difficult, if not impossible. Imagine a simple task that is performed often. As you walk by a desk, you reach down and pick up a pencil that is sitting on the corner. Simple, right? Now, imagine a robot doing it. First, most robots are stationary to maintain positional accuracy. A robot that is out of left-to-right positioning (think of it as movement in a straight line) by only half an inch will miss the pencil. The robot also has a rotational orientation (think of it as turning at the waist), which is measured in degrees. If the robot misses its rotational start point by only a degree, it will not grasp the pencil.

Now assume that someone walked by and bumped the desk. A slight movement of the pencil will make it difficult for the robot to be successful. These are a few of the problems that need to be overcome in assembly and inspection if robots are to be successful. Development of high-resolution vision systems will certainly help to solve these problems.

People can often work in spaces with limited access. Compare your arm with a robot's arm. Many people, if they cup their hand, can put it through a 3½-inch diameter hole and can get a part of their forearm through the same hole. A 5-inch diameter hole would allow the arm, up to the shoulder, to pass through. Once inside, a person can bend an elbow, rotate a forearm and wrist, and move fingers. The arm is an excellent blend of strength and flexibility in a small package. A robot arm can have greater strength than the human arm, or it can be smaller than the human arm, but it has not yet attained the same blend of strength, size, and flexibility.

Robot technology will continue to improve, and new application areas will develop, but robots will not eliminate people. Following is a summary of the advantages people have over robots:

1. Ability to think and devise new ways to solve problems
2. Greater speed in executing tasks
3. Ability to cope with limited or uncertain information
4. More flexibility
5. Ability to manage complex operations
6. Ability to gain access to areas that may be difficult for robots

People will be used for development and planning, where their creativity and thinking can be applied to deal with complex tasks. Robots will be used in repetitive tasks that require some flexibility and tasks that may be hard, dirty, or dangerous to people.

Justification of Robots

Many things that are technologically possible are not economical to implement. There are still many tasks that robots could be used for, but are not because they cannot be justified financially. How can managers determine which jobs are candidates for robot application?

Many factors should be considered before detailed analysis of a specific application can begin. Several considerations are listed below.

1. Direct labor savings
   - A robot does not receive an hourly wage or fringe benefits.
   - A robot does not require incentive pay, shift premiums, or overtime premiums.
2. Increased productivity
   - In the long run, the robot's steady pace and high reliability will increase throughput.
   - Consistent high quality will reduce rejected and reworked parts.
   - Lost production for absenteeism may be eliminated.
   - Low performance caused by poor motivation and job dissatisfaction will be eliminated.
3. Material savings
   - Less material will be consumed because the process is consistent.
   - In spray painting, less overspray may occur.

- In welding, less overwelding occurs.
- In polishing metal, the consistent pressure applied by the robot attendant can lead to a longer life for the grinding wheel.

4. Facility and equipment
   - In some cases, floor-space requirements can be reduced.
   - Consistent use and less abuse of the equipment being tended by the robot may lead to longer machine life and fewer repairs.

When considering using a robot for spot welding, management should compare the costs of a manual solution with the costs of a robot solution. A robot work station is likely to achieve savings in labor, material, and rework costs, while reducing scrap and increasing weld quality. The robot has a high degree of repeatability and can remember complex instructions with ease. On the negative side, a robot is likely to have a much higher investment cost for each work station. It is important to determine whether the robot's operating advantages will cover the additional investment.

In addition to the quantitative data, information about improved quality and decreased delivery lead time should be considered. Has the robot allowed the organization to increase capacity? Even though a robot is slower than a person in performing a job, the robot has more endurance and can continue to work at a steady pace for long periods of time. In many cases, this consistent performance allows the robot's capacity over the long run to be greater than the person's.

A robot is spot welding body parts on an automobile assembly line. *Courtesy: Cincinnati Milacron, Inc.*

Also, investments in robots are often undertaken as part of an overall automation effort to improve an organization's competitive position. Managers should carefully look for synergistic effects when automation projects are combined. For example, some automation projects may require a person to remember several complex sets of instructions and to recognize when to apply them. A robot can easily "memorize" complex instructions. If a simple recognition system can be developed for the robot, then applying the instructions is not difficult. Remembering detail is not the strength of the human mind, so a robot may be used even if it does not have a decided cost advantage.

Ethical Considerations in Robot Applications

In most cases, when a robot is selected to do a job, a person could be employed to do that job. Some people have argued and will continue to argue that taking away the opportunity to work is morally wrong. Should technology be applied when some people are not employed?

In an ideal environment, all people would be working at jobs that best utilized their skills so they could attain job satisfaction and be able to maximize their earnings. Because earnings must be translated into purchasing power in order to be meaningful, the other important factor to consider when evaluating a robotic application is the cost of services and goods. In other words, the productivity of the work force should be high so that workers' earnings would permit them to purchase the goods and services they require. From an economic perspective, if applying robot to a particular job would be more productive than using a person to do it, then the costs of providing a particular service or good will be reduced.

What happens to the displaced person? In the real world, the job loss is not one-for-one; that is, each time a robot is used, it is not true that one less person is employed. Someone at the robot manufacturer will be responsible for designing and building the robot, someone else will be responsible for transporting and installing the robot, and someone at the facility will be responsible for maintenance. The robot application may have eliminated a machine-tending or welding job (manual work), but it has created work for a group of people with higher skill requirements (intellectual work). If the product is now priced lower because of the productivity improvement, then more people can afford to buy it, which stimulates demand and allows the organization to be more competitive, which could further stimulate demand. When enough of these automation efforts are aggregated, more jobs may actually be created than lost.

A productive and efficient economy leads to the creation of new services and goods, which further enhances job opportunities. The problem with this type of job creation is that the job often has a high intellectual work content and a low manual work content. The displaced worker may not have the necessary training and education to do the newly created job.

Replacing a person with a robot application or initiating other automation efforts that displace people is not, in our opinion, an ethical problem. As Isaac Asimov said, when a robot displaces a person, the job is beneath the dignity of a human being simply because a robot can do it. One of the ethical issues seems to be this: Does the displaced worker have the basic skills (high school education) that will enable him or her to be trained for a more intellectual job? Has our educational system been effective? The chance of this person's finding another high-paying, low-skill manufacturing job is very low because those jobs are rapidly being eliminated. Consider another ethical issue: Does this person have an opportunity for additional training that allows him or her to qualify for another position? The important ethical questions seem to be the following: (1) Do people have the basic education that provides them with opportunities for advanced education and job training and (2) Is the advanced education and training easily accessible to these people? The organization's moral responsibility seems to be to prepare its work force for the shift from manual to intellectual work.

The Impact of Computer-Based Information Systems

Computer-based information systems are important to success for most organizations, but the full power of information has not yet been realized. The uses and potential uses of information systems are important to operations managers and are discussed at many points in this text.

How will computer-based information systems affect the role of people?

1. All business disciplines, including marketing, accounting, and finance, as well as operations, will require people with more computer training. People may not need to know how to write computer programs, but they will need to know how to use information systems. The following aspects of computer knowledge may be important:
   - A general knowledge of computer use and application
   - Hands-on experience with microcomputer software
   - Knowledge of the methods and procedures for developing information systems
   - The ability to create data bases on microcomputers
   - The ability to access large data bases and extract needed information
   - A general understanding of computer networking (linking computers)
2. This knowledge will be gained through existing educational programs and increasing on-the-job training and development. Operations managers should become proficient in information processing.

INTEGRATING THE SYSTEM

Information Systems to Gain a Competitive Edge

Companies such as American Hospital Supply, Krogers Supermarkets, USA Today, Merrill Lynch, General Electric, Allen Bradley, and Federal Express are examples of companies described in this text that use information and information-processing capabilities to move ahead of their competition. In earlier chapters, we have described production planning and scheduling systems that use information-processing capabilities to improve operations. We have also discussed the use of information to control inventory, reduce cost, and improve quality. Access to information needed to answer questions about the status of a customer's orders, daily production, product availability, machine maintenance, and so on is important for managing operations successfully. Once again, these computer-based systems will raise the level of expertise required to become a successful manager. People will be required to design, build, and use these systems. Without people, these systems will not work effectively.

3. Managers will be required to obtain a "big-picture" view of operations and a broad base of knowledge about how the various parts fit together. This is the systems approach that is stressed throughout this text. Managers with such a broad base of knowledge will be in greater demand than are narrowly trained experts.
4. There will be fewer, better-trained staff, helping to make that part of the organization more responsive to change.
5. Direct labor forces will be greatly reduced. Certain types of indirect labor will also decline because of automation efforts discussed in previous sections and because of increasing use of computers to control operations. Routine decisions on the shop floor will be made and transmitted by networking (tying together) the different steps in the production process.
6. Some types of indirect labor will tend to increase as more equipment maintenance, better planning, and more computer controls are required. The costs for such labor will be partially offset by reductions in clerical staff that formerly shuffled paper back and forth between departments.

Information systems, especially those that are computer based, are a very important part of an organization. Chapter 19 will discuss creating information systems to manage and control operations. It will also elaborate on information systems to support decision making, information needs for MRP II, computer control of production systems, and cost control systems.

PEOPLE BUILD COMPETITIVE ADVANTAGE

The major asset of an organization is its people. People and their degree of motivation have more to do with an organization's success than any other single factor. Great care should be taken in selecting, training, and motivating people.

Training and Development

The rapidly changing technological environment is forcing private industry and government agencies to increase support for training and retraining. Training is a way of improving employees' skills for better on-the-job performance; it also indicates an interest in employees' welfare, which may improve motivation.

Establishing training programs that satisfy the diverse needs of an organization requires a broad range of skills. A maintenance supervisor on a production line requires different knowledge than a sales representative. Here are some key points that can be followed in establishing training programs.

1. A clear set of objectives should be established for the program. These objectives will be useful in program development, as well as in a follow-up evaluation.
2. Experts involved in designing training programs should not be exclusively relied on to develop the program. To keep the trainee's interest, any training program requires a blend of presentation skills and relevant content. Training experts may be used to organize presentations, but they should work with

INTEGRATING THE SYSTEM

Understanding Organizational Behavior Is a Key to Operations

Before graduation, business students are required to study human relations in the organization, a subject usually called organizational behavior. The ideas of training and developing employees, communicating effectively, instilling positive motivation, and providing leadership are important for the organization and are keys to successful operations. In most organizations, a majority of the people are involved in marketing or operations, so it makes sense to work hard in both areas to improve worker involvement and motivation.

For many years, these concepts have been successfully applied to salespersons and marketing managers. Imagine how the motivation level of a sales force would drop if management did not invest in their future through training, did not listen to their suggestions, and did not treat them as intelligent human beings.

Many organizations have only recently begun to realize that these factors are very important for getting the highest level of performance from people in operations. Imagine how the motivation and performance of operations personnel would increase if management invested in their future, listened and took action on their suggestions, and treated them as intelligent human beings.

people in the relevant areas, such as maintenance or sales, to ensure that the content is appropriate.

3. If the training is designed to upgrade the skills of trainees who already have some experience at the position, these people should be consulted. They often have a good understanding of what they need to know to do the job.
4. The trainees should be convinced that the programs are designed with their best interests and the company's best interests in mind. No one will believe that an organization is involved in training solely for the welfare of the employee. On the other hand, trainees will not learn effectively if they do not see how they can benefit personally.
5. The training program should be evaluated. Training programs are expensive, with estimates of training costs by industrial and government organizations topping $100 billion per year. Although evaluation of training programs is usually difficult because many of the results are intangible, that should not stop managers from evaluation efforts.
6. The information gathered in the evaluation process should be used to provide feedback to the designers of future training programs. This effort is often overlooked or poorly attempted.

Leadership

What is leadership? Can it be learned, or is it only possible to cultivate the natural ability existing within each individual? When you next meet with a group of friends, try to determine who is the group leader. Who tends to get things moving? To whom do the others look for direction? What is it about that person that makes him or her a leader?

Leadership has long been studied by experts, but no clear definition of leadership has emerged. Lacking definitions or prescriptions for leadership, we list some characteristics that we feel good leaders possess.

1. Good leaders are good listeners. Listening is becoming a lost art in today's fast-paced society. Listening carefully to subordinates and superiors will usually give a manager a better idea of the problem and the potential solution than an equal amount of talking. Listening carefully usually allows a manager to ask better questions and to pull out other relevant information. It shows both subordinates and superiors that the manager is genuinely interested in them and the problem or opportunity at hand.
2. Good leaders are decision makers. Decisions need to be made, and good leaders are willing to make them and then commit resources to implement them. They do not study problems to death because they are afraid of making a mistake.
3. Good leaders may be able to do everything well, but they do not do everything. Delegation of responsibility and authority is critical to effective leadership. First, no one person, no matter how talented, can perform every task under his or her control. Second, if leaders attempt to do everything, their subordinates will have little confidence in their own abilities. They will always be looking over their shoulders to see what the boss thinks.
4. Good leaders have ultimate responsibility for all decisions made by them or their subordinates. Leaders do not hide behind their subordinates when a poor decision is made. If a leader gives someone a job to do and he or she is unsuccessful, the leader's judgment is most certainly in question. When a subordinate fails, a leader needs to take appropriate action. This could range from a private talk with a subordinate to dismissal for repeated problems.
5. Good leaders act on suggestions. That does not mean that a leader can implement every idea that someone puts forth. Good leaders act on ideas that are consistent with the organization's overall goals and provide positive feedback. But they do not ignore ideas that are not acted on. They discuss unused suggestions with the people who made them so that both leader and subordinates understand why there is no fit.
6. Good leaders provide clear direction and feedback on past decisions. One way of avoiding many ideas that do not meet the organization's goals is to provide subordinates with a translation of those goals into terms that are meaningful to them, such as improving quality, reducing customer lead time, or reducing shipping costs. Most subordinates want to work toward the goals of the organization as long as they perceive that it is in their best interest to do so and they have been shown the direction. Providing clear direction leads to a discussion of communication.

Communication

One of the most important skills that a manager can possess and, unfortunately, one that students and managers find the most difficult to master is effective communication. All organizations are based on the ability to communicate. In fact, organizations could not exist without communication. Marketing talks with finance, finance with accounting, and accounting with operations. Within operations, information flows from entering customer orders through production and shipping. Feedback on product quality should reach the product designer, the operations manager, and the direct-labor employee.

Readers who remember that computer-based information systems help to shoulder part of the communications burden may say, "Yes, but communications will not be as important in the future." But these systems manage only low-level transfers of information. More complex decisions and decision making will still require communication of ideas. It is our contention that communications will become more important as organizations attempt to respond rapidly to customer and competitive changes. Certainly, the speed and accuracy of communication need to increase if the organization is to remain competitive.

People in organizations should be able to communicate verbally and in writing. Presenting ideas to others is one way for employees to demonstrate that they have what it takes to move up the organization and take on new responsibility. We have sat in many meetings where the decisions were based on who made the best presentation, not who had the best idea. The quality of the presentation and the quality of the idea are hard to separate.

Motivation

There are always two ways of looking at a problem. How can I find a way to solve it, and how can I find a reason not to?

Motivation is an inner state that directs behavior toward a goal. It is a set of factors that cause people to behave in certain ways. No amount of intelligence can make up for poor motivation. Yet people with only average intelligence can go far beyond their expectations if they are motivated.

Motivation is a powerful force that can drive people to do things that are physically and intellectually far beyond their perceived capabilities. When properly controlled and channeled in the right direction, motivation can boost an individual's and an organization's performance. On the other hand, negative motivation can be a destructive force that no amount of careful planning or automation can overcome.

SUMMARY

- Computers, information, and manufacturing technology will have a significant impact on reshaping organizations.
- Productivity gains at Shenandoah Life are part of a powerful synergism taking root in the United States that pairs people with automation.
- Factories run by high-tech information-processing capabilities and robots depend on people more than ever before.
- To compete in global markets, companies are installing work systems that emphasize broad-based jobs, teamwork, participative managers, and multiskilled workers.
- Future organizations will be more flexible and more responsive to change. They will have to respond to rapidly changing markets with high-quality products that fit specific customer needs.

- CAD and CAM will provide engineers with the ability to rapidly design and build products in response to customer needs. These functions will be done more quickly and with fewer people.
- Expert systems will allow managers and engineers to spend less time dealing with routine decisions and to concentrate their efforts on developing systems that improve performance. This will be accomplished with fewer and more highly trained people.
- Robots will replace people in many jobs that require limited thinking power. Organizations will have to take advantage of people's intellect if they want to be competitive in world markets.
- Computer-based information systems will assist labor and management in making better decisions. Organizations will continue to expand their information-processing resources in order to leverage their employees' time.
- Training and development programs, improved leadership skills, better communications, and motivation hold the keys to building an organization by building its people base. This is true in operations, as well as in all other parts of the organization.

CAREER PROFILE

Ronald Niemesh

Material Manager
Inland Tool and Manufacturing

Inland Tool and Manufacturing is located in Detroit, Michigan, and is a supplier to the automotive industry. Ronald Niemesh is responsible for material management. He directs a staff that handles order-entry processing, and he develops the master production schedule, prepares the production schedule, purchases materials and services, and manages shipping and receiving. Niemesh and his staff are responsible for almost everything that moves in the plant. He reports to the plant manager. The next step in his career could be to plant manager.

Education and Experience

Niemesh has had extensive training in material requirements planning, master scheduling, and material control. Recently, he completed his M.B.A. with emphasis in management and industrial relations. He is working toward certification (CPIM) by the American Production and Inventory Control Society (APICS). Niemesh also credits listening carefully to people and their problems as an important part of his training.

Previously, Niemesh was the special projects coordinator for Sharon Manufacturing Company. In that position, he analyzed data regarding scrap generation, salvage and parts reworking, inventory levels, and overall production efficiency. Before becoming special projects coordinator, he held positions as production supervisor, scheduler, material control manager, operations manager, and plant superintendent at Sharon Manufacturing.

QUESTIONS

1. Summarize the key impacts that changes in technology will have on the organization.

2. How will the role of people change within the organization as new technologies are introduced?

3. How can teamwork be used to increase productivity?

4. What will be the impact of computer-aided design and computer-aided manufacturing on the role of people in operations?

5. What will be the impact of expert systems on the role of people in operations?

6. What will be the impact of robots on the role of people in operations?

7. When do robots possess an advantage over people, and when do people have the advantage?

8. How will the application of computer-based information systems change the role of people in the organization?

9. Why is training and development necessary if an organization wants to gain a competitive edge?

10. What are some important points in building training programs?

11. Describe some of the attributes required for developing leadership.

12. Why are communication skills important?

MINI-CASES

Tebbin Tubing, Inc.

Elizabeth Tebbin, president of Tebbin Tubing (TT), has recently decided to automate the company's production lines. To make tubing, TT takes flat steel plate, bends it in a circle, and welds the seam. The company produces very large diameter pipe that is used in oil pipelines. Presently, the company has a six-month backlog of orders and has lost considerable business to its competitors. Building another manual production line will cost about $2,000,000.

Present operations require large amounts of manual setup and manual welding. Weldment must be added to the outside and the inside of the seam. With people doing the welding, the following problems arise: (1) the inside and outside seams must be welded sequentially because of the danger to the person on the inside, (2) the inside weld is often rough and requires a large amount of hand grinding, and (3) after welding the inside, a large amount of splatter must be cleaned up.

The new approach would use a robot welder to weld the seam on the inside and outside at the same time. A smoother weld would be achieved that would require less grinding and have less splatter. It is estimated that the processing time for a one-foot length of pipe would be reduced from 70 minutes to 30 minutes. As a result, output will more than double. It is also estimated that the average for rework time per foot of pipe would drop from three minutes to one minute.

The problem that TT's management faces is that no one in the organization is familiar with robot applications and how they can be justified to the company's board of directors. You have been hired as a consultant to outline some of the key issues involved in robot application. The company has posed several questions about robots and has compiled the following data. (All data are for one production line.) Assume that the company will continue to run two shifts for a total of sixteen hours per day, five days per week.

Initial cost of robot	$400,000
Operating cost of robot (excluding material costs)	$3.00/hour
Feet of pipe welded with robot	2/hour
Direct labor wages saved with robot	$17.00/hour
Weldment saved with robot	$1.50/hour
Life of robot without significant expense for upgrade	5 years

1. Describe the type of applications for which robots can perform better than people.

2. Describe applications for which people are better suited than robots.

3. What are the key areas for justifying robot applications? Describe them in detail.

4. With the information given earlier, make a recommendation to TT management about automating the line. Give as much detail as possible.

Magic Airlines

Airlines are faced with deregulation problems, an increased number of mergers and acquisitions, declining fares, and increasing passenger traffic. Magic Airlines has been flying for more than forty years, but currently it and many other airlines are under tremendous pressure to cut costs. Presently, Magic pays the following average salaries: over $90,000 to airline pilots, more than $35,000 to mechanics, and $30,000 to flight attendants. Since deregulation, new entrants have opted for nonunion shops and have been successful. Some existing carriers have won concessions from their unions. These low-cost airlines often pay mechanics and flight attendants $20,000 or less.

In the past, Magic has been very profitable. However, recent dramatic declines in fares have pushed the company into a loss position. Magic's executives have tried to bargain with union leaders to take wage cuts to improve Magic's competitiveness. These talks have often lead to unfriendly exchanges between management and labor. Union leaders and the rank and file are becoming more distressed with management positions.

Meanwhile, Magic's president has received a 10 percent salary increase, raising his salary to more than $400,000. The company has over forty vice-presidents, carryovers from the days of regulated airfares. Perks for executives and their families have not been reduced. Faced with more losses in the coming quarter, how can Magic improve its short- and long-term profit position?

1. How is Magic's position different from that of other airlines?

2. Do you think that Magic's management has treated the unions fairly in putting most of the blame for high costs on the unions?

3. Devise an approach that would allow Magic to get wage concessions from the unions.

SELECTED BIBLIOGRAPHY

Annual Research Review of the Robotics Institute 1985. Pittsburgh: Carnegie-Mellon University, 1986.

Arnold, Hugh J., and Feldman, Daniel C. *Organizational Behavior.* New York: McGraw-Hill, 1986.

Cherns, Albert. "The Principles of Sociotechnical Design." *Human Relations* 29, no. 8 (August 1976): 783–792.

Cherns, Albert. *Sociotechnics.* London: Malaby Press, 1976.

De Greene, Kenyon B. *Sociotechnical Systems: Factors in Analysis, Design, and Management.* Englewood Cliffs, N.J.: Prentice-Hall, 1973.

Engelberger, Joseph F. *Robotics in Practice.* New York: AMACOM, 1980.

Ettlie, John E.; Bridges, William P.; and O'Keefe, Robert D. "Organization Strategy and Structural Differences for Radical Versus Incremental Innovation." *Management Science* 30, no. 6 (June 1984): 682–695.

Galbraith, Jay R. "Designing the Innovating Organization." *Organizational Dynamics* (AMACOM) (Winter 1982): 5–25.

Gibson, Cyrus F. *Managing Organizational Behavior.* Homewood, Ill.: Irwin, 1980.

Griffin, Ricky W., and Moorhead, Gregory. *Organizational Behavior.* Boston: Houghton Mifflin, 1986.

Groover, Mikell P. *Automation, Production Systems, and Computer-Aided Manufacturing.* Englewood Cliffs, N.J.: Prentice-Hall, 1980.

Harmon, Paul, and King, David. *Expert Systems: Artificial Intelligence in Business.* New York: Wiley, 1985.

Huber, George P. "The Nature and Design of Post-Industrial Organizations." *Management Science* 30, no. 8 (August 1984): 928–951.

Industrial Robots: A Summary and Forecast. Naperville, Ill.: Tech Tran Corporation, 1983.

Keen, P., and Morton, M. S. *Decision Support Systems: An Organizational Perspective.* Reading, Mass.: Addison-Wesley, 1978.

Organ, Dennis W., and Hamner, W. Clay. *Organizational Behavior: An Applied Psychological Approach.* Plano, Tex.: BPI, 1982.

Pasmore, William A., and Sherwood, John J. *Sociotechnical Systems: A Sourcebook.* La Jolla, Calif.: University Associates, 1978.

Susman, Gerald I., and Chase, Richard B. "A Sociotechnical Analysis of the Integrated Factory." *Journal of Applied Behavioral Science* 22, no. 3 (1986): 257–270.

Szilagyi, Andrew D., and Wallace, Marc J. *Organizational Behavior and Performance.* Glenview, Ill.: Scott, Foresman, 1987.

Timm, Paul R., and Peterson, Brent D. *People at Work: Human Relations in Organizations*. St. Paul, Minn.: West, 1986.

Turban, Efraim. *Decision Support and Expert Systems: Management Support Systems*. New York: Macmillan, 1990.

Wexley, Kenneth N., and Latham, Gary P. *Developing and Training Human Resources in Organizations*. Glenview, Ill.: Scott, Foresman, 1981.

Chapter 19

Creating Information Systems to Manage and Control Operations

CHAPTER OUTLINE

LEARNING OBJECTIVES

After completing this chapter, you should be able to

- Define the term *information* and describe the importance of information in supporting decision making.
- Explain how an organization's performance is determined by the decisions it makes.
- Discuss the importance of information systems and explain why they need to be cost-effective.
- Describe the information requirements of the operations function in designing a production system, planning the system, and managing and controlling the system.
- Describe how information systems can be developed to control material flow, beginning with customer order entry and following through to shop floor controls.
- Explain the importance of gathering performance data to provide feedback to managers.
- Describe the role of bar coding in material control.
- Discuss the ways in which computer systems can be developed to control equipment. This includes the application of local area networks in building integrated computer control systems.
- Understand accounting system information in order to control costs.

OPERATIONS IN ACTION

Getting Better Information Faster Leads to Better Decisions

The information business is getting to be big business. One such information business is Lloyd's Maritime Data Network, which monitors both the cargoes and the movements of all commercial ocean-going vessels. Hundreds of shippers use data provided by the network to make better deals when chartering ships. Shippers who use this service can save hundreds of thousands of dollars by knowing which ships are available and where they are going.

Another information business, the Philadelphia-based Institute for Science Information, scans and indexes about 7,000 scientific and medical journals for about 300,000 customers, including doctors, research scientists, and business people. Customers can quickly scan the institute's vast array of information and select only the information that meets their needs.

Telerate, another company in the information business, gathers financial information and sells it to stockbrokers and traders, who have to make quick decisions. Information electronically delivered to a trader's desk gives the trader an edge.

Information is a key to building a successful organization. Organizations whose business is to gather, process, and deliver information need to understand the market and current technology. Organizations that use these services should evaluate the advantages of buying information and compare these with the costs of acquiring it.[1]

INFORMATION

Information is data that have been gathered, classified, organized, and analyzed in a way that makes them useful for decision making. For example, data could be a list of all customer orders for microcomputer software. To transform data into information, a manager or data analyst might group the orders by type of software, such as word-processing, data-base, and communications software; sort the orders by region of the country; and calculate the average number of software packages ordered per customer. These actions would make the data more useful for forecasting sales, determining shipping schedules, and planning distribution.

Information Systems Support Decision Making

An **information system** is a mechanism for gathering, classifying, organizing, storing, analyzing, and disseminating information. The objective of an information system is to help managers make better decisions. Information is an essential part of decision making, and decision making, in turn, is the most critical task that organizations perform. It is not an exaggeration to say that an organization's position (its value in the stock market) is a direct result of the decisions the organization has made. If you find it difficult to see why this is true, think about the ways in which decisions and decision making affect your life. Decisions regarding education, physical activities, diet, marriage, investments, and so on have shaped and will continue to shape your life. Information and the methods used to collect it will play a critical role in determining your future. The same is true for organizations.

Organizations constantly make decisions that affect performance. For example, an organization might have to decide whether or not to invest in new technology and facilities. If it decides to make the investment, the organization must decide whether to raise the capital through equity (stocks) or borrowing (bonds). If the choice is stocks, the organization must decide what kind of stock to offer, what the selling price should be, and so on. All of these decisions will have an impact on the organization's performance, and the quality of each decision will be influenced by the timeliness and quality of the information provided.

As Exhibit 19.1 implies, an organization relies on the information it gathers and the people who use it in decision making. An organization's status with respect to products, market share, and profits, as well as its ability to respond to threats and opportunities in its environment, are direct results of past decisions. The links between information, decisions, and organizational performance are real and important.

An information system must support a broad range of decisions from many functional areas. Exhibit 19.2 indicates several areas of decision making and some of the key decisions within each area.

OPERATIONS IN ACTION

Nickel Plate Railroad: Decision to Extend Freight Service

The Nickel Plate Railroad has been asked to bring ten empty railcars to and haul ten full railcars from the Woodville Lime plant each day. Although there is an existing rail line from Nickel Plate's main line into the plant, the track would require major improvements before service could begin. Nickel Plate must make the following decisions about extending service to Woodville Lime:

- Does Nickel Plate want this kind of business?
- What price should it charge?
- What length of contract should it seek?
- Who should be responsible for upgrading the track?
- Who should be responsible for maintaining the track?
- Could this contract lead to more work?

Nickel Plate needs the following information to make the decisions listed above:

- The cost of upgrading the track
- The cost of providing the service
- The probability that Woodville Lime will remain in business
- Woodville Lime's present financial position
- The market for Woodville Lime's product—is it stable, declining, or increasing?

The following problems could arise as a result of poor information:

- Nickel Plate could lose money on the contract because it underestimated labor requirements for the job.
- Woodville Lime could go out of business because of declining demand for its products, leaving Nickel Plate with unneeded track.
- An unexpected increase in demand from other customers could make it difficult for Nickel Plate to continue serving Woodville Lime.

To avoid these problems, Nickel Plate management must gather and analyze as much relevant data as possible to make an effective decision on whether or not to provide rail service to the Woodville Lime plant.

Exhibit 19.1 The Importance of People and Information to an Organization's Success

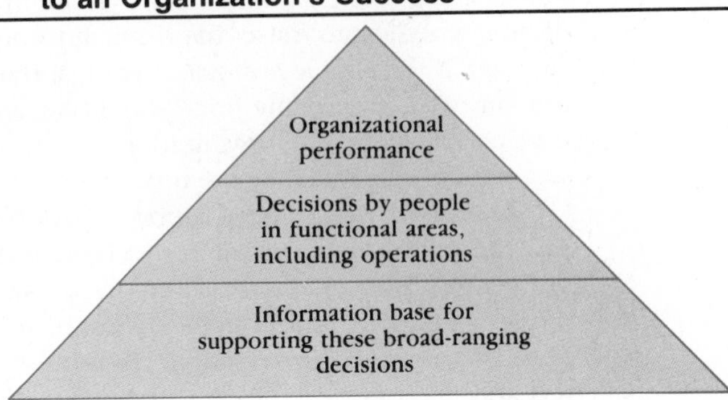

Exhibit 19.2 Information Systems Support Decision Making

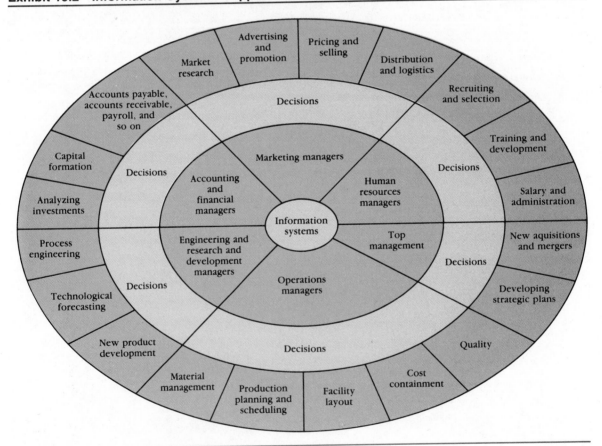

Information systems

Marketing managers
Accounting and financial managers
Human resources managers
Engineering and research and development managers
Top management
Operations managers

Decisions
Decisions
Decisions
Decisions
Decisions
Decisions

Market research
Advertising and promotion
Pricing and selling
Distribution and logistics
Recruiting and selection
Training and development
Salary and administration
New aquisitions and mergers
Developing strategic plans
Quality
Cost containment
Facility layout
Production planning and scheduling
Material management
New product development
Technological forecasting
Process engineering
Analyzing investments
Capital formation
Accounts payable, accounts receivable, payroll, and so on

Computers are playing a greater role in collecting data and in processing and accessing information. Although most of the systems we will discuss in this chapter can function without computers, computers make information processing and accessing easier and faster. But a computer is not a substitute for a well-designed information system. A poorly designed information system that uses a computer will simply allow an organization to make mistakes at a faster pace.

Dealing with Imperfect Information

Managers must often deal with imperfect information. For example, in one case, an important piece of information may not be available. In another case, the accuracy of the information may be uncertain. But mangers should not use these problems as an excuse for avoiding a decision. If the information is unavailable or unreliable, managers should use their judgment, experience, and any related information to attempt to estimate the missing information. Managers can prepare different scenarios to test the outcome of a decision, or they can apply decision trees, which have been discussed in previous chapters.

Example

Let us return to the Nickel Plate Railroad situation described above. It is unlikely that Nickel Plate could gather conclusive information about the longevity of the Woodville Lime plant. How can Nickel Plate's managers make a decision without conclusive information? In this case, they can estimate their operating profit and compare it with the investment they must make to extend railway service to Woodville. To begin, assume the alternatives are to extend railway service to Woodville or not. Nickel Plate's management should consider some reasonable possibilities for Woodville's longevity and then estimate the probability of each. The following table uses Nickel Plate's estimates based on three possible events:

Event	Probability	Nickel Plate's Operating Profit
Woodville fails after one year	.1	$10,000
Woodville fails after three years	.2	45,000
Woodville is operating after five years	.7	80,000
	1.0	

By analyzing information on the service's cost and selling price, it is possible to estimate operating profit for each potential length of service—in this case, one, three, and five years. Assumptions are made in calculating these profits, as they are in any model. For example, an assumption is made in the model that the lime plant will not fail within six months.

A decision tree is one way to handle unknown or uncertain data. The decision tree in Exhibit 19.3 can help Nickel Plate's management visualize the problem and determine the expected value of extending service. The expected value of operating profit shown in the decision tree is $66,000.

$$\text{Expected value of operating profit} = .1(\$10{,}000) + .2(\$45{,}000) + .7(\$80{,}000)$$
$$= \$66{,}000$$

Exhibit 19.3 Decision Tree for Nickel Plate

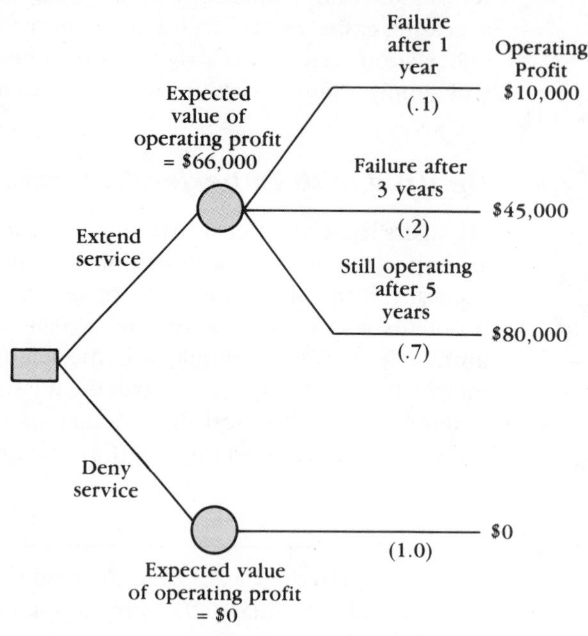

The expected profit potential is thus $66,000. Nickel Plate should then estimate the investment required to bring the rail line up to operating standards. With estimates of operating profit and investment, the company's managers could calculate a return on investment to help them make the decision.

Cost-Effective Information Systems

As discussed earlier in this chapter, information is critical to the success of any organization. However, management's goal should not be information at any price. Managers need appropriate information at a reasonable cost so they can make effective and efficient decisions regarding the operations of their organizations. There are two sides to the information equation, the cost of acquiring it and the benefits of using it. If an organization spends more to acquire information than it gains from using it, then an information system is not cost-effective. If an organization does this repeatedly, it will eventually be out of business.

To ensure that information systems are cost-effective, managers who make decisions about quality, inventory, production planning, or other operating areas should (1) participate actively in the design of their information system, (2) decide what information is to be captured by their information system, and (3) be aware of and control the cost of their information system. When the development and creation of information systems is decentralized, the managers who make the operating decisions are also the ones who decide how much information should be gathered to answer a question or solve a problem. These managers are in the best position to evaluate the costs of acquiring more information and the benefits gained by using it.

With a centralized information system, the costs and benefits of the system are often split between two different groups within the organization. The costs and the development of the information system are controlled by a centralized information system staff, but the benefits gained from using the information are known by the operating managers. This approach can be a formula for creating information systems that are too costly and not responsive to the organization's needs. On the one hand, changes may not be made as rapidly as they should be because the information systems staff understands only the cost side of the information equation. They do not fully understand the benefits of acquiring the information. On the other hand, inappropriate changes may be requested by the operating managers because they do not fully understand the amount of time or the costs needed to make a change. They may request a change that is not cost-effective. To respond to these problems, many organizations are decentralizing data processing operations so that users develop the software. This approach, sometimes called end-user computing, is often applied on networks of microcomputers.

INFORMATION REQUIREMENTS IN OPERATIONS

The information requirements in operations are extensive. The initial chapters of this text described decisions involving the development of new products, the design of new processes for making those products, capacity determination, facility location and layout, and job design. All of these decisions require information. A review of the outlines for Chapters 3 through 9 may help you recall the large number of decisions described in these chapters and the amount of information needed to make them. These decisions require the design and development of information systems to aid in decision making. Exhibit 19.4 summarizes the key decisions in these areas and lists some of the information needed to make them.

Planning for operations, which was discussed in Section II of this text, requires information about customer needs, staffing levels, material availability, equipment reliability, and existing demands on the facility. Scheduling requires information about material, equipment, employee training, maintenance, and availability of labor. A review of the outlines for Chapters 10 through 14 may help you recall the decisions and required information for these areas.

The remainder of this chapter focuses on using information systems to manage and control operations. Management and control of operations involve (1) guiding the production process so that actual production is directed toward the goals described in the organizational plan and (2) collecting and feeding back information about performance. The purposes of providing feedback are to evaluate the effectiveness of management in guiding the actual production phase, to determine the reasonableness of current plans and schedules, and to consider the appropriateness of the design of the production system. Performance review implies control of operations, through evaluation, feedback, and corrective action.

Exhibit 19.4 Key Decisions in System Design

Decisions	Information
Forecast of demand	Historical sales data
Product design	Customer requirements Production capabilities Historical cost data
Capacity determination	Production rates for departments Product flow Product yield
Facility location	Transportation costs Variable production costs Investment Revenue Sales volume Qualitative factors
Process selection	Production volume Lists of available technology Production cost data
Facility layout	Activity level between departments Material-handling costs
Job design and work measurement	Precedence relationships Product design parameters Process design parameters

To provide direction and performance feedback, an information system should focus on the material, the facility and equipment, and the people needed in the production process. The factors to consider include

1. Inventory level
2. Quality
3. Role of people in the organization
4. Material flows
5. Utilization of facility and equipment
6. Actual production volume
7. Production costs

Inventory control, quality management, and the role of people in organizations are discussed in earlier chapters (Chapters 15 through 18), and the coverage is not repeated here. The other factors are discussed here.

COORDINATING AND MONITORING MATERIAL FLOWS

In a production system, information helps managers control the physical flow of material. In this section, we use the example of Lima Locomotive Works, previously described in Chapter 15, to discuss the design of an information system to be used to monitor and direct material flows. The material flows for Lima Locomotive are illustrated in Exhibit 19.5. In our example, we cover the key elements of the information system in order to provide guidelines for its development. These key elements are as follows:

Exhibit 19.5 Material Flow for Lima Locomotive

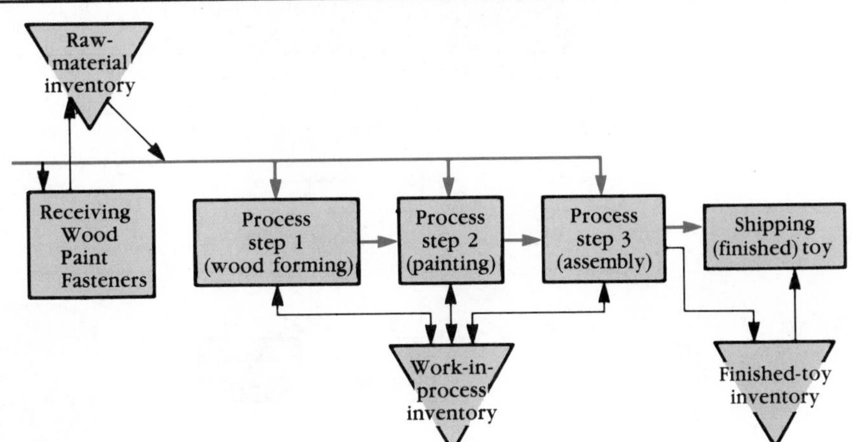

1. Managing customer orders
2. Planning production
3. Procuring materials
4. Preparing equipment
5. Scheduling production
6. Controlling the shop floor

To simplify our discussion, we will use the term *product* to refer to a finished product and the term *part* to refer to a component part used in making the finished product.

An overview of the information flow for Lima Locomotive is shown in Exhibit 19.6. In the exhibit, the boxes represent decisions or actions and the cylinders represent stored data. In a computer-based system, the boxes represent computer programs and the cylinders represent computer files or data bases. We will refer to this exhibit many times as we trace the information flows through the organization. In the discussion that follows, the numbers in brackets refer to the boxes that are similarly marked in Exhibit 19.6. We begin with customer open orders.

Managing Customer Orders

The information stream begins with the receipt of a customer order [1], specifying the product desired and the quantity demanded. Additional information, such as the company name, the ship-to address, and the due date, is usually included on the order and will be entered into the system for later use. The file that results is usually called the **customer open-order file.** A sample customer order is shown in Exhibit 19.7.

To manage customer open orders effectively, the system should have the capability to add, change, and delete orders, as well as to provide an up-to-date look at any order. Quick access to a customer's **order status** for the purpose of

Exhibit 19.6 Information System for Managing and Controlling Operations

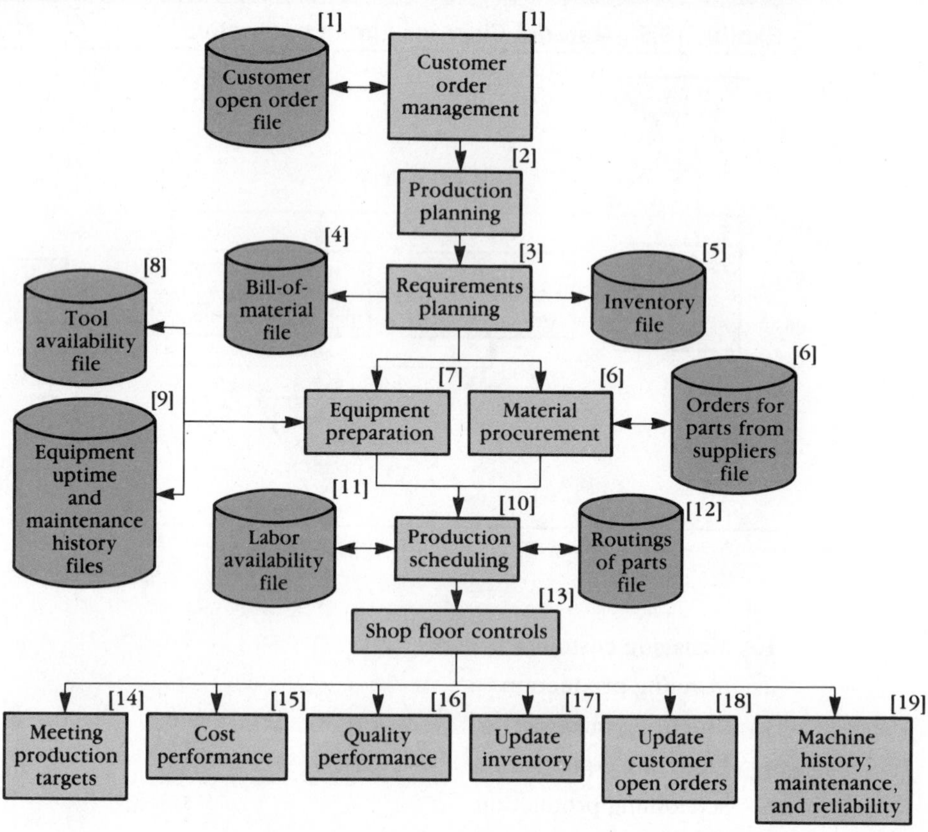

Exhibit 19.7 Customer Order for Lima Locomotive Works

From: Gamble Toys for Us 2846 W. North St. Upper Saddle River, NJ		To: Lima Locomotive Works 509 North Elizabeth Lima, Oregon	Purchase Order #4217 Order Date 10/4 Shipping Date 12/1	
Quantity	**Product Number**	**Description**	**Unit Cost**	**Total**
1,000	5424	Red locomotive made from maple	$13.49	$13,490.00
5,000	5629	Green locomotive made from oak	$14.29	$71,450.00
3,000	5721	Black "old-time" locomotive made from maple	$13.79	$41,370.00
				$126,310.00
		Ship to: Gamble Warehouse Division 1214 Main St. Memphis, TN		

responding promptly to inquiries is critical for building strong and effective relationships with customers.

In addition, the customer open orders should be updated to reflect progress that orders make through the facility. Some typical order-status possibilities include complete and ready to ship, waiting for a special paint color that has not yet arrived, and held for changes in product design.

Planning Production

Not every order in the open-order file will necessarily be put into the production plan immediately. Production-planning personnel develop policies and rules that guide the selection process. A production plan may look several weeks or months into the future and is not as detailed as a schedule. For more details on how production plans are formed, review the appropriate sections in Chapters 10 and 11 on planning.

A production plan [2] becomes the guide for directing operations. Material procurement, equipment preparation, and the detailed production scheduling follow logically from requirements planning, as shown in Exhibit 19.6. The status of a customer order should be updated once it enters the production plan. Lima Locomotive's production plan for November is shown in Exhibit 19.8.

Procuring Materials

Once an order enters the production plan, efforts should begin to ensure the timely delivery of materials. This implies that materials should be available as they

Exhibit 19.8 Lima Locomotive Works Production Plan for November

Date prepared: 10/15

First Week (November 3-7)

Customer	Product Number	Quantity
Gott	8321	1,500
Buswack	8321	5,000
Wyler	5424	2,000

Second Week (November 10-14)

Customer	Product Number	Quantity
Crocker	5629	5,000
Buswack	5424	4,000

Third Week (November 17-21)

Customer	Product Number	Quantity
Gamble	5629	2,500
Gamble	5424	1,000
Wyler	5629	4,500

Fourth Week (November 24-28)

Customer	Product Number	Quantity
Gamble	5721	3,000
Gamble	5629	2,500
Crocker	5424	3,500

Exhibit 19.9 Bill of Materials

Product number: 5721
Description: Black "Old-time" Locomotive (Maple)

Component Parts and Subassemblies
(Indented to reflect product structure

Part Number	Quantity	Description
29743	1	Body subassembly
44166	1	Main body
00986	1	Maple block
49176	1	Smokestack
46258	1	Cowcatcher
01440	1 oz.	Wood glue (for stack and cowcatcher
26451	1	Rear wheel subassembly
53771	2	Rear wheel
54601	1	Real axle
06684	2	Metal staple (to attach whe to axle)
22166	3	Front wheel subassembly
53600	2	Front wheel
54200	1	Front axle
06684	2	Metal stable (to attach whe to axle)
06920	8	Metal fastener (to hold wheel subassembly to body)
02115	6 oz.	Antique black paint

are needed. Efforts should be made to minimize inventory levels and keep delays due to part shortages or late delivery at or very close to zero.

Whether an organization is using material requirements planning (MRP), just-in-time (JIT), or another material-management method, material procurement depends on knowing the

1. Quantity of finished product required (the production plan).
2. Parts required to make the product from the bill of materials (BOM).
3. Amount of inventory that is not committed to other customer orders.

Beginning with the production plan, requirements planning [3] looks at the BOM file [4] to determine the parts and the quantity of each required to make a finished product. For purposes of illustration, we will examine the Gamble order for product number 5721, the black "old-time" locomotive, which is planned for production during the last week in November.

The BOM shown in Exhibit 19.9 lists all the required parts for the old-time locomotive, as well as the tools and fixtures needed to make the parts. Engineer-

Exhibit 19.9 continuing

Tools and Fixtures

Tool Number	Description
T4321	Band-saw blade
T5693	Router bit
F6341	Fixture to hold locomotive for painting

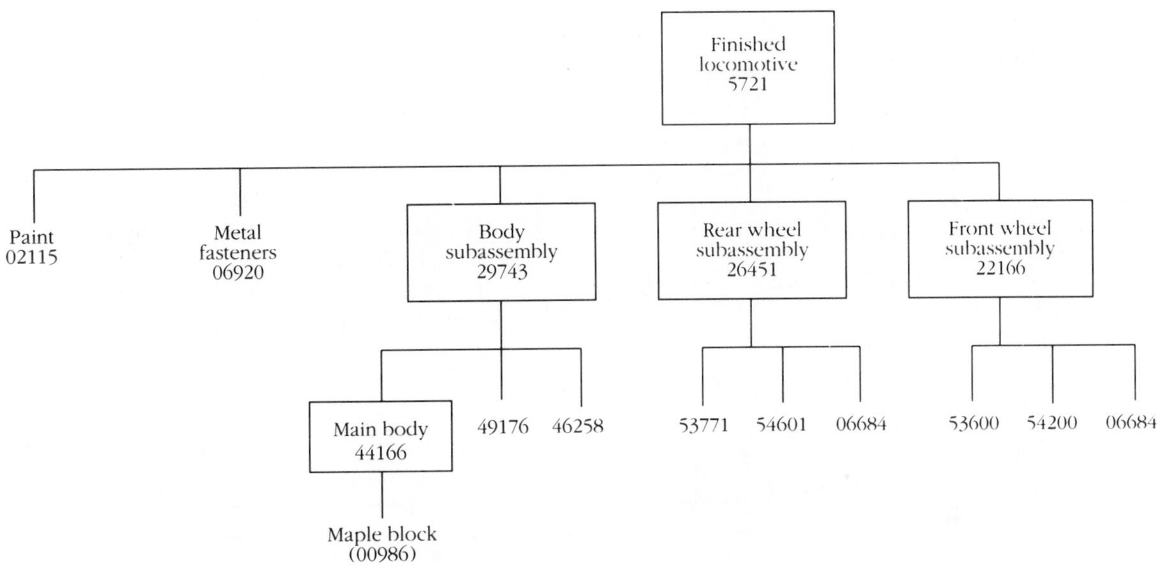

ing would prepare such a BOM when the product is designed. The product structure to the right of the BOM shows how the locomotive is to be assembled. It indicates which parts require processing and assembly and which parts are to be purchased. In this example, a box around a part or subassembly indicates in-house production.

Once the requirements are determined, inventory [5] that has not been committed to production is deducted from the part requirements, and the net requirements are determined. Orders for the parts to be purchased [6] and the parts to be manufactured are determined. Exhibit 19.10 shows an example of the information contained in the inventory file, and Exhibit 19.11 shows a sample purchase order. An order was placed for 2,500 maple blocks, rather than 3,000, because the inventory file shows 500 blocks available for production.

At this point, production has not actually taken place, nor has a firm schedule been made. In this example, today's date is October 15, and the black old-time locomotive (product number 5721) does not appear in the production plan until November 24–28. Actual production for the third week in October was planned several weeks ago.

Exhibit 19.10 Inventory File (Raw Material, Work in Process, Finished Goods, and Tools and Supplies)

Raw Materials

Part Number	Quantity	Description
00986	500	Block of maple 12" x 4" x 3"
06920	10,000	Metal fastener to hold subassembly to body
06684	50,000	Metal staple
.	.	.
.	.	.
.	.	.

Work in Process

Part Number	Quantity	Description
47121	100	Main body of standard locomotive
26068	500	Body subassembly for standard locomotive (unpainted)
29844	1,000	Body subassembly for standard locomotive (painted)
26451	100	Real wheel subassembly
.	.	.
.	.	.
.	.	.

Preparing Equipment

It is essential that equipment availability [7] be considered when preparing a production plan. It is unreasonable to prepare a plan that cannot be carried out because of insufficient capacity. For example, during the last week in November, Lima Locomotive Works is not able to produce the 1,000 locomotives (product number 5424) and 2,500 of the 5,000 locomotives (product number 5629) ordered by Gamble for a December 1 delivery (see Exhibits 19.7 and 19.8). Production of these locomotives had to be shifted to the third week in November to fit within the capacity constraint of the facility, which is approximately 9,000 units per week.

Tool Availability

Preparing equipment also incudes planning for any special tool requirements [8]. Just as orders for component parts are made, stocks of tools and fixtures need to be checked and orders generated as needed. Tools should be repaired or otherwise prepared in advance to avoid unnecessary delays.

An information system can help answer many questions. For example, the people responsible for preparing equipment might ask: Where is the tool located

Exhibit 19.10 continuing

Finished Goods

Part Number	Quantity	Description
5629	500	Green standard locomotive (oak)
8321	800	Red old-time locomotive (oak)
.	.	.
.	.	.
.	.	.

Tools and Fixtures

Part Number	Quantity	Description
T4321	12	Band-saw blade
T5693	7	Router bit
F6341	5	Paint fixture for old-time locomotive
F2149	6	Paint fixture for standard locomotive
.	.	.
.	.	.
.	.	.

Exhibit 19.11 Purchase Order

To:
Lima Locomotive Works
509 North Elizabeth
Lima, Oregon

To:
Beck Block Corp.
301 W. Third Street
Delphos, Montana

Purchase Order #12793

Quantity	Product Number	Description	Unit Cost	Total
2,500	76824*	Maple block 12" x 4" x 3"	$1.50	$3,750.00

*The part number here would be Beck Block's number, which will not be the same part number used by Lima Locomotive (00986 is Lima Locomotive's number).

within the facility? What is its present status: ready, needs minor repair, needs to be sent outside for complete rework? How long before the tool will be ready for production?

Maintenance and Equipment Uptime

Preparing equipment and making production plans require that an accurate maintenance history and estimates of equipment uptime [9] be kept. The proper maintenance of equipment is essential to smooth running operations. Estimates of equipment uptime are needed to determine available capacity. If equipment is expected to be unavailable 5 percent of the time, this needs to be known.

Scheduling Production

Production scheduling [10] was defined earlier in the text as determining who will make the products and which materials and equipment will be used. The important points here are how decision makers (schedulers, in this case) get the information to help them make the decision and how they transfer the schedule to all relevant parts of the operation.

In addition, information about labor availability [11] and routings [12] is required. Labor includes both the people directly involved in production activities (direct labor) and the support personnel. The material-handling function, maintenance, and the tool shop need to be staffed for the desired level of production.

Routings define the machines or processes that materials pass through in order to make a product. Several machines must work on the locomotive before the 12" × 4" × 3" block of wood can be turned into a finished product. The steps in that process define the routes. A scheduler must know the routes before a successful schedule can be prepared.

A sample schedule for assembly is shown in Exhibit 19.12. After the schedule is determined for all operations, the information must be transferred to several

Exhibit 19.12 Production Schedule for Assembly, October 17

```
First Shift: Wayne Wade   First Assembly Station
             Al Friemoth  Second Assembly Station
```

First Station		
Product	Quantity	
5721	250	See bill of materials for required parts
5424	250	See bill of materials for required parts

Second Station		
Product	Quantity	
5424	500	See bill of materials for required parts

departments. The following list illustrates how the release of a schedule affects the information available and the decisions made:

1. The status of a customer's order changes from waiting to be scheduled to scheduled. When the customer calls to inquire, a quick check of the customer open-order file will give the date the order is scheduled for production.
2. A list of who will work, their hours, and their assignments needs to be posted so people know when and where they are expected to work.
3. Materials needed to begin the process are either released from raw-material inventory or arrive just-in-time. The timely arrival of materials is aided by working closely with suppliers to ensure that deliveries will be made consistently. Lima Locomotive should share its production schedules with its suppliers.
4. Any adjustments or changes to equipment are communicated with the department responsible for machine preparation. Needed machine setups are planned ahead of time, based on the production schedule.
5. Department supervisors in woodworking, assembly, and painting should have the schedule so they can work to meet it.

Now the schedule is ready to be executed. Systems are developed to control the execution of the schedule and to report the results of actual operations, which may be substantially different from the schedule.

Controlling the Shop Floor

Shop floor controls [13] can be viewed as having two major parts. First, many decisions must be made regarding the details of actually making the product, and much information must be passed around the shop floor to help make those decisions. Second, it is necessary to report the actual performance results.

Decision Making on the Shop Floor

Decisions to deviate from the schedule often have to be made on the shop floor because of unexpected problems. For example, some of the following situations could arise for Lima Locomotive:

1. The woodworking department has completed one batch of bodies for an order. If assembly cannot keep pace, there is very little logic in continuing to make train bodies until the assembly department can catch up.
2. Unexpectedly, some of the maple blocks used in making the bodies are rejected because of poor surface quality. Should the blocks be reworked? Should the blocks be sent back to the supplier? If so, should production shift to a different order, or should oak, which is more expensive than maple, be used instead? Managers require information to choose one of the options.
3. One of the band saws breaks down. Will production be slowed until it is fixed? Is there a backup band saw that can be used? Can the band saw cuts be done on a different machine? What will the impact on production be if the band saw is out of operation for one day or two days?
4. The woodworking department is nearly finished with the wood pulled from stock this morning and needs more. How much should be pulled? Where is

the inventory stored? Which stock should be pulled? Lima Locomotive wants to use the older inventory first.

The list above describes only a few of the situations that might occur on the shop floor. Some of the questions that arise are straightforward and easy to answer. Others require more time and thought.

Gathering Performance Data

Operations managers need to gather actual performance data on production so that they can evaluate performance. These performance data can be grouped into several categories.

1. Production volume [14]: The actual amount produced for each product is collected. This amount will be compared with planned production volume. The comparison of actual and planned production will be described later in this chapter.
2. Costs [15]: The amount of labor, material, and machine time consumed in making the products is collected so that actual costs can be compared with budgeted costs.
3. Quality [16]: Information about product quality is collected so that probable causes of any defects can be identified and investigated. It is necessary to find the causes of quality defects and fix them at the source to have a real solution to a quality problem.
4. Inventory [17]: Inventory status is updated. Raw materials are depleted to reflect consumption and increased to reflect incoming materials. Changes in work-in-process and finished-goods inventory are made accordingly.
5. Customer order status [18]: The customer order file is changed to indicate that an order has been completed and is being held in finished-goods inventory or has been shipped to the customer.
6. Maintenance and reliability [19]: Maintenance performed on equipment, as well as machine failures, is noted so that a history can be built. This will be useful in planning future operations and in taking actions to prevent recurrences.

Most of the information gathered in the steps above is fed back to management to improve operations. Information about actual production volumes, costs, quality, inventory, customer satisfaction, and equipment is used to determine why problems occurred and to make better decisions in the future.

The Role of Bar Coding in Material Control

Some information system designs put computer terminals in the hands of the equipment operators or supervisors, allowing them quick access to information regarding materials, equipment status, customer orders, and so on. Information systems also allow for the quick and easy collection of data. In many cases, data are automatically gathered by devices that monitor the operations and store the results in the computer.

Increasingly, customers are requesting or requiring that parts they accept for delivery have a bar-coded label attached. This label contains such information as the part number, the quantity shipped, and the supplier's name. Upon receiving the shipment, the customer can read the bar codes with a scanning device and enter that data directly into the computer-based information system, thus eliminating delays and errors in entering the data. A unique identification number should be on the label to avoid entering the same set of parts twice.The bar-coded label remains on the container of parts until these parts are used in production.

The bar codes attached to finished goods provide an important way to track these goods until they are delivered to the customer. If the supplier uses bar-coded labels for parts produced internally, the tracking of work-in-process inventory can also be fast and easy. If the supplier's incoming parts arrive with bar-coded labels, then the supplier can track parts from the beginning to the end of the production process.

Bar Coding Applied to Lima Locomotive. To illustrate the application of bar coding, consider the Lima Locomotive example shown in Exhibit 19.13. Our discussion will start with Lima's customers and work back to its suppliers. Lima

Exhibit 19.13 Applying Bar-Coded Labels in Lima Locomotive Works' Production Process

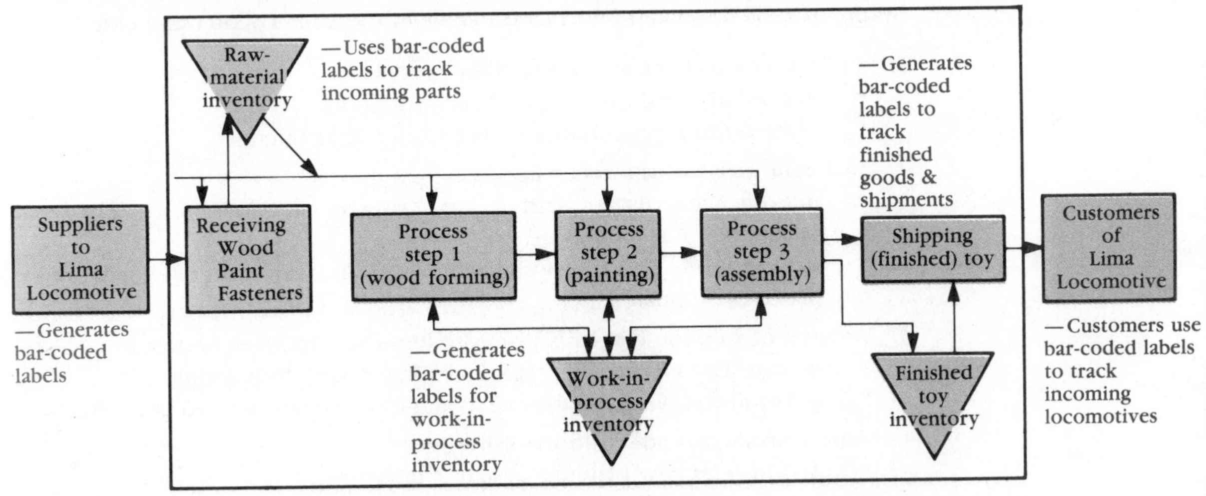

Locomotive's customers use the bar-coded labels printed by Lima Locomotive to track incoming locomotives. Lima Locomotive, in turn, uses the bar-coded labels to track its finished-goods inventory (locomotives).

If partially finished locomotives are stored as work-in-process inventory, then bar-coded labels should be generated to track them. If the locomotives move through the production line without delay, which is preferred, then bar-coded labels are not needed because the locomotives are in transition for a very short time.

If Lima Locomotive's suppliers generate bar-coded labels for incoming materials, such as paint, staples, and wood, then Lima can use these labels to track materials. With this link, Lima Locomotive can track material from the beginning to the end of its production.

Bar Coding and Just-in-Time. Can bar-coded labels and just-in-time (JIT), with its kanban cards, work together? The answer is yes. Visualize the Lima Locomotive example running with JIT production. The kanban ticket is the internal device for moving materials quickly from incoming parts to finished products ready for delivery. Bar-coded labels may not be used until the locomotives are boxed and ready for shipment to customers. At that point, bar-coded labels can be printed and attached to the shipping containers. Incoming parts to Lima Locomotive could also have bar codes that allow them to be tracked until used. This approach is becoming common in the automotive industry, as auto makers are going to JIT production and requiring bar-coded labels on incoming parts.

Summary

At the beginning of this section, we stated that managers should be capable of coordinating the physical flow of materials through the facility with the flow of information required to monitor their progress. Exhibit 19.5 showed the physical flow of materials for Lima Locomotive, and Exhibit 19.6 showed the information flows. These flows must be integrated if Lima Locomotive is to be successful.

The following list describes a few situations that require coordination between material flows and information flows in the Lima Locomotive case:

1. Orders for products are released for production.
   - *Action:* Materials are released for production.
   - *Information:* Schedules are sent to the departments.
2. Materials arrive at the receiving area.
   - *Action:* Materials are sent to raw-material inventory or travel to the production line as needed.
   - *Information:* The appropriate inventory file, raw materials or work-in-process, is updated.
3. A batch of wooden blocks is processed into locomotives bodies.
   - *Action:* The locomotive bodies are transferred to painting.
   - *Information:* Order status, cost, and quality statistics are updated.
4. A new product is added to the sales line.
   - *Action:* The new product design is developed.
   - *Information:* The BOM and routing of parts are developed.

5. A customer order for a product that is in stock is received.
   - *Action:* The product is shipped from finished-goods inventory.
   - *Information:* The customer open-order file and finished-goods inventory file are updated.

The preceding list of situations is obviously not exhaustive, nor do the action and information examples fully describe the situations. Nevertheless, these situations illustrate the importance of an organized information system to monitor and control operations and to measure performance.

DESIGNING INTEGRATED COMPUTER SYSTEMS FOR EQUIPMENT CONTROL

We have already discussed systems for coordinating and monitoring materials. Another function of an information system is equipment control. In an integrated production environment, the equipment may be controlled by computers. In such an environment, computers control the process at several levels, as illustrated in Exhibit 19.14.

Programmable Controllers

At the lowest level of a computerized integrated production system, programmable controllers manage the actions of machines. On a drill press, for example, a controller can dictate the speed of the rotating drill bit and the force applied to the object being drilled. A **programmable controller** can remember instructions (the program) and transfer those instructions to the machine.

Exhibit 19.14 Computer System for Equipment Control

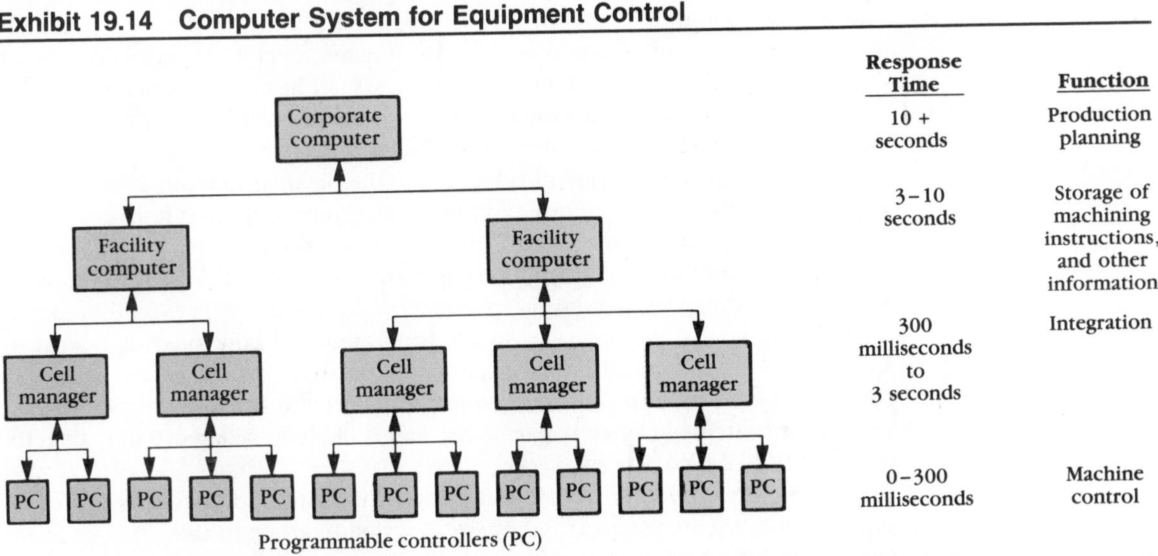

Programmable controllers and robots serve different functions. For a milling machine, the robot and the robot's microprocessor provide the brawn and the brains for tending a machine (loading and unloading it). But the robot does not operate the milling machine in the sense of giving it instructions. Instead, a programmable controller is dedicated to that task. It can control the speed at which the machine runs and the feed rate of the part being milled. To operate efficiently, a milling machine requires large amounts of data and almost instantaneous response time. Such quick responses cannot be provided by the corporate or facility computers. These computers have many other duties that make them unsuitable for machine tending. Thus, a dedicated programmable controller serves this purpose.

Cell Managers

Because most facilities require more than one or two machines to make products, most facilities have several programmable controllers. For efficient operation, these controllers need to be integrated. If a drill press and a milling machine are required to complete a certain operation, information must be transferred between the two steps. Before computer-based automation, people (operators) provided the integration. Without people as machine operators, computers must integrate the various operations. Computers that provide this integration are called **cell managers.**

A cell manager is likely to be a microcomputer or a small minicomputer. It is responsible for integrating the equipment working on the same part or on the same family of parts. The cell manager coordinates material and information flows between machines within the cell. It knows when a machine is idle and when totransfer work from one machine to the next. It also serves as a communications link between the programmable controllers and the facility computer.

The Facility Computer

The facility computer, sometimes called the facility host, is likely to be a large microcomputer or minicomputer that coordinates several cell managers. In addition to coordination, the facility computer, which has a large storage capacity, is likely to be used to hold information that the smaller cell manager and the even smaller programmable controller do not have room for.

This information is downloaded from the facility computer as needed. **Downloading** is moving information from one computer, usually larger in size, to another computer. For example, the instructions needed by the milling machine for parts not presently being produced may reside on the facility computer. When one of those parts goes into production, the instructions would be downloaded through the cell manager to the programmable controller. A typical response time for downloading is three to ten seconds, which is acceptable for switching between parts, but unreasonable for direct machine control. The tool change for switching from one part to another is likely to take more time than the downloading of instructions.

The facility computer has other functions in addition to its role as part of the equipment control system. The system described earlier in this chapter in the section on information systems for coordinating and monitoring material flows would be most likely to use the facility computer. The accounting system could use this computer as well.

The Corporate Computer

The corporate computer, probably a mainframe, serves many purposes. Its role in integrating operations is to download information to the facility computer. These interactions do not occur frequently and may include sales and marketing information to be used in preparing production plans.

Information is not always transferred from top to bottom. Typically, detailed performance data are collected at the lowest level and then transferred to the next level. The data are summarized and passed up the information chain. The people at corporate headquarters are not interested in how long it took to make one part but may be interested in the production rate achieved during the week.

Networking

The linkage of programmable controllers, cell managers, facility computers, and the corporate computer is referred to as a network. **Networking** is linking together one or more computer devices so they can transfer data. This transfer occurs quickly, and communications through a network are said to take place in "real time."

The specific type of network described here is a local area network. A **local area network (LAN)** connects devices within a restricted area, often the same building. The best-known network is Ethernet, which has been successfully used to build the kind of LAN described here. The application of LANs to facility

OPERATIONS IN ACTION

AT&T: Building a Digital Switching Center with a Computer-Controlled Factory

At its Oklahoma City factory, AT&T is building all of the company's digital switching centers and all of its computers except the personal computers. No two of the switching centers are alike. Digital switching centers are used in universities, large companies, or any installation that has its own telephone system and more than about 1,000 phone lines. They enable the rapid transfer of calls within the organization and between the organization and the telephone system in total.

At AT&T, the production lines have unmanned work stations, with robots and other flexible automation equipment performing the work. There is extensive computer control of all manufacturing, assembly, testing, and reporting activities. Computers control the action of the robots, coordinate the material flow on the production line, and gather information about the factory's performance. The information system at Oklahoma City is computer-based, and the facility is rapidly moving toward a paperless office.[2]

automation is not yet widespread. However, LANs are becoming increasingly popular, and significant applications in the future appear to be certain.

Computer technology, including both networking concepts and integrated automation systems, can also be applied to service operations. Computer process controls in banking operations and in mail handling and sorting have been implemented successfully for many years.

OFFICE AUTOMATION AND ITS ROLE IN OPERATIONS

Office automation is the application of electronic and electromechanical devices to office procedures for the purpose of increasing productivity. Office automation includes storage and manipulation of data as well as communications

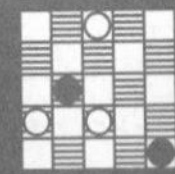

GAINING STRATEGIC ADVANTAGE WITH NETWORKS

Networking Boosts Productivity, Once the Problems Are Overcome

Organizations engaged in serving travelers, providing health care, and manufacturing goods are realizing that computer networks can be an important tool for increasing productivity and managing information. The Westin St. Francis Hotel in San Francisco has obtained 33 percent more work from its word-processing department since it installed a network. Work flows more smoothly within the department, and fewer mistakes are made.

After overcoming hardware, software, and organization problems, Johns Hopkins Hospital in Baltimore, Maryland, has successfully implemented an Ethernet network. The hospital staff started with computers made by four different manufacturers, including IBM and DEC, and four different operating systems. In addition to different hardware and software, each department had its own differently designed data base. In order for each department to access and work with a centralized data base, the hardware had to be linked, the different operating systems had to be made to communicate, and the departments had to agree on a design for a central data base.

The major advantages of Johns Hopkins' implementation of the network are more accurate records and improved productivity. Before there was a centralized data base and access through the network, departmental data bases did not agree, and some information had to be entered several times in several different departmental data bases. Now, most information is entered only once and updated as needed.

A Midwest parts manufacturer for the automotive industry has successfully linked machines, programmable controllers, and cell managers to the facility's computer using Ethernet. Each day, the facility's computer receives updated sales requirements directly from the corporate computer system. The benefits of the network have been reduced direct labor, fewer middle managers and supervisors, and better control of inventory and shipments.

Several problems must be overcome in developing networks. Simple problems like installation of the wrong wire, insufficient employee training, and faulty software can frustrate managers and delay implementation. In spite of these problems, customers are being drawn to networks at an accelerated pace.[3]

capabilities. The electronic office typically has word-processing capabilities, electronic mail, and electronic calendars. In addition, it may include such features as video mail, audioconferencing, and videoconferencing.

In an integrated information system, the office automation system is linked to the data bases that contain the information about material flows. With this direct link, reports on operations can be prepared electronically and sent electronically to people within the facility or at corporate headquarters. It is also possible to access information about machine uptime from the systems for monitoring equipment. Office automation is not an information-creating function. It is a tool for organizing information that already exists.

MEETING PRODUCTION TARGETS

Earlier in the text, we defined effectiveness as getting a job done and efficiency as doing the job while consuming a reasonable level of resources. In this section, we consider the development of ways to evaluate effectiveness.

Meeting production targets is a relatively simple concept to understand. The number of units scheduled for production merely needs to be compared with the number of units actually produced. This comparison can be made over any time period—a year, a month, a week, a day, an hour—and for any department, plant, or group of plants. Comparisons can be made for one product or for several products. The operating budget for the time period in question would show the planned production.

We will use the example of Miser Brake Shop to clarify our discussion of meeting production targets. Miser's activity report for August is shown below.

Service	Actual Production	Planned Production	Variance
Brake jobs	36	44	−8
Mufflers	220	200	20
Shock absorbers	88	120	−32
Tune-ups	128	140	−12

The report shows that, in August, Miser had unfavorable variances (the negative figures) for three services, which means that the actual production was less than the planned or budgeted production. The **variance** is the difference between the actual and the planned (budgeted) amounts. The concept of a variance can be applied to anything that can be planned, including costs and sales.

Variance analysis is a retrospective analysis of performance to help determine the causes for the differences. Let's consider the negative variance for brake jobs to see how it might have occurred.

1. Competitors ran specials on brakes during the month, and several customers canceled their appointments with Miser. This can be verified from the appointment log. Management should examine its price for this service.
2. During the third week of the month, two key employees were absent due to illness, and several customers could not be served. Management should look at training that would allow more people to do brake work.

3. No brake appointments were scheduled for three days because the shop manager thought that the brake technicians would be on vacation. As a result, the brake technicians had to do lower-profit muffler work.
4. The equipment used for doing brake work malfunctioned, and repairs took two days, causing the cancellation of several appointments.

A variance does not tell management which of these alternatives or combination of alternatives explains the difference. It simply gives a clue about where to begin looking.

For variance analysis to be useful, an information system needs to be developed to capture both the actual work and the planned work. The actual volume is part of the data collected by the shop floor control system. The planned volume can be obtained from the production plan, discussed earlier in this chapter.

ACCOUNTING INFORMATION SYSTEMS AND COST CONTROL

In addition to having flexible operations that produce a variety of high-quality products to meet specific customer needs and delivering those products in a timely manner, an organization must have a system to gather information about product cost and disseminate that information for the purpose of cost control. In most organizations, management accountants, information system professionals, and operations managers work together to develop such a system.

Example

Metro Maid is a residential house-cleaning service. The company hires mostly part-time employees. For a fixed fee per home, Metro Maid will provide an agreed-on cleaning service on a weekly or biweekly basis. The fee and the contracted service are set by the company owners who visit each home, write the contract, and bid the job. Metro Maid provides all the equipment (sweepers, buckets, mops, etc.) and all the cleaning supplies. The company's annual sales have increased from $1.5 million to $1.9 million, yet profits have declined from $85,000 to $50,000.

The owners are finding it difficult to understand the reasons for the declining profits during this period of growth. They have decided to design a system to gather information needed to track costs. Management has compiled the following list of questions that should be addressed:

1. How long should it take to mop 100 square feet of kitchen floor? The idea of setting a standard time for a task was discussed in Chapter 9 on job design and work measurement. If the standard time is not set correctly, the job may be bid too low or too high because the standard time is multiplied by the hourly wage rate to get the estimated cost.
2. How much actual time is being consumed? If the actual time exceeds the standard, then actual costs will exceed standard or budgeted costs, causing the organization to lose money. The actual time could be greater than the standard time because the worker was not properly trained, the standard time was not accurately estimated, or the worker is not putting forth enough effort.

3. Is the equipment being replaced more frequently than accounted for in the bid? Have equipment repair costs exceeded expectation? Has the work force been properly trained in using the equipment?
4. Are the supplies, such a floor waxes and cleansers, being used as expected in the bid?

The owners of Metro Maid can develop an information system that collects data on equipment repair expenses, equipment replacement costs, time spent on each job, supplies consumed, and other costs. These can be compared to the bid or budgeted costs of operations to give the owners some insights into how the organization's resources are being consumed.

In operations, the concept of a responsibility center can be used to monitor and control costs. The Metro Maid example illustrates some of the questions that can arise in controlling costs. The following steps are necessary to develop a cost control system:

1. Planning
2. Budgeting
3. Actual operations and data collection
4. Analysis and reporting

This system begins when the production plans are prepared. Typical questions to be answered include these: How does the organization propose to allocate its resources over the next year or longer? Will one product line be dropped and another take its place? How will dollars be invested to upgrade facilities?

An **operating budget** is a plan expressed in quantitative terms that covers a specific period of time, usually one year. In the budget process, each plan is translated into specific terms that relate to the appropriate responsibility center.

During actual operations, the shop floor control system, which was described earlier in this chapter, would collect data on labor costs, material, and overhead

INTEGRATING THE SYSTEM

Establishing Responsibility Centers

Management accountants have developed a concept called responsibility centers for tracking organizational performance. A **responsibility center** is a part or subsystem of the organization that is responsible for and contributes to performance. For example, a hospital may treat its emergency room or X-ray department as a responsibility center. Both incur revenue and costs. By tracking revenue and costs for each center, management can determine whether each department is operating profitably. Furthermore, if management knows the investment in facilities and equipment for each department, it can calculate a return on investment for that business unit. By pinpointing problems and developing solutions, management can make decisions that improve an organization's performance.

so these costs can be traced to the appropriate account. Labor costs and material costs would be tracked separately. The plant could be subdivided into responsibility centers.

Analyzing the results involves the comparison of actual to budgeted expenses. It requires the communication of the results to the responsible manager in a way that motivates improved performance. Managers need to maintain efficiency, high product quality, short delivery lead times, and flexible systems for meeting the increasing demand for a greater variety of products.

Activity Accounting for Estimating Product Cost

Many faculty members in business schools and practicing managers are concerned about the accuracy of cost accounting data provided by traditional cost accounting systems. In the traditional approach, full production costs are assigned to each product by measuring and assigning the variable labor and material costs, plus allocating a share of the overhead cost. The amount of overhead allocated to a product is often based on direct labor hours.

Because of productivity improvements and investments in automated equipment, direct labor hours in many organizations have declined. In some cases, the direct labor hour per unit produced is zero. As direct labor hours shrink, the accuracy of allocating overhead based on labor hours is more and more difficult to accept. Some have suggested that because automation is increasing, allocating overhead based on the machine hours used by a product is a logical alternative. Many companies are now recognizing that the increase in overhead is not caused solely or even substantially by the rise in depreciation charges on the new equipment. Other factors, such as product variety, are causing overhead to increase.

One approach that is being used is activity accounting. **Activity accounting** collects financial and operating data and allocates costs based on the nature and the extent of business activities. Activity accounting focuses on assigning costs to a product based on the activities performed to produce, distribute, or support it. Costs are assigned to activity centers and to products using a cost driver. A **cost driver** is an action or condition that directly influences and creates costs. For example, the number of setups required is one cost driver, and the number of parts produced is another.

In a traditional accounting system, a single cost driver, such as direct labor, is used. In an activity accounting system, multiple cost drivers are used. Within the same organization, different products may have different sets of cost drivers. In this way, overhead allocations more accurately reflect the way costs are actually incurred.

USING INFORMATION SYSTEMS FOR COMPETITIVE ADVANTAGE

Information systems are critical to organizational success because an organization's performance is a direct result of the decisions its people make. Decision making is a direct result of the information available, so an organization that has better information is in a position to outperform its competitors.

Many organizations are using information systems for competitive advantage. For example, the SABRE computer-based reservation system developed by American Airlines has given the company an advantage over other airlines in booking flights and attracting customers. Black and Decker's production planning and control system, which blends MRP II with just-in-time, has given it an edge over foreign and domestic competition.

The use of information systems to gain competitive advantage in service operations has grown dramatically. The Inventory Location Service allows air carriers to specify the parts needed for repairing and servicing planes. The system has a data base of suppliers, and the system automatically generates a request-for-quotation letter to potential suppliers. Brokers have developed software that matches people seeking mortgages with mortgage-granting institutions. The software analyzes the buyer's credit rating and gives conditional approval.

SUMMARY

- Information is data that have been gathered, classified, organized, and analyzed in a way that makes them useful for decision making.
- The objective of an information system is to help people make better decisions.
- Managers need the right information at a reasonable cost. Managers should compare the cost of gathering information with the benefits of using it.
- The information requirements in managing operations are extensive. Information is needed for making design, planning, and operating decisions.
- Information systems for coordinating and monitoring material flows require information on managing customer orders, transmitting production plans, managing material procurement systems, transmitting information for preparing equipment, and transmitting production schedules.
- Performance information needs to be collected and fed back to managers to evaluate performance.
- Computer systems that control production equipment can have multiple levels of control. These systems include programmable controllers, cell managers, facility computers, and corporate computers. This hierarchical system allows information to be passed from level to level using networking.
- Accounting systems can be used to gather data that assist managers in cost control.

CAREER PROFILE

John F. Joslin

Executive Vice-President, Administrative Sector
Society Bank and Trust

John F. Joslin is the executive vice-president of the Administrative Sector and reports directly to the chairman, president, and chief executive officer of Society

Bank and Trust, Frederick A. Deal. Society Bank and Trust resulted from the merger of Trustcorp Bank, Ohio, which was formerly Toledo Trust, and Society Corporation on January 5, 1990. In his present position, Joslin is responsible for the areas of legal services, human resources, controllership, information services, operations, facilities, security, and purchasing.

Education and Experience

Before beginning his career at Toledo Trust Company, Joslin earned a bachelor's degree in art with a major in history, served in the U.S. Navy, and earned an M.B.A. He began his career at Toledo Trust as a commercial credit analyst in 1975, quickly rising to be manager of corporate services, operations, and administration. In 1984, he became the vice-president of bank services, which included loan and credit card operations; trust operations; checking, savings, IRA, and certificate of deposit operations; check processing; and corporate services, which included sales and operations, cash management products, data-processing services, and automated clearinghouse functions.

SOLVED PROBLEMS

1. Steinway Publishing is trying to decide whether a new textbook will be successful in the market. The company's contribution (selling price − unit variable cost) on each text is $8.00, and the fixed costs are $190,000. After sending the textbook to outside reviewers and the company's editorial staff, the acquisition editor makes the following assessment. (If the book sells well, it will be revised in three years. If not, it will be dropped.)

Event	Probability	Three Years of Sales
Very successful	.3	50,000 books
Successful	.5	36,000 books
Moderately successful	.15	24,000 books
Flop	.05	10,000 books

a. What are the contributions for each event?

Solution

Very successful	(50,000 books) ($8.00/book) =	$400,000
Successful	(36,000 books) ($8.00/book) =	288,000
Moderately successful	(24,000 books) ($8.00/book) =	192,000
Flop	(10,000 books) ($8.00/book) =	80,000

b. Draw a decision tree, and label each event.

Solution

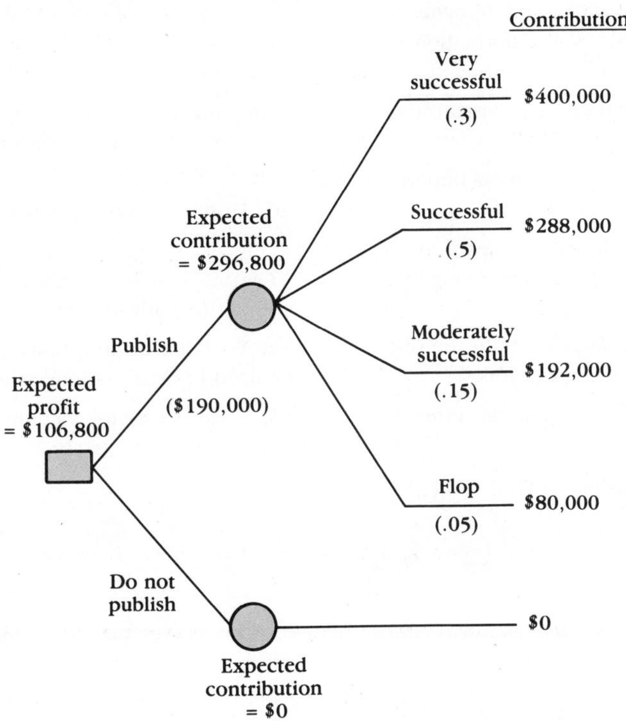

c. What are the expected values of the book's contribution and profit?

Solution

$$\text{Expected value contribution} = .3(400{,}000) + .5(288{,}000) + .15(192{,}000) + .05(80{,}000)$$

$$= \$296{,}800$$

$$\text{Expected value of profit} = \$296{,}800 - \$190{,}000$$

$$= \$106{,}800$$

d. Based on this analysis, which alternative would you recommend?

Solution

Because Steinway makes these decisions many times, it is appropriate for the company to make the decision based on the expected value of profit. We would recommend that Steinway publish the book because of its strong profit potential.

QUESTIONS

1. Define the terms *information* and *information system*. What is the objective of an information system?

2. Why is information important to an organization? Give some examples.

3. Explain how managers can deal with imperfect information.

4. Summarize the information requirements for designing, planning, and managing and controlling operations.

5. Why is it important to coordinate both the physical flow of material and the information flow?

6. Provide an overview of the information system for controlling material flows.

7. Why is it important to gather performance data? How can these data be used?

8. Describe the role of bar coding in material control.

9. Describe a typical computer system for equipment control. Explain why these systems are necessary as people are replaced with robots and programmable controllers.

10. How can office automation play a role in operations?

11. How can information systems be used to gain competitive advantage?

12. What are responsibility centers, and how can they be used in organizations to control costs?

13. What is activity accounting?

PROBLEMS

1. Pfizer Pharmaceutical is trying to estimate the profit potential for a new drug that the company would like to put on the market. Sales have been estimated for the new product called percodine.

Event	Probability	Estimated Sales (Units per Year)
High demand	.4	2,000,000
Moderate demand	.3	1,250,000
Low demand	.3	500,000

a. If the contribution per unit is $.60, what is the total contribution Pfizer is expected to make in the first year?
b. If sales in the second year equal first-year sales, what is the total contribution Pfizer would be expected to make over the two-year period?
c. If second-year sales increase over first-year sales by 10 percent and the unit contribution increases by $.10, what is the total contribution Pfizer would be expected to make over the two-year period?

2. Hicksville Memorial is trying to decide whether or not the hospital should open a center for sleep therapy. The hospital will charge $400 per person for treatment sessions lasting ten weeks. The hospital's variable costs are $75 per attendee. The annual fixed costs are $200,000. After a marketing study of the area, management has made the following estimates:

Event	Probability	Number of People Served per Year
High usage	.15	1,000
Moderate usage	.6	700
Low usage	.25	450

a. What are the profits for each event?
b. Draw a decision tree that represents the decision.
c. What would you recommend to the hospital?

3. Long Island, New York, is considering investing in a new tourist attraction. The annual fixed costs of the attraction are $8,850,000. The admission fee is $4.00 per person, and the variable costs are practically zero. Market Research, Inc., has recently studied the viability of this unusual attraction and has predicted the following results:

Event	Probability	Number of People Served
Extremely successful	.1	3,400,000
Very successful	.2	3,000,000
Successful	.5	2,700,000
Moderately successful	.15	2,500,000
Failure	.05	1,800,000

a. Should Long Island invest in the new attraction?
b. List some of the assumptions of the model.

4. Trumble Travel Agency is trying to organize a series of Caribbean cruises. The travel agency is uncer-

tain as to the size of ship that it should lease. Management is considering 1,000-, 700-, 400-, and 200-passenger ships.

Ship Size	Profit ($/Passenger)	Cost ($/Unused Capacity)
1,000	200	80
700	180	75
400	150	70
200	120	65

The ship can make thirty trips per season, and the lease is for only one year. The distribution of demand is given here.

Demand (Passengers)	Probability
1,000	.1
800	.4
700	.2
600	.2
500	.1

a. To maximize its profit, which size ship should Trumble lease for next year?

b. Would there be an advantage to leasing two smaller ships?

MINI-CASES

Kalida Cooperative

Kalida Cooperative produces electricity for farms and small rural communities. It is trying to decide whether or not to invest in another natural gas-fired boiler and another steam-driven turbine. The total investment would be $20 million. Increasing demand has forced the cooperative to purchase more electricity from neighboring utilities. This electricity costs more than the electricity generated by the cooperative.

Recently, demand by the cooperative's members has grown at 3 percent per year, which is far above the national average. The cooperative attributes this increase in demand to the number of people moving from urban to rural areas. Kalida will satisfy future demand even if it continues to purchase electricity from external sources. Following is the cooperative's estimate of demand for the next five years:

Demand Growth per Year for Year 1 Only	Demand Growth per Year for Years 2–5	Probability
1%	1.5%	.05
2	2.0	.2
3	3.0	.45
4	3.5	.2
5	4.0	.1

To interpret this table, assume that when demand in the first year is 1 percent, it is followed by a demand in years 2–5 of 1.5 percent, and so on. In statistical terms, the probability that demand in years 2–5 is 1.5 percent, given that demand in year 1 is 1 percent, is 1.0.

Presently, the cooperative has the capacity to generate 75 percent of its annual demand, which is 200 million kilowatt-hours. The present cost of cooperative-generated electricity is $.063 per kilowatt-hour. The cost of each kilowatt-hour purchased outside is $.085. The new unit would increase the capacity of the cooperative by 100 million kilowatt-hours per year.

1. What are the decision alternatives?

2. Draw a decision tree that lays out the decision alternatives and the possible events.

3. For each different projected growth rate, calculate the expected savings from generating electricity internally rather than purchasing. Do this for a five-year time period.

4. Would you recommend investing in the extra capacity based on the savings over the five-year period?

5. Assuming that the growth in demand for electricity in years 2 through 5 continues far into the future, would this be a good investment?

6. List the assumptions you have made in calculating the expected savings. How do those assumptions affect the analysis and your decision?

Clyde's Cameras

Clyde's Cameras fabricates the components for and assembles a complete line of cameras for professional photographers at its Mexico City plant. Carla Clyde, the owner and manager of the company, has been concerned for some time about the efficiency of her plant and the overall quality of the finished products. Recently, competition from producers in the Far East has cut into the company's profit margin.

Two years ago, the company invested in a computer system, similar to the one described in Exhibit

19.6, to assist management in increasing operating efficiency, reducing lead time for customer orders, and improving product quality. During implementation, several problems developed, so the system was not fully operational until six months ago. With the new system fully functioning, operating efficiency has remained unchanged, lead times have increased, and product quality has declined. Purchased parts are not available when final assembly is scheduled to take place. Tooling for some of the equipment is also not available. The system has not achieved its goals, and Clyde would like to determine why. She has hired you as a consultant to examine the situation and to offer suggestions for improving the system's effectiveness.

1. What portion or portions of the system described in Exhibit 19.6 are most likely to be creating problems for Clyde? Describe why these areas are likely causes.

2. What suggestions might you make to Clyde?

SELECTED BIBLIOGRAPHY

Berliner, Callie, and Brimson, James A. *Cost Management for Today's Advanced Manufacturing*. Boston: Harvard Business School Press, 1988.

Bruns, W. J., Jr., and Kaplan, Robert S., eds. *Accounting and Management: Field Study Perspectives*. Boston: Harvard Business School Press, 1987. pp. 204–228.

Cooper, Robin. "You Need a New Cost System When. . . ." *Harvard Business Review*, 77, no. 1 (January–February 1989): 77–82.

Davis, Gordon B., and Olson, Margrethe H. *Management Information Systems: Conceptual Foundations, Structure, and Development*. New York: McGraw-Hill, 1985.

Essick, Edward L. *Essentials of Computer Data Processing*. Chicago: Science Research Associates, 1984.

Ives, Blake, and Learmonth, Gerard P. "The Information System as a Competitive Weapon." *Communications of the ACM* 27, no. 12 (December 1984): 1193–1201.

Materna, Anthony T. "Local Area Networks in Corporate Planning," *Managerial Planning*, November/December 1984, pp. 32–41.

McGarry, Susan L. "Networking Has a Job to Do in the Factory." *Data Communications*, February 1985, 119–128.

McLeod, Raymond, Jr. *Management Information Systems*. Chicago: Science Research Associates, 1986.

Murdick, Robert G., and Munson, John C. *MIS Concepts and Design*. Englewood Cliffs, N.J.: Prentice-Hall, 1986.

Owens, Thomas, and Edwards, Perry. *Information Processing Today*. Santa Rosa, Calif.: Burgess Communications, 1986.

Rackoff, N.; Wiseman, C.; and Ullrich, W. "Information Systems for Competitive Advantage: Implementation of a Planning Process." *MIS Quarterly* 9, no. 4 (December 1985): 285–294.

Sprague, Ralph H., Jr., and McNurlin, Barbara C. *Information Systems Management in Practice*. Englewood Cliffs, N.J.: Prentice Hall, 1986.

Vollmann, Thomas E. *Manufacturing Planning and Control System*. Homewood, Ill.: Irwin, 1988.

Chapter 20

Future Directions for Operations Management

CHAPTER OUTLINE

LEARNING OBJECTIVES

After completing this chapter, you should be able to

- List the major changes that will be occurring in the field of production/operations management.
- Explain how the global marketplace impacts on operations activities.
- Discuss the effects of unification of the European Economic Community.
- Describe challenges and opportunities resulting from changes in iron curtain countries.
- List and discuss the major areas of increased competition.
- Explain what is meant by a service factory.
- Discuss how computers and automation will be used.
- Describe changes that will occur in information flows.
- Explain some of the changes in work-force management.
- Discuss how companies will be more integrated.
- Explain changes that will occur in quality management.
- Describe some changes that will occur in the management of service operations.

OPERATIONS IN ACTION

Allen-Bradley: Moving CIM into the Corporate Strategy

Allen-Bradley manufactures automation controls—everything from contactors and relays for starting motors to programmable logic controllers (PLCs) for directing the activities of flexible manufacturing systems. One part of A-B's competitive strategy has been to produce the component parts for factory automation. However, trying to sell customers on adopting its ideas for computer-integrated manufacturing was difficult because A-B did not have a working model to demonstrate.

At the same time, Allen-Bradley found that its motor contactors and control relays were not competitive in the world market because of price. After considering the idea of moving production overseas, A-B finally struck on the idea of developing the kind of CIM facility it had been trying to sell its customers on and using that facility to make contactors and relays at low cost.

Using a multidisciplinary team approach, Allen-Bradley simultaneously designed a new product and the facility to produce it. By combining those activities, it took only two years before the new product was being manufactured, instead of the usual seven.

Today, the World Contractor Assembly Facility at Allen-Bradley's headquarters in Milwaukee is a showplace for the company's automation products and concepts. However, it also can produce 125 different product variations at the rate of 600 units per hour with no direct labor. Further, production cost is 60 percent less than for manual assembly. As a result, Allen-Bradley does 25 percent of its business outside North America.[1]

INTRODUCTION

After getting this far in the book, you should be aware that many changes have occurred in the operations management area within the last few years. For those of us in the field of production/operations management, this is very exciting time, but also a difficult one. When MRP was first introduced some thirty years ago, it was a revolutionary idea. But at least we had a long time to evaluate and consider the impact of MRP in the P/OM area before another revolutionary idea came along. That situation has changed. Today, we have many new concepts and techniques (and new acronyms) appearing each year—JIT, CWQC, CIM. These are all complex ideas, and it will be many years before the influence of each is fully evaluated. But in the meantime we are sure that other new ideas and methods will appear on the horizon.

Most of this change is being brought about by the ever-accelerating pace of worldwide competition and by the increasing rate of technological advancement. It used to be that companies generally competed only with other companies in their own country. And each of those companies usually had a reasonable share of the market, with little change from one year to the next. Competition was often based more on marketing strength in a certain region than on price or quality. But that situation has changed as we enter what can truly be called a world marketplace. It was the Europeans first and then the Japanese who stepped up the pace. Today, the Koreans are also coming into the market with low-priced, high-quality products, further increasing the whirlwind of competition.

As that competitive pace increases, companies will search ever more diligently for ways to increase productivity, improve quality, and cut costs. For us, it is extremely exciting to see just how ingenious people can be in finding better ways to produce goods and services. Throughout this book, we have used real examples to indicate how today's companies are changing and improving their operations activities to become more competitive.

But reducing costs and improving quality are not the whole issue. Another shift that we see occurring in the marketplace is an increased rate of change. Totally new products, new designs, and new technologies are constantly being introduced at an ever-increasing pace. To meet these changes, companies must maintain a high level of flexibility; they must be able to quickly change to a new design or a new product—or even change the business they are in.

By the time you read this book, there will probably be new ideas in the P/OM area that did not even exist when we were writing. Of course, we can't know what those will be. However, we would like to peek at the crystal ball for a while and let you know what we think the major trends will be in P/OM as we move into the twenty-first century.

GLOBALIZATION

We are already in a global marketplace. Almost anywhere in the world, it is possible to find products manufactured in other countries. In fact, even services are becoming available internationally. This trend will continue as organizations look for ways to expand their markets and as consumers throughout the world demand greater selection, quality, value, and lower cost from the goods and services they purchase and as they care less about where those products originated.

Planning for Global Operations and Markets

Companies can no longer plan based on a small geographic area. Today, any business—no matter how large or how small—is just as likely to buy its parts and materials from an overseas supplier as from one down the block. Further, even small companies are selling to overseas markets.

This means that strategic plans must be based on a global strategy, not just a local one. Goods and services produced must be designed to meet the needs of a worldwide market in which many different standards and customs prevail. Further, marketing plans must be designed to appeal to consumers in each target market. What works in Indianapolis, Indiana, may not work in Nakajo, Japan.

Unfortunately, many companies that operate in different countries do so on a multinational basis, instead of a global one. In other words, instead of taking a global approach, these companies treat their operations in one country as separate and independent from their operations in other countries. This leads to duplication and inefficiencies.

Companies with facilities throughout the world must also plan their production on a global basis. For example, shifts in demand may mean that a company's factory in Taiwan has excess capacity to meet that area's demand, while one in

France is overloaded in trying to meet European demand. By planning on a global basis, worldwide capacity can be used to meet worldwide demand.

A Single European Market

In 1992, the Single Market program of the European Economic Community (EEC) will go into effect. At that time, much of Western Europe will become like a single country, in terms of trade, as product standards are made uniform, border controls are eased, and customs duties are dropped.

These changes will have a major impact as companies in EEC countries can no longer rely on national trade barriers to protect them from competition. Within the EEC, products will be redesigned for the common market, not just individual countries, and quality standards will be notched up to those of the global marketplace.

The Dropping of the Iron Curtain

In Eastern Europe, dramatic changes will also be occurring as communism is replaced by democratic capitalism. The people in those countries, as East Germany has shown, have a tremendous pent-up demand for Western goods and services. However, the economies of most East European countries are in a shambles, and few of their organizations can compete on a worldwide basis. A major challenge will be to bring the manufacturing and service organizations in Eastern Europe up to the level of worldwide competition. However, this challenge also opens up exciting possibilities for joint ventures and overseas investment.

Increasing Foreign Ownership

At present, half of all companies in Canada have non-Canadian ownership. However, Canada is not alone as, throughout the world, companies and individuals look beyond their own shores for investment opportunities. We expect this continuing trend to produce some significant changes. Probably the most obvious one will be that more managers who can function in an international environment will be needed.

Further, ideas and techniques developed in one country will spread more quickly to others. For example, Kawasaki's use of JIT at its plant in Lincoln, Nebraska, helped spur increased interest in that philosophy within the United States.

However, foreign ownership will also have a negative side as managers within a foreign-owned company find their advancement possibilities limited by their nationality. Companies must find ways to either open international opportunities for advancement or keep managers happy when they can advance no farther.

Increasing Need for Ethical Behavior

Unfortunately, the conduct of business in much of the world still depends on bribes and kickbacks. This situation probably will not change soon, and businesses operating internationally will be faced with ethical dilemmas. To remove any doubt about how a manager should deal with such situations, many companies have adopted policies that prohibit bribes or kickbacks of any kind. Such companies have usually found they can still do business without resorting to such unethical behavior.

As companies come under increased competitive pressure in the world market, managers may be tempted to pursue other types of unethical behavior, such as marketing unsafe products or endangering the safety of employees. Although such actions may work in the short run, they are usually disastrous in the long run. Thus, managers will have to be ever more diligent about maintaining a high level of ethical behavior.

INCREASED COMPETITION

With the worldwide marketplace, we have seen a significant increase in competition and in the standards a company must meet if it is to compete in that marketplace. In fact, the term *world class* is often used when referring to companies that are capable of meeting those standards. We expect the standards for worldwide competition to increase even further, with particular emphasis in the following areas.

Shorter Lead Times

At its World Contactor Assembly Facility in Milwaukee, Allen-Bradley accepts customer orders one day and shops out the finished product the next. While there are still many companies where the lead time from order to finished product is measured in months, such companies will be at an increasing disadvantage. According to recent surveys, the one thing that consumers hate most is having to wait. Increasingly, customers will come to expect goods and services to be delivered with very short lead times.

Increased Flexibility

To meet the customer expectations of short lead times, companies will have to be very flexible. This will mean switching from making one product to making another very quickly. In fact, small batch sizes may become the norm.

Further, customers will expect fast response to their changing needs. Thus, not only must a product be provided quickly, but also a company must be quick to produce a new product to meet those changing needs.

Reduced Costs

Sears ran into trouble when it found that customers no longer bought its products at the regular price, but waited for those items to go on sale. However, even the "everyday low prices" offered by discount stores such as Wal-Mart may not be good enough. In fact, Sam Walton, founder of Wal-Mart, has started Sam's Wholesale Club as one way of offering even lower prices.

Increasingly, customers expect and demand low prices. To compete effectively and stay in business, companies will have to cut costs. For example, Japanese auto manufacturers have been able to avoid significant price increases in the

U. S. market—in spite of significant appreciation of the yen relative to the dollar—by continuing to cut their manufacturing costs.

Service Factories

Richard Chase has introduced the concept of a "service factory"[2]—that is, a factory that in addition to producing a good also provides services for its customers. Chase has proposed four types of service factory:

1. *Laboratory:* experiments with new products and techniques and provides data to customers about product quality, flexibility, etc.
2. *Consultant:* provides technical expertise and assistance for solving customers' problems.
3. *Showroom:* uses the factory to show off a company's products and processes or to demonstrate concepts.
4. *Dispatcher:* provides fast delivery of replacement parts and replenishment of spare parts inventory.

Although no company yet has developed a full-fledged service factory, several are well on the way. For example, Chapparal Steel works closely with customers when problems occur with its products and even undertakes experiments, at its own expense, to find steel formulations that will better meet its customers' needs.

Operations in the Organizational Strategy

Throughout this book, we have emphasized the importance of operations as part of an organization's competitive strategy. We foresee that this will become even more important. In the past, companies developed a competitive strategy and then expected the operations function to join in step with the rest of the organization. However, some companies are beginning to realize that operations must be involved in the development of that strategy from the very beginning.

Furthermore, the organization's strategy must be based on the capabilities of operations. For example, a company with highly automated, high-volume equipment will usually compete best on the basis of price. For such a company, trying to develop a competitive strategy based on product customization will lead to failure unless major investments are made in new plant facilities and equipment.

COMPUTER INTEGRATION AND AUTOMATION

Computer-integrated manufacturing (CIM) is a topic that we have discussed extensively in this book. However, you should realize that as we write, CIM is more a concept than a reality. Very few companies have been able to achieve what could truly be called a successful CIM system. But many companies are moving in that direction—among them, General Motors, Allen-Bradley, General Electric, and Hughes Aircraft. We think this trend will continue as it becomes increasingly important that companies coordinate all parts of the organization.

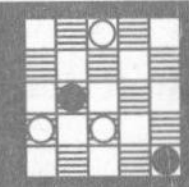

GAINING STRATEGIC ADVANTAGE AT WAL-MART

Providing Service and Low Prices

Most people don't expect to get good service at a discount store. Instead, they are just looking for the product they want at the lowest price. But Wal-Mart competes by providing customers with both what they expect and what they don't expect.

As soon as you walk into a Wal-Mart, you'll know something is different because one of the employees, the "people greeter," will welcome you to Wal-Mart. But this person isn't really an employee; he or she is an "associate," a term applied to everyone who works at Wal-Mart.

But just because Wal-Mart is friendly doesn't mean the company isn't on the ball. Wal-Mart uses technology extensively to track sales trends, replenish inventory, and notify its stores about what is happening. For example, the scanners at checkout counters continuously keep track of sales of each product. From that information, inventory records are constantly updated by computer.

Using satellites, each store can transmit orders to the company's headquarters in Bentonville, Arkansas. Again using computers, replenishment orders can be scheduled to arrive at the store within thirty-six hours by ordering shipments from a distribution center, which uses laser scanners to route goods along eleven miles of conveyors. If some items are not selling, orders from suppliers can be cut off and information transmitted back to stores via the company's TV satellite system.[3]

Because of the increasing complexity of organizational activities, much of that coordination will have to be through the computer.

Understanding Interrelationships

Coordination in the operations area will be of prime importance. As of now, we don't have good methods for determining the interrelationships among various operations decisions. For example, what product mix provides the highest rate of machine utilization? Which production plan will eventually give us the best workforce utilization? For the time being, we must deal with each decision in a sequential manner, first developing a production plan and then working down to the final schedule. In the future, companies will need better ways of determining how each decision will affect their operations activities. In fact, going even further, the entire organization will need to be involved so that marketing can immediately determine how its plans affect operations and how operations, in turn, will influence the finance function.

In order to achieve this level of coordination, the computer will be used heavily. For instance, we are already beginning to see companies using computer simulation to evaluate the effects of various scheduling options. We think this trend will continue further to the point where the computer will be used as a tool for optimizing all operations activities, from long-range planning to dispatching.

Flexibility and Consistency

A second reason that we see for increased us of computer integration and automation is to improve flexibility. Companies must become increasingly able to adapt quickly to changes in demand or technology. There will be a need to develop and produce new products in less and less time. Doing this will require computer power combined with flexible automation systems.

The third reason is that companies will need more consistency in their operations activities. By consistency, we mean the ability to perform the same activity over and over in the same time and with the same results. In order to coordinate operations activities, it will be essential that times to perform various tasks be known and that those tasks always be done in the same way, which will mean high levels of automation.

Judicious Use of Automation

Automation can greatly improve the quality, consistency, and productivity of a production process. However, applied without adequate forethought, automation can actually cause more problems than it solves. Unfortunately, there has been a recent trend to automate simply for the sake of automation. Companies that really did not need robots have gone out and bought them—often with disastrous results. However, we believe that trend is now changing.

Many companies have begun to realize that automation is not necessarily the panacea it was originally thought to be. For example, General Motors had originally planned its Saturn plant to be a highly automated facility. Based on its experiences at other plants, GM has decided to reduce the level of automation and place more emphasis on worker involvement to increase productivity.

However, this does not mean that the use of automation will decrease. On the contrary, we think it will increase. However, the trend will be first to improve the productivity of existing systems and then to automate only those operations that can benefit further by the use of automation.

INFORMATION FLOWS

An increased need for coordination will also mean an increased need for information to flow among various parts of the organization. It will also mean that much more information will be collected than previously.

For example, consider a job shop type of production process. In that type of situation, information flow is extremely important so that machine operators know exactly which job they should be working on at any given time. Likewise, management must be constantly aware of how jobs are progressing through the shop and the status of each machine so they can plan the production schedule and make changes when problems occur.

Today, the trend is toward production systems that will have the flexibility of a job shop, but be able to produce at a rate closer to that of an assembly line. This blending of advantages from two different types of processes places a strong emphasis on the fast flow of information to and from machines and work centers.

Increased Communication

However, collecting information just for information's sake will not be enough. The purpose of information is to provide communication. In the past, different parts of a company have not communicated well with one another, and companies have not been in touch with their customers. With the increasing availability of information technology, we will begin to see companies that truly use that technology to bring everyone closer together. Information will serve to get all parts of the company communicating and working together. At the same time, the company will know much better what its customers want and be able to meet those wants.

The Accounting Information System

Traditionally, accounting has been the way a company kept score. However, with increased production speed, fast changeovers, and small batch sizes, the accounting system often cannot keep up. Further, the focus on cost minimization will require that companies know precisely what each part and each product cost to produce.

Companies are just now beginning to search for ways of handling this problem, such as activity-based cost accounting. However, computer systems and real-time data collection capabilities will ease the problem. We foresee that companies will eventually have accounting information systems that will be able to show minute by minute what a company's costs are as it is actually making the product.

WORK–FORCE MANAGEMENT

In spite of the emphasis we have placed on the increased use of automation and computers, we still believe that people will continue to be the single most important part of any organization. In fact, the role played by people will change greatly, due, in part, to computer integration and automation.

The Industrial Revolution is probably not yet over in the sense that people are still doing many jobs that machines could do better. This is not an antipeople statement. But if one observes how people have been employed historically, much of the time the work force was simply a source of horsepower. That is changing as machines take over the more menial and dangerous activities. In fact, it is projected that by the next century facilities will exist that can run with only a few people in managerial and design roles.

As this trend continues, people will be more important, not for their physical abilities, but for their abilities to think, make decisions, and develop new ideas. Already, companies are finding that their work force is a valuable source of problem-solving skills. Many of the most successful companies today are not those that are highly automated, but those that have given their employees an important role in the decision-making process.

As machines take over the manual labor, people will become more involved with the designing, planning, and problem-solving activities. This will have a major impact on work-force management. Instead of telling the employees what to do, managers will fill more of a supportive role, guiding, assisting, and representing their work force. The organizational climate will no longer be the boss-worker type of relationship, but will become more of a cooperative one, with each individual playing his or her own, but equally important, role. Such changes may require extensive retraining as employees are shifted from manual-labor jobs to ones that involve working with or maintaining computerized systems. Likewise, managers will need more training in participative methods for getting employees involved in the decision-making process.

Work-force Flexibility

We mentioned earlier in this chapter that one major factor on which companies will compete is flexibility. This will also require that their work forces be flexible. Already many Japanese companies cross-train workers so they can perform several different jobs. This gives the company the ability to move workers around from one area to another as needed. Fast-food operations, such as Burger King, have been using cross-training for some time, and some retail stores are also beginning to focus on work-force flexibility.

Fellow Employees as Customers

Maryland Bank, N. A. (MBNA), is one of the largest credit card issuers in the United States. When MBNA hires new employees, it emphasizes its slogan, "We want people who like people." Likewise, the New United Motor Manufacturing, Inc. (NUMMI) plant in Fremont, California, spent hours interviewing and testing each prospective employee before hiring. Both of these cases reflect a trend toward finding employees who can work well with others.

A major emphasis in organizations is becoming customer service. However, many companies are realizing that employees in one part of the company are also customers of employees in another part of the company. Thus, many companies are spreading the idea that every employee should treat every other employee like a customer. The idea is that if employees in a company can meet the needs of other employees, then they are much more likely to meet the needs of final customers as well.

SYSTEM INTEGRATION

Most of the prognostications we have made so far relate primarily to the operations function. However, the operations activities are going to become less distinct from the other parts of an organization. In the past, marketing, personnel, finance, and operations were all very independent activities. Now that situation is changing. We are already seeing companies in which marketing is performing activities historically done by operations, or operations is doing things that finance used to do.

What is occurring is that companies are realizing that an effective organization must be coordinated to compete effectively. As we have discussed previously, actions taken by one part of an organization will almost invariably have an impact on other parts of that organization. In the past, the full effect of those impacts has not been considered. But as computer power gives organizations the ability to communicate and analyze data, it will also give them the ability to analyze the probable future results of various decision alternatives and to determine how those results would influence the entire business.

Further Integration of Marketing and Operations

We have mentioned in many places in this book the importance of having marketing and operations work closely together. We believe this trend will continue, and, in fact, the dividing line between marketing and operations will become very indistinct. Some companies already use factory workers to help sell the product since those people often know more about it than anyone. Increasingly, marketing and operations will work together as a team to meet the customer's needs.

QUALITY MANAGEMENT

Quality is already extremely important. But it is going to become even more important in the future. We have only begun to scratch the surface in finding ways of monitoring, controlling, and improving quality. Already, some companies have begun to emphasize quality and to work at measuring it. For those companies, quality is becoming a way of life for the entire organization.

This trend will continue as we move away from having a separate quality control department and move toward quality's becoming a major concern of every part of the organization. Once again, this means more integration of the entire organizational system.

Many organizations have begun to realize that quality is something that must be built into the product, not inspected in. But only a few companies have really begun to do much about it. We think there will be an increasing emphasis on designing operations systems that are made to produce zero defects. At the same time, there will be much more emphasis on monitoring quality throughout the process. Too many companies still perform inspections only at selected points in the process. Instead, we see more movement toward continuous monitoring and control.

This ties in, then, with our previous comments about increased emphasis on information. Companies will collect and analyze much more data than they are now. Much of the data will have to do with quality measurements and the identification of problem causes.

GREATER FOCUS ON SERVICES

Seventy percent of the labor force in the United States is employed in services. Accordingly, throughout this book, we have discussed service organizations and described how their operations are managed. However, you may come away with the feeling that most of the emphasis has been on manufacturing. The reason for that is that the concepts and techniques are much more developed for manufacturing operations than for service operations.

Thus, there is a great need to develop more procedures and techniques for designing, planning, and managing service operations. Some of the more important areas that we foresee getting increased attention are these.

A Better Understanding of Services

Manufacturing activities are well defined and can be classified. However, we do not have such a good understanding of the types of service organizations and how they can be classified. In manufacturing, it is very easy for us to identify the product being produced. However, in services, there often is no tangible product. In fact, we may not always be sure what that product is. Thus, we will need to develop a better understanding of service operations.

Quality of Service

Likewise, the area of quality is much more developed in manufacturing than in services. In manufacturing, we can often measure quality quite easily. But in services, because the product is intangible, it is not so easy to measure. Some companies, as mentioned in Chapter 17, are beginning to develop ways of measuring quality of services. However, we still have much farther to go in that direction.

Integration of Manufacturing and Services

We have already mentioned the concept of a service factory. Increasingly, companies that manufacture a tangible product will begin to realize there needs to be a major service component associated with the product. That service may include the obvious things, such as fast repair, or it may also include the less obvious, such as helping the customer use the product appropriately or even incorporating customers' preferences into the product design.

OPERATIONS IN ACTION

Four Seasons Hotels: Staying in Touch with the Customer

Four Seasons Hotels runs a chain of twenty-two luxury hotels, including the Pierre in New York and Ritz-Carlton in Chicago. The company, which has its headquarters in Toronto, has seven regional vice-presidents, each of whom must also be general manager of a hotel in his or her region.

The company's president also keeps in touch with what is happening in the hotels by talking with housekeepers and other hotel employees. However, Four Seasons does more than that to stay in touch with its customers. For example, it is installing an information system that will maintain data about each guest so that each hotel can provide the right kind of pillow or satisfy any other requirements whenever a guest returns.

The length to which Four Seasons will go to please its guests is indicated by the story of a doorman in Toronto. While loading a guest's belongings into a taxi, the doorman inadvertently left out the person's briefcase. When it was learned the guest needed that briefcase the next day, the doorman caught a plane to Washington, D. C., and delivered the briefcase in person. That doorman was later named employee of the year.[4]

SUMMARY

- Competitive pressures will force companies to improve quality and cut costs.
- An increased rate of change means that companies must have the flexibility to keep up with that change.
- Companies will have to plan for global production and make products that serve global needs.
- The dropping of barriers in Europe in 1992 will mean increased competition and larger markets.
- The elimination of communist regimes in Eastern Europe will open up new markets, but will require major overhauling of the industries in those countries.
- Competition will increase and be based on short lead time, flexibility, and low cost.
- A service factory provides services in addition to producing a good.
- Operations will play a greater role in corporate strategy.
- Computers will be used to develop a better understanding of interrelationships among parts of a company.
- Automation will increase flexibility and improve consistency, but must be used judiciously.
- Greater information flow will improve communication within the company and between the company and its customers.
- Accounting information systems will be improved to truly represent costs on a real-time basis.
- Employees will be able to perform more jobs, will increasingly be involved in decisions, and will work together better.
- There will be more integration of functional areas, especially marketing and operations.
- Quality will continue to be important as we find better ways to measure it.
- There will be more emphasis on services and efforts to better understand service operations.
- Manufacturers will be more service-oriented.

CAREER PROFILE

John Wolf
Vice-President and General Manager
MD-90/MD-80/DC-9
McDonnell Douglas Corporation

Educational Background and Career Steps

John Wolf's background is in electrical engineering, which he studied at the bachelor's and master's levels at the University of Missouri at Rolla. While a student, Wolf started working for McDonnell Douglas Corporation through its cooperative education program. That experience introduced him to all parts of the corporation, and, after graduation, Wolf went to work for McDonnell Douglas, doing R&D work in astronautics.

Even though Wolf's background is in engineering, he moved rapidly into managerial roles, first in subsystem management, then system management, and finally program management. At that point, Wolf was moved to a different unit of the corporation, McDonnell Douglas Electronics Company, as the heir apparent to the general manager. During the two years before he moved into that position, Wolf worked as vice-president for program management and as executive vice-president.

Wolf had to develop a strategic market perspective for his roles in program management. This perspective paid off when he became general manager of the 1,500-employee McDonnell Douglas Electronics Company and increased its sales from $100 million to $130 million.

After that position, Wolf became executive vice-president of operations for McDonnell Aircraft Company, where he was responsible for overseeing all operational activities related to production of the three high-performance military aircraft that McDonnell Aircraft Company manufactures. Those activities ranged from material procurement and quality assurance to human resources and information management.

Current Position and Duties

After McDonnell Douglas restructured into business units built around products, Wolf was named vice-president and general manager in charge of the company's MD-90, MD-80, and DC-9 aircraft. In that position, he is no longer responsible for just operations activities, but must oversee all functional areas, including design, development, finance, and contracts, related to those products.

Under Wolf's direction a great deal of emphasis has been placed on total quality management. Within that framework, employees are organized by teams, and each component of the aircraft has its own business unit responsible for human resources management and relationships with suppliers. By developing cooperative relationships with the union and with suppliers, the company has been able to greatly improve its performance. One measure of that performance is the time it takes to build an airplane, which has been reduced by 30 percent under Wolf's management.

QUESTIONS

1. Compare two fast-food restaurants, such as Wendy's and McDonald's. Describe some ways that the operations decisions of each have been influenced by competitive strategies.

2. Select any organization, and diagram the information flows that take place between different functional areas of that organization. How do you think those flows will change in the future.?

3. Some individuals predict that by the next century, there will be only half a dozen or so auto makers left in the world. List some strategies that you think are going to be important for today's auto makers if they are to survive. What are the operations implications of those strategies?

4. You may have seen the following quotation from the comic strip Pogo: "We have met the enemy and they is us." In the past, many companies have operated that way. Traditionally, operations and marketing have been at odds because operations wanted few products and long production runs, while marketing wanted to meet every customer whim. Operations and finance have fought because operations wanted new equipment and large inventories, while finance wanted to spend little money and carry low inventories. Discuss

how a more cooperative environment can develop through an overall competitive strategy.

5. Select a simple device that you can take apart. How easy do you think it was to produce? Suggest some ways that its production could be simplified without adversely affecting quality.

6. Select some tangible good you own, and explain how the intangible elements of service related to that product have affected your impression of the product's quality.

7. Provide an example of a company in which you have seen employees performing more than one job.

8. During a day, count how many goods or services you use that are provided by companies outside the country in which you are a student.

9. Give examples of the impact that international trade has on operations management.

10. List some reasons other than labor cost that motivate companies to locate their facilities overseas.

11. Explain the impact that a lower value for the U. S. dollar relative to other world currencies would have on U. S. operations activities.

12. Describe the four types of service factories proposed by Chase.

13. Can you think of other services that might be provided by a manufacturer?

14. Describe how product design activities relate to organizational strategy.

15. Explain some future ways that operations will be integrated with marketing, finance, human resources management, and engineering.

16. Obtain examples from popular publications that describe how a company has given its employees more decision-making authority.

17. Why is flexibility going to become important for tomorrow's organizations?

SELECTED BIBLIOGRAPHY

Chase, Richard B., and Garvin, David A. "The Service Factory." *Harvard Business Review* 67, no.4 (July–August 1989): 61–69.

Crosby, Philip B. *Leading*. New York: McGraw-Hill, 1990.

Ettlie, John E.; Burstein, Michael C.; and Fiegenbaum, Avi. *Manufacturing Strategy*. Boston: Kluwer, 1990.

Hayes, Robert H.; Wheelwright, Steven C.; and Clark, Kim B. *Dynamic Manufacturing*. New York: Free Press, 1988.

Murdick, Robert G.; Render, Barry; and Russell, Roberta S. *Service Operations Management*. Boston: Allyn and Bacon, 1990.

Peters, T. *Thriving on Chaos: Handbook for a Management Revolution*. New York: Knopf, 1987.

Endnotes

Chapter 2

1. Based on Richard Brandt and Otis Port, "How Automation Could Save the Day," *Business Week,* March 3, 1986, pp. 72–74; and "LTV Aircraft Products Group: Only the Beginning...," *Industry Week,* March 21, 1988, pp. 50–54.
2. For more information, see Wickham Skinner, "The Focused Factory," *Harvard Business Review* 52, no. 3 (May–June 1974): 114–121.
3. Based on "Electrolux Corp.: Octupling Sales with Automation," *Industry Week,* March 21, 1988, pp. 34–36.
4. This definition of CAM was given by Computer Aided Manufacturing International.

Chapter 3

1. Based on Todd Vogel, Mark Ivey, and Mimi Bluestone, "The Big Spill's Big Chill," *Business Week,* May 1, 1989, pp. 102–103.
2. Based, respectively, on the following: Michael Schroeder, "Has Aluminum Climbed Off Its Roller Coaster," *Business Week,* May 1, 1989, pp. 106–111; David Lieberman, "Dow Jones Still Sluggish, Still Optimistic," *Business Week,* May 1, 1989, pp. 114–117; and Mark Maremont, "A Sky-High Bet on the Plane-Leasing Business," *Business Week,* May 1, 1989, p. 120.

Chapter 4

1. Based on Russell Mitchell, "How Ford Hit the Bull's-Eye with Taurus," *Business Week,* June 30, 1986, pp. 69–70; and Bro Uttal, "Speeding, New Ideas to Market," *Fortune,* March 2, 1987, pp. 62–66.
2. Gene Sylinsky, "The High Tech Race," *Fortune,* October 13, 1986, p. 26.
3. Based on Brian Dumaine, "Turbulence Hits the Air Couriers," *Fortune,* July 21, 1986, pp. 101–106. Many facts were provided through conversations with managers at Federal Express.

Chapter 5

1. Based on Katherine M. Hafner, Dan Cook, Gary Geipel, Stewart Toy, and Patrick Houston, "There Are Two Kinds of Supermarkets: The Quick and the Dead," *Business Week,* August 11, 1986, pp. 62–63.

Chapter 6

1. Some facts are based on James B. Treece and John Hoerr, "Shaking Up Detroit," *Business Week,* August 14, 1989, pp. 74–80.
2. Based on Jeremy Main, "A Rust Belt City Takes on a Shine," *Fortune,* November 10, 1986, pp. 116–128.
3. For a more detailed discussion of problems with on-site expansion, see Roger W. Schmenner, "Looking Beyond the Obvious in Plant Location," *Harvard Business Review* 57, no. 1, (January–February 1979) pp. 126–132.
4. William H. Miller, "U.S. Manufacturing on Whose Turf?" *Industry Week,* September 5, 1988, pp. 53–81; and Elizabeth Weiner, Dean Foust, and Dori Jones Yang, "Why Made-in-America Is Back in Style," *Business Week,* November 7, 1988, pp. 116–120.

Chapter 8

1. Based on John Merwin, "A Tale of Two Worlds," *Forbes,* June 16, 1986, pp. 101–106. One of the authors has also toured both the Honda and the Jeep facilities.
2. Jonathan Kastein and John Hoerr, "Volvo's Radical New Plant: 'The Death of the Assembly Line'?" *Business Week,* August 28, 1989, pp. 92–93.

Chapter 9

1. These steps are based on James H. Greene, *Operations Management: Productivity and Profit* (Reston, Va.: Reston, 1984.)
2. Based on George H. Labovitz, "Manager's Journal: Speed on the Cycle Helps Companies Win the Race," *Wall Street Journal,* October 30, 1989, p. A12.
3. MOST is a registered trademark of H. B. Maynard and Company, Inc.
4. Based on A. D. Sharplin, "Lincoln Electric Company," in George A. Steiner, John B. Miner, and Edmund R. Gray, *Management Policy and Strategy: Text, Readings, and Cases* 2ed. (New York, N.Y.: McMillan, 1982); Nancy J. Perry, "Here Come Richer, Riskier Pay Plans," *Fortune,* December 19, 1988, pp. 51–58; "Alcoa Will Start Cash Profit-Sharing Plan for Salaried Workers," *Wall Street Journal,* September 15, 1988, p. 12; Jacob

M. Schlesinger, "GM's Offer to UAW Expected to Include Lump-Sum Raises with Links to Output," *Wall Street Journal,* August 12, 1987, p. 4; and Laurie Hays, "All Eyes on DuPont's Incentive-Pay Plan," *Wall Street Journal,* December 5, 1988, p. B1.

Chapter 10

1. Based on Paul Ingrassia and Bradley A. Stertz, "Ford's Strong Sales Raise Agonizing Issue of Additional Plants," *Wall Street Journal,* October 26, 1988, p. A1; Melinda Grenier Guiles and Krystal Miller, "Mazda and Mitsubishi-Chrysler Venture Cut Output, Following Big Three's Lead," *Wall Street Journal,* January 12, 1990, p. A2; Neal Templin, "U.S. Auto Sales Stage a Spotty January Rally," *Wall Street Journal,* February 6, 1990, p. A2; James R. Healey, "Spring Car Shortage New Worry," *USA Today,* February 7, 1990, p. 1A; and Jacqueline Mitchell, "Auto Makers Carefully Watch Quarter Output," *Wall Street Journal,* February 9, 1990, p. A2.
2. See Terry Hill, *Manufacturing Strategy: Text and Cases* (Homewood, Ill.: Irwin, 1989).
3. Based on Milton Humphreys, "The Renaissance of Thomasville Furniture," in *APICS 32d International Conference Proceedings* (Falls Church, Va.: American Production and Inventory Control Society, 1989), pp. 651–653.
4. Based on Marj Charlier, "Keystone Is Heady Success, Coors Says, Citing Fantasy Ads, Rival Beers' Woes," *Wall Street Journal,* February 2, 1990, p. B4; and Ellen Neuborne, "Buyers in a Lather over Sensor," *USA Today,* February 5, 1990, p. 1B.
5. Based on Michael J. McCarthy, "Restaurants Search for Winning Recipes," *Wall Street Journal,* January 29, 1990, p. B1; and Richard Gibson, "Burger King Aims to Revamp Drive-throughs," *Wall Street Journal,* March 29, 1990, p. B1.

Chapter 11

1. Based on Anthony Ramirez, "Boeing's Happy, Harrowing Times," *Fortune,* July 17, 1989, pp. 40–45; and Howard Banks, "Sitting Pretty," *Forbes,* January 8, 1990, p. 123.
2. This phrase was coined by Thomas E. Vollmann, William L. Berry, and D. Clay Whybark, *Manufacturing Planning and Control Systems* (Homewood, Ill.: Irwin, 1984).
3. Based on Paul Cissel, "Ben & Jerry's Adds to Its Recipe for Success," *P&IM Review with APICS News,* February 1989, pp. 37–40.
4. Based on Fred Tolbert, "Personal Computer-Based DRP: The Way To Go," in *APICS 32d International Conference Proceedings* (Falls Church, Va.: American Production and Inventory Control Society, 1989), pp. 134–137.

Chapter 12

1. Based on Dexter Hutchins, "Having a Hard Time with Just-in-Time," *Fortune,* June 9, 1986, pp. 64–66; Mehran Sepehri, *Just-in-Time, Not Just in Japan* (Falls Church, Va.: American Production and Inventory Control Society, 1986); and John A. Conway, "Harley Back in Gear," *Forbes,* April 20, 1987, p. 8.
2. Henry Ford, *Today and Tomorrow* Garden City: Garden City Publishing, 1926.
3. Robert W. Hall, *Driving the Productivity Machine* (Falls Church, Va.: American Production and Inventory Control Society, 1981). Note: This formula is based on the dual-card system. However, it may be easily modified for the single-card system by eliminating T_p from the calculation.
4. To see what we mean, just look back at some of the planned order releases under MRP in Chapter 11. Those planned order releases almost invariably became large and irregularly spaced by the time we reached the component parts or raw materials level. This was caused by batch production in the master schedule.
5. Robert W. Hall, *Zero Inventories* (Homewood, Ill.: Dow Jones–Irwin, 1983).
6. Based on Mehran Sepehri, *Just-in-Time, Not Just in Japan* (Falls Church, Va.: American Production and Inventory Control Society, 1986).
7. Based on Robert B. Vollum, "Improving on JIT Success with Constraint Management and Synchronous Flow: A Case Study," in *APICS 32d International Conference Proceedings* (Falls Church, Va.: American Production and Inventory Control Society, 1989), pp. 583–584.

Chapter 13

1. Based on Marc R. Lambrecht and Freddy Van den Wijngaert, "A Microcomputer System for MRP and Scheduling in Essochem," *Production and Inventory Management* 26, no. 4 (1985): pp. 59–69.
2. Based on William Baldwin, "Industrial Chic," *Forbes,* November 27, 1989, p. 96.
3. Based on Robert L. Rose, "American Airlines' Fixer of Broken Schedules," *Wall Street Journal,* June 28, 1988, p. 31; and Laurie McGinley, "Public

Outcries Move Airports to Cut Noise," *Wall Street Journal,* April 9, 1990, p. B1.

Chapter 14

1. Based on "PertMaster Helps Change the Face of British Airways," ***Industrial Management and Data Systems,*** March–April 1986, pp. 6–7.
2. Based on Brian Dumaine, "How Managers Can Succeed Through Speed," *Fortune,* February 13, 1989, pp. 54–59.

Chapter 15

1. John H. Sheridan, "Betting on a Single Source," *Industry Week,* February 1, 1988, pp. 31–36; and Thomas M. Rohan, "Supplier-Customer Links Multiplying," *Industry Week,* April 17, 1989, p. 28.
2. Based on Tom Ichniowski, "Hechinger's: Nobody Does It Better in Do-It-Yourself," *Business Week,* May 5, 1986, p. 96.

Chapter 16

1. Based on Gary J. Finke, "Determining Target Inventories of Wood Chips Using Risk Analysis," *Interfaces* 14, no. 5 (September–October 1984): pp. 53–58.
2. Based on Subrata N. Chakravarty, "Will Toys 'B' Great?" *Forbes,* February 22, 1988, pp. 37–39.
3. Based on Gail Bronson, "Billion-Dollar Brainstorm," *Forbes,* October 19, 1987, p. 98.
4. E. A. Silver and H. C. Meal, "A Heuristic for Selecting Lot Size Requirements for the Case of a Deterministic Time-Varying Demand Rate and Discrete Opportunities for Replenishment," ***Production and Inventory Management*** 14, no. 2 (1973): pp. 64–74.

Chapter 17

1. Based on Joel Dreyfuss, "Victories in the Quality Crusade," *Fortune,* October 11, 1988, pp. 80–88; and Ned Hamson, "Excellence & Quality," *Forbes,* April 16, 1990, pp. 78–87.
2. John M. Groocock, *The Chain of Quality* (New York: Wiley, 1986), p. 250.
3. Philip B. Crosby, *Quality Without Tears* (New York: McGraw-Hill, 1984), p. 99.
4. W. Edwards Deming, *Quality, Productivity, and Competitive Position* (Cambridge, Mass.: MIT Press, 1982).
5. John M. Groocock, *The Chain of Quality* (New York: Wiley, 1986), p. 250.
6. This material is based on the discussion of total quality control presented in Richard J. Schonberger, *Japanese Manufacturing Techniques* (New York: Free Press, 1982).
7. Bando Satoshi, "Qualitative Change in the Labor Movement," *Japan Echo* 8 (1981): pp. 30–37.
8. Based on Thomas A. Stewart, "Westinghouse Gets Respect at Last," *Fortune,* July 3, 1989, pp. 92–98.
9. Based on Genichi Taguchi: and Don Clausing, "Robust Quality," ***Harvard Business Review 68,*** no. 1 (January–February 1990): pp. 65–75.
10. Based on Lawrence P. Sullivan, "The Seven Stages in Company-Wide Quality Control," *Quality Progress* 19, no. 5 (May 1986): pp. 77–83.
11. Joseph Anthony, "What Will You Do?" *National Geographic Traveler* (March–April 1990): pp. 24–26.
12. Based on John Paul Newport, Jr., "American Express: Service That Sells," *Fortune,* November 20, 1989, pp. 80–89; and Jolie Solomon, "How a CEO Expresses His Devotion to Quality," *Wall Street Journal,* April 20, 1990, p. B1.

Chapter 18

1. Based on Russell Mitchell, "Boldly Going Where No Robot Has Gone Before," *Business Week,* December 22, 1986, p. 45.

Chapter 19

1. Based on Ann R. Field and Catherine L. Harris, "The Information Business," *Business Week,* August 25, 1986, pp. 82–90.
2. "One-a-Day at $3.5 Million a Pop," *Industry Week,* March 21, 1988, pp. 60–62.
3. Based on John W. Wilson, "Suddenly the Heavyweights Smell Money in Computer Networks," *Business Week,* April 27, 1987, pp. 110–111; and John W. Wilson and Zach Schiller, "The Nerve-racking Job of Setting Up a Network," *Business Week,* April 27, 1987, pp. 112–114.

Chapter 20

1. Based on "CIM at Allen-Bradley," *Allen-Bradley HORIZONS* 3, no. 1 (1986): pp. 14–19.
2. Richard B. Chase and David A. Garvin, "The Service Factory," *Harvard Business Review* 67, no. 1 (July–August 1989): pp. 61–69.
3. Based on John Huey, "Wal-Mart: Will It Take Over the World?" *Fortune,* January 30, 1989, pp. 52–61.
4. Based on Patricia Sellers, "Getting Customers to Love You," *Fortune,* March 13, 1989, pp. 38–49; Faye Rice, "Hotels Fight for Business Guests," *Fortune,* April 23, 1990, pp. 265–274; and Lionel Tiger, "When 'Corporate' and 'Culture' Clash," *Wall Street Journal,* April 9, 1990, p. A10.

Glossary

ABC analysis A classification scheme for inventory items so that those 20 percent of items (A items) that account for the top 80 percent of dollar usage receive the most attention.

Absolute quota Limits the entry of a service or good into a country for a period of time.

Acceptable quality level (AQL) The percentage of defective units that would be acceptable in a batch.

Acceptance sampling A statistical procedure in which samples are used to determine whether an entire lot meets acceptable quality standards.

Activity accounting Collects financial and operating data and allocates costs based on the nature and extent of business activity.

Activity matrix Organizes and displays the movement of people, parts, or other factors between departments.

Activity-on-arc (AOA) representation A method for representing project networks in which each arc corresponds to an activity.

Activity-on-node (AON) representation A method for representing project networks in which each node corresponds to an activity.

Additive model for analyzing a time series Is a method for combining the components of a time series. With this approach, the factors (trend, seasonal, cyclical, and random) are added.

Aggregate planning A term used to mean medium-range operations planning. A first rough-cut approximation at determining how existing resources of people and facilities should be used to meet projected demand.

Aggregation Refers to the combining of products into groups or families for planning purposes.

Allowance Time required for personal time, rest, and delays as a percentage of normal time.

Analysis Is a step in design which separates the whole into its parts in order to determine their nature, proportion, function, and relationship.

Annual fixed costs Are costs that do not vary with volume. These costs are incurred during the year and can include supervisory labor, utilities, and support staff.

Arc An arrow in a precedence diagram or project network that connects together two nodes.

Assembly line Is a process where discrete parts are put together to make a finished product. It is a high volume operation that produces products that are very similar in features and performance.

Assignable causes Causes of variation in the output of a process that can be assigned to factors such as tool wear, material from different suppliers, etc.

Automated Guided Vehicle Systems (AGVS) Are driverless and flexible transportation devices resembling a forklift truck which can transport parts between manufacturing cells.

Automated Storage and Retrieval System Is a computerized system for storing and retrieving parts or tools.

Availability Is the amount of time that a system or product is ready to operate divided by total time—i.e., the sum of uptime and downtime.

Available to promise The number of units in a master schedule not yet committed to customer orders.

Backward scheduling An approach to scheduling that starts from a desired due date and works backward.

Batch Is a term used to describe a production process that does not have sufficient volume from a single product to fully use the facility. In this case, the facility produces several products to build sufficient volume.

Bill-of-materials (BOM) Describes the type and quantity of each component part needed to build one unit of a product.

Blanket purchase requisition A document authorizing a vendor to provide a specified quantity or number of parts or raw materials over a specified period of time.

Bottleneck Is the department, work station, or operation that restricts the flow of product through the production system. A bottleneck department restricts the flow of product from upstream departments and starves downstream departments.

Branch An arrow in a precedence diagram or project network that connects together two nodes.

Break-even point (BEP) Is the volume required to be produced and sold so that profit is zero. This is the zero profit point in the cost-volume profit model.

Buffer Any backlog that is used purposely to avoid running out of parts or material.

Build-up method Is an approach to forecasting that starts at the bottom of an organization and makes an overall estimate by adding together estimates from each element.

Business plan A medium-range statement of planned sales, production, and inventory levels, usually in terms of dollars, on a monthly basis.

C-kanban A kanban that authorizes the movement of materials from one location to another.

Capacity Is a measure of the organization's ability to provide customers with the demanded services or goods, in the amount requested and in a timely manner. Capacity is the maximum rate of production.

Capacity-constrained resource A work center or machine that is being utilized near its capacity.

Capacity requirements planning (CRP) The process of estimating total capacity that will be required at each work center or machine, based on the master schedule and MRP.

Capital budget Indicates planned expenditures for plant and equipment.

Carrying costs The variable costs associated with keeping inventory.

Cause-and-effect diagram A diagram that is used in problem-solving to list all the possible causes of a problem, usually divided into materials, equipment, methods, and personnel.

Cell manager Is a computer that links together several programmable controllers. Cell managers store information including computer instructions which are too large to keep on the programmable controller. A cell manager coordinates information flows between machines in a manufacturing cell.

Cellular manufacturing Is the physical layout of the facility into compact groups of machines that are responsible for producing families of parts.

Center-of-gravity method See load-distance method.

Changeover time Is the time required to change the facility/equipment from making one product to making the next product.

Closed-loop MRP A variation of MRP in which feedback about execution of production plans is provided so MRP can be updated to reflect reality.

Coding and classification Is a method used to determine a family of parts in a group technology study. Each part is assigned a code which defines the size, shape, metal type, machining operations and other factors.

Coefficient of correlation Is a measure of the strength of a relationship between variables. If there is no relationship the coefficient of correlation will be zero. A perfect positive correlation is 1.0 and a perfect negative correlation is -1.0.

Companywide quality control (CWQC) An approach to quality control that emphasizes all aspects of quality throughout the company, including, especially, service to the customer.

Competitive advantage Is an organization's special abilities, such as shorter delivery lead-times or higher quality products, which gives it an edge on its competition.

Computer Aided design (CAD) Is the effective use of the computer to create or modify an engineering design. An interactive CAD terminal can be used for dimensional analysis, interference checking between two or more objects, stress analysis, and examining cross-sections of the part.

Computer Aided Manufacturing (CAM) Is the effective use of computer technology in the management, control, and operations of the production facility through either direct or indirect computer interface with the physical and human resources. (This definition of CAM was given by Computer Aided Manufacturing International.) CAM systems include monitoring the production process and the operation of machines by machines.

Computer Aided Process Planning (CAPP) Is an expert system which can generate routings and machining instructions for parts.

Computer Assisted Instruction (CAI) Is self-paced, computer guided learning. It can help organizations to quickly and economically upgrade people skills.

Computer integrated manufacturing (CIM) Blends recent developments in manufacturing with information technology to achieve a competitive advantage.

Computer numerically controlled (CNC) Is a machining system that utilizes a dedicated computer to store programs. The programs control the machine so it can shape the finished part.

Constraints Functions in a linear programming problem that limit our actions.

Consuming the master schedule A concept in which the master schedule can be envisioned as moving from mostly forecasts to mostly customer orders as time gets closer to the present.

Continuous flow process Does not identify individual units, rather the products are mixed and flow together in a continuous stream. Oil refining is a good example of a continuous flow process.

Control Is gathering information in order to evaluate, feedback, and take corrective action.

Conveyance kanban A kanban that authorizes the movement of materials from one location to another.

Corner point The intersection of constraint lines in graphical solution of a linear programming problem.

Correlation analysis Measures the degree of relationship between two variables.

Cost-volume-profit model Is a simple model of an organization that uses estimates of costs, revenues, volume sold, and volume produced in order to estimate profit.

Crash cost The cost of completing a project activity in its crash time.

Crash time The shortest possible time in which a project activity can be completed.

Critical path A path in a CPM diagram that consists of all activities with the least slack. These are activities that must be watched the closest.

Critical path method (CPM) A procedure for analyzing projects to determine the earliest and latest started and ending dates and the critical path.

Critical ratio A measure of the ratio between time until an order is due and the processing time remaining.

CRP The process of estimating total capacity that will be required at each work center or machine, based on the master schedule and MRP.

Customer Is the buyer of a service or good.

Customer open order file Contains information about a customer order including the customer's name, the type of product, quantity demanded, due date, and shipping address.

Cycle counting A procedure in which inventory of an item is counted at least once during an order cycle.

Cycle time Is the amount of time required to produce one unit. It is the time it takes from the start of the nth unit to the start of the n + 1 unit.

Cyclical fluctuations Are changes that occur periodically in a fixed period of more that one year. These are often referred to as the business-cycle effects.

Decision support systems (DDS) Are systems that allow managers to easily access information stored in a database and provide easy-to-use tools for analysis.

Delphi Technique Use a panel of experts and surveys to build consensus regarding future events.

Demand management The process of identifying all sources of demand and reflecting them in the master schedule.

Dependent demand Demand (usually for components or raw materials) that depends upon production of a finished product.

Dependent variable Is the variable in regression analysis which is being perdicted.

Designing the system Includes all the decisions necessary to establish the facilities and information systems required to produce the service or good.

Deterministic simulation A simulation in which every change that occurs is according to fixed values, not random.

Dispatching The assignment of priorities and selection of jobs for processing at a work center.

Distribution requirements planning (DRP) Is a system for determining the quantity of products needed within the distribution system. DRP uses forecasts of customers' orders to estimate the quantity of materials to have available at the distribution centers. Demands at the distribution centers, in turn, are aggregated to determine requirements at regional warehouses which influence requirements at supplying facilities.

Distribution resource planning A modification of distribution requirements planning that resembles MRP II.

Distribution system Is material handling between suppliers and customers. It involves moving materials between facilities and has a physical and an informational component. Distribution systems weave together customers and suppliers in a chain that takes the most basic materials like iron ore, crude oil, and lumber and transforms them into consumer products like power boats, toasters, and furniture.

Dollar usage The unit value of an item multiplied by its annual usage, in units.

Downloading Is moving information from one computer, usually larger in size, to another computer. For example, the instructions needed by the milling machine for parts not presently being produced may reside on the plant host. When that part is going into production, the instructions would be down loaded through the cell manager to the programmable controller.

Drum A term used in synchronous manufacturing to identify the machine or work center that will determine production rate for the entire production system.

Dual-card kanban system A pull system that uses both C-kanbans and P-kanbans to carefully control WIP inventory.

Dummy activity An imaginary activity that must be used in AOA project network diagrams to clarify precedence relationships.

Durability Is the ability of a product to function when subjected to hard and frequent use.

Economic order quantity (EOQ) An amount to order at one time that theoretically minimizes total annual cost of ordering and holding inventory.

Economies of scale This doctrine states that there is a most efficient size for a facility and there is a most efficient size for the firm.

Economies of scope Are economies of scale across products. Economies of scope implies building the volume necessary to cover fixed costs by producing a variety of products on the same equipment.

Effective Means the system achieves the desired results.

Efficient Means the system uses a "reasonable" amount of effort (inputs) to achieve the desired outputs.

Electronic transfer Uses phone lines as data circuits to move information between two computers.

Element A segment of a task.

Ergonomics The design of workplaces, furniture, machines, tools and other items so that the physical limitations and capabilities of people are taken into account.

Event In a project network, an event is the beginning or end of an activity.

Event-oriented simulation A simulation in which time is incremented only as events occur.

Expediting Is the monitoring of supplier deliveries of materials which have become critical for the customer.

Expert System (ES) Is defined as a computer program that uses knowledge and inference procedures to solve problems that are difficult enough to require significant human expertise for their solution. The knowledge and the inference procedures are attempts to create a model of the best practitioners in the field.

Extreme point The intersection of constraint lines in graphical solution of a linear programming problem.

Facility layout Is the physical arrangement of the work space including the position of departments or work groups with respect to one another and how the work space within a department is arranged.

Facility location Is the placement of a facility with respect to customers, suppliers, and other facilities with which it interfaces.

Factory focus A strategy that argues each facility a company operates should be focused to produce a particular type of product that is designed to compete based on a certain strategic plan.

Family of parts Is a group of parts that require similar machining operations.

Feasible region The area that satisfies all constraints in graphical solution of a linear programming problem.

Final assembly schedule (FAS) Like a master schedule except that it is usually done only a week ahead of time and it indicates exact option combinations for each finished product to be produced.

Finished goods inventories Are final products awaiting customer acceptance and delivery.

Finite loading An approach to machine loading that considers available capacity.

Fishbone chart A diagram that is used in problem-solving to list all the possible causes of a problem, usually divided into materials, equipment, methods, and personnel.

Fixture A device for holding parts so a worker's hands may be used for other activities.

Flexibility Is the ability to change between products or customers with minimal costs and delays.

Flexible manufacturing systems (FMS) Use computer and information technology to integrate material handling, robotics, and Computer Aided Process Planning (CAPP) with cellular manufacturing.

Flow process chart Used for analyzing the movements of a worker or the flow of materials through a process.

Flow time The total time it takes to produce a good or service.

Focused factories Are smaller operations producing fewer products. They do not attempt to achieve low costs through economies of scale (i.e., spreading fixed costs over a large volume). Focused factories achieve low costs through better control (i.e., eliminating waste), and ease of managing a smaller operation (i.e., fewer people involved).

Forecasting Is an attempt to predict the future.

Forward Scheduling An approach to scheduling that starts from the present time and schedules each job to start at the earliest possible moment.

Freezing the master schedule A policy that prevents changes in the master schedule within a certain time period from the present.

Functional areas Are the parts or subsystems of an organization such as accounting, marketing, finance, and engineering.

Gantt load chart A graphic device for indicating the schedule of jobs on equipment or facilities.

Goal programming A variation of linear programming that allows for multiple objectives in which all objectives cannot necessarily be achieved.

Go/no-go gages Inspection tools that can be used to quickly determine whether a part meets specifications.

Goods Are physical products.

Graphical approach A method of aggregate planning that uses a graph to indicate cumulative demand for the product versus cumulative production.

Graphical method Is a way to predict the trend factor in a time series.

Gross requirements In MRP, the total demand for an item during a time bucket.

Group incentive system A payment or bonus plan that rewards an entire group for increased productivity.

Group technology The grouping together of parts or products into families by processing operations so that all members of a family are processed in a miniature factory, called a GT cell, to maximize efficiency.

GT The grouping together of parts or products into families by processing operations so that all members of a family are processed in a miniature factory called a GT cell.

GT cell A group of machines, usually arranged in a U-shaped layout, used to process only a family of parts requiring similar operations.

Hard automation Is used to describe processes which have very limited flexibility.

Hiring costs Include expenses associated with finding qualified personnel, interviewing and training them, and then any productivity losses involved before they become proficient at the job.

Historical data in work measurement The use of data about past worker performance to develop time standards.

Holding costs The variable costs associated with keeping inventory.

Horizontal expansion of work Giving a person more tasks or more jobs to perform.

House of quality A diagram used to convert customer attributes desired in a product to engineering characteristics, parts characteristics, and process details.

Human engineering (ergonomics) Is the consideration of people in the design of products, facilities and the environment that people use.

Indented bill of material A bill of material in which components are indented from the item they go into.

Independent demand Demand for a part or product that is not dependent upon a production plan.

Independent variable Is a variable in regression analysis which is used to predict the dependent variable.

Index number for MOST A number corresponding to 10 TMUs, representing how difficult or time-consuming a motion is.

Infinite loading An approach to machine loading that does not take capacity considerations into account.

Information Data which has been gathered, classified, organized, and analyzed in a way that makes it useful for decision making.

Information system Is a mechanism for gathering, classifying, organizing, storing, analyzing, and disseminating information.

Input/output control A method for managing work flow and queue lengths by comparing input to a machine with output from it.

Instantaneous replenishment Replenishment of inventory such that all units ordered are placed into inventory at the same time.

Interplant orders In some companies, one plant is a supplier for another. Orders to the supplier are termed interplant orders.

Inventory Is material which is stored in anticipation of some future use. Inventory can be used as an alternative to future production. It is created when production (procurement in the case of purchased parts) exceeds consumption.

Inventory Control Is the effort to maintain inventory levels and costs within acceptable limits. It includes models that determine how much and when to order inventory as well as systems for monitoring inventory levels for management evaluation and decision making.

Ishikawa chart A diagram that is used in problem-solving to list all the possible causes of a problem, usually divided into materials, equipment, methods, and personnel.

Job enlargement An employee's job is expanded to include several tasks.

Job enrichment Providing a person with more decision-making authority to increase job satisfaction.

Job rotation To periodically shift workers from one job to another.

Job shop Is a facility capable of producing a wide variety of products in very small volumes. The production facility is general purpose and flexible enough to meet a variety of needs.

Job specialization A job design in which each employee performs only a particular narrowly defined task.

Just-in-time (JIT) Can be used as a basis for planning and scheduling, yet is more properly viewed as a strategy for designing manufacturing systems that are responsive to customer requirements. Applying JIT forces a reexamination of operating philosophy. The JIT philosophy focuses on reducing lead times, reducing set-up times and improving product quality to minimize raw material, work-in-process and finished goods inventory.

Kanban A Japanese word meaning "visible record." In manufacturing it is a card that is used to indicate when more materials are needed in a pull system.

Key policies Are methods or guidlies for achieving an organization's goals.

Knowledge engineers Build expert systems. They help human experts structure the problem by interpreting and integrating human answers, drawing analogies, posing examples and bringing out conceptual differences.

Labor productivity Is a measure of the efficiency of labor. It is the number of units produced per labor hour.

Layoff costs Include any severance pay or state-mandated payments into an unemployment compensation fund when employees are terminated or laid off.

Lead time Is the difference between the time the order is placed and the delivery of the product.

Lead-time offsetting The process of taking lead time into account for planning purposes.

Learning curve Indicates how the time required per unit of product decreases as the cumulative number of units produced increases.

Learning factor Indicates the percentage of time required to produce unit number 2n compared to the time for unit n.

Left-hand/right-hand chart Lists precisely what each hand is doing at all times during the performance of a task.

Level assembly schedule A final assembly schedule that involves producing a specified sequence of products so that production of each is matched with expected daily demand.

Leverage When referring to operations and productivity it means to make the work force more productive through the use of better tools.

Life cycle costing Is considering the cost of a product over its useful life not just the purchase price. When two alternatives are compared, which one has the lower total cost? Total cost includes purchase price, maintenance costs, and operating expense.

Linear programming A mathematical technique that can solve any resource allocation problem so long as that problem can be stated in terms of linear functions.

Line balancing The procedure in which tasks along an assembly line are assigned to work stations so each has approximately the same amount of work.

Line flow processes Are high volume operations. Two examples of line flow processes are continuous flow processes and assembly lines.

Line functions Are functions that transfer authority and decision-making responsibility from top management to the level of facility supervisor in operations and salesperson in marketing.

Load The total capacity requirements placed on a machine or work center during a specified period of time.

Load-distance method Is used to measure the proximity of a facility to its customers, suppliers, and other facilities with which it interacts.

Loading An approach to scheduling that tries to take capacity utilization into account.

Load profile A diagram that indicates the work load being placed on each work center.

Load report A graphical representation of the load on a machine or work center over time.

Local area network (LAN) Is a network that connects devices over a restricted area, often within the same building.

Long-range planning Involves activities that are planned to occur eighteen months or more in the future.

Loss function In quality management, the measure of loss to society associated with deviation of a process from its target output value.

Lot A quantity of material or number of units produced or processed at one time (a batch).

Lot-for-lot A lot sizing rule used in MRP in which planned order releases are equated to net requirements by time bucket.

Lot sizing The process of determining how much of an item should be ordered or produced at one time.

Lot tolerance percent defective (LTPD) The percentage of defective units in a batch that would definitely be unacceptable.

Lowest final cost Is the lowest total cost of the product including the purchase price, shipping and receiving costs, costs to rework defective products, and costs for special processing that would not be necessary if another supplier were used.

Low-level coding A procedure in which level numbers are assigned to parts in the bill of materials, starting at level 0 for the finished product. A part that appears at more than one level would be assigned the lowest level (highest number) at which it appears.

Lumpy demand Demand (usually for components or raw materials) that depends upon production of a finished product.

Machine Constrained The machine is holding back production. The equipment is operating for all the available time at its best speed while the operator has some idle time.

Machining instructions Are the procedures and specifications for each machine in the sequence.

Macro job design Involves the environment in which the job is performed, how the employee relates to the rest of the organization, and how much autonomy there is in performing the job tasks.

Maintainability Is the ease with which a product can be returned to its operating state after it has failed.

Make-to-order company A company that produces only to customer orders.

Make-to-stock company A company that produces for inventory and meets customer orders from inventory.

Managing and controlling the system Includes the execution of production plans and measuring, evaluating, and providing feedback on performance.

Manufacturability Is the ease with which a product can be produced.

Manufacturing Is a production process that produces goods.

Manufacturing cell A group of machines, usually arranged in a U-shaped layout, used to process only a family of parts requiring similar operations. See cellular manufacturing.

Manufacturing Resource Planning (MRP II) Is an integrated decision support system that ties together departments such as engineering, finance, personnel, manufacturing and marketing via a computer-based dynamic simulation model. MRP II works within the limits of an organization's present production system and with known orders and demand forecasts.

Market research Is the study of consumer needs so the organization can determine new markets for existing products and discover demand for new products.

Market share Is an organization's sales in a market divided by the total sales.

Master production schedule (MPS) A specific statement of exactly what, usually in terms of individual end items or product models, will be produced in each time period. Usually these time periods are weeks, although they may be days or even hours.

Master scheduler A person whose job is to develop the master production schedule.

Material handling Includes systems for moving materials within the facility. It implies a physical component (equipment to perform the task) and an information component (decisions about when and how much should be moved).

Material management Includes decisions regarding the procurement, control, handling, storage, and distribution of materials.

Material requirements planning (MRP) A way of scheduling the ordering or production of parts or raw materials so they will be available when needed to meet the master schedule.

Materials Are the physical items which are necessary to produce the goods and services we consume.

Mean Absolute Deviation (MAD) Is the average of the absolute differences between the forecasted and actual value of the variable being forecast.

Mean Squared Error (MSE) Is the average of all the squared errors. The differences between the actual value of a variable and the forecasted value are squared, added together and divided by the number of observations.

Medium-range planning Concerned with the time between six months and eighteen months ahead.

Method of overall factors A procedure for rough-cut capacity planning that uses historical accounting data to estimate the number of standard hours required per unit.

Methods analysis Methods and techniques concerned only with the physiological aspects of a job—how easy the job is to do, how quickly the person can work.

Methods improvement Methods and techniques concerned only with the physiological aspects of a job—how easy the job is to do, how quickly the person can work.

Methods-time measurement A system of predetermined time standards. Standard motions require a predetermined number of time measurement units (TMUs).

Micro job design Involves a detailed analysis of tasks and the way those tasks are performed.

Mixed-model sequencing The production of different products in small batches on the same equipment following a repeating cycle.

Mixed strategy An aggregate planning strategy that combines two or more of the pure strategies.

Model Is an abstraction from the real problem of the key variables and relationships in order to simplify the problem. The purpose of modeling is to provide the user with a better understanding of the problem, and with a means of manipulating the results for "what if" analysis.

Monte Carlo simulation The use of random numbers to simulate a real system.

MOST Stands for Maynard Operation Sequence Technique. MOST is based on MTM, but is much faster and easier to use.

Motivation Is an inner state that directs behavior towards a goal.

Move time The material handling time between work centers.

Movement An individual motion that comprises elements of a task.

MRP A way of scheduling the ordering or production of parts or raw materials so they will be available when needed to meet the master schedule.

MRP II Another name for Manufacturing Resource Planning.

MTM Stands for Methods Time Measurement and was developed by Dr. H. B. Maynard. Under this system, each movement has been determined to take a certain number of Time Measurement Units (TMUs).

Multiple regression analysis Uses two or more (independent variables) to predict the dependent variable.

Multiplicative model for analyzing a time series Is a method for combining the components of a time series. With this approach the factors (trend, seasonal, cyclical, and random) are multiplied.

Networking Is linking together one or more computer devices so they can transfer data. This transfer occurs quickly and communications are said to take place in "real time."

Node A circle in a precedence diagram or project network.

Nonlinear programming Mathematical procedures related to linear programming, but which do not require that all functions be linear.

Normal cost The cost of completing a project activity in its normal time.

Normal time The time that a project or an activity takes under normal conditions.

Objective function The function in a linear programming problem that includes the variables and indicates what is to be achieved.

Off-loading Involves taking a part that would ordinarily be processed on one machine and processing it on another machine that has available capacity.

Office automation Is the application of electronic and electromechanical devices to office procedures with the purpose of increasing productivity. This includes storage of data, manipulation, and communications.

Operating budget Is part of a plan for production. It includes estimates of material, labor, and other facilities costs necessary to meet the forecasted production goal.

Operating characteristic curve (OC curve) A graph indicating the probability of accepting a batch as a function of the percentage of defective units in the batch.

Operating leverage Is replacing variable costs of production, usually labor, with fixed costs. This action causes profits to rise rapidly as volume increases because the incremental costs (variable costs/unit) are low.

Operationalizing the strategic plan Converting the strategic plan into detailed plans for each functional area.

Operations Are the processes by which people, capital, and material (inputs) are combined to produce the services and goods we consume (outputs). Operations employ labor and management (people), and use facilities and equipment (capital) to change materials into finished good (farm tractors) or to provide services (computer software development).

Operations management Is decision-making involving the many factors which affect operations. Decisions that need to be made might include which products to produce, how large a facility to build, and how many people to hire on first shift.

Operator-machine chart Records the way that an operator interacts with one or more machines and the amount of idle time (either operator or machine) that will occur.

Order backlog A stream of orders that are waiting to be started into production.

Ordering cost The variable costs associated with replenishing inventory.

Order point The level of inventory at which a company should order more to avoid a possible stockout.

Order status Is the ability to query the customer orders to determine if the order has been completed, scheduled, or is waiting to be produced and the reasons the order is waiting.

Order-up-to level In a periodic review inventory control system, the level to which a replenishment order should bring on-hand plus on-order inventory.

Order-winning criteria Criteria such as price or quality that consumers use in making purchase decisions.

Organizational structure Is the formal relationship between different function areas or subsystems.

Outsourcing Is contracting with another company to do work that was once done by the organization itself.

P-kanban A kanban that authorizes the production of more parts in a pull system.

Pallet Is a storage device, usually made of wood, that allows a fork-lift truck to easily pick up the parts by picking up the entire pallet.

Panel of experts Is an approach to forecasting that involves people who are knowledgeable about the subject. This group attempts to make a forecast by building consensus.

Pareto analysis A procedure for identifying which problems are most important.

PERT A procedure for analyzing projects when activity durations may vary randomly.

Piece-rate plan An employee compensation plan in which pay is based on the number of units produced.

Plan Is a list of actions that management expects to take. A plan is a basis for allocating the organization's resources to deal with opportunities and problems present in the environment.

Planned receipts In MRP, a quantity expected to be received in a given time bucket based on an order that is planned, but not yet released.

Planned order release An order to either the shop or a supplier, planned to be released for a given amount during a time bucket in MRP.

Planning horizon A length of time into the future for which plans are developed.

Planning the system Defines the way in which an organization expects its physical facilities, people, and materials to meet projected customer demand and the organization's objectives.

Precedence diagram Is a series of nodes which represent activities and arcs or lines which indicate the sequence of operations.

Preemptive pricing A strategy based on the learning curve that involves short-term losses but long-term gains.

Proactive strategy A strategy that emphasizes efforts to modify the environment, rather than simply reacting to that environment.

Probability-based simulation Simulation in which values of certain variables vary randomly according to some probability distribution.

Process Describes the way in which the product is made.

Process batch The number of units of a given part that are processed consecutively on a given machine or work center.

Process capability A measure of the ability of a process to consistently maintain specifications.

Process design Describes how the product will be made.

Process generator A mathematical function that generates random numbers according to a given probability distribution.

Process selection Is a series of decisions that include technical or engineering issues and volume or scale issues.

Process technology Is the application of knowledge to improve the process.

Product Can be either a good or a service.

Product design Is the determination of the characteristics and features of the product, i.e., how does it function?

Product facility strategy One facility is responsible for producing one product or product line and shipping that product all over the country and around the world.

Production chain Is a mechanism that takes basic materials—such as trees, crude oil, iron ore, and sand—all the way to finished products—such as houses, automobiles, and microcomputers. A microcomputer, for example, has parts that are (1) molded from plastic which is derived from crude oil, (2) shaped from steel which comes from iron ore, and (3) made of glass which is made from sand.

Production flow analysis (PFA) Is a method for determining families of parts. In this systematic analysis, the production sequence for each part, the machining operations for each part, and the characteristics of the material are used. From these data, similarities can be determined and parts can be divided into families.

Production kanban A kanban that authorizes the production of more parts in a pull system.

Production scheduling See scheduling.

Productivity Output divided by input.

Product layout Is the physical arrangement of facilities so that products move along one path. There is little product variation so equipment is arranged to minimize material movement and to reduce material handling costs.

Product mix Is the percent of total demand or output that is devoted to each product.

Product technology Is the application of knowledge to improve the product.

Program evaluation and review technique (PERT) A procedure for analyzing projects when activity durations may vary randomly.

Programmable controller Has the properties of a computer. It can remember instructions (a program), and transfer those instructions to the machine. On a drill press for example, a programmable controller can control the speed of the rotating drill bit and the force applied against the object being drilled.

Project Is a process for making one-of-a-kind products. Most large construction jobs are projects. Many service jobs can be categorized as projects. Installing new computer hardware, adding major new computer software, or implementing a new management planning and control system all could qualify as projects.

Projected ending inventory In MRP, the inventory level expected to be on hand at the end of a time bucket.

Prototype Is a model of a product. It could be a working model, a model reduced in scale, or a mock-up of the product.

Pull system An approach to manufacturing in which materials are pulled through processing based on actual requirements for those materials.

Purchasing Is the activity of acquiring services and goods for the organization. It includes all the activities necessary for filling the organization's long- and short-term needs.

Pure strategies Three strategies for medium-range operations planning: vary the workforce, vary workforce utilization, and use inventory to absorb demand fluctuations.

Push system An approach to manufacturing that forces materials through processing based on a schedule.

Quality The degree of conformance of all the relevant features and characteristics of a product to all of the aspects of a customer's need, limited by the price and delivery that he or she will accept.

Quality assurance Any activities related to making sure that quality is maintained at the desired level.

Quality audit An evaluation of all aspects related to quality and procedures for assuring quality.

Quality circle (QC) A group of employees who meet, usually weekly, to identify and solve problems related to their work.

Quality function deployment A procedure for spreading the voice of the customer throughout a company in determining how products should be designed and processes operated.

Queue A waiting line.

Queue time The time a job spends waiting to be processed at a work center.

Random fluctuations Are other types of small variations that may result from many different factors.

Rating factor How fast or slow the worker being observed in a time study performed the task in relation to an average worker.

Raw materials inventories Are goods purchased and stored for later use in the production process.

Reactive strategy A planning strategy that merely responds to the environment.

Reduced cost An output from linear programming that indicates how much the objective function would change if a variable with value of zero were to have its value increased by one unit.

Regional facility strategy Each facility is assigned a market area and each facility produces a complete line of products for that area.

Regression analysis Is a method to predict the value of one variable base on the value of one or more other variables.

Relative advantage Is the difference between the lowest-cost producer and the next-lowest-cost producer.

Reliability Is the length of time that a product will function before it fails.

Request for quotes Is a notice which indicates that an organization wants to gather price information for the purpose of making a purchase.

Responsibility center Is a part or subsystem of the organization which is responsible for and contributes to performance. Information about the revenues generated and the costs consumed by each responsibility center are collected so that the manager of the center can be evaluated.

Review interval The time between one review of inventory and the next in a periodic review inventory control system.

Robot Is a reprogrammable, multifunctional manipulator designed to move materials, parts, tools or specialized devices through variable programmed motions for the performance of a variety of tasks.

Rope A term used in synchronous manufacturing to indicate methods of communication between the drum and other machines or work centers.

Rough-cut capacity planning Used to determine whether sufficient overall production capacity will exist to meet the master production schedule.

Rounding out capacity Is adding capacity to a bottleneck department to increase the capacity of a system by bringing the capacity of the bottleneck department into balance with the other departments.

Routing Is a sequence of machines or processes in which a part travels in order to be properly finished.

Routing sheet A document used in manufacturing to indicate the sequence of operations, machines, or work centers that a part or product must follow.

Run time Actual processing time for a job.

Run-out Time The period of time before a company will run out of a particular product.

Safety stock An extra amount added to the order point as a buffer against stockout possibilities.

Scanlon plan Employees are rewarded for their cost reduction efforts. Any reduction in the labor cost per unit of output is reflected in an employee bonus, which is based on a ratio of total labor costs to the value of output.

Scheduled receipts In MRP, a quantity for which an order has already been released and which is planned for receipt during a given time bucket.

Scheduling A final, detailed determination of the times employees will work, the sequence in which goods or services will be provided, and the operating times for machines.

Seasonal complements Products with seasonal demand patterns that are opposite or nearly so.

Seasonal variation Reflects forces that act periodically in a fixed period of one year or less.

Secular trend Reflects forces that are responsible for growth or decline over a long period of time.

Selected time The average time it took the worker being observed in a time study to perform the task.

Sequencing A step in the scheduling process in which the ordering of jobs or work is determined.

Service level The percentage of inventory replenishment orders that are received before a stockout occurs.

Service parts Parts that are ordered and produced as replacement parts in units already sold.

Services Are intangible products.

Set-up Is the preparation of a machine to perform the required operations on a part.

Setup time The time to get a machine ready to process a job.

Shadow price An output from linear programming that indicates how much the objective function would increase if the right-hand side of a constraint were increased by one unit.

Short-range planning Goes up to about six months into the future.

Simple regression analysis Uses only one variable (independent variable) to predict the dependent variable.

Simplex method A mathematical procedure, usually programmed on a computer, for solving linear programming problems.

Simulation The use of mathematical procedures to represent a real system.

Single-card kanban system A pull system that uses only the C-kanban. Actual production may be scheduled using MRP.

Slack time A figure representing how much leeway each activity in a project has in its starting time or duration.

Slack variable A variable in linear programming that indicates how much capacity is unused in a $\leq$ type constraint.

SMED (Single Minute Exchange of Dies) Setup time for changing dies in a press that takes less than 10 minutes.

Sociopsychological factors Include more than just how a job is done, but also how the employee feels about that job.

Sociotechnical systems Are organizations that blend social (people) aspects and technology. A sociotechnical system is not interested in optimizing the technical system but in joint optimization of the social and technical aspects in the organization.

Staff functions Assist the line functions, operations and marketing in completing their tasks.

Standard container A container used in pull systems to control inventory. Each standard container holds a specified number of units.

Standard error of the coefficient Is a standard deviation for a coefficient estimated by regression analysis.

Standard error of the estimate It is a measure of the amount of scatter around the regression line. It is the difference between each observed value, Y^o, and the estimated value, Y^e.

Standard-hour system In an incentive plan each job has a standard time. Whenever an employee performs that job, they are paid based on the standard time—regardless of how long it actually took them to do the job.

Standard time Expressed in terms of time per unit (e.g., 3.75 minutes per part) or units per time period (e.g., 16 parts per hour). This represents the time it should take to perform a task under ordinary conditions, allowing for rest periods, fatigue, and other unavoidable delays.

Statement of work In project management, a statement describing the objectives to be achieved and work to be done.

Stationary time series Is one that does not have a trend component.

Statistical process control (SPC) The use of statistical methods to determine when a process is out of control before defects are produced.

Statistical quality control (SQC) The use of statistical methods to avoid accepting or producing defects.

Steady-state conditions Conditions that prevail in a system after any start-up variations have disappeared.

Stockout A condition that occurs when no more inventory of an item is left.

Strategic planning Essentially concerned with determining how the organization will compete effectively in the marketplace. The strategic plan specifies what market the company is in and how it will compete effectively in the marketplace.

Strategy Consists of the organizational goals and the methods for implementing the goals, called key policies. Strategy defines how an organization chooses to compete within the framework dictated by the external environment.

Sub-contracting Is buying parts or sub-assemblies from outside suppliers whenever a company's capacity is insufficient to meet its needs from internal production.

Supplier Is the seller of a service or good. A supplier is sometimes referred to as a vendor.

Supplier certification Is the verification of supplier performance in various categories such as quality, lead time, and reliability in meeting promised delivery dates.

Supply inventories Are materials which are not part of the finished product but are consumed either in production or in tasks in other departments.

Survey Is a systematic effort to elicit information from specific groups and is usually conducted via a written questionnaire or phone interview.

Synchronous Manufacturing A manufacturing philosophy that focuses on bottlenecks and plans production to maximize utilization of the bottlenecks.

Synergy Is cooperative (teamwork) actions where the actions taken together have a greater effect than the sum of the individual effects. The whole is greater than the sum of its parts.

Synthesis Is putting the parts or elements together to form a whole. In analysis, each part is examined and answers to questions are determined. In synthesis, the parts are combined in a way that addresses the interaction between those parts. The concept behind synthesis is to make the best decision for overall performance of a system, not to optimize one part.

System Is a group of items, events or actions in which no item, event or action occurs independently of at least one other. Accordingly, no item that is studied in isolation will act in the same way it would in the normal environment.

Systematic layout planning Use codes that describe the importance of having two departments close together to arrive at an appropriate job shop layout.

System cycle time Refers to a series of operations or departments linked in a continuous flow process. It is the time between the nth unit and the n + 1 unit existing the line. It is determined by the department with the longest cycle time.

Tabular method A method for aggregate planning that utilizes a table based on the transportation method.

Tacit judgement Is a method for determining families of parts. It involves the visual review of design drawings and specifications for similarities. This process is usually easy to do and can result in good families of parts, if relatively few parts are involved.

Taguchi methods Experimental design techniques used to identify those factors that cause output from a process to deviate from a target value.

Tariff rate quotas Are tariffs that increase with the volume that is imported.

Tariffs Are extra charges placed on goods or services that are imported into the home country.

Task A clearly defined activity that makes up a job.

Technology Is the application of knowledge, usually in the form of recently developed tools, processes, and procedures, to solve problems.

Test market Is a special kind of survey. The forecaster arranges for the placement of a new product or an existing product that has been modified. Data on actual sales are collected.

Time bucket A period of time, usually a week, in which demand and requirements are grouped for master scheduling and material requirements planning.

Time Measurement Unit Equal to .00001 hour, or .036 seconds.

Time-oriented simulation An approach to simulation in which time is constantly incremented by a fixed amount.

Time phasing The process used in material requirements planning of determining requirements by time period.

TMU Equal to .00001 hour, or .036 seconds.

Total preventive maintenance An approach to equipment maintenance that emphasizes prevention of breakdowns, maintenance each day, and operator responsibility for maintenance.

Total quality control An approach to quality control that emphasizes quality at the source by placing responsibility on all parts of the organization to build quality into the product.

Trade embargoes Eliminate trade between two countries for a period of time. Trade could be eliminated entirely or in a specific product or product line.

Transfer batch The number of units of a given part that are transferred at one time from one machine or work center to another.

Transfer line Is a sophisticated set of machines that are able to perform a complex set of operations without human operators. Transfer lines have very limited flexibility. A transfer line in the automotive industry can take a raw casting of an engine block in one end and produce a machined engine block from the other without operator intervention. However, the same transfer line cannot produce eight, six, and four cylinder engines.

Transportation method A mathematical procedure for solving certain types of linear programming problems that often involve transportation of materials.

Two-hand operation chart Lists precisely what each hand is doing at all times during the performance of a task.

Type I error An error in acceptance sampling in which a good lot is rejected.

Type II error An error in acceptance sampling in which a bad lot is accepted.

U-shaped layout A layout of facilities or equipment in the shape of a U. This layout improves teamwork, reduces material handling, and provides better flow of materials.

Utilization factor In queuing, the proportion of time the system will have at least one customer.

Variables Such as X_1 and X_2 are used to represent things we want to determine.

Vendor Is the seller or supplier of a service or good.

Vertical expansion of the job Giving workers responsibility for planning many of their own activities and, to some extent, allowing them to make decisions related to the job they are performing.

Vertical loading Giving workers responsibility for planning many of their own activities and, to some extent, allowing them to make decisions related to the job they are performing.

Visual inspection When referring to group technology see the definition for tacit judgement.

Voluntary import quotas Are agreements between governments that limit the import of services and goods.

Wage incentive plan A procedure that ties an employee's pay to productivity.

Wait time The time a job spends waiting before being moved to the next work center.

WIP A term used to denote work-in-process inventory.

Work breakdown structure A list of individual activities or tasks that make up a project and the precedence relationships among them.

Work centers See work stations.

Work improvement Methods and techniques concerned only with the physiological aspects of a job—how easy the job is to do, how quickly the person can work.

Work-in-process inventories Are products which the organization has partially completed.

Work measurement A tool that is used to determine the amount of time a work activity, or task, should take under ordinary conditions.

Work physiology The study of people's bodily reactions under working conditions.

Work sampling Used in developing an estimate of the percentage of time a worker spends on different activities.

Work stations Are places where individuals perform tasks on a product.

Yield Is the ratio between the quantity of output to the quantity of input.

Formulas

Activity level, distance, cost model for determining layout

Objective function = Minimize $\sum_{i=1}^{n}\sum_{j=1}^{n} A_{ij}D_{ij}C_{ij}$ for all $i \neq j$

where

A_{ij} = the activity level from department i to department j; $i = 1, \ldots, n$ and $j = 1, \ldots, n$, where n is the number of departments

D_{ij} = the distance from department i to department j

C_{ij} = the cost per unit distance from department i to department j

Additive time series model

$$Y = T + S + C + R$$

where

T = Trend

S = Seasonal variation

C = Cyclical fluctuations

R = Random fluctuations

Average number of units waiting

$$\text{Single server model } L_q = \frac{\lambda^2}{\mu(\mu - \lambda)}$$

$$\text{Multiserver model } L_q = \frac{P(0)(\lambda/\mu)^s \rho}{s!(1 - \rho)^2}$$

where

$P(0)$ = probability of being idle

ρ = utilization factor

λ = average arrival rate

μ = average service rate

s = number of servers

Average time spent waiting

$$\text{Single server model } W_q = \frac{\lambda}{\mu(\mu - \lambda)}$$

$$\text{Multiserver model } W_q = \frac{L_q}{\lambda}$$

where

λ = average arrival rate

μ = average service rate

s = number of servers

L_q = Average number of units waiting

Base-rate Wage

Base-rate wage = base rate × hours worked

c charts

$$UCL_c = \bar{c} + 3\sigma_c$$

$$LCL_c = \bar{c} - 3\sigma_c$$

where

$\bar{c}$ = mean number of defects per sample when process is in control

σ_c = standard deviation of mean number of defects in a sample

Capacity

Capacity/period = (maximum production rate/hour) × (number of hours worked/period)

$$\text{Capacity} = \frac{H}{C}$$

where

H = hours worked per period

C = cycle time

Critical ratio

$$\text{Critical ratio } (CR) = \frac{\text{Time until due date}}{\text{Processing time remaining}}$$

Cycle time

$$C = \frac{1}{PR}$$

where

PR = production rate

Days of inventory

Days of inventory

$$= \frac{\text{Average inventory investment} \times \text{Days per year}}{\text{Annual cost of goods sold}}$$

Distance between two points

$$d_i^2 = \Delta x_i^2 + \Delta y_i^2$$

where

d_i = the distance between any two points
Δx_i = the distance between those points as measure along the X-axis
Δy_i = the distance between those points as measured along the Y-axis.

Earliest finish time

Earliest finish time (EF) = Earliest start (ES) + duration

Economic order quantity (EOQ)

$$EOQ = \sqrt{\frac{2DC_o}{C_h}}$$

where

C_h = Variable cost of holding a unit of inventory
D = Demand rate
C_o = Variable cost of ordering more inventory

Economic production quantity (EPQ)

$$EPQ = \sqrt{\frac{2DC_o}{C_h(1 - d/p)}}$$

where

C_h = Variable cost of holding a unit of inventory
D = Demand rate per year
C_o = Variable cost of ordering more inventory
d = Demand rate per day
p = Production rate per day

Expected time in PERT

$$t_e = \frac{a+4m+b}{6}$$

where

t_e = expected activity duration
a = optimistic time
m = most likely time
b = pessimistic time

Exponential smoothing

$$\begin{aligned}
f_{t+1} &= x_t \\
f_{t+2} &= A(x_{t+1}) + (1 - A)f_{t+1} \\
f_{t+3} &= A(x_{t+2}) + (1 - A)f_{t+2} \\
&\vdots \\
f_{t+n} &= A(x_{t+n-1}) + (1 - A)f_{t+n-1}
\end{aligned}$$

where

f_t = forecast for time period t.
x_t = actual for time period t.
n = some number of periods in the future
$0 \leq A \leq 1$

Forecast error

$$\text{Total forecast error} = \sum_{t=1}^{n} (x_t - f_t)$$

where

f_t = forecast for period t.
x_t = actual for period t.
n = number of periods

Inventory turnover ratio

Inventory turnover ratio

$$= \frac{\text{Annual cost of goods sold}}{\text{Average inventory investment.}}$$

Latest start time

Latest start time = Latest finish time (LF) − duration

Learning Curve

$$Y_n = Y_1 n^b$$

where

Y_n = the time it will take to produce the nth unit
Y_1 = the time it took to produce the first unit
n = the unit number
r = learning factor

$$b = \frac{\log r}{\log 2}$$

Load-distance or center of gravity method

$$x_f = \frac{\sum_{i=1}^{n}(a_i)(x_i)}{\sum_{i=1}^{n}(a_i)} \qquad y_f = \frac{\sum_{i=1}^{n}(a_i)(y_i)}{\sum_{i=1}^{n}(a_i)}$$

where

x_f = distance along the X axis from the origin to the center of gravity

y_f = distance along the Y axis from the origin to the center of gravity

a_i = the activity level (load) from the ith location to the proposed facility

x_i = the coordinate on the X axis for the ith customer

y_i = the coordinate on the Y axis for the ith customer

$$LD = \sum_{i=1}^{n}(a_i)(d_i)$$

where

LD = the total load distance for any proposed location

d_i = distance from a proposed location to the ith location.

Mean Absolute Deviation (*MAD*)

$$MAD = \frac{\sum_{t=1}^{n}|x_t - f_t|}{n}$$

where

x_t = actual value for time period t where $t = 1, \ldots, n$.

f_t = forecasted value for time period t, where $t = 1, \ldots, n$.

n = number of observations for which data are available.

Mean Squared Error (*MSE*)

$$MSE = \frac{\sum_{t=1}^{n}(x_t - f_t)^2}{n}$$

where

x_t = actual value for time period t where $t = 1, \ldots, n$

f_t = forecasted value for time period t where $t = 1, \ldots, n$

n = number of observations for which data are available

Moving average

$$f_{t+1} = \frac{\sum_{i=0}^{n-1}(x_{t-i})}{n}$$

where

f_{t+1} = the forecast for time period $t + 1$, that is, the next time period

x_{t-i} = the observed value for period $t - i$, where t is the last period for which data are available and $i = 0, \ldots, n - 1$.

n = the number of time periods in the average

Multiplicative time series model

$$Y = T \times S \times C \times R$$

where

T = Trend

S = Seasonal variation

C = Cyclical fluctuations

R = Random fluctuations

Normal Time

Normal Time (NT) = Cycle Time (CT) × Rating Factor

where

Cycle Time = Average of observed times

Number of kanbans

$$y = \frac{D(T_w + T_p)(1 + X)}{a}$$

where

y = total number of kanban cards needed

D = planned usage rate for the part

T_w = average waiting time for replenishment of parts

T_p = average production time for a standard container of parts

X = a policy variable set by r

a = capacity of a standar

Operating ratio

$$\text{Operating ratio} = \frac{\text{Capacity consumed}}{\text{Capacity available}} \times 100$$

Order-up-to level (*S*)

$$S = D(R + M) + s$$

where

D = Demand rate
R = Review interval
M = Lead time
s = Safety stock

Order period (Period order quantity for *MRP*)

$$\text{Order period} = \frac{EOQ}{D}$$

where

EOQ = Economic order quantity
D = Demand rate

Order point

$$\text{Order point } (r) = dm + s$$

where

d = Demand rate
m = Lead time
s = Safety stock

***p* charts**

$$UCL_p = \bar{p} + 3\sigma_p$$
$$LCL_p = \bar{p} - 3\sigma_p$$

where

$\bar{p}$ = mean proportion defective when the process is in control
σ_p = standard deviation of mean proportion defective

Percent idle time

$$\begin{array}{c}\text{Balance delay}\\ \text{(percent idle time)}\end{array} = \frac{\text{idle time}}{\text{time available in the line}}(100)$$

$$= \frac{(m)(C) - \sum_{i=1}^{n} t_i}{(m)(C)}(100)$$

where

m = actual number of stations in the balance
C = cycle time
$\sum_{i=1}^{n} t_i$ = total task time required to assemble one unit

Piece-rate Wage

$$\text{Piece-rate wage} = \text{piece rate} \times \text{number of pieces}$$

Probability of being idle

$$\text{Single server model } P(0) = 1 - \frac{\lambda}{\mu}$$

$$\text{Multiserver model } P(0) = \frac{1}{\sum_{n=0}^{s-1} \frac{(\lambda/\mu)^n}{n!} + \frac{(\lambda/\mu)^s}{s!(1 - \lambda/\mu s)}}$$

where

λ = average arrival rate
μ = average service rate
s = number of servers

Probability of completing project by a given time

$$z = \frac{T' - T}{\sqrt{\Sigma\sigma_{cp}^2}}$$

where

z = number of standard deviations from mean in standardized normal probability distribution table, Chapter 14 Appendix
T' = desired completion time
T = sum of expected durations for critical path activities
$\Sigma\sigma_{cp}^2$ = sum of variances for critical path activities

Production rate

$$\text{Production rate} = \frac{\text{(number of units produced)}}{\text{(amount of time)}}$$

$$\text{Production rate} = \frac{\text{capacity}}{H}$$

$$\text{Production rate} = \frac{1}{C}$$

where

C = cycle time
H = number hours worked

Productivity

$$\text{Productivity} = \frac{\text{output}}{\text{input}}$$

Profit

$$P = SP(X_s) - [FC + VC(X_p)]$$

where

SP = selling price per unit

X_s = number of units sold

FC = fixed costs

VC = variable cost per unit

X_p = number of units produced

Profit point

$$X = \frac{P + FC}{C}$$

$$X = \frac{P + FC}{WC}$$

where

P = profit

FC = fixed costs

C = contribution per unit

WC = weighted contribution per unit

***R* chart**

$$UCL_R = D_4\bar{R}$$

$$LCL_R = D_3\bar{R}$$

where

$\bar{R}$ = mean of sample ranges when process is in control

D_3 = value from table of Exhibit 17.9

D_4 = value from table of Exhibit 17.9

Regression analysis (multiple)

$$Y = a + b_1X_1 + b_2X_2 + \ldots b_kX_k$$

where

Y = the dependent variable. It depends on the variables X_1 thru X_k and the model parameters $a, b_1, b_2, \ldots b_k$, *where k* is the number of independent variables. (Equations for the parameters are not given here. Rather, you are encouraged to use an available computer package, such as SPSSX™, SAS™, MINITAB™, or a microcomputer package, to do necessary calculations.)

X_i = an independent variable, with $i = 1, \ldots, k$.

Each independent variable will have n observations or data points.

Regression analysis (simple)

$$Y = a + b(X)$$

where

Y = the dependent variable. It depends on the variable X and the model parameters a and b.

X = the independent variable.

n = the number of data points in the sample

r = the coefficient of correlation

$s_{y/x}$ = standard error of the estimate

$$b = \frac{n\Sigma XY - \Sigma X\Sigma Y}{n\Sigma X^2 - (\Sigma X)^2}$$

$$a = \frac{\Sigma Y}{n} - b\frac{\Sigma X}{n}$$

$$r = \frac{n\Sigma XY - \Sigma X\Sigma Y}{\sqrt{[n\Sigma X^2 - (\Sigma X)^2][n\Sigma Y^2 - (\Sigma Y)^2]}}$$

$$s_{y/x} = \sqrt{\frac{\Sigma Y^2 - a\Sigma Y - b\Sigma XY}{n - 2}}$$

Required cycle time

$$\text{Required cycle time} = \frac{\text{Working time per day}}{\text{Units required per day}}$$

Review interval (*R*)

$$R = \frac{EOQ}{D}$$

where

EOQ = Economic order quantity

D = Demand rate

Run-out time

$$\text{Run-out time} = \frac{\text{Current inventory}}{\text{Usage rate}}$$

Safety stock

Continuous Review:

$$\text{Safety stock} = z\sigma_L$$

where

z = number of standard deviations from the mean required to obtain the desired service level

σ_L = standard deviation of demand during lead time

Periodic Review:

$$\text{Safety stock} = z\sigma_{I+L}$$

where

z = number of standard deviations from the mean required to obtain the desired service level

σ_{I+L} = standard deviation of demand during review interval plus lead time

Scanlon Plan

$$\text{Bonus} = \text{allowed payroll} - \text{labor costs}$$

where

$$\text{Allowed payroll} = \text{profit-sharing ratio} \times \text{value of output}$$

$$\text{Profit-sharing ratio} = \frac{\text{base period labor costs}}{\text{value of output}}$$

Slack time

$$\begin{aligned}\text{Slack time} &= \text{Latest start time } (LS) - \text{Earliest start time } (ES) \\ &= \text{Latest finish time } (LF) - \text{Earliest finish time } (EF)\end{aligned}$$

Standard deviation of mean number of defects in a sample

$$\sigma_c = \sqrt{\bar{c}}$$

where

$\bar{c}$ = mean number of defectives per sample when process is in control

Standard deviation of mean proportion defective

$$\sigma_p = \sqrt{\frac{\bar{p}(1-\bar{p})}{n}}$$

where

$\bar{p}$ = mean proportion defective

n = sample size

Standard deviation of sample means

$$\sigma_{\bar{x}} = \frac{\sigma}{\sqrt{n}}$$

where

σ = process standard deviation

n = sample size

Standard-hour Wage

$$\text{Standard-hour wage} = \text{Standard time} \times \text{Wage rate} \times \text{units}$$

Standard time

$$\text{Standard Time } (ST) = \text{Normal Time } (NT) \times \text{Allowance}$$

Theoretical minimum number of work stations

$$N = \frac{\sum_{i=1}^{n} t_i}{C}$$

where

N = theoretical minimum number of work stations

t_i = task time for element i, where $i = 1, \ldots, n$ tasks

$\sum_{i=1}^{n} t_i$ = total task time required to assemble one unit

C = cycle time for the balance

Total annual variable costs of inventory

EOQ Model:

$$\text{Total annual variable costs} = (Q/2)C_h + (D/Q)C_o$$

where

Q = Order quantity

C_h = Variable cost of holding a unit of inventory

D = Demand rate

C_o = Variable cost of ordering more inventory

EPQ Model:

$$\text{Total annual variable costs} = \frac{Q(1-d/p)}{2}C_h + \frac{D}{Q}C_o$$

where

Q = Production quantity

C_h = Variable cost of holding a unit of inventory

D = Annual demand rate

C_o = Variable cost of setting up for production

d = daily demand rate

p = daily production rate

Total cost

$$TC = FC + (VC)(X_p)$$

where

TC = total cost

FC = fixed costs

VC = variable cost per unit

X_p = number of units produced

Total revenue

$$TR = (SP)(X_s)$$

where

TR = total revenue

SP = selling price per unit

X_s = number of units sold

Tracking signal

$$\text{Tracking signal} = \frac{\sum_{t=1}^{n}(x_t - f_t)}{MAD}$$

where

x_t = actual for period t

f_t = forecast for period t

MAD = Mean Absolute Deviation

Utilization factor (of a facility in queuing)

Single server model $\rho = \lambda/\mu$

Multiserver model $\rho = \lambda/s\mu$

where

ρ = utilization factor

λ = average arrival rate

μ = average service rate

s = number of servers

Variance

Variance = balanced cost − actual cost

Variance of activity duration in *PERT*

$$\sigma^2 = \left(\frac{b - a}{6}\right)^2$$

where

σ^2 = variance of activity duration

a = optimistic time

b = pessimistic time

Weighted contribution

$$WC = \sum_{i=1}^{n} M_i(SP_i - VC_i)$$

where

WC = weighted contribution per unit

M_i = product mix as a percentage of total sales for product i, where $i = 1, \ldots, n$ for n different products or product lines

SP_i = selling price for product i

VC_i = variable cost for product i

Weighted moving average

$$f_{t+1} = \sum_{i=0}^{n-1}(w_{t-i})(x_{t-i})$$

where

f_{t+1} = the forecast for time period $t + 1$, that is, the next time period

x_{t-i} = the observed value for period $t - i$, where t is the last period for which data are available and $i = 0, \ldots, n - 1$.

w_{t-i} = the weight for period $t - i$, where t is the last period for which data are available and $i = 0, \ldots, n - 1$. The weights for all n periods must sum to 1.0.

***X*-bar chart**

$$UCL_{\bar{x}} = \bar{\bar{X}} + A_2\bar{R}$$

$$LCL_{\bar{x}} = \bar{\bar{X}} - A_2\bar{R}$$

where

$\bar{R}$ = mean of sample ranges when process is in control

A_2 = value from table of Exhibit 17.9

Yield

$$\text{Yield} = \frac{\text{quantity of output}}{\text{quantity of input}}$$

Index